Best Plays of the
EARLY AMERICAN THEATRE
1787–1911

EDITED BY
John Gassner

IN ASSOCIATION WITH
Mollie Gassner

DOVER PUBLICATIONS, INC.
MINEOLA, NEW YORK

Bibliographical Note

This Dover edition, first published in 2000, is an unabridged reprint
of *Best Plays of the Early American Theatre,* originally published by
Crown Publishers, Inc., in 1967.

Library of Congress Cataloging-in-Publication Data

Best plays of the early American theatre, 1787–1911 / edited by John
Gassner in association with Mollie Gassner.
     p. cm.
Includes bibliographical references (p.).
ISBN 0-486-41098-6 (pbk.)
     1. American drama. I. Gassner, John, 1903–1967. II. Gassner,
Mollie.

PS625 .B47 2000
812.008—dc21

                                                            00-027931

Manufactured in the United States by Courier Corporation
41098602
www.doverpublications.com

For

DOROTHY and ROBERT M. KLUGER

Affectionately,

Mais où sont les neiges d'antan?

TABLE OF CONTENTS

	PAGE
PREFACE: "1714-1916"	IX
INTRODUCTION: BEFORE O'NEILL	XI
THE PLAYS AND THEIR AUTHORS	XXVIII
A SELECTIVE BIBLIOGRAPHY	XLVII

THE CONTRAST (1787)
Royall Tyler ... 1

SUPERSTITION (1824)
James N. Barker ... 38

CHARLES THE SECOND (1824)
John Howard Payne and Washington Irving ... 73

FASHION (1845)
Anna Cora Mowatt ... 97

UNCLE TOM'S CABIN (1852)
George L. Aiken ... 136

THE OCTOROON (1859)
Dion Boucicault ... 185

THE COUNT OF MONTE CRISTO (1883)
Charles Fechter ... 216

THE MOUSE-TRAP (1889)
William Dean Howells ... 262

SECRET SERVICE (1896)
William Gillette ... 277

THE GREAT DIVIDE (1906)
William Vaughn Moody ... 361

THE NEW YORK IDEA (1906)
Langdon Mitchell ... 398

THE TRUTH (1907)
Clyde Fitch ... 458

THE WITCHING HOUR (1907)
Augustus Thomas 511

SALVATION NELL (1908)
Edward Sheldon 557

THE EASIEST WAY (1909)
Eugene Walter 617

THE SCARECROW (1911)
Percy MacKaye 677

PREFACE: "1714-1916"

THE PRESENT VOLUME REPRESENTS a first attempt (there may be a second, in due time) to close a considerable gap in the *Best American Plays* series, since the previously published volumes have represented drama on the American stage after the climax of the avant-garde "Little Theatre" movement marked by the beginnings of the Provincetown Players in 1915 and the emergence of O'Neill in 1916 as a produced playwright. The year 1714 is remembered as the date of *Androborus*, by Robert Hunter, a governor of the New York colony, the first play to be published in America. Two hundred years later, after a long and, in the main, commercially flourishing career, American theatre enters the twentieth century. The modernizing trend that had started about a decade earlier is on the verge of bursting into bloom with the establishment of no fewer than three adventurous New York "little theatre groups," the most important of which to American playwriting is the Provincetown Players.

No other claims are being made here for the present compilation that will not be self-evident. And no apologies, either, for omissions that will occur to anyone familiar with the field other than that a number of these were necessitated by escalating printing costs. Only a supplementary volume will satisfy the editors' historical interest. Scholars will certainly have to go to larger collections, such as the expensive three-volume *Representative Plays by American Dramatists* (1765–1917) edited decades ago by the late Montrose J. Moses (now reprinted by Benjamin Blom in New York) and the vast and valuable *America's Lost Plays*, originally published in twenty volumes by the Princeton University Press under the general editorship of the late Barrett H. Clark, and now republished in ten double volumes by the Indiana University Press.

In any event, the general reader is not being deprived by us of masterpieces. He is, instead, being spared some embarrassment, since much of our early dramatic literature, regardless of its apparent vigor on the stage at one time, is almost subliterary. Quite often the dialogue, especially when it reproduces dialect, would be found downright painful to read. We have tried to spare the reader the most traumatic examples, although we have to trust to his historical interest to tolerate some excrescences of sentimentality along with their clichés and stereotypes of characterization. As for dialogue, it is wise to put the best rather than the worst construction on it and to imagine hearing it spoken by the best actors of a vanished age.

The text published here, we must say at once, is for the general reader, and certainly not for the antiquarian, the precisionist, or the specialist-scholar. We have made no thoroughgoing attempt to arrive at an indisputable text, and we have arrived at a format consistent with that of the plays in the previously published volumes of the *Best American Plays* series. In many instances, moreover, we have removed cumbersome and redundant pre-modern stage directions such as those found in the old-fashioned acting editions. We have borne in mind our primary intention, which was to provide a rapidly readable introduction to some of the plays of the period before 1916.

As for the present collection, the best policy to follow, we thought, would be to mingle familiar but historically important plays with less well-known pieces, such as James N. Barker's *Superstition* of the year 1824, which may be regarded as a period anticipation of Arthur Miller's *The Crucible*, and a hitherto unavailable work such as Edward Sheldon's *Salvation Nell*, which appears to have made an impression on the young Eugene O'Neill. One historically important piece not included in this volume, since our original list of plays had to be amputated for reasons of space, is James M. Herne's *Margaret Fleming*. But our regret was diminished by the reflection that the original text was destroyed in a conflagration and that the only available version was reconstructed from memory by the author's widow. For a play that stage historians have regarded as the first Ibsenite work of the American theatre (that Herne knew a realistic Ibsen play when he wrote *Margaret Fleming* is actually doubtful), it seems to us singularly mild. And George Henry Boker's somewhat unrepresentative tragedy with a Renaissance background, *Francesca da Rimini*, which we should have liked to include for its relative literary distinction, has been rather easily available.

In conclusion, we are grateful to a number of friends and associates for their help. To Travis Bogard of the University of California and Richard L. Moody for suggestions. To Mrs. Catherine MacKaye Barnes for the permission to include her distinguished father's play *The Scarecrow* and for information about him. To Miss Helen D. Willard and Miss Penelope D. Hull of the Houghton Library at Harvard University who made a typescript of Edward Sheldon's *Salvation Nell* available to us, and to Theodore Sheldon for permission to print *Salvation Nell*. And to Herbert Michelman and Naomi Rosenbach of Crown Publishers.

J.G., M.G.

INTRODUCTION: BEFORE O'NEILL

THE SIXTEEN PLAYS INCLUDED in the present volume are dramatic pieces produced before the advent of the so-called modern phase of the American theatre. It is commonly held that this event began with the discovery of O'Neill and the establishment of the avant-garde associated with that discovery, the Provincetown and the Washington Square Players in 1915. It is difficult to dissent from this view, although it is not impossible to hedge it with a qualification or two.

Not to make a mystery of this matter, let us simply say that the "changeover" from the old to the new style was somewhat less radical than most of us have tended to think during the past half century. It may actually be humbling to realize that our playwrights' average performance since 1950 has made distinctions between the period before and after 1915 less conducive than they used to be to complacency. Also, more than a few Pulitzer Prize winners of the 1920's seemed as dated by 1955 or 1965 as plays from the period 1870 and 1915 seemed to be by 1925. Thirty years of theatre history are enough to date almost any play that is not an unmistakable masterpiece or an extraordinarily seminal failure.

An inevitable selection such as *The Contrast*, at the beginning of our period, celebrated an early sloughing off of aristocratic pretentiousness in favor of republican virtue. Another selection, *Fashion*, a success at the midpoint of our "pre-modern" period, brings us to themes and views about which we apparently fail to acquire much certainty. It seems that we must reassure ourselves repeatedly that the attractions of Europe are a snare and a delusion. This theme recurs even in

the 1920's and 1930's, in such plays as Elmer Rice's *The Left Bank* and the Sidney Howard dramatization of Sinclair Lewis's novel *Dodsworth*. If criticism in such plays aims a shaft or two at American manners, it is for succumbing to the temptation of pseudorefinement when true refinement is easily ascertainable in an honest native breast resounding with our "native wood-notes wild."

There are flies in every national ointment, of course, but social vanities are not the most aggravating of these. They are productive of comedy of manners, at which Americans are supposedly not at all adept. In the early American theatre, however, some of our writers were still sustained by the tradition of eighteenth-century social satire in the manner of Sheridan and his lesser brethren of the British theatrical establishment. Moreover, until the middle of the last century, when *Fashion* took hold, national consciousness was not ruffled in the theatre to a degree that could make the practice of comedy of manners anomalous or grossly inappropriate. Some sort of recovery of the genre of social comedy was also to take place about half a century later, when memories of civil war were fading. By then we were moving into the twentieth century, and after the vogue of the transitional figure of Clyde Fitch we would move (or at least start moving) into precincts of so-called twentieth-century sophistication with Philip Barry and S. N. Behrman. It is this transition that is necessarily represented in our collection by a late Clyde Fitch play, *The Truth* (1907), and Langdon Mitchell's *The New York Idea* (1906).

These two pieces, and their predecessors *The Contrast* and *Fashion*, are not exactly new to anyone even moderately familiar with our early pre-modern stage history. But it would be virtually impossible to dispense with them in a volume that would do some modicum of justice to the period between 1775 and 1915. Moreover, the very limitations of this period's theatre could not be demonstrated without the presence of these plays. It is important for us to understand these limitations if we are to judge not only the past but the present.

It will be apparent only from a reading or, indeed, an alert rereading of these (and a few other) comedies that in the areas represented by them we moved forward after 1915 far less remarkably than we once complimented ourselves on doing. Especially in the 1920's and 1930's (but to a degree even later) we thought we had made enormous strides in high comedy. But this occurred far less often and less unambiguously than we thought. The above-mentioned plays will not be found vastly superior to comedies written after 1915, once some allowance is made for archaisms of idiom, sentiment, and milieu. It is necessary to cite exceptions to this generalization when one remembers Behrman's *The Second Man* and *End of Summer*, Sherwood's *Reunion in Vienna*, O'Neill's *Ah Wilderness!* and Barry's *The Philadelphia Story*. But to judge their levels of excellence by those attained by Shaw, Chekhov, O'Casey, Giraudoux, Brecht, and Pirandello across the sea would be disastrous to our self-esteem. We have lacked the animus or the ferment to which their vastly greater originality and artistry are attributable. If Royall Tyler was an inferior Sheridan of the eighteenth century, writers of the twentieth-century American comedy have been very inferior Shaws, Chekhovs, O'Caseys, Giraudouxs, and Pirandellos. It would be idle to contend that plays such as *The Second Man* and *The Philadelphia Story* do not mark

an advance over *The Contrast* and *Fashion* in complexity of argument or point of view were it not that progress has been at a snail's pace by comparison with the best British and Continental European work in the genre of comedy.

What has been seen in the case of comedy also becomes apparent in serious drama. In character study the progress marked by such plays in our collection as *The Great Divide* and *The Easiest Way* in the first decade of our century over plays written half a century earlier is admissible. Our progress as viewed in the perspective of another half a century that has witnessed such work as *A Streetcar Named Desire* and *Who's Afraid of Virginia Woolf?* is also by no means negligible. Yet the last-mentioned advance can leave one with mixed feelings when we reflect that the gain has been more in the modes of frankness of expression, which is a social manifestation, than in fine realizations or significant penetration into characters. And this, too, becomes most apparent when we look for a gauge of achievement beyond our shores; when we measure the Williams and Albee dramas by the standards set by *The Father*, *Miss Julie*, *The Dance of Death*, *Hedda Gabler*, and *The Master Builder*.

In the present volume we can also observe some effort to touch upon the social tensions of nineteenth-century America, for we include here such representative pieces as *The Octoroon* and *Uncle Tom's Cabin*, which attained much popularity in the decade before the Civil War. The evasions and sentimentalities in these pieces can embarrass the reader. But the embarrassment may be alleviated by the reflection that, except for changes in style and taste, a softness of intellect actually never departed from our theatre even in plays that came after the conclusion of the First World War.

In war plays such as *What Price Glory?* that caused an explosion in the theatre of the 1920's and in dramas of social conscience and sociological interest in the 1930's, the voices of protest were louder and distinctly more gruff. But the orientation was not radically different. The main appeal was not directed at the head but at the heart; we displayed little aptitude for "drama of ideas," we were "sympathetic" rather than analytical. This continued to be the case even in plays produced in subsequent decades. Hardheadedness has somehow frequently seemed to us close to hardheartedness. There have been more than traces of this inclination in our plays to let idealism that starts out as sentimental humanitarianism but may end in napalm-bombing take precedence over analysis, irony, and "distanced" thinking. Our political history, whether viewed from the "right" or the "left," has provided instances of this tendency ever since our confrontation with problems connected with the American Indian and the Negro slave. Our theatrical history seems but a reflection of the same mode of response, and symptomatic of it has been *Death of a Salesman*, which contains an unmistakable indictment of its mediocre hero's success-worship but the total effect of which is a sympathetic identification with Willy Loman.

On close analysis it will be found that even the pervasive realism of *Street Scene* and *Awake and Sing*, the sociological concern of *Dead End*, and the revolutionary ferment of *Waiting for Lefty* were, strictly considered, sentimental. Can one arrive at a contrary conclusion, especially after taking cognizance of the bracing irony and distanced objectivity of much transatlantic social drama, of which *The Weavers*, *The Vultures* (Becque's *Les Corbeaux*), *The Cherry Orchard*, *Heartbreak House*, *The Madwoman of Chaillot*, and *The Good Woman of Setzuan* are a few examples?

Another play revolving around a subject of concern to our historical consciousness is James N. Barker's *Superstition*, a drama of the year 1824 that anticipated Arthur Miller's *The Crucible* by some 130 years in treating Puritan repressiveness and witchcraft trials. Despite marked difference of styles, it cannot be said that the later work departed radically from Barker's early drama in a pitying concern with injured innocence and a patent employment of plot contrivance, especially in the melodramatic malice of a principal personage as the cause of the undoing of worthy characters. If *The Crucible* is undoubtedly the superior play, it is superior mainly in more sophisticated employment of sentiment (both plays, for example, make little, if any, incisive use of irony) and the very goal of tragedy is sentimentalized in both plays, though with theoretically commendable intentions, in Proctor's concern in *The Crucible* with his "name" as the issue that results in his heroically sacrificing his life. Both Barker's play of the year 1824 and Miller's of the year 1953 belong to the same mainstream of romanticism, a fact that would be quickly apparent from a comparison with Brecht's *Galileo*.

Comparisons such as those proposed in the preceding paragraphs need not be pursued further, however, because of one palpable fact. The plays in the present compilation, like many of the plays in the post-1915 *Best American Plays* series, are essentially manifestations of the same motivation to provide either "entertainment" or "thrills" for the workaday theatre. Theoretically, of course, there is much more window dressing of intellectuality and "art" in the later works, as in Maxwell Anderson's 1935 poetic tragedy *Winterset* by comparison with, say, Augustus Thomas's 1907 effective trial melodrama *The Witching Hour* (which has its own, but much less ostentatious, window dressing of amateur psychology); or, to take another example, in Anderson's poetic fantasy of the year 1936, *High Tor*, with its phantom Henrik Hudson crew, by comparison with, say, Joseph Jefferson's London and New York "hit" of the years 1865–1866 *Rip Van Winkle*. To our playgoing public of the 1930's, as well as subsequently, the difference was understandably enormous. But even so, the motive of trying to capitalize on as many showmanly effects as possible was substantially the same.

But even if it is possible to dissent somewhat from this generalization (Maxwell Anderson's motives in *Winterset* included righteous indignation over a miscarriage of justice and a resolve to write at all costs an exalting verse tragedy about an event of his own day), there can be no denying that the primary interest of American playwriting was generally opportunistic. The object in the nineteenth century was to supply stage pieces for actor-managers. Readers and potential producers of plays in the present volume would do well to think of them as commodities designed for the stage. By refraining from cerebral exercises of explication, we shall reap the reward of honesty. We shall look upon all but a few of the plays as artifacts, to be enjoyed as such. We shall then observe how they were contrived—by what means and to what degree of journeyman's success. We shall not measure the result by the factitious success of contemporary writers who have pretended to themselves that they were not serving Moloch. Most of the authors in the present volume harbored no such delusions.

This was not less the case when Boucicault contrived a melodrama on slavery in the South such as *The Octoroon* in 1859 than when the successful actor William Gillette fabricated the Civil War spy drama (called by a historian of the stage "Gillette's most significant play") *Secret Service* and

starred in it in 1896; or when the man of letters Washington Irving collaborated with the man of the theatre John Howard Payne (of "Home, Sweet Home" fame) in the writing of a typical nineteenth-century romantic pseudo-historical comedy, *Charles the Second*, in 1824, which held the stage for a long time with its blithe, compactly structured, intrigue. Rightly, the highest praise reserved for these stage pieces was well "constructed." Only by reading a play of deft artisanship devised solely for theatrical effect can a reader some seventy years later understand what critics of a vanished generation could have meant in commending a play such as *Secret Service* for "effortlessly achieved development" and "reality of characters."

Plays fashioned for standardized thrills of false accusation, imprisonment, escape, and long-nursed vengeance, such as the various dramatizations of Alexander Dumas's *The Count of Monte Cristo*, were obviously of ancient vintage by the time the actor Charles Fechter provided a version in 1883. As the basis of a vehicle for Eugene O'Neill's actor-manager father James, it still served to make the latter's fortune in the twentieth century.

Fechter was solely one of the "minions" of the theatre. William Dean Howells was certainly not one of these, and is remembered in histories of American literature as the author of early realistic novels such as *The Rise of Silas Lapham* (1885) and *A Hazard of New Fortunes* (1896), as well as the champion of the greater European realism that, as he put it, "feels in every nerve the equality of things and the unity of men." Yet his contribution to dramatic literature consisted chiefly of a series of short workaday "afterpieces," like *The Mouse-Trap* (1889), which belong solely to the theatre of "entertainment"; and if Howells was not actually adept at show business it was not for want of trying, but because he could not quite shake off his novelistic discursiveness. Howells registers a typical "pre-modern" nineteen-century split in sensibility that made it possible for him to hold elevated standards for fiction and critical writing while treating the theatre as "show business." He reflects the same schizoid attitude that made it possible for the more or less educated British public to throng to the lectures of a Carlyle and read the book-sized reviews of a Macaulay, not to mention the triple-decker galleons of Victorian fiction, and yet to expose themselves to Victorian farces and melodramas apparently without wincing.

Finally, confining ourselves to the plays collected here, we cannot acclaim a revolution in taste or attitude even in a relatively late play like *Salvation Nell* (1908), in which Edward Sheldon anticipated the background naturalism of O'Neill's *Anna Christie*. In *Salvation Nell* we are never far from the sentiment of moral reform or redemption from sin that still meant almost uniformly all departures from licensed connubial bliss and strict monogamy. As a Shavian literary critic once remarked, the Victorians had reduced the decalogue to a monologue, though there were writers and playgoers in the first decade of our century who weren't Victorians. And that leaves us with only one more play, Percy MacKaye's *The Scarecrow* (1911), to be accounted for here. Its merits have been frequently noted, even if it shows its period, especially in the optimism of its viewpoint (since love can turn even a scarecrow into a man!), and its "symbolist" style of theatre—which was soon to vanish, along with other noble esthetic and humanist causes, in the holocaust of World War I. In *The Scarecrow* the world of fancy is still well ordered, no matter how free the author's invention. It is soon to be supplanted by the anarchic and fragmented nightmare world of Expressionism presented in

our theatre of the 1920's by O'Neill's *The Emperor Jones* and *The Hairy Ape*.

THEATRE BEFORE 1916

Theatre in America produced no masterpieces, not even near masterpieces, of dramatic writing, but began to accumulate the multifarious elements that make up theatrical history as early as the second half of the seventeenth century. It became as eventful in the next century as one could expect in an expanding nation. It was a borrowed theatre for about a century, but an increasingly busy one in which unquestionably new native dramatic literature was greatly overshadowed by show business. And, operating without national or local subsidy throughout its history and well into our times, it could not be anything but show business for better or worse. Plays pirated from nineteenth-century Europe or adapted from European plays by authors working for not always scrupulous managements or actor-managers were simply regarded as common property. Shakespeare's masterpieces were usually treated merely as vehicles for a star actor to be taken on tour by him with or without supporting casts from Europe or the eastern seaboard.

Still, it is essential to realize that since present-day rival forms of entertainment such as movies and television were unavailable, the theatre was the one medium of communication, aside from public readings, concerts, and lectures, that could bring Americans even a modicum of culture above the level of acrobatics or, at most, minstrel shows. A play did not need to be homespun for this purpose; the performance of a foreign play, in fact, could be appreciated as one way of alleviating the playgoer's sense of cultural inferiority. Therefore European dramas drawn from history and romance were bound to be greatly in demand, and adapters had a ready call for their talents of patchwork accommodation. At the same time, there was considerable demand for writers, actors, and managers who could satisfy the opposite need to assert national pride by acclaiming native virtue; many a salvo was fired by them in honor of plain living, forthright speaking, unvarnished manliness, incorruptible womanliness, and innocent, though occasionally deluded, maidenliness. The patriotic theatre was no less popular when it contrasted New World probity with Old World parasitism, or the "Protestant ethic" of upright assiduity in the pursuit of wealth with Old World idleness and specious urbanity. While devious European elegance and American frontier vigor vied for the public interest, the theatre was a profitable business indeed, until the last decades of the nineteenth century.

After insignificant early attempts to write and stage plays following the return of Charles II to the English throne (we at least know the title of one play, William Darby's *Ye Bare and Ye Cubb* on view in Virginia in 1665), there is still little report about theatre in America until the second half of the eighteenth century. We have a political satire, *Androborus*, written in 1714 by the royal governor of the New York colony, Robert Hunter, and we have nothing else to report except occasional attempts to give public performances in Philadelphia (1723), in New York (George Farquhar's late Restoration comedy *The Recruiting Officer* at the New Theatre in 1732), and in Charleston, South Carolina (Thomas Otway's Restoration tragedy *The Orphan*, 1736). We know about the building of theatres in Williamsburg, Virginia, and elsewhere after 1716. We know something about the playing of a professional Walter Murray and Thomas Kean "Virginia" company in Philadelphia, New York, and Williamsburg in 1759. We know more about Lewis Hallam's "Company of Comedians" from London, which began an American tour with a production of *The Merchant of Venice* on September 15, 1752, and fell afoul of the colonial authorities, who looked upon playacting with a jaundiced eye. We know that the company disbanded in Jamaica, after Lewis Hallam's death there; that it was reassembled by the actor-manager David Douglass, who married Hallam's widow, and brought to New York; and that it opened in 1759 with Nicholas Rowe's historical drama *Jane Shore*, billed as a moral entertainment in order to satisfy the noble scruples of the city fathers.

David Douglass, who discreetly renamed his troupe the "American Company," became a mighty builder of theatres; and at one of these in Philadelphia, the Southwark Theatre, he presented, in 1767, the first American play to be produced by a professional company. It was Thomas Godfrey's "heroic tragedy" *The Prince of Parthia*, the first of a long line of American plays dealing with British history. But native American subjects were already exerting a parallel attraction. About a year before *The Prince of Parthia* production, the reading public had available to it a play about an Indian subject, *Ponteach; or The Savages of America*, attributed to a Major Robert Rogers.

Playwriting became polemical during the American Revolution, the pro-American view being sustained with particular perseverance by Mrs. Mercy Otis Warren in satirical farces, actually written by or attributed to her, such as *The Group* in 1775 and *The Blockheads* in 1776. In little more than a decade (in 1787), however, it was possible to produce sophisticated American comedy such as Royall Tyler's *The Contrast*, and in this sprightly work, acclaimed as the first professionally staged American comedy on an American subject, we encounter the British high-comedy or comedy-of-manners tradition that had reached its peak ten years before in Sheridan's *The School for Scandal*. Today we are unlikely to be impressed by the sentiments that moved "Candour," *The Daily Advertiser*'s drama critic, to applaud the American author as "a man of genius" and Tyler's sentiments as "the effusions of an honest patriot heart expressed with energy and eloquence." (It may be worth noting that several years later, in Boston, *The Contrast* was presented as "A Moral Lesson in Five Parts.") But the rest of the review can serve to remind us that the critical faculty was rather well developed, at least in New York in 1787. Standards of daily reviewing 180 years later would not appear to be more acute. But in 1787 a critic was still in the eighteenth century, when the romantic solvent of sentimentalism had not yet altogether dissolved the critical faculty.

After the five-day run of *The Contrast* in New York, the American theatre begins moving ahead quite rapidly with the enterprise of one unusual man, William Dunlap (1766–1839), who was not only the first American professional playwright (whereas Tyler, who inspired him to write his first play, was a lawyer) but also a theatrical manager who assumed control of the Old American Company in 1798. In the same year, after the opening of his new Park Theatre in New York, Dunlap produced his own adaptation of the inordinately popular German playwright Kotzebue's *The Stranger*. The signal success of this venture ("We think that no piece, since *The School for Scandal* has made so favorable an impression upon the public as this comedy," wrote *The Commercial Advertiser*) encouraged the author to make more depredations on Kotzebue's material; in a period of several seasons Dunlap presented no fewer than nineteen of this author's fabrications.

Nevertheless, he went bankrupt as a manager as a result of a series of mishaps, and closed the Park Theatre in 1805. He retired from theatre management altogether in 1812. In his other career, that of playwriting, he was virtually indefatigable and notably resourceful, writing native plays in numerous genres ranging from farce to tragedy, and proving himself especially adept in adapting melodramas by Pixérécourt and other popular French playwrights. Some of his original plays, especially his historical drama *André* (1798), which deals with the execution of Major André as a British spy during the American Revolutionary War, are still remembered by students of the American stage. When Dunlap came to publish his *History of the American Theatre* in 1832, no one writing in America had a better claim to being an authority on the subject and to having obtained a good deal of his information at first hand; his book was inevitably a personal history.

There seems to be no doubt that by the beginning of the new century the theatre, particularly at the "Park" in New York, could count on a fairly loyal following, a fact for which Dunlap was mostly responsible. Washington Irving, the first eminent American professional essayist, reviewing for *The Morning Chronicle* under the nom de plume "Jonathan Oldstyle," reflected a growing taste when he wrote in 1801: "There is no place of public amusement of which I am so fond as the theatre. . . . I find there is no play, however poor or ridiculous, from which I cannot derive some entertainment." And that crudity is urbanely conveyed by Irving when he reports, for example, that at a performance of a piece called *The Battle of Hexham; or Days of Old* the Queen appeared at the rise of the curtain, followed by a courtier, and that they "talked for some time" so unintelligibly that he could not understand the drift of their discourse. Later on, when he saw some banditti carousing and singing an inelegant song, he learned "that there had been, or was, or would be, a battle," and then observed the wife of the captain of the banditti "looking for her errant husband and being reunited with him at the fall of the curtain." Curtains gave the reviewer some trouble, it would seem, and "Jonathan Oldstyle" expressed the wish that the management would use "a *drop* scene at the close of the acts" so that one would be able to ascertain the termination of the play "by the green curtain." At the performance of this piece, he was "indebted to the polite bows of the actors for this pleasing information."

Jonathan Oldstyle's comments on the audience are also anything but complimentary. He indicates that the shortcomings of the performances were apt to be made up by the liveliness of the gallery in the customary manner of imitations of "the whistles and yells of every kind of animal" (a compensation for "the want of music" in the performance, "as the gentlemen of our orchestra are very economic of their favours"), and a barrage of apples, nuts, and gingerbreads aimed at the heads of the honest people in the pit of the theatre. There were also other distractions for the friends of the theatre, such as the dripping of the candle grease from the chandelier on the clothes of occupants of the pit, and a host of strapping fellows standing with their dirty boots on the seats of the benches until at the ringing of a bell for the second time to signalize the beginning of the play they were called to order with cries of "Down, down—hats off."

Irving's recommendations to the theatre in New York, printed the year before, had not been heeded by 1801, and they were not to be for many years, although he had worded them tersely enough:

To the actors—less etiquette, less fustian, less buckram.

To the orchestra—new music, and more of it.

To the pit—patience, clear benches, and *umbrellas.*

To the boxes—less affectation, less noise, less coxcombs.

To the gallery—less grog, and *better constables;*—and

To the whole house, inside and out, a total reformation.

"And so much for the Theatre," he concluded, while refraining from making recommendations concerning the plays themselves—perhaps out of charity and possibly out of hopelessness.

All this did not dissuade the public from giving growing support to the stage. A powerful stimulus to playgoing was the invasion of the New World by actors from the Old World ever since the arrival of the Hallam Company, even though it was still possible in the early nineteenth century in New York for a young lady, the daughter of a Presbyterian churchman, to be severely penalized for attending a performance at the Park Theatre. Her own father pronounced the sentence the following Sunday: "Eliza Spring, having recently visited one of those profane and sinful places of carnal recreation, commonly called theatres, is hereby cut off from the communion of the Church of Christ."

Theatres in New York, Boston, New Haven, and Philadelphia found support among the wealthy citizens and the ladies eager to display their charms from the lower tiers of the boxes. A circuit system enlarged the playgoing public by touring plays in other cities of the eastern seaboard, such as Providence, Newport, Baltimore, and Washington. In the fall of 1810 came the historically important visit of George Frederick Cooke of the Drury Lane Theatre, which had been arranged by the actor Thomas Abthorpe Cooper, who had assumed the management of the Park Theatre, and by Stephen Price, who had become co-manager in 1808. Exceedingly temperamental and alcoholic, the great Cooke engaged for the season of 1810–1811 at a salary of $14,000 (plus three benefit nights), played in the United States for two years, often with success between bouts with the bottle.

After the War of 1812, Stephen Price brought more actors from England to revive the failing fortunes of the Park Theatre once more. An important visit was that of the handsome and versatile twenty-five-year-old James William Wallack, who made his American debut in 1818 in *Macbeth*. Wallack settled permanently in New York and became one of America's leading actor-managers during a career on the stage that lasted over forty years. Another memorable visit was that of England's most gifted romantic actor, Edmund Kean, who opened his American tour in the fall of 1820 with *Richard III*, followed by *Hamlet* and *Othello*, giving some of the explosive performances that made Coleridge say that watching Kean was like reading Shakespeare by flashes of lightning.

In October, 1821, the rebuilt Park Theatre opened with the New York debut of the erratic Drury Lane and Covent Garden actor Junius Brutus Booth, the father of Edwin and John Wilkes Booth. About a year later, the Park company was augmented by a visit of the British star actor Charles Mathews, who won great success in New York and on tour in 1822–1823, chiefly with his talent for comedy (inevitably he played Falstaff in *Henry IV*). Other English actors to visit the United States were Edmund Kean's son Charles, in 1831; Charles Kemble and his daughter, the lovely Fanny Kemble, who proved a sensation at the Park Theatre; and William Charles Macready, the distinguished tragedian known for his performances as *Richard III*, *Coriolanus*, and *Hamlet*, who first acted in the United States in 1826–1827

and whose return engagement in 1849, after his unfortunate rivalry with the American star Edwin Forrest, was punctuated on May 10 by the sanguinary Astor Place Riot in New York. (See Richard Moody's excellent book *The Astor Place Riot*, Indiana University Press, 1958.)

By then, the American stage had also acquired noteworthy native actors such as John Howard Payne, who was also notable as a playwright; James H. Hackett, and George Handel Hill, who impersonated Yankee characters; Edwin Forrest, who after his New York debut in 1826 achieved great popularity with his forceful acting in heroic roles; Charlotte Cushman, who made her New York debut in 1836 as Lady Macbeth; and the Philadelphia-born Joseph Jefferson, best known for his playing of the title-character Rip in a dramatization of Washington Irving's tale *Rip Van Winkle*. Native or foreign born, these celebrated performers represented the star system in its palmiest decades. Its chief contribution to the country's theatre consisted of attracting audiences with widely publicized personalities. Its disadvantages lay in its neglect of the production as a whole, careless casting of secondary roles, indifference to the development of good supporting actors, and insufficient rehearsal time. The star system, of course, made ensemble playing wholly impossible.

By the middle of the century a reaction was overdue. It resulted in the rise of resident companies in various cities; and their experienced actors, who were used to playing together and meshing their talents, could play without a star on tour or could give him valuable support whenever he was available. Several managers, most notably James William Wallack, launched resident companies in New York, and a famous one known as the Wallack Company, performing at Wallack's Theatre, had a long career from 1852 to 1887 under him and later under his actor-son Lester Wallack. The son was joined at one time or another by such celebrities as Rose Coghlan, Charles Coghlan, E. H. Sothern, and Maurice Barrymore (1848–1905), the Cambridge-educated British father of Lionel, Ethel, and John Barrymore.

In the midst of all theatrical activity (to which one must add such folksy showmanship as showboat performances started by William Chapman on the Ohio and Mississippi rivers in 1831 and minstrel shows or blackface acts which came into vogue in the 1840's), the playwrights, inadequately paid and unprotected by copyright laws, fared poorly. But they compensated with assiduity for what they lacked in status and, often, in talent. It is impossible to know where to begin and where to stop in summarizing their ceaseless activity, and even a partial list of their original plays, translations, and adaptations would make a fulsome chronicle.

Many plays amounted to little more than dramatized journalism, often weighed down with romantic embroidery in treatments of the American Revolution and later wars. Many dealt with the remoter past. Among these were James Nelson Barker's *Superstition* in 1824 and Cornelius Matthews' *Witchcraft, or The Martyrs of Salem* in 1848, both set in colonial times. Romantic matter decked out in blank verse multiplied considerably, culminating in the best literary play, George Henry Boker's tragedy *Francesca da Rimini*, in 1855. Some playwrights wrote both tragedy and comedy in verse, notably John Howard Payne (1791–1852), who succeeded in 1818 with his tragic *Brutus; or The Fall of Tarquin* and his comic venture in collaboration with Washington Irving six years later, *Charles the Second*. One of the best comedies, and one with Shakespearian rather than Restoration overtones, was Nathaniel Parker Willis's *Tortesa the Usurer* (1839),

rather extravagantly praised by Edgar Allan Poe in a magazine article for its "naturalness, truthfullness, appropriateness upon all occasions of sentiment and language; a manly vigor and breath in the conception of character." And, six years later, in 1845, came Anna Cora Mowatt's *Fashion; or, Life in New York*, the outstanding early American comedy of manners.

An assiduous romantic writer for the stage was Robert Montgomery Bird (1806–1854), whose most highly regarded pieces, both winners of play contests sponsored by the actor-manager Edwin Forrest, are his tragedies *The Gladiator* (1831), a salute to Spartacus and freedom, and *The Broker of Bogota* (1834), a melodramatic treatment of tensions between a righteous father and a dissolute, rebellious son. And the theatrical marketplace was virtually glutted with a variety of plays on American types of character, most notably the Yankee, a homespun but shrewd character who played major or minor roles under such names as Jonathan Postfree, Jonathan Ploughboy, Solon Shingle, Lot Sap Sago, and Deuteronomy Dutiful in numerous undistinguished plays such as *Jonathan Postfree; or, The Honest Yankee* (1807), *The First Rose; or, American Farmers* (1825), *The People's Lawyer* (1839), *Yankee Land* (circa 1835), and *The Vermont Wool Dealer* (1840). Other generic types also figured in plays of local color and history, especially the noble Indian in James Nelson Barker and George Washington Parke Curtis's Pocahontas plays respectively titled *The Indian Princess* (1808) and *Pocahontas; or, The Settlers of Virginia* (1830) and in John Augustus Stone's prize-winning tragedy of romantic bombast *Metamora; or, The Last of the Wampanoags* (1892) in which Edwin Forrest, the donor of the $500 prize, performed profitably for some thirty-five years.

Reflecting national trends, too,

were plays dealing with early waves of immigration and extracting ethnic humor from the immigrant Irish and German; with the opening up of the West, the gold rush, and the westward trek of the Mormons in the years 1846–1848; and with the growth of the temperance movement, which began in Boston in the 1820's and came to be remembered in the theatre for two lugubrious plays culminating in the reform of their alcoholic principals, later revived only to be travestied— namely, W. H. Smith's *The Drunkard; or, The Fallen Saved* (1844) and William W. Pratt's *Ten Nights in a Bar Room* (1858). And the great issue of Negro slavery was also an inevitable subject for the stage after 1850, most notably in Boucicault's melodrama *The Octoroon; or, Life in Louisiana* (1859) and the dramatization of Harriet Beecher Stowe's antislavery novel *Uncle Tom's Cabin*, by George L. Aiken, first presented at Troy, New York, in September, 1852.

The most significant phase of American theatrical history began with the consequences of the antislavery agitation reflected in these productions. A new, or "new-old," era began with the Civil War, and presumably came to an end with the First World War in 1914–1918. After the Civil War we find ourselves on familiar dramatic terrain, the well trodden one of alleged realism, and can no longer suspend judgment or mollify criticism by making an antiquarian's allowance for something rather quaint in content or style. As for the drama's leanings toward realism in matter or manner, our American playwrights run up against the formidably high standards of late-nineteenth- and early-twentieth-century dramatists such as Ibsen, Strindberg, Shaw, and Chekhov. As a result, we are perhaps still most at ease with plays to which we cannot even remotely presume to apply such standards, such as the

various dramatic versions of *The Count of Monte Cristo* or plays such as *The Witching Hour* from which we can banish high standards of realism on the grounds that melodramatic or farcical intentions alone have any bearing on whatever merits can be found in the work.

In both play production and playwriting some achievements in realism were nevertheless fairly new in their time and place. In stage production realistic scenery actually reached formidable degrees of verisimilitude. Numerous sensational events were presented on the stage, and spectacles later considered the provenance of the Hollywood celluloid industry became familiar in the theatre. They reached their zenith in the reign of David Belasco (1859–1931), who allowed nothing to stand in the way of his resolve to astonish audiences with his virtuosity as a producer and stage director. In his production of *The Governor's Lady*, he duplicated a Child's restaurant on the stage; and he bought a setting directly from a cheap boardinghouse and set it up intact for his production of Eugene Walter's *The Easiest Way*, so great was his devotion to literal realism, which he transformed into a cult like almost anything else he displayed in the theatre. George Jean Nathan, the stormy petrel of dramatic criticism, wrote in 1917, "—by way of bequeathing to himself an air of aloof austerity and monastic meditation, he discarded the ordinary habiliments of commerce and by the simple device of turning his collar hind end foremost, made of himself a sort of Broadway Rasputin."

But Belasco was only one of a large number of actors, actor-managers, playwright-managers, or simply managers who sustained a busy, often profitable, and occasionally—alas, *very* occasionally—significant enterprise. Steele MacKaye (1842–1894) was particularly noteworthy for his technical innovations. This theatre manager and stage director, who had begun by studying art and theatre in Paris, promoted such innovations as a device for overhead lighting and an elevator stage for changing scenes efficiently. More successful and influential was the Brooklyn-born Augustin Daly, the subject of much interest to theatre historians and of an excellent scholarly study, Marvin Felheim's *The Theater of Augustin Daly*. As Mr. Felheim's Preface states "One will find that the the only dates of importance in Augustin Daly's life which were not directly connected with the theatre were his birth in 1838 and the death of his two sons in 1885"; and perhaps one should add, his *own* death in 1899, but for the fact that just before he died on June 7 in Paris he was actually engaged "on business connected with the lease of his London theatre."

Starting as a dramatic critic for New York newspapers, he moved into the field of playwriting, in long concealed collaboration with his jurist-brother Joseph, winning much success with the melodrama *Under the Gaslight* in 1867 and with other adaptations (about 90 of these) from French and German plays beginning in 1862 with *Leah the Forsaken*, a sentimental play about the persecution of the Jews in an eighteenth-century Austrian village. One of his most impressive adaptations was from the Sarah Bernhardt Paris success *Frou-Frou* by Henri Meilhac and Ludovic Halévy.

But it was as a producer and director that Augustin Daly made the greatest dent in the theatre, and this not merely with the variety of his productions but with his large reliance on realism in stagecraft and scenic effect. He opened his first theatre, the Fifth Avenue, in 1869, and then a few years later "Daly's," where he developed a famous stock company in which he starred such celebrated performers as Ada Rehan, Clara Morris, Fanny Davenport, and John Drew. He even took his company to London and displayed its prowess with considerable success in another Daly's theatre, which he opened there in 1893.

The American theatre, lacking subsidy and an institutional basis, continued to be a complex of private managements dependent upon the aims and ambitions of individuals like Daly. Among these was his namesake Arnold Daly (1875–1927), the actor and producer best known for introducing the American public to early Shaw plays such as *Candida*, *Mrs. Warren's Profession*, and *You Never Can Tell*. Another was Richard Mansfield (1857–1907), who came to the United States at the age of twenty-five as an actor. He starred in *Cyrano de Bergerac*, introduced Shaw to the public with his production of *Arms and the Man* in 1894, and gave him his first financial success in both England or America by touring *The Devil's Disciple*. He also presented the first professional production of *Peer Gynt* in English. Clyde Fitch wrote *Beau Brummel* for him, and Mansfield wrote several plays himself.

Minnie Maddern Fiske (1865–1932), who started as a child actress and worked herself up to soubrette and ingenue roles with great success, became a force in the American theatre after her marriage to the editor, playwright, and dramatic critic Harrison Grey Fiske. Often under his management but actually as his co-producer, and as an actress famous for her realistic acting, she served the theatre creditably in productions of a dramatization of Thomas Hardy's novel *Tess of the D'Urbervilles*, Hauptmann's *Hannele* (with Schnitzler's *The Green Cockatoo* serving as curtain raiser), and Ibsen's *The Pillars of Society, Ghosts, Rosmersholm*, and *Hedda Gabler*. She also did well by American playwrights who exhibited any sort of literary or dramatic distinction, notably in producing and appearing in Langdon Mitchell's comedy *The New York Idea* (1906) and Edward Sheldon's "lower depths" drama *Salvation Nell* (1908), although she is perhaps remembered simply as America's leading producer-actress until the advent of Eva Le Gallienne as the producer-actress of the New York Civic Repertory Theatre in 1926. (A good study of her career is Archie Binns's *Mrs. Fiske, and the American Theatre*, Crown Publishers, New York, 1955.)

There were many other entrepreneurs of the stage who contributed to the entertainment of the nation. Mention must be made of at least a few of them. One of the outstanding managers was Albert M. Palmer (1838–1905), who, as manager of the Union Square Theatre in New York from 1872 to 1883, presented such star performers as Clara Morris and Richard Mansfield and the plays of such prominent nineteenth-century American playwrights as William Gillette, Steele MacKaye, and Augustus Thomas. Daniel Frohman (1851–1940) and his brother Charles (1860–1915), who went down with the *Lusitania* in the famous sea disaster, were indefatigable managers. The former took control of the Lyceum Theatre of New York in 1887. In 1890, the latter started the Charles Frohman Stock Company, which occupied the Empire Theatre with distinction. The brothers, producing plays separately or in partnership, starred such well known performers as Maude Adams, Ethel Barrymore, Otis Skinner, Margaret Anglin, Henry Miller, William Faversham, James K. Hackett, Effie Shannon, Henrietta Crossman, and May Robson.

The Harvard-educated Winthrop Ames (1871–1937), who left the publishing business to take over the Castle Square Opera House of Boston in 1904 and four years later became the managing director of the New Theatre and the Booth Theatre in New York, deserves to be cited for productions of Shakespeare and modern dramas

well into the 1920's. William Brady (1863–1950), now best remembered for his production of Elmer Rice's realistic slum-tenement drama *Street Scene* in 1929, started acting in San Francisco, built and managed theatres, and presented English and American plays in forthright fashion with great success. Arthur Hopkins (1878–1950) began producing in 1912 with the mildly expressionistic drama *Poor Little Rich Girl* by Eleanor Gates, and went on to present some of the most avant-garde productions of the 1910's and 1920's, such as Elmer Rice's *On Trial* (the first successful play employing the cinematic flashback method of play construction), Tolstoy's *Redemption* (under the title of *The Living Corpse*) with John Barrymore in the leading part, *Macbeth* (with Robert Edmond Jones's symbolist settings), and O'Neill's *The Hairy Ape*. And the roster of managers must, of course, include the "Shuberts"—J. J. and Lee Shubert—who created a vast empire of theatres and directly or indirectly produced numerous plays.

Virtually up to the advent of O'Neill and the spread of the avant-garde groups associated with it, there could be no doubt that we had an actors' and actor-managers' theatre in America, which was substantially also the case in England right up to the Edwardian age of George Alexander, Beerbohm Tree, and Forbes-Robertson. As a *Times Literary Supplement* article (December 22, 1950) put it, it is necessary to recognize the fact "that there is not only an art of the drama, there is also an art of the stage" (it is also an unfortunate fact that the two arts don't always agree), and the author of the article made a point that could just as well have been made concerning American show business: "In the Edwardian theatre, audiences were agog for something contributed by the actor over and above the author's contribution of his imagined character, and the actor-managers did their best to give it to them." In the latter part of the nineteenth century, moreover, even playwrights could not but realize that their texts were secondary not only to the art of the performer but also to the production effects or spectacularity the growing technical facilities of the age were making possible. A practical playwright such as Boucicault, who had started to exploit local color in his native Ireland and continued to do so in the United States, which became the country of his adoption, exerted himself to supply a "big" production scene in every play. The melodramas that proved most profitable owed their attractiveness not merely to suspenseful situations but also to the visual effects associated with them. The classic example is the Augustin Daly production *Under the Gaslight* (1867), in which the virtuous heroine pursued by a villain she has been resisting for some time sees her protector tied to the railroad tracks and rescues him from certain death just in time. It was from the nineteenth-century melodramas, fantasies, and pantomimes or panoramas that the general public derived its taste for the early motion pictures as developed between 1895 and 1925 by the cinema pioneers E. S. Porter and D. W. Griffith, who evolved their techniques in part from the new staging devices of the nineteenth century. (See *Stage to Screen*, by A. H. Nicholas Vardac, Harvard University Press, 1949.)

A "playwright's theatre," in which the drama itself was to be the primary interest, had yet to be born. The playwright was fortunate when he was the recipient of benefactions from a popular actor-manager such as Edwin Forrest above and beyond the fee to which he was legally entitled, since he normally sold all rights to his plays for a lump sum. Nevertheless, there were developments in the American drama itself; and while these cannot really be reduced to a single line of ascent, a variety of tendencies became apparent after 1850.

Thus, the regional life of the country began to find expression beyond the mere exploitation of the "stage Yankee," and this tendency continued to be operative even in the 1920's and 1930's in Paul Green's plays of the South, Sidney Howard's local-color dramas associated with several regions (California in *They Knew What They Wanted*, Maine in *Ned McCobb's Daughter*, the Midwest in *Alien Corn*, and New York in *Lucky Sam McCarver*), and Owen Davis (New England in *Icebound* and, with his son Donald, *Ethan Frome*). Outstanding in the late nineteenth century are the actor-producer-playwright James A. Herne's New England plays, such as his collaboration with David Belasco *Hearts of Oak* (1879), *Sag Harbor* (1899), and, above all, *Shore Acres* (1892), a melodrama rich in local color and dialect. An example is Uncle Nat's sympathetic speech to his niece when she tells him her father doesn't want to catch her speaking to the young man she fancies: "You musn't let'm ketch yeh. (*Chuckling*) Law sakes, ef I couldn't spark a fellah athout my father ketchin' me at it, I'd bag my head." *The Old Homestead* (1886) by Denman Thompson was another popular New England drama, unfortunately outdated by its sentimentality.

The expanding West was an even more abundant source of local realism as well as romanticism. Frank Murdock's *Davy Crockett* (1872) dealt with one of the favorite backwoods heroes of American history and legend, who continued to provide some impetus to American playwriting as late as the 1930's and 1940's. He reappeared in H. R. Hayes's *The Ballad of Davy Crockett*, produced by the Federal Theatre, and Edwin Justus Mayer's *Sunrise in My Pocket*, a beautifully written paean to the American democratic ideal produced by Margo Jones in her Dallas arena-theatre. Augustus Thomas successfully represented life in the Midwest with *In Mizzoura* (1893) and the Far West with *Arizona* (1899). One especially successful play of the Far West, David Belasco's *The Girl of the Golden West* (1905), revolving around the devotion of a plucky girl for a highwayman, even crossed the Atlantic to become the opera by Puccini.

Because southern authors were drawn to Civil War romanticism and because the Negro they liked to depict remained a stereotyped character, the Deep South was less realistically portrayed until the 1920's and 1930's when the one-act plays of Paul Green and long plays by him, such as *In Abraham's Bosom* and *The House of Connelly*, began to give that region dramatic importance. City life, and especially the world of the immigrant and various ethnic groups, whether native or foreign-born, also contributed local color to the stage. This world has been dramatically productive ever since the "Mulligan Guard" farces of Irish immigrant life produced by Edward Harrigan and Tony Hart in the 1870's. That the subject was not exhausted even in the mid-1960's was made gratifyingly evident by the success of William Alfred's drama *Hogan's Goat*, revolving around political careers among the Irish in late-nineteenth-century Brooklyn. This play appeared in New York a full thirty years after Bronx Jewish life supplied the texture of Clifford Odets' social drama *Awake and Sing!* in 1935.

Another important development, in fact, produced dramas of social transition, problems, and conflicts that took the theatre beyond merely descriptive realism of localities, as in regional drama, and beyond general descriptions of characters and manners as found in the plays of social relations by William Dean Howells and Henry James. Realism of character was combined with "drama of ideas" by James A. Herne (1839–1901) in his most important play, *Margaret Fleming* (1890). Although the play, at least in the memorially reconstructed version available to us, is a pallid piece of realism by comparison with the work of Ibsen and other turn-of-the-century European playwrights, it was found unacceptable by average critical standards in America, and the few who favored the play spoke but vaguely of its "truth to life." In matters of morality, somewhat challenged by Herne when he made his heroine Margaret accept an illegitimate baby fathered by her weak-willed husband (whom she even "forgives"), there wasn't much else to be expected from the American stage even in the 1890's. Perhaps the most forceful review of the work was written from a conservative point of view by the critic Edward A. Dithmar for the *New York Times* (December 10, 1891). He complained that the play was "the quintessence of the commonplace"; that its language was "the colloquial English of the shops and streets and the kitchen fire-place"; and that its characters were "the everyday nonentities that some folks like to forget when they go to the theatre." He concluded that "the stage would be a stupid and useless thing if such plays as *Margaret Fleming* were to prevail." It did not "prevail," but its realism of detail, including a movement on Margaret's part to give suck to the illegitimate baby, soon became familiar enough in the American theatre to be commonplace.

The drama of social tension and conflict carried that theatre further into the modern world, though with less than remarkable results in artistry or intellectual stimulation. In 1899, Herne himself provided one of these works, *The Reverend Griffith Davenport*, the drama of a liberal clergyman in the South who opposes slavery; but we have only one act left of this play, apparently the first nonromantic Civil

War treatment. Steele MacKaye provided one social drama in 1887, *Paul Kauvar, or Anarchy*, sympathetic to the radicals who had been condemned the year before as the instigators of the "Haymarket Riot" in Chicago. (The subject was still considered alive in the late 1930's, and yielded a spirited verse drama by the young poet Norman Rosten, written under the supervision of Professor Kenneth Rowe at the University of Michigan.)

Social drama began to be written with considerable emphasis on economic realities by Bronson Howard (1842–1908), whose popular success was the romantic Civil War melodrama *Shenandoah*. Business life was combined with social comedy in Howard's most distinguished pieces, *Young Mrs. Winthrop* (1882) and *The Henrietta* (1887), a somewhat satirical treatment of financial rivalries. Monopolistic practices and financial manipulations became a target, and Charles Klein's *The Lion and the Mouse* aroused interest in 1905 with a treatment of the subject. The rising conflicts of capital and labor became the theme of a number of treatments sympathetic to the underdog. *Baron Rudolf* (1881) was an early treatment by Bronson Howard; Augustus Thomas provided one, *The New Blood*, in 1894; and in 1911 Edward Sheldon wrote the best known social drama before the 1920's, *The Boss*. Political corruption was another popular turn-of-the-century theme; Charles Klein dealt with it not only in *The Lion and the Mouse* but also in *The District Attorney* (1895), and toward the end of the next decade Clyde Fitch treated it with some vigor in *The City* (1909) before arriving at a sentimental happy ending. The Negro racial problem began to be confronted with the Herne drama *The Reverend Griffith Davenport* and, ten years later, with Edward Sheldon's *The Nigger* (1909), in which a candidate for the governorship of a southern state discovers that he has Negro blood in his veins and resolves to make his Negro descent public.

The genre we call social drama was to have a respectable future in our theatre. It acquired sophistication in the 1920's, and dramatic as well as ideological militancy in the depression period of the 1930's. The sophistication was apparent not only in the choice of subject matter but in more or less expressionistic stylization. It was employed satirically in Elmer Rice's *The Adding Machine*, Kaufman and Connelly's *Beggar on Horseback*, and John Howard Lawson's *Processional;* and seriously in O'Neill's *The Hairy Ape*, Lawson's semi-Freudian *Roger Bloomer*, and Sophie Treadwell's treatment of the much publicized Ruth Snyder murder trial in *Machinal*. The militancy mounted, along with sociology and social comedy, in the early pieces of Clifford Odets, starting with *Waiting for Lefty* in 1935, and in plays by Sidney Kingsley, Irwin Shaw, Lillian Hellman, S. N. Behrman, Robert Sherwood, Maxwell Anderson, Elmer Rice, and others.

In the forty-year period between 1880 and 1920, social drama was still a feeble plant, ill-nourished by the authors' sentimentality and timidity, as well as by the narrow compass of their ideas and imagination. Only in the limited area of social comedy did the modern orientation proceed with some zest and with theatrical and, at times, even literary skill. Here it is possible to cite some Clyde Fitch comedies, especially the melodramatic yet also satirical picture of New York "society" *The Climbers* (1901), *The Girl with the Green Eyes* (1902), and *The Truth* (1907). The culmination of these exercises in acute observation and conversational vivacity is generally considered to be *The New York Idea* (1906), Langdon Mitchell's bright comedy of divorce and marriage.

But just as early social drama

continued to be overshadowed by melodrama, so the genre of high comedy was subordinated to farce. It remains to be noted only that the results were not always dreadful once the validity of this popular genre of entertainment is granted. Not all American melodrama is as trashy as *East Lynne*, the notorious dramatization of the Mrs. Henry Wood novel in 1863. Not all were dependent on the spectacularity of the scenery and stage action, as in the case of the William Young 1899 dramatization of the Lew Wallace historical novel *Ben Hur*, which stunned its audiences with a hair-raising chariot race staged on treadmills. Boucicault's Civil War spy play *Belle Lamar* (1874), like Gillette's *Secret Service*, had dramatic verve, as did later Elmer Rice's *On Trial* (1914), Bayard Veiller's crime-detection play *Within the Law* (1912), and George M. Cohan's farce-melodrama *Seven Keys to Baldpate* (1913). Not all the farces were shopworn from the start, a fact that cannot surprise French admirers of Feydeau and Labiche or, for that matter, anyone who realizes that the nineteenth century was the golden age of farce as well as melodrama in England and on the European Continent. The last decades of the century in the American theatre were replete with well contrived farces such as William Gillette's busy *Too Much Johnson* and Charles Hoyt's farce-satire *A Texas Steer*, aptly subtitled "Money Makes the Mare Go" (1890). The early decades of the next century were not poorer in farce so long as they had stage pieces such as Byron Ongley's *Brewster's Millions* (1906) and George M. Cohan's *Broadway Jones* (1912), not to mention

the George S. Kaufman collaborations of the early 1920's.

Whatever may be said against these popular types of dramatic entertainment, to which we were soon to add the American musical and musical comedies (anticipated in 1866 by *The Black Crook*) that supplanted Central European operetta, we rarely found viable alternatives in the art of poetic drama often proposed by literary-minded critics and teachers. After Boker's *Francesca da Rimini* in 1855, nothing particularly distinguished in verse or poetic prose appeared on the American stage as a practical piece of playwriting with the exception of Josephine Peabody's mild enough symbolist literary effort, *The Piper* (1910), Belasco's fantasy *The Return of Peter Grimm* (1911), and most notably Percy MacKaye's *The Scarecrow* (1908). The only alternatives to melodrama and farce were the earlier mentioned comedies of manners and social drama and some high-minded realistic plays by William Vaughn Moody and Edward Sheldon, notably the former's *The Great Divide* and *The Faith Healer* and the latter's *Salvation Nell*, to some extent an anticipation in 1908 of O'Neill's brand of romantic realism in *Anna Christie*.

We simply cannot escape the conclusion that genuinely modern drama, which had begun in continental Europe in the 1860's with Ibsen's *Brand* and *Peer Gynt* and in England in the 1890's with Bernard Shaw's early plays, had barely started on the American stage before the arrival of Eugene O'Neill's first major dramas, *Beyond the Horizon* and *Anna Christie*.

THE PLAYS AND THEIR AUTHORS

THE CONTRAST

THE BOSTON-BORN, HARVARD-EDUCATED ROYALL TYLER (1757–1826), who also received a degree from Yale in 1777, would have been a man of some distinction even if he had never written a single play. He became a major in the Continental Army and was aide-de-camp to General Benjamin Lincoln during the Shays' Rebellion. He joined the bar in 1780, served between 1807 and 1813 as a Chief Justice of the Supreme Court of the State of Vermont, and taught at the University of Vermont from 1811 to 1814 as Professor of Jurisprudence. But on going to New York on official business in 1787, he developed an interest in the early American stage there, and wrote *The Contrast* for performance by the American Company under the management of Lewis Hallam and John Henry at the John Street Theatre, and thus became the author of the first American comedy dealing with native characters to be performed by professional actors. The play, in which the popular comic part of Jonathan was played by the company's leading low comedian, Thomas Wignell, was successful enough to be played several times again in New York and to be performed subsequently in other American cities. It has continued to attract production, and was presented in the 1950's on television by the Ford Foundation Radio and TV Workshop's "Omnibus" program.

A month after the premiere, Tyler had another production in New York, the comic opera *May-Day in Town; or, New York in an Uproar*, also at the John Street Theatre, and in 1797 he had a satire on land speculation, *A Georgia Spec; or, Land in the Moon*, on the boards, first in Boston and then in New York. (Neither play has survived.) Tyler wrote a number of other plays, three on Biblical themes, and a fourth, a satire based on Don Quixote. But only *The Contrast* has continued to attest the talent of its author; and the success of the rustic dialect-speaking servant Jonathan began the vogue of the so-called homespun "Yankee" stock character or "stage Yankee" in the American theatre to which many plays were devoted. An excellent book has been written on this subject by Francis Hodge of the University of Texas, *Yankee Theatre: The Image of America on the Stage: 1825–1850* (University of Texas Press, Austin, Texas, 1964).

The following comments on *The Contrast* appeared in the critic "Candour's" review of the play on April 18, 1787, in *The Daily Advertiser* of New York, indicating the development of some critical alertness in the theatrical capital of the young republic:

> The characters are drawn with spirit, particularly Charlotte's; the dialogue is easy, sprightly, and often witty, but wants the pruning knife very much. The author has made frequent use of soliloquies, but I must own, I think, injudiciously; Maria's song and her reflections after it are pretty, but certainly misplaced. Soliloquies are seldom so conducted as not to wound probability. If we ever talk to ourselves, it is when the mind is much engaged in some very interesting subject, and never to make calm reflections on indifferent things. . . . Colonel Manly's advice to America, tho' excellent is yet liable to the same

blame, and perhaps greater. A man can never be supposed to be in conversation with himself, to point out examples of imitation to his countrymen. . . .

A Prologue spoken by Thomas Wignell, and written, it was announced, by "a Young Gentleman of New York" (could it have been the author himself, who modestly had himself listed as merely "A Citizen of the United States" on the title page of the published play?), expresses the same national self-consciousness that *The Daily Advertiser*'s review does:

> EXULT each patriot heart!—this night is shewn
> A piece, which we may fairly call our own;
> Where the proud titles of "My Lord! Your Grace!"
> To humble Mr. and plain Sir give place.
> Our Author pictures not from foreign climes
> The fashions, or the follies of the times;
> But has confin'd the subject of his work
> To the gay scenes—the circles of New-York.
> On native themes his Muse displays her pow'rs;
> If ours the faults, the virtues too are ours.
> Why should our thoughts to distant countries roam,
> When each refinement may be found at home?
> Who travels now to ape the rich or great,
> To deck an equipage and roll in state;
> To court the graces, or to dance with ease,
> Or by hypocrisy to strive to please?
> Our free-born ancestors such arts despis'd;
> Genuine sincerity alone they priz'd;
> Their minds, with honest emulation fir'd,
> To solid good—not ornament—aspir'd;
> Or, if ambition rous'd a bolder flame,
> Stern virtue throve, where indolence was shame.
>
> But modern youths, with imitative sense,
> Deem taste in dress the proof of excellence;
> And spurn the meanness of your homespun arts,
> Since homespun habits would obscure their parts;
> Whilst all, which aims at splendour and parade,
> Must come from Europe, and be ready made.
> Strange! we should thus our native worth disclaim,
> And check the progress of our rising fame.
> Yet once, whilst imitation bears the sway,
> Aspires to nobler heights, and points the way,
> Be rous'd, my friends! his bold example view;
> Let your own Bards be proud to copy you!
> Should rigid critics reprobate our play,
> At least the patriotic heart will say,
> "Glorious our fall, since in a noble cause.
> "The bold attempt alone demands applause."
> Still may the wisdom of the Comic Muse
> Exalt your merits, or your faults accuse.

SUPERSTITION

THE PHILADELPHIA-BORN JAMES NELSON BARKER (1784–1858), five of whose ten plays survived from the early 19th century, was a poet, dramatist, and public figure. He distinguished himself in the War of 1812, in which he became a captain of an artillery regiment. He was elected Mayor of Philadelphia in 1819, served there as Collector of the Port for nearly a decade, and held the post of Comptroller of the United States Treasury until his death in Washington. (His varied activities are described in an informative study, Paul H. Musser's *James Nelson Barker*, published in 1929.)

Barker's versatility is reflected in his dramatic output. Among the plays he is known to have written, some are comedies; and one of these, *Tears and Smiles*, presented in Philadelphia in 1807, helped to establish the convention of the stage "Yankee" with a successor, named Nathan Yank, to Tyler's comic servant Jonathan. One play was a dramatization of Walter Scott's narrative poem *Marmion; or, the Battle of Flodden Field;* another, perhaps the first produced American play to glorify the Indian and to deal with the story of Pocahontas, *The Indian Princess; or, La Belle Sauvage* (1808), was an opera; still another was a journalistic work, *The Embargo, or, What News?* (1808), supporting the Embargo Act forbidding American ships to engage in foreign trade during the war between England and France.

His continued interest in comedy was attested to by the production of *How to Try a Lover*, a stage version of a French picaresque novel written in 1817 but first staged in 1836 in Philadelphia. But his outstanding play is *Superstition*, a tragedy in verse based on an early American subject, which was produced in Philadelphia in 1824. A romantic drama with historical and social elements, it was also an early indictment of Puritan intolerance and of superstition in colonial New England. It was also the culmination of Barker's most distinguishing characteristic as a playwright—namely, his concern with American subjects and problems.

CHARLES THE SECOND

JOHN HOWARD PAYNE (1791–1852) developed a passion for the stage at an early age and became an actor in 1806 at the age of fifteen. He went to England in 1813, but on failing to win much attention in London with his acting he started to translate and adapt plays for the Drury Lane management, and very soon he had the good fortune to collaborate with the great actor Edmund Kean on the romantic historical drama *Brutus; or, The Fall of Tarquin.* It turned into a misfortune when Payne was accused of plagiarism. Later, he was even imprisoned for debt after an unsuccessful season as manager of Sadler's Wells.

But by 1821 Fortune's wheel brought him back into favor with the production of the melodrama *Thérèse, the Orphan of Geneva*. Two years later he succeeded again in 1823 with *Clari; or, The Maid of Milan* (long remembered for the song "Home, Sweet Home"), quickly followed in 1824 by his collaboration with Washington Irving on the comedy *Charles the Second*, which was produced both in London and New York and came to be considered the best comedy of the early American theatre. It was freely based on a French play (Alexandre Duval's *La*

Jeunesse de Henri V of the year 1805) which revolved around the French monarch Henry V rather than Charles II of England. Payne, who spent time in Paris observing the French theatre, was indeed constantly drawing on its resources of melodrama and comedy. *Charles the Second* became a favorite vehicle for star performers, while discriminating early critics appreciated its smooth construction and polished dialogue, probably the result of the collaboration with Irving, who preferred to keep his participation in the work a secret.

Payne wrote or adapted many other plays, both comedies and tragedies or melodramas, and his busy career has been the subject of a number of studies. It is especially to be noted that despite his abundant writing he was unable to benefit greatly from his labors. He felt himself persecuted in England for his democratic sympathies (for having "so strongly asserted my American principles," he declared in 1835), and because of inadequate copyright protection he did not fare better financially in America, even though numerous plays by him were produced there regularly. He was better rewarded by his country when he was appointed American Consul at Tunis from 1842 to 1845 and from 1851 to the time of his death. Arthur Hobson Quinn in his *History of the American Drama* provides a good summary of Payne's work in the theatre: "He went to the French drama of his time or a little earlier for much of his inspiration. So did other dramatists in England. . . . Originality in its greatest sense was not his. His prime characteristic was a capacity for borrowing what would be theatrically effective, and reshaping it to make of it a new thing."

WASHINGTON IRVING (1783–1859), the well-known New York City essayist, critic, humorist, storyteller, and author of travel books, histories, and biographies, was America's first major literary figure. His collaborations with Payne on *Charles the Second* and several other less well-known plays were peripheral to his main literary activities.

FASHION

ANNA CORA MOWATT RITCHIE (1819–1870), born into a cultivated New York family, was married to a well-to-do lawyer, James Mowatt, at the age of fifteen. At seventeen she wrote a first play, apparently for private delectation (*The Gypsy Wanderer; or, The Stolen Child*), and after traveling for her health, published another play, *Gulzara; or, The Persian Star*, in 1840. She had also shown an aptitude for acting ever since childhood. But it was only when her husband, many years her senior, lost both health and fortune that she turned to the theatre, at first with public readings and then with the writing of a play, *Fashion; or Life in New York*, which opened in 1845 to instant success at the famous Park Theatre of New York. It was still a minor success when revived in the same city in 1924, and it has been performed frequently since then in community and university theatres. She also published fiction, succeeding especially in 1844, with the novel *The Fortune Hunter* later translated into German.

Since authorship of even a successful play was an insufficient source of income, she went on the stage, making her first public appearance in a production of Bulwer-Lytton's romantic play *The Lady of Lions* at the Park Theatre in June, 1845. In 1847, she had a second successful piece on the boards, *Armand, the Child of the People*, a comedy and melodrama set in the reign of Louis XV and written partly in verse, which she presented successfully in London in 1849 at the Theatre

Royal, where she also produced *Fashion* about a year later. She returned to America in 1850, married William F. Ritchie, a Virginia journalist, after her first husband's death in 1851, and continued to appear on the stage until illness caused her to retire in 1854. In the same year she published her *Autobiography*, an important book to theatre historians, which was followed a year later by semi-auto-biographical stories of the stage, *Mimic Life; or, Before and Behind the Curtain.*

Fashion was the subject of two reviews by Edgar Allan Poe in the *Broadway Journal*, on March 29 and April 5, 1845. They are unusually interesting examples of early American dramatic criticism.

In the first review Poe was sharply critical, writing that *Fashion* is "theatrical but not dramatic." He added:"It is a pretty well-arranged selection from the usual routine of stage characters, and stage manœuvres, but there is not one particle of any nature beyond greenroom nature about it. No such events ever happened, in fact, or ever could happen, as happen in *Fashion*. Our fault-finding is on the score of deficiency in verisimilitude—in natural art—that is to say, in art based on the natural laws of man's heart and understanding."

In the second review, Poe was considerably more generous. He declared: "In one respect, perhaps, we have done Mrs. Mowatt unintentional injustice. We are not quite sure, upon reflection, that her entire thesis is not an original one. We can call to mind no drama, just now, in which the design can probably be stated as the satirizing of fashion *as* fashion. . . . [Had Poe forgotten Sheridan, or, for that matter, Tyler, whose influence is pronounced in *Fashion?*] We are delighted to find, in the reception of Mrs. Mowatt's comedy, the clearest indications of a revival of the American drama—that is to say of an earnest disposition to see it revived." He also praised the Park Theatre production, because "whatever management and an excellent company could do for the comedy has been done."

The Epilogue spoken at the production conveys the gay spirit of the work too well to be overlooked:

EPILOGUE

PRUDENCE.	I told you so! And now you hear and see.
	I told you *Fashion* would the fashion be!
TRUEMAN.	Then both its point and moral I distrust.
COUNT JOLIMAITRE.	Sir, is that liberal?
HOWARD.	Or is it just?
TRUEMAN.	The guilty have escaped!
TIFFANY.	Is, therefore, sin
	Made charming? Ah! there's punishment within.
	Guilt ever carries his own scourge along.
GERTRUDE.	Virtue her own reward!
TRUEMAN.	You're right, I'm wrong.
MRS. TIFFANY.	How we have been deceived!
PRUDENCE.	I told you so.
SERAPHINA.	To lose at once a title and a beau!
COUNT JOLIMAITRE.	A *count* no more, I'm no more of *account*.
TRUEMAN.	But to a nobler title you may mount,
	And be in time—who knows?—an honest man!
COUNT JOLIMAITRE.	Eh, Millinette?
MILLINETTE.	Oh, *oui*—I know you can!

GERTRUDE. (*To the audience*) But ere we close the scene, a word with you—
           We charge you answer—Is this picture true?
           Some little mercy to our efforts show,
           Then let the world your honest verdict know.
           Here let it see portrayed its ruling passion,
           And learn to prize at its just value—*Fashion.*

UNCLE TOM'S CABIN

HARRIET BEECHER STOWE's antislavery novel *Uncle Tom's Cabin; or, Life among the Lowly*, first published serially and then in book form in 1852, sold over 300,000 copies during the first year of publication. It became the most popular work of fiction in its time, and exerted a strong influence on the nation. The book was quickly translated into several languages and was frequently republished. It was extravagantly praised, attacked, and defended—defended, in fact, by the author herself against allegations of misrepresentation in a book published in 1853 under the title *A Key to Uncle Tom's Cabin*. It is not surprising, therefore, that it should have been quickly dramatized. This dramatization, by an actor named C. W. Taylor, was promptly presented in New York in August, 1852. It was also promptly denounced. In his invaluable book *Theatre, U.S.A.* (McGraw-Hill Book Company, New York, 1959), Barnard Hewitt quotes a New York *Herald* editorial dated September, 1852, which declares that the production was "a sad blunder" and that if the American stage becomes "the deliberate agent in the cause of abolitionism, with the sanction of the public, and their approbation, the peace and harmony of the Union will soon be ended." The editorial went on to "advise all concerned to drop the play of *Uncle Tom's Cabin* at once and forever."

That the Taylor dramatization was indeed withdrawn after only eleven performances did not, however, deter the manager of a stock company in Troy, New York, George C. Howard, from ordering another dramatization of the novel from one of his actors, also a playwright, George L. Aiken (1830–1876); and this new version, first produced at Troy in September, 1852, opened in New York on September 27, 1853, for a run of over two hundred performances. Aiken himself played two roles in this production; George Howard appeared as St. Clair, Mrs. Howard as Topsy, and his apparently extremely talented six- or seven-year-old daughter Cordelia as the pathetic, if not indeed bathetic, Little Eva. The play created a sensation, and was enthusiastically received by the New York public, which was greatly moved by it. The production was subsequently toured by Howard and his company down the eastern seaboard as far as Baltimore and as far west as St. Louis, and was eventually taken to England.

For Professor Hewitt the New York production had historical consequences aside from its influence on antislavery sentiment in America. He reports that *Uncle Tom's Cabin* was one of the few plays to be performed *without an afterpiece* and that "it drew into the theatre a whole new audience composed of the deeply religious for whom the theatre had hitherto been, in Jonathan's words, 'the devil's stamping ground.' Finding *Uncle Tom's Cabin* edifying, many came back to see other 'moral' dramas." Elsewhere, in a fine article, "Uncle Tom and Uncle Sam: New Light from an Old Play," published in the *Quarterly Journal of Speech*, February, 1951 (Vol. 37, No. 1), Hewitt takes issue with latter-day detractors, declaring that "The play, like the novel, has many characters, and in spite of the necessarily sketchy treatment which they receive, it is amazing how alive they are," and levels the barb of his criticism on the dialogue, much of it "lifted almost verbatim from the novel." He points especially to the effective characterization of the passionately freedom-loving George, to Tom's dignity, and to the portrayal of St. Clare as an "intellectual, sensitive, world-weary Southerner."

It is well to remember, however, that an important factor in the success of *Uncle Tom's Cabin* before the era of the motion picture was its spectacularity, particularly the tableaux of the Ohio River scene, called "The Escape from the Frozen River," which presents Eliza's flight across the frozen Ohio with the bloodhounds almost within reach of her, and the "Allegory" at the end, after Uncle Tom's death, showing him on his way to Heaven with two angels swinging the Pearly Gates open for him, other angels behind the gates, and the previously deceased St. Clare and Little Eva extending their hands lovingly toward him. (See *The Ohio State University Collection Bulletin* No. 10, pages 31–39, "Scenery and Staging of Uncle Tom's Cabin: The Allegory and the Ohio River Scenes," by Mary Ann Fruth.) An illuminating account of the popularity of the Aiken play and of the reactions to it appears in Monroe Lippman's "Uncle Tom and His Poor Relations: American Slavery Plays," in *Southern Speech Journal*, Spring, 1963 (Vol. 28, No. 3).

THE OCTOROON

USUALLY considered by Americans the maturest of the numerous plays of the Dublin-born Dion Boucicault (1820–1890), *The Octoroon* was a climax in a career that extended well before and considerably after its first production in New York's Winter Garden on December 5, 1859, on the very eve of the Civil War. Educated at London University and elsewhere, and apprenticed to an engineer for a while, Boucicault brought to the theatre a lively fancy and a liking for mechanics that later served him well in inventing stage effects. It is characteristic of him that he combined playwriting with a strongly professional involvement with stage production almost from the start.

He appears to have begun his acting career in 1837 (perhaps some four years earlier) and written his first play about the same time. A few years later, in the spring of 1841, his second play, *London Assurance*, opened successfully in 1841. This comedy marked the beginning of a playwriting career that yielded as many as 125 plays and brought their volatile author (known "for the Celtic lash of his tongue" and "the French barb of his pen," according to a contemporary) fortune, misfortune, and charges of plagiarism. So busy was Boucicault that a contemporary leader of the theatre in England, Squire Bancroft, recalled the playwright-producer's own notion of an appropriate epitaph on himself: "Dion Boucicault; his first holiday."

In 1853, after his marriage to an actress who became the leading lady of many of his productions, he came to the United States, where he spent the greater part of his life indefatigably writing, adapting, and producing plays and touring in them. A considerable number of these were set in Ireland. The best known of these are *The Colleen Bawn* in 1860, *Arrah-Na-Pogue* in 1864, and *The Shaughraun* in 1874. He also turned out a number of successful dramatizations of nineteenth-century novels. But for American stage historians his most important pieces are those that dealt with American life. The most successful or important were *The Poor of New York*, produced in December, 1857, with a sensational fire scene on the stage, and *The Octoroon*, loosely based on the novel *The Quadroon* by

Mayne Reid, which was published in New York in 1856. An interesting report on a conflict over the production of the play will be found in the article *The Octoroon War* by Sheldon Faulkner, published in the *Educational Theatre Journal* of March, 1963.

As late as 1961, a century after its first presentation, *The Octoroon* was still considered by New York reviewers an interesting piece of theatre when staged by Stuart Vaughan for the New York Phoenix Theatre led by Norris Houghton and T. Edward Hambleton. Richard Watts, Jr., published an appreciative Sunday article, "The Basic Appeal of *The Octoroon*," in the New York *Post* of February 12, 1961, from which we quote the following paragraphs with his kind permission:

> Some of its theatrics do seem excessive to us now, and Mr. Vaughan was understandably not averse to taking advantage of their humorous possibilities, but, on the whole, it is still a play of sturdy dramatic values and it deserves to be seen far more for its intrinsic merits than for its occasional sins of innocence against modern sophistication.
>
> John Mason Brown recently told me of a persuasive theory he has about *The Octoroon*. He likes to think of it as an American variation on *The Cherry Orchard*, written by a man of talent rather than by one of genius. In its sympathetic depiction of a collapsing social order, the gracious old lady who is losing her plantation to a rising new class is Boucicault's Mme. Ranevsky, while Lopahin, Chekhov's representative of this new class, is divided into two characters, both of them Northerners: the ruthless scoundrel scheming evilly to take over the estate, and the kindly, bumbling and sententious overseer who is trying to save it.
>
> There happily can be no charges of plagiarism here, since *The Octoroon* was written half a century before *The Cherry Orchard* and it is doubtful that Chekhov ever even heard of Boucicault. This baleful possibility having been dissipated, the similarity may be more cheerfully noted. Boucicault's plantation with its charming, generous, doomed masters and devoted slaves is as dramatic if not so subtle a symbol of a dying class in an outmoded society as the estate of Mme. Ranevsky, where the death knell was heard in the sound of the axe chopping down the cherry tree and the loyal old serf, Firs, was forgotten and left to die alone.
>
> It is a highly romanticized slave plantation that the author dramatized, in which all the white Southerners are kind and noble and only the Yankee is vile. Boucicault was a frankly commercial playwright and didn't believe in offending more potential customers than was necessary. But he was also a skillful craftsman, and, while his idealization of slave-owners may have originated from box-office reasons, it likewise served a valuable dramatic purpose. The abomination of slavery as an institution is emphasized rather than softened because the participants in the horrors of a slave auction are basically kind-hearted men.

THE COUNT OF MONTE CRISTO

THE triumph of the actor-manager James O'Neill's productions of *Monte Cristo*, in which he played the hero some six thousand times, was one of the last gasps of old-fashioned, simplistic romanticism in the American theatre. The contrast between this unsophisticated drama of villainy perpetrated and punished and the unconventional quasi-naturalistic and expressionist plays of the star-actor's son Eugene O'Neill spans the distance between two eras of stage history, the Victorian and the modern, in the United States.

It may be observed that the play was in a technical sense by no means an American drama. The well-known novel from which it was taken was Alexander Dumas's *The Count of Monte Cristo*, in which neither the events nor the characters were even remotely American. The French author, moreover, had been the first to carve a play out of it himself, under the abbreviated title *Monte Cristo*, a play divided into so many acts (twenty of them) and requiring so large a cast that its failure was assured. The marvel is not only that it should have been produced but that the French production should have actually reached the Drury Lane Theatre in London, no doubt on the strength of the novel's inordinate reputation. The dramatization was divided into two parts and had to be presented on two successive nights.

This was in the year 1848. Twenty years later, the English actor-manager Ben Webster presented a different and evidently more manageable dramatization by Charles Fechter at the Adelphi Theatre in London, but with no greater success. About the same time a third attempt to wrestle with the problem of adaptation, by a Thomas H. Lacy, also made no impact on the English stage. Other versions were made for the American stage, and the first, presented in New York, had a fairly good run as early as 1848. Other New York productions are reported for the years 1863, 1864, and 1868.

In 1870, Charles Fechter, working with a collaborator, Arthur Leclerq, made a second adaptation, which was first seen in Boston. After several unsuccessful attempts, Fechter, in his capacity of actor-manager, presented and played in this version in New York in 1873 and 1877. Fechter died in 1879. But his version, subjected to modifications over the years, was destined to have a long life as a result of the interest of the American impresario John Stetson. The latter cast the young James O'Neill in the part of Dantès in a new production that opened in New York on February 12, 1883. Within two years, O'Neill gained possession of the play by purchase from John Stetson, and made it his own as a star vehicle that brought him popularity and wealth. No "final" version of the script can possibly be established for a play that underwent so many revisions and was probably pared down by O'Neill himself for the purpose of touring in it. But it is not too much to claim the play for America, so long as James O'Neill continued to present it. A link with the modern American theatre was established when the young Eugene O'Neill joined his father's production of *Monte Cristo.* An essay on the possible influence of this production, though not specifically by the play as presented here, John Henry Raleigh's "Eugene O'Neill and the Escape from the Château D'If" will be found in *Eugene O'Neill: A Collection of Critical Essays*, edited by John Gassner and published by Prentice-Hall in 1964, pages 7–22.

NOTE: The text played by James O'Neill that was in Eugene O'Neill's possession appeared in Volume XVI (edited by J. B. Russak) of *America's Lost Plays* under the general editorship of Barrett H. Clark, published by Princeton University, 1941, and reprinted by the Indiana University Press. It also appeared in Barrett H. Clark's *Favorite American Plays*. The text contains stage directions customary in Victorian playing scripts, such as "Exit L. U. E.," "Crosses to R," and "Enters R. U. E." A slightly different version was given by Eugene O'Neill to the Museum of the City of New York. Another acting version, the early dramatization by Thomas H. Lacy, was published in two editions by Samuel French in London. Portions of this version are reprinted in the version presented here.

THE MOUSE-TRAP

WILLIAM DEAN HOWELLS (1837–1920), the author of this and other early dramatic trifles, owes his considerable reputation to radically different work. He distinguished himself as an editor of the influential *Atlantic Monthly*, a critic (most notably in his book *Criticism and Fiction* in 1891), an essayist, and a novelist. He is now best remembered for his moderately realistic novels *The Rise of Silas Lapham* (1885), *A Hazard of New Fortunes* (1890), and *The Quality of Mercy* (1892).

For the theatre, Howells wrote some twenty-five mostly unproduced short farces, of which *The Mouse-Trap* is one. He also wrote a number of full-length plays, such as *A Counterfeit Presentment*, *A True Hero*, and *The Unexpected Guests*, as well as dramatizations of his own novels, *A Foregone Conclusion* and *The Rise of Silas Lapham*. His most important contribution to the American theatre was his criticism (in his magazine pieces, "The Editor's Study" and "The Editor's Easy Chair") of the asides, soliloquies, and contrivances of conventional plays, and his call for realistic situations and dialogue. But his best playwriting appears in his well-written short entertainments, such as *The Elevator* (1885), *The Garroters* (1886), and *Five o'Clock Tea* (1889), *A Likely Story* (1889), and the sophisticated little farce *The Mouse-Trap* (1889), all first published in *Harper's Weekly* and later *Harper's Magazine*, which proved notably popular with readers.

SECRET SERVICE

WILLIAM GILLETTE (1855–1937) first established himself in the theatre as an actor. But not content with an acting career alone and attending classes at the City College of New York, Harvard, and Boston University in search of an ampler education than the stage could provide, he began to write plays as well as to perform in them. His first stage piece, *The Professor*, was produced successfully in New York at the Madison Square Theatre in 1881. Gillette played the main part in it as a professor who is idolized by girls. Another play, *Esmeralda*, a collaboration with Francis Hodgson Burnett, revolved about a domineering woman who is ultimately defied by a daughter in love with a young man whom the ambitious mother has considered ineligible. The play opened in 1881, ran for almost a year in New York, and continued to be performed now and then for nearly twenty years. Gillette turned his attention profitably to the Civil War with *Held by the Enemy*, first presented in Brooklyn in 1886, and the subject was the familiar one of honor versus love, while the plot involved the discovery of a high-minded southern spy. The same theme was developed by Gillette more richly in *Secret Service* after several other productions, including the cleverly written plot-filled farce *Too Much Johnson*.

First tried out in 1895 in Philadelphia, the superior Civil War spy drama *Secret Service* opened in a revised version in 1896 in New York with Gillette filling the principal role of Captain Thorne. In 1897, the play also had productions in London and Paris. Gillette wrote some twelve other plays after *Secret Service*, but without any particular distinction except in the case of his successful free adaptation of Conan Doyle's *Sherlock Holmes*, which opened in 1899 with Gillette in the title role.

Walter Prichard Eaton's comments on *Secret Service* in an essay "On Reading Plays" are instructive:

> Here is a play which in its day, as performed by the author, was intensely exciting, and which had a pronounced influence on the growth of a native realistic drama in our country. The text is printed from Gillette's own prompt-book and embodies both the spoken dialogue and directions for all the gestures and movements. You will note that in the telegraph office scene especially, the stage directions often occupy double or triple the space of the dialogue.... What the actors *did* was of more importance in creating the illusion and excitement than what they *said*. Hence a study of this play becomes a study not of literature, of the arrangement of words, but of construction, of how Gillette planned the actions and movements of his characters to achieve his effects.

THE GREAT DIVIDE

ONE of the most distinguished contributors to turn-of-the-century American drama was the Indiana-born poet, scholar, and university teacher William Vaughn Moody (1869–1910), who is remembered for two plays written during a short life, *The Great Divide* and *The Faith Healer*. After doing some schoolteaching, Moody entered Harvard, took two degrees and taught there for a year, and then spent the next seven years at the University of Chicago. Thereafter he maintained only a loose connection with the English Department of this major institution while he traveled abroad, wrote and edited books, and published poetry until his untimely death. He also wrote verse plays of modest distinction, *The Masque of Judgment* (1900), a piece revolving around the conflict between Man and God, *The Fire-Bringer* (1904), dealing with Prometheus' conflict with the Olympian gods on behalf of humanity, and the fragment *The Death of Eve*, published posthumously. His prose plays were, however, decidedly more effective than these essentially literary exercises. His last play, *The Faith Healer*, a more or less psychological drama of conflict between obsessive religious faith and human love, first presented in St. Louis in 1909, was nonetheless not particularly successful.

The earlier written prose play *The Great Divide*, first presented in Chicago and then in New York in 1906 (three years later also in London), came closer to direct dramatic experience even if *The Faith Healer* has had staunch champions who consider it to be the better work. *The Great Divide* was based, indeed, on actual events. According to Arthur Hobson Quinn, Moody learned about them from his wife: "She had heard the story of a girl of her acquaintance who had gone with her brother to a cabin in the West, had been left alone and had been attacked by three men. She had appealed to one to save her from the others and had agreed to marry him. The marriage did not turn out successfully, and resulted in a divorce." The original title of *The Great Divide*, which was first called *The Sabine Woman*, refers to this story as a parallel to the legendary Rape of the Sabine Women in early Roman history or legend.

In Moody's dramatic version, the woman's puritanical resistance, the result of her New England breeding, is overcome at last by her love for the vigorous devil-may-care man to whom she had been forced to yield in the "wild" West. Moody even went a step further toward a realistic treatment of the emotions when he made the latter, Stephen Ghent, say to the reluctant heroine Ruth: "Does it gall you the way we came together. You asked me that night what brought me, and I told you whiskey, and sun, and the devil. Well, I tell you now I'm thankful on my knees for all three. Does it rankle in your mind that I took you when I could get you, by main strength and fraud? I guess most good women are taken that way, if they only knew."

We are not far here from a modern frankness still rare when the play was produced. Moreover, when Moody revised the play and published it, he omitted a reference in the first act to Ghent's going through the formality of marrying Ruth. Even in the original version, as noted by the drama critic of the New York *Sun* (October 4, 1906), the play seemed a bold departure from conventional American drama. The reviewer declared, after the opening night at the Princess Theatre, that it "is so bold and vital in theme, so subtly veracious, and unaffectedly strong in the writing, that it is very hard in the few moments left by a tardy if excellent performance [in which Margaret Anglin and Henry Miller were principals] to speak of it in terms at once of justice and of moderation." Even in the year 1959, while conceding that *The Great Divide* had faults, the stage historian Barnard Hewitt could still consider it "a landmark in the development of our native drama."

THE NEW YORK IDEA

THE PHILADELPHIA-BORN LANGDON MITCHELL (1862–1935) had the proper qualifications for writing a society comedy of some literary distinction. He was the son of a prominent physician, Dr. S. Weir Mitchell, who was also a novelist. He attended St. Paul's School in Concord, New Hampshire, was educated abroad for a period of years, then studied law at Harvard and at Columbia University, and was admitted to the bar.

Mitchell indulged his literary bent by the time he reached his majority, publishing poetry and drama in 1885 in a volume titled *Sylvian and Other Poems*. A second book of verse came out in 1894, and a collection of stories, *Love in the Backwoods*, in 1896. After having dramatized his father's novel *The Adventures of François* unsuccessfully, he undertook to dramatize Thackeray's famous Victorian novel *Vanity Fair* under the title of *Becky Sharp*. Mrs. Fiske presented and played in it with great success in 1899 and revived it a decade later; the Player's Club also revived it in New York in 1929. It is probably this success that inspired a second bout with a Thackeray novel, *Pendennis*, in 1916.

Mrs. Fiske also produced *The New York Idea* in 1906 with her husband, and played the leading part in it. It was revived with Grace George in the same part during the 1915–1916 New York season. The play, which combines comedy with farce, still gave evidence of liveliness, if not life, when it was given by the Harvard Summer Players under the direction of George Hamblin at the Loeb Theatre during the summer of 1963, and Howard Taubman, then the New York *Times* drama critic, was still impressed with such quips as one character's description of another as "shaking and quaking like an automobile in ecstasy." Ten years after the New York premiere Max Reinhardt produced it in German in Berlin under the title of *Jonathanstochter*, and the comedy was translated into several other languages.

It was the first Mrs. Fiske presentation that was the outstanding production, with Mrs. Fiske in the part of John Karslake's divorced wife, Cynthia Karslake, and with other parts played by Charles Harbury as Philip Phillimore, Dudley Clinton as his brother The Reverend Matthew Phillimore, Emily Stevens as Phillimore's sister, William B. Mack as his cousin, Marian Lea as his divorced wife, George Arliss as Sir Wilfrid Cates-Darby, John Mason as John Karslake, and Dudley Digges as his valet. The well-cast play seemed rather bold in its day, and the reviewer for *Life* magazine reflected a characteristic ambivalence in his November 29, 1906, review, as the following paragraphs will indicate:

> *The New York Idea* is very up to date. It makes fun of a religion which tries to make form take the place of truth. This is embodied in a fashionable clergyman who wears a gold cross on his watch-chain and books a tip on the races. It makes love and sentiment largely the result of previousiy imbibed high-balls. Its heroines are actuated by no higher motives than feminine spite, jealousy and craving for new sensations. Of course it is exaggerated, and, as it is entirely farcical and satirical, should not be taken too seriously. At the same time it voices one man's notions of social evils and is preached from the broad pulpit of the stage. Gentlemen like Mr. Mitchell do not appreciate, perhaps, the power of the medium at their command, and, therefore, do not stop to think that they should be careful, very careful, how they use it, lest they should sow evil in minds not able to understand the good they intend. He uses his medium to voice his discontent and stir up anarchy, when more thoughtfully and better studied, he might be quite as humorous and help to a rational solution of evils we all condemn.
>
> The play is admirably acted. Mrs. Fiske herself still persists in faults of delivery which, with her artistic intelligence, she should be ashamed of. Her position is too firmly fixed to make it necessary for her to resort to any tricks of manner, and she lets them give the lie to the expertness and cleverness she has at her command. At the same time Mr. Mitchell has given her such a thoroughly artificial character to delineate that artificiality is not entirely out of place. The same description fits the Vida of which Marion Lea makes a triumph of characterization. Mr. Arliss's Englishman in America is a finished creation, and Mr. Clinton's clergyman of the "Four Hundred" is very clever exaggeration. Mr. John Mason is, as always, a perfectly satisfactory gentleman of the world. The remainder of the cast deserves more than passing mention for its excellencies.
>
> *The New York Idea* isn't half as serious as a commentary on its teachings might suggest. It is laughable throughout and very well staged and acted.

THE TRUTH

PERHAPS the most consistently productive American author of comedies before the 1920's was Clyde Fitch (1865–1909), relegated since then to the rank of second-class playwrights. In view of his great productivity of thirty-odd original pieces and over twenty dramatizations and adaptations, this may be a tempting conclusion. Nevertheless, if the commercial theatre must have its hack writers, Fitch usually brought some literary facility and good observation of manners and character traits to his assignments. He was a well-educated man, a graduate of Amherst College, who had contracted an attachment to the theatre at an early age.

To fulfill his ambitions he moved to New York and before long received a commission from the popular actor-manager Richard Mansfield to write a play for him. Fitch obliged with his comedy of England's most famous dandy, *Beau Brummel*, which Mansfield produced in 1890. The play was successful, as well as a second play produced in the same year, *Frédérick Lemaître*, starring Henry Miller. Play after play followed these two productions. He once worked on five plays at the same time to satisfy the great demand for his work; and in one year, 1901, flourishing beyond all previous expectations on the part of American playwrights, he had four plays running simultaneously in New York theatres.

Fitch was singularly skilled in his craft; he believed in rapidity and brevity of writing as recipes for playmaking, while priding himself on putting truth of individual and social life on the stage. It was an extremely limited kind of truth, however, and only a few of the plays have retained some interest for later generations. One of these was *The Climbers*, which lives up to its title, since it deals with social climbing in New York. It even struck a serious note or two, as in the case of one character's reference to the twentieth century as "the Era of Egotism."

The Climbers was produced in 1901. It was followed in 1902 by *The Girl with the Green Eyes*, a comedy about a woman's extreme jealousy, which gives rise to a variety of complications before the inevitable happy resolution of the play. In the next few years, as well as earlier, Fitch added to his output a large number of social comedies, melodramas, and plays of historical interest and period color, the best of the latter being perhaps *Captain Jinks of the Horse Marines*, produced in 1901. His last important play was *The City*, presented in New York in 1909, after his death. The last important play produced during his lifetime was the comedy *The Truth*. Although the production of 1907 was a failure, Fitch reached the peak of his powers in this genial comedy of manners.

Fitch was a man who generally inspired among his contemporaries a favorable view of his attainments and influence. This generous estimate of Fitch is well reflected in Walter Prichard Eaton's summation of the playwright in his book *At the New Theatre and Others*, published in 1910:

> Admitting . . . his limitations, his half-failures and incomplete realizations, we must at the same time admit his positive merits and, striking the balance, judge him as one whose contributions to stage literature possessed considerable truth and value of themselves, and have been of even more significance as influence and example. . . .
> A man of the actual theatre, with the failings as well as the virtues of a man of the theatre, without the consciousness of a prophet's call

nor the intellectual assurance of a self-appointed leader, Clyde Fitch led by his practical success as a maker of popular plays which were also truthful plays. That those plays obeyed the tendency of the times and led the theatre still farther from poetry and true romance there is no question. The pendulum had to swing. It is still swinging. The mission of the theatre to-day is to give reflective realism a full and fair trial. So far as he could, Mr. Fitch instinctively made his plays realistic, he commented upon the life about him by showing it on the stage as he saw it, often through the glass of a kindly irony. . . .

THE WITCHING HOUR

VERY much the workaday playwright, and a decidedly proficient one, Augustus Thomas (1857–1934), the son of a St. Louis physician who dabbled in the theatre in New Orleans, developed an early interest in the stage. He began to write plays at the age of fourteen, and organized an amateur theatre company by the time he was seventeen. His interest was unswerving even when he began to write for newspapers and to edit and publish one of them, the Kansas City *Mirror*, himself. He continued to write plays, and he even established a professional actors' company, which he took on tour with a dramatization of a novel, *Editha's Burglar*, in 1883.

In several of his most vivid pieces, he exploited an interest in regional drama. Among these were *Alabama* (1891) and *Arizona* (1899). But he was equally efficient in contriving other melodramas and comedies, and in *The Copperhead* he wrote one of the best Civil War spy dramas with considerable feeling and understanding. It opened in 1918 with Lionel Barrymore in the main role. In still other dramas, he capitalized on current interests, concerning himself with the double standard and with the subject of mental healing in an effective drama, *As a Man Thinks* (1911), and with mental telepathy, a subject on which he had obtained some knowledge almost twenty years earlier when he had acted as advance publicist in St. Louis for a mind reader rather ostentatiously called Washington Irving Bishop. He employed this interest effectively in the murder-trial drama *The Witching Hour*, first presented in Providence, Rhode Island, and then in New York in 1907. He also wrote another play on the same subject, *The Harvest Moon*, produced in 1909, in which an aunt poisons a sensitive girl's mind. Thomas published a vivid account of his career in the autobiography *The Print of My Remembrance* in 1922.

SALVATION NELL

EDWARD SHELDON (1886–1946) was considered the white hope of the American theatre during the first dozen years of the twentieth century before he was struck down in 1915 by a paralyzing illness, and even then he was revered and consulted by fellow playwrights. Born in Chicago and educated at Harvard, he was alternately a realist and a romanticist in his work; or, rather, his observation of background details and situation was realistic while his sentiments were idealistic and romantic.

Sheldon had barely qualified for his Master of Arts degree at Harvard and graduated from George Pierce Baker's "47 Workshop" there when he obtained his first success in the theatre with his drama of common life, *Salvation Nell*, in Mrs. Fiske's production. A year later he aroused attention with a melodrama of race conflict *The Nigger*, involving a young southern politician's discovery that he is of mixed blood, and in 1911 with his play on political corruption, *The Boss*. These realistic plays were followed in 1913 by the successful romantic drama *Romance*, in which the popular actress Doris Keene starred triumphantly in England as well as in the United States.

Sheldon returned to realism in 1926 with the Belasco production of *Lulu Belle*, a collaboration with Charles MacArthur, in which the passion of the white hero for a Negro girl was represented against a slum background. But *Salvation Nell*, despite its patently sentimental tone, was Sheldon's most vividly realistic work. It is published here for the first time.

Its impact on the theatre in 1908 is conveyed by a review in the January issue of *Theatre Magazine*, from which the following passages are taken:

> "Salvation Nell" is from the heart of the times. It is, first of all, a triumph of stage management and acting, the intelligence of its production far exceeding the meager expression of what it involves as contained in the text of the manuscript from which the play was built. This is obvious. There are many things in a play that do not depend upon the written word, and which cannot be expressed by it. The only way in which the uncommon realism of this play could have been obtained was by stage management. . . .
>
> A scrubwoman in a barroom of a disreputable kind, in a part of the city of New York where there is congested evil, is roughly and insultingly handled by a loafer, who is killed by her man in the brawl that follows. He is sent to the penitentiary. She comes under the influence of one of the Salvation Army workers and enlists with them. She is good at heart, seen to be so at once, faithful in her relations with the Bowery brute with whom she is in the unwedded state. Is her character and condition unfit for the stage? We think not. Are the incidents seen in the barroom and in the areaways of the slums too gross for audiences? We think not. The intent is not to entertain us with the disagreeable or to make us acquainted with vice for our amusement. It is all incidental to the pity and sympathy which it should evoke.

A particularly vivid scene, described by the critic Walter Prichard Eaton, was one in which "a scrub woman in a barroom" held her drunken lover's head in her lap for fully ten minutes without a word" and moved the critic with her "silent pathos."

THE EASIEST WAY

THE EASIEST WAY, BY EUGENE WALTER (1874–1941), was an outstanding David Belasco production of the year 1909 and was considered downright sensational in its day. The relatively bold, if hardly profound, handling of the subject of the efforts of a kept woman, spoiled by a man of wealth, to leave her mode of life after falling in love with a young newspaper reporter, followed by her relapse into "the easiest way," drew the kind of enthusiasm that Arthur Wing Pinero's *The Second Mrs. Tanqueray* (1893) had drawn in England some fifteen years earlier. The very presentation of the subject, not to mention the last line of the actress-heroine Laura Murdock: "Dress up my body and paint my face. I'm going to Rector's to make a hit—and to hell with the rest!" was still a bold gambit in the American theatre of the first decade of our century. Writes the historian of American manners, Lloyd Morris, "Impressed by its unhappy ending, but ignoring its inconsistencies and sentimentality, most of the critics and many playgoers praised it as an important American drama. . . . It represented, at the time, an immense advance toward the social realism of Ibsen and other European dramatists."

For the manager-director Belasco and for perceptive critics (then not particularly conspicuous in number), the realism was primarily the superficial one of scenic illusion. Belasco prided himself on it, writing, "I went to the meanest theatrical boarding house I could find in the Tenderloin district and bought the entire interior of one of its most dilapidated rooms—patched furniture, threadbare carpet, tarnished and broken gas fixtures, tumbledown cupboards, dingy doors and window casing, and even the faded paper on the walls." For Belasco, indeed, realism consisted of the photographic realism he painstakingly and expensively secured for the setting of this and other plays, such as *The Governor's Lady* with its sensational Childs' Restaurant "complete even to griddle cakes"; he spoke glowingly of "the importance and emphasis I place upon every minute detail which makes for truth in my theatre." As the playwright George Middleton, who knew Belasco, wrote, "He had no broad culture and was unaware of social and economic readjustments in the world about him. He produced no play, I recall, which reflected the new moralities touching on man and society . . . he would dare a bit, as in *The Easiest Way*, but the revolutionary [*sic*] *Doll's House* or any plays which suggested the claims of mild feminism were beyond him. With few exceptions, the American plays he did were amiably unimportant though the best of their kind."

Eugene Walter was himself not a remarkably avant-garde writer and intellectual. He started as a regular journalist on a Cleveland paper and later wrote for the New York *Sun*. He also served the commercial theatre as an advance promotion agent. And as a playwright with a flair for reporting action, he favored strong melodramatic situations. His first successful play, *The Undertow* (1907), was a sentimental account of a straightforward woman's success in securing mercy for her thieving, weakling husband from his "hard-as-nails" employer, a steamship captain. A year later, Walter succeeded with *The Wolf*, a realistically staged melodrama set in a Canadian forest full of howling wolves. He drew closer to contemporary social realities in *Fine Feathers* (1913), his last play of any possible claim to importance, when he showed a uxorious man conniving in a shady business enterprise with an unscrupulous contractor.

The impression originally created by *The Easiest Way*, which carried the genteel subtitle "An American Play Concerning a Particular Phase of New York Life," is well recorded in a review written by the queasy dramatic critic Alan Dale, in the New York *American* (January 20, 1909). Some excerpts from it follow:

> A weak little drama of a vacuous, aimless woman, too puerile to be moral, and almost too cowardly to be brazenly immoral, pitted against two lovers—one a type of the bestial Broadway booze-feeder, represent-

ing immorality, the other the figure of a vigorous Lothario, suggesting non-morality—made out a sensational case at the Stuyvesant Theatre last night, in a play called *The Easiest Way*. It purported to sketch the familiar picture of the theatre-woman, struggling for her virtue amid the alleged temptations of Broadway—temptations that are popularly supposed to begin at the lobster-palace. It did sketch this picture, with daubs of color, splashes of verity and a dazzling varnish of candor at which a sophisticated audience laughed last night, at which a less sophisticated audience might feel impelled to grieve. But this is a big community, and there are all sorts of people in it. The duty of the critic need not be to preach. Let him tell, and be satisfied at that.

In the dialogue last night the sophisms of a courtesan, bold and untrammeled, were received as though they were outbursts of pure comedy, priceless gems of uncorroded wit, while the interjectional profanity of one of the men was rippled out as though it were the prettiest persiflage of an intelligent commentator. But there are all sorts of people, and all sorts of plays for them. At the outset it may be said that *The Easiest Way* is not a play for the Young Person....

At the end she [the actress-heroine] is left by the reporter to her unshakable affinity, and—to Rector's. One wonders all the time why the genial Broadway bloke was so cussedly addicted to such a whining, flabby little imbecile. But such things are. Such things have been shown to be. Such things are continually being shown to be. Men commit murder—only for fast women, never for the good ones, or the intelligent ones, or the bright ones. One wonders just the same. It is one's privilege to wonder. Laura Murdock is a despicable type, but a real one. So is the Broadway beast. The only absurdity is the reportorial lover, who is ridiculously drawn.

THE SCARECROW

THE author of numerous plays and volumes of poetry, Percy MacKaye (1875–1956) was the son of the celebrated stage innovator, producer, and playwright Steele MacKaye. Like his father, on whom he wrote a valuable monograph, he was a man of much cultivation (he was educated at Harvard and at the University of Leipzig) and of daring imagination. He taught at a private school for several years (1900–1906) and lectured during the next half dozen years at Harvard, Yale, Columbia, and other universities. He was appointed to the first American fellowship in poetry and drama, at Miami University in Oxford, Ohio, in 1920. He contributed to almost every kind of theatre, including pageantry and opera, and was rewarded with much recognition, including honorary degrees, in the course of a long and distinguished career.

Several of his published books dealt directly with the theatre: *The Playhouse and the Play* (1909), *The Civic Theatre in Relation to the Redemption of Leisure* (1912), and *Community Drama* (1917). He was a forerunner of Paul Green and other champions of community and pageant drama. Among his noteworthy contributions in this area, described by him as Communal Dramas or Masques and Pageant-Rituals, were *The Gloucester Pageant*, "*The Canterbury Pilgrims*" with music composed by Walter Damrosch, performed with 1,500 citizens of

Gloucester, Massachusetts, in 1909; *Sanctuary*, a "bird masque," produced in 1913 at the Meriden, New Hampshire, bird sanctuary and subsequently in many other communities; *Caliban, by the Yellow Sands*, written to commemorate the tercentenary of Shakespeare's death, and performed in New York at the City College Stadium from May 25 to June 5, 1916 and the next year at the Harvard Stadium. And related to these ventures in the 1920's were a number of writings with a Kentucky mountaineering background, most notably his effective folk drama *This Fine-Pretty World*. It was presented at the pioneering Neighborhood Playhouse "little theatre" in New York in December, 1923, to much acclaim by Hamlin Garland, the poet Edwin Arlington Robinson, Kenneth MacGowan, and other distinguished writers, as well as by the New York press.

In a sense his dramatic masterpiece *The Scarecrow* is also a folk drama, just as the Nathaniel Hawthorne story *Feathertop* upon which it was freely based is essentially a folktale. *The Scarecrow*, it is true, was a culmination of the author's romantic endeavors in a number of spiritually elevated plays such as *The Canterbury Pilgrims* (1902), produced in 1909 and turned into an opera in 1917 with music by Reginald de Koven: *Fenris the Wolf*, a verse drama presented by the famous acting couple Sothern and Marlowe in 1906; and *Sappho and Phaon*, staged in New York in 1907. But, with the addition of a somewhat philosophical view suggested by the full title, *The Scarecrow, or The Glass of Truth: A Tragedy of the Ludicrous*, this play proved to be a vivid re-creation of a New England folk background as sublimated by a poet's imagination.

It was first produced by the Harvard Dramatic Club at Brattle Hall in Cambridge on December 7, 1909, and then in New York at the Garrick Theatre on January 17, 1911, with Frank Reicher in the main role of the Scarecrow "Lord Ravensbane." The play, later revived in New York, was also presented in England at the Theatre Royal of Bristol on November 30, 1914. It was translated into French in 1910 under the title of *L'Epouvantail*, and into German under the title of *Die Vogelscheue* by Walter Fischer of the University of Pennsylvania and produced in 1914 at the Deutsches Theater in Berlin under the direction of the celebrated Max Reinhardt.

Percy MacKaye continued to write verse and drama long after the success of his *Scarecrow*. The most ambitious as well as the most remarkable of his works came many years later when he published his huge drama, the "Hamlet Tetralogy" in 1949. Entitled *The Mystery of Hamlet, King of Denmark*, it was produced by the Pasadena Players under Gilmor Brown's direction at Pasadena, California. Brooks Atkinson acclaimed these four plays as a major achievement, writing in the New York *Times* that "Only a professional poet, living in a singing world of his own, could write so many pages with so much passion, in the grand manner of the classics." Its author, who had won the Shelley Memorial Prize in 1942, received the Fellowship of the Academy of American Poets in 1948.

A SELECTIVE BIBLIOGRAPHY

Since the present volume is not intended to supplant scholarly studies of the early American theatre and drama, the following selective bibliography barely skims the surface of the subject. Special bibliographies are available in a number of volumes listed below:

Anderson, John, *The American Theatre in New York*. New York: Dial Press, 1938.

Brown, T. A., *A History of the New York Stage from the First Performances in 1732 to 1901*. 3 vols. New York: Dodd, Mead, and Company, 1903.

Coad, Oral Sumner, and Mimsi Edwin, *The American Stage*. Vol. 14, *The Pageant of America*. New Haven: Yale University Press, 1929.

Dickinson, Thomas H., *Playwrights of the New American Theater*. New York: The Macmillan Company, 1925.

Downer, Alan, *Fifty Years of American Drama: 1900–1950*. Chicago: Henry Regnery Company, 1951. The first two chapters deal penetratively with pre-1920 period.

———(editor), *American Drama and Its Critics*. New York: The University of Chicago Press, 1965. The first four essays, by Heme, Howells, Eaton, and Haneker, bear upon the pre-1920 drama.

Dunlap, William, *A History of the American Theatre*. New York: J. & J. Harper, 1832. Available in reprints.

Felheim, Marvin, *The Theater of Augustin Daly*. Cambridge, Mass.: Harvard University Press, 1956.

Gassner, John, and Ralph Allen, *Theatre and Drama in the Making*. Boston: Houghton Mifflin Company, 1946. See Part Seven for source material on "The American Drama and Theatre, 1800–1930."

Gagey, Edmond, *Revolution in American Drama*. New York: Columbia University Press, 1947. See the first chapter.

Gilbert, Douglas, *American Vaudeville: Its Life and Times*. New York: Whittlesey House, 1940.

Hartman, John Geoffrey, *The Development of American Social Comedy from 1787 to 1936*. Philadelphia: University of Pennsylvania Press, 1939.

Hewitt, Barnard, *Theatre, U.S.A. 1668–1957*. New York: McGraw-Hill Company, 1959.

Hodge, Francis, *Yankee Theatre: The Image of America on the Stage, 1825–1850*. Austin, Tex.: University of Texas Press, 1964.

Hornblow, Arthur, *A History of the Theatre in America*. Philadelphia: J. B. Lippincott Company, 1919.

Hughes, Glenn, *A History of the American Theatre, 1700–1950*. New York: S. French, 1951.

Ireland, Joseph N., *Records of the New York Stage from 1750 to 1860*. 2 vols. New York: T. H. Morrell, 1866–1867.

Jefferson, Joseph, *The Autobiography of Joseph Jefferson*. New York: The Century Company, 1890.

Kinney, Wister Payne, *George Pierce Baker and the American Theatre*. Cambridge: Harvard University Press, 1954. See pages 1-198.

Krows, Arthur Edwin, *Play Production in America*. New York: Henry Holt and Company, 1916. A valuable introduction to the subject of play production before 1916.

Lovell, John, *Digests of Great American Plays*. New York: Thomas Y. Crowell Company, 1961. Valuable digests of pre-1920 plays on pages 1 to 193.

Mates, Julian, *The American Musical Stage Before 1800*. New Brunswick: Rutgers University Press, 1962.

Mayorga, Margaret G., *A Short History of the American Drama*. New York: Dodd, Mead & Company, 1932.

Meserve, Walter J., *An Outline History of American Drama*. Totawa, N. J.: Littlefield, Adams and Co., 1965.

Moody, Richard, *America Takes the Stage: Romanticism in American Drama, 1750-1900*. Bloomington, Ind.: Indiana University Press, 1955.

————(editor), *Dramas from the American Theatre 1762-1909*. Cleveland: World Publishing Company, 1966.

————, *Edwin Forrest: First Star of the American Stage*. New York: Alfred A. Knopf, 1960.

————, *The Astor Place Riot*. Bloomington, Ind.: Indiana University Press, 1959.

Morris, Lloyd, *Curtain Time: The Story of the American Theatre*. New York: Random House, 1953.

Moses, Montrose J., *The American Dramatist*. Boston: Little, Brown, and Company, 1925.

————, and John Mason Brown, *The American Theatre as Seen by Its Critics*. New York: W. W. Norton, 1934.

Odell, George C. D., *Annals of the New York Stage*. 15 vols. New York: Columbia University Press, 1927-1949.

Quinn, Arthur Hobson, *A History of the American Drama: From the Beginnings to the Civil War*. New York:Appleton-Century-Crofts,Inc., 1943.

————, *A History of the American Drama: From the Civil War to the Present Day*. New York: Appleton-Century-Crofts, Inc., 1936.

————, *Representative American Plays*. 7th revised and enlarged edition. New York: Appleton-Century-Crofts, 1953.

Rowell, George, *The Victorian Theatre: A Survey*. London: Oxford University Press, 1956. Suggested for comparison with the American theatre during the same period.

————(editor), *Nineteenth Century Plays*. London: Oxford University Press, 1953. For comparative study.

Seilhamer, George O., *History of the American Theatre*. 3 vols. Philadelphia: Globe Printing House, 1888-1891.

Smith, Cecil, *Musical Comedy in America*. New York: Theatre Arts Books, 1950.

Taubman, Howard, *The Making of the American Theatre*. New York: Coward McCann, 1965.

BEST PLAYS
OF THE
EARLY AMERICAN THEATRE

From the Beginning to 1916

THE CONTRAST

Royall Tyler

First performed at the John Street Theatre in New York by the American Company on April 16, 1787.

COLONEL MANLY	CHARLOTTE
DIMPLE	MARIA
VAN ROUGH	LETITIA
JESSAMY	JENNY
JONATHAN	SERVANTS

SCENE: New York.

ACT ONE

SCENE ONE

An Apartment at CHARLOTTE's. CHAR-
LOTTE *and* LETITIA *discovered.*

———

LETITIA. And so, Charlotte, you really think the pocket-hoop unbecoming.

CHARLOTTE. No, I don't say so: It
may be very becoming to saunter
round the house of a rainy day; to
visit my grand-mamma, or go to
Quakers' meeting: but to swim in a
minuet, with the eyes of fifty well-
dressed beaux upon me, to trip it in
the Mall, or walk on the battery, give
me the luxurious, jaunty, flowing,
bell-hoop. It would have delighted
you to have seen me the last evening,
my charming girl! I was dangling o'er
the battery with Billy Dimple; a knot
of young fellows were upon the platform; as I passed them I faultered
with one of the most bewitching false
steps you ever saw, and then recovered
myself with such a pretty confusion,
flirting my hoop to discover a jet
black shoe and brilliant buckle. Gad!
how my little heart thrilled to hear
the confused raptures of—"*Demme,
Jack, what a delicate foot!*" "*Ha! General, what a well-turn'd*—"

LETITIA. Fie! fie! Charlotte (*Stopping her mouth*), I protest you are
quite a libertine.

CHARLOTTE. Why, my dear little
prude, are we not all such libertines?
Do you think, when I sat tortured two
hours under the hands of my friseur,
and an hour more at my toilet, that
I had any thoughts of my aunt Susan,
or my cousin Betsey? though they are
both allowed to be critical judges of
dress.

LETITIA. Why, who should we dress

to please, but those who are judges of
its merit?

CHARLOTTE. Why a creature who
does not know *Buffon* from *Souflee*—
Man!—my Letitia—Man! for whom we
dress, walk, dance, talk, lisp, languish,
and smile. Does not the grave Spectator assure us, that even our much
bepraised diffidence, modesty, and
blushes, are all directed to make ourselves good wives and mothers as fast
as we can. Why, I'll undertake with
one flirt of this hoop to bring more
beaux to my feet in one week, than
the grave Maria, and her sentimental
circle, can do, by sighing sentiment
till their hairs are grey.

LETITIA. Well, I won't argue with
you; you always out talk me; let us
change the subject. I hear that Mr.
Dimple and Maria are soon to be
married.

CHARLOTTE. You hear true. I was
consulted in the choice of the wedding
clothes. She is to be married in a
delicate white sattin, and has a monstrous pretty brocaded lutestring for
the second day. It would have done
you good to have seen with what an
affected indifference the dear sentimentalist turned over a thousand
pretty things, just as if her heart did
not palpitate with her approaching
happiness, and at last made her
choice, and arranged her dress with
such apathy, as if she did not know
that plain white sattin, and a simple
blond lace, would shew her clear skin,
and dark hair, to the greatest advantage.

LETITIA. But they say her indifference to dress, and even to the gentleman himself, is not entirely affected.

CHARLOTTE. How?

LETITIA. It is whispered, that if
Maria gives her hand to Mr. Dimple,
it will be without her heart.

CHARLOTTE. Though the giving the heart is one of the last of all laughable considerations in the marriage of a girl of spirit, yet I should like to hear what antiquated notions the dear little piece of old fashioned prudery has got in her head.

LETITIA. Why you know that old Mr. John-Richard-Robert-Jacob-Isaac-Abraham-Cornelius Van Dumpling, Billy Dimple's father (for he has thought fit to soften his name, as well as manners, during his English tour), was the most intimate friend of Maria's father. The old folks, about a year before Mr. Van Dumpling's death, proposed this match: the young folks were accordingly introduced, and told they must love one another. Billy was then a good natured, decent, dressing young fellow, with a little dash of the coxcomb, such as our young fellows of fortune usually have. At this time, I really believe she thought she loved him; and had they then been married, I doubt not, they might have jogged on, to the end of the chapter, a good kind of a singsong lack-a-daysaical life, as other honest married folks do.

CHARLOTTE. Why did they not then marry?

LETITIA. Upon the death of his father, Billy went to England to see the world, and rub off a little of the patroon rust. During his absence, Maria like a good girl, to keep herself constant to her *nown true-love,* avoided company, and betook herself, for her amusement, to her books, and her dear Billy's letters. But, alas! how many ways has the mischievous demon of inconstancy of stealing into a woman's heart! Her love was destroyed by the very means she took to support it.

CHARLOTTE. How?—Oh! I have it—

some likely young beau found the way to her study.

LETITIA. Be patient, Charlotte—your head so runs upon beaux.— Why she read *Sir Charles Grandison, Clarissa Harlowe,* Shenstone, and the *Sentimental Journey;* and between whiles, as I said, Billy's letters. But as her taste improved, her love declined. The contrast was so striking betwixt the good sense of her books, and the flimsiness of her love-letters, that she discovered she had unthinkingly engaged her hand without her heart; and then the whole transaction managed by the old folks, now appeared so unsentimental, and looked so like bargaining for a bale of goods, that she found she ought to have rejected, according to every rule of romance, even the man of her choice, if imposed upon her in that manner—Glary Harlowe would have scorned such a match.

CHARLOTTE. Well, how was it on Mr. Dimple's return? Did he meet a more favourable reception than his letters?

LETITIA. Much the same. She spoke of him with respect abroad, and with contempt in her closet. She watched his conduct and conversation, and found that he had by travelling acquired the wickedness of Lovelace without his wit, and the politeness of Sir Charles Grandison without his generosity. The ruddy youth who washed his face at the cistern every morning, and swore and looked eternal love and constancy, was now metamorphosed into a flippant, pallid, polite beau, who devotes the morning to his toilet, reads a few pages of Chesterfield's letters, and then minces out, to put the infamous principles in practice upon every woman he meets.

CHARLOTTE. But, if she is so apt at conjuring up these sentimental bugbears, why does she not discard him at once?

LETITIA. Why, she thinks her word too sacred to be trifled with. Besides, her father, who has a great respect for the memory of his deceased friend, is ever telling her how he shall renew his years in their union, and repeating the dying injunctions of old Van Dumpling.

CHARLOTTE. A mighty pretty story! And so you would make me believe, that the sensible Maria would give up Dumpling manor, and the all-accomplished Dimple as a husband, for the absurd, ridiculous reason, forsooth, because she despises and abhors him. Just as if a lady could not be privileged to spend a man's fortune, ride in his carriage, be called after his name, and call him her *nown dear lovee* when she wants money, without loving and respecting the great he-creature. Oh! my dear girl, you are a monstrous prude.

LETITIA. I don't say what I would do; I only intimate how I suppose she wishes to act.

CHARLOTTE. No, no, no! A fig for sentiment. If she breaks, or wishes to break, with Mr. Dimple, depend upon it, she has some other man in her eye. A woman rarely discards one lover, until she is sure of another.— Letitia little thinks what a clue I have to Dimple's conduct. The generous man submits to render himself disgusting to Maria, in order that she may leave him at liberty to address me. (*Aside, and rings a bell.*) I must change the subject.

(*Enter* SERVANT.)

Frank, order the horses to.— Talking of marriage—did you hear that Sally Bloomsbury is going to be married next week to Mr. Indigo, the rich Carolinian?

LETITIA. Sally Bloomsbury married! —Why, she is not yet in her teens.

CHARLOTTE. I do not know how that is, but, you may depend upon it, 't is a done affair. I have it from the best authority. There is my aunt Wyerley's Hannah (you know Hannah—though a black, she is a wench that was never caught in a lie in her life) ; now Hannah has a brother who courts Sarah, Mrs. Catgut the milliner's girl, and she told Hannah's brother, and Hannah, who, as I said before, is a girl of undoubted veracity, told it directly to me, that Mrs. Catgut was making a new cap for Miss Bloomsbury, which, as it was very dressy, it is very probable is designed for a wedding cap: now, as she is to be married, who can it be to, but to Mr. Indigo? Why, there is no other gentleman that visits at her papa's.

LETITIA. Say not a word more, Charlotte. Your intelligence is so direct and well grounded, it is almost a pity that it is not a piece of scandal.

CHARLOTTE. Oh! I am the pink of prudence. Though I cannot charge myself with ever having discredited a tea-party by my silence, yet I take care never to report any thing of my acquaintance, especially if it is to their credit—*discredit,* I mean—until I have searched to the bottom of it. It is true, there is infinite pleasure in this charitable pursuit. Oh! how delicious to go and condole with the friends of some backsliding sister, or to retire with some old dowager or maiden aunt of the family, who love scandal so well, that they cannot forbear gratifying their appetite at the expence of the reputation of their nearest relations! And then to return full fraught with a rich collection of circumstances, to retail to the next circle of our acquaintance 'under the strongest injunctions of secrecy—ha, ha, ha!—interlarding the melancholy tale with so many doleful shakes of the head, and more doleful, "Ah! who would have thought it! so amiable, so prudent a young lady, as we all thought her, what a monstrous pity! well, I have nothing to charge myself with; I acted the part of a friend, I warned her of the principles of that rake, I told her what would be the consequence; I told her so, I told her so."— Ha, ha, ha!

LETITIA. Ha, ha, ha! Well, but Charlotte, you don't tell me what you think of Miss Bloomsbury's match.

CHARLOTTE. Think! why I think it is probable she cried for a plaything, and they have given her a husband. Well, well, well, the puling chit shall not be deprived of her plaything: 't is only exchanging London dolls for American babies— Apropos, of babies, have you heard what Mrs. Affable's high-flying notions of delicacy have come to?

LETITIA. Who, she that was Miss Lovely?

CHARLOTTE. The same; she married Bob Affable of Schenectady. Don't you remember?

SERVANT (enters). Madam, the carriage is ready.

LETITIA. Shall we go to the stores first, or visiting?

CHARLOTTE. I should think it rather too early to visit; especially Mrs. Prim: you know she is so particular.

LETITIA. Well, but what of Mrs. Affable?

CHARLOTTE. Oh, I'll tell you as we go; come, come, let us hasten. I hear Mrs. Catgut has some of the prettiest caps arrived you ever saw. I shall die if I have not the first sight of them. (Exeunt.)

SCENE TWO

A room in VAN ROUGH's house. MARIA sitting disconsolate at a table, with books, etc.

Song[1]

The sun sets in night, and the stars
  shun the day;
But glory remains when their lights
  fade away!
Begin, ye tormentors! your threats
  are in vain,
For the son of Alknomook shall
  never complain.

Remember the arrows he shot from
  his bow;
No—the son of Alknomook will
  never complain.
Remember your chiefs by his hatchet laid low:
Why so slow?—do you wait till I
  shrink from the pain?

Remember the wood where in ambush we lay;
And the scalps which we bore from
  your nation away:
Now the flame rises fast, you exult
  in my pain;
But the son of Alknomook can
  never complain.

I go to the land where my father is
  gone;
His ghost shall rejoice in the fame
  of his son:
Death comes like a friend, he relieves me from pain;
And thy son, Oh Alknomook! has
  scorn'd to complain.

[1] This popular song of the period was published in New York under the title of Alknomook and carried the subtitle "The Death Song of the Cherokee Indians."

There is something in this song which ever calls forth my affections. The manly virtue of courage, that fortitude which steels the heart against the keenest misfortunes, which interweaves the laurel of glory amidst the instruments of torture and death, displays something so noble, so exalted, that in despite of the prejudices of education, I cannot but admire it, even in a savage. The prepossession which our sex is supposed to entertain for the character of a soldier is, I know, a standing piece of raillery among the wits. A cockade, a lapell'd coat, and a feather, they will tell you, are irresistible by a female heart. Let it be so.— Who is it that considers the helpless situation of our sex, that does not see we each moment stand in need of a protector, and that a brave one too. Formed of the more delicate materials of nature, endowed only with the softer passions, incapable, from our ignorance of the world, to guard against the wiles of mankind, our security for happiness often depends upon their generosity and courage:— Alas! how little of the former do we find. How inconsistent! that man should be leagued to destroy that honour, upon which solely rests his respect and esteem. Ten thousand temptations allure us, ten thousand passions betray us; yet the smallest deviation from the path of rectitude is followed by the contempt and insult of man, and the more remorseless pity of woman: years of penitence and tears cannot wash away the stain, nor a life of virtue obliterate its remembrance. Reputation is the life of woman; yet courage to protect it is masculine and disgusting; and the only safe asylum a woman of delicacy can find is in the arms of a man of honour. How naturally, then,

should we love the brave, and the generous; how gratefully should we bless the arm raised for our protection, when nerv'd by virtue, and directed by honour! Heaven grant that the man with whom I may be connected—may be connected!—Whither has my imagination transported me—whither does it now lead me?—Am I not indissolubly engaged by every obligation of honour, which my own consent, and my father's approbation can give, to a man who can never share my affections, and whom a few days hence it will be criminal for me to disapprove—to disapprove! would to heaven that were all—to despise. For, can the most frivolous manners, actuated by the most depraved heart, meet, or merit, anything but contempt from every woman of delicacy and sentiment?

VAN ROUGH (*without*). Mary!

MARIA. Ha, my father's voice— Sir!—

VAN ROUGH (*enters*). What, Mary, always singing doleful ditties, and moping over these plaguy books.

MARIA. I hope, Sir, that it is not criminal to improve my mind with books; or to divert my melancholy with singing at my leisure hours.

VAN ROUGH. Why, I don't know that, child; I don't know that. They us'd to say when I was a young man, that if a woman knew how to make a pudding, and to keep herself out of fire and water, she knew enough for a wife. Now, what good have these books done you? have they not made you melancholy? as you call it. Pray, what right has a girl of your age to be in the dumps? haven't you every thing your heart can wish; an't you going to be married to a young man of great fortune; an't you going to have the quit-rent of twenty miles square?

MARIA. One hundredth part of the land, and a lease for life of the heart of a man I could love, would satisfy me.

VAN ROUGH. Pho, pho, pho! child; nonsense, downright nonsense, child. This comes of your reading your story-books; your Charles Grandisons, your Sentimental Journals, and your Robinson Crusoes, and such other trumpery. No, no, no! child, it is money makes the mare go; keep your eye upon the main chance, Mary.

MARIA. Marriage, Sir, is, indeed, a very serious affair.

VAN ROUGH. You are right, child; you are right. I am sure I found it so to my cost.

MARIA. I mean, Sir, that as marriage is a portion for life, and so intimately involves our happiness, we cannot be too considerate in the choice of our companion.

VAN ROUGH. Right, child; very right. A young woman should be very sober when she is making her choice, but when she has once made it, as you have done, I don't see why she should not be as merry as a grig; I am sure she has reason enough to be so— Solomon says, that "there is a time to laugh, and a time to weep"; now a time for a young woman to laugh is when she has made sure of a good rich husband. Now a time to cry, according to you, Mary, is when she is making choice of him: but, I should think that a young woman's time to cry was when she despaired of *getting* one.—Why, there was your mother now; to be sure when I popp'd the question to her she did look a little silly; but when she had once looked down on her apron-strings, as all modest young women us'd to do, and drawled out ye-s, she was as brisk and as merry as a bee.

MARIA. My honoured mother, Sir, had no motive to melancholy; she married the man of her choice.

VAN ROUGH. The man of her choice! And pray, Mary, an't you going to marry the man of your choice—what trumpery notion is this?— It is these vile books. (*Throwing them away*) I'd have you to know, Mary, if you won't make young Van Dumpling the man of *your* choice, you shall marry him as the man of *my* choice.

MARIA. You terrify me, Sir. Indeed, Sir, I am all submission. My will is yours.

VAN ROUGH. Why, that is the way your mother us'd to talk. "My will is yours, my dear 'Mr. Van Rough, my will is yours": but she took special care to have her own way though for all that.

MARIA. Do not reflect upon my mother's memory, Sir—

VAN ROUGH. Why not, Mary, why not? She kept me from speaking my mind all her *life*, and do you think she shall henpeck me now she is *dead* too? Come, come; don't go to sniveling: be a good girl, and mind the main chance. I'll see you well settled in the world.

MARIA. I do not doubt your love, Sir; and it is my duty to obey you.— I will endeavor to make my duty and inclination go hand in hand.

VAN ROUGH. Well, well, Mary; do you be a good girl, mind the main chance, and never mind inclination.— Why, do you know that I have been down in the cellar this very morning to examine a pipe of Madeira which I purchased the week you were born, and mean to tap on your wedding day.— That pipe cost me fifty pounds sterling. It was well worth sixty pounds; but I over-reached Ben Bulkhead, the supercargo: I'll tell you the

whole story. You must know that—
SERVANT (*enters*). Sir, Mr. Transfer,
the broker, is below. (*Exit.*)
VAN ROUGH. Well, Mary, I must go.—
Remember, and be a good girl, and
mind the main chance. (*Exit.*)
MARIA (*alone*). How deplorable is
my situation! How distressing for a
daughter to find her heart militating
with her filial duty! I know my father
loves me tenderly, why then do I
reluctantly obey him? Heaven knows!
with what reluctance I should oppose
the will of a parent, or set an example
of filial disobedience; at a parent's
command I could wed awkwardness
and deformity. Were the heart of my
husband good, I would so magnify his
good qualities with the eye of con-
jugal affection that the defects of
his person and manners should be
lost in the emanation of his virtues.
At a father's command, I could embrace poverty. Were the poor man
my husband, I would learn resignation to my lot; I would enliven our
frugal meal with good humour, and
chase away misfortune from our cottage with a smile. At a father's command, I could almost submit to what
every female heart knows to be the
most mortifying, to marry a weak
man, and blush at my husband's folly
in every company I visited.— But to
marry a depraved wretch, whose only
virtue is a polished exterior; who is
actuated by the unmanly ambition of
conquering the defenceless; whose
heart, insensible to the emotions of
patriotism, dilates at the plaudits of
every unthinking girl: whose laurels
are the sighs and tears of the miserable victims of his specious behav-
iour.— Can he, who has no regard
for the peace and happiness of other
families, ever have a due regard for
the peace and happiness of his own?

Would to heaven that my father were
not so hasty in his temper! Surely, if
I were to state my reasons for declin-
ing this match, he would not compel
me to marry a man—whom, though
my lips may solemnly promise to
honour, I find my heart must ever
despise. (*Exit.*)

ACT TWO

SCENE ONE

Enter CHARLOTTE *and* LETITIA.

———

CHARLOTTE (*at entering*). Betty, take
those things out of the carriage and
carry them to my chamber; see that
you don't tumble them.— My dear,
I protest, I think it was the homeliest
of the whole. I declare I was almost
tempted to return and change it.
LETITIA. Why would you take it?
CHARLOTTE. Didn't Mrs. Catgut say
it was the most fashionable?
LETITIA. But, my dear, it will never
sit becomingly on you.
CHARLOTTE. I know that; but did
not you hear Mrs. Catgut say it was
fashionable?
LETITIA. Did you see that sweet airy
cap with the white sprig?
CHARLOTTE. Yes, and I longed to
take it; but, my dear, what could I
do?— Did not Mrs. Catgut say it was
the most fashionable; and if I had not
taken it, was not that awkward gawky,
Sally Slender, ready to purchase it
immediately?
LETITIA. Did you observe how she
tumbled over the things at the next
shop, and then went off without purchasing any thing, nor even thanking
the poor man for his trouble?— But
of all the awkward creatures, did you

see Miss Blouze, endeavouring to thrust her unmerciful arm into those small kid gloves?

CHARLOTTE. Ha, ha, ha, ha!

LETITIA. Then did you take notice, with what an affected warmth of friendship she and Miss Wasp met? when all their acquaintances know how much pleasure they take in abusing each other in every company?

CHARLOTTE. Lud! Letitia, is that so extraordinary? Why, my dear, I hope you are not going to turn sentimentalist.— Scandal, you know, is but amusing ourselves with the faults, foibles, follies and reputations of our friends—indeed, I don't know why we should have friends if we are not at liberty to make use of them. But no person is so ignorant of the world as to suppose, because I amuse myself with a lady's faults, that I am obliged to quarrel with her person, every time we meet; believe me, my dear, we should have very few acquaintances at that rate.

(SERVANT *enters and delivers a letter to* CHARLOTTE, *and goes out.*)

CHARLOTTE. You'll excuse me, my dear. (*Opens it and reads to herself.*)

LETITIA. Oh, quite excusable.

CHARLOTTE. As I hope to be married, my brother Henry is in the city.

LETITIA. What, your brother, Colonel Manly?

CHARLOTTE. Yes, my dear; the only brother I have in the world.

LETITIA. Was he never in this city?

CHARLOTTE. Never nearer than Harlem Heights, where he lay with his regiment.

LETITIA. What sort of a being is this brother of yours? If he is as chatty, as pretty, as sprightly as you, half the belles in the city will be pulling caps for him.

CHARLOTTE. My brother is the very

counterpart and reverse of me: I am gay, he is grave; I am airy, he is solid; I am ever selecting the most pleasing objects for my laughter, he has a tear for every pitiful one. And thus, whilst he is plucking the briars and thorns from the path of the unfortunate, I am strewing my own path with roses.

LETITIA. My sweet friend, not quite so poetical, and little more particular.

CHARLOTTE. Hands off, Letitia. I feel the rage of simile upon me; I can't talk to you in any other way. My brother has a heart replete with the noblest sentiments, but then, it is like —it is like—Oh! you provoking girl, you have deranged all my ideas—it is like—Oh! I have it—his heart is like an old maiden lady's band-box; it contains many costly things, arranged with the most scrupulous nicety, yet the misfortune is that they are too delicate, costly, and antiquated for common use.

LETITIA. By what I can pick out of your flowery description, your brother is no beau.

CHARLOTTE. No, indeed; he makes no pretension to the character. He'd ride, or rather fly, an hundred miles to relieve a distressed object, or to do a gallant act in the service of his country; but, should you drop your fan or bouquet in his presence, it is ten to one that some beau at the farther end of the room would have the honour of presenting it to you, before he had observed that it fell. I'll tell you one of his antiquated, anti-gallant notions.— He said once in my presence, in a room full of company— would you believe it—in a large circle of ladies, that the best evidence a gentleman could give a young lady of his respect and affection was to endeavour in a friendly manner to rectify her foibles. I protest I was crimson to the eyes, upon reflecting that I was known as his sister.

LETITIA. Insupportable creature! tell a lady of her faults! If he is so grave, I fear I have no chance of captivating him.

CHARLOTTE. His conversation is like a rich old fashioned brocade, it will stand alone; every sentence is a sentiment. Now you may judge what a time I had with him, in my twelve months' visit to my father. He read me such lectures, out of pure brotherly affection, against the extremes of fashion, dress, flirting, and coquetry, and all the other dear things which he knows I doat upon, that, I protest, his conversation made me as melancholy as if I had been at church; and heaven knows, though I never prayed to go there but on one occasion, yet I would have exchanged his conversation for a psalm and a sermon. Church is rather melancholy, to be sure; but then I can ogle the beaux, and be regaled with "here endeth the first lesson"; but his brotherly *here*, you would think, had no end. You captivate him! Why, my dear, he would as soon fall in love with a box of Italian flowers. There is Maria now, if she were not engaged, she might do something.— Oh! how I should like to see that pair of penserosos together, looking as grave as two sailors' wives of a stormy night, with a flow of sentiment meandering through their conversation like purling streams in modern poetry.

LETITIA. Oh! my dear fanciful—

CHARLOTTE. Hush! I hear some person coming through the entry.

SERVANT (*enters*). Madam, there's a gentleman below who calls himself Colonel Manly; do you chuse to be at home?

CHARLOTTE. Shew him in. (*Exit SERVANT.*) Now for a sober face.

MANLY (*enters*). My dear Charlotte, I am happy that I once more enfold you within the arms of fraternal affection. I know you are going to ask (amiable impatience!) how our parents do—the venerable pair transmit you their blessing by me—they totter on the verge of a well-spent life, and wish only to see their children settled in the world, to depart in peace.

CHARLOTTE. I am very happy to hear that they are well. (*Coolly*) Brother, will you give me leave to introduce you to our uncle's ward, one of my most intimate friends.

MANLY (*saluting* LETITIA). I ought to regard your friends as my own.

CHARLOTTE. Come, Letitia, do give us a little dash of your vivacity; my brother is so sentimental, and so grave, that I protest he'll give us the vapours.

MANLY. Though sentiment and gravity, I know, are banished the polite world, yet, I hoped, they might find some countenance in the meeting of such near connections as brother and sister.

CHARLOTTE. Positively, brother, if you go one step further in this strain, you will set me crying, and that, you know, would spoil my eyes; and then I should never get the husband which our good papa and mamma have so kindly wished me—never be established in the world.

MANLY. Forgive me, my sister—I am no enemy to mirth; I love your sprightliness; and I hope it will one day enliven the hours of some worthy man; but when I mention the respectable authors of my existence—the cherishers and protectors of my helpless infancy, whose hearts glow with such fondness and attachment, that they would willingly lay down their lives for my welfare, you will excuse me if I am so unfashionable as to speak of them with some degree of respect and reverence.

CHARLOTTE. Well, well, brother; if you won't be gay, we'll not differ; I will be as grave as you wish. (*She affects gravity.*) And so, brother, you have come to the city to exchange some of your commutation notes for a little pleasure.

MANLY. Indeed, you are mistaken; my errand is not of amusement, but business; and as I neither drink nor game, my expences will be so trivial, I shall have no occasion to sell my notes.

CHARLOTTE. Then you won't have occasion to do a very good thing. Why, there was the Vermont General —he came down some time since, sold all his musty notes at one stroke, and then laid the cash out in trinkets for his dear Fanny. I want a dozen pretty things myself; have you got the notes with you?

MANLY. I shall be ever willing to contribute as far as it is in my power, to adorn, or in any way to please my sister; yet, I hope, I shall never be obliged for this to sell my notes. I may be romantic, but I preserve them as a sacred deposit. Their full amount is justly due to me, but as embarrassments, the natural consequences of a long war, disable my country from supporting its credit, I shall wait with patience until it is rich enough to discharge them. If that is not in my day, they shall be transmitted as an honourable certificate to posterity, that I have humbly imitated our illustrious WASHINGTON, in having exposed my health and life in the service of my country, without reaping any other reward than the glory of conquering in so arduous a contest.

CHARLOTTE. Well said heroics. Why, my dear Henry, you have such a lofty way of saying things, that I protest I almost tremble at the thought of introducing you to the polite circles in the city. The belles would think you were a player run mad, with your head filled with old scraps of tragedy; and, as to the beaux, they might admire, because they would not understand you.—But, however, I must, I believe, venture to introduce you to two or three ladies of my acquaintance.

LETITIA. And that will make him acquainted with thirty or forty beaux.

CHARLOTTE. Oh! brother, you don't know what a fund of happiness you have in store.

MANLY. I fear, sister, I have not refinement sufficient to enjoy it.

CHARLOTTE. Oh! you cannot fail being pleased.

LETITIA. Our ladies are so delicate and dressy.

CHARLOTTE. And our beaux so dressy and delicate.

LETITIA. Our ladies chat and flirt so agreeably.

CHARLOTTE. And our beaux simper and bow so gracefully.

LETITIA. With their hair so trim and neat.

CHARLOTTE. And their faces so soft and sleek.

LETITIA. Their buckles so tonish and bright.

CHARLOTTE. And their hands so slender and white.

LETITIA. I vow, Charlotte, we are quite poetical.

CHARLOTTE. And then, brother, the faces of the beaux are of such a lily white hue! None of that horrid robustness of constitution, that vulgar corn-fed glow of health, which can only serve to alarm an unmarried lady with apprehensions, and prove a melancholy memento to a married one, that she can never hope for the happiness of being a widow. I will say this to the credit of our city beaux, that such is the delicacy of their complexion, dress, and address, that, even had I no reliance upon the honour of the dear Adonises, I would trust myself in any possible situation with them, without the least apprehensions of rudeness.

MANLY. Sister Charlotte!

CHARLOTTE. Now, now, now brother (*Interrupting him*), now don't go to spoil my mirth with a dash of your gravity; I am so glad to see you, I am in tip-top spirits. Oh! that you could be with us at a little snug party. There is Billy Simper, Jack Chassé, and Colonel Van Titter, Miss Promonade, and the two Miss Tambours, sometimes make a party, with some other ladies, in a side-box at the play. Everything is conducted with such decorum —first we bow round to the company in general, then to each one in particular, then we have so many inquiries after each other's health, and we are so happy to meet each other, and it is so many ages since we last had that pleasure, and, if a married lady is in company, we have such a sweet dissertation upon her son Bobby's chincough, then the curtain rises, then our sensibility is all awake, and then by the mere force of apprehension, we torture some harmless expression into a double meaning, which the poor author never dreamt of, and then we have recourse to our fans, and then we blush, and then the gentlemen jog one another, peep under the fan, and make the prettiest remarks; and then we giggle and they simper, and they giggle and we simper, and then the curtain drops, and then for nuts and oranges, and then we bow, and it's pray Ma'am take it, and pray Sir keep it, and oh! not for the world, Sir: and then the curtain rises again, and then we blush, and giggle, and simper, and bow, all over again. Oh! the sentimental charms of a side-box conversation! (*All laugh.*)

MANLY. Well, sister, I join heartily with you in the laugh; for, in my opinion, it is as justifiable to laugh at folly, as it is reprehensible to ridicule misfortune.

CHARLOTTE. Well, but brother, positively, I can't introduce you in these clothes: why, your coat looks as if it were calculated for the vulgar purpose of keeping yourself comfortable.

MANLY. This coat was my regimental coat in the late war. The public tumults of our state have induced me to buckle on the sword in support of that government which I once fought to establish. I can only say, sister, that there was a time when this coat was respectable, and some people even thought that those men who had endured so many winter campaigns in the service of their country, without bread, clothing, or pay, at least deserved that the poverty of their appearance should not be ridiculed.

CHARLOTTE. We agree in opinion entirely, brother, though it would not have done for me to have said it: it is the coat makes the man respectable. In the time of the war, when we were almost frightened to death, why, your coat was respectable, that is, fashionable; now another kind of coat is fashionable, that is, respectable. And pray direct the tailor to make yours the height of the fashion.

MANLY. Though it is of little consequence to me of what shape my coat is, yet, as to the height of the fashion, there you will please to excuse me, sister. You know my sentiments on that subject. I have often lamented the advantage which the French have over us in that particular. In Paris, the fashions have their dawnings, their routine and declensions, and depend as much upon the caprice of the day as in other countries; but there every lady assumes a right to deviate from the general *ton*, as far as will be of advantage to her own appearance. In America, the cry is, what is the fashion? and we follow it, indiscriminately, because it is so.

CHARLOTTE. Therefore it is, that when large hoops are in fashion, we often see many a plump girl lost in the immensity of a hoop petticoat, whose want of height and *em-bonpoint* would never have been remarked in any other dress. When the high headdress is the mode, how then do we see a lofty cushion, with a profusion of gauze, feathers, and ribband, supported by a face no bigger than an apple; whilst a broad full-faced lady, who really would have appeared tolerably handsome in a large headdress, looks with her smart chapeau as masculine as a soldier.

MANLY. But remember, my dear sister, and I wish all my fair countrywomen would recollect, that the only excuse a young lady can have for going extravagantly into a fashion, is, because it makes her look extravagantly handsome.—Ladies, I must wish you a good morning.

CHARLOTTE. But, brother, you are going to make home with us.

MANLY. Indeed, I cannot. I have seen my uncle, and explained that matter.

CHARLOTTE. Come and dine with us, then. We have a family dinner about half past four o'clock.

MANLY. I am engaged to dine with the Spanish ambassador. I was introduced to him by an old brother officer; and instead of freezing me with a cold card of compliment to dine with him ten days hence, he, with the true old Castilian frankness, in a friendly manner, asked me to dine with him today—an honour I could not refuse. Sister, adieu—Madam, your most obedient— (*Exit.*)

CHARLOTTE. I will wait upon you to the door, brother; I have something particular to say to you. (*Exit.*)

LETITIA (*alone*). What a pair!— She the pink of flirtation, he the essence of everything that is *outré* and gloomy.— I think I have completely deceived Charlotte by my manner of speaking of Mr. Dimple; she's too much the friend of Maria to be confided in. He is certainly rendering himself disagreeable to Maria, in order to break with her and proffer his hand to me. This is what the delicate fellow hinted in our last conversation. (*Exit.*)

SCENE TWO

The Mall.

———

JESSAMY (*enters*). Positively this Mall is a very pretty place. I hope the city won't ruin it by repairs. To be sure, it won't do to speak of in the same day with Ranelagh or Vauxhall; however, it's a fine place for a young fellow to display his person to advantage. Indeed, nothing is lost here; the girls have taste, and I am very happy to find they have adopted the elegant London fashion of looking back, after a genteel fellow like me has passed them. Ah! who comes here? This, by his awkwardness, must be the Yankee colonel's servant. I'll accost him.

(*Enter* JONATHAN.)

Votre très—humble serviteur, Monsieur. I understand Colonel Manly, the Yankee officer, has the honour of your services.

JONATHAN. Sir!—

JESSAMY. I say, Sir, I understand that Colonel Manly has the honour of having you for a servant.

JONATHAN. Servant! Sir, do you take me for a neger—I am Colonel Manly's waiter.

JESSAMY. A true Yankee distinction, egad, without a difference. Why, Sir, do you not perform all the offices of a servant? Do you not even blacken his boots?

JONATHAN. Yes; I do grease them a bit sometimes; but I am a true blue son of liberty, for all that. Father said I should come as Colonel Manly's waiter to see the world, and all that; but no man shall master me: my father has as good a farm as the colonel.

JESSAMY. Well, Sir, we will not quarrel about terms upon the eve of an acquaintance, from which I promise myself so much satisfaction—therefore *sans cérémonie*—

JONATHAN. What?—

JESSAMY. I say, I am extremely happy to see Colonel Manly's waiter.

JONATHAN. Well, and I vow, too, I am pretty considerably glad to see you—but what the dogs need of all this outlandish lingo? Who may you be, Sir, if I may be so bold?

JESSAMY. I have the honour to be Mr. Dimple's servant, or, if you please, waiter. We lodge under the same roof, and should be glad of the honour of your acquaintance.

JONATHAN. You a waiter! By the living jingo, you look so topping, I took you for one of the agents to Congress.

JESSAMY. The brute has discernment notwithstanding his appearance.— Give me leave to say I wonder then at your familiarity.

JONATHAN. Why, as to the matter of that, Mr.—pray, what's your name?

JESSAMY. Jessamy, at your service.

JONATHAN. Why, I swear we don't make any great matter of distinction in our state, between quality and other folks.

JESSAMY. This is, indeed, a levelling principle. I hope, Mr. Jonathan, you have not taken part with the insurgents.

JONATHAN. Why, since General Shays has sneaked off, and given us the bag to hold, I don't care to give my opinion; but you'll promise not to tell—put your ear this way—you won't tell?— I vow, I did think the sturgeons were right.

JESSAMY. I thought, Mr. Jonathan, you Massachusetts men always argued with a gun in your hand.— Why didn't you join them?

JONATHAN. Why, the colonel is one of those folks called the Shin—shin—dang it all, I can't speak them lignum vitæ words—you know who I mean—there is a company of them—they wear a China goose at their buttonhole—a kind of gilt thing.— Now the colonel told father and brother—you must know there are, let me see—there is Elnathan, Silas, and Barnabas, Tabitha—no, no, she's a she—tarnation, now I have it—there's Elnathan, Silas, Barnabas, Jonathan, that's I—seven of us, six went into the wars, and I stayed at home to take care of mother. Colonel said that it was a burning shame for the true blue Bunker-hill sons of liberty, who had fought Governor Hutchinson, Lord North, and the Devil, to have any hand in kicking up a cursed dust against a government, which we had every mother's son of us a hand in making.

JESSAMY. Bravo!— Well, have you been abroad in the city since your arrival? What have you seen that is curious and entertaining?

JONATHAN. Oh! I have seen a power of fine sights. I went to see two marble-stone men and a leaden horse, that stands out in doors in all weathers; and when I came where they was, one had got no head, and t' other weren't there. They said as how the leaden man was a damn'd tory, and that he took wit in his anger and rode off in the time of the troubles.

JESSAMY. But this was not the end of your excursion.

JONATHAN. Oh, no; I went to a place they call Holy Ground. Now I counted this was a place where folks go to meeting; so I put my hymnbook in my pocket, and walked softly and grave as a minister; and when I came there, the dogs a bit of a meeting-house could I see. At last I spied a young gentlewoman standing by one of the seats, which they have here at the doors—I took her to be the deacon's daughter, and she looked so kind, and so obliging, that I thought I would go and ask her the way to lecture, and would you think it—she called me dear, and sweeting, and honey, just as if we were married; by the living jingo, I had a month's mind to buss her.

JESSAMY. Well, but how did it end?

JONATHAN. Why, as I was standing talking with her, a parcel of sailor men and boys got round me, the snarl headed curs fell a-kicking and cursing of me at such a tarnal rate, that, I vow, I was glad to take to my heels and split home, right off, tail on end like a stream of chalk.

JESSAMY. Why, my dear friend, you are not acquainted with the city; that girl you saw was a— (*Whispers.*)

JONATHAN. Mercy on my soul! was that young woman a harlot!— Well, if this is New York Holy Ground, what must the Holy-day Ground be!

JESSAMY. Well, you should not judge of the city too rashly. We have a number of elegant fine girls here, that make a man's leisure hours pass very agreeably. I would esteem it an honour to announce you to some of them.— Gad! that announce is a select word; I wonder where I picked it up.

JONATHAN. I don't want to know them.

JESSAMY. Come, come, my dear friend, I see that I must assume the honour of being the director of your amusements. Nature has given us passions, and youth and opportunity stimulate to gratify them. It is no shame, my dear Blueskin, for a man to amuse himself with a little gallantry.

JONATHAN. Girl huntry! I don't altogether understand. I never played at that game. I know how to play hunt the squirrel, but I can't play anything with the girls; I am as good as married.

JESSAMY. Vulgar, horrid brute! Married, and above a hundred miles from his wife, and think that an objection to his making love to every woman he meets! He never can have read, no, he never can have been in a room with a volume of the divine Chesterfield.— So you are married?

JONATHAN. No, I don't say so; I said I was as good as married, a kind of promise.

JESSAMY. As good as married!—

JONATHAN. Why, yes; there's Tabitha Wymen, the deacon's daughter, at home, she and I have been courting a great while, and folks say as how we are to be married; and so I broke a piece of money with her when we parted, and she promised not to spark it with Solomon Dyer while I am gone. You wouldn't have me false to my true love, would you?

JESSAMY. May be you have another reason for constancy; possibly the young lady has a fortune? Ha! Mr. Jonathan, the solid charms; the chains of love are never so binding as when the links are made of gold.

JONATHAN. Why, as to fortune, I must needs say her father is pretty dumb rich; he went representative for our town last year. He will give her—let me see—four times seven is— seven times four—nought and carry one—he will give her twenty acres of land—somewhat rocky though—a Bible, and a cow.

JESSAMY. Twenty acres of rock, a Bible, and a cow! Why, my dear Mr. Jonathan, we have servant maids, or, as you would more elegantly express it, wait'resses, in this city, who collect more in one year from their mistresses' cast clothes.

JONATHAN. You don't say so!—

JESSAMY. Yes, and I'll introduce you to one of them. There is a little lump of flesh and delicacy that lives at next door, wait'ress to Miss Maria; we often see her on the stoop.

JONATHAN. But are you sure she would be courted by me?

JESSAMY. Never doubt it; remember a faint heart never—blisters on my tongue—I was going to be guilty of a vile proverb; flat against the authority of Chesterfield.— I say there can be no doubt that the brilliancy of your merit will secure you a favourable reception.

JONATHAN. Well, but what must I say to her?

JESSAMY. Say to her! why, my dear friend, though I admire your profound knowledge on every other subject, yet, you will pardon my saying, that your want of opportunity has made the female heart escape the poignancy of your penetration. Say to her!— Why, when a man goes acourting, and hopes for success, he must begin with doing, and not saying.

JONATHAN. Well, what must I do?

JESSAMY. Why, when you are introduced you must make five or six elegant bows.

JONATHAN. Six elegant bows! I understand that; six, you say? Well—

JESSAMY. Then you must press and kiss her hand; then press and kiss, and so on to her lips and cheeks; then talk as much as you can about hearts, darts, flames, nectar and ambrosia— the more incoherent the better.

JONATHAN. Well, but suppose she should be angry with I?

JESSAMY. Why, if she should pretend—please to observe, Mr. Jonathan —if she should pretend to be offended, you must— But I'll tell you how my master acted in such a case: He was seated by a young lady of eighteen upon a sofa, plucking with a wanton hand the blooming sweets of youth and beauty. When the lady thought it necessary to check his ardour, she called up a frown upon her lovely face so irresistibly alluring that it would have warmed the frozen bosom of age: "Remember," said she, putting her delicate arm upon his, "remember your character and my honour." My master instantly dropped upon his knees, with eyes swimming with love, cheeks glowing with desire, and in the gentlest modulation of voice, he said— "My dear Caroline, in a few months our hands will be indissolubly united at the altar; our hearts I feel are already so—the favours you now grant as evidence of your affection, are favours indeed; yet when the ceremony is once past, what will now be received with rapture will then be attributed to duty."

JONATHAN. Well, and what was the consequence?

JESSAMY. The consequence!— Ah! forgive me, my dear friend, but you

New England gentlemen have such a laudable curiosity of seeing the bottom of every thing—why, to be honest, I confess I saw the blooming cherub of a consequence smiling in its angelic mother's arms, about ten months afterwards.

JONATHAN. Well, if I follow all your plans, make them six bows, and all that; shall I have such little cherubim consequences?

JESSAMY. Undoubtedly.— What are you musing upon?

JONATHAN. You say you'll certainly make me acquainted?— Why, I was thinking then how I should contrive to pass this broken piece of silver—won't it buy a sugar-dram?

JESSAMY. What is that, the love-token from the deacon's daughter?— You come on bravely. But I must hasten to my master. Adieu, my dear friend.

JONATHAN. Stay, Mr. Jessamy—must I buss her when I am introduced to her?

JESSAMY. I told you, you must kiss her.

JONATHAN. Well, but must I buss her?

JESSAMY. Why, kiss and buss, and buss and kiss, is all one.

JONATHAN. Oh! my dear friend, though you have a profound knowledge of all, a pugnancy of tribulation, you don't know everything. (*Exit.*)

JESSAMY (*alone*). Well, certainly I improve; my master could not have insinuated himself with more address into the heart of a man he despised.— Now will this blundering dog sicken Jenny with his nauseous pawings, until she flies into my arms for very ease. How sweet will the contrast be, between the blundering Jonathan, and the courtly and accomplished Jessamy!

ACT THREE

SCENE ONE

DIMPLE'S *room.*

DIMPLE (*discovered at a toilet, reading*). "Women have in general but one object, which is their beauty." Very true, my lord; positively very true. "Nature has hardly formed a woman ugly enough to be insensible to flattery upon her person." Extremely just, my lord; every day's delightful experience confirms this. "If her face is so shocking that she must, in some degree, be conscious of it, her figure and air, she thinks, make ample amends for it." The sallow Miss Wan is a proof of this.— Upon my telling the distasteful wretch, the other day, that her countenance spoke the pensive language of sentiment, and that Lady Wortley Montague declared, that if the ladies were arrayed in the garb of innocence, the face would be the last part which would be admired, as Monsieur Milton expresses it, she grin'd horribly a ghastly smile. "If her figure is deformed, she thinks her face counterbalances it."

(*Enter* JESSAMY *with letters.*)

DIMPLE. Where got you these, Jessamy?

JESSAMY. Sir, the English packet is arrived.

(DIMPLE *opens and reads a letter enclosing notes.*)

"Sir,

"I have drawn bills on you in favour of Messrs. Van Cash and Co. as per margin. I have taken up your note to Col. Piquet, and discharged your debts to my Lord Lurcher and Sir Harry Rook. I herewith enclose you copies of the bills, which I have no doubt will be immediately honoured. On failure, I shall empower some lawyer in your country to recover the amounts.

"I am, Sir,
"Your most humble servant,
"JOHN HAZARD."

Now, did not my lord expressly say that it was unbecoming a well-bred man to be in a passion, I confess I should be ruffled. (*Reads*.) "There is no accident so unfortunate, which a wise man may not turn to his advantage; nor any accident so fortunate, which a fool will not turn to his disadvantage." True, my lord: but how advantage can be derived from this, I can't see. Chesterfield himself, who made, however, the worst practice of the most excellent precepts, was never in so embarrassing a situation. I love the person of Charlotte, and it is necessary I should command the fortune of Letitia. As to Maria!—I doubt not by my *sang-froid* behavior I shall compel her to decline the match; but the blame must not fall upon me. A prudent man, as my lord says, should take all the credit of a good action to himself, and throw the discredit of a bad one upon others. I must break with Maria, marry Letitia, and as for Charlotte—why, Charlotte must be a companion to my wife.— Here, Jessamy! (*Enter* JESSAMY.)

DIMPLE (*folds and seals two letters*). Here, Jessamy, take this letter to my love. (*Gives him one*.)

JESSAMY. To which of your honour's loves?— Oh! (*Reading*) to Miss Letitia, your honour's rich love.

DIMPLE. And this (*Delivering another*) to Miss Charlotte Manly. See that you deliver them privately.

JESSAMY (*going*). Yes, your honour.

DIMPLE. Jessamy, who are these strange lodgers that came to the house last night?

JESSAMY. Why, the master is a Yankee colonel; I have not seen much of him; but the man is the most unpolished animal your honour ever disgraced your eyes by looking upon. I have had one of the most *outré* conversations with him!— He really has a most prodigious effect upon my risibility.

DIMPLE. I ought, according to every rule of Chesterfield, to wait on him and insinuate myself into his good graces.— Jessamy, wait on the colonel with my compliments, and if he is disengaged, I will do myself the honour of paying him my respects.— Some ignorant unpolished boor—

JESSAMY (*goes off and returns*). Sir, the colonel is gone out, and Jonathan, his servant, says that he is gone to stretch his legs upon the Mall— Stretch his legs! what an indelicacy of diction!

DIMPLE. Very well. Reach me my hat and sword. I'll accost him there, in my way to Letitia's, as by accident; pretend to be struck with his person and address, and endeavour to steal into his confidence. Jessamy, I have no business for you at present. (*Exit*.)

JESSAMY (*taking up the book*). My master and I obtain our knowledge from the same source—though, gad! I think myself much the prettier fellow of the two. (*Surveying himself in the glass*) That was a brilliant thought, to insinuate that I folded my master's letters for him; the folding is so neat, that it does honour to the operator. I once intended to have insinuated that I wrote his letters too; but that was before I saw them; it won't do now; no honour there, positively.— "Nothing looks more vulgar (*Reading affectedly*), ordinary, and illiberal, than ugly, uneven, and ragged nails; the ends of which should be kept even and clean, not tipped with black, and cut in small segments of circles"— Segments of circles! surely my lord did not consider that he wrote for the beaux. Segments of circles! what a crabbed term! Now I dare answer, that my master, with all his learning, does not know that this means, according to the present mode, to let the nails grow long, and then cut them off even at top. *(Laughing without)*[2] Ha! that's Jenny's titter. I protest I despair of ever teaching that girl to laugh; she has something so execrably natural in her laugh, that I declare it absolutely discomposes my nerves. How came she into our house!— *(Calling)* Jenny!

(Enter JENNY.*)*

JESSAMY. Prythee, Jenny, don't spoil your fine face with laughing.
JENNY. Why, mustn't I laugh, Mr. Jessamy?
JESSAMY. You may smile; but, as my lord says, nothing can authorise a laugh.
JENNY. Well, but I can't help laughing— Have you seen him, Mr. Jessamy? Ha, ha, ha!
JESSAMY. Seen whom?—
JENNY. Why, Jonathan, the New England colonel's servant. Do you know he was at the play last night, and the stupid creature don't know where he has been. He would not go to a play for the world; he thinks it was a show, as he calls it.
JESSAMY. As ignorant and unpolished as he is, do you know, Miss Jenny, that I propose to introduce him to the honour of your acquaintance.

2 That is laughter off stage, which Jessamy hears and comments on.

JENNY. Introduce him to me! for what?
JESSAMY. Why, my lovely girl, that you may take him under your protection, as Madam Rambouillet did young Stanhope; that you may, by your plastic hand, mould this uncouth cub into a gentleman. He is to make love to you.
JENNY. Make love to me!—
JESSAMY. Yes, Mistress Jenny, make love to you; and, I doubt not, when he shall become domesticated in your kitchen, that this boor, under your auspices, will soon become *un amiable petit Jonathan.*
JENNY. I must say, Mr. Jessamy, if he copies after me, he will be vastly monstrously polite.
JESSAMY. Stay here one moment, and I will call him.—Jonathan!— *(Calling)* Mr. Jonathan!—
JONATHAN *(within).* Holla! there.— *(Entering)* You promise to stand by me—six bows you say. *(Bows.)*
JESSAMY. Mrs. Jenny, I have the honour of presenting Mr. Jonathan, Colonel Manly's waiter, to you. I am extremely happy that I have it in my power to make two worthy people acquainted with each other's merit.
JENNY. So, Mr. Jonathan, I hear you were at the play last night.
JONATHAN. At the play! why, did you think I went to the devil's drawing room!
JENNY. The devil's drawing room!
JONATHAN. Yes; why an't cards and dice the devil's device; and the playhouse, the shop where the devil hangs out the vanities of the world, upon the tenterhooks of temptation. I believe you have not heard how they were acting the old boy one night, and the wicked one came among them sure enough; and went right off in a storm, and carried one quarter

of the playhouse with him. Oh! no, no, no! you won't catch me at a playhouse, I warrant you.

JENNY. Well, Mr. Jonathan, though I don't scruple your veracity, I have some reasons for believing you were there; pray, where were you about six o'clock?

JONATHAN. Why, I went to see one Mr. Morrison, the *hocus pocus* man; they said as how he could eat a case knife.

JENNY. Well, and how did you find the place?

JONATHAN. As I was going about here and there, to and again, to find it, I saw a great crowd of folks going into a long entry, that had lanterns over the door; so I asked a man, whether that was not the place where they played *hocus pocus?* He was a very civil kind man, though he did speak like the Hessians; he lifted up his eyes and said—"they play *hocus pocus* tricks enough there, Got knows, mine friend."

JENNY. Well—

JONATHAN. So I went right in, and they showed me away clean up to the garret, just like a meetinghouse gallery. And so I saw a power of topping folks, all sitting round in little cabbins, just like father's corncribs—and then there was such a squeaking with the fiddles, and such a tarnal blaze with the lights, my head was near turned. At last the people that sat near me set up such a hissing—hiss—like so many mad cats; and then they went thump, thump, thump, just like our Peleg threshing wheat, and stampt away, just like the nation; and called out for one Mr. Langolee—I suppose he helps act the tricks.

JENNY. Well, and what did you do all this time?

JONATHAN. Gor, I—I liked the fun, and so I thumpt away, and hiss'd as lustily as the best of 'em. One sailor-looking man that sat by me, seeing me stamp, and knowing I was a cute fellow, because I could make a roaring noise, clapt me on the shoulder and said, you are a damned hearty cock, smite my timbers! I told him so I was, but I thought he need not swear so, and make use of such naughty words.

JESSAMY. The savage!—Well, and did you see the man with his tricks?

JONATHAN. Why, I vow, as I was looking out for him, they lifted up a great green cloth, and let us look right into the next neighbour's house. Have you a good many houses in New York made so in that 'ere way?

JENNY. Not many, but did you see the family?

JONATHAN. Yes, swamp it; I see'd the family.

JENNY. Well, and how did you like them?

JONATHAN. Why, I vow they were pretty much like other families—there was a poor, good-natured, curse of a husband, and a sad rantipole of a wife.

JENNY. But did you see no other folks?

JONATHAN. Yes. There was one youngster, they called him Mr. Joseph; he talked as sober and as pious as a minister; but like some ministers that I know, he was a sly tike in his heart for all that: He was going to ask a young woman to spark it with him, and—the Lord have mercy on my soul!—she was another man's wife.

JESSAMY. The Wabash!

JENNY. And did you see any more folks?

JONATHAN. Why they came on as thick as mustard. For my part, I thought the house was haunted. There was a soldier fellow, who talked about his row de dow dow, and courted a young woman; but of all the cute folk I saw, I liked one little fellow—

JENNY. Aye! who was he?

JONATHAN. Why, he had red hair, and a little round plump face like mine, only not altogether so handsome. His name was Darby—that was his baptizing name, his other name I forgot. Oh! it was, Wig—Wag—Wagall, Darby Wag-all—pray, do you know him?—I should like to take a sling with him, or a drap of cyder with a pepper pod in it, to make it warm and comfortable.

JENNY. I can't say I have that pleasure.

JONATHAN. I wish you did, he is a cute fellow. But there was one thing I didn't like in that Mr. Darby; and that was, he was afraid of some of them 'ere shooting irons, such as your troopers wear on training days. Now, I'm a true born Yankee American son of liberty, and I never was afraid of a gun yet in all my life.

JENNY. Well, Mr. Jonathan, you were certainly at the playhouse.

JONATHAN. I at the playhouse!—Why didn't I see the play then?

JENNY. Why, the people you saw were players.

JONATHAN. Mercy on my soul! did I see the wicked players?—Mayhap that 'ere Darby that I liked so, was the old serpent himself, and had his cloven foot in his pocket. Why, I vow, now I come to think on 't, the candles seemed to burn blue, and I am sure where I sat it smelt tarnally of brimstone.

JESSAMY. Well, Mr. Jonathan, from your account, which I confess is very accurate, you must have been at the playhouse.

JONATHAN. Why, I vow I began to smell a rat. When I came away, I went to the man for my money again: "You want your money," says he. "Yes," says I. "For what," says he. "Why," says I, "no man shall jocky me out of my money; I paid my money to see sights, and the dogs a bit of a sight have I seen, unless you call listening to people's private business a sight." "Why," says he, "it is the School for Scandalization."—"The School for Scandalization!—Oh, ho! no wonder you New York folks are so cute at it, when you go to school to learn it": and so I jogged off.

JESSAMY. My dear Jenny, my master's business drags me from you; would to heaven I knew no other servitude than to your charms.

JONATHAN. Well, but don't go; you won't leave me so.—

JESSAMY. Excuse me. (Aside to him) Remember the cash. (Exit.)

JENNY. Mr. Jonathan, won't you please to sit down. Mr. Jessamy tells me you wanted to have some conversation with me.

(Having brought forward two chairs, they sit.)

JONATHAN. Ma'am!—

JENNY. Sir!—

JONATHAN. Ma'am!—

JENNY. Pray, how do you like the city, Sir?

JONATHAN. Ma'am!—

JENNY. I say, Sir, how do you like New York?

JONATHAN. Ma'am!—

JENNY. The stupid creature! but I must pass some little time with him, if it is only to endeavour to learn whether it was his master that made such an abrupt entrance into our house, and my young mistress's heart, this morning. (Aside) As you don't seem to like to talk, Mr. Jonathan—do you sing?

JONATHAN. Gor, I—I am glad she

asked that, for I forgot what Mr. Jessamy bid me say, and I dare as well be hanged as act what he bid me do, I'm so ashamed. (*Aside*) Yes, Ma'am, I can sing—I can sing "Mear," "Old Hundred," and "Bangor."

JENNY. Oh! I don't mean psalm tunes. Have you no little song to please the ladies; such as "Roslin Castle" or "The Maid of the Mill"?

JONATHAN. Why, all my tunes go to meeting tunes, save one, and I count you won't altogether like that 'ere.

JENNY. What is it called?

JONATHAN. I am sure you have heard folks talk about it, it is called "Yankee Doodle."

JENNY. Oh! it is the tune I am fond of; and, if I know anything of my mistress, she would be glad to dance to it. Pray, sing?

JONATHAN (*he sings*).

Father and I went up to camp,
Along with Captain Goodwin;
And there we saw the men and boys,
As thick as hasty pudding.
    Yankee Doodle do, etc.

And there we saw a swamping gun,
Big as log of maple,
On a little deuced cart,
A load for father's cattle.
    Yankee Doodle do, etc.

And every time they fired it off
It took a horn of powder,
It made a noise—like father's gun,
Only a nation louder.
    Yankee Doodle do, etc.

There was a man in our town,
His name was—

No, no, that won't do. Now, if I was with Tabitha Wymen and Jemima Cawley, down at father Chase's, I

shouldn't mind singing this all out before them—you would be affronted if I was to sing that, though that's a lucky thought; if you should be affronted, I have something dang'd cute, which Jessamy told me to say to you.

JENNY. Is that all! I assure you I like it of all things.

JONATHAN. No, no; I can sing more, some other time, when you and I are better acquainted, I'll sing the whole of it—no, no—that's a fib—I can't sing but a hundred and ninety verses: our Tabitha at home can sing it all.— (*Sings.*)

Marblehead's a rocky place,
And Cape-Cod is sandy;
Charleston is burnt down,
Boston is the dandy.
    Yankee Doodle do, etc.

I vow, my own town song has put me into such topping spirits, that I believe I'll begin to do a little, as Jessamy says we must when we go a courting—(*Runs and kisses her.*) Burning rivers! cooling flames! red hot roses! pignuts! hasty pudding and ambrosia!

JENNY. What means this freedom! (*Striking him*) you insulting wretch.

JONATHAN. Are you affronted?

JENNY. Affronted! with what looks shall I express my anger?

JONATHAN. Looks! why, as to the matter of looks, you look as cross as a witch.

JENNY. Have you no feeling for the delicacy of my sex?

JONATHAN. Feeling! Gor, I—I feel the delicacy of your sex pretty smartly (*Rubbing his cheek*), though, I vow, I thought when you city ladies courted and married, and all that, you put feeling out of the question. But I want to know whether you are really affronted, or only pretend to be so? 'Cause, if you are certainly right down affronted, I am at the end of my tether;—Jessamy didn't tell me what to say to you.

JENNY. Pretend to be affronted!

JONATHAN. Aye, aye, if you only pretend, you shall hear how I'll go to work to make cherubim consequences. (*He runs up to her.*)

JENNY. Begone, you brute!

JONATHAN. That looks like mad; but I won't lose my speech. My dearest Jenny—your name is Jenny, I think? My dearest Jenny, though I have the highest esteem for the sweet favours you have just now granted me—Gor, that's a fib though, but Jessamy says it is not wicked to tell lies to the women. (*Aside*) I say, though I have the highest esteem for the favours you have just now granted me, yet, you will consider, that as soon as the dissolvable knot is tied, they will no longer be favours, but only matters of duty, and matters of course.

JENNY. Marry you! you audacious monster! get out of my sight, or rather let me fly from you. (*Exit hastily.*)

JONATHAN. Gor! she's gone off in a swinging passion, before I had time to think of consequences. If this is the way with your city ladies, give me the twenty acres of rock, the Bible, the cow, and Tabitha, and a little peaceable bundling.

SCENE TWO

The Mall. MANLY *enters.*

———

MANLY. It must be so, Montague! and it is not all the tribe of Mandevilles shall convince me, that a nation, to become great, must first become dissipated. Luxury is surely the bane of a nation: Luxury! which enervates both soul and body, by opening a thousand new sources of enjoyment, opens, also, a thousand new sources of contention and want: Luxury! which renders a people weak at home, and accessible to bribery, corruption, and force from abroad. When the Grecian states knew no other tools than the axe and the saw, the Grecians were a great, a free, and a happy people. The kings of Greece devoted their lives to the service of their country, and her senators knew no other superiority over their fellow citizens than a glorious pre-eminence in danger and virtue. They exhibited to the world a noble spectacle,—a number of independent states united by a similarity of language, sentiment, manners, common interest, and common consent, in one grand mutual league of protection.—And, thus united, long might they have continued the cherishers of arts and sciences, the protectors of the oppressed, the scourge of tyrants, and the safe asylum of liberty: But when foreign gold, and still more pernicious, foreign luxury, had crept among them, they sapped the vitals of their virtue. The virtues of their ancestors were only found in their writings. Envy and suspicion, the vices of little minds, possessed them. The various states engendered jealousies of each other; and, more unfortunately, growing jealous of their great federal council, the Amphictyons, they forgot that their common safety had existed, and would exist, in giving them an honourable extensive prerogative. The common good was lost in the pursuit of private interest; and that people, who, by uniting, might have stood against the world in arms, by dividing, crumbled into ruin;—their name is now only known in the page of the historian, and what they once were, is all we have left to admire. Oh! that America! Oh! that my country, would in this her day, learn the things which belong to her peace!

DIMPLE (*enters*). You are Colonel Manly, I presume?

MANLY. At your service, Sir.

DIMPLE. My name is Dimple, Sir. I have the honour to be a lodger in the same house with you, and hearing you were in the Mall, came hither to take the liberty of joining you.

MANLY. You are very obliging, Sir.

DIMPLE. As I understand you are a stranger here, Sir, I have taken the liberty to introduce myself to your acquaintance, as possibly I may have it in my power to point out some things in this city worthy your notice.

MANLY. An attention to strangers is worthy a liberal mind, and must ever be gratefully received. But to a soldier, who has no fixed abode, such attentions are particularly pleasing.

DIMPLE. Sir, there is no character so respectable as that of a soldier. And, indeed, when we reflect how much we owe to those brave men who have suffered so much in the service of their country, and secured to us those inestimable blessings that we now enjoy, our liberty and independence, they demand every attention which gratitude can pay. For my own part, I never meet an officer, but I embrace him as my friend, nor a private in distress, but I insensibly extend my charity to him. (*Aside*) I have hit the Bumpkin off very tolerably.

MANLY. Give me your hand, Sir! I do not proffer this hand to everybody; but you steal into my heart. I hope I am as insensible to flattery as most men; but I declare (it may be my weak side), that I never hear the name of soldier mentioned with respect, but I ex-

perience a thrill of pleasure, which I never feel on any other occasion.

DIMPLE. Will you give me leave, my dear colonel, to confer an obligation on myself, by shewing you some civilities during your stay here, and giving a similar opportunity to some of my friends?

MANLY. Sir, I thank you; but I believe my stay in this city will be very short.

DIMPLE. I can introduce you to some men of excellent sense, in whose company you will esteem yourself happy; and, by way of amusement, to some fine girls, who will listen to your soft things with pleasure.

MANLY. Sir, I should be proud of the honour of being acquainted with those gentlemen—but, as for the ladies, I don't understand you.

DIMPLE. Why, Sir, I need not tell you, that when a young gentleman is alone with a young lady, he must say some soft things to her fair cheek —indeed, the lady will expect it. To be sure, there is not much pleasure, when a man of the world and a finished coquette meet, who perfectly know each other; but how delicious is it to excite the emotions of joy, hope, expectation, and delight, in the bosom of a lovely girl, who believes every tittle of what you say to be serious.

MANLY. Serious, Sir! In my opinion, the man, who, under pretensions of marriage, can plant thorns in the bosom of an innocent, unsuspecting girl, is more detestable than a common robber, in the same proportion, as private violence is more despicable than open force, and money of less value than happiness.

DIMPLE (*aside*). How he awes me by the superiority of his sentiments. As you say, Sir, a gentleman should be cautious how he mentions marriage.

MANLY. Cautious, Sir! No person more approves of an intercourse between the sexes than I do. Female conversation softens our manners, whilst our discourse, from the superiority of our literary advantages, improves their minds. But, in our young country, where there is no such thing as gallantry, when a gentleman speaks of love to a lady, whether he mentions marriage, or not, she ought to conclude, either that he meant to insult her, or, that his intentions are the most serious and honourable. How mean, how cruel, is it, by a thousand tender assiduities, to win the affections of an amiable girl, and though you leave her virtue unspotted, to betray her into the appearance of so many tender partialities, that every man of delicacy would suppress his inclination towards her, by supposing her heart engaged! Can any man, for the trivial gratification of his leisure hours, affect the happiness of a whole life! His not having spoken of marriage may add to his perfidy, but can be no excuse for his conduct.

DIMPLE. Sir, I admire your sentiments—they are mine. The light observations that fell from me, were only a principle of the tongue; they came not from the heart—my practice has ever disapproved these principles.

MANLY. I believe you, Sir. I should with reluctance suppose that those pernicious sentiments could find admittance into the heart of a gentleman.

DIMPLE. I am now, Sir, going to visit a family, where, if you please, I will have the honour of introducing you. Mr. Manly's ward, Miss Letitia, is a young lady of immense fortune; and his niece, Miss Charlotte Manly, is a young lady of great sprightliness and beauty.

MANLY. That gentleman, Sir, is my uncle, and Miss Manly my sister.

DIMPLE (aside). The devil she is! Miss Manly your sister, Sir? I rejoice to hear it, and feel a double pleasure in being known to you. (Aside) Plague on him! I wish he was at Boston again with all my soul.

MANLY. Come, Sir, will you go?

DIMPLE. I will follow you in a moment, Sir. (Exit MANLY.) Plague on it! this is unlucky. A fighting brother is a cursed appendage to a fine girl. Egad! I just stopped in time; had he not discovered himself, in two minutes more I should have told him how well I was with his sister.—Indeed, I cannot see the satisfaction of an intrigue, if one can't have the pleasure of communicating it to our friends. (Exit.)

ACT FOUR

SCENE ONE

CHARLOTTE's apartment. CHARLOTTE leads in MARIA.

———

CHARLOTTE. This is so kind, my sweet friend, to come to see me at this moment. I declare, if I were going to be married in a few days, as you are, I should scarce have found time to visit my friends.

MARIA. Do you think then that there is an impropriety in it?—How should you dispose of your time?

CHARLOTTE. Why, I should be shut up in my chamber; and my head would so run upon—upon—upon the solemn ceremony that I was to pass through—I declare it would take me above two hours merely to learn that little monosyllable—Yes. Ah! my dear, your sentimental imagination does not conceive what that little tiny word implies.

MARIA. Spare me your raillery, my sweet friend; I should love your agreeable vivacity at any other time.

CHARLOTTE. Why this is the very time to amuse you. You grieve me to see you look so unhappy.

MARIA. Have I not reason to look so?

CHARLOTTE. What new grief distresses you?

MARIA. Oh! how sweet it is, when the heart is borne down with misfortune, to recline and repose on the bosom of friendship! Heaven knows, that, although it is improper for a young lady to praise a gentleman, yet I have ever concealed Mr. Dimple's foibles, and spoke of him as of one whose reputation I expected would be linked with mine: but his late conduct towards me has turned my coolness into contempt. He behaves as if he meant to insult and disgust me; whilst my father, in the last conversation on the subject of our marriage, spoke of it as a matter which laid near his heart, and in which he would not bear contradiction.

CHARLOTTE. (aside). This works well: oh! the generous Dimple. I'll endeavour to excite her to discharge him. But, my dear friend, your happiness depends on yourself: Why don't you discard him? Though the match has been of long standing, I would not be forced to make myself miserable: No parent in the world should oblige me to marry the man I did not like.

MARIA. Oh! my dear, you never lived with your parents, and do not know what influence a father's frowns have upon a daughter's heart. Besides, what have I to allege against Mr. Dimple, to justify myself to the world? He carries himself so smoothly, that every one would impute the blame to me,

and call me capricious.

CHARLOTTE. And call her capricious! Did ever such an objection start into the heart of woman? For my part, I wish I had fifty lovers to discard, for no other reason, than because I did not fancy them. My dear Maria, you will forgive me; I know your candour and confidence in me; but I have at times, I confess, been led to suppose, that some other gentleman was the cause of your aversion to Mr. Dimple.

MARIA. No, my sweet friend, you may be assured, that though I have seen many gentlemen I could prefer to Mr. Dimple, yet I never saw one that I thought I could give my hand to, until this morning.

CHARLOTTE. This morning!

MARIA. Yes!—one of the strangest accidents in the world. The odious Dimple, after disgusting me with his conversation, had just left me when a gentleman, who, it seems, boards in the same house with him, saw him coming out of our door, and the houses looking very much alike, he came into our house instead of his lodgings; nor did he discover his mistake until he got into the parlour, where I was: he then bowed so gracefully; made such a genteel apology, and looked so manly and noble!—

CHARLOTTE (aside). I see some folks, though it is so great an impropriety, can praise a gentleman, when he happens to be the man of their fancy.

MARIA. I don't know how it was—I hope he did not think me indelicate—but I asked him, I believe, to sit down, or pointed to a chair. He sat down, and instead of having recourse to observations upon the weather, or hackneyed criticisms upon the theatre, he entered readily into a conversation worthy a man of sense to speak, and a lady of delicacy and sentiment to hear. He was not strictly handsome, but he spoke the language of sentiment, and his eyes looked tenderness and honour.

CHARLOTTE. Oh! (*Eagerly*) you sentimental grave girls, when your hearts are once touched, beat us rattles a bar's length. And so, you are quite in love with this he-angel?

MARIA. In love with him! How can you rattle so, Charlotte? am I not going to be miserable? (*Sighing*) In love with a gentleman I never saw but one hour in my life, and don't know his name!—No: I only wished that the man I shall marry may look, and talk, and act, just like him. Besides, my dear, he is a married man.

CHARLOTTE. Why, that was good natured.—He told you so, I suppose, in mere charity, to prevent your falling in love with him?

MARIA (*peevishly*). He didn't tell me so; he looked as if he was married.

CHARLOTTE. How, my dear, did he look sheepish?

MARIA. I am sure he has a susceptible heart, and the ladies of his acquaintance must be very stupid not to—

CHARLOTTE. Hush! I hear some person coming.

LETITIA (*enters*). My dear Maria, I am happy to see you. Lud! what a pity it is that you have purchased your wedding clothes.

MARIA. I think so. (*Sighing.*)

LETITIA. Why, my dear, there is the sweetest parcel of silks come over you ever saw. Nancy Brilliant has a full suit come; she sent over her measure, and it fits her to a hair; it is immensely dressy, and made for a court-hoop. I thought they said the large hoops were going out of fashion.

CHARLOTTE. Did you see the hat?—

Is it a fact, that the deep laces round the border is still the fashion?

DIMPLE (*within*). Upon my honour, Sir!

MARIA. Ha! Dimple's voice! My dear, I must take leave of you. There are some things necessary to be done at our house.—Can't I go through the other room?

(*Enter* DIMPLE *and* MANLY.)

DIMPLE. Ladies, your most obedient.

CHARLOTTE. Miss Van Rough, shall I present my brother Henry to you? Colonel Manly, Maria—Miss Van Rough, brother.

MARIA. Her brother! (*Turns and sees* MANLY.) Oh! my heart! The very gentleman I have been praising.

MANLY. The same amiable girl I saw this morning!

CHARLOTTE. Why, you look as if you were acquainted.

MANLY. I unintentionally intruded into this lady's presence this morning, for which she was so good as to promise me her forgiveness.

CHARLOTTE (*aside*). Oh! ho! is that the case! Have these two penserosos been together? Were they Henry's eyes that looked so tenderly?—And so you promised to pardon him? and could you be so good natured?—have you really forgiven him? I beg you would do it for my sake. (*Whispering loud to* MARIA) But, my dear, as you are in such haste, it would be cruel to detain you: I can show you the way through the other room.

MARIA. Spare me, my sprightly friend.

MANLY. The lady does not, I hope, intend to deprive us of the pleasure of her company so soon.

CHARLOTTE. She has only a mantuamaker who waits for her at home. But, as I am to give my opinion of the dress, I think she cannot go yet.

We were talking of the fashions when you came in; but I suppose the subject must be changed to something of more importance now.—Mr. Dimple, will you favour us with an account of the public entertainments?

DIMPLE. Why, really, Miss Manly, you could not have asked me a question more *malapropos*. For my part, I must confess, that to a man who has travelled, there is nothing that is worthy the name of amusement to be found in this city.

CHARLOTTE. Except visiting the ladies.

DIMPLE. Pardon me, Madam; that is the avocation of a man of taste. But, for amusement, I positively know of nothing that can be called so, unless you dignify with that title the hopping once a fortnight to the sound of two or three squeaking fiddles, and the clattering of the old tavern windows, or sitting to see the miserable mummers, whom you call actors, murder comedy, and make a farce of tragedy.

MANLY. Do you never attend the theatre, Sir?

DIMPLE. I was tortured there once.

CHARLOTTE. Pray, Mr. Dimple, was it a tragedy or a comedy?

DIMPLE. Faith, Madam, I cannot tell; for I sat with my back to the stage all the time, admiring a much better actress than any there—a lady who played the fine woman to perfection—though, by the laugh of the horrid creatures around me, I suppose it was comedy. Yet, on second thoughts, it might be some hero in a tragedy, dying so comically as to set the whole house in an uproar.—Colonel, I presume you have been in Europe?

MANLY. Indeed, Sir, I was never ten leagues from the continent.

DIMPLE. Believe me, Colonel, you have an immense pleasure to come; and when you shall have seen the brilliant exhibitions of Europe, you will learn to despise the amusements of this country as much as I do.

MANLY. Therefore I do not wish to see them; for I can never esteem that knowledge valuable, which tends to give me a distaste for my native country.

DIMPLE. Well, Colonel, though you have not travelled, you have read.

MANLY. I have, a little: and by it have discovered that there is a laudable partiality, which ignorant, untravelled men entertain for everything that belongs to their native country. I call it laudable;—it injures no one; adds to their own happiness; and, when extended, becomes the noble principle of patriotism. Travelled gentlemen rise superior, in their own opinion, to this: but, if the contempt which they contract for their country is the most valuable acquisition of their travels, I am far from thinking that their time and money are well spent.

MARIA. What noble sentiments!

CHARLOTTE. Let my brother set out from where he will in the fields of conversation, he is sure to end his tour in the temple of gravity.

MANLY. Forgive me, my sister. I love my country; it has its foibles undoubtedly—some foreigners will with pleasure remark them—but such remarks fall very ungracefully from the lips of her citizens.

DIMPLE. You are perfectly in the right. Colonel—America has her faults.

MANLY. Yes, Sir; and we, her children, should blush for them in private, and endeavour, as individuals, to reform them. But, if our country has its errors in common with other countries, I am proud to say America, I mean the United States, has displayed virtues and achievements which modern nations may admire, but of which they have seldom set us the example.

CHARLOTTE. But, brother, we must introduce you to some of our gay folks, and let you see the city, such as it is. Mr. Dimple is known to almost every family in town—he will doubtless take a pleasure in introducing you.

DIMPLE. I shall esteem every service I can render your brother an honour.

MANLY. I fear the business I am upon will take up all my time, and my family will be anxious to hear from me.

MARIA (*aside*). His family! But what is it to me that he is married! Pray, how did you leave your lady, Sir?

CHARLOTTE (*observing her anxiety*). My brother is not married; it is only an odd way he has of expressing himself.—Pray, brother, is this business, which you make your continual excuse, a secret?

MANLY. No, sister: I came hither to solicit the honourable Congress that a number of my brave old soldiers may be put upon the pension list, who were, at first, not judged to be so materially wounded as to need the public assistance.—My sister says true: (*to* MARIA) I call my late soldiers my family.—Those who were not in the field in the late glorious contest, and those who were, have their respective merits; but, I confess, my old brother-soldiers are dearer to me than the former description. Friendships made in adversity are lasting; our countrymen may forget us; but that is no reason why we should forget one another. But I must leave you; my time of engagement approaches.

CHARLOTTE. Well, but brother, if you will go, will you please to conduct my fair friend home? You live in the same street—I was to have gone with her myself— (*Aside*) A lucky thought.

MARIA. I am obliged to your sister, Sir, and was just intending to go. (*Going.*)

MANLY. I shall attend her with pleasure. (*Exits with* MARIA, *followed by* DIMPLE *and* CHARLOTTE.)

MARIA. Now, pray don't betray me to your brother.

CHARLOTTE (*just as she sees him make a motion to take his leave*). One word with you, brother, if you please. (*She follows them out.*)

(*Manent*[3] DIMPLE *and* LETITIA.)

DIMPLE. You received the billet I sent you, I presume?

LETITIA. Hush!—Yes.

DIMPLE. When shall I pay my respects to you?

LETITIA. At eight I shall be unengaged.

(*Re-enter* CHARLOTTE.)

DIMPLE (*to* CHARLOTTE). Did my lovely angel receive my billet?

CHARLOTTE. Yes.

DIMPLE. What hour shall I expect with impatience?

CHARLOTTE. At eight I shall be at home, unengaged.

DIMPLE. Unfortunate! I have a horrid engagement of business at that hour.—Can't you finish your visit earlier, and let six be the happy hour?

CHARLOTTE. You know your influence over me. (*They go out severally.*)

SCENE TWO

VAN ROUGH's *house.*

———

VAN ROUGH (*alone*). It cannot possibly be true! The son of my old

---

[3] Remain [on stage].

friend can't have acted so unadvised-
ly. Seventeen thousand pounds! in
bills!—Mr. Transfer must have been
mistaken. He always appeared so prudent, and talked so well upon money-
matters, and even assured me that he
intended to change his dress for a
suit of clothes which would not cost
so much, and look more substantial,
as soon as he married. No, no, no! it
can't be; it cannot be.—But, however,
I must look out sharp. I did not care
what his principles or his actions were,
so long as he minded the main chance.
Seventeen thousand pounds!—If he
had lost it in trade, why the best men
may have ill-luck; but to game it
away, as Transfer says—why, at this
rate, his whole estate may go in one
night, and, what is ten times worse,
mine into the bargain. No, no; Mary
is right. Leave women to look out in
these matters; for all they look as if
they didn't know a journal from a
ledger, when their interest is concerned, they know what's what; they
mind the main chance as well as the
best of us.—I wonder Mary did not
tell me she knew of his spending his
money so foolishly. Seventeen thousand pounds! Why, if my daughter
was standing up to be married, I
would forbid the banns, if I found it
was to a man who did not mind the
main chance.—Hush! I hear somebody coming. 'T is Mary's voice: a
man with her too! I shouldn't be sur-
prized if this should be the other
string to her bow.—Aye, aye, let them
alone; women understand the main
chance.—Though, i' faith, I'll listen a
little. (*Retires into a closet.*)

(*Enter* MANLY *leading in* MARIA.)

MANLY. I hope you will excuse my
speaking upon so important a subject, so abruptly; but the moment I
entered your room, you struck me as
the lady whom I had long loved in
imagination, and never hoped to see.

MARIA. Indeed, Sir, I have been led
to hear more upon this subject than
I ought.

MANLY. Do you then disapprove my
suit, Madam, or the abruptness of my
introducing it? If the latter, my peculiar situation, being obliged to leave
the city in a few days, will, I hope,
be my excuse; if the former, I will
retire: for I am sure I would not give
a moment's inquietude to her, whom
I could devote my life to please. I am
not so indelicate as to seek your immediate approbation; permit me only
to be near you, and by a thousand
tender assiduities to endeavour to excite a grateful return.

MARIA. I have a father, whom I
would die to make happy—he will
disapprove—

MANLY. Do you think me so ungenerous as to seek a place in your
esteem without his consent? You must
—you ever ought to consider that man
as unworthy of you, who seeks an
interest in your heart, contrary to a
father's approbation. A young lady
should reflect that the loss of a lover
may be supplied, but nothing can
compensate for the loss of a parent's
affection. Yet, why do you suppose
your father would disapprove? In our
country, the affections are not sacrificed to riches, or family aggrandize-
ment:—should you approve, my family is decent, and my rank honourable.

MARIA. You distress me, Sir.

MANLY. Then I will sincerely beg
your excuse for obtruding so disagreeable a subject and retire. (*He starts
to leave.*)

MARIA. Stay, Sir! your generosity
and good opinion of me deserve a
return; but why must I declare what,
for these few hours, I have scarce

suffered myself to think?—I am—

MANLY. What?—

MARIA. Engaged, Sir—and, in a few days, to be married to the gentleman you saw at your sister's.

MANLY. Engaged to be married! And have I been basely invading the rights of another? Why have you permitted this?—Is this the return for the partiality I declared for you?

MARIA. You distress me, Sir. What would you have me say? You are too generous to wish the truth: ought I to say that I dared not suffer myself to think of my engagement, and that I am going to give my hand without my heart?—Would you have me confess a partiality for you? If so, your triumph is complete; and can be only more so, when days of misery, with the man I cannot love, will make me think of him whom I could prefer.

MANLY (after a pause). We are both unhappy; but it is your duty to obey your parent—mine to obey my honour. Let us, therefore, both follow the path of rectitude; and of this we may be assured, that if we are not happy, we shall, at least, deserve to be so. Adieu! I dare not trust myself longer with you.

(They go out severally.)

ACT FIVE

Scene One

DIMPLE's lodgings, JESSAMY meeting JONATHAN.

———

JESSAMY. Well, Mr. Jonathan, what success with the fair?

JONATHAN. Why, such a tarnal cross tike you never saw!—You would have counted she had lived upon crab apples and vinegar for a fortnight. But what the rattle makes you look so tarnation glum?

JESSAMY. I was thinking, Mr. Jonathan, what could be the reason of her carrying herself so coolly to you.

JONATHAN. Coolly, do you call it? Why, I vow, she was fire-hot angry: may be it was because I buss'd her.

JESSAMY. No, no, Mr. Jonathan; there must be some other cause: I never yet knew a lady angry at being kissed.

JONATHAN. Well, if it is not the young woman's bashfulness, I vow I can't conceive why she shouldn't like me.

JESSAMY. May be it is because you have not the Graces, Mr. Jonathan.

JONATHAN. Grace! Why, does the young woman expect I must be converted before I court her?

JESSAMY. I mean graces of person; for instance, my lord tells us that we must cut off our nails even at top, in small segments of circles—though you won't understand that—In the next place, you must regulate your laugh.

JONATHAN. Maple-log seize it! don't I laugh natural?

JESSAMY. That's the very fault, Mr. Jonathan. Besides, you absolutely misplace it. I was told by a friend of mine that you laughed outright at the play the other night, when you ought only to have tittered.

JONATHAN. Gor! I—what does one go to see fun for if they can't laugh?

JESSAMY. You may laugh—but you must laugh by rule.

JONATHAN. Swamp it—laugh by rule! Well, I should like that tarnally.

JESSAMY. Why you know, Mr. Jonathan, that to dance, a lady to play with her fan, or a gentleman with his cane, and all other natural motions, are regulated by art. My master has composed an immensely pretty gamut, by which any lady, or gentleman, with a few years' close application, may learn to laugh as gracefully as if they were born and bred to it.

JONATHAN. Mercy on my soul! A gamut for laughing—just like fa, la, sol?

JESSAMY. Yes. It comprises every possible display of jocularity, from an *affettuoso* smile to a *piano* titter, or full chorus *fortissimo* ha, ha, ha! My master employs his leisure-hours in marking out the plays, like a cathedral chanting-book, that the ignorant may know where to laugh; and that pit, box, and gallery may keep time together, and not have a snigger in one part of the house, a broad grin in the other, and a damned grum look in the third. How delightful to see the audience all smile together, then look on their books, then twist their mouths into an agreeable simper, then altogether shake the house with a general ha, ha, ha! loud as a full chorus of Handel's, at an Abbey-commemoration.

JONATHAN. Ha, ha, ha! that's dang'd cute, I swear.

JESSAMY. The gentlemen, you see, will laugh the tenor; the ladies will play the countertenor; the beaux will squeak the treble; and our jolly friends in the gallery a thorough bass, ho, ho, ho!

JONATHAN. Well, can't you let me see that gamut?

JESSAMY. Oh! yes, Mr. Jonathan; here it is. (*Takes out a book.*) Oh! no, this is only a titter with its variations. Ah, here it is. (*Takes out another.*) Now you must know, Mr. Jonathan, this is a piece written by Ben Jonson, which I have set to my master's gamut. The places where you must smile, look grave, or laugh outright, are marked below the line. Now look over me:

"There was a certain man"—now you must smile.

JONATHAN. Well, read it again; I warrant I'll mind my eye.

JESSAMY. "There was a certain man, who had a sad scolding wife"—now you must laugh.

JONATHAN. Tarnation! That's no laughing matter, though.

JESSAMY. "And she lay sick a-dying" —now you must titter.

JONATHAN. What, snigger when the good woman's a-dying! Gor, I—

JESSAMY. Yes; the notes say you must—"And she asked her husband leave to make a will"—now you must begin to look grave—"and her husband said"—

JONATHAN. Ay, what did her husband say?—Something dang'd cute, I reckon.

JESSAMY. "And her husband said, you have had your will all your lifetime, and would you have it after you are dead too?"

JONATHAN. Ho, ho, ho! There the old man was even with her; he was up to the notch—ha, ha, ha!

JESSAMY. But, Mr. Jonathan, you must not laugh so. Why, you ought to have tittered *piano,* and you have laughed *fortissimo.* Look here; you see these marks, A. B. C. and so on; these are the references to the other part of the book. Let us turn to it, and you will see the directions how to manage the muscles. This (*Turns over.*) was note D you blundered at.— "You must purse the mouth into a smile, then titter, discovering the lower part of the three front upper teeth."

JONATHAN. How! read it again.

JESSAMY. "There was a certain man"—very well!—"who had a sad scolding wife"—why don't you laugh?

JONATHAN. Now, that scolding wife sticks in my gizzard so pluckily, that

I can't laugh for the blood and nowns of me. Let me look grave here, and I'll laugh your belly full where the old creature's a-dying.—

JESSAMY. "And she asked her husband"—(*Bell rings*.) My master's bell! he's returned, I fear—Here, Mr. Jonathan, take this gamut; and, I make no doubt but with a few years' close application you may be able to smile gracefully.

(*They go out severally.*)

SCENE TWO

CHARLOTTE's *apartment.*

———

MANLY (*enters*). What, no one at home? How unfortunate to meet the only lady my heart was ever moved by, to find her engaged to another, and confessing her partiality for me! Yet engaged to a man who, by her intimation, and his libertine conversation with me, I fear, does not merit her. Aye! there's the sting; for, were I assured that Maria was happy, my heart is not so selfish but that it would dilate in knowing it, even though it were with another.—But to know she is unhappy!—I must drive these thoughts from me. Charlotte has some books; and this is what I believe she calls her little library. (*Enters a closet.*)

(*Enter* DIMPLE *leading* LETITIA.)

LETITIA. And will you pretend to say, now, Mr. Dimple, that you propose to break with Maria? Are not the banns published? Are not the clothes purchased? Are not the friends invited? In short, is it not a done affair?

DIMPLE. Believe me, my dear Letitia, I would not marry her.

LETITIA. Why have you not broke with her before this, as you all along deluded me by saying you would?

DIMPLE. Because I was in hopes she would ere this have broke with me.

LETITIA. You could not expect it.

DIMPLE. Nay, but be calm a moment; 't was from my regard to you that I did not discard her.

LETITIA. Regard to me!

DIMPLE. Yes; I have done everything in my power to break with her, but the foolish girl is so fond of me that nothing can accomplish it. Besides, how can I offer her my hand, when my heart is indissolubly engaged to you?—

LETITIA. There may be reason in this; but why so attentive to Miss Manly?

DIMPLE. Attentive to Miss Manly! For heaven's sake, if you have no better opinion of my constancy, pay not so ill a compliment to my taste.

LETITIA. Did I not see you whisper her to-day?

DIMPLE. Possibly I might—but something of so very trifling a nature, that I have already forgot what it was.

LETITIA. I believe, she has not forgot it.

DIMPLE. My dear creature, how can you for a moment suppose I should have any serious thoughts of that trifling, gay, flighty coquette, that disagreeable—

(*Enter* CHARLOTTE.)

DIMPLE. My dear Miss Manly, I rejoice to see you; there is a charm in your conversation that always marks your entrance into company as fortunate.

LETITIA. Where have you been, my dear?

CHARLOTTE. Why, I have been about to twenty shops, turning over pretty things, and so have left twenty visits unpaid. I wish you would step into the carriage and whisk round, make my apology, and leave my cards where our friends are not at home; that you know will serve as a visit. Come, do go.

LETITIA (*aside*). So anxious to get me out! but I'll watch you.—Oh! yes, I'll go; I want a little exercise.—Positively (DIMPLE *offering to accompany her*), Mr. Dimple, you shall not go, why, half my visits are cake and caudle visits; it won't do, you know, for you to go.— (*Exit, but returns to the door in the back scene and listens.*)

DIMPLE. This attachment of your brother to Maria is fortunate.

CHARLOTTE. How did you come to the knowledge of it?

DIMPLE. I read it in their eyes.

CHARLOTTE. And I had it from her mouth. It would have amused you to have seen her! She that thought it so great an impropriety to praise a gentleman that she could not bring out one word in your favour, found a redundancy to praise him.

DIMPLE. I have done everything in my power to assist his passion there: your delicacy, my dearest girl, would be shocked at half the instances of neglect and misbehaviour.

CHARLOTTE. I don't know how I should bear neglect; but Mr. Dimple must misbehave himself, indeed, to forfeit my good opinion.

DIMPLE. Your good opinion, my angel, is the pride and pleasure of my heart; and if the most respectful tenderness for you and an utter indifference for all your sex, besides, can make me worthy of your esteem, I shall richly merit it.

CHARLOTTE. All my sex besides, Mr. Dimple—you forgot your tête-à-tête with Letitia.

DIMPLE. How can you, my lovely angel, cast a thought on that insipid, wry-mouthed, ugly creature!

CHARLOTTE. But her fortune may have charms?

DIMPLE. Not to a heart like mine. The man who has been blessed with the good opinion of my Charlotte, must despise the allurements of fortune.

CHARLOTTE. I am satisfied.

DIMPLE. Let us think no more on the odious subject, but devote the present hour to happiness.

CHARLOTTE. Can I be happy, when I see the man I prefer going to be married to another?

DIMPLE. Have I not already satisfied my charming angel that I can never think of marrying the puling Maria. But, even if it were so, could that be any bar to our happiness; for, as the poet sings—

"Love, free as air, at sight of human ties,
"Spreads his light wings, and in a moment flies."

Come then, my charming angel! why delay our bliss! The present moment is ours; the next is in the hand of fate. (*Kissing her.*)

CHARLOTTE. Begone, Sir! By your delusions you had almost lulled my honour asleep.

DIMPLE. Let me lull the demon to sleep again with kisses. (*He struggles with her; she screams.*)

MANLY (*enters*). Turn, villain! and defend yourself.— (*Draws.* VAN ROUGH *enters and beats down their swords.*)

VAN ROUGH (*holding* DIMPLE). Is the devil in you? are you going to murder one another?

DIMPLE. Hold him, hold him—I can command my passion.

JONATHAN (*enters*). What the rattle ails you? Is the old one in you? Let the colonel alone, can't you? I feel chock full of fight—do you want to kill the colonel?—

MANLY. Be still, Jonathan; the gentleman does not want to hurt me.

JONATHAN. Gor! I—I wish he did; I'd shew him Yankee boys' play, pretty quick—Don't you see you have frightened the young woman into the *hystrikes?*

VAN ROUGH. Pray, some of you explain this; what has been the occasion of all this racket?

MANLY. That gentleman can explain it to you; it will be a very diverting story for an intended father-in-law to hear.

VAN ROUGH. How was this matter, Mr. Van Dumpling?

DIMPLE. Sir — upon my honour — all I know is, that I was talking to this young lady, and this gentleman broke in on us, in a very extraordinary manner.

VAN ROUGH. Why, all this is nothing to the purpose. (*To* CHARLOTTE) Can you explain it, Miss?

LETITIA (*entering through the back scene*). I can explain it to that gentleman's confusion. (*To* VAN ROUGH) Though long betrothed to your daughter, yet allured by my fortune, it seems (with shame do I speak it), he has privately paid his addresses to me. I was drawn in to listen to him by his assuring me that the match was made by his father without his consent, and that he proposed to break with Maria, whether he married me or not. But whatever were his intentions respecting your daughter, Sir, even to me he was false; for he has repeated the same story, with some cruel reflections upon my person, to Miss Manly.

JONATHAN. What a tarnal curse!

LETITIA. Nor is this all, Miss Manly. When he was with me this very morning, he made the same ungenerous reflections upon the weakness of your mind as he has so recently done upon the defects of my person.

JONATHAN. What a tarnal curse and damn too!

DIMPLE (*aside*). Ha! since I have lost Letitia, I believe I had as good make it up with Maria—Mr. Van Rough, at present I cannot enter into particulars; but, I believe I can explain everything to your satisfaction in private.

VAN ROUGH. There is another matter, Mr. Van Dumpling, which I would have you explain—pray, Sir, have Messrs. Van Cash and Co. presented you those bills for acceptance?

DIMPLE (*aside*). The deuce! Has he heard of those bills! Nay, then, all's up with Maria, too; but an affair of this sort can never prejudice me among the ladies; they will rather long to know what the dear creature possesses to make him so agreeable. (*To* MANLY) Sir, you'll hear from me.

MANLY. And you from me, Sir.—

DIMPLE. Sir, you wear a sword.—

MANLY. Yes, Sir—This sword was presented to me by that brave Gallic hero, the Marquis de La Fayette. I have drawn it in the service of my country, and in private life, on the only occasion where a man is justified in drawing his sword, in defence of a lady's honour. I have fought too many battles in the service of my country to dread the imputation of cowardice. —Death from a man of honour would be a glory you do not merit; you shall live to bear the insult of man, and the contempt of that sex whose general smiles afforded you all your happiness.

DIMPLE. You won't meet me, Sir?— Then I'll post you for a coward.

MANLY. I'll venture that, Sir.—The reputation of my life does not depend upon the breath of a Mr. Dimple. I would have you to know, however, Sir, that I have a cane to chastise the insolence of a scoundrel, and a sword and the good laws of my country, to protect me from the attempts of an assassin.—

DIMPLE. Mighty well! Very fine, indeed!—ladies and gentlemen, I take my leave, and you will please to observe, in the case of my deportment, the contrast between a gentleman, who has read Chesterfield and received the polish of Europe, and an unpolished, untraveled American. (*Exit.*)

MARIA (*enters*). Is he indeed gone?—

LETITIA. I hope never to return.

VAN ROUGH. I am glad I heard of those bills; though it's plaguy unlucky: I hoped to see Mary married before I died.

MANLY. Will you permit a gentleman, Sir, to offer himself as a suitor to your daughter? Though a stranger to you, he is not altogether so to her, or unknown in this city. You may find a son-in-law of more fortune, but you can never meet with one who is richer in love for her, or respect for you.

VAN ROUGH. Why, Mary, you have not let this gentleman make love to you without my leave?

MANLY. I did not say, Sir—

MARIA. Say, Sir!—I—the gentleman, to be sure, met me accidentally.

VAN ROUGH. Ha, ha, ha! Mark me, Mary; young folks think old folks to be fools; but old folks know young folks to be fools.—Why, I knew all about this affair:—This was only a cunning way I had to bring it about—Hark ye! I was in the closet when you and he were at our house. (*Turns to the company.*) I heard that little baggage say she loved her old father, and would die to make him happy! Oh! how I loved the little baggage!—And you talked very prudently, young

man. I have inquired into your character, and find you to be a man of punctuality and mind the main chance. And so, as you love Mary, and Mary loves you, you shall have my consent immediately to be married. I'll settle my fortune on you, and go and live with you the remainder of my life.

MANLY. Sir, I hope—

VAN ROUGH. Come, come, no fine speeches; mind the main chance, young man, and you and I shall always agree.

LETITIA. I sincerely wish you joy (*Advancing to* MARIA); and hope your pardon for my conduct.

MARIA. I thank you for your congratulations, and hope we shall at once forget the wretch who has given us so much disquiet, and the trouble that he has occasioned.

CHARLOTTE. And I, my dear Maria— how shall I look up to you for forgiveness? I, who, in the practice of the meanest arts, have violated the most sacred rights of friendship? I can never forgive myself, or hope charity from the world, but I confess I have much to hope from such a brother; and I am happy that I may soon say, such a sister.—

MARIA. My dear, you distress me; you have all my love.

MANLY. And mine.

CHARLOTTE. If repentance can entitle me to forgiveness, I have already much merit; for I despise the littleness of my past conduct. I now find, that the heart of any worthy man cannot be gained by invidious attacks upon the rights and characters of others—by countenancing the addresses of a thousand—or that the finest assemblage of features, the greatest taste in dress, the genteelest address, or the most brilliant wit, cannot eventually secure a coquette from contempt and ridicule.

MANLY. And I have learned that probity, virtue, honour, though they should not have received the polish of Europe, will secure to an honest American the good graces of his fair countrywoman, and, I hope, the applause of *the public.*

SUPERSTITION

James N. Barker

First performed at the Chestnut Theatre in Philadelphia
on March 12, 1824.

SIR REGINALD EGERTON	EDWARD
GEORGE EGERTON	BOY
RAVENSWORTH	SECOND JUDGE
WALFORD	OFFICER
CHARLES	VILLAGERS
THE UNKNOWN	INDIANS
JUDGE	ISABELLA
FIRST VILLAGER	MARY
SECOND VILLAGER	ALICE
MESSENGER	LUCY
FIRST OFFICER	FEMALE VILLAGERS
SECOND OFFICER	

ACT ONE

Scene One

*New England, about the year 1675.
A village at a little distance. In front,
on the left of the stage, the cottage of
RAVENSWORTH; a handsome rustic
building. A large mansion, on an
eminence nearer the village, on the
right. Enter from the cottage, MARY
and ALICE.*

MARY. Nay, come away, dear Alice,
     every moment
Of your brief visit must be wholly
     mine;
Let's leave our fathers to their grave
     discourse
Of witch and wizard, ere we laugh
     outright.
ALICE. It is a subject that the country
     round
Deems a most solemn one.
MARY.   True: but to me,
'T is not the less absurd on that
     account.
ALICE. This levity's misplac'd: your fa-
     ther claims
Your love and reverence—
MARY.   And I do revere him,
And love him dearly, Alice; do I not?
How often have I striven to melt his
     sternness;
And, when my heart was sick of its
     own cares,
Lock'd up my selfish sorrows from his
     view,
And tried, by every filial endearment,
To win his smiles. E'en when his
     brow was darkest;
I've brav'd its terrors; hung upon his
     neck,
And spoken of my mother: O how
     sweet
It were methought even to weep with
     him.

ALICE. You're an enthusiast, Mary. Ah,
     beware,
Lest this impetuous current of your
     feeling
Urge you, one day, against the peril-
     ous rock.
MARY. I'm young, and youth is ardent,
     and should be
Cheerful, and full of bright and sun-
     ny thoughts;
I would be if I dared. You, too, are
     young,
Yet may be happy; for you have a
     parent
Who, tho' he guide you safely down
     the stream,
Does not, like angry pilots, chide e'en
     louder
Than the loud storm.
ALICE.   His high and holy office
May, haply give to your good father's
     manner
A grave solemnity, perhaps, a harsh-
     ness—
MARY. And why a harshness? Sure, ah
     sure, Religion
Descends not like the vulture in its
     wrath;
But rather like the mild and gentle
     dove,
Emblem of peace and harbinger of
     joy,
Love in its eye and healing on its
     wing;
With pure and snowy plumage, downy
     soft,
To nestle in the bosom of its votaries.
ALICE. I cannot argue; I'm content to
     follow
Where e'er our fathers lead. For you,
     I fear
You've learn'd too much from this
     mysterious stranger.
MARY. O Alice, join not you with the
     slanderous crowd
Against a noble lady, whom you know
     not.

For me, be satisfied I never more
Perhaps, shall see her: I've obeyed
my father;
And must, tho' it should break my
heart: tho' Charles—(*Pauses and
crosses.*)
ALICE. And what of Charles?
MARY.   Her son—
ALICE.   I know: her son,
And what of him?
MARY.   This very day, 't is said,
He will be here—
ALICE. Expell'd, they say, from college.
MARY. Disgrac'd— 'T is false: Charles
cannot be disgrac'd;
If envy, persecution, drive him thence,
They but disgrace themselves, and
not poor Charles.
ALICE. Mary?
MARY.   Yes; take my secret; take it
quickly,
Or it will burst my heart.
ALICE.   Nay, but be calm.
MARY. You shall know all—surely you'll
pity, Alice,
And perhaps, pardon me. Three years
ago
When Charles's mother first came
here to live;
From England, was it not—the vil-
lage then
Had scarce begun to hate her, for as
yet
She had not lavish'd charities abroad,
To purchase up ingratitude and envy.
Being her nearest neighbour, (my
dear mother
Was then alive,) there rose at once
between us
That intercourse which neighbour-
hood compels
At times, e'en with the most reserv-
ed. The lady,
I know not why, unless out of her
goodness,
Graced me with her regard, and
when my mother

Died, she took the desolate child to
her bosom.
ALICE. 'T was kindly done.
MARY.   O she was goodness all,
Her words, so sweet and soothing; as
she spoke,
Alice, methought I saw my sainted
mother
Lean o'er the bright edge of a silvery
cloud
And smile upon her happy orphan
girl—
And there was Charles, so busy still
around me,
Exhausting all his boyish gallantries,
With brotherly affection.—
ALICE.   Charles, still Charles?
MARY. Can I forget it!—
ALICE.   Nay, go on.
MARY.   The winter
Soon pass'd away, and then the spring
came on
With all its flowers, and still the
earliest blossom
Was cull'd for me. O, we were then
so happy—
I always lov'd the spring. Young
nature then
Came to me like a play-mate. Ere the
snows
Had left the hills, I've often wand-
er'd forth,
And, all impatient for the verdure,
clear'd
A patch of infant green; or even
turn'd
With mighty effort, some recumbent
stone,
To find the fresh grass under it.
ALICE.   This is childish.
MARY. I was a child, then—would I
were e'en now,
As then I was—my life, I fear, will
prove
A wintry waste with no green spot
to cheer it.
ALICE. More visionary still.

MARY. Well, to my story:—
My father took me home, I think it was
About the time you came into the village,
Fell superstition now had spread around.
Reports—I scarce know what they meant—arose
Concerning Isabella; and my father
Made gloomier by my mother's death, and yielding
His strong mind to the doctrine of the times,
Grew daily still more stern, until at length,
At peril of his curse, he bade me never
To hold communion with that family.
ALICE. And you obeyed?
MARY. All that I could, I did.
But O the tales they tell—the horrid stories—
Her very virtues they distort to crimes.
And for poor Charles, his manliness and spirit,
The gayety of youth and innocence,
In him are vices. Could I help defending,
Knowing them as I did:—all others hating,
Could I help loving!
ALICE. Loving, Mary?
MARY. Ay; most deeply, strongly loving
Charles and his mother.
ALICE. But sure you have not seen this Charles?
MARY. Not often.—
Nay, frown not, friend, for how could I avoid it,
When chance insisted on an interview?
ALICE. Have ye met lately?
MARY. Yes.
ALICE. What pass'd between you?
MARY. A plight of faith: A vow to live or die,

Each for the other.
ALICE. Lost, lost girl.
MARY. Why, ay,
It may be so; if so, 't is Heaven's will.
You have my secret, Alice.
(*Enter from the house,* RAVENS-
WORTH *and* WALFORD.)
ALICE. Peace; our fathers.
(*They retire into house.*)
RAVENSWORTH. No, Walford, no: I have no charity
For what you term the weakness of our nature.
The soul should rise above it. It was this
That made the fathers of this land prevail,
When man and the elements opposed, and win
Their heritage from the heathen.
WALFORD. True; the times
Impos'd a virtue, almost superhuman.
But surely, the necessity is pass'd
For trampling on our nature.
RAVENSWORTH. We have grown
Luke-warm in zeal, degenerate in spirit;—
I would root out with an unsparing hand,
The weeds that choke the soil;—
pride and rank luxury
Spring up around us; alien sectaries,
Spite of the whip and axe, infest our limits;
Bold infidelity, dark sorcery—
WALFORD. Nay,
Nay, Ravensworth—
RAVENSWORTH. I tell thee, Walford, yea:
The powers of darkness are at work among us.
Not distant we have seen the fagot blaze,
And soon the stake may ask its victim here.

WALFORD. What victim point you at?

RAVENSWORTH. Turn your eye—thither
Upon yon haughty mansion—you
have heard?—

WALFORD. Much idle rumour.

RAVENSWORTH.   Do you deem it so.
Whence then, and who is this im-
perious dame
That holds herself above her fellow
creatures,
And scorns our church's discipline:
her means—
Her business here?

WALFORD.   The ignorant and envious
May find, in her superior intellect—
E'en in her ample wealth and proud
reserve—
Food for their hate, and therefore
their suspicion;
But for us, Ravensworth—

RAVENSWORTH.   No more, ere long,
These questions must be answer'd.

WALFORD.   Be it so;
I shall be ready in all lawful ways
To seek the truth.

RAVENSWORTH. 'T is well, we soon
may need you.
What public tidings hear you?

WALFORD.   That King Philip
Our savage foe, after his late defeat,
Has gained his rocky hold, where he
now lies,
With scarce a fragment of his former
force.

RAVENSWORTH. Where are our troops?

WALFORD.   They watch the enemy.

RAVENSWORTH. They should have fol-
lowed up their victory,
To the extermination of the heathen.—
Has there aught chanc'd in the village?

WALFORD.   There have arrived
Two persons from the court of Charles.

RAVENSWORTH.   More vanity!
What do they here?

WALFORD.   The elder, it is said,
Brings letters to the government.

RAVENSWORTH.   Charles Stuart,

Is growing much concern'd about the
people
His family have scourg'd, hunted
and driven
From shed and shelter in their native
land.
We needs must thank that most
paternal care
That, when the expos'd infant climbs
to manhood,
Comes for the first time, then, to
claim his service.

WALFORD. You broach a startling topic
—But the day wears—
Fare thee well, Ravensworth.

RAVENSWORTH.   Farewell, farewell.
(*Exit* WALFORD.)
Timid, weak-minded man.
(*Enter* MARY, *from house.*)
                Come hither, daughter.

MARY. Father! (*Running to him.*)

RAVENSWORTH. What mean these tears?

MARY.   I cannot check them.

RAVENSWORTH. They do displease me,
tears can only flow
From frailty or from folly, dry them
straight,
And listen to me. I have heard, the
son
Of this strange woman is returning
home,
And wil again pollute our neighbourhood;
Remember my command, and shun
his presence
As you would shun the adder. If report
Err not, his course of boyhood has
been run
Without one gleam of virtue to redeem
The darkness of his vices.

MARY.   I'll obey—
To the utmost of my power.—But,
my dear father,
May not report err sometimes? You
were wont

To instruct me never to withhold the truth;
And fearlessly to speak in their defence,
Whom I could vindicate from calumny;
That to protect the innocent, the absent—

RAVENSWORTH. How's this! the innocent—and calumny?
And whence do you presume to throw discredit
On general report.— What can you know?

MARY. Not much perhaps, of late: while I remain'd
At his mother's—he was in his boyhood then;
I knew him well; and there's one incident
Much dwelt on to his prejudice, that I
Was witness to—if you would bid me tell it.

RAVENSWORTH. O, by all means, come, your romance.

MARY. 'T is truth.
It was a wintry day, the snow was deep,
And the chill rain had fallen and was frozen,
That all the surface was a glittering crust.—
We were all gather'd in the lady's hall,
That overlook'd the lawn; a poor stray fawn
Came limping toward us. It had lost, perhaps,
Its dam, and chas'd by cruel hunters, came
To seek a refuge with us. Every bound
The forlorn creature made, its little feet
Broke through the crust, and we could mark that one

Of its delicate limbs was broken. A rude boy
Follow'd it fast, as it would seem, to kill it;
I could not choose but wish its life were sav'd,
And at the word Charles ran and took it up,
And gave it to me, and I cherish'd it
And bound its broken limb up; and it liv'd,
And seem'd to thank me for my care of it.

RAVENSWORTH. But was this all? Was not the village lad
Assailed and beaten?

MARY. He was rude and churlish,
And would have forc'd the animal from Charles.
And tho' 't was on his mother's grounds, Charles proffer'd him
The price of the fawn. But nothing would content him,
And he struck Charles; he was a larger boy,
But did not prove the stronger—so he went
And made the village all believe his story,
That Charles had robb'd and beaten him, for Charles
Had none to speak for him.

RAVENSWORTH. No more of this—
And never let me hear the name you've utter'd
Pass from your lips again. It is enough
I know this youth for a lewd libertine;
The woman, for a scoffer at things sacred,
At me, and at my functions—and perhaps,
Given to practices, that yet may need
A dreadful expiation. Get you gone,
And on your knees petition that you may not

Deserve my malediction.

MARY.   I obey.

(*Exit* MARY, *into cottage, followed by* RAVENSWORTH; *enter* GEORGE EGERTON, *followed by* SIR REGINALD, *both in shooting costume.*)

GEORGE. By Heaven a lovely creature!

SIR REGINALD.   Softly, George,
Is this the game you point at? Have
    a care,
You're not in London now, where
    our gay monarch
Sets such a fine example in these
    matters.
They'll have no poaching here, that
    I can tell you,
Among their wives and daughters.
    These same roundheads,
That crop their hair so short—a
    plague upon 'em—
Will cut your ears as close, if you're
    caught meddling.

GEORGE. Why, what a heathen region
    have we come to.
What a deuce, uncle, did you bring
    me here for?
To shoot at bears and panthers;
    pleasant sport;
No women: zounds; I'll back to
    court again—
No women!

SIR REGINALD. None: the old they burn
    for witches,
The young they keep clos'd up (like
    flies in amber)
In adamantine ice.—

GEORGE.   They should be hang'd
For treason against nature. Let the
    old ones
Freeze, 'tis their charter; but youth
    should have fire.

SIR REGINALD. They've good laws here
    for gallants—t' other day
They put a man i' the stocks be-
    cause he kiss'd
His wife o' Sunday.

GEORGE.   They were in the right.

Kiss his own wife! it is a work-day
    business;
Play-days and holy-days are made
    for lovers.

SIR REGINALD. To lay hands on a maid
    here's present death.

GEORGE. It might be so in London, and
    no lives lost:
The law were a dead letter there—

SIR REGINALD.   And widows
May not be spoken to, under the pain
Of fine and pillory.

GEORGE.   Uncle, let's embark,
Tho' for the north pole; their clime is
    too cold—
Or to some catholic country, where
    a man
May have flesh sometimes: here 'tis
    always Lent.

SIR REGINALD. No: you must stay, your
    stomach must endure it.

GEORGE. I' faith, dear uncle, being a
    cavalier,
A gentleman of honour and of breed-
    ing,
I marvel much you could come hither;
    but
The greater wonder is you'd have
    me with you,
Knowing my humour.

SIR REGINALD.   Troth, my gentle
    nephew,
Knowing your humour, I could do
    no better
Than take you from the sphere of
    Charles's court;
From Rochester, and his dissolute
    companions,
To cool your blood here in the wilder-
    ness.

GEORGE. Well! there may come a time.

SIR REGINALD.   As for my voyage,
Perhaps it was a royal jest; or haply
My clothes had grown too rusty for
    the court,
Or Charles was tired of the old
    cavalier,

Who had fought some battles for
him, and consum'd
Some certain paltry acres—all he
had—
And having left no vacant place at
court,
He sent me here Ambassador.
GEORGE.   But uncle,
Is that your character?
SIR REGINALD.   Much the same thing,
In Christian countries, nephew; I'm
a spy.
GEORGE. The devil!
SIR REGINALD. Yes; we read in ancient
history,
Of Kings and Emperors, who have
kept the men
Who help'd them to the Throne
(by simply putting
Their fathers out o' the way)—about
their persons,
As their prime friends. But Charles,
being advis'd
That this was in bad taste, and took
place only
In semi-barbarous courts, finds it
decorous
To grow a little angry with the per-
sons
That kill'd his father. And being told,
besides,
That his most loving and beloved
subjects
This side the water—who, by the way,
he never
Thought of before—had given food
and shelter
To certain of the regicides, he sends
me
To—
GEORGE. Well, Sir?
SIR REGINALD. Nothing. Come, 'tis
growing late.
We must regain our cottage. In the
morning,
We leave the village.
GEORGE.   'Gad, with all my soul—

And so to England?
SIR REGINALD. Not so fast, good Spring-
al,
We must have patience yet. Come,
let's begone.
GEORGE. I'll see her in the morning,
tho' they hang me.
(*Exeunt,* GEORGE *looking back.*)

ACT TWO

SCENE ONE

*A forest. In the background an in-
sulated caverned rock. Night. The*
UNKNOWN *enters by a bridge formed
of the trunk of a tree, which is let
down from the rock. His dress is of
skins; his general appearance, wild—
but his air and manner dignified. He
is armed.*

UNKNOWN. Yes: it is near the dawn—
the dawn! when man
Again shall greet his fellow man, and
nature
Through all her living kingdom
shall rejoice.
I only of the human race, condemn'd
To shun my species, and in caves of
night
Shut out the common day. Ye glori-
ous stars,
I gaze on you—I look on you, ye
Heavens,
With an unblenching eye. You read
the heart,
And you can judge the act. If I was
wrong;
If innocent blood rest on me—here
I stand
To pay the dreadful forfeiture,—let
fall
In drops of fire your red-hot venge-
ance on me.

Am I a murderer? Is the mark of
Cain
Imprinted on my front!—I would
not murmur—
But as I am but man, forgive it
Heaven.
Torn from the beings that I fondly
lov'd.—
For nineteen years an outlaw and a
wanderer—
Proscribed and hunted like the raven-
ing wolf—
A price set on my felon head—A
felon!
Am I so, Heaven! Did these wounds,
receiv'd
In thy holy cause, stream with a
felon's blood,
Was it a felon's courage nerved my
arm,
A felon's zeal that burn'd within
my heart?
Yet this I could endure—but when
I think
Of thee, my child—my daughter—
Ha! a step!
Perhaps, a beast of prey! I fear not
that,
The panther is my co-mate and my
brother;
Man only is mine enemy—He comes.
(*Retires into cave.*)
(*Enter* CHARLES, *in a neat hunting
dress of green, cap, etc., a short sword,
or* couteau-de-chasse, *slung, and a gun
in his hand.*)
CHARLES. Each step I take but plunges
me the deeper
In this wild labyrinth.— Here's a
pretty scene
For those whose love o' the pictur-
esque, could make them
Forget their bed and supper. My
poor mother
Will be so disappointed—and, dear
Mary,
Will not your hopes, too, rise with
the lark: I'll on,

But whither? May I not be straying
further:
I must needs make my couch e'en
here.— What's this?
A bridge; and further on, methinks,
a cavern,
'T will serve— But hold—perhaps I
shall disturb
Some wild beast in his lair. Tut! 'tis
some hunter
Has made his cabin here—I'll try.
(*Goes to cavern.*)
UNKNOWN.   Pass not.
(*Enters from cave.*)
CHARLES. You speak commandingly.
UNKNOWN. And may, when strangers
Intrude upon my privacy. That cave
Is mine, my castle.
CHARLES.   It must be confess'd
You play the Castellain right courte-
ously.
UNKNOWN. No trifling, boy. Are you a
spy?—What are you?
CHARLES. My answer's here. (*Levelling
his gun.*)
UNKNOWN.   Tut, overweening child,
Level thy weapon at the timid deer
That fears thy puny skill. The
wither'd leaf
Stirr'd by the falling nut, or passing
breeze,
Startles as much as does thy idle
menace.
CHARLES. To prove it is not idle—
UNKNOWN.   Hold, rash boy;
If but this tube is rais'd, thou perish'st.
For years, as many as thou tell'st of
life,
I've wielded it.
CHARLES. I've had some practice, too.
UNKNOWN. Do you provoke your fate!
— But hold; no, no—
**Thought 't were my sole security, no
blood.**
He spoke of his mother too; I'll not
deprive
The mother of her child— Hear me,
bold youth.

'Tis meet that I should know so much of thee,

As to be well assur'd thou com'st not hither,

At this dark hour, for evil purpose —tell me—

I do not now command, but I request thee—

Wherefore this visit?

CHARLES. Now, sir, that your question
Is one a gentleman may give reply to,
I'll frankly tell you. I've a mother lives,
I trust, in the next town. A short time since
I left her, for the second time, for college,
To make a second trial for the honours,
I think, with due humility, I'd merited.
Their worships as before play'd with my patience,
Till I grew tired of it, and told them so,
In good round terms. Glad of the fit excuse,
They just discover'd then, I was too wild
For their strait limits, and so they expell'd me.

UNKNOWN. You speak but lightly of a circumstance
That an ingenuous and aspiring youth,
And, such you seem, might well think serious.

CHARLES. I cannot be a hypocrite, and deem
The acts of solemn folly serious.
When I shall cease to scorn malevolence
And learn to reverence cant and superstition,
Then, not till then, I'll weep at my expulsion.

UNKNOWN. But to your tale.

CHARLES. 'Tis told: I turn'd my back

On my grave censors; seized my hunter's arms,

And struck in to the wilderness for home;

Which by the forest route I hoped to reach

Ere the light closed to-day. I was deceived.

Night came upon me; yet, I travell'd on,

For by a civil horseman that pass'd by
I had sent letters bidding them expect me.

Briefly, when I had fairly lost myself
I met a hunter, whose bark cabin stands
A few miles hence. He put me in the track,
And pointed out a certain star to steer by;
But passing clouds, and intervening boughs,
And perhaps thoughts of home, and those at home,
Marr'd my astronomy. I lost my star,
And then I lost my path, and then myself.
And so, through swamp and thicket, brake and bramble,
I've scrambled on thus far—and, there's my story.

UNKNOWN. Your way was perilous—
Did you meet nothing?

CHARLES. Not much. Sometimes a snake I trod on coil'd
Around my leg, but I soon shook him off;
A howl at times approach'd—and as I pass'd,
The brake stirr'd near me with some living thing
Beside myself—but this was all.

UNKNOWN. 'T was wrong,
Rashly to tempt these dangers. If your air
Deceive me not, you are of foreign birth.

CHARLES. Not four years since, we left
our native England.

UNKNOWN. England!

CHARLES. But why's a mystery. We're
not known
Nor understood here; we're of another
world.

UNKNOWN. Your name?

CHARLES.   'Tis Charles Fitzroy.

UNKNOWN.   Fitzroy! Your mother's?

CHARLES. You're somewhat curious;
Isabella.

UNKNOWN. Ha!

CHARLES.   What is it moves you?

UNKNOWN.   Isabella, say you?

CHARLES. This strong emotion—

UNKNOWN.   It is nothing, nothing.—
Or—is it strange that I should feel
emotion
At the sad tale you tell?

CHARLES.   Sad tale!

UNKNOWN.   I wander.—
I've been a solitary man so long
That—'Tis no matter.— What dost
think me, youth?

CHARLES. A hunter who loves freedom
and the forest;
Who'd rather kill his venison in the
wood
Than toil for it in the town. Am I
not right?

UNKNOWN. 'Tis true—I am—a hunter—

CHARLES.   But a strange one.—
But come, sir, will you put me on my
way?

UNKNOWN. Will you not rather enter
my poor cave
And take its shelter till the morning
breaks?
'T will not be long.

CHARLES.   I cannot lose a moment
In selfish rest, while those who love
me suffer.

UNKNOWN. Give me your hand then.
I'm your friend.

CHARLES.   I thank you.

'Tis the first cordial grasp I've had
from man.

UNKNOWN. Poor youth! But hold—
Give me your solemn promise
To keep this meeting secret.

CHARLES.   I hate secrets;
Lovers alone should have them.

UNKNOWN.   There are reasons:—
I cannot now disclose them—solemn
reasons—
I do implore you—

CHARLES.   Sir, be satisfied;
I'll not reveal it.

UNKNOWN.   Nor allude to it,
However press'd—Nor give the dark-
est hint
That such a man as I exist!

CHARLES.   I promise.

UNKNOWN. I'm satisfied. Your words
are from the heart.
Fidelity and truth sit on your brow.
The blush of morn begins to tinge
the east;
You are not far from home; you'll
soon embrace
Your mother, Charles. Come, this
way lies the path. (*Exeunt.*)

SCENE TWO

An open wood near the cottage of
RAVENSWORTH. *Early dawn.—Enter*
GEORGE EGERTON.

———

GEORGE. Poor uncle! little does your
vision dream,
(Being abed) what ramble I'm upon.
A hopeful enterprize, this of my uncle's—
To tame me in a wild wood. Ay, and
then
His bug-bear stories of the laws—
confound 'em,
Last night they spoil'd the sweetest
vision for me;
Methought I saw this beauteous puritan,

The parson's daughter; well, I woo'd
and won—
A thing of course—But going to
embrace her,
I hugg'd—my pillow, think you? no;
a pillory!
Well: I'm resolved in spite of dream
and omen,
To see her, if I can, before we go.
I've three hours, good; and three
hours may do much.—
By Vulcan, the intruding and lame
God,
My uncle limping this way! Gout
confound him.
A royal oak! Bend your umbrageous
branches,
And saving me, be twice immortalized.
(*Conceals himself in a tree. Enter* SIR
REGINALD.)
SIR REGINALD. 'Sblood! the young re-
bel, what a march he's led me!
Tortur'd too, all the route, like a
poor prisoner
By my own natural enemy the gout.
The worst of't I cannot find the
rascal,
I've been around the house. And I'd
ha' sworn
That was his mark. If I but catch
him—Hey!
(*Enter* MARY.)
A pretty girl—I' faith, a pretty girl!
I'll speak to her, I will; there's no
one near—
Hem! Save you lady—
MARY (*who is anxiously looking another
way*). Would you aught with me,
sir!
SIR REGINALD. Aught? Yes, egad: a
very pretty girl—
My dear, I—that is—
GEORGE. So, so, my grave uncle.—
SIR REGINALD. I meant to say—'t is
somewhat early, child,
For youth like yours—She's beautiful
by gad:—

To leave your downy slumbers—
GEORGE. Poetry!
MARY. It is my custom, sir—But age
like yours
May suffer from the chill air of the
morning.
GEORGE. A brave girl, faith:
MARY (*aside*). 'Tis one of those
strange persons,
My father spoke of—would that he
would go.
SIR REGINALD. Why, as you say, my dear
—that is—in fact—
GEORGE. Nay, charge again, brave
cavalier.
SIR REGINALD. In truth then,
My errand here so early, was to seek
A runagate nephew.
GEORGE (*aside*). Meaning me.—
SIR REGINALD. A rascal!
Pray, lady, have you met him?
MARY. Sir, I know not
The person you enquire for.
SIR REGINALD. I'll describe him.
GEORGE. Now for a flattering portrait.
SIR REGINALD (*aside*). I'll disgust her
Lest he, perchance, should meet her
—He's a fellow
Of an indifferent person, which his
tailor
Cannot make handsome; yet he thinks
himself
The only true Adonis. He has language
If you can understand it. When he
speaks,
'Tis in a lisp or oath. His gait's be-
tween
A swagger and a dance. His grin's
from France,
His leer from Cyprus. He's a Turk
in morals,
And is of that religion no man
knows of:
In fine, he's as ridiculous as danger-
ous—
A mongrel thing; a slip of the cox-
comb, madam,

Grafted upon the rake.

MARY.   Sir, you describe
A monster.

SIR REGINALD. You have hit it: that is
he,
Should he approach you shun him.

MARY.   Sir, I shall.

GEORGE (aside). Here's a kind uncle:
but I'll be reveng'd.

(SIR REGINALD bows and exits.)

MARY. He should have come last night:
yet here's the morning,
And yet he comes not. He cannot
have pass'd me.
Is it because this is his homeward
path
That I am loitering here? I fear it
is—
O, I am most imprudent—most forgetful—
I fear most sinful.

GEORGE (descending, and comes down
the stage on the left). Now he's
out of sight.
And now for the encounter—Madam,
your slave.
Nay start not; I am not the monster,
lady,
That gouty person pictur'd. Did you
know him
But half so well as I, you'd not believe him,
Or did you but know me, but half
so well
As I would have you, and you would
believe him
To be the most transcendent of
romancers.
Bunyan's book, madam, is true history
To that he speaks. He was a soldier
once,
But was cashier'd for lying. Mande-
ville,
The greatest liar of antiquity,
May be hereafter quoted as authentic,
When he's believ'd—And I'm his
nephew, too!

A pleasant jest: he kept the wild
beasts, madam,
In London, till they turn'd him off
for stealing
The lion's supper—Yet a single moment.

MARY. What would you, sir?

GEORGE.   You see, before you, lady,
The most unfortunate young fellow
breathing,
Banish'd to this strange country for
the crime
Of being too susceptible—and sentenc'd
To die a lingering death upon the rack
Unless your smile reprieve him.

MARY.   This is strange:
I do not understand you.

GEORGE.   If my words
Lack meaning, lady, look into my eyes,
And thro' them to my heart, and
see enshrin'd
Your worshipp'd image there—

MARY.   Most wonderful,
What language is't you speak, sir?

GEORGE.   Ma'am: what language?
English, I think. The pretty simple-
ton!
Bred in the woods, to her a metaphor
Is Heathen Greek. Madam, those
foolish figures
Are all the mode at court; and mean,
my dear,
In simple phrase—

MARY.   I pray, sir, let me pass—

GEORGE. Not yet, my child—

MARY.   Sure 'tis a madman.

GEORGE.   True,
And therefore treat me soothingly
and kindly,
For of all madmen your mad lover's
maddest.
Do you not fear me?

MARY.   No.

GEORGE.   Why, then you love me.
Come; I have seen such clouds before; they tell
Of coming sunshine—nay, you must
not go.—

I will be monstrous kind to thee and
love thee
Most constantly—
MARY.   Release me.
GEORGE.   Ay, and take thee
To England, child, and make thee
'there, my dear,
The envy of thy sex.
MARY.   If you're a gentleman—
GEORGE. The conscious grove would
blush its green leaves red
Should I give back [give up].
MARY.   Do you not fear the laws?
GEORGE. Nor law nor gospel now—
Come, come, 'tis folly—
MARY. O Heav'n: help, help!
(*Enter* CHARLES, *comes down to
center.*)
CHARLES.   Ruffian, unhand the lady!
GEORGE. So peremptory, boy?
CHARLES.   Do you delay?
(*Throws him off.*)
GEORGE. Curse on my haste: I have
forgot my sword.
MARY. O Charles!
CHARLES. My dearest Mary; my be-
lov'd!
(MARY *retires upstage.*)
GEORGE. Hum; is it so? But s'death! I
mustn't bear it.
Hark ye, Sir.
CHARLES.   Well, Sir.
GEORGE.   I shall find a time.—
CHARLES. Best make it.
GEORGE.   When?
CHARLES. Two hours hence, in the
grove
East of the village.
GEORGE.   I shall meet you there.
But look ye, sir, be punctual: I've
engagements.
CHARLES. I shall not fail you.
GEORGE.   'Gad, a pretty fellow.
I'll pink him first, and then I'll
patronize him. (*Exit.*)
MARY. O Charles! what pass'd between
you? surely, surely
You will not honour him with

further notice.
CHARLES. Speak not of him—he is not
worth a thought—
We can employ our time to better
purpose.
Tell me, have yet the calumnies
against me,
Found shelter here?
MARY. You know they have not,
Charles.
But I have much to tell you—We
must part!
Heav'n! is not that my father? Oh,
it is!
He comes this way; but has not yet
descried us—
Ah! fly, fly quickly!
CHARLES.   Fly?
MARY.   Yes, if you wish
That we should ever meet—
CHARLES.   But shall we meet!
MARY. That way—behind the trees—O
quickly, quickly!
(CHARLES *goes up.*)
CHARLES (*from the grove*). But tell
me, Mary, will you walk this way
In the evening?
MARY.   It is impossible; my father
Forbids my walks—
CHARLES. Why then, one place remains
—One only—I will visit you
tonight—
You do not answer—Shall I?
MARY.   O begone!
(*Exit* CHARLES, *behind the trees.*)
Did I consent? I fear he'll think I did.
My father comes—should be have
seen us part!
Am I the guilty creature that I feel?
He's here—I cannot look him in the
face.
(*Enter* RAVENSWORTH, *who looks at*
MARY *sternly for some time.*)
RAVENSWORTH. 'Tis well; that air of
shame becomes you well,
Is this your duty? Did I not forbid
These lonely walks? But get you home;
anon,

I'll talk with you.
MARY (*as she goes out*). He did not
see him!
RAVENSWORTH.   Home. (*Exeunt.*)

SCENE THREE

An apartment at ISABELLA'*s. Enter*
ISABELLA, *meeting* LUCY.

———

ISABELLA. Speak; is he yet in sight?
LUCY.   No, madam.
ISABELLA.   Go,
O! go again, good Lucy, and be swift
When he appears. (*Exit* LUCY.) My
     poor, poor boy! my Charles—
To be thus treated, and thy gentle
     heart
So full of kindness to all living crea-
     tures:
To have thy aspirations after fame
Thus rudely scorn'd, thy youthful
     hopes thus blighted!
But he deserves it not; there's com-
     fort yet,
And he may rise above it.—Not yet
     come.
He promis'd, and he would not break
     his word,
And to his mother, without serious
     cause—
The way is full of peril, and I know
His temper shuns not danger. Graci-
     ous Heav'n!
If I should lose him—him, the only
     being—
(*Enter* LUCY, *hastily.*)
Now, Lucy, quick!
LUCY.   Madam, he is in sight;
And flying up the avenue.
ISABELLA.   Thank Heaven!
(*Enter* CHARLES.)
CHARLES. Mother!
ISABELLA. My son. (*Falls into his
     arms.*)
CHARLES.   My ever dearest mother!
ISABELLA. O Charles, how could you

thus delay your coming?
The night was pass'd in watch.
CHARLES.   I grieve to know it.
I was benighted in the forest, Mother,
And lost my way.
ISABELLA. Alas! thou art spent with
     toil.
CHARLES. Not much.
ISABELLA.   Poor Charles: And so
     they have expelled thee—
Expell'd!
CHARLES. Nay, pry'thee let us forget it.
ISABELLA.   Wretches!
I could have borne all else—but to
     disgrace thee—
To spurn thee from them—thee!
I could endure
The daily persecutions that assail me
With patience and with firmness—
But I have thee.
Come, let us in: you need rest and
     refreshment.
You shall not leave me soon again,
     my son—
I am a child without you.
CHARLES (*aside*). My poor mother.
ISABELLA. But let us in—
CHARLES.   I'll follow you, my mother.
I will but give an order. (*Exit* ISA-
     BELLA.) Edward.
EDWARD (*enters*).   Sir.
CHARLES. Go, get my rapier ready,
     wrap it close,
And some hour hence, not later,
     choose a time,
And speed with it to the wood, east
     of the village,
There wait my coming.
EDWARD.   Yes, sir.
CHARLES.   But be sure
That no one see it.
EDWARD.   I'll be careful, sir. (*Exits.*)
ISABELLA (*enters*). Fie, sir; is this your
     breeding? must I wait?
CHARLES. Forgive me, madam, I am
     ready now.
(*Exeunt.*)

ACT THREE

Scene One

An open wood. Enter CHARLES, *followed by* EDWARD.

———

CHARLES. Give me the sword; remain at the edge of the wood;
If any one approach, haste to inform me.
(*Exit* EDWARD.)
I am here first, 'tis well. My mother thinks
It is a softer interview I seek;
And while she cautioned me, her sad smile seem'd
To sanction what she fear'd. My dear, kind mother.
And should I fall—well: it would be my fate.
We are but barques upon the sea of life,
And when the storm is up, we greet the port,
Or meet the rock, as destiny determines,
Spite of our feeble efforts. Mary, too!
These thoughts are not in season.
Here's my man.
(*Enter* GEORGE EGERTON, *hastily.*)
Well met, sir.
GEORGE. Sir, I kiss your hands. I' faith,
I've had a race to get here. My wise uncle
Hung round me like a bride in the first month—
Or rather like a wife in the second year,
When jealousy commences. —Come on, sir.
CHARLES. Best breathe awhile; I have the advantage of you.
GEORGE. You will not keep it long. My greater skill
Will give me still the odds.
CHARLES. It may be so,
Yet you may be deceived. My masters flatter'd

Or I, too, have some science.
GEORGE. I'm glad of it;
For you're a pretty fellow, and deserve
To fall with credit. Come, sir, to your guard.
We shall be interrupted.
CHARLES. Better so,
Than that we fight unfairly. You pant still, sir.
GEORGE. You are a soul of honour, and, were't possible—
But no; the person of an Egerton
Must never' be profan'd. Come, sir, *en garde.*
CHARLES. If you will have it so.
GEORGE. I will.
CHARLES. Come on then.
(*They fight.* GEORGE *is wounded.*)
GEORGE. I'm pink'd egad; who would have thought it? 'Sdeath!
I'm out of practice.
CHARLES. Here, sir, on this bank.
Your head against this tree—Your wound's not deep
I hope. How feel you now?
GEORGE. I' faith, but faintly.
(*Enter* EDWARD.)
EDWARD. There is a gentleman approaching, sir.
GEORGE. It is my uncle, like a keen old sportsman,
In at the death. Pry'thee begone, my friend,
'T were well you were not known.
CHARLES. This handkerchief—
So, press it close—I'll haste to send you aid.—
But for the lady's fame, and your own honour,
The cause of this our meeting is a secret.
GEORGE. It shall be so: I thank you. But away!
(*Exeunt* CHARLES *and* EDWARD.)
That's a fine lad. But where i' the devil's name,
Learn'd he to fence? I wonder, now

I think on't,
Who'll write my epitaph. My uncle can't,
He has no genius. I would do't myself,
Had I an amanuensis: let me see—
Hic jacet— (*Faints.*)
SIR REGINALD (*enters*).   Gracious
Heav'n, what is this!
My nephew bleeding, dead! no, he but faints,
With loss of blood. Soft, he revives;
why, nephew—
My poor mad George, how fares it?
GEORGE.   How d' ye, uncle?
Is't day or night? Faith my eyes twinkle strangely.
SIR REGINALD. Cheerly, George, cheerly, we'll do well enough—
What shall I do?—But how came this about?
Was't fairly done?
GEORGE.   According to the rules.
Should I die, uncle, and my adversary
E'er be discover'd, testify for him—
He kill'd me like a gentleman and Christian.
SIR REGINALD. A duel! ah, George, George. But zounds! do the round-heads
Fight duels too! a pretty school I've chosen
To teach you prudence in! will no one come!
(*Enter* TWO MEN, *with a bier.*)
Ah, you are welcome, set it down, so, so.
GEORGE. A pretty ominous conveyance, this.
SIR REGINALD. I pry'thee hold thy peace, and get thee in.
GEORGE. A grain of opium now, were worth a jewel,
Uncle, I'll never fight again without it.
SIR REGINALD. Be quiet, George—you waste your strength. So, so.
(*The* MEN *take him up and are about moving.*)

GEORGE. Head foremost if you please, my worthy friends;
'Tis but fair play—heels first perhaps, tomorrow.
(*The* MEN *carry him a few paces.*)
Halt, if it please ye, gentlemen, one moment.
Two hobbles more and I'm defunct.
—Pray, general,
Drill those recruits to the step. In camp, now, uncle,
It were a pleasure to be carried out.
SIR REGINALD. Wilt hold thy peace then?
GEORGE.   Yes.—The left foot, uncle—
SIR REGINALD. Now, gentlemen, at the word "march" lift up
The left foot each of you, and so move on.
GEORGE. Right, uncle.
SIR REGINALD.   Hold your tongue. March!
GEORGE.   Ay; so, so.
(*Exeunt.*)

SCENE TWO

The village. Enter CHARLES *and* EDWARD.

————

CHARLES. Can it be true! the savages so near?
EDWARD. It is so said.
CHARLES.   Edward, do you return,
And see the unfortunate gentleman I wounded
Placed in security. I'll hasten home.
(*Exit* EDWARD.)
My first care is my mother—then for Mary! (*Exits.*)
(*Enter* WALFORD, *meeting* ALICE.)
WALFORD. Whence this alarm?
ALICE.   O father, we are lost.
A hunter has come in nigh dead with speed,
With tidings that the savages are coming.

WALFORD. How near?

ALICE. Alas! a few miles from the village.

WALFORD. Is't possible! can they have thus eluded
Our watchful troops! we must prepare—O welcome!

(*Enter* RAVENSWORTH.)
Heard you the fearful tidings, Ravensworth?

RAVENSWORTH. I have, and will you now believe, our sins
Bring these afflictions on us? We have murderers
Lurking among us.

WALFORD. How!

RAVENSWORTH. This moment pass'd me
The relative of the Knight, Sir Reginald;
Dying, or dead.

WALFORD. Whose was the act?

RAVENSWORTH. Whose was't?
The act of him, whose every act is crime.
The son of this dark woman.

WALFORD. How is it known?

RAVENSWORTH. His sword and handkerchief stain'd both with blood,
And mark'd with his vile name, were found in the wood.
He has not been one day yet in the village,
And lo! these visitations. On the instant
He must be dealt with.

WALFORD. First for our defence—
What do you counsel?

RAVENSWORTH. Prayer and sacrifice.

WALFORD. 'Tis too late now, we must take other means.

(*The* VILLAGERS *enter, exhibiting signs of wild affright.*)

WALFORD. Hark ye, my friend, have messengers been sent
To warn the scatter'd settlers round?

FIRST VILLAGER. They have.

WALFORD. Why rings not the alarum bell!

FIRST VILLAGER. I know not,
Unless the exposed position of the church—

WALFORD. Go, some of you and do it.
—Hasten, friends,
Seize every man his arms.

(*Exeunt* VILLAGERS.)

RAVENSWORTH. Behold where comes
In all her pride, one of the moving causes
Of all this horror—mark with what an air,
How tranquil and compos'd she looks around
Upon the growing evil—safe, 'midst the fury
Of her own tempest.

(*As he speaks, enter* ISABELLA; *the women shrink from her in fear.* ALICE *gazes upon her with interest;* RAVENSWORTH *fixes his eyes sternly upon her. She remains unmoved.*)

WALFORD. Ravensworth, forbear.
Is this a time.—

(*Enter* SECOND VILLAGER.)
Now, friend, what news have you?

SECOND VILLAGER. They have begun to issue from the wood.

SIR REGINALD (*enters*). What is this I hear? the savage approaching!
Now plague upon this gout!—But I've an arm left
That yet can wield a sword.

WALFORD. Your nephew, Sir,
May need your care. You're strange to our wild warfare.

SIR REGINALD. True; I'd forgot poor George. They'll cut thro' me
Before they get a hair of him.

(*Retires.*)
(*Re-enter* FIRST VILLAGER.)

WALFORD. How now?

FIRST VILLAGER. We've rallied at the church; but want a leader.

WALFORD. You shall not want one longer.

ALICE. O, my father!

WALFORD. Heav'n bless you, my dear daughter. Follow me.

(*Exit* WALFORD, *followed by* VIL-LAGERS. *Distant yell. The alarm bell rings, a few distant and straggling shots heard. Houses at a distance beginning to blaze; a pause of the bell.*)

RAVENSWORTH. Now, where's your son?

ISABELLA. Gone, Sir, to save your daughter.

RAVENSWORTH. My daughter! I'd forgot.—Is she not here.

(*Runs wildly around. Bell rings. The shots are nearer and more frequent. The blaze increases.*)

RAVENSWORTH. My daughter! where, O where's my daughter!

(*Enter* CHARLES, *bearing* MARY.)

CHARLES. There, Sir.

(RAVENSWORTH *receives her, and for a moment yields to his paternal feeling. But instantly withdraws from* CHARLES *with a scowl.* CHARLES, *after affectionately recognizing his mother, rushes out.* ALICE *joins* MARY; *who is prevented from addressing* ISABELLA, *by her father's frown.* ISABELLA *maintains her dignity and composure. Alarm continues, shouts, yells, etc. The* VILLAGERS *enter in disorder, followed by* CHARLES *and* WALFORD.)

CHARLES. One effort more.

WALFORD. It is impossible, Panic has seiz'd them all and we must perish.

(*The bell has ceased. A dreadful yell. The* VILLAGERS *turn and are about to fly in despair.*)

UNKNOWN (*enters*). Turn back for shame—as ye are men, turn back! As ye are husbands, fathers, turn, and save From death and violation those ye love.—If this not move you, as ye are Christian men And do believe in God, tempt not his wrath By doubting thus his providence. Behold I am sent to save you.

OMNES. Save us, save us.

WALFORD. Say, What shall we do; we're ready to obey thee.

UNKNOWN. Front then and bear yourselves like men—'Tis well. The savage sees us rally; and the pause His caution grants, secures us the advantage.

(*He passes rapidly along the line, dividing them into three bodies. Then addresses* WALFORD *and* CHARLES.)

This band be yours—this yours— Quick, lead them forth, And each by a rapid circuit, turn the foe By either flank. This will I lead myself Against his front—holding him thus in check Until I hear the horn sound your arrival— Then while perplex'd he hesitates between us, Rush to the onset all—close on the heathen, And shower destruction on him— haste away.

(*Exeunt* UNKNOWN, WALFORD, *and* CHARLES, *leading their bands.*)

ISABELLA. How awful is this pause, that but precedes The shock that may o'erwhelm us. God, to thee, The mother turns. Not for myself, Not for my sinful self—but for my son— My innocent son I plead. Cut him not off In the blossom of his days.

RAVENSWORTH. Mark, if the hag Mutter not, even now, her incantations.

(*A few scattering shots heard.*)

The fronts have met, and from the

forest coverts,
Exchange their cautious fire.

(*A bugle sounds, answered by another from a different quarter. Shouts, yells, a general and continued discharge of musketry. Shouts and bugles.*)

RAVENSWORTH. The crisis has arrived
—the fire has ceased,
And now the closer work of death
commences.

(*To a* BOY, *who ascends the tree.*)
Ascend yon tree, and say what thou
observest.

BOY. I see them now. The Indians
stand dismay'd.
We're pouring now upon them from
the forest,
From every side.—Now, now the Indians turn—
They meet—they close—they're struggling man to man.
Sword, knife and tomahawk are
glancing.

ISABELLA. Heaven!
Protect, protect my Charles!

ALICE.   Save my dear father.

(*Shout.*)

RAVENSWORTH. What shout is that?
Hear ye the savage yell?

BOY. No, no, 't was ours—we've conquer'd—and they come,
Dragging their prisoners with them.
Here's my father.

(*Enter* FIRST VILLAGER *shouting* "*Victory,*" *meets and caresses the* BOY. *General shout, bugles. Enter* WALFORD, CHARLES, VILLAGERS, *with* INDIAN PRISONERS. *They arrange themselves on each side; the* INDIANS *in the background.* CHARLES *flies to his mother, who sinks on her knees in his embrace.* ALICE *joins her father, various groups formed.* MARY *manifests much interest for* CHARLES, *who regards her tenderly.* RAVENSWORTH *preserves his suspicious and reserved demeanour. Enter the* UNKNOWN. *He passes down the center.*

All gaze on him with awe, and stretch forth their hands towards him, bending their bodies.)

UNKNOWN. No; not to me this homage
—not to man
Is your this day's deliverance owing.
There—
To heaven address your gratitude.
To God
Stretch forth your hands and raise
your swimming eyes.
Before Jehovah bend your bodies down,
And from your humble hearts pour
out the flood
Of Thankfulness. It was his care
that watch'd,
His eye that saw; his arm that smote
the heathen—
His be the praise and glory.

(*All bend in adoration. The* UNKNOWN *casts a glance at* ISABELLA, *and exclaims as he goes out.*) Yes; 'tis she.

(*Exit* UNKNOWN. *After a short pause, they raise their heads and look around anxiously for the* UNKNOWN. *Enter* SIR REGINALD.)

WALFORD. Has this thing been? Where
is he? did he pass you?

SIR REGINALD. Who?

WALFORD.   Our mysterious leader—

SIR REGINALD.   I saw him not.

WALFORD. Was't an earthly being?

ALICE.   O my father!
It was not mortal.

CHARLES.   In the fight his arm,
Like the fierce lightning wither'd
where it fell.

SIR REGINALD. You speak of wonders!

RAVENSWORTH.   Woman, what think
you—
Was it an angel—or a fiend?

WALFORD.   What mean you?

(ISABELLA *turns from him proudly.* CHARLES *represses his anger on exchanging glances with* MARY.)

RAVENSWORTH. You'll know anon.
Walford, you bleed. (*Crosses to*

WALFORD.)

WALFORD.   A trifle.

RAVENSWORTH. *He* does not bleed—

WALFORD.   I think not; yet he dar'd
The thickest of the fight.

RAVENSWORTH.   Can you not see?
Do you but mark?

WALFORD. Your meaning is most dark.

RAVENSWORTH. The murkiest night
must fly before the day;
Illusion, strong as Hell must yield to
Truth.
You understand me not—No matter
—come—
Let these vile heathens be securely
plac'd
To await their certain death—then
to the temple—
There, to the Throne of Mercy to
present
Our sacrifice of prayer and of thanks-
giving.
(*Exeunt* CHARLES, ISABELLA, *and
others.*)

ACT FOUR

SCENE ONE[1]

Before the house of RAVENSWORTH.
Enter RAVENSWORTH *from the house,
meeting* WALFORD.

———

RAVENSWORTH. You come in happy
time; I would have sought you.
Walford, my soul is sick, even to death,
To look upon the miseries our sins
Bring down upon us. But I am re-
solv'd;—
This day's events at length have
steel'd my heart
Against the accursed cause; who must
not longer
Pollute, unquestion'd thus, our whole-

———

[1] This scene was omitted in the stage production.

some air.

WALFORD. You know the cause then?

RAVENSWORTH. Who can know this
woman,
This Isabella, and be ignorant!
But she must answer it—the time is
come;
She and her son must answer for
their deeds.
And since my letters to the government
Have fail'd to bring their aid—our-
selves, my friend,
Must call them to the judgment seat.

WALFORD.   Not so;
Your efforts have been crown'd with
sad success.
Commissioners have even now ar-
riv'd.—
I came to let you know it.

RAVENSWORTH.   Thanks, my friend,
You make me happy.

WALFORD.   Happy, Ravensworth!

RAVENSWORTH. And should I not rejoice that guilt like theirs
Should cease to spread its poison thro'
the land?

WALFORD. Where shall we find the evidence of guilt?

RAVENSWORTH. The trial shall produce
it, doubt it not;
Meantime, methinks the general belief
In their dark crimes; the universal
horror
Inspir'd e'en by their presence—as
if nature
Shudder'd instinctively at what was
monstrous,
And hostile to its laws, were, of
themselves,
A ground to rest the charge on.

WALFORD.   Ah, my friend,
If reason in a mind like yours, so
form'd,
So fortified by knowledge, can bow
down
Before the popular breath, what shall
protect

From the all-with'ring blasts of super-
stition
The unthinking crowd, in whom cre-
dulity,
Is ever the first born of ignorance?
RAVENSWORTH. Walford, what meanest
thou by superstition!
Is there in our religion aught forbid-
ding
Belief in sorcery! Look thro' this land,
Or turn thine eyes abroad—are not
the men
Most eminent for piety and knowl-
edge—
The shining lights of a benighted age,
Are they not, too, believers?
WALFORD.   There have been,
In every age, among the learn'd,
divines,
Statesmen, philosophers, astronomers,
Who have upheld with much ability,
The errors they believ'd in. Abstract
points
In science, may be safely tolerated,
Altho' erroneous—But there may be
doctrines,
So fatal in their influence, that, until
Their truth is manifest, 't were well
not cast them,
With lavish hand, among the multitude.
RAVENSWORTH. And is not sorcery
manifest as day?
Have not our senses testified unto it?
WALFORD. We have heard infant wit-
nesses aver it,
And seen them while they seem'd
to suffer it;
We have heard wretches in despair
confess it,
And have seen helpless creatures
perish for it;
And yet—
RAVENSWORTH.   What yet?
WALFORD.   O Ravensworth! these
things
Have happened: on a day of gloom
and terror,

When but to doubt was danger, to
deny, death;
When childish petulance, e'en idiocy,
Were gravely listened to, when mere
suspicion,
Could, with a hint destroy, and coward
malice,
With whispers, reach'd at life; when
frenzy's flame,
Like fire in tow, ran thro' the minds
of men,
Fann'd by the breath of those in
highest places,
E'en from the bench, yea, from the
sacred desk.
RAVENSWORTH. Hold, Walford, I have
held thee as my friend,
For many years, beware—
WALFORD.   I know thy power
Over the multitude, but fear it not.
I have discharged my duty, fare
thee well.
RAVENSWORTH. Stay, Walford, thou
art honest, but mistaken,
We will dispute no more. But tell
me, friend,
Have the commissioners enquired for
me?
WALFORD. They have. Before they en-
ter on their duties,
They'd have thy counsel.
RAVENSWORTH.   They shall have it
straight,
I'll go to them at once. 'T is almost
night—
There is no hour to lose. I pray
thee, Walford,
As I may haply, be detain'd abroad,
Let thy good Alice stay here with
my daughter
Till my return.
WALFORD.   Most willingly. I'll haste,
And bring her hither.
RAVENSWORTH.   Nay, we'll
go together.
(*Exeunt.*)

SCENE TWO

An apartment at ISABELLA'*s. Enter*
ISABELLA *and* CHARLES.

ISABELLA. Ungrateful people!
CHARLES.   Had they not presum'd
To cloud your clear name with their
viperous breath,
I could forgive them. 'T was not for
the herd
I drew my sword.
ISABELLA. Unthankful wretches; what!
Upon the very act that saved their
lives,
To found a charge that might en-
danger thine!
CHARLES. 'T is even so: I am in
league, it seems,
With fiends, so say their worships;
and the stranger,
Is no less, than the prince of fiends
himself.
Nothing is too ridiculous for those
Whom bigotry has brutaliz'd, I laugh
At their most monstrous folly.
ISABELLA.   But such folly,
When it infects the crowd, is dangerous.
Already we've had proof what dreadful
acts
Their madness may commit, and
each new day
The frenzy spreads. We are suspect-
ed too—
Then your imprudent duel—O my son,
We must remove from hence.
CHARLES.   Remove, from hence?
ISABELLA. Yes; ere the monsters catch
us in the toils
They are preparing.
CHARLES.   Mother, you were wont
To bear a mind whose firmness could
resist
Your sex's common weaknesses!
ISABELLA.   I know not
How it is, Charles, but dark and sad
forebodings

Hang o'er my subdued spirit; and
I tremble
E'en for thy life.
CHARLES.   Banish those thoughts, my
mother.
ISABELLA. I try, but cannot.—Yes; we
will hence, my son.
Tho' on the verge, perhaps, of that
discovery
The hope of which has held me here
so long,
We will begone tomorrow.
CHARLES.   So soon, mother?
ISABELLA. You do not wish it. Charles,
a mother's eye
Can penetrate the heart. The gentle
Mary—
She will be left behind—is it not so?
But this is boyish, you are yet too
young
To entertain such fantasies—and then
You know her father—sadder still my
son;
Well, we'll not cross the ocean—
we'll but seek
The nearest spot that is inhabited
By rational beings. And besides, your
youth
Will wear a year or two. How say you,
Charles,
Are you contented?
CHARLES.   You're the best of mothers.
And were my heart strings fasten'd
to the spot,
I'd with you, tho' they sunder'd.
But you spoke
A moment since, of some discovery
You were near making: what dis-
covery?
ISABELLA. It was an inadvertence—
CHARLES.   Must I never
Hope to enjoy your confidence?
ISABELLA.   Not now—
Another time, my son.
CHARLES.   Another time—
'T is ever thus you put my questions by.
Rather forbid me e'er again to ask

Of what so much concerns me, and
I promise
However hard the task, I will obey
you.
I trust you have ne'er found me dis-
obedient!
ISABELLA. You have been all a
mother's heart could wish.
You ask but what you have a right
to ask,
And I have always purposed a fit
time—
When that your age were ripe
enough—
CHARLES. Well, mother,
Has not that time arrived?
ISABELLA. Your age, dear Charles,
Has scarce reach'd manhood yet. 'T
is true, your courage,
Your conduct amidst danger—manly
virtues—
Are well approv'd. Your judgment
too—so much,
A mother may believe and say—is far
Beyond the years you count. But
there's a quality;
A virtue it may be, which is the
growth
Only of minds well disciplin'd; which
looks
On human actions with a liberal eye.
That knows the weakness of the
human heart,
Because it feels it; and will not con-
demn
In others, what itself is conscious of—
That will not with the tyrant pre-
judice,
Without allowance or extenuation,
Yea, without hearing pass its dread-
ful sentence.
CHARLES. And am I such a one?[2]
thanks to my nature,

Which I feel is not quite so vile.
My breeding,
Which has been liberal. Nay thanks
to those
Who daily here exhibit its deformity,
I scorn this monster prejudice.
ISABELLA. And yet—
Should you—I could not live if you
should hate me.
CHARLES. Hate you, my mother? Had
not all your actions
Been, as I've seen them, noble; all
your precepts
As I have ever found them, full of
goodness,
Could I recall the tenderness you've
shewn
Towards me, and cease to love you.—
Never, never!
All crimes however great, dwindle to
atoms
Near filial ingratitude; the heart
That is that monster's throne, ne'er
knew a virtue.
ISABELLA. Ah! how shall I commence!
—What would you know.
CHARLES. Why you left England? Why
in this wilderness,
Amidst a race that scorn, that shun
and loathe us,
You linger out existence? Chiefly,
Mother (*Taking her hand.*),
Who is my father?
ISABELLA (*turning away*). Ah!
CHARLES. In our own England,
At school, among my frank and
laughing mates,
When they have put this question,
it was done
In merry mood, and I could bear
it—well—
Although I could not answer it; but
here,

---

[2] This passage, apparently confused, should
perhaps read: Thanks to my nature,
Which I feel is not so vile, and to my
breeding,

Which has been liberal—nay, thanks to
those
Who daily here exhibit its deformity—
I scorn this monster prejudice.

O mother—to these cold and selfish beings,
Their smooth tongues dipp'd in bitterness, their eyes
Scowling suspicion—what can I reply?

ISABELLA. Poor boy, poor boy! Well, Charles, the time is come
And if my spirits fail not—you shall know all.
Your father—but I cannot, no, I cannot
Commence my story there.—I was left, Charles,
Without a parent's care, just at that age
That needs it most. I had ne'er known my mother,
And was scarce fifteen when my father's fate
Forc'd him to abandon child and home and country;
For he had been a patriot, as he deemed it,
Or, as his destiny decreed, a traitor.—
He fled to this New World.

CHARLES.   Does he yet live?

ISABELLA. Alas! I know not, rumours came to England
That he survived. It was to find my father,
And on my knees implore his benediction;—
Haply, should he forgive, to minister
Unto his age's comfort—I came hither.

CHARLES. 'T is strange, if living, he should seek concealment,
After the general amnesty.

ISABELLA.   O! Charles;
He was excepted in that Act of Mercy;
He had done that, the king might never pardon.

CHARLES. Unhappy man!

ISABELLA. Most true.—But let me haste
To close my dark recital. I was plac'd
In charge of a kinsman—a perfidious villain
Whose avarice sold, betrayed me.—

O my son,
It is not fit thy ears should hear the tale,
And from my lips. I wept, implor'd, resisted—
Riches and pleasure tempted me in vain
Coupled with shame. But hellish craft at length
Triumph'd over credulous vanity—
The altar
Was made the scene of sacrilegious mockery,
The holy vestments of the priest, became
A profane masking habit—

CHARLES.   Power of Justice!
Could you behold this and forbear to strike!

ISABELLA. The illusion vanish'd, and I fled, I fled
In horror and in madness.

CHARLES.   Dreadful, dreadful!

ISABELLA. It was thy birth that sav'd me from destruction—
I had thee to live for, and I liv'd; deep hid
In solitude, under an assum'd name,
Thou wer't rear'd, Charles, amidst thy mother's tears.

CHARLES. An assum'd name—in solitude—Shame, shame!
Why not unmask the villain to the world,
And boldly challenge what was yours?

ISABELLA.   His rank—

CHARLES. No rank should shield injustice. Quick, inform me
Who was the wretch? Give me the villain's name.

ISABELLA. He was thy father, Charles.

CHARLES.   In the sight of Heaven
I here disclaim and curse—

ISABELLA.   Forbear, forbear—
Or curse me too—

CHARLES.   His name, his name—

ISABELLA.   You will destroy me! (*She*

falls into his arms.)

CHARLES. What have I done? I will be calm—forgive me.

LUCY (*enters*). A person from the village, madam, asks
To be admitted to your presence.

ISABELLA. How! Does he declare his business?

LUCY. He declines it, Until he see yourself.

ISABELLA. Admit him, Lucy. (*Exit* LUCY.)

CHARLES. Madam, you tremble still, let me support you.

ISABELLA. No; I must learn to overcome this weakness.

(*Enter* MESSENGER.)

Now, Sir, I'm she you ask for—to your business.

MESSENGER. My business is with both. You, Isabella
And Charles, surnam'd Fitzroy, are cited both,
By a commission of the government,
To attend them at their session on the morrow
At nine in the morning.

CHARLES. And to what purpose?

MESSENGER. That You'll learn from them, farewell. (*Exit.*)

CHARLES. Why farewell, gravity.

ISABELLA. What can this mean?

CHARLES. They do not know themselves.

ISABELLA. I fear I've been too tardy.

CHARLES. Nay, 't is nothing. To question us, perhaps, upon our means,
And pack us from the parish, nothing more.
But, madam, you were interrupted, ere I learn'd the name—

ISABELLA. Not at this moment, Charles.

CHARLES. Well then, enough of sorrow for today—
I will return anon, and laugh with you

At the absurdities of these strange people.
At supper we'll discuss our plans for the future.
We may be happy yet.—

ISABELLA. But whither go you?

CHARLES. I ought to visit him I wounded, madam,
And perhaps I may gather in the village,
Something that may concern us— and perhaps—

ISABELLA. Well do not be long absent; it is night.

CHARLES. I will not, madam: I shall soon return. (*Exit.*)

ISABELLA. He does not feel the danger, his frank spirit,
His careless youth, disdains it. We must fly.—

(*Enter* LUCY.)

Bid Edward, with all speed, prepare the horses,
Then follow to my chamber. We must prepare
In all haste, for a journey—

LUCY. Madam, a journey— Tonight?

ISABELLA. Tonight: it is most necessary. So, bid Edward
Be secret.

LUCY. He is here.

EDWARD. (*within*). You cannot pass. (*Enter* EDWARD.)

ISABELLA. What noise is this?

EDWARD. Madam, in spite of me They press into your presence.

ISABELLA. We are lost! (*Enter several* OFFICERS.)

FIRST OFFICER. For that we do we have sufficient warrant.

ISABELLA. What means this rudeness?

FIRST OFFICER. Answer; where's your son?

ISABELLA. He is not in the house.

FIRST OFFICER (*to* ATTENDANTS *who go*

out). Go you, make search.

ISABELLA. Again I ask, what is your business here?

FIRST OFFICER. Read. (*He hands her a paper.*)

ISABELLA. Gracious Heav'n! Is this the charge against us!
But why this second visit! we are cited
To answer in the morning.

FIRST OFFICER.   But the judges
Ha've chang'd their mind. Your chamber is your prison
'Til you are sent for. We'll attend you thither.

ISABELLA. But one word with my servant—

FIRST OFFICER.   Not one word;
It is forbidden, come—

ISABELLA. My son, my son!

(*She exchanges significant looks with* LUCY, *and exits guarded.*)

LUCY (*going*). I understand.

SECOND OFFICER. And so do we—our duty.
You are not to stir hence, nor hold discourse
One with another. Lead them in— away.

(OFFICERS *lead off* LUCY *and* EDWARD.)

SCENE THREE

Before the house of RAVENSWORTH. —*Enter* MARY *from house.*

MARY. He does not come. I do not wish it, sure—
At least I ought not. But has he forgotten?—
That is impossible.—Perhaps he fears—
O no! Charles never fears—should he not come—
I ought to hope he could not—ah! a figure,
Stealing between the trees—should

it be he?
But may it not be a stranger! ah, let me fly:
(*Exit, into the house.*)

CHARLES (*enters cautiously*). 'T was she, her white robe, emblem of her innocence,
Dispels the darkness of the libertine night,
And all around her's purity and brightness.
She is alone. As I pass'd thro' the village
I learn'd her father was in council there.—
She is alone and unprotected quite—
She loves me and confides in me— be that,
Tho' passion mount to madness, her protection.
The door is fasten'd, right; a common guest
Comes by a common passage— there are posterns
And wickets for the lover. Let me try.
(*Exit behind the house.*)

SCENE FOUR

A chamber; a window in the flat; a light burning near the window. MARY *discovered, a book in her hand.*

MARY. I cannot read—my thoughts are all confusion,
If it be he, will he not think the light
Was plac'd designedly. I will remove it.
(*Goes towards the window, and starts when* CHARLES *appears at it.*)

CHARLES. Be not alarm'd, my Mary: it is I.

MARY. O Charles, how could you?—

CHARLES.   How could I refrain
When that the beacon light so fairly blaz'd
From steering to this haven?

MARY. There! I fear'd
You would presume to think—
CHARLES. But I think nothing—
Presume, know nothing, but that
thou, my Mary,
Art the divinest creature on the earth
And I the happiest—O my best,
my dearest,
That thou might'st live forever near
this heart;
And why not there forever! What
prevents it,
What can—what shall? My beaute-
ous, my beloved.
MARY. No more;
This warmth alarms me—hear me,
Charles—
I've given to thee my heart and
maiden vow,
O, be content—and—leave me—
CHARLES. Leave thee, Love?
MARY. Before you teach me to despise
myself;
Ere you yourself despise me.
CHARLES. Have I, Mary,
Have I deserv'd that from thee? Lo,
I'm calm—
And gaze upon thee as the pilgrim
looks
Upon the shrine he kneels at; the
pure stars
Look not on angels with a holier light.
MARY. I do believe you, Charles—but
O this meeting,
So rash, so—
CHARLES. 'T was presumptuous in
me, Mary,
I do confess it.
MARY. Still you mistake me, Charles,
I do not say I did not wish you
here—
Yet I must wish you gone. It is so
wrong—
I am so much to blame—
CHARLES. I will not stay,
To give you pain.
MARY. But do not go in anger—

CHARLES. Anger! at you!
MARY. A happier time will come—
Each moment now is full of peril,
Charles;
My father may return, and should
he find you!—
CHARLES. One word and I will leave
you. You will hear,
To-morrow, that we've left this
place for ever.
MARY. How, Charles?
CHARLES. My mother has resolv'd to
fly
The persecutions that surround her
here
And we depart tomorrow—if we may—
For we're already cited—
MARY. Heav'ns! for what?
CHARLES. It can be nothing surely.
But, dear Mary,
Tho' absent, ah, remember there is
one
Who lives for you alone.
MARY. Charles, can you doubt it?
CHARLES. And should there, Mary,
should there come an hour
Propitious to our loves; secure and
safe—
Suspicion dead, her eye, nor ear
to mark us—
And should the lover that adores you,
Mary,
Appear at that blest hour, with cer-
tain means
To bear you far from cruelty and
slav'ry,
To love and happiness?—
MARY. No more, no more—
CHARLES. Would you consent?
MARY. O tempt me not to sin—
'T would break my father's heart—
CHARLES. Give me your promise.
(*Enter* RAVENSWORTH, WALFORD,
ALICE.)
MARY (*observing her father*). Unhand
me, oh unhand me—Father,
father!

(*She faints in* CHARLES' *arms.*)

RAVENSWORTH. Thy father's here to save thee, hapless girl,
And hurl confusion on thy base betrayer.

CHARLES (*attending only to* MARY). She's dead, she's dead!

RAVENSWORTH. Haste, tear her from his arms
Ere the pollution of his touch destroy her.

(ALICE *and* WALFORD *convey* MARY *out.*)

CHARLES (*gazing after her*). And have I killed her!

RAVENSWORTH. Wretch, and do you mourn
Over the clay, that would have kill'd the soul?

WALFORD (*re-enters*). She has reviv'd and calls for thee, my friend.

CHARLES. She lives, she lives! Then I defy my fate.

RAVENSWORTH. Outcast from Heav'n, thy doom is near at hand.
Walford, we'll strait convey him to the church,
Where by this time the judges have assembled,
To try his sinful mother.

CHARLES.   How? my mother!
And have ye laid your sacrilegious hands
Upon my mother?

RAVENSWORTH.   Silence, wretched youth.
I will but see my daughter meantime Walford,
Guard well your prisoner.

CHARLES.   Guard me! heartless father,
That feelest not the ties of blood and nature—
Think you, at such an hour, I'd quit my mother?

(*Exeunt* RAVENSWORTH, CHARLES, *and* WALFORD.)

ACT FIVE

SCENE ONE

A wood. Stage dark. Enter the UNKNOWN.

———

UNKNOWN. At length, unseen by human eye, I've gain'd
Her neighbourhood. The village lies before me;
And on the right rises the eminence
On which she dwells—She dwells! who dwells? O heart
Hold till thou art assur'd. Such were the features,
The stately form of her, whose cherish'd image,
Time spares my widow'd heart, fresh and unchang'd.—
I must be satisfied.— The night has fallen
Murky and thick; and in the western Heavens,
The last of day was shrouded in the folds
Of gathering clouds, from whose dark confines come,
At intervals, faint flashes, and the voice
Of muttering thunder: there will be a storm.
How is it that I feel, as never yet
I felt before, the threatening elements;
My courage is bow'd down and cowers, as though
The lowering canopy would fall in streams
Of death and desolation. Dark portents,
Hence! There's a Heaven beyond the tempest's scope,
Above the clouds of death. Wing your flight thither,
Thoughts—hopes, desires; there is your resting place. (*Exit.*)

SCENE TWO

The interior of the church, arranged as a Hall of Justice. Passages lead to doors on each side of the desk. The JUDGES *seated at the desk.* CHARLES *stands on the left, near the* JUDGES. ISABELLA *nearer the front; on the same side* RAVENSWORTH, WALFORD, MARY, *and* ALICE; *on the opposite side,* VILLAGERS, OFFICERS, *etc.*

JUDGE. Ye have heard the charge—but ere ye answer to it
Bethink ye well. Confession may do much
To save you from the penalty; or mitigate
Your punishment. Denial must deprive you
Of every hope of mercy.—Answer then—
And first, you, madam.
ISABELLA.   Sorcery! Gracious Heaven!
Is it necessary, in this age of light,
And before men and Christians, I should deny
A charge so monstrous!
JUDGE.   Answer to the question.
ISABELLA. We are not guilty then; so aid us Heaven!
JUDGE. Speak for yourself alone. Will you disclose
Who—what ye are?
ISABELLA.   I am a gentlewoman—
More I cannot disclose.
JUDGE.   Say, wherefore, madam,
You came among us?
ISABELLA.   Sir, I came to seek
A father.
JUDGE.   Who is he?
ISABELLA.   I dare not name him.
RAVENSWORTH. Mark you, how she prevaricates?
JUDGE.   What evidence
Have you against this woman?

RAVENSWORTH.   Ye all remember
The terror and despair that fill'd each bosom
When the red comet, signal of Heaven's wrath,
Shook its portentous fires above our heads.
Ye all have seen, and most of ye have felt
The afflictions which this groaning land is vex'd with—
Our smiling fields wither'd by blight and blast,
The fruitful earth parch'd into eddying dust,—
On our fair coast the strewings of wreck'd commerce;
In town and city, fire and pestilence,
And famine, walking their destroying rounds—
Our peaceful villages, the scene of slaughter,
Echoing the savage yell, and frenzied shriek
Of maid and matron, or the piercing wail
Of widows and of orphans—
JUDGE.   We deplore
The evils you recite; but what avails
Their repetition here, and how do they
Affect the cause in question?
RAVENSWORTH.   Shall we forget
That worldly pride and irreligious lightness,
Are the provoking sins, which our grave synod
Have urg'd us to root out? Turn then to her,
Swelling with earth-born vanity, to her
Who scorns religion and its meek professors;
And, to this hour—until compell'd, ne'er stood
Within these holy walls.
JUDGE.   Yet this is nothing,
Touching the charge against her—you must be

Less vague and general. Produce your proofs.

RAVENSWORTH. There are two witnesses at hand; her servants—
Who have confess'd she had prepared to fly
This very night—a proof most clear and potent
Of conscious guilt. But why refer to this!
Each one that hears me is a witness of it,
It is the village horror. Call, at random,
One from the crowd, and mark if he will dare
To doubt the thing I speak of.
JUDGE.   'T must not be,
Nor can we listen further.
ISABELLA.   I beseech you
Let him proceed; let him endeavour still
To excite the passions of his auditors;
It will but shew how weak he deems his proof
Who lays such stress on prejudice. I fear not,
But I can answer all his accusations.
If I intended flight—need I remind you
Of what your fathers—what yourselves have done?
It was not conscious guilt bade them or you
Escape from that you felt was persecution—
If I have thought the manner of my worship
A matter between Heaven and my conscience,
How can ye blame me, who in caves and rocks
Shunning the church, offer'd your secret prayers?
Or does my state offend? Habit and taste
May make some difference, and humble things

Seem great to those more humble; yet I have used
My little wealth in benefits. Your saints
Climb'd to high places—Cromwell to the highest—
As the sun seeks the eminence from which
He can diffuse his beams most bounteously.
RAVENSWORTH. The subtle power she serves does not withhold
The aid of sophistry.
ISABELLA.   I pray my judges
To shield me from the malice of this man,
And bring me to the trial. I will meet it,
As it concerns myself with firm indifference;
But as it touches him whom I exist in,
With hope that my acquittal shall dissolve
The fetters of my son.
RAVENSWORTH (aside).   That must not be.
JUDGE. Bring forth your proofs, and let the cause proceed.
RAVENSWORTH. Perhaps it is the weakness of the father
Prompts the suggestion—But I have bethought me,
It were most fit this youth should first be dealt with,
'Gainst whom there are a host of witnesses
Ready to testify—unless his actions,
Obvious and known, are proof enough
—his life
Which is a course of crime and profligacy,
Ending, with contemplated rape and murder.
ISABELLA. What do I hear?
JUDGE. How say you? rape and murder!
RAVENSWORTH. The victim of his bloody purpose lingers

Upon the verge of death—Here are
   the proofs
That point out the assassin!
   (*Showing the sword and handker-
chief, which are held by a* VILLAGER
who is standing near him.)
             For the violence—
Myself, my daughter here—
MARY.   O father, father!
JUDGE. These things are terrible. But
   you forget,
They are not now the charge.
RAVENSWORTH.   What matters it,
Whether by hellish arts of sorcery
He wrought upon the maiden—or
   with force
Attempted violation—Let him an-
   swer—
Denying one, he but admits the other.
JUDGE. Bid him stand forth. We wait
   your answer, youth.
CHARLES. You wait in vain— I shall
   not plead.
JUDGE.   Not plead!
RAVENSWORTH (*aside*). This is beyond
   my hopes.
ISABELLA.   O Charles, my son!
JUDGE. What do you mean?
CHARLES. Simply, sir, that I will not
Place myself on my trial here.
JUDGE.   Your reason?
Do you question then the justice of
   the court?
RAVENSWORTH. He does, no doubt he
   does.
CHARLES.   However strong
Might be the ground for question—
   't is not that
Determines me to silence.
JUDGE.   If you hope
To purchase safety by this con-
   tumacy;
'T is fit you be aware that clinging
   there,
You may pull ruin on your head.
CHARLES.   I know
The danger I incur, but dare to meet it.

ISABELLA. O Charles, reflect—
CHARLES.   Mother my soul is fixed;
They shall not call yon maiden to
   the bar.
Tremble not, weep not, pure and
   timid soul,
They shall not question thee.
RAVENSWORTH. Hence with thy spells—
Take thine eyes off my child, ere her
   weak frame
Yield to the charm she shakes with—
   hence I say!
   (MARY *attempts to speak, but is
prevented by her father.*)
JUDGE. Prisoner, attend: at once in-
   form the court
Of all you know concerning the
   strange being,
Who, like a supernatural visitant,
Appear'd this day among us. What
   connexion
Subsists between you?
CHARLES.   None. I know him not.
RAVENSWORTH. And yet this morning,
   ere the dawn had broken,
They were both seen together in the
   forest,
Holding mysterious converse. Here's
   a witness
Who will avouch the fact; and that
   the stranger
With the first day-beam, vanished
   from his sight.
ISABELLA (*aside*). He never told me
   this. Can he have met him?
JUDGE. Look on these things. They are
   mark'd with your name,
And stain'd with blood. They were
   found near the spot
Where a poor wretch lay bleeding.
   Can you explain it?
CHARLES. They are mine—I do con-
   fess it. I encounter'd
A person near that spot, and wound-
   ed him
In honourable duel. Nothing more
Can I explain.

MARY (*struggling*). O father, let me speak.

RAVENSWORTH. Silence! Now answer me, and let the powers
Of darkness, that sustain you in your pride,
Yield and abandon you unto your fate.
Did you not, robber-like, this night break in
My unguarded house, and there with ruffian force
Attempt the honour of this maiden?

ISABELLA.   Heaven!

RAVENSWORTH. D'ye hesitate! you dare not answer nay?
For here are witnesses to your confusion,
Who saw you clasp her in your vile embrace,
And heard her shrieks for help. Nay, here's the maiden,
Who will herself aver it.

MARY.   Father, father!

RAVENSWORTH (*attempting to lead her forward*). Come forth, my child.

CHARLES.   Forbear! it shall not need.

RAVENSWORTH. Do you confess?

CHARLES.   What e'er you will.

ISABELLA.   'T is past.

(MARY *faints in the arms of* ALICE.)

RAVENSWORTH. Hear ye this, Judges! People, hear ye this?

(*Storm commences.*)

And why do we delay! His doom were death,
Disdaining, as he has, to make his plea
To the charge of sorcery. Now, his full confession,
Which ye have heard, dooms him a second time.

(*Storm increases; thunder and lightning.*)

Then why do ye delay? The angry Heavens—
Hark, how they chide in thunder!
Mark their lightnings.

(*The storm rages; the* JUDGES *rise; all is confusion; the* PEOPLE *and two* OFFICERS *gather around* CHARLES; OFFICERS *seize him.*)

ISABELLA.   Save him!
O Heaven! As ye are men, have mercy!

RAVENSWORTH. No; not beneath this roof: among the tombs,
Under the fury of the madden'd sky;
Fit time and place!

CHARLES (*as they are dragging him out*). Mary; my mother! Mary!

ISABELLA. My son!

(*Leans nearly fainting in* LUCY'S *arms.*)

MARY (*reviving*). Who calls me? Ah! What would ye do?
He's innocent—he's my betroth'd— my husband!
He came with my consent—he's innocent!

RAVENSWORTH. Listen not to her; 'tis his hellish magic
Speaks in her voice—away!

MARY (*fainting*).   O Charles, my Charles!—

(*They bear* CHARLES *out. The storm continues.*)

RAVENSWORTH. It is accomplish'd.

UNKNOWN (*enters*). What? what is accomplish'd?

RAVENSWORTH. Who'rt thou that ask'st?

UNKNOWN. Nay, answer me. They tell
Of dreadful deeds ye are performing here.—
How's this! Has death been here among you?

RAVENSWORTH. Yes,
Whatever thou may'st be, death has been here
Guided by Heaven's vengeance.

UNKNOWN.   Who is this?
'T is she, 't is she! Dost know me, Isabella?

ISABELLA. Is it not—?

UNKNOWN.   'T is thy father.
ISABELLA.   Father, father!
Have I then found thee! But my son!
    my son!
UNKNOWN. Unhappy child, be calm—
    I know thy story,
And do forgive and bless thee.
ISABELLA (*struggling to speak*). Thanks,
    my father.—
But—
UNKNOWN. What means this?
ISABELLA. O, for a moment's strength—
Haste—haste—they murder him—my
    son—
UNKNOWN. Thy son,
    O, where?
ISABELLA. There—there—O Heaven! it
    is too late!
    (*They enter with a bier, carrying*
CHARLES. The UNKNOWN *leads* ISABEL-
LA *slowly towards it.*)
SIR REGINALD (*enters*). O fatal tardi-
    ness! and yet I came
The instant that I learned it. Bloody
    monsters!
How will ye answer this? Behold
    these papers,
They're from the king! They bid
    me seek a lady,
Nam'd Isabella, whom he espoused
    in secret
And her son Charles Fitzroy—And is
    it thus—
    (*Enter* GEORGE EGERTON, *pale and
weak.*)
O George, look there!
GEORGE.   O, brave, unhappy youth!
My generous foe, my honourable con-
    queror!
MARY (*reviving*). Nay, ye shall not de-
    tain me—I will go,
And tell them all. Before I could not
    speak
My father held me here fast by the
    throat.
Why will you hold me? they will
    murder him—

Unless I speak for him. He spoke for
    me—
He sav'd my honour! Ah! what's here?
    O Heaven!
'T is he—is he asleep?—No, it is not
    he.—
I'd think 't were he, but that his eyes
    are swoll'n
Out of their sockets—and his face is
    black
With settled blood.—It is a murder'd
    man
You've brought me to—and not my
    Charles—my Charles!
He was so young and lovely.—Soft,
    soft, soft!
Now I remember.—They have made
    you look so,
To fright me from your love. It will
    not do—
I know you well enough—I know
    those lips
Tho' I have never touch'd them.
    There, love, there,
It is our nuptial kiss. They shall not
    cheat us—
Hark in thine ear how we will laugh
    at them.
    (*She leans her head down on the
body, as if whispering.*)
SIR REGINALD. Alas! poor maniac.
    (ISABELLA *who, supported by her
father, had been bending over the body
in mute despair, is now sinking.*)
UNKNOWN.   Daughter—Isabella—
ISABELLA (*looking up in his face*).
    Father—
UNKNOWN.   You will not leave me,
    Isabella?
ISABELLA. I would remain to comfort
    you, my father,
But there's a tightness here.—For
    nineteen years
He was my only stay on earth—my
    good,
My duteous son. Ere I found thee,
    my father,

The cord was snapp'd—Forgive me—
(*Falls, and is received in the arms
of* LUCY.)
UNKNOWN.   Bless thee, child—
I will not linger long behind thee.
(*The storm subsides.*)
SIR REGINALD.   Sir,
If you're that lady's father, I have
    here
A pardon for you from the king.
UNKNOWN.   I thank him;
But it is now too late.—She's gone.
    —The world
Has nothing left for me—deep in the
    wilderness,
I'll seek a grave, unknown, unseen
    by man.—
WALFORD. How fares your hapless
    friend?
ALICE.   Her cold cheek rests
Against his cheek—not colder—
WALFORD.   Place your hand
Upon her heart: is there no beating

there?
ALICE. There is no beating there—She's
    dead!
RAVENSWORTH.   Dead, dead!—
(RAVENSWORTH, *who thro' this
scene, had shewn the signs of stern and
settled despair, occasionally casting his
eyes upon his daughter, or raising them
to Heaven, but withdrawing them
again in utter hopelessness, now sinks
groaning into the arms of* WALFORD.
ISABELLA *is on her knees, on the upper
side of the bier, leaning on* LUCY. *The*
UNKNOWN, *with his hands clasp'd,
bends over his daughter.* ALICE *is kneeling at the side of her friend.* SIR RE-
GINALD *and* GEORGE EGERTON *stand
near the head of the bier.* LUCY *and*
EDWARD *behind their mistress. The
background filled up by the* JUDGES,
VILLAGERS, *etc. The curtain falls amidst
a burst of the storm, accompanied by
thunder and lightning.*)

CHARLES THE SECOND

John Howard Payne and Washington Irving

First performed in the United States at the Park Theatre in New York on October 25, 1824.

KING CHARLES II	LADY CLARA
ROCHESTER	MARY, *adopted daughter of* COPP
EDWARD, *a page*	SERVANTS
CAPTAIN COPP	TWO PAGES

ACT ONE

SCENE ONE

The Royal Palace.—Enter ROCHESTER *and* LADY CLARA.

LADY CLARA. Yes, my lord, her majesty will have it, that you are the chief cause of the king's irregularities.

ROCHESTER. Oh, I'll warrant it: and of his not loving her, too—is it not so?

LADY CLARA. I did not say that; but, in truth, my lord, your continual jests on the married state—

ROCHESTER. Heaven bless it!

LADY CLARA. Your continual ridicule of married men—

ROCHESTER. Heaven help them!

LADY CLARA. Your licentious example, and still more licentious poetry—

ROCHESTER. What's coming next?

LADY CLARA. All these, I say, make you the most dangerous of men.

ROCHESTER. Dangerous! My dear Lady Clara, you make me vain.

LADY CLARA. It is well known that you are the king's prime companion in all his excesses.

ROCHESTER. What, is my loyalty to be made my reproach? Must I not stand by my monarch in all his moods? Would you have me weep, when my sovereign laughs? Would you have me whine, when my sovereign calls for a jolly song? No, no, my lady, that might have done in the days of Praise-God-Barebones and the Roundheads; but times are altered.— We have a merry monarch to reign over us—A merry monarch makes a merry court—so God save the jovial king, and send him boon companions!

LADY CLARA (*laughing*). I see it is in vain to reason with you.

ROCHESTER. Then give over the attempt.—Let us talk of something of a nearer and a dearer interest—of your merits and my most ardent flame.

LADY CLARA. Ah, me! I fear, like many other of your flames, it will but end in smoke.—You talk of being desperately in love,—what proof have you ever given?

ROCHESTER. What proof? Am I not ready to give the greatest proof a man can offer—to lay down this sweet bachelor life, and commit matrimony for your sake?

LADY CLARA. Well, this last, I must say, coming from a Rochester, is a most convincing proof. I have heard *you* out, listen now to *me*. (ROCHESTER *bows*.) I will propose a bargain.—If, by your ascendancy over the king, you can disgust him with these nocturnal rambles, and bring him back to reason—

ROCHESTER. Your ladyship forgets one of my talents.

LADY CLARA. Which is it?

ROCHESTER. That of getting myself banished two or three times a year.

LADY CLARA. And if the woman you profess to love should offer to *partake* your exile?—

ROCHESTER. I am a lost man—I surrender.—That last shot reached my heart.

LADY CLARA (*sighing*). Ah, my lord— if that heart were only worth your head!—Well, is it agreed?

ROCHESTER. It is your will—I undertake the sacrifice—but, madam, bear in mind my recompense.

LADY CLARA. You may hope for everything. Adieu, my lord.—I now begin to believe in your passion, since you are willing to make a sacrifice to it, even of your follies. (*Exit.*)

ROCHESTER (*alone*). A pretty task I have undertaken, truly! I—Rochester —become reformer! And, then, the convert I have to work upon! Charles, who glories in all kinds of rambling frolics!—True, he has had none but pleasant adventures as yet.—If I should trick him into some ridiculous dilemma?—My whole life has been a tissue of follies, and I am called a man of wit. I am now to attempt a rational act, and I shall be called a madman!—Well, be it so—matrimony will be sure to bring me to my senses.

(*Enter* EDWARD, *languidly*.)

ROCHESTER. Ah! here comes my young protégé—How downcast he seems! How now, Edward, what's the matter with you, boy?

EDWARD (*sighing*). Nothing, my lord.

ROCHESTER. Good heaven, what a sigh to heave up nothing with! Tell me the truth this instant. Hast thou dared to fall in love?

EDWARD. I hope, my lord, there is no harm in indulging an honest attachment.

ROCHESTER. An honest attachment! A young half-fledged page about court, who has hardly tried his wings in the sunshine of beauty, to talk of an honest attachment. Why, thou silly boy, is this the fruit of all the lessons I have given thee?

EDWARD. Did not your lordship tell me, that one of the first duties of a page was to be zealous in his devotion to the fair?

ROCHESTER. Yes; but I told thee to skim over the surface of beauty, just dipping your wings, like a swallow, not plumping in like a goose—I told you to hover from flower to flower like a butterfly, not to bury yourself in one like a bee. An honest attachment!—What a plebeian phrase!—There's a wife and seven children in the very sound of it.

EDWARD. My lord, I know your talent for putting things in a whim-sical light, but, could you see the object of my passion—

ROCHESTER. Nay, a truce with all description.—But who, pray, is the object of this honest attachment?

EDWARD (*embarrassed*). My lord!

ROCHESTER. One of the maids of honour, I'll be bound, who has privately been petting you with sweet-meats, and lending you love-tales.

EDWARD. No, my lord.

ROCHESTER. Some veteran belle about court, too well known to the veteran beaux, and anxious to take in a new comer.

EDWARD. No such thing, my lord.

ROCHESTER. Pray, then, give me some clue. What is the name of your beauty?

EDWARD. Her name, my lord, is Mary.

ROCHESTER. Mary! a very pretty, posy-like name—And what sequestered spot may the gentle Mary embellish with her presence?

EDWARD. She lives at the Tav—Nay, my lord, promise not to laugh.

ROCHESTER. Far be it from me to laugh in so serious a matter. Come, the residence of this fair one?

EDWARD. Why, then, my lord, she inhabits the tavern of the Grand Admiral, in Wapping.

ROCHESTER. Usquebaugh and to-bacco! the tavern of the Grand Admiral!—Ha! ha! ha!—An honest attachment for some pretty bar-maid!

EDWARD. No, my lord, no bar-maid, I assure you. Her uncle keeps the tavern.

ROCHESTER (*with mock gravity*). Oh, I ask pardon, then she is heiress apparent to the tap-room, and you no doubt look forward to rise in the state through the dignities of drawer, tapster, and head-waiter, until you succeed to the fair hand of the niece, and the copper nose of the uncle, and rule with spigot in hand over the fair realms of Wapping. You, who I flattered myself would have made the torment and delight of all the pretty women at court—*you* to be so completely gulled at the very outset,—the dupe of a green girl, and some old rogue of a publican!

EDWARD. Indeed, indeed, my lord, you do the uncle injustice. He is a perfectly honest, upright man—an old captain of a cruiser.

ROCHESTER. Worse and worse! Some old buccaneer, tired of playing the part of a monster at sea, has turned shark on shore. And do you dare to appear in such a house with the dress of a royal page?

EDWARD. Oh! I have taken care to avoid that. I have introduced myself into the house as a music-master.

ROCHESTER. And your musical name, gentle sir?

EDWARD. Georgini, at your service.

ROCHESTER. Ha! ha! ha! very soft and Italianish—I'll warrant this heroine bar-maid will turn out some unknown princess, carried off by the old buccaneer landlord, in one of his cruisings.

EDWARD. Your lordship is joking; but, really, at times, I think she is not what she seems.

ROCHESTER. Ha! ha! ha! I could have sworn it. But silence—I hear his majesty dismount. Run to where your duty calls—we'll take another opportunity to discuss the merits of this Wapping Princess.

EDWARD (*goes out, muttering*). There's many a true thing said in jest. I am certain her birth· is above her condition. (*Exit.*)

ROCHESTER. I must see this paragon of barmaids—She must be devilish pretty! The case admits of no delay—I'll see her this very evening. Hold! Why not fulfil my promise to Lady Clara at the same time? It is decided:—I'll give his majesty my first lesson in morals this very night. But, he comes.

CHARLES (*enters*). Good day, my lord!—What, musing! I never see thee with that air of grave cogitation, but I am sure there is some mischief devising.

ROCHESTER. On the contrary, I am vehemently tempted to reform.

CHARLES. Reform! ha! ha! ha! why, man, no one will credit thy conversion! Is not thy name a by-word? Do not mothers frighten their daughters with it, as formerly with that of **Beelzebub? Is not thy appearance in a neighborhood a signal for all the** worthy burghers to bar their windows and put their womankind under lock and key?—Art thou not, in melancholy truth, the most notorious scapegrace in the kingdom?

ROCHESTER. Heaven forefend that in anything I should take precedence of your majesty.

CHARLES. But what proof do you give of your conversion?

ROCHESTER. The most solemn—I am going to be married.

CHARLES. Married!—And who, pray, is the lady you have an idea of rendering miserable?

ROCHESTER. The Lady Clara.

CHARLES. The Lady Clara! The brilliant, the discreet, the virtuous Lady Clara! She marry Rochester! ha! ha! ha!

ROCHESTER. Ah, my liege, heaven has given her a superabundance of virtues.—She will be able to make a very virtuous man of me with her superfluity.

CHARLES. Well, when thou art married, I will undertake to write thy epithalamium.

ROCHESTER. Then your majesty may at once invoke the Muses. All is settled. (*With great gravity*) As soon as the rites are solemnized, I shall quit the court, and its mundane pleasures, and retire with my lovely bride to my castle at Rochester, under permission of my creditors, the faithful garrison of that fortress.

CHARLES. What! is your castle again in pledge?

ROCHESTER. No, my liege, not again. It has never, to my knowledge, been exactly out of keeping. A castle requires a custodian.

CHARLES. Ah, Rochester! Rochester! Thou art an extravagant dog. I see I shall be called on to pay these usurers at last.

ROCHESTER. Your majesty is ever bounteous. I should not have dared to solicit, and certainly shall not presume to decline.

CHARLES. Ha! ha! Thou art an arrant juggler, and hast an admirable knack of extracting a gift out of an empty hand. But, to business,—where shall we pass the night?

ROCHESTER (*assuming a serious air*). I must beg your majesty to excuse me this evening—I have an engagement of a grave and important nature.

CHARLES. Grave and important! Thou liest, Rochester, or thine eyes speak false and whither does this grave engagement take thee?

ROCHESTER. To the tavern of the Grand Admiral in Wapping!

CHARLES. I thought it was some such haunt. And the object of this business?

ROCHESTER. A young girl, beautiful as an angel, and virtuous as a dragon —about whom there hangs a mystery that I must investigate.

CHARLES. A mysterious beauty! It is a case for royal scrutiny—I will investigate it myself.

ROCHESTER. But, my liege—

CHARLES. No buts. Provide disguises. We will go together. (*With mock gravity*) I like to study human nature in all its varieties, and there is no school equal to a tavern. There's something of philosophy in this—one often gets a useful lesson in the course of a frolic.

ROCHESTER (*aside*). It shall go hard but your majesty shall have one tonight. (*Aloud.*) Ah, how few, except myself, give your majesty credit for your philosophy! And yet, by many, I am considered the partaker of your majesty's excesses.

CHARLES. Partaker! what a calumny! you are the promoter of them.

ROCHESTER. The world will judge me in this instance with even more severity than your majesty has done, should any disagreeable adventure be the result.

CHARLES. Psha! I take the consequences on myself. Provide two seamen's dresses, a purse well filled, and arrange everything for nine precisely. Till then, farewell. (*Exit.*)

ROCHESTER. I will attend your majesty. So! the plot is in train. I'll off to Lady Clara, and report progress. Let me see. This night the lesson. To-morrow my disgrace. Within eight days my marriage, and then, at my leisure, to repent and reform. (*Exit.*)

ACT TWO

SCENE ONE

Outside of COPP's *Tavern, the Grand Admiral. A view of the Thames and Wapping.—Enter* MARY *from the house.*

———

VOICES (*within*). Wine! wine! house!

—waiter!—more wine, ho! Huzza! huzza! huzza!

MARY. What a noise those sailors make in the bar-room—nothing but singing, and laughing, and shouting—I should like to take a peep at them—but no—my uncle forbids me to show myself in the public rooms—he scarcely lets me be seen by the guests—he brings me up more like a young lady than the niece of a tavern keeper.— (*Walks about restless.*) Heigho! what a tiresome long day! what shall I do with myself? what can be the matter with me? I wonder what can keep Mr. Georgini away? For three days he has not been here to give me a lesson—no matter— (*Pettishly*) —I don't care—I shall forget all my singing, that's certain—he was just teaching me such a pretty song, too—all about love—I'll try it— (*Attempts to sing.*) —no, I can't—it's all out of my head—well, so much the better! I suppose he is teaching it to some fine lady scholar—let him, I don't care—I don't believe he'll find her so apt a scholar.

Song

Oh! not when other eyes may read
My heart upon my cheek,
Oh! not when other ears can hear
Dare I of love to speak—
But when the stars rise from the sea,
Oh then I think of thee, dear love!
Oh then I think of thee.

When o'er the olives of the dell
The silent moonlight falls,
And when upon the rose, the dew
Hangs scented coronals,
And buds close on the chestnut tree,
Oh then I think of thee, dear love!
Oh then I think of thee.

COPP (*enters*). What, Mary, my little blossom, what cheer? what cheer? Keep close, my little heart—why do you stir out of port? Here be cruisers abroad.

MARY. Who are those people, Uncle, that make such a noise?

COPP. Two hearty blades—mad roysters—oons how they drink. I was obliged to part company, old cruiser as I am, or they would soon have had me on my beam ends.

MARY. Are they sailors, Uncle?

COPP. To be sure they are: who else would fling about money as they do, and treat a whole bar-room? The tallest in particular is a very devil. Hollo, Captain Copp, cries he every minute, another bottle to treat my brother tars.

MARY. By their swaggering about so, they must be very rich.

COPP. Pho, child, 't is n't the deepest laden ships that make the most rolling.

MARY. But they spend their money so freely.

COPP. A sure sign that it's running out. The longest cable must come to an end. He that pays out fastest, will soonest be brought up with a round turn.

MARY. To what ship do they belong?

COPP. That's more than I can say. Suppose they're a couple of man of war's men just paid off, who think they've a Spanish mine in each pocket— (*Shout of laughter from within.*) Ah, the jolly tars! I was just the same at their age.

MARY. I should like to have a look at them.

COPP. Avast, there—what, trust thee in the way of two such rovers? No, no, I recollect too well what it was to get on shore after a long voyage. The first glimpse of a petticoat—whew! up boarding pikes and grappling irons!— (*Recollecting himself*) Ahem—no, no, child, mustn't venture in these latitudes.

MARY. Ah, my good uncle, you are always so careful of me.

COPP. And why not? What else have I in the whole world to care for, or to care for me? Thou art all that's left to me out of the family fleet—a poor slight little pinnace. I've seen the rest, one after another, go down; it shall go hard but I'll convoy thee safe into port.

MARY. I fear I give you a great deal of trouble, my dear uncle.

COPP. Thou'rt the very best lass in the whole kingdom, and I love thee as I loved my poor brother; that's because you're his very image. To be sure, you haven't his jolly nose, and your little mouth is but a fool to his. But then, there are his eyes, and his smile, and the good humoured cut of his face— (*Sighing*) —poor Philip! What! I'm going again, like the other night.— (*Wiping his eyes*) Psha! let's change the subject, because, d'ye see, sensibility and all that, it does me no good—none—so let's talk of something else. What makes thee so silent of late, my girl? I've not heard a song from thee these three days!

MARY. It's three days since I've seen my music-master.

COPP. Well, and can't you sing without him?

MARY. Without him I can't sing well.

COPP. And what's become of him?

MARY (*pettishly*). I can't tell, it's very tiresome. If he did not mean to come again, he might have said so.

COPP. Oddsfish, neglect thee—neglect his duty!—I'll break him on the spot. Thou shalt have another master, my girl.

MARY (*eagerly*). Oh, no, on no account; I dare say he is not well, some accident has happened. Besides, there is no other teacher in town equal to him, he sings with such feeling.

COPP. Ah! girl, if I had my old messmate, Jack Rattlin, here, he'd teach thee to sing. He had a voice—faith it would make all the bottles dance, and glasses jingle on the table!—Talk of feeling! Why, when Jack would sit of an evening on the capstan when on watch, and sing about sweethearts and wives, and jolly tars, and true lovers' knots, and the roaring seas, and all that; smite my timbers, but it was enough to melt the heart of a grampus. Poor Jack, he taught me the only song I ever knew, it's a main good one though— (*Sings a stave.*)

———

In the time of the Rump,
As old Admiral Trump,
With his broom swept the chops of
the Channel:
And his crew of Tenbreeches,
Those Dutch sons of—

———

MARY (*putting her hand on his mouth*). Oh, Uncle, Uncle, don't sing that horrible rough song.

COPP. Rough? that's the beauty of it. It rouses one up, pipes all hands to quarters like a boatswain's call. Go in, Mary, but go in at the other door; don't go near the bar: go up to your own room, my dear, and your music-master will come to you presently, never fear.

(*Exit* MARY.)

VOICE (*within*). Hollo—house! Waiter! Captain Copp! another bottle, my hearty fellow.

COPP. There they go again! I can't stand it any longer. I am an old cruiser, and can't hear an engagement without longing to be in the midst of it. Avast, though (*Stopping short*), these lads are spending too much money. Have a care, friend Copp, don't sink the sailor in the publican; don't let a free-hearted tar ruin himself in thy house—no, no, faith. If they want more wine they shall have it; but they shall drink as messmates, not as guests. So have at you, boys; it's my turn to treat now.— (*Exit.*)

SCENE TWO

A room in COPP'S *house.*

———

MARY (*enters*). How provoking this absence of Mr. Georgini! It would be serving him right to let my uncle discharge him: but then I should like just to learn that song he is teaching me—hark!—How my heart beats! Hark! I'll wager it's Georgini—I have a gift of knowing people before I see them—my heart whispers me—

(*Enter* EDWARD, *as* GEORGINI.)

MARY. So, sir, you are come at last, are you? I had supposed you did not intend to come any more, and was about to look out for another teacher.

EDWARD. Pardon me for my absence —you have no idea what I have suffered.

MARY (*with anxiety*). Suffered!— Have you been ill, then?

EDWARD. Very ill—

MARY. Indeed! and what was your complaint?

EDWARD (*smiling*). The not seeing you.

MARY (*half piqued, half pleased*). Mighty fine, sir; it is a complaint that you might have cured in a moment.— I have been angry, sir—very angry at your neglect—don't smile, sir—I won't be laughed at—

EDWARD. Laugh at you!—Can you suspect me of such a thing?—I do but smile from the pleasure of seeing you again—nothing but circumstances that I could not control caused my absence.

MARY (*softening*). Well, it's very

provoking to be interrupted in one's lessons just in the middle of a new song—I'll warrant you've been teaching it all over town.

EDWARD. Indeed, I teach it to no one but yourself—for no one else can do it such justice.

MARY (*smiling*). Nay, now you are flattering—have you brought it with you?

EDWARD. Here it is—if you please, we will sing it at once.

MARY. Yes—but—but—don't look so steadily at me while I sing—it puts me out; and then—and then—I don't know what I'm singing.

EDWARD. What!—have you fear of me, then?

MARY. Oh! yes; I fear that I may not please you.

EDWARD (*apart*). Amiable innocence! for the world would I not betray thee.

Duetto

Love one day essayed to gain
Entrance into Beauty's bower,
Many a toil, and many a chain,
Guarded round the precious flower.
But Love laid aside his bow,
Veiled his wing, hid his dart,
Entered more than Beauty's bower,
Entered also Beauty's heart.
Hence was the sweet lesson learnt,
Fond hearts never should despair,
Kept with truth, and led by hope,
What is there Love may not dare?

(*Enter* COPP, *a little gay, singing.*)

"In the time of the Rump," &c. Aha! master crotchet and quaver, so you've come at last, have you? What the deuce did you stay away for, and let my little girl get out of tune?

EDWARD. Oh! I have explained all, sir, and made my peace.

COPP. Ah, she's a forgiving little

baggage, and amazing fond of music—why, she's always on the lookout for you an hour before the time.

MARY. Never mind, Uncle. Are your strange companions here still?

COPP. Here still? ay, and likely to stay here—ha! ha! ha!—no getting rid of them—they're a couple of devils, of right down merry devils, ha! ha! ha!—They've flustered me a little, i' faith.

EDWARD. You seem to have a great deal of company in the house, sir; I'll take my leave.

COPP. You shall take no such thing—you shall take tea with us, my little semibreve, and we'll have a lesson of music too. Oddsfish! you shall give me a lesson—I am confoundedly out of practice, and can't turn my old song for the life of me. (*Begins.*) "In the time of the Rump"—

MARY. Never mind the song now, Uncle, we must have tea first, and Mr. Georgini will help me make it.

COPP. Ay, faith, and we'll add a bowl of punch and a flask of old Madeira to make a set out—my two messmates in the other room are to be of the party.

MARY. What, those wild sailors who have been keeping the house in an uproar?

COPP. To be sure—they're good lads, though they have a little of the devil in them.—They asked to clink the cup with me, and you know I can't well refuse, by trade, to clink the cup with any one. In troth, they had put me in such rare good humour—ha! ha! ha!—that I could not refuse them for the life of me.

MARY. But they are such a couple of harebrains—

COPP. Oh! don't be afraid—they are rough, but good-natured—sailor-like: besides, am not I always within hail? One of them, I see, is heaving in sight

already. Come with me, my girl, and help to prepare the punch and get the tea—*you*, my king of crotchets, will stay and receive our guests—make yourself at home.— (*Sings as he goes.*) "In the time of the Rump"— (*Exeunt* COPP *and* MARY.)

EDWARD. Here's a transformation! from a court page behold me master of ceremonies at a Wapping tavern! (*Starts.*) Good heaven! whom have we here? The Earl of Rochester in that rude garb!

ROCHESTER (*enters*). The shouts of those jolly fellows began to turn my brain—his majesty is in fine humour to get into a scrape; and if he does, to make his difficulties more perplexing, I have secured his purse, so that he cannot bribe his way out of them—Hey! Edward?

EDWARD (*confused*). My lord Rochester—

ROCHESTER. Silence, you rogue! I am no lord here, no Rochester. I am a seaman—my name Tom Taffrel. The king, my messmate, is Jack Mizen.

EDWARD. The king with you!—(*Aside*) I see it all—he's after Mary—ah! I am lost.

ROCHESTER. Don't be alarmed, friend Georgini; none but the most innocent motives have brought us here—

EDWARD. Innocent motives bring you and the king, at night, to a tavern in Wapping, where there is a beautiful girl? Ah! my lord, my lord—

ROCHESTER. Nay, to convince you that you have nothing to fear, I permit you to remain with us— (*Aside*) He may assist my scheme— (*Aloud*) You must play off your character of music-master upon the king.

EDWARD. Impossible! His majesty will recognise my features.

ROCHESTER. Psha! you have not been a page a month; he probably has not seen your face three times. But take care how you act; the least indiscretion on your part—

EDWARD. Ah! my lord, I am too much interested in keeping the secret.

ROCHESTER. That is not all. In whatever situation the king may find himself, whatever chagrin he may suffer, I forbid you to assist him in the slightest manner. You are to see in him only the sailor, Jack Mizen.

EDWARD. Should his majesty chance to incur any danger, my lord, I can never be passive. In such case, I have but one course.

ROCHESTER. There *can* be no danger —I shall myself watch over his safety.

EDWARD. That decides me—I think I apprehend the object, and will obey your lordship.

ROCHESTER. The king approaches— Silence! let each resume his part.

CHARLES (*enters*). Well, messmate, shall we soon see this marvellous beauty?

EDWARD (*apart*). So—this is his majesty's innocent motive!

ROCHESTER. Peace, friend Jack, here's one of her admirers—her music-master—

CHARLES. Ah! you teach the young lady music, do you? (*Looking earnestly at him*) Zounds! how like he is to the page you gave me lately.

EDWARD (*apart*). Ah! my face strikes him.

ROCHESTER. Hum—I can't say I see much resemblance. He is taller than Edward, and older, and the expression of his countenance is not the same.

CHARLES. No, no, not altogether, but there is a something—

ROCHESTER. Why, to tell the truth, the page had a wild fellow for a father—and, your majesty knows, likenesses are stamped at random about the world sometimes.

CHARLES (*laughing*). I understand— duplicate impressions—like enough.

(*Enter* MARY *and* SERVANT *with tea.*)

MARY (*to* SERVANT). Set the table in this room.

CHARLES (*to* ROCHESTER). By heaven, she's a divinity!

EDWARD (*low to* ROCHESTER). What does he say?

ROCHESTER (*to* EDWARD). That your divinity is a devilish fine girl.

CHARLES (*to* ROCHESTER). Amuse this confounded singing-master. I wish to have a duo with his mistress.—He'll only mar music.

ROCHESTER (*to* EDWARD, *with an air of great business*). My good Mr. Georgini, I have something particular to say to you— (*Drawing him to a corner*) His majesty (*Suppressing a laugh*) fancies that you are uncomfortable, and requests me to amuse you.

EDWARD. Yes, that he may have Mary all to himself— (*Drawing near her.*)

ROCHESTER (*drawing him back*). Come, don't be childish. What, you pretend to follow my lessons and want complaisance! (CHARLES *has been making advances to* MARY, *who appears at first a little shy.*)

CHARLES. Do let me assist you, my pretty lass.

MARY. Don't trouble yourself, sir; Mr. Georgini is to help me make tea.

EDWARD (*breaking from* ROCHESTER). I am here, madam—what can I do to help you?

CHARLES (*puts the kettle, as if accidentally, against his hand. Dryly*). Take care, young man, you may scald your fingers.

ROCHESTER (*drawing* EDWARD *back, and speaking low*). Why, what a plague, boy, are you doing?

(CHARLES *continues to assist* MARY *mingling little gallantries, and blun-*

dering in attempts to assist.)

EDWARD (*aside, and struggling with* ROCHESTER). I shall go mad!

MARY. Oh, dear sir, you're so kind, you quite put me out— (*Laughing*) — hey!—you have taken my hand instead of the teapot. I will not say you are awkward, sir, but really, you have the oddest manner of assisting—nay—let go my hand, I beg.

CHARLES. By Heaven, it is a beautiful one!

MARY. Nay, nay—pray, sir.— (*Withdrawing her hand with smiling confusion.—Apart.*) Upon my word, I don't see any thing so very rude in these people.

EDWARD (*endeavoring to get away from* ROCHESTER). Let me go, I entreat you; I can stand this no longer.

ROCHESTER (*holding him, and suppressing a laugh*). Psha! man, if you think to marry, or rise at court, you must learn to be deaf and blind upon occasion.

CHARLES (*in rather an under-tone to* MARY). And how is it possible so pretty a lass should not be married?

MARY. Married—bless me! I never thought of such a thing.

CHARLES. No? never? and yet surrounded by lovers.

MARY. Lovers! I haven't one, sir.

CHARLES. Indeed! and what is that young man, fidgeting yonder?

MARY. He?—he is my singing-master, sir.

CHARLES. And he sings to some purpose, I'll warrant.

MARY. Delightfully.

CHARLES. And gives you a love-song now and then?

MARY. Oh, often, often.

CHARLES. I thought so—he has it in his countenance.

EDWARD (*to* ROCHESTER). You *must* let me go—you see I am wanted.

ROCHESTER. Upon my word, they are getting on amazingly well without you.

CHARLES (*to* MARY). And so you are fond of music, my pretty lass?

MARY. Oh, I love it of all things.

CHARLES. A pretty hand to beat time with. (*Taking her hand.*)

MARY. Sir— (*Withdrawing it.*)

CHARLES. And as pretty a little mouth to warble a love-song. I warrant, there come none but sweet notes from these lips. (*Offers to kiss her.*)

MARY (*resisting*). Sir, give over—let me go, sir.—Mr. Georgini—help, help!

(EDWARD *bursts from* ROCHESTER, *who is laughing. At this moment* COPP *enters.*)

COPP. Avast there, messmate! what the devil, yard arm and yard arm with my niece!

(CHARLES *desists, a little confused—* EDWARD *approaches* MARY.)

MARY (*flurried*). I am glad you are come, Uncle—this rude stranger—

COPP (*taking her arm under his*). Thunder and lightning—what! insult Captain Copp's niece in his own house! Fire and furies!

CHARLES (*pretending to be a little gay*). I insult your niece, messmate? Since when has an honest tar's kissing a pretty girl been considered an insult? As to the young woman, if she takes offence at a piece of sailor civility, why, I ask pardon, that's all.

COPP (*softened*). Oh, as to a piece of civility, d'ye see, that alters the case; but, guns and blunderbusses! if any one should dare—

ROCHESTER. Come, come, Uncle Copp, what a plague! you were a youngster once, and a frolicsome one, I'll warrant. I see it in your eye— what—didst ever think it a crime to kiss a pretty girl in a civil way.

COPP. No, no, in a civil way, no,

certainly; I can make allowance when a lad and a lass, and a bottle, come pretty near each other—odds fish—you say right, at your age, I was a rattler myself.—Come, Mary, no harm done. Come, lads, take your seats— (*They seat themselves.* EDWARD *attempts to place himself by* MARY.—CHARLES *interferes, and takes the place.*) Come, my girl, pour out the tea—I'll fill out the punch, and we'll have a time of it, i'faith—Come, I'll give you a jolly song to begin with— (*Sings.*)

In the time of the Rump,
As old Admiral Trump—

MARY (*apart*). That odious song!—come, Uncle, never mind the song, take a cup of tea— (*Offering one.*)

COPP. What, drown my song and myself in warm water? ha! ha! no, faith—not while there's a drop in the punch bowl.

(MARY *helps* EDWARD *and* ROCHESTER, *omitting* CHARLES.)

CHARLES (*low to* MARY). Am I then excluded?

MARY (*looking down*). I thought punch would be more to your liking, sir.

CHARLES. Then punch be it—Come, clink with me, neighbour Copp—clink with me, my boy.

COPP. Oh! I'm not proud, I'll clink with anybody—that's to say, mind ye, when the liquor is good, and there's a good fellow in the case.

CHARLES (*rising*). Well, here goes—To the health of Mary, the fair maid of Wapping.

COPP. With all my heart, here's to her health—the darling child—Oh! messmate, there you touch a soft corner of my heart—did you but know how I love this little girl. Psha! I'm a foolish old fellow, and when I have

got punch, and sensibility, and all that on board—Come, let's talk of something else.

MARY. My dear uncle—

CHARLES. I don't wonder at your loving her, I can't help feeling a kind of admiration for her myself— (*Offering to take her hand.*)

COPP. Softly, shipmate, no grappling —admire at a distance as much as you please, but hands off. Come, my lads, a merry song—I love to sing when I drink. (*Sings.*)

In the time of the Rump,
As old Admiral Trump—

MARY. Not that song, my dear uncle —I entreat—

COPP. Ah, I recollect—ha! ha! my poor song; ha! ha!—well, well, since you don't like me to sing, sing it for me yourself, Mary.

CHARLES. Ay, a song from the charming Mary (*Significantly*), I dare say your master has some pretty love-song for you.

EDWARD. Oh, yes—I have brought one of the latest in vogue—one by the most fashionable poet of the day—the Earl of Rochester.

COPP. Rochester? fire and fury—roast Rochester! a rascally rogue!—the devil take Rochester, and his song, too!

CHARLES. Bravo! Captain Copp—another broadside, old boy.

ROCHESTER. Why, what the deuce, neighbor—has your powder magazine taken fire? Why, what has Rochester done to you, to occasion such a terrible explosion?

COPP. What's that to you? What have you to do with my family secrets? Rochester! His very name makes my blood boil—

MARY. My dear uncle, be calm. You

promised never to speak on this subject.

ROCHESTER. Why, what connexion can there be between you and Rochester?

COPP. No matter, he has been put to the proof, that's enough. (*To* MARY) Don't be uneasy—I'll say no more about it, my girl. You know me —when I say mum, that's enough.

CHARLES. This affair seems curious—I must have an explanation. (*With an air of authority*) It is my pleasure—

COPP. Your pleasure, quotha—and who the devil are you? You're a pleasant blade. (*Sturdily*) But it's not my pleasure, messmate, look ye.

CHARLES (*recollecting himself*). I mean to say, that I feel a deep interest in your welfare.

COPP (*gruffly*). Thank ye, thank'e, —but I am not used to such warm friends on such short acquaintance. (*Apart*) I wonder is it myself, or my niece, this chap has fallen in love with at first sight?

CHARLES (*apart to* ROCHESTER). I am curious to know what charge they have against you.

ROCHESTER (*apart to* CHARLES). And so am I, and I'll make this old buccaneer speak plain, before we leave him.

CHARLES. You have misunderstood me, friend Copp. I am no defender of Rochester. I know him to be a sad fellow.

COPP. As destitute of feeling as a stockfish.

EDWARD. He is a great genius, however.

COPP. He is an evil genius, I know.

EDWARD. He has a very clear head—

COPP. But a very black heart.

ROCHESTER. This Rochester is a sad light-headed fellow, that's notorious; but will you have the goodness, my blunt Captain Copp, to mention one heartless act of his?

COPP (*loudly*). Ay, that I will. Is it not a burning shame—

MARY. My dear uncle, you forget your promise.

COPP. Let me alone, girl, let me alone—you've nothing to fear; I have you under convoy.

ROCHESTER. Out with it, what is his crime?

COPP. Crime! Is it not a burning shame, I say, to disclaim his own niece —to keep from her every stiver of her little fortune, and leave her to pass her days in a tavern, when she has a right to inhabit a palace?

EDWARD (*eagerly*). What do I hear?

ROCHESTER. What, and is this young woman the niece? How can that be?

COPP. Simply enough. Her father, Philip Copland, married a sister of Lord Rochester.

ROCHESTER (*apart*). Philip Copland is indeed the name.

CHARLES. This is most singular. And this Philip Copland was your brother?

COPP. Ay, but worth a dozen of me —a steady man, an able officer, an ornament of the regular navy. I was always a wild dog, and never took to learning—ran away from school—shipped myself on board a privateer. In time I became captain, and returned from my last cruise just in time to receive poor Philip's last breath—his sand was almost run out. "Brother," said he, "I feel that my cruising is over; but there's my little girl. Take care of her for my sake, and never bother the Rochesters again."— "Brother," said I, "it's a bargain; tip us your fist on it, and die in peace, like a good Christian." He grasped my hand, and gave it a gentle squeeze. I would have shook his, but it grew cold in mine, and poor Philip was no more! (*With great feeling.*)

MARY. My dear uncle.— (*Laying her hand on his shoulder.*)

COPP (*rousing himself*). But the girl was left, the girl was left (*Embracing her*) ; and (*Taking her arm under his*) —and I'll keep my word to my poor brother, and take care of *her* as long as I have breath in my body.

CHARLES. Well, brother Tom, what do *you* think of all this?

ROCHESTER. It touches me to the soul.

CHARLES. And so you took home the child?

MARY. Oh! yes: and my uncle's bounty and kindness have taken care of his poor girl ever since.

COPP. Oh! you should have seen what a little thing it was,—a little chubby-faced thing of four years old, no higher than a handspike. Now she's a grown girl.

CHARLES. And you have given her a good education, it appears?

COPP. And why not? What tho' *I'm* a dunce, that's no reason that Mary Copland should be a fool. Her father was a man of parts.

CHARLES. And you have given up your voyages for her?

COPP. To be sure. Could I have a child running after me about deck? I sold my ship, and bought this tavern, where I receive none but good fellows, who drink, and smoke, and talk to me of voyages and battles all day long.

CHARLES. But ambition might have induced you—

COPP. Ambition! you don't know me; my only ambition is to marry my niece to some honest citizen, and give her a dower of one thousand pounds, with as much more when old Captain Copp takes his long nap.

ROCHESTER (*apart*). Generous fellow! (*Aloud*) Let me advise you to apply to the Earl of Rochester.

EDWARD. Oh! yes, *he* will provide *an* honorable match for your niece.

MARY (*piqued*). Much obliged, Mr. Georgini, but nobody asked your advice.

COPP. Apply to him!—no—no—I'll have nothing to do with the Rochesters.

CHARLES. But why not apply to the king himself?

COPP. Oddsfish! they say he is not much better—he's a wild devil—a great friend of Rochester—and birds of a feather, you know—

CHARLES (*apart*). Now comes my turn.

ROCHESTER. True enough, Captain Copp; they say he is a rover—rambles about at night—frolics in taverns.

COPP. Well, let him cruise, so he does not cruise into my waters. He's a desperate rogue among the petticoats, they say—well, I like a merry heart, wherever it beats.—Charley has some good points, and if I could but give him a piece of my mind—

CHARLES. What would it be, friend Copp?

COPP. To keep more in port, anchor himself at home, and turn that fellow, Rochester, adrift—there might then be some hopes of him.—But, come, 't is getting late—now, friends, it's time to turn out, and turn in—these are late hours for the Grand Admiral— come, a parting cup. (*To* MARY) See that the fires are out, my girl, and all hands ready for bed.

MARY. I will, but no more drinking, Uncle.

COPP. Well, well—no more—only one parting cup.

MARY. Only one—recollect, you have promised—no more. (*Exit* MARY.)

COPP. Only this last drop.—Come, my lads, this farewell cup, and then you must push your boats.

ROCHESTER. Now to execute my plan. (*Makes signs that the king will pay.*) Hist, Captain Copp! (*Whispers while* CHARLES *is drinking.*)

COPP. Ay, ay, all right.

ROCHESTER (*low to* EDWARD). Follow me quietly—I've something to say to you. (*Apart, and chuckling as he goes out*) Now, brother Jack, I think you'll soon find yourself among the breakers! (*Exit, followed by* EDWARD.)

COPP. Now, messmate, let's square accounts— (*Handing a paper*); here's a note of your expenses—you see I charge nothing for the last two bottles —nor for the tea-table—that's my treat.

CHARLES (*looking over the paper*). Um! wine—punch—wine—punch—total five pounds ten—a mere trifle!

COPP. Do you call that a trifle?— Gad, messmate, you must have made good prizes in your last cruise—or you've high wages, mayhap.

CHARLES (*laughing*). Ay, ay, I'm pretty well paid—Here, Tom Taffrel, pay Copp's bill, and let's be off.— (*Looks round.*) Hey—where is he?

COPP. Oh! he went off in a great hurry—he said he had to be aboard ship, but that you would pay the bill.

CHARLES. With all my heart. (*Apart*) It's odd that he should leave me alone —my raillery has galled him.—Poor Rochester (*Laughing*), how ill some people take a joke! (*Feels in his pockets.*) Five pounds ten, you say?

COPP. Just so—five pounds ten.

CHARLES (*searching in all his pockets*). Well! this is the oddest thing —I am certain I had my purse.

COPP (*apart*). My neighbour seems rather in a quandary.

CHARLES (*feeling more eagerly*). Some one has picked my pocket.

COPP. Avast there, friend—none but honest people frequent the Grand Ad-miral. (*Apart*) I begin to suspect this spark, who spends so freely, is without a stiver in his pocket.

CHARLES. All I know, is, that one of these honest people must have taken my purse.

COPP. Come, come, messmate—I am too old a cruiser to be taken in by so shallow a manœuvre—I understand all this—your companion makes sail—you pretend to have been robbed—it's all a cursed privateering trick—clear as day.

CHARLES. Friend Copp—if you will wait till tomorrow, I'll pay you double the sum.

COPP. Double the sum!!—thunder and lightning! what do you take me for?—Look ye, neighbour, to an honest tar in distress, my house and purse are open—to a jolly tar who wants a caper, and has no coin at hand, drink today and pay tomorrow is the word —but to a sharking land lubber, that hoists the colours of a gallant cruiser, to play off the tricks of a pirate, old Copp will show him his match any day.

CHARLES. A land lubber?

COPP. Ay, a land lubber.—D'ye think I can't see through you, and your shallow sailor phrases.—Who the devil are you?—none of the captains know you—what ship do you belong to?

CHARLES. What ship? why, to—to— (*Apart*) what the deuce shall I say?

COPP. A pretty sailor, truly—not know the name of his ship—a down-right swindler—a barefaced impudent swindler—comes into my house, kicks up a bobbery, puts every thing in an uproar—treats all the guests—touzles my niece—and then wants to make off without paying.

CHARLES (*apart*). How shall I get out of this cursed scrape?—Oh, happy thought, my watch—(*Aloud*) hearkee, Captain Copp—if I haven't money, may be this will do as well—what say you to my watch as pledge?

COPP (*taking the watch*). Let me see it—um—large diamonds. (*Shaking his head.*)

CHARLES (*gayly*). Well—that's worth your five pounds ten—hey?

COPP. Um—I don't know that:—if the diamonds are *false*, it is not worth so much—if *real*, none but a great lord could own it—(*Turning quick to him*), —how did you come by this watch?

CHARLES. It's my own.

COPP. Your own! A common sailor own a watch set with large diamonds! I'll tell you what, messmate, it's my opinion as how you stole this watch.

CHARLES. Stole it? Give back my watch, fellow, or I'll—

COPP. Softly, my lad, keep cool, or I'll have you laid by the heels in a twinkling.

CHARLES (*apart*). What a bull-dog! Well, sir, what do you intend to do?

COPP. Lock you up here for the present, and have you lodged in limbo immediately.

CHARLES. Will you not listen to reason?

COPP (*going*). Yes, through the keyhole! (*From the door*) You shall have news of me presently, my fine fellow. (*Exit.*)

CHARLES. Was ever monarch in such a predicament?—a prisoner in a tavern—to be presently dragged through the streets as a culprit—and tomorrow sung in lampoons, and stuck up in caricatures all through the city—What is to be done? This Copp seems a man of probity, suppose I avow myself to him? Um! will he credit me, and will he keep the matter secret? This sturdy veteran may be an old cruiser under the Commonwealth: if

so, what have I not to apprehend? Alone—unarmed, at midnight. (*Shaking his head*) Charles! Charles! wilt thou never learn wisdom? Yes; let me but get out of *this* scrape, and I renounce these rambling humours for ever. (*A noise of unlocking the door*) Hark! some one comes.

(*Enter* EDWARD *and* MARY. *Several servants quaintly dressed, and armed, appear at the door.*)

MARY. Place yourselves outside and guard the passages.

CHARLES. They are placing sentinels.

EDWARD (*apart*). The earl has given me my lesson: no flinching.

MARY. I am afraid to go near him. I wish my uncle had not set us this task.— (MARY *is armed with an old cutlass,* EDWARD *with a long rusty pistol or carbine.*)

EDWARD. Be not afraid, I am here to defend you.

CHARLES (*advancing*). What! my pretty Mary in arms?

MARY. Ah, don't come near me! What a ferocious ruffian it is!

CHARLES (*gallantly*). Was that delicate hand made to grasp so rude a weapon?

EDWARD (*low to* MARY). Don't let him touch your hand, or you are lost.

MARY (*drawing back*). He does not look so very ferocious, neither. Fie, sir, fie! what, steal the jewels of the crown?

CHARLES. Is it, then, known already?

MARY. Yes, indeed, all is known. My uncle took the watch to our neighbour, the jeweller, who knew it instantly. It belongs to his royal majesty himself.

CHARLES. Confusion!

EDWARD (*low to* MARY). You hear he confesses— (*Aloud*) Well, Captain Copp will be here presently with the magistrate. Here will be a fine piece of work. All Wapping is already in an uproar.

CHARLES (*eagerly*). My friends, it is of the highest importance that I should escape before they come.

MARY. I have not a doubt of it. Oh! you culprit!

CHARLES (*with insinuation*). And would Mary, the pretty Mary, see me dragged to prison? I won't believe it. That sweet face bespeaks a gentle heart.

MARY. Poor creature! I can't but pity him.

CHARLES (*with gallantry*). I never saw a pretty woman yet, that would not help a poor fellow in distress— (*Apart*) She yields. But I need other bribes for my gentleman—I have it— my ring. (*Aloud*) Assist me to escape, and take this ring as a pledge of what I will do. It is of great value.

MARY. What a beautiful diamond ring! How it sparkles! Don't touch it, Georgini, it's a stolen ring.

EDWARD. And for that very reason I take it. We can return both together to the right owner.

MARY (*apart to* EDWARD). He certainly has something genteel in his air. This unfortunate man may, perhaps, belong to decent people.

CHARLES. I do indeed; my family is considered very respectable. Ah, bless that sweet face! I knew a hard heart could not belong to it.

EDWARD (*apart*). Egad, I must get him off, or he'll win his pretty jailor, culprit as she thinks him.

MARY (*taking* EDWARD *apart*). How penitent he seems, and his countenance is rather amiable too! What will they do with him?

EDWARD (*carelessly*). Hum—why, they'll hang him, of course.

MARY. Heavens! will they touch his life? oh, horrible! and so good looking

a man! I would not have his death upon my mind for the whole world. (*Earnestly.*)

CHARLES (*who has been traversing the apartment uneasily, and eyeing them occasionally*). Will this consultation never end! I dread the arrival of the officers.

MARY (*aloud*). Let us assist him to escape!

CHARLES. Thanks, my generous girl: there's nothing like a petticoat in time of trouble.

EDWARD. How shall we get him off? The door is guarded.

CHARLES. Ay, but the window.

EDWARD (*eagerly*). No, not the window, you may hurt yourself.

CHARLES (*surprised*). You are very considerate, my friend.

MARY. Oh! it is not very high, and opens into a lane that leads to the river.

CHARLES (*opening the window*). Psha! it's nothing; with your assistance, I shall be on the ground in an instant.

MARY. It is, perhaps, very wrong in me to let you escape; but I beg you to listen to a word of advice.

CHARLES. Oh, yes, I hear you.

MARY. It is on condition that you change your course of life.

CHARLES. Yes, yes, I'll change it, I warrant you.

MARY. And not drink, nor rove about this way at night.

CHARLES. Not for the world.

MARY. And steal no more, for it will bring you to a shameful end.

CHARLES (*getting out of the window, assisted by* MARY). An excellent sermon! But I must *steal*—one kiss to impress it on my memory!

EDWARD. Did he steal a kiss, Mary?

MARY. Oh, yes, he did indeed.

EDWARD. Stop thief! stop thief!

CHARLES (*descending outside*). Tell Uncle Copp to put it in the bill!

EDWARD. I hear them coming. (*Looks out of the window.*) He's safe down--he's off— (*Apart*) —now I'm easy.

MARY. But what shall we say to my uncle?

EDWARD. I'll manage that; only say as I say, and fear nothing.

COPP (*heard outside the door*). This way—this way.

EDWARD. Stop thief! stop thief! (*To* MARY) Cry out as I do.

MARY (*feebly*). Stop the thief! stop the thief! I can't.

COPP (*enters with a double-barrelled gun, followed by two servants*). Hollo —what the devil's to pay here?

EDWARD. The culprit has jumped out of the window.

MARY. Oh, yes, out of the window!

COPP. Thunder and lightning! why didn't you stop him?

EDWARD. *I* was too far off. The young lady attempted, but he kissed her, and leaped out like a greyhound.

COPP. Fire and furies!—kissed her?

MARY. Yes, Uncle, but he didn't hurt me.

EDWARD. And he said you might put it in the bill.

COPP. Guns and blunderbusses! this is running up an account with a vengeance. (*Looking out of the window*) I see something in the offing; we may overhaul him yet. Come along, all hands to the chase! Get to your room, Mary, there's no knowing what might happen if this pirate should fall foul of you again. Come along—away with you all—divide at the street door— scour the three passages—I'll show him what it is to come in the way of an old cruiser!— (*Bustle—*COPP *fires off his gun out of the window after* CHARLES. *Curtain falls.*)

ACT THREE

SCENE ONE

The Royal Palace.

EDWARD (*enters, in his habit, as a page*). I've had a hard scramble of it, to get here, and dress in time. The king must arrive presently, though my light heels have given me a good start of him. Hark! a noise in the king's private staircase—Softly, then, softly. (*Seats himself in an armchair at the door of the king's chamber, and pretends to sleep.*)

CHARLES (*enters, his dress in disorder*). Confound the city! what a journey it is!

EDWARD (*aside*). Especially to foot passengers.

CHARLES. I began to think I should never find the palace. (*Sitting down*) Phew! I shall not forget this night in a hurry. Forced to escape like a thief, —to risk my neck from a window,— hunted about the streets by that old buccaneer and his crew! Egad! I fancy I can hear old Copp's voice, even now, like a huntsman giving the view-halloo, as I doubled about the mazes of Wapping.

EDWARD (*aside, and suppressing a laugh*). A royal hunt, truly!

CHARLES. Well, thank fortune, I am safe home at last, and seen by nobody but my confidential valet.

EDWARD (*aside*). And the most discreet of pages.

CHARLES (*seeing* EDWARD). So, the page already in waiting. Deuce take him! he is exactly in the door-way of my chamber. So, so! Lady Clara coming! Oh, then, all's over!

LADY CLARA (*enters, goes to* EDWARD). What! asleep at this hour, Edward?

EDWARD. I beg your pardon, my lady —I am waiting his majesty's rising.

LADY CLARA. You will come, and let the queen know when the king is visible. (*Perceives* CHARLES.) Heavens! your majesty in this dress?

CHARLES (*affecting an unembarrassed air*). What! it amuses you, ha! ha! My regular morning dress, I assure you. I have taken a whim for gardening lately, and, every morning, by day-light, I am on the terrace, planting, transplanting, and training. Oh! you should see how busy I am, particularly among the roses.

LADY CLARA. I have no doubt your majesty has an eye for every fresh one that blows.—But, how quiet you have been in these pursuits!

CHARLES. One does not want all the world to know of one's caprices. But what has procured me the pleasure of seeing your ladyship so early?

LADY CLARA. The queen, sire, knowing how deeply you were immersed in affairs of state, last night sent me to enquire how your majesty had slept.

CHARLES. Very restless—very restless —I tumbled and tossed about sadly.

LADY CLARA. Ah! why does not your majesty take more care of yourself? You devote yourself too much to your people. This night-work will be too much for you.

CHARLES. Why, yes, if it were often as severe as last night.

LADY CLARA. Indeed, your majesty must give up these midnight labours to your ministers.

CHARLES (*apart*). To my ministers, ha! ha! Egad! I should like to see old Clarendon and Ormond hob or nobbing with Uncle Copp, struggling for kisses with Mary, and scouring the lanes of Wapping at full speed.— (*Aloud*) Well, my Lady Clara, have you anything further to communicate?

LADY CLARA. Might I presume, I have a favour to request of your majesty. An author, in whose cause I take a warm interest, has offended a person high in power, and is threatened with a prosecution.

CHARLES. The blockhead! let him write against me only, and they'll never trouble him.

LADY CLARA. His pardon depends upon your majesty—would you but deign to sign it!

CHARLES (*apart*). Sinner that I am, it would but ill become me to be severe.— (*Aloud*) Lady Clara, you look amazingly well this morning—I can refuse you nothing.—(*Signs the paper.*) And now, to make my toilette—(*Aside*) —Safe at last! she suspects nothing.

LADY CLARA (*smiling*). He thinks he has deceived me.—Oh, these men, these men! how they will impose upon us easy, simple, *knowing* women!

(*Exeunt* LADY CLARA *and* EDWARD. *Enter* COPP *and* MARY.)

COPP. Oddsfish! I never knew such a piece of work to get into a house before. If that good-looking gentlewoman had not seen us from the window, and taken our part, hang me, if I don't think they would have turn'd us adrift.

MARY. What beautiful rooms!

COPP. Gingerbread finery! I would not change the bar-room of the Grand Admiral for the best of them. But what a bother to give a watch back to the right owner! Why, there's no finding the king in his own house.—Now, for my part, I always stand on the threshold, and if any one comes, there's my hand.—Tip us your bone, says I, and make yourself welcome.— That's what I call acting like a king of good fellows.

MARY. Oh, Uncle, I have always heard say, that the king is very kind and affable; and, I dare say, when you hand him back his watch, he will behave with generosity.

COPP. Generosity! Why, dost think, girl, I'd take a reward? No, no!—They say Charley's not overstocked with the shiners.—I want none of them. To be sure, he may do the civil thing—he may ask us to stay, and take pot-luck, perhaps.

MARY. Pot-luck, Uncle!

COPP. Ay, in a friendly way, d'ye see? And I don't care if I did, if it were only to see how royalty messed. But, where the deuce is the king to be found? Oh! yonder is a fine gim-crack young gentleman, who, perhaps, can tell us—I'll hail him. Yo-ho! mess-mate! (*Exit, hallooing after* EDWARD.)

MARY. What a beautiful place this is! But, without content, grandeur is not to be envied. The humble and the good, may be as happy in a cottage as a palace.

MARY (*recitative*).

Thrice beautiful! Alas! that here
Should ever come a frown or tear;
But not beneath the gilded dome
Hath happiness its only home.

Not in the pictured halls,
Not amid marble walls
Will young Love dwell.

Love's home's the heart alone,
That heart, too, all his own,
Else, Love, farewell!

COPP (*enters, pulling in* EDWARD, *who tries to hide his face*). Come along, young man—don't be so bashful —you needn't mind us.

EDWARD (*aside*). Let me put on a steady face— (*Aloud*) —You come to speak to his majesty?

MARY. Yes, Sir, we come— (*Apart*)

—Dear uncle, those features—how my heart beats!—Did you ever see such a resemblance, Uncle?

COPP (*looking at* EDWARD). Odds-fish! he is like, indeed!—But it can't be him!

MARY. I like Mr. Georgini's face better—it is more animated.

COPP. Don't talk to me of that Georgini. Didst not tell me, he took a ring of that land-pirate?—and, then, to disappear so suddenly.—Fire and fury! if I catch him—

EDWARD. No swearing in the king's palace.

COPP. Well, well, true; no swearing. But, thunder and lightning! what keeps the king so long?

EDWARD. I think I hear him. Step into that apartment—a lady will introduce you.

COPP. Ah! the same that I saw at the window;—very well. But, I say, Mister, don't keep me waiting. Just hint to the king, that I've no time to lose. Tell him, there's a launch at Wapping to-day—busy times at the Grand Admiral.

MARY. Let us retire, Uncle. I dare say we shall be sent for in good time.

COPP. Very well, very well. But, do think of the Grand Admiral—all aback for want of me. If the king loses his watch again, the devil take me— Oh! I forgot—I mustn't swear in the king's palace. (*Exeunt* COPP *and* MARY.)

EDWARD. This will be a whimsical court presentation, truly! His majesty's perplexities are not yet over.

CHARLES (*enters, in his riding dress*). Has Rochester appeared?

EDWARD. Not yet, Sire.

CHARLES (*apart*). What could be his motive for the cruel trick he played me?

EDWARD. Your majesty asked for Lord Rochester; here he comes with

Lady Clara.

CHARLES. Pish! Lady Clara is one too many here. I shall not be able to explain myself before her. No matter —he shall not escape me.

(*Enter* ROCHESTER *and* LADY CLARA.)

ROCHESTER. May I venture to ask, if your majesty has passed a comfortable night?

CHARLES. Indifferent, my lord— (*Low, to him*) —Traitor!

LADY CLARA (*smiling*). I understood his lordship had assisted your majesty in your labours.

ROCHESTER. Not throughout, my lady. An accident obliged me to leave his majesty in rather a moment of perplexity.

CHARLES (*angrily*). Yes, his lordship left the whole weight of—business—upon my shoulders.

ROCHESTER. I doubt not your majesty got through with your usual address.

CHARLES (*apart*). Perfidious varlet! (*Aloud*) My lord, you will please to present yourself in my study at two o'clock. I have something particular to say to you.

ROCHESTER. Deign to dispense with my attendance, sire. I quit London in a few moments for my estate, as I mentioned yesterday. I am a great offender.—It is time to exile myself from court, and turn hermit.

CHARLES (*harshly*). I approve the project; but will take the liberty of choosing your hermitage myself.

ROCHESTER (*low to* LADY CLARA). The king is furious against me.

LADY CLARA. Courage, my lord—all will end well.

COPP (*shouting outside*). What the devil is the meaning of this? Am I to be kept here all day?

CHARLES. What uproar is that?

LADY CLARA. Oh! two persons, whom I met this morning, seeking to speak with his majesty, on some personal concern. As I know him to be so accessible to the people, I undertook to present them.

CHARLES. Just now it is impossible.

LADY CLARA. I am very sorry, especially on the young girl's account.

CHARLES. A young girl, did you say?

LADY CLARA. Beautiful as an angel!

CHARLES. Oh! since you take such interest in her, Lady Clara— (*To* EDWARD) Show them in.

(*Enter* COPP *and* MARY.)

EDWARD (*preceding them*). Come in —his majesty consents to hear you.

COPP. I'm taken all aback—my courage begins to fail me.

MARY. What have you to fear, my dear uncle? (*Keeps her eyes modestly cast down.*)

COPP. Fear! it isn't fear, look ye. But, somehow, I never fell in with a king before in all my cruisings.

CHARLES (*apart*). Copp and his niece! here's a pretty rencontre. (*He summons up his dignity.*)

COPP. Well, I suppose I must begin. —Oddsfish! I had it all settled in my head, and now, the deuce a word can I muster up.

MARY. Come, Uncle, courage! I never saw you so cast down before.

COPP. Well, then, what I have to say is this—Mr. King.— (*Low*) Hey, Mary, what is it I had to say?

CHARLES. What is your name, my good friend?

COPP. Copp, at your service; that is to say, Copland, or Captain Copp, as they call me. And here's Mary, my niece, who, though I say it, is one of the best girls— (*While talking, he looks down and fumbles with his cap.*)

MARY. But, that's not the point, Uncle.

COPP. Eh! true, very true, always

keep to the point, like a good helms-man. First and foremost, then, you must know, my lord—when I say my lord, I mean your majesty.

CHARLES (*apart*). Egad, he's as much puzzled as I was, to give an account of myself.

COPP (*still looking down*). In finis—primo to begin—you must know, then, that I command, that is to say, I keep the Grand Admiral, as honest a tavern as your majesty would wish to set your foot in—none but good company ever frequent it, excepting when a rogue or so drops in, in disguise—last night, for instance, a couple of gallows knaves, saving your majesty's presence —Ah! if I could only lay eyes on them again—I should know 'em, wherever I saw 'em—one in particular had a confounded hanging look—a man about the height of— (*Eyeing* ROCH-ESTER, *stops short*.) Mary! Mary! if there isn't one of the very rogues!

MARY. My dear uncle, hush, for heaven's sake! (*Apart*) That wine is still in his head.

CHARLES (*apart*). Rochester's face seems to puzzle him.

COPP. I'll say no more; for the more I look— (*Low to* MARY) hang me, if it isn't himself.

MARY. Hush, I entreat you—I will speak for you— (*Takes his place, her eyes still modestly cast down*.) My uncle has thought it his duty to in-form your majesty that two strangers came to his house last night, and after calling for a great deal of wine, were unable to pay, and went off, leaving a valuable watch in pledge, which has proved to belong to your majesty.

(ROCHESTER *and* LADY CLARA *in bye play express great delight at the man-ner of* MARY.)

COPP (*apart, rubbing his hands*). Oh! bless her! she talks like a book.

MARY. My uncle being an honest man, has brought the watch to your majesty.

COPP. Yes, by St. George, and here it is. The sharpers, to be sure, have run off with five pounds ten of my money, but that's neither here nor there—I don't say that, because I ex-pect you to pay it, you know.—In short, without more palaver (*Crossing, and giving it*), here's the watch— (*Glances at the king, stops short, and gives a long whistle*.) whew! (*Treads softly back*.)—(*Low to* MARY) Smite my timbers! if it be n't the other rogue!

MARY. What ails you, Uncle? surely, you are losing your senses to speak thus of his majesty!

COPP (*low to her*). Majesty, or no majesty, I'll put my hand in the fire on 't he's the other.

CHARLES. The watch is certainly mine.

LADY CLARA (*smiling significantly at* ROCHESTER). Your majesty's?

ROCHESTER (*affecting astonishment*). Your majesty's watch?

CHARLES. Even so; and I might have lost it, but for this man's honesty. (*Looking sternly at* ROCHESTER) I shall be more on my guard in future.

MARY (*looking at* CHARLES *and* ROCHESTER). The voice and the face are astonishingly alike. But it is im-possible.

COPP (*rapping his forehead*). I have it—I see how it is.— (*Low to* MARY) We've made a pretty kettle of fish of it. The king, you know, is said to cruise under false colours.

MARY. Mercy on me! what will be-come of us?

COPP (*to* MARY). Let me alone—it's one of the king's mad frolics—but never you mind—I'll get *you* off— (*Aloud*) Your majesty will not be angry with my little fool of a niece. The two strangers might be very worthy people—many a man has a gallows look, and is an honest fellow for all that.—The truth is, they were a brace of merry wags.—Besides, if I had known for certain, I wouldn't for the world—ha! ha!—because, d'ye see—honour bright—mum! (*Turns to* MARY.) Come, I think I've got you pretty well out of the scrape, hey?

CHARLES. Captain Copp, I am aware of all that passed at your house.

COPP. Ah! your majesty knows, that he who cracks a joke must not complain if he should chance to pinch his fingers.

CHARLES. True, Captain. But was there not question of one Rochester?

COPP. Why, craving your majesty's pardon, I did let slip some hard truths about him.

ROCHESTER. And do you know him of whom you spoke so bluntly?

COPP. Not I, thank heaven! But I only said, what everybody says—and what everybody says, you know, must be true.

CHARLES. Spoken like an oracle—and did not you say, that this pretty lass was his niece?

COPP. Ay, as to that matter, I'll stick to that, proof in hand. Make a reverence, Mary, and no thanks to Rochester for the relationship.

CHARLES. I will take care that he shall make a suitable provision for his niece, or provide her an honourable husband.

ROCHESTER. I can assure your majesty you only anticipated his intentions.

COPP. Avast there!—I don't give up my girl.

ROCHESTER. But you will choose a match suited to her noble family.

COPP. I'll choose for her an honest man; but no ranticumscout companion to suit that Earl of Rochester you talk of.—(*Chuckling and winking*) To tell the truth between friends, and

all in confidence, I had a match in my eye, a young music-master.—Nay, don't blush, girl—I know there was a sneaking kindness in the case.

CHARLES. I oppose that match. That young man received a ring last night, but has not had the honesty, like Captain Copp, to seek the owner.

(MARY *involuntarily springs forward to defend* EDWARD *against the charge, which* LADY CLARA *and* ROCHESTER *observe and smile at.*)

EDWARD (*advancing*). He only waited a suitable moment to return it to your majesty. (*He kneels and presents it.*)

CHARLES. How! Edward!—The resemblance is no longer a wonder.

COPP. What, little crotchet and quaver! Aha! ha! ha! there's witchcraft in all this.

MARY. Oh, heavens! Georgini a gentleman! But my heart knew it.

CHARLES. It is in vain, Lady Clara, to attempt concealment. Behold the heroes of the adventure.

LADY CLARA. Pardon me, sire, I knew it all along—I was in the plot.

CHARLES. How?

LADY CLARA. Her majesty, the queen, was at the head of it. If the earl be guilty, it is we who induced him, and should undergo the punishment.

CHARLES. I understand the whole. But the treachery of this earl I cannot forgive. He shall not obtain my pardon.

LADY CLARA (*producing a paper*). It is already obtained. Your majesty, ever merciful, has signed it.

CHARLES. What! he, too, is the author for whom you have interested yourself.—Ha! ha! ha! fairly taken in at all points. Rochester, thou hast conquered.

(ROCHESTER *kneels.*)

COPP (*passionately*). Thunder and

lightning! this man Rochester!—come along, girl, come along!

MARY. What, can he be that hard-hearted man? He does not look so cruel, Uncle.

COPP (*taking her under his arm*). Come along, girl, come along.

ROCHESTER. One moment, Captain Copp. (COPP *stops, and looks fiercely at him.*) It is true, I am Rochester—a sad fellow, no doubt, since all the world says so—but there is one griev-ous sin which I will not take to my conscience, for it is against beauty. I am not the Rochester who dis-claimed this lovely girl—he was my predecessor, and is dead.

COPP (*sternly*). Dead!—gone to his long reckoning.— (*Pauses.*) May Heav-en deal kindlier with him than he did with this orphan child!

MARY. That's my own uncle!

CHARLES. I have pardoned you, Rochester; but my eyes are opened to the follies which I have too fre-quently partaken. From this night I abjure them.

ROCHESTER. And I, my liege (*Bowing to* LADY CLARA), will mortify myself with matrimony, and hope to reform into a very rational and submissive husband. (*He takes* LADY CLARA's *hand.*)

CHARLES. There yet remains a party to be disposed of. What say you, Captain Copp?—What say you, my Lord of Rochester? Must we not find a husband for our niece?

COPP. Fair and softly, your majesty—craving your majesty's pardon, I can't give up my right over my little girl. This lord is an uncle—I can't gainsay it; but he's a new-found uncle.—I have bred her, and fed her, and been her uncle all her life, haven't I, Mary?

MARY. Oh, sir, you have been a father to me!

COPP. My good little girl—my darl-ing girl.—Take thee away from thy own uncle? Pshaw! Ha! ha! I shall grow silly and soft again! Ha! ha!

CHARLES. You are right, Captain—you alone ought to dispose of her. But I hope to propose a match that shall please all parties.—What think you of my page—the music-master, who brought back the ring? I shall present him with a commission in my own regiment.

EDWARD. Oh! so much goodness!

COPP. Your majesty has fathomed my own wishes.

ROCHESTER. And mine.

EDWARD (*approaching* MARY). And mine.

MARY. And— (*Extending her hand*) —and mine.

COPP. So, here we are, all safe in port, after last night's squall. Odds-fish! I feel so merry!—my girl's provided for—I have nothing now to care for—I'll keep open house at the Grand Admiral—I'll set all my liquor a-tap—I'll drown all Wapping in wine and strong beer—I'll have an illumina-tion—I'll make a bonfire of the Grand Admiral—I'll give up business for the rest of my life—I'll sing "In the time of the Rump"—

(MARY *runs down and stops him.*)

CHARLES. Captain Copp, I am your debtor—five pounds ten?—accept this watch as a mark of my esteem. The ring I reserve for the lovely Mary. (*Putting it on her finger*) And now (*Beckoning all the characters to the front with an air of mystery*), let me particularly enjoin on all present, the most profound secrecy in regard to **our whimsical adventures at Wapping.**

COPP (*clapping his finger to his lips*). **Honour bright!—Mum!**

FASHION

Anna Cora Mowatt

First performed at the Park Theatre in New York
on March 24, 1845.

ADAM TRUEMAN

COUNT JOLIMAITRE, *a fashionable European importation*

COLONEL HOWARD, *an officer in the
United States Army*

MR. TIFFANY, *a New York merchant*

T. TENNYSON TWINKLE, *a modern poet*

AUGUSTUS FOGG, *a drawing room appendage*

SNOBSON, *a rare species of confidential
clerk*

ZEKE, *a colored servant*

MRS. TIFFANY, *a lady who imagines herself fashionable*

PRUDENCE, *a maiden lady of a certain
age*

MILLINETTE, *a French lady's maid*

GERTRUDE, *a governess*

SERAPHINA TIFFANY, *a belle*

ACT ONE

Scene One

*A splendid Drawing Room in the
House of* MRS. TIFFANY. *Open folding
doors, discovering* [*revealing*] *a Conservatory. On either side glass windows
down to the ground. Doors on right and
left. Mirror, couches, ottomans, a table
with albums, beside it an arm chair.*
MILLINETTE *is dusting furniture.* ZEKE
is in a dashing livery, scarlet coat.

ZEKE. Dere's a coat to take de eyes
ob all Broadway! Ah! Missy, it am de
fixin's dat make de natural *born* gemman. A libery for ever! Dere's a pair
ob insuppressibles to 'stonish de colored
population.

MILLINETTE (*very politely*). Oh, *oui*,
Monsieur Zeke. (*Aside*) I not *comprend* one word he say!

ZEKE. I tell 'ee what, Missy, I'm
'stordinary glad to find dis a bery
'spectabul like situation! Now, as
you've made de acquaintance ob dis
here family, and dere you've had a
supernumerary advantage ob me—
seeing dat I only receibed my appointment dis morning. What I wants to
know is your publicated opinion, privately expressed, ob de domestic circle.

MILLINETTE. You mean vat *espèce*,[1]
vat kind of personnes are Monsieur
and Madame Tiffany? Ah! Monsieur
is not de same ting as Madame—not
at all.

ZEKE. Well, I s'pose he ain't altogether.

MILLINETTE. Monsieur is man of
business—Madame is lady of fashion.
Monsieur make de money—Madame
spend it. Monsieur nobody at all—

Madame everybody altogether. Ah!
Monsieur Zeke, de money is all dat is
nécessaire in dis country to make one
lady of fashion. Oh! it is quite anoder
ting in *la belle France!*

ZEKE. A bery lucifer explanation.
Well, now we've disposed ob de heads
ob de family, who come next?

MILLINETTE. First, dere is Mademoiselle Seraphina Tiffany. Mademoiselle
is not at all one proper *personne.*
Mademoiselle Seraphina is one coquette. Dat is not de mode in *la belle
France;* de ladies, dere, never learn *la
coquetterie* until dey do get one husband.

ZEKE. I tell 'ee what, Missy, I dis-
reprobate dat proceeding altogeder!

MILLINETTE. Vait! I have not tell you
all *la famille* yet. Dere is Ma'mselle
Prudence—Madame's sister, one very
bizarre personne. Den dere is Ma'mselle
Gertrude, but she not anybody at all;
she only teach Mademoiselle Seraphina
la musique.

ZEKE. Well now, Missy, what's your
own special defunctions?

MILLINETTE. I not understand, Monsieur Zeke.

ZEKE. Den I'll amplify. What's de
nature ob your exclusive services?

MILLINETTE. Ah, *oui! je comprend.*
I am Madame's *femme de chambre*—
her lady's maid, Monsieur Zeke. I
teach Madame *les modes de Paris,* and
Madame set de fashion for all New
York. You see, Monsieur Zeke, dat it
is me, *moi-même,*[2] dat do lead de
fashion for all de American *beau
monde!*

ZEKE. Yah! yah! yah! I hab de idea
by de heel. Well now, p'raps you can
'lustrify my officials?

MILLINETTE. Vat you will have to do?
Oh! much tings, much tings. You vait
on de table—you tend de door—you

_____
[1] *espèce*—species, sort.

[2] *moi-même*—myself.

clean de boots—you run de errands—you drive de carriage—you rub de horses—you take care of de flowers—you carry de water—you help cook de dinner—you wash de dishes—and den you always remember to do everything I tell you to!

ZEKE. Wheugh, am dat *all?*

MILLINETTE. All I can t'ink of now. To-day is Madame's day of reception, and all her grand friends do make her one *petite* visit. You mind run fast ven de bell do ring.

ZEKE. Run? If it wasn't for dese superfluminous trimmings, I tell 'ee what, Missy, I'd run—

MRS. TIFFANY (*outside*). Millinette!

MILLINETTE. Here comes Madame! You better go, Monsieur Zeke.

ZEKE (*aside*). Look ahea, Massa Zeke, doesn't dis open rich! (*Exit* ZEKE.)

(*Enter* MRS. TIFFANY, *dressed in the most extravagant height of fashion.*)

MRS. TIFFANY. Is everything in order, Millinette? Ah! very elegant, very elegant, indeed! There is a *jenny-says-quoi*[3] look about this furniture—an air of fashion and gentility perfectly bewitching. Is there not, Millinette?

MILLINETTE. Oh, *oui,* Madame!

MRS. TIFFANY. But where is Miss Seraphina? It is twelve o'clock; our visitors will be pouring in, and she has not made her appearance. But I hear that nothing is more fashionable than to keep people waiting.—None but vulgar persons pay any attention to punctuality. Is it not so, Millinette?

MILLINETTE. Quite *comme il faut.*[4] —Great personnes always do make little personnes wait, Madame.

MRS. TIFFANY. This mode of receiving visitors only upon one specified day of the week is a most convenient cus-tom! It saves the trouble of keeping the house continually in order and of being always dressed. I flatter myself that *I* was the first to introduce it amongst the New York *ee-light.* You are quite sure that it is strictly a Parisian mode, Millinette?

MILLINETTE. Oh, *oui,* Madame; entirely *mode de Paris.*

MRS. TIFFANY. This girl is worth her weight in gold. (*Aside*) Millinette, how do you say *armchair* in French?

MILLINETTE. *Fauteuil,* Madame.

MRS. TIFFANY. *Fo-tool!* That has a foreign—an out-of-the-wayish sound that is perfectly charming—and so genteel! There is something about our American words decidedly vulgar. *Fowtool!* how refined. *Fowtool! Armchair!* what a difference!

MILLINETTE. Madame have one *charmante* pronunciation. *Fowtool* (*Mimicking aside*) charmante, Madame!

MRS. TIFFANY. Do you think so, Millinette? Well, I believe I have. But a woman of refinement and of fashion can always accommodate herself to everything foreign! And a week's study of that invaluable work—*French Without a Master,* has made me quite at home in the court language of Europe! But where is the new valet? I'm rather sorry that he is black, but to obtain a white American for a domestic is almost impossible; and they call this a free country! What did you say was the name of this new servant, Millinette?

MILLINETTE. He do say his name is Monsieur Zeke.

MRS. TIFFANY. Ezekiel, I suppose. Zeke! Dear me, such a vulgar name will compromise the dignity of the whole family. Can you not suggest something more aristocratic, Millinette? Something *French!*

---

3 *je ne sais quoi*—I know not what.

4 *comme il faut*—in good taste.

MILLINETTE. *Oh, oui,* Madame; *Adolph* is one very fine name.

MRS. TIFFANY. A-dolph! Charming! Ring the bell, Millinette! (MILLINETTE *rings the bell.*) I will change his name immediately, besides giving him a few directions. (*Enter* ZEKE. MRS. TIFFANY *addresses him with great dignity.*) Your name, I hear, is *Ezekiel.*—I consider it too plebeian an appellation to be uttered in my presence. In future you are called A-dolph. Don't reply— never interrupt me when I am speaking. A-dolph, as my guests arrive, I desire that you will inquire the name of every person, and then announce it in a loud, clear tone. That is the fashion in Paris.

(MILLINETTE *retires up the stage.*)

ZEKE. Consider de office discharged, Missus. (*Speaking very loudly.*)

MRS. TIFFANY. Silence! Your business is to obey and not to talk.

ZEKE. I'm dumb, Missus!

MRS. TIFFANY (*pointing up stage*). A-dolph, place that *fowtool* behind me.

ZEKE (*looking about him*). I habn't got dat far in de dictionary yet. No matter, a genus gets his learning by nature. (*Takes up the table and places it behind* MRS. TIFFANY, *then expresses in dumb show great satisfaction.* MRS. TIFFANY, *as she goes to sit, discovers the mistake.*)

MRS. TIFFANY. You dolt! Where have you lived not to know that *fow-tool* is the French for *armchair?* What ignorance! Leave the room this instant. (MRS. TIFFANY *draws forward an armchair and sits.* MILLINETTE *comes forward suppressing her merriment at* ZEKE's *mistake and removes the table.*)

ZEKE. Dem's de defects ob not having a libery education. (*Exit.*)

(PRUDENCE *peeps in.*)

PRUDENCE. I wonder if any of the fine folks have come yet. Not a soul, — I knew they hadn't. There's Betsy all alone. (*Walks in.*) Sister Betsy!

MRS. TIFFANY. Prudence! how many times have I desired you to call me *Elizabeth? Betsy* is the height of vulgarity.

PRUDENCE. Oh! I forgot. Dear me, how spruce we do look here, to be sure —everything in first rate style now, Betsy. (MRS. TIFFANY *looks at her angrily.*) *Elizabeth,* I mean. Who would have thought, when you and I were sitting behind that little mahogany- colored counter, in Canal Street, making up flashy hats and caps—

MRS. TIFFANY. Prudence, *what do* you mean? Millinette, leave the room.

MILLINETTE. *Oui,* Madame. (MILLI- NETTE *pretends to arrange the books upon a side table, but lingers to listen.*)

PRUDENCE. But I always predicted it, —I always told you so, Betsy,—I always said you were destined to rise above your station!

MRS. TIFFANY. Prudence! Prudence! have I not told you that—

PRUDENCE. No, Betsy, it was *I* that told *you,* when we used to buy our silks and ribbons of Mr. Antony Tiffany— "talking Tony," you know we used to call him, and when you always put on the finest bonnet in our shop to go to his—and when you stayed so long smiling and chattering with him, I always told you that *something* would grow out of it—and didn't it?

MRS. TIFFANY. Millinette, send Seraphina here instantly. Leave the room.

MILLINETTE. *Oui,* Madame. So dis Americaine lady of fashion vas one *milliner?* Oh, vat a fine country for *les marchands des modes!*[5] I shall send for all my relation by de next packet! (*Aside.*)

_____

[5] *les marchands des modes* — fashionable shopkeepers.

(*Exit* MILLINETTE.)

MRS. TIFFANY. Prudence! never let me hear you mention this subject again. Forget what we *have* been, it is enough to remember that we *are* of the *upper ten thousand!*

(PRUDENCE *goes up and sits down. Enter* SERAPHINA, *very extravagantly dressed.*)

MRS. TIFFANY. How bewitchingly you look, my dear! Does Millinette say that that head dress is strictly Parisian?

SERAPHINA. Oh, yes, Mamma, all the rage! They call it a *lady's tarpaulin,* and it is the exact pattern of one worn by the Princess Clementina at the last court ball.

MRS. TIFFANY. Now, Seraphina, my dear, don't be too particular in your attentions to gentlemen not eligible. There is Count Jolimaitre, decidedly the most fashionable foreigner in town, —and so refined,—so much accustomed to associate with the first nobility in his own country that he can hardly tolerate the vulgarity of Americans in general. You may devote yourself to him. Mrs. Proudacre is dying to become acquainted with him. By the by, if she or her daughters should happen to drop in, be sure you don't introduce them to the Count. It is not the fashion in Paris to introduce—Millinette told me so.

(*Enter* ZEKE.)

ZEKE (*in a very loud voice*). Mister T. Tennyson Twinkle!

MRS. TIFFANY. Show him up. (*Exit* ZEKE.)

PRUDENCE. I must be running away! (*Going.*)

MRS. TIFFANY. Mr. T. Tennyson Twinkle—a very literary young man and a sweet poet! It is all the rage to patronize poets! Quick, Seraphina, hand me that magazine.—Mr. Twinkle writes for it.

(SERAPHINA *hands her the magazine;* MRS. TIFFANY *seats herself in an armchair and opens the book.*)

PRUDENCE (*returning*). There's Betsy trying to make out that reading without her spectacles. (*Takes a pair of spectacles out of her pocket and hands them to* MRS. TIFFANY.) There, Betsy, I knew you were going to ask for them. Ah! they're a blessing when one is growing old!

MRS. TIFFANY. What do you mean, Prudence? A woman of fashion *never* grows old! Age is always out of fashion.

PRUDENCE. Oh, dear! what a delightful thing it is to be fashionable. (*Exit* PRUDENCE. MRS. TIFFANY *resumes her seat.*)

(*Enter* TWINKLE. *He salutes* SERAPHINA.)

TWINKLE. Fair Seraphina! the sun itself grows dim,
Unless you aid his light and shine on him!

SERAPHINA. Ah! Mr. Twinkle, there is no such thing as answering you.

TWINKLE (*looks around and perceives* MRS. TIFFANY). The "New Monthly Vernal Galaxy." Reading my verses by all that's charming! (*Aside*) Sensible woman! I won't interrupt her.

MRS. TIFFANY (*rising and coming forward*). Ah! Mr. Twinkle, is that you? I was perfectly *abîmé*[6] at the perusal of your very *distingué* verses.

TWINKLE. I am overwhelmed, Madam. Permit me. (*Taking the magazine*) Yes, they do read tolerably. And you must take into consideration, ladies, the rapidity with which they were written. Four minutes and a half by the stop watch! The true test of a poet is the *velocity* with which he composes. Really they do look very prettily, and they read tolerably—*quite* tolerably— *very* tolerably—especially the first verse.

6 *abîmé*—sunk, overcome.

(*Reads.*) "To Seraphina T——."

SERAPHINA. Oh! Mr. Twinkle!

TWINKLE (*reads*). "Around my heart"—

MRS. TIFFANY. How touching! Really, Mr. Twinkle, quite tender!

TWINKLE (*recommencing*). "Around my heart"—

MRS. TIFFANY. Oh, I must tell you, Mr. Twinkle! I heard the other day that poets were the aristocrats of literature. That's one reason I like them, for I do dote on all aristocracy!

TWINKLE. Oh, Madam, how flattering! Now pray lend me your ears! (*Reads.*) "Around my heart thou weavest"—

SERAPHINA. That is such a *sweet* commencement, Mr. Twinkle!

TWINKLE (*aside*). I wish she wouldn't interrupt me! (*Reads.*) "Around my heart thou weavest a spell"—

MRS. TIFFANY. Beautiful! But excuse me one moment, while I say a word to Seraphina! (*Aside to* SERAPHINA) Don't be too affable, my dear! Poets are very ornamental appendages to the drawing room, but they are always as poor as their own verses. They don't make eligible husbands!

TWINKLE. Confound their interruptions! (*Aside*) My dear Madam, unless you pay the utmost attention you cannot catch the ideas. Are you ready? Well, now you shall hear it to the end! (*Reads.*) "Around my heart thou weavest a spell

"Whose"—

(*Enter* ZEKE.)

ZEKE. Mister Augustus Fogg! (*Aside*) A bery misty lookin' young gemman?

MRS. TIFFANY. Show him up, Adolph! (*Exit* ZEKE.)

TWINKLE. This is too much!

SERAPHINA. Exquisite verses, Mr. Twinkle—exquisite!

TWINKLE. Ah, lovely Seraphina! your smile of approval transports me to the summit of Olympus.

SERAPHINA. Then I must frown, for I would not send you so far away.

TWINKLE. Enchantress! (*Aside*) It's all over with her.

(*Retire up and converse.*)

MRS. TIFFANY. Mr. Fogg belongs to one of our oldest families—to be sure he is the most difficult person in the world to entertain, for he never takes the trouble to talk, and never notices anything or anybody—but then I hear that nothing is considered so vulgar as to betray any emotion, or to attempt to render oneself agreeable!

(*Enter* MR. FOGG, *fashionably attired but in very dark clothes.*)

FOGG (*bowing stiffly*). Mrs. Tiffany, your most obedient. Miss Seraphina, yours. How d'ye do, Twinkle?

MRS. TIFFANY. Mr. Fogg, how do you do? Fine weather—delightful, isn't it?

FOGG. I am indifferent to weather, Madam.

MRS. TIFFANY. Been to the opera, Mr. Fogg? I hear that the *bow monde* make their *debutt* there every evening.

FOGG. I consider operas a bore, Madam.

SERAPHINA (*advancing*). You must hear Mr. Twinkle's verses, Mr. Fogg!

FOGG. I am indifferent to verses, Miss Seraphina.

SERAPHINA. But Mr. Twinkle's verses are addressed to me!

TWINKLE. Now pay attention, Fogg! (*Reads.*)—"Around my heart thou weavest a spell

"Whose magic I"—

(*Enter* ZEKE.)

ZEKE. Mister—No, he say he ain't no Mister—

TWINKLE. "Around my heart thou weavest a spell

"Whose magic I can never tell!"

MRS. TIFFANY. Speak in a loud, clear tone, A-dolph!

TWINKLE. This is terrible!

ZEKE. Mister Count Jolly-made-her!

MRS. TIFFANY. Count Jolimaitre! Good gracious! Zeke, Zeke—A-dolph I mean.—Dear me, what a mistake! (*Aside*) Set that chair out of the way —put that table back. Seraphina, my dear, are you all in order? Dear me! dear me! Your dress is so tumbled! (*Arranges her dress.*) What are you grinning at? (*To* ZEKE) Beg the Count to *honor* us by walking up! (*Exit* ZEKE.) Seraphina, my dear (*Aside to her*), remember now what I told you about the Count. He is a man of the highest,—good gracious! I am so flurried; and nothing is so ungenteel as agitation! what will the Count think! Mr. Twinkle, pray stand out of the way! Seraphina, my dear, place yourself on my right! Mr. Fogg, the conservatory—beautiful flowers—pray amuse yourself in the conservatory.

FOGG. I am indifferent to flowers, Madam.

MRS. TIFFANY. Dear me! the man stands right in the way—just where the Count must make his *entray!* (*Aside*) Mr. Fogg,—pray—

(*Enter* COUNT JOLIMAITRE, *very dashingly dressed, wears a moustache.*)

MRS. TIFFANY. Oh, Count, this unexpected honor—

SERAPHINA. Count, this inexpressible pleasure—

COUNT JOLIMAITRE. Beg you won't mention it, Madam! Miss Seraphina, your most devoted!

MRS. TIFFANY. What condescension! (*Aside*) Count, may I take the liberty to introduce—Good gracious! I forgot. (*Aside*) Count, I was about to remark that we never introduce in America. All our fashions are foreign, Count.

(TWINKLE, *who has stepped forward* to be introduced, *shows great indignation.*)

COUNT JOLIMAITRE. Excuse me, Madam, our fashions have grown antediluvian before you Americans discover their existence. You are lamentably behind the age—lamentably! 'Pon my honor, a foreigner of refinement finds great difficulty in existing in this provincial atmosphere.

MRS. TIFFANY. How dreadful, Count! I am very much concerned. If there is anything which I can do, Count—

SERAPHINA. Or I, Count, to render your situation less deplorable—

COUNT JOLIMAITRE. Ah! I find but one redeeming charm in America—the superlative loveliness of the feminine portion of creation—(*Aside*) and the wealth of their obliging papas.

MRS. TIFFANY. How flattering! Ah! Count, I am afraid you will turn the head of my simple girl here. She is a perfect child of nature, Count.

COUNT JOLIMAITRE. Very possibly, for though you American women are quite charming, yet, demme, there's a deal of native rust to rub off!

MRS. TIFFANY. *Rust?* Good gracious, Count! where do you find any rust? (*Looks about the room.*)

COUNT JOLIMAITRE. How very unsophisticated!

MRS. TIFFANY. Count, I am so much ashamed—pray excuse me! Although a lady of large fortune, and one, Count, who can boast of the highest connections, I blush to confess that I have never travelled,—while you, Count, I presume are at home in all the courts of Europe.

COUNT JOLIMAITRE. *Courts?* Eh? Oh, yes, Madam, very true. I believe I am pretty well known in some of the courts of Europe—(*Aside, crossing*) *police courts.* In a word, Madam, I had seen enough of civilized life—

wanted to refresh myself by a sight of barbarous countries and customs—had my choice between the Sandwich Islands and New York—chose New York!

MRS. TIFFANY. How complimentary to our country! And, Count, I have no doubt you speak every conceivable language? You talk English like a native.

COUNT JOLIMAITRE. Eh, what? Like a native? Oh, ah, demme, yes, I am something of an Englishman. Passed one year and eight months with the Duke of Wellington, six months with Lord Brougham, two and a half with Count d'Orsay—knew them all more intimately than their best friends—no heroes to me—hadn't a secret from me, I assure you—(*Aside*) *especially of the toilet.*

MRS. TIFFANY (*aside to* SERAPHINA). Think of that, my dear! Lord Wellington and Duke Broom!

SERAPHINA (*aside to* MRS. TIFFANY). And only think of Count d'Orsay, Mamma! I am so wild to see Count d'Orsay!

COUNT JOLIMAITRE. Oh! a mere man milliner. Very little refinement out of Paris! Why, at the very last dinner given at Lord—Lord Knowswho, would you believe it, Madam, there was an individual present who wore a *black* cravat and took *soup twice!*

MRS. TIFFANY. How shocking! the sight of him would have spoilt my appetite! (*Aside to* SERAPHINA) Think what a great man he must be, my dear, to despise lords and counts in that way. I must leave them together. (*Aside*) Mr. Twinkle, your arm. I have some really very *foreign exotics* to show you.

TWINKLE. I fly at your command. (*Aside, and glancing at the* COUNT) I wish all her exotics were blooming in their native soil!

MRS. TIFFANY. Mr. Fogg, will you accompany us? My conservatory is well worthy a visit. It cost an immense sum of money.

FOGG. I am indifferent to conservatories, Madam; flowers are such a bore!

MRS. TIFFANY. I shall take no refusal. Conservatories are all the rage, —I could not exist without mine! Let me show you,—let me show you.

(*Places her arm through* MR. FOGG's, *without his consent. Exeunt* MRS. TIFFANY, FOGG, *and* TWINKLE *into the conservatory, where they are seen walking about.*)

SERAPHINA. America, then, has no charms for you, Count?

COUNT JOLIMAITRE. Excuse me— some exceptions. I find you, for instance, particularly charming! Can't say I admire your country. Ah! if you had ever breathed the exhilarating air of Paris, ate creams at Tortoni's, dined at the Café Royale, or if you had lived in London—felt at home at St. James's, and every afternoon driven a couple of Lords and a Duchess through Hyde Park, you would find America—where you have no kings, queens, lords, nor ladies—insupportable!

SERAPHINA. Not while there was a Count in it?

(*Enter* ZEKE, *very indignant.*)

ZEKE. Where's de Missus?

(*Enter* MRS. TIFFANY, FOGG, *and* TWINKLE, *from the conservatory.*)

MRS. TIFFANY. Whom do you come to announce, A-dolph?

ZEKE. He said he wouldn't trust me —no, not eben wid so much as his name; so I wouldn't trust him up stairs, den he ups wid *his stick* and I *cuts mine.*

MRS. TIFFANY (*aside*). Some of Mr. Tiffany's vulgar acquaintances. I shall die with shame. A-dolph, inform him that I am *not at home*. (*Exit* ZEKE.) My nerves are so shattered, I am ready to sink. Mr. Twinkle, that *fow tool*, if you please!

TWINKLE. What? What do you wish, Madam?

MRS. TIFFANY (*aside*). The ignorance of these Americans! Count, may I trouble you? That *fow tool*, if you please!

COUNT JOLIMAITRE (*aside*). She's not talking English, nor French, but I suppose it's American.

TRUEMAN (*outside*). Not at home!

ZEKE. No, Sar—Missus say she's not at home.

TRUEMAN. Out of the way, you grinning . . .

(*Enter* ADAM TRUEMAN, *dressed as a farmer, a stout cane in his hand, his boots covered with dust.* ZEKE *jumps out of his way as he enters. Exit* ZEKE.)

TRUEMAN. Where's this woman that's not *at home* in her own house? May I be shot! if I wonder at it! I shouldn't think she'd ever feel *at home* in such a showbox as this! (*Looks round.*)

MRS. TIFFANY (*aside*). What a plebeian looking old farmer! I wonder who he is? Sir—(*Advancing very agitatedly*) what do you mean, Sir, by this *ow*dacious conduct? How dare you intrude yourself into my parlor? Do you know who I am, Sir? (*With great dignity*) You are in the presence of Mrs. Tiffany, Sir!

TRUEMAN. Antony's wife, eh? Well now, I might have guessed that—ha! ha! ha! for I see you make it a point to carry half your husband's shop upon your back! No matter; that's being a good helpmate—for he carried the whole of it once in a pack on his own shoulders—now you bear a share!

MRS. TIFFANY. How dare you, you impertinent, *ow*dacious, ignorant old man! It's all an invention. You're talking of somebody else. (*Aside*) What will the Count think!

TRUEMAN. Why, I thought folks had better manners in the city! This is a civil welcome for your husband's old friend, and after my coming all the way from Catteraugus to see you and yours! First a grinning nigger tricked out in scarlet regimentals—

MRS. TIFFANY. Let me tell you, Sir, that liveries are all the fashion!

TRUEMAN. The fashion, are they? To make men wear the *badge of servitude* in a free land,—that's the fashion, is it? Hurrah, for republican simplicity! I will venture to say now, that you have your coat of arms too!

MRS. TIFFANY. Certainly, Sir; you can see it on the panels of my *voyture*.[7]

TRUEMAN. Oh! no need of that. I know what your escutcheon must be! A bandbox *rampant* with a bonnet *couchant*, and a peddlar's pack *passant*! Ha, ha, ha! that shows both houses united!

MRS. TIFFANY. Sir! you are most profoundly ignorant,—what do you mean by this insolence, Sir? (*Aside*) How shall I get rid of him?

TRUEMAN (*aside, looking at* SERAPHINA). I hope that is not Gertrude!

MRS. TIFFANY. Sir, I'd have you know that—Seraphina, my child, walk with the gentlemen into the conservatory.

(*Exeunt* SERAPHINA, TWINKLE, FOGG *into conservatory.*)

Count Jolimaitre, pray make due allowances for the errors of this rustic! I do assure you, Count— (*Whispers to him.*)

TRUEMAN (*aside*). Count! She calls that critter with a shoe brush over his mouth, Count! To look at him, I

---

7 *voiture*—carriage.

should have thought he was a tailor's walking advertisement!

COUNT JOLIMAITRE (*addressing* TRUEMAN *whom he has been inspecting through his eyeglass*). Where did you say you belonged, my friend? Dug out of the ruins of Pompeii, eh?

TRUEMAN. I belong to a land in which I rejoice to find that you are a foreigner.

COUNT JOLIMAITRE. What a barbarian! He doesn't see the honor I'm doing his country! Pray, Madam, is it one of the aboriginal inhabitants of the soil? To what tribe of Indians does he belong—the Pawnee or Choctaw? Does he carry a tomahawk?

TRUEMAN. Something quite as useful, —do you see that? (*Shakes his stick.*)

(COUNT *runs behind* MRS. TIFFANY.)

MRS. TIFFANY. Oh, dear! I shall faint! Millinette! (*Approaches.*) Millinette!

(*Enter* MILLINETTE, *without advancing into the room.*)

MILLINETTE. *Oui*, Madame.

MRS. TIFFANY. A glass of water!

(*Exit* MILLINETTE.)

Sir (*Crossing to* TRUEMAN), I am shocked at your plebeian conduct! This is a gentleman of the highest standing, Sir! He is a *Count*, Sir!

(*Enter* MILLINETTE, *bearing a salver with a glass of water. In advancing towards* MRS. TIFFANY, *she passes in front of the* COUNT, *starts and screams. The* COUNT, *after a start of surprise, regains his composure, plays with his eye glass, and looks perfectly unconcerned.*)

MRS. TIFFANY. What is the matter? What *is* the matter?

MILLINETTE. Not'ing, not'ing,—only — (*Looks at* COUNT *and turns away her eyes again.*) only—not'ing at all!

TRUEMAN. Don't be afraid, girl! Why, did you never see a live Count before? He's tame,—I dare say your mistress there leads him about by the ears.

MRS. TIFFANY. This is too much! Millinette, send for Mr. Tiffany instantly!

(*Crosses to* MILLINETTE, *who is going.*)

MILLINETTE. He just come in, Madame!

TRUEMAN. My old friend! Where is he? Take me to him,—I long to have one more hearty shake of the hand!

MRS. TIFFANY (*crosses to him*). Count, honor me by joining my daughter in the conservatory, I will return immediately.

(COUNT *bows and walks towards conservatory*, MRS. TIFFANY *following part of the way and then returning to* TRUEMAN.)

TRUEMAN. What a Jezebel! These women always play the very devil with a man, and yet I don't believe such a damaged bale of goods as *that* (*Looking at* MRS. TIFFANY) has smothered the heart of little Antony!

MRS. TIFFANY. This way, Sir, sal vous plait.

(*Exit with great dignity.*)

TRUEMAN. *Sal vous plait.* Ha, ha, ha! We'll see what Fashion has done for him. (*Exit.*)

ACT TWO

SCENE ONE

Inner apartment of MR. TIFFANY'S *Counting House.* MR. TIFFANY, *seated at a desk looking over papers.* MR. SNOBSON, *on a high stool at another desk, with a pen behind his ear.*

———

SNOBSON (*rising, advances to the*

front of the stage, regards TIFFANY, *shrugs his shoulders, and says aside*). How the old boy frets and fumes over those papers, to be sure! He's working himself into a perfect fever—exactly—therefore *bleeding's* the prescription! So here goes! Mr. Tiffany, a word with you, if you please, Sir?

TIFFANY (*sitting still*). Speak on, Mr. Snobson, I attend.

SNOBSON. What I have to say, Sir, is a matter of the first importance to the credit of the concern—*the credit* of the concern, Mr. Tiffany!

TIFFANY. Proceed, Mr. Snobson.

SNOBSON. Sir, you've a handsome house—fine carriage—servant in livery —feed on the fat of the land—everything first rate—

TIFFANY. Well, Sir?

SNOBSON. My salary, Mr. Tiffany!

TIFFANY. It has been raised three times within the last year.

SNOBSON. Still it is insufficient for the necessities of an honest man—mark me, an *honest* man, Mr. Tiffany.

TIFFANY (*crossing, says aside*). What a weapon he has made of that word! Enough—another hundred shall be added. Does that content you?

SNOBSON. There is one other subject, which I have before mentioned, Mr. Tiffany,—your daughter—what's the reason you can't let the folks at home know at once that I'm to be *the man?*

TIFFANY (*aside*). Villain! And must the only seal upon this scoundrel's lips be placed there by the hand of my daughter? Well, Sir, it shall be as you desire.

SNOBSON. And Mrs. Tiffany shall be informed of your resolution?

TIFFANY. Yes.

SNOBSON. Enough said! That's the ticket! The CREDIT *of the concern's safe*, Sir! (*Returns to his seat.*)

TIFFANY (*aside*). How low have I bowed to this insolent rascal! To rise himself he mounts upon my shoulders, and unless I can shake him off he must crush me!

(*Enter* TRUEMAN.)

TRUEMAN. Here I am, Antony, man! I told you I'd pay you a visit in your money-making quarters. (*Looks around.*) But it looks as dismal here as a cell in the States' prison!

TIFFANY (*forcing a laugh*). Ha, ha, ha! States' prison! You are so facetious! Ha, ha, ha!

TRUEMAN. Well, for the life of me I can't see anything so amusing in that! I should think the States' prison plaguy uncomfortable lodgings. And you laugh, man, as though you fancied yourself there already.

TIFFANY. Ha, ha, ha!

TRUEMAN (*imitating him*). Ha, ha, ha! What on earth do you mean by that ill-sounding laugh, that has nothing of a laugh about it! This *fashion*-worship has made heathens and hypocrites of you all! *Deception* is your household God! A man laughs as if he were crying, and cries as if he were laughing in his sleeve. Everything is something else from what it seems to be. I have lived in your house only three days, and I've heard more lies than were ever invented during a Presidential election! First your fine lady of a wife sends me word that she's not at home—I walk up stairs, and she takes good care that *I* shall not be *at home*—wants to turn me out of doors. Then *you* come in—take your old friend by the hand—whisper, the deuce knows what, in your wife's ear, and the tables are turned in a tangent! Madam curtsies—says she's enchanted to see me—and orders her grinning servant to show me a room.

TIFFANY. We were exceedingly happy to welcome you as our guest!

TRUEMAN. Happy? *You* happy? Ah, Antony! Antony! that hatchet face of yours, and those criss-cross furrows tell quite another story! It's many a long day since you were *happy* at anything! You look as if you'd melted down your flesh into dollars, and mortgaged your soul in the bargain! Your warm heart has grown cold over your ledger—your light spirits heavy with calculation! You have traded away your youth—your hopes—your tastes, for wealth! and now you *have* the wealth you coveted, what does it profit you? Pleasure it cannot buy; for you have lost your *capacity* for enjoyment—Ease it will not bring; for the love of gain is never satisfied! It has made your counting-house a penitentiary, and your home a fashionable *museum* where there is no niche for you! You have spent so much time *ciphering* in the one, that you find yourself at last a very *cipher* in the other! See me, man! seventy-two last August!—strong as a hickory and every whit as sound!

TIFFANY. I take the greatest pleasure in remarking your superiority, Sir.

TRUEMAN. Bah! no man takes pleasure in remarking the superiority of another! Why the deuce, can't you speak the truth, man? But it's not the *fashion* I suppose! I have not seen one frank, open face since—no, no I can't say that either, though lying *is* catching! There's that girl, Gertrude, who is trying to teach your daughter music—but Gertrude was bred in the country!

TIFFANY. A good girl; my wife and daughter find her very useful.

TRUEMAN. Useful? Well, I must say you have queer notions of *use!*—But come, cheer up, man! I'd rather see one of your old smiles, than know you'd realized another thousand! I hear you are making money on the true, American, high pressure system—better go slow and sure—the more steam, the greater danger of the boiler's bursting! All sound, I hope? Nothing rotten at the core?

TIFFANY. Oh, sound—quite sound!

TRUEMAN. Well, that's pleasant—though I must say you don't look very pleasant about it!

TIFFANY. My good friend, although I am solvent, I may say, perfectly solvent—yet you—the fact is, you can be of some assistance to me!

TRUEMAN. That's the *fact* is it? I'm glad we've hit upon one *fact* at last! Well—(SNOBSON, *who during this conversation has been employed in writing, but stops occasionally to listen, now gives vent to a dry chuckling laugh.*)

TRUEMAN. Hey? What's that? Another of those deuced ill-sounding, city laughs! (*Sees* SNOBSON.) Who's that perched up on the stool of repentance —eh, Antony?

SNOBSON (*aside and looking at* TIFFANY's *seat*). The old boy has missed his text there—*that's* the stool of repentance!

TIFFANY. One of my clerks—my confidential clerk!

TRUEMAN. Confidential? Why he looks for all the world like a spy—the most inquisitorial, hang-dog face— ugh! the sight of it makes my blood run cold! Come (*crosses.*), let us talk over matters where this critter can't give us the benefit of his opinion! Antony, the next time you choose a confidential clerk, take one that carries his credentials in his face—those in his pocket are not worth much without!

(*Exeunt* TRUEMAN *and* TIFFANY.)

SNOBSON (*jumping from his stool and advancing*). The old prig has got the tin, or Tiff would never be so civil! All right—Tiff will work every shiner into the concern—all the better for me! Now I'll go and make love to Seraphina. The old woman needn't try to knock me down with any of her French lingo! Six months from today if I ain't driving my two footmen tandem, down Broadway—and as fashionable as Mrs. Tiffany herself, then I ain't the trump I thought I was! that's all. (*Looks at his watch.*) Bless me! eleven o'clock and I haven't had my julep yet! Snobson, I'm ashamed of you! (*Exit.*)

SCENE TWO

The interior of a beautiful conservatory; walk through the center; stands of flower pots in bloom; a couple of rustic seats. GERTRUDE, *attired in white, with a white rose in her hair; watering the flowers.* COLONEL HOWARD *regarding her.*

HOWARD. I am afraid you lead a sad life here, Miss Gertrude?

GERTRUDE (*turning round gaily*). What! amongst the flowers? (*Continues her occupation.*)

HOWARD. No, amongst the thistles, with which Mrs. Tiffany surrounds you; the tempests, which her temper raises!

GERTRUDE. They never harm me. Flowers and herbs are excellent tutors. I learn prudence from the reed, and bend until the storm has swept over me!

HOWARD. Admirable philosophy! But still this frigid atmosphere of fashion must be uncongenial to you? Accustomed to the pleasant companionship of your kind friends in Geneva, surely you must regret this cold exchange?

GERTRUDE. Do you think so? Can you suppose that I could possibly prefer a ramble in the woods to a promenade in Broadway? A wreath of scented wild flowers to a bouquet of these sickly exotics? The odour of new-mown hay to the heated air of this crowded conservatory? Or can you imagine that I could enjoy the quiet conversation of my Geneva friends, more than the edifying chit-chat of a fashionable drawing room? But I see you think me totally destitute of taste?

HOWARD. You have a merry spirit to jest thus at your grievances!

GERTRUDE. I have my *mania*—as some wise person declares that all mankind have—and mine is a love of independence! In Geneva, my wants were supplied by two kind old maiden ladies, upon whom I know not that I have any claim. I had abilities, and desired to use them. I came here at my own request; for here I am no longer dependent! *Voilà tout,*[8] as Mrs. Tiffany would say.

HOWARD. Believe me, I appreciate the confidence you repose in me!

GERTRUDE. Confidence! Truly, Colonel Howard, the *confidence* is entirely on your part, in supposing that I confide that which I have no reason to conceal! I think I informed you that Mrs. Tiffany only received visitors on her reception day—she is therefore not prepared to see you. Zeke—Oh! I beg his pardon—Adolph, made some mistake in admitting you.

HOWARD. Nay, Gertrude, it was not Mrs. Tiffany, nor Miss Tiffany, whom I came to see; it—it was—

GERTRUDE. The conservatory perhaps? I will leave you to examine the flowers at leisure! (*Crosses.*)

HOWARD. Gertrude—listen to me. (*Aside*) If I only dared to give utterance to what is hovering upon my lips! Gertrude!

GERTRUDE. Colonel Howard!

HOWARD. Gertrude, I must—must—

---

8 *voilà tout*—that's all.

GERTRUDE. Yes, indeed you *must,* must leave me! I think I hear somebody coming—Mrs. Tiffany would not be well pleased to find you here—pray, pray leave me—that door will lead you into the street. (*Hurries him out through door; takes up her watering pot, and commences watering flowers, tying up branches, etc.*) What a strange being is man! Why should he hesitate to say—nay, why should I prevent his saying, what I would most delight to hear? Truly man *is* strange—but woman is quite as incomprehensible! (*Walks about gathering flowers.*)

(*Enter* COUNT JOLIMAITRE.)

COUNT JOLIMAITRE. There she is—the bewitching little creature! Mrs. Tiffany and her daughter are out of earshot. I caught a glimpse of their feathers floating down Broadway, not ten minutes ago. Just the opportunity I have been looking for! Now for an engagement with this captivating little piece of prudery! 'Pon honor, I am almost afraid she will not resist a *Count* long enough to give value to the conquest. (*Approaching her*) Ma belle petite, were you gathering roses for me?

GERTRUDE (*starts on first perceiving him, but instantly regains her self-possession*). The roses here, Sir, are carefully guarded with thorns—if you have the right to gather, pluck for yourself!

COUNT JOLIMAITRE. Sharp as ever, little Gertrude! But now that we are alone, throw off this frigidity, and be at your ease.

GERTRUDE. Permit me to *be alone,* Sir, that I *may* be at my ease!

COUNT JOLIMAITRE. Very good, *ma belle,* well said! (*Applauding her with his hands*) Never yield too soon, even to a *title!* But as the old girl may find her way back before long, we may as well come to particulars at once. I love you; but that you know already. (*Rub-*

bing *his eyeglass unconcernedly with his handkerchief*) Before long I shall make Mademoiselle Seraphina my wife, and, of course, you shall remain in the family!

GERTRUDE (*indignantly*). Sir—

COUNT JOLIMAITRE. 'Pon my honor you shall! In France we arrange these little matters without difficulty!

GERTRUDE. But I am an *American!* Your conduct proves that you are not one! (*Going.*)

COUNT JOLIMAITRE (*preventing her*). Don't run away, my immaculate *petite Americaine!* Demme, you've quite overlooked my condescension—the difference of our stations—you a species of upper servant—an orphan—no friends.

(*Enter* TRUEMAN *unperceived.*)

GERTRUDE. And therefore more entitled to the respect and protection of every *true gentleman!* Had you been one, you would not have insulted me!

COUNT JOLIMAITRE. My charming little orator, patriotism and declamation become you particularly! (*Approaches her.*) I feel quite tempted to taste—

TRUEMAN (*thrusting him aside*). An American hickory-switch! (*Strikes him.*) Well, how do you like it?

COUNT JOLIMAITRE (*aside*). Old matter-of-fact! Sir, how dare you?

TRUEMAN. My stick has answered that question!

GERTRUDE. Oh! now I am quite safe!

TRUEMAN. Safe! not a bit safer than before! All women would be safe, if they knew how virtue became them! As for you, Mr. Count, what have you to say for yourself? Come, speak out!

COUNT JOLIMAITRE. Sir—aw—aw— you don't understand these matters!

TRUEMAN. That's a fact! Not having had *your* experience, I don't believe I *do* understand them!

COUNT JOLIMAITRE. A piece of pleasantry—a mere joke—

TRUEMAN. A joke was it? I'll show you a joke worth two of that! I'll teach you the way we natives joke with a puppy who don't respect an honest woman! (*Seizes him.*)

COUNT JOLIMAITRE. Oh! oh! demme —you old ruffian! let me go. What do you mean?

TRUEMAN. Oh! a piece of pleasantry —a mere joke—very pleasant isn't it? (*Attempts to strike him again; COUNT struggles with him. Enter MRS. TIFFANY hastily, in her bonnet and shawl.*)

MRS. TIFFANY. What *is* the matter? I am perfectly *abîmé* with terror. Mr. Trueman, what has happened?

TRUEMAN. Oh! we have been *joking!*

MRS. TIFFANY (*to COUNT, who is re-arranging his dress*). My dear Count, I did not expect to find you here—how kind of you!

TRUEMAN. Your *dear* Count has been showing his *kindness* in a very *foreign* manner. Too *foreign* I think, he found it to be relished by an *unfashionable native!* What do you think of a puppy, who insults an innocent girl all in the way of *kindness?* This Count of yours --this importation of—

COUNT JOLIMAITRE. My dear Madam, demme, permit me to explain. It would be unbecoming—demme—particular unbecoming of you—aw—aw— to pay any attention to this ignorant person. (*Crosses to TRUEMAN.*) Anything that he says concerning a man of my standing—aw—the truth is, Madam—

TRUEMAN. Let us have the truth by all means,—if it is only for the novelty's sake!

COUNT JOLIMAITRE (*turning his back to TRUEMAN*). You see, Madam, hoping to obtain a few moments' private conversation with Miss Seraphina—with *Miss Seraphina* I say and—aw—and

knowing her passion for flowers, I found my way to your very tasteful and *recherché*[9] conservatory. (*Looks about him approvingly.*) Very beautifully arranged—does you great credit, madam! Here I encountered this young person. She was inclined to be talkative; and I indulged her with—with a—aw—demme—a few *commonplaces!* What passed between us was mere *harmless badinage*—on *my* part. You, madam, you —so conversant with our European manners—you are aware that when a man of fashion—that is, when a woman —a man is bound—amongst noblemen, you know—

MRS. TIFFANY. I comprehend you perfectly — *parfittement* [parfaitement], my dear Count.

COUNT JOLIMAITRE (*aside*). 'Pon my honor, that's very obliging of her.

MRS. TIFFANY. I am shocked at the plebeian forwardness of this conceited girl!

TRUEMAN (*walking up to COUNT*). Did you ever keep a reckoning of the lies you tell in an hour?

MRS. TIFFANY. Mr. Trueman, I blush for you! (*Crosses to TRUEMAN.*)

TRUEMAN. Don't do that—you have no blushes to spare!

MRS. TIFFANY. It is a man of rank whom you are addressing, Sir!

TRUEMAN. A rank villain, Mrs. Antony Tiffany! A *rich one* he would be, had he as much *gold* as *brass!*

MRS. TIFFANY. Pray pardon him, Count; he knows nothing of how *ton!*

COUNT JOLIMAITRE. Demme, he's beneath my notice. I tell you what, old fellow—(TRUEMAN *raises his stick as* COUNT *approaches, the latter starts back.*) the sight of him discomposes me —aw—I feel quite uncomfortable—aw —let us join your charming daughter? I can't do you the honor to shoot you,

---

9 *recherché*—refined.

Sir—(*To* TRUEMAN) you are beneath me—a nobleman can't fight a commoner! Good bye, old Truepenny! I—aw—I'm insensible to your insolence!

(*Exeunt* COUNT *and* MRS. TIFFANY.)

TRUEMAN. You won't be insensible to a cow hide in spite of your nobility! The next time he practises any of his foreign fashions on you, Gertrude, you'll see how I'll wake up his sensibilities!

GERTRUDE. I do not know what I should have done without you, sir.

TRUEMAN. Yes, you do—you know that you would have done well enough! Never tell a lie, girl! not even for the sake of pleasing an old man! When you open your lips let your heart speak. Never tell a lie! Let your face be the looking-glass of your soul—your heart its clock—while your tongue rings the hours! But the glass must be clear, the clock true, and then there's no fear but the tongue will do its duty in a woman's head!

GERTRUDE. You are very good, Sir!

TRUEMAN. That's as it may be—(*Aside*) How my heart warms towards her! Gertrude, I hear that you have no mother?

GERTRUDE. Ah! no, Sir; I wish I had.

TRUEMAN (*aside, and with emotion*). So do I! Heaven knows, so do I! And you have no father, Gertrude?

GERTRUDE. No, Sir—I often wish I had!

TRUEMAN (*hurriedly*). Don't do that, girl! don't do that! Wish you had a mother—but never wish that you had a father again! Perhaps the one you had did not deserve such a child!

(*Enter* PRUDENCE.)

PRUDENCE. Seraphina is looking for you, Gertrude.

GERTRUDE. I will go to her. (*Crosses.*) Mr. Trueman, you will not permit me to thank you, but you cannot prevent my gratitude! (*Exit.*)

TRUEMAN (*looking after her*). If falsehood harbours there, I'll give up searching after truth!

(*Crosses, retires up the stage musingly, and commences examining the flowers.*)

PRUDENCE (*aside*). What a nice old man he is to be sure! I wish he would say something! (*Crosses, walks after him, turning when he turns—after a pause*) Don't mind *me*, Mr. Trueman!

TRUEMAN. Mind you? Oh! no, don't be afraid (*Crosses.*)—I wasn't minding you. Nobody seems to mind you much!

(*Continues walking and examining the flowers*—PRUDENCE *follows.*)

PRUDENCE. Very pretty flowers, ain't they? Gertrude takes care of them.

TRUEMAN. Gertrude? So I hear—(*Advancing*) I suppose you can tell me now who this Gertrude—

PRUDENCE. Who she's in love with? I *knew* you were going to say that! I'll tell you all about it! Gertrude, she's in love with—Mr. Twinkle! and he's in love with her. And Seraphina she's in love with Count Jolly—what-d' ye-call-it: but Count Jolly don't take to her at all—but Colonel Howard—he's the man—he's desperate about her!

TRUEMAN. Why you feminine newspaper! Howard in love with that quintessence of affectation! Howard—the only, frank, straightforward fellow that I've met since—I'll tell him my mind on the subject! And Gertrude hunting for happiness in a rhyming dictionary! The girl's a greater fool than I took her for!

PRUDENCE. So she is—you see I know all about them!

TRUEMAN. I see you do! You've a wonderful knowledge—wonderful—of *other people's concerns!* It may do here, but take my word for it, in the county of Catteraugus you'd get the name of a great *busy-body*. But perhaps you know that too?

PRUDENCE. Oh! I always know what's coming. I feel it beforehand all over me. I knew something was going to happen the day you came here——and what's more I can always tell a married man from a single—I felt right off that you were a bachelor!

TRUEMAN. Felt right off I was a bachelor did you? you were sure of it — sure? — quite sure? (PRUDENCE *assents delightedly*.) Then you felt wrong!—a bachelor and a widower are not the same thing!

PRUDENCE. Oh! but it all comes to the same thing—a widower's as good as a bachelor any day! And besides I knew that you were a farmer *right off*.

TRUEMAN. On the spot, eh? I suppose you saw cabbages and green peas growing out of my hat?

PRUDENCE. No, I didn't—but I knew all about you. And I knew—(*Looking down and fidgeting with her apron*) I knew you were for getting married soon! For last night I dream't I saw your funeral going along the streets, and the mourners all dressed in white. And a funeral is a sure sign of a wedding, you know! (*Nudges him with her elbow*.)

TRUEMAN (*imitating her voice*). Well I can't say that I *know* any such thing! you know! (*Nudges her back*.)

PRUDENCE. Oh! it does, and there's no getting over it! For my part, I like farmers—and I know all about setting hens and turkeys, and feeding chickens, and laying eggs, and all that sort of thing!

TRUEMAN (*aside*). May I be shot! if mistress newspaper is not putting in an advertisement for herself! This is your city mode of courting I suppose, ha, ha, ha!

PRUDENCE. I've been west, a little;

but I never was in the county of Catteraugus, myself.

TRUEMAN. Oh! you were not? And you have taken a particular fancy to go there, eh?

PRUDENCE. Perhaps I shouldn't object—

TRUEMAN. Oh!—ah!—so I suppose. Now pay attention to what I am going to say, for it is a matter of great importance to yourself.

PRUDENCE. Now it's coming— (*Aside*) I know what he's going to say!

TRUEMAN. The next time you want to tie a man for life to your apron-strings, pick out one that don't come from the county of Catteraugus—for greenhorns are scarce in those parts, and modest women plenty! (*Exit*.)

PRUDENCE. Now who'd have thought he was going to say that! But I won't give him up yet—I won't give him up. (*Exit*.)

ACT THREE

SCENE ONE

MRS. TIFFANY'S *Parlor. Enter* MRS. TIFFANY, *followed by* MR. TIFFANY.

TIFFANY. Your extravagance will ruin me, Mrs. Tiffany!

MRS. TIFFANY. And your stinginess will ruin me, Mr. Tiffany! It is totally and *toot a fate*[10] impossible to convince you of the necessity of *keeping up appearances*. There is a certain display which every woman of fashion is forced to make!

TIFFANY. And pray who made *you* a woman of fashion?

MRS. TIFFANY. What a vulgar ques-

[10] *tout à fait*—completely.

tion! All women of fashion, Mr. Tiffany—

TIFFANY. In this land are *self-constituted*, like you, Madam—and *fashion* is the cloak for more sins than charity ever covered! It was for *fashion's* sake that you insisted upon my purchasing this expensive house—it was for *fashion's* sake that you ran me in debt at every exorbitant upholsterer's and extravagant furniture warehouse in the city—it was for *fashion's* sake that you built that ruinous conservatory—hired more servants than they have persons to wait upon—and dressed your footman like a harlequin!

MRS. TIFFANY. Mr. Tiffany, you are thoroughly plebeian, and insufferably *American*, in your grovelling ideas! And, pray, what was the occasion of these very *mal-ap-pro-pos* remarks? Merely because I requested a paltry fifty dollars to purchase a new style of head-dress—a *bijou*[11] of an article just introduced in France.

TIFFANY. Time was, Mrs. Tiffany, when you manufactured your own French head-dresses—took off their first gloss at the public balls, and then sold them to your shortest-sighted customers. And all you knew about France, or French either, was what you spelt out at the bottom of your fashion plates— but now you have grown so fashionable, forsooth, that you have forgotten how to speak your mother tongue!

MRS. TIFFANY. Mr. Tiffany, Mr. Tiffany! Nothing is more positively vulgarian—more *unaristocratic* than any allusion to the past!

TIFFANY. Why I thought, my dear, that *aristocrats* lived principally upon the past—and traded in the market of fashion with the bones of their ancestors for capital?

MRS. TIFFANY. Mr. Tiffany, such

11 *bijou*—jewel.

vulgar remarks are only suitable to the counting house, in my drawing room you should—

TIFFANY. Vary my sentiments with my locality, as you change your *manners* with your *dress!*

MRS. TIFFANY. Mr. Tiffany, I desire that you will purchase Count d'Orsay's *Science of Etiquette,* and learn how to conduct yourself—especially before you appear at the grand ball, which I shall give on Friday!

TIFFANY. Confound your balls, Madam; they make *footballs* of my money, while you dance away all that I am worth! A pretty time to give a ball when you know that I am on the very brink of bankruptcy!

MRS. TIFFANY. So much the greater reason that nobody should suspect your circumstances, or you would lose your credit at once. Just at this crisis a ball is absolutely *necessary* to save your reputation! There is Mrs. Adolphus Dashaway—she gave the most splendid fête of the season—and I hear on very good authority that her husband has not paid his baker's bill in three months. Then there was Mrs. Honeywood—

TIFFANY. Gave a ball the night before her husband shot himself—perhaps you wish to drive me to follow his example?

MRS. TIFFANY. Good gracious! Mr. Tiffany, how you talk! I beg you won't mention anything of the kind. I consider black the most unbecoming color. I'm sure I've done all that I could to gratify you. There is that vulgar old torment, Trueman, who gives one the lie fifty times a day—haven't I been very civil to him?

TIFFANY. Civil to his *wealth,* Mrs. Tiffany! I told you that he was a rich, old farmer—the early friend of my father—my own benefactor—and that I had reason to think he might assist me in my present embarrassments. Your civility was *bought*—and like most of your *own* purchases has yet to be *paid* for.

MRS. TIFFANY. And will be, no doubt! The condescension of a woman of fashion should command any price. Mr. Trueman is insupportably indecorous—he has insulted Count Jolimaitre in the most outrageous manner. If the Count was not so deeply interested—so *abîmé* with Seraphina, I am sure he would never honor us by his visits again!

TIFFANY. So much the better—he shall never marry my daughter!—I am resolved on that. Why, Madam, I am told there is in Paris a regular matrimonial stock company, who fit out indigent dandies for this market. How do I know but this fellow is one of its creatures, and that he has come here to increase its dividends by marrying a fortune?

MRS. TIFFANY. Nonsense, Mr. Tiffany. The Count, the most fashionable young man in all New York—the intimate friend of all the dukes and lords in Europe—not marry my daughter? Not permit Seraphina to become a Countess? Mr. Tiffany, you are out of your senses!

TIFFANY. That would not be very wonderful, considering how many years I have been united to you, my dear. Modern physicians pronounce lunacy infectious!

MRS. TIFFANY. Mr. Tiffany, he is a man of fashion—

TIFFANY. Fashion makes fools, but cannot *feed* them. By the bye, I have a request—since you are bent upon ruining me by this ball, and there is no help for it—I desire that you will send an invitation to my confidential clerk, Mr. Snobson.

MRS. TIFFANY. Mr. Snobson! Was there ever such an *you-nick* demand! Mr. Snobson would cut a pretty figure amongst my fashionable friends! I shall do no such thing, Mr. Tiffany.

TIFFANY. Then, Madam, the ball shall not take place. Have I not told you that I am in the power of this man? That there are circumstances which it is happy for you that you do not know—which you cannot comprehend,—but which render it essential that you should be civil to Mr. Snobson? Not you merely, but Seraphina also? He is a more appropriate match for her than your foreign favorite.

MRS. TIFFANY. A match for Seraphina, indeed! (*Crosses.*) Mr. Tiffany, you are determined to make a *fow pas*.

TIFFANY. Mr. Snobson intends calling this morning.

MRS. TIFFANY. But, Mr. Tiffany, this is not reception day—my drawing-rooms are in the most terrible disorder—

TIFFANY. Mr. Snobson is not particular—he must be admitted.

(*Enter* ZEKE.)

ZEKE. Mr. Snobson.

(*Enter* SNOBSON, *exit* ZEKE.)

SNOBSON. How dye do, Marm? (*Crosses.*) How are you? Mr. Tiffany, your most!—

MRS. TIFFANY (*formally*). *Bung jure. Comment vow portè vow,*[12] *Monsur Snobson?*

SNOBSON. Oh, to be sure—very good of you—fine day.

MRS. TIFFANY (*pointing to a chair with great dignity*). *Sassoyez vow,*[13] *Monsur Snobson.*

SNOBSON. I wonder what she's driving at? I ain't up to the fashionable lingo yet! (*Aside*) Eh? what? Speak a little louder, Marm?

_____

[12] *comment vous portez-vous?*—how are you?

[13] *asseyez-vous*—be seated.

MRS. TIFFANY. What ignorance! (*Aside.*)

TIFFANY. I presume Mrs. Tiffany means that you are to take a seat.

SNOBSON. Exactly—very obliging of her—so I will. (*Sits.*) No ceremony amongst friends, you know—and likely to be nearer—you understand? *O. K.,* all correct. How *is* Seraphina?

MRS. TIFFANY. Miss Tiffany is not visible this morning.

SNOBSON. Not visible? (*Jumping up*) I suppose that's the English for can't see her? Mr. Tiffany, Sir—(*Walking up to him*) what am I to understand by this *de-fal-ca-tion,* Sir? I expected your word to be as good as your bond—beg pardon, Sir—I mean *better*—considerably better—no humbug about it, Sir.

TIFFANY. Have patience, Mr. Snobson. (*Rings bell.*)

(*Enter* ZEKE.)

Zeke, desire my daughter to come here.

MRS. TIFFANY (*coming down*). Adolph, — I say, Adolph — (ZEKE *straightens himself and assumes foppish airs, as he turns to* MRS. TIFFANY.)

TIFFANY. Zeke.

ZEKE. Don't know any such nigga, Boss.

TIFFANY. Do as I bid you instantly, or off with your livery and quit the house!

ZEKE. Wheugh! I'se all dismission! (*Exit.*)

MRS. TIFFANY. A-dolph, A-dolph! (*Calling after him.*)

SNOBSON (*aside*). I brought the old boy to his bearings, didn't I though! Pull that string, and he is sure to work right. Don't make any stranger of me, Marm—I'm quite at home. If you've got any odd jobs about the house to do up, I sha'nt miss you. I'll amuse myself with Seraphina when she comes—we'll get along very cosily by ourselves.

MRS. TIFFANY. Permit me to inform you, Mr. Snobson, that a French mother never leaves her daughter alone with a young man—she knows your sex too well for that!

SNOBSON. Very *dis*-obliging of her—but as we're none French—

MRS. TIFFANY. You have yet to learn, Mr. Snobson, that the American *ee-light*—the aristocracy—the *how-ton*—as a matter of conscience, scrupulously follow the foreign fashions.

SNOBSON. Not when they are foreign to their interests, Marm—for instance —(*Enter* SERAPHINA). There you are at last, eh, Miss? How d'ye do? Ma said you weren't visible. Managed to get a peep at her, eh, Mr. Tiffany?

SERAPHINA. I heard you were here, Mr. Snobson, and came without even arranging my toilette; you will excuse my negligence?

SNOBSON. Of everything but *me,* Miss.

SERAPHINA. I shall never have to ask your pardon for *that,* Mr. Snobson.

MRS. TIFFANY. Seraphina—child—really—

(*As she is approaching* SERAPHINA, MR. TIFFANY *plants himself in front of his wife.*)

TIFFANY. Walk this way, Madam, if you please. (*Aside*) To see that she fancies the surly fellow takes a weight from my heart.

MRS. TIFFANY. Mr. Tiffany, it is highly improper and not at all *distingué* to leave a young girl—

(*Enter* ZEKE.)

ZEKE. Mr. Count Jolly-made-her!

MRS. TIFFANY. Good gracious! The Count—Oh, dear!—Seraphina, run and change your dress,—no there's not time! A-dolph, admit him. (*Exit* ZEKE.) Mr. Snobson, get out of the way, will you? Mr. Tiffany, what are you doing at home at this hour?

(*Enter* COUNT JOLIMAITRE, *ushered by* ZEKE.)

ZEKE (*aside*). Dat's de genuine article ob a gemman. (*Exit.*)

MRS. TIFFANY. My dear Count, I am overjoyed at the very sight of you.

COUNT JOLIMAITRE. Flattered myself you'd be glad to see me, Madam—knew it was not your *jour de réception*.

MRS. TIFFANY. But for you, Count, all days—

COUNT JOLIMAITRE. I thought so. Ah, Miss Tiffany, on my honor, you're looking beautiful.

SERAPHINA. Count, flattery from you—

SNOBSON. What? Eh? What's that you say?

SERAPHINA (*aside to him*). Nothing but what etiquette requires.

COUNT JOLIMAITRE (*regarding* MR. TIFFANY *through his eyeglass*). Your worthy Papa, I believe? Sir, your most obedient.

(MR. TIFFANY *bows coldly;* COUNT *regards* SNOBSON *through his glass, shrugs his shoulders, and turns away.*)

SNOBSON (*to* MRS. TIFFANY). Introduce me, will you? I never knew a Count in all my life—what a strange-looking animal!

MRS. TIFFANY. Mr. Snobson, it is not the fashion to introduce in France!

SNOBSON. But, Marm, we're in America. (MRS. TIFFANY *crosses to* COUNT. *Aside*) The woman thinks she's somewhere else than where she is —she wants to make an *alibi?*

MRS. TIFFANY. I hope that we shall have the pleasure of seeing you on Friday evening, Count?

COUNT JOLIMAITRE. Really, madam, my invitations—my engagements—so numerous—I can hardly answer for myself: and you Americans take offence so easily—

MRS. TIFFANY. But, Count, everybody expects you at our ball—you are the principal attraction—

SERAPHINA. Count, you *must* come!

COUNT JOLIMAITRE. Since you insist —aw—aw—there's no resisting you, Miss Tiffany.

MRS. TIFFANY. I am so thankful. How can I repay your condescension! (COUNT *and* SERAPHINA *converse.*) Mr. Snobson, will you walk this way? —I have *such* a cactus in full bloom —remarkable flower! Mr. Tiffany, pray come here—I have something particular to say.

TIFFANY. Then speak out, my dear— (*Aside to her*) I thought it was highly improper just now to leave a girl with a young man?

MRS. TIFFANY. Oh, but the Count—that is different!

TIFFANY. I suppose you mean to say there's nothing of *the* man about him?

(*Enter* MILLINETTE *with a scarf in her hand.*)

MILLINETTE (*aside*). Adolph tell me he vas here. Pardon, Madame, I bring dis scarf for Mademoiselle.

MRS. TIFFANY. Very well, Millinette; you know best what is proper for her to wear.

(MR. *and* MRS. TIFFANY *and* SNOBSON *retire up; she engages the attention of both gentlemen.* MILLINETTE *crosses towards* SERAPHINA, *gives the* COUNT *a threatening look, and commences arranging the scarf over* SERAPHINA'S *shoulders.*)

MILLINETTE. Mademoiselle, *permettez-moi.* (*Aside to* COUNT) *Perfide!* If Mademoiselle vil stand *tranquille* one *petit moment.* (*Turns* SERAPHINA'S *back to the* COUNT, *and pretends to arrange the scarf. Aside to* COUNT) I must speak vid you to-day, or I tell all —you find me at de foot of de stair ven you go. *Prends garde!*[14]

---

14 *Prends garde!*—take care!

SERAPHINA. What is that you say, Millinette?

MILLINETTE. Dis scarf make you so very beautiful, Mademoiselle—*Je vous salue, mes dames. (Curtsies. Exit.)*

COUNT JOLIMAITRE (*aside*). Not a moment to lose! Miss Tiffany, I have an unpleasant—a particularly unpleasant piece of intelligence—you see, I have just received a letter from my friend—the—aw—the Earl of Airshire; the truth is, the Earl's daughter—beg you won't mention it—has distinguished me by a tender *penchant.*

SERAPHINA. I understand—and they wish you to return and marry the young lady; but surely you will not leave us, Count?

COUNT JOLIMAITRE. If *you* bid me stay—I shouldn't have the conscience —I couldn't *afford* to tear myself away. (*Aside*) I'm sure that's honest.

SERAPHINA. Oh, Count!

COUNT JOLIMAITRE. Say but one word —say that you shouldn't mind being made a Countess—and I'll break with the Earl to-morrow.

SERAPHINA. Count, this surprise— but don't think of leaving the country, Count—we could not pass the time without you! I—yes—yes, Count—I do consent!

COUNT JOLIMAITRE (*aside, while he embraces her*). I thought she would! Enchanted, rapture, bliss, ecstasy, and all that sort of thing—words can't express it, but you understand. But it must be kept a secret—positively it *must!* If the rumor of our engagement were whispered abroad—the Earl's daughter—the delicacy of my situation, aw—you comprehend? It is even possible that our nuptials, my charming Miss Tiffany, *our nuptials* must take place in private!

SERAPHINA. Oh, that is quite impossible!

COUNT JOLIMAITRE. It's the latest fashion abroad—the very latest. Ah, I knew that would determine you. Can I depend on your secrecy?

SERAPHINA. Oh, yes! Believe me.

SNOBSON (*coming forward in spite of* MRS. TIFFANY's *efforts to detain him*). Why, Seraphina, haven't you a word to throw to a dog?

TIFFANY (*aside*). I shouldn't think she had after wasting so many upon a puppy.

(*Enter* ZEKE, *wearing a three-cornered hat.*)

ZEKE. Missus, de bran-new carriage am below.

MRS. TIFFANY. Show it up—I mean, Very well, A-dolph. (*Exit* ZEKE.) Count, my daughter and I are about to take an airing in our new *voyture,* —will you honor us with your company?

COUNT JOLIMAITRE. Madam, I—I have a most *pressing* engagement. A letter to write to the *Earl of Airshire*— who is at present residing in the *Isle of Skye.* I must bid you good morning.

MRS. TIFFANY. Good morning, Count. (*Exit* COUNT.)

SNOBSON. *I'm* quite at leisure (*Crosses to* MRS. TIFFANY.) Marm. Books balanced—ledger closed—nothing to do all the afternoon,—I'm for you.

MRS. TIFFANY (*without noticing him*). Come, Seraphina, come!

(*As they are going,* SNOBSON *follows them.*)

SNOBSON. But, Marm—I was saying, Marm, I am quite at leisure—not a thing to do; have I, Mr. Tiffany?

MRS. TIFFANY. Seraphina, child— your red shawl—remember—Mr. Snobson, *bon swear!*

(*Exit, leading* SERAPHINA.)

SNOBSON. Swear! Mr. Tiffany, Sir, am I to be fobbed off with a *bon swear?* D — n it, I will swear!

TIFFANY. Have patience, Mr. Snobson, if you will accompany me to the counting house—

SNOBSON. Don't count too much on me, Sir. I'll make up no more accounts until these are settled! I'll run down and jump into the carriage in spite of her *bon swear.* (*Exit.*)

TIFFANY. You'll jump into a hornet's nest, if you do! Mr. Snobson, Mr. Snobson! (*Exit after him.*)

SCENE TWO

Housekeeper's room. Enter MILLINETTE.

———

MILLINETTE. I have set dat *bête,*[15] Adolph, to vatch for him. He say he would come back so soon as Madame's *voiture* drive from de door. If he not come—but he vill—he vill—he *bien étourdi,*[16] but he have *bon coeur.*[17] (*Enter* COUNT.)

COUNT JOLIMAITRE. Ah! Millinette, my dear, you see what a good-natured dog I am to fly at your bidding—

MILLINETTE. Fly? Ah! *trompeur!*[18] Vat for you fly from Paris? Vat for you leave me—and I love you so much? Ven you sick—you almost die—did I not stay by you—take care of you—and you have no else friend? Vat for you leave Paris?

COUNT JOLIMAITRE. Never allude to disagreeable subjects, *mon enfant!* I was forced by uncontrollable circumstances to fly to the land of liberty—

MILLINETTE. Vat you do vid all de money I give you? The last sou I had —did I not give you?

COUNT JOLIMAITRE (*aside*). I dare

———
15 *bête*—beast.
16 *bien étourdi*—quite a scatter-brain.
17 *bon coeur*—a good heart.
18 *trompeur*—deceiver.

say you did, *ma petite*—wish you'd been better supplied! Don't ask any questions here—can't explain now— the next time we meet—

MILLINETTE. But, ah! ven shall ve meet—ven? You not deceive me, not any more.

COUNT JOLIMAITRE. Deceive you! I'd rather deceive myself—I wish I could! (*Aside*) I'd persuade myself you were once more washing linen in the Seine!

MILLINETTE. I vil tell you ven ve shall meet—On Friday night Madame give one grand ball—you come *sans doute*—den ven de supper is served— de Americans tink of noting else ven de supper come—den you steal out of de room, and you find me here—and you give me one grand *explanation!* (*Enter* GERTRUDE, *unperceived.*)

COUNT JOLIMAITRE. Friday night— while supper is serving—*parole d'honneur* I will be here—I will explain every thing—my sudden departure from Paris—my—demme, my countship—every thing! Now let me go—if any of the family should discover us—

GERTRUDE (*who during the last speech has gradually advanced*). They might discover more than you think it advisable for them to know!

COUNT JOLIMAITRE. The devil!

MILLINETTE. *Mon Dieu!* Mademoiselle Gertrude!

COUNT JOLIMAITRE (*recovering himself*). My dear Miss Gertrude, let me explain—aw—aw—nothing is more natural than the situation in which you find me—

GERTRUDE. I am inclined to believe that, Sir.

COUNT JOLIMAITRE. Now—'pon my honor, that's not fair. Here is Millinette will bear witness to what I am about to say—

GERTRUDE. Oh, I have not the slightest doubt of that, Sir.

COUNT JOLIMAITRE. You see, Millinette happened to be lady's-maid in the family of—of—the Duchess Château d'Espagne—and I chanced to be a particular friend of the Duchess— *very particular* I assure you! Of course I saw Millinette, and she, demme, she saw me! Didn't you, Millinette?

MILLINETTE. Oh! *oui*—Mademoiselle, I knew him ver' vell.

COUNT JOLIMAITRE. Well, it is a remarkable fact that—being in correspondence with this very Duchess—at this very time—

GERTRUDE. That is sufficient, Sir—I am already so well acquainted with your extraordinary talents for improvisation, that I will not further tax your invention—

MILLINETTE. Ah! Mademoiselle Gertrude do not betray us—have pity!

COUNT (*assuming an air of dignity*). Silence, Millinette! My word has been doubted—the word of a nobleman! I will inform my friend, Mrs. Tiffany, of this young person's audacity. (*Going.*)

GERTRUDE. His own weapons alone can foil this villain! (*Aside*) Sir—Sir —Count! (*At last word the* COUNT *turns.*) Perhaps, Sir, the least said about this matter the better!

COUNT JOLIMAITRE (*delightedly*). The least said? We won't say anything at all. She's coming round—couldn't resist me. (*Aside*) Charming Gertrude—

MILLINETTE. *Quoi?* Vat that you say?

COUNT JOLIMAITRE (*aside to her*). My sweet, adorable Millinette, hold your tongue, will you?

MILLINETTE (*aloud*). No, I vill not! If you do look so from.out your eyes at her again, I vill tell all!

COUNT JOLIMAITRE (*aside*). Oh, I never could manage two women at once,—jealousy makes the dear creatures so spiteful. The only valor is in flight! Miss Gertrude, I wish you good morning. Millinette, *mon enfant, adieu.* (*Exit.*)

MILLINETTE. But I have one word more to say. Stop, Stop! (*Exit after him.*)

GERTRUDE (*musingly*). Friday night, while supper is serving, he is to meet Millinette here and explain—what? This man is an impostor! His insulting me—his familiarity with Millinette— his whole conduct—prove it. If I tell Mrs. Tiffany this she will disbelieve me, and one word may place this so-called Count on his guard. To convince Seraphina would be equally difficult, and her rashness and infatuation may render her miserable for life. No—she shall be saved! I must devise some plan for opening their eyes. Truly, if I *cannot* invent one, I shall be the first woman who was ever at a loss for a stratagem—especially to punish a villain or to shield a friend. (*Exit.*)

ACT FOUR

SCENE ONE

Ballroom splendidly illuminated. A curtain hung at the further end. MR. *and* MRS. TIFFANY, SERAPHINA, GERTRUDE, FOGG, TWINKLE, COUNT, SNOBSON, COLONEL HOWARD, *a number of guests—some seated, some standing. As the curtain rises, a cotillion is danced;* GERTRUDE *dancing with* HOWARD, SERAPHINA *with* COUNT.

COUNT JOLIMAITRE (*advancing with* SERAPHINA *to the front of the stage*). To-morrow then—to-morrow—I may salute you as my bride—demme, my

Countess!

(*Enter* ZEKE, *with refreshments.*)

SERAPHINA. Yes, to-morrow.

(*As the* COUNT *is about to reply,* SNOBSON *thrusts himself in front of* SERAPHINA.)

SNOBSON. You said you'd dance with me, Miss—now take my fin, and we'll walk about and see what's going on.

(COUNT *raises his eyeglass, regards* SNOBSON, *and leads* SERAPHINA *away;* SNOBSON *follows, endeavoring to attract her attention, but encountering* ZEKE, *bearing a waiter of refreshments; stops him, helps himself, and puts some in his pockets.*)

Here's the treat! get my to-morrow's luncheon out of Tiff.

(*Enter* TRUEMAN, *yawning and rubbing his eyes.*)

TRUEMAN. What a nap I've had, to be sure! (*Looks at his watch.*) Eleven o'clock, as I'm alive! Just the time when country folks are comfortably *turned in,* and here your grand *turnout* has hardly begun yet. (*To* TIFFANY, *who approaches.*)

GERTRUDE (*advancing*). I was just coming to look for you, Mr. Trueman. I began to fancy that you were paying a visit to dream-land.

TRUEMAN. So I was, child—so I was —and I saw a face—like yours—but brighter!—even brighter. (*To* TIFFANY) There's a smile for you, man! It makes one feel that the world has something worth living for in it yet! Do you remember a smile like that, Antony? Ah! I see you don't—but I do—I do! (*Much moved.*)

HOWARD (*advancing*). Good evening, Mr. Trueman. (*Offers his hand.*)

TRUEMAN. That's right, man; give me your whole hand! When a man offers me the tips of his fingers, I know at once there's nothing in him worth seeking beyond his fingers' ends.

(TRUEMAN *and* HOWARD, GERTRUDE *and* TIFFANY *converse.*)

MRS. TIFFANY (*advancing*). I'm in such a fidget lest that vulgar old fellow should disgrace us by some of his plebeian remarks! What it is to give a ball, when one is forced to invite vulgar people!

(MRS. TIFFANY *advances towards* TRUEMAN; SERAPHINA *stands conversing flippantly with the gentlemen who surround her; amongst them is* TWINKLE, *who having taken a magazine from his pocket, is reading to her, much to the undisguised annoyance of* SNOBSON.)

Dear me, Mr. Trueman, you are very late—quite in the fashion, I declare!

TRUEMAN. Fashion! And pray what is *fashion,* madam? An agreement between certain persons to live without using their souls! to substitute etiquette for virtue—decorum for purity—manners for morals! to affect a shame for the works of their Creator! and expend all their rapture upon the works of their tailors and dressmakers!

MRS. TIFFANY. You have the most *ow-tray* ideas, Mr. Trueman—quite rustic, and deplorably *American!* But pray walk this way.

(MRS. TIFFANY *and* TRUEMAN *go up stage.*)

COUNT JOLIMAITRE (*advancing to* GERTRUDE, HOWARD *a short distance behind her*). Miss Gertrude—no opportunity of speaking to you before— in demand you know!

GERTRUDE (*aside*). I have no choice, I must be civil to him. What were you remarking, Sir?

COUNT JOLIMAITRE. Miss Gertrude— charming Ger—(*Aside*) Aw—aw—I never found it so difficult to speak to a woman before.

GERTRUDE. Yes, a very charming ball —many beautiful faces here.

COUNT JOLIMAITRE. Only one!—aw —aw—one—the fact is—(*Talks to her in dumb show.*)

HOWARD. What could old Trueman have meant by saying she fancied that puppy of a Count—that paste jewel thrust upon the little finger of society.

COUNT JOLIMAITRE. Miss Gertrude— aw—'pon my honor—you don't understand — really — aw — aw — will you dance the polka with me?

(GERTRUDE *bows and gives him her hand; he leads her to the set forming;* HOWARD *remains looking after them.*)

HOWARD. Going to dance with him too! A few days ago she would hardly bow to him civilly—could old Trueman have had reasons for what he said? (*Retires up.*)

(*Dance, the polka;* SERAPHINA, *after having distributed her bouquet, vinaigrette, and fan amongst the gentlemen, dances with* SNOBSON.)

PRUDENCE (*peeping in as dance concludes*). I don't like dancing on Friday; something strange is always sure to happen! I'll be on the look out. (*Remains peeping and concealing herself when any of the company approach.*)

GERTRUDE (*advancing hastily*). They are preparing the supper—now if I can only dispose of Millinette while I unmask this insolent pretender! (*Exit.*)

PRUDENCE (*peeping*). What's that she said? It's coming!

(*Re-enter* GERTRUDE, *bearing a small basket filled with bouquets; approaches* MRS. TIFFANY; *they walk to the front of the stage.*)

GERTRUDE. Excuse me, Madam—I believe this is just the hour at which you ordered supper?

MRS. TIFFANY. Well, what's that to you! So you've been dancing with the Count—how dare you dance with a nobleman—*you?*

GERTRUDE. I will answer that question half an hour hence. At present I have something to propose, which I think will gratify you and please your guests. I have heard that at the most elegant balls in Paris, it is customary—

MRS. TIFFANY. What? what?

GERTRUDE. To station a servant at the door with a basket of flowers. A bouquet is then presented to every lady as she passes in—I prepared this basket a short time ago. As the company walk in to supper, might not the flowers be distributed to advantage?

MRS. TIFFANY. How *distingué!* You are a good creature, Gertrude—there, run and hand the *bokettes* to them yourself! You shall have the whole credit of the thing.

GERTRUDE (*aside*). Caught in my own net! But, Madam, *I* know so little of fashions—Millinette, being French herself, will do it with so much more grace. I am sure Millinette—

MRS. TIFFANY. So am I. She will do it a thousand times better than you —there go call her.

GERTRUDE (*giving basket*). But, Madam, pray order Millinette not to leave her station till supper is ended—as the company pass out of the supper room she may find that some of the ladies have been overlooked.

MRS. TIFFANY. That is true—very thoughtful of you, Gertrude. (*Exit* GERTRUDE.) What a *recherché* idea! (*Enter* MILLINETTE.) Here, Millinette, take this basket. Place yourself there, and distribute these *bokettes* as the company pass in to supper; but remember not to stir from the spot until supper is over. It is a French fashion you know, Millinette. I am so delighted to be the first to introduce it—it will be all the rage in the *bow-monde!*

MILLINETTE (*aside*). *Mon Dieu!* dis vill ruin all! Madame, Madame, let me tell you, Madame, dat in France, in Paris, it is de custom to present *les bouquets* ven every body first come—long before de supper. Dis vould be *outré! barbare!* not at all *la mode!* Ven dey do come in—dat is de fashion in Paris!

MRS. TIFFANY. Dear me! Millinette, what is the difference? besides I'd have you to know that Americans always improve upon French fashions! here, take the basket, and let me see that you do it in the most *you-nick* and genteel manner.

(MILLINETTE *poutingly takes the basket and retires up stage. A march. Curtain hung at the further end of the room is drawn back, and discloses a room, in the centre of which stands a supper table, beautifully decorated and illuminated; the company promenade two by two into the supper room;* MILLINETTE *presents bouquets as they pass;* COUNT *leads* MRS. TIFFANY.)

TRUEMAN (*encountering* FOGG, *who is hurrying alone to the supper room*). Mr. Fogg, never mind the supper, man! Ha, ha! ha! Of course you are indifferent to suppers!

FOGG. Indifferent! suppers—oh, ah —no, Sir—suppers? no—no—I'm not indifferent to suppers! (*Hurries away towards table.*)

TRUEMAN. Ha, ha, ha! Here's a new discovery I've made in the fashionable world! Fashion don't permit the critters to have *heads* or *hearts,* but it allows them stomachs! (*To* TIFFANY, *who advances*) So it's not fashionable to *feel,* but it's fashionable to *feed,* eh, Antony? ha, ha, ha!

(TRUEMAN *and* TIFFANY *retire towards supper room. Enter* GERTRUDE, *followed by* ZEKE.)

GERTRUDE. Zeke, go to the supper room instantly—whisper to Count Joli-maitre that all is ready, and that he must keep his appointment without delay—then watch him, and as he pass-es out of the room, place yourself in front of Millinette in such a manner, that the Count cannot see her nor she him. Be sure that they do not see each other—every thing depends upon that. (*Crosses.*)

ZEKE. Missey, consider dat business brought to a scientific conclusion. (*Exit into supper room.*)

(*Exit* GERTRUDE.)

PRUDENCE (*who has been listening*). What can she want of the Count? I always suspected that Gertrude, because she is so merry and busy! Mr. Trueman thinks so much of her too—I'll tell him this! There's something wrong—but it all comes of giving a ball on a Friday! How astonished the dear old man will be when he finds out how much I know! (*Advances timidly towards the supper room.*)

SCENE TWO

Housekeeper's room; dark stage; table, two chairs. Enter GERTRUDE, *with a lighted candle in her hand.*

———

GERTRUDE. So far the scheme prospers! And yet this imprudence—if I fail? Fail! to lack courage in a difficulty, or ingenuity in a dilemma, are not woman's failings!

(*Enter* ZEKE, *with a napkin over his arm, and a bottle of champagne in his hand.*)

Well, Zeke—Adolph!

ZEKE. Dat's right, Missey; I feels just now as if dat was my legitimate title; dis here's de stuff to make a nigger feel like a gemman!

GERTRUDE. But he is coming?

ZEKE. He's coming! (*Sound of a champagne cork heard.*) Do you hear dat, Missey? Don't it put you all in a froth, and make you feel as light as a cork? Dere's nothing like the *union brand,* to wake up de harmonies ob de heart. (*Drinks from bottle.*)

GERTRUDE. Remember to keep watch upon the outside—do not stir from the spot; when I call you, come in quickly with a light—now, will you be gone!

ZEKE. I'm off, Missey, like a champagne cork wid de strings cut. (*Exit.*)

GERTRUDE. I think I hear the Count's step. (*Crosses, stage dark; she blows out candle.*) Now if I can but disguise my voice, and make the best of my French. (*Enter* COUNT.)

COUNT JOLIMAITRE. Millinette, where are you? How am I to see you in the dark?

GERTRUDE (*imitating* MILLINETTE'S *voice in a whisper*). Hush! *parle bas.*[19]

COUNT JOLIMAITRE. Come here and give me a kiss.

GERTRUDE. *Non—non* (*Retreating alarmed,* COUNT *follows.*) make haste, I must know all.

COUNT JOLIMAITRE. You did not use to be so deuced particular.

ZEKE (*without*). No admission, gemman! Box office closed, tickets stopped!

TRUEMAN (*without*). Out of my way; do you want me to try if your head is as hard as my stick?

GERTRUDE. What shall I do? Ruined, ruined! (*She stands with her hands clasped in speechless despair.*)

COUNT JOLIMAITRE. Halloa! they are coming here, Millinette! Millinette, why don't you speak? Where can I hide myself? (*Running about stage, feeling for a door.*) Where are all your closets? If I could only get out—or get in somewhere; may I be smothered in a clothes' basket, if you ever catch me in such a scrape again! (*His hand accidentally touches the knob of a door opening into a closet.*) Fortune's favorite yet! I'm safe! (*Gets into closet and closes door.*)

(*Enter* PRUDENCE, TRUEMAN, MRS.

[19] *parle bas*—speak low.

TIFFANY, *and* COLONEL HOWARD, *followed by* ZEKE, *bearing a light; lights up.*)

PRUDENCE. Here they are, the Count and Gertrude! I told you so! (*Stops in surprise on seeing only* GERTRUDE.)

TRUEMAN. And you see what a lie you told!

MRS. TIFFANY. Prudence, how dare you create this disturbance in my house? To suspect the Count too—a nobleman!

HOWARD. My sweet Gertrude, this foolish old woman would—

PRUDENCE. Oh! you needn't talk—I heard her make the appointment—I know he's here—or he's been here. I wonder if she hasn't hid him away! (*Runs peeping about the room.*)

TRUEMAN (*following her angrily*). You're what I call a confounded—troublesome—meddling—old—prying—(*As he says the last word,* PRUDENCE *opens closet where the* COUNT *is concealed.*) Thunder and lightning!

PRUDENCE. I told you so.

(*They all stand aghast;* MRS. TIFFANY, *with her hands lifted in surprise and anger;* TRUEMAN, *clutching his stick;* HOWARD, *looking with an expression of bewildered horror from the* COUNT *to* GERTRUDE.)

MRS. TIFFANY (*shaking her fist at* GERTRUDE). You depraved little minx! this is the meaning of your dancing with the Count!

COUNT JOLIMAITRE (*stepping from the closet and advancing*). I don't know what to make of it! Millinette not here! Miss Gertrude—oh! I see—a disguise—the girl's desperate about me—the way with them all.

TRUEMAN. I'm choking—I can't speak—Gertrude—no—no—it is some horrid mistake! (*Partly aside, changes his tone suddenly.*) The villain! I'll hunt the truth out of him, if there's any in—(*Crosses, approaches* COUNT *threateningly.*) Do you see this stick? You made its first acquaintance a few days ago; it is time you were better known to each other. (*As* TRUEMAN *attempts to seize him,* COUNT *escapes, and shields himself behind* MRS. TIFFANY, TRUEMAN *following.*)

COUNT JOLIMAITRE. You ruffian! would you strike a woman?—Madam —my dear Madam—keep off that barbarous old man, and I will explain! Madam, with—aw—your natural *bon gout*—aw—your fashionable refinement —aw—your—aw—your knowledge of *foreign customs*—

MRS. TIFFANY. Oh! Count, I hope it ain't a *foreign custom* for the nobility to shut themselves up in the dark with young women? We think such things *dreadful* in *America.*

COUNT JOLIMAITRE. Demme—aw— hear what I have to say, Madam—I'll satisfy all sides—I am perfectly innocent in this affair—'pon my honor I am! That young lady shall inform you that I am so herself!—can't help it, sorry for her. (*Aside*) Old matter-of-fact won't be convinced any other way, —that club of his is so particularly unpleasant! Madam, I was summoned here *malgré moi,*[20] and not knowing whom I was to meet—Miss Gertrude, favor the company by saying whether or not you directed—that—aw—aw— that colored individual to conduct me here?

GERTRUDE. Sir, you well know—

COUNT JOLIMAITRE. A simple yes or no will suffice.

MRS. TIFFANY. Answer the Count's question instantly, Miss.

GERTRUDE. I did—but—

COUNT JOLIMAITRE. You hear, Madam—

TRUEMAN. I won't believe it—I can't!

—————
[20] *malgré moi*—despite myself.

Here, you (*to Zeke*), stop rolling up your eyes, and let us know whether she told you to bring that critter here?

ZEKE. I'se refuse to gib ebidence; dat's de device ob de skilfullest counsels of de day! Can't answer, Boss—neber git a word out ob dis child—Yah! yah! (*Exit.*)

GERTRUDE. Mrs. Tiffany—Mr. Trueman, if you will but have patience—

TRUEMAN. Patience! Oh, Gertrude, you've taken from an old man something better and dearer than his patience—the one bright hope of nineteen years of self-denial—of nineteen years of— (*Throws himself upon a chair, his head leaning on table.*)

MRS. TIFFANY. Get out of my house, you *owdacious*—you ruined—you *abîmé* young woman!— You will corrupt all my family. Good gracious! don't touch me,—don't come near me. Never let me see your face after to-morrow. Pack. (*Goes up.*)

HOWARD. Gertrude, I have striven to find some excuse for you—to doubt—to disbelieve—but this is beyond all endurance! (*Exit.*)

(*Enter* MILLINETTE *in haste.*)

MILLINETTE. I could not come before —(*Stops in surprise at seeing the persons assembled.*) Mon Dieu! vat does dis mean?

COUNT JOLIMAITRE (*aside to her*). Hold your tongue, fool! You will ruin everything, I will explain to-morrow. Mrs. Tiffany—Madam—my dear Madam, let me conduct you back to the ball-room. (*She takes his arm.*) You see I am quite innocent in this matter; a man of my standing, you know,—aw, aw—you comprehend the whole affair. (*Exit* COUNT *leading* MRS. TIFFANY.)

MILLINETTE. I will say to him von vord, I will! (*Exit.*)

GERTRUDE. Mr. Trueman, I beseech you—I insist upon being heard,—I claim it as a right!

TRUEMAN. Right? How dare you have the face, girl, to talk of rights? (*Comes down.*) You had more rights than you thought for, but you have forfeited them all! All right to love, respect, protection, and to not a little else that you don't dream of. Go, go! I'll start for Catteraugus to-morrow,—I've seen enough of what fashion can do! (*Exit.*)

PRUDENCE (*wiping her eyes*). Dear old man, how he takes on! I'll go and console him! (*Exit.*)

GERTRUDE. This is too much! How heavy a penalty has my imprudence cost me!—his esteem, and that of one dearer—my home—my— (*Burst of lively music from ball-room.*) They are dancing, and I—I should be weeping, if pride had not sealed up my tears. (*She sinks into a chair. Band plays the polka behind, till Curtain falls.*)

ACT FIVE

SCENE ONE

MRS. TIFFANY'S *drawing room— same scene as Act One.* GERTRUDE *seated at a table, with her head leaning on her hand; in the other hand she holds a pen. A sheet of paper and an inkstand before her.*

——

GERTRUDE. How shall I write to them? What shall I say? Prevaricate I cannot—(*Rises and comes forward.*) and yet if I write the truth—simple souls! how can they comprehend the motives for my conduct? Nay—the truly pure see no imaginary evil in others! It is only vice, that reflecting its own image, suspects even the innocent. I have no time to lose—I must prepare them for my return. (*Resumes her seat and writes.*) What a true pleasure there is in daring to be frank! (*After writing a few lines more, pauses.*) Not so frank either,—there is one name that I cannot mention. Ah! that he should suspect—should despise me. (*Writes.*)

(*Enter* TRUEMAN.)

TRUEMAN. There she is! If this girl's soul had only been as fair as her face, —yet she dared to speak the truth,—I'll not forget that! A woman who refuses to tell a lie has one spark of heaven in her still. (*Approaches her.*) Gertrude (GERTRUDE *starts and looks up.*), what are you writing there? Plotting more mischief, eh, girl?

GERTRUDE. I was writing a few lines to some friends in Geneva.

TRUEMAN. The Wilsons, eh?

GERTRUDE (*surprised, rising*). Are you acquainted with them, Sir?

TRUEMAN. I shouldn't wonder if I was. I suppose you have taken good care not to mention the dark room— that foreign puppy in the closet—the pleasant surprise—and all that sort of thing, eh?

GERTRUDE. I have no reason for concealment, Sir! for I have done nothing of which I am ashamed!

TRUEMAN. Then I can't say much for your modesty.

GERTRUDE. I should not wish you to say more than I deserve.

TRUEMAN (*aside*). There's a bold minx!

GERTRUDE. Since my affairs seem to have excited your interest—I will not say *curiosity,* perhaps you even feel a desire to inspect my correspondence? There (*Handing the letter*) I pride myself upon my good nature,—you may like to take advantage of it?

TRUEMAN (*aside*). With what an air she carries it off! Take advantage of it?

So I will. (*Reads.*) What's this? "French chambermaid—Count—impostor—infatuaticn—Seraphina — Millinette—disguised myself—expose him." Thunder and lightning! I see it all! Come and kiss me, girl! (GERTRUDE *evinces surprise.*) No, no—I forgot—it won't do to come to that yet! She's a rare girl! I'm out of my senses with joy! I don't know what to do with myself! Tol, de rol, de rol, de ra. (*Capers and sings.*)

GERTRUDE (*aside*). What a remarkable old man! Then you do me justice, Mr. Trueman?

TRUEMAN. I say I don't! Justice? You're above all dependence upon justice! Hurrah! I've found one true woman at last? *True?* (*Pauses thoughtfully.*) Humph! I didn't think of that flaw! Plotting and manoeuvering—not much truth in that? An honest girl should be above stratagems!

GERTRUDE. But my *motive*, Sir, was good.

TRUEMAN. That's not enough—your *actions* must be *good* as well as your *motives!* Why could you not tell the silly girl that man was an impostor?

GERTRUDE. I did inform her of my suspicions—she ridiculed them; the plan I chose was an imprudent one, but I could not devise—

TRUEMAN. I hate devising! Give me a woman with the *firmness* to be *frank!* But no matter—I had no right to look for an angel out of Paradise; and I am as happy—as happy as a Lord! that is, ten times happier than any Lord ever was! Tol, de rol, de rol! Oh! you—you—I'll thrash every fellow that says a word against you!

GERTRUDE. You will have plenty of employment then, Sir, for I do not know of one just now who would speak in my favor!

TRUEMAN. Not *one*, eh? Why, where's your dear Mr. Twinkle? I know all about it—can't say that I admire your choice of a husband! But there's no accounting for a girl's taste.

GERTRUDE. Mr. Twinkle! Indeed you are quite mistaken!

TRUEMAN. No—really? Then you're not taken with him, eh?

GERTRUDE. Not even with his rhymes.

TRUEMAN. Hang that old mother meddle-much! What a fool she has made of me. And so you're quite free, and I may choose a husband for you myself? Heart-whole, eh?

GERTRUDE. I—I—I trust there is nothing *unsound* about my heart.

TRUEMAN. There it is again. Don't prevaricate, girl! I tell you an *evasion* is a *lie in contemplation,* and I hate lying! Out with the truth! Is your heart *free* or not?

GERTRUDE. Nay, Sir, since you *demand* an answer, permit *me* to demand by what right you ask the question?

(*Enter* HOWARD.)

Colonel Howard here!

TRUEMAN. I'm out again! What's the Colonel to her? (*Retires up.*)

HOWARD (*crosses to her*). I have come, Gertrude, to bid you farewell. To-morrow I resign my commission and leave this city, perhaps for ever. You, Gertrude, it is you who have exiled me! After last evening—

TRUEMAN (*coming forward to* HOWARD). What the plague have you got to say about last evening?

HOWARD. Mr. Trueman!

TRUEMAN. What have you got to say about last evening? and what have you to say to that little girl at all? It's Tiffany's precious daughter you're in love with.

HOWARD. Miss Tiffany? Never! I never had the slightest pretension—

TRUEMAN. That lying old woman! But I'm glad of it! Oh! Ah! Um!

(*Looks significantly at* GERTRUDE *and then at* HOWARD.) I see how it is. So you don't choose to marry Seraphina, eh? Well now, whom do you choose to marry? (*Glancing at* GERTRUDE.)

HOWARD. I shall not marry at all!

TRUEMAN. You won't? (*Looks at them both again.*) Why, you don't mean to say that you don't like— (*Points with his thumb to* GERTRUDE.)

GERTRUDE. Mr. Trueman, I may have been wrong to boast of my good nature, but do not presume too far upon it.

HOWARD. You like frankness, Mr. Trueman, therefore I will speak plainly. I have long cherished a dream from which I was last night rudely awakened.

TRUEMAN. And that's what you call speaking plainly? Well, I differ with you! But I can guess what you mean. Last night you suspected Gertrude there of—(*Angrily*) of what no man shall ever suspect her again while I'm above ground! You did her injustice— it was a mistake! There, now that matter's settled. Go, and ask her to forgive you—she's woman enough to do it! Go, go!

HOWARD. Mr. Trueman, you have forgotten to whom you dictate.

TRUEMAN. Then you won't do it? you won't ask her pardon?

HOWARD. Most undoubtedly I will not—not at any man's bidding. I must first know—

TRUEMAN. You won't do it? Then if I don't give you a lesson in politeness—

HOWARD. It will be because you find me your *tutor* in the same science. I am not a man to brook an insult, Mr. **Trueman! but we'll not quarrel in presence of the lady.**

TRUEMAN. Won't we? I don't know that—

GERTRUDE. Pray, Mr. Trueman— Colonel Howard, pray desist, Mr.

Trueman, for my sake! (*Takes hold of his arm to hold him back.*) Colonel Howard, if you will read this letter it will explain everything. (*Hands letter to* HOWARD, *who reads.*)

TRUEMAN. He don't deserve an explanation! Didn't I tell him that it was a mistake? Refuse to beg your pardon! I'll teach him, I'll teach him!

HOWARD (*after reading*). Gertrude, how have I wronged you!

TRUEMAN. Oh, you'll beg her pardon now? (*Between them.*)

HOWARD. Hers, Sir, and yours! Gertrude, I fear—

TRUEMAN. You needn't—she'll forgive you. You don't know these women as well as I do,—they're always ready to pardon; it's their nature, and they can't help it. Come along, I left Antony and his wife in the dining room; we'll go and find them. I've a story of my own to tell! As for you, Colonel, you may follow. Come along. Come along! (*Leads out* GERTRUDE, *followed by* HOWARD.)

(*Enter* MR. *and* MRS. TIFFANY, MR. TIFFANY *with a bundle of bills in his hand.*)

MRS. TIFFANY. I beg you won't mention the subject again, Mr. Tiffany. Nothing is more plebeian than a discussion upon economy—nothing more *ungenteel* than looking over and fretting over one's bills!

TIFFANY. Then I suppose, my dear, it is quite as ungenteel to *pay* one's bills?

MRS. TIFFANY. Certainly! I hear the *ee-light* never condescend to do anything of the kind. The honor of their invaluable patronage is sufficient for the persons they employ!

TIFFANY. *Patronage* then is a newly invented food upon which the working classes fatten? What convenient appetites poor people must have! Now listen to what I am going to say. As soon as my daughter marries Mr. Snobson—

(*Enter* PRUDENCE, *a three-cornered note in her hand.*)

PRUDENCE. Oh, dear! oh, dear! what shall we do! Such a misfortune! Such a disaster! Oh, dear! oh, dear!

MRS. TIFFANY. Prudence, you are the most tiresome creature! What *is* the matter?

PRUDENCE (*pacing up and down the stage*). Such a disgrace to the whole family! But I always expected it. Oh, dear! oh, dear!

MRS. TIFFANY (*following her up and down the stage*). What are you talking about, Prudence? Will you tell me what has happened?

PRUDENCE (*still pacing*, MRS. TIFFANY *following*). Oh! I can't, I can't! You'll feel so dreadfully! How could she do such a thing! But I expected nothing else! I never did, I never did!

MRS. TIFFANY (*still following*). Good gracious! what do you mean, Prudence? Tell me, will you tell me? I shall get into such a passion! What *is* the matter?

PRUDENCE (*still pacing*). Oh, Betsy, Betsy! That your daughter should have come to that! Dear me, dear me!

TIFFANY. Seraphina? Did you say Seraphina? What has happened to her? What has she done? (*Following* PRUDENCE *up and down the stage on the opposite side from* MRS. TIFFANY.)

MRS. TIFFANY (*still following*). What has she done? what *has* she done?

PRUDENCE. Oh! something dreadful—dreadful—shocking!

TIFFANY (*still following*). Speak quickly and plainly—you torture me by this delay—Prudence, be calm, and speak! What is it?

PRUDENCE (*stopping*). Zeke just told me—he carried her travelling trunk

himself—she gave him a whole dollar! Oh, my!

TIFFANY. Her trunk? where? where?

PRUDENCE. Round the corner!

MRS. TIFFANY. What did she want with her trunk? You are the most vexatious creature, Prudence! There is no bearing your ridiculous conduct!

PRUDENCE. Oh, you will have worse to bear—worse! Seraphina's gone!

TIFFANY. Gone! where?

PRUDENCE. Off!—eloped—eloped with the Count! Dear me, dear me! I always told you she would!

TIFFANY. Then I am ruined! (*Stands with his face buried in his hands.*)

MRS. TIFFANY. Oh, what a ridiculous girl! And she might have had such a splendid wedding! What could have possessed her?

TIFFANY. The devil himself possessed her, for she has ruined me past all redemption! Gone, Prudence, did you say gone? Are you *sure* they are gone?

PRUDENCE. Didn't I tell you so! Just look at this note—one might know by the very fold of it—

TIFFANY (*snatching the note*). Let me see it! (*Opens the note and reads.*) "My dear Ma—When you receive this I shall be a *countess!* Isn't it a sweet title? The Count and I were forced to be married privately, for reasons which I will explain in my next. You must pacify Pa, and put him in a good humour before I come back, though now I'm to be a countess I suppose I shouldn't care!" Undutiful huzzy! "We are going to make a little excursion and will be back in a week.

"Your dutiful daughter—Seraphina."

A man's curse is sure to spring up at his own hearth—here is mine! The sole curb upon that villain gone, I am wholly in his power! Oh! the first downward step from honor—he who takes it cannot pause in his mad descent and is sure to be hurried on to ruin!

MRS. TIFFANY. Why, Mr. Tiffany, how you do take on! And I dare say to elope was the most fashionable way after all!

(*Enter* TRUEMAN, *leading* GERTRUDE, *and followed by* HOWARD.)

TRUEMAN. Where are all the folks? Here, Antony, you are the man I want. We've been hunting for you all over the house. Why—what's the matter? There's a face for a thriving city merchant! Ah! Antony, you never wore such a hang-dog look as that when you trotted about the country with your pack upon your back! Your shoulders are no broader now—but they've a heavier load to carry—that's plain!

MRS. TIFFANY. Mr. Trueman, such allusions are highly improper! What would my daughter, *the Countess,* say!

GERTRUDE. The Countess? Oh! Madam!

MRS. TIFFANY. Yes, the Countess! My daughter Seraphina, the Countess *dee* Jolimaitre! What have you to say to that? No wonder you are surprised after your *recherché, abîmé* conduct! I have told you already, Miss Gertrude, that you were not a proper person to enjoy the inestimable advantages of my patronage. You are dismissed—do you understand? Discharged!

TRUEMAN. Have you done? Very well, it's my turn now. Antony, perhaps what I have to say don't concern you as much as some others—but I want you to listen to me. You remember, Antony (*His tone becomes serious.*), a blue-eyed, smiling girl—

TIFFANY. Your daughter, Sir? I remember her well.

TRUEMAN. None ever saw her to forget her! Give me your hand, man. There—that will do! Now let me go on. I never coveted wealth—yet twenty

years ago I found myself the richest farmer in Catteraugus. This cursed money made my girl an object of speculation. Every idle fellow that wanted to feather his nest was sure to come courting Ruth. There was one—my heart misgave me the instant I laid eyes upon him—for he was a city chap, and not over fond of the truth. But Ruth—ah! she was too pure herself to look for guile! His fine words and his fair looks—the old story—she was taken with him—I said, "no"—but the girl liked her own way better than her old father's—girls always do! and one morning—the rascal robbed me—not of my money, he would have been welcome to that—but of the only treasure I cherished—my daughter!

TIFFANY. But you forgave her!

TRUEMAN. I did! I knew she would never forgive herself—that was punishment enough! The scoundrel thought he was marrying my gold with my daughter—he was mistaken! I took care that they should never want; but that was all. She loved him—what will not woman love? The villain broke her heart—mine was tougher, or it wouldn't have stood what it did. A year after they were married, he forsook her! She came back to her old home—her old father! It couldn't last long—she pined—and pined—and—then—she died! Don't think me an old fool—though I am one—for grieving won't bring her back. (*Bursts into tears.*)

TIFFANY. It was a heavy loss!

TRUEMAN. So heavy, that I should not have cared how soon I followed her, but for the child she left! As I pressed that child in my arms, I swore that my unlucky wealth should never curse it, as it had cursed its mother! It was all I had to love—but I sent it away—and the neighbors thought it was dead. The girl was brought up tenderly but humbly by my wife's relatives in Geneva. I had her taught true independence—she had hands—capacities—and should use them! Money should never buy her a husband! for I resolved not to claim her until she had made her choice, and found the man who was willing to take her for herself alone. She turned out a rare girl! and it's time her old grandfather claimed her. Here he is to do it! And there stands Ruth's child! Old Adam's heiress! Gertrude, Gertrude!—my child! (GERTRUDE *rushes into his arms.*)

PRUDENCE (*after a pause*). Do tell; I want to know! But I knew it! I always said Gertrude would turn out somebody, after all!

MRS. TIFFANY. Dear me! Gertrude an heiress! My dear Gertrude, I always thought you a very charming girl—quite *you-nick*—an heiress! (*Aside*) I must give her a ball! I'll introduce her into society myself—of course an heiress must make a sensation!

HOWARD (*aside*). I am too bewildered even to wish her joy. Ah! there will be plenty to do that now—but the gulf between us is wider than ever.

TRUEMAN. Step forward, young man, and let us know what you are muttering about. I said I would never claim her until she had found the man who loved her for herself. I *have* claimed her—yet I never break my word—I think I *have* found that man! and here he is. (*Strikes* HOWARD *on the shoulder.*) Gertrude's yours! There—never say a word, man—don't bore me with your thanks—you can cancel all obligations by making that child happy! There—take her!—Well, girl, and what do you say?

GERTRUDE. That I rejoice too much at having found a parent for my first act to be one of disobedience! (*Gives*

her hand to HOWARD.)

TRUEMAN. How very dutiful! and how disinterested!

(TIFFANY *paces the stage, exhibiting great agitation.*)

PRUDENCE (*to* TRUEMAN). All the *single folks* are getting married!

TRUEMAN. No they are not. You and I are single folks, and we're not likely to get married.

MRS. TIFFANY. My dear Mr. Trueman—my sweet Gertrude, when my daughter, the Countess, returns, she will be delighted to hear of this *deenooment!* I assure you that the Countess will be quite charmed!

GERTRUDE. The Countess? Pray, Madam, where *is* Seraphina?

MRS. TIFFANY. The Countess *dee* Jolimaitre, my dear, is at this moment on her way to—to Washington! Where after visiting all the fashionable curiosities of the day—including the President—she will return to grace her native city!

GERTRUDE. I hope you are only jesting, Madam? Seraphina is not married?

MRS. TIFFANY. Excuse me, my dear, my daughter had this morning the honor of being united to the Count *dee* Jolimaitre!

GERTRUDE. Madam! He is an impostor!

MRS. TIFFANY. Good gracious! Gertrude, how can you talk in that disrespectful way of a man of rank? An heiress, my dear, should have better manners! The Count—

(*Enter* MILLINETTE, *crying.*)

MILLINETTE. Oh! Madame! I will tell **everyting — oh! dat *monstre!* He break my heart!**

MRS. TIFFANY. Millinette, what is the matter?

MILLINETTE. Oh! he promise to marry me—I love him much—and now

Zeke say he run away vid Mademoiselle Seraphina!

MRS. TIFFANY. What insolence! The girl is mad! Count Jolimaitre marry my *femmy de chamber!*

MILLINETTE. Oh! Madame, he is not one Count, not at all! Dat is only de title he go by in dis country. De foreigners always take de large title ven dey do come here. His name *à Paris* vas Gustave Treadmill. But he not one Frenchman at all, but he do live one long time *à Paris.* First he live vid Monsieur Vermicelle—dere he vas de head cook! Den he live vid Monsieur Tire-nez, de barber! After dat he live wid Monsieur le Comte Frippon-fin— and dere he vas le Comte's valet! Dere, now I tell everyting I feel one great deal better!

MRS. TIFFANY. Oh! good gracious! I shall faint! Not a Count! What will everybody say? It's no such thing! I say he *is* a Count! One can see the foreign *jenny says quoi* in his face! Don't you think I can tell a Count when I see one? I say he *is* a Count!

(*Enter* SNOBSON, *his hat on—his hands thrust in his pocket—evidently a little intoxicated.*)

SNOBSON. I won't stand it! I say I won't!

TIFFANY (*rushing up to him, aside*). Mr. Snobson, for heaven's sake—

SNOBSON. Keep off! I'm a hard customer to get the better of! You'll see if I don't come out strong!

TRUEMAN (*quietly knocking off* SNOBSON's *hat with his stick*). Where are your manners, man?

SNOBSON. My business ain't with you, Catteraugus; you've waked up the wrong passenger!—Now the way I'll put it into Tiff will be a caution. I'll make him wince! That extra mint julep has put the true pluck in me.

(*Aside*) Now for it! Mr. Tiffany, Sir —you needn't think to come over me, Sir—you'll have to get up a little earlier in the morning before you do *that,* Sir! I'd like to know, Sir, how you came to assist your daughter in running away with that foreign loafer? It was a downright swindle, Sir. After the conversation I and you had on that subject she wasn't your property, Sir.

TRUEMAN. What, Antony, is that the way your city clerk bullies his boss?

SNOBSON. You're drunk, Catteraugus —don't expose yourself—you're drunk! Taken a little too much toddy, my old boy! Be quiet! I'll look after you, and they won't find it out. If you want to be busy, you may take care of my *hat* —I feel so deuced weak in the chest, I don't think I *could* pick it up myself. —(*Aside*) Now to put the screws to Tiff. Mr. Tiffany, Sir—you have broken your word, as no virtuous individual—no honorable member—of— the—com—mu—ni—ty—

TIFFANY. Have some pity, Mr. Snobson, I beseech you! I had nothing to do with my daughter's elopement! (*Aside to him*) I will agree to anything you desire—your salary shall be doubled—trebled—

SNOBSON (*aloud*). No you don't. No bribery and corruption.

TIFFANY. I implore you to be silent. (*Aside to him*) You shall become partner of the concern, if you please —only do not speak. You are not yourself at this moment.

SNOBSON. Ain't I, though? I feel *twice* myself. I feel like two Snobsons rolled into one, and I'm chock full of the spunk of a dozen! Now Mr. Tiffany, Sir—

TIFFANY. I shall go distracted! (*Aside to him*) Mr. Snobson, if you have one spark of manly feeling—

TRUEMAN. Antony, why do you stand

disputing with that drunken jackass? **Where's your servant? Let him kick the critter out, and be of use for once in his life.**

SNOBSON. Better be quiet, Catteraugus. This ain't your hash, so keep your spoon out of the dish. Don't expose yourself, old boy.

TRUEMAN. Turn him out, Antony!

SNOBSON. He daren't do it! Ain't I up to him? Ain't he in my power? Can't I knock him into a cocked hat with a word? And now he's got my steam up—I *will* do it!

TIFFANY (*beseechingly*). Mr. Snobson—my friend—

SNOBSON. It's no go—steam's up—and I don't stand at anything!

TRUEMAN. You won't *stand* here long unless you mend your manners—you're not the first man I've *upset* because he didn't know his place.

SNOBSON. I know where Tiff's place is, and that's in the *States' Prison!* It's bespoke already. He would have it! He wouldn't take pattern of me, and behave like a gentleman! He's a *forger,* Sir! (TIFFANY *throws himself into a chair in an attitude of despair; the others stand transfixed with astonishment.*) He's been forging Dick Anderson's endorsements of his notes these ten months. He's got a couple in the bank that will send him to the wall anyhow—if he can't make a raise. I took them there myself! Now you know what he's worth. I said I'd expose him, and I have done it!

MRS. TIFFANY. Get out of the house! You ugly little drunken brute, get out! It's not true. Mr. Trueman, put him out; you have got a stick—put him out!

(*Enter* SERAPHINA, *in her bonnet and shawl—a parasol in her hand.*)

SERAPHINA. I hope Zeke hasn't delivered my note. (*Stops in surprise at seeing the persons assembled.*)

MRS. TIFFANY. Oh, here is the Countess! (*Advances to embrace her.*)

TIFFANY (*starting from his seat, and seizing* SERAPHINA *violently by the arm*). Are—you—married?

SERAPHINA. Goodness, Pa, how you frighten me! No, I'm not married, quite.

TIFFANY. Thank heaven.

MRS. TIFFANY (*drawing* SERAPHINA *aside*). What's the matter? Why did you come back?

SERAPHINA. The clergyman wasn't at home—I came back for my jewels—the Count said nobility couldn't get on without them.

TIFFANY. I may be saved yet! Seraphina, my child, you will not see me disgraced—ruined! I have been a kind father to you—at least I have tried to be one—although your mother's extravagance made a *madman* of me! The Count is an impostor—you seemed to like him—(*Pointing to* SNOBSON. *Aside*) Heaven forgive me! Marry *him* and save *me.* You, Mr. Trueman, you will be my friend in this hour of extreme need—you will advance the sum which I require—I pledge myself to return it. My wife—my child—who will support them were I—the thought makes me frantic! You will aid me? You had a child yourself.

TRUEMAN. But I did not *sell* her—it was her own doings. Shame on you, Antony! Put a price on your own flesh and blood! Shame on such foul traffic!

TIFFANY. Save me—I conjure you—for my father's sake.

TRUEMAN. For your *father's son's* sake I will *not* aid you in becoming a greater villain than you are!

GERTRUDE. Mr. Trueman—Father, I should say—save him—do not embitter our happiness by permitting this calamity to fall upon another—

TRUEMAN. Enough—I did not need

your voice, child. I am going to settle this matter my own way. (*Goes up to* SNOBSON—*who has seated himself and fallen asleep—tilts him out of the chair.*)

SNOBSON (*waking up*). Eh? Where's the fire?' Oh! it's you, Catteraugus.

TRUEMAN. If I comprehend aright, you have been for some time aware of your principal's forgeries? (*As he says this, he beckons to* HOWARD, *who advances as witness.*)

SNOBSON. You've hit the nail, Catteraugus! Old chap saw that I was up to him six months ago; left off throwing dust into my eyes—

TRUEMAN. Oh, he did!

SNOBSON. Made no bones of forging Anderson's name at my elbow.

TRUEMAN. Forged at your elbow? You saw him do it?

SNOBSON. I did.

TRUEMAN. Repeatedly.

SNOBSON. Re—pea—ted—ly.

TRUEMAN. Then you, Rattlesnake, if he goes to the States' Prison, you'll take up your quarters there too. You are an accomplice, an *accessory!*

(TRUEMAN *walks away and seats himself;* HOWARD *rejoins* GERTRUDE. SNOBSON *stands for some time bewildered.*)

SNOBSON. The deuce, so I am! I never thought of that! I must make myself scarce. I'll be off! Tif, I say, Tif! (*Going up to him and speaking confidentially*) that drunken old rip has got us in his power. Let's give him the slip and be off. They want men of genius at the West—we're sure to get on! You—you can set up for a writing master, and teach copying *signatures;* and I—I'll give lectures on *temperance!* You won't come, eh? Then I'm off without you. Good bye, Catteraugus! Which is the way to California? (*Steals off.*)

TRUEMAN. There's one debt your city owes me. And now let us see what other nuisances we can abate. Antony, I'm not given to preaching, therefore I shall not say much about what you have done. Your face speaks for itself, —the crime has brought its punishment along with it.

TIFFANY. Indeed it has, Sir! In one *year* I have lived a *century* of misery.

TRUEMAN. I believe you, and upon one condition I will assist you—

TIFFANY. My friend—my first, ever kind friend—only name it!

TRUEMAN. You must sell your house and all these gew gaws, and bundle your wife and daughter off to the country. There let them learn economy, true independence, and home virtues, instead of foreign follies. As for yourself, continue your business—but let moderation, in future, be your counsellor, and let *honesty* be your confidential clerk.

TIFFANY. Mr. Trueman, you have made existence once more precious to me! My wife and daughter shall quit the city tomorrow, and—

PRUDENCE. It's all coming right! It's all coming right! We'll go to the county of Catteraugus. (*Walks up to* TRUEMAN.)

TRUEMAN. No, you won't,—I make that a stipulation, Antony; keep clear of Catteraugus. None of your fashionable examples there!

(JOLIMAITRE *appears in the conservatory and peeps into the room unperceived.*)

COUNT JOLIMAITRE. What can detain Seraphina? We ought to be off!

MILLINETTE (*turns round, perceives him, runs and forces him into the room*). Here he is! Ah, Gustave, mon cher Gustave! I have you now and we never part no more. Don't frown, Gustave, don't frown—

TRUEMAN. Come forward, Mr.

Count! and for the edification of fashionable society confess that you're an impostor.

COUNT JOLIMAITRE. An impostor? Why, you abominable old—

TRUEMAN. Oh, your feminine friend has told us all about it, the cook—the valet—barber and all that sort of thing. Come, confess, and something may be done for you.

COUNT JOLIMAITRE. Well, then, I do confess I am no count; but really, ladies and gentlemen, I may recommend myself as the most capital cook.

MRS. TIFFANY. Oh, Seraphina!

SERAPHINA. Oh, Ma! (*They embrace and retire up stage.*)

TRUEMAN. Promise me to call upon the whole circle of your fashionable acquaintances with your own advertisements and in your cook's attire, and I will set you up in business to-morrow. Better turn stomachs than turn heads!

MILLINETTE. But you will marry me?

COUNT JOLIMAITRE. Give us your hand, Millinette! Sir, command me for the most delicate *pâté*—the daintiest *croquette à la royale*—the most transcendent *omelette soufflée* that ever issued from a French pastrycook's oven. I hope you will pardon my conduct, but I heard that in America, where you pay homage to titles while you profess to scorn them—where *Fashion* makes the basest coin current—where you have no kings, no princes, no *nobility*—

TRUEMAN. Stop there! I object to your use of that word. When justice is found only among lawyers—health **among physicians — and patriotism** among politicians, *then* may you say that there is no *nobility* where there are no titles! But we *have* kings, princes, and nobles in abundance—of *Nature's stamp*, if not of *Fashion's*— we have honest men, warmhearted and brave, and we have women—gentle, fair, and true, to whom no *title* could add *nobility*.

UNCLE TOM'S CABIN

George L. Aiken
Based on the novel by Harriet Beecher Stowe.

Produced for the first time at the Troy (New York) Museum in 1852.

UNCLE TOM	QUIMBO
GEORGE HARRIS	DOCTOR
GEORGE SHELBY	WAITER
ST. CLARE	HARRY
PHINEAS FLETCHER	EVA
GUMPTION CUTE	ELIZA
MR. WILSON	MARIE
DEACON PERRY	CASSY
SHELBY	OPHELIA
HALEY	CHLOE
LEGREE	TOPSY
TOM LOKER	ADOLF
MARKS	MANN
SAMBO	SKEGGS

ACT ONE

SCENE ONE

Plain chamber. Enter ELIZA, *meeting* GEORGE HARRIS.

———

ELIZA. Ah! George, is it you? Well, I am so glad you've come. (GEORGE HARRIS *regards her mournfully.*) Why don't you smile, and ask after Harry?

GEORGE HARRIS (*bitterly*). I wish he'd never been born!—I wish I'd neven been born myself!

ELIZA (*sinking her head upon his breast and weeping*). Oh George!

GEORGE HARRIS. There now, Eliza, it's too bad for me to make you feel so. Oh! how I wish you had never seen me—you might have been happy!

ELIZA. George! George! how can you talk so? What dreadful thing has happened, or is going to happen? I'm sure we've been very happy till lately.

GEORGE HARRIS. So we have, dear. But oh! I wish I'd never seen you, nor you me.

ELIZA. Oh, George! how can you?

GEORGE HARRIS. Yes, Eliza, it's all misery! misery! The very life is burning out of me! I'm a poor, miserable, forlorn drudge! I shall only drag you down with me, that's all! What's the use of our trying to do anything—trying to know anything—trying to be anything? I wish I was dead!

ELIZA. Oh! now, dear George, that is really wicked. I know how you feel about losing your place in the factory, and you have a hard master; but pray be patient—

GEORGE HARRIS. Patient! Haven't I been patient? Did I say a word when he came and took me away—for no earthly reason—from the place where everybody was kind to me? I'd paid him truly every cent of my earnings, and they all say I worked well.

ELIZA. Well, it *is* dreadful; but, after all, he is your master you know.

GEORGE HARRIS. My master! And who made him my master? That's what I think of. What right has he to me? I'm as much a man as he is! What right has he to make a dray-horse of me?—to take me from things I can do better than he can, and put me to work that any horse can do? He tries to do it; he says he'll bring me down and humble me, and he puts me to just the hardest, meanest, and dirtiest work, on purpose.

ELIZA. Oh, George! George! you frighten me. Why, I never heard you talk so. I'm afraid you'll do something dreadful. I don't wonder at your feelings at all; but oh! do be careful—for my sake, for Harry's.

GEORGE HARRIS. I have been careful, and I have been patient, but it's growing worse and worse—flesh and blood can't bear it any longer. Every chance he can get to insult and torment me he takes. He says that though I don't say anything, he sees that I've got the devil in me, and he means to bring it out; and one of these days it will come out, in a way that he won't like, or I'm mistaken.

ELIZA. Well, I always thought that I must obey my master and mistress, or I couldn't be a Christian.

GEORGE HARRIS. There is some sense in it in your case. They have brought you up like a child—fed you, clothed you, and taught you, so that you have a good education—that is some reason why they should claim you. But I have been kicked and cuffed and sworn at, and what do I owe? I've paid for all my keeping a hundred times over. I won't bear it!—no, I *won't!* Master will find out that I'm one whipping won't tame. My day will come yet, if he don't look out!

ELIZA. What are you going to do? Oh! George, don't do anything wicked; if you only trust in heaven and try to to do right, it will deliver you.

GEORGE HARRIS. Eliza, my heart's full of bitterness. I can't trust in heaven. Why does it let things be so?

ELIZA. Oh, George! we must all have faith. Mistress says that when all things go wrong to us, we must believe that heaven is doing the very best.

GEORGE HARRIS. That's easy for people to say who are sitting on their sofas and riding in their carriages; but let them be where I am—I guess it would come some harder. I wish I could be good; but my heart burns and can't be reconciled. You couldn't, in my place, you can't now, if I tell you all I've got to say; you don't know the whole yet.

ELIZA. What do you mean?

GEORGE HARRIS. Well, lately my master has been saying that he was a fool to let me marry off the place—that he hates Mr. Shelby and all his tribe—and he says he won't let me come here any more, and that I shall take a wife and settle down on his place.

ELIZA. But you were married to *me* by the minister, as much as if you had been a white man.

GEORGE HARRIS. Don't you know I can't hold you for my wife if he chooses to part us? That is why I wish I'd never seen you—it would have been better for us both—it would have been better for our poor child if he had never been born.

ELIZA. Oh! but my master is so kind.

GEORGE HARRIS. Yes, but who knows? —he may die, and then Harry may be sold to nobody knows who. What pleasure is it that he is handsome and smart and bright? I tell you, Eliza, that a sword will pierce through your soul for every good and pleasant thing your child is or has. It will make him worth too much for you to keep.

ELIZA. Heaven forbid!

GEORGE HARRIS. So, Eliza, my girl, bear up now, and good-by, for I'm going.

ELIZA. Going, George! Going where?

GEORGE HARRIS. To Canada; and when I'm there I'll buy you—that's all the hope that's left us. You have a kind master that won't refuse to sell you. I'll buy you and the boy—heaven helping me, I will!

ELIZA. Oh, dreadful! If you should be taken?

GEORGE HARRIS. I won't be taken, Eliza—I'll *die* first! I'll be free, or I'll die.

ELIZA. You will not kill yourself?

GEORGE HARRIS. No need of that; they will kill me, fast enough. I will never go down the river alive.

ELIZA. Oh, George! for my sake, do be careful. Don't lay hands on yourself, or anybody else. You are tempted too much, but don't. Go, if you must, but go carefully, prudently, and pray heaven to help you!

GEORGE HARRIS. Well, then, Eliza, hear my plan. I'm going home quite resigned, you understand, as if all was over. I've got some preparations made, and there are those that will help me; and in the course of a few days I shall be among the missing. Well, now, good-by.

ELIZA. A moment—our boy.

GEORGE HARRIS (*choked with emotion*). True, I had forgotten him; one last look, and then farewell!

ELIZA. And heaven grant it be not forever! (*Exeunt.*)

Scene Two

A dining room. Table and chairs

center. Dessert, wine, etc., on table.
SHELBY *and* HALEY *discovered at table.*

———

SHELBY. That is the way I should arrange the matter.

HALEY. I can't make trade that way —I positively can't, Mr. Shelby. (*Drinks.*)

SHELBY. Why, the fact is, Haley, Tom is an uncommon fellow! He is certainly worth that sum anywhere— steady, honest, capable, manages my whole farm like a clock!

HALEY. You mean honest, as niggers go. (*Fills glass.*)

SHELBY. No; I mean, really, Tom is a good, steady, sensible, pious fellow. He got religion at a camp-meeting, four years ago, and I believe he really *did* get it. I've trusted him since then, with every thing I have—money, house, horses, and let him come and go round the country, and I always found him true and square in everything.

HALEY. Some folks don't believe there is pious niggers, Shelby, but *I* do. I had a fellow, now, in this yer last lot I took to Orleans—'twas as good as a meetin' now, really, to hear that critter pray; and he was quite gentle and quiet like. He fetched me a good sum, too, for I bought him cheap of a man that was 'bliged to sell out, so I realized six hundred on him. Yes, I consider religion a valeyable thing in a nigger, when it's the genuine article and no mistake.

SHELBY. Well, Tom's got the real article, if ever a fellow had. Why, last fall I let him go to Cincinnati alone, to do business for me and bring home five hundred dollars. "Tom," says I to him, "I trust you, because I think you are a Christian—I know you wouldn't cheat." Tom comes back sure enough, I knew he would. Some low fellows, they say, said to him—"Tom, why don't you make tracks for Canada?" "Ah, master trusted me, and I couldn't," was his answer. They told me all about it. I am sorry to part with Tom, I must say. You ought to let him cover the whole balance of the debt and you would, Haley, if you had any conscience.

HALEY. Well, I've got just as much conscience as any man in business can afford to keep, just a little, you know, to swear by, as 'twere; and then I'm ready to do anything in reason to 'blige friends, but this yer, you see, is a leetle too hard on a fellow—a leetle too hard!

SHELBY. Well, then, Haley, how will you trade?

HALEY. Well, haven't you a boy or a girl that you could throw in with Tom?

SHELBY. Hum! none that I could well spare; to tell the truth, it's only hard necessity makes me willing to sell at all. I don't like parting with any of my hands, that's a fact.

(HARRY *runs in.*)

Hulloa! Jim Crow! (*Throws a bunch of raisins towards him.*) Pick that up now!

(HARRY *does so.*)

HALEY. Bravo, little 'un! (*Throws an orange, which* HARRY *catches. He sings and dances around the stage.*) Hurrah! Bravo! What a young 'un! That chap's a case, I'll promise. Tell you what, Shelby, fling in that chap, and I'll settle the business. Come, now, if that ain't doing the thing up about the rightest!

(ELIZA *enters. Starts on beholding* HALEY, *and gazes fearfully at* HARRY, *who runs and clings to her dress, showing the orange, etc.*)

SHELBY. Well, Eliza?

ELIZA. I was looking for Harry, please, sir.

SHELBY. Well, take him away, then.

(ELIZA *grasps the child eagerly in her*

arms, and casting another glance of apprehension at HALEY, *exits hastily.*)

HALEY. By Jupiter! there's an article, now. You might make your fortune on that ar gal in Orleans any day. I've seen over a thousand in my day paid down for gals not a bit handsomer.

SHELBY. I don't want to make my fortune on her. Another glass of wine. (*Fills the glasses.*)

HALEY (*drinks and smacks his lips*). Capital wine—first chop. Come, how will you trade about the gal? What shall I say for her? What'll you take?

SHELBY. Mr. Haley, she is not to be sold. My wife wouldn't part with her for her weight in gold.

HALEY. Ay, ay! women always say such things, 'cause they hain't no sort of calculation. Just show 'em how many watches, feathers, and trinkets one's weight in gold would buy, and that alters the case, I reckon.

SHELBY. I tell you Haley, this must not be spoken of—I say no, and I mean no.

HALEY. Well, you'll let me have the boy, tho'; you must own that I have come down pretty handsomely for him.

SHELBY. What on earth can you want with the child?

HALEY. Why, I've got a friend that's going into this yer branch of the business—wants to buy up handsome boys to raise for the market. Well, what do you say?

SHELBY. I'll think the matter over and talk with my wife.

HALEY. Oh, certainly, by all means; but I'm in a devil of a hurry and shall want to know as soon as possible what I may depend on. (*Rises and puts on his overcoat, which hangs on a chair. Takes hat and whip.*)

SHELBY. Well, call up this evening, between six and seven, and you shall have my answer.

HALEY. All right. Take care of yourself, old boy! (*Exits.*)

SHELBY. If anybody had ever told me that I should sell Tom to those rascally traders, I should never have believed it. Now it must come for aught I see, and Eliza's child too. So much for being in debt, heigho! The fellow sees his advantage and means to push it. (*Exits.*)

SCENE THREE

Snowy landscape. UNCLE TOM'S *cabin.—Snow on roof. Practicable door and window. Dark stage. Music.*

———

ELIZA (*enters hastily, with* HARRY *in her arms*). My poor boy! they have sold you, but your mother will have you yet! (*Goes to cabin and taps on window.*)

CHLOE (*appears at window with a large white nightcap on*). Good Lord! what's that? My sakes alive if it ain't Lizy! Get on your clothes, old man, quick! I'm gwine to open the door.

(*The door opens and* CHLOE *enters followed by* UNCLE TOM *in his shirt sleeves holding a tallow candle.*)

TOM (*holding the light towards* ELIZA). Lord bless you! I'm skeered to look at ye, Lizy! Are ye tuck sick, or what's come over ye?

ELIZA. I'm running away, Uncle Tom and Aunt Chloe, carrying off my child! Master sold him!

TOM *and* CHLOE. Sold him!

ELIZA. Yes, sold him! I crept into the closet by mistress' door tonight and heard master tell mistress that he had sold my Harry and you, Uncle Tom, both, to a trader, and that the man was to take possession tomorrow.

CHLOE. The good lord have pity on us! Oh! it don't seem as if it was true. What has he done that master should sell *him?*

ELIZA. He hasn't done anything—it isn't for that. Master don't want to sell, and mistress—she's always good. I heard her plead and beg for us, but he told her 'twas no use—that he was in this man's debt, and he had got the power over him, and that if he did not pay him off clear, it would end in his having to sell the place and all the people and move off.

CHLOE. Well, old man, why don't you run away, too? Will you wait to be toted down the river, where they kill niggers with hard work and starving? I'd a heap rather die than go there, any day! There's time for ye, be off with Lizy—you've got a pass to come and go any time. Come, bustle up, and I'll get your things together.

TOM. No, no—I ain't going. Let Eliza go—it's her right. I wouldn't be the one to say no—t'aint in nature for her to stay; but you heard what she said? If I must be sold, or all the people on the place, and everything go to rack, why, let me be sold. I s'pose I can bear it as well as any one. Mas'r always found me on the spot—he always will. I never have broken trust, nor used my pass no ways contrary to my word, and I never will. It's better for me to go alone, than to break up the place and sell all. Mas'r ain't to blame, and he'll take care of you and the poor little 'uns! (*Overcome.*)

CHLOE. Now, old man, what is you gwine to cry for? Does you want to break this old woman's heart? (*Crying.*)

ELIZA. I saw my husband only this afternoon, and I little knew then what was to come. He told me he was going to run away. Do try, if you can, to get word to him. Tell him how I went and why I went, and tell him I'm going to try and find Canada. You must give my love to him, and tell him if I never see him again on earth, I trust we shall meet in heaven!

TOM. Dat is right, Lizy, trust in the Lord—he is our best friend—our only comforter.

ELIZA. You won't go with me, Uncle Tom?

TOM. No; time was when I would, but the Lord's given me a work among these yer poor souls, and I'll stay with 'em and bear my cross with 'em till the end. It's different with you—it's more'n you could stand, and you'd better go if you can.

ELIZA. Uncle Tom, I'll try it!

TOM. Amen! The Lord help ye! (*Exit ELIZA and HARRY.*)

CHLOE. What is you gwine to do, old man! What's to become of you?

TOM (*solemnly*). Him that saved Daniel in the den of lions—that saved the children in the fiery furnace—Him that walked on the sea and bade the winds be still—He's alive yet! and I've faith to believe he can deliver me.

CHLOE. You is right, old man.

TOM. The Lord is good unto all that trust him, Chloe.

(*They go into the cabin.*)

SCENE FOUR

Room in tavern by the riverside. A large window in flat, through which the river is seen, filled with floating ice. Moonlight. Table and chairs brought on.

———

PHINEAS (*enters*). Chaw me up into tobaccy ends! how in the name of all that's onpossible am I to get across that yer pesky river? It's a reg'lar blockade of ice! I promised Ruth to meet her tonight, and she'll be into my har if I don't come. (*Goes to window.*) Thar's a conglomerated prospect for a loveyer! What in creation's to be done? That thar river looks like a permiscuous ice-cream shop come to an awful state of friz. If I war on the adjacent bank, I wouldn't care a tee-total atom. Rile up, you old varmint, and shake the ice off your back!

ELIZA (*enters with* HARRY). Courage, my boy—we have reached the river. Let it but roll between us and our pursuers, and we are safe! (*Goes to window.*) Gracious powers! the river is choked with cakes of ice!

PHINEAS. Holloa, gal!—what's the matter? You look kind of streaked.

ELIZA. Is there any ferry or boat that takes people over now?

PHINEAS. Well, I guess not; the boats have stopped running.

ELIZA (*in dismay*). Stopped running?

PHINEAS. Maybe you're wanting to get over—anybody sick? Ye seem mighty anxious.

ELIZA. I—I—I've got a child that's very dangerous. I never heard of it till last night, and I've walked quite a distance today, in hopes to get to the ferry.

PHINEAS. Well, now, that's onlucky; I'm re'lly consarned for ye. Thar's a man, a piece down here, that's going over with some truck this evening, if he duss to; he'll be in here to supper tonight, so you'd better set down and wait. That's a smart little chap. Say, young 'un, have a chaw tobaccy? (*Takes out a large plug and a bowie knife.*)

ELIZA. No, no! not any for him.

PHINEAS. Oh! he don't use it, eh? Hain't come to it yet? Well, I have. (*Cuts off a large piece, and returns the plug and knife to pocket.*) What's the matter with the young 'un? He looks kind of white in the gills!

ELIZA. Poor fellow! he is not used to walking, and I've hurried him on so.

PHINEAS. Tuckerd, eh? Well, there's a little room there, with a fire in it. Take the baby in there, make yourself comfortable till that thar ferryman shows his countenance—I'll stand the damage.

ELIZA. How shall I thank you for such kindness to a stranger!

PHINEAS. Well, if you don't know how, why, don't try; that's the teetotal. Come, vamose!

(*Exit* ELIZA *and* HARRY.)

Chaw me into sassage meat, if that ain't a perpendicular fine gal! she's a reg'lar A No. 1 sort of female! How'n thunder am I to get across this re-frigerated stream of water? I can't wait for that ferryman.

(*Enter* MARKS.)

Halloa! what sort of a critter's this? (*Advances.*) Say, stranger, will you have something to drink?

MARKS. You are excessively kind: I don't care if I do.

PHINEAS. Ah! he's a human. Holloa, thar! bring us a jug of whisky in-stantaneously, or expect to be teetotally chawed up! Squat yourself, stranger, and go in for enjoyment. (*They sit at table.*) Who are you, and what's your name?

MARKS. I am a lawyer, and my name is Marks.

PHINEAS. A land shark, eh? Well, I don't think no worse on you for that. The law is a kind of necessary evil; and it breeds lawyers just as an old stump does fungus. Ah! here's the whisky.

(*Enter* WAITER, *with jug and tum-blers. Places them on table.*)

Here, you—take that shin-plaster. (*Gives bill.*) I don't want any change —thar's a gal stopping in that room— the balance will pay for her—d'ye hear?—vamose! (*Exit* WAITER.—*Fills glass.*) Take hold, neighbor Marks— don't shirk the critter. Here's hoping your path of true love may never have an ice-choked river to cross! (*They drink.*)

MARKS. Want to cross the river, eh?

PHINEAS. Well, I do, stranger. Fact is, I'm in love with the teetotalist pretty girl, over on the Ohio side, that ever wore a Quaker bonnet. Take another swig, neighbor.

(*Fills glasses, and they drink.*)

MARKS. A Quaker, eh?

PHINEAS. Yes—kind of strange, ain't it? The way of it was this:—I used to own a grist of niggers—had 'em to work on my plantation, just below here. Well, stranger, do you know I fell in with that gal—of course I was considerably smashed—knocked into a pretty conglomerated heap—and I told her so. She said she wouldn't hear a word from me so long as I owned a nigger!

MARKS. You sold them, I suppose?

PHINEAS. You're teetotally wrong, neighbor. I gave them all their freedom, and told 'em to vamose!

MARKS. Ah! yes—very noble, I dare say, but rather expensive. This act won you your lady-love, eh?

PHINEAS. You're off the track again, neighbor. She felt kind of pleased about it, and smiled, and all that; but she said she could never be mine unless I turned Quaker! Thunder and earth! what do you think of that? You're a lawyer—come, now, what's your opinion? Don't you call it a knotty point?

MARKS. Most decidedly. Of course you refused.

PHINEAS. Teetotally; but she told me to think better of it, and come tonight and give her my final conclusion. Chaw me into mince meat, if I haven't made up my mind to do it!

MARKS. You astonish me!

PHINEAS. Well, you see, I can't get along without that gal—she's sort of

fixed my flint, and I'm sure to hang fire without her. I know I shall make a queer sort of Quaker, because you see neighbor, I ain't precisely the kind of material to make a Quaker out of.

MARKS. No, not exactly.

PHINEAS. Well, I can't stop no longer. I must try to get across that candaverous river some way. It's getting late—take care of yourself neighbor lawyer. I'm a teetotal victim to a pair of black eyes. Chaw me up to feed hogs, if I'm not in a ruinatious state! (*Exits.*)

MARK. Queer genius, that, very!

(*Enter* TOM LOKER.)

So you've come at last.

LOKER. Yes. (*Looks into jug.*) Empty! Waiter! more whisky!

(*WAITER enters with jug, and removes the empty one.*)

HALEY (*enters*). By the land! if this yer ain't the nearest, now, to what I've heard people call Providence! Why, Loker, how are ye?

LOKER. The devil! What brought you here, Haley?

HALEY (*sitting at table*). I say, Tom, this yer's the luckiest thing in the world. I'm in a devil of a hobble, and you must help me out!

LOKER. Ugh! aw! like enough. A body may be pretty sure of that when you're glad to see 'em, or can make something off of 'em. What's the blow now?

HALEY. You've got a friend here—partner, perhaps?

LOKER. Yes, I have. Here, Marks—here's that ar fellow that I was with in Natchez.

MARKS (*grasping* HALEY's *hand*). Shall be pleased with his acquaintance. Mr. Haley, I believe?

HALEY. The same, sir. The fact is, gentlemen, this morning I bought a young'un of Shelby up above here. His mother got wind of it, and what does she do but cut her lucky with him; and I'm afraid by this time that she has crossed the river, for I tracked her to this very place.

MARKS. So, then, ye're fairly sewed up, ain't ye? He! he! he! it's neatly done, too.

HALEY. This young'un business makes lots of trouble in the trade.

MARKS. Now, Mr. Haley, what is it? Do you want us to undertake to catch this gal?

HALEY. The gal's no matter of mine—she's Shelby's—it's only the boy. I was a fool for buying the monkey.

LOKER. You're generally a fool!

MARKS. Come now, Loker, none of your huffs; you see, Mr. Haley's a-puttin' us in a way of a good job. I reckon: just hold still—these yer arrangements are my forte. This yer gal, Mr. Haley—how is she?—what is she?

(ELIZA appears, with HARRY, listening.)

HALEY. Well, white and handsome—well brought up. I'd have given Shelby eight hundred or a thousand, and then made well on her.

MARKS. White and handsome—well brought up! Look here, now, Loker, a beautiful opening. We'll do a business here on our own account. We does the catchin'; the boy, of course, goes to Mr. Haley—we takes the gal to Orleans to speculate on. Ain't it beautiful?

(They confer together.)

ELIZA. Powers of mercy, protect me! How shall I escape these human bloodhounds? Ah! the window—the river of ice! That dark stream lies between me and liberty! Surely the ice will bear my trifling weight. It is my only chance of escape—better sink beneath the cold waters, with my child locked in my arms, than have him torn from me and sold into bondage. He sleeps upon my breast.—Heaven, I put my trust in thee! (Gets out of window.)

MARKS. Well, Tom Loker, what do you say?

LOKER. It'll do!

(Strikes his hand violently on the table. ELIZA screams. They all start to their feet. ELIZA disappears. Music, chord.)

HALEY. By the land, there she is now! (They all rush to the window.)

MARKS. She's making for the river!

LOKER. Let's after her!

(Music. They all leap through the window. Change.)

SCENE FIVE

Snow landscape. Music.

———

ELIZA (enters with HARRY, hurriedly). They press upon my footsteps—the river is my only hope. Heaven grant me strength to reach it, ere they overtake me! Courage, my child!—we will be free—or perish! (Rushes off, as music continues.)

(Enter LOKER, HALEY, and MARKS.)

HALEY. We'll catch her yet; the river will stop her!

MARKS. No, it won't, for look! she has jumped upon the ice! She's a brave gal, anyhow!

LOKER. She'll be drowned!

HALEY. Curse that young 'un! I shall lose him, after all.

LOKER. Come on, Marks, to the ferry!

HALEY. Aye, to the ferry!—a hundred dollars for a boat!

(Music. They rush off.)

SCENE SIX

The entire depth of stage, representing the Ohio River, is filled with floating ice.

———

(ELIZA *appears, with* HARRY, *on a cake of ice, and floats slowly across.* HALEY, LOKER, *and* MARKS *on bank, observing.* PHINEAS *on opposite bank.*)

ACT TWO

SCENE ONE

A handsome parlor.

MARIE (*reclining on a sofa, looking at a note*). What can possibly detain St. Clare? According to this note, he should have been here a fortnight ago. (*Noise of carriage outside*) I do believe he has come at last.

EVA (*runs in*). Mamma! (*Throws her arms around* MARIE'S *neck and kisses her.*)

MARIE. That will do—take care, child —don't you make my head ache! (*Kisses her languidly.*)

(*Enter* ST. CLARE, OPHELIA, *and* TOM, *nicely dressed.*)

ST. CLARE. Well, my dear Marie, here we are at last. The wanderers have arrived, you see. Allow me to present my cousin, Miss Ophelia, who is about to undertake the office of our housekeeper.

MARIE (*rising to a sitting posture*). I am delighted to see you. How do you like the appearance of our city?

EVA (*running to* OPHELIA). Oh! is it not beautiful? My own darling home! —is it not beautiful?

OPHELIA. Yes, it is a pretty place, though it looks rather old and heathenish to me.

ST. CLARE. Tom, my boy, this seems to suit you?

TOM. Yes, mas'r, it looks about the right thing.

ST. CLARE. See here, Marie, I've brought you a coachman, at last, to order. I tell you, he is a regular hearse for blackness and sobriety, and will drive you like a funeral, if you wish. Open your eyes, now, and look at him. Now, don't say I never think about you when I'm gone.

MARIE. I know he'll get drunk.

ST. CLARE. Oh! no he won't. He's warranted a pious and sober article.

MARIE. Well, I hope he may turn out well; it's more than I expect, though.

ST. CLARE. Have you no curiosity to learn how and where I picked up Tom?

EVA. *Uncle* Tom, Papa; that's his name.

ST. CLARE. Right, my little sunbeam!

TOM. Please, mas'r, that ain't no 'casion to say nothing 'bout me.

ST. CLARE. You are too modest, my modern Hannibal. Do you know Marie, that our little Eva took a fancy to Uncle Tom—whom we met on board the steamboat—and persuaded me to buy him?

MARIE. Ah! she is so odd.

ST. CLARE. As we approached the landing, a sudden rush of the passengers precipitated Eva into the water—

MARIE. Gracious heavens!

ST. CLARE. A man leaped into the river, and, as she rose to the surface of the water, grasped her in his arms, and held her up until she could be drawn on the boat again. Who was that man, Eva?

EVA. Uncle Tom! (*Runs to him. He lifts her in his arms. She kisses him.*)

TOM. The dear soul!

OPHELIA (*astonished*). How shiftless!

ST. CLARE (*overhearing her*). What's the matter now, pray?

OPHELIA. Well, I want to be kind to everybody, and I wouldn't have anything hurt, but as to kissing—

ST. CLARE. Niggers! that you're not up to, hey?

OPHELIA. Yes, that's it—how can she?

ST. CLARE. Oh! bless you, it's nothing when you are used to it!

OPHELIA. I could never be so shiftless!

EVA. Come with me, Uncle Tom, and I will show you about the house.

TOM. Can I go, mas'r?

ST. CLARE. Yes, Tom; she is your little mistress—your only duty will be to attend to her!

(TOM *bows and exits.*)

MARIE. Eva, my dear!

EVA. Well, mamma?

MARIE. Do not exert yourself too much!

EVA. No, mamma! (*Runs out.*)

OPHELIA (*lifting up her hands*). How shiftless!

(ST. CLARE *sits next to* MARIE *on sofa.* OPHELIA *next to* ST. CLARE.)

ST. CLARE. Well, what do you think of Uncle Tom, Marie?

MARIE. He is a perfect behemoth!

ST. CLARE. Come, now, Marie, be gracious, and say something pretty to a fellow!

MARIE. You've been gone a fortnight beyond the time!

ST. CLARE. Well, you know I wrote you the reason.

MARIE. Such a short, cold letter!

ST. CLARE. Dear me! the mail was just going, and it had to be that or nothing.

MARIE. That's just the way; always something to make your journeys long and letters short!

ST. CLARE. Look at this. (*Takes an elegant velvet case from his pocket.*) Here's a present I got for you in New York—a daguerreotype of Eva and myself.

MARIE (*looks at it with a dissatisfied air*). What made you sit in such an awkward position?

ST. CLARE. Well, the position may be a matter of opinion but what do you think of the likeness?

MARIE (*closing the case snappishly*). If you don't think anything of my opinion in one case, I suppose you wouldn't in another.

OPHELIA (*sententiously, aside*). How shiftless!

ST. CLARE. Hang the woman! Come, Marie, what do you think of the likeness? Don't be nonsensical now.

MARIE. It's very inconsiderate of you, St. Clare, to insist on my talking and looking at things. You know I've been lying all day with the sick headache, and there's been such a tumult made ever since you came, I'm half dead!

OPHELIA. You're subject to the sick headache, ma'am?

MARIE. Yes, I'm a perfect martyr to it!

OPHELIA. Juniper-berry tea is good for sick headache; at least, Molly, Deacon Abraham Perry's wife, used to say so; and she was a great nurse.

ST. CLARE. I'll have the first juniper-berries that get ripe in our garden by the lake brought in for that special purpose. Come, cousin, let us take a stroll in the garden. Will you join us, Marie?

MARIE. I wonder how you can ask such a question, when you know how fragile I am. I shall retire to my chamber, and repose till dinner time. (*Exits.*)

OPHELIA (*looking after her*). How shiftless!

ST. CLARE. Come, cousin! (*As he goes out*) Look out for the babies! If I step upon any body, let them mention it.

OPHELIA. Babies under foot! How shiftless!

Scene Two

A garden. TOM *is seated on a bank, with* EVA *on his knee—his buttonholes are filled with flowers, and* EVA *is hanging a wreath around his neck. Music at opening of scene. Enter* ST. CLARE *and* OPHELIA, *observing.*

EVA. Oh, Tom! you look so funny.

TOM (*sees* ST. CLARE *and puts* EVA *down*). I begs pardon, mas'r, but the young missis would do it. Look yer, I'm like the ox, mentioned in the good book, dressed for the sacrifice.

ST. CLARE. I say, what do you think, Pussy? Which do you like the best—to live as they do at your uncle's, up in Vermont, or to have a houseful of servants, as we do?

EVA. Oh! of course our way is the pleasantest.

ST. CLARE (*patting her head*). Why so?

EVA. Because it makes so many more round you to love, you know.

OPHELIA. Now, that's just like Eva—just one of her odd speeches.

EVA. Is it an odd speech, Papa?

ST. CLARE. Rather, as this world goes, Pussy. But where has my little Eva been?

EVA. Oh! I've been up in Tom's room, hearing him sing.

ST. CLARE. Hearing Tom sing, hey?

EVA. Oh, yes! he sings such beautiful things, about the New Jerusalem, and bright angels, and the land of Canaan.

ST. CLARE. I dare say; it's better than the opera, isn't it?

EVA. Yes; and he's going to teach them to me.

ST. CLARE. Singing lessons, hey? You are coming on.

EVA. Yes, he sings for me, and I read to him in my Bible, and he explains what it means. Come, Tom. (*She takes his hand and they exit.*)

ST. CLARE (*aside*). Oh, Evangeline! Rightly named; hath not heaven made thee an evangel to me?

OPHELIA. How shiftless! How can you let her?

ST. CLARE. Why not?

OPHELIA. Why, I don't know; it seems so dreadful.

ST. CLARE. You would think no harm in a child's caressing a large dog even if he was black; but a creature that can think, reason, and feel, and is immortal, you shudder at. Confess it, cousin. I know the feeling among some of you Northerners well enough. Not that there is a particle of virtue in our not having it, but custom with us does what Christianity ought to do: obliterates the feeling of personal prejudice. You loathe them as you would a snake or a toad, yet you are indignant at their wrongs. You would not have them abused but you don't want to have anything to do with them yourselves. Isn't that it?

OPHELIA. Well, cousin, there may be some truth in this.

ST. CLARE. What would the poor and lowly do without children? Your little child is your only true democrat. Tom, now, is a hero to Eva; his stories are wonders in her eyes; his songs and Methodist hymns are better than an opera, and the traps and little bits of trash in his pockets a mine of jewels, and he the most wonderful Tom that ever wore a black skin. This is one of the roses of Eden that the Lord has dropped down expressly for the poor and lowly, who get few enough of any other kind.

OPHELIA. It's strange, cousin; one might almost think you was a *p, ofessor,* to hear you talk.

ST. CLARE. A professor?

OPHELIA. Yes, a professor of religion.

ST. CLARE. Not at all; not a professor as you town folks have it, and, what is worse, I'm afraid, not a *practicer*, either.

OPHELIA. What makes you talk so, then?

ST. CLARE. Nothing is easier than talking. My forte lies in talking, and yours, cousin, lies in doing. And speaking of that puts me in mind that I have made a purchase for your department. There's the article now. Here, Topsy! (*Whistles.*)

(TOPSY *runs on.*)

OPHELIA. Good gracious! what a heathenish, shiftless-looking object, St. Clare, what in the world have you brought that thing here for?

ST. CLARE. For you to educate, to be sure, and train in the way she should go. I thought she was rather a funny specimen in the Jim Crow line. Here, Topsy, give us a song, and show us some of your dancing.

(TOPSY *sings a verse and dances a breakdown.*)

OPHELIA (*paralyzed*). Well, of all things! If I ever saw the like!

ST. CLARE (*smothering a laugh*). Topsy, this is your new mistress— I'm going to give you up to her. See now that you behave yourself.

TOPSY. Yes, mas'r.

ST. CLARE. You're going to be good, Topsy, you understand?

TOPSY. Oh, yes, mas'r.

OPHELIA. Now, St. Clare, what upon earth is this for? Your house is so full of these plagues now, that a body can't set down their foot without treading on 'em. I get up in the morning and find one asleep behind the door, and see one black head poking out from under the table—one lying on the door mat, and they are moping and mowing and grinning between all the railings, and tumbling over the kitchen floor! What on earth did you want to bring this one for?

ST. CLARE. For you to educate— didn't I tell you? You're always preaching about educating, I thought I would make you a present of a fresh caught specimen, and let you try your hand on her and bring her up in the way she should go.

OPHELIA. I don't want her, I am sure; I have more to do with 'em now than I want to.

ST. CLARE. That's you Christians, all over. You'll get up a society, and get some poor missionary to spend all his days among just such heathen; but let me see one of you that would take one into your house with you, and take the labor of their conversion upon yourselves.

OPHELIA. Well, I didn't think of it in that light. It might be a real missionary work. Well, I'll do what I can. (*Advances to* TOPSY.) She's dreadful dirty and shiftless! How old are you, Topsy?

TOPSY. Dunno, missis.

OPHELIA. How shiftless! Don't know how old you are? Didn't anybody ever tell you? Who was your mother?

TOPSY (*grinning*). Never had none.

OPHELIA. Never had any mother? What do you mean? Where was you born?

TOPSY. Never was born.

OPHELIA. You musn't answer me in that way. I'm not playing with you. Tell me where you was born, and who your father and mother were?

TOPSY. Never was born, tell you; never had no father, nor mother, nor nothin'. I war raised by a speculator, with lots of others. Old Aunt Sue used to take car on us.

ST. CLARE. She speaks the truth, cousin. Speculators buy them up cheap, when they are little, and get them raised for the market.

OPHELIA. How long have you lived with your master and mistress?

TOPSY. Dunno, missis.

OPHELIA. How shiftless! Is it a year, or more, or less?

TOPSY. Dunno, missis.

ST. CLARE. She does not know what a year is; she don't even know her own age.

OPHELIA. Have you ever heard anything about heaven, Topsy? (TOPSY *looks bewildered and grins.*) Do you know who made you?

TOPSY. Nobody, as I knows on, he, he, he! I 'spect I growed. Don't think nobody never made me.

OPHELIA. The shiftless heathen! What can you do? What did you do for your master and mistress?

TOPSY. Fetch water—and wash dishes—and rub knives—and wait on folks—and dance breakdowns.

OPHELIA. I shall break down, I'm afraid, in trying to make anything of you, you shiftless mortal!

ST. CLARE. You find virgin soil there, cousin; put in your own ideas. You won't find many to pull up. (*Exit, laughing.*)

OPHELIA (*takes out her handkerchief. A pair of gloves falls.* TOPSY *picks them up slyly and puts them in her sleeve.*) Follow me, you benighted innocent!

TOPSY. Yes, missis.

(*As* OPHELIA *turns her back to her, she seizes the end of the ribbon she wears around her waist, and twitches it off.* OPHELIA *turns and sees her as she is putting it in her other sleeve.* OPHELIA *takes ribbon from her.*)

OPHELIA. What's this? You naughty, wicked girl, you've been stealing this?

TOPSY. Laws! why, that ar's missis' ribbon, a'nt it? How could it got caught in my sleeve?

OPHELIA. Topsy, you naughty girl, don't you tell me a lie—you stole that ribbon!

TOPSY. Missis, I declare for't, I didn't—never seed it till dis yer blessed minnit.

OPHELIA. Topsy, don't you know it's wicked to tell lies?

TOPSY. I never tells no lies, missis; it's just de truth I've been telling now and nothing else.

OPHELIA. Topsy, I shall have to whip you, if you tell lies so.

TOPSY. Laws missis, if you's to whip all day, couldn't say no other way. I never seed dat ar—it must a got caught in my sleeve. (*Blubbers.*)

OPHELIA (*seizes her by the shoulders*). Don't you tell me that again you barefaced fibber! (*Shakes her. The gloves fall on stage.*) Then you, my gloves too—you outrageous young heathen! (*Picks them up.*) Will you tell me, now, you didn't steal the ribbon?

TOPSY. No, missis; stole de gloves, but didn't steal de ribbon. It was permiskus.

OPHELIA. Why, you young reprobate!

TOPSY. Yes—I's knows I's wicked!

OPHELIA. Then you know you ought to be punished. (*Boxes her ears.*) What do you think of that?

TOPSY. He, he, he! De Lord, missus; dat wouldn't kill a 'skeeter. (*Runs off laughing.* OPHELIA *follows indignantly.*)

SCENE THREE

The tavern by the river.—Table and chairs. Jug and glasses on table. On flat is a printed placard, headed: "Four Hundred Dollars Reward — Runaway—George Harris!"

PHINEAS (*seated at table*). So yer I am; and a pretty business I've undertook to do. Find the husband of the gal that crossed the river on the ice two or three days ago. Ruth said I must do it, and I'll be teetotally chawed up if I don't do it. I see they've offered a reward for him dead or alive. How in creation am I to find the varmint? He isn't likely to go round looking natural, with a full description of his hide and figure staring him in the face. (*Enter* MR. WILSON.) I say, stranger, how are ye? (*Rises and comes forward.*)

WILSON. Well, I reckon.

PHINEAS. Any news? (*Takes out plug and knife.*)

WILSON. Not that I know of.

PHINEAS (*cutting a piece of tobacco and offering it*). Chaw?

WILSON. No, thank ye—it don't agree with me.

PHINEAS. Don't, eh? (*Putting it in his own mouth*) I never felt any the worse for it.

WILSON (*sees placard*). What's that?

PHINEAS. Nigger advertised. (*Advances toward it and spits on it.*) There's my mind upon that.

WILSON. Why, now stranger, what's that for?

PHINEAS. I'd do it all the same to the writer of that ar paper, if he was here. Any man that owns a boy like that, and can't find any better way of treating him, than branding him on the hand with the letter H, as that paper states, *deserves* to lose him. Such papers as this ar' a shame to old Kaintuck! that's my mind right out, if anybody wants to know.

WILSON. Well, now, that's a fact.

PHINEAS. I used to have a gang of boys, sir—that was before I fell in love —and I just told 'em:—"Boys," says I, "run now! Dig! put! jest when you want to. I never shall come to look after you!" That's the way I kept mine.

Let 'em know they are free to run any time, and it jest stops their wanting to. It stands to reason it should. Treat 'em like men, and you'll have men's work.

WILSON. I think you are altogether right, friend, and this man described here is a fine fellow—no mistake about that. He worked for me some half dozen years in my bagging factory, and he was my best hand, sir. He is an ingenious fellow, too; he invented a machine for the cleaning of hemp—a really valuable affair; it's gone into use in several factories. His master holds the patent of it.

PHINEAS. I'll warrant ye; holds it, and makes money out of it, and then turns round and brands the boy in his right hand! If I had a fair chance, I'd mark him, I reckon, so that he'd carry it *one* while!

GEORGE HARRIS (*enters disguised, speaking as he enters*). Jim, see to the trunks. (*Sees* WILSON.) Ah! Mr. Wilson here?

WILSON. Bless my soul, can it be?

GEORGE HARRIS (*advances and grasps his hand*). Mr. Wilson, I see you remember me, Mr. Butler, of Oaklands, Shelby County.

WILSON. Ye—yes—yes—sir.

PHINEAS. Holloa! there's a screw loose here somewhere. That old gentleman seems to be struck into a pretty considerable heap of astonishment. May I be teetotally chawed up! if I don't believe that's the identical man I'm arter. (*Goes to* GEORGE.) How are ye, George Harris?

GEORGE HARRIS (*starting back and thrusting his hands into his breast*). You know me?

PHINEAS. Ha, ha, ha! I rather conclude I do; but don't get riled, I an't a bloodhound in disguise.

GEORGE HARRIS. How did you discover me?

PHINEAS. By a teetotal smart guess. You're the very man I want to see. Do you know I was sent after you?

GEORGE HARRIS. Ah! by my master?

PHINEAS. No; by your wife.

GEORGE HARRIS. My wife! Where is she?

PHINEAS. She's stopping with a Quaker family over on the Ohio side.

GEORGE HARRIS. Then she is safe?

PHINEAS. Teetotally!

GEORGE HARRIS. Conduct me to her.

PHINEAS. Just wait a brace of shakes and I'll do it. I've got to go and get the boat ready. 'Twon't take me but a minute—make yourself comfortable till I get back. Chaw me up! but this is what I call doing things in short order. (*Exit.*)

WILSON. George!

GEORGE HARRIS. Yes, George!

WILSON. I couldn't have thought it!

GEORGE HARRIS. I am pretty well disguised, I fancy; you see I don't answer to the advertisement at all.

WILSON. George, this is a dangerous game you are playing; I could not have advised you to it.

GEORGE HARRIS. I can do it on my own responsibility.

WILSON. Well, George, I suppose you're running away—leaving your awful master, George (I don't wonder at it); at the same time, I'm sorry, George, yes, decidedly. I think I must say that it's my duty to tell you so.

GEORGE HARRIS. Why are you sorry, sir?

WILSON. Why to see you, as it were, setting yourself in opposition to the laws of your country.

GEORGE HARRIS. *My* country! What country have *I* but the grave? And I would to heaven that I was laid there!

WILSON. George, you've got a hard master, in fact he is—well, he conducts himself reprehensibly—I can't pretend to defend him. I'm sorry for you, now; it's a bad case—very bad; but we must all submit to the indications of providence, George, don't you see?

GEORGE HARRIS. I wonder, Mr. Wilson, if the Indians should come and take you a prisoner away from your wife and children, and want to keep you all your life hoeing corn for them, if you'd think it your duty to abide in the condition in which you were called? I rather imagine that you'd think the first stray horse you could find an indication of providence, shouldn't you?

WILSON. Really, George, putting the case in that somewhat peculiar light— I don't know—under those circumstances—but what I might. But it seems to me you are running an awful risk. You can't hope to carry it out. If you're taken it will be worse with you than ever; they'll only abuse you, and half kill you, and sell you down river.

GEORGE HARRIS. Mr. Wilson, I know all this. I *do* run a risk, but—(*Throws open coat and shows pistols and knife in his belt.*) There! I'm ready for them. Down South I never *will* go! no, if it comes to that, I can earn myself at least six feet of free soil—the first and last I shall ever own in Kentucky!

WILSON. Why, George, this state of mind is awful—it's getting really desperate. I'm concerned. Going to break the laws of your country?

GEORGE HARRIS. My country again! Sir, I haven't any country any more than I have any father. I don't want anything of *your* country, except to be left alone—to go peaceably out of it; but if any man tries to stop me, let him take care, for I am desperate. I'll fight for my liberty, to the last breath I breathe! You say your fathers did it, if it was right for them, it is right for me!

WILSON (*walking up and down and fanning his face with a large yellow silk handkerchief*). Blast 'em all! Haven't I always said so—the infernal old cusses! Bless me! I hope I an't swearing now! Well, go ahead, George, go ahead. But be careful, my boy; don't shoot anybody, unless—well, you'd *better* not shoot—at least I wouldn't *hit* anybody, you know.

GEORGE HARRIS. Only in self-defense.

WILSON. Well, well. (*Fumbling in his pocket*) I suppose, perhaps, I an't following my judgment—hang it, I won't follow my judgment. So here, George. (*Takes out a pocketbook and offers* GEORGE *a roll of bills.*)

GEORGE HARRIS. No, my kind, good sir, you've done a great deal for me, and this might get you into trouble. I have money enough, I hope, to take me as far as I need it.

WILSON. No; but you must, George. Money is a great help everywhere, can't have too much, if you get it honestly. Take it, do take it, *now* do, my boy!

GEORGE HARRIS (*taking the money*). On condition, sir, that I may repay it at some future time, I will.

WILSON. And now George, how long are you going to travel in this way? Not long or far I hope? It's well carried on, but too bold.

GEORGE HARRIS. Mr. Wilson, it is *so bold,* and this tavern is so near, that they will never think of it; they will look for me on ahead, and you yourself wouldn't know me.

WILSON. But the mark on your hand?

GEORGE HARRIS (*draws off his glove and shows scar*). That is a parting mark of Mr. Harris' regard. Looks interesting, doesn't it? (*Puts on glove again.*)

WILSON. I declare, my very blood runs cold when I think of it—your condition and your risks!

GEORGE HARRIS. Mine has run cold a good many years; at present, it's about up to the boiling point.

WILSON. George, something has brought you out wonderfully. You hold up your head, and move and speak like another man.

GEORGE HARRIS (*proudly*). Because I'm a *freeman!* Yes, sir; I've said "master" for the last time to any man. *I'm free!*

WILSON. Take care! You are not sure; you may be taken.

GEORGE HARRIS. All men are free and equal *in the grave,* if it comes to that Mr. Wilson.

PHINEAS (*enters*). Them's my sentiments, to a teetotal atom, and I don't care who knows it! Neighbor, the boat is ready, and the sooner we make tracks the better. I've seen some mysterious strangers lurking about these diggings, so we'd better put.

GEORGE HARRIS. Farewell, Mr. Wilson, and heaven reward you for the many kindnesses you have shown the poor fugitive!

WILSON (*grasping his hand*). You're a brave fellow, George. I wish in my heart you were safe through, though —that's what I do.

PHINEAS. And ain't I the man of all creation to put him through, stranger? Chaw me up if I don't take him to his dear little wife, in the smallest possible quantity of time. Come, neighbor, let's vamose.

GEORGE HARRIS. Farewell, Mr. Wilson.

WILSON. My best wishes go with you, George. (*Exit.*)

PHINEAS. You're a trump, old Slow-and-Easy.

GEORGE HARRIS (*looking off*). Look! look!

PHINEAS. Consarn their picters, here they come! We can't get out of the house without their seeing us.

We're teetotally treed!

GEORGE HARRIS. Let us fight our way through them!

PHINEAS. No, that won't do; there are too many of them for a fair fight —we should be chawed up in no time. (*Looks round and sees trap door.*) Holloa! here's a cellar door. Just you step down here a few minutes, while I parley with them. (*Lifts trap.*)

GEORGE HARRIS. I am resolved to perish sooner than surrender! (*Goes down trap.*)

PHINEAS. That's your sort! (*Closes trap and stands on it.*) Here they are!

(*Enter* HALEY, MARKS, LOKER, *and three* MEN.)

HALEY. Say, stranger, you haven't seen a runaway darkey about these parts, eh?

PHINEAS. What kind of a darkey?

HALEY. A mulatto chap, almost as light-complexioned as a white man.

PHINEAS. Was he a pretty good-looking chap?

HALEY. Yes.

PHINEAS. Kind of tall?

HALEY. Yes.

PHINEAS. With brown hair?

HALEY. Yes.

PHINEAS. And dark eyes?

HALEY. Yes.

PHINEAS. Pretty well dressed?

HALEY. Yes.

PHINEAS. Scar on his right hand?

HALEY. Yes, yes.

PHINEAS. Well, I ain't seen him.

HALEY. Oh, bother! Come, boys, let's search the house. (*Exeunt.*)

PHINEAS (*raises trap*). Now, then, neighbor George.

(GEORGE *enters, up trap.*)

Now's the time to cut your lucky.

GEORGE HARRIS. Follow me, Phineas. (*Exit.*)

PHINEAS. In a brace of shakes. (*Closing trap.*)

(HALEY, MARKS, LOKER, *etc., re-enter.*)

HALEY. Ah! he's down in the cellar. Follow me, boys! (*Thrusts* PHINEAS *aside, and rushes down trap, followed by the others.*)

PHINEAS (*closes trap and stands on it*). Chaw me up! but I've got 'em all in a trap. (*Knocking below*) Be quiet, you pesky varmints! (*Knocking*) They're getting mighty oneasy. (*Knocking*) Will you be quiet, you savagerous critters!

(*The trap is forced open.* HALEY *and* MARKS *appear.* PHINEAS *seizes a chair and stands over trap.*)

Down with you or I'll smash you into apple-fritters!

SCENE FOUR

A plain chamber.

TOPSY (*outside*). You go 'long. No more nigger dan you be! (*Enters— shouts and laughter without—looks off.*) You seem to think yourself white folks. You ain't nerry one—black *nor* white. I'd like to be one or turrer. Law! you niggers, does you know you's all sinners? Well, you is—everybody is. White folks is sinners too—Miss Feely says so—but I 'spects niggers is the biggest ones. But Lor! ye ain't any on ye up to me. I's so awful wicked there can't nobody do nothin' with me. I used to keep old missis a-swarin at me haf de time. I 'spects I's de wickedest critter in de world.

(*Song and dance introduced.*)

EVA (*enters*). Oh, Topsy! Topsy! you have been very naughty again.

TOPSY. Well, I'spects I have.

EVA. What makes you do so?

TOPSY. I dunno; I'spects it's cause I's so wicked.

EVA. Why did you spoil Jane's earrings?

TOPSY. 'Cause she's so proud. She called me a little black imp and turned up her pretty nose at me 'cause she is whiter than I am. I was gwine by her room, and I seed her coral earrings lying on de table, so I threw dem on de floor, and put my foot on 'em, and scrunches 'em all to little bits—he! he! he! I's so wicked.

EVA. Don't you know that was very wrong?

TOPSY. I don't car'! I despises dem what sets up for fine ladies, when dey ain't nothing but cream-colored niggers! Dere's Miss Rosa—she gives me lots of 'pertinent remarks. T'other night she was gwine to a ball. She put on a beau'ful dress dat missis give her —wid her hair curled, all nice and pretty. She hab to go down de back stairs—dey am dark—and I puts a pail of hot water on dem, and she put her foot into it, and den she go tumbling to de bottom of de stairs, and de water go all ober her, and spile her dress, and scald her dreadful bad! He! he! he! I's so wicked!

EVA. Oh! how could you!

TOPSY. Don't dey despise me cause I don't know nothing? Don't dey laugh at me 'cause I'm brack, and dey ain't?

EVA. But you shouldn't mind them.

TOPSY. Well, I don't mind dem; but when dey are passing under my winder, I trows dirty water on 'em, and dat spiles der complexions.

EVA. What does make you so bad, Topsy? Why won't you try and be good? Don't you love anybody, Topsy?

TOPSY. Can't recommember.

EVA. But you love your father and mother?

TOPSY. Never had none, ye know, I telled ye that, Miss Eva.

EVA. Oh! I know; but hadn't you any brother, or sister, or aunt, or—

TOPSY. No, none on 'em—never had nothing nor nobody. I's brack—no one loves me!

EVA. Oh! Topsy, I love you! (*Laying her hand on* TOPSY's *shoulder*) I love you because you haven't had any father, or mother, or friends. I love you, and I want you to be good. I wish you would try to be good for my sake.

(TOPSY *looks astonished for a moment, and then bursts into tears.*)

Only think of it, Topsy—*you* can be one of those spirits bright Uncle Tom sings about!

TOPSY. Oh! dear Miss Eva—dear Miss Eva! I will try—I will try. I never did care nothin' about it before.

EVA. If you try, you will succeed. Come with me. (*Goes and takes* TOPSY's *hand.*)

TOPSY. I will try; but den, I's so wicked!

(*Exit* EVA, *followed by* TOPSY, *crying.*)

SCENE FIVE

Chamber. Enter GEORGE HARRIS, ELIZA, *and* HARRY.

———

GEORGE HARRIS. At length, Eliza, after many wanderings, we have been united.

ELIZA. Thanks to these generous Quakers, who have so kindly sheltered us.

GEORGE HARRIS. Not forgetting our friend Phineas.

ELIZA. I do indeed owe him much. 'Twas he I met upon the icy river's bank, after that fearful, but successful attempt, when I fled from the slave-trader with my child in my arms.

GEORGE HARRIS. It seems almost incredible that you could have crossed the river on the ice.

ELIZA. Yes, I did. Heaven helping me, I crossed on the ice, for they were behind me—right behind—and there was no other way.

GEORGE HARRIS. But the ice was all in broken-up blocks, swinging and heaving up and down in the water.

ELIZA. I know it was—I know it; I did not think I should get over, but I did not care—I could but die if I did not! I leaped on the ice, but how I got across I don't know; the first I remember, a man was helping me up the bank —that man was Phineas.

GEORGE HARRIS. My brave girl! you deserve your freedom—you have richly earned it!

ELIZA. And when we get to Canada I can help you to work, and between us we can find something to live on.

GEORGE HARRIS. Yes, Eliza, so long as we have each other, and our boy. Oh, Eliza, if these people only knew what a blessing it is for a man to feel that his wife and child belong to *him!* I've often wondered to see men that could call their wives and children *their own,* fretting and worrying about anything else. Why, I feel rich and strong, though we have nothing but our bare hands. If they will only let me alone now, I will be satisfied—thankful!

ELIZA. But we are not quite out of danger; we are not yet in Canada.

GEORGE HARRIS. True; but it seems as if I smelt the free air, and it makes me strong!

PHINEAS (*enters, dressed as a Quaker, with a snuffle*). Verily, friends, how is it with thee?—hum!

GEORGE HARRIS. Why, Phineas, what means this metamorphosis?

PHINEAS. I've become a Quaker, that's the meaning on't.

GEORGE HARRIS. What—you?

PHINEAS. Teetotally! I was driven to it by a strong argument, composed of a pair of sparkling eyes, rosy cheeks, and pouting lips. Them lips would persuade a man to assassinate his grandmother! (*Assumes the Quaker tone again.*) Verily, George, I have discovered something of importance to the interests of thee and thy party, and it were well for thee to hear it.

GEORGE HARRIS. Keep us not in suspense!

PHINEAS. Well, after I left you on the road, I stopped at a little, lone tavern, just below here. Well, I was tired with hard driving, and after my supper I stretched myself down on a pile of bags in the corner, and pulled a buffalo hide over me—and what does I do but get fast asleep.

GEORGE HARRIS. With one ear open, Phineas?

PHINEAS. No, I slept ears and all for an hour or two, for I was pretty well tired; but when I came to myself a little, I found that there were some men in the room, sitting round a table, drinking and talking; and I thought, before I made much muster, I'd just see what they were up to, especially as I heard them say something about the Quakers. Then I listened with both ears and found they were talking about you. So I kept quiet, and heard them lay off all their plans. They've got a right notion of the track we are going tonight, and they'll be down after us, six or eight strong. So, now, what's to be done?

ELIZA. What *shall* we do, George?

GEORGE HARRIS. I know what I shall do! (*Takes out pistols.*)

PHINEAS. Ay—ay, thou seest, Eliza, how it will work—pistols—phitz—poppers!

ELIZA. I see; but I pray it come not to that!

GEORGE HARRIS. I don't want to involve any one with or for me. If you will lend me your vehicle, and direct me, I will drive alone to the next stand.

PHINEAS. Ah! well, friend, but thee'll need a driver for all that. Thee's quite welcome to do all the fighting thee knows; but I know a thing or two about the road that thee doesn't.

GEORGE HARRIS. But I don't want to involve you.

PHINEAS. Involve me! Why, chaw me—that is to say—when thee does involve me, please to let me know.

ELIZA. Phineas is a wise and skillful man. You will do well, George, to abide by his judgment. And, oh! George, be not hasty with these—young blood is hot! (*Laying her hand on pistols.*)

GEORGE HARRIS. I will attack no man. All I ask of this country is to be left alone, and I will go out peaceably. But I'll fight to the last breath before they shall take from me my wife and son! Can you blame me?

PHINEAS. Mortal man cannot blame thee, neighbor George! Flesh and blood could not do otherwise. Woe unto the world because of offenses, but woe unto them through whom the offense cometh! That's gospel, teetotally!

GEORGE HARRIS. Would not even you, sir, do the same, in my place?

PHINEAS. I pray that I be not tried; the flesh is weak—but I think my flesh would be pretty tolerably strong in such a case; I ain't sure, friend George, that I shouldn't hold a fellow for thee, if thee had any accounts to settle with him.

ELIZA. Heaven grant we be not tempted.

PHINEAS. But if we are tempted too much, why, consarn 'em! let them look out, that's all.

GEORGE HARRIS. It's quite plain you was not born for a Quaker. The old nature has its way in you pretty strong yet.

PHINEAS. Well, I reckon you are pretty teetotally right.

GEORGE HARRIS. Had we not better hasten our flight?

PHINEAS. Well, I rather conclude we had; we're full two hours ahead of them, if they start at the time they planned, so let's vamose. (*Exeunt.*)

SCENE SIX

A rocky pass in the hills. Large set rock and platform.

———

PHINEAS (*without*). Out with you in a twinkling, every one, and up into these rocks with me! run *now*, if you *ever* did run!

(*Music.* PHINEAS *enters, with* HARRY *in his arms.* GEORGE *supporting* ELIZA.) Come up here; this is one of our old hunting dens. Come up.

(*They ascend the rock*).

Well, here we are. Let 'em get us if they can. Whoever comes here has to walk single file between those two rocks, in fair range of your pistols—d'ye see?

GEORGE HARRIS. I do see. And now, as this affair is mine, let me take all the risk, and do all the fighting.

PHINEAS. Thee's quite welcome to do the fighting, George; but I may have the fun of looking on, I suppose. But see, these fellows are kind of debating down there, and looking up, like hens when they are going to fly up onto the roost. Hadn't thee better give 'em a word of advice, before they come up, jest to tell 'em handsomely they'll be shot if they do.

(LOKER, MARKS, *and three* MEN *enter.*)

MARKS. Well, Tom, your coons are fairly treed.

LOKER. Yes, I see 'em go up right here; and here's a path—I'm for going right up. They can't jump down in a hurry, and it won't take long to ferret 'em out.

MARKS. But, Tom, they might fire at us from behind the rocks. That would be ugly, you know.

LOKER. Ugh! always for saving your

skin, Marks. No danger, niggers are too plaguy scared!

MARKS. I don't know why I shouldn't save my skin, it's the best I've got; and niggers do fight like the devil sometimes.

GEORGE HARRIS (*rising on the rock*). Gentlemen, who are you down there and what do you want?

LOKER. We want a party of runaway niggers. One George and Eliza Harris, and their son. We've got the officers here, and a warrant to take 'em too. D'ye hear? An't you George Harris, that belonged to Mr. Harris, of Shelby County, Kentucky?

GEORGE HARRIS. I am George Harris. A Mr. Harris, of Kentucky, did call me his property. But now I'm a freeman, standing on heaven's free soil! My wife and child I claim as mine. We have arms to defend ourselves and we mean to do it. You can come up if you like, but the first one that comes within range of our bullets is a dead man.

MARKS. Oh, come—come, young man, this ain't no kind of talk at all for you. You see we're officers of justice. We've got the law on our side, and the power and so forth; so you'd better give up peaceably, you see—for you'll certainly have to give up at last.

GEORGE HARRIS. I know very well that you've got the law on your side, and the power; but you haven't got us. We are standing here as free as you are, and by the great power that made us we'll fight for our liberty till we die!

(*During this,* MARKS *draws a pistol and, when he concludes, fires at him.* ELIZA *screams.*)

GEORGE HARRIS. It's nothing, Eliza; I am unhurt.

PHINEAS (*drawing* GEORGE *down*). Thee'd better keep out of sight with thy speechifying; they're teetotal mean scamps.

LOKER. What did you do that for, Marks?

MARKS. You see, you get jist as much for him dead as alive in Kentucky.

GEORGE HARRIS. Now, Phineas, the first man that advances I fire at; you take the second, and so on. It won't do to waste two shots on one.

PHINEAS. But what if you don't hit?

GEORGE HARRIS. I'll try my best.

PHINEAS. Creation! chaw me up if there a'nt stuff in you!

MARKS. I think I must have hit some on 'em. I heard a squeal.

LOKER. I'm going right up for one. I never was afraid of niggers, and I an't a going to be now. Who goes after me?

(*Music.* LOKER *dashes up the rock.* GEORGE *fires. He staggers for a moment, then springs to the top.* PHINEAS *seizes him. A struggle.*)

PHINEAS. Friend, thee is not wanted here! (*Throws* LOKER *over the rock.*)

MARKS (*retreating*). Lord help us— they're perfect devils!

(*Music.* MARKS *and* PARTY *run off.* GEORGE *and* ELIZA *kneel in an attitude of thanksgiving, with the* CHILD *between them.* PHINEAS *stands over them exulting.*)

ACT THREE

SCENE ONE

Chamber. Enter ST. CLARE, *followed by* TOM.

_____

ST. CLARE (*giving money and papers to* TOM). There, Tom, are the bills and the money to liquidate them.

TOM. Yes, mas'r.

ST. CLARE. Well, Tom, what are

you waiting for? Isn't all right there?

TOM. I'm 'fraid not, mas'r.

ST. CLARE. Why, Tom, what's the matter? You look as solemn a coffin.

TOM. I feel very bad, mas'r. I allays have thought that mas'r would be good to everybody.

ST. CLARE. Well, Tom, haven't I been? Come, now, what do you want? There's something you haven't got, I suppose, and this is the preface.

TOM. Mas'r allays been good to me. I haven't nothing to complain of on that head; but there is one that mas'r isn't good to.

ST. CLARE. Why, Tom, what's got into you? Speak out—what do you mean?

TOM. Last night, between one and two, I thought so. I studied upon the matter then—mas'r isn't good to *himself*.

ST. CLARE. Ah! now I understand; you allude to the state in which I came home last night. Well, to tell the truth, I *was* slightly elevated—a little more champagne on board than I could comfortably carry. That's all, isn't it?

TOM (*deeply affected, clasping his hands and weeping*). All! Oh! my dear young mas'r, I'm 'fraid it will be *loss of all*—all, body and soul. The good book says "it biteth like a serpent and stingeth like an adder," my dear mas'r.

ST. CLARE. You poor, silly fool! I'm not worth crying over.

TOM. Oh, mas'r! I implore you to think of it before it gets too late.

ST. CLARE. Well, I won't go to any more of their cursed nonsense, Tom —on my honor, I won't. I don't know why I haven't stopped long ago; I've always despised *it*, and myself for it. So now, Tom, wipe up your eyes and go about your errands.

TOM. Bless you, mas'r. I feel much better now. You have taken a load from poor Tom's heart. Bless you!

ST. CLARE. Come, come, no blessings; I'm not so wonderfully good, now. There, I'll pledge my honor to you, Tom, you don't see me so again.

(*Exit* TOM.)

I'll keep my faith with him, too.

OPHELIA (*outside*). Come along, you shiftless mortal!

ST. CLARE. What new witchcraft has Topsy been brewing? That commotion is of her raising, I'll be bound.

OPHELIA (*enters, dragging in* TOPSY). Come here now; I will tell your master.

ST. CLARE. What's the matter now?

OPHELIA. The matter is that I cannot be plagued with this girl any longer. It's past all bearing; flesh and blood cannot endure it. Here I locked her up and gave her a hymn to study; and what does she do but spy out where I put my key, and has gone to my bureau, and got a bonnet-trimming and cut it all to pieces to make dolls' jackets! I never saw anything like it in my life!

ST. CLARE. What have you done to her?

OPHELIA. What have I done? What haven't I done? Your wife says I ought to have her whipped till she couldn't stand.

ST. CLARE. I don't doubt it. Tell me of the lovely rule of woman. I never saw above a dozen women that wouldn't half kill a horse or servant, either, if they had their own way with them—let alone a man.

OPHELIA. I am sure, St. Clare, I don't know what to do. I've taught and taught—I've talked till I'm tired; I've whipped her, I've punished her in every way I could think of, and still she's just what she was at first.

ST. CLARE. Come here, Tops, you monkey!

(TOPSY *goes to* ST. CLARE, *grinning*.) What makes you behave so?

TOPSY. 'Spects it's my wicked heart—

Miss Feely says so.

ST. CLARE. Don't you see how much Miss Ophelia has done for you? She says she has done everything she can think of.

TOPSY. Lor', yes, mas'r! old missis used to say so, too. She whipped me a heap harder, and used to pull my ha'r, and knock my head agin the door; but it didn't do me no good. I 'spects if they's to pull every spear of ha'r out o' my head, it wouldn't do no good neither—I's so wicked! Laws! I's nothin' but a nigger, no ways!

OPHELIA. Well, I shall have to give her up; I can't have that trouble any longer.

ST. CLARE. I'd like to ask you one question.

OPHELIA. What is it?

ST. CLARE. Why, if your doctrine is not strong enough to save one heathen child, that you can have at home here, all to yourself, what's the use of sending one or two poor missionaries off with it among thousands of just such? I suppose this girl is a fair sample of what thousands of your heathen are.

OPHELIA. I'm sure I don't know; I never saw such a girl as this.

ST. CLARE. What makes you so bad, Tops? Why won't you try and be good? Don't you love any one, Topsy?

TOPSY (*comes down*). Dunno nothing 'bout love; I loves candy and sich, that's all.

OPHELIA. But, Topsy, if you'd only try to be good, you might.

TOPSY. Couldn't never be nothing but a nigger, if I was ever so good. If I could be skinned and come white, I'd try then.

ST. CLARE. People can love you, if you are black, Topsy. Miss Ophelia would love you, if you were good.

(TOPSY *laughs*.)

Don't you think so?

TOPSY. No, she can't b'ar me, 'cause I'm a nigger—she'd's soon have a toad touch her. There can't nobody love niggers, and niggers can't do nothin'! I don't car'! (*Whistles*.)

ST. CLARE. Silence, you incorrigible imp, and begone!

TOPSY. He! he! he! didn't get much out of dis chile! (*Exit*.)

OPHELIA. I've always had a prejudice against Negroes, and it's a fact—I never could bear to have that child touch me, but I didn't think she knew it.

ST. CLARE. Trust any child to find that out, there's no keeping it from them. But I believe all the trying in the world to benefit a child, and all the substantial favors you can do them, will never excite one emotion of gratitude, while that feeling of repugnance remains in the heart. It's a queer kind of a fact, but so it is.

OPHELIA. I don't know how I can help it—they are disagreeable to me, this girl in particular. How can I help feeling so?

ST. CLARE. Eva does, it seems.

OPHELIA. Well, she's so loving. I wish I was like her. She might teach me a lesson.

ST. CLARE. It would not be the first time a little child had been used to instruct an old disciple, if it were so. Come, let us seek Eva, in her favorite bower by the lake.

OPHELIA. Why, the dew is falling, she mustn't be out there. She is unwell, I know.

ST. CLARE. Don't be croaking, cousin —I hate it.

OPHELIA. But she has that cough.

ST. CLARE. Oh, nonsense, of that cough—it is not anything. She has taken a little cold, perhaps.

OPHELIA. Well, that was just the way Eliza Jane was taken—and Ellen—

ST. CLARE. Oh, stop these hobgoblin, nurse legends. You old hands get so wise that a child cannot cough or sneeze but you see desperation and ruin at hand. Only take care of the child, keep her from the night air, and don't let her play too hard, and she'll do well enough. (*Exeunt.*)

SCENE TWO

The flat represents the lake. The rays of the setting sun tinge the waters with gold. A large tree. Beneath this a grassy bank, on which EVA *and* TOM *are seated side by side.* EVA *has a Bible open on her lap. Music.*

TOM. Read dat passage again, please, Miss Eva?

EVA (*reading*). "And I saw a sea of glass, mingled with fire." (*Stopping suddenly and pointing to lake*) Tom, there it is!

TOM. What, Miss Eva?

EVA. Don't you see there? There's a "sea of glass mingled with fire."

TOM. True enough, Miss Eva. (*Sings.*)

Oh, had I the wings of the morning,
I'd fly away to Canaan's shore;
Bright angels should convey me home,
To the New Jerusalem.

EVA. Where do you suppose New Jerusalem is, Uncle Tom?

TOM. Oh, up in the clouds, Miss Eva.

EVA. Then I think I see it. Look in those clouds, they look like great gates of pearl; and you can see beyond them —far, far off—it's all gold! Tom, sing about "spirits bright."

TOM (*sings*).

I see a band of spirits bright,
That taste the glories there;
They are all robed in spotless white,
And conquering palms they bear.

EVA. Uncle Tom, I've seen *them*.

TOM. To be sure you have; you are one of them yourself. You are the brightest spirit I ever saw.

EVA. They come to me sometimes in my sleep—those spirits bright—

They are all robed in spotless white,
And conquering palms they bear.

Uncle Tom, I'm going there.

TOM. Where Miss Eva?

EVA (*pointing to the sky*). I'm going there, to the spirits bright, Tom; I'm going before long.

TOM. It's jest no use tryin' to keep Miss Eva here; I've allays said so. She's got the Lord's mark in her forehead. She wasn't never like a child that's to live—there was always something deep in her eyes.

(*Rises and comes forward.* EVA *also comes forward, leaving Bible on bank.*)

ST. CLARE (*enters*). Ah! my little pussy, you look as blooming as a rose! You are better nowadays, are you not?

EVA. Papa, I've had things I wanted to say to you a great while. I want to say them now, before I get weaker.

ST. CLARE. Nay, this is an idle fear, Eva; you know you grow stronger every day.

EVA. It's all no use, Papa, to keep it to myself any longer. The time is coming that I am going to leave you, I am going, and never to come back.

ST. CLARE. Oh, now, my dear little Eva! you've got nervous and low-spirited; you mustn't indulge such gloomy thoughts.

EVA. No, Papa, don't deceive yourself, I am *not* any better; I know it perfectly well, and I am going before long. I am not nervous—I am not low-spirited. If it were not for you, Papa and my friends, I should be perfectly happy. I want to go—I long to go!

ST. CLARE. Why, dear child, what has made your poor little heart so sad? You have everything to make you happy that could be given you.

EVA. I had rather be in heaven! There are a great many things here that make me sad—that seem dreadful to me; I had rather be there; but I don't want to leave you—it almost breaks my heart!

ST. CLARE. What makes you sad, and what seems dreadful, Eva?

EVA. I feel sad for our poor people; they love me dearly, and they are all good and kind to me. I wish, Papa, they were all free!

ST. CLARE. Why, Eva, child, don't you think they are well enough off now?

EVA (*not heeding the question*). Papa, isn't there a way to have slaves made free? When I am dead, Papa, then you will think of me, and do it for my sake?

ST. CLARE. When you are dead, Eva? Oh, child, don't talk to me so. You are all I have on earth!

EVA. Papa, these poor creatures love their children as much as you do me. Tom loves his children. Oh, do something for them!

ST. CLARE. There, there darling; only don't distress yourself, and don't talk of dying, and I will do anything you wish.

EVA. And promise me, dear father, that Tom shall have his freedom as soon as— (*Hesitating*) — I am gone!

ST. CLARE. Yes, dear, I will do anything in the world—anything you could ask me to. There, Tom, take her to her chamber, this evening air is too chill for her. (*Music. Kisses her.*)

(*Tom takes* EVA *in his arms, and they exit.*)

ST. CLARE (*gazing mournfully after* EVA). Has there ever been a child like Eva? Yes, there has been; but their names are always on gravestones, and their sweet smiles, their heavenly eyes, their singular words and ways, are among the buried treasures of yearning hearts. It is as if heaven had an especial band of angels, whose office it is to sojourn for a season here, and endear to them the wayward human heart, that they might bear it upward with them in their homeward flight. When you see that deep, spiritual light in the eye when the little soul reveals itself in words sweeter and wiser than the ordinary words of children, hope not to retain that child; for the seal of heaven is on it, and the light of immortality looks out from its eyes! (*Music. Exit.*)

SCENE THREE

A corridor. Proscenium doors onstage. Music. Enter TOM; *he listens at door and then lies down.*

OPHELIA (*enters with candle*). Uncle Tom, what alive have you taken to sleeping anywhere and everywhere, like a dog, for? I thought you were one of the orderly sort, that liked to lie in bed in a Christian way.

TOM (*rises, mysteriously*). I do, Miss Feely, I do, but now—

OPHELIA. Well, what now?

TOM. We mustn't speak loud; Mas'r St. Clare won't hear on't; but Miss Feely, you know there must be somebody watchin' for the bridegroom.

OPHELIA. What do you mean, Tom?

TOM. You know it says in Scripture, "At midnight there was a great cry made, behold, the bridegroom cometh!" That's what I'm spectin' now, every night, Miss Feely, and I couldn't sleep out of hearing, no ways.

OPHELIA. Why, Uncle Tom, what

makes you think so?

TOM. Miss Eva, she talks to me. The Lord, he sends his messenger in the soul. I must be thar, Miss Feely; for when that ar blessed child goes into the kingdom, they'll open the door so wide, we'll all get a look in at the glory!

OPHELIA. Uncle Tom, did Miss Eva say she felt more unwell than usual tonight?

TOM. No; but she told me she was coming nearer—thar's them that tells it to the child, Miss Feely. It's the angels—it's the trumpet sound afore the break o' day!

OPHELIA. Heaven grant your fears be vain! Come in Tom. (*Exeunt.*)

SCENE FOUR

EVA's *chamber.* EVA *is on a couch. A table stands near the couch with a lamp on it. The light shines upon* EVA's *face, which is very pale. Scene half dark.* UNCLE TOM *is kneeling near the foot of the couch.* OPHELIA *stands at the head.* ST. CLARE *at back. Scene opens to plaintive music. After a strain, enter* MARIE, *hastily.*

MARIE. St. Clare! Cousin! Oh! what is the matter now?

ST. CLARE (*hoarsely*). Hush! she is dying!

MARIE (*sinking on her knees, beside* TOM). Dying!

ST. CLARE. Oh! if she would only wake and speak once more. (*Bending over* EVA) Eva, darling!

EVA (*uncloses her eyes, smiles, raises her head, and tries to speak*).

ST. CLARE. Do you know me, Eva?

EVA (*throwing her arms feebly about his neck*). Dear Papa. (*Her arms drop and she sinks back.*)

ST. CLARE. Oh, heaven! this is dreadful! Oh! Tom, my boy, it is killing me!

TOM. Look at her, mas'r. (*Points to* EVA).

ST. CLARE. Eva! (*A pause*) She does not hear. Oh, Eva! tell us what you see. What is it?

EVA (*feebly smiling*). Oh! love! joy! peace! (*Dies.*)

TOM. Oh! bless the Lord! it's over, dear mas'r, it's over.

ST. CLARE (*sinking on his knees*). Farewell, beloved child! the bright eternal doors have closed after thee. We shall see thy sweet face no more. Oh! woe for them who watched thy entrance into heaven when they shall wake and find only the cold, gray sky of daily life and thou gone forever.

(*Solemn music, slow curtain.*)

ACT FOUR

SCENE ONE

A street in New Orleans. Enter GUMPTION CUTE, *meeting* MARKS.

———

CUTE. How do ye dew?

MARKS. How are you?

CUTE. Well, now, squire, it's a fact that I am dead broke and busted up.

MARKS. You have been speculating, I suppose?

CUTE. That's just it and nothing shorter.

MARKS. You have had poor success, you say?

CUTE. Tarnation bad, now I tell you. You see I came to this part of the country to make my fortune.

MARKS. And you did not do it?

CUTE. Scarcely. The first thing I tried my hand at was keeping school. I opened an academy for the instruction of youth in the various branches of orthography, geography, and other graphies.

MARKS. Did you succeed in getting any pupils?

CUTE. Oh, lots on 'em! and a pretty set of dunces they were too. After the first quarter, I called on the respectable parents of the juveniles, and requested them to fork over. To which they politely answered—don't you wish you may get it?

MARKS. What did you do then?

CUTE. Well, I kind of pulled up stakes and left those diggins. Well then I went into Spiritual Rappings for a living. That paid pretty well for a short time, till I met with an accident.

MARKS. An accident?

CUTE. Yes; a tall Yahoo called on me one day, and wanted me to summon the spirit of his mother—which, of course, I did. He asked me about a dozen questions which I answered to his satisfaction. At last he wanted to know what she died of—I said, "Cholera." You never did see a critter so riled as he was. "Look yere, stranger," said he, "it's my opinion that you're a pesky humbug! for my mother was blown up in a steamboat!" With that he left the premises. The next day the people furnished me with a conveyance, and I rode out of town.

MARKS. Rode out of town?

CUTE. Yes; on a rail!

MARKS. I suppose you gave up the spirits, after that?

CUTE. Well, I reckon I did; it had such an effect on my spirits.

MARKS. It's a wonder they didn't tar and feather you.

CUTE. There was some mention made of that, but when they said *feathers,* I felt as if I had wings and flew away.

MARKS. You cut and run?

CUTE. Yes; I didn't like their company and I cut it. Well, after that I let myself out as an overseer on a cotton plantation. I made a pretty good thing of that, though it was dreadful trying to my feelings to flog the darkies; but I got used to it after a while, and then I used to lather 'em like Jehu. Well, the proprietor got the fever and ague and shook himself out of town. The place and all the fixings were sold at auction and I found myself adrift once more.

MARKS. What are you doing at present?

CUTE. I'm in search of a rich relation of mine.

MARKS. A rich relation?

CUTE. Yes, a Miss Ophelia St. Clare. You see, a niece of hers married one of my second cousins—that's how I came to be a relation of hers. She came on here from Vermont to be housekeeper to a cousin of hers, of the same name.

MARKS. I know him well.

CUTE. The deuce you do!—well, that's lucky.

MARKS. Yes, he lives in this city.

CUTE. Say, you just point out the locality, and I'll give him a call.

MARKS. Stop a bit. Suppose you shouldn't be able to raise the wind in that quarter, what have you thought of doing?

CUTE. Well, nothing particular.

MARKS. How should you like to enter into a nice, profitable business—one that pays well?

CUTE. That's just about my measure —it would suit me to a hair. What is it?

MARKS. Nigger catching.

CUTE. Catching niggers! What on airth do you mean?

MARKS. Why, when there's a large reward offered for a runaway darkey, we goes after him, catches him, and gets the reward.

CUTE. Yes, that's all right so far— but s'pose there ain't no reward offered?

MARKS. Why, then we catches the darkey on our own account, sells him, and pockets the proceeds.

CUTE. By chowder, that ain't a bad speculation!

MARKS. What do you say? I want a partner. You see, I lost my partner last year, up in Ohio—he was a powerful fellow.

CUTE. Lost him! How did you lose him?

MARKS. Well, you see, Tom and I—his name was Tom Loker—Tom and I were after a mulatto chap, called George Harris, that run away from Kentucky. We traced him through the greater part of Ohio, and came up with him near the Pennsylvania line. He took refuge among some rocks, and showed fight.

CUTE. Oh! then runaway darkies show fight, do they?

MARKS. Sometimes. Well, Tom—like a headstrong fool as he was—rushed up the rocks, and a Quaker chap, who was helping this George Harris threw him over the cliff.

CUTE. Was he killed?

MARKS. Well, I didn't stop to find out. Seeing that the darkies were stronger than I thought, I made tracks for a safe place.

CUTE. And what became of this George Harris?

MARKS. Oh! he and his wife and child got away safe into Canada. You see, they will get away sometimes, though it isn't very often. Now what do you say? You are just the figure for a fighting partner. Is it a bargain?

CUTE. Well, I rather calculate our teams won't hitch, no how. By chowder, I hain't no idea of setting myself up as a target for darkies to fire at—that's a speculation that don't suit my constitution.

MARKS. You're afraid, then?

CUTE. No, I ain't; it's against my principles.

MARKS. Your principles—how so?

CUTE. Because my principles are to keep a sharp lookout for No. 1. I shouldn't feel wholesome if a darkey was to throw me over the cliff to look after Tom Loker. (*Exeunt arm in arm.*)

SCENE TWO

Gothic chamber. Slow music. ST. CLARE *is seated on sofa.* TOM *is also present.*

———

ST. CLARE. Oh! Tom, my boy, the whole world is as empty as an egg shell.

TOM. I know it, mas'r, I know it. But oh! if mas'r could look up—up where our dear Miss Eva is—

ST. CLARE. Ah, Tom! I do look up; but the trouble is, I don't see anything when I do. I wish I could. It seems to be given to children and poor, honest fellows like you, to see what we cannot. How comes it?

TOM. Thou hast hid from the wise and prudent, and revealed unto babes; even so, Father, for so it seemed good in thy sight.

ST. CLARE. Tom, I don't believe—I've got the habit of doubting—I want to believe and I cannot.

TOM. Dear mas'r, pray to the good Lord: "Lord, I believe, help thou my unbelief."

ST. CLARE. Who knows anything about anything? Was all that beautiful love and faith only one of the ever-shifting phases of human feeling, having nothing real to rest on, passing away with the little breath! And is there no more Eva—nothing?

TOM. Oh! dear mas'r, there is. I know it; I'm sure of it. Do, do, dear mas'r, believe it!

ST. CLARE. How do you know there is, Tom? You never saw the Lord.

TOM. Felt Him in my soul, mas'r—feel Him now! Oh, mas'r! when I was sold away from my old woman and the children, I was jest a'most broken up—I felt as if there warn't nothing left—and then the Lord stood by me, and He says, "Fear not, Tom," and He brings light and joy into a poor fellow's soul—makes all peace; and I's so happy, and loves everybody, and feels willin' to be jest where the Lord wants to put me. I know it couldn't come from me, 'cause I's a poor, complaining creature—it comes from above, and I know He's willin' to do for mas'r.

ST. CLARE (*grasping* TOM's *hand*). Tom, you love me!

TOM. I's willin' to lay down my life this blessed day for you.

ST. CLARE (*sadly*). Poor, foolish fellow! I'm not worth the love of one good, honest heart like yours.

TOM. Oh, mas'r! there's more than me loves you—the blessed Saviour loves you.

ST. CLARE. How do you know that, Tom?

TOM. The love of the Saviour passeth knowledge.

ST. CLARE (*turns away*). Singular! that the story of a man who lived and died eighteen hundred years ago, can affect people so yet. But He was no man. (*Rises.*) No man ever had such long and living power. Oh! that I could believe what my mother taught me, and pray as I did when I was a boy! But, Tom, all this time I have forgotten why I sent for you. I'm going to make a freeman of you. Go have your trunk packed, and get ready to set out for Kentucky.

TOM (*joyfully*). Bless the Lord!

ST. CLARE (*dryly*). You haven't had such very bad times here, that you need be in such a rapture, Tom.

TOM. No, no, mas'r, 'tain't that; it's being a *freeman*—that's what I'm joyin' for.

ST. CLARE. Why, Tom, don't you think, for your own part, you've been better off than to be free?

TOM. No, *indeed*, Mas'r St. Clare—no, indeed!

ST. CLARE. Why, Tom, you couldn't possibly have earned by your work such clothes and such living as I have given you.

TOM. I know all that, Mas'r St. Clare—mas'r's been too good; but I'd rather have poor clothes, poor house, poor everything, and have 'em *mine*, than have the best, if they belonged to somebody else. I had *so*, mas'r; I think it's natur', mas'r.

ST. CLARE. I suppose so, Tom; and you'll be going off and leaving me in a month or so—though why you shouldn't no mortal knows.

TOM. Not while mas'r is in trouble. I'll stay with mas'r as long as he wants me, so as I can be any use.

ST. CLARE (*sadly*). Not while I'm in trouble, Tom? And when will my trouble be over?

TOM. When you are a believer.

ST. CLARE. And you really mean to stay by me till that day comes? (*Smiling and laying his hand on* TOM's *shoulder*) Ah, Tom! I won't keep you till that day. Go home to your wife and children, and give my love to all.

TOM. I's faith to think that day will come—the Lord has a work for mas'r.

ST. CLARE. A work, hey? Well, now, Tom, give me your views on what sort of a work it is—let's hear.

TOM. Why, even a poor fellow like me has a work; and Mas'r St. Clare, that has larnin', and riches, and friends, how much he might do for the Lord.

ST. CLARE. Tom, you seem to think the Lord needs a great deal done for him.

TOM. We does for him when we does for his creatures.

ST. CLARE. Good theology, Tom. Thank you, my boy; I like to hear you talk. But go now, Tom, and leave me alone. (TOM goes.) That faithful fellow's words have excited a train of thoughts that almost bear me, on the strong tide of faith and feeling, to the gates of that heaven I so vividly conceive. They seem to bring me nearer to Eva.

OPHELIA (outside). What are you doing there, you limb of Satan? You've been stealing something, I'll be bound. (OPHELIA drags in TOPSY.)

TOPSY. You go 'long, Miss Feely, 'tain't none o' your business.

ST. CLARE. Heyday! what is all this commotion?

OPHELIA. She's been stealing.

TOPSY (sobbing). I hain't neither.

OPHELIA. What have you got in your bosom?

TOPSY. I've got my hand dar.

OPHELIA. But what have you got in your hand?

TOPSY. Nuffin'.

OPHELIA. That's a fib, Topsy.

TOPSY. Well, I 'spects it is.

OPHELIA. Give it to me, whatever it is.

TOPSY. It's mine—I hope I may die this bressed minute, if it don't b'long to me.

OPHELIA. Topsy, I order you to give me that article; don't let me have to ask you again.

(TOPSY reluctantly takes the foot of an old stocking from her bosom and hands it to OPHELIA.) Sakes alive! what is all this? (Takes from it a lock of hair, and a small book, with a bit of crape twisted around it.)

TOPSY. Dat's a lock of ha'r dat Miss Eva give me—she cut it from her own beau'ful head herself.

ST. CLARE (takes book). Why did you wrap this (Pointing to crape) around the book?

TOPSY. 'Cause—'cause—'cause 'twas Miss Eva's. Oh! don't take 'em away, please! (Sits down and, putting her apron over her head, begins to sob vehemently.)

OPHELIA. Come, come, don't cry; you shall have them.

TOPSY (jumps up joyfully and takes them). I wants to keep 'em 'cause dey makes me good; I ain't half so wicked as I used to was. (Runs off.)

ST. CLARE. I really think you can make something of that girl. Any mind that is capable of a real sorrow is capable of good. You must try and do something with her.

OPHELIA. The child has improved very much; I have great hopes of her.

ST. CLARE. I believe I'll go down the street, a few moments, and hear the news.

OPHELIA. Shall I call Tom to attend you?

ST. CLARE. No, I shall be back in an hour. (Exits.)

OPHELIA. He's got an excellent heart, but then he's so dreadful shiftless. (Exits.)

SCENE THREE

Front chamber.

———

TOPSY (enters). Dar's somethin' de matter wid me—I isn't a bit like myself. I haven't done anything wrong since poor Miss Eva went up in de skies and left us. When I's gwine to do anything wicked, I tinks of her, and somehow I can't do it. I's getting to be good, dat's a fact I 'spects when I's dead I shall be turned into a little brack angel.

OPHELIA (*enters*). Topsy, I've been looking for you; I've got something very particular to say to you.

TOPSY. Does you want me to say the catechism?

OPHELIA. No, not now.

TOPSY (*aside*). Golly! dat's one comfort.

OPHELIA. Now, Topsy, I want you to try and understand what I am going to say to you.

TOPSY. Yes, missis, I'll open my ears drefful wide.

OPHELIA. Mr. St. Clare has given you to me, Topsy.

TOPSY. Den I b'longs to you, don't I? Golly! I thought I always belonged to you.

OPHELIA. Not till today have I received any authority to call you my property.

TOPSY. I's your property, am I? Well, if you say so, I 'spects I am.

OPHELIA. Topsy, I can give you your liberty.

TOPSY. My liberty?

OPHELIA. Yes, Topsy.

TOPSY. Has you got 'um with you?

OPHELIA. I have, Topsy.

TOPSY. Is it clothes or wittles?

OPHELIA. How shiftless! Don't you know what your liberty is, Topsy?

TOPSY. How should I know when I never seed 'um?

OPHELIA. Topsy, I am going to leave this place; I am going many miles away—to my own home in Vermont.

TOPSY. Den what's to become of dis chile?

OPHELIA. If you wish to go, I will take you with me.

TOPSY. Miss Feely, I doesn't want to leave you no how, I loves you, I does.

OPHELIA. Then you shall share my home for the rest of your days. Come, Topsy.

TOPSY. Stop, Miss Feely; does dey hab any oberseers in Varmount?

OPHELIA. No, Topsy.

TOPSY. Nor cotton plantations, nor sugar factories, nor darkies, nor whipping, nor nothing?

OPHELIA. No, Topsy.

TOPSY. By Golly! de quicker you is gwine de better den.

TOM (*enters, hastily*). Oh, Miss Feely! Miss Feely!

OPHELIA. Gracious me, Tom! what's the matter?

TOM. Oh, Mas'r St. Clare! Mas'r St. Clare!

OPHELIA. Well, Tom, well?

TOM. They've just brought him home and I do believe he's killed.

OPHELIA. Killed?

TOPSY. Oh, dear! what's to become of de poor darkies now?

TOM. He's dreadful weak. It's just as much as he can do to speak. He wanted me to call you.

OPHELIA. My poor cousin! Who would have thought of it? Don't say a word to his wife, Tom; the danger may not be so great as you think; it would only distress her. Come with me; you may be able to afford some assistance. (*Exeunt.*)

SCENE FOUR

Handsome chamber. ST. CLARE *is seated on sofa.* OPHELIA, TOM, *and* TOPSY *are clustered around him.* DOCTOR *is back of sofa, feeling his pulse. Scene opens to slow music.*

ST. CLARE (*raising himself feebly*). Tom—poor fellow!

TOM. Well, mas'r?

ST. CLARE. I have received my death wound.

TOM. Oh, no, no, mas'r!

ST. CLARE. I feel that I am dying—Tom, pray!

TOM (*sinking on his knees*). I do pray, mas'r! I do pray!

ST. CLARE (*after a pause*). Tom, one thing preys upon my mind—I have forgotten to sign your freedom papers. What will become of you when I am gone?

TOM. Don't think of that, mas'r.

ST. CLARE. I was wrong, Tom, very wrong, to neglect it. I may be the cause of much suffering to you hereafter. Marie, my wife—she—oh!—

OPHELIA. His mind is wandering.

ST. CLARE (*energetically*). No! it is coming *home* at last! (*Sinks back.*) at last! at last! Eva, I come! (*Dies.*)

(*Music, slow curtain.*)

ACT FIVE

SCENE ONE

An auction mart. UNCLE TOM *and* EMMELINE *at back.* ADOLF, SKEGGS, MARKS, MANN, *and various spectators are also present.* MARKS *and* MANN *come forward.*

———

MARKS. Hulloa, Alf! what brings you here?

MANN. Well, I was wanting a valet, and I heard that St. Clare's lot was going; I thought I'd just look at them.

MARKS. Catch me ever buying any of St. Clare's people. Spoilt niggers, every one—impudent as the devil.

MANN. Never fear that; if I get 'em, I'll soon have their airs out of them —they'll soon find that they've another kind of master to deal with than St. Clare. 'Pon my word, I'll buy that fellow—I like the shape of him. (*Pointing to* ADOLF.)

MARKS. You'll find it'll take all you've got to keep him—he's deucedly extravagant.

MANN. Yes, but my lord will find that he *can't* be extravagant with me. Just let him be sent to the calaboose a few times, and thoroughly dressed down, I'll tell you if it don't bring him to a sense of his ways. Oh! I'll reform him, up hill and down, you'll see. I'll buy him, that's flat.

(*Enter* LEGREE; *he goes up and looks at* ADOLF, *whose boots are nicely blacked.*)

LEGREE. A nigger with his boots blacked—bah! (*Spits on them.*) Holloa, you! (*To* TOM) Let's see your teeth. (*Seizes* TOM *by the jaw and opens his mouth.*) Strip up your sleeve and show your muscle. (TOM *does so.*) Where was you raised?

TOM. In Kintuck, mas'r.

LEGREE. What have you done?

TOM. Had care of mas'r's farm.

LEGREE. That's a likely story. (*Turns to* EMMELINE.) You're a nice-looking girl enough. How old are you? (*Grasps her arm.*)

EMMELINE (*shrieking*). Ah! you hurt me.

SKEGGS. Stop that, you minx! No whimpering here. The sale is going to begin. (*Mounts the rostrum.*) Gentlemen, the next article I shall offer you today is Adolf, late valet to Mr. St. Clare. How much am I offered?

(*Various bids are made.* ADOLF *is knocked down to* MANN *for eight hundred dollars.*)

Gentlemen, I now offer a prime article —the quadroon girl, Emmeline, only fifteen years of age, warranted in every respect.

(EMMELINE *is sold to* LEGREE *for one thousand dollars.*)

Now, I shall close today's sale by offering you the valuable article known as

Uncle Tom, the most useful nigger ever raised. Gentlemen in want of an overseer, now is the time to bid.

(*As before.* TOM *is sold to* LEGREE *for twelve hundred dollars.*)

LEGREE. Now look here, you two belong to me.

(TOM *and* EMMELINE *sink on their knees.*)

TOM. Heaven help us, then!

(*Music.* LEGREE *stands over them exulting.*)

SCENE TWO

The garden of MISS OPHELIA'*s house in Vermont. Enter* OPHELIA *and* DEACON PERRY.

———

DEACON. Miss Ophelia, allow me to offer you my congratulations upon your safe arrival in your native place. I hope it is your intention to pass the remainder of your days with us?

OPHELIA. Well, Deacon, I have come here with that express purpose.

DEACON. I presume you were not over-pleased with the South?

OPHELIA. Well, to tell you the truth, Deacon, I wasn't; I liked the country very well, but the people there are so dreadful shiftless.

DEACON. The result, I presume, of living in a warm climate.

OPHELIA. Well, Deacon, what is the news among you all here?

DEACON. Well, we live on in the same even jog-trot pace. Nothing of any consequence has happened—Oh! I forgot. (*Takes out his handkerchief.*) I've lost my wife; my Molly has left me. (*Wipes his eyes.*)

OPHELIA. Poor soul! I pity you, Deacon.

DEACON. Thank you. You perceive I bear my loss with resignation.

OPHELIA. How you must miss her tongue!

DEACON. Molly certainly was fond of talking. She always would have one last word—heigho!

OPHELIA. What was her complaint, Deacon?

DEACON. A very mild and soothing one, Miss Ophelia; she had a severe attack of the lockjaw.

OPHELIA. Dreadful!

DEACON. Wasn't it? When she found she couldn't use her tongue, she took it so much to heart that it struck to her stomach and killed her. Poor dear! Excuse my handkerchief; she's been dead only eighteen months.

OPHELIA. Why, Deacon, by this time you ought to be setting your cap for another wife.

DEACON. Do you think so, Miss Ophelia?

OPHELIA. I don't see why you shouldn't—you are still a good-looking man, Deacon.

DEACON. Ah! well, I think I do wear well—in fact, I may say remarkably well. It has been observed to me before.

OPHELIA. And you are not much over fifty?

DEACON. Just turned of forty, I assure you.

OPHELIA. Hale and hearty?

DEACON. Health excellent—look at my eye! Strong as a lion—look at my arm!! A No. 1 constitution—look at my leg!!!

OPHELIA. Have you no thoughts of choosing another partner?

DEACON. Well, to tell you the truth, I have.

OPHELIA. Who is she?

DEACON. She is not far distant. (*Looks at* OPHELIA *in a languishing manner.*) I have her in my eye at this present moment.

OPHELIA (*aside*). Really, I believe

he's going to pop. Why, surely, Deacon, you don't mean to—

DEACON. Yes, Miss Ophelia, I do mean; and believe me, when I say— (*Looking off*) The Lord be good to us, but I believe there is the devil coming!

TOPSY (*runs on with bouquet; she is now dressed very neatly*). Miss Feely, here is some flowers dat I hab been gathering for you. (*Gives bouquet.*)

OPHELIA. That's a good child.

DEACON. Miss Ophelia, who is this young person?

OPHELIA. She is my daughter.

DEACON (*aside*). Her daughter! Then she must have married a colored man off South. I was not aware that you had been married, Miss Ophelia?

OPHELIA. Married! Sakes alive! what made you think I had been married?

DEACON. Good gracious. I'm getting confused. Didn't I understand you to say that this—somewhat tanned— young lady was your daughter?

OPHELIA. Only by adoption. She is my adopted daughter.

DEACON. O—oh! (*Aside*) I breathe again.

TOPSY (*aside*). By Golly! dat old man's eyes stick out of 'um head dre'ful. Guess he never seed anything like me afore.

OPHELIA. Deacon, won't you step into the house and refresh yourself after your walk?

DEACON. I accept your polite invitation. (*Offers his arm.*) Allow me.

OPHELIA. As gallant as ever, Deacon. I declare, you grow younger every day.

DEACON. You can never grow old, madam.

OPHELIA. Ah, you flatterer! (*Exeunt.*)

TOPSY. Dar dey go, like an old goose and gander. Guess dat ole gemblemun feels kind of confectionary—rather sweet on my old missis. By Golly! she's been dre'ful kind to me ever since I come away from de South; and I loves her, I does, 'cause she takes such car' on me and gives me dese fine clothes. I tries to be good too, and I's getting 'long 'mazin' fast. I's not so wicked as I used to was. (*Looks out.*) Holloa! dar's someone comin' here. I wonder what he wants now. (*Retires, observing.*)

CUTE (*enters, very shabby, with a small bundle, on a stick, over his shoulder*). By chowder, here I am again. Phew, it's a pretty considerable tall piece of walking between here and New Orleans, not to mention the wear of shoe-leather. I guess I'm about done up. If this streak of bad luck lasts much longer, I'll borrow sixpence to buy a rope, and hang myself right straight up! When I went to call on Miss Ophelia, I swow if I didn't find out that she had left for Vermount; so I kind of concluded to make tracks in that direction myself and as I didn't have any money left, why I had to foot it, and here I am in old Varmount once more. They told me Miss Ophelia lived up here. I wonder if she will remember the relationship. (*Sees* TOPSY.) By chowder, there's a darkey. Look here, Charcoal!

TOPSY (*comes forward*). My name isn't Charcoal—it's Topsy.

CUTE. Oh! your name is Topsy, is it, you juvenile specimen of Day & Martin?

TOPSY. Tell you I don't know nothin' 'bout Day & Martin. I's Topsy and I belong to Miss Feely St. Clare.

CUTE. I'm much obleeged to you, you small extract of Japan, for your information. So Miss Ophelia lives up there in the white house, does she?

TOPSY. Well, she don't do nothin' else.

CUTE. Well, then, just locomote your pins.

TOPSY. What—what's dat?

CUTE. Walk your chalks!

TOPSY. By Golly! dere ain't no chalk 'bout me.

CUTE. Move your trotters.

TOPSY. How you does spoke! What you mean by trotters?

CUTE. Why, your feet, Stove Polish.

TOPSY. What does you want me to move my feet for?

CUTE. To tell your mistress, you ebony angel, that a gentleman wishes to see her.

TOPSY. Does you call yourself a gentleman? By Golly! you look more like a scar'crow.

CUTE. Now look here, you Charcoal, don't you be sassy. I'm a gentleman in distress; a done-up speculator; one that has seen better days—long time ago—and better clothes too, by chowder! My creditors are like my boots—they've no soles. I'm a victim to circumstances. I've been through much and survived it. I've taken walking exercise for the benefit of my health; but as I was trying to live on air at the same time, it was a losing speculation, 'cause it gave me such a dreadful appetite.

TOPSY. Golly! you look as if you could eat an ox, horns and all.

CUTE. Well, I calculate I could, if he was roasted—it's a speculation I should like to engage in. I have returned like the fellow that run away in Scripture; and if anybody's got a fatted calf they want to kill, all they got to do is to fetch him along. Do you know, Charcoal, that your mistress is a relation of mine?

TOPSY. Is she your uncle?

CUTE. No, no, not quite so near as that. My second cousin married her niece.

TOPSY. And does you want to see Miss Feely?

CUTE. I do. I have come to seek a home beneath her roof, and take care of all the spare change she don't want to use.

TOPSY. Den just you follow me, mas'r.

CUTE. Stop! By chowder, I've got a great idee. Say, you Day & Martin, how should you like to enter into a speculation?

TOPSY. Golly! I doesn't know what a spec—spec—cu—what-do-you-call-'um am.

CUTE. Well, now, I calculate I've hit upon about the right thing. Why should I degrade the manly dignity of the Cutes by becoming a beggar—expose myself to the chance of receiving the cold shoulder as a poor relation? By chowder, my blood biles as I think of it! Topsy, you can make my fortune, and your own, too. I've an idee in my head that is worth a million of dollars.

TOPSY. Golly! is your head worth dat? Guess you wouldn't bring dat out South for de whole of you.

CUTE. Don't you be too severe, now, Charcoal; I'm a man of genius. Did you ever hear of Barnum?

TOPSY. Barnum! Barnum! Does he live out South?

CUTE. No, he lives in New York. Do you know how he made his fortin?

TOPSY. What is him fortin, hey? Is it something he wears?

CUTE. Chowder, how green you are!

TOPSY (*indignantly*). Sar, I hab you to know I's not green; I's black.

CUTE. To be sure you are, Day & Martin. I calculate, when a person says another has a fortune, he means he's got plenty of money, Charcoal.

TOPSY. And did he make the money?

CUTE. Sartin sure, and no mistake.

TOPSY. Golly! now I thought money always growed.

CUTE. Oh, git out! You are too cute you are cuterer than I am and I'm

Cute by name and cute by nature. Well, as I was saying Barnum made his money by exhibiting a *woolly* horse; now wouldn't it be an all-fired speculation to show you as the woolly gal?

TOPSY. You want to make a sight of me?

CUTE. I'll give you half the receipts, by chowder!

TOPSY. Should I have to leave Miss Feely?

CUTE. To be sure you would.

TOPSY. Den you hab to get a woolly gal somewhere else, Mas'r Cute. (*Runs off.*)

CUTE. There's another speculation gone to smash, by chowder! (*Exit.*)

SCENE THREE

A rude chamber. TOM *is discovered, in old clothes, seated on a stool. He holds in his hand a paper containing a curl of* EVA's, *hair. The scene opens to the symphony of "Old Folks at Home."*

TOM. I have come to de dark places; I's going through de vale of shadows. My heart sinks at times and feels just like a big lump of lead. Den it gits up in my throat and chokes me till de tears roll out of my eyes; den I take out dis curl of little Miss Eva's hair, and the sight of it brings cal'm to my mind and I feels strong again. (*Kisses the curl and puts it in his breast—takes out a silver dollar, which is suspended around his neck by a string.*) Dere's de bright silver dollar dat Mas'r George Shelby gave me the day I was sold away from old Kentuck, and I've kept it ever since. Mas'r George must have grown to be a man by this time. I wonder if I shall ever see him again.

(*Song: "Old Folks at Home." Enter* LEGREE, EMMELINE, SAMBO, *and* QUIMBO.)

LEGREE. Shut up, you black cuss! Did you think I wanted any of your infernal howling? (*Turns to* EMMELINE.) We're home. (EMMELINE *shrinks from him. He takes hold of her ear.*) You didn't ever wear earrings?

EMMELINE (*trembling*). No, master.

LEGREE. Well, I'll give you a pair, if you're a good girl. You needn't be so frightened; I don't mean to make you work very hard. You'll have fine times with me and live like a lady; only be a good girl.

EMMELINE. My soul sickens as his eyes gaze upon me. His touch makes my very flesh creep.

LEGREE (*turns to* TOM, *and points to* SAMBO *and* QUIMBO). Ye see what ye'd get if ye'd try to run off. These yer boys have been raised as track niggers and they'd just as soon chaw one on ye up as eat their suppers; so mind yourself. (*To* EMMELINE) Come, mistress, you go in here with me. (*Taking* EMMELINE's *hand.*)

EMMELINE (*withdrawing her hand and shrinking back*). No, no! let me work in the fields; I don't want to be a lady.

LEGREE. Oh! you're going to be contrary, are you? I'll soon take all that out of you.

EMMELINE. Kill me, if you will.

LEGREE. Oh! you want to be killed, do you? Now come here, you Tom, you see I told you I didn't buy you jest for the common work; I mean to promote you and make a driver of you, and tonight ye may jest as well begin to get yer hand in. Now ye jest take this yer gal, and flog her; ye've seen enough on't to know how.

TOM. I beg mas'r's pardon—hopes mas'r won't set me at that. It's what I a'nt used to—never did, and can't do—no way possible.

LEGREE. Ye'll larn a pretty smart

chance of things ye never did know before I've done with ye. (*Strikes* TOM *with whip, three blows. Music chord each blow.*) There! now will ye tell me ye can't do it?

TOM. Yes, mas'r! I'm willing to work night and day, and work while there's life and breath in me; but this yer thing I can't feel it right to do, and, mas'r, I *never* shall do it, *never!*

LEGREE. What! ye black beast! tell *me* ye don't think it right to do what I tell ye! What have any of you cussed cattle to do with thinking what's right? I'll put a stop to it. Why, what do ye think ye are? May be ye think yer a gentleman, master Tom, to be telling your master what's right and what a'nt! So you pretend it's wrong to flog the gal?

TOM. I think so, mas'r; 'twould be downright cruel, and it's what I never will do, mas'r. If you mean to kill me, kill me; but as to raising my hand agin any one here, I never shall—I'll die first!

LEGREE. Well, here's a pious dog at last, let down among us sinners— powerful holy critter he must be. Here, you rascal! you make believe to be so pious, didn't you never read out of your Bible, "Servants, obey your masters"? An't I your master? Didn't I pay twelve hundred dollars, cash, for all there is inside your cussed old black shell? An't you mine, body and soul?

TOM. No, no! My soul a'nt yours, mas'r; you haven't bought it—ye can't buy it; it's been bought and paid for by one that is able to keep it, and you can't harm it!

LEGREE. I can't? we'll see, we'll see! Here, Sambo! Quimbo! give this dog such a breaking in as he won't get over this month!

EMMELINE. Oh, no! you will not be so cruel—have some mercy! (*Clings to* TOM.)

LEGREE. Mercy? you won't find any in this shop! Away with the black cuss! Flog him within an inch of his life!

(*Music.* SAMBO *and* QUIMBO *seize* TOM *and drag him up stage.* LEGREE *seizes* EMMELINE, *and throws her aside. She falls on her knees, with her hands lifted in supplication.* LEGREE *raises his whip, as if to strike* TOM.)

SCENE FOUR

Plain chamber. Enter OPHELIA, *followed by* TOPSY.

———

OPHELIA. A person inquiring for me, did you say, Topsy?

TOPSY. Yes, missis.

OPHELIA. What kind of a looking man is he?

TOPSY. By golly! he's very queer-looking man, anyway; and den he talks so dre'ful funny. What does you think? —yah! yah! he wanted to 'sibite me as de woolly gal! yah! yah!

OPHELIA. Oh! I understand. Some cute Yankee, who wants to purchase you, to make a show of—the heartless wretch!

TOPSY. Dat's just him, missis; dat's just his name. He tole me dat it was Cute—Mr. Cute Speculashum—dat's him.

OPHELIA. What did you say to him, Topsy?

TOPSY. Well, I didn't say much, it was brief and to the point—I tole him I wouldn't leave you, Miss Feely, no how.

OPHELIA. That's right, Topsy; you know you are very comfortable here— you wouldn't fare quite so well if you went away among strangers.

TOPSY. By golly! I know dat; you takes care on me, and makes me good.

I don't steal any now, and I don't swar, and I don't dance breakdowns. Oh! I isn't so wicked as I used to was.

OPHELIA. That's right, Topsy; now show the gentleman, or whatever he is, up.

TOPSY. By golly! I guess he won't make much out of Miss Feely. (*Exits.*)

OPHELIA. I wonder who this person can be? Perhaps it is some old acquaintance, who has heard of my arrival, and who comes on a social visit.

CUTE (*enters*). Aunt, how do ye do? Well, I swan, the sight of you is good for weak eyes. (*Offers his hand.*)

OPHELIA (*coldly drawing back*). Really, sir, I can't say that I ever had the pleasure of seeing you before.

CUTE. Well, it's a fact that you never did. You see I never happened to be in your neighborhood afore now. Of course you've heard of me? I'm one of the Cutes—Gumption Cute, the first and only son of Josiah and Maria Cute, of Oniontown, on the Onion River in the north part of this ere State of Varmount.

OPHELIA. Can't say I ever heard the name before.

CUTE. Well then, I calculate your memory must be a little ricketty. I'm a relation of yours.

OPHELIA. A relation of mine! Why, I never heard of any Cutes in our family.

CUTE. Well, I shouldn't wonder if you never did. Don't you remember your niece, Mary?

OPHELIA. Of course I do. What a shiftless question!

CUTE. Well, you see, my second cousin, Abijah Blake, married her an' you see that makes me a relation of yours.

OPHELIA. Rather a distant one, I should say.

CUTE. By chowder! I'm *near* enough, just at present.

OPHELIA. Well, you certainly are a sort of connection of mine.

CUTE. Yes, kind of sort of.

OPHELIA. And of course you are welcome to my house, as long as you choose to make it your home.

CUTE. By chowder! I'm booked for the next six months—this isn't a bad speculation.

OPHELIA. I hope you left all your folks well at home?

CUTE. Well, yes, they're pretty comfortably disposed of. Father and Mother's dead, and Uncle Josh has gone to California. I am the only representative of the Cutes left.

OPHELIA. There doesn't seem to be a great deal of *you* left. I declare, you are positively in rags.

CUTE. Well, you see, the fact is, I've been speculating—trying to get banknotes—specie-rags, as they say—but I calculate I've turned out rags of another sort.

OPHELIA. I'm sorry for your ill luck, but I am afraid you have been shiftless.

CUTE. By chowder! I've done all that a fellow could do. You see, somehow, everything I take hold of kind of bursts up.

OPHELIA. Well, well, perhaps you'll do better for the future; make yourself at home. I have got to see to some household matters, so excuse me for a short time. (*Aside*) Impudent and shiftless. (*Exit.*)

CUTE. By chowder! I rather guess that this speculation will hitch. She's a good-natured old critter; I reckon I'll be a son to her while she lives, and take care of her valuables arter she's a defunct departed. I wonder if they keep the vittles in this ere room? Guess not. I've got extensive accommodations for all sorts of eatables, I'm a regular vacuum, throughout—pockets and all.

I'm chuckfull of emptiness. (*Looks out.*) Holloa! who's this elderly individual coming upstairs? He looks like a compound essence of starch and dignity. I wonder if he isn't another relation of mine. I should like a rich old fellow now for an uncle.

DEACON (*enters*). Ha! a stranger here!

CUTE. How d'ye do?

DEACON. You are a friend to Miss Ophelia, I presume?

CUTE. Well, I rather calculate that I am a leetle more than a friend.

DEACON (*aside*). Bless me! what can he mean by those mysterious words? Can he be her—no I don't think he can. She said she hasn't—well, at all events, it's very suspicious.

CUTE. The old fellow seems kind of stuck up.

DEACON. You are a particular friend to Miss Ophelia, you say?

CUTE. Well, I calculate I am.

DEACON. Bound to her by any tender tie?

CUTE. It's something more than a tie—it's a regular double-twisted knot.

DEACON. Ah! just as I suspected. (*Aside*) Might I inquire the nature of that tie?

CUTE. Well, it's the natural tie of relationship.

DEACON. A relation—what relation?

CUTE. Why, you see, my second cousin, Abijah Blake, married her niece, Mary.

DEACON. Oh! is that all?

CUTE. By chowder, ain't that enough?

DEACON. Then you are not her husband?

CUTE. To be sure I ain't. What put that ere idee into your cranium?

DEACON (*shaking him vigorously by the hand*). My dear sir, I'm delighted to see you.

CUTE. Holloa! you ain't going slightly insane, are you?

DEACON. No, no fear of that; I'm only happy, that's all.

CUTE. I wonder if he's been taking a nipper?

DEACON. As you are a relation of Miss Ophelia's, I think it proper that I should make you my confidant; in fact, let you into a little scheme that I have lately conceived.

CUTE. Is it a speculation?

DEACON. Well, it is, just at present; but I trust before many hours to make it a surety.

CUTE. By chowder! I hope it won't serve you the way my speculations have served me. But fire away, old boy, and give us the prospectus.

DEACON. Well, then, my young friend, I have been thinking, ever since Miss Ophelia returned to Vermont, that she was just the person to fill the place of my lamented Molly.

CUTE. Say, you, you couldn't tell us who your lamented Molly was, could you?

DEACON. Why, the late Mrs. Perry, to be sure.

CUTE. Oh! then the lamented Polly was your wife?

DEACON. She was.

CUTE. And now you wish to marry Miss Ophelia?

DEACON. Exactly.

CUTE (*aside*). Consarn this old porpoise if I let him do me out of my living. By chowder! I'll put a spoke in his wheel.

DEACON. Well, what do you say? will you intercede for me with your aunt?

CUTE. No! bust me up if I do!

DEACON. No?

CUTE. No, I tell you. I forbid the banns. Now, ain't you a purty individual, to talk about getting married, you old superannuated Methuselah specimen of humanity! Why, you've got one foot in eternity already, and t'other ain't fit to stand on. Go home and go to bed! have your head shaved, and send for a lawyer to make your will, leave your property to your heirs—if you hain't got any, why leave it to me —I'll take care of it, and charge nothing for the trouble.

DEACON. Really, sir, this language to one of my standing, is highly indecorous—it's more, sir, than I feel willing to endure, sir. I shall expect an explanation, sir.

CUTE. Now, you see, old gouty toes, you're losing your temper.

DEACON. Sir, I'm a deacon; I never lost my temper in all my life, sir.

CUTE. Now, you see, you're getting excited; you had better go; we can't have a disturbance here!

DEACON. No, sir! I shall not go, sir! I shall not go until I have seen Miss Ophelia. I wish to know if she will countenance this insult.

CUTE. Now keep cool, old stick-in-the-mud! Draw it mild, old timber-toes!

DEACON. Damn it all, sir, what—

CUTE. Oh! only think, now, what would people say to hear a deacon swearing like a trooper?

DEACON. Sir—I—you—this is too much, sir.

CUTE. Well, now, I calculate that's just about my opinion, so we'll have no more of it. Get out of this! start your boots, or by chowder! I'll pitch you from one end of the stairs to the other.

OPHELIA (enters). Hoity toity! What's the meaning of all these loud words.

CUTE (together with DEACON). Well, you see, Aunt—

DEACON (together with CUTE). Miss Ophelia, I beg—

CUTE. Now, look here, you just hush your yap! How can I fix up matters if you keep jabbering?

OPHELIA. Silence! for shame, Mr. Cute. Is that the way you speak to the deacon?

CUTE. Darn the deacon!

OPHELIA. Deacon Perry, what is all this?

DEACON. Madam, a few words will explain everything. Hearing from this person that he was your nephew, I ventured to tell him that I cherished hopes of making you my wife, whereupon he flew into a violent passion, and ordered me out of the house.

OPHELIA. Does this house belong to you or me, Mr. Cute?

CUTE. Well, to you, I reckon.

OPHELIA. Then how dare you give orders in it?

CUTE. Well, I calculated that you wouldn't care about marrying old half a century there.

OPHELIA. That's enough; I will marry him; and as for you (points), get out.

CUTE. Get out?

OPHELIA. Yes; the sooner the better.

CUTE. Darned if I don't serve him out first, though.

(*Music.* CUTE *makes a dash at* DEACON, *who gets behind* OPHELIA. TOPSY *enters with a broom and beats* CUTE *around stage.* OPHELIA *faints in* DEACON'S *arms.* CUTE *falls, and* TOPSY *butts him, kneeling over him. Quick drop of curtain.*)

ACT SIX

SCENE ONE

Dark landscape. An old, roofless shed. TOM *is in shed, lying on some old cotton bagging.* CASSY *kneels by his side, holding a cup to his lips.*

CASSY. Drink all ye want. I knew how it would be. It isn't the first time I've been out in the night, carrying water to such as you.

TOM (*returning cup*). Thank you, missis.

CASSY. Don't call me missis. I'm a miserable slave like yourself—a lower one than you can ever be! It's no use, my poor fellow, this you've been trying to do. You were a brave fellow. You had the right on your side; but it's all in vain for you to struggle. You are in the Devil's hands; he is the strongest, and you must give up.

TOM. Oh! how can I give up?

CASSY. You see *you* don't know anything about it; I do. Here you are, on a lone plantation, ten miles from any other, in the swamps; not a white person here who could testify, if you were burned alive. There's no law here that can do you, or any of us, the least good; and this man! there's no earthly thing that he is not bad enough to do. I could make one's hair rise, and their teeth chatter, if I should only tell what I've seen and been knowing to here; and it's no use resisting! Did I *want* to live with him? Wasn't I a woman delicately bred? and he!—Father in Heaven! what was he and is he? And yet I've lived with him these five years, and cursed every moment of my life, night and day.

TOM. Oh, heaven! have you quite forgot us poor critters?

CASSY. And what are these miserable low dogs you work with, that you should suffer on their account? Every one of them would turn against you the first time they get a chance. They are all of them as low and cruel to each other as they can be; there's no use in your suffering to keep from hurting them!

TOM. What made 'em cruel? If I

give out I shall get used to it and grow, little by little, just like 'em. No, no, missis, I've lost everything, wife, and children, and home, and a kind master, and he would have set me free if he'd only lived a day longer—I've lost everything in *this* world, and now I can't lose heaven, too: no, I can't get to be wicked besides all.

CASSY. But it can't be that He will lay sin to our account; he won't charge it to us when we are forced to it; he'll charge it to them that drove us to it. Can I do anything more for you? Shall I give you some more water?

TOM. Oh, missis! I wish you'd go to Him who can give you living waters!

CASSY. Go to him! Where is he? Who is he?

TOM. Our Heavenly Father!

CASSY. I used to see the picture of him, over the altar, when I was a girl, but *he isn't here!* there's nothing here but sin, and long, long despair! There, there, don't talk any more, my poor fellow. Try to sleep, if you can. I must hasten back, lest my absence be noted. Think of me when I am gone, Uncle Tom, and pray, pray for me.

SCENE TWO

Street in New Orleans.

GEORGE SHELBY (*enters*). At length my mission of mercy is nearly finished, I have reached my journey's end. I have now but to find the house of Mr. St. Clare, repurchase old Uncle Tom, and convey him back to his wife and children in old Kentucky. Some one approaches; he may, perhaps, be able to give me the information I require. I will accost him.

(*Enter* MARKS.)

Pray, sir, can you tell me where Mr. St. Clare dwells.

MARKS. Where I don't think you'll be in a hurry to seek him.

GEORGE SHELBY. And where is that?

MARKS. In the grave!

GEORGE SHELBY. Stay, sir! you may be able to give me some information concerning Mr. St. Clare.

MARKS. I beg pardon, sir, I am a lawyer; I can't afford to give anything.

GEORGE SHELBY. But you would have no objections to selling it?

MARKS. Not the slightest.

GEORGE SHELBY. What do you value it at?

MARKS. Well, say five dollars, that's reasonable.

GEORGE SHELBY. There they are. (*Gives money.*) Now answer me to the best of your ability. Has the death of St. Clare caused his slaves to be sold?

MARKS. It has.

GEORGE SHELBY. How were they sold?

MARKS. At auction—they went dirt cheap.

GEORGE SHELBY. How were they bought—all in one lot?

MARKS. No, they went to different bidders.

GEORGE SHELBY. Was you present at the sale?

MARKS. I was.

GEORGE SHELBY. Do you remember seeing a Negro among them called Tom.

MARKS. What, Uncle Tom?

GEORGE SHELBY. The same—who bought him?

MARKS. A Mr. Legree.

GEORGE SHELBY. Where is his plantation?

MARKS. Up in Louisiana, on the Red River; but a man never could find it, unless he had been there before.

GEORGE SHELBY. Who could I get to direct me there?

MARKS. Well, stranger, I don't know of any one just at present, 'cept myself, could find it for you; it's such an out-of-the-way sort of hole; and if you are a mind to come down handsomely, why, I'll do it.

GEORGE SHELBY. The reward shall be ample.

MARKS. Enough said, stranger; let's take the steamboat at once. (*Exeunt.*)

SCENE THREE

A rough chamber.

———

LEGREE (*enters and sits*). Plague on that Sambo, to kick up this yer row between him and the new hands.

(CASSY *steals on and stands behind him.*)

The fellow won't be fit to work for a week now, right in the press of the season.

CASSY. Yes, just like you.

LEGREE. Hah! you she-devil! you've come back, have you? (*Rises.*)

CASSY. Yes, I have; come to have my own way, too.

LEGREE. You lie, you jade! I'll be up to my word. Either behave yourself, or stay down in the quarters and fare and work with the rest.

CASSY. I'd rather, ten thousand times, live in the dirtiest hole at the quarters, than be under your hoof!

LEGREE. But you are under my hoof, for all that, that's one comfort; so sit down here and listen to reason. (*Grasps her wrist.*)

CASSY. Simon Legree, take care! (LEGREE *lets go his hold.*) You're afraid of me, Simon, and you've reason to be; for I've got the Devil in me!

LEGREE. I believe to my soul you have. After all, Cassy, why can't you be friends with me, as you used to?

CASSY (*bitterly*). Used to!

LEGREE. I wish, Cassy, you'd behave

yourself decently.

CASSY. *You* talk about behaving decently! and what have you been doing? You haven't even sense enough to keep from spoiling one of your best hands, right in the most pressing season, just for your devilish temper.

LEGREE. I was a fool, it's fact, to let any such brangle come up, but when Tom set up his will he had to be broke in.

CASSY. You'll never break *him* in.

LEGREE. Won't I? I'd like to know if I won't! He'd be the first nigger that ever come it round me! I'll break every bone in his body but he shall give up.

(*Enter* SAMBO, *with a paper in his hand, stands bowing.*)

LEGREE. What's that, you dog?

SAMBO. It's a witch thing, mas'r.

LEGREE. A what?

SAMBO. Something that niggers gits from witches. Keep 'em from feeling when they's flogged. He had it tied round his neck with a black string.

(LEGREE *takes the paper and opens it.—A silver dollar drops on the stage, and a long curl of light hair twines around his finger.*)

LEGREE. Damnation. (*Stamping and writhing, as if the hair burned him*) Where did this come from? Take it off! burn it up! burn it up! (*Throws the curl away.*) What did you bring it to me for?

SAMBO (*trembling*). I beg pardon, mas'r; I thought you would like to see um.

LEGREE. Don't you bring me any more of your devilish things. (*Shakes his fist at* SAMBO, *who runs off.* LEGREE *kicks the dollar after him.*) Blast it! where did he get that? If it didn't look just like—whoo! I thought I'd forgot that. Curse me if I think there's any such thing as forgetting anything, any how.

CASSY. What is the matter with you, Legree? What is there in a simple curl of fair hair to appall a man like you—you who are familiar with every form of cruelty.

LEGREE. Cassy, tonight the past has been recalled to me—the past that I have so long and vainly striven to forget.

CASSY. Has aught on this earth power to move a soul like thine?

LEGREE. Yes, for hard and reprobate as I now seem, there has been a time when I have been rocked on the bosom of a mother, cradled with prayers and pious hymns, my now seared brow bedewed with the waters of holy baptism.

CASSY (*aside*). What sweet memories of childhood can thus soften down that heart of iron?

LEGREE. In early childhood a fair-haired woman has led me, at the sound of Sabbath bells, to worship and to pray. Born of a hard-tempered sire, on whom that gentle woman had wasted a world of unvalued love, I followed in the steps of my father. Boisterous, unruly and tyrannical, I despised all her counsel, and would have none of her reproof, and, at an early age, broke from her to seek my fortunes on the sea. I never came home but once after that, and then my mother, with the yearning of a heart that must love something, and had nothing else to love, clung to me, and sought with passionate prayers and entreaties to win me from a life of sin.

CASSY. That was your day of grace, Legree; then good angels called you, and mercy held you by the hand.

LEGREE. My heart inly relented; there was a conflict, but sin got the victory, and I set all the force of my rough nature against the conviction of my conscience. I drank and swore, was wilder and more brutal than ever. And one night, when my mother, in the last agony of her despair, knelt at my feet, I spurned her from me, threw her senseless on the floor, and with brutal curses fled to my ship.

CASSY. Then the fiend took thee for his own.

LEGREE. The next I heard of my mother was one night while I was carousing among drunken companions. A letter was put in my hands. I opened it, and a lock of long, curling hair fell from it, and twined about my fingers, even as that lock twined but now. The letter told me that my mother was dead, and that dying she blest and forgave me! (*Buries his face in his hands.*)

CASSY. Why did you not even then renounce your evil ways?

LEGREE. There is a dread, unhallowed necromancy of evil, that turns things sweetest and holiest to phantoms of horror and afright. That pale, loving mother—her dying prayers, her forgiving, love—wrought in my demoniac heart of sin only as a damning sentence, bringing with it a fearful looking for of judgment and fiery indignation.

CASSY. And yet you would not strive to avert the doom that threatened you.

LEGREE. I burned the lock of hair and I burned the letter; and when I saw them hissing and crackling in the flame, inly shuddered as I thought of everlasting fires! I tried to drink and revel, and swear away the memory; but often in the deep night, whose solemn stillness arraigns the soul in forced communion with itself, I have seen that pale mother rising by my bedside, and felt the soft twining of that hair around my fingers, 'till the cold sweat would roll down my face, and I would spring from my bed in horror—horror! (*Falls in chair. After a pause*) What the devil ails me? Large drops of sweat stand on my forehead, and my heart beats heavy and thick with fear. I thought I saw something white rising and glimmering in the gloom before me, and it seemed to bear my mother's face! I know one thing; I'll let that fellow Tom alone, after this. What did I want with his cussed paper? I believe I am bewitched sure enough! I've been shivering and sweating ever since! Where did he get that hair? It couldn't have been that! I *burn'd* that up, I know I did! It would be a joke if hair could rise from the dead! I'll have Sambo and Quimbo up here to sing and dance one of their dances, and keep off these horrid notions. Here, Sambo! Quimbo! (*Exit.*)

CASSY. Yes, Legree, that golden tress was charmed; each hair had in it a spell of terror and remorse for thee, and was used by a mightier power to bind thy cruel hands from inflicting uttermost evil on the helpless! (*Exit.*)

SCENE FOUR

Street. Enter MARKS, *meeting* CUTE, *who enters dressed in an old faded uniform.*

————

MARKS. By the land! stranger, but it strikes me that I've seen you somewhere before.

CUTE. By chowder! do you know now, that's just what I was going to say?

MARKS. Isn't your name Cute?

CUTE. You're right, I calculate. Yours is Marks, I reckon.

MARKS. Just so.

CUTE. Well, I swow, I'm glad to see you. (*They shake hands.*) How's your wholesome?

MARKS. Hearty as ever. Well, who would have thought of ever seeing you again. Why, I thought you was in Vermont?

CUTE. Well, so I was. You see I went

there after that rich relation of mine—but the speculation didn't turn out well.

MARKS. How so?

CUTE. Why, you see, she took a shine to an old fellow—Deacon Abraham Perry—and married him.

MARKS. Oh, that rather put your nose out of joint in that quarter.

CUTE. Busted me right up, I tell you. The Deacon did the handsome thing, though; he said if I would leave the neighborhood and go out south again, he'd stand the damage. I calculate I didn't give him much time to change his mind, and so, you see, here I am again.

MARKS. What are you doing in that soldier rig?

CUTE. Oh, this is my sign.

MARKS. Your sign?

CUTE. Yes; you see, I'm engaged just at present in an all-fired good speculation, I'm a Fillibusterow.

MARKS. A what?

CUTE. A Fillibusterow! Don't you know what that is? It's Spanish for Cuban Volunteer; and means a chap that goes the whole porker for glory and all that ere sort of thing.

MARKS. Oh! you've joined the order of the Lone Star!

CUTE. You've hit it. You see I bought this uniform at a second-hand clothing store, I puts it on and goes to a benevolent individual and I says to him—appealing to his feelings—I'm one of the fellows that went to Cuba and got massacred by the bloody Spaniards. I'm in a destitute condition—give me a trifle to pay my passage back, so I can whop the tyrannical cusses and avenge my brave fellow sogers what got slewed there.

MARKS. How pathetic!

CUTE. I tell you it works up the feelings of benevolent individuals dreadfully. It draws tears from their eyes and

money from their pockets. By chowder! one old chap gave me a hundred dollars to help on the cause.

MARKS. I admire a genius like yours.

CUTE. But I say, what are you up to?

MARKS. I am the traveling companion of a young gentleman by the name of Shelby, who is going to the plantation of a Mr. Legree on the Red River, to buy an old darkey who used to belong to his father.

CUTE. Legree—Legree? Well, now, I calculate I've heard that ere name afore.

MARKS. Do you remember that man who drew a bowie knife on you in New Orleans?

CUTE. By chowder! I remember the circumstance just as well as if it was yesterday; but I can't say that I recollect much about the man, for you see I was in something of a hurry about that time and didn't stop to take a good look at him.

MARKS. Well, that man was this same Mr. Legree.

CUTE. Do you know, now, I should like to pay that critter off?

MARKS. Then I'll give you an opportunity.

CUTE. Chowder! how will you do that?

MARKS. Do you remember the gentleman that interfered between you and Legree?

CUTE. Yes—well?

MARKS. He received the blow that was intended for you, and died from the effects of it. So, you see, Legree is a murderer, and we are only witnesses of the deed. His life is in our hands.

CUTE. Let's have him right up and make him dance on nothing to the tune of Yankee Doodle!

MARKS. Stop a bit. Don't you see a chance for a profitable speculation?

CUTE. A speculation! Fire away,

don't be bashful, I'm the man for a speculation.

MARKS. I have made a deposition to the Governor of the state of all the particulars of that affair at Orleans.

CUTE. What did you do that for?

MARKS. To get a warrant for his arrest.

CUTE. Oh! and have you got it?

MARKS. Yes; here it is. (*Takes out paper.*)

CUTE. Well, now, I don't see how you are going to make anything by that bit of paper.

MARKS. But I do. I shall say to Legree, I have got a warrant against you for murder; my friend, Mr. Cute, and myself are the only witnesses who can appear against you. Give us a thousand dollars, and we will tear the warrant and be silent.

CUTE. Then Mr. Legree forks over a thousand dollars, and your friend Cute pockets five hundred of it, is that the calculation?

MARKS. If you will join me in the undertaking.

CUTE. I'll do it, by chowder!

MARKS. Your hand to bind the bargain.

CUTE. I'll stick by you thro' thick and thin.

MARKS. Enough said.

CUTE. Then shake. (*They shake hands.*)

MARKS. But I say, Cute, he may be contrary and show fight.

CUTE. Never mind, we've got the law on our side, and we're bound to stir him up. If he don't come down handsomely we'll present him with a necktie made of hemp!

MARKS. I declare you're getting spunky.

CUTE. Well, I reckon, I am. Let's go and have something to drink. Tell you what, Marks, if we don't get *him,* we'll have his hide, by chowder! (*Exeunt, arm in arm.*)

Rough chamber. Enter LEGREE, *followed by* SAMBO.

———

LEGREE. Go and send Cassy to me.

SAMBO. Yes mas'r. (*Exit.*)

LEGREE. Curse the woman! she's got a temper worse than the devil! I shall do her an injury one of these days, if she isn't careful.

(*Re-enter* SAMBO, *frightened.*) What's the matter with, you black scoundrel?

SAMBO. S'help me, mas'r, she isn't dare.

LEGREE. I suppose she's about the house somewhere?

SAMBO. No, she isn't, mas'r; I's been all over de house and I can't find nothing of her nor Emmeline.

LEGREE. Bolted, by the Lord! Call out the dogs! saddle my horse! Stop! are you sure they really have gone?

SAMBO. Yes, mas'r; I's been in every room 'cept the haunted garret and dey wouldn't go dere.

LEGREE. I have it! Now, Sambo, you jest go and walk that Tom up here, right away!

(*Exit* SAMBO.)

The old cuss is at the bottom of this yer whole matter; and I'll have it out of his infernal black hide, or I'll know the reason why! I *hate* him—I *hate* him! And isn't he *mine?* Can't I do what I like with him? Who's to hinder, I wonder?

(TOM *is dragged on by* SAMBO *and* QUIMBO.)

LEGREE (*grimly confronting* TOM). Well, Tom, do you know I've made up my mind to *kill* you?

TOM. It's very likely, mas'r.

LEGREE. *I—have—done—just—that —thing,* Tom, unless you'll tell me what do you know about these yer gals? (TOM *is silent.*)

D'ye hear? Speak!

TOM. I hain't got anything to tell, mas'r.

LEGREE. Do you dare to tell me, you old black rascal, you don't know? Speak! Do you know anything?

TOM. I know, mas'r; but I can't tell anything. *I can die!*

LEGREE. Hark ye, Tom! ye think, 'cause I have let you off before, I don't mean what I say; but, this time, I have made *up my mind,* and counted the cost. You've always stood it out agin me; now, I'll *conquer ye or kill ye!* one or t'other. I'll count every drop of blood there is in you, and take 'em, one by one, 'till ye give up!

TOM. Mas'r, if you was sick, or in trouble, or dying, and I could save you, I'd *give* you my heart's blood; and, if taking every drop of blood in this poor old body would save your precious soul, I'd give 'em freely. Do the worst you can, my troubles will be over soon; but if you don't repent yours won't never end.

LEGREE (*strikes* TOM *down with the butt of his whip*). How do you like that?

SAMBO. He's most gone, mas'r!

TOM (*rises feebly on his hands*). There ain't no more you can do. I forgive you with all my soul. (*Sinks back, and is carried off by* SAMBO *and* QUIMBO.)

LEGREE. I believe he's done for finally. Well, his mouth is shut up at last—that's one comfort.

(*Enter* GEORGE SHELBY, MARKS, *and* CUTE.)

Strangers! Well what do you want?

GEORGE SHELBY. I understand that you bought in New Orleans a Negro named Tom.

LEGREE. Yes, I did buy such a fellow, and a devil of a bargain I had of it, too! I believe he's trying to die, but I don't know as he'll make it out.

GEORGE SHELBY. Where is he? Let me see him!

SAMBO. Dere he is! (*Points off, at* TOM.)

LEGREE. How dare you speak? (*Drives* SAMBO *and* QUIMBO *off.*)

(GEORGE *exits.*)

CUTE. Now's the time to nab him.

MARKS. How are you, Mr. Legree?

LEGREE. What the devil brought you here?

MARKS. This little bit of paper. I arrest you for the murder of Mr. St. Clare. What do you say to that?

LEGREE. This is my answer! (*Makes a blow at* MARKS, *who dodges, and* CUTE *receives the blow—he cries out and runs off.* MARKS *fires at* LEGREE, game's up!

(*Falls dead.* QUIMBO *and* SAMBO *return and carry him off, laughing.* GEORGE SHELBY *enters, supporting* TOM. *Music. They advance to front and* TOM *falls.*)

GEORGE SHELBY. Oh! dear Uncle Tom! do wake—do speak once more! look up! Here's Master George—your own little Master George. Don't you know me?

TOM (*opening his eyes and speaking in a feeble tone*). Mas'r George! Bless de Lord! it's all I wanted! They hav'n't forgot me! It warms my soul; it does my old heart good! Now I shall die content!

GEORGE SHELBY. You shan't die! you mustn't die, nor think of it. I have come to buy you, and take you home.

TOM. Oh, Mas'r George, you're too late. The Lord has bought me, and is going to take me home.

GEORGE SHELBY. Oh! don't die. It

will kill me—it will break my heart to think what you have suffered, poor, poor fellow!

TOM. Don't call me, poor fellow! I *have* been poor fellow; but that's all past and gone now. I'm right in the door, going into glory! Oh, Mas'r George! *Heaven has come! I've got the* victory; the Lord has given it to me! Glory be to His name! (*Dies.*)

(*Solemn music.* GEORGE *covers* UN-CLE TOM *with his cloak, and kneels over him. Clouds work on and con-* ceal them, and then work off.)

SCENE SIX

Gorgeous clouds, tinted with sun-light. EVA, *robed in white, is discovered on the back of a milk-white dove, with expanded wings, as if just soaring up-ward. Her hands are extended in benediction over* ST. CLARE *and* UNCLE TOM, *who are kneeling and gazing up to her. Expressive music. Slow curtain.*

THE OCTOROON

Dion Boucicault

First performed at the Winter Garden Theatre in
New York on December 6, 1859.*

GEORGE PEYTON	JACKSON
SALEM SCUDDER	OLD PETE
MR. SUNNYSIDE	PAUL, *a boy slave*
JACOB M'CLOSKY	SOLON
WAHNOTEE	MRS. PEYTON
LAFOUCHE	ZOE
CAPTAIN RATTS	DORA SUNNYSIDE
COLONEL POINTDEXTER	GRACE
JULES THIBODEAUX	MINNIE
JUDGE CAILLOU	DIDO

---

* For the date of December 6 (usually given as December 5), see Albert E.
Johnson's "Dion Boucicault: Man and Fable," *Educational Theatre Journal,* December, 1954, p. 313. The Winter Garden Management announced on December 5, 1859,
that the play "would not be shown until the following evening because the new
drama required special rehearsals and new scenery and machinery." The author, who
built and operated the Winter Garden himself, was probably responsible for this
one-day delay, since he supervised the production of his own plays and, as Johnson
observes, was greatly concerned with technical details as well as with the performances.

ACT ONE

The scene opens on a view of the Plantation Terrebonne, in Louisiana. A branch of the Mississippi is seen winding through the estate. A low-built but extensive planter's dwelling, surrounded with a veranda, and raised a few feet from the ground, occupies the left side. On the right stand a table and chairs. GRACE *is discovered sitting at breakfast-table with the Negro children.*

SOLON (*enters, from the house*). Yah! you bomn'ble fry—git out—a gen'leman can't pass for you.

GRACE (*seizing a fly whisk*). Hee!—ha git out! (*She drives the children away. In escaping, they tumble against* SOLON, *who falls with the tray; the children steal the bananas and rolls that fall about.*)

PETE (*who is lame, enters; he carries a mop and pail*). Hey! laws a massey! why, clar out! drop dat banana! I'll murder this yer crowd. (*He chases children about; they leap over railing at back.*)

(*Exit* SOLON.)

Dem little niggers is a judgment upon dis generation.

GEORGE (*enters, from the house*). What's the matter, Pete?

PETE. It's dem black trash, Mas'r George; dis ere property wants claring; dem's getting too numerous round: when I gets time I'll kill some on 'em, sure!

GEORGE. They don't seem to be scared by the threat.

PETE. Stop, you varmin! stop till I get enough of you in one place!

GEORGE. Were they all born on this estate?

PETE. Guess they nebber was born—dem tings! what, dem?—get away! Born here—dem darkies? What, on Terrebonne!. Don't b'lieve it, Mas'r George; dem black tings never was born at all; dey swarmed one mornin' on a sassafras tree in the swamp; I cotched 'em; dey ain't no 'count. Don't believe dey'll turn out niggers when dey're growed; dey'll come out sunthin' else.

GRACE. Yes, Mas'r George, dey was born here; and old Pete is fonder on 'em dan he is of his fiddle on a Sunday.

PETE. What? dem tings—dem? get away. (*Makes blow at the children.*) Born here! dem darkies! What, on Terrebonne? Don't b'lieve it, Mas'r George—no. One morning dey swarmed on a sassafras tree in de swamp, and I cotched 'em all in a sieve—dat's how dey come on top of dis yearth—git out, you—ya, ya! (*Laughs.*)

(*Exit* GRACE.)

MRS. PEYTON (*enters from the house*). So, Pete, you are spoiling those children as usual!

PETE. Dat's right, missus! gib it to ole Pete! he's allers in for it. Git away dere! Ya! if dey ain't all lighted, like coons, on dat snake fence, just out of shot. Look dar! Ya, ya! Dem debils. Ya!

MRS. PEYTON. Pete, do you hear?

PETE. Git down dar! I'm arter you! (*Hobbles off.*)

MRS. PEYTON. You are out early this morning, George.

GEORGE. I was up before daylight. We got the horses saddled, and galloped down the shell road over the Piney Patch; then coasting the Bayou Lake, we crossed the long swamps, by Paul's Path, and so came home again.

MRS. PEYTON (*laughing*). You seem already familiar with the names of every spot on the estate.

(*Enter* PETE, *who arranges breakfast.*)

GEORGE. Just one month ago I quitted Paris. I left that siren city as I would have left a beloved woman.

MRS. PEYTON. No wonder! I dare say you left at least a dozen beloved women there, at the same time.

GEORGE. I feel that I departed amid universal and sincere regret. I left my loves and my creditors equally inconsolable.

MRS. PEYTON. George, you are incorrigible. Ah! you remind me so much of your uncle, the judge.

GEORGE. Bless his dear old handwriting, it's all I ever saw of him. For ten years his letters came every quarterday, with a remittance and a word of advice in his formal cavalier style; and then a joke in the postscript, that upset the dignity of the foregoing. Aunt, when he died, two years ago, I read over those letters of his, and if I didn't cry like a baby—

MRS. PEYTON. No, George; say you wept like a man. And so you really kept those foolish letters?

GEORGE. Yes; I kept the letters, and squandered the money.

MRS. PEYTON (*embracing him*). Ah! why were you not my son—you are so like my dear husband.

SCUDDER (*enters*). Ain't he! Yes—when I saw him and Miss Zoe galloping through the green sugar crop, and doing ten dollars' worth of damage at every stride, says I, how like his old uncle he do make the dirt fly.

GEORGE. O, aunt! what a bright, gay creature she is!

SCUDDER. What, Zoe! Guess that you didn't leave anything female in Europe that can lift an eyelash beside that gal. When she goes along, she just leaves a streak of love behind her. It's a good drink to see her come into the cotton fields—the niggers get fresh on the sight of her. If she ain't worth her

weight in sunshine you may take one of my fingers off, and choose which you like.

MRS. PEYTON. She need not keep us waiting breakfast, though. Pete, tell Miss Zoe that we are waiting.

PETE. Yes, missus. Why, Minnie, why don't you run when you hear, you lazy crittur?

(*Minnie runs off*).

Dat's de laziest nigger on dis yere property. (*Sitting down*) Don't do nuffin.

MRS. PEYTON. My dear George, you are left in your uncle's will heir to this estate.

GEORGE. Subject to your life interest and an annuity to Zoe, is it not so?

MRS. PEYTON. I fear that the property is so involved that the strictest economy will scarcely recover it. My dear husband never kept any accounts, and we scarcely know in what condition the estate really is.

SCUDDER. Yes, we do, ma'am; it's in a darned bad condition. Ten years ago the judge took as overseer a bit of Connecticut hardware called M'Closky. The judge didn't understand accounts—the overseer did. For a year or two all went fine. The judge drew money like Bourbon whisky from a barrel, and never turned off the tap. But out it flew, free for everybody or anybody to beg, borrow, or steal. So it went, till one day the judge found the tap wouldn't run. He looked in to see what stopped it, and pulled out a big mortgage. "Sign that," says the overseer; "it's only a formality." "All right," says the judge, and away went a thousand acres; so at the end of eight years, Jacob M'Closky, Esquire, finds himself proprietor of the richest half of Terrebonne—

GEORGE. But the other half is free.

SCUDDER. No, it ain't; because, just then, what does the judge do, but hire another overseer—a Yankee—a Yankee named Salem Scudder.

MRS. PEYTON. O, no, it was—

SCUDDER. Hold on, now! I'm going to straighten this account clear out. What was this here Scudder? Well, he lived in New York by sittin' with his heels up in front of French's Hotel, and inventin'—

GEORGE. Inventing what?

SCUDDER. Improvements—anything, from a stay-lace to a fire-engine. Well, he cut that for the photographing line. He and his apparatus arrived here, took the judge's likeness and his fancy, who made him overseer right off. Well, sir, what does this Scudder do but introduces his inventions and improvements on this estate. His new cotton gins broke down, the steam sugar-mills burst up, until he finished off with his folly what Mr. M'Closky with his knavery began.

MRS. PEYTON. O, Salem! how can you say so? Haven't you worked like a horse?

SCUDDER. No, ma'am, I worked like an ass—an honest one, and that's all. Now, Mr. George, between the two overseers, you and that good old lady have come to the ground; that is the state of things, just as near as I can fix it.

(ZOE sings without.)

GEORGE. 'Tis Zoe.

SCUDDER. O, I have not spoiled that anyhow. I can't introduce any darned improvement there. Ain't that a cure for old age; it kinder lifts the heart up, don't it?

MRS. PEYTON. Poor child! what will become of her when I am gone? If you haven't spoiled her, I fear I have. She has had the education of a lady.

GEORGE. I have remarked that she is treated by the neighbors with a kind of familiar condescension that annoyed me.

SCUDDER. Don't you know that she is the natural daughter of the judge, your uncle, and that old lady thar just adored anything her husband cared for; and this girl, that another woman would 'a' hated, she loves as if she'd been her own child.

GEORGE. Aunt, I am prouder and happier to be your nephew and heir to the ruins of Terrebonne, than I would have been to have had half Louisiana without you.

ZOE (enters from the house). Am I late? Ah! Mr. Scudder, good morning.

SCUDDER. Thank'ye. I'm from fair to middlin', like a bamboo cane, much the same all the year round.

ZOE. No; like a sugar cane; so dry outside, one would never think there was so much sweetness within.

SCUDDER. Look here: I can't stand that gal! if I stop here, I shall hug her right off. (He sees PETE, who has set his pail down up stage, and gone to sleep on it.) If that old nigger ain't asleep, I'm blamed. Hillo! (He kicks pail from under PETE, and lets him down. Exit.)

PETE. Hi! Debbel's in de pail! Whar's breakfass?

(Enter SOLON and DIDO with coffee-pot and dishes.)

DIDO. Bless'ee, Missey Zoe, here it be. Dere's a dish of penpans—jess taste, Mas'r George—and here's fried bananas; smell 'em do, sa glosh.

PETE. Hole yer tongue, Dido. Whar's de coffee? (He pours it out.) If it don't stain de cup, your wicked ole life's in danger, sure! dat right! black as nigger; clar as ice. You may drink dat, Mas'r George. (Looks off.) Yah! here's Mas'r Sunnyside, and Missey Dora, jist drove up. Some of you niggers run and hole de hosses; and take dis, Dido. (He gives her coffeepot to hold, and hobbles off, followed by SOLON and DIDO.)

(Enter SUNNYSIDE and DORA.)

SUNNYSIDE. Good day, ma'am. (*He shakes hands with George.*) I see we are just in time for breakfast. (*He sits.*)

DORA. O, none for me; I never eat. (*She sits.*)

GEORGE (*aside*). They do not notice Zoe. (*Aloud*) You don't see Zoe, Mr. Sunnyside.

SUNNYSIDE. Ah! Zoe, girl; are you there?

DORA. Take my shawl, Zoe. (ZOE *helps her.*) What a good creature she is.

SUNNYSIDE. I dare say, now, that in Europe you have never met any lady more beautiful in person, or more polished in manners, than that girl.

GEORGE. You are right, sir; though I shrank from expressing that opinion in her presence, so bluntly.

SUNNYSIDE. Why so?

GEORGE. It may be considered offensive.

SUNNYSIDE (*astonished*). What? I say, Zoe, do you hear that?

DORA. Mr. Peyton is joking.

MRS. PEYTON. My nephew is not acquainted with our customs in Louisiana, but he will soon understand.

GEORGE. Never, Aunt! I shall never understand how to wound the feelings of any lady; and, if that is the custom here, I shall never acquire it.

DORA. Zoe, my dear, what does he mean?

ZOE. I don't know.

GEORGE. Excuse me, I'll light a cigar. (*He goes up.*)

DORA (*aside to* ZOE). Isn't he sweet! O, dear, Zoe, is he in love with anybody?

ZOE. How can I tell?

DORA. Ask him, I want to know; don't say I told you to inquire, but find out. Minnie, fan me, it is so nice— and his clothes are French, ain't they?

ZOE. I think so; shall I ask him that too?

DORA. No, dear. I wish he would make love to me. When he speaks to one he does it so easy, so gentle; it isn't bar-room style; love lined with drinks, sighs tinged with tobacco—and they say all the women in Paris were in love with him, which I feel *I* shall be. Stop fanning me; what nice boots he wears.

SUNNYSIDE (*to* MRS. PEYTON). Yes, ma'am, I hold a mortgage over Terrebonne; mine's a ninth, and pretty near covers all the property, except the slaves. I believe Mr. M'Closky has a bill of sale on them. O, here he is.

(*Enter* M'CLOSKY.)

SUNNYSIDE. Good morning, Mr. M'Closky.

M'CLOSKY. Good morning, Mr. Sunnyside; Miss Dora, your servant.

DORA (*seated*). Fan me, Minnie.— (*Aside*) I don't like that man.

M'CLOSKY (*aside*). Insolent as usual. —(*Aloud*) You begged me to call this morning. I hope I'm not intruding.

MRS. PEYTON. My nephew, Mr. Peyton.

M'CLOSKY. O, how d'ye do, sir? (*He offers his hand,* GEORGE *bows coldly. Aside*) A puppy—if he brings any of his European airs here we'll fix him.— (*Aloud*) Zoe, tell Pete to give my mare a feed, will ye?

GEORGE (*angrily*). Sir!

M'CLOSKY. Hillo! did I tread on ye?

MRS. PEYTON. What is the matter with George?

ZOE (*takes fan from* MINNIE). Go, Minnie, tell Pete; run! (*Exit* MINNIE.)

MRS. PEYTON. Grace, attend to Mr. M'Closky.

M'CLOSKY. A julep, gal, that's my breakfast, and a bit of cheese.

GEORGE (*aside to* MRS. PEYTON). How can you ask that vulgar ruffian to your table!

MRS. PEYTON. Hospitality in Europe is a courtesy; here, it is an obligation.

We tender food to a stranger, not because he is a gentleman, but because he is hungry.

GEORGE. Aunt, I will take my rifle down to the Atchafalaya. Paul has promised me a bear and a deer or two. I see my little Nimrod yonder, with his Indian companion. Excuse me, ladies. Ho! Paul! (*He enters house.*)

PAUL (*outside*). I'ss, Mas'r George. (*Enter* PAUL *with the Indian.*)

SUNNYSIDE. It's a shame to allow that young cub to run over the swamps and woods, hunting and fishing his life away instead of hoeing cane.

MRS. PEYTON. The child was a favorite of the judge, who encouraged his gambols. I couldn't bear to see him put to work.

GEORGE (*returning with rifle*). Come, Paul, are you ready?

PAUL. I'ss, Mas'r George. O, golly! ain't that a pooty gun.

M'CLOSKY. See here, you imp; if I catch you, and your redskin yonder, gunning in my swamps, I'll give you rats, mind. Them vagabonds, when the game's about, shoot my pigs.

(GEORGE *goes into house.*)

PAUL. You gib me rattan, Mas'r Clostry, but I guess you take a berry long stick to Wahnotee. Ugh, he make bacon of you.

M'CLOSKY. Make bacon of me, you young whelp! Do you mean that I'm a pig? Hold on a bit. (*He seizes whip and holds* PAUL.)

ZOE. O, sir! don't, pray, don't.

M'CLOSKY (*slowly lowering his whip*). Darn you, redskin, I'll pay you off some day, both of ye. (*He returns to table and drinks.*)

SUNNYSIDE. That Indian is a nuisance. Why don't he return to his nation out West?

M'CLOSKY. He's too fond of thieving and whiskey.

ZOE. No; Wahnotee is a gentle, honest creature, and remains here because he loves that boy with the tenderness of a woman. When Paul was taken down with the swamp fever the Indian sat outside the hut, and neither ate, slept, nor spoke for five days, till the child could recognize and call him to his bedside. He who can love so well is honest—don't speak ill of poor Wahnotee.

MRS. PEYTON. Wahnotee, will you go back to your people?

WAHNOTEE. Sleugh.

PAUL. He don't understand; he speaks a mash-up of Indian and Mexican. Wahnotee Patira na sepau assa wigiran?

WAHNOTEE. Weal Omenee.

PAUL. Says he'll go if I'll go with him. He calls me Omenee, the Pigeon, and Miss Zoe is Ninemoosha, the Sweetheart.

WAHNOTEE (*pointing to* ZOE). Ninemoosha.

ZOE. No, Wahnotee, we can't spare Paul.

PAUL. If Omenee remain, Wahnotee will die in Terrebonne.

(*During the dialogue,* WAHNOTEE *has taken* GEORGE'S *gun.*)

GEORGE (*enters*). Now I'm ready. (GEORGE *tries to regain his gun;* WAHNOTEE *refuses to give it up;* PAUL *quietly takes it from him and remonstrates with him.*)

DORA. Zoe, he's going; I want him to stay and make love to me; that's what I came for today.

MRS. PEYTON. George, I can't spare Paul for an hour or two; he must run over to the landing; the steamer from New Orleans passed up the river last night, and if there's a mail they have thrown it ashore.

SUNNYSIDE. I saw the mailbags lying in the shed this morning.

MRS. PEYTON. I expect an important letter from Liverpool; away with you, Paul; bring the mailbags here.

PAUL. I'm 'most afraid to take Wahnotee to the shed, there's rum there.

WAHNOTEE. Rum!

PAUL. Come, then, but if I catch you drinkin', O, laws a mussey, you'll get snakes! I'll gib it you! now mind. (*Exits with Indian.*)

GEORGE. Come, Miss Dora, let me offer you my arm.

DORA. Mr. George, I am afraid, if all we hear is true, you have led a dreadful life in Europe.

GEORGE. That's a challenge to begin a description of my feminine adventures.

DORA. You have been in love, then?

GEORGE. Two hundred and forty-nine times! Let me relate you the worst cases.

DORA. No! no!

GEORGE. I'll put the naughty parts in French.

DORA. I won't hear a word! O, you horrible man! go on. (GEORGE *and* DORA *go into the house.*)

M'CLOSKY. Now, ma'am, I'd like a little business, if agreeable. I bring you news; your banker, old Lafouche, of New Orleans, is dead; the executors are winding up his affairs, and have foreclosed on all overdue mortgages, so Terrebonne is for sale. Here's the *Picayune* (*Producing paper*) with the advertisement.

ZOE. Terrebonne for sale!

MRS. PEYTON. Terrebonne for sale, and you, sir, will doubtless become its purchaser.

M'CLOSKY. Well, ma'am, I s'pose there's no law agin my bidding for it. The more bidders, the better for you. You'll take care, I guess, it don't go too cheap.

MRS. PEYTON. O, sir, I don't value the place for its price, but for the many happy days I've spent here; that landscape, flat and uninteresting though it may be, is full of charm for me; those poor people, born around me, growing up about my heart, have bounded my view of life; and now to lose that homely scene, lose their black, ungainly faces! O, sir, perhaps you should be as old as I am, to feel as I do, when my past life is torn away from me.

M'CLOSKY. I'd be darned glad if somebody would tear my past life away from *me*. Sorry I can't help you, but the fact is, you're in such an all-fired mess that you couldn't be pulled out without a derrick.

MRS. PEYTON. Yes, there is a hope left yet, and I cling to it. The house of Mason Brothers, of Liverpool, failed some twenty years ago in my husband's debt.

M'CLOSKY. They owed him over fifty thousand dollars.

MRS. PEYTON. I cannot find the entry in my husband's accounts; but you, Mr. M'Closky, can doubtless detect it. Zoe, bring here the judge's old desk; it is in the library.

(*Exit* ZOE *to the house.*)

M'CLOSKY. You don't expect to recover any of this old debt, do you?

MRS. PEYTON. Yes; the firm has recovered itself, and I received a notice two months ago that some settlement might be anticipated.

SUNNYSIDE. Why, with principal and interest this debt has been more than doubled in twenty years.

MRS. PEYTON. But it may be years yet before it will be paid off, if ever.

SUNNYSIDE. If there's a chance of it, there's not a planter round here who wouldn't lend you the whole cash, to keep your name and blood amongst us. Come, cheer up, old friend.

MRS. PEYTON. Ah! Sunnyside, how good you are; so like my poor Peyton.

(*Exit* MRS. PEYTON *and* SUNNYSIDE *to the house.*)

M'CLOSKY. Curse their old families—they cut me—a bilious, conceited, thin lot of dried-up aristocracy. I hate 'em. Just because my grandfather wasn't some broken-down Virginia transplant, or a stingy old Creole, I ain't fit to sit down to the same meat with them. It makes my blood so hot I feel my heart hiss. I'll sweep these Peytons from this section of the country. Their presence keeps alive the reproach against me that I ruined them. Yet, if this money should come! Bah! There's no chance of it. Then, if they go, they'll take Zoe—she'll follow them. Darn that girl; she makes me quiver when I think of her; she's took me for all I'm worth.

(*Enter* ZOE *from house, with the desk.*)

O, here, do you know what the annuity the old judge left you is worth today? Not a picayune.

ZOE. It is surely worth the love that dictated it; here are the papers and accounts. (*Putting the desk on the table.*)

M'CLOSKY. Stop, Zoe; come here! How would you like to rule the house of the richest planter on Atchafalaya—eh? or say the word, and I'll buy this old barrack, and you shall be mistress of Terrebonne.

ZOE. O, sir, do not speak so to me!

M'CLOSKY. Why not! look here, these Peytons are bust; cut 'em; I am rich, jine me; I'll set you up grand, and we'll give these first families here our dust, until you'll see their white skins shrivel up with hate and rage; what d'ye say?

ZOE. Let me pass! O, pray, let me go!

M'CLOSKY. What, you won't, won't ye? If young George Peyton was to make you the same offer, you'd jump at it pretty darned quick, I guess. Come, Zoe, don't be a fool; I'd marry you if I could, but you know I can't; so just say what you want. Here, then, I'll put back these Peytons in Terrebonne, and they shall know you done it; yes, they'll have you to thank for saving them from ruin.

ZOE. Do you think they would live here on such terms?

M'CLOSKY. Why not? We'll hire out our slaves, and live on their wages.

ZOE. But I'm not a slave.

M'CLOSKY. No; if you were I'd buy you, if you cost all I'm worth.

ZOE. Let me pass!

M'CLOSKY. Stop.

SCUDDER (*enters*). Let her pass.

M'CLOSKY. Eh?

SCUDDER. Let her pass! (*He takes out his knife. Exit* ZOE *to house.*)

M'CLOSKY. Is that you, Mr. Overseer? (*He examines paper.*)

SCUDDER. Yes, I'm here, somewhere, interferin'.

M'CLOSKY (*sitting*). A pretty mess you've got this estate in—

SCUDDER. Yes—me and Co.—we done it; but, as you were senior partner in the concern, I reckon you got the big lick.

M'CLOSKY. What d'ye mean?

SCUDDER. Let me proceed by illustration. (*Sits.*) Look thar! (*Points with his knife off*) D'ye see that tree?—it's called a live oak, and is a native here; beside it grows a creeper; year after year that creeper twines its long arms round and round the tree—sucking the earth dry all about its roots—living on its life—overrunning its branches, until at last the live oak withers and dies out. Do you know what the niggers round here call that sight? they call it the Yankee hugging the Creole.

M'CLOSKY. Mr. Scudder, I've listened to a great many of your insinuations, and now I'd like to come to an understanding what they mean. If you want a quarrel!—

SCUDDER. No, I'm the skurriest crittur at a fight you ever see; my legs have been too well brought up to stand and see my body abused; I take good care of myself, I can tell you.

M'CLOSKY. Because I heard that you had traduced my character.

SCUDDER. Traduced! Whoever said so lied. I always said you were the darndest thief that ever escaped a white jail to misrepresent the North to the South.

M'CLOSKY (raises hand to back of his neck). What!

SCUDDER. Take your hand down— take it down. (M'CLOSKY lowers his hand.) Whenever I gets into company like yours, I always start with the advantage on my side.

M'CLOSKY. What d'ye mean?

SCUDDER. I mean that before you could draw that bowie knife, you wear down your back, I'd cut you into shingles. Keep quiet, and let's talk sense. You wanted to come to an understanding, and I'm coming thar as quick as I can. Now, Jacob M'Closky, you despise me because you think I'm a fool; I despise you because I know you to be a knave. Between us we've ruined these Peytons; you fired the judge, and I finished off the widow. Now, I feel bad about my share in the business. I'd give half the balance of my life to wipe out my part of the work. Many a night I've laid awake and thought how to pull them through, till I've cried like a child over the sum I couldn't do; and you know how darned hard 't is to make a Yankee cry.

M'CLOSKY. Well, what's that to me?

SCUDDER. Hold on, Jacob, I'm coming to that—I tell ye, I'm such a fool —I can't bear the feeling, it keeps at

me like a skin complaint, and if this family is sold up—

M'CLOSKY. What then?

SCUDDER (rising). I'd cut my throat —or yours—yours I'd prefer.

M'CLOSKY. Would you now? why don't you do it?

SCUDDER. 'Cos I's skeered to try! I never killed a man in my life—and civilization is so strong in me I guess I couldn't do it—I'd like to, though!

M'CLOSKY. And all for the sake of that old woman and that young puppy —eh? No other cause to hate—to envy me—to be jealous of me—eh?

SCUDDER. Jealous? what for?

M'CLOSKY. Ask the color in your face: d'ye think I can't read you, like a book? With your New England hypocrisy, you would persuade yourself that it was this family alone you cared for; it ain't—you know it ain't—'t is the "Octoroon"; and you love her as I do; and you hate me because I'm your rival—that's where the tears come from, Salem Scudder, if you ever shed any—that's where the shoe pinches.

SCUDDER. Wal, I do like the gal; she's a—

M'CLOSKY. She's in love with young Peyton; it made me curse whar it made you cry, as it does now; I see the tears on your cheeks now.

SCUDDER. Look at 'em, Jacob, for they are honest water from the well of truth. I ain't ashamed of it—I do love the gal; but I ain't jealous of you, because I believe the only sincere feeling about you is your love for Zoe, and it does your heart good to have her image thar; but I believe you put it thar to spile. By fair means I don't think you can get her, and don't you try foul with her, 'cause if you do, Jacob, civilization be darned, I'm on you like a painter, and when I'm drawed out I'm pizin. (Exit SCUDDER to house.)

M'CLOSKY. Fair or foul, I'll have her —take that home with you! (*He opens desk.*) What's here—judgments? yes, plenty of 'em: bill of costs; account with Citizens' Bank—what's this? "Judgment, $40,000, 'Thibodeaux against Peyton,'"—surely, that is the judgment under which this estate is now advertised for sale— (*He takes up paper and examines it.*) yes, "Thibodeaux against Peyton, 1838." Hold on! whew! this is worth taking to—in this desk the judge used to keep one paper I want—this should be it. (*Reads.*) "The free papers of my daughter Zoe, registered February 4th, 1841." Why, Judge, wasn't you lawyer enough to know that while a judgment stood against you it was a lien on your slaves? Zoe is your child by a quadroon slave, and you didn't free her; blood! if this is so, she's mine! this old Liverpool debt—that may cross me— if it only arrive too late—if it don't come by this mail—Hold on! this letter the old lady expects—that's it; let me only head off that letter, and Terrebonne will be sold before they can recover it. That boy and the Indian have gone down to the landing for the post-bags; they'll idle on the way as usual; my mare will take me across the swamp, and before they can reach the shed, I'll have purified them bags —ne'er a letter shall show this mail. Ha, ha!—(*Calls.*) Pete, you old turkey-buzzard, saddle my mare. Then, if I sink every dollar I'm worth in her purchase, I'll own that Octoroon.

ACT TWO

The wharf with goods, boxes, and bales scattered about—a camera on a stand; DORA *being photographed by* SCUDDER, *who is arranging photographic apparatus,* GEORGE *and* PAUL *looking on at back.*

———

SCUDDER. Just turn your face a leetle this way—fix your—let's see—look here.
DORA. So?
SCUDDER. That's right. (*Putting his head under the darkening apron*) It's such a long time since I did this sort of thing, and this old machine has got so dirty and stiff, I'm afraid it won't operate. That's about right. Now don't stir.
PAUL. Ugh! she looks as though she war gwine to have a tooth drawed!
SCUDDER. I've got four plates ready, in case we miss the first shot. One of them is prepared with a self-developing liquid that I've invented. I hope it will turn out better than most of my notions. Now fix yourself. Are you ready?
DORA. Ready!
SCUDDER. Fire!—one, two, three. (SCUDDER *takes out watch.*)
PAUL. Now it's cooking; laws mussey! I feel it all inside, as if I was at a lottery.
SCUDDER. So! (*Throws down apron.*) That's enough. (*Withdrawing slide, turns and sees* PAUL.) What! what are you doing there, you young varmint! Ain't you took them bags to the house yet?
PAUL. Now, it ain't no use trying to get mad, Mas'r Scudder. I'm gwine! I only come back to find Wahnotee; whar is dat ign'ant Ingiun?
SCUDDER. You'll find him scenting round the rum store, hitched up by the nose. (*Goes into the room.*)
PAUL (*calling at the door*). Say, Mas'r Scudder, take me in dat telescope?
SCUDDER (*inside the room*). Get out, you cub! clar out!

PAUL. You got four of dem dishes ready. Gosh, wouldn't I like to hab myself took! What's de charge, Mas'r Scudder? (*He runs off.*)

SCUDDER (*enters from the room*). Job had none of them critters on his plantation, else he'd never ha' stood through so many chapters. Well, that has come out clear, ain't it? (*Showing the plate.*)

DORA. O, beautiful! Look, Mr. Peyton.

GEORGE (*looking*). Yes, very fine!

SCUDDER. The apparatus can't mistake. When I travelled round with this machine, the homely folks used to sing out, "Hillo, mister, this ain't like me!" "Ma'am," says I, "the apparatus can't mistake." "But, mister, that ain't my nose." "Ma'am, your nose drawed it. The machine can't err—you may mistake your phiz but the apparatus don't." "But, sir, it ain't agreeable." "No, ma'am, the truth seldom is."

PETE (*enters, puffing*). Mas'r Scudder! Mas'r Scudder!

SCUDDER. Hillo! what are you blowing about like a steamboat with one wheel for?

PETE. *You* blow, Mas'r Scudder, when I tole you: dere's a man from Noo Aleens just arriv'd at de house, and he's stuck up two papers on de gates: "For sale—dis yer property," and a heap of oder tings—an he seen missus, and arter he shown some papers she burst out crying—I yelled; den de corious of little niggers dey set up, den de hull plantation children—de live stock reared up and created a purpiration of lamentation as did de ole heart good to har.

DORA. What's the matter?

SCUDDER. He's come.

PETE. Dass it—I saw 'm!

SCUDDER. The sheriff from New Orleans has taken possession—Terrebonne is in the hands of the law.

ZOE (*enters*). O, Mr. Scudder! Dora! Mr. Peyton! come home—there are strangers in the house.

DORA. Stay, Mr. Peyton: Zoe, a word! (*She leads her forward—aside*) Zoe, the more I see of George Peyton the better I like him; but he is too modest—that is a very impertinent virtue in a man.

ZOE. I'm no judge, dear.

DORA. Of course not, you little fool; no one ever made love to you, and you can't understand; I mean, that George knows I am an heiress; my fortune would release this estate from debt.

ZOE. O, I see!

DORA. If he would only propose to marry me I would accept him, but he don't know that, and he will go on fooling, in his slow European way, until it is too late.

ZOE. What's to be done?

DORA. You tell him.

ZOE. What? that he isn't to go on fooling in his slow—

DORA. No, you goose! twit him on his silence and abstraction—I'm sure it's plain enough, for he has not spoken two words to me all the day; then joke round the subject, and at last speak out.

SCUDDER. Pete, as you came here, did you pass Paul and the Indian with the letter-bags?

PETE. No, sar; but dem vagabonds neber take the 'specable straight road, dey goes by de swamp. (*Exits up the path.*)

SCUDDER. Come, sir!

DORA (*to* ZOE). Now's your time. —(*Aloud*) Mr. Scudder, take us with you—Mr. Peyton is so slow, there's no getting him on. (*Exit* DORA *and* SCUDDER.)

ZOE. They are gone!—(*Glancing at* GEORGE) Poor fellow, he has lost all.

GEORGE. Poor child! how sad she

looks now she has no resource.

ZOE. How shall I ask him to stay?

GEORGE. Zoe, will you remain here? I wish to speak to you.

ZOE (*aside*). Well, that saves trouble.

GEORGE. By our ruin you lose all.

ZOE. O, I'm nothing; think of yourself.

GEORGE. I can think of nothing but the image that remains face to face with me; so beautiful, so simple, so confiding, that I dare not express the feelings that have grown up so rapidly in my heart.

ZOE (*aside*). He means Dora.

GEORGE. If I dared to speak!

ZOE. That's just what you must do, and do it at once, or it will be too late.

GEORGE. Has my love been divined?

ZOE. It has been more than suspected.

GEORGE. Zoe, listen to me, then. I shall see this estate pass from me without a sigh, for it possesses no charm for me; the wealth I covet is the love of those around me—eyes that are rich in fond looks, lips that breathe endearing words; the only estate I value is the heart of one true woman, and the slaves I'd have are her thoughts.

ZOE. George, George, your words take away my breath!

GEORGE. The world, Zoe, the free struggle of minds and hands is before me; the education bestowed on me by my dear uncle is a noble heritage which no sheriff can seize; with that I can build up a fortune, spread a roof over the heads I love, and place before them the food I have earned; I will work—

ZOE. Work! I thought none but colored people worked.

GEORGE. Work, Zoe, is the salt that gives savor to life.

ZOE. Dora said you were slow; if she could hear you now—

GEORGE. Zoe, you are young; your mirror must have told you that you are beautiful. Is your heart free?

ZOE. Free? of course it is!

GEORGE. We have known each other but a few days, but to me those days have been worth all the rest of my life. Zoe, you have suspected the feeling that now commands an utterance—you have seen that I love you.

ZOE. Me! you love *me?*

GEORGE. As my wife—the sharer of my hopes, my ambitions, and my sorrows; under the shelter of your love I could watch the storms of fortune pass unheeded by.

ZOE. *My* love! *My* love? George, you know not what you say! *I* the sharer of your sorrows—your wife! Do you know what I am?

GEORGE. Your birth—I know it. Has not my dear aunt forgotten it—she who had the most right to remember it? You are illegitimate, but love knows no prejudice.

ZOE (*aside*). Alas! he does not know, he does not know! and will despise me, spurn me, loathe me, when he learns who, what, he has so loved.— (*Aloud*) George, O, forgive me! Yes, I love you —I did not know it until your words showed me what has been in my heart; each of them awoke a new sense, and now I know how unhappy—how very unhappy I am.

GEORGE. Zoe, what have I said to wound you?

ZOE. Nothing; but you must learn what I thought you already knew. George, you cannot marry me; the laws forbid it!

GEORGE. Forbid it?

ZOE. There is a gulf between us, as wide as your love, as deep as my despair; but, O, tell me, say you will pity me! that you will not throw me from you like a poisoned thing!

GEORGE. Zoe, explain yourself—your language fills me with shapeless fears.

ZOE. And what shall I say? I—my mother was—no, no—not her! Why should I refer the blame to her? George, do you see that hand you hold? look at these fingers; do you see the nails are of a bluish tinge?

GEORGE. Yes, near the quick there is a faint blue mark.

ZOE. Look in my eyes; is not the same color in the white?

GEORGE. It is their beauty.

ZOE. Could you see the roots of my hair you would see the same dark, fatal mark. Do you know what that is?

GEORGE. No.

ZOE. That is the ineffaceable curse of Cain. Of the blood that feeds my heart, one drop in eight is black—bright red as the rest may be, that one drop poisons all the flood; those seven bright drops give me love like yours—hope like yours—ambition like yours—life hung with passions like dewdrops on the morning flowers; but the one black drop gives me despair, for I'm an unclean thing—forbidden by the laws—I'm an Octoroon!

GEORGE. Zoe, I love you none the less; this knowledge brings no revolt to my heart, and I can overcome the obstacle.

ZOE. But *I* cannot.

GEORGE. We can leave this country, and go far away where none can know.

ZOE. And your mother, she who from infancy treated me with such fondness, she who, as you said, has most reason to spurn me, can she forget what I am? Will she gladly see you wedded to the child of her husband's slave? No! she would revolt from it, as all but you would; and if I consented to hear the cries of my heart, if I did not crush out my infant love, what would she say to the poor girl on whom she had bestowed so much? No, no!

GEORGE. Zoe. must we immolate our lives on her prejudice?

ZOE. Yes, for I'd rather be black than ungrateful! Ah, George, our race has at least one virtue—it knows how to suffer!

GEORGE. Each word you utter makes my love sink deeper into my heart.

ZOE. And I remained here to induce you to offer that heart to Dora!

GEORGE. If you bid me do so I will obey you—

ZOE. No, no! if you cannot be mine, O, let me not blush when I think of you.

GEORGE. Dearest Zoe! (*Exit* GEORGE *and* ZOE. *As they exit,* M'CLOSKY *rises from behind a rock and looks after them.*)

M'CLOSKY. She loves him! I felt it—and how she can love! (*Advances.*) That one black drop of blood burns in her veins and lights up her heart like a foggy sun. O, how I lapped up her words, like a thirsty bloodhound! I'll have her, if it costs me my life! Yonder the boy still lurks with those mailbags; the devil still keeps him here to tempt me, darn his yellow skin! I arrived just too late, he had grabbed the prize as I came up. Hillo! he's coming this way, fighting with his Injiun. (*Conceals himself.*)

PAUL (*enters, wrestling with* WAHNOTEE). It ain't no use now: you got to gib it up!

WAHNOTEE. Ugh!

PAUL. It won't do! You got dat bottle of rum hid under your blanket—gib it up now, you—. Yar! (*Wrenching it from him*) You nasty, lying Injiun! It's no use you putting on airs; I ain't gwine to sit up wid you all night and you drunk. Hillo! war's de crowd gone? And dar's de 'paratus—O, gosh, if I could take a likeness ob dis child! Uh—uh, let's have a peep. (*Looking through camera*) O, golly! yar, you Wahnotee!

you stan' dar, I see you. Ta demine usti. (*He looks at* WAHNOTEE *through the camera;* WAHNOTEE *springs back with an expression of alarm.*)

WAHNOTEE. No tue Wahnotee.

PAUL.. Ha, ha! he tinks it's a gun. You ign'ant Injiun, it can't hurt you! Stop, here's dem dishes—plates—dat's what he call 'em, all fix: I see Mas'r Scudder do it often—tink I can take likeness—stay dere, Wahnotee.

WAHNOTEE. No, carabine tue.

PAUL. I must operate and take my own likeness too—how debbel I do dat? Can't be ober dar an' here too—I ain't twins. Ugh! ach! 'Top; you look, you Wahnotee; you see dis rag, eh? Well when I say go, den lift dis rag like dis, see! den run to dat pine tree up dar (*Points.*) and back ag'in, and den pull down de rag so, d'ye see?

WAHNOTEE. Hugh!

PAUL. Den you hab glass ob rum.

WAHNOTEE. Rum!

PAUL. Dat wakes him up. Coute, Wahnotee in omenee dit go Wahnotee, poina la fa, comb a pine tree, la revieut sala, la fa.

WAHNOTEE. Firewater!

PAUL. Yes, den a glass ob firewater; now den. (*Throwing mailbags down and sitting on them*) Pret, now den go.

(WAHNOTEE *raises the apron and runs off.* PAUL *sits for his picture—* M'CLOSKY *appears.*)

M'CLOSKY. Where are they? Ah, yonder goes the Indian!

PAUL. De time he gone just 'bout enough to cook dat dish plate.

M'CLOSKY. Yonder is the boy—now is my time! What's he doing; is he asleep? (*Advancing*) He is sitting on my prize! darn his carcass! I'll clear him off there —he'll never know what stunned him. (*He takes Indian's tomahawk and steals to* PAUL.)

PAUL. Dam dat Injiun! is dat him creeping dar? I daren't move fear to spile myself. (M'CLOSKY *strikes him on the head—he falls dead.*)

M'CLOSKY. Hooraw; the bags are mine—now for it!—(*Opening the mailbags*) What's here? Sunnyside, Pointdexter, Jackson, Peyton; here it is—the Liverpool postmark, sure enough!— (*Opening letter—reads.*) "Madam, we are instructed by the firm of Mason and Co., to inform you that a dividend of forty per cent. is payable on the first proximo, this amount in consideration of position, they send herewith, and you will find enclosed by draft to your order, on the Bank of Louisiana, which please acknowledge—the balance will be paid in full, with interest, in three, six, and nine months—your drafts on Mason Brothers at those dates will be accepted by La Palisse and Compagnie, N. O., so that you may command immediate use of the whole amount at once, if required. Yours, etc., James Brown." What a find! this infernal letter would have saved all. (*During the reading of the letter, he remains nearly motionless under the focus of the camera.*) But now I guess it will arrive too late—these darned U. S. mails are to blame. The Injiun! he must not see me. (*Exits rapidly.*)

(WAHNOTEE *runs on, and pulls down the apron. He sees* PAUL, *lying on the ground, and speaks to him, thinking that he is shamming sleep. He gesticulates and jabbers to him and moves him with his feet, then kneels down to rouse him. To his horror he finds him dead. Expressing great grief he raises his eyes and they fall upon the camera. Rising with a savage growl, he seizes the tomahawk and smashes the camera to pieces. Going to* PAUL *he expresses in pantomime grief, sorrow, and fondness, and takes him in his arms to carry him away.*)

ACT THREE

A room in MRS. PEYTON's *house showing the entrance on which an auction bill is pasted.* SOLON *and* GRACE *are there.*

PETE (*outside*). Dis way—dis way.

(*Enter* PETE, POINTDEXTER, JACKSON, LAFOUCHE, *and* CAILLOU.)

PETE. Dis way, gen'l'men; now, Solon—Grace—dey's hot and tirsty—sangaree, brandy, rum.

JACKSON. Well, what d'ye say, Lafouche—d'ye smile?

(*Enter* THIBODEAUX *and* SUNNYSIDE.)

THIBODEAUX. I hope we don't intrude on the family.

PETE. You see dat hole in dar, sar? I was raised on dis yar plantation—nebber see no door in it—always open, sar, for stranger to walk in.

SUNNYSIDE. And for substance to walk out.

RATTS (*enters*). Fine southern style that, eh!

LAFOUCHE (*reading the bill*). "A fine, well-built old family mansion, replete with every comfort."

RATTS. There's one name on the list of slaves scratched, I see.

LAFOUCHE. Yes; No. 49, Paul, a quadroon boy, aged thirteen.

SUNNYSIDE. He's missing.

POINTDEXTER. Run away, I suppose.

PETE (*indignantly*). No, sar; nigger nebber cut stick on Terrebonne; dat boy's dead, sure.

RATTS. What, Picayune Paul, as we called him, that used to come aboard my boat?—poor little darkey, I hope not; many a picayune he picked up for his dance and nigger songs, and he supplied our table with fish and game from the Bayous.

PETE. Nebber supply no more, sar—nebber dance again. Mas'r Ratts, you hard him sing about de place where de good niggers go, de last time.

RATTS. Well!

PETE. Well, he gone dar hisself; why I tink so—'cause we missed Paul for some days, but nebber tout nothin' till one night dat Injiun Wahnotee suddenly stood right dar 'mongst us—was in his war paint, and mighty cold and grave—he sit down by de fire. "Whar's Paul?" I say—he smoke and smoke, but nebber look out ob de fire; well knowing dem critters, I wait a long time—den he say, "Wahnotee great chief"; den I say nothing—smoke anoder time—last, rising to go, he turn round at door, and say berry low—O, like a woman's voice he say, "Omenee Pangeuk"—dat is, Paul is dead—nebber see him since.

RATTS. That redskin killed him.

SUNNYSIDE. So we believe; and so mad are the folks around, if they catch the redskin they'll lynch him sure.

RATTS. Lynch him! Darn his copper carcass, I've got a set of Irish deck-hands aboard that just loved that child; and after I tell them this, let them get a sight of the redskin, I believe they would eat him, tomahawk and all. Poor little Paul!

THIBODEAUX. What was he worth?

RATTS. Well, near on five hundred dollars.

PETE (*scandalized*). What, sar! You p'tend to be sorry for Paul, and prize him like dat! Five hundred dollars! (*To* THIBODEAUX) T'ousand dollars, Massa Thibodeau.

SCUDDER (*enters*). Gentlemen, the sale takes place at three. Good morning, Colonel. It's near that now, and there's still the sugar-houses to be inspected. Good day, Mr. Thibodeaux—shall we drive down that way? Mr.

Lafouche, why, how do you do, sir? you're looking well.

LAFOUCHE. Sorry I can't return the compliment.

RATTS. Salem's looking a kinder hollowed out.

SCUDDER. What, Mr. Ratts, are you going to invest in swamps?

RATTS. No; I want a nigger.

SCUDDER. Hush.

PETE. Eh! wass dat?

SCUDDER. Mr. Sunnyside, I can't do this job of showin' round the folks; my stomach goes agin it. I want Pete here a minute.

SUNNYSIDE. I'll accompany them certainly.

SCUDDER (*eagerly*). Will ye? Thank ye; thank ye.

SUNNYSIDE. We must excuse Scudder, friends. I'll see you round the estate.

(*Enter* GEORGE *and* MRS. PEYTON.)

LAFOUCHE. Good morning, Mrs. Peyton.

(*All salute.*)

SUNNYSIDE. This way, gentlemen.

RATTS (*aside to* SUNNYSIDE). I say, I'd like to say summit soft to the old woman; perhaps it wouldn't go well, would it?

THIBODEAUX. No; leave it alone.

RATTS. Darn it, when I see a woman in trouble, I feel like selling the skin off my back.

(*Exit* THIBODEAUX, SUNNYSIDE, RATTS, POINTDEXTER, GRACE, JACKSON, LAFOUCHE, CAILLOU, SOLON.)

SCUDDER (*aside to* PETE). Go outside there; listen to what you hear, then go down to the quarters and tell the boys, for I can't do it. O, get out.

PETE. He said "I want a nigger." Laws, mussey! What am goin' to cum ob us! (*Exits slowly, as if trying to conceal himself.*)

GEORGE. My dear aunt, why do you not move from this painful scene? Go with Dora to Sunnyside.

MRS. PEYTON. No, George; your uncle said to me with his dying breath, "Nellie, never leave Terrebonne," and I never *will* leave it, till the law compels me.

SCUDDER. Mr. George, I'm going to say somethin' that has been chokin' me for some time. I know you'll excuse it. Thar's Miss Dora—that girl's in love with you; yes, sir, her eyes are startin' out of her head with it: now her fortune would redeem a good part of this estate.

MRS. PEYTON. Why, George, I never suspected this!

GEORGE. I did, Aunt, I confess, but—

MRS. PEYTON. And you hesitated from motives of delicacy?

SCUDDER. No, ma'am; here's the plan of it. Mr. George is in love with Zoe.

GEORGE. Scudder!

MRS. PEYTON. George!

SCUDDER. Hold on, now! things have got so jammed in on top of us, we ain't got time to put kid gloves on to handle them. He loves Zoe, and has found out that she loves him. (*Sighing*) Well, that's all right; but as he can't marry her, and as Miss Dora would jump at him—

MRS. PEYTON. Why didn't you mention this before?

SCUDDER. Why, because *I* love Zoe, too, and I couldn't take that young feller from her; and she's jist living on the sight of him, as I saw her do; and they so happy in spite of this yer misery around them, and they reproachin' themselves with not feeling as they ought. I've seen it, I tell you; and darn it, ma'am, can't you see that's what's been a hollowing me out so—I beg your pardon.

MRS. PEYTON. O, George—my son, let me call you—I do not speak for my own sake, nor for the loss of the estate, but for the poor people here: they will be sold, divided, and taken away—they have been born here. Heaven has denied me children; so all the strings of my heart have grown around and amongst them, like the fibres and roots of an old tree in its native earth. O, let all go, but save them! With them around us, if we have not wealth, we shall at least have the home that they alone can make—

GEORGE. My dear mother—Mr. Scudder—you teach me what I ought to do; if Miss Sunnyside will accept me as I am, Terrebonne shall be saved: I will sell myself, but the slaves shall be protected.

MRS. PEYTON. *Sell* yourself, George! Is not Dora worth any man's—

SCUDDER. Don't say that, ma'am; don't say that to a man that loves another gal. He's going to do an heroic act; don't spile it.

MRS. PEYTON. But Zoe is only an Octoroon.

SCUDDER. She's won this race agin the white, anyhow; it's too late now to start her pedigree. (*As* DORA *enters*) Come, Mrs. Peyton, take my arm. Hush! here's the other one: she's a little too thoroughbred—too much of the greyhound; but the heart's there, I believe.

(*Exeunt* SCUDDER *and* MRS. PEYTON.)

DORA. Poor Mrs. Peyton.

GEORGE. Miss Sunnyside, permit me a word: a feeling of delicacy has suspended upon my lips an avowal, which—

DORA (*aside*). O, dear, has he suddenly come to his senses?

(*Enter* ZOE, *stopping at back.*)

GEORGE. In a word, I have seen and admired you!

DORA (*aside*). He has a strange way of showing it. European, I suppose.

GEORGE. If you would pardon the abruptness of the question, I would ask you, Do you think the sincere devotion of my life to make yours happy would succeed?

DORA (*aside*). Well, he has the oddest way of making love.

GEORGE. You are silent?

DORA. Mr. Peyton, I presume you have hesitated to make this avowal because you feared, in the present condition of affairs here, your object might be misconstrued, and that your attention was rather to my fortune than myself. (*A pause*) Why don't he speak? —I mean, you feared I might not give you credit for sincere and pure feelings. Well, you wrong me. I don't think you capable of anything else but—

GEORGE. No, I hesitated because an attachment I had formed before I had the pleasure of seeing you had not altogether died out.

DORA (*smiling*). Some of those sirens of Paris, I presume. (*Pausing*) I shall endeavor not to be jealous of the past; perhaps I have no right to be. (*Pausing*) But now that vagrant love is— eh, faded—is it not? Why don't you speak, sir?

GEORGE. Because, Miss Sunnyside, I have not learned to lie.

DORA. Good gracious—who wants you to?

GEORGE. I do, but I can't do it. No, the love I speak of is not such as you suppose—it is a passion that has grown up here since I arrived; but it is a hopeless, mad, wild feeling, that must perish.

DORA. Here! since you arrived! Impossible: you have seen no one; whom can you mean?

ZOE (*advancing*). Me.

GEORGE. Zoe!

DORA. You!

ZOE. Forgive him, Dora; for he knew no better until I told him. Dora, you are right. He is incapable of any but sincere and pure feelings—so are you. He loves me—what of that? You know you can't be jealous of a poor creature like me. If he caught the fever, were stung by a snake, or possessed of any other poisonous or unclean thing, you could pity, tend, love him through it, and for your gentle care he would love you in return. Well, is he not thus afflicted now? I am his love—he loves an Octoroon.

GEORGE. O, Zoe, you break my heart!

DORA. At college they said I was a fool—I must be. At New Orleans, they said, "She's pretty, very pretty, but no brains." I'm afraid they must be right; I can't understand a word of all this.

ZOE. Dear Dora, try to understand it with your heart. You love George; you love him dearly; I know it; and you deserve to be loved by him. He will love you—he must. His love for me will pass away—it shall. You heard him say it was hopeless. O, forgive him and me!

DORA (weeping). O, why did he speak to me at all then? You've made me cry, then, and I hate you both! (Exits through room.)

(Enter MRS. PEYTON and SCUDDER, M'CLOSKY and POINTDEXTER.)

M'CLOSKY. I'm sorry to intrude, but the business I came upon will excuse me.

MRS. PEYTON. Here is my nephew, sir.

ZOE. Perhaps I had better go.

M'CLOSKY. Wal, as it consarns you, perhaps you better had.

SCUDDER. Consarns Zoe?

M'CLOSKY. I don't know; she may as well hear the hull of it. Go on, Colonel—Colonel Pointdexter, ma'am—the mortgagee, auctioneer, and general agent.

POINTDEXTER. Pardon me, madam, but do you know these papers? (He hands the papers to MRS. PEYTON.)

MRS. PEYTON (taking them). Yes, sir; they were the free papers of the girl Zoe; but they were in my husband's secretary. How came they in your possession?

M'CLOSKY. I—I found them.

GEORGE. And you purloined them?

M'CLOSKY. Hold on, you'll see. Go on, Colonel.

POINTDEXTER. The list of your slaves is incomplete—it wants one.

SCUDDER. The boy Paul—we know it.

POINTDEXTER. No, sir, you have omitted the Octoroon girl, Zoe.

MRS. PEYTON. } Zoe!
ZOE.   } Me!

POINTDEXTER. At the time the judge executed those free papers to his infant slave, a judgment stood recorded against him; while that was on record he had no right to make away with his property. That judgment still exists: under it and others this estate is sold today. Those free papers ain't worth the sand that's on 'em.

MRS. PEYTON. Zoe a slave! It is impossible!

POINTDEXTER. It is certain, madam: the judge was negligent, and doubtless forgot this small formality.

SCUDDER. But the creditors will not claim the gal?

M'CLOSKY. Excuse me; one of the principal mortgagees has made the demand.

(Exeunt M'CLOSKY and POINTDEXTER.)

SCUDDER. Hold on yere, George Peyton; you sit down there. You're trembling so, you'll fall down directly. This blow has staggered me some.

MRS. PEYTON. O, Zoe, my child! don't think too hard of your poor father.

ZOE. I shall do so if you weep. See, I'm calm.

SCUDDER. Calm as a tombstone, and with about as much life. I see it in your face.

GEORGE. It cannot be! It shall not be!

SCUDDER. Hold your tongue—it must. Be calm—darn the things; the proceeds of this sale won't cover the debts of the estate. Consarn those Liverpool English fellers, why couldn't they send something by the last mail? Even a letter, promising something—such is the feeling round amongst the planters. Darn me, if I couldn't raise thirty thousand on the envelope alone, and ten thousand more on the postmark.

GEORGE. Zoe, they shall not take you from us while I live.

SCUDDER. Don't be a fool; they'd kill you, and then take her, just as soon as —stop: old Sunnyside, he'll buy her; that'll save her.

ZOE. No, it won't; we have confessed to Dora that we love each other. How can she then ask her father to free me?

SCUDDER. What in thunder made you do that?

ZOE. Because it was the truth, and I had rather be a slave with a free soul, than remain free with a slavish, deceitful heart. My father gives me freedom —at least he thought so. May Heaven bless him for the thought, bless him for the happiness he spread around my life. You say the proceeds of the sale will not cover his debts. Let me be sold then, that I may free his name. I give him back the liberty he bestowed upon me; for I can never repay him the love he bore his poor Octoroon child, on whose breast his last sigh was drawn, into whose eyes he looked with the last gaze of affection.

MRS. PEYTON. O, my husband! I thank Heaven you have not lived to see this day.

ZOE. George, leave me! I would be alone a little while.

GEORGE. Zoe! (*Turns away, overpowered.*)

ZOE. Do not weep, George. Dear George, you now see what a miserable thing I am.

GEORGE. Zoe!

SCUDDER. I wish they could sell *me!* I brought half this ruin on this family, with my all-fired improvements. I deserve to be a nigger this day—I feel like one, inside. (*Exit* SCUDDER.)

ZOE. Go now, George—leave me— take her with you.

(*Exit* MRS. PEYTON *and* GEORGE.)

A slave! a slave! Is this a dream—for my brain reels with the blow? He said so. What! then I shall be sold—sold! and my master—O! (*She falls on her knees, with her face in her hands.*) No — no master but one. George — George—hush—they come! save me! No, (*Looks off.*) 't is Pete and the servants—they come this way. (*Enters the inner room.*)

(*Enter* PETE, GRACE, MINNIE, SOLON, DIDO, *and all* NEGROES.)

PETE. Cum yer now—stand round, 'cause I've got to talk to you darkies— keep dem chil'n quiet—don't make no noise, de missus up dar har us.

SOLON. Go on, Pete.

PETE. Gen'l'men, my colored frens and ladies, dar's mighty bad news gone round. Dis yer prop'ty to be sold—old Terrebonne—whar we all been raised, is gwine—dey's gwine to tak it away— can't stop here nohow.

ALL. O-o!—O-o!

PETE. Hold quiet, you trash o' niggers! tink anybody wants you to cry? Who's you to set up screeching?—be quiet! But dis ain't all. Now, my cullud brethren, gird up your lines, and listen —hold on yer bref—it's a comin'. We t'ought dat de niggers would belong to de ole missus, and if she lost Terrebonne, we must live dere allers, and we would hire out, and bring our wages to ole Missus Peyton.

ALL. Ya! ya! Well—

PETE. Hush! I tell ye, 't ain't so—we can't do it—we've got to be sold—

ALL. Sold!

PETE. Will you hush? she will har you. Yes! I listen dar jess now—dar was ole lady cryin'—Mas'r George— ah! you seen dem big tears in his eyes. O, Mas'r Scudder, he didn't cry zackly; both ob his eyes and cheek look like de bad Bayou in low season—so dry dat I cry for him. (*Raising his voice*) Den say de missus, " 'T ain't for de land I keer, but for dem 'poor niggers—dey'll be sold—dat wot stagger me." "No," say Mas'r George, "I'd rather sell myself fuss; but dey shan't suffer, nohow —I see 'em dam fuss."

ALL. O, bless 'um! Bless Mas'r George.

PETE. Hole yer tongues. Yes, for you, for me, for dem little ones, dem folks cried. Now, den, if Grace dere wid her chil'n were all sold, she'll begin screechin' like a cat. She didn't mind how kind old judge was to her; and Solon, too, he'll holler, and break de ole lady's heart.

GRACE. No, Pete; no, I won't. I'll bear it.

PETE. I don't tink you will any more, but dis here will; 'cause de family spile Dido, dey has. She nebber was worth much a' dat nigger.

DIDO. How dar you say dat, you black nigger, you? I fetch as much as any odder cook in Louisiana.

PETE. What's the use of your takin' it kind, and comfortin' de missus' heart, if Minnie dere, and Louise, and Marie, and Julie is to spile it?

MINNIE. We won't, Pete; we won't.

PETE (*to the men*). Dar, do ye hear dat, ye mis'able darkies; dem gals is worth a boat load of kinder men dem is. Cum, for de pride of de family, let every darky look his best for the judge's sake—dat ole man so good to us, and dat ole woman—so dem strangers from New Orleans shall say, Dem's happy darkies, dem's a fine set of niggers; every one say when he's sold, "Lor' bless dis yer family I'm gwine out of, and send me as good a home."

ALL. We'll do it, Pete; we'll do it.

PETE. Hush! hark! I tell ye dar's somebody in dar. Who is it?

GRACE. It's Missy Zoe. See! see!

PETE. Come along; she har what we say, and she's cryin' for us. None o' ye ign'rant niggers could cry for yerselves like dat. Come here quiet: now quiet.

(*Exeunt* PETE *and all the* NEGROES, *slowly.*)

ZOE (*who is supposed to have overheard the last scene, enters*). O! must I learn from these poor wretches how much I owe, and how I ought to pay the debt? Have I slept upon the benefits I received, and never saw, never felt, never knew that I was forgetful and ungrateful? O, my father! my dear, dear father! forgive your poor child. You made her life too happy, and now these tears will flow. Let me hide them till I teach my heart. O, my—my heart! (*Exits, with a low, wailing, suffocating cry.*)

(*Enter* M'CLOSKY, LAFOUCHE, JACKSON, SUNNYSIDE, *and* POINTDEXTER.)

POINTDEXTER (*looking at his watch*). Come, the hour is past. I think we may begin business. Where is Mr. Scudder?

JACKSON. I want to get to Ophelensis tonight.

DORA (*enters*). Father, come here.

SUNNYSIDE. Why, Dora, what's the matter? Your eyes are red.

DORA. Are they? thank you. I don't care, they were blue this morning, but it don't signify now.

SUNNYSIDE. My darling! who has been teasing you?

DORA. Never mind. I want you to buy Terrebonne.

SUNNYSIDE. Buy Terrebonne! What for?

DORA. No matter—buy it!

SUNNYSIDE. It will cost me all I'm worth. This is folly, Dora.

DORA. Is my plantation at Comptableau worth this?

SUNNYSIDE. Nearly—perhaps.

DORA. Sell it, then, and buy this.

SUNNYSIDE. Are you mad, my love?

DORA. Do you want *me* to stop here and *bid* for it?

SUNNYSIDE. Good gracious, no!

DORA. Then I'll do it if you don't.

SUNNYSIDE. I will! I will! But for Heaven's sake go—here comes the crowd. (*Exit* DORA.) What on earth does that child mean or want?

(*Enter* SCUDDER, GEORGE, RATTS, CAILLOU, PETE, GRACE, MINNIE, *and all the* NEGROES. *A large table is in the center of the background.* POINTDEXTER *mounts the table with his hammer, his clerk sitting at his feet. The Negro mounts the table from behind. The rest sit down.*)

POINTDEXTER. Now, gentlemen, we shall proceed to business. It ain't necessary for me to dilate, describe or enumerate; Terrebonne is known to you as one of the richest bits of sile in Louisiana, and its condition reflects credit on them as had to keep it. I'll trouble you for that piece of baccy, Judge—thank you—so, gentlemen, as life is short, we'll start right off. The first lot on here is the estate in block, with its sugar-houses, stock, machines, implements, good dwelling-houses and furniture. If there is no bid for the estate and stuff, we'll sell it in smaller lots. Come, Mr. Thibodeaux, a man has a chance once in his life—here's yours.

THIBODEAUX. Go on. What's the reserve bid?

POINTDEXTER. The first mortgagee bids forty thousand dollars.

THIBODEAUX. Forty-five thousand.

SUNNYSIDE. Fifty thousand.

POINTDEXTER. When you have done joking, gentlemen, you'll say one hundred and twenty thousand. It carried that easy on mortgage.

LAFOUCHE. Then why don't you buy it yourself, Colonel?

POINTDEXTER. I'm waiting on your fifty thousand bid.

CAILLOU. Eighty thousand.

POINTDEXTER. Don't be afraid: it ain't going for that, Judge.

SUNNYSIDE. Ninety thousand.

POINTDEXTER. We're getting on.

THIBODEAUX. One hundred—

POINTDEXTER. One hundred thousand bid for this mag—

CAILLOU. One hundred and ten thousand—

POINTDEXTER. Good again—one hundred and—

SUNNYSIDE. Twenty.

POINTDEXTER. And twenty thousand bid. Squire Sunnyside is going to sell this at fifty thousand advance tomorrow. (*Looking round*) Where's that man from Mobile that wanted to give one hundred and eighty thousand?

THIBODEAUX. I guess he ain't left home yet, Colonel.

POINTDEXTER. I shall knock it down to the Squire—going—gone—for one hundred and twenty thousand dollars. (*Raising hammer*) Judge, you can raise the hull on mortgage—going for half its value. (*Knocking on the table*) Squire Sunnyside, you've got a pretty bit o' land, Squire. Hillo, darkey, hand me a smash dar.

SUNNYSIDE. I got more than I can work now.

POINTDEXTER. Then buy the hands along with the property. Now, gentlemen, I'm proud to submit to you the

finest lot of field hands and house servants that was ever offered for competition: they speak for themselves, and
do credit to their owners. (*Reading*)
"No. 1, Solon, a guest boy, and a good
waiter."

PETE. That's my son—buy him,
Mas'r Ratts; he's sure to sarve you well.

POINTDEXTER. Hold your tongue!

RATTS. Let the old darkey alone—
eight hundred for that boy.

CAILLOU. Nine.

RATTS. A thousand.

SOLON. Thank you, Mas'r Ratts: I
die for you, sar; hold up for me, sar.

RATTS. Look here, the boy knows and
likes me, Judge; let him come my way?

CAILLOU. Go on—I'm dumb.

POINTDEXTER. One thousand bid.
He's yours, Captain Ratts, *Magnolia*
steamer.

(SOLON *goes and stands behind*
RATTS.)
"No. 2, the yellow girl, Grace, with two
children—Saul, aged four, and Vic-
toria, five." (*They get on table.*)

SCUDDER. That's Solon's wife and
children, Judge.

GRACE (*to* RATTS). Buy me, Mas'r
Ratts, do buy me, sar?

RATTS. What in thunder should I do
with you and those devils on board my
boat?

GRACE. Wash, sar—cook, sar—anyting.

RATTS. Eight hundred agin, then—
I'll go it.

JACKSON. Nine.

RATTS. I'm broke, Solon—I can't
stop the Judge.

THIBODEAUX. What's the matter,
Ratts? I'll lend you all you want. Go
it, if you're a mind to.

RATTS. Eleven.

JACKSON. Twelve.

SUNNYSIDE. O, O!

SCUDDER (*to* JACKSON). Judge, my
friend. The Judge is a little deaf.

Hello! (*Speaking in his ear trumpet*)
This gal and them children belong to
that boy Solon there. You're bidding to
separate them, Judge.

JACKSON. The devil I am! (*Rising*)
I'll take back my bid, Colonel.

POINTDEXTER. All right, Judge; I
thought there was a mistake. I must
keep you, Captain, to the eleven hundred.

RATTS. Go it.

POINTDEXTER. Eleven hundred—going—going—sold! "No. 3, Pete, a house
servant."

PETE. Dat's me—yer, I'm comin'—
stand around dar. (*Tumbles upon the
table.*)

POINTDEXTER. Aged seventy-two.

PETE. What's dat? A mistake, sar—
forty-six.

POINTDEXTER. Lame.

PETE. But don't mount to nuffin—kin
work cannel. Come, Judge, pick up.
Now's your time, sar.

JACKSON. One hundred dollars.

PETE. What, sar? me! for me—look
ye here! (*He dances.*)

GEORGE. Five hundred.

PETE. Mas'r George—ah, no, sar—
don't buy me—keep your money for
some udder dat is to be sold. I ain't no
'count, sar.

POINTDEXTER. Five hundred bid—it's
a good price. He's yours, Mr. George
Peyton. (*Pete goes down.*) "No. 4, the
Octoroon girl, Zoe."

(*Enter* ZOE, *very pale, and stands on
table.* M'CLOSKY *who hitherto has taken
no interest in the sale, now turns his
chair.*)

SUNNYSIDE (*rising*). Gentlemen, we
are all acquainted with the circumstances of this girl's position, and I feel
sure that no one here will oppose the
family who desires to redeem the child
of our esteemed and noble friend, the
late Judge Peyton.

ALL. Hear! bravo! hear!

POINTDEXTER. While the proceeds of this sale promises to realize less than the debts upon it, it is my duty to prevent any collusion for the depreciation of the property.

RATTS. Darn ye! You're a man as well as an auctioneer, ain't ye?

POINTDEXTER. What is offered for this slave?

SUNNYSIDE. One thousand dollars.

M'CLOSKY. Two thousand.

SUNNYSIDE. Three thousand.

M'CLOSKY. Five thousand.

GEORGE. Demon!

SUNNYSIDE. I bid seven thousand, which is the last dollar this family possesses.

M'CLOSKY. Eight.

THIBODEAUX. Nine.

ALL. Bravo!

M'CLOSKY. Ten. It's no use, Squire.

SCUDDER. Jacob M'Closky, you shan't have that girl. Now, take care what you do. Twelve thousand.

M'CLOSKY. Shan't I! Fifteen thousand. Beat that any of ye.

POINTDEXTER. Fifteen thousand bid for the Octoroon.

DORA (*enters*). Twenty thousand.

ALL. Bravo!

M'CLOSKY. Twenty-five thousand.

ALL (*groan*). O! O!

GEORGE. Yelping hound—take that. (*He rushes on* M'CLOSKY. M'CLOSKY *draws his knife.*)

SCUDDER (*darting between them*). Hold on, George Peyton—stand back. This is your own house; we are under your uncle's roof; recollect yourself. And, strangers, ain't we forgetting there's a lady present? (*The knives disappear.*) If we can't behave like Christians, let's try and act like gentlemen. Go on, Colonel.

LAFOUCHE. He didn't ought to bid against a lady.

M'CLOSKY. O, that's it, is it? Then I'd like to hire a lady to go to auction and buy my hands.

POINTDEXTER. Gentlemen, I believe none of us have two feelings about the conduct of that man; but he has the law on his side—we may regret, but we must respect it. Mr. M'Closky has bid twenty-five thousand dollars for the Octoroon. Is there any other bid? For the first time, twenty-five thousand—last time! (*Brings hammer down.*) To Jacob M'Closky, the Octoroon girl, Zoe, twenty-five thousand dollars.

ACT FOUR

SCENE. *The wharf. The steamer,* Magnolia, *alongside, a bluff rock.* RATTS *discovered, superintending the loading of ship. Enter* LAFOUCHE *and* JACKSON.

JACKSON. How long before we start, captain?

RATTS. Just as soon as we put this cotton on board.

(*Enter* PETE, *with a lantern, and* SCUDDER, *with notebook.*)

SCUDDER. One hundred and forty-nine bales. Can you take any more?

RATTS. Not a bale. I've got engaged eight hundred bales at the next landing, and one hundred hogsheads of sugar at Patten's Slide—that'll take my guards under—hurry up thar.

VOICE (*outside*). Wood's aboard.

RATTS. All aboard then.

(*Enter* M'CLOSKY.)

SCUDDER. Sign that receipt, Captain, and save me going up to the clerk.

M'CLOSKY. See here—there's a small freight of turpentine in the fore hold there, and one of the barrels leaks; a spark from your engines might set the ship on fire, and you'll go with it.

RATTS. You be darned! Go and try it, if you've a mind to.

LAFOUCHE. Captain, you've loaded up here until the boat is sunk so deep in the mud she won't float.

RATTS (*calling off*). Wood up thar, you Pollo—hang on to the safety valve —guess she'll crawl off on her paddles. (*Shouts heard.*)

JACKSON. What's the matter?

SOLON (*enters*). We got him!

SCUDDER. Who?

SOLON. The Injiun!

SCUDDER. Wahnotee? Where is he? D'ye call running away from a fellow catching him?

RATTS. Here he comes.

ALL. Where? Where?

(*Enter* WAHNOTEE. *They are all about to rush on him.*)

SCUDDER. Hold on! stan' round thar! no violence—the crittur don't know what we mean.

JACKSON. Let him answer for the boy then.

M'CLOSKY. Down with him—lynch him.

ALL. Lynch him!

(*Exit* LAFOUCHE.)

SCUDDER. Stan' back, I say! I'll nip the first that lays a finger on him. Pete, speak to the redskin.

PETE. Whar's Paul, Wahnotee? What's come ob de child?

WAHNOTEE. Paul wunce—Paul pangeuk.

PETE. Pangeuk—dead!

WAHNOTEE. Mort!

M'CLOSKY. And you killed him? (*They approach him.*)

SCUDDER. Hold on!

PETE. Um, Paul reste?

WAHNOTEE. Hugh view. (*Goes.*) Paul reste ci!

SCUDDER. Here, stay! (*Examines the ground.*) The earth has been stirred here lately.

WAHNOTEE. Weenee Paul. (*He points down, and shows by pantomime how he buried* PAUL.)

SCUDDER. The Injun means that he buried him there! Stop! here's a bit of leather. (*Drawing out the mailbags*) The mailbags that were lost! (*Sees the tomahawk in* WAHNOTEE's *belt—draws it out and examines it.*) Look! here are marks of blood—look thar, redskin, what's that?

WAHNOTEE. Paul! (*Makes a sign that* PAUL *was killed by a blow on the head.*)

M'CLOSKY. He confesses it; the Indian got drunk, quarrelled with him, and killed him.

LAFOUCHE (*re-enters with smashed apparatus*). Here are evidences of the crime; this rum-bottle half emptied— this photographic apparatus smashed— and there are marks of blood and footsteps around the shed.

M'CLOSKY. What more d'ye want— ain't that proof enough? Lynch him!

ALL. Lynch him! Lynch him!

SCUDDER. Stan' back, boys! He's an Injiun—fair play.

JACKSON. Try him, then—try him on the spot of his crime.

ALL. Try him! Try him!

LAFOUCHE. Don't let him escape!

RATTS. I'll see to that. (*Drawing revolver*) If he stirs, I'll put a bullet through his skull, mighty quick.

M'CLOSKY. Come, form a court then, choose a jury—we'll fix this varmin.

(*Enter* THIBODEAUX *and* CAILLOU.)

THIBODEAUX. What's the matter?

LAFOUCHE. We've caught this murdering Injiun, and are going to try him.

(WAHNOTEE *sits, rolled in blanket.*)

PETE. Poor little Paul—poor little nigger!

SCUDDER. This business goes agin me,

Ratts—'t ain't right.

LAFOUCHE. We're ready; the jury's impanelled—go ahead—who'll be accuser?

RATTS. M'Closky.

M'CLOSKY. Me?

RATTS. Yes; you was the first to hail Judge Lynch.

M'CLOSKY. Well, what's the use of argument whar guilt sticks out so plain; the boy and Injiun were alone when last seen.

SCUDDER. Who says that?

M'CLOSKY. Everybody—that is, I heard so.

SCUDDER. Say what you know—not what you heard.

M'CLOSKY. I know then that the boy was killed with that tomahawk—the redskin owns it—the signs of violence are all round the shed—this apparatus smashed—ain't it plain that in a drunken fit he slew the boy, and when sober concealed the body yonder?

ALL. That's it—that's it.

RATTS. Who defends the Injiun?

SCUDDER. I will; for it is agin my natur' to b'lieve him guilty; and if he be, this ain't the place, nor you the authority to try him. How are we sure the boy is dead at all? There are no witnesses but a rum bottle and an old machine. Is it on such evidence you'd hang a human being?

RATTS. His own confession.

SCUDDER. I appeal against your usurped authority. This lynch law is a wild and lawless proceeding. Here's a pictur' for a civilized community to afford; yonder, a poor, ignorant savage, and round him a circle of hearts, white with revenge and hate, thirsting for his blood: you call yourselves judges—you ain't—you're a jury of executioners. It is such scenes as these that bring disgrace upon our Western life.

M'CLOSKY. Evidence! Evidence! Give us evidence. We've had talk enough; now for proof.

ALL. Yes, yes! Proof, proof!

SCUDDER. Where am I to get it? The proof is here, in my heart.

PETE (who has been looking about the camera). 'Top, sar! 'Top a bit! O, laws-a-mussey, see dis! here's a pictur' I found stickin' in that yar telescope machine, sar! look, sar!

SCUDDER. A photographic plate.

(PETE holds his lantern up.) What's this, eh? two forms! The child —'t is he! dead—and above him—Ah! ah! Jacob M'Closky, 't was you murdered that boy!

M'CLOSKY. Me?

SCUDDER. You! You slew him with that tomahawk; and as you stood over his body with the letter in your hand, you thought that no witness saw the deed, that no eye was on you—but there was, Jacob M'Closky, there was. The eye of the Eternal was on you—the blessed sun in heaven, that, looking down, struck upon this plate the image of the deed. Here you are, in the very attitude of your crime!

M'CLOSKY. 'T is false!

SCUDDER. 'T is true! the apparatus can't lie. Look there, jurymen. (Showing plate to jury) Look there. O, you wanted evidence—you called for proof —Heaven has answered and convicted you.

M'CLOSKY. What court of law would receive such evidence? (Going.)

RATTS. Stop! this would! You called it yourself; you wanted to make us murder that Injiun; and since we've got our hands in for justice, we'll try it on you. What say ye? shall we have one law for the redskin and another for the white?

ALL. Try him! Try him!

RATTS. Who'll be accuser?

SCUDDER. I will! Fellow citizens, you are convened and assembled here under a higher power than the law. What's the law? When the ship's abroad on the ocean, when the army is before the enemy, where in thunder's the law? It is in the hearts of brave men, who can tell right from wrong, and from whom justice can't be bought. So it is here, in the wilds of the West, where our hatred of crime is measured by the speed of our executions—where necessity is law! I say, then, air you honest men? air you true? Put your hands on your naked breasts, and let every man as don't feel a real American heart there, bustin' up with freedom, truth, and right, let that man step out—that's the oath I put to ye—and then say, Darn ye, go it!

ALL. Go on! Go on!

SCUDDER. No! I won't go on; that man's down. I won't strike him, even with words. Jacob, your accuser is that picter of the crime—let that speak—defend yourself.

M'CLOSKY (drawing knife). I will, quicker than lightning.

RATTS. Seize him, then!

(They rush on M'CLOSKY, and disarm him.)

He can fight though he's a painter: claws all over.

SCUDDER. Stop! Search him, we may find more evidence.

M'CLOSKY. Would you rob me first, and murder me afterwards?

RATTS (searching him). That's his programme—here's a pocket-book.

SCUDDER (opening it). What's here? Letters! Hello! To "Mrs. Peyton, Terrebonne, Louisiana, United States." Liverpool postmark. Ho! I've got hold of the tail of a rat—come out. (Reads.) What's this? A draft for eighty-five thousand dollars, and credit on Palisse and Co., of New Orleans, for the balance. Hi! the rat's out. You killed the boy to steal this letter from the mailbags—you stole this letter, that the

money should not arrive in time to save the Octoroon; had it done so, the lien on the estate would have ceased, and Zoe be free.

ALL. Lynch him! Lynch him! Down with him!

SCUDDER. Silence in the court: stand back, let the gentlemen of the jury retire, consult, and return their verdict.

RATTS. I'm responsible for the crittur—go on.

PETE (to WAHNOTEE). See, Injiun; look dar, (Showing him the plate) see dat innocent; look, dar's de murderer of poor Paul.

WAHNOTEE. Ugh! (Examining the plate.)

PETE. Ya! as he? Closky tue Paul—kill de child with your tomahawk dar: 't wasn't you, no—ole Pete allus say so. Poor Injiun lub our little Paul.

(WAHNOTEE rises and looks at M'CLOSKY—he is in his war paint and fully armed.)

SCUDDER. What say ye, gentlemen? Is the prisoner guilty, or is he not guilty?

ALL. Guilty!

SCUDDER. And what is to be his punishment?

ALL. Death! (All advance.)

WAHNOTEE (crosses to M'CLOSKY). Ugh!

SCUDDER. No, Injiun; we deal out justice here, not revenge. 'T ain't you he has injured, 't is the white man, whose laws he has offended.

RATTS. Away with him—put him down the aft hatch, till we rig his funeral.

M'CLOSKY. Fifty against one! O! if I had you one by one alone in the swamp, I'd rip ye all. (He is borne off in boat, struggling.)

SCUDDER. Now, then, to business.

PETE (re-enters from boat). O, law, sir, dat debil Closky, he tore hisself from de gen'lam, knock me down, take my light, and trows it on de turpentine barrels, and de shed's all afire!

(*Fire seen.*)

JACKSON (*re-entering*). We are catching fire forward: quick, cut free from the shore.

RATTS. All hands aboard there—cut the starn ropes—give her headway!

ALL. Ay, ay!

(*Cry of "Fire" heard—engine bells heard—steam whistle noise.*)

RATTS. Cut all away, for'ard—overboard with every bale afire.

(*The steamer moves off with the fire still blazing.*)

M'CLOSKY. (*re-enters, swimming*). Ha! have I fixed ye? Burn! burn! that's right. You thought you had cornered me, did ye? As I swam down, I thought I heard something in the water, as if pursuing me—one of them darned alligators, I suppose—they swarm hereabout—may they crunch every limb of ye. (*Exits.*)

(WAHNOTEE *is seen swimming. He finds trail and follows* M'CLOSKY. *The steamer floats on at back, burning.*)

ACT FIVE

SCENE ONE

Negroes' quarters.

———

ZOE (*enters*). It wants an hour yet to daylight—here is Pete's hut—(*Knocks.*) He sleeps—no: I see a light.

DIDO (*enters from hut*). Who dat?

ZOE. Hush, Aunty 'T is I—Zoe.

DIDO. Missey Zoe? Why you out in de swamp dis time ob night; you catch de fever sure—you is all wet.

ZOE. Where's Pete?

DIDO. He gone down to de landing last night wid Mas'r Scudder; not come back since—kint make it out.

ZOE. Aunty, there is sickness up at the house; I have been up all night beside one who suffers, and I remembered that when I had the fever you gave me a drink, a bitter drink, that made me sleep—do you remember it?

DIDO. Didn't I? Dem doctors ain't no 'count; dey don't know nuffin.

ZOE. No; but you, Aunty, you are wise—you know every plant, don't you, and what it is good for?

DIDO. Dat you drink is fust rate for red fever. Is de folks' head bad?

ZOE. Very bad, Aunty; and the heart aches worse, so they can get no rest.

DIDO. Hold on a bit, I get you de bottle. (*Exits.*)

ZOE. In a few hours that man, my master, will come for me: he has paid my price, and he only consented to let me remain here this one night, because Mrs. Peyton promised to give me up to him to-day.

DIDO (*re-enters with phial*). Here 't is—now you give one timble-full—dat's nuff.

ZOE. All there is there would kill one, wouldn't it?

DIDO. Guess it kill a dozen—nebber try.

ZOE. It's not a painful death, Aunty, is it? You told me it produced a long, long sleep.

DIDO. Why you tremble so? Why you speak so wild? What you's gwine to do, missey?

ZOE. Give me the drink.

DIDO. No. Who dat sick at de house?

ZOE. Give it to me.

DIDO. No. You want to hurt yourself. O, Miss Zoe, why you ask old Dido for dis pizen?

ZOE. Listen to me. I love one who is here, and he loves me—George. I sat outside his door all night—I heard his sighs—his agony—torn from him by my coming fate; and he said, "I'd rather see her dead than his!"

DIDO. Dead!

ZOE. He said so—then I rose up, and stole from the house, and ran down to the bayou: but its cold, black, silent stream terrified me—drowning must be so horrible a death. I could not do it. Then, as I knelt there, weeping for courage, a snake rattled beside me. I shrunk from it and fled. Death was there beside me, and I dared not take it. O! I'm afraid to die; yet I am more afraid to live.

DIDO. Die!

ZOE. So I came here to you; to you, my own dear nurse; to you, who so often hushed me to sleep when I was a child; who dried my eyes and put your little Zoe to rest. Ah! give me the rest that no master but One can disturb —the sleep from which I shall awake free! You can protect me from that man—do let me die without pain.

DIDO. No, no—life is good for young t'ing like you.

ZOE. O! good, good nurse: you will, you will.

DIDO. No—g' way.

ZOE. Then I shall never leave Terrebonne—the drink, nurse; the drink; that I may never leave my home—my dear, dear home. You will not give me to that man? Your own Zoe, that loves you, Aunty, so much, so much. (*She gets the phial.*) Ah! I have it.

DIDO. No, missey. O! no—don't.

ZOE. Hush! (*Runs off.*)

DIDO. Here, Solon, Minnie, Grace. (*They enter.*)

ALL. Was de matter?

DIDO. Miss Zoe got de pizen. (*Exits.*)

ALL. O! O! (*Exeunt.*)

SCENE TWO

In a canebrake bayou, on a bank, *with a canoe nearby,* M'CLOSKY *is seen asleep.*

M'CLOSKY. Burn, burn! blaze away! How the flames crack. I'm not guilty; would ye murder me? Cut, cut the rope—I choke—choke—Ah! (*Wakes.*) Hello! where am I? Why, I was dreaming—curse it! I can never sleep now without dreaming. Hush! I thought I heard the sound of a paddle in the water. All night, as I fled through the canebrake, I heard footsteps behind me. I lost them in the cedar swamp— again they haunted my path down the bayou, moving as I moved, resting when I rested—hush! there again!— no; it was only the wind over the canes. The sun is rising. I must launch my dug-out, and put for the bay, and in a few hours I shall be safe from pursuit on board of one of the coasting schooners that run from Galveston to Matagorda. In a little time this darned business will blow over, and I can show again. Hark! there's that noise again! If it was the ghost of that murdered boy haunting me! Well—I didn't mean to kill him, did I? Well, then, what has my all-cowardly heart got to skeer me so for? (*He gets in canoe and rows off.* WAHNOTEE *appears in another canoe. He gets out and finds trail and paddles off after* M'CLOSKY.)

SCENE THREE

A cedar swamp. Enter SCUDDER *and* PETE.

SCUDDER. Come on, Pete, we shan't reach the house before midday.

PETE. Nebber mind, sa, we bring good news—it won't spile for de keeping.

SCUDDER. Ten miles we've had to walk, because some blamed varmin on-hitched our dugout. I left it last night all safe.

PETE. P'r'aps it floated away itself.

SCUDDER. No; the hitching line was cut with a knife.

PETE. Say, Mas'r Scudder, s'pose we go in round by de quarters and raise de darkies, den dey cum long wid us, and we 'proach dat ole house like Gin'ral Jackson when he took London out dar.

SCUDDER. Hello, Pete, I never heard of that affair.

PETE. I tell you, sa—hush!

SCUDDER. What?

PETE. Was dat?—a cry out dar in the swamp—dar again!

SCUDDER. So it is. Something forcing its way through the undergrowth—it comes this way—it's either a bear or a runaway nigger. (*He draws a pistol.* M'CLOSKY *rushes on, and falls at* SCUD-DER's *feet.*)

SCUDDER. Stand off—what are ye?

PETE. Mas'r Clusky.

M'CLOSKY. Save me—save me! I can go no farther. I heard voices.

SCUDDER. Who's after you?

M'CLOSKY. I don't know, but I feel it's death! In some form, human, or wild beast, or ghost, it has tracked me through the night. I fled; it followed. Hark! there it comes—it comes—don't you hear a footstep on the dry leaves!

SCUDDER. Your crime has driven you mad.

M'CLOSKY. D'ye hear it—nearer—nearer—ah!

(WAHNOTEE *rushes on, and attacks* M'CLOSKY.)

SCUDDER. The Injuin! by thunder.

PETE. You'se a dead man, Mas'r Clusky—you got to b'lieve dat.

M'CLOSKY. No—no. If I must die, give me up to the law; but save me from the tomahawk. You are a white man; you'll not leave one of your own blood to be butchered by the redskin?

SCUDDER. Hold on now, Jacob; we've got to figure on that—let us look straight at the thing. Here we are on the selvage of civilization. It ain't our side, I believe, rightly; but Nature has said that where the white man sets his foot, the red man and the black man shall up sticks and stand around. But what do we pay for that possession? In cash? No—in kind—that is, in protection, forbearance, gentleness, in all them goods that show the critters the difference between the Christian and the savage. Now, what have you done to show them the distinction? for, darn me, if I can find out.

M'CLOSKY. For what I have done, let me be tried.

SCUDDER. You have been tried—honestly tried and convicted. Providence has chosen your executioner. I shan't interfere.

PETE. O, no; Mas'r Scudder, don't leave Mas'r Closky like dat—don't, sa —'t ain't what good Christian should do.

SCUDDER. D' ye hear that, Jacob? This old nigger, the grandfather of the boy you murdered, speaks for you— don't that go through you? D' ye feel it? Go on, Pete, you've waked up the Christian here, and the old hoss responds. (*He throws bowie knife to* M'CLOSKY.) Take that, and defend yourself.

(*Exeunt* SCUDDER *and* PETE. WAH-NOTEE *faces him. They fight.* M'CLOSKY *runs off,* WAHNOTEE *follows him.— Screams outside.*)

SCENE FOUR

Parlor at Terrebonne.

———

ZOE (*enters*). My home, my home! I must see you no more. Those little flowers can live, but I cannot. Tomorrow they'll bloom the same—all will be here as now, and I shall be cold. O! my life, my happy life; why has it been so bright?

(*Enter* MRS. PEYTON *and* DORA.)

DORA. Zoe, where have you been?

MRS. PEYTON. We felt quite uneasy about you.

ZOE. I've been to the Negro quarters. I suppose I shall go before long, and I wished to visit all the places, once again, to see the poor people.

MRS. PEYTON. Zoe, dear, I'm glad to see you more calm this morning.

DORA. But how pale she looks, and she trembles so.

ZOE. Do I? (*Enter* GEORGE.) Ah! he is here.

DORA. George, here she is.

ZOE. I have come to say good-by, sir; two hard words—so hard, they might break many a heart; mightn't they?

GEORGE. O, Zoe! can you smile at this moment?

ZOE. You see how easily I have become reconciled to my fate—so it will be with you. You will not forget poor Zoe! but her image will pass away like a little cloud that obscured your happiness a while—you will love each other; you are both too good not to join your hearts. Brightness will return amongst you. Dora, I once made you weep; those were the only tears I caused anybody. Will you forgive me?

DORA. Forgive you— (*Kisses her.*)

ZOE. I feel you do, George.

GEORGE. Zoe, you are pale. Zoe!— she faints!

ZOE. No; a weakness, that's all—a little water. (DORA *gets some water.*) I have a restorative here—will you pour it in the glass? (DORA *attempts to take it.*) No; not you—George. (GEORGE *pours the contents of the phial into glass.*) Now, give it to me. George, dear George, do you love me?

GEORGE. Do you doubt it, Zoe?

ZOE. No! (*She drinks.*)

DORA. Zoe, if all I possess would buy your freedom, I would gladly give it.

ZOE. I am free! I had but one Master on earth, and he has given me my freedom!

DORA. Alas! but the deed that freed you was not lawful.

ZOE. Not lawful—no—but I am going to where there is no law—where there is only justice.

GEORGE. Zoe, you are suffering—your lips are white—your cheeks are flushed.

ZOE. I must be going—it is late. Farewell, Dora. (*Retires.*)

PETE (*outside*). Whar's Missus— whar's Mas'r George?

GEORGE. They come.

SCUDDER (*enters*). Stand around and let me pass—room thar! I feel so big with joy, creation ain't wide enough to hold me. Mrs. Peyton, George Peyton, Terrebonne is yours. It was that rascal M'Closky— but he got rats, I swow— he killed the boy, Paul, to rob this letter from the mailbags—the letter from Liverpool you know—he sot fire to the shed—that was how the steamboat got burned up.

MRS. PEYTON. What d' ye mean?

SCUDDER. Read—read that. (*He gives letter to them.*)

GEORGE. Explain yourself.

SUNNYSIDE (*enters*). Is it true?

SCUDDER. Every word of it, Squire. Here, you tell it, since you know it. If I was to try, I'd bust.

MRS. PEYTON. Read, George. Terrebonne is yours.

(*Enter* PETE, DIDO, SOLON, MINNIE, *and* GRACE.)

PETE. Whar is she—whar is Miss Zoe?

SCUDDER. What's the matter?

PETE. Don't ax me. Whar's de gal? I say.

SCUDDER. Here she is—Zoe!—water —she faints.

PETE. No—no. 'T ain't no faint— she's a dying, sa: she got pizon from old Dido here, this mornin'.

GEORGE. Zoe!

SCUDDER. Zoe! is this true?—no, it ain't—darn it, say it ain't. Look here, you're free, you know; nary a master to hurt you now: you will stop here as long as you're a mind to, only don't look so.

DORA. Her eyes have changed color.

PETE. Dat's what her soul's gwine to do. It's going up dar, whar dere's no line atween folks.

GEORGE. She revives.

ZOE (*on the sofa*). George—where— where—

GEORGE. O, Zoe! what have you done?

ZOE. Last night I overheard you weeping in your room, and you said, "I'd rather see her dead than so!"

GEORGE. Have I then prompted you to this?

ZOE. No; but I loved you so, I could not bear my fate; and then I stood between your heart and hers. When I am dead she will not be jealous of your love for me, no laws will stand between us. Lift me; so— (GEORGE *raises her head.*) —let me look at you, that your face may be the last I see of this world. O! George, you may, without a blush, confess your love for the Octoroon. (*She dies.* GEORGE *lowers her head gently and kneels beside her.*)

THE COUNT OF MONTE CRISTO

Charles Fechter

Dramatization of the novel of Alexandre Dumas.

Played under the title *Monte Cristo* by James
O'Neill; first produced on February 12, 1883, at
Booth's Theatre, New York.*

EDMUND DANTÈS	FARIA
MOREL	GOVERNOR
DANGLARS	SENTINEL
NOIRTIER	FIRST GAOLER
CADEROUSSE	SECOND GAOLER
FERNAND	BRIGADIER
FISHERMAN	ALBERT DE MORCERF
MAN	SAILOR
VILLEFORT	MLLE. DANGLARS
FIRST AGENT	MERCÉDÈS
SECOND AGENT	CARCONTE
GERMAIN, *a servant*	WOMAN

* Edited for reading (without nineteenth-century stage indications) by MOLLIE GASSNER.
For the original acting version exactly as left by James O'Neill, the reader is referred to
Volume 16 of *America's Lost Plays*, edited by J. B. Russak, Princeton University Press.
Reprinted by the Indiana University Press, Volume 8.

PROLOGUE[1]

[*A garret, window with climbing plants.* DANTÉS *discovered seated,* LA CARCONTE *standing.*

LA CARCONTE. You seem very melancholy today, Father Dantés.

DANTÉS. I grow so impatient for my son's return, he has been so long absent.

LA CARCONTE. The voyage of *The Pharaon* always is a lengthy one, but its owner, Monsieur Morel, is expecting her now daily, in fact, does not know one hour from another but he may see her enter the harbor.

DANTÉS (*rising*). Ah! my dear Edmond, what joy to me when I shall again hold you to my heart.

LA CARCONTE. Well, well, have patience, and as I have told you, expect him every hour now.

DANTÉS. Patience when awaiting the only stay—the only joy of my aged life!

LA CARCONTE. But, Father Dantés, I came to you now expecting that I should meet here, my drunken rogue, Caderousse.

DANTÉS. I have not seen him today.

LA CARCONTE. Then he is at the tavern again, the lazy—and such a good trade as he has, if he would but work, but he won't, and so all his customers are leaving him one after the other, and soon he will be without either money or credit.

DANTÉS. Then why do you not quit Marseilles, you have a small property at Cales, your birthplace, and there—

LA CARCONTE. I return to Cales—it would be the death of me; you know that I was nearly dead before I left it.

DANTÉS. Yes, true, poor woman, the ague and fever—but you are better now?

LA CARCONTE. Oh, yes, quite recovered, and provided I do not return, to have another dose of that unwholesome air—

DANTÉS. Well, well, let us hope there may be no occasion for your return, Caderousse may reform—

LA CARCONTE. Hark! I hear footsteps on the stairs, it is he perhaps.

EDMOND DANTÉS (*without*). Father! Father!

DANTÉS. Oh, heaven, my son, Edmond! Edmond!, etc.]

ACT ONE

SCENE ONE

A tavern at the edge of a cliff with a balustrade, with the harbor and the city of Marseilles in the background. FISHERMEN *and* PEASANTS *are drinking, and the clamor of voices grows as the curtain rises.*

MAN. 'Tis she—'tis she!

WOMAN. I tell you 'tis not.

MAN. I tell you it is!

WOMAN. A ship in sight!

(*Enter* MOREL *and* CARCONTE.)

MOREL (*to the crowd*). Friends, yonder comes a rich cargo, and all must today partake of my good fortune. (*Gives them money and goes upstage.*)

CARCONTE. Is not my husband here? Did he not come out with you?

MOREL. No.

CARCONTE. The drunken sot, he is in some low wineshop!

[1] The prologue in brackets is from the Thomas H. Lacy dramatization made before 1870 and published under the description "French's Acting Edition (Late Lacy's)." Reproduced here for its value as exposition. (Dantés has an accent *aigu* and not an accent *grave* in this edition, and the hero's first name is spelled "Edmond.")

MOREL (*looking through a telescope*). Here come the officers of health and customs along with my supercargo. Douglass, how is it that Edmund is not with them? The captain usually lets him land before getting into harbor.

FISHERMAN. Look, Monsieur Morel, the flag is half-mast!

MOREL. Good heavens, it is! What can it mean? What can have happened on board?

FISHERMAN. Some chief officer dead, no doubt.

MOREL. It can't be Edmund Dantès! Here is Danglars! We shall know all from him.

(*Enter* DANGLARS.)

Speak, Danglars, what means the flag lowered?

DANGLARS. I am sorry, sir, to be the bearer of bad news. The captain is dead.

MOREL. What, my dear old friend?

DANGLARS. He died of brain fever that carried him off in a few hours after we left Naples. 'Tis unfortunate, Monsieur Morel, very unfortunate. Such a captain is not easily found to look properly after the interests of such a house as yours, it needs an old and experienced seaman.

MOREL. A man need not be an absolute veteran to understand his business. What did Edmund Dantès do in this emergency?

DANGLARS. Dantès! (*Aside*) Now for him! (*Aloud*) Oh, Monsieur Morel, the captain was scarcely dead, he was scarcely at the bottom of the sea, when Dantès assumed the command and caused us to lose a day at Elba, instead of steering for Marseilles direct.

MOREL. To take command of the vessel was his duty as mate, but to lose a day at Elba, there he was wrong. (*Coldly*) I shall take the account from him,

and soon know the merits of the case.

DANGLARS. Very good, Monsieur Morel. Edmund is young, but I believe in his honesty.

MOREL. And I am assured of it. I will go and meet him. (*Exit.*)

CARCONTE (*to* DANGLARS). Caught are ye? I'm not sorry to see you getting into hot water. You have been the bane of my husband. (*Going upstage*) Edmund will avenge me.

DANGLARS. Not so fast, they laugh best, who laugh last.

NOIRTIER (*entering and stopping at* CARCONTE). Your pardon. May I ask, madame, is not that the ship *Pharaon*?

CARCONTE. It is, sir, and I am going to see her come into the harbor.

NOIRTIER. Can you inform me where to find the captain?

CARCONTE. Go to the bay of Naples, and you will find him at the bottom. (*Exit.*)

NOIRTIER. Is the woman mad?

DANGLARS. She spoke the truth, sir. We lost our captain on the voyage, and his body lies where Carconte told you.

NOIRTIER. And after his death, who took charge of the ship?

DANGLARS. The mate.

NOIRTIER. His name?

DANGLARS. Edmund Dantès.

NOIRTIER. And is he alive?

DANGLARS (*sighing*). Quite alive!

NOIRTIER. Where could I find him?

DANGLARS. On board at present. In an hour's time, at the Reserve Inn. Any matter that I can answer in his stead?

NOIRTIER (*going*). I merely wished a little information about the vessel's course this voyage.

DANGLARS. I can give you that.

NOIRTIER. You?

DANGLARS. I am the supercargo on board the *Pharaon*. What do you wish to know?

NOIRTIER. Only whether the ship made land on the voyage.

DANGLARS. Yes. (*Looking mysteriously around*) On the Isle of Elba!

NOIRTIER. Thank you. (*Walks away.*)

DANGLARS. Well—

NOIRTIER. What?

DANGLARS. Is that all?

NOIRTIER. That is all.

DANGLARS. I thought you wanted—

NOIRTIER. Thank you. (*Exit.*)

DANGLARS. Something not quite straight here! That man came looking for the letter that Edmund received at Elba from the hands of the exiled emperor. Let me only be sure, and then—

CADEROUSSE (*looking out of inn*). Wife gone? Then, I may show myself.

DANGLARS. Caderousse!

CADEROUSSE. Danglars! Hurrah! We'll crack a bottle in honor of your safe return.

DANGLARS. You're drunk.

CADEROUSSE. Drunk, of course, I am —and proud of it! So much the worse for them that are afraid of wine, that is because they are afraid of speaking the truth. I'll engage you never get drunk. (*A ship is glimpsed moving from the right.*) *

DANGLARS. Idiot!

CADEROUSSE. Am I? You're afraid to let your heart—ain't I complimentary? I say "your heart!"—you're afraid to let it disclose its thoughts, but I, never! I drink so much as ever I like— as much as I can—and then I open the floodgates of truth and avow I love wine, hate work, and pray for widowhood! Come on, have a glass. You won't? Well, give me your arm. You see, my head is light, but my legs are like pillars of lead. You never feel that way for you drink water like a

---

* The stage direction in the James O'Neill manuscript reads, "*Ship works on from R.*"

---

shark. (*Sings.*) "The bottle for me, the pump for thee!"

DANGLARS (*looking off*). Who is that pretty girl?

CADEROUSSE. Don't you know Mercédès, our brave Edmund's betrothed? Here comes the *Pharaon* into port, look at her—isn't she pretty? (*Exit into the tavern with* DANGLARS. *A ship is seen coming into port.* MERCÉDÈS *and* FERNAND *enter.*)

FERNAND. Mercédès, for the last time, will you answer me?

MERCÉDÈS. You are your own enemy to ask me again.

FERNAND. Answer me a hundred times more, that I may at last believe it. Tell me that you scorn my love— that my life, my death are nothing to you—that you reject my hand, my heart! Ah, Mercédès, what have I done that you should kill thus?

MERCÉDÈS. Blame me not, Fernand, blame yourself. From the very first, I told you, "Fernand, I love you as a brother, but ask not, hope not more, for my heart is given to another."— Did I say so, Fernand?

FERNAND. Yes, oh, yes. But, you know Mercédès, it is a sacred law amongst us Catalans, to intermarry.

MERCÉDÈS. Not a law, merely a custom, Fernand, that is all. Fernand, I will never be yours because I love another, and I am his!

FERNAND. You?

MERCÉDÈS. His! Fernand, do you hear? His, in the sight of Heaven, and whilst I live I cannot be another's without guilt.

FERNAND. I will kill him!

MERCÉDÈS. You will not! Fernand, what would it profit you? To find my friendship turned to hate? To know that in killing him, you had killed me?

FERNAND. The sea has not your constancy, Mercédès—a sailor's is a dangerous trade, and the ocean a vast grave. The sea will do my business.

MERCÉDÈS. You have a bad heart, Fernand. I blush to be your relative and to bear your name, but even were I to lose him, I should know that he died loving me, and I would die loving him.

FERNAND. But, if he were to forget you?

MERCÉDÈS. Forget me?

FERNAND. Aye, the ship is in port, why is he not here?

MERCÉDÈS. Heavens!

FERNAND. Ah, at last you know what jealousy is! It is fearful is it not?

MERCÉDÈS. Fernand!

FERNAND. I am avenged, Mercédès, he has forgotten you.

EDMUND (off stage). Mercédès!

MERCÉDÈS. 'Tis false, Fernand, he is here! (Enter EDMUND, and she flies to him, whereupon FERNAND half draws the knife he is carrying.)

FERNAND (controlling himself). No, it would kill her!

EDMUND. Mercédès, my beloved Mercédès! (Noticing FERNAND) Oh, I did not know you had a companion; who is this man?

MERCÉDÈS. My cousin, Fernand Mondego, the man whom after you, I love best in the world.

EDMUND. Then he is my friend. Brother of Mercédès, here is my hand! (Advances, offering his hand, but FERNAND refuses it.)

MERCÉDÈS. Fernand!

FERNAND (approaching MERCÉDÈS). No, no, it is too much! I cannot! Adieu, Mercédès, adieu! (He rushes off.)

EDMUND (looking after him). Mercédès, that man will cause us misfortune.

MERCÉDÈS. Misfortune? No, Edmund, now reunited, no misfortune can befall us. But, thou knowest not how I have suffered in thy absence, the nights I have passed. How I have prayed when the seas—now so calm, so smiling on thy return—roared dashing on the rocks when thou were away. And hast thou no thought of me?

EDMUND. Thought of thee? Oh, what should I have thought of! Art thou not my Providence, my guardian angel, my life itself? When the tempest howled, when the sea and wind were raging, thy prayers were to thy patron saint, beloved one. My prayers were to Mercédès, and my prayers were heard. The storm abated, the sea grew calm, and believed in thee! Ah, Monsieur Morel!

MOREL (entering). Yes. Monsieur Morel, not quite welcome, eh? He might have chosen his time better. Aye, aye, but there is little time to lose, happiness so rarely visits us here below, that when it passes by our portal we must seize it in its flight. But, I thought of you—everything is ready—I have had all the papers duly prepared. In the commerce of life there are so few honest debtors, Edmund, you are now in funds and must make prompt payment.

EDMUND. Thanks, Monsieur Morel, for judging me so truly. Yes, I repay in ready coin the noble trust of my Mercédès. I place in her hand my present, my future, my life, my soul, they are thine, Mercédès, thine forever, my beloved wife!

(DANGLARS and CADEROUSSE enter.)

CADEROUSSE (to EDMUND). Well, my boy, have you forgotten your friends?

EDMUND. Oh, how fares it, Caderousse? Bless you!

CADEROUSSE. And where are you going like that?

EDMUND. Where happy people go, my friend, straight before them without caring what rises in the distance, or what lies behind them—au revoir! (*He leaves with Mercédès.*)

CADEROUSSE. There's a case of hearty love, if ever I saw one, but nothin' like love of the bottle! (*He goes out.*)

DANGLARS. Here are the ship's papers.

MOREL.(*sitting at the table and looking at the papers*). All right, thanks. All complete and regular. I have only to sign the several returns.

DANGLARS. You have not spoken to Edmund Dantès, Monsieur Morel, I hope he gave you a satisfactory reason for anchoring at Elba?

MOREL. I forgot all about that.

DANGLARS. Then he has given you the emperor's letter?

MOREL. The emperor's letter?

DANGLARS. Yes, the letter he received at Elba from the emperor's own hand. His Majesty Louis XVIII is not given to jesting with the friends of the ex-emperor, and I supposed the letter was for you.

MOREL. For me?

DANGLARS. For whom can Edmund have brought it?

MOREL. He never said a word to me about it.

DANGLARS. In that case, Monsieur Morel, say nothing to Edmund of what I have told you—I may have been mistaken. I should feel very sorry to get him into a mess.

MOREL. There are your papers and the entries signed—let this affair of Edmund's rest. He must have nothing to trouble him on his wedding day.

DANGLARS. His wedding day?

MOREL. Let the crew of the *Pharaon* know of their captain's marriage.

DANGLARS. Edmund, the captain?

MOREL. Yes, that is my marriage present to him. (*He walks out.*)

DANGLARS. Indeed? You have not got your captain's epaulettes yet, Edmund Dantès, nor will your next voyage be on board the *Pharaon*.

(CADEROUSSE *and* FERNAND *enter.*)

CADEROUSSE. Come along, my hearty, what's the odds? A woman lost and two bottles won! Come, have a glass —nothing makes one so thirsty as jealousy. Come along!

FERNAND. Let me alone, Caderousse, I won't drink.

DANGLARS. Not drink, young man? 'Tis only whining lovers that don't drink.

CADEROUSSE. Oh, he is one, and whining. He met his love in his rival's arms.

FERNAND. He is not her husband yet.

DANGLARS. He will be this evening.

FERNAND. This evening?

DANGLARS. The wedding is to take place at your house, Caderousse, at the Reserve. I shall be there, we shall all be there. (*To* FERNAND) You will be of the party, I presume?

FERNAND (*furious*). I? I would rather see them both dead!

CADEROUSSE (*knocking on the table*). Waiter, some more wine!

DANGLARS. If your rival could be got rid of without killing him, you would spare Mercédès's feelings—and Dantès need not die.

CADEROUSSE (*drinking*). Why should Dantès die? I won't have Dantès die; he is a fine fellow. Here's to your health, Edmund!

FERNAND (*angrily*). Caderousse!

DANGLARS. He's drunk; never mind him. Suppose you put between Edmund and Mercédès the walls of a prison—it would part them quite as effectively as a tombstone.

FERNAND. Edmund in prison!

CADEROUSSE (*drinking and following them dreamily*). Why? Why put Dantès in prison? I won't have Dantès in prison! I love Edmund; here's to your health, Edmund.

DANGLARS. Hold your noise!

CADEROUSSE. I shall drink his health if I like.

FERNAND. But how to get him into prison?

CADEROUSSE (*pushing away the papers*). Take away all this rubbish, Danglars. It belongs to you, these are the weapons you're accustomed to. There is what can kill a man more surely than lying in wait for him with a knife in some dark corner.

DANGLARS. The vagabond says true enough.

FERNAND. How so?

CADEROUSSE. I have a greater dread of a pen and an ink bottle, and a sheet of paper, than I have of a sword and pistol and—a bottle of wine.

DANGLARS. Do you understand?

FERNAND (*as all sit at table,* CADEROUSSE *singing*). No.

DANGLARS. Fill his glass.

(FERNAND *fills* CADEROUSSE's *glass.*)

FERNAND. Well?

DANGLARS. Well, this drunkard has pointed out the way. If I bore a grudge against Dantès, if I wanted to rid myself of him, I would take this sheet of paper, I would dip this pen in the ink, and I would write thus—with the left hand to disguise the writing—a piece of information in these words—(*Writes with left hand.*)

FERNAND (*anxiously, reading over him*). "To the Procureur du Roi!"

DANGLARS (*pointing to* CADEROUSSE). Is he asleep?

FERNAND. He sleeps—proceed.

DANGLARS (*writing*). "The Procureur du Roi is informed that a man named Edmund Dantès who arrived from Smyrna today, touched at the Isle of Elba, where he was intrusted by the usurper Napoleon with a letter for the Bonapartist Committee. The letter will be found either on his person, or in his cabin on board the *Pharaon.* —Signed, A Friend to the Throne and Religion."—The letter is placed in the hands of the Procureur du Roi, and the business is done.

CADEROUSSE (*who has awakened*). The business is done, but 'tis a rascally business!

DANGLARS (*startled, but recovering*). For which I shall not make myself responsible. (*He crumples the letter and throws it at* FERNAND's *feet.*) There, take it. Danglars will not be the bearer.

FERNAND. But I will! (*He picks it up and leaves.*)

CADEROUSSE. Where's he off to in such a hurry?

DANGLARS. To Mercédès's cottage, no doubt.

CADEROUSSE. To Mercédès's cottage —do you think I am blind drunk? He is off to the city. What does he want in the city?

DANGLARS. How should I know?

CADEROUSSE (*looking to the ground*). And the letter—where's the letter?

DANGLARS. What letter?

CADEROUSSE. The letter. The letter informing against Dantès. The letter you threw down there, where is it? I want that letter! I must have the letter! (*Takes a glass which* DANGLARS *fills for him.*) Ah, how well you know me—here's your health.

DANGLARS. Just in time—here they come.

(EDMUND, MOREL, *and* CREW *of* Pharaon *enter.*)

EDMUND. Monsieur Morel, all is prepared at the Reserve according to your orders. Caderousse, your wife wants you to arrange the table, supper will be ready in an hour.

(*During the cheering* NOIRTIER *enters, and having* EDMUND *pointed out* to him by DANGLARS, *touches his shoulder.*)

NOIRTIER. May I speak a word to you?

EDMUND. With me?

NOIRTIER. You are the mate of the *Pharaon*?

EDMUND (*coming forward*). I am, may I know your pleasure?

NOIRTIER. I understand your ship cast anchor at the Isle of Elba?

EDMUND. She did.

NOIRTIER. And you landed there?

EDMUND. I did.

NOIRTIER. To execute a commission entrusted to your captain.

EDMUND. Who died on the voyage, yes.

NOIRTIER. The emperor has made you the bearer of a letter.

EDMUND. How know you that?

NOIRTIER. With orders to deliver it to a man unknown to you, who would accost you?

EDMUND. Yes.

NOIRTIER. I am he.

EDMUND. The description corresponds exactly. Your name then, is—I have asked your name!

NOIRTIER. It is for you to begin—and halve it.

EDMUND. True. N.o.i.r.—

NOIRTIER. T.i.e.r.

EDMUND. Right.

NOIRTIER. Now, give me the letter.

EDMUND. I thought it of too great importance to carry about me, and left it in my cabin on board.

NOIRTIER. You can get it at once?

EDMUND. To go and return would take me, altogether, an hour.

NOIRTIER. Then go for an hour. I will await you here.

EDMUND. Would it be the same to you to come for it to the Reserve Inn?

NOIRTIER. Why so?

EDMUND. Because I am going to be married there within an hour to the fair girl you see yonder, and I should be sorry to fail in attendance.

NOIRTIER. I can understand.

EDMUND. At the Reserve, then?

NOIRTIER. At the Reserve Inn.

EDMUND. In an hour from this. (*Goes upstage and disappears.*)

NOIRTIER. In an hour from this—pretty, very! (*Exit.*)

DANGLARS (*having overheard this conversation*). And my letter will be there in time! (SAILORS *drink and cheer, as the scene changes.*)

SCENE TWO

VILLEFORT *in his office. A writing table heaped with papers is near the door at the back.* GERMAIN *and two* POLICE *enter.*

———

VILLEFORT. First with you—what intelligence?

FIRST AGENT. The man we seek has been traced. He has been in the port, landed from a fishing boat, and shortly afterwards in the village of Catalans.

VILLEFORT. Does he answer the description sent from the Prefecture in Paris?

FIRST AGENT. Assuredly. "About forty years of age, long black hair, combed back, black whiskers and moustache, meeting—wears a long sourtout buttoned up to his chin, and decorated with the Legion of Honor. Hat with a wide leaf."

VILLEFORT (*looking over the paper*). Just so! Is he in custody?

FIRST AGENT. Not yet, but he has been followed. We shall have him before night.

VILLEFORT. Good. He is described as being a most dangerous conspirator, and a very likely person to be mixed up in this affair of Dantès, denounced to me in this anonymous letter. (*To the other* AGENT) What have you done in his case?

SECOND AGENT. Arrested him as he was getting into the *Pharaon's* boat to go on board.

VILLEFORT. Was the letter found on him?

SECOND AGENT. No, sir. I have brought him here, whilst my comrades went to search his cabin.

VILLEFORT. Bring him in.

(*Exit* SECOND AGENT.)

And see you to the immediate arrest of the other.

(*Exit* FIRST AGENT.)

There is plainly some connection between these two affairs. (*Reading* DANGLARS' *letter*) "The Procureur du Roi is informed that a man named Edmund Dantès, who arrived from Smyrna today, touched at the Isle of Elba, where he was entrusted by the usurper, Napoleon, with a letter for the Bonapartist Committee. The letter will be found either on his person or in his cabin on board the *Pharaon*."

(*The* SECOND AGENT *enters with* EDMUND.)

SECOND AGENT. This is the Procureur du Roi.

EDMUND. The Procureur du Roi!

VILLEFORT. Come forward.

(EDMUND *advances and bows to the* AGENT.)

Await my orders.

(*The* AGENT *leaves.*)

EDMUND. What the deuce am I wanted for?

VILLEFORT. Your name?

EDMUND. Edmund Dantès!

VILLEFORT. Your occupation?

EDMUND. Mate of the ship *Pharaon.*

VILLEFORT. And you were arrested when going on board. How did you intend acting after visiting the *Pharaon?*

EDMUND. I intended returning as quickly as possible to the Reserve. I have been expected there this hour past.

VILLEFORT. What for?

EDMUND. To get married—that's all.

VILLEFORT. Go on.

EDMUND. To what purpose, may I ask? If justice will condescend to inform me in what matter she wants me to enlighten her, I will tell her all I know—only promising her I know very little.

VILLEFORT. Your political opinions are said to be very violent.

EDMUND. My political opinions? Violent? Why, I'm almost ashamed to say I have no political opinions at all. My profession of faith is very concise; I love my father, I respect Monsieur Morel. I trust in Heaven, and I adore Mercédès—that is my political creed, Monsieur Procureur, it cannot be very interesting to justice.

VILLEFORT. 'Tis strange.

EDMUND. What is?

VILLEFORT. This accusation against you.

EDMUND. On account of my opinions?

VILLEFORT. Even so.

EDMUND. Gracious me, how stupid! Oh, I beg pardon.

VILLEFORT. Have you any great enemy to your knowledge? (*He looks at the letter.*) There must be someone who wishes you ill, very ill.

EDMUND. Well, possibly so. You know men better than I do, but if that "someone" be amongst those I love, I have no wish to know who he is, that I may not have to despise him.

VILLEFORT. You appear to be such an honest-minded lad that in your case I will forego the ordinary cases. (*Handing him the letter*) Read your denunciation—do you know the writing?

EDMUND. No, I do not know this writing. I see at once it is a counterfeit hand. I am indeed most fortunate in having to deal with a man like yourself, for my accuser is a fearful enemy.

VILLEFORT. How much truth is there in this paper?

EDMUND. There is truth, and no truth. There lies the guile, the venom of the charge.

VILLEFORT. How is that?

EDMUND. It is true that I arrived from Smyrna, it is true that I cast anchor at Elba, it is true that I received a letter from the emperor's hand, but I was ignorant of any plot, and was totally unconscious of furthering any conspiracy.

VILLEFORT. Yet, you went out of your course to touch at Elba; you therefore called there expressly of your own will, in the teeth of your owner's orders. This bears a very serious appearance.

EDMUND. I see too well it does, but it was not of my own doing and a very few words will explain it.

VILLEFORT. Proceed. (*He sits down.*)

EDMUND. Well then, on leaving Naples where I believe he had an interview with Murat, our captain fell ill of brain fever. He grew rapidly worse, and feeling himself dying and his senses about to desert him, he called me to his side. "Dantès," he said, "swear to me by your honor as a sailor, by your faith in Heaven, by your love for me, to discharge when I am gone, the mission I shall confide to you, and with which I was entrusted. Do not hesitate, Edmund, my body's rest, my soul's salvation, my honor are at stake!"—and the tears coursed down his bronzed and burning cheek. I could demur no longer. I swore. Then, with his ring, he gave

me a packet, commanded me to steer for the Island of Elba. To land at Port Farrajo, to have the ring conveyed to the emperor and to place the packet in his own hands. In a few moments he was dead. I reached Elba. I had the ring conveyed to the emperor—I gave him the packet. He entrusted me with a letter which a stranger he described would ask me for on landing at Marseilles. As soon as I arrived, the stranger presented himself, and I was on my way to get the letter, left in my cabin, when I was arrested. This is the truth, the whole truth, by my honor as a sailor, by my love for Mercédès, by my father's life!

VILLEFORT (*rising*). Yes, I believe you. You are surely innocent.

EDMUND. Thanks, monsieur, adieu, and thanks. (*Starting to go.*)

VILLEFORT. Stay—where are you going?

EDMUND. I am going away.

VILLEFORT. But you are not free yet.

EDMUND. You say I am innocent—how are the guilty treated?

VILLEFORT. That is just what you and I are going to consider.

EDMUND. You and I?

VILLEFORT. Yes.

EDMUND. I am very much afraid our views about justice are widely different.

VILLEFORT. Let us try.

EDMUND. First of all, if I am to have a voice in the matter, I acquit myself as an innocent man.

VILLEFORT. I agree.

EDMUND. And I give myself full discharge.

VILLEFORT. Granted—on one condition.

EDMUND. I impose no conditions on myself.

VILLEFORT. But, you are not the sole judge in the case.

EDMUND. Quite right.

VILLEFORT. There are two of us.

EDMUND. Unfortunately.

VILLEFORT. And we must be unanimous.

EDMUND. I have said that would be difficult. Your condition?

VILLEFORT. You are not to speak to any person whatsoever of your interview with the emperor.

EDMUND. I agree.

VILLEFORT. You are not to say a word of what has passed between ourselves.

EDMUND. Granted.

VILLEFORT. Finally, you pledge your word of honor to present yourself at my first summons.

EDMUND. I swear it.

VILLEFORT. You see I am not too hard.

EDMUND. I do not complain.

VILLEFORT. Very kind. Were you to see that stranger again?

EDMUND. Yes, at the Reserve.

VILLEFORT. Off with you, then, wait for him there—let him accost you.

EDMUND. But how about the letter he is coming to claim?

VILLEFORT. My men will give it to him.

EDMUND. What? (*A bell is heard.*)

VILLEFORT. Silence! Someone comes.

GERMAIN (*entering*). A stranger, sir, wishes particularly to see you on business of the greatest importance.

VILLEFORT (*writing at table*). Impossible, I am engaged! I can't see him. Let him demand an interview in writing. (*As* GERMAIN *leaves,* VILLEFORT *hands* EDMUND *a letter.*) Go at once by that door. On your way, leave this note at the guardhouse.

EDMUND (*aside*). Well, I'm on pretty good terms with justice. 'Tis well to have friends in every quarter. (*He leaves.*)

GERMAIN (*enters*). This man insists on seeing you. He says, sir, if you knew who he was—

NOIRTIER (*enters*). It is I.

VILLEFORT. My brother! (*To* GERMAIN) Go! (GERMAIN *leaves.*)

NOIRTIER. It appears you did not expect me. Is it the custom among the present nobility for younger brothers to make their elder brothers wait in the anteroom?

VILLEFORT. Good heavens!

NOIRTIER. What is the matter with you?

VILLEFORT. The very description!

NOIRTIER. What description?

VILLEFORT (*troubled*). The description of your person sent down from Paris, and which I myself have furnished here for the police.

NOIRTIER. So, you have given my description to the police, eh? Not very kind on your part, my younger brother—but when a son of a general of the empire becomes Procureur du Roi of His Majesty, Louis the XVIII, his first act is naturally to disown his family. His first thought to disembarrass himself of them.

VILLEFORT. You insult me!

NOIRTIER. Truth, then, is offensive to you?

VILLEFORT. What is it you want of me?

NOIRTIER. A few moments' shelter from your own bloodhounds who are now on my track, thanks to the description you had the goodness to supply them.

VILLEFORT (*sitting down*). Did I know that it referred to you? Did I know that you were still conspiring?

NOIRTIER. And what the devil would you have me do? Everyone is not blessed with your turncoat talent. That comes to you from your lady mother, whose name I thank you for adopting: since at least you do not disgrace that of our common father, who had made her his second wife. But, what am I about? I am accusing you, whilst you are the judge. I ask pardon, Monsieur le Procureur. You said that I was conspiring.

VILLEFORT. I hold the proofs.

NOIRTIER. Against whom do I conspire?

VILLEFORT. Against the king.

NOIRTIER. Correct to syllable! Allow me to congratulate you on your police. I never thought they were so sharp.

VILLEFORT. But you cannot remain in this house.

NOIRTIER. I have no desire to do so. I mean to depart directly.

VILLEFORT. And whither do you think of going?

NOIRTIER. That is my business.

VILLEFORT. How will you get out?

NOIRTIER. By the door, of course.

VILLEFORT. In the daylight?

NOIRTIER. In the daylight.

VILLEFORT. And in the midst of the men who are dogging you?

NOIRTIER. In the midst of them.

VILLEFORT. But, they will arrest you.

NOIRTIER. They will let me pass in peace. And they will also most respectfully salute me. (*Goes toward the bell.*)

VILLEFORT. What are you doing?

NOIRTIER. Ringing for your servant. (*As he rises,* GERMAIN *enters.*) What is your name, my man.

GERMAIN. Germain.

NOIRTIER. Then Germain, take this Napoleon (*Gives him a coin.*) ; 'tis the picture of the usurper, and I fear lest its possession compromise me. Now, show me to your master's dressing room, and then go and spend that bit of gold as fast as ever you can.

(GERMAIN *looks dubious.*)

VILLEFORT. Do as the gentleman tells you. (*As* GERMAIN *and* NOIRTIER *leave,*

he sinks in chair.) Great heavens, is the hateful past of my family to haunt me ever on my aspiring path? Is this elder brother, proud and contemptuous, to come everlastingly between me and the goal of my ambition? What were life and fortune had this occurred in Paris—had the prefect of police sent the notification to any other official than myself? Should the arrest be effected under my immediate order, I were disgraced forever! How shall I throw them off the scent? How contrive his escape?—Who is there? (FIRST AGENT *enters.*) What do you want?

FIRST AGENT. I ask your pardon, Monsieur le Procureur, your instructions have been faithfully observed. We are certain that the fugitive is in the street and we have his escape quite cut off. I come for a warrant to search the houses all around.

NOIRTIER (*enters, changed in appearance*). Give it, Villefort, prompt action against the king's enemies!

VILLEFORT. You?

NOIRTIER (*aside*). Take care, you will betray yourself! (*To* AGENT) So, my friend, you have lit on this fellow—at least you have recognized him?

FIRST AGENT. Yes, long, black hair and whiskers, wide-leaved hat, military surtout with the ribbon of the "Legion."

NOIRTIER. It would be impossible to be deceived. There is nothing so handy as an accurate description. (SECOND AGENT *enters.*) It positively rains police agents today!

SECOND AGENT (*giving* VILLEFORT *a letter*). The letter found on board.

VILLEFORT (*aside*). For him—addressed to Noïrtier—if any but I had read it. (*Aside to* NOIRTIER) Away—away! Quit Marseilles instantly or you will betray us both.

NOIRTIER. Well, I'll intrude no longer. To work Villefort; search, arrest, imprison! I—I shall be off to dinner. (AGENTS *bow to him.*) Did I not tell you so? Your servant, gentlemen. (*He goes out.*)

VILLEFORT. And this Dantès knows his person—has seen this letter—knows his name. A word from him can ruin me. (*To the* AGENTS) Go with a strong party to the Reserve Inn instantly. There you will find the young sailor you apprehended this afternoon.

FIRST AGENT. Edmund Dantès?

VILLEFORT. Yes. Arrest him—let him be conveyed at once to the dungeons of the Château d'If and kept in strict and most careful detention. There is the order to the governor. (*Signs and gives the paper to the* AGENTS, *who leave. Tears up letter to* NOIRTIER.) This letter destroyed, the mouth of the young sailor sealed, no trace remains of the pernicious secret. And now to work, Villefort, to work.

SCENE THREE

The Reserve Inn overlooking the sea. A long table is laid out under an arbor of vines. MOREL, MERCÉDÈS, DANGLARS, CADEROUSSE, CARCONTE, FISHERMAN, *and* SAILORS *are on stage.* CADEROUSSE *drinks from bottle before putting it on the table.* CARCONTE *is superintending setting of table.*

———

CARCONTE. An hour behind time—my dinner will be spoilt.

CADEROUSSE. And the wine will be so warm it won't be drinkable.

MERCÉDÈS. What can have happened to him—what can have happened to him?

MOREL. Come, come, no tears, no lamentations. He has but gone to the ship to bring up doubtless some hand-some presents he purchased at Smyrna for his bride.

CADEROUSSE (*touching* DANGLARS *on the shoulder*). Is this then, part of the trick you concerted with Fernand?

DANGLARS (*uneasy*). What trick?

CADEROUSSE. The letter this afternoon.

DANGLARS. What letter! The one I tore up?

CADEROUSSE. You didn't tear it up, you threw it into a corner, and then when Fernand left, it was gone.

DANGLARS. You don't know what you are saying. You were drunk.

CADEROUSSE. Maybe so, but this sobers me. 'Tis a piece of rascality and I'll tell all about it.

DANGLARS (*catching his arm*). You had better keep quiet.

SAILOR (*shouts*). Here is the mate—here is Monsieur Edmund!

DANGLARS (*aside*). What's this, released?

EDMUND (*enters*). Yes, my friends, here is the mate! I am sorry I am so late, but it really was not my fault. I was not absent willingly, believe me.

MERCÉDÈS. What was the matter? Whence come you?

EDMUND. From the office of the Procureur du Roi.

MERCÉDÈS. What were you doing there?

EDMUND. That, my love of a future wife, is precisely what I am forbidden to tell you. I am on the most friendly footing with justice, and should any of you ever be accused of swallowing his own ship, or running away with the Château d'If, I'll be answerable for his acquittal. (*Laughs.*) But come, let us make up for lost time. Is all ready for the ceremony?

ALL. Yes, yes!

MOREL. Now, my friends, you join me in a cheer for the commander of the *Pharaon,* Edmund Dantès, her captain!

ALL. Hurrah for our captain!

EDMUND. Captain?

MOREL. Here is your commission signed by me, which gives you the *Pharaon.*

EDMUND. O Monsieur Morel—O Mercédès—oh, my father! See, the tears are in my eyes. Oh, dear wife, dear friends, speak my thanks to my benefactor—I cannot say them, I cannot speak!

ALL. Vive Monsieur Morel!

CADEROUSSE. All is ready for the happy couple.

MOREL. Come on then.

EDMUND (*embracing* MERCÉDÈS). I would not give this hour of my life for all the riches of Peru. (POLICE AGENT *and* NOIRTIER *enter.*)

AGENT. Stop. Which of you is named Edmund Dantès?

EDMUND (*coming forward*). I am he.

AGENT. In the name of the law, I arrest you.

EDMUND. Good heavens!

MERCÉDÈS. My Edmund!

NOIRTIER (*aside*). The bearer of Napoleon's letter arrested? I did well to change my outward man!

EDMUND. Whither am I to be taken?

AGENT. To the Château d'If.

EDMUND. I am lost!

DANGLARS (*aside*). You are indeed! (*The* AGENTS *seize* DANTÈS, *while* MOREL *keeps back the* SAILORS; MERCÉDÈS *falls into* MOREL'*s arms.*)

ACT TWO

SCENE ONE

Eighteen years after the preceding act. An apartment in the house of the Count de Morcerf; ball music within.

MOREL *and a* SERVANT *enter.* MOREL *is greatly aged, and is poorly dressed.*

———

SERVANT. Have the goodness to wait here, sir.

MOREL. I did not know there was company, or— (*Looking at dress.*)

SERVANT. A ball to celebrate my master's return from Jamaica.[2] (*He leaves.*)

MOREL (*looking at a letter in his hand*). "General, the Count de Morcerf." So, the letter I received is signed, but I know no person by that name. (*Reading*) "Hearing that M. Morel is in Paris, a person with whom he was acquainted many years since, and whose hand I have the honor to solicit, entreats his advice, before forming her decision. In full reliance on his prudence and sincerity, I anxiously await his visit and commit my happiness to his hand. Signed, Count de Morcerf." Who is the Count de Morcerf? Who is the person he speaks of?

MERCÉDÈS (*entering*). It is I, dear Monsieur Morel! Do you not remember me?

MOREL. Your features are not unfamiliar to me, madame, but I cannot immediately— (*Struck by a recollection.*) No, no, it cannot be!

MERCÉDÈS. Your hand—your hand! It is I, indeed.

MOREL. Mercédès—Mercédès Mondego!

MERCÉDÈS. Yes, Mercédès the Catalan. Mercédès, the bride and widow of our poor Edmund who disappeared eighteen years ago. Eighteen years of mourning and tears!

MOREL. But, madame, this style of dress. In whose house am I?

MERCÉDÈS. In my cousin Fernand's.

MOREL. The Catalan?

———

[2] Thus in the O'Neill acting version. Janina is what is meant.

MERCÉDÈS. Yes. The poor fisherman of former days.

MOREL. Can it be so?

MERCÉDÈS. All is fortune and misfortune in this world, dear Monsieur Morel. Fernand is now Count de Morcerf, and this evening is the celebration of his return and his elevation to the peerage.

MOREL (showing the letter). It was he then, that wrote to me?

MERCÉDÈS. Yes.

MOREL. And it is you whom he seeks to marry?

MERCÉDÈS. Yes.

MOREL. And you wish to consult me?

MERCÉDÈS. Yes.

MOREL. Truly, madame, I cannot see wherein my opinion is necessary, nor do I believe I can possibly give an opinion.

MERCÉDÈS. Why?

MOREL. You said but now, "All is fortune and misfortune in this world." Eighteen years have passed since your bridegroom was torn from your arms as he led you to the altar. Our poor lamented Edmund, whose father perished of grief and misery. Eighteen years have passed since you, too, disappeared. I find you today, but him I never found—no, notwithstanding my daily search, my hourly prayers. He rots in an unhallowed ground—you preside at the fête given in honor of your future husband's return. You said well, "All is fortune and misfortune in this world!"

MERCÉDÈS. Monsieur Morel, when you have listened to me, you will bitterly regret the cruel words that have escaped you.

MOREL. Madame.

MERCÉDÈS. Call me Mercédès as in the old time—the name I have borne bravely and amid all my wretchedness have never dishonored. Were my Edmund living, were he this instant standing beside us, he might proudly join his hand in mine and find no cause to blush. I wear these robes for the first time today, and when I have told you all, if you so counsel me, I will lay them aside without regret, and resume the Catalan rags I wore yesterday.

MOREL. What mean you?

MERCÉDÈS. That when Edmund was torn from my arms—as you thought to remind me, as if I ever could forget—I also disappeared. They had bereaved me at the foot of the altar of the father of my child. Aye, our marriage was not the union of two loving souls alone, it was the reparation of a fault. A son was born to me—none knew the place of my retreat but Fernand who discovered it. Yet, knowing my deep sorrow, and fearing to intrude on my privacy, he enlisted as a soldier and sent me in a farewell letter, the money paid to him for this generous transaction. The sum was sufficient for my son's early requirements. For me, I needed nothing but to find Edmund again. I went forth—but what have I done, what have I suffered, Heaven only knows! Not a prison, but I have visited it. Not a man in power but I have knelt before him. Onward from day to day, from town to town, wheresoever I deemed a sign, begging on the road to attain my aim!

MOREL. Poor soul! And your child?

MERCÉDÈS. Fernand by that time had risen to be a captain—had placed my boy in a military college. The war of independence broke out in Greece—Fernand accepted service under the Pasha of Jamaica[3] to discipline his troops. Fernand—his last defender—received from the expiring pasha a

[3] Thus in the O'Neill acting version. Janina is what is meant.

casket of priceless jewels, the foundation of his present fortunes, arrived but yesterday in Paris with the rank of general; he is now Count de Morcerf and peer of France. I am still, and if such is your advice I will ever remain, Mercédès the Catalan, the widow of Edmund Dantès, the poor sailor wrongfully imprisoned.

MOREL. What would you of me?

MERCÉDÈS. In a few months my son, Edmund's son, will leave St. Cyr a lieutenant. In a few months I will have to tell him, "thy name is Albert Mondego, the base-born," or "thou art Albert Mondego, Viscount de Morcerf," the title by which Fernand will recognize him on espousing me. But, mark me, nothing on earth should compel me to this marriage, were there a single ray of hope that Edmund could be found. Oh, say, do you believe that Edmund still lives?

MOREL. Alas!

MERCÉDÈS. Have you ascertained nothing?

MOREL. Nothing.

MERCÉDÈS. He never reappeared at Marseilles?

MOREL. Never.

MERCÉDÈS. Then you, no more than I, have discovered nothing?

MOREL. Absolutely nothing. And yet I went direct to Monsieur Villefort; when at my urgent entreaty he visited the Château d'If whither Edmund was taken a first, he learned that the prisoner had been transferred by superior orders.

MERCÉDÈS. Transferred?

MOREL. Yes, transferred. There is something mysterious and fearful in this dire affair.

MERCÉDÈS. Can Edmund be dead?

MOREL. Doubtless, my child, and now listen to me. Let not the lover's heart silence the mother's. Your son's future claims your care. He has been brought up under the name of Mondego which is Fernand's name as well as yours. He will remain ever ignorant of his birth—none will suspect it— every career is open to him, and if I may judge by the noble conduct Fernand has displayed, the Count de Morcerf will prove a father to your boy. (FERNAND, *in uniform, appears.*)

FERNAND. Well spoken, Monsieur Morel! Accept my thanks for your kindly and correct opinion of me. I have shown that, hoping for no reward, I look upon Albert Mondego as my son, and I now solicit the right of securing to him my fortune and my titles. In the name of your child, Mercédès, I ask your hand!

MERCÉDÈS. Fernand, you know that I respect and honor you—you know that I should be proud to endow my son with a name so honorably acquired, but—

FERNAND. Hold, Mercédès! I am aware of your objection ere you utter it, and I reverence it. So long as there is the faintest chance of your beholding Edmund Dantès again in life you shrink from wedding another—is it not so? You are right, I should despise you, did you otherwise, and could my love for you be greater than it is, I would love you all the more for the sacred refusal.

MERCÉDÈS (*kissing his hand*). You are generous and good!

MOREL. Count, suffer me to clasp your loyal hand! You have a generous heart.

FERNAND. Nay, my worthy friend, I love! And I would prove I merit some small return. Let us now seek united, what you have singly sought in vain; Villefort, for whom I have obtained the nomination to the ministry of justice, can refuse me nothing.

He is now in the house—he expects this evening a special officer of prisons whom he dispatched to examine all goal registers, and search out the name of Dantès, so that we may hope to learn the poor captain's fate today. Here comes Villefort—withdraw, Mercédès, none should salute you in this mansion but as the Countess de Morcerf. Return to your apartments, we will rejoin you there as I learn the result of the inquiry.

MERCÉDÈS. You will come soon?

FERNAND. Without delay.

(*Exit* MERCÉDÈS. *Enter* VILLEFORT, *aged and careworn.*)

VILLEFORT. Do I intrude?

FERNAND. By no means, dear Villefort. On the contrary we were impatient to see you. This is the former master of the unfortunate Dantès—I longed to introduce him to you.

VILLEFORT. Oh, we are old acquaintances. Monsieur Morel, if I mistake not.

MOREL. You remember me, sir?

VILLEFORT. I could never have forgotten the object of your inquiries.

MOREL. Yes, to detect the wretch who procured the incarceration of an innocent, honest youth—blighting his felicity, and crushing out his life—and all through vile, secret schemes.

VILLEFORT. Enough, enough.

FERNAND (*to* MOREL, *who seems surprised at both*). Of course, good sir, we are all indignant at the cause, but it is the fact we have to grapple with. What has become of Dantès? That is the problem to be solved, deeds are now required, not words. Am I right, Villefort?

VILLEFORT. Unquestionably, Count. And I am ready to serve you to the utmost of my power.

MOREL. Oh, thanks! You will recover him and restore him to those who love him, who pined for him so many long years?

VILLEFORT. If it be in my power, I swear to do so. (MOREL *and* FERNAND *retire a little, conversing.*) Yes, if the inspector, on whom I can rely, shall report to me that Dantès is alive, I will set him free. (*A* SERVANT *enters and speaks to* FERNAND.)

FERNAND (*approaching* VILLEFORT). The inspector you commissioned is below. Not finding you at home, he has come on here to take your orders for tomorrow.

MOREL. O sir, do not go by halves. See him at once and spare us another night of anxious sorrow.

VILLEFORT. Well, Count, if you can let me have this room without interruption, and my man brought here without passing among the other guests—

FERNAND. I was about proposing so.

MOREL. I am most grateful for your consideration.

FERNAND (*to* SERVANT). Bring him by the garden stairs, and see that no one enters this room but by Monsieur de Villefort's orders. (SERVANT *leaves.*) Now, monsieur, you are home, we will leave you. Monsieur Morel and I will wait the result of your interview in another room. You will terminate our suspense as soon as possible.

VILLEFORT. Be assured I will. (FERNAND *and* MOREL *leave as a* SERVANT *enters, introducing* NOIRTIER *disguised.*) If Dantès live, and I release him, and this brother of mine turn not up before I am appointed minister, my conscience will be calm and my career secure.

SERVANT (*to* NOIRTIER). This way.

VILLEFORT. Come in, Fooyar. (*To* SERVANT) Leave us. (*As the* SERVANT *leaves,* VILLEFORT *locks the door.*) We are alone—well?

NOIRTIER (*facing him*). Well, good brother, how are you?

VILLEFORT. You—alive?

NOIRTIER. Does it inconvenience you?

VILLEFORT. Whence come you?

NOIRTIER. From a prison inspection in pursuance of orders issued by you. Am I not your humble servant?

VILLEFORT. That dress?

NOIRTIER. Was that of your worthy Fooyar. I see you recognize it—it is rather tight fitting I grant, your agents are so wretchedly fed—but under the present reign of repression we must accustom ourselves to a little squeezing. This is a fine trade you made me take to.

VILLEFORT. I?

NOIRTIER. Certainly. That fellow Fooyar had always a penchant for firing the second barrel when he was sent out for game. He came upon me on the road to Marseilles whither I was going to embark for Italy to superintend a Carbonari meeting which takes place in a fortnight. I saw directly that he knew me and was making for the police station, of course. I therefore arrested him.

VILLEFORT. You?

NOIRTIER. Assuredly. Would you have me allow him to arrest me? I am too careful of your position—too regardful of my own person to suffer myself to be collared and handed over to justice by a rascal of that kind. He raised his hand against me—I felled him to the ground with a single push. He fired his pistol—I killed him with a blow of my stick—so should such beggars die. I took his clothes and papers, saw your name, found the affair interesting, and proceeded on the mission your understrapper would have pursued, had I not shortened his career.

VILLEFORT. And you have been inspecting prisons?

NOIRTIER. Only one. I know you a little better than you know Fooyar. I went direct to the Château d'If.

VILLEFORT. What?

NOIRTIER. This grows interesting, does it not?

VILLEFORT. Why did you go to the Château d'If?

NOIRTIER. Because your main instructions to Fooyar were to ferret out whether a certain individual was alive or dead. One Edmund Dantès, apprehended in the year 1815, and I strongly suspect it was your handiwork—for I know you thoroughly.

VILLEFORT. Speak lower—for mercy's sake, speak lower!

NOIRTIER. Ah, we are within hearing, are we? Lower then, it shall be. I know how disagreeable it would be to have one's character known when such as yours. Come nearer then, and hearken. (VILLEFORT *approaches trembling*, NOIRTIER *speaks commandingly*.) Your conduct in this whole affair is infamous!

VILLEFORT. Infamous?

NOIRTIER. I repeat the word, infamous! That lad was innocent, but he had my secret, and the secret being fraught with ruin to your position, you sacrificed that man—and that man I will have free!

VILLEFORT. He lives, then?

NOIRTIER. Yes, he lives. He languishes in that horrid dungeon into which your selfishness thrust him—but again I say, I will have him free. I give you one month: in a month I shall have returned from Rome—in a month you will find me on the Marseilles road at the Inn of the Pont du Gard, in a disguise of which you shall have timely notice. You will come there, bringing to me Dantès liberated, likewise a passport authorizing us both to pass freely and without fear throughout France.

VILLEFORT. But, this man now embittered by me, soon to be inspired by you —this man boiling over with revenge would be my ruin, my destruction!

NOIRTIER. It is my will that he be set free.

VILLEFORT. It would be my death!

NOIRTIER. It is my will!

VILLEFORT. An end then, to agony and torture! This shall come to a close. I will drag you down with me! You, Dantès and I shall be engulfed together. I shall deliver you up to justice!

NOIRTIER. Me?

VILLEFORT. Yes, you!

NOIRTIER. Do it, and for once in your life you will evince a spark of courage. (*He walks over to the bell-rope and pulls at it violently.*)

VILLEFORT. What are you about?

NOIRTIER. Summoning your myrmidons. (*Doors are heard opening.*) Come, denounce me.

VILLEFORT. No, no, stop! I agree to all, I obey your will.

NOIRTIER. In a month?

VILLEFORT. In a month.

NOIRTIER. At the Inn of the Pont du Gard?

VILLEFORT. At the Inn of the Pont du Gard.

(*SERVANTS enter through one doorway; FERNAND and MOREL, through another.*)

FERNAND. Anything the matter?

NOIRTIER. Nothing. My master giving final orders. Monsieur de Villefort, I am your most respectful servant. (*He bows low and leaves, the servant follows him.*)

FERNAND. Well, what news?

VILLEFORT. News? (*Recovering himself gradually*) Alas, gentlemen, I have sorry tidings.

(MERCÉDÈS *appears on threshold.*)

MOREL. Of our poor prisoner?

VILLEFORT. Of him.

MOREL. Speak! Better cruel certainty than this horrid doubt.

VILLEFORT. Hope to see Edmund Dantès no more; his sufferings are over.

ALL. Dead?

(FERNAND *supports* MERCÉDÈS, *who is falling.*)

FERNAND. Be careful, think of your child.

MERCÉDÈS (*throwing herself in his arms*). Oh, Fernand, Fernand!

FERNAND. Yes, yes, lean on this heart, which will never fail you.

MERCÉDÈS. Fear not, Fernand, I will be firm. From this day forth, I bid farewell to mourning and devote myself to my child. Fernand when you will, I am your wife.

VILLEFORT. Count!

FERNAND. Oh, I ask pardon. Allow me to present you the Countess de Morcerf. I hope shortly to introduce my son.

VILLEFORT. Madame, I was in ignorance.

FERNAND. Monsieur Morel, will you conduct the countess to her rooms? I will go bid my guests farewell and return shortly. (*He watches* MERCÉDÈS *and* MOREL *leave.*)

VILLEFORT (*aside*). My brother must not reappear—Dantès must die! Tomorrow I'll start for the Château d'If.

FERNAND (*returns*). And now, Monsieur de Villefort, I am at your service.

VILLEFORT (*taking his arm*). And pray, how old is your son?

FERNAND. Nearly eighteen.

VILLEFORT. The countess is a charming woman. (*They both leave.*)

SCENE TWO

Two cells in the Château d'If at night. The cells, occupied by FARIA *and* EDMUND, *are separated by a thick wall, excavated in its thickness for their escape, opening by a hole into each cell. Above the cells, there is a rampart where the guards pace.* EDMUND *stands in the opening of the wall, while* FARIA *is kneeling near the hole leading to it. The* SENTINEL *paces to and fro on the rampart as the clock strikes eleven.*

FARIA (*whispering*). Well?

EDMUND. Only the thickness of the flag between us and the sky! between us and liberty! I can hear the tread of the sentinel above.

FARIA. So that by detaching one or two stones—

EDMUND (*close to him*). The flag falls! And if we can seize the precise moment when the sentinel passes, he falls with it, too, we gag him, bind him fast, both climb through the aperture, and before they are up to change the guard, we shall have swum the coast and be free. Where are the ropes and the gag?

FARIA. There, under my bed.

EDMUND. Liberty at last!

FARIA. Yes, at last! After eighteen years of struggle, of incessant toil. Never shall I forget the patience, the devotion you brought to this rough task, when my enfeebled limbs were powerless to assist you. From this day forth, Edmund, you are my son, my heir.

EDMUND. My father!

FARIA. Think not it is an idle word, the Abbé Faria has never lied. Not towards our deliverance alone have you labored with such ardor, but towards our fortune—a colossal, incalculable fortune!

EDMUND (*aside*). Relapsed into his old delusion!

FARIA. Dantès, you are a noble-hearted man, you never laugh in my face as the rest do, but you say to yourself "This man is mad." Do not deny it, I read your thoughts. Is it true?

EDMUND. It is true.

FARIA. Good. I expected that reply from your frankness. What hour was it that struck when you were there?

EDMUND. Eleven.

FARIA. At midnight the guard is relieved, and we shall then have two hours before us ere they can perceive your escape, if it succeed. We have yet an hour to wait. Attend to me now, and you shall be satisfied that the wealth I speak of is no phantom, that the Abbé Faria is not the maniac he is thought to be.

EDMUND. I am all attention.

FARIA. I have often in our conversation dwelt upon the history of the Borgias, have I not? You remember the poisons by whose agency they made themselves heirs of the cardinals who died around them. My ancestor, Cardinal Spada, of whom I am the last descendant, was one of their victims. But, knowing them of old, he had buried his treasure in a place unknown to that age, and of which he was the proprietor—the Island of Monte Cristo. Therefore when the hour of his death arrived, when the Borgias came to search out his immense and renowned treasure, nothing was found in his palace. No gold, no jewels, nothing but an old breviary, in which was written "to my heirs."

EDMUND. Well?

FARIA. Well; its trifling value rendered its sale worthless, this worn old breviary remained in our family, but nobody thought of searching out the meaning of the words "to my heirs" written by the cardinal on his death-bed. At last the book fell to me, and for years, Edmund, I used to turn over the pages again and again—convinced that the breviary contained the mystery of the missing treasure. Finally one evening, feeling that the book was driving me mad, I flung it into the fire. The page on which the words were written was its first page, and the flames which had already seized upon the remainder of the book, made it radiate to my eyes, some other characters appeared upon the surface. I snatched the page from the fire and read, written in a sympathetic ink which at once became visible on exposure to strong heat, these lines— "Fearing from my knowledge of the Borgias, that they hope by my poisoning to secure my fortune speedily, I hid all that I possess in ingots, coined money, jewels, diamonds and trinkets, in the secret grottos of my Island of Monte Cristo. This treasure will be found on raising the twentieth rock, counting in a straight line from the little creek, eastward, and I bequeath it to my heirs."

EDMUND. This is a fairy tale!

FARIA. Here is the page, Edmund, it is reality!

EDMUND. Ah, let me once be free, and thou shalt be happy then, Mercédès.

FARIA. Your bride? Are you quite sure to find her on your return, my son?

EDMUND. Dead? Do you believe she is dead?

FARIA. You have been a captive, Edmund, for eighteen years, and oblivion is a tomb as sure as clay.

EDMUND. She forget me? Mercédès unfaithful? Oh, my father, doubt of Heaven—doubt of Providence—doubt of your own being—but never doubt Mercédès. My faith, my life, my happiness are all her. Do I cling to liberty, do I cling to life? No—I cling to Mercédès. I would fain live, I would fain be free, but for her. To see her, to regain her, and then to die if die I must, upon her last kiss.

FARIA. So may it be! And now, Edmund, that the hour of freedom is about to strike, think of vengeance. I have satisfied your mind by a clear train of inference—from the details you gave me—that Danglars was the denouncer. That he wrote the fatal letter and that Fernand was the bearer. That the renegade Villefort entombed you alive because he had his position to preserve, and therefore he who could denounce his brother must be extinguished. Villefort, Fernand, Danglars—let those three names be engraved upon your memory.

EDMUND. Hush! I hear footsteps upon the rampart!

FARIA. The sentinel no doubt.

EDMUND (in a low voice). Give me the ropes, it is time we have all ready. I will live, I will regain my liberty—for thee, Mercédès. (He takes the rope and goes into the excavation, as GOVERNOR, VILLEFORT and SENTINEL enter from above.)

GOVERNOR. There you will find the prisoner Dantès.

EDMUND (to FARIA). They are speaking of me!

VILLEFORT. Is he in number seventeen?

EDMUND. I know that voice.

GOVERNOR. Yes, he was brought to us with written instructions enjoining most rigorous treatment.

VILLEFORT. Yes, I know. (Aside) Mine! He must perish at any cost. But, how?

SENTINEL (stops them). I ask your pardon, Governor.

GOVERNOR. What is it?

SENTINEL. We are on guard every other day, as you know.

GOVERNOR. Yes.

SENTINEL. I went on guard forty-eight hours since.

GOVERNOR. Well?

SENTINEL. I walked on my usual beat, but I never found it sound so hollow before.

GOVERNOR. Indeed?

VILLEFORT. Where?

SENTINEL. Here. (*Striking flagstone with the butt of his gun.*)

EDMUND. Discovered!

VILLEFORT. What cell is under this flag?

GOVERNOR. Number seventeen, the cell of the very man so specially commended.

EDMUND. We are lost!

VILLEFORT (*to* GOVERNOR). Let the sentinel be reinforced by two soldiers, let all three be on the alert. (*To the* SOLDIERS) You are not to interrupt the prisoner in his attempt, but as soon as he raises the flag and believes himself safe, fire on him without mercy! Let his release come by death of his own procuring.

EDMUND. I am accursed!

VILLEFORT. Bear in mind what I have told you—go away now.

SENTINEL (*looking at* GOVERNOR). But—

VILLEFORT. Obey my orders!

(*The* GOVERNOR *and* VILLEFORT *depart.*)

EDMUND. Villefort! I thought I knew that voice. (*Goes into* FARIA's *cell.*) Oh, my father—my father—

FARIA (*when the* SENTINEL *leaves*). I have heard all, my son. Do you now doubt my words? Villefort, Fernand and Danglars—those are the three wretches who have destroyed you.

EDMUND. And escape is now impossible!

FARIA. You are mistaken, Edmund. This last blow kills me, but it insures your liberty, your fortune—it makes you master of the tormentors!

EDMUND. What say you?

FARIA. Do you know how they bury him who dies here?

EDMUND. No.

FARIA. They enclose him in a sack, fasten a shot to his feet, and throw him into the sea.

EDMUND. Horrible!

FARIA. I am dying, Edmund, they will give me such a burial. Thanks to the communication between the cells, you can take my place.

EDMUND. No, no, no, no!

FARIA. Silence! Obey me, it is the last wish of a dying man. Raise my bed—there in the foot which I have hollowed out, you will find a knife. Take it; when thrown into the waves, you will cut open the sack in which you are wrapped and swim to shore. You will then be free, and the treasures of Monte Cristo will be yours. I give them to you. Ah—death is upon me!

EDMUND. No, no, you shall not die! I will save you!

FARIA. They are coming, go. (*He cries out with pain.* EDMUND *goes into his cell, and the* GOVERNOR *and* GAOLER *enter.*)

GOVERNOR (*examining* FARIA). Well? Dead!

SECOND GAOLER (*enters*). What has happened here?

FIRST GAOLER. Yes, he is dead. Get a sack, I'll prepare the ball.

GOVERNOR. Come. (*They depart.*)

EDMUND (*in his cell*). You were right, noble Faria. I will take your place. I must live. I have the wicked to punish and the good to reward. Your will be done! (*The cell sinks; a platform is discovered, sea and rocks are seen beneath a stormy sky. Thunder is heard.*)

SCENE THREE

Platform of the Château d'If. Steps cut in the rock, leading to a sort of jetty from the second floor. Door of secret dungeons on first floor. Enter two GAOLERS *carrying a sack enveloping a form.*

———

FIRST GAOLER. Are you ready?

SECOND GAOLER. Ready! (*They swing the sack into the sea down steps.*)

FIRST GAOLER. An ugly night on the sea.

SECOND GAOLER. Aye, under, too.

(*They recross stage, and leave the prison. The moon breaks out, lighting up a projecting rock.* EDMUND *rises from the sea, he is dripping, a knife in his hand, some shreds of sack adhering to it.*)

EDMUND (*on the rock*). Saved! Mine, the treasures of Monte Cristo! The world is mine!

ACT THREE

Interior of the Inn Pont du Gard. Staircase leading to gallery with doors. CADEROUSSE, CARCONTE, BRIGADIER, *and* GENDARMES *are drinking at a table.*

———

CADEROUSSE. I tell you, 'tis as I say!

CARCONTE (*hands under her apron, dress tattered, she is seen before a fire*). Hold your tongue, Caderousse, you'll never rest until you drag down more ill-luck upon us, just as you did with your mad talk about Dantès' arrest.

CADEROUSSE. Poor fellow!

CARCONTE. Will you hold your peace?

CADEROUSSE. He was a brave lad I tell you, but what is the good of being honest? Would you think it, because I proclaimed too loudly that I would answer for his innocence, I saw my establishment of the Reserve closed by the police.

BRIGADIER. Caderousse, don't talk politics.

CARCONTE. You cursed chatterer, do you want to take the bread again out of our mouths? Do you want to have this inn shut up, too?

CADEROUSSE. Oh, your inn is a fine one, a profitable inn indeed, this Pont du Gard! We cannot sell three bottles of six-sous wine a day. However, there's an end to it now, we are to be sold out tomorrow because of the unpaid taxes.

BRIGADIER. If the job that brought us to your inn succeeds—the arrest of a desperate character by order of Monsieur Villefort—and as you can assist us, if the arrest is effected this evening, you will not be sold out tomorrow.

CADEROUSSE. Rather vague, but the promise is made. Is it true?

BRIGADIER. On the honor of a gendarme. (*A noise is heard.*) Some cavalier is arrived! (*Goes to the door, and looks out.*)

CADEROUSSE. A traveller, not likely he will stop here. He will pass on. It is fair time at Beaucaire.

CARCONTE (*who has gone to the door*). No, he stops, he ties up his horse.

BRIGADIER (*to* MEN). Attention!

(*The* MEN *rise.*)

CARCONTE. Why, there are two!

BRIGADIER. On one horse, too!

CADEROUSSE (*looking out*). So there are. A young officer, quite a boy—and a priest!

BRIGADIER. A priest?

CARCONTE. Aye, like the raven, he brings no good luck. (*She crosses to the fire.*)

CADEROUSSE. Hold your tongue, woman. Here they are! (EDMUND *enters dressed as the abbé, with* ALBERT DE MORCERF *in uniform, kepi in hand, giving precedence to* EDMUND.)

ALBERT. You were looking for the Inn of the Pont du Gard, we are at it, Father, and I am delighted that I have been able to be of assistance to you on the road.

EDMUND. Thank you.

BRIGADIER (*to* EDMUND). You were looking for this inn?

EDMUND. Yes.

BRIGADIER. And you intend making a halt here?

EDMUND (*smiling*). If you have no objection.

BRIGADIER. Your name.

EDMUND. The Abbé Busoni.

BRIGADIER. Your papers? (EDMUND *hesitates.*)

ALBERT (*with a show of importance*). Here are mine!

BRIGADIER. Unnecessary, you are an officer and—

ALBERT. And he is a priest—two professions each alike sufficient against an imputation of untruth. If you suspect one, you must suspect the other —take my papers!

BRIGADIER. But—

ALBERT. My name is Albert, Viscount de Morcerf.

CADEROUSSE (*aside*). Fernand's son!

ALBERT. I am on my way to Marseilles to embark for Algiers, to join my regiment under orders to take the field. Here is my route on the road, take it I say, and let pass the man of peace.

BRIGADIER. Lieutenant, I ask pardon. (*He takes the papers.*) But I have a serious duty on hand. Have either of you passed any other travellers on the road, coming in this direction?

ALBERT. There was a sort of hawker who assisted the abbé to get up behind me on my horse, and who asked for the Pont du Gard Inn.

CADEROUSSE. Another coming? This is miraculous!

BRIGADIER. A hawker?

ALBERT. Yes. A strolling jeweller, or something of that sort.

BRIGADIER. A jeweller!

ALBERT. By what he told us, he was going to the fair at Beaucaire.

CADEROUSSE. It is old Johannes. I had quite forgotten him. He stops here every year.

BRIGADIER (*aside, to the* MEN). It is our man more likely. This is the character we are to look for. We'll report to Monsieur Villefort. (*Salutes.*) Lieutenant and company, I salute you.

ALBERT (*salutes comically*). Brigadier and gendarmes, I salute you.

(*The* BRIGADIER *and* GENDARMES *depart.*)

Come, my veteran (*To* CADEROUSSE), give my horse a rub-down and a feed of oats. And you, my good lady (*To* CARCONTE), let us have a bottle of your best to drink the stirrup cup.

CARCONTE (*gets a bottle from the sideboard*). Directly!

CADEROUSSE (*as he goes out*). Fernand's son a viscount and an officer? Fernand a general and a peer of France? What's the good of being virtuous. (*He departs.*)

CARCONTE (*puts bottle and glasses on table*). Here's the wine. (*Exit.*)

ALBERT. Thank you. Your health, Father, may I have the happiness of meeting you again on my return from the war.

EDMUND. Thanks, my son, and may your wish be accomplished. I shall rejoice greatly to see you safe and sound again. Why do you look at me thus?

ALBERT. Oh, pardon.

EDMUND. Make no excuse, I am unknown to you, so exercise your right of question.

ALBERT. Well then, I look at you and vainly try to recognize you.

EDMUND. Have we seen each other before?

ALBERT. No, I believe not.

EDMUND. What then?

ALBERT. Although my reason clearly tells me that we have met today for the first time, it seems to me as though we were acquainted before—before united—where I know not. But consider two formerly separated in past ages, meeting in future generations. I experience when near you, feelings akin to those their souls must experience. I love you! Yes, from the moment I met you on the way, I felt the necessity of hastening to your aid, of being some service to you. When as you rode behind, your arms entwined me, a strange emotion thrilled my heart, a tear of delight sprang to my eye. But, you will perhaps laugh at me, and it is in spite of myself, as forced from me by a divine power, that I give you this confidence, I love you more than I love my father, almost as I love my mother!

EDMUND. A sainted woman must she be, to have endowed you with a heart so true, with such noble candor. You ought, indeed to love her for thus rearing you.

ALBERT. Alas, she did not rear me. She was far away, doubtless with my father whom I saw myself but at rare and long intervals. It is only within the last year that they have both returned to France where my father holds a high rank—that it has been given to me to know my mother. But, we have redeemed the lost time. Let all the ills of humanity fall on me—let my heart cease to beat—let all on earth cease to live—but let her be rich,

bright and happy, be it at the price of my life—aye, of my eternal peace!

EDMUND (embracing him). The first genial drops that have fallen from mine eyes in well nigh twenty years. They flow from my heart, refreshing and consoling it. Thou, to whom I owe them, child, I thank you.

CADEROUSSE (entering). The viscount's horse is ready.

EDMUND. So soon?

(CARCONTE comes slowly downstairs.)

ALBERT. Are you not going to Marseilles? Shall we not be on the road together?

EDMUND. No, impossible. Your duty calls you at once on shipboard. Mine detains me here. Perhaps we shall never meet again.

ALBERT. Oh, do not say that!

EDMUND. 'Tis like all else in life, but if in this world's pilgrimage you chance to meet my brother—

ALBERT. Your brother?

EDMUND. Monte Cristo.

ALBERT. What a singular appellation!

EDMUND. Monte Cristo is a little desert island that you encounter on your way to Palermo.

ALBERT. Oh, yes, I remember.

EDMUND. It is infested with pirates and smugglers. My brother, immensely rich, purchased it from Tuscany, and of this mite of rock he is lord paramount. Both pirates and smugglers yield obedience to his decrees and term him King of the Isle. In Epris he is called Sinbad, the sailor—in Rome, Busoni—and he will shortly be known in France under the name of Monte Cristo.

ALBERT. I long to see him.

EDMUND. Have you a card?

ALBERT. Yes.

EDMUND. Give it to me.

ALBERT. Here. (Gives it to EDMUND,

who tears it in half.) What is that for?

EDMUND. For a token of recognition.

ALBERT. Between your brother and me?

EDMUND. Yes. The presenter of the other half will be the Count of Monte Cristo. Trust in him as you confide in me.

ALBERT. If he resembles you, he shall be well received.

EDMUND (*offers his hand*). Farewell.

ALBERT. Nay, au revoir. (*Exit.*)

CARCONTE (*going to the fire*). The kiss of the black coat is a Judas kiss; mind the one this priest has given you does not work you woe, young man.

EDMUND (*to* CADEROUSSE). And now a word with you.

CADEROUSSE. You wish to speak to me?

EDMUND. Yes.

CARCONTE. Take care how you answer.

EDMUND. Is your name Caderousse?

CADEROUSSE. From my birth.

EDMUND. You lived in Marseilles?

CADEROUSSE. For forty years.

EDMUND. And were innkeeper there?

CADEROUSSE. Yes, as I now am here.

EDMUND. You knew there a young sailor named Dantès.

CARCONTE. See, now!

CADEROUSSE. See what? I don't shame to say that I knew Edmund, why should I be afraid? I am an honest man, I have done wrong to no one.

EDMUND. So much the better for you if it be so, for sooner or later believe me, the honest man will meet his reward and the wicked be punished.

CADEROUSSE. It is part of your trade to say that. For my part, I don't see that Providence troubles itself much about my honesty.

EDMUND. You shall judge for yourself presently. Did you really love this Dantès?

CADEROUSSE. Edmund—did I love him? 'Twas because I stood up for him after his arrest that I find myself brought to this plight, and I would willingly lose a finger off my right hand to save him from prison or to hear tidings of him. Have you seen him?

EDMUND. Yes.

CADEROUSSE. How is he? What is he doing? Is he happy?

EDMUND. He is dead.

CADEROUSSE. Dead?

EDMUND. Edmund Dantès is dead.

CADEROUSSE. Poor boy!

EDMUND. Wait! Providence may sometimes seem to slumber as regards the good—

CADEROUSSE. And sleep sound methinks.

EDMUND. It is but to prove them, and its awakening is terrible to the guilty, believe me. As surely as they will be punished, you will be rewarded.

CADEROUSSE. I should like a substantial proof.

EDMUND (*producing paper parcel*). Behold it!

CADEROUSSE. What is that?

EDMUND. Look and see.

CADEROUSSE (*opens parcel*). A stone!

EDMUND. A diamond!

CADEROUSSE. Of such size?

CARCONTE. A diamond? Impossible! A diamond of that size would be worth—

EDMUND. Fifty thousand francs.

CADEROUSSE. And this is worth?

EDMUND. Fifty thousand francs.

CADEROUSSE. Really and truly?

EDMUND. On my solemn word.

CARCONTE. From whom then did you have it?

EDMUND. From Dantès.

CADEROUSSE. Our Edmund? And who was to have it?

EDMUND (*taking the stone*). You

shall know presently.

CARCONTE. Ah, you are taking it back.

EDMUND. Listen to me. In the hour of his eternal farewell in prison, Dantès said to me, "I had three good friends and an affianced wife," whose name was—I cannot remember the name of his betrothed.

CADEROUSSE. Mercédès—

EDMUND. Yes, that was it. Pray give me a glass of water!

CADEROUSSE. Here.

EDMUND (drinking). Thanks—where was I?

CADEROUSSE. At "three good friends and his betrothed"—whose name was Mercédès.

EDMUND. Right. "You will go to Marseilles"—you are to understand it is Dantès who speaks.

CADEROUSSE. Exactly so.

EDMUND. You will divide the price of this diamond into five parts.

CADEROUSSE. Five parts? You mentioned only four persons—three friends and his betrothed.

EDMUND. Because I ascertained at Nismes that the fifth was dead. The fifth was Dantès' father.

CADEROUSSE. That is true, the poor man is dead.

EDMUND. Aye, dead! Without his child to close his eyes, without embracing his son or knowing his fate! He doubtless died of grief.

CADEROUSSE. Of starvation!

EDMUND. Of starvation!

CARCONTE. Be cautious.

CADEROUSSE. I will speak! What more can they do, now that they have ruined me and killed Edmund, and caused his father's death? I tell you he died of starvation!

EDMUND. Oh, horrible, horrible!

CADEROUSSE. After his son was arrested, Dantès took to his bed, which he never left. Monsieur Morel brought the first physician in Marseilles to see him; he left also on the table, showing it to me, a red silk purse full of gold so that the old man wanted for nothing. But all the money in the purse went to the doctor's visits—the old man let it go and never ceased to smile. One day at length the smile left his face, but his eyes were clear and open, looking to the Heavens—he was dead.

EDMUND (swallowing some water). Thanks! And this red silk purse that Morel left filled with money?

CADEROUSSE. I found only a scrap of paper in it with two lines, "For Edmund if he lives—a memorial of Morel's kindness."

EDMUND (aside). I will remember the good, my father, and I will not forget the bad. (Aloud) And you say it was Danglars, you say it was Fernand—

CADEROUSSE. I never mentioned them.

EDMUND. Who threw the son into a dungeon, and drove the father to death, broken-hearted and starved.

CADEROUSSE. I never said a word of the sort.

CARCONTE. You see—you see—

EDMUND. Denial is useless, I know all. Caderousse, you were by him when one of those wretches wrote the letter denouncing Edmund to the Procureur du Roi!

CADEROUSSE. You know? I—

EDMUND. He wrote that letter with his left hand, and Fernand himself took it to Marseilles.

CADEROUSSE. True, true, but forgive me, Father—and may Edmund from Heaven forgive me. I had been made drunk, and nearly lost all sense.

EDMUND. I know it, Edmund knew it and forgave you.

CADEROUSSE (*on knees*). And remorse has pursued me ever since, day and night.

EDMUND. Rise and answer me. What has become of Fernand, of Danglars?

CADEROUSSE. Fernand is a general, a count—a peer of France.

EDMUND. Fernand Mondego?

CADEROUSSE. The same.

EDMUND. By what means?

CADEROUSSE. That, no one knows.

EDMUND (*aside*). I'll know it! (*Aloud*) And Danglars?

CADEROUSSE. Danglars, after robbing Monsieur Morel of the cargo of two vessels that were not insured and that were empty as everyone believes, set up as a banker at Nismes, then at Lyons, finally at Paris, where he is king at present among the financial celebrities. His daughter is engaged to the son of Fernand and Mercédès.

EDMUND. Mercédès married? Mercédès married to Edmund's denouncer —uniting her son to the Danglars?

CADEROUSSE. It is so. Sophie Danglars is to marry the young Viscount de Morcerf.

EDMUND. What! No, I am mistaken. Not the young man who was here just now?

CADEROUSSE. Yes, the son of Fernand and Mercédès, now the Viscount de Morcerf.

EDMUND (*aside*). And I grasped his hand and pressed him to my heart! Oh, woe to him! His father must love him, may well be proud of him—it is through his child I will strike Fernand. I will kill his son! (*Aloud*) Take the diamond, it is yours.

CARCONTE. All ours?

EDMUND. Yes, the heritage is yours, and may you be as upright in prosperity as you have been in adversity.

CADEROUSSE. And are you leaving us?

EDMUND. Yes. I have need of air, of space, of liberty. (*Aside*) I'll go pray at my father's grave and regain strength to live—strength to reward and to punish. (*Aloud*) You shall see me soon again. I shall return to demand—

CADEROUSSE. What, the diamond?

EDMUND. No. The little red purse which Morel gave to old Dantès, who bequeathed it to his son. Adieu! (*Takes his leave.*)

CADEROUSSE. Carconte, are we dreaming?

CARCONTE. No—I hold the diamond in my hand. But what if it is a false one?

CADEROUSSE. You are always so superstitious! Why should he have given us a false one?

CARCONTE. To extract your information without paying for it, simpleton.

CADEROUSSE. We shall soon see that.

CARCONTE. How?

CADEROUSSE. It is now the fair at Beaucaire. Old Johannes, the rich jeweller who stops here every year and makes such rich purchases there, shall value it—buy it, perhaps.

CARCONTE. You think so?

CADEROUSSE. I do, indeed.

CARCONTE. But fifty thousand francs is money.

CADEROUSSE. Nothing to him. He has always double that, at least, in his pockets. What makes your eyes sparkle so?

CARCONTE. Nothing. I was only thinking that he often sleeps here on his way to Beaucaire.

CADEROUSSE. Well?

CARCONTE. And—oh, nothing you would understand.

CADEROUSSE. I am only afraid I understand you too well. (*A knock is heard at the door.*)

CARCONTE. Be silent, there's a knock at the door.

CADEROUSSE. No, 'tis the wind. (*Knock.*)

CARCONTE. Can't you hear it?

CADEROUSSE. Yes.

CARCONTE. It must be Johannes.

CADEROUSSE. Now I say wife, no nonsense.

CARCONTE. Pshaw! Go open the door.

(NOIRTIER, *dressed as a Jewish peddler, appears.*)

NOIRTIER. Good evening, good people.

CADEROUSSE. Thank heaven, it's not Johannes.

CARCONTE. Pshaw! Go open the door. Don't you like my good friend Johannes?

CADEROUSSE. Oh, yes, but—

CARCONTE. But we did not expect him so soon and his room is not ready.

NOIRTIER. Then get it ready, for I am here in his stead.

CARCONTE. You?

NOIRTIER. Yes, I. I have bought his stock and I am on my way to the fair at Beaucaire with my merchandise. Oh, I have money to pay my way, look here—and here—and here! (*He shows them gold and notes.*) Without reckoning the trinkets and jewelry in my box. (*Aside*) And the millions of francs to start my journal. (*Aloud*) Come, good people, you won't lose by your change of customers. (*Goes to the fire.*)

CADEROUSSE (*to* CARCONTE). You see these gentry are always in funds; he will be able to buy our diamond.

CARCONTE. Try him.

NOIRTIER (*at the fire*). Well, are you making any arrangements about me?

CADEROUSSE. Just what we were doing good monsieur—monsieur—

NOIRTIER (*rising*). Solomon Van Gripp.

CADEROUSSE. A pretty name.

NOIRTIER. It inspires immediate confidence.

CARCONTE (*going to cupboard*). Here is wine.

NOIRTIER. Have you nothing to eat?

CARCONTE. Not much. but we can give you—

CADEROUSSE (*making signs to her*). No, no, no, he can't eat that.

CARCONTE. Why?

CADEROUSSE. His name is Solomon.

CARCONTE. Oh, the devil!

NOIRTIER. Well, what meat have you in the house?

CADEROUSSE. Meat?

NOIRTIER. Yes.

CADEROUSSE. We have only cabbage.

NOIRTIER (*sadly*). Oh!

CADEROUSSE. And bacon.

NOIRTIER (*brightening*). Ha!

CADEROUSSE. But you said your name was Solomon—

NOIRTIER. I see. Never mind, my fine fellow, when I take it from your hands it won't come from a hog. Ha, ha, ha! Clever, that, isn't it? (*Aside*) I am becoming as great an ass in this disguise as Johannes himself.

(CARCONTE *sets the table,* CADEROUSSE *takes* NOIRTIER *to the light to show him the diamond.*)

CADEROUSSE. What is your opinion of this?

NOIRTIER (*opens the paper, goes to the table*). What is it, a diamond?

CARCONTE. Is it a genuine diamond?

NOIRTIER. It is indeed. What a stone! Magnificent! Must be worth—

CARCONTE. Fifty thousand francs.

NOIRTIER. At least.

CADEROUSSE (*to* CARCONTE). You see?

CARCONTE. Will you buy it?

NOIRTIER (*in a natural voice*). I— why should I?

CARCONTE. How you spoke that! Without a trace of accent.

NOIRTIER (*aside*). Near betraying

myself! (*Aloud*) I am never a Jew that, eh? (*Aside*) I must stick close in business. Ha, ha, ha! Clever said, to my part, or be discovered and undone. (*Aloud*) Yes, I will take it. I will give you—I am a plain, downright man of business—I never go from my word—I will give you forty thousand francs, ready money.

CADEROUSSE. How, forty thousand?

NOIRTIER. Yes, I never haggle—never.

CARCONTE. But you said fifty thousand.

NOIRTIER. I?

CARCONTE. Yes, you.

NOIRTIER. Never.

CADEROUSSE. You said it was worth fifty thousand francs.

NOIRTIER. Your wife said so.

CADEROUSSE. And you added, "at least."

NOIRTIER. Then I did not say fifty thousand francs.

CADEROUSSE. But you said more.

NOIRTIER. Then I will give you forty thousand.

CADEROUSSE. Ah!

NOIRTIER. I never go from my word. I am a plain, downright man of business. I'll now have something to eat. (*Does so. In an aside*) I think I have got myself pretty well out of this.

CADEROUSSE (*to* CARCONTE). Well, shall we let him have it?

CARCONTE. It is worth more than that.

CADEROUSSE. We'll keep it, then. I'll go to the fair and see some dealers.

NOIRTIER. Well, have you made up your minds?

CADEROUSSE. Yes, to sell it to somebody else.

NOIRTIER. Just as you please, only you won't find somebody else so easy to deal with as me.

CARCONTE. Oh, as to that—

NOIRTIER (*eating*). Somebody else will ask you where you got such a stone.

CARCONTE (*to* CADEROUSSE). That is true.

CADEROUSSE (*drawing her into a corner*). What do you say to it?

CARCONTE. I say it's hard, but we must let him have it.

CADEROUSSE (*to* NOIRTIER). Come, it's settled, the jewel is yours.

NOIRTIER. And here is your money. Count it.

CARCONTE (*to* CADEROUSSE). What are those rags?

CADEROUSSE. Bank notes, to be sure.

CARCONTE. Are they of value?

CADEROUSSE. As good as gold, and more portable.

CARCONTE. Be cautious.

CADEROUSSE. Be quiet!

NOIRTIER. Now my good people, will you get my room ready?

CARCONTE. Take our room, Monsieur Solomon, the bed is better, and I wish you to sleep comfortably. (*She looks at* CADEROUSSE.)

NOIRTIER. I must not say nay, for I am dropping with fatigue. (*Thunder and lightning*) Oh, what weather. (*Aside*) I don't wonder it makes Villefort late. (*Looking at his watch*) Ten o'clock. If within two hours a gentleman does not come whom I am expecting, and who will give my name when he asks to see me, you will awaken me, for I shall have to go out to Marseilles tonight.

CARCONTE (*who has lit candle*). What, take the road again tonight? And in such weather?

NOIRTIER. I fear neither wind nor weather.

CADEROUSSE. But robbers?

NOIRTIER (*showing pistols*). Here are a pair of trusty dogs who bark and bite at the same instant—ready for those who may covet your diamond, Caderousse.

CARCONTE (*aside*). Armed! (*Aloud*)

Are you coming?

NOIRTIER. I'll follow you. (*Goes upstairs to chamber, seen through.*) Good night, Caderousse.

CADEROUSSE. Good night. (NOIRTIER *leaves after* CARCONTE.) I am glad he is armed. Carconte made me shudder with her notions. She's a dreadful woman; her gloomy words strike into you one by one like the stab of a knife. I'm all of a shiver still. Luckily he's armed, so there's nothing to fear.

VILLEFORT (*has entered dripping wet; touches* CADEROUSSE *on shoulder*). Are you alone?

CADEROUSSE. Who is there?

VILLEFORT. Silence, fellow.

CADEROUSSE. Monsieur de Villefort?

VILLEFORT. Silence!

CARCONTE (*from above*). Did you call?

CADEROUSSE. I—no. (VILLEFORT *signals for silence.*)

CARCONTE. Who are you talking with?

CADEROUSSE. Nobody. I am talking with myself.

CARCONTE. Idiot!

VILLEFORT. What is your wife doing up there?

CADEROUSSE. She is taking a traveller to our room.

VILLEFORT. Who is he?

CADEROUSSE. A jeweller who came this evening.

VILLEFORT. About nine o'clock was it not?

CADEROUSSE. Thereabouts.

VILLEFORT. Is it Johannes who is in the habit of stopping here?

CADEROUSSE. No, not he.

VILLEFORT. Then this one travels under the name of Solomon Van Gripp.

CADEROUSSE. Is not that his name?

VILLEFORT. Answer me!

CADEROUSSE. That was the name he gave. He told us to wait up for a person who would come to inquire for him, and desired us to call him at midnight if the other did not come.

VILLEFORT. Did he offer you a bargain? Be careful.

CADEROUSSE. I don't know what you mean.

VILLEFORT. No lies! The gendarmes are on the watch, and at the slightest signal—

CADEROUSSE. I see it all! This vagabond priest has informed against us just as Carconte thought. So, you want to arrest us for the affair of the diamond?

VILLEFORT (*aside*). What is this?

CADEROUSSE. Mercy, Monsieur le Procureur, if it was stolen I know nothing of it. It was given to me and I sold it for forty thousand francs to the Jew upstairs. But I'll give up the money. 'Tis very hard, don't harm us.

VILLEFORT. You were given a diamond of that value? Speak lower.

CADEROUSSE. Yes.

VILLEFORT. By whom?

CADEROUSSE. By a priest.

VILLEFORT. What for?

CADEROUSSE. For inquiries I answered him about Dantès.

VILLEFORT. The prisoner Dantès?

CADEROUSSE. Yes. Edmund, who is dead.

VILLEFORT. Is he dead?

CADEROUSSE. Yes.

VILLEFORT. Who told you so?

CADEROUSSE. The priest that brought me his legacy.

VILLEFORT. Where, how did he die?

CADEROUSSE. That he did not tell me. He gave me the diamond as his representative, and that is all.

VILLEFORT. You swear it?

CADEROUSSE. I swear it.

VILLEFORT. Are you to see this priest again?

CADEROUSSE. He is to return for a purse I promised him.

VILLEFORT *(aside)*. I shall know who he is. *(Aloud)* You sold this diamond to the man who has gone to sleep there?

CADEROUSSE. For forty thousand francs, yes.

(CARCONTE *creeps down;* VILLEFORT *sits down,* CADEROUSSE *before him.)*

VILLEFORT. This traveller is of a very confiding disposition.

CADEROUSSE. How so?

VILLEFORT. To go to bed here in a lonely inn, by the side of a canal, so convenient of hiding all traces of a crime. In fact, were you not an honest man—nobody saw him enter—nobody would see him go out—you would regain possession of the diamond, keeping at the same time the price you have received for it. You would let the sale of your own goods and furniture take place tomorrow as if you were reduced to your last sou. None would suspect you, and you would be richer by ninety thousand francs.

CARCONTE *(coming between them and putting her elbows on the table, chin on hands)*. To say nothing about the money he has about him.

VILLEFORT. You were here?

CARCONTE. And have heard all, and I agree with you.

CADEROUSSE. How?

CARCONTE. You must be very honest—and that man very unsuspecting.

CADEROUSSE. It would be nefarious!

CARCONTE. Since the Procureur du Roi advises it.

VILLEFORT. I?

CARCONTE. Don't speak so loud. He has not gone to sleep yet and may hear you.

VILLEFORT *(in trepidation)*. Oh, heavens!

CARCONTE *(to* VILLEFORT*)*. Listen to me, and let us treat as equal to equal, since we have the same object.

VILLEFORT. We!

CARCONTE. Bah! Don't you suppose I see clearer than this idiot here. You have a motive—such as it is—and I do not care to know it—for wishing to dispose of this traveller.

VILLEFORT. I!

CARCONTE. In plain words, you want to have him murdered. But, say so plainly, that I must know there is nothing to be dreaded from the law afterwards.

VILLEFORT. Is he armed?

CADEROUSSE. He has pistols.

CARCONTE. Can he see clearly in the dark? Stuff!

VILLEFORT. But you will see no clearer.

CARCONTE. As if we did not know our own room.

CADEROUSSE. I won't have anything to do with it.

CARCONTE. Then I will do it alone. And you will be no less my accomplice, and you will keep silent through fear.

CADEROUSSE. I'll give him warning— I'll call him— *(As he is about to go upstairs,* CARCONTE *takes her handkerchief and gags him.)*

CARCONTE. Now, give him warning. Now, call him.

VILLEFORT. Oh, great heavens, whither am I fallen?

CARCONTE. Seize his hand, quick! We must tie him fast. (VILLEFORT *does so, stupefied.* CARCONTE *ties* CADEROUSSE'S *hand with his neckcloth. A stir is heard in* NOIRTIER'S *room. They stand alarmed.)*

NOIRTIER *(calling from his room)*. Good night, good people, good night.

VILLEFORT. His voice, 'tis his voice.

CARCONTE. Good night. *(Light goes out.)* He's going to bed—now to work.

(*They throw a cloak over* CADEROUSSE *and carry him into the chimney corner.* CARCONTE *gets hatchet, she and* VILLEFORT *regard each other a moment.*) Do you promise me we shall never be brought to trouble? And we shall have all the money he has about him.

VILLEFORT (*almost speechless with terror*). Yes!

CARCONTE. And you will guarantee our escape hence?

VILLEFORT. Yes, yes, but go, go!

CARCONTE. Watch the door that none may enter. Do not come to me unless I call. (*She goes upstairs, listens.*)

VILLEFORT (*in a low voice*). Well?

CARCONTE. He sleeps. (*She opens the door, slips in; a chair is heard falling. There is noise of a struggle in the room.*)

NOIRTIER (*from the room*). Who is there? (VILLEFORT *goes to the table, snatches a knife; a shot is heard and* CARCONTE *comes out bleeding, falls on the stairs, breaking her fall on the railing, through which her head can be seen hanging.*)

VILLEFORT. She has failed—she has failed. (*Dashes forward with knife. Comes face to face with* NOIRTIER, *who enters from the room. He has thrown off his disguise.*)

NOIRTIER (*offering his breast*). Strike then! See, I offer you my breast defenseless. Strike to my heart! (*Advancing;* VILLEFORT *recoils.*) Coward, thou hast not even the courage of a vulgar criminal. Thou need'st hire assassins and yet payest them not. What, must thy brother die that it may remain unknown he were of thy family? I am not so proud, and I shall deliver my good brother up to the executioner. (*Goes toward the door.*)

VILLEFORT. Since you force me to it, then— (*He rushes at him, and is held back by* CADEROUSSE, *who has released himself.*)

CADEROUSSE. Not so!

NOIRTIER. Wretch!

CADEROUSSE. Help—help!

VILLEFORT. Will you be silent? (*He breaks from him and rushes for* NOIRTIER, *but stops before* EDMUND, *who enters.*) I am lost!

NOIRTIER (*to* GENDARMES *who enter*). Seize that man!

VILLEFORT. Not alive, at least! (*Stabs himself, falls dead.*)

EDMUND (*behind him, pointing to the body*). "One!"

ACT FOUR

The Count de Morcerf's conservatory. [*Music is heard.*] *Discovered at the rise of the curtain,* FERNAND, ALBERT, *and* MERCÉDÈS *are in evening dress;* FERNAND *is receiving guests.* CADEROUSSE *is wearing a livery.*

———

MERCÉDÈS (*to* ALBERT). Are you certain the Count of Monte Cristo is in Paris?

ALBERT. Yes, dear mother, he arrived this evening about the same time I did. He seems to have followed my steps.

MERCÉDÈS. Why then did he not accept your invitation to our family dinner? I should have wished to communicate with the preserver of my son's life.

ALBERT. A previous engagement compelled him to refuse, at least such was the answer he gave my servant, was it not, Gaspardo?

CADEROUSSE. Yes, sir. The count regretted that he was unable to sit at General de Morcerf's table, but would do himself the honor of offering his excuses in person this evening.

ALBERT (*to* MERCÉDÈS). You hear?

MERCÉDÈS. I fear he will not come.

ALBERT. Oh, he will come, I will answer for that. We have his promise.

CADEROUSSE. Any further commands, sir?

ALBERT. No. Remain in the salon and announce the count when he arrives.

MERCÉDÈS (*to* CADEROUSSE, *who bows as he is going out*). You are not French?

CADEROUSSE. I, madame?

MERCÉDÈS. You are not from Marseilles?

CADEROUSSE. I am said to be a native of Naples, and was resident in Africa when I entered your son's service.

MERCÉDÈS. Your name is—?

CADEROUSSE. Gaspardo.

MERCÉDÈS. Gaspardo what?

CADEROUSSE. Simply Gaspardo, I am in Paris for the first time.

MERCÉDÈS. Very good. I must be mistaken. (CADEROUSSE *bows.* DANGLARS *and his daughter, led by* FERNAND, *enter.*)

ALBERT. Danglars and his daughter!

CADEROUSSE (*aside*). Danglars, the backguard! Well, Edmund will have them all in his net. (*He leaves.*)

FERNAND (*to* MADEMOISELLE DANGLARS). What a charming dress! No one has such taste.

DANGLARS. You should compliment me, I know what it cost.

MLLE. DANGLARS. Don't deceive yourself, Father, you don't even suspect it.

DANGLARS. Capital!

MERCÉDÈS (*to* MADEMOISELLE DANGLARS). Whom are you looking for?

ALBERT. I wager I can guess.

MLLE. DANGLARS (*giving him her hand*). Oh, some new silliness, no doubt.

ALBERT. Not in the least. I am not in question.

MLLE. DANGLARS. Well?

ALBERT. You were about to ask—

MLLE. DANGLARS. What?

ALBERT. If it were true—

MLLE. DANGLARS. Go on.

ALBERT. That the Count de Monte Cristo was coming.

MLLE. DANGLARS. You have won your wager, you guess correctly.

ALBERT. He is coming.

MLLE. DANGLARS. Bravo!

DANGLARS (*coming down*). And it is already known who he is.

MERCÉDÈS. Indeed?

DANGLARS. Yes. He is a Polish refugee who has served in the Egyptian army and also organized a pearl fishery in Ceylon. The king, enchanted, gave him I don't know how many purses, and the same year he fished up six million of pearls.

ALBERT (*laughing*). Excellent!

MLLE. DANGLARS. That is not it at all. His name is Zaccone, he is a Maltese—he has served in India—he worked a silver mine in Thessaly—and he has now come to Paris to establish artificial sea-water baths in the Champs Elysées. (*All laugh.*) It is true, I assure you.

ALBERT. In the name of wonder, who has told you all this?

MLLE. DANGLARS. The prefect of police. Some unusual splendor awakened his attention, and the count must answer his inquiries this evening.

ALBERT. Poor Monte Cristo, threatened to be arrested for being a vagabond as well as being too rich!

DANGLARS. Well, the train his princess sports—

MERCÉDÈS. What princess?

DANGLARS. She was with him this evening at the opera.

ALBERT. Monte Cristo at the opera this evening?

DANGLARS. Certainly.

MLLE. DANGLARS. Opposite the prefect's box, where we were.

MERCÉDÈS (*aside*). And for such a

trifling motive he refused our invitation—'tis strange!

FERNAND. But who tells you this woman is a princess?

DANGLARS. Why, everybody. But see, here is Noirtier, editor of the *Imperial*. As a well-informed journalist, he can probably enlighten us.

NOIRTIER (*enters and bows*). Madame la Comtesse—General— (*Shaking hands*) Albert, welcome back, my dear boy. Glad to see you safe and well. (*The music stops.*)

ALBERT. Thanks, dear friend.

DANGLARS. You come just in time.

NOIRTIER (*looking at him*). So? Many persons ought not to come at all.

DANGLARS. Do you say that for me?

NOIRTIER. Decidedly.

DANGLARS. 'Tis worth while indeed, to be a subscriber to your journal.

NOIRTIER. You read my paper without understanding it—I report your speeches without listening to them.

DANGLARS. Impertinent. (MADEMOISELLE DANGLARS *runs to him.*)

MERCÉDÈS. Gentlemen!

NOIRTIER. Oh, don't be alarmed, madame, this is quite allowable, such are the curiosities of the press literature nowadays. It is no longer necessary to write good French, to have talents and convictions. Be slanderous and coarse, and you will print off four hundred thousand copies—write slang and you will be elected deputy, and you will make your fortune in twelve months. Now, in what way can I serve you?

MLLE. DANGLARS. We want to know from you—

NOIRTIER. Sixty-seven.

MLLE. DANGLARS. What sixty-seven?

NOIRTIER. I mean you are the sixty-seventh person who has asked me the same question.

MLLE. DANGLARS. But you don't know yet what mine is.

NOIRTIER. My dear young lady, you must have a very poor opinion of my understanding. You were going to ask me, whence comes, and what is the name of the fair Greek whom Monte Cristo accompanied this evening to the opera. Is it not so?

MLLE. DANGLARS (*greatly surprised*). It is.

NOIRTIER. Well. (*Mysteriously, as all gather round.*) I absolutely know nothing about it!

ALL. Ah!

DANGLARS. That is rather too strong.

NOIRTIER. I was even ignorant of the count's arrival in Paris.

DANGLARS. Why, your own journal was the first to announce it!

NOIRTIER. Do you believe that I read my journal? Thank you, it is quite enough to write it. All I know of the count is, he saved the life of this brave young man—and that I love him for having preserved to us a good soldier and an honorable man—a rarity in these money-hunting days.

MLLE. DANGLARS. It seems odd that a soldier should be saved by a civilian on the field of battle.

NOIRTIER. Yes, and unusual, too.

ALBERT. The count has peculiar notions. In place of making war on men, he makes it on wild beasts, and says their bites are less dangerous.

NOIRTIER. A man that knows the world.

ALBERT. In Africa he is called the tiger-slayer.

DANGLARS. A queer employment.

NOIRTIER. Less easy work than jobbing in the funds, eh?

MLLE. DANGLARS. Don't interrupt.

NOIRTIER. I am dumb. Proceed.

ALBERT. One day on the razzia, ambitious to win my spurs in the field, I dashed in pursuit of a body of Arabs without perceiving I was separated from my men, who themselves were surrounded on all sides. I was surrounded, seized. You know the delightful religious notions of the Arab gentry—they believe that their good angels carry them off after death to Mahomet's Paradise by the tuft of hair they grow on their skull. So, to debar their enemies from that celestial trip, they neatly sever their heads from their bodies.

MLLE. DANGLARS. How shocking!

ALBERT. An ugly prospect, I confess, and when I think of it I cannot help slightly shuddering. I already felt the fatal blade on my neck, and I commended my soul to Heaven—my last prayer to my mother—when a shot rang out behind us, and the man who held me dropped dead at my side. The circle opened as if by magic around my preserver. "The tiger-slayer!" they cried, and in a twinkling I was behind the stranger's saddle on his Arab steed which bore us like the wind from the murderous band. We soon heard the spahi bugles and I said to the cavalier, "There are my men, I am saved and I owe my life to you." "You owe me nothing," he replied. "You rode behind me as did my brother behind you on his road to Marseilles." Then, reaching me a torn card, the other half of which I had by me, he said "I am the Count de Monte Cristo; we are quits, adieu." "Shall I not see you again?" said I, detaining him. "Yes, at the Hôtel de Morcerf, on your next leave." "But, should I be killed in the war?" "You will not die on the field," he replied with a strange smile, "and on the day of your death you will find me before you—adieu." The next minute my soldiers were around me, whilst he disappeared in a cloud of dust.

(*Music is heard.*)

MLLE. DANGLARS. A perfect romance.

MERCÉDÈS (*hanging on* ALBERT). It is like a dream.

DANGLARS. Are you sure of him this evening?

ALBERT. Yes, for he promised me.

DANGLARS. Promises are air—a traveller's word.

NOIRTIER. As good as a stock jobber's.

DANGLARS. I'll bet he won't come.

CADEROUSSE (*enters and announces*). His excellency, the Count of Monte Cristo.

NOIRTIER. You have lost; I wonder who will pay?

(EDMUND *enters*, MERCÉDÈS *watches him and shrinks back.*)

MERCÉDÈS. Oh—how he has aged!

FERNAND. Who?

MERCÉDÈS. Look! (*Points to* EDMUND.)

FERNAND. The count—do you know him?

MERCÉDÈS. I—I—can't tell. I know not— (ALBERT *has gone over to* EDMUND *and offers his hand.*)

EDMUND (*not taking it*). Pray present me to the Countess de Morcerf.

ALBERT (*leading him to her*). My mother, this is he.

MERCÉDÈS (*mastering her emotion*). Sir, but for you I should be in tears and desolation—bless you! (*Aside, as* EDMUND *bows*) Oh, yes, I was mistaken. He never could be so changed.

FERNAND. Welcome amongst us, Count, the preserver to this house of its only heir, has a right to our eternal gratitude. (EDMUND *bows without replying.*)

MERCÉDÈS (*looking after him*). Oh, that look.

EDMUND. You praise me too highly.

MERCÉDÈS (*aside*). His voice, too!

EDMUND. To spare a mother's sorrow by saving the "only heir" of whom her husband is so justly proud is simply discharging an act of common humanity.

NOIRTIER. Count, you utter noble sentiments. I read your aim in life.

EDMUND. Do you?

MERCÉDÈS (aside). No, 'tis impossible. It would be too fearful.

ALBERT. Allow me, Count, to present you to Mademoiselle Danglars, my betrothed. (He bows.)

DANGLARS. My daughter.

EDMUND. And your name is—

DANGLARS. Danglars is my name.

EDMUND. Aye, Danglars and Company.

DANGLARS. Eh?

EDMUND. Is not that your firm?

DANGLARS (looking at MADEMOISELLE DANGLARS). As banker it is—but—

EDMUND. Oh, I have only to do with the banker, and I am glad, that I may hand you this letter of credit.

DANGLARS. From the house of Franch and Rossi at Rome. I will see you tomorrow on the subject.

MERCÉDÈS (aside). No, that tone, that bearing—no, it is a freak of my imagination. But why did he refuse to sit at our table? Oh, I shall know if it is a determination.

DANGLARS (after reading the letter). 'Tis impossible—'tis downright madness.

ALL. What? (Music stops.)

DANGLARS. The contents of this letter.

EDMUND. What is there so extraordinary in that letter?

DANGLARS. It gives the Count of Monte Cristo unlimited credit in my house.

ALL. Well?

DANGLARS. Don't you understand? —"unlimited."

EDMUND. Is the phrase good French?

DANGLARS (sneeringly). Oh, quite correct as regards grammar, but not as regards competency.

EDMUND. Is not the house of Franch and Rossi safe?

DANGLARS. I say nothing of them.

EDMUND. On the contrary, pray tell me, are they in a bad state? I have some millions in their hands and—

DANGLARS. Their bank is of the highest standing, but—

EDMUND. But—?

DANGLARS. But their letter is so vague!

EDMUND. Well?

DANGLARS. That seems absurd!

EDMUND. Meaning to say, you will not honor it.

DANGLARS. "Decline where there is any doubt," say the wise. And as I doubt, I decline.

EDMUND. Through wisdom or insolvency?

DANGLARS. Sir!

EDMUND. Sir?

DANGLARS. My capital has never yet been questioned by any man.

EDMUND. Then I will be the first to do so.

DANGLARS. You?

EDMUND. I!

DANGLARS. You know nothing of business.

EDMUND. That is a question. (He joins the others.) Pray excuse this ridiculous scene which I unwillingly introduce, but my self-respect requires that this single hesitation should be explained.

DANGLARS (aside). Can he know my position?

EDMUND. You lost five million francs yesterday by the fall, ten on the Spanish loan. You must find fifty for the newly announced railway—add to that forty you must have for current transactions, and it gives a total of one hundred and five million francs.

You see, I do not reckon badly for a man who knows nothing of business.

DANGLARS (*aside*). He knows all!

EDMUND. Do these few petty millions engaged prevent your opening credit with me?

DANGLARS (*aside*). If I hesitate, I am lost!

EDMUND. Well?

DANGLARS. I will prove to you the contrary, sir. Fix the sum you wish to draw, and even were you to require a million francs—

EDMUND. A million! And what use do you think a million would be to me? If I wanted a measly million, I should open no account at all. I always carry a million in treasury bonds in some corner of my pocketbook—see? (*Showing them*) Oh, no, how can I tell what whims may seize me, and what sums I may require? Be prepared for ten or fifteen millions at first sight.

DANGLARS (*aside*). I am ruined!

NOIRTIER (*in a low tone*). Ask him for the diamonds of his Greek companion as guarantee.

EDMUND. What are you saying?

NOIRTIER. The deuce! You have sharp ears!

EDMUND. I can read the eye—when Haidee is spoken of.

FERNAND. Haidee!

EDMUND. Yes, my slave.

FERNAND. Your slave?

EDMUND. Certainly, since I have bought her.

FERNAND. Danglars gave her out to be a princess.

EDMUND. She is one in reality, General. Hers is a sad and terrible history.

FERNAND (*aside*). Oh, heavens!

EDMUND (*all gather round him*). Great and powerful was the vizier her father—so powerful and great that the Sultan's self grew jealous of him and decreed his death. But the palace guard was entrusted to a French officer whom the vizier had loaded with kindness, and he slept in peace, relying on the gratitude and loyalty of the very man who sold him to his foes! And on a dark and fearful night, the assassins were introduced into a lower room beneath the kiosk, and when Haidee's father awoke at the untimely noise, a dull explosion was heard, and the boards under his feet flew in slivers around his head. Not daring to confront the lion face to face, the traitor had killed him through the flooring—and in a whirlwind of flames, as if Hell itself opened beneath his feet, fell Ali Tebelin, Haidee's father—Pasha of Janina!

MERCÉDÈS. Janina? Why, that is—

FERNAND (*aside to her*). Not a word, silence, or you will undo me!

MERCÉDÈS (*aside*). O saints above—could he be the man?

FERNAND. And do you know the name of the trai—of the man who sold the pasha to his murderers?

EDMUND. I know—I know that he received as the price of his treachery a vast fortune and his master's daughter, whom he doubtless lacked the courage to kill, for he sold her to the slave merchant from whom I bought her at Constantinople.

ALBERT. But this villain, this wretched coward, this traitor, was he not punished?

EDMUND. Not yet.

ALBERT. No?

EDMUND. Rest satisfied, he will be!

NOIRTIER. And if I can assist in so doing, you can depend on me.

EDMUND (*taking his hand*). Thanks.

FERNAND (*aside*). Is the hour of retribution come?

CADEROUSSE (*announces*). His excellency, the Greek Ambassador.

FERNAND (*aside*). He, too!

EDMUND (*aside*). He has kept his promise.

MERCÉDÈS. Go, receive him, Fernand, I wish to speak to the count.

FERNAND. You?

MERCÉDÈS. Go! Albert—

(FERNAND *leaves*, ALBERT *crosses to* MERCÉDÈS.)

I have always warned you against new acquaintances, do you know who this Monte Cristo is?

ALBERT. A perfect gentleman, as you can see for yourself.

MERCÉDÈS. Has the count ever clasped your hand?

ALBERT. Never.

MERCÉDÈS. Has he ever called you friend?

ALBERT. No.

MERCÉDÈS. And he has refused to sit at the same table with you?

ALBERT. Mother!

MERCÉDÈS. Leave us—take Danglars and his daughter with you. I wish to be alone with this man.

(ALBERT *goes to* DANGLARS *and* MADEMOISELLE DANGLARS, EDMUND *talking to* NOIRTIER.)

If it be not Edmund, can it be his avenging angel? But I am not guilty— O Heaven, protect my son, watch over my child.

MLLE. DANGLARS (*to* ALBERT). And is the ambassador in costume?

ALBERT. From head to foot.

MLLE. DANGLARS. Will you present me to him?

ALBERT. Yes, and your father, too.

DANGLARS. Come along then, quick.

MLLE. DANGLARS. Give me your arm.

(MADEMOISELLE DANGLARS, ALBERT *and* DANGLARS *take their leave*.)

MERCÉDÈS. Monsieur Noirtier—

NOIRTIER. Madame— (*To* EDMUND) Excuse me. (*He goes over to her.*)

EDMUND (*to* CADEROUSSE). Well?

CADEROUSSE. The newspaper is on the card table where Danglars is sure to find it.

EDMUND. Good.

CADEROUSSE. And shall be put into Albert's hand at the fitting time.

EDMUND. You will take the *Etoile* to Danglars when I tell you.

CADEROUSSE (*touches his pocket*). I have it here.

EDMUND. Silence, we are observed.

NOIRTIER (*bowing to* MERCÉDÈS). I obey, madame.

MERCÉDÈS. I shall know what to depend on.

EDMUND. You have not gone to receive the Greek Ambassador, madame; his wonderful accounts of Esperus and the reign of Ali Tebelin would interest you, I am certain. May I take you to the salon?

MERCÉDÈS. No, the heat is oppressive —I feel weak already—my head swims — (*Leans on* EDMUND, *she is silent*.)

EDMUND. The powerful scent those flowers exhale is dangerous—go in.

MERCÉDÈS. No, thanks. I feel better. There is a touching Arabian custom which you must know, and of which I was recently reminding my son—

EDMUND (*aside*). Fernand's son!

MERCÉDÈS. It makes eternal friends of those who partake of the same meal; shall we share together? You still refuse?

EDMUND. We are in France, madame, not in Arabia. Here one can by paying for them, find bread and salt perhaps, but eternal friendship is an unknown feast.

MERCÉDÈS. You refuse?

EDMUND. I refuse.

(MERCÉDÈS *lets her hand drop.*)

Madame—

MERCÉDÈS. What has steeled your heart to act thus? What motive impels you?

EDMUND (*coldly*). I cannot tell.

MERCÉDÈS (*wildly*). I will then—you seek revenge.

EDMUND. I?

MERCÉDÈS. Yes, for an enforced deed—for an act of which you know not the motive, and which you tax with guilt. You seek revenge on a woman.

EDMUND. No, no, not on her. If she has the fortitude to be happy, may she be so. It is he that I would reach!

MERCÉDÈS. He?

EDMUND. Yes, the traitor who stepped between her and me. Oh, fear nothing, I will not touch him—Providence will strike him when the hour comes.

MERCÉDÈS. By ruining his fortune, is it not?

EDMUND (*with irony*). No.

MERCÉDÈS. By degrading him in the army?

EDMUND. No.

MERCÉDÈS. By accusing him loudly before the chamber of peers, of treason and murder?

EDMUND. No, no, a thousand times no. That but touches his honor, and what is that to such a man? 'Tis at his heart I shall aim—'tis in his heart he shall be struck!

MERCÉDÈS (*with a low cry*). Unhappy man, I understand you—you would kill my son.

EDMUND (*in a rage*). Yours—and his!

MERCÉDÈS. O madman! This son, this child, my beloved Albert, is—

ALBERT (*enters with paper in hand*). Mother!

MERCÉDÈS (*to* EDMUND). Not a word before him!

ALBERT. Mother, the count is looking for you, he wishes you to join him in detaining Danglars, who wants rudely to take away his daughter.

MERCÉDÈS (*embracing* ALBERT). Love him, too—respect him above all others,

and if any quarrel should arise between you, be thou silent. Do thou submit, and come—come to me and tell me all.

EDMUND. Madame!

MERCÉDÈS (*seizing his arm*). I rely upon your honor, no provocation from you? This night you shall know all. Fear no longer. (*She goes into the salon, leaving them face to face.*)

ALBERT. Count—

EDMUND. What is it?

ALBERT. I have a great service to ask at your hands.

EDMUND. At mine?

ALBERT. Yes. Oh, don't refuse me, I feel that you would bring me harm.

EDMUND. What is it?

ALBERT. I am about to fight a duel.

EDMUND. You?

ALBERT. I.

EDMUND. A serious one?

ALBERT. A mortal one.

EDMUND. With whom?

ALBERT. With Noirtier.

EDMUND. This is madness. He might be your father—he is a most respected politician, a man whose honor and integrity—

ALBERT. It is not a question of his honor, but mine. The name I bear—

EDMUND. And does Noirtier attack that honor?

ALBERT. In his journal of today—here is a copy.

EDMUND. And what does he say in his journal?

ALBERT. It is horrible. (*Reads.*) "From a correspondent at Janina—" (*Stops, unable to proceed.*)

EDMUND (*aside*). The journal put in Danglars' way by Caderousse! (*Aloud*) What says the correspondent at Janina?

ALBERT. I cannot—read for yourself—it is too frightful. (*He sits down.*)

EDMUND (*reading*). "From a correspondent at Janina it is now ascertained as a fact that the brave Ali Tebelin who was massacred in his castle was betrayed and given up to his enemies by the French officer whose fortune he had made, and whose name was Fernand." What of that?

ALBERT (*getting up*). Now do you understand?

EDMUND. I understand your agitation, but still I do not see what there is to challenge Noirtier.

ALBERT. I required of him to retract his calumny.

EDMUND. And he refused?

ALBERT. No.

EDMUND. Well?

ALBERT. But he added a condition.

EDMUND. What was it?

ALBERT. Of his being first convinced that the statement was false.

EDMUND. And then you challenge him?

ALBERT. And he will either retract this odious lie or I will kill him.

EDMUND. Now, what would you ask of me?

ALBERT. First, that you would receive Noirtier's answer.

EDMUND. I will do so.

ALBERT. Then—and this is the service I ask you not to refuse—to be my second in case of a duel.

EDMUND. Be it so.

ALBERT. Ah, Count, you said truly to me when you saved my life, "You will not perish in a battle, boy, and on the day of your death you will find me before you."—You keep your word.

EDMUND. I always do.

ALBERT (*looking off*). My father and Danglars—let them know nothing.

EDMUND. Rest satisfied. (*He leaves, bowing to* FERNAND *and* DANGLARS, *who enter.*)

FERNAND. Now, sir, we are alone—alone with my son, who is as much in-

terested as I am—who has an equal right with me to call you to account for the scandal created by your refusal.

DANGLARS. I have nothing to do with the scandal—I was leaving quietly with my daughter—you set the countess on us, we were detained. You force me to explain, and I simply say read the *Imperial* of today. It will be less unpleasant for you, and make it easier for me.

ALBERT. Have you read the *Imperial*?

FERNAND. What is it all about, Albert, what does he allude to?

ALBERT. To a vile slander, Father. They say, Father, they dare to say that you, whose loyal services are so well known, whose bravery and valor have been so highly recompensed by the king, they say—oh, pardon me for repeating such infamies!—they say to enrich yourself, in a word, for a price, like the lowest traitors, you sold and assassinated your benefactor.

FERNAND. Oh! Who said so?

ALBERT (*giving him the papers*). See here, and as for you who have hawked this lie—

DANGLARS. It is my fault if the journal gives the name of the Count de Morcerf in full?

ALBERT. Thou liest! They do not give his name. (*Taking the paper*) Look!

DANGLARS. The *Imperial* does not, but the *Étoile* does.

(CADEROUSSE *enters with the paper.*)

ALBERT. 'Tis false!

CADEROUSSE (*to* DANGLARS). Here, sir, is the number of the *Étoile* you asked for.

DANGLARS. Ah, here it is! (*He tears off the cover;* ALBERT *snatches the paper.*)

ALBERT (*reads excitedly*). "The French officer alluded to in the Janina correspondence of the *Imperial* and mentioned under the name of Fernand, now bears the title of Count de Morcerf, and is a member of the chamber of peers."

FERNAND. And who sends the journals in such good time?

DANGLARS. How do I know? Here is the cover.

FERNAND (*reading*). "The Count de Monte Cristo."

ALBERT. He? Oh, this will drive me mad.

(EDMUND *and* NOIRTIER *enter.*)

Here they are at last.

NOIRTIER. Albert, my child, be calm.

ALBERT. Do you retract, Noirtier, do you defend my father?

NOIRTIER. I regret to say that I cannot without forfeiting honor. I have acquired the sad proof of the allegation.

ALBERT. From whom have you the proofs?

NOIRTIER. From the Ambassador of Greece himself. (FERNAND *staggers against the wall.*)

ALBERT. Furnished before witnesses, no doubt.

NOIRTIER. Albert!

ALBERT (*drawing off his glove*). Answer!

NOIRTIER. Before the Count of Monte Cristo, who represented you.

ALBERT (*mockingly*). Who represented me? Indeed, and what reply did that noble friend make to this accusation?

NOIRTIER. That he could not doubt it, as he himself had it from Haidee.

(MERCÉDÈS *appears.*)

ALBERT (*with uplifted glove to* EDMUND). Ah, the wretched coward!

EDMUND (*seizing his wrist and glove, he turns to* FERNAND). Revenge is mine, Fernand—I hold thy heart in my hand.

ALBERT (*with dignity*). You have a firm wrist, sir; tomorrow we shall see if you have as firm a heart.

EDMUND. Tomorrow I will return your glove from a pistol, wrapped around a bullet.

MERCÉDÈS (*aside to* EDMUND). You will not do so, Edmund.

EDMUND (*looking at* FERNAND). I will!

MERCÉDÈS. You will not harm a hair of his head!

EDMUND. I will kill him!

MERCÉDÈS. You will not even fight him.

EDMUND. I will kill him.

MERCÉDÈS. Try—he is your son!

ACT FIVE

The forest of Vincennes. Woodcutter's hut, the door facing front.

———

EDMUND (*enters, followed by* NOIRTIER *with swords and* DANGLARS *with pistols*). Are we arrived?

DANGLARS. Yes.

EDMUND. This is the spot fixed for the duel between Albert and me?

NOIRTIER. This is the spot.

DANGLARS. But, thanks to your haste, we are considerably before the time mentioned.

EDMUND. I expect someone here whom I must see before I die.

NOIRTIER. Die!

EDMUND. Is not this a duel to the death?

NOIRTIER. But you are acknowledged to be the best swordsman, the first shot of the day. Your reputation makes the best duellist tremble, and—

EDMUND. And I could kill Albert at my pleasure—is it not so?

NOIRTIER. Assuredly.

EDMUND. Well, Albert will leave the ground uninjured—and you will have, my good friend, to carry me off to my last home.

NOIRTIER. Look you now, I have followed you throughout the ball last night, watched you throughout the challenge, and comprehended that you had a great act to accomplish, and I feel convinced that you act in justice.

EDMUND. Yes, I thought so, too.

NOIRTIER. Why, then, speak of death?

EDMUND. It is not time to answer your questions. Before I cross swords with Albert, or confront him, you shall know all.

NOIRTIER. Let it be so. (*He walks up to* DANGLARS.)

EDMUND (*alone, resting on a fallen tree*). It is all over now; the edifice built so slowly, reared with such trouble and labor falls at a blow—at a woman's breath—at a child's mere name. (*Looking upward*) Oh, Thou art great and powerful, and I reel under Thy mighty hand, and submit to Thy eternal justice. How Thou dost lower us all to our level, when we proudly essay to soar into Thy Kingdom. I aspired to be Thy avenger, and Thou hast shown me by Villefort's dreadful end how Thy time has come. Thou knowest how to punish. Led by a mean and selfish jealousy, I sought to strike Fernand cruelly to the heart by slaying his son, and it is my heart Thou strikest, and before my weapon Thou placest mine own child. 'Tis justice, and I shall fall beneath that same weapon with which I meant to slay. I am prepared to die.

DANGLARS. Someone approaches.

EDMUND. Can it be Albert already?

NOIRTIER. No, it is his new servant.

EDMUND (*aside*). Caderousse at last!

(CADEROUSSE *enters.*)

NOIRTIER. How did you leave him?

CADEROUSSE. Alas, full of rage and spite—he spent the whole night practic-ing with a pistol, shooting at a mark.

NOIRTIER. You have the choice of weapons, Count, and must take—

EDMUND. The pistol, Noirtier, and give the boy a fair chance.

NOIRTIER. 'Tis madness!

EDMUND. No, 'tis resignation, and you'll approve of it when you know all.

NOIRTIER. We'll see. (*He leaves with* DANGLARS.)

EDMUND (*to* CADEROUSSE). Now, we are alone.

CADEROUSSE. I have seen her.

EDMUND. You have?

CADEROUSSE. Yes.

EDMUND. And you have told her?

CADEROUSSE. All. How you were betrayed—Danglars' letter—Fernand's perfidy—even my involuntary share in the infamous plot.

EDMUND. And she has forgiven me my hateful project of revenge—does she not despise me?

CADEROUSSE. She reveres and loves you.

EDMUND. Oh, say not that, courage will fail me, I should lack the strength to die.

CADEROUSSE. She has abjured the base hypocrite Fernand, who for twenty years has defrauded her of her esteem and respect, as he robbed his benefactor of wealth and life. She rose, pale but firm and noble. From a secluded chest she drew her long-abandoned Catalan dress, and in those garments, unpurchased by the wages of treachery and murder, she will leave Fernand's mansion.

EDMUND. What?

CADEROUSSE. "Tell Edmund this," did she add, "and while he lives—whose tainted name I and my son bear, let the secret I confided to Edmund concerning Albert remain sacred—I trust his honor"—and she handed me this medal, snatched from your neck in the last embrace when the felon's deed dragged you to prison.

EDMUND (*embracing him*). Ah, Mercédès, we are both condemned in this world!

CADEROUSSE. Master!

EDMUND. Enough of this, listen. You will go to Marseilles—you will bear my last wishes—

CADEROUSSE. Your last?

EDMUND. Keep silence and mark me. Here is a letter for Morel. It informs him of the spot where he will find the red silk purse which he left filled with gold for the wants of my poor old father. Its present contents will save Morel from bankruptcy. In a few days a new *Pharaon* which I have built, and which old Penelon himself has laden with the treasures of Monte Cristo, will bravely enter the port of Marseilles. She holds millions—their fortune—that of Morel, and the future fortune of Albert and Mercédès when they come; take the letter and go.

CADEROUSSE. Here is Albert.

EDMUND. Go, he must not see you. (CADEROUSSE *leaves*.) And now let the dead reenter his tomb! The spectre fade away in the shade of night. (AL-BERT, DANGLARS, *and* NOIRTIER *appear*.)

DANGLARS (*looking at his watch*). You are late, Viscount.

ALBERT (*saluting him*). I ask pardon, gentlemen, for causing you to wait. An interview with my mother detained me, and I beg of you to accept her excuses and mine.

NOIRTIER. But I do not see your seconds, Albert.

ALBERT. They are needless, my esteemed friend. My arrival alone suffices for what must pass between the count and myself. Remain, Noirtier. The presence of one man of honor is necessary at our conversation.

DANGLARS. Sir?

NOIRTIER (*detaining him*). Your pardon, you are not spoken of.

ALBERT (*to* EDMUND). Count, I harshly challenged you last night. I thought it my duty to repress a calumny. Today, that which I thought to be a slander, has become a terrible truth. The Count de Morcerf is struck off the roll of peers, and the General Fernand is degraded. But, it is not the treachery of the officer Mondego toward the Pasha that makes me ready to excuse you—it is the foulness of the fisherman Fernand toward you that bows me with shame. It is for your eighteen years of incarceration that I humbly ask your pardon! (*He kneels before* EDMUND.)

EDMUND. Albert—sir—

ALBERT. Yes, I proclaim it publicly. You were justified in revenging yourself on my father, and I, the son of Mercédès, I thank you for having sought revenge on him. (*He kneels again.*)

EDMUND (*aside*). Ah, your heart is there, Mercédès. (FERNAND *appears at back.*)

ALBERT. An angel from Heaven alone could have saved us from death. That angel came in my mother's form, if not to make us friends—that is impossible—at least to make two men of honor who esteem each other, regard their conscience more dearly than their vanity.

DANGLARS. Ah, all ends with an apology, does it?

ALBERT (*to* DANGLARS). And if anyone should doubt the motive which urges me, I shall speedily correct his opinion.

FERNAND (*confronting him*). Even mine, Viscount de Morcerf?

ALBERT. My father!

ALL. Morcerf!

FERNAND (*to* NOIRTIER *and* DANG-

LARS). I have not to do with you, but with this man. (*To* EDMUND) To this public insulter, who knows everyone and whom no one knows. Who then, are you, demon? You, who have clothed me in shame and contempt. You, who have by the light of Hell, read every page in my past life?

ALBERT (*covers his face with his hands*). Ah, Heaven!

FERNAND. Come, who are you? Yesterday you called yourself Monte Cristo—in Italy, Busoni. In Epirus—I know not—I can't recollect. But of these hundred names you give yourself, which is your real one? That I may spit it in your face while I plunge my sword in your heart, or send a bullet crashing through your skull. Have you a name you dare avow?

EDMUND (*calmly*). Fernand, of the hundred names you mention, you have forgotten one. I have but to pronounce it to strike you to my feet. Fernand, look me well in the eye. We have met but once—but look at me.

FERNAND. Oh! 'Tis impossible.

EDMUND. You guessed at once, because Heaven at this moment lights them with a spark of its own fire.

FERNAND. You alive, and knowing all?

EDMUND. All!

FERNAND. And you did not kill me?

EDMUND. No. But I have told Mercédès all.

FERNAND. Ah, wretch, defend yourself! (*He throws the pistols to him.*)

EDMUND (*pushing the pistol away with his foot*). Fernand, you can murder me, but I shall not fight you.

FERNAND. If you will have it, then— (*He cocks the pistol as* MERCÉDÈS *rushes between them and stops him.*)

MERCÉDÈS. Assassin!

FERNAND. Ah—she? I am accursed! (*He runs into the hut, and a shot is heard within.* MERCÉDÈS *and* ALBERT *run to the hut.*)

ALBERT (*supporting* MERCÉDÈS). Mother!

MERCÉDÈS. Dead!

EDMUND. "Two!" (*To* DANGLARS, *taking the sword*) Your turn, now, defend yourself!

NOIRTIER. Hold!

EDMUND. Back, Noirtier, I can kill this man, and this man shall die!

MERCÉDÈS. Edmund—

DANGLARS. Edmund Dantès! (*He springs for the sword.*)

EDMUND. Ha, you know me now. Noirtier, be witness that I grant the honor of a duel to that viper whom I have the right to crush beneath my heel. It was that serpent who crawled beneath all those villainies, his venom that has poisoned all those lives! Danglars, your time has come! You are going to die. (*As he is rolling up his sleeve,* DANGLARS *makes a thrust at him.* NOIRTIER *throws it off with his cane.*)

NOIRTIER. Coward! Go in, Edmund, and kill the villain. I will act as umpire!

DANGLARS. You forget my secret thrust.

EDMUND. No, for Heaven fights on my side and nerves my arm! I tell you, Danglars, you are going to die.

NOIRTIER. *En garde!*

EDMUND. *En garde!* (*They cross swords.*)

MERCÉDÈS (*to* ALBERT). On your knees, child, and pray for him. Albert, Albert—pray. Soon you shall know your birth—soon I can tell you all.

DANGLARS (*making a pass*). Hit!

EDMUND. Nothing. Your foul stroke is known! Now, Danglars, you are a dead man.

DANGLARS (*lunging at him*). Have at thee!

EDMUND (*runs him through*). Die!

DANGLARS. Ha! (*Dies and rolls at his feet.*)

EDMUND. "Three!"

MERCÉDÈS. Your prayers have saved your father's life, Albert—you are his son!

CURTAIN

[4][FERNAND (*in the utmost terror*). Edmond Dantés! Dantés, whom I buried in a living tomb—thou art not human, but a devil—whom I will send to his native hell! (*He attacks* DANTÉS, *a fierce and rapid combat.* FERNAND *is disarmed, and pierced through, falls at the back, between the doors which open on the stage.*)

DANTÉS. Thus falls the last and worst of my enemies—Peace now and good will to all mankind, for the vengeance of Monte Cristo is no more. (*He closes the doors, concealing the body.*)

(*Enter* MAXIMILIAN, *leading* VALENTINE; *she wears a bridal veil, is clothed in white, wears a coronet of roses.*)

MAXIMILIAN. My protector, my benefactor!

DANTÉS. My children, pardon me that I delayed your happiness, 'twas but to ensure its permanence. My task is accomplished. I have punished the wicked, have recompensed the good! If I have erred, O, Heaven, have mercy on me!—and in Thy infallible balance, may the good that I have done outweight the evil I have wrought!

(ALBERT *and* MERCÉDÈS *appear through the door at the right,* MERCÉDÈS *wears the Catalan dress of first act.* ALBERT *plainly dressed.*)

MERCÉDÈS. Edmond!

DANTÉS. Mercedés!

MERCÉDÈS. Edmond! I go! bestow on me your pardon; on my son, your blessing. (*She passes* ALBERT *over to* MONTE CRISTO *who embraces him.*)

MERCÉDÈS. Ah! (*Joyfully*) Oh! Heaven, I thank thee that I have beheld that which I had never hoped to see; (*Leading* ALBERT *slowly towards downstage right*) farewell, Edmond, farewell!

DANTÉS. Farewell!

(HAYDÉE *glides from behind the curtains into the arms of* MONTE CRISTO.)

HAYDÉE. I have heard all. O, my lord, Heaven has made me younger than her, that I may have the happiness longer to love you! (*Tableau, and curtain.*)]

---

[4] The bracketed lines that follow are from the "Late Lacy" version, reproduced here to indicate a variant ending.—MAXIMILIAN is the son of the ruined merchant MOREL, and HAYDÉE is the daughter of Ali Pacha (Pasha) of Janina, whom DANTÉS took under his protection after the death of her father in battle, and who loves DANTÉS although many years younger than he.

THE MOUSE-TRAP[*]

William Dean Howells

MRS. SOMERS   MRS. CURWEN

MR. CAMPBELL   MRS. BEMIS

JANE   MRS. ROBERTS

MRS. MILLER

---

[*] Circa 1889. Presented before 1904 by Margaret Robertson (Dame Madge Kendal).

SCENE ONE

In her drawing room, MRS. AMY
SOMERS, *young, pretty, stylish, in the
last evanescent traces of widowhood,
stands confronting* MR. WILLIS CAMP-
BELL. *She has a newspaper in her hand,
folded to the width of a single column,
which she extends toward him with an
effect of indignant menace.*

————

MRS. SOMERS. Then you acknowledge
that it is yours?

CAMPBELL. I acknowledge that I
made a speech before the legislative
committee on behalf of the anti-
suffragists. You knew I was going to
do that. I don't know how they've reported it.

MRS. SOMERS (*with severity*). Very
well, then; I will read it: "Willis
Campbell, Esq., was next heard on behalf of the petitioners. He touched
briefly upon the fact that the suffrage
was evidently not desired by the vast
majority of educated women."

CAMPBELL. You've always said they
didn't want it.

MRS. SOMERS. That is not the
point. (*Reading*) "And many of them
would feel it an onerous burden, and
not a privilege."

CAMPBELL. Well, didn't you—

MRS. SOMERS. Don't interrupt!
(*Reading*) "Which would compel
them, at the cost of serious sacrifices,
to contend at the polls with the ignorant classes who would be sure to exercise the right if conferred."

CAMPBELL. That was your own argument, Amy. They're almost your own
words.

MRS. SOMERS. That isn't what I object to. (*Reading*) "Mr. Campbell
then referred in a more humorous
strain to the argument, frequently used
by the suffragists, that every taxpayer

should have the right to vote. He said
that he objected to this, because it implied that nontaxpayers should not
have the right to vote, which would deprive of the suffrage a large body of
adoptive citizens, who voted at all the
elections with great promptness and assiduity. He thought the exemption of
women from some duties required of
men by the State fairly offset the loss
of the ballot in their case, and that until
we were prepared to send ladies to battle we ought not to oblige them to go
to the polls. Some skirmishing ensued
between Mr. Campbell and Mr. Wil-
lington, on the part of the suffragists,
the latter gentleman affirming that in
great crises of the world's history wom-
en had shown as much courage as
men, and the former contending that
this did not at all affect his position,
since the courage of women was in high
degree a moral courage, which was not
evoked by the ordinary conditions of
peace or war, but required the immi-
nence of some extraordinary, some vital
emergency."

CAMPBELL. Well, what do you object
to in all that?

MRS. SOMERS (*tossing the paper on
the table and confronting him with her
head lifted and her hands clasped upon her left side*). Everything! It is an
insult to women.

CAMPBELL. *Woman,* you mean. I
don't think *women* would mind it.
Who's been talking to you, Amy?

MRS. SOMERS. Nobody. It doesn't
matter who's been talking to me. That
is not the question.

CAMPBELL. It's the question I asked.

MRS. SOMERS. It isn't the question *I*
asked. I wish simply to know what you
mean by that speech.

CAMPBELL. I wish you knew how
pretty you look in that dress. (MRS.
SOMERS *involuntarily glances down at*

the skirt of it on either side and rearranges it a little, folding her hands again as before.) But perhaps you do.

MRS. SOMERS (*with dignity*). Will you answer my question?

CAMPBELL. Certainly. I meant what I said.

MRS. SOMERS. Oh, you did! Very well, then! When a woman stands by the bedside of her sick child, and risks her life from contagion, what kind of courage do you call that?

CAMPBELL. Moral.

MRS. SOMERS. And when she remains in a burning building or a sinking ship —as they often do—and perishes, while her child is saved, what kind of courage is it?

CAMPBELL. Moral.

MRS. SOMERS. When she seizes an axe and defends her little ones against a bear or a wolf that's just bursting in the cabin door, what kind of courage does she show?

CAMPBELL. Moral.

MRS. SOMERS. Or when her babe crawls up the track, and she snatches it from the very jaws of the cowcatcher—

CAMPBELL. Oh, hold on now, Amy! Be fair! It's the engineer who does that; he runs along the side of the locomotive, and catches the smiling infant up, and lays it in the mother's arms as the train thunders by. His name is usually Hank Rollins. The mother is always paralyzed with terror.

MRS. SOMERS. Of course she is. But in those other cases, how does her courage differ from a man's? If hers is always moral, what kind of courage does a man show when he faces the cannon?

CAMPBELL. Immoral. Come, Amy, are you trying to prove that women are braver than men? Well, they are. I never was in any danger yet that I didn't wish I was a woman, for then I should have the courage to face it, or else I could turn and run without disgrace. All that I said in that speech was that women haven't so much nerve as men.

MRS. SOMERS. They have more.

CAMPBELL. Nerves—yes.

MRS. SOMERS. No, nerve. Take Dr. Cissy Gay, that little, slender delicate, sensitive thing: what do you suppose she went through when she was studying medicine and walking the hospitals, and all those disgusting things? And Mrs. J. Plunkett Harmon: do you mean to say that *she* has no nerve, facing all sorts of audiences, on the platform, everywhere? Or the Reverend Lily Barber, living down all that ridicule and going quietly on in her work—

CAMPBELL. Oh, *they've* been talking to you.

MRS. SOMERS. They have *not!* And if they have, Dr. Gay is as much opposed to suffrage as you are.

CAMPBELL. As *I?* Aren't you opposed to it, too?

MRS. SOMERS. Of course I am. Or I was till you made that speech.

CAMPBELL. It wasn't exactly intended to convert you.

MRS. SOMERS. It has placed me in a false position. Everybody knows, or the same as knows, that we're engaged—

CAMPBELL. Well, I'm not ashamed of it, Amy.

MRS. SOMERS (*severely*). No matter! And now it will look as if I had no ideas of my own, and was just swayed about any way by you. A woman is despicable that joins with men in ridiculing women.

CAMPBELL. Who's been saying that?

MRS. SOMERS. No one. It doesn't matter who's been saying it. Mrs. Mervane has been saying it.

CAMPBELL. Mrs. Mervane?

MRS. SOMERS. Yes, Mrs. Mervane, that you're always praising and admiring so for her good sense and her right ideas. Didn't you say she wrote as logically and forcibly as a man?

CAMPBELL. Yes, I did.

MRS. SOMERS. Very well, then, she says that if anything could turn her in favor of suffrage it is that speech of yours. She says it's a subtle attack upon the whole sex.

CAMPBELL. Well, I give it up! You are all alike. You take everything personally, in the first place, and then you say it's an attack on all women. Couldn't I make this right by publishing a card to acknowledge your physical courage before the whole community, Amy? Then your friends would have to say that I had recognized the pluck of universal womanhood.

MRS. SOMERS. No, sir; you can't make it right now. And I'm sorry, sorry, *sorry* I signed the antisuffrage petition. Nothing will ever teach men to appreciate women till women practically assert themselves.

CAMPBELL. That sounds very much like another quotation, Amy.

MRS. SOMERS. And they must expect to be treated as cowards till they show themselves heroes. And they must first of all have the ballot.

CAMPBELL. Oh!

MRS. SOMERS. Yes. Then, and not till then, men will acknowledge their equality in all that is admirable in both. Then there will be no more puling insolence about moral courage and vital emergencies to evoke it.

CAMPBELL. I don't see the steps to this conclusion, but the mastermind of Mrs. J. Plunkett Harmon reaches conclusions at a bound.

MRS. SOMERS. It *wasn't* Mrs. Harmon.

CAMPBELL. Oh, well, the Reverend Lily Barber, then. You needn't tell me *you* originated that stuff, Amy. But I submit for the present. Think it over, my dear, and when I come back tomorrow—

MRS. SOMERS. Perhaps you had better not come back tomorrow.

CAMPBELL. Why?

MRS. SOMERS. Because—because I'm afraid we are not in sympathy. Because if you thought that I needed some vital emergency to make me show that I was ready to die for you any moment—

CAMPBELL. *Die* for me? I want you to live for me, Amy.

MRS. SOMERS. —and the emergency never came, you would despise me.

CAMPBELL. Never!

MRS. SOMERS. If you have such a low opinion of women generally—

CAMPBELL. *I* a low opinion of women!

MRS. SOMERS. You said they were cowards.

CAMPBELL. I didn't say they were cowards. And if I seemed to say so, it was my misfortune. I honestly and truly think, Amy, that when a woman is roused she isn't afraid of anything in heaven or on—(*He stops abruptly, and looks toward the corner of the room.*)

MRS. SOMERS. What is it?

CAMPBELL. Oh, nothing. I thought I saw a mouse.

MRS. SOMERS. A mouse! (*She flings herself upon him and clutches him with convulsive energy. Then suddenly freeing him, she leaps upon a chair and stoops over to hold her train from the floor.*) Oh, drive it out, drive it out! Don't *kill* it. Oh—e-e-e-e! *Drive* it out! Oh, what shall I do? Oh, Willis, love, jump on a chair! Oh, horrid little dreadful reptile! Oh, *drive* it out!" (*In uttering these appeals, MRS.*

SOMERS *alternately looses her hold upon her train in order to clasp her face in her hands, and then uncovers her face to seize her train.*) Oh, is it *gone?* Come here, Willis, and let me hold your hand! Or no! Drive it, drive it, *drive* it out!

CAMPBELL (*going about the room in deliberate examination*). *I* can't find it. I guess it's gone into its hole again.

MRS. SOMERS. No, it hasn't! It hasn't got any hole here. It must have come in from somewhere else. Oh, I *hope* I shall have a little wisdom *some* time, and never, never, never have cake and wine brought into the drawing room again, no matter *how* faint with walking any one is. Of course, it was the smell of the fruit and crumbs attracted it; and they might just as well take the horsecars; but they said they had walked all the way to get me to sign the suffrage petition, and when I said I'd signed the antisuffrage, of course I had to offer them something; I couldn't do less. Have you driven it out?

CAMPBELL. I've done my best. But I can't find it, and I can't drive it out till I *do* find it.

MRS. SOMERS. It's run into the fireplace. Rattle the tongs! (CAMPBELL *goes to the fireplace and rattles the tongs against the shovel,* MRS. SOMERS, *meanwhile, covering her face.*) Ow— ugh—e-e-e-e! Is it gone? (*She uncovers her eyes.*)

CAMPBELL. It never was there.

MRS. SOMERS. Yes, it was, Willis. Don't tell me it wasn't! Where else was it if it wasn't there? Look under that book table!

CAMPBELL. Which one?

MRS. SOMERS. That one with the shelf coming down almost to the carpet. Poke under it with the poker! (*As* CAMPBELL *obeys, she again hides her face.*) U-u-u-gh! Is it gone *now?*

CAMPBELL. It wasn't there.

MRS. SOMERS. Poke hard! Bang against the mopboard! Bang!

CAMPBELL (*poking and banging*). There! I tell you it never was there.

MRS. SOMERS (*uncovering her face*). Oh, what shall I do? It must be somewhere in the room, and I never can breathe till you've found it. Bang again!

CAMPBELL. Nonsense! It's gone long ago. Do you suppose a mouse of any presence of mind or self-respect would stay here after all this uproar? (*He restores the tongs to their stand with a clash.*)

MRS. SOMERS (*responsive to the clash*). Ow!

CAMPBELL (*advancing toward her and extending his hand*). Come, Amy; get down now. I must be going.

MRS. SOMERS (*in horror*). Get down? Going?

CAMPBELL. Certainly. I can't stay here all day. I've got to follow that mouse out into the street and have him arrested. It's a public duty.

MRS. SOMERS. Don't throw ridicule on it! (*After a moment*) You know I can't let you go till I've seen that mouse leave this room. Go all round and stamp in the corners. (*She covers her face again.*) Ugh!

CAMPBELL. How are you going to see him leave the room if you won't look? He's left long ago. *I* wouldn't stay if I was a mouse. And I've got to go, anyway.

MRS. SOMERS (*uncovering her face*). No! I beg, I *command* you to stay, or I shall never get out of this room alive. You *know* I sha'n't. (*A ring at the street door is heard.*) Oh, *dear,* what shall I do? I've told Jane I would see anybody that called, and now I daren't step my foot to the floor! What *shall* I do?

CAMPBELL (*with authority*). You must get down. There's no mouse here, I tell you; and if people come and find you standing on a chair in your drawing room, what will they think?

MRS. SOMERS. I can kneel on it. (*She drops to her knees on the chair.*) There!

CAMPBELL. That's no better. It's worse.

MRS. SOMERS (*listening to the party at the door below, which the maid has opened*). 'Sh! I want to make out who it is. 'Sh! Yes—it is! (*After listening.*) Yes; it's Mrs. Miller and Lou Bemis and Mrs. Curwen! I don't see how they happen to come together, for Mrs. Miller and Mrs. Curwen perfectly hate each other. Oh, yes! I know! They're all on the way to Mrs. Ransom's reception; he's showing his pictures and some of her things—horrid daubs; I don't see how she can have the face— and they've met here by accident. 'Sh! She's showing them into the reception room. Yes, that's quite right. (MRS. SOMERS *delivers these sentences in a piercing whisper of extreme volubility.*) Now, as soon as she brings up their cards, I'll say I'm not at all well— that I'm engaged—just going out. No, that won't do. I *must* be sick. Anything else would be perfectly insulting after saying that I was at home; and Jane has got to go back and tell them she forgot that I had gone to bed with a severe headache. (*As* JANE *appears at the drawing room door, and falters at sight of* MRS. SOMERS *kneeling on her chair, that lady beckons her to her, frowning, shaking her head, and pressing her finger on her lip to enforce silence, and takes the cards from her, while she continues in whisper.*) Yes. All right, Jane! Go straight back and tell them you forgot I had gone to bed with a perfectly blinding

headache; and don't let another soul into the house. Mr. Campbell saw a mouse, and I can't get down till he's caught it. Go!

SCENE TWO

JANE (*after a moment of petrification*). A mouse! In the room here? Oh, my goodness gracious me! (*She leaps upon the chair next to* MRS. SOMERS, *who again springs to her feet.*)

MRS. SOMERS. Did you *see* it? Oh, e-e-e-e!

JANE. W-o-o-o-o! I don't know! Where was it? Oh, yes, I thought— (*They clutch each other convulsively and blend their cries, at the sound of which the ladies in the reception room below come flocking upstairs into the drawing room.*)

THE LADIES (*at sight of* MRS. SOMERS *and her servant*). What is it? What is it?

MRS. SOMERS. Oh, there's a *mouse* in the room. Oh, jump on chairs!

MRS. MILLER (*vaulting into the middle of the sofa*). A mouse!

MRS. BEMIS (*alighting upon a slight reception chair*). Oh, not in *this* room, Mrs. Somers! *Don't* say it!

MRS. CURWEN (*with a laugh of mingled terror and enjoyment from the top of the table where she finds herself*). Where is it?

MRS. SOMERS. I don't know. I didn't see it. But, oh; it's here somewhere. Mr. Campbell saw it, and Jane did when she came up with your cards, and he's been trying to drive it out, but he can't even *budge* it; and—

CAMPBELL (*desperately*). Ladies, there isn't any mouse here! I've been racketing round here with the shovel and tongs all over the room, and the mouse is gone. You can depend upon that. You're as safe here as you would be in your own rooms.

MRS. SOMERS. How can you say such a thing? No, I won't be responsible if anything happens. The mouse is in this room. No one has seen it go out, and it's here still.

MRS. BEMIS (*balancing herself with difficulty on her chair*). Oh, dear! how tippy it is! I'm sure it's going to break.

MRS. CURWEN. Get up here with me, Mrs. Bemis. We can protect each other.

MRS. MILLER. You would both fall off. Better come here on the sofa, Mrs. Bemis.

MRS. CURWEN. The mouse could run up that ottoman sofa as easily as the ground.

MRS. MILLER (*covering her face*). Oh, how can you say such a thing?

MRS. BEMIS. Oh, I know I'm going to fall!

MRS. SOMERS. Willis, for shame! Help her!

CAMPBELL. But how—how can I help—

MRS. SOMERS. Get her another chair.

CAMPBELL. Oh! (*He pushes a large armchair toward* MRS. BEMIS, *who leaps into it with a wild cry, spurning the reception chair half across the room in her flight.*)

MRS. BEMIS. Oh, thank you, thank you, Mr. Campbell! Oh, I shall always bless you!

MRS. CURWEN. Yes, you have saved all our lives. Where there's a man, I don't care for a thousand mice.

MRS. MILLER. Oh, how very frank!

MRS. CURWEN. Yes, I'm nothing if not open-minded.

CAMPBELL (*surveying her with amusement and interest*). I don't believe you're very much scared.

MRS. BEMIS. Oh yes, she is, Mr. Campbell. She keeps up that way, and then the first thing she faints.

MRS. CURWEN. Not on center tables, my dear; there isn't room.

CAMPBELL (*with increasing fascination*). Why don't you get down and set the rest an example of courage.

MRS. CURWEN. I prefer to set the example here; it's safer.

CAMPBELL. You look like the statue of some goddess on her altar—or saint—

MRS. CURWEN. Thank you. If you will say victim, I will agree with you. Say Iphigenia. But the others are too much. I draw the line at goddesses and saints.

CAMPBELL. And *you're* afraid of mice, too?

MRS. CURWEN. To be sure, I am.

CAMPBELL. Well, there is no mouse down here—nothing but a miserable man. Now, will you get down?

MRS. SOMERS. Mrs. Curwen, don't think of it! He's just saying it. The mouse *is* there. (*To* CAMPBELL) You are placing us all in a very ridiculous position.

CAMPBELL. I am sorry for that; I am, indeed. I give you my word of honor that I don't believe there's any mouse in the room.

MRS. SOMERS. But Jane saw it.

CAMPBELL. She *thought* she saw it, but I don't think she did. A lion would have been scared out by this time. (*A ring at the door is heard.*)

MRS. SOMERS. There, Jane, there's someone ringing! You must go to the door.

JANE (*throwing her apron over her head*). Oh, please, Mrs. Somers, I can't go! I'm so afraid of mice!

MRS. SOMERS. Nonsense! You *must* go. It's perfectly ridiculous your pretending not.

JANE. Oh, I couldn't, Mrs. Somers! I was always so from a child. I can't bear 'em.

MRS. SOMERS. This is disgraceful. Do you mean to say that you won't do what I ask you? Very well, then; you can *go!* You needn't stay the week out; I will pay you, and you can go at once. Do you understand?

JANE. Yes, I do, and I'd be glad to go this very minute, but I don't dare to get down.

MRS. SOMERS. But why shouldn't you get down? There isn't the least danger. Is there any danger now, Mr. Campbell?

CAMPBELL. Not the least in the world. Mouse gone long ago.

MRS. SOMERS. There!

JANE. I can't help it. There are so many in the dining room—

MRS. SOMERS. In *my* dining room? Oh, my goodness! Why didn't you tell me before?

JANE. And one ran right over my foot.

MRS. SOMERS. Your foot? Oh, I wonder that you live to tell it! Why haven't you put traps? Where's the cat?

JANE. The cook's spoiled the cat, feeding it so much.

MRS. MILLER. Yes, that's the worst of cooks: they always spoil cats.

MRS. BEMIS. They overfeed them.

MRS. MILLER. And then, of course, the cats are worth nothing as mousers. I had a cat— (*The bell sounds again.*)

MRS. SOMERS. There! Some one *must* go.

CAMPBELL. Why, *I'll* go to the door.

MRS. SOMERS. And leave *us* here? Never! How can you propose such a thing? If you dare to go I shall die. Don't think of such a thing.

JANE. The cook will go, if they keep ringing. Oh! ugh! hu, hu! When ever shall I get out of this?

MRS. SOMERS. Stop crying, Jane! Be calm! You're perfectly safe. You may be glad it's no worse. 'Sh! There's the cook going to the door at last. Who can it be? Listen!

JANE (*clutching* MRS. SOMERS). Oh! ugh! W-o-o-o-o!

ALL THE LADIES. E-e-e-e!

MRS. SOMERS. What's the *matter,* Jane? Let me go! *What's* the matter?

JANE. Oh, I thought I was falling— right down in among it!

MRS. AGNES ROBERTS (*calling up from below*). What in the world *is* it, Amy?

CAMPBELL. Oh, my prophetic soul, my sister!

MRS. SOMERS (*shouting*). Is that you, Agnes? Don't come up! Don't come up, for your *life!* Don't come up, unless you wish to perish instantly. Oh, it's dreadful, your coming now. Keep away! Go right straight out of the house, unless you wish to fling your life away.

THE OTHER LADIES. Don't come! Don't come! Keep away! It will do no good.

SCENE THREE

MRS. ROBERTS (*mounting the stairs, as if lured to her doom by an irresistible fascination*). Not come? Keep away? Who's talking? What is it? Oh, Amy, what is it? (*As she reaches the stair-landing space before the drawing room and looks in, where* CAMPBELL *stands in the middle of the floor with his hands in his pockets and despair in his face.*) You here, Willis? What are you doing? What is it? (*Her eye wanders to the ladies trembling in their several refuges, and a dawning apprehension makes itself seen in her face.*)

———

What is—Oh, it is—it isn't—it isn't a—mouse! Oh, *Amy!* Amy! Amy! Oh, how *could* you let me come right into the room with it? Oh, I never can forgive you! I thought it was somebody getting killed. Oh, why didn't you *tell* me it was a mouse? (*She alights on the piano-stool, and keeps it from rocking by staying herself with one hand on the piano-top.*)

CAMPBELL. Now look here, Agnes—

MRS. ROBERTS. Hush! Don't speak to me, Willis! You unnatural, cruel, heartless— Why did *you* let me come in? I wonder at you, Willis! If you had been *half* the brother you ought to be— Oh, dear, dear! I know how you will go away and laugh now and tell everybody. I suppose you think it corroborates that silly speech of yours before the legislative committee that's wounded all your best friends so, and that I've been talking myself perfectly dumb defending you about. (MRS. ROBERTS *unconsciously gives a little push for emphasis, and the stool revolves with her.*) E-e-e-e; Oh, Amy, how can you have one of these old-fashioned, horrid, whirling things, fit for nothing but boarding-house parlors!

MRS. SOMERS (*with just pique*). I'm very sorry you don't like my piano-stool, Agnes. I keep it because it was my poor mother's; but if you'll give me due notice another time I'll try to have a different—

MRS. ROBERTS (*bursting into tears*). Oh, don't say another word, Amy dear! I'm so ashamed of myself that I can hardly breathe now!

CAMPBELL. And I'm ashamed of you, too, Agnes! Get down off that stool, and behave yourself like a sensible woman. (*He goes toward her as if to lift her down.*) The mouse is gone long ago. And if it was here, it wouldn't bite you.

MRS. ROBERTS (*repelling him with one hand while she clings insecurely to the piano with the other*). Bite? Do you suppose I care for a mouse's

biting, Willis? I wouldn't care for the bite of an elephant. It's the *idea*. Can't you understand?

THE OTHER LADIES. Oh, yes, it's the idea.

MRS. SOMERS. Yes, I told him in the first place, Agnes, that it was the *idea* of a mouse.

MRS. CURWEN. It's the innate repugnance.

CAMPBELL. It's the enmity put between the mouse that tempted Eve and the woman—

MRS. ROBERTS. Don't be—sacrilegious, Willis! Don't, for your own sake!

MRS. SOMERS. Yes, it's very easy to make fun of the Bible.

MRS. ROBERTS. Or woman. And the wit is equally contemptible in either case.

MRS. MILLER. Other animals feel about mice just as we do. I was reading only the other day of an elephant —your mentioning an elephant reminded me of it, Mrs.—

MRS. ROBERTS. Oh!

THE OTHER LADIES. E-e-e-e!

MRS. SOMERS. What is it?

MRS. ROBERTS. Nothing. I thought I was going to fall. Go on, Mrs. Miller.

MRS. MILLER. Oh, it's merely that the elephant was asleep, and a mouse ran up its trunk—

ALL THE LADIES. Horrors!

MRS. MILLER. And the poor creature sprang up in the greatest alarm, and bellowed till it woke the whole menagerie. It simply shows that it isn't because women are nervously constituted that they're afraid of mice, for the nervous organism of an elephant—

MRS. SOMERS. The first time I went to Europe I found a mouse in one of my trunks. It was a steamer trunk that you push under the berth, and I've perfectly loathed them ever since.

MRS. BEMIS. Once in a farmhouse, where we were staying the summer, a mouse ran right across the table.

ALL THE LADIES. Oh!

MRS. CURWEN. One morning I found one in the bathtub.

ALL THE LADIES. *Oh*, Mrs. Curwen!

MRS. CURWEN. We'd heard it scrambling round all night. It was stone-dead.

ALL THE LADIES. Hideous!

CAMPBELL. Why, bless my soul, if the mouse was dead—

MRS. SOMERS. Then it was ten times as bad as if it was alive. Can't you understand? It's the *idea*. But, oh, don't let's talk of it any more, ladies! Let's talk of something else. Agnes, are you going to Mrs. Ransom's?

MRS. ROBERTS. I've been. Nearly everybody's coming away.

MRS. MILLER. Why, what time is it, Mrs. Somers?

MRS. SOMERS. I don't know.

CAMPBELL (*looking at his watch*). It's ten minutes of six, and I've missed my appointment.

MRS. CURWEN. And if we don't go now we shall miss the reception.

MRS. BEMIS. Papa was very particular I should go, because he couldn't.

MRS. MILLER. We must go at once.

MRS. SOMERS. Oh, I'm so sorry! Jane, go down with the ladies.

JANE. Oh, *please*, Mrs. Somers!

MRS. MILLER. But how are we to go? We are imprisoned here. We cannot get away. You must do something.

MRS. CURWEN. It is your house, Mrs. Somers. You are responsible.

MRS. SOMERS. But what can I do? I can't get down myself. And if I did, what good would it do?

MRS. ROBERTS. For shame, Willis, to laugh!

CAMPBELL. I wasn't laughing. I was merely smiling aloud.

MRS. ROBERTS. It's the same thing. You ought to think of something.

MRS. SOMERS. Oh, yes, do, Willis. Think of something for my—for goodness' sake, and I will always thank you. You're so ingenious.

CAMPBELL. Well, in the first place, I don't believe there's any mouse in the room.

MRS. SOMERS. That is nonsense; Jane saw it. Is that all your ingenuity amounts to?

MRS. ROBERTS (*electrically*). Amy, I have an idea!

MRS. SOMERS. Oh, Agnes! How *like* you!

MRS. ROBERTS. Not at all. It's the simplest thing in the world. It's the only way. And no thanks to Willis, either.

ALL THE LADIES. Well? Well? Well?

MRS. ROBERTS. It's just this: all make a rush, one after another, and the rest scream. And Willis must keep beating the floor.

MRS. SOMERS. How perfectly magnificent! Well, Agnes, you *have* got your wits about you! It is the very thing! Now, Mrs. Curwen, if you will jump down and make a rush—

MRS. CURWEN. It's for you to make the rush first, Mrs. Somers. You are the hostess.

MRS. SOMERS. Yes, but I'm not going, don't you see? I've sent my card to Mrs. Ransom.

MRS. CURWEN. Then, Mrs. Miller, will you, please—

MRS. MILLER. Mrs. Bemis is nearest the door. I think she will wish to start first.

MRS. BEMIS. No; I will wait for the rest.

MRS. SOMERS. That is a good idea. They ought to all rush together, not one after another. Don't you think so, Agnes?

MRS. ROBERTS. Yes, that was what I meant. And we ought to all scream just before they start, so as to scare it.

MRS. SOMERS. Oh, how capital! You *have* got a brain, Agnes! *Now* I begin to believe we shall live through it. And Mr. Campbell ought to beat the floor first, oughtn't he?

CAMPBELL. I haven't got anything to to beat it with. (*He looks about the room.*) But I can go down and get my cane.

ALL. No!

MRS. SOMERS. Jane will go down and get it for you.

JANE. Oh, I couldn't, Mrs. Somers!

CAMPBELL. Perhaps the poker—but it would spoil your carpet.

MRS. SOMERS. No matter for the carpet; you can beat it into—pulp. (*Campbell gets the poker and beats the carpet in different places.*) Harder! Beat harder!

MRS. ROBERTS. You're not beating at all, Willis. You're just—temporizing. (CAMPBELL *wildly thrashes the carpet.*)

MRS. SOMERS. There! That is something like. Now scream, Agnes! Scream, Mrs. Curwen! Mrs. Miller, Lou, scream, please!

ALL. E-e-e-e!

MRS. SOMERS. But nobody started!

MRS. CURWEN. I didn't believe the rest would start, and so *I* didn't.

MRS. MILLER. I was sure no one else would start.

MRS. BEMIS. So was I.

MRS. ROBERTS. We must have faith in one another, or else the plan's a failure. Now all scream! (*They scream.*)

MRS. SOMERS. E-e-e-e! Keep beating the carpet, Willis! Hard, hard, hard! (*The other* LADIES *all leap down from their perches, and rush screaming out of the drawing room, followed by* JANE —*with a whoop that prolongs itself into the depths of the basement, after the retreating wails and hysterical*

laughter of the ladies have died out through the street door.*) Oh, wasn't it splendid! It was a perfect success!

SCENE FOUR

CAMPBELL (*leaning on his poker and panting with exhaustion*). They got out alive.

MRS. SOMERS. And it was all Agnes' idea. Why, Agnes is gone, too!

CAMPBELL. Yes, Agnes is gone. I think it was a ruse of hers to save her own life. She's quite capable of it.

MRS. SOMERS (*with justice*). No, I don't think that. She was just carried away by the excitement of the moment.

CAMPBELL. At any rate, she's gone. And now, Amy, don't you think you'd better get down?

MRS. SOMERS (*in astonishment*). Get *down?* Why, you must be crazy. How can I get down if it's still there?

CAMPBELL. What?

MRS. SOMERS. The mouse.

CAMPBELL. But it *isn't* there, my dear. You saw for yourself that it wasn't there.

MRS. SOMERS. Did you see it run out?

CAMPBELL. No; but—

MRS. SOMERS. Very well, then, it's there still. Of course it is. I wouldn't get down for worlds.

CAMPBELL. Oh, good Heavens! Do you expect to spend the rest of your life up there in that chair?

MRS. SOMERS. I don't know. I shall not get down till I see that mouse leave this room.

CAMPBELL (*desperately*). Well, then, I must make a clean breast of it. There never was any mouse here.

MRS. SOMERS. What do you mean?

CAMPBELL. I mean that when we were talking—arguing—about the physical courage of women, I thought I would try a mouse. It's succeeded only too well. I'll never try another.

MRS. SOMERS. And could you really be guilty of such a cruel—

CAMPBELL. Yes.

MRS. SOMERS. Shameless—

CAMPBELL. I was.

MRS. SOMERS. Despicable deception?

CAMPBELL. It was vile, I know, but I did it.

MRS. SOMERS. I don't believe it. No, rather than believe that of *you*, Willis, I would believe there were a million mice in the room.

CAMPBELL. Amy, indeed—

MRS. SOMERS. No; if you could deceive me then, you can deceive me now. If you could say there was a mouse in the room when there wasn't, you are quite capable of saying there isn't when there is. You are just saying it now to get me to get down.

CAMPBELL. Upon my honor, I'm not.

MRS. SOMERS. Oh, don't talk to me of honor! The honor of a man who could revel—yes, *revel*—in the terrors of helpless women—

CAMPBELL. No, no; I'd no idea of it, Amy.

MRS. SOMERS. You will please not address me in that way, Mr. Campbell. You have forfeited all right to do so.

CAMPBELL. I know it. What I did was very foolish and thoughtless.

MRS. SOMERS. It was very low and ungentlemanly. I suppose you will go away and laugh over it with your—associates.

CAMPBELL. Why not say my ruffianly accomplices at once, Amy? No, I assure you that unless you tell of the affair, nobody shall ever hear of it from me. It's too disastrous a victory. I'm hoist by my own petard, caught in my own mouse-trap. There is such a thing as succeeding too well.

MRS. SOMERS. I should *think* you would be ashamed of it. Suppose you

have shown that women are nervous and excitable, does that prove anything?

CAMPBELL. Nothing in the world.

MRS. SOMERS. Very likely some of us will be sick from it. I dare say you think that would be another triumphant argument.

CAMPBELL. I shouldn't exult in it.

MRS. SOMERS. I don't know when I shall ever get over it myself. I have had a dreadful shock.

CAMPBELL. I'm sorry with all my heart—I am, indeed. I had no conception that you cared so much for mice—despised them so much.

MRS. SOMERS. Oh, yes, laugh, do! It's quite in character. But if you have such a contempt for women, of course you wouldn't want to *marry* one.

CAMPBELL. Yes, I should, my dear. But *only* one.

MRS. SOMERS. Very well, then! You can find some *other* one. All is over between *us*. Yes! I will send you back the precious gifts you have lavished upon me, and I will thank you for mine. A man who can turn the sex that his mother and sister belong to into ridicule can have no real love for his wife. I am glad that I found you out in time.

CAMPBELL. Do you really mean it, Amy?

MRS. SOMERS. Yes, I mean it. And I hope it will be a lesson to you. If you find any other poor, silly, trusting creature that you can impose yourself upon for a gentleman as you have upon me, I advise you to reserve your low, vulgar, boyish tricks till after she is helplessly yours, or she may tear your hateful ring from her finger and fling it— (*She attempts to pull a ring from her finger, but it will not come off.*) Never mind! I will get it off with a little soap-suds; and then—

CAMPBELL. Oh, no, my dear! Come, I can allow for your excitement, but I can't stand everything, though I admit everything. When a man has said he's played a silly part he doesn't like to be told so, and as for imposing myself upon you for a gentleman—you must take that back, Amy.

MRS. SOMERS. I do. I take it back. There hasn't been any imposture. I *knew* you were not a gentleman.

CAMPBELL. Very good! Then I'm not fit for a lady's company, and I don't deny, though you're so hard upon me, that you're a lady, Amy. Good-by. (*He bows, and walks out of the room.*)

MRS. SOMERS (*sending her voice after him in a wail of despair*). Willis!

CAMPBELL (*coming back*). Well?

MRS. SOMERS. I can't let you go. (*He runs toward her, but she shrinks back on her chair against the wall.*) No, no!

CAMPBELL (*hesitating*). Why did you call me back, then?

MRS. SOMERS. I—I didn't call you back; I just said—Willis.

CAMPBELL. This is unworthy—even of *you.*

MRS. SOMERS. Oh!

CAMPBELL. Do you admit that you have been too severe?

MRS. SOMERS. I don't know. What did I say?

CAMPBELL. A number of pleasant things: that I was a fraud, and no gentleman.

MRS. SOMERS. Did I say that?

CAMPBELL. Yes, you did.

MRS. SOMERS. I must have been very much incensed against you. I beg your pardon for—being so angry.

CAMPBELL. That won't do. I don't care how angry you are if you don't call me names. You must take them back.

MRS. SOMERS. Do you see my handkerchief anywhere about on the carpet?

CAMPBELL (*looking about, and then finding it*). Yes; here it is. (*He hands it to her, and she bends forward and takes it from him at arm's-length, whipping it nervously out of his hand.*) What's the matter?

MRS. SOMERS. Oh, nothing—nothing! Will you please give me my fan from the table there? (*He obeys, and she catches it from him as she has caught the handkerchief.*) Thank you! Keep away, please!

CAMPBELL (*angrily*). Really, this is too much. If you are afraid of touching me—

MRS. SOMERS. No, I don't mind touching you; that isn't it. But if you stood so near, don't you see, it might run up *you* and jump on to *me.*

CAMPBELL. What might?

MRS. SOMERS. You know. The mouse.

CAMPBELL. The mouse! There *is* no mouse.

MRS. SOMERS. That's what you said before.

CAMPBELL. Well, it's true. There isn't any mouse, and there never was.

MRS. SOMERS. There's the *idea.* And that's all I ever cared for.

CAMPBELL. Well, what are you going to do? I can't kill the idea of a mouse, and I can't drive it out of the room.

MRS SOMERS. I don't know what I'm going to do. I suppose I shall die here. (*She presses her handkerchief to her eyes.*) I shall never get out of the room alive. Then I hope you will be satisfied.

CAMPBELL. Amy, how can you say such things to me?

MRS. SOMERS. Oh, I suppose you're fond of me in your contemptuous way. I never denied that. And I'm sorry, I'm sure, if I wounded your feelings by anything I said.

CAMPBELL. Then you admit that I am a gentleman?

MRS. SOMERS. I didn't say that.

CAMPBELL. And I can't be satisfied with less. I'll own that I've been stupid, but I haven't been ungentlemanly. I can't remain unless you do.

MRS. SOMERS. And do you think threatening me is gentlemanly?

CAMPBELL. That isn't the question. Do you think I'm a gentleman?

MRS. SOMERS. You're what the *world* calls a gentleman—yes.

CAMPBELL. Do *you* think I'm one?

MRS. SOMERS. How can I tell? I can't think at all, perched up here.

CAMPBELL. Why don't you get down, then?

MRS. SOMERS. You know very well why.

CAMPBELL. But you'll have to get down some time. You can't stay there always.

MRS. SOMERS. Why should you care?

CAMPBELL. You know I do care. You know that I love you dearly, and that I can't bear to see you in distress. Shall I beat the carpet, and you scream and make a rush?

MRS. SOMERS. No; I haven't the strength for that. I should drop in a faint as soon as I touched the floor.

CAMPBELL. Oh, good Heavens! What am I going to do, then?

MRS. SOMERS. I don't know. You got me into the trouble. I should think you could get me out of it.

CAMPBELL (*after walking distractedly up and down the room*). There's only one way that I can think of, and if we're not engaged any longer it wouldn't do.

MRS. SOMERS (*yielding to her curiosity, after a moment's hesitation*). What is it?

CAMPBELL. Oh, unless we're still engaged, it's no use proposing it.

MRS. SOMERS. Can't you tell me without?

CAMPBELL. Impossible.

MRS. SOMERS (*looking down at her fan*). Well, suppose we are still engaged, then? (*Looking up*) Yes, say we *are* engaged.

CAMPBELL. It's to carry you out.

MRS. SOMERS (*recoiling a little*). Oh! Do you think that would be very nice?

CAMPBELL. Yes, I think it would. We can both scream, you know.

MRS. SOMERS. Yes?

CAMPBELL. And then you fling yourself into my arms.

MRS. SOMERS. Yes?

CAMPBELL. And I rush out of the room with you.

MRS. SOMERS (*with a deep breath*). I would never do it in the world.

CAMPBELL. Well, then, you must stay where you are.

MRS. SOMERS (*closing her fan*). You're not strong enough. (*She puts her handkerchief into her pocket.*) You would be sure to fall. (*She gathers her train in one hand.*) Well, then, look the other way! (CAMPBELL *turns his face aside and waits.*) No, I can't do it.

CAMPBELL (*retiring wrathfully to the other side of the room*). What shall we do, then?

MRS. SOMERS (*after reflection*). I don't know what we shall do. But if I were a man—

CAMPBELL. Well, if you were a man—

MRS. SOMERS. Don't you think Mrs. Curwen is fascinating?

CAMPBELL. *She* does.

MRS. SOMERS. You must admit she's clever? And awfully stylish?

CAMPBELL. I don't admit anything of the kind. She's always posing. I think she made herself ridiculous standing there on the table.

MRS. SOMERS (*fondly*). Oh, do you think so? You are very severe.

CAMPBELL. Come, now, Amy, what

has all this got to do with it?

MRS. SOMERS. Nothing. But if I were a man—

CAMPBELL. Well?

MRS. SOMERS. Well, in the first place, I wouldn't have got you wrought up so.

CAMPBELL. Well, but if you had! Suppose you had done all that I've done, and that I was up there in your place standing on a chair and wouldn't let you leave the room, and wouldn't get down and walk out, and wouldn't allow myself to be carried, what should you do?

MRS. SOMERS (*who has been regarding him attentively over the top of her fan, which she holds pressed against her face*). Why, I suppose if you wouldn't let me help you willingly—*I should use violence.*

CAMPBELL. You witch! (*As he makes a wild rush upon her, the curtain, which in the plays of this author has a strict regard for the* convenances, *abruptly descends.*)

SECRET SERVICE

William Gillette

First presented at the Garrick Theatre in New York on October 5, 1896.

GENERAL NELSON RANDOLPH, *commanding in Richmond*

MRS. GENERAL VARNEY, *wife of a Confederate officer of high rank*

EDITH VARNEY, *her daughter*

WILFRED VARNEY, *her youngest son*

CAROLINE MITFORD, *from across the street*

LEWIS DUMONT, *United States Secret Service—known in Richmond as Captain Thorne*

HENRY DUMONT, *United States Secret Service—*LEWIS DUMONT'*s brother*

MR. BENTON ARRELSFORD, *Confederate Secret Service*

MISS KITTRIDGE, *sewing for the hospitals*

MARTHA, *Negro house servant*

JONAS, *Negro house servant*

LIEUTENANT MAXWELL, *President's detail*

LIEUTENANT FORAY, *first operator, military telegraph lines*

LIEUTENANT ALLISON, *second operator, military telegraph lines*

LIEUTENANT TYREE, *artillery*

LIEUTENANT ENSING, *artillery*

SERGEANT WILSON

SERGEANT ELLINGTON

CORPORAL MATSON

CAVALRY ORDERLY

ARTILLERY ORDERLY

HOSPITAL MESSENGER

FIRST WAR DEPARTMENT MESSENGER

SECOND WAR DEPARTMENT MESSENGER

THIRD WAR DEPARTMENT MESSENGER

FOURTH WAR DEPARTMENT MESSENGER

TELEGRAPH OFFICE MESSENGER A

TELEGRAPH OFFICE MESSENGER B

EDDINGER

ACT ONE

The scene is a drawing room in GENERAL VARNEY's house on Franklin Street in Richmond. Eight o'clock.

A richly furnished room.—Southern characteristics.

(Fireplace on the left side. A wide door or arch up left or left center set diagonally, open to a front hall. The portieres on this door or arch draw, completely closing the opening. A stairway is seen through this door or arch, in the hall, at the back, ascending from a landing a few steps high back of the center of the opening, and rising off to the left. Entrance to the front hall—which communicates with other parts of the house, or via front door to the street, is off left below stairs. Entrance to the dining room and kitchen below stairs. Both of these openings are back of the wide door or arch. A wide door up center opens to a back parlor which is being used for women who come there to sew and work for hospitals. In elaborate production, when the doors are opened, these women are seen in the room at the back, seated at tables working. Two double French windows on the right side, one up stage set oblique, and one down, both opening to a wide veranda. There is shrubbery beyond the veranda and vines on the balustrade and the posts of the veranda—which must be in the line of sight for the whole house outside the upper of these two windows. Both these windows are "French," extending down to the floor, and opening and closing on hinges. They also have curtains or draperies which can easily be drawn to cover them. Below the window down right, a writing desk and a chair. Between these windows stand a pedestal and a vase of flowers to be knocked over by THORNE in Act Four. A chair near the pedestal. A chair and a cabinet right of center door against wall. Table up center or trifle left of center, on which is a lamp and vase of flowers. Couch down right center. Small table and two chairs left center. Chair each side of the fireplace at the left. Hall seat in the hall. Pedestal and statue on the landing in the hall. Dark or nearly dark outside the windows right with moonlight effect. The lights are on in the hall outside the door up left and in the room up center but are not glaring. The light in the room itself is full on but is shaded so that it gives a subdued effect. No fire is in the fireplace. The portieres on both windows closed at the rise. Windows are closed at the rise.

At the rise of the curtain, low, distant boom of cannonading rolls in the distance and quiets down—then is heard again.)

MISS KITTRIDGE, one of the women who is sewing for the hospitals, enters. She stops, listens to the sound of cannon with some anxiety—and crosses to the window up right and looks out. Flashes on her face. She turns and goes down toward the table at the left. She gathers up the pieces of cloth and linen rags that are on the table. Looks toward the window again. Then she takes the cloth off at the door up center, closing it carefully after her.

Sound of a heavy door closing outside up left.

Enter at the door from dining-room WILFRED VARNEY, a boy of about sixteen—impetuous—Southern—black-eyed—dark hair. He is fairly well dressed, but in a suit that has evident-

ly been worn for some time and is of a dark shade. He comes rapidly into the room, looking about. Goes to the door which he opens a little way and looks off. Closes it, goes to window up right. Throws open the portieres and windows and looks anxiously off. Red flashes on backing. Distant boom and low thunder of cannon.

Enter MARTHA, *an old Negro servant, through the door at the foot of the stairs.* WILFRED, *turning, sees her, and crosses toward her.*

———

WILFRED. Where's Mother?

MARTHA. She's up staars with Mars Howard, sah.

WILFRED. I've got to see 'er!

MARTHA. Mars Howard he's putty bad dis ebenin'—I dunno's she'd want to leave 'im—I'll go up an' see what she says. (*Goes out and up the stairway.*)

(WILFRED, *left alone, moves restlessly about, especially when low rumble of distant cannon is heard. Effect of passing artillery in the street outside. On hearing it, he hurries to the window and looks out, continuing to do so while the sounds of the passing guns, horses, and men are heard. While he is at the window,* MRS. VARNEY *comes down the stairway and enters. She is quiet, pale, with white or nearly white hair and a rather young face. Her dress is black and, though rich, is plain. Not in the least "dressy" or fashionable. In manner, she is calm and self-possessed. She stops and looks at* WILFRED *a moment. He turns and sees her.* MARTHA *follows her down the stairway and goes out the door at foot of the stairway.*)

WILFRED (*goes toward* MRS. VARNEY). Howard isn't worse is he?

MRS. VARNEY (*meeting* WILFRED *near center*). I'm afraid so.

WILFRED. Anything I can do?

MRS. VARNEY (*shakes head*). No—no. —We can only wait—and hope. (WILFRED *walks away a little, as if he could not quite say the thing on his mind.*) I'm thankful there's a lull in the cannonading. Do they know why it stopped?

(*Boom of cannon—a low distant rumble.*)

WILFRED. It hasn't stopped altogether—don't you hear?

MRS. VARNEY. Yes, but compared to what it was yesterday—you know it shook the house. Howard suffered dreadfully!

WILFRED (*suddenly faces her*). So did I, Mother! (*Slight pause. Low boom of cannon.*)

MRS. VARNEY. You!

WILFRED. When I hear those guns and know the fighting's on, it makes me—

MRS. VARNEY (*goes toward table; interrupting quickly*). Yes, yes—we all suffered—we all suffered dear! (*Sits right of table.*)

WILFRED. Mother—you may not like it but you must listen—(*Going toward her*)—you must let me tell you how—

MRS. VARNEY. Wilfred! (*He stops speaking. She takes his hand in hers tenderly. After a brief pause*) I know.

WILFRED (*low pleading voice*). But it's true Mother! I can't stay back here any longer! It's worse than being shot to pieces! I can't do it!

(MRS. VARNEY *looks steadily into* WILFRED'S *face but says nothing. Soon she turns away a little as if she felt tears coming into her eyes.*) Why don't you speak?

MRS. VARNEY (*turning to him; a faint attempt to smile*). I don't know what to say.

WILFRED. Say you won't mind if I go down there and help 'em!

MRS. VARNEY. It wouldn't be true!

WILFRED. I can't stay here!

MRS. VARNEY. You're so young!

WILFRED. No younger than Tom Kittridge—no younger than Ell Stuart —nor cousin Stephen—nor hundreds of the fellows fighting down there!— See Mother—they've called for all over eighteen—that was weeks ago! The seventeen call may be out any minute —the next one after that takes me! Do I want to stay back here till they *order* me out! I should think not! (*Walks about. Stops and speaks to* MRS. VAR-NEY.) If I was hit with a shell an' *had* to stay it would be different! But I can't stand this—I can't do it Mother!

MRS. VARNEY (*rising and going to him*). I'll write to your Father.

WILFRED. Why that'll take forever! You don't know where his Division is —they change 'em every day! I can't wait for you to write.

MRS. VARNEY (*speaks finally*). I couldn't let you go without his consent! You must be patient! (WILFRED *starts slowly across toward door at left, with head lowered in disappointment —but not ill-naturedly.* MRS. VARNEY *looks yearningly after him a moment as he moves away, then goes toward him.*) Wilfred! (WILFRED *turns and meets her and she holds him and smooths his hair a little with her hand.*) Don't feel bad that you have to stay here with your mother a little longer!

WILFRED. Aw—no—it isn't that!

MRS. VARNEY. Darling boy—I know it! You want to fight for your country —and I'm proud of you! I want my sons to do their duty! But with your father commanding a brigade at the front and one boy lying wounded— perhaps mortally— (*Pause.* MRS. VAR-NEY *turns and moves away a few steps toward the right.*)

WILFRED (*after pause, goes to her*). You will write to Father to-night— won't you?

MRS. VARNEY. Yes—yes! I'll write to him.

(*Doorbell is heard ringing in distant part of the house.* WILFRED *and* MRS. VARNEY *both listen.* MARTHA *enters from dining room and crosses outside door on her way to the front door. Heavy sound of door. In a moment she returns and stands in the wide doorway.*)

MARTHA. Hit's one o' de men fum de hossiple ma'am.

(WILFRED *hurries to door and exits to see the messenger.*)

MRS. VARNEY. We've just sent all the bandages we have, Martha.

MARTHA. He says dey's all used up, an' two more trains juss come in crowded full o' wounded sojers—an' mos' all of 'em dreful bad!

MRS. VARNEY. Is Miss Kittridge here yet?

MARTHA. Yass'm, she's yeah.

MRS. VARNEY. Ask her if they've got enough to send. Even if it's only a little, let them have it. What they need most is bandages.

MARTHA (*crossing toward door*). Yaas'm. (*Exits.*)

(MRS. VARNEY *goes toward the door from the front hall. Stops near the door and speaks a word to* MESSENGER *who is waiting at front door outside to attract his attention—then beckons him.*)

MRS. VARNEY. Oh— (*Beckoning*) Come in please! (*She moves toward center.*)

(MESSENGER *appears at the door from the front hall. He is a crippled soldier in battered Confederate uniform. His left arm is in a sling.*) What hospital did you come from?

MESSENGER (*remains near door*). The

Winder, ma'am.

MRS. VARNEY. Have you been to St. Paul's? You know the ladies are working there to-night.

MESSENGER. Yes—but they hain't a-workin' for the hospitals, ma'am—they're a-making sandbags for the fortifications.

MRS. VARNEY. I do hope we can give you something.

MESSENGER. Yes ma'am.

(MISS KITTRIDGE *enters at door up center, bringing a small bundle of lint, etc.*—MRS. VARNEY *moves down and soon seats herself on couch.*)

MISS KITTRIDGE. This is all there is now. (*She hands the package to the* MESSENGER.) If you'll come back in an hour we'll have more.

(MESSENGER *takes package and exits at door to front hall. Sound of heavy door closing outside.*)

We're all going to stay to-night, Mrs. Varney. There's so many more wounded come in it won't do to stop now.

MRS. VARNEY (*on couch*). No no—we mustn't stop.

MISS KITTRIDGE. Is—is your son—is there any change?

MRS. VARNEY. I'm afraid the fever's increasing.

MISS KITTRIDGE. Has the surgeon seen him this evening?

MRS. VARNEY. No—oh no! (*Shaking her head*) We couldn't ask him to come twice—with so many waiting for him at the hospital.

MISS KITTRIDGE. But they couldn't refuse *you* Mrs. Varney!—There's that man going right back to the hospital! I'll call him and send word that— (*Starting toward the door.*)

MRS. VARNEY (*rises*). No no—I can't let you!

MISS KITTRIDGE (*stops and turns to* MRS. VARNEY *in surprise*). Not for—your own son?

MRS. VARNEY. Think how many own sons must be neglected to visit mine twice!

(*Sound of door outside. Enter* EDITH VARNEY *at door from dining room, a light quick entrance, coming from outside, hat in hand as if taking it off as she comes in.*)

MRS. VARNEY (*meeting* EDITH). Edith dear! How late you are! You must be tired to death!

EDITH. Oh no I'm not!—Besides, I haven't been at the hospital *all* day. Good-by Miss Kittridge—I want to tell Mama something.

MISS KITTRIDGE. O dear! (*Turning up*) I'll get out of hearing right quick! (*Goes out.*)

EDITH (*up to door lightly and calling after* MISS KITTRIDGE). I hope you don't mind!

MISS KITTRIDGE (*as she exits*). Mercy no—I should think not! (EDITH *closes the door and goes to* MRS. VARNEY, *taking her down stage to chair right of table.* MRS. VARNEY *sits in chair and* EDITH *on stool close to her, in front of the table.*)

EDITH. Mama—what do you think? What *do* you think?

MRS. VARNEY. What is it dear?

EDITH. I've been to see the President!

MRS. VARNEY. Mr. Davis!

EDITH. Um hm! (*Assent*) An' I asked him for an appointment for Captain Thorne on the War Department Telegraph Service—an' he gave it to me—a Special Commission Mama —appointing him to duty here in Richmond—a very important position —so now he won't have to be sent back to the front—an' it'll be doing his duty just the same!

MRS. VARNEY. But Edith—you don't—

EDITH. Yes it will, Mama! The President told me they needed a man who understood telegraphing and who was of high enough rank to take charge of the Service! And you know Cap'n Thorne is an expert! Since he's been here in Richmond he's helped 'em in the telegraph office over an' over again—Lieutenant Foray told me so! (MRS. VARNEY *slowly rises and moves away. After a slight pause*) Now Mama, you're going to scold an' behave dreadfully—an' you mustn't—because it's all fixed—an' there's no trouble — an' the commission'll be sent over here in a few minutes—just as soon as it can be made out! An' the next time he comes I'm to hand it to him myself! (*Turns and moves away a little beyond the table.*)

MRS. VARNEY (*moves back toward table*). He's coming this evening.

EDITH (*turns quickly and looks at* MRS. VARNEY *an instant before speaking—then in low voice*). How do you know?

MRS. VARNEY (*moving toward table*). This note came half an hour ago. (*Reaching toward the note to get it for* EDITH. EDITH, *however, sees the note instantly, and impulsively snatches it.*)

EDITH. Has it been here—all this time? (*Takes note from the already opened envelope as she pauses and eagerly glances at it.*)

MRS. VARNEY (*after a moment*). You see what he says—this'll be his last call.—He's got his orders to leave. (*Sits right of table.*)

EDITH (*sitting on couch*). Why it's too ridiculous! Just as if the Commission from the President wouldn't supersede everything! It puts him at the head of the Telegraph Service! He'll be in the command of the Department!—He says— (*Glancing at note*) "good-by call" does he! All the better—it'll be that much more of a surprise. (*Rising and going toward* MRS.

VARNEY) Now Mama, don't you breathe—I want to tell him myself!

MRS. VARNEY. But Edith dear—I don't quite approve of your going to the President about this.

EDITH (*changing from light manner to earnestness*). But listen, Mama—I couldn't go to the War Department people—Mr. Arrelsford's there in one of the offices—and ever since I refused him you know how he's treated me!— (*Slight deprecatory motion from* MRS. VARNEY) If I'd applied for the appointment there he'd have had it refused—and he'd have got them to order Cap'n Thorne away right off—I know he would—and— (*Stands motionless, as she thinks of it.*) That's where his orders to go came from!

MRS. VARNEY. But my dear—

EDITH. It is, Mama! (*Slight pause*) Isn't it lucky I got that commission today! (*Emphasis on "Isn't."*)

(*Doorbell rings in distant part of the house.* JONAS *appears above door from dining room and goes to front door.* MRS. VARNEY *moves up stage a little, waiting to see who it is.* EDITH *listening. Heavy sound of door closing outside.* JONAS *enters at the door from the hall.*)

JONAS (*coming down right of* MRS. VARNEY). It's a officer, ma'am. He says he's fum de President—an'— (*Hands a card to* MRS. VARNEY.) he's got ter see Miss Edith pussonully.

EDITH (*going up center a little; low voice*). It's come, Mama!

MRS. VARNEY (*rises and goes up center*). Ask the gentleman in. (JONAS *exits at door.* MRS. VARNEY *gives* EDITH *the card.*)

EDITH (*after a glance at the card*). Oh yes!

MRS. VARNEY (*low voice*). Do you know who it is?

EDITH (*low voice*). No! But he's

from the President so it must be the Commission!

JONAS (*enters from the hall. He comes on a little way, bowing someone in.* LIEUTENANT MAXWELL *follows. He is a very dashing young officer, handsome, polite, and dressed in a showy and perfectly fitting uniform.* JONAS *goes out door to dining room.* MRS. VARNEY *advances a little.*)

LIEUT. MAXWELL. Good evening. (*Bowing.* MRS. VARNEY *bows slightly. To* MRS. VARNEY) Have I the honah of addressing Miss Varney?

MRS. VARNEY. I am Mrs. Varney, sir. (*Emphasizing "Mrs." a little.*)

LIEUT. MAXWELL (*bowing to* MRS. VARNEY). Madam—I'm very much afraid this looks like an intrusion on my part, but I come from the President and he desires me to see Miss Varney personally!

MRS. VARNEY (*inclining her head graciously*). Anyone from the President could not be otherwise than welcome.—This is my daughter. (*Indicating* EDITH.)

LIEUT. MAXWELL (*bows to* EDITH *and she returns the salutation. He then walks across to her, taking a large brown envelope from his belt*). Miss Varney, the President directed me to deliver this into your hands—with his compliments. (*Handing the envelope to* EDITH) He is glad to be able to do this not only at your request, but as a special favor to your father, General Varney.

EDITH (*taking envelope*). Oh thank you!

MRS. VARNEY. Won't you be seated, Lieutenant?

EDITH (*in front*). O yes—do! (*Holds envelope pressed very tight against her side.*)

LIEUT. MAXWELL. Nothing would please me so much I assure you—but I'm compelled to be back at the President's house right away—I'm on duty this evening.—Would you mind writing me off a line or two Miss Varney —just to say you have the communication?

EDITH. Why certainly!— (*Takes a step or two toward desk at right.*) You want a receipt—I— (*Stops, hesitating, then turns and crosses toward door.*) I'll go upstairs to my desk—it won't take a minute! (*Turns at door.*) And—could I put in how much I thank the President for his kindness?

LIEUT. MAXWELL. I'm very sure he'd be more than pleased! (EDITH *exits and hastens up the stairway.*)

MRS. VARNEY (*moving forward slowly*). We haven't heard so much cannonading today, Lieutenant. Do they know what it means?

LIEUT. MAXWELL (*going forward with* MRS. VARNEY). I don't think they're quite positive ma'am, but they can't help lookin' for a violent attack to follow.

MRS. VARNEY. I don't see why it should quiet down before an assault!

LIEUT. MAXWELL. It might be some signal, ma'am, or it might be they're moving their batteries to open on a special point. They're tryin' ev'ry way to break through our defenses—ev'ry way they know!

(*Doorbell rings in distant part of house.*)

MRS. VARNEY. It's very discouraging! (*Seats herself right of table.*) We can't seem to drive them back this time!

LIEUT. MAXWELL. No ma'am, but we're holding 'em where they are! They're no nearer now than they were six weeks ago, an' they'll never get in unless they do it by some scurvy trick —that's where the danger lies!

(*Heavy sound of door outside*)

EDITH (*coming lightly and quickly*

down the stairway, enters with a note in her hand, and without the official envelope, which she has left in her room). Is Lieutenant Maxwell— (Seeing him with MRS. VARNEY *and going toward him)* O yes!

(LIEUTENANT MAXWELL *moves to meet* EDITH.)

JONAS (*enters from the hall as* EDITH *reaches center, showing in* CAPTAIN THORNE. *As he stands back for* THORNE *to pass*). Will you jess kinely step dis way, suh!

(MRS. VARNEY *rises and moves down in front of and then up left of table.* MAXWELL *meets* EDITH.)

EDITH (*meeting* MAXWELL). I didn't know but you— (*She stops—hearing* JONAS—*and quickly turns, looking off left.*) Oh!—Captain Thorne!

(CAPTAIN THORNE *enters from hall, meeting and shaking hands with* EDITH. THORNE *wears the uniform of a Confederate Captain of Artillery. It is somewhat worn and soiled.* LIEUTENANT MAXWELL *turned and moved up a little on* EDITH'*s entrance, remaining a little right of center.* JONAS *exits to dining room.* EDITH *gives* THORNE *her hand briefly.*)
We were expecting you!—Here's Captain Thorne, Mama!

(MRS. VARNEY *moves up to meet* THORNE, *shaking hands with him graciously.* EDITH *turns away and goes to* LIEUTENANT MAXWELL. THORNE *and* MRS. VARNEY *move near small table and converse.*)
I wasn't so very long writing it, was I, Lieutenant? (*She hands* LIEUTENANT MAXWELL *the note.*)

LIEUT. MAXWELL. I've never seen a quicker piece of work, Miss Varney. (*Putting the note in belt or pocket*) When you want a clerkship ovah at the Government offices you must shorely let me know!

EDITH (*smilingly*). You'd better not commit yourself—I might take you at your word!

LIEUT. MAXWELL. Nothing would please me so much I'm sure! All you've got to do is just to apply!

EDITH. Lots of the girls are doing it—they have to, to live! Aren't there a good many where you are?

LIEUT. MAXWELL. Well, we don't have so many as they do over at the Treasury. I believe there are more ladies there than men!

MRS. VARNEY (*comes down a little*). Perhaps you gentlemen have met!— (*Glancing toward* LIEUTENANT MAXWELL *and back to* THORNE. THORNE *shakes head a little and takes a step forward, facing* MAXWELL.) Cap'n Thorne—Lieutenant Maxwell.

THORNE (*slight inclination of head*). Lieutenant.

LIEUT. MAXWELL (*returning bow pleasantly*). I haven't had that pleasure—though I've heard the Cap'n's name mentioned several times!

THORNE. Yes?

(MRS. VARNEY *and* EDITH *are looking at* MAXWELL.)

LIEUT. MAXWELL (*as if it were rather amusing*). In fact, Cap'n, there's a gentleman in one of our offices who seems mighty anxious to pick a fight with you!

(EDITH *is suddenly serious, and a look of apprehension spreads over* MRS. VARNEY'*s face.*)

THORNE (*easily*). Pick a fight! Really! Why, what office is that, Lieutenant?

LIEUT. MAXWELL (*slightly annoyed*). The War Office, sir!

THORNE. Oh, dear! I didn't suppose you had anybody in the *War* Office who wanted to fight!

LIEUT. MAXWELL (*almost angry*). An' why not, sir?

THORNE (*easily*). Well, he'd hardly

be in an office would he—at a time like this?

LIEUT. MAXWELL (*trying to be light again*). I'd better not tell him that, Cap'n—he'd certainly insist on havin' you out!

THORNE (*moving down left center with* MRS. VARNEY). That would be too bad—to interfere with the gentleman's office hours! (THORNE *and* MRS. VARNEY *move down left center near table—in conversation.*)

LIEUT. MAXWELL (*to* EDITH). He doesn't believe it, Miss Varney—but it's certainly true, an' I dare say you know who the—

EDITH (*quickly interrupting* MAX-WELL, *in a low voice*). Please don't, Lieutenant! — I — (*An apprehensive glance toward* THORNE) I'd rather not— (*With a slight catch of breath*) —talk about it!

LIEUT. MAXWELL (*after short pause of surprise*). Yes, of course!—I didn't know there was any—

EDITH (*interrupting again, with attempt to turn it off*). Yes! (*A rather nervous effort to laugh lightly*) —You know there's always the weather to fall back on!

LIEUT. MAXWELL (*picking it up easily*). Yes—an' mighty bad weather too —most of the time!

EDITH (*laughingly*). Yes—Isn't it!

(*They laugh a little and go on talking and laughing to themselves, moving toward right upper window for a moment and soon move across toward door as if* MAXWELL *were going.*)

MRS. VARNEY (*back of table, right of* THORNE). From your note, Captain Thorne, I suppose you're leaving us soon. Your orders have come.

THORNE (*back of table, left of* MRS. VARNEY). Yes—Mrs. Varney, they have. —I'm very much afraid this 'll be my last call.

MRS. VARNEY. Isn't it rather sudden? It seems to me they ought to give you a little time.

THORNE (*slight smile*). We have to be ready for anything, you know!

MRS. VARNEY (*with a sigh*). Yes—I know!—It's been a great pleasure to have you drop in on us while you were here. We shall quite miss your visits.

THORNE (*a slight formality in manner*). Thank you, Mrs. Varney—I shall never forget what they've been to me.

(MAXWELL *is taking leave of* EDITH.)

EDITH. Lieutenant Maxwell is going, Mama!

MRS. VARNEY. So soon! Excuse me a moment, Captain! (*Goes hurriedly toward* MAXWELL. THORNE *goes down left of table near mantel.*) I'm right sorry to have you hurry away, Lieutenant. We shall hope for the pleasure of seeing you again. (*Right of* MAX-WELL.)

LIEUT. MAXWELL. I shall certainly call, Mrs. Varney—if you'll allow me.— (*Goes toward door.*) —Cap'n! (*Salutes* THORNE *from near door.*)

THORNE (*turning from mantel, half salute*). Lieutenant!

LIEUT. MAXWELL. Miss Varney! Mrs. Varney! (*Bowing to each. Exits to hall.*)

MRS. VARNEY (*follows* MAXWELL *off, speaking as she goes*). Now remember, Lieutenant, you're to come sometime when duty doesn't call you away so soon!

(EDITH *turns and moves slowly to table up center on* MAXWELL's *exit.*)

LIEUT. MAXWELL (*outside, voice getting more distant*). Trust me to attend to that, Mrs. Varney!

(*Sound of heavy door closing.*)

THORNE (*moving toward* EDITH *who is at small table*). Shall I see Mrs. Varney again?

EDITH (*getting a rose from vase on table up center*). Oh, yes—you'll see her again!

THORNE (*at the little table near EDITH, on her left*). I haven't long to stay.

EDITH. Oh—not long!

THORNE. No—I'm sorry to say.

EDITH (*moving slowly down left center*). Well—do you know—I think you have more time than you really think you have! It would be odd if it turned out that way—wouldn't it? (*Plays with the flower in her hand.*)

THORNE (*moves as EDITH does*). Yes —but it won't turn out that way.

EDITH. Yes—but you— (*She stops as THORNE is taking the rose from her hand—which she was holding up in an absent way as she talked. THORNE at the same time holds the hand she had it in. She lets go of the rose and draws away her hand. Slight pause, and then, a little embarrassed.*) You know—you can sit down if you want to! (*Indicating chair at left of table.*)

THORNE (*smiles a little*). Yes—I see. (*He has the rose.*)

EDITH (*sits right of table*). You'd better!—I have a great many things to say!

THORNE. Oh—you have!

EDITH (*nodding; her left hand on the table*). Yes.

THORNE. I have only one.

EDITH (*looking up at him*). And— that is—?

THORNE (*leaning toward her over table, covering her hand with his*). Good-by.

EDITH. But I don't really think you'll have to say it!

THORNE (*earnestly, looking down into her eyes*). I know I will!

EDITH (*low voice, more serious*). Then it'll be because you want to!

THORNE (*quickly*). Oh, no! It will

be—because I must.

EDITH (*rising slowly and looking at him a little mischievously as she does so*). Oh—because you must! (THORNE nods a little—saying "yes" with his lips. EDITH *walks toward center thinking how to tell him. He watches her. She suddenly turns back and goes to table.*) You don't know some things I do! (*She sits in chair right of table.*)

THORNE (*laughing a little at first*). I think that's more than likely, Miss Varney! (*Moves to left of table and seats himself in chair facing EDITH.*) Would you mind telling me a few so I can somewhat approach you in that respect?

EDITH (*seriously*). I wouldn't mind telling you one, and that is, it's very wrong for you to think of leaving Richmond yet!

THORNE. Ah—but you don't—

EDITH (*breaking in, quickly*). Oh, yes, I do!

THORNE (*looking up at her, amused*). Well—what?

EDITH. Whatever you were going to say! Most likely it was that there's something or other I don't know about!—But I know this— (*Looking away, eyes lowered a little*) You were sent here only a few weeks ago to recover from a very bad wound— (THORNE *looks down and a little front quickly.*) —and you haven't nearly had time for it yet!

THORNE (*as if amused*). Ha, ha—yes. (*Looking up at EDITH with usual expression*) I do look as if the next gentle breeze would blow me away, don't I?

EDITH (*turning to him earnestly, half rising*). No matter how you look, you ought not—Oh— (*Rising fully, turning away from him*) You're just making fun of it like you always do! (*Goes up center a little. Turns to*

THORNE *again a little up center.*) No matter! You can make all the fun you like, but the whole thing is settled and you aren't going away at all!

THORNE (*has risen with* EDITH *and stands near table left center watching her smilingly, his hat in left hand*). Oh—I'm *not!*

EDITH. No—you're *not!* Doesn't that surprise you?

THORNE. Well rather! (*Puts hat on table and moves up near* EDITH, *going back of table.*) Now you've gone into the prophesying business perhaps you wouldn't mind telling me what I am going to do?

EDITH (*up center a little, turning to him*). I wouldn't mind at all—an' it's this—you see I've been to the— (*Hesitates.*) Now! I'm almost afraid to tell you!

THORNE (*near* EDITH, *left of her*). Don't tell me Miss Varney—because it's true that my orders have come— I'm leaving tonight.

EDITH (*looks at* THORNE *an instant, then turns and sits on couch. Turns and looks at him from there, after an instant*). Where—to the front?

THORNE (*moving easily to the couch where* EDITH *sits*). Well— (*Little laugh*) you see we—(*Sits on couch near* EDITH.) we can't always tell where orders will take us Miss Varney.

EDITH. But listen! Supposing there were other orders—from a higher authority—appointing you to duty here?

THORNE (*eyes lowered*). It wouldn't make any difference.

EDITH (*sudden alarm*). You don't— you don't mean you'd go—in spite of them?

(THORNE *raises his eyes to hers in slight surprise and looks at her an instant. Then he nods affirmatively.*) But if it proved your first order was a mistake—and— (*In her earnestness,* she makes a little motion with her left hand within his reach.)

THORNE (*catching her hand and holding it close in both of his*). My first order isn't a mistake Miss Varney.—I—I don't suppose I shall ever see you— (*He stops suddenly—then rises quickly, moves a little, stands facing toward window.*)

EDITH (*after watching* THORNE *until he is motionless, rises and crosses up to left of him; with a new apprehension*). Is it—is it something dangerous?

THORNE (*turning to* EDITH *and speaking lightly*). Well I hope so— enough to make it interesting!

EDITH (*low voice*). Don't be angry if I ask you again about your orders— I—Oh I must know!

THORNE. Why?

EDITH. Tell me!—Please tell me!

THORNE. I can't do that Miss Varney.

EDITH. You needn't! I know!

(THORNE *gives a very slight apprehensive glance to down left but instantly back to her.*) They're sending you on some mission where death is almost certain! They'll sacrifice your life because they know you are fearless and will do *anything!* There's a chance for you to stay here in Richmond and be just as much use —and I'm going to ask you to do this! It isn't *your* life alone—there are other lives to think of—that's why I ask you! —It may not sound well—but—you see—

THORNE (*catching her hands passionately*). Ah, my dear one—my dear —my darling—how can I— (*Suddenly stops. Recovers control of himself.*) No! (*Head turned slightly away*) You shan't have this against me too!

EDITH. Oh, no! No! I could never have anything against you!—What do you mean?

THORNE (*holding her hands close*). I mean that I must go—my business is elsewhere—I ought never to have seen you or spoken to you—but I had to come to this house—and you were here—and now it's only you in the— (*Stops. Releases her hands. Turns blindly right. Then turns toward door.*) Your mother—I'll say good-by to her!

EDITH (*stepping quickly in his way*). No!—You must listen! (THORNE *stops before her.*) They need you here in Richmond more than anywhere else— the President told me so himself!— Your orders are to stay! You are given a Special Commission on the War Department Telegraph service, and you—

THORNE (*quickly, decisively, but in subdued voice*). No, no! I won't take it! I couldn't take it, Miss Varney!

EDITH. You'll do that much for me!

THORNE (*seizing her hands again*). It's for you that I'll do nothing of the kind! If you ever think of me again remember that I refused it!

EDITH (*breaking into* THORNE'S *last few words*). You can't refuse! It's the President's request—it's his order! (*Breaking away from him and going toward door*) Please wait a minute! I left it upstairs and you'll see for yourself that—

THORNE. Don't get it Miss Varney! (*Following her*) I won't look at it!

EDITH (*stops and turns*). But I want you to see what it is! It puts you at the head of everything! You have entire control! When you see it I know you'll accept! Please wait! (EDITH *exits at door and runs lightly up the stairway.*)

THORNE (*following her toward stairway*). Miss Varney—I can't—

EDITH (*as she goes*). Oh, yes, you can! (THORNE *stands looking up the stair-way after* EDITH *for an instant. Then turns and hurries down to the table and, seizing his hat and the rose, starts rapidly up toward the door, as if to go. As* THORNE *starts down for hat, sound of heavy door closing outside.* CAROLINE MITFORD *skips in lightly, crossing in front of* THORNE—*who has stepped out of the way. She is breathless from having run across the street. Her dress is made of her great-grand-mother's wedding gown—as light and pretty as possible—with a touch of the old-fashioned in cut and pattern. She is very young and charming.*)

CAROLINE (*comes in quickly, stops abruptly*). Oh!—Cap'n Thorne!

THORNE (*saluting mechanically*). Miss Mitford! (*Turns and looks up the stairway again.*)

CAROLINE (*saluting*). Yes of co'se— I forgot!—How lucky this is! You're just the very person I wanted to see! (*Going toward couch*) I'll tell you all about it in just a minute! Good-ness me! (*Sits on couch.*) I'm all out o' breath—just runnin' ovah from our house! (*Devotes herself to breathing for a moment.*)

THORNE (*going quickly down to* CAROLINE). Miss Mitford—would you do something for me!

CAROLINE. Why, of co'se I would!

THORNE (*rapidly*). Thank you very much!—Tell Miss Varney when she comes down—Just say good-night for me and tell her I've gone!

CAROLINE (*pretending astonish-ment*). Why I wouldn't do such a thing for the wide wide world! It would be a wicked dreadful lie—be-cause you *won't* be gone!

THORNE. Well I'm sorry you look at it that way.—Good-night Miss Mit-ford! (*Turns to go.*)

CAROLINE (*jumping to her feet and running round on his left between him and the door).* No, no!—You don't seem to understand! I've got something to say to you!

THORNE *(hurriedly).* Yes—I understand that all right—but some other time! *(Trying to pass* CAROLINE.)

CAROLINE *(detaining him).* No, no, no!—Wait! *(*THORNE *stops.)* There isn't any other time! It's to-night!— We're going to have a Starvation Party!

THORNE. Good heavens—another of those things!

CAROLINE. Yes, we are! It's goin' to be ovah at mah house this time! Now we'll expect you in half an hour. *(Her finger up to emphasize the time.)*

THORNE. Thank you very much, Miss Mitford, but I can't come! *(Indicating off left)* I've got to be—

CAROLINE *(interrupting).* N—n—n— *(Until she quiets him)* Now that wouldn't do at all! You went to Mamie Jones's! Would you treat me like that?

THORNE. Mamie Jones—that was last week Thursday— *(*CAROLINE *trying to stop him with "now—now—now!" etc.)* and her mother— *(*CAROLINE *louder with "now—now!"—*THORNE *raises his voice above the din.)* Her mother — *(As* CAROLINE *is still going on, he gives up and turns front in despair.)*

CAROLINE *(when quiet has come, very distinctly).* Now, there isn't any use o' talkin'!

THORNE. Yes, I see that!

CAROLINE. Didn't you promise to obey when I gave orders? Well these are orders!

THORNE *(turning to her for a last attempt).* Yes, but this time—

CAROLINE. This time is just the same as all the other times only *worse!* *(Turns away and goes to back of table and picks up something from table.* THORNE *turns and goes a little way*

toward right center, as if discouraged.)

CAROLINE *(without turning).* Besides that, she expects it.

THORNE *(turns and looks across at* CAROLINE). What did you say?

CAROLINE *(at table, smelling a flower daintily, facing front).* I say she expects it—that's all!

THORNE. Who do you mean? *(Moves toward her inquiringly.)*

CAROLINE *(turns and looks at him).* Who?

THORNE *(assent).* Um hm!

CAROLINE *(innocently).* Who expects you?

THORNE *(assent again).* Ah ha!

CAROLINE. Why, Edith of co'se! Who did you s'pose I was talkin' about all this time?

THORNE. You mean—you mean she expects me to— *(Slight motion of hand toward door.)*

CAROLINE. Why, of co'se she does!— Just to take her ovah that's all!— Goodness me—you needn't *stay* if you don't want to! Now I'll go an' tell her you're waiting—that's what I'll do! *(Starts toward door. Stops and turns.)* You won't go now? *(Emphasize "go.")*

THORNE *(hesitating).* Well—e—I—I— If she expects it, Miss Mitford. *(Moves up toward* CAROLINE.) I'll wait an' take her over—but I can't stay at your party a minute!

CAROLINE. I *thought* you'd come to your senses some time or other!—You don't seem to quite realize what you've got to do!—See here, Mr. Captain— *(Taking hold of the left sleeve of his coat and bringing him down center a little way)* Was she most ready?

THORNE. Well—e—how do I—how—

CAROLINE. What dress did she have on?

THORNE. Dress?—Why, I hardly—

CAROLINE. Oh, you *men!* Why, she's only got two!

THORNE (*relieved*). Yes—well then, very likely this was one of them, Miss Mitford!

CAROLINE (*starting toward door*). Oh, no mattah—I'm going up anyhow!

(THORNE *moves up as* CAROLINE *goes.* CAROLINE *stops near door and turns back to* THORNE.)

Cap'n Thorne—you can wait out there on the veranda! (*Pointing to window.*)

THORNE (*glances where she points, then to her*). Yes of course—but if I wait right here I can see her when she—

CAROLINE (*majestically*). Those are orders! (THORNE *looks at her an instant—then salutes and wheels about, making complete military turn to right and marches toward the window at right.* CAROLINE *is watching him admiringly. Speaks as* THORNE *reaches right center.*) It's cooler outside, you know!

THORNE (*turning to her at up right center and standing in stiff military attitude*). Pardon me, Miss Mitford—orders never have to be explained!

CAROLINE. That's right!—I take back the explanation! (*Taking one step to her right as she gives an odd little salute.*)

THORNE (*with deferential salute in slight imitation of hers, but with step to his left*). That's right, Miss Mitford —take it back! (*Turns and is reaching to pull aside curtains of window up right with right hand.*)

CAROLINE. And—oh, yes—Cap'n! (THORNE *turns to her again questioningly—right hand still holding curtain behind him. A peremptory order.*) Smoke! (*For an instant,* THORNE *does not understand. Then he sees it and relapses at once into easy manner, stepping forward a little and feeling* with right hand in breast of coat front for cigar—turning somewhat to front.)

THORNE (*as above*). Oh—ha, ha— (*Smiling*) you mean one of those Nashville sto—

CAROLINE. Silence, sir! (THORNE *looks at her quickly.*) Orders never have to be explained!

THORNE (*with a salute*). Right again, Miss Mitford—orders never have to be explained! (*Salutes, turns, and goes off at window up right.*)

CAROLINE (*looks admiringly after* THORNE). He's splendid! If Wilfred was only like that! (*Moves slowly, thinking it over.*) But then—our engagement's broken off anyhow, so what's the diff!—Only—if he was like that I'd—no! I don't think I would either! (*Shakes her head.*) No!—Still —I must say it would make a heap of difference! An' then if he was like that— (*In same tone, seeing* MRS. VARNEY *close to her*) Why, howdy do!

MRS. VARNEY (*entered earlier from the front hall, and noticing* CAROLINE, *has come down to her on her left*). Why, Caroline dear, what are you talking about all to yourself?

CAROLINE (*confused*). Oh—just—I was just saying you know—that—why I don't know—I don't really know what I was goin' to—e—Do you think it's goin' to rain?

MRS. VARNEY. Dear me, child—I haven't thought about it!—Why what have you got on? Is that a new dress?

CAROLINE. New *dress!* Well I should think it was—I mean *is!* These are my great-grandmother's mother's weddin' clothes! Aren't they just the most beaufleist you ever saw! Just in the nick of time too! I was on my very last rags, an' I didn't know what to do—an' Mama gave me a key and told me to look in an old horsehair trunk in the attic—an' I did—and these were in it! (*Takes a dance step or two, holding skirt out.*) Just in time for the Starvation Party to-night! Ran ovah to show it to Edith—where is she?

MRS. VARNEY. She won't be over tonight, I'm afraid.

CAROLINE. Oh, yes she will!

MRS. VARNEY. But I've just come down, dear!

CAROLINE. Yes, but I'm just going up, dear! (*Turns and runs up the stairway, disappearing at the upper landing.*)

MRS. VARNEY (*alone a moment. After a little she moves forward in thought, then turns to desk and prepares to write a letter. Suddenly* CAROLINE *races down the stairs again and runs lightly on.* MRS. VARNEY *looks up surprised.* CAROLINE *hurries across toward window, as if going out*). You see, Caroline, it was no use!

CAROLINE (*turning*). No use! (*Comes down in front of couch near* MRS. VARNEY.)

MRS. VARNEY (*at desk*). Why, you don't mean—in this short time—

CAROLINE. Goodness me! I didn't stop to argue with her—I just *told* her!

MRS. VARNEY. Told her what, child!

CAROLINE. Why—that Cap'n Thorne was waitin' for her out yere on the v'randah!

MRS. VARNEY. But she isn't going, is she?

CAROLINE. Well, I wouldn't like to say for sure— (*Moving nearer* MRS. VARNEY *and in lower voice*) but you just watch which dress she has on when she comes down! Now, I'll go out there an' tell him she'll be down in a minute—then the whole thing's finished up all round! (*Turns and goes around couch and toward window, speaking as she goes.*) I have more work getting people fixed up so they can come to my party than it

would take to run a blockade into Savannah every fifteen minutes! (*She runs lightly off at window.*)

(MRS. VARNEY *looks after* CAROLINE *with a smile and then, taking some paper and envelopes in her hand, rises and moves as if to go to door. Enter* WILFRED *at door from hall, coming in as though he wished to avoid being seen, and looking up the stairway as he enters. He carries a large bundle stuffed loosely under his coat, which is done up in a paper. He turns quickly on seeing* MRS. VARNEY *and makes a very slight movement as if to better conceal the package he carries. Stands looking at her.*)

MRS. VARNEY. What have you got there, Wilfred?

WILFRED. Here?

MRS. VARNEY. Yes—under your coat.

WILFRED. Oh—this! (*Tapping the place where his coat protrudes*) Why, it's only a—that is, it's one of the—e— Have you written that letter yet?

MRS. VARNEY. No, dear, I've been too busy. But I'm going to do it right now. (MRS. VARNEY *goes across to door. Near the door, she glances round a little anxiously at* WILFRED. *He is looking at her. Then she turns, exits, and goes up the stairway.* WILFRED *turns away after she has gone. Glances round room. Goes to table and begins to undo the package cautiously. He has hardly more than loosened the paper when* CAROLINE *appears at window up right.*)

CAROLINE (*speaking off, at window up right*). Those are orders Cap'n— an' orders never have to be explained!

(WILFRED *hurriedly stuffs the loosened bundle inside his coat again.*)

THORNE (*outside the window up right*). Right you are Miss Mitford! I'll see that they're carried out!

(CAROLINE *enters through window,*

closing it after her, but does not close the portieres. WILFRED *is about to start toward down left.* CAROLINE, *turning from window, sees* WILFRED. *Both stand an instant.*)

CAROLINE (*after the pause*). Good evening (*With emphasis*) Mr. Varney!

WILFRED (*coldly*). Good evening (*With emphasis*) Miss Mitford!

(*Both start rapidly toward door, but, as it brings them toward each other, stop simultaneously in order to avoid meeting in the doorway.*)

CAROLINE. Excuse me—I'm in a great hurry!

WILFRED. That's plain enough! (*Looks at her.*) Another party (*With contemptuous emphasis*) I reckon!

CAROLINE. You reckon perfectly correct—it *is* another party! (*Turns and moves slowly down toward center.*)

WILFRED. Dancing! (*Moves down left center.*)

CAROLINE. Well—what of it! What's the matter with dancing, I'd like to know!

WILFRED. Nothing's the matter with it—if you want to *do* it! (*Stands looking away to down left.*)

CAROLINE. Well, I want to *do* it fast enough if that's all you mean! (*Turns away little toward right.*)

WILFRED (*an emphatic turn toward her*). But I must say it's a pretty way to carry on—with the sound of the cannon not six miles away!

(WILFRED *is dead in earnest not only in this scene but throughout the entire performance. To give the faintest idea that he thinks there is anything humorous about his lines or behavior would be inexcusable.*)

CAROLINE (*turning back to him*). Well, what do you want us to do—sit down and cry about it?—A heap o' good *that* would do now, wouldn't it?

WILFRED. Oh—I haven't time to talk about it! (*Turns, as if to go.*)

CAROLINE. Well it was you who started *out* to talk about it—I'm right sure *I* didn't!

WILFRED (*stops dead on* CAROLINE'*s speech and, after a quick glance to see that no one is near, goes to her*). You needn't try to fool me! I know well enough how you've been carrying on since our engagement was broken off! Half a dozen officers proposing to you —a dozen for all I know!

CAROLINE. What difference does it make? I haven't got to *marry* 'em, have I?

WILFRED. Well— (*Twist of head*) it isn't very nice to go on like that I must say—proposals by the wholesale! (*Turning away.*)

CAROLINE. Goodness gracious— what's the use of talking to me about it? *They're* the ones that propose—*I* don't!

WILFRED (*turning on her*). Well, what do you let 'em *do* it for?

CAROLINE. How can I help it?

WILFRED. Ho! (*Sneer*) Any girl can help it!—You helped it with *me* all right!

CAROLINE. Well— (*An odd little glance to floor in front*) that was different!

WILFRED. And ever since you threw me ovah—

CAROLINE (*looking up at him indignantly*). Oh!—I *didn't* throw you ovah —you just *went* ovah! (*Turns away a little.*)

WILFRED. Well, I went over because you walked off alone with Major Sillsby that night we were at Drury's Bluff an' encouraged him to propose—(CAROLINE *looks round in wrath.*) Yes— (*Advancing*) encouraged him!

CAROLINE. Of co'se I did! I didn't want 'im hangin' round forever, did I? That's the on'y way to finish 'em off!

WILFRED. You want to finish too many of 'em off! Nearly every officer in the Seventeenth Virginyah, I'll be sworn!

CAROLINE. Well, what do you want me to do—string a placard round my neck saying "No proposals received here—apply at the office!" Would that make you feel any better?

WILFRED (*throwing it off with pretended carelessness*). Oh—it doesn't make any difference to me what you do! (*Turns away.*)

CAROLINE. Well, if it doesn't make any difference to you, it doesn't even make as much as that to me! (*Turns and goes to couch; sits on left end of it.*)

WILFRED (*turning on her again*). Oh —it doesn't! I think it *does*, though!— You looked as if you enjoyed it pretty well while the Third Virginyah was in the city!

CAROLINE (*jumping to her feet*). Enjoyed it! I should think I did! I just love every one of 'em! They're on their way to the front! They're going to fight for us—an'—an' die for us—an' I *love* 'em! (*Turns front.*)

WILFRED. Well, why don't you accept one of 'em an' done with it!

CAROLINE. How do you know but what I'm going to?

WILFRED (*goes toward her a little*). I suppose it'll be one of those *smart* young fellows with a cavalry uniform!

CAROLINE. It'll be *some* kind of a uniform—I can tell you that! It won't be anybody that stays here in Richmond—

WILFRED (*unable to say anything for a few seconds, looks about room helplessly, and then speaks in low voice*). Now I see what it was! I had to stay in Richmond—an' so you—an' so—

CAROLINE (*in front of couch*). Well— (*Looking down, playing with some-*

thing with her foot*) that made a heap o' difference! (*Looks up; different tone*) Why, I was the on'y girl on Franklin Street that didn't have a—a— (*Hesitates.*) —someone she was engaged to at the front! The on'y one! Just *think* what it was to be out of it like that! (WILFRED *simply looks at her.*) Why, you've no idea what I suffered! Besides, it's our—it's our *duty* to help all we can!

WILFRED (*looking up toward front*). Help! (*Thinking of the trousers under his coat.*)

CAROLINE. Yes—help! There aren't many things we girls can do—I know that well enough! But Colonel Woodbridge—he's one o' Morgan's men, you know—well he told Mollie Pickens that the boys fight *twice* as well when they have a—a sweetheart at home!

WILFRED (*glances quickly about as he thinks*). He said *that*, did he!

CAROLINE. Yes—an' if we can make 'em fight twice as well why we just ought to do it—that's all! We girls can't do much but we can do *something!*

WILFRED (*short pause; he makes an absent-minded motion of feeling the package under his arm*). You're in earnest, are you?

CAROLINE. Earnest!

WILFRED. You really want to help— all you can!

CAROLINE. Well, I should think I *did!*

WILFRED. Yes—but do you *now?*

CAROLINE. Of co'se—that's what I say!

WILFRED. An' if I was— (*Glances around cautiously.*) —if I was going to join the army—would you help *me?*

CAROLINE (*looking front and down; slight embarrassment*). Why, of co'se I would—if it was anything I could (*With slight emphasis*) do!

WILFRED (*earnestly, quite near her*). Oh, it's something you can *do*, all right!

CAROLINE (*hardly daring to look up*). What is it?

WILFRED (*unrolling a pair of old gray army trousers, taking them from under his coat so that they unfurl before her*). Cut these off! (*Short pause.* CAROLINE *looks at trousers.* WILFRED *looking at her.* WILFRED *soon goes on very earnestly, holding trousers before his own legs to measure.*) They're about twice too long! All you got to do is to cut 'em off about there, an' sew up the ends so they won't ravel out!

CAROLINE (*the idea beginning to dawn on her*). Why, they're for the Army! (*Taking trousers and hugging them to her, legs hanging down.*)

WILFRED. Sh!—Don't speak so loud, for heaven's sake! (*A glance back, as if afraid of being overheard*) I've got a jacket here too! (*Shows her a small army coat.*) Nearly a fit—came from the hospital—Johnny Seldon wore it —he won't want it any more, you know—an' he was just about my size!

CAROLINE (*in a low voice*). No—he won't want it any more. (*Stands thinking.*)

WILFRED (*after a slight pause*). Well! —What is it!—I thought you said you wanted to help!

CAROLINE (*quickly*). Oh, yes—I do! I do!

WILFRED. Well go on—what are you waiting for?

CAROLINE (*near end of couch*). Yes! Yes! (*Hurriedly drops on knees on floor and takes hold, spreading trousers out exactly and patting them smooth.*) This is the place isn't it? (*Pointing to near the knees.*)

WILFRED. No—not up there—Here! (*Indicating about five inches from the bottom of the trouser leg.*)

CAROLINE. Oh, yes—I see! (*Hurriedly snatches pins from her dress. Puts one in mouth and one in place* WILFRED *indicates. All very rapid and earnest. Takes hold of other leg of trousers. Speaking as if pin in mouth. Innocently, without looking up*) The other one just the same? (*A musical rise to voice at end of this.* WILFRED *does not deign to reply.* CAROLINE, *hearing nothing, looks up at him.*) Oh, yes, o' co'se! (*She quickly puts pin in other leg of trousers. From this time on,* CAROLINE'*s demeanor toward* WILFRED *is entirely changed because he is going to join the army.* CAROLINE, *on floor with trousers and coat, takes hold of the work with enthusiasm— very busy—pins—etc.—etc.*) Do you see any scissors around anywhere! (WILFRED *dashes about looking on tables, after throwing jacket on end of couch.*) This won't never tear— (*Trying to tear off the trousers' leg*) —for all I can do!

WILFRED (*first looking on table and picking up the paper jacket was wrapped in. Getting a work-basket from table up center and quickly bringing it*). There must be some in here! (*Hands the scissors out of the basket to* CAROLINE. *As she reaches up from her position on the floor to take them, she looks in* WILFRED'*s face an instant, then quickly down to work again. Then she works with head down.* WILFRED *leaves wrapping paper up stage out of the way. Brief pause.* CAROLINE *working.* WILFRED *standing near center, looking down at her.*)

CAROLINE (*on her knees near couch. Low voice, not looking up at him*). When are you goin' to wear 'em?

WILFRED (*rather gruffly*). When they're cut off!

CAROLINE (*looks up at him. Thread

or scissors in mouth). You mean—
you're really—

WILFRED (*assent*). Um hm!

CAROLINE. But your mother—

WILFRED. She knows.

CAROLINE. Oh!

WILFRED. She's going to write the
General tonight.

CAROLINE. But how about if he
won't let you?

WILFRED (*with boyish determination, but keeping voice down*). I'll go
just the same!

CAROLINE (*suddenly jumps to her
feet, dropping everything on the floor
and catches his hand*). Oh, I'm so
glad! Why, it makes another thing of
it! When I said that about staying in
Richmond I didn't know! Oh, I *do*
want to help all I can!

WILFRED (*who has been regarding
her burst of enthusiasm rather coldly*).
You do!

CAROLINE. Indeed—indeed I do!

WILFRED. Then cut those off for
heaven's sake!

CAROLINE. Oh, yes! (*She catches up
trousers, jacket, etc., and sits quickly
on lounge and excitedly paws them
over.*) Where shall I cut 'em?

WILFRED. The same place—I haven't
grown any!

CAROLINE. Dear me—I don't know
where it was!

WILFRED. You stuck some pins in!

CAROLINE (*finding pins*). Oh, yes—
here they are! (*Seizing the trousers
and going to work, soon cutting off
one of the legs.*)

WILFRED. That's it!

CAROLINE. When did you say she
was going to write?

WILFRED. To-night.

CAROLINE (*looking up with distrust*).
She doesn't want you to go, does she?

WILFRED. I don't reckon she does—
very much!

CAROLINE. She'll tell him not to let
you!

WILFRED (*looks at her with wide-
open eyes*). No!

CAROLINE. That's the way they always do!

WILFRED. The devil!

CAROLINE. I should think so!

WILFRED. What can I do?

CAROLINE. Write to him yourself!

WILFRED. Good idea!

CAROLINE. Then you can just tell
him what you like!

WILFRED. I'll tell him I *can't* stay
here!

CAROLINE (*excitedly rising, letting
the jacket fall on floor at one side*).
Tell him you're coming anyhow!

WILFRED. I will!

CAROLINE. Whether he says so or
not!

WILFRED. Then he'll say so won't he?

CAROLINE. O' co'se he will—there
ain't anythin' else to say!

WILFRED. I'll do it! (*Starts to go
up left. Stops and goes back to
CAROLINE.*) Say—you're pretty good!
(*Catching one of CAROLINE's hands
impulsively, as CAROLINE looks down
at work on floor.*) I'll go upstairs an'
write it now! (*Starts toward door.
CAROLINE watches him. He turns back
and she looks quickly down again.*)
Finish those things as soon as you
can an' leave 'em here—in the hall
closet! (*Indicating outside left.*)

CAROLINE (*nodding her head*). Yes—
I will.

WILFRED. An' don't let anyone see
'em whatever you do!

CAROLINE (*shaking her head*). No—
I won't.

(*WILFRED hurries off at door to the
front hall. CAROLINE looks after him
with expression of ecstasy—lapsing into dreaminess as she turns to front.
Suddenly recollects with a start and*

a little "O" and slipping down on floor near couch, she goes excitedly to work on the trousers, cutting at the other leg with violence and rapidity, getting it nearly cut through so that later it dangles by a few threads. Suddenly she stops work and listens. Then with great haste she gathers up all the things she can, leaving the jacket, however, where it fell, and jumps to her feet with them in her arms, hugging the confused bundle close against her and hastily tucking in portions that hang out so that MRS. VARNEY *won't see what it is.*)

MRS. VARNEY (*comes down the stairway and into the room*). Oh, Caroline—you haven't gone yet!

CAROLINE. Not quite!—I mean not yet!—It doesn't begin for an hour, you know!

MRS. VARNEY. What doesn't begin?

CAROLINE. The party!

MRS. VARNEY. Oh—then you have plenty of time! (*Turning as if to go up center.*)

CAROLINE (*hastening across toward door, with her arms full of things*). Yes—but I'll have to go now sure enough! (*She drops the scissors.*)

MRS. VARNEY (*turning*). You dropped your scissors, dear!

CAROLINE. Oh! (*Coming back for them*) I—I thought I heard something! (*In picking them up, she lets the cut-off end of a trouser leg fall but does not notice it and goes toward door.*)

MRS. VARNEY. What are you making, Caroline?

CAROLINE (*turning near door*). Oh—I—I was just altering a dress—that's all! (*Turning to go.*)

MRS. VARNEY (*stooping and picking up the piece of trouser leg*). Here Carrie!—you dropped a—a— (*Looks at it.*)

CAROLINE (*hurrying to* MRS. VARNEY *and snatching the piece—stuffing it in with rest*). Oh, yes!—Ha, ha! (*Looks at* MRS. VARNEY *an instant. The other piece of the trouser leg is hanging by its shred in full sight.*) That—that was one of the *sleeves!* (*Turns and hurries off at door near foot of stairway.*)

(MRS. VARNEY, *after a moment, turns and goes toward door. Seeing something on the couch, she stops and goes to pick it up. On coming to it, she finds the soldier's little gray jacket left by* CAROLINE *in her hasty scramble. She stoops and picks it up and stands for a moment looking at it. After a brief pause, the sound of the hurried opening of front door and tramp of heavy feet in the hall are heard.* MRS. VARNEY *looks up, letting the coat fall on the couch.* MR. BENTON ARRELSFORD *is seen in the hall. He is a tall, fine-looking, Southern man of about thirty-five or forty, dressed in citizen's clothes—black frock coat, of rather distinguished appearance. He is seen outside door hurriedly placing a guard of Confederate soldiers at doors outside and also at foot of stairway.* MRS. VARNEY, *much surprised, moves toward door.* MR. ARRELSFORD, *at the same time and as noiselessly as possible, hastens into the room.*)

MRS. VARNEY (*as he enters*). Mr. Arrelsford!

ARRELSFORD (*comes quickly across to* MRS. VARNEY. *Speaks in a low voice and rapidly*). I was obliged to come in without ceremony, Mrs. Varney. You'll understand when I tell you what it is!

MRS. VARNEY. And those men— (*Motions toward guard outside door.*)

ARRELSFORD (*in a low voice*). They're on guard at the doors out there!

MRS. VARNEY (*in a low voice*). On

guard!—You mean that in this house you—

ARRELSFORD. I'm very much afraid, Mrs. Varney, that we've got to put you to a little inconvenience. (*Glances about cautiously, as* MRS. VARNEY *stands astonished.*) Is there anybody in that room? (*Pointing to door.*)

MRS. VARNEY. Yes.

ARRELSFORD. Who?

MRS. VARNEY. There are quite a number of ladies there—sewing for the hospitals.

ARRELSFORD. Kindly come this way a little. (*Going with* MRS. VARNEY) One of your servants has got himself into trouble, Mrs. Varney, an' we're compelled to have him watched!

MRS. VARNEY. One of my servants!— Why, what kind of trouble?

ARRELSFORD (*in a low voice*). Pretty serious, ma'am—that's the way it looks now!—You've got an old white-haired niggah here—

MRS. VARNEY. You mean Jonas?

ARRELSFORD. I believe that's his name!

MRS. VARNEY. You *suspect* him of something!

ARRELSFORD (*keeping voice down*). We don't suspect—we *know* what he's done! (*Glances round before going on.*) He's been down in the Libby Prison under pretense of selling something to the Yankees we've got in there, an' he now has on his person a written communication from one of those Yankees which he intends to deliver to another one that's here in Richmond! (ARRELSFORD *goes around in front of table and up to door.*)

MRS. VARNEY (*stands motionless a second; she soon recovers*). Send for the man! (*Starting to move up stage and toward left*) Let us see if there's any truth in such a—

ARRELSFORD (*up to upper corner of table, quickly stopping her*). No! Not yet! (*Glances quickly round at doors and windows—then speaks in lowered voice but with great intensity and clearness.*) I've got to get that paper! If he's alarmed he'll destroy it! I've got to have it! It's the clue to one o' their cursed plots! They've been right close on this town for months—trying to make a break in our defenses and get in. This is some rascally game they're at to weaken us from the inside!—Two weeks ago we got word from one of our agents over there in the Yankee lines telling us that two brothers—Lewis and Henry Dumont— have been under Secret Service orders to do some rascally piece of work here in Richmond. We had close descriptions of these two men but we've never been able to lay our hands on 'em till last night!

MRS. VARNEY (*a little nearer* ARRELSFORD, *intense whisper*). You've got them?

ARRELSFORD (*low voice, but intense*). We've got one o' them! An' it won't take long to run down the othah!

MRS. VARNEY (*in a low voice*). The one—the one you caught—was he here in Richmond?

ARRELSFORD (*in a low voice*). No—he was brought in last night with a lot o' men we captured making a raid.

MRS. VARNEY. You mean he was taken prisoner?

ARRELSFORD (*nods affirmatively, glances round*). Let himself be taken! That's one of their tricks for getting through our lines when they want to bring a message or give some signal.

MRS. VARNEY. They—they actually get into Libby Prison?

ARRELSFORD (*in a low voice, great intensity*). Yes! (*Indistinctly between his teeth*) Damn them! But we were on the lookout for this man an' we spotted him mighty quick! I gave orders not to search him or take away his clothes but to put him in with the others and keep the closest watch on him that was ever kept on a man! Here was one of the Dumont brothers an' we knew from his coming in that the othah must be here in the city waiting to hear from him, an' he'd send him a message the first chance he got!

MRS. VARNEY (*in a low voice*). But, Jonas!—How could he—

ARRELSFORD (*low and intense*). Easy enough!—Easy *enough!* He comes down to Libby to sell goubers to the prisoners—we let 'im pass in—he fools around awhile until he gets a chance to brush against this man Dumont— we're watching, an' we see a bit of paper pass between 'em! The old nigger's got that paper on 'im now, ma'am, an' besides these men in heah I've got a dozen more on the outside watching him through the windows! (*Turns and moves up glancing off up left with some anxiety.*)

MRS. VARNEY (*after slight pause, turns and speaks in an intense but subdued voice—almost whisper*). The man he gives it to! *He's* the one we want!

ARRELSFORD (*approaching her quickly, low voice but intense*). Yes—but I can't wait long! If the niggah sees a man or hears a sound he'll destroy it before we can jump in on 'im—an' I *must* have that paper! (*Strides quickly up,* MRS. VARNEY *following a step or two. Speaking off in low but sharp voice*) Corporal!

(CORPORAL *enters from the hall. He salutes and stands in the large arched doorway.*)
How is it now?

CORPORAL (*in a low voice*). All quiet, sir!

(ARRELSFORD *and* MRS. VARNEY *face each other.*)

ARRELSFORD (*low, intense*). It won't do to wait—I've *got* to get that paper! It's the key to the game they're trying to play an' we must have it!

MRS. VARNEY (*intense, half whisper*). No no—the man who's going to play it! Get *him!*

ARRELSFORD (*low, intense*). That paper the nigger's got might give us a clue! If not I'll make him tell who it was *for*—damn it I'll shoot it out of him! (*Turns to* CORPORAL.) How quick can you get at him from that door! (*Pointing to door right of stairway.*)

CORPORAL (*no salute, in a low voice*). It's through a hallway, sir—and across the dining room.

ARRELSFORD (*low voice*). Well, take two men and—

MRS. VARNEY (*interrupting, touching* ARRELSFORD *to stop him, in a low voice*). Why not keep your men out of sight and let me send for him— here?

ARRELSFORD (*after a second's thought, in a low voice*). That's better—we'll get 'im in here! While you're talking to him they can nab him from behind! (*Turns to* CORPORAL.) You heard!

CORPORAL (*low voice*). Yes, sir.

ARRELSFORD (*low voice*). Keep your men out of sight—get 'em back there in the hall—an' while we're making him talk send a man down each side and pin him! Hold 'im stiff! He mustn't destroy any paper he's got! Look out for that!

(CORPORAL *salutes and exits with men. After exit of* CORPORAL *and* MEN, MRS. VARNEY *moves swiftly to left side, and taking the bell cord in her hand, turns toward* ARRELSFORD. *Pause. Both are motionless for four seconds.*)

MRS. VARNEY (*after the pause. Low voice, but distinct.*) Now Mr. Arrelsford?

ARRELSFORD (*low voice*). Yes.

(MRS. VARNEY *rings the bell. Short pause. Enter* MARTHA *from dining room. She stands below the doorway.*)

MRS. VARNEY (*near mantel*). Is there anyone I can send to the hospital, Martha?

MARTHA. Luther's out yere, mam.

MRS. VARNEY. Luther? (*Considers.*) No—he's too small. I don't want a boy.

MARTHA. Jonas is yere, mam—if you want him.

MRS. VARNEY. Oh, Jonas—yes! Tell him to come here right away.

MARTHA. Yaas'm. (*Exits to dining room.*)

(MRS. VARNEY *sits on couch.* ARRELSFORD *waits. Old* JONAS *appears at the door from dining room. He is a thick-set gray-haired old Negro. He comes a few steps into the room.* MRS. VARNEY *looks at* JONAS *and he at her. At first, he is entirely unsuspecting, but in a moment, seeing* ARRELSFORD, *his eyes shift restlessly for an instant.*)

MRS. VARNEY (*on couch*). Jonas—

JONAS. Yes 'm.

MRS. VARNEY. Have you any idea why I sent for you?

JONAS. I heers you was wantin' to sen' to de hossiple, ma'am.

(CORPORAL *and* MEN *enter very quietly from the hall and on to behind* JONAS.)

MRS. VARNEY. Oh—then Martha told you?

(CORPORAL *motions to* MEN *and two instantly step forward, one on each side of* JONAS, *and stand there motionless.*)

JONAS. Wall, she didn't ezzackly say whut you— (*Sees man each side of him and stops in the midst of his speech. He does not start, but is frozen*

with terror. Expression of face scarcely changes. Soon he lowers his eyes and then begins stealthily to get his right hand toward his inside breast pocket.*)

(CORPORAL *gives a sharp order. The two* MEN *instantly seize* JONAS. CORPORAL *quickly feels in his pockets.* JONAS *struggles desperately, but, in an instant, the* CORPORAL *has the paper, which he hands, with a salute, to* ARRELSFORD. MRS. VARNEY *has risen as* MEN *seized* JONAS.)

ARRELSFORD (*right of* MEN *and* JONAS). See if there's anything more! (ARRELSFORD *stands watching the search.*)

(CORPORAL *quickly searches* JONAS— *feeling rapidly along body, arms, down each leg, etc.,* MEN *raising his arms above head, etc., for the purpose. Pushes fingers down into slippers, which are sufficiently loose for this. After the search* MEN *release* JONAS *and stand guard one on each side of him.*)

CORPORAL (*rises and comes to salute*). That's all, sir!

(ARRELSFORD *turns quickly away to lamp on table, opening the paper as he does so.* MRS. VARNEY *watches him intently.* ARRELSFORD *reads the paper quickly and at once wheels round on* JONAS, *coming down right of him.*)

ARRELSFORD (*low voice, but sharp and telling*). Who was this for? (JONAS *stands silent.*) If you don't tell, it's going to be mighty bad for you! (JONAS *stands silent. After a pause,* ARRELSFORD *turns to* MRS. VARNEY.) I'm right sorry, ma'am, but it looks like we've got to shoot 'im! (*Eyeing* JONAS *a moment—then goes down center.*) Corporal! (*Motions* CORPORAL *to approach.* CORPORAL *steps to* ARRELSFORD *on salute. To* CORPORAL, *in a low voice.*) Take him outside and get it out of him! String him up till he talks! You understand! (CORPORAL *salutes and is about to turn.*) Here! (CORPORAL *turns back to* ARRELSFORD *on salute.* ARRELSFORD *glances toward the windows at right and then to left.*) Go down on that side—back of the house! (*Indicating up left*) And keep it quiet! Nobody must know of this! Not a soul!

(CORPORAL *salutes again and goes up to* MEN. *Gives a low-voiced order.* MEN *turn on order and march* JONAS *off at door to the hall. All very quick with military precision. The* CORPORAL *goes with them.* ARRELSFORD *stands watching exit of* JONAS *and* MEN *until they are gone and the sound of the closing of heavy front door is heard outside. He then turns to* MRS. VARNEY. ARRELSFORD *and* MRS. VARNEY *keep voices down to nearly a whisper in the coming scene—but speak with the utmost force and intensity.*)

MRS. VARNEY (*indicating the paper in* ARRELSFORD's *hand*). Was there anything in that—

ARRELSFORD (*near* MRS. VARNEY). We've got the trick they want to play!

MRS. VARNEY. But not the *man*—not the man who is to *play* it?

ARRELSFORD. I didn't say that!

MRS. VARNEY. You mean there's a clue—*to him?*

ARRELSFORD. I mean there's a clue to him!

MRS. VARNEY. Will it answer? Do you know who it is? Do you—

ARRELSFORD (*interrupting*). As plain as if we had his name!

MRS. VARNEY. Thank God! (*Motionless an instant, then she extends her hand for the paper.*) Let me see! (AR-RELSFORD *momentarily hesitates, then hands her the paper. She looks at paper, then reads it aloud—not too easily.*) "ATTACK TONIGHT—

PLAN 3—USE TELEGRAPH."— (*Slight motion or sound from* ARRELS-FORD *to quiet her, and a quick glance about. After the glance about by* AR-RELSFORD, *she goes on in low voice.*) What does it mean?

ARRELSFORD (*takes paper from her; in a low voice but incisive*). They attack to-night!—The place where they strike is indicated by "Plan 3." (*Finger on the words on paper in his hand.*)

MRS. VARNEY. Plan three?

ARRELSFORD. He knows what they mean by that!—It's arranged beforehand!

MRS. VARNEY. And—the last—the last there! (*Excited motion toward the paper in* ARRELSFORD's *hands*) "Use Telegraph"?—What does that—

ARRELSFORD. He's to use our War Department Telegraph Lines to send some false order and weaken that position—the one they indicate by "Plan Three"—so they can break through and come down on the city!

MRS. VARNEY. Oh! (*A breathless exclamation of indignation. A second's pause, then suddenly*) But the *man*—the man who is to do this—there's nothing about *him!*

ARRELSFORD. There *is* something about him!

MRS. VARNEY (*rapidly, almost run together*). What? Where? I don't see it!

ARRELSFORD. "Use Telegraph"! (*A pause. Both stand motionless regarding each other.* ARRELSFORD *goes on after playing this pause to the limit.*) We know every man on the Telegraph Service—and every man of them's true! But there's some who want to get on that service that we don't know quite so well!

MRS. VARNEY (*indicating the paper*). He would be one—of course!

ARRELSFORD. There aren't so very many! (*These speeches given suggestively, with slight pause after each. All very low voiced and intense.*) It isn't *every* man that's an expert!—The niggah brought this paper to *your* house, Mrs. Varney!

MRS. VARNEY. My— (*Hesitates, beginning to realize.*) —my house you say!

ARRELSFORD. For more than a month your daughter has been working to get an appointment for someone on the Telegraph Service—perhaps *she* could give us some idea— (*Stops in the midst of speech and stands looking at* MRS. VARNEY.)

(*A moment's pause.—Suddenly* MRS. VARNEY *turns and hurries to window up right and quickly pulls curtains together, turning and facing back to* ARRELSFORD *at same instant.*)

ARRELSFORD (*almost whisper, but with utmost intensity*). IS HE THERE? (MRS. VARNEY *nods affirmatively. She then comes down toward* ARRELSFORD.) Could he hear what we said?

MRS. VARNEY (*shakes head negatively. Almost whisper*). He's at the further end! (*Comes back to right of* ARRELSFORD. ARRELSFORD *glances at windows nervously.* MRS. VARNEY, *after a pause, in low voice.*) You have a description you say!

ARRELSFORD (*nods affirmatively*). At the office.

MRS. VARNEY. Then this man—this Captain Thorne—

ARRELSFORD (*breaking in savagely but in low voice*). There *is* no Captain Thorne! This fellow you have in your house is Lewis Dumont! (*Short pause.*)

MRS. VARNEY. You mean—he came here to—

ARRELSFORD (*with vindictive fury breaking through in spite of himself, yet voice subdued almost to a sharp whisper*). He came to this town—he came to this house—knowing your position and the influence of your name —for the sole purpose of getting some hold on our Department Telegraph Lines!—He's corrupted your servants— he's thick with the men in the telegraph office—what he hasn't done God A'mighty knows! But Washington ain't the only place where there's a Secret Service! We've got one here in Richmond! Oh— (*A shake of his head*) two can play at that game—an' it's my move now! (*Goes up a few steps.*)

(*Enter* EDITH VARNEY *running rapidly down the stairway up left and in at door. She wears a white dress and has in her hand the large official envelope which she took upstairs at the end of her first scene.* ARRELSFORD *goes toward windows up right.*)

EDITH (*as she runs down the stairway*). Mama! Mama!—Quick, Mama! (MRS. VARNEY *hurries toward door to meet her.* ARRELSFORD *turns in surprise, looking toward door.* EDITH *meeting* MRS. VARNEY.) Under my window—in the garden—they're hurting someone frightfully—I'm sure they are! Oh—come! (*Starting toward door to lead the way.* MRS. VARNEY *stands looking at* EDITH. EDITH *stops surprised that* MRS. VARNEY *does not follow.*) If you aren't coming, I'll go myself! (*Turning to go*) It's terrible!

MRS. VARNEY. Wait, Edith! (EDITH *stops and turns back to* MRS. VARNEY. MRS. VARNEY *goes to her.*) I must tell you something—it will be a terrible shock, I'm afraid! (EDITH *moves down with* MRS. VARNEY. ARRELSFORD *turns away a little, standing watching window.*) A man we trusted as a friend has shown himself a treacherous conspirator against us!

EDITH (*after a slight pause. Low voice*). Who? (*Pause.* MRS. VARNEY *cannot bring herself to speak the name.*) Who is it?

ARRELSFORD (*swinging round on her. Low voice, suppressed vindictiveness*). It is the gentleman, Miss Varney, whose attentions you have been pleased to accept in the place of mine!

(*Short pause.* EDITH *white and motionless, looking at* ARRELSFORD. *Soon she turns her face appealingly to her mother.* MRS. VARNEY *nods slowly in affirmation.*)

EDITH (*low voice*). Is it Mr. Arrelsford who makes this accusation?

ARRELSFORD (*breaking out hotly but speaking in suppressed voice*). Yes—since you wish to know! From the first I've had my suspicions that this— (*He stops on seeing* EDITH'*s move toward the window up right.* EDITH, *on cue "Yes," quickly thrusts envelope containing commission into belt or waist of her dress, and starts rapidly toward the window up right.* ARRELSFORD *breaks off in his speech and steps before her. Low voice, speaking rapidly.*) Where are you going?

EDITH (*low voice*). For Captain Thorne.

ARRELSFORD (*low voice*). Not now!

EDITH (*turning with flashing indignation on* ARRELSFORD). Mr. Arrelsford, if this is something you're afraid to say to him—don't you *dare* say it to me!

ARRELSFORD (*indignantly, in a low voice*). Miss Varney, if you—

MRS. VARNEY (*interrupting quickly, in a low voice*). Edith—listen to me! (EDITH *turns quickly to* MRS. VARNEY.) Mr. Arrelsford has good reasons for not meeting Captain Thorne just now!

EDITH. I should think he had! (*Quick turn back to* ARRELSFORD) The man who said that to his face wouldn't *live* to speak again!

MRS. VARNEY. My dear, you don't—

EDITH. Mama—this man has left his desk in the War Department so that he can have the pleasure of persecuting me! He's never attempted anything in the active service before! And when I ask him to face the man he accuses he turns like a coward!

ARRELSFORD (*angrily, but keeping voice down*). Mrs. Varney, if she thinks—

EDITH (*low voice*). I think nothing! I *know* that a man of Captain Thorne's character is above suspicion!

ARRELSFORD (*low voice*). His character! (*Sneeringly*) Where did he come from?—Who is he?

EDITH (*low voice*). Who are you?

ARRELSFORD. That's not the question!

EDITH (*low voice*). Neither is it the question who *he* is! If it were I'd answer it—the answer above all others —he's a soldier who has fought and been wounded for his country!

ARRELSFORD (*low voice but incisive*). We're not so sure of that!

EDITH (*after a pause of indignation*). He brought us letters from General Stonewall Jackson and from—

ARRELSFORD (*quick and sharp*). Jackson was killed before his letter was presented!

EDITH. What does that signify if he wrote it?

ARRELSFORD. Nothing— (*With vindictive fury*) *if* he wrote it!

EDITH. Mr. Arrelsford—if you mean—

MRS. VARNEY (*goes to* EDITH, *putting her hand on* EDITH'*s arm, in a low voice*). Listen, Edith! They have proofs of a conspiracy on our Government Telegraph Lines.

(ARRELSFORD *says "Sh" and goes to*

window. EDITH *turns from* ARRELSFORD *and looks before her, listening on mention of "Telegraph Lines."* MRS. VARNEY *leads* EDITH *a little left of center.* ARRELSFORD *stands near window.*)

A treacherous conspiracy on the War Department lines to the front. Two men in the Northern Secret Service have been sent here to carry it out. One is in Libby Prison. He's just been brought in—and he allowed himself to be taken prisoner so as to get in here and bring a message to the other. Our old Jonas went there to-day—secretly took that message from him and brought it here! (EDITH *turns toward* MRS. VARNEY *sharply.*) Yes, Edith—he brought it to this house! We've just had Jonas in and found that paper on him!

(ARRELSFORD *quietly moves down right, looking off through curtains at windows down right.*)

EDITH (*rapidly, desperately, in low voice*). But he hasn't said it was for— (*Heavy sound of front door closing.*)

ARRELSFORD (*low voice but incisively*). Not yet—but he will!

(EDITH *looks at* ARRELSFORD, *not comprehending. Enter* CORPORAL *from hall. He stands on salute. Ladies turn to him.* EDITH *breathless with anxiety.* MRS. VARNEY *calm but intent.*—ARRELSFORD *goes quickly across to the* CORPORAL, *speaks in a low voice.*)

Well what does he say?

CORPORAL (*low voice*). Nothing!— He won't speak!

ARRELSFORD (*sharply, but voice subdued*). Won't speak! What have you done?

CORPORAL. Strung him up three times and—

ARRELSFORD (*enraged, but keeping his voice down*). Well, string him up again! If he won't speak shoot it out

of him! Kill the dog! (*Comes blindly down left.* CORPORAL *salutes and exits at door to front hall.* ARRELSFORD *turns to ladies, coming down back of table.*) We don't need the niggah's evidence —there's enough without it! (*Takes his hat from table.*)

EDITH (*in a low voice*).There is nothing!

ARRELSFORD (*left of table, low voice*). By twelve o'clock to-night you'll have all the proof you want!

EDITH (*low voice*). There's no proof at all!

ARRELSFORD (*low voice*). I'll show it to you at the telegraph office! Do you dare go there with me?

EDITH (*low voice*). Dare! (*Moves toward him.*) I *will* go with you!

ARRELSFORD (*low voice*). I'll call for you in half an hour! (*Goes toward door.*)

EDITH. Wait! (ARRELSFORD *stops and turns to her.*) What are you going to do?

ARRELSFORD (*comes down back of table. Low voice but incisive*). I'm going to let him get this paper! When he looks at it he'll know what they want him to do—and then we'll see him try to do it!

EDITH. You're going to spy on him— hound him like a criminal!

ARRELSFORD. I'm going to prove what he *is!*

EDITH. Then prove it openly! Prove it at once! It's a shame to let a suspicion like that rest on an honorable man! Let him come in here and—

ARRELSFORD (*low voice*). Impossible! (*Goes down left of table a little.*)

EDITH (*low voice*). Then do something else,but do it now! (*Turning away, goes up center a little, speaks desperately.*) We must know that he —that he's innocent! We must know that! (*A thought. Turns to* ARRELS-

FORD.) You say— (ARRELSFORD *makes a movement to go.*) Wait! *Wait!* (AR-RELSFORD *stops.*)
You say the man in Libby Prison is his brother—that's what you said—his brother! Bring him here! Go to the prison and bring that man here!

ARRELSFORD (*speaking across the table, with a subdued exclamation*). What!

EDITH. Let them meet! Bring them face to face! Then you can see wheth-er—

ARRELSFORD (*low voice, speaking rapidly*). You mean— bring them to-gether here?

EDITH. Yes! Here!—Anywhere! Wherever you please!

ARRELSFORD. As if the prisoner was trying to escape?

EDITH. Any way you like—but end it!

ARRELSFORD. When?

EDITH. Now! Now!—I won't have such a suspicion as that hanging over him!

ARRELSFORD (*after an instant's thought*). I'm willing to try that!—(*With a motion toward windows*) Can you keep him here?

EDITH (*scarcely more than a move-ment of lips*). Yes.

ARRELSFORD. It won't be more than half an hour.—Be out there on the veranda.—When I tap on the glass bring him into this room and leave him alone! You understand—*alone!*

EDITH (*hardly more than a whisper*). Yes. (*Turns away toward front.*)

ARRELSFORD (*goes rapidly toward door. Stops and turns near door*). I rely on you Miss Varney to give him no hint or sign that we suspect—

MRS. VARNEY (*interrupting* ARRELS-FORD *indignantly*). Mr. Arrelsford!

(EDITH *does not notice anything.* AR-RELSFORD *stands an instant, then bows* stiffly and exits to the hall. Sound of closing of heavy door outside, shortly after his disappearance. EDITH *stands where she was as if stunned.* MRS. VAR-NEY *remains, looking after* ARRELSFORD —then turns to EDITH.)

EDITH (*after pause, not looking round, nearly whispers*). Mama! (*Reaches out her hand as if feeling for help or support.* MRS. VARNEY *comes to* EDITH *and takes her hand.*) Mama!

MRS. VARNEY (*low voice*). I'm here, Edith!

(*Pause.* EDITH *thinking of some-thing—her eyes wide open, staring vacantly before her.*)

EDITH (*holding tight to* MRS. VAR-NEY's *hand*). Do you think—do you think—that could be what he meant? (MRS. VARNEY *looking intently at* EDITH.) The Commission I got for him—this afternoon—you know!

MRS. VARNEY (*low voice*). Yes—yes!

EDITH. The Commission—from the President—for the —for the Telegraph Service! He—he—refused to take it!

MRS. VARNEY. Refused!

EDITH (*nodding a little, hardly able to speak*). He said—he said it was for me that he could not!

MRS. VARNEY (*sudden deep em-phasis*). It's true then!

EDITH (*turning quickly to* MRS. VAR-NEY *and trying to stop her by putting her hand over her mouth. Speaking rapidly, breathlessly—yet not in loud voice*). No, no! Don't say it!—Don't say it!

MRS. VARNEY (*putting* EDITH's *hand away*). Yes!

EDITH. Oh, no!

MRS. VARNEY. Infamous traitor! They ought to lash him through the streets of Richmond!

EDITH (*impulsively trying to stop* MRS. VARNEY). No, Mama! No—no—no! (*She stops. A moment's pause.*

She realizes the truth. Speaks in almost a whisper.) Yes—yes— (*Fainter and fainter*) Yes—yes— (*Stops, pauses, stands erect, looks about, makes very slight motion asking* MRS. VARNEY *to leave her.*)

(MRS. VARNEY *turns quietly and leaves the room, going out the door to the front hall.* EDITH *stands supporting herself without knowing that she does so—one hand on a table or back of chair. Soon coming to herself, she turns and goes toward the window. When near center, she hesitates, stands there a moment looking toward the window, then brushes her hand quickly across her eyes and takes the President's Commission from her waist or belt. She looks at it a moment, folds it slowly and puts it back again. Walks to the window, throws aside the curtains and pushes it open. Upon* EDITH *pushing open the window,* CAPTAIN THORNE *outside at some distance, makes a noise with chair as though he rose and pushed or set it back, and the sound of his footsteps outside approaching the window briskly follows at once.* EDITH *moves away from the window and to the table, and stands there looking across at the window for an instant, but soon turning away, so that she is not looking at* THORNE *as he enters. After footsteps and after* EDITH *is motionless,* CAPTAIN THORNE *walks easily and unsuspiciously into the room, glancing about as he does so—not seeing* EDITH *until he is a little way in. Upon seeing her, he stops an instant where he is, and then goes directly across to her and is about to take her hand as he speaks.*)

THORNE (*coming to* EDITH). Miss Varney—

EDITH (*quickly snatching her hand away and shrinking backward a step*

or two. *Speaks rapidly, breathlessly, with almost a gasp*). No—don't touch me! (*A second's pause. She recovers almost instantly.*) Oh—it was you! (*Smiling as if at her own stupidity.*) Why, how perfectly absurd I am! (*Crossing in front of* THORNE *and going to window*) I'm sure I ought to be ashamed of myself! (*Turns to him.*) Do come out a minute—on the veranda.—I want to talk to you about a whole lot o' things! There's half an hour yet before the party! (*Turning to go*) Isn't it a perfectly lovely evening! (*She exits at the window with forced gaiety of manner, disappearing in the darkness.*)

(THORNE *stands looking at* EDITH *when she first speaks. As she crosses, he is looking down a little but looks slowly up toward front and turns a little after her crossing, looking at her as she stands for a moment in the window. After her exit, he slowly turns toward front and his eyes glance about, as he weighs the chances.*)

EDITH (*after brief pause for above—calling gaily from outside, not too near the window, with emphasis*). Oh, Cap'n Thorne!

(THORNE *turns quickly, looking off right again. Hesitates an instant. Makes up his mind. Walks rapidly to window. A very slight hesitation there, without stopping. Exits at window.*)

ACT TWO

The same room. Nine o'clock. Furniture as before. Electric calciums for strong moonlight outside both windows. Portieres are closed at both windows.

MRS. VARNEY *discovered seated at desk down right. She is not busy with anything but sits there to see that no one goes out to the veranda. Sound of closing of door outside. Enter* MISS KITTRIDGE *from the hall. The door at center stands ajar as if she had recently come out.*

———

MRS. VARNEY. Was it the same man?

MISS KITTRIDGE (*pausing*). No—they sent another this time.

MRS. VARNEY. Did you have anything ready?

MISS KITTRIDGE. Oh, yes—I gave him quite a lot. We've all been at the bandages—that's what they need most.

(MRS. VARNEY *rises. Seems preoccupied. Goes across up left and looks off.* MISS KITTRIDGE *watches her rather anxiously.*)

Did you want anything, Mrs. Varney?

MRS. VARNEY (*turning*). No—I—nothing, thank you. (MISS KITTRIDGE *is turning to go, but stops when* MRS. VARNEY *speaks again.* MRS. VARNEY *goes nearer to* MISS KITTRIDGE.) Perhaps it would be just as well if any of the ladies want to go, to let them out the other way—through the dining room I mean. We're expecting someone here on important business.

MISS KITTRIDGE. I'll see to it, Mrs. Varney.

MRS. VARNEY. Thank you. (*Exit* MISS KITTRIDGE *at center door.* MRS. VARNEY *stands a moment, then goes down left and rings bell. Then goes slowly up center, waiting. Enter* MARTHA *at door from dining room.*) Did Miss Caroline go home?

MARTHA (*near door*). No 'm—she's been out yere in de kitchen fur a while.

MRS. VARNEY. In the kitchen!

MARTHA. Yaas 'm.

MRS. VARNEY. What has she been doing?

MARTHA. She been mostly sewin' and behavin' mighty strange about sumfin' a great deal o' de time. I bleeve she gittin' ready to go home now.

MRS. VARNEY. Ask her to come here a moment.

MARTHA. Yaas 'm. (*Turns and exits to dining room.*)

(MRS. VARNEY *waits a little, then goes forward a few steps. Enter* CAROLINE *from dining room. She comes into the room trying to look perfectly innocent.*)

MRS. VARNEY. Caroline— (CAROLINE *goes down center with* MRS. VARNEY. *She is expecting to hear something said about the sewing she has been doing.*) Are you in a hurry to get home? Because if you can wait a few minutes while I go up stairs to Howard, it will be a great help.

CAROLINE (*looking round in some doubt*). You want me to—just wait?

MRS. VARNEY. Yes.—You see I— (*Hesitates a little.*) —I don't want anyone to go out on the veranda—just now.

CAROLINE (*doubtfully*). Oh.

MRS. VARNEY. Edith and—and—

CAROLINE. —And Captain Thorne— (MRS. VARNEY *nods very slightly.*) (*Suddenly comprehending.*) Oh, yes! (*Glances toward windows.*) I know how *that* is!—I'll attend to it, Mrs. Varney!

MRS. VARNEY. Yes—if you will—just while I'm upstairs—it won't be long! (*Goes to door and turns.*) Be careful won't you, dear! (*Exits and goes up the stairway.*)

CAROLINE. Careful!—Well I should think so! As if I didn't know enough for that! (*Goes toward window, pauses. Her face is radiant with the imagined romance of the situation. Goes to window and peeps out slyly through curtains. After a moment, she turns, an idea having occurred to her, and quickly rolls the couch across before the window. Kneels on it with her back to the audience and tries to peep through curtains again. Enter* WILFRED VARNEY *from the front hall, coming in cautiously and as if he had been watching for an opportunity. He stops just within the door and looks back up stairway. He has on the trousers which* CAROLINE *fixed for him in the previous act, and also the Army Jacket.* CAROLINE *rises, turns from the couch, and sees* WILFRED. *He turns to her. She stands adoring him in his uniform. These clothes are not by any means new. The trousers must be all right as to length, though showing strange folds and awkwardness at bottom from being cut off and sewed by an amateur. But on no account must there be anything grotesque or laughable.*)

CAROLINE (*in a subdued exclamation as she sees* WILFRED *in uniform*). Oh!

WILFRED (*low voice—speaking from door*). Mother isn't anywhere around, is she?

CAROLINE. She—she just went upstairs.

WILFRED. I'm not running away—but if she saw me with these things on she might feel funny.

CAROLINE (*half to herself*). She might not feel so very funny!

WILFRED. Well— (*Going over to desk and taking papers and letters from pockets*) —you know how it is with a feller's mother. (CAROLINE *nods affirmatively.* WILFRED *business of hurriedly finding letter among others—feeling in different pockets for it—so that he speaks without much thinking*

about what he says.) Other people don't care—but mothers—well—they're different.

CAROLINE (*absently*). Yes— other people don't care! (*Moves over toward left. The thought of* WILFRED *actually going gives her a slight sinking of the heart at which she herself is surprised.*)

WILFRED. I've written that letter to the General!—Here it is—on'y I've got to end it off some way! (*Pulls a chair sideways to desk and half sits on it, intent on finishing the letter. Business with pen, etc., and running hand into his hair impetuously.*) I'm not going to say "Your loving son" or any such rubbish as that! It would be an almighty let-down! I *love* him of course —that's all right, you know—but this isn't that kind of a letter! (*Pointing out writing on letter and speaking as if he supposed* CAROLINE *was at his shoulder*) I've been telling him— (*Looking around, he sees that* CAROLINE *is standing at a considerable distance, looking at him.*) —What's the matter?

CAROLINE. Nothing—! That is—I was only—

WILFRED. I thought you wanted to help!

CAROLINE (*quickly*). Oh, yes— I do! I do! (*Goes, at once, to* WILFRED *at desk.* WILFRED *looks in her face an instant. A slight pause. Stammering*) The—the— (*Indicating his trousers by a little gesture*) —are they how you wanted 'em?

WILFRED. What?

CAROLINE. Those things. (*Points to trousers* WILFRED *is wearing.*)

WILFRED (*glances at legs*). Oh— they're all right!—Fine!—Now about this letter—tell me what you think! (*Turns to letter again.*)

CAROLINE. Tell me what you said!

WILFRED. Want to hear it?

CAROLINE. I've got to, haven't I? How could I help you if I didn't know what it was all about!

WILFRED. You're pretty good! (*Looks at her briefly.*) You *will* help me, won't you? (*Catching hold of her right hand as she stands near him on his left.*)

CAROLINE. O' co'se I will— (*After an instant's pause draws hand away from him.*) —about the letter!

WILFRED. That's what I mean!—It's mighty important, you know! Everything depends on it!

CAROLINE. Well, I should *think* so! (CAROLINE *gets chair from between windows and pulls it around near* WILFRED *on his left, and sits looking over the letter while he reads.*)

WILFRED. I just gave it to him strong!

CAROLINE. That's the *way* to give it to him!

WILFRED. You can't fool round with *him* much! He means business! But he'll find out I mean business too!

CAROLINE. That's right—everybody means business!—What did you say?

WILFRED. I said this!— (*Reads letter.*) "General Ranson Varney—Commanding Division Army of Northern Virginia—Dear Papa! This is to notify you that I want you to let me come right now! If you don't I'll come anyhow—that's all! The seventeen call is almost out—the sixteen comes next an' I'm not going to wait for it! Do you think I'm a damned coward? Tom Kittridge has gone! He was killed yesterday at Cold Harbor. Billy Fisher has gone. So has Cousin Stephen and he ain't sixteen. He lied about his age but I don't want to do that unless you make me. Answer this right now or not at all!"

CAROLINE. That's *splendid!*

WILFRED (*surprised and delighted*). Do you think so?

CAROLINE. It's just the thing!

WILFRED. But how 'm I going to end it?

CAROLINE. Why just end it!

WILFRED. How?

CAROLINE. Sign your name.

WILFRED. Nothing else?

CAROLINE. What else is there?

WILFRED. Just "Wilfred"?

CAROLINE. O' co'se!

WILFRED (*looks at her an instant, then turns suddenly to desk and writes his name*). That's the thing! (*Holds it up.*) Will the rest of it do?

CAROLINE. Do! I should think so! (*Rising*) I wish he had it now! (*Goes toward center.*)

WILFRED (*rising*). So do I!—It might take two or three days! (*Moves toward center.*) I *can't* wait that long!— Why the Seventeen call might— (*Stops. Thinks frowningly.*)

CAROLINE (*suddenly turning*). I'll tell you what to do!—Telegraph! (WILFRED *looks at her; she at him. After an instant, he glances at the letter.*)

WILFRED. Whew! (*A whistle*) I haven't got money enough!

CAROLINE. 'T won't take so very much!

WILFRED. Do you know what they're charging now? Over seven dollars a word!

CAROLINE. Let 'em charge! We can cut it down so there's only a few words an' it means just the same! (*They both go at the letter each holding it on his or her side.*) You know the address won't cost a thing!

WILFRED. Won't it?

CAROLINE. No! They never do! There's a heap o' money saved right now! We can use that to pay for the rest! (WILFRED *looks at her a little puzzled.*) What comes next? (*Both look over the letter.*)

WILFRED (*looks at letter*). "Dear Papa"—

CAROLINE. Leave that out! (*Both scratch at it with pens or pencils.*)

WILFRED. I didn't care much for it anyway!

CAROLINE. He knew it before.

WILFRED. Of course he did!—I'm glad it's out!

CAROLINE. So 'm I!—What's next? (*Reading*) "This-is-to-notify-you-that-I-want-you-to-let-me-come-right-now." We might leave out that last "to."

WILFRED and CAROLINE (*reciting it off together experimentally to see how it reads without the "to"*). "I-want-you—let-me-come-right-now." (*After instant's thought both shake heads.*)

WILFRED (*shaking head*). No!

CAROLINE (*shaking head*). No!

WILFRED. It doesn't sound right.

CAROLINE. That's only a little word anyhow!

WILFRED. So it is. What's after that? (*Both eagerly look at letter.*)

CAROLINE. Wait—here it is! (*Reads.*) "If-you-don't — I'll — come — anyhow —that's—all." (*They consider.*)

WILFRED. We might leave out "that's all."

CAROLINE (*quickly*). No! Don't leave that out! It's very important. It doesn't seem so but it is! It shows—(*Hesitates.*) well—it shows that's all there is about it! That one thing might convince him!

WILFRED. We've got to leave out something!

CAROLINE. Yes—but not that! Perhaps there's something in the next! (*Reads.*) "The-seventeen-call-is-almost-out"—That's *got* to stay!

WILFRED (*reads*). "The-sixteen-comes-next."

CAROLINE. *That's* got to stay!

WILFRED (*shaking head*). Yes!

CAROLINE (*taking it up*). "And-I'm-not-going-to-wait-for-it!" (*Shaking her head without looking up*) No! No!

WILFRED (*shaking head*). No!

CAROLINE. We'll find something in just a minute! (*Reading*) "Do-you-think-I'm-a-damned-coward!" (*Both look up from the letter simultaneously and gaze at each other in silence for an instant.*)

WILFRED (*after the pause*). We might leave out the—

CAROLINE (*breaking in on him with almost a scream*). No! (*They again regard each other.*)

WILFRED (*after the pause*). That "damn" 's going to cost us seven dollars and a half!

CAROLINE. It's *worth* it! Why it's the best thing you've got in the whole thing! Your papa's a general in the army! He'll *understand* that! What's next? I know there's something now.

WILFRED (*reads*). "Tom-Kittridge-has-gone. He-was-killed-yesterday-at-Cold-Harbor."

CAROLINE (*slight change in tone, a little lower*). Leave out that about his (*Very slight catch of breath*) about his being killed.

WILFRED (*looking at CAROLINE*). But he was!

CAROLINE (*suddenly very quiet*). I know he was—but you haven't got to tell him the news, have you?

WILFRED. That's so! (*They both cross off the words.*)

CAROLINE (*becoming cheerful again*). How does it read now? (*They are both looking over the letter.*)

WILFRED. It reads just the same—except that about Tom Kittridge.

CAROLINE (*looking at WILFRED astonished*). Just the same! After all this work!

(*They look at one another rather*

astounded, then suddenly turn to the letter again and study over it earnestly. Sound of doorbell in distant part of house. Soon after MARTHA *crosses outside, coming from door right of stairway and disappearing into the dining room. Sound of door. A moment later she enters from the front hall and goes up the stairway carrying a large envelope.* WILFRED *and* CAROLINE *are so absorbed in work that they do not observe the bell or* MARTHA'S *movements.*)

CAROLINE (*looking up from letter*). Everything else has got to stay!

WILFRED. Then we can't telegraph —it would take hundreds of dollars!

CAROLINE (*with determination*). Yes, we can! (WILFRED *looks at her. She takes the letter.*) I'll send it! (*Backing up a little toward door.*)

WILFRED. How can you—

CAROLINE. Never you mind!

WILFRED (*follows her up a little*). See here! (*Taking hold of the letter*) I'm not going to have you spending money!

CAROLINE. Ha—no danger! I haven't got any to spend!

WILFRED (*releases hold on letter*). Then what are you going to do?

CAROLINE (*turning toward door with letter*). Oh—I know! (*Turns toward* WILFRED.) I reckon Douglass Stafford 'll send it for me!

WILFRED (*quickly to her*). No, he won't! (*They face each other.*)

CAROLINE (*surprised*). What's the reason he won't?

WILFRED (*slight pause*). If he wants to send it for *me* he can—but he won't send it for *you!*

CAROLINE. What do you care so long as he sends it?

WILFRED (*looking at* CAROLINE, *slight change of tone*). Well—I care!— that's enough! (*They look at each*

other, then both lower eyes, looking in different directions.*)

CAROLINE. Oh, well—if you feel like that about it—! (*Turns away.*)

WILFRED (*eyes lowered*). That's the way I feel! (*Pause.* WILFRED *looks up at her, then moves toward her.*) You —you won't give up the idea of helping me because I feel like that—will you?

CAROLINE (*impulsively, with start and turns toward* WILFRED). Mercy, no—I'll help you all I can— (WILFRED *impulsively takes her hand as if in gratitude and so quick that she draws it away and goes on with only a slight break.*) —about the letter!

WILFRED. That's what I mean! (*They stand an instant,* CAROLINE *looking down,* WILFRED *at her.*)

CAROLINE (*suddenly turning toward desk*). I'm going to see if we can't leave out something else! (*Sits at desk.* WILFRED *goes near her and stands looking over her, intent on the letter.*)

(*Enter* MRS. VARNEY, *coming down the stairway and into the room. She has an open letter in her hand. Also brings a belt and cap rolled up together. She pauses near the door and motions someone who is outside to come in—then comes in a little way.* MARTHA *follows her down and exits through door at the right of stairway. Enter an* ORDERLY *from the hall just from his horse after a long ride. Dusty, faded, and bloody uniform; yellow stripes. Face sunburned and grim. He stands near the door waiting, without effort to be precise or formal, but nevertheless being entirely soldierly.* MRS. VARNEY *waits until he enters.*)

MRS. VARNEY (*turning to* WILFRED). Wilfred!

(WILFRED *and* CAROLINE *turn quick-*

ly. They both stare motionless for a moment.)
Here's a letter from your Father. He sent it by the orderly.

(WILFRED *moves a step or two toward* MRS. VARNEY *and stands looking at her.* CAROLINE *slowly rises with her eyes on* MRS. VARNEY.)

(MRS. VARNEY *continues to speak calmly but with the measured quietness of one who is controlling herself.*) He tells me— (*She stops a little but it is only her voice that fails. Holds letter toward* WILFRED.) You read it!

(WILFRED, *after a glance at* CAROLINE, *steps quickly to* MRS. VARNEY *and takes the letter. Reads it,* MRS. VARNEY *looking away a little as he does so.* CAROLINE'S *eyes upon* WILFRED *as he reads.—The* ORDERLY *facing to the right on an oblique line with the door.* WILFRED *finishes very soon—only two or three seconds necessary. He glances at the* ORDERLY, *then hands the letter to his mother as he steps across to him.*)

WILFRED (*standing before the* ORDERLY). The General says I'm going back with you!

ORDERLY (*saluting*). His orders, sir!

WILFRED. When do we start?

ORDERLY. Soon as you can, sir—I'm waiting!

WILFRED. We'll make it right now! (WILFRED *turns and walks quickly to his mother.*) You won't mind, Mother?

MRS. VARNEY (*does not speak, but quietly strokes the hair back from his forehead with a trembling hand—and only once. She then hands him the belt and cap. Old and worn cap. Belt that has seen service. In a low voice*). Your brother wanted you to take these—I told him you were going.

(WILFRED *takes them. Puts on the*

belt at once.*) He says he can get another belt—when he wants it. You're to have his blanket too—I'll get it. (*She goes past* WILFRED *and out the door to the hall.*)

(WILFRED *finishes adjusting the belt. —*CAROLINE *is motionless but now looking down at the floor—facing nearly front.*)

WILFRED (*suppresses excitement*). Fits as if it was made for me! (*To* ORDERLY) I'll be with you in a jiffy! (WILFRED *goes to* CAROLINE.) We won't have to send that now— (*Indicating letter they have been working on*), will we? (WILFRED *stands on her left.* CAROLINE *shakes her head a little without looking up—then slowly raises left hand in which she has the letter and holds it out to him, her eyes still on the floor.* WILFRED *takes the letter mechanically and keeps it in his hand during the next few lines, tearing it up absent-mindedly.*) You're pretty good—to help me like you did! You can help me again if you—if you want to! (CAROLINE *raises her eyes and looks at him.*) I'd like to fight twice as well if— (*Hesitates.* CAROLINE *looks at him an instant longer and then looks down without speaking.*) Good-by! (WILFRED *holds out his hand.* CAROLINE *puts her hand in his without looking at him.*) Perhaps you'll write to me about—about helping me fight twice as well! I wouldn't mind if you telegraphed! That is—if you telegraphed that you would! (*Slight pause.* WILFRED *holding* CAROLINE'S *hand boyishly.* CAROLINE *looking down.* WILFRED *trying to say something but not finding the words.— Enter* MRS. VARNEY *at door from front hall.* WILFRED *hears her and turns— leaving* CAROLINE *and meeting his mother near center. She brings an army blanket rolled up and tied.* WIL-FRED *takes it and slings it over his shoulder.*) Good-by Mother! (*He kisses her rather hurriedly.* MRS. VAR-NEY *stands passive.*) You won't mind, will you! (WILFRED *goes at once to* ORDERLY.) Ready, sir! (*Saluting.* OR-DERLY *turns and marches out through the door at the left.* WILFRED *follows the* ORDERLY. *Brief pause.*)

(*The opening and heavy closing of the outside door is heard, and then it is still.* MRS. VARNEY *is the first to move. She turns and walks slowly up a few steps, her back to the audience, but with no visible emotion. It is as if her eyes were filled with tears and she turned away. When* MRS. VARNEY *stops,* CAROLINE *moves a little, her eyes still down, walking slowly across toward the door.* MRS. VARNEY *hears her and turns in time to speak just before she reaches the door.*)

MRS. VARNEY. Going, dear? (CARO-LINE *nods her head a little without looking round.*) Oh, yes! (*Speaks with a shade of forced cheerfulness.*) Your party, of course! You ought to be there! (CAROLINE *stops and speaks back into the room without looking at* MRS. VARNEY.)

CAROLINE (*subdued voice. With a sad little shake of head*). There won't —there won't be any party to-night. (*Goes out the door to the front hall.*)

MRS. VARNEY (*after an instant's wait, starts toward the door*). Caroline! Stop a moment! (*At door*) I don't want you to go home alone! (*She goes and rings the bell.*)

CAROLINE (*from outside*). Oh, I don't mind!

(*Sounds of front door and heavy steps of men outside.* MRS. VARNEY *goes up left center looking off, and then retreats a little. Enter* ARRELS-FORD *and two* SOLDIERS *at the door*

from the hall. ARRELSFORD *motions* MEN *to stand at the door and goes quickly to* MRS. VARNEY.)

ARRELSFORD (*in a low voice*). Is he—? (*Motions toward the window.*)

MRS. VARNEY (*to* ARRELSFORD, *hardly above a whisper*). Yes!

CAROLINE (*enters*). Oh, Mrs. Varney —there's a heap o' soldiers out yere! You don't reckon anything's the mattah, do you?

(MARTHA *enters at door right of stairway.* ARRELSFORD *goes back of* MRS. VARNEY, *and looks through curtains of window.*)

MRS. VARNEY (*hastening to* CARO-LINE). Sh!—No—there's nothing the matter! Martha, I want you to go home with Miss Mitford—at once! (*Urging* CAROLINE *off*) Good night, dear! (*Kissing her.*)

CAROLINE. Good night! (*Looks up into* MRS. VARNEY'S *face.*) You don't reckon she could go with me to— (*Hesitates.*) to somewhere else, do you?

MRS. VARNEY. Why, where do you want to go?

CAROLINE. Just to—just to the telegraph office!

(ARRELSFORD *turns sharply and looks at* CAROLINE *from window.*)

MRS. VARNEY. Now! At this time of night!

CAROLINE. I've *got* to! Oh, it's very important business!

(ARRELSFORD *watches* CAROLINE.)

MRS. VARNEY. Of course, then, Martha must go with you! Good night!

CAROLINE. Good night! (*Exit* CARO-LINE *and* MARTHA *at door to the hall.*)

MRS. VARNEY (*calling off*). Martha, don't leave her an instant!

MARTHA (*from outside*). No 'm—I'll take care! (MARTHA *does not come into room for foregoing scene. She remains back of archway. Heavy sound of outside door.*)

ARRELSFORD (*going up quickly—low, sharp voice*). What is she going to do at the telegraph office?—What is it?

MRS. VARNEY (*going down a little—low voice*). I've no (*Accenting first syllable*) idea!

ARRELSFORD (*low voice*). Has she had any conversation with him? (*Motion toward right.*)

MRS. VARNEY (*low voice*). Why—they were talking together here—early this evening! But it isn't possible that Caroline could have any—

ARRELSFORD (*interrupting, in a low voice*). Anything is possible! (*Goes over to* CORPORAL *quickly, passing back of* MRS. VARNEY. MRS. VARNEY *moves as* ARRELSFORD *crosses at back.*) Have Eddinger follow that girl! She's going to the telegraph office.—Don't let her get any dispatch off until I see it! Make no mistake about that! (CORPORAL *exits with a salute at door. Brief pause.* ARRELSFORD *turns to* MRS. VARNEY.) Are they both out there? (*Motioning toward veranda.*)

MRS. VARNEY (*low tone*). Yes!—Did you bring the man from Libby Prison?

ARRELSFORD (*low voice*). The guard's holding him out in the street. When she gets Thorne in here and leaves him alone I'll have them bring him up to that window (*Pointing to window*) and then shove him into the room.

(CORPORAL *re-appears at the door and awaits further orders.* ARRELSFORD *and* MRS. VARNEY *continue in low tones.*)

MRS. VARNEY. Where shall I—

ARRELSFORD. Out there (*Pointing left and going toward door a little*) where you can get a view of this room!

MRS. VARNEY. But if he sees me—

ARRELSFORD. He won't if it's dark in the hall! (*Turns to* CORPORAL *and gives order in low distinct voice.*) Shut off those lights out there! (*Indicating lights outside the door or archway up left.* CORPORAL *exits. An instant later the lights outside go off.*) We can close these curtains, can't we?

MRS. VARNEY. Yes.

(ARRELSFORD *draws curtains or portieres across at door or archway.* CORPORAL *and* MEN *are out of sight behind the drawn curtains.*)

ARRELSFORD (*turning to front*). I don't want much light in here! (*Indicating drawing room.* ARRELSFORD *goes to table and turns down the lamp.* MRS. VARNEY *turns down lamp on desk. Stage is in dim light.* ARRELSFORD *carefully moves couch away from window and opens portieres of window. Almost in a whisper*) Now open those curtains!—Carefully!—Don't attract attention! (*Indicating window.*)

(MRS. VARNEY *very quietly draws back the curtains to window. Moonlight streams through window, covering as much of stage as possible. Moonlight also strong on backing and also across room from there.*)

ARRELSFORD (*moving over up left center; speaking across to* MRS. VARNEY *after the lights are down*). Are those women in there yet? (*Indicating door up center.*)

MRS. VARNEY. Yes.

ARRELSFORD. Where's the key?

(MRS. VARNEY *moves noiselessly to the door.*)
Is it on this side?

(MRS. VARNEY *turns and nods affirmatively.*)
Lock the door!

(MRS. VARNEY *turns the key as noiselessly as possible.* EDITH *suddenly appears at window, coming on quickly and closing the window after her.* MRS. VARNEY *and* ARRELSFORD *both turn and stand looking at her.*)

EDITH (*stretching out left hand toward* MRS. VARNEY. *Very low voice, but breathlessly*). Mama!

(MRS. VARNEY *hurries forward with her.* EDITH *on her right.* ARRELSFORD *remains, looking on.*)

I want to speak to you!

ARRELSFORD (*low tone, stepping forward*). We can't wait!

EDITH. You must! (ARRELSFORD *moves back protestingly.* EDITH *turns to* MRS. VARNEY. *Almost a whisper*) I can't—I can't do it! Oh—let me go!

MRS. VARNEY (*very low voice*). Edith! You were the one who—

EDITH (*almost a whisper*). I was sure then!

MRS. VARNEY. Has he confessed?

EDITH (*quickly*). No, no! (*Glances toward* ARRELSFORD.)

ARRELSFORD (*low voice, sharp*). Don't speak so loud!

MRS. VARNEY (*low voice*). What is it, Edith—you *must* tell me!

EDITH (*almost a whisper*). Mama—he loves me! (*Breathless*) —Yes—and I—Oh—let someone else do it!

MRS. VARNEY. You don't mean that you—

(ARRELSFORD *comes forward quickly.*)

EDITH (*seeing* ARRELSFORD *approach, goes to him*). No, no! Not now! Not now!

MRS. VARNEY (*low voice*). More reason now than ever!

ARRELSFORD (*low voice*). We *must* go on!

EDITH (*turning desperately upon* ARRELSFORD. *Low voice*). Why are *you* doing this?

ARRELSFORD (*low voice*). Because I please!

EDITH (*low voice, but with force*). You never pleased before! Hundreds of suspicious cases have come up—hundreds of men have been run down

—but you preferred to sit at your desk in the War Department!

MRS. VARNEY (*low voice*). Edith!

ARRELSFORD (*low voice*). We won't discuss that now!

EDITH (*low voice*). No—we'll end it! I'll have nothing more to do with the affair!

ARRELSFORD (*low voice*). You won't!

MRS. VARNEY (*low voice*). Edith—!

EDITH (*low voice*). Nothing at all!—Nothing!—Nothing!

ARRELSFORD (*low voice but with vehemence*). At your own suggestion, Miss Varney, I agreed to a plan by which we could criminate this friend of yours—or establish his innocence. At the critical moment—when everything's ready, you propose to withdraw—making it a failure and perhaps allowing him to escape altogether!

MRS. VARNEY (*low voice*). I can't allow you to do this Edith!

EDITH (*low voice, desperately*). He's there!—the man is there—at the further end of the veranda! What more do you want of me!

ARRELSFORD (*low voice, sharp, intense*). Call him into this room! If anyone else should do it he'd· suspect —he'd be on his guard!

EDITH (*after pause, low voice*). Very well—I'll call him into this room. (*Turning away as if to do so.*)

ARRELSFORD (*low voice*). One thing more!

(EDITH *turns back to him.*)

I want him to have this paper! (*Holding out paper that was taken from* JONAS *in Act One*) Tell him where it came from—tell him the old niggah got it from a prisoner in Libby!

EDITH (*quietly, low voice*). Why am I to do this?

ARRELSFORD (*low but very strong*). Why not? If he's innocent where's the harm?—If not—if he's what I think he is—the message on that paper will send him to the telegraph office to-night and that's just where we want him!

EDITH (*low voice*). I never promised that!

ARRELSFORD (*hard sharp voice though subdued*). Do you still believe him innocent?

(*Pause.* EDITH *slowly raises her head erect and looks* ARRELSFORD *full in the face.*)

EDITH (*almost whisper*). I still—believe him—innocent!

ARRELSFORD. Then why are you afraid to give him this? (*Indicating paper.*)

(*Pause.* EDITH *turns to* ARRELSFORD *and stretches out her hand for the paper.* ARRELSFORD *puts the paper in* EDITH's *hand.* ARRELSFORD *and* MRS. VARNEY *watch her. She turns and moves up a few steps toward the window. Stops and stands listening to the noise of a chair being set back on the veranda.*)

EDITH (*low voice*). Captain Thorne's coming.

ARRELSFORD (*going to door and holding curtains back*). This way, Mrs. Varney!—Quick!—Quick! (ARRELSFORD *and* MRS. VARNEY *hasten off, closing portieres after them.*)

(EDITH *moves and stands near table. Sound of* THORNE's *footsteps on veranda outside windows.* EDITH *slowly turns toward the window and stands looking at it with a fascinated dread.* THORNE *opens the window and enters at once, coming a few steps into the room. He stops and stands an instant looking at* EDITH *as she looks strangely at him. Then he goes to her.*)

THORNE (*low voice, near* EDITH). Is anything the matter?

EDITH (*slightly shakes her head before speaking in nearly a whisper*).

Oh (*With emphasis*) no! (*Stands looking up in his face.*)

THORNE (*low voice*). You've been away a long time!

EDITH (*low voice*). Only a few minutes!

THORNE (*low voice*). Only a few years.

EDITH (*easier*). Oh—if that's a few years— (*Turning away a little*) what a lot of time there is!

THORNE (*low voice*). There's only to-night!

EDITH (*turning to him, a breathless interrogation*). What!

THORNE (*taking her hands and drawing her into his arms*). There's only to-night and you in the world!—Oh—see what I've been doing! I came here determined not to tell you that I love you—I love you—I love you—and for the last half hour I've been telling you nothing else! Ah, my darling—there's only to-night and you!

EDITH (*in a breathless whisper*). No, no—you mustn't! (*A quick apprehensive glance around toward left and back*) —not now! (*Her head is turned a little away from him.*)

THORNE (*still holding her, is motionless an instant. Then he gives a lightning-quick glance about and almost instantly his eyes are back to her. He slowly releases her and stands back a step. In a low voice*). Don't mind what I said, Miss Varney—I must have forgotten myself. Believe me I came to make a friendly call and—and say good-by. (*Bowing slightly*) Permit me to do so now. (*Turns at once and walks toward door to the hall.*)

EDITH (*quickly across as* THORNE *goes*). Oh!—Cap'n Thorne! (*This is timed to stop* THORNE *just before he reaches the closed portieres of door.* THORNE *turns and looks at* EDITH. *Cal-*

cium light from window on him. EDITH *is trying to be natural but her lightness is somewhat forced.)* Before you go I— *(Slight quiver in her voice)* —I wanted to ask your advice about something! *(She stands near center, turned a little to front.)*

THORNE *(looks at her motionless an instant, then turns his head slowly toward the portieres on his left. Turns back to* EDITH *again and at once moves to her. As he comes to* EDITH*).* Yes?

EDITH. What do you think—this means? *(Holds the piece of paper out toward* THORNE *but avoids looking in his face.)*

THORNE *(stepping quickly to her and taking the paper easily).* Why, what is it? *(A half-glance at the paper as he takes it.)*

EDITH. It's a— *(Hesitates slightly. Recovers at once and looks up at him brightly.)* That's what I want you to tell me.

THORNE *(looking at the paper).* Oh —you don't know!

EDITH *(shaking her head slightly).* No. *(Stands waiting—eyes averted.* THORNE *glances quickly at her an instant on peculiar tone of "no.")*

THORNE *(looking again at the paper).* A note from someone?

EDITH. It might be.

THORNE *(glancing about).* Well, it's pretty dark here! *(Sees the low-turned lamp on desk and crosses to it.)* If you'll excuse me I'll turn up this lamp a little— *(Comes to desk.)* then we can see what it is. *(Turns up lamp.)* There we are! *(Looks at paper, holding it down in light from lamp. Reads as if with much difficulty.)* "Attack . . . . to-night" . . . . There's something about "Attack to-night"—*(Turns easily to* EDITH.*)* Could you make out what it was?

*(*EDITH *shakes head negatively. Her*

lips move, but she cannot speak. She turns away.* THORNE *looks at her a second, then a slow turn of head, glancing up stage. Then quickly turns to examine the paper again.)*

"Attack . . . to-night . . . plan . . . three." *(Looks up to front as if considering. Repeats.)* Plan three! *(Considering again. Slight laugh)* Well— this thing must be a puzzle of some kind, Miss Varney. *(Turning to* EDITH.*)*

EDITH *(slowly, in a strained voice, as if forcing herself to speak).* It was taken from a Yankee prisoner!

THORNE *(instantly coming from former easy attitude into one showing interest and surprise. Looking at* EDITH*).* So!—Yankee prisoner, eh? *(While speaking he is holding paper in right hand as if to look at it again when he finishes speaking to* EDITH.*)*

EDITH. Yes—down in Libby!—He gave it to one of our servants—old Jonas!

THORNE *(turning quickly to paper).* Why, here—this might be something— *(Looks again at the paper.)* "Attack to-night—plan three—use Telegraph—" *(Second's pause. He looks up front.)* Use telegraph! *(Turns quickly to* EDITH *and goes toward her.)* This might be something important, Miss Varney! Looks like a plot on our Department Telegraph Lines! Who did Jonas give it to?

EDITH. No one!

THORNE. No one! — Well — how — how —

EDITH. We took it away from him!

THORNE. Oh! *(An "Oh!" meaning "What a pity!" Starting at once as if to cross above* EDITH *to door to the hall)* That was a mistake!

EDITH *(detaining him. Speaks rapidly, in almost a whisper).* What are you going to do?

THORNE *(strong, determined).* Find

that nigger and make him tell who this paper was for—he's the man we want! (*Going to hall.*)

EDITH (*turning quickly to him*). Cap'n Thorne—they've lied about you!

THORNE (*wheeling round like a flash and coming quickly to her*). Lied about me! What do you mean? (*Seizing her hands and looking in her face to get the answer there.*)

EDITH (*quick, breathless, very low, almost a whisper*). Don't be angry—I didn't think it would be like this!

THORNE (*with great force*). Yes—but what have you done?

EDITH (*breaking loose from him*). No!

THORNE (*as she crosses before him, trying to detain her*). But I must know!

(*Sound of heavy outside door and of steps and voices in the hall—"Here!" "This way!" etc.*)

CORPORAL (*speaking outside door*). This way! Look out on that side, will you?

(THORNE, *on hearing* CORPORAL, *etc., backs away, keeping his eyes on door and at same time snatching revolver from holster. Stands motionless, eyes on door, revolver ready.*)

EDITH. Oh! (*Going rapidly*) —I don't want to be here! (*She exits and goes upstairs out of the way of the soldiers.*)

(*Enter at once on exit of* EDITH, CORPORAL *with two* MEN. *They cross rapidly toward window up right,* CORPORAL *leading and carrying a lighted lantern.* THORNE, *seeing* CORPORAL, *at once breaks position and moves across towards center as* MEN *cross, watching* CORPORAL *who is directing his* MEN.)

CORPORAL (*near window*). Out here! Look out now!

(*The* MEN *exit at window.*)

THORNE (*quick on* CORPORAL's *speech so as to stop him*). What is it, Corporal? (*Putting revolver back into holster,* THORNE *stands in light from window, facing* CORPORAL.)

CORPORAL (*turning and saluting*). Prisoner, sir—broke out o' Libby! We've run him down the street—he turned in here somewhere! If he comes in that way (*Indicating the window down right*) would you be good enough to let us know!

THORNE. Go on, Corporal! (*Starts across to window.*) I'll look out for this window!

(*Exit* CORPORAL *through window up right.* THORNE *strides rapidly to window down right. Pushes curtains back each side and stands within the window looking off. Right hand on revolver in holster. Left hand holding curtains back. Moonlight through windows on right across stage. Dead pause for an instant. Suddenly the two* MEN *who crossed with* CORPORAL *appear at window up right holding* HENRY DUMONT. *With a sudden movement, they force him on through the window into the room and disappear quickly outside.* DUMONT *stands an instant where he landed. Looks back through window, not comprehending what is going on. He gives a quick glance about the room.* DUMONT *wears a worn and tattered uniform of a United States Cavalry private. He is pale as from lack of food—but not emaciated or ill. Hold this Tableau:* THORNE *standing motionless just within the window down right, his eyes sharply watching off to right, his hand on the butt of his revolver;* DUMONT *up right center holding position he came to on being forced into the room, with enough light through window*

*to show the blue of his uniform.
After a second's pause* DUMONT *turns
from the window and looks slowly
about the room, taking in the various
points like a caged animal, turning
his head very slowly as he looks one
way and another. Soon he moves a few
steps and pauses. Turns and makes
out a doorway up left center and, after
a glance around, he walks rapidly toward it. Just before he reaches the
door, the blades of four bayonets come
down into position between the drawn
curtain or portieres, barring his exit
there. Light from outside strikes across
on blades of the bayonets. Very slight
steely click of bayonets striking together as they come down into position.* DUMONT *stops instantly and
stands motionless.* THORNE *turns
sharply on click of bayonets, looking
into room, and advancing a few steps
in as he does so, coming to a stand
with right hand on chair that is near,
and trying to see who it is on the
opposite side of the room. Bayonets
withdrawn at once after they are
shown.* DUMONT *turns from the door
and begins to move slowly down along
the wall. Just as he is coming around
table down left, he sees* THORNE *and
stops dead.—Both men motionless,
their eyes upon each other. Hold it
several seconds.* DUMONT *makes a start
as if to escape through window up
right, moving toward it.)*

THORNE *(giving a quick and loud
order as* DUMONT *starts toward window).* Halt!—You're a prisoner!

(DUMONT, *after instant's hesitation
on* THORNE's *order, starts rapidly toward window again.* THORNE *heads
him off, meets and seizes him, ordering, as he heads* DUMONT *off)* Halt!
I say!

(DUMONT *grapples with* THORNE *and
the two men struggle together, moving*

*quickly down stage, very close to
front—getting as far as possible from
those who are watching them.* THORNE
*continues in a loud voice, as they
struggle down stage.)*
Here's your man, Corporal! What
are you waiting for! Here's your man
I say!

DUMONT *(when they are down as
far as possible, holding* THORNE *motionless an instant and hissing out
between his teeth, without pause or
inflection on the words).* ATTACK
TO-NIGHT—PLAN THREE—TEL-
EGRAPH—DO YOU GET IT?

THORNE *(quick on it).* YES!

*(This dialogue is shot at each other
with great force and rapidity—and so
low that people outside the door
could not hear.)*

DUMONT *(low voice, almost a whisper).* They're watching us! Shoot me
in the leg!

THORNE *(holding* DUMONT *motionless).* No, no! I can't do that!

DUMONT. You must!

*(They are struggling desperately—
but with little movement.)*

THORNE *(quick on it).* I can't shoot
my own brother!

DUMONT. It's the only way to throw
'em off the scent!

THORNE. Well, I won't do it anyhow!

DUMONT. If you won't do it I will!
Give me that gun! *(Pushing left arm
out to get revolver.)*

THORNE *(holding* DUMONT's *arm
back motionless).* No, no, Harry!
You'll hurt yourself!

DUMONT *(struggling to get revolver).*
Let me have it!

*(They are now struggling in real
desperation, moving quickly up center as they do so, coming into light
from windows.)*

THORNE *(calling out as he struggles*

with DUMONT). Here's your man Corporal! What's the matter with you! (DUMONT *gets hold of* THORNE's *revolver and pulls it out of holster.*)
THORNE (*as* DUMONT *holds him and is getting revolver. Loud, aspirated, sharp*). Look out, Harry! You'll hurt yourself! (*Gets his right hand on revolver to hold it.* DUMONT *manages with his left hand to wrench* THORNE's *hand loose from the revolver and hold it up while he seizes the weapon with his right hand and pulls it out of the holster. At the same time, he shoves* THORNE *off. As* DUMONT *throws him off*) Look out! (DUMONT *back quickly —with same motion—the revolver in his right hand. Before* THORNE *can recover and turn* DUMONT *fires. There is a quick sharp scream from ladies behind portieres.* DUMONT *staggers and falls, holding the revolver in his hand until he is down and then releasing it, so that it lies on the floor near him.* THORNE *back against chair—which he was flung against.*) Harry—you've shot yourself! (*Instantly on this, he dives for the revolver that* DUMONT *has dropped and gets it, coming up on same motion with it in right hand and stands in careless attitude just over* DUMONT's *body. Men's voices heard outside up left and outside windows.*)

(*Instantly on* THORNE *stooping to snatch up revolver, enter* ARRELSFORD *and* MEN *followed by* EDITH, MRS. VAR-NEY, *and* MISS KITTRIDGE *through the portieres, and up right, the* CORPORAL *and* MEN *from windows.* ARRELSFORD *runs at once to table and turns up the lamp. Others stand on tableau—*MRS. VARNEY *and* EDITH *at left,* MISS KITT-RIDGE *up left.* MEN *in doorway and near window. Bright lights fall instantly on* ARRELSFORD *reaching the lamp.*)

ARRELSFORD, MRS. VARNEY, EDITH, MISS KITTRIDGE, CORPORAL, MEN (*as they enter*). Where is he!—What has he done!—He's shot the man!—This way now! (*These different exclamations from the different characters and nearly together as they rush into the room, but quieting down at once as they see* THORNE *standing over* DU-MONT.)
THORNE (*instantly on people stopping quiet. With easy swing of revolver, he brings it up to put back into holster*). There's your prisoner, Corporal—look out for him! (*Stands, putting revolver back into holster.*)

ACT THREE

The War Department Telegraph Office. Ten o'clock.

Plain and somewhat battered and grimy room on the second floor of a public building. Moldings and stuccowork broken and discolored. Stained and smoky walls. Large windows, the glass covered with grime and cobwebs. Plaster fallen or knocked from walls and ceiling in some places. All this from neglect—not from bombardment. The building was once a handsome one, but has been put to war purposes. Very large and high double doors up right center obliqued. These doors open to a corridor showing plain corridor-backing of a public building. This door must lead off well to right so that it shall not interfere with window showing street up left center. Three wide French windows up left and left center obliqued a little and opening down to floor, with balcony outside extending right and left and showing several massive white columns, bases at balcony and extending up out of sight as if for several stories above. Part of the building with columns shown in perspective, as if a wing. Backing of windows showing night view of city roofs and buildings as from height of second floor. Large disused fireplace with elaborate marble mantel in bad repair and very dirty on right side behind telegraph tables. Door up center opening to cupboard with shelves on which are battery jars and telegraph office truck of various kinds. Room lighted by gas on right above right telegraph table, several burners branching from a main pipe and all to turn on and off easily by means of one cock in main pipe, just above the telegraph table. Show evening through windows up left—dark, with lights of buildings very faint and distant, keeping general effect outside window of darkness in order to avoid distracting attention from interior of room. Electric calciums (moonlight) to throw on at windows up left center and left on cues, and also to hold on the massive white columns and on the characters who go out on the balcony. Corridor outside door up right center not strongly illuminated. In the room itself, there is fair but not brilliant light. Plain, solid table with telegraph instruments down right center. Another plain plank table with instruments along wall at right side. Table down right center braced to look as if fastened securely to the floor. Also see that wire connections are properly made from all the instruments in the room to wires running up the wall on right side, thence across along ceiling to up left center and out through broken lights in half circle windows above the French windows at up left center. This large bunch of wires leading out, in plain sight, is most important. Large office clock over mantel set at ten o'clock at opening and to run during the Act.

Two instruments, A. and D., on table down right center. A. is at right end of table and is the only one regularly used at that table, D. being for emergency. Two instruments, B. and C., on long table at right against fireplace. B. is at lower end of table. C. at upper end. One chair at table down right center. Two chairs at table right. One chair up center. No sound of cannonading in this Act.

At opening there are two Operators at work, one at table down right center, one at table on right side. They are in old gray uniforms, but in shirt sleeves. Coats are hung up or thrown on chairs. Busy click-effect of instruments from an instant before curtain rises, and continues. After first continued clicking for a moment, there are occasional pauses. TELEGRAPH OFFICE MESSENGERS A. and B. near door up right center. THIRD WAR DEPARTMENT MESSENGER in front of door center talking to FOURTH WAR DEPARTMENT MESSENGER. SECOND WAR DEPARTMENT MESSENGER looking out of middle window over left.

—

SECOND OPERATOR [LIEUT. ALLISON] (at table right—instrument B.—finishing writing a dispatch). Ready here! (MESSENGER A. steps quickly forward and takes dispatch.) Department! The Secretary must have it to-night! (MESSENGER salutes and exits quickly at door up right center with dispatch.— Short pause.—Other MESSENGERS standing at attention.)

FIRST OPERATOR [LIEUT. FORAY] (at table down right center—instrument A.). Ready here! (MESSENGER B. steps quickly down and takes dispatch from FIRST OPERATOR). To the President— General Watson—marked private!

(MESSENGER B. *salutes, exits quickly.*)

(*Scene continues a short time as before. Busy clicking of instruments. Calls of sentries far below in the square.* SECOND OPERATOR *moves to another instrument when it begins to click and answers call.*)

FIRST MESSENGER (*enters hurriedly with dispatch*). Major Bridgman!

FIRST OPERATOR (*looking up from work*). Bridgman! Where's that?

FIRST MESSENGER (*glances at dispatch*). Longstreet's Corps.

FIRST OPERATOR. That's yours, Allison. (*Resumes work at instrument* A.)

(SECOND OPERATOR *holds out hand for dispatch.* FIRST MESSENGER *gives it to him and exits.* SECOND OPERATOR *sends message on instrument* B. *Sound of band of music in distance increasing very gradually.* MESSENGERS *go to windows and look out, but glance now and then at* OPERATORS.)

SECOND MESSENGER (*opens window and looks out while music is coming on and still distant*). What's that going up Main Street?

THIRD MESSENGER (*looks out*). Richmond Grays!

SECOND *and* FOURTH MESSENGERS (*together*). No! (MESSENGERS *look out through middle window.*)

SECOND MESSENGER. That's what they are, sure enough!

THIRD MESSENGER. They're sending 'em down the river!

SECOND MESSENGER. Not tonight!

FOURTH MESSENGER. Seems like they was, though!

THIRD MESSENGER. I didn't reckon they'd send the Grays out without there was something going on!

FOURTH MESSENGER. How do you know but what there is?

SECOND MESSENGER. To-night! Why good God! It's as quiet as a tomb!

FOURTH MESSENGER. I reckon that's what's worrying 'em! It's so damned unusual!

(*Sound of band gradually dies away.*)

FIRST OPERATOR (*before music is quite off, finishes a dispatch from instrument* A. *and calls*). Ready here!

(THIRD MESSENGER *comes to him and takes dispatch.*)

Department—from General Lee—duplicate to the President!

(THIRD MESSENGER *salutes and exits quickly. Business goes on.—Enter an* ORDERLY, *who goes quickly down to* FIRST OPERATOR. SECOND *and* FOURTH MESSENGERS *stand talking near windows.*)

ORDERLY (*salutes*). The Secretary would like to know if there's anything from General Lee come in since nine o'clock this evening.

FIRST OPERATOR. Just sent one over an' a duplicate went out to the President.

ORDERLY. The President's with the Cabinet yet—he didn't go home! They want an operator right quick over there to take down a cipher.

FIRST OPERATOR (*calling out to* SECOND OPERATOR). Got anything on, Charlie?

SECOND OPERATOR. Not right now!

FIRST OPERATOR. Well, go over to the Department—they want to take down a cipher.

(SECOND OPERATOR *gets coat and exits, putting coat on as he goes, followed by the* ORDERLY *who came for him. Business and click of instruments goes on.—Doors up right center are opened from the outside by a couple of young officers in showy and untarnished uniforms, who stand in most polite attitudes waiting for a lady to pass in.* FIRST OPERATOR *very busy writing at table, taking message from instrument* A.)

FIRST YOUNG OFFICER. Right this way, Miss Mitford!

SECOND YOUNG OFFICER. Allow me, Miss Mitford! *This* is the Department Telegraph office!

(CAROLINE MITFORD *enters. The* YOUNG OFFICERS *follow her in.* MARTHA *enters after the officers, and waits near door.*)

CAROLINE (*as she comes in, she speaks in rather subdued manner and without vivacity, as if her mind were upon what she came for*). Thank you!

FIRST YOUNG OFFICER. I'm afraid you've gone back on the Army, Miss Mitford!

CAROLINE (*looks at* FIRST YOUNG OFFICER). Gone where?

SECOND YOUNG OFFICER. Seems like we ought to a' got a salute as you went by!

CAROLINE. Oh, yes! (*Salutes in perfunctory and absent-minded manner and turns away glancing about room and moving a step or two.*) Good evening! (*Nodding to one of the* MESSENGERS.)

SECOND MESSENGER (*touching cap and stepping quickly to* CAROLINE). Good evening, Miss Mitford! Could we do anything for you in the office to-night?

(FIRST MESSENGER *remains near window.*)

CAROLINE. I want to send a telegram!

(*The three* OFFICERS *stand looking at* CAROLINE, *quieted for a moment by her serious tone.*)

SECOND YOUNG OFFICER. I'm afraid you've been havin' bad news, Miss Mitford?

CAROLINE. No— (*Shaking her head*) No! I mean—not specially.

FIRST YOUNG OFFICER. Maybe some friend o' yours has gone down to the front!

CAROLINE (*beginning to be interested*). Well, supposing he had—would you call that bad news?

FIRST YOUNG OFFICER. Well, I didn't know as you'd exactly like to—

CAROLINE. Then let me tell you—as you didn't know—that *all* my friends go down to the front!

SECOND YOUNG OFFICER. I hope not *all*, Miss Mitford!

CAROLINE. Yes—all! If they didn't they wouldn't *be* my friends!

FIRST YOUNG OFFICER. But some of us are obliged to stay back here to take care of you.

CAROLINE. Well there's altogether too many trying to take care of me! You're all discharged!

(THIRD MESSENGER *enters and joins* FOURTH MESSENGER *near upper window.* OFFICERS *fall back a little, looking rather foolish but entirely good-natured.*)

SECOND YOUNG OFFICER. Well—if we're really discharged, Miss Mitford, looks like we'd have to go!

FIRST YOUNG OFFICER. Yes—but we're mighty sorry to see you in such bad spirits, Miss Mitford!

SECOND YOUNG OFFICER *and* SECOND MESSENGER (*murmuring nearly together*). Yes, indeed we are, Miss Mitford!

CAROLINE (*turning on them*). Would you like to put me in real good spirits?

FIRST YOUNG OFFICER. Would we!

SECOND YOUNG OFFICER. You try us once!

SECOND MESSENGER. I reckon there ain't anything we'd like bettah!

CAROLINE. Then I'll tell you *just* how to do it!

(*They listen eagerly.*)

Start out this very night and never stop till you get to where my friends are—lying in trenches and ditches and earth-works between us and the Yankee guns!

SECOND YOUNG OFFICER, FIRST YOUNG OFFICER, SECOND MESSENGER (*remonstrating*). But really, Miss—You don't mean— (*etc.*)

CAROLINE. Fight Yankees a few days and lie in ditches a few nights till those uniforms you've got on look like they'd been some *use* to somebody! If you're so mighty anxious to do something for me, *that's* what you can do! (*Turning away*) It's the only thing I want!

(*The* YOUNG OFFICERS *stand rather discouraged an instant.*)

FIRST OPERATOR (*business*). Ready here! (THIRD MESSENGER *steps quickly to table.*) Department! Commissary General's office! (THIRD MESSENGER *salutes, takes dispatch, and exits.* SECOND MESSENGER *returns to* FOURTH MESSENGER *during this and stands with him near window.*)

(MESSENGER A. *enters quickly and comes to* FIRST OPERATOR, *handing him a dispatch, and at once makes his exit.* FIRST *and* SECOND YOUNG OFFICERS *exit dejectedly, after this* MESSENGER.)

CAROLINE (*with a determined air to* FIRST OPERATOR *when she sees an opportunity, accenting "Oh"*). Oh, Lieutenant Foray!

FIRST OPERATOR (*turns and rises quickly with half salute;* CAROLINE *gives a little attempt at a military salute*). Beg your pardon, Miss! (*Gets his coat, on chair or table, and hastily starts to put it on.*) I didn't know—

CAROLINE. No, no—don't! I don't mind. You see—I came on *business!*

FIRST OPERATOR (*puts on coat*). Want to send something out?

CAROLINE. Yes! That's it.—I mean I do.

FIRST OPERATOR (*goes to her*). 'Fraid we can't do anything for you here!

This is the War Department, Miss.

CAROLINE. I know that—but it's the on'y way to send, an' I—

(*Sudden loud click of instrument* B. FIRST OPERATOR *turns and listens.*)

FIRST OPERATOR. Excuse me a minute, won't you? (*Going to lower instrument on table and answering. Writing down message, etc.*)

CAROLINE. Yes—I will. (*A trifle disconcerted, stands uneasily. Speaks absently while she watches him.*) I'll— excuse you—of co'se.

FIRST OPERATOR. Ready here! (SECOND MESSENGER *goes quickly to the* FIRST OPERATOR.) Department! Quick as you can—they're waiting for it! (SECOND MESSENGER *takes dispatch, salutes, and exits.* FIRST OPERATOR *rises and goes to* CAROLINE. *To* CAROLINE) Now, what was it you wanted us to do, Miss?

CAROLINE. Just to (*Short gasp*) to send a telegram.

FIRST OPERATOR. I reckon it's private business?

CAROLINE (*looking at him with wide-open eyes*). Ye—yes! It's—private! —Oh, yes—I should *say* so!

FIRST OPERATOR. Then you'll have to get an order from someone in the department. (*Goes to back of table and picks up papers.*)

CAROLINE. That's what I thought (*Taking out a paper*), so I got it. (*Hands it to* OPERATOR.)

FIRST OPERATOR (*glancing at paper*). Oh—Major Selwin!

CAROLINE. Yes—he—he's one of my—

FIRST OPERATOR. It's all right, then! (*Instrument* B. *calls. Quickly picks up a small sheet of paper and a pen and places them on table near* CAROLINE *and pushes chair up, with almost the same movement.*) You can write it here, Miss.

CAROLINE. Thank you. (*Sits at table,*

looks at small sheet of paper, picks out large sheet, smooths it out. She starts writing.)

(FIRST OPERATOR *returns to table, answers call, and sits—writes hurriedly, taking down dispatch.* CAROLINE *earnestly writing—pausing an instant to think once or twice and a nervous glance toward* FIRST OPERATOR. FIRST OPERATOR *very busy.* MARTHA *standing motionless, waiting—her eyes fixed on the telegraph instruments.* CAROLINE *starts and draws away suspiciously on loud click of instrument* A. *near her. Moves over to side of table, looking suspiciously at the instrument. Puts pen in mouth, gets ink on tongue, makes wry face. After writing, she carefully folds up her dispatch and turns down a corner.* FIRST OPERATOR, *when nearly through, motions to* FOURTH MESSENGER *and speaks hurriedly.)*

FIRST OPERATOR (*still writing*). Here! (FOURTH MESSENGER *comes quickly.*) Department! Try to get it in before the President goes! (*Handing* FOURTH MESSENGER *dispatch.* FOURTH MESSENGER *salutes and exits.* FIRST OPERATOR *rising, to* CAROLINE) Is that ready yet, Miss?

CAROLINE (*rising, hesitating, getting left of and a little above table right center*). Yes, but I— (*Finally starts to hand it up to him.*) Of course you've— (*Hesitates.*) You've got to *take* it!

FIRST OPERATOR (*near* CAROLINE, *a brief puzzled look at her*). Yes, of course.

(*She hands him the dispatch. He opens it at once.*)

CAROLINE (*sharp scream*). Oh! (*Quickly seizes the paper out of his hand. They stand looking at each other.*) Why, I didn't tell you to *read* it!

FIRST OPERATOR (*after look at her*). Well, what did you want?

CAROLINE. I want you to *send* it!

FIRST OPERATOR. How am I going to send it if I don't read it?

CAROLINE (*after looking at him in consternation*). Do—you—mean—to—say—

FIRST OPERATOR. I've got to spell out every word! Didn't you know that?

CAROLINE (*sadly, and shaking her head from side to side*). Oh—I must have—but I— (CAROLINE *pauses, trying to think what to do.*) —you see—

FIRST OPERATOR. Would there be any harm in my—

CAROLINE (*turning on him with sudden vehemence*). Why, I wouldn't have you see it for worlds! My gracious! (*She soon opens the dispatch and looks at it.*)

FIRST OPERATOR (*good-naturedly*). Is it as bad as all that!

CAROLINE. Bad! It isn't bad at all! On'y—I only don't want it to get out all over the town—that's all.

FIRST OPERATOR. It won't ever get out from this office, Miss. (CAROLINE *looks steadfastly at him.*) We wouldn't be allowed to mention anything outside!

CAROLINE (*a doubtful look at him*). You wouldn't?

FIRST OPERATOR. No, Miss. All sorts of private stuff goes through here.

CAROLINE (*with new hope*). Does it?

FIRST OPERATOR. Every day! Now, if that's anything important—

CAROLINE (*impulsively*). Oh, yes—it's (*Recovering herself*) —it is!

FIRST OPERATOR. Then I reckon you'd better trust it to me.

CAROLINE (*looks at* OPERATOR *a moment*). Ye—yes—I reckon I had! (*She hesitatingly hands him her telegram.* FIRST OPERATOR *takes the paper and at once turns to the table, as if to send it on instrument* B. *She speaks quickly.*) Oh, stop! (FIRST OPERATOR

turns and looks at her from table.)
Wait till I— (*Turns and goes up stage toward door hurriedly.*) I don't want to be here—while you *spell out every word!* Oh, no—I couldn't *stand* that!

(FIRST OPERATOR *stands good-naturedly waiting.* CAROLINE *takes hold of* MARTHA *to start out of door with her. Enter* EDDINGER, *a private in a gray uniform.* CAROLINE *and* MARTHA *stand back out of his way. He glances at them and at once goes to the* FIRST OPERATOR, *salutes, and hands him a written order and goes in front of table, wheels and stands at attention.* FIRST OPERATOR *looks at the order, glances at* EDDINGER, *then at* CAROLINE. CAROLINE *and* MARTHA *move as if to go.*)

FIRST OPERATOR. Wait a minute, please! (CAROLINE *and* MARTHA *stop and turn toward* FIRST OPERATOR.) Are you Miss Mitford?

CAROLINE. Yes—I'm Miss Mitford!

FIRST OPERATOR. I don't understand this! Here's an order just come in to hold back any dispatch you give us.

CAROLINE (*after looking speechless at* FIRST OPERATOR *a moment*). Hold back any—hold back—

FIRST OPERATOR. Yes, Miss. And that ain't the worst of it!

CAROLINE. Wh—what else is there? (*Comes down a little way looking at* FIRST OPERATOR *with wide-open eyes.* MARTHA *remains near door.*)

FIRST OPERATOR. This man has orders to take it back with him. (*There is a slight pause.*)

CAROLINE (*rather weakly*). Take it back with him? (*Brief pause—then suddenly with great animation*) Take what back with him?

FIRST OPERATOR (*near table*). Your dispatch, Miss.

(CAROLINE *simply opens mouth and slowly draws in her breath.*)

There must be some mistake, but that's what the orders say.

CAROLINE (*with unnatural calmness*). And where does it say to take it back to?

FIRST OPERATOR (*looks at the order*). The name is Arrelsford! (*Brief pause.*)

CAROLINE. The order is for that man— (*Indicating* EDDINGER) to take my dispatch back to Mr. Arrelsford?

FIRST OPERATOR. Yes, Miss.

CAROLINE. An' does it say in there what I'm to be doin' in the meantime?

FIRST OPERATOR (*shakes head*). No, Miss.

CAROLINE. That's too bad!

FIRST OPERATOR. I'm right sorry this has occurred, Miss, and—

CAROLINE. Oh—there isn't any occasion yet for your feeling sorry—because it hasn't occurred! And besides that, it isn't goin' to occur! (*Becoming excited*) When it does you can go aroun' bein' sorry all you like! Have you got the faintest idea that I'm goin' to let him take my telegram away with him and show it to that man! Do you suppose—

MARTHA (*coming forward a step from near the door. Breaking in, in a voice like a siren*). No—sir! You ain't a goin' ter do it—you can be right sure you ain't!

FIRST OPERATOR. But what can I do, Miss?

CAROLINE (*advancing*). It's perfectly simple what you can do—you can either send it or hand it back to me—that's what you can do!

MARTHA (*calling out*). Yes, suh— that's the very best thing you can do! An' the sooner you do it the quicker it'll be done—I kin tell you that right now!

FIRST OPERATOR. But this man has come here with orders to—

CAROLINE (*going defiantly to* EDDIN-

GER *and facing him*). Well, this man can go straight back and report to Mr. Arrelsford that he was unable to carry out his orders! (*Defiant attitude toward* EDDINGER) That's what *he* can do!

MARTHA (*now thoroughly roused and coming to a sense of her responsibility*). Let 'im take it! Let 'im take it ef he wants to so pow'fle bad! Just let the other one there give it to 'im —an' then see 'im try an' git out through this do' with it! (*Standing solidly before door, with folded arms and ominously shaking head.* MARTHA *talks and mumbles on, half to herself.*) I want to see him go by! I'm just a' waitin' fur a sight o' him gittin' past dis do'! That's what I'm waitin' fur! (*Goes on talking half to herself, quieting down gradually.*) I'd like to know what they s'pose it was I come aroun' yere for anyway—these men with their orders an' fussin' an'—

FIRST OPERATOR (*when quiet is restored*). Miss Mitford, if I was to give this dispatch back to you now it would get me into a heap o' trouble.

CAROLINE. What kind of trouble?

FIRST OPERATOR. Might be prison— might be shot!

CAROLINE. You mean to say they might—

FIRST OPERATOR. Sure to do one or the other!

CAROLINE. Just for givin' me back my own writin'?

FIRST OPERATOR. That's all.

CAROLINE (*after looking silently at* FIRST OPERATOR *a moment*). Then you'll have to keep it!

FIRST OPERATOR (*after slight pause*). Thank you, Miss Mitford!

CAROLINE (*a sigh, reconciling herself to the situation*). Very well—that's understood! You don't give it back to me—an' you *can't* give it to him—

so nobody's disobeying any orders at all! (*Turning up and getting a chair, bringing it forward*) And that's the way it stands! (*Banging chair down close to* EDDINGER *and directly between him and the* FIRST OPERATOR. *Then plumps herself down on the chair and facing right, looks entirely unconcerned.*) I reckon I can stay here as long as he can! (*Half to herself*) I haven't got much to do!

FIRST OPERATOR. But Miss Mitford—

CAROLINE. Now, there ain't any good o' talkin'! If you've got any telegraphin' to do you better do it. I won't disturb you!

(*Rapid steps heard in corridor outside. Enter* MR. ARRELSFORD *hurriedly, somewhat flushed and excited. He looks hastily about.*)

ARRELSFORD. What's this! Didn't he get here in time?

FIRST OPERATOR. Are you Mr. Arrelsford?

ARRELSFORD. Yes. (*Sharp glance at* CAROLINE) Are you holding back a dispatch?

FIRST OPERATOR. Yes, sir.

ARRELSFORD. Why didn't he bring it?

FIRST OPERATOR. Well—Miss Mitford— (*Hesitates. A motion toward* CAROLINE.)

ARRELSFORD (*comprehending*). Oh! Eddinger! (EDDINGER *wheels, facing him.*) Report back to Corporal Matson. Tell him to send a surgeon to General Varney's house on Franklin Street. He's to attend to a Yankee prisoner there who was shot—if he isn't dead by this time! (*Moves, as* EDDINGER *goes.* CAROLINE *turns and looks at* ARRELSFORD *on hearing cue "prisoner," rising at same time and pushing chair back.* EDDINGER *salutes and exits quickly.* ARRELSFORD *turns and starts toward* FIRST OPERATOR.)

Let me see what that dispatch—

(FIRST OPERATOR *stands with* CAROLINE's *dispatch in his hand.* CAROLINE *steps quickly in front of* ARRELSFORD. ARRELSFORD *stops in some surprise at* CAROLINE's *sudden move.*)

CAROLINE (*facing* ARRELSFORD). I expect you think you're going to get my telegram an' read it?

ARRELSFORD. I certainly intend to do so!

CAROLINE. Well, there's a great big disappointment loomin' up right in front of you!

ARRELSFORD (*with suspicion*). So! You've been trying to send out something you don't want us to see!

CAROLINE. What if I have?

ARRELSFORD. Just this! You won't send it—and I'll see it! (*About to pass* CAROLINE) This is a case where—

CAROLINE (*steps in front of* ARRELSFORD *again so that he has to stop*). This is a case where you ain't goin' to read my private writin'— (*Stands looking at him with blazing eyes.*)

ARRELSFORD. Lieutenant—I have an order here putting me in charge! Bring that dispatch to me!

(FIRST OPERATOR *is about to move toward* ARRELSFORD *with the dispatch, when* MARTHA *steps down in front of him with ponderous tread and stands facing him.*)

MARTHA (*facing* FIRST OPERATOR). Mistah Lieutenant can stay juss about whar he is! (*Brief pause.*)

ARRELSFORD (*to* FIRST OPERATOR). Is that Miss Mitford's dispatch in your hand?

FIRST OPERATOR. Yes, sir!

ARRELSFORD. Read it!

(CAROLINE *turns with a gasp of horror.* MARTHA *turns in slow anger.* FIRST OPERATOR *stands surprised for an instant.*)
Read it out!

CAROLINE. You shan't do such a thing! You have no right to read a private telegram— (*etc.*)

MARTHA (*speaking with* CAROLINE). No sah! He ain't no business to read her letters—none whatsomever! (*etc.*)

ARRELSFORD (*angrily*). Silence!

(CAROLINE *and* MARTHA *stop talking.*)
If you interfere any further with the business of this office I'll have you both put under arrest! (*To* FIRST OPERATOR) Read that dispatch!

(CAROLINE *gasps breathless at* ARRELSFORD, *then turns and buries her face on* MARTHA's *shoulder, sobbing.*)

FIRST OPERATOR (*reads with some difficulty*). "Forgive me—Wilfred—darling—please—forgive—me—and—I—will—help—you—all—I—can."

ARRELSFORD. That dispatch can't go! (*Turns and moves left a few steps.*)

CAROLINE (*turning and facing* ARRELSFORD). That dispatch *can* go! An' that dispatch *will* go!

(ARRELSFORD *turns and looks at* CAROLINE. MARTHA *moves, ready to exit, turning toward* ARRELSFORD.)
I know someone whose orders even *you* are bound to respect and someone who'll come here with me an' see that you *do* it!

ARRELSFORD. I can show good and sufficient reasons for what I do!

CAROLINE. Well, you'll have to show good and sufficienter reasons than you've shown to me—I can tell you *that*, Mr. Arrelsford!

ARRELSFORD. I give my reasons to my *superiors* Miss Mitford!

CAROLINE. Then you'll have to go 'round givin' 'em to everybody in *Richmond*, Mr. Arrelsford! (*Saying which,* CAROLINE *makes a deep curtsy and turns and sweeps out through doors, followed in the same spirit by* MARTHA, *who turns at the door and*

also makes a profound curtsy to
ARRELSFORD, *going off haughtily.*)

(FIRST OPERATOR *sits down at table
and begins to write.* ARRELSFORD *looks
after* CAROLINE *an instant and then
goes rapidly over to* FIRST OPERATOR.)

ARRELSFORD. Let me see that dispatch!

FIRST OPERATOR (*slight doubt*). You
said you had an order, sir?

ARRELSFORD (*impatiently*). Yes—yes!
(*Throws order down on telegraph
table.*) Don't waste time!

FIRST OPERATOR (*picks up order and
looks closely at it, being careful to
show no haste*). Department order, sir?

ARRELSFORD (*assenting shortly*). Yes
—yes!

FIRST OPERATOR. I suppose you're
Mr. Arrelsford all right?

ARRELSFORD. Of course!

FIRST OPERATOR. We have to be pretty careful here. (*Hands him* CARO-
LINE's *telegram and goes on writing.*
ARRELSFORD *takes* CAROLINE's *telegram
eagerly and reads it. Thinks an instant.*)

ARRELSFORD. Did she seem nervous
or excited when she handed this in?

FIRST OPERATOR. She certainly did!

ARRELSFORD. Anxious not to have it
seen?

FIRST OPERATOR. Anxious! I should
say so! She didn't want *me* to see it!

ARRELSFORD. We've got a case on
here and she's mixed up in it!

FIRST OPERATOR. But that dispatch
is to young Varney—the General's son!

ARRELSFORD. So much the worse if
he's mixed up in it. The lying scoundrel has made dupes of all of them—
and this Mitford girl too!

FIRST OPERATOR. Who's that sir?

ARRELSFORD. Well—no matter now.
You'll know before long! It's one of
the ugliest affairs we ever had! I had
them put me on it and I've got it

down pretty close! We'll end it right
here in this office inside of thirty
minutes!

(*Enter a* PRIVATE. *He goes, at once,
to* ARRELSFORD.)

ARRELSFORD (*to* PRIVATE). Well,
what is it?

PRIVATE. The lady's here, sir!

ARRELSFORD. Where is she?

PRIVATE. Waiting down below—at
the front entrance.

ARRELSFORD. Did she come alone?

PRIVATE. Yes, sir.

ARRELSFORD. Show her the way up.
(PRIVATE *salutes and exits.* ARRELS-
FORD *goes to* FIRST OPERATOR.) I suppose you've got a revolver there?

(FIRST OPERATOR *brings up revolver
in matter-of-fact way from shelf
beneath table with left hand and lays
it on table at his left without looking
up at* ARRELSFORD, *and scarcely interrupting his writing.*)
I'd rather handle this thing myself—
but I might call on you. Be ready—
that's all!

FIRST OPERATOR. Yes, sir.

ARRELSFORD. Obey any orders you
get an' send out all dispatches unless
I stop you.

FIRST OPERATOR. Very well, sir. (*Soon
puts revolver back on shelf beneath
table.*)

(*Doors are opened by the* PRIVATE
last on, and EDITH *is shown in.* ARRELS-
FORD *meets her. The* PRIVATE *exits.*
EDITH *stops a little way down from
doors and looks at* ARRELSFORD. *She
is slightly breathless—not from exertion but owing to the situation.*)

EDITH. I—I accepted your invitation,
Mr. Arrelsford!

ARRELSFORD. I'm greatly obliged,
Miss Varney! As a matter of justice to
me it was—

EDITH (*interruption*). I didn't come
here to oblige you! I came to see—I

came to see that no more— (*A slight break before she can speak the word*) murders are committed in order to satisfy your singular curiosity.

(ARRELSFORD *waits, and then goes near* EDITH.)

ARRELSFORD (*low voice*). Is the man dead?

EDITH (*turning and looking at* ARRELSFORD *steadily*). The man is dead.

(ARRELSFORD *stands a few seconds looking at* EDITH, *then turns front slowly. Turns to her again.*)

ARRELSFORD (*with cutting emphasis but low voice*). It's a curious thing, Miss Varney, that a Yankee prisoner more or less should make so much difference to you! They're dying down in Libby by the hundreds!

EDITH. At least they're not killed in our houses—before our very eyes! (*Turns and moves.*)

(*Enter an* ORDERLY *who is a Special Agent of the War Department. He comes quickly in and goes to* ARRELSFORD. *Glances toward* FIRST OPERATOR *and quickly back to* ARRELSFORD.)

ARRELSFORD (*low voice*). Where is he? Have you kept track of him?

ORDERLY (*low voice*). He's coming up Fourth Street, sir!

ARRELSFORD (*low voice*). Where has he been?

ORDERLY (*low voice*). To his quarters on Cary Street. We got in the next room and watched him through a transom.

ARRELSFORD (*low voice*). What was he doing? What was it?

ORDERLY (*low voice*). Working at some papers or documents.

ARRELSFORD (*low voice*). Could you see them? Could you see what it was?

ORDERLY (*low voice*). Headings looked like orders from the War Department.

ARRELSFORD (*low voice*). He's com-

ing in here with forged orders!

ORDERLY (*low voice*). Yes, sir.

ARRELSFORD (*low voice*). His game is to get control of these wires and then send out dispatches to the front that'll take away a battery or division from some vital point!

ORDERLY (*low voice*). Looks like it, sir.

ARRELSFORD (*low voice*). And that vital point is what the Yankees mean by "Plan Three"! That's where they'll hit us. (*Glances round quickly, considering. Goes above line of middle window. Turns to* ORDERLY.) Is there a guard in this building?

ORDERLY (*going near* ARRELSFORD, *in a low voice*). Not inside—there's a guard in front and sentries around the barracks over in the square.

ARRELSFORD (*low voice*). They could hear me from this window, couldn't they?

ORDERLY (*low voice*). The *guard* could hear you, sir. (*A glance toward doors*) He must be nearly here by this time—you'd better look out!

EDITH (*low voice*). Where shall I go?

ARRELSFORD (*low voice*). Outside here on the balcony—I'll be with you!

EDITH (*low voice*). But—if he comes to the window! He may come here and look out!

ARRELSFORD (*low voice*). We'll go along to the next window and step in there—out of sight. (*To* ORDERLY) See if the window of the Commissary-General's office is open.

(ORDERLY *crosses* ARRELSFORD *and steps quickly through middle window, and goes off along balcony. He returns at once, re-entering through middle window.*)

ORDERLY. The next window's open, sir.

ARRELSFORD. That's all I want of you—report back to Corporal Matson.

Tell him to get the body of that prisoner out of the Varney house—he knows where it's to go!

ORDERLY. Very well, sir! (*Salutes and exits.*)

ARRELSFORD (*to* EDITH). This way, please. (*Conducts* EDITH *out through middle window to the balcony. She exits.* ARRELSFORD *is closing the window to follow, when he sees a* MESSENGER *enter, and thereupon he stops just in the window, keeping out of sight of* MESSENGER *behind window frame.*)

(*Enter* FIRST MESSENGER. *He takes his position, waiting for message as before.* ARRELSFORD *eyes him sharply an instant, then comes into room a step or two.*)

ARRELSFORD (*from near window*). Where did you come from?

FIRST MESSENGER. War Department, sir.

ARRELSFORD. Carrying dispatches?

FIRST MESSENGER. Yes, sir.

ARRELSFORD. You know me, don't you?

FIRST MESSENGER. I've seen you at the office, sir.

ARRELSFORD. I'm here on Department business. All you've got to do is to keep quiet about it! (*Exit* ARRELSFORD *through middle window, which he closes after him, and then disappears from view along balcony.*)

(*Enter* SECOND MESSENGER. *He takes his place with* FIRST MESSENGER. FIRST OPERATOR *is busy at table. A moment's wait. Enter* CAPTAIN THORNE. *As he comes in, he gives one quick glance about the room but almost instantly to front again, so that it would hardly be noticed. He wears cap and carries an order in his belt. Goes at once to table and faces* FIRST OPERATOR. FIRST OPERATOR, *on seeing* THORNE, *rises with off hand salute.*)

THORNE (*saluting*). Lieutenant! (*Hands* FIRST OPERATOR *the order he carried in his belt.*)

FIRST OPERATOR (*takes the order, opens and looks at it*). Order from the Department. (*Looking closely at the order.*)

THORNE (*motionless*). I believe so. (*A quick glance at doors as* OPERATOR *is looking at the order.*)

FIRST OPERATOR. They want me to take a cipher dispatch ovah to the President's house.

THORNE (*moving to take* FIRST OPERATOR'S *place at table, pulls chair back a little and tosses cap over on table*). Yes—I'm ordered on here till you get back. (*Goes to place back of table and stands arranging things on the table.*)

FIRST OPERATOR (*at table, looking front*). That's an odd thing. They told me the President was down here with the Cabinet! He must have just now gone home, I reckon.

THORNE (*standing at table, arranging papers, etc.*). Looks like it. If he isn't there you'd better wait. (*Looking through a bunch of dispatches as he speaks.*)

FIRST OPERATOR (*gets his cap from table and puts it on*). Yes—I'll wait! (*Pause*) You'll have to look out for Allison's wires, Cap'n—he was called ovah to the Department.

THORNE (*stops his eyes to front an instant, on mention of* ALLISON, *easy manner again*). Ah, ha—Allison.

FIRST OPERATOR. Yes.

THORNE. Be gone long? (*Throwing used sheets in waste-basket and arranging a couple of large envelopes ready for quick use.*)

FIRST OPERATOR. Well, you know how it is—they generally whip around quite a while before they make up their minds what they want to do. I don't expect they'll trouble you much! It's as quiet as a church down the river. (*Starting toward doors.*)

THORNE (*seeing a cigar on the table near instrument*). See here—wait a minute—you'd better not walk out and leave a— (FIRST OPERATOR *stops and turns back to* THORNE.) Oh, well —no matter—it's none of my business! (*Tapping with the end of a long envelope on table where the cigar is*) Still, if you want some good advice, that's a dangerous thing to do!

FIRST OPERATOR (*coming nearer*). Why, what is it, Cap'n?

THORNE. That!— (*Striking at cigar with envelope*) Leave a cigar lying around this office like that! (*Picks it up, and lights a match.*) Anybody might walk in here any minute and take it away! (*About to light cigar*) I can't watch your cigars all day— (*Lighting cigar.*)

FIRST OPERATOR (*grinning*). Oh!— Help yourself, Cap'n!

THORNE (*suddenly snatching cigar out of mouth and looking at it*). What's the matter with it?—Oh well— I'll take a chance. (*Puts it in his mouth and resumes lighting.*)

FIRST OPERATOR (*hesitates a moment then goes nearer to* THORNE *and says in a low voice*). Oh, Cap'n,—if there's any trouble around here you'll find a revolver under there. (*Indicating shelf under table.*)

THORNE (*stops lighting cigar an instant, letting match blaze in his hand, eyes motionless to front. At once resumes nonchalance—finishing lighting cigar*). What about that? What makes you think— (*Pulling in to light cigar*) there's going to be trouble?

FIRST OPERATOR. Oh, well, there might be!

THORNE (*tossing match away*). Been having a dream?

FIRST OPERATOR. Oh, no—but you never can tell! (*Starts up toward doors.*)

THORNE (*cigar in mouth; going at papers again*). That's right! You never can tell. (*A thought*) But see here— hold on a minute! (*Reaching down and getting revolver from shelf and tossing it on table*) If you never can tell you'd better take that along with you. I've got one of my own. (*Rather sotto voce*) I can tell!

(*Click of instrument* A. THORNE *answers on instrument* A. *and slides into chair.*)

FIRST OPERATOR. Well, if you've got one here, I might as well. (*Takes revolver.*) Look out for yourself, Cap'n! (*Goes up. Instrument* A. *begins clicking off a message.*)

THORNE (*sits at table listening and ready to take down what comes*). Same to you old man—and many happy returns of the day! (*Exit* FIRST OPERATOR. THORNE *writes message and briefly addresses a long envelope. Instrument* A. *stops receiving as* THORNE *addresses envelope.* THORNE *O.K.'s dispatch and puts it in envelope, which he quickly seals.*) Ready here! (FIRST MESSENGER *goes to* THORNE *and salutes.*) Quartermaster-General. (*Handing dispatch to* MESSENGER.)

FIRST MESSENGER. Not at his office, sir!

THORNE. Find him—he's got to have it!

FIRST MESSENGER. Very well, sir! (*Salutes and exits quickly.*)

(*Brief pause. Silence. No instruments clicking.* THORNE *eyes front. After a moment, he turns slowly, looking to see if there is a* MESSENGER *there. Sees there is one without looking entirely around. A second's wait. Instrument* C. *begins to click.* THORNE *rises and, going to instrument* C., *answers call—drops into chair—writes message*

—puts it in envelope—and O.K.'s call, etc.)

THORNE. Ready here! (SECOND MESSENGER *goes quickly and salutes.*) Secretary of the Treasury—marked private.—Take it to his house. (*Begins to read a dispatch he twitched off from a file.*)

SECOND MFSSENGER. He's down yere at the cabinet, sir.

THORNE. Take it to his house and wait till he comes!

(SECOND MESSENGER *salutes and exits, closing doors after him.—On the slam of doors after exit of* MESSENGER, THORNE *crushes dispatch in his right hand and throws it to floor—and wheels front—his eyes on the instrument, all in one quick movement. Then he rises and with cat-like swiftness springs to the doors and listens— opens one of the doors a little and looks off. He closes it quickly, turning and moving swiftly, and opens the door to cupboard, glancing in, then moves to the windows. Pushes the window open a little and looks off to balcony, beginning at same time to unbuckle belt and unbutton coat. Turns and moves down toward the telegraph table, at same time throwing belt down, and taking off coat. Glances back, looking to see that a document is in breast pocket of coat, letting audience see that it is there. He lays coat over back of chair, with document in sight so that he can get it without delay. Takes revolver from right hip pocket and quickly but quietly lays it on the table, just to right of instrument* A. *and then seizes key of that instrument and gives a certain call: (—.... .. ...). Waits. A glance rapidly to left. He is standing at table, cigar in mouth. Makes the call again: (—.... .. ...). Waits again. Gives the call third time:*

(—.... .. ...). Goes to lower end of table and half sits on it, folding arms, eyes on instrument, chewing cigar, with a glance or two up stage, but his eyes back quickly to instrument. Slides off table, takes cigar out of his mouth and gives the call again: (—.... .. ...). Puts cigar in mouth again, turning and walking and looking about. Soon he carelessly throws some scraps of torn paper—which he took from pocket—off up stage. Just as he throws papers, the call is answered: (—........ ..). THORNE *is back at the table in an instant and telegraphing rapidly, cigar in mouth. When he has sent for about five seconds, steps are heard in corridor outside.* THORNE *quickly strikes a match, which is close at hand, and sinks into the chair, appearing to be lazily lighting his cigar as a* MESSENGER *comes in the door.* FOURTH MESSENGER *enters as soon as he hears match strike. He delivers a dispatch, which he extends toward* THORNE *as he salutes.)*

FOURTH MESSENGER. Secretary of War, Cap'n! Wants to go out right now!

(THORNE *tosses away match, takes dispatch and opens it.* FOURTH MESSENGER *salutes, turns, and starts toward doors.*)

THORNE. Here! Here! What's all this! (*Looking at the dispatch.* FOURTH MESSENGER *returns to* THORNE, *salutes.*) Is that the Secretary's signature? (*Indicating a place on the dispatch which he holds in his hand.*)

FOURTH MESSENGER. Yes, sir—I saw him sign it.

THORNE (*looks closely at the signature. Turns it so as to get gas light. Turns and looks sharply at the* MESSENGER. *Writing*). Saw him sign it, did you?

FOURTH MESSENGER. Yes, sir.

THORNE *(turns and laying dispatch on table begins to O.K. it. Writing).* Got to be a little careful to-night!

FOURTH MESSENGER. I can swear to that one sir. *(Salutes, turns, and exits.)*

(THORNE listens for exit of MESSENGER, the dispatch in his left hand. Instantly on slam of doors, he puts cigar down at end of table, rises, laying the dispatch down flat on table. Quickly folds and very dexterously and rapidly cuts off the lower part of the paper—which has the signature of the Secretary of War upon it—with a paper knife, and holds it between his teeth while he tears the rest of the order in pieces, which he is on the point of throwing into waste-basket, when he stops and changes his mind, stuffing the torn-up dispatch into his trousers pocket. Picks up coat from back of chair and takes the document out of inside breast pocket. Opens it out on table and quickly pastes to it the piece of the real order bearing the signature, wipes quickly with handkerchief, puts handkerchief back into trousers pocket, picks up cigar which he laid down on table and puts it in mouth, at same time sitting and at once beginning to telegraph rapidly on instrument A. THORNE is intent, yet vigilant. While THORNE is pasting dispatch, ARRELSFORD appears outside windows, on balcony at side of columns. He motions off toward left. EDITH also comes into view. ARRELSFORD points toward THORNE, calling her attention to what he is doing. They stand at the window watching THORNE, the strong moonlight bringing them out sharply. After a few seconds, ARRELSFORD accidentally makes a slight noise with latch of window. Instantly on this faint click of latch, THORNE stops telegraphing and sits absolutely motionless—his eyes front. ARRELSFORD and EDITH disappear instantly and noiselessly on balcony. Dead silence. After a motionless pause, THORNE begins to fumble among papers on the table with his left hand, soon after raising the dispatch or some other paper with that hand in such a way that it will screen his right hand and the telegraph instrument on the key of which it rests, from an observer on the left. While he appears to be scanning this paper or dispatch with the greatest attention, his right hand slowly slips off the telegraph key and toward his revolver which lies just to the right of the instrument. Reaching it, he very slowly moves it over the right edge of the table, and down against his right leg. He then begins to push things about on the table with his left hand as if looking for something, and soon rises as if not able to find it, and looks still more carefully, keeping the revolver close against his right leg, out of sight from the windows. He looks about on table and glances over to table on right as if looking for what he wanted there, puts cigar down on table before him— after about to do so once and taking a final puff—and steps over to table at right, still looking for something and now—as he turns right—shifting revolver around in front of him. As he looks about among papers on table, he raises left hand carelessly to the cock of the gas bracket and suddenly shuts off light. Stage dark. Instantly on lights off, THORNE drops on one knee behind table—facing toward left and revolver—with table for a rest— covering windows up left. Light from windows gauged to strike across to THORNE at table with revolver. After holding it a short time, he begins slowly to edge up stage, first seizing

chair with his coat on it, and crouching behind it, then moving up from that, crouched with revolver ready and eyes on windows up until within reach of doors. Reaching behind him —without taking eyes or revolver off windows—he finds big heavy bolt and suddenly slides it, thus locking the doors on the inside. From doors, THORNE glides with a dash—throwing aside the chair in the way—at the door of cupboard which opens down stage and hinges on its left side. With motion of reaching it, he has it open—if not already open—and pushes it along before him as he moves left toward window. When moving slowly behind this door with his eyes and revolver on window, the telegraph instrument down right center suddenly gives two or three sharp clicks. THORNE makes an instantaneous turn covering the instrument with revolver. Seeing what it was, he turns left again. Just as he gets door nearly wide open against wall at back, he dashes at the upper window up left and bangs it open with his left hand, covering all outside with revolver in his right. In an instant he sees that no one is there, and straightens up—looking. He makes a quick spring past first window, stopping close behind the upright between first and second windows, and at same time banging these windows open and covering with revolver. Sees no one. Looks this way and that. Makes quick dash outside and covers over balustrade—as if someone might be below. In again quick. Looks about with one or two quick glances. Concludes he must have been mistaken, and starts down toward table. Stops after going two or three steps and looks back. Turns and goes rapidly down to table. Picks up cigar with left hand. Puts revolver at right end of table with right hand, and gets a match with that hand. Stands an instant looking left. Strikes match and is about to relight cigar. Pause—eyes front. Match burning. Listening. Looks left. Lights cigar. As he is lighting cigar, thinks of gas being out, and stepping to right, turns it on and lights it with match he used for cigar. Lights full on. THORNE turns quickly, looking left as lights come on. Then steps at once —after glancing quickly about room— to telegraph table, puts down cigar near upper right corner of table with left hand and begins to telegraph with left hand, facing front. Sudden sharp report of revolver outside through lower window, with crash of glass, and on it ARRELSFORD springs in from middle window, with revolver in his hand. THORNE does not move on shot except quick recoil from instrument, leaning back a little, expression of pain an instant. His left hand—with which he was telegraphing—is covered with blood. He stands motionless an instant. Eyes then down toward his own revolver. Slight pause. He makes a sudden plunge for it, getting it in his right hand. At same instant, quick turn on ARRELSFORD but before he can raise the weapon ARRELSFORD covers him with revolver and THORNE stops where he is, holding position.)

ARRELSFORD (covering THORNE). Drop it! (Pause) Drop that gun or you're a dead man! Drop it, I say! (A moment's pause. THORNE gradually recovers to an erect position, looking easily front, and puts revolver on the table, picking up cigar with same hand and putting it casually into his mouth as if he thought he'd have a smoke after all, instead of killing a man. He then gets handkerchief out of pocket with right hand and gets *hold of a corner of it, not using his left.—*ARRELSFORD *advances a step or two, lowering revolver, but holding it ready.*) Do you know why I didn't kill you like a dog just now?

THORNE (*low voice, as he twists handkerchief around his wounded hand*). Because you're such a damn bad shot.

ARRELSFORD. Maybe you'll change your mind about that!

THORNE (*speaks easily and pleasantly*). Well, I hope so, I'm sure. It isn't pleasant to be riddled up this way, you know!

ARRELSFORD. Next time you'll be riddled somewhere else besides the hand! There's only one reason why you're not lying there now with a bullet through your head!

THORNE. Only one, eh?

ARRELSFORD. Only one!

THORNE (*still fixing hand and sleeve*). Do I hear it?

ARRELSFORD. Simply because I gave my word of honor to someone outside there that I wouldn't kill you now!

(THORNE, *on hearing "Someone outside there," turns and looks at* ARRELSFORD *with interest.*)

THORNE (*taking cigar out of mouth and holding it in right hand as he moves toward* ARRELSFORD). Ah! Then it isn't a pleasant little tête-à-tête between ourselves! You have someone with you! (*Stopping, coolly facing* ARRELSFORD.)

ARRELSFORD (*sarcastically*). I *have* someone with me, Captain Thorne! Someone who takes quite an interest in what you're doing to-night!

THORNE. Quite an interest, eh! That's kind, I'm sure. (*Knocking the ashes from his cigar with a finger of right hand*) Is the gentleman going to stay out there all alone on the cold balcony, or shall I have the pleasure

(*Enter* EDITH *from balcony through the upper window, where she stands supporting herself by the sides. She is looking toward right as of intending to go, but not able, for a moment, to move. Avoids looking at* THORNE.) of inviting him in here and having a charming little three-handed— (*Glancing toward left, he sees* EDITH *and stops motionless with eyes toward left. After a moment he turns front and holds position.*)

EDITH (*does not speak until after* THORNE *looks front, low voice*). I'll go, Mr. Arrelsford!

ARRELSFORD. Not yet, Miss Varney!

EDITH (*coming blindly into the room a few steps, as if to get across to the doors*). I don't wish to stay—any longer! (*Moves toward right.*)

ARRELSFORD. One moment please! We need you!

EDITH (*stopping*). For what?

ARRELSFORD. A witness.

EDITH. You can send for me. I'll be at home. (*About to start toward door.*)

ARRELSFORD (*sharply*). I'll have to detain you till I turn him over to the guard—it won't take a moment! (*Steps to the middle window, still keeping an eye on* THORNE, *and calls off in loud voice.*) Corporal o' the guard! Corporal o' the guard! Send up the guard, will you?

(EDITH *shrinks back, not knowing what to do.*)

VOICE (*outside in distance, as if down below in the street*). What's the matter up there! Who's calling the guard!

ARRELSFORD (*at window*). Up here! Department Telegraph! Send 'em up quick!

VOICES (*outside, in distance as before*). Corporal of the Guard Post Four! (*Repeated more distant*) Corporal of the Guard Post Four! (*Repeated again, almost inaudible*) Corporal of the Guard Post Four! Fall in the guard! Fall in! (*These orders gruff, indistinct, distant. Give effect of quick gruff shouts of orders barely audible.' If* VOICES *seem close at hand, it will be disastrous.*)

EDITH (*turning suddenly upon* AR-, RELSFORD). I'm going, Mr. Arrelsford —I don't *wish* to be a witness!

ARRELSFORD (*after an instant's look at* EDITH, *suspecting the reason for her refusal*). Whatever your *feelings* may be, Miss Varney, we can't permit you to refuse!

EDITH (*with determination*). I do refuse! If you won't take me down to the street I'll find the way out myself! (*Stops as she is turning to go, on hearing the* GUARD *outside.*)

(*Sound of* GUARD *outside running through lower corridors. Tramp of men coming up stairway and along hallways outside.* THORNE *holds position, looking steadily front, cigar in right hand.*)

ARRELSFORD (*loud voice to stop* EDITH). You can't get out—the guard is here! (*With revolver, his eyes on* THORNE.)

(EDITH *stands an instant and then as the* GUARD *is heard nearer in the corridor outside, she moves up to window and remains there until sound of* GUARD *breaking in the door. Then she makes her exit to the balcony, disappearing so as to attract no attention.*)

(*Shouting across to* THORNE *above noise of* GUARD.) I've got you about where I want you at last!

(THORNE *motionless. Sound of hurried tread of men outside, as if coming on double quick toward the doors on the bare floor of corridor.*)

You thought you was almighty smart —but you'll find we can match your tricks every time!

(*Sound of the* GUARD *coming outside, suddenly ceases close to the doors.*)

SERGEANT OF THE GUARD (*close outside door*). What's the matter here! Let us in!

THORNE (*loud, incisive voice. Still facing front*). Break down the door, Sergeant! Break it down! (*As he calls, he begins to back up stage.*)

(OFFICERS *and* MEN *outside at once begin to smash in the door with the butts of their muskets.*)

ARRELSFORD (*surprised*). What are you saying about it!

THORNE. You want 'im in here, don't you?

ARRELSFORD (*moves up a little as* THORNE *does, and covers him with revolver; through noise of smashing door*). Stand where you are!

(THORNE *has backed up until nearly between* ARRELSFORD *and the door, so that the latter cannot fire on him without hitting others. But he must stand a trifle to right of line the men will take in rushing across to* ARRELSFORD.)

THORNE (*facing* ARRELSFORD). Smash in the door! What are you waiting for! Smash it in, Sergeant! (*Keeps up this call till doors break down and men rush in. Doors are quickly battered in and* SERGEANT *and* MEN *dash through and into the room.* THORNE, *continuing without break from last speech, above all the noise, pointing to* ARRELSFORD *with left hand.*) Arrest that man! (SERGEANT OF THE GUARD *and six* MEN *spring forward past* THORNE *and seize* ARRELSFORD *before he can recover from his astonishment, throwing him backward and nearly down in the first struggle, but pulling him to his feet and holding him fast.—As soon as there is quiet,* THORNE *moves down center.*) He's got in here with a revolver and he's playing hell with it!

ARRELSFORD. Sergeant—my orders are—

THORNE (*facing* ARRELSFORD). Damn your orders! You haven't got orders to shoot everybody you see in this office!

(ARRELSFORD *makes a sudden effort to break loose.*)

Get his gun away—he'll hurt himself! (*Turns, at once, and goes to the table right center, putting his coat in better position on back of chair, and then getting things in shape on the table, at same time putting cigar back in mouth and smoking.* SERGEANT *and* MEN *twist the revolver out of* ARRELSFORD'S *hands.*)

ARRELSFORD (*continuing to struggle and protest*). Listen to me! Arrest him! He's sending out a false—

SERGEANT OF THE GUARD. Now that'll do! (*Silencing* ARRELSFORD *roughly by hand across his mouth. To* THORNE) What's it all about, Cap'n?

THORNE (*standing at table arranging things*). All about! I haven't got the slightest (*Sudden snatch of cigar out of mouth with right hand and then to* SERGEANT, *as if remembering something*) He says he came out of some office! Sending out dispatches here he began letting off his gun at me. (*Turns back, arranging things on table.*) Crazy lunatic!

ARRELSFORD (*struggling to speak*). It's a lie! Let me speak—I'm from the—

SERGEANT OF THE GUARD (*quietly to avoid laugh*). Here! That'll do now! (*Silencing* ARRELSFORD. *To* THORNE) What shall we do with him?

THORNE (*tossing things into place on table with one hand*). I don't care a damn—get him out o' here—that's all I want!

SERGEANT OF THE GUARD. Much hurt, Cap'n?

THORNE (*carelessly*). Oh, no—did one hand up a little—I can get along with the other all right. (*Sits at table and begins telegraphing.*)

ARRELSFORD (*struggling desperately*). Stop him! He's sending a—Wait! Ask Miss Varney! She saw him! Ask her! Ask Miss Varney! (*Speaks wildly—losing all control of himself.*)

SERGEANT OF THE GUARD (*breaking in on* ARRELSFORD). Here! Fall in there! We'll get him out. (*The guard quickly falls in behind* ARRELSFORD, *who is still struggling.*) Forward—

OFFICER (*strides in quickly—in a loud voice, above the noise*). Halt! The General! (OFFICER *remains standing near doors.*)

SERGEANT OF THE GUARD (*to* MEN). Halt! (MEN *on motion from* SERGEANT *stand back, forming a double rank behind* ARRELSFORD, *two men holding him in front rank. All facing to center.*)

(*Enter* MAJOR GENERAL NELSON RANDOLPH,* *striding in at doors.* CAROLINE *comes to doors after the* GENERAL, *and stands just within.* ARRELSFORD *has been so astonished and indignant at his treatment that he can't find his voice at first.* OFFICERS *salute as* GENERAL RANDOLPH *comes in.* THORNE *goes on working instrument at table, cigar between his teeth. He has the dispatch with signature pasted on it, spread on table before him.*)

GENERAL RANDOLPH (*comes in and stops*). What's all this about refusing to send Miss Mitford's telegram! Is it some of your work, Arrelsford?

ARRELSFORD (*breathless, violent, excited*). General!—They've arrested me! —A conspiracy!—A— (*Sees* THORNE

* Erroneously listed as Major General *Harrison* Randolph in the 1898 edition, published by Samuel French, Inc., and in later editions, including the text in Arthur Hobson Quinn's *Representative American Plays.*

working at telegraph instrument.)
Stop that man—for God's sake stop
him before it's too late!

(CAROLINE *makes an unnoticed
exit.*)

GENERAL RANDOLPH. Stop him! What
do you mean?

THORNE (*rising quickly with salute,
timed to speak on cue*). He means me,
sir! He's got an idea some dispatch
I'm sending out is a trick of the
Yankees!

ARRELSFORD (*excitedly*). It's a conspiracy. He's an impostor—a—a—

THORNE (*subdued voice*). Why, the
man must have gone crazy, General!
(THORNE *stands motionless.*)

ARRELSFORD. I came here on a case
for—

GENERAL RANDOLPH (*sharply*). Wait!
—I'll get at this! (*To* SERGEANT, *without turning to him*) What was he
doing?

SERGEANT OF THE GUARD (*saluting*).
He was firing on the Cap'n, sir.

ARRELSFORD. He was sending out a
false order to weaken our lines at
Cemetery Hill and I—Ah! (*Suddenly
recollecting*) Miss Varney! (*Looking
excitedly about*) She was here—she
saw it all!

GENERAL RANDOLPH (*gruffly*). Miss
Varney!

ARRELSFORD. Yes, sir!

GENERAL RANDOLPH. The General's
daughter?

ARRELSFORD (*nodding affirmatively
with excited eagerness*). Yes, sir!

GENERAL RANDOLPH. What was she
doing here?

ARRELSFORD. She came to see for herself whether he was guilty or not!

GENERAL RANDOLPH. Is this some personal matter of yours?

ARRELSFORD. He was a visitor at
their house—I wanted her to know!

GENERAL RANDOLPH. Where is she

now? Where is Miss Varney?

ARRELSFORD (*looking about excitedly*). She must be out there on the
balcony! Send for her! Send for her!

GENERAL RANDOLPH (*after looking
at* ARRELSFORD *in silence for a few
seconds*). Sergeant! (SERGEANT *steps
down and salutes* GENERAL RANDOLPH.)
Step out there on the balcony. Present
my compliments to Miss Varney and
ask her to come in!

(SERGEANT *salutes and steps quickly
out on the balcony through middle
window. Walks off along balcony and
disappears. Re-appears walking back
as far as balcony goes. Turns and re-
enters room.*)

SERGEANT OF THE GUARD (*saluting*).
No one there, sir!

(THORNE *turns quietly and, opening
instrument* A., *begins to send dispatch,
picking up the forged order with left
hand, as if sending from that copy
and telegraphing with right.*)

ARRELSFORD. She must be there!
She's in the next office! The other
window. Tell him to— (*Sees* THORNE
working at instrument A.) Ah! (*Almost a scream*) Stop him! He's sending it now!

GENERAL RANDOLPH (*to* THORNE).
One moment, Cap'n! (THORNE *stops.
Salutes. Drops dispatch in left hand
to table. Pause for an instant, all holding their positions.* GENERAL RANDOLPH,
after above pause, to ARRELSFORD)
What have you got to do with this?

ARRELSFORD. It's a Department Case!
They assigned it to me!

(THORNE *picks up the forged dispatch and examines it.*)

GENERAL RANDOLPH. What's a Department Case?

ARRELSFORD. The whole plot—to
send the order—it's the Yankee Secret
Service! His brother brought in the
signal to-night!

(GENERAL RANDOLPH *looks sharply at* ARRELSFORD.)

THORNE (*very quiet and matter-of-fact*). This ought to go out, sir—it's very important.

GENERAL RANDOLPH. Go ahead with it!

(THORNE *salutes and quickly turns to instrument* A., *dropping dispatch on table, and begins sending rapidly as he stands before the table, glancing at the dispatch as he does so as if sending from it.*)

ARRELSFORD (*seeing what is going on*). No, no! It's a—

GENERAL RANDOLPH. Silence!

ARRELSFORD (*excitedly*). Do you know what he's telling them!

GENERAL RANDOLPH. No!—Do you?

ARRELSFORD. Yes! If you'll—

GENERAL RANDOLPH (*to* THORNE). Wait!

(THORNE *stops telegraphing, coming at once to salute, military position a step back from table facing front.*) Where's that dispatch?.

(THORNE *goes to* GENERAL RANDOLPH *and hands him the dispatch with salute, then back a step.* GENERAL RANDOLPH *takes the dispatch. To* ARRELSFORD) What was it? What has he been telling them? (*Looks at dispatch in his hand.*)

ARRELSFORD (*excitedly*). He began to give an order to withdraw Marston's Division from its present position!

GENERAL RANDOLPH. That is perfectly correct.

ARRELSFORD. Yes—by that dispatch—but that dispatch is a forgery!

(THORNE *with a look of surprise turns sharply toward* ARRELSFORD.) It's an order to withdraw a whole division from a vital point! A false order! He wrote it himself!

(THORNE *stands as if astounded.*)

GENERAL RANDOLPH. Why should he write it? If he wanted to send out a false order he could do it without setting it down on paper, couldn't he?

ARRELSFORD. Yes—but if any of the operators came back they'd catch him doing it! With that order and the Secretary's signature he could go right on! He could even order one of *them* to send it!

GENERAL RANDOLPH. How did he get the Secretary's signature?

ARRELSFORD. He tore it off from a genuine dispatch!—Why, General—look at that dispatch in your hand! The Secretary's signature is *pasted on!* I saw him do it!

THORNE. Why—they often come that way! (*Turns toward front.*)

ARRELSFORD. He's a liar! They never do!

THORNE (*turns on "liar," and the two men glare at each other a moment. Recovering himself*). General, if you have any doubts about that dispatch, send it back to the War Office and have it verified!

(ARRELSFORD *is so thunderstruck that he starts back a little, unable to speak. Stands with his eyes riveted on* THORNE *until cue of telegraph click below.*)

GENERAL RANDOLPH (*speaks slowly, his eyes on* THORNE). Quite a good idea! (*Brief pause*) Sergeant! (*Holding out the dispatch.* SERGEANT OF THE GUARD *salutes and waits for orders.*) Take this dispatch over to the Secretary's office and— (*Sudden loud click of telegraph instrument* A. *on table.* GENERAL RANDOLPH *stops, listening. To* THORNE) What's that?

(ARRELSFORD *looking at the instrument.* THORNE *stands motionless excepting that he took his eyes off* AR-RELSFORD *and looked across, listening.*)

THORNE (*after slight wait*). Adjutant-General Chesney.

GENERAL RANDOLPH. From the front?

THORNE. Yes, sir.

GENERAL RANDOLPH. What does he say?

THORNE (*turns and steps to the table and gives quick signal on instrument* A. *closing circuit to receive, and then stands erect listening, eyes toward front*). His compliments, sir— (*Pause. Continued click of instrument*) He asks— (*Pause. Continued click of instrument*) for the rest— (*Pause. Continued click of instrument*) of that dispatch— (*Pause. Continued click of instrument which then stops.*) It's of vital importance. (THORNE *stands motionless.*)

GENERAL RANDOLPH (*after very slight pause abruptly turns and hands the dispatch back to* THORNE). Let him have it! (THORNE *hurries salute, takes dispatch, sits at table, and begins sending.*)

ARRELSFORD. General—if you—

GENERAL RANDOLPH (*sharply to* ARRELSFORD). That's enough! We'll have you examined at headquarters!

(*Hurried steps in corridor outside; the* FIRST OPERATOR *enters quickly. He is breathless and excited.*)

ARRELSFORD (*catching sight of* FIRST OPERATOR *as he comes in*). Ah! Thank God! There's a witness! He was sent away on a forged order! Ask him! Ask him!

(*Pause.* FIRST OPERATOR *looks at others, surprised.* THORNE *is telegraphing grimly and desperately.*)

GENERAL RANDOLPH (*after instant's pause during which click of instrument is heard*). Wait a moment, Cap'n!

(THORNE *stops telegraphing, sits motionless, hand on the key, eyes straight front.—An instant of dead silence.*) (*To* FIRST OPERATOR, *gruffly*) Where did you come from?

FIRST OPERATOR (*not understanding what is going on, salutes*). There was some mistake, sir!

(ARRELSFORD *gives gasp of triumph quickly on cue. Brief pause of dead silence.*)

GENERAL RANDOLPH. Mistake, eh?— Who made it?

FIRST OPERATOR. I got an order to go to the President's house, and when I got there the President—!

THORNE (*rising at telegraph table, on cue "President's house"*). This delay will be disastrous, sir! Permit me to go on—if there's any mistake we can rectify it afterwards! (*Turns to instrument and begins sending, as he stands before it.*)

ARRELSFORD (*cry of remonstrance*). No!

GENERAL RANDOLPH (*who has not given heed to* THORNE'S *speech, to* FIRST OPERATOR). Where did you get the order?

ARRELSFORD. He's at it again, sir!

GENERAL RANDOLPH (*suddenly sees what* THORNE *is doing*). Halt there! (THORNE *stops telegraphing.*) What are you doing! I ordered you to wait!

THORNE (*turns to* GENERAL RANDOLPH). I was sent here to attend to the business of this office and that business is going on! (*Turning again, as if to telegraph.*)

GENERAL RANDOLPH (*his temper rising*). It is not going on, sir, until I'm ready for it!

THORNE (*turning back to the* GENERAL). My orders come from the War Department—not from you! This dispatch came in half an hour ago— they're calling for it—and it's my business to send it out! (*Turning at end of speech and seizing the key, he endeavors to rush off the rest of the dispatch.*)

GENERAL RANDOLPH. Halt! (THORNE *goes on telegraphing.—To* SERGEANT

OF THE GUARD) Sergeant! (SERGEANT *salutes.*) Hold that machine there! *(Pointing at telegraph instrument.— SERGEANT OF THE GUARD and two MEN spring quickly across to right. SERGEANT rushes against THORNE with arm across his breast forcing him over against chair and table on right—chair a little away from table to emphasize with crash as THORNE is flung against it—and holds him there. The two MEN cross bayonets over instrument and stand motionless. All done quickly, business-like, and with as little disturbance as possible. GENERAL RANDOLPH speaks to THORNE.)* I'll have you court-martialed for this!

THORNE *(breaking loose from SERGEANT)*. You'll answer yourself, sir, for delaying a dispatch of vital importance!

GENERAL RANDOLPH *(sharply)*. Do you mean that!

THORNE. I mean that! And I demand that you let me proceed with the business of this office!

GENERAL RANDOLPH. By what authority do you send that dispatch?

THORNE. I refer you to the Department!

GENERAL RANDOLPH. Show me your order for taking charge of this office!

THORNE. I refer you to the Department! *(Stands motionless.)*

(EDITH *appears at upper window, coming on from balcony, and moves a little into room. SERGEANT OF THE GUARD remains at table when THORNE breaks away from him.)*

GENERAL RANDOLPH. By God, then I'll go to the Department! *(Swings round and strides a little way.)* Sergeant! (SERGEANT OF THE GUARD *salutes.*) Leave your men on guard there and go over to the War Office— my compliments to the Secretary and will he be so good as to—

ARRELSFORD *(suddenly breaking out, on seeing EDITH)*. Ah! General! *(Pointing to EDITH)* Another witness! Miss Varney! She was here! She saw it all!

(THORNE, *on ARRELSFORD's mention of another witness, glances quickly toward EDITH, and at once turns front and stands motionless, waiting. GENERAL RANDOLPH turns left and sees EDITH.)*

GENERAL RANDOLPH *(bluffly touching hat)*. Miss Varney!

(EDITH *comes forward a little.*) Do you know anything about this?

EDITH *(speaks in low voice)*. About what, sir?

GENERAL RANDOLPH. Mr. Arrelsford here claims that Captain Thorne is acting without authority in this office and that you can testify to that effect.

EDITH *(very quietly, in low voice)*. Mr. Arrelsford is mistaken—he has the highest authority.

(ARRELSFORD *aghast.* GENERAL RANDOLPH *surprised.* THORNE *listening, motionless.)*

GENERAL RANDOLPH *(after an instant's pause)*. What authority has he?

EDITH *(drawing the Commission, used in Act One, from her dress. While her voice is low and controlled, it trembles slightly, and she has to pause a little twice)*. The authority— of the President—of the Confederate States of America! *(Handing the Commission to GENERAL RANDOLPH. GENERAL RANDOLPH takes the Commission and at once opens and examines it. EDITH stands a moment where she was, looking neither at ARRELSFORD nor THORNE, then stands back of others, out of the way.)*

GENERAL RANDOLPH *(looking at the Commission)*. What's this! Major's Commission! Assigned to duty on the Signal Corps! In command of the Telegraph Department!

ARRELSFORD (*breaking out*). That Commission—let me explain how she —I beg you to—

GENERAL RANDOLPH. That'll do!—I suppose this is a forgery too?

ARRELSFORD. Let me tell you, sir—

GENERAL RANDOLPH. You've told me enough! Sergeant—take him to headquarters!

SERGEANT OF THE GUARD (*quick salute*). Fall in there! (*Motioning* MEN *at instrument.* MEN *at instrument hurry across and fall into rank.*) Forward march!

(SERGEANT *and* GUARD *quickly rush* ARRELSFORD *across to doors and off, the* SERGEANT *shouting to him to keep quiet, and continuing until out of hearing.*)

ARRELSFORD (*resisting and protesting as he is forced across and off*). No! —For God's sake, General—listen to me! It's the Yankee Secret Service! Never mind me, but don't let that dispatch go out! He's a damned Yankee Secret Agent! His brother brought in the signal to-night! (*Etc.*)

(*Sounds of footsteps of the* GUARD *and voices of* ARRELSFORD *and* SERGEANT *dying away down the corridor outside. Short pause.* THORNE *motionless through above.* GENERAL RANDOLPH *goes and looks across at* THORNE.)

GENERAL RANDOLPH (*gruffly*). Cap'n Thorne!

(THORNE *comes to erect military position. Goes to the* GENERAL, *saluting.*)

It's your own fault, Cap'n! If you'd had the sense to mention this before we'd have been saved a damned lot o' trouble!—There's your Commission! (*Handing Commission to* THORNE, *who takes it saluting.* GENERAL *turns to go.*) I can't understand why they have to be so cursed shy about their Secret Service Orders! (*Goes toward door. Stops and speaks to* FIRST OPERATOR, *who is standing near door.*) Lieutenant! (FIRST OPERATOR *salutes.*) Take your orders from Major Thorne. (*Turns and goes heavily off, very much out of temper.* GENERAL *must on no account emphasize "Major."*)

(FIRST OPERATOR *goes and sits at telegraph table on extreme right, going to work on papers. No noise.* THORNE *stands facing left, Commission in his right hand, until the* GENERAL *is off. Turns head slowly around, watching to see when the* GENERAL *is gone—at the same time crushing the Commission in his right hand. After exit of* GENERAL, *he instantly glides to telegraph instrument* A. *and begins sending with right hand—still holding Commission in it.* EDITH *comes quickly to* THORNE *on his left and very near him.*)

EDITH (*speaks breathlessly, in a half whisper*). Cap'n Thorne!

(THORNE *stops telegraphing—hand still on key—but does not look at her.*) (*She goes on in low voice, hurried—breathless.*) That Commission—gives you authority—long enough to escape from Richmond!

THORNE. Escape! After all this! Impossible! (*Seizes key and begins to send.*)

EDITH. Oh!—You wouldn't do it—now!

(THORNE *instantly stops telegraphing and looks at her.*)

I brought it—*to save your life!* I didn't think you'd use it—*for anything else!* Oh—you wouldn't!

(THORNE *stands looking at her. Sudden sharp call from instrument* A. *He instantly turns back to it. His hand moves to grasp it, hovers uncertainly over it as he hesitates.* EDITH *sees his hand at the key again, covers her face* and moans, at the same time turning away. She moves to the doors and goes out. THORNE *stands in a desperate struggle with himself as instrument* A. *is clicking off the same signal that he made when calling up the front. He almost seizes the key—then resists—and finally, with a bang of right fist on the table, turns and strides across room, the Commission crushed in his right hand.*)

FIRST OPERATOR (*who has been listening to calls of instrument* A. *on table, rising at right as* THORNE *comes to a stop*). They're calling for that dispatch, sir! What shall I do?

THORNE (*turning quickly*). Send it!

(FIRST OPERATOR *drops into seat at table and begins sending, at same time spreading out the dispatch which he is sending from near left end of table.* THORNE *stands motionless an instant. As* OPERATOR *begins to send, he turns round a little, slowly and painfully, right arm up across eyes in a struggle with himself. Suddenly, he breaks away and dashes toward table.*) No, no—stop! (*Seizes the dispatch from the table in his right hand, which still has the Commission crumpled in it.*) I can't do it! I can't do it! (FIRST OPERATOR *rises in surprise on* THORNE *seizing the dispatch, and stands facing him.—*THORNE *points at instrument unsteadily.*) Revoke the order! It was a mistake!— I refuse to act under this Commission! (*Throwing the papers in his right hand down on the floor—then turns away and walks uncertainly up toward left center—turning there and after slight hesitation walking across to doors up right center—pausing an instant as he supports himself with hand on the upper door as it stands open— then exits unsteadily at doors and passes out of sight down the corridor.*)

ACT FOUR

Eleven o'clock. Drawing room at GENERAL VARNEY'S. *This is the same set as in Acts One and Two.—The furniture is somewhat disordered as if left as it was after the disturbances at the close of Act Two.—Couch is up right where* ARRELSFORD *put it end of Act Two. Nothing is broken or upset. Half light in room. Lamps lighted but not strong. See that portieres on windows down right are closed. Thunder of distant cannonading and sounds of volleys of musketry and exploding shells on very strong at times during this act. Quivering and rather subdued flashes of light (the artillery is some miles distant) shown at windows right on cues. Violent and hurried ringing of church bells in distant parts of the city—deep, low tones booming out like fire bells. Sounds of hurried passing in the street outside of bodies of soldiers—artillery— cavalry, etc., on cues, with many horse-hoof and rattling gun carriage and chain effects—shouting to horses— orders, bugle calls, etc.*

Note: This thunder of cannonading, shelling fortifications, musketry, flashes, etc., must be kept up during the act, coming in now and then where it will not interfere with dialogue, and so arranged that the idea of a desperate attack will not be lost. Possible places for this effect are noted in the manuscript.

At rise of curtain, thunder of artillery and flashes of light now and then. Ringing of church and fire bells in distance.

CAROLINE *is discovered in window up right, shrinking back against curtains and looking out through the window in a terrified way.*

———

MRS. VARNEY (*enters after coming hurriedly down the stairway*). Caroline! (CAROLINE *goes to her. She takes* CAROLINE *forward a little.*) Tell me what happened? She won't speak! Where has she been? Where was it?

CAROLINE (*frightened*). It was at the telegraph office!

MRS. VARNEY. What did she do? What happened there? Do try to tell!

(*Flashes—cannonading—bells, etc., kept up strong. Effect of passing artillery begins in the distance very faint.*)

CAROLINE. Oh, I *don't* know! How can I tell? I was afraid and ran out!

(*Alarm bell is very strong.*)

It's the alarm bell, Mrs. Varney—to call out the reserves!—That's to call out the reserves!

MRS. VARNEY. Yes—yes, I know it, dear! (*A glance of anxiety toward windows right*) They're making a terrible attack to-night. Lieutenant Maxwell was right! That quiet spell was the signal!

(*Artillery effect is louder.*)

CAROLINE (*goes timidly to window up right. Turning to* MRS. VARNEY *and speaking above the noise, which is not yet on full*). It's another regiment of artillery goin' by! They're sendin' 'em all over to Cemetery Hill! That's where the fighting is! Cemetery Hill!

(*Effect on loud.* CAROLINE *watches from window.* MRS. VARNEY *goes and rings bell.—As artillery effect dies away,* MARTHA *enters door from dining room.*)

MRS. VARNEY (*to* MARTHA). Go up and stay with Miss Edith till I come. Don't leave her a moment, Martha—not a moment!

MARTHA. No 'm—I won't. (*She turns and hastens off and up the stairway.*)

(*Alarm bell and cannon on strong.*)

MRS. VARNEY. Do close the curtains, Caroline!

CAROLINE (*closes the window curtains at right*). I'm afraid they're goin' to have a right bad time to-night! (*Going to* MRS. VARNEY.)

MRS. VARNEY. Indeed, I'm afraid so! —Now try to think, dear, who was at the telegraph office? Can't you tell me something?

CAROLINE (*shaking her head*). No— only—they arrested Mr. Arrelsford!

MRS. VARNEY. Mr. Arrelsford! Why you don't mean that he was—that he was actually arrested!

CAROLINE. Yes, I do—an' I was glad of it!—An' General Randolph—he came—I went an' brought him there— an' Oh—he was in a frightful temper!

MRS. VARNEY. And Edith—now you can tell me—what did *she* do?

CAROLINE. I can't, Mrs. Varney—I don't know! I just waited for her outside—an' when she came out she couldn't speak—an' then we hurried home! That's all I know, Mrs. Varney —truly!

(*Loud ringing of doorbell in another part of the house.* CAROLINE *and* MRS. VARNEY *turn toward door. Noise of heavy steps outside and* ARRELSFORD *almost immediately strides into the room, followed by two* PRIVATES, *who stand at the door.* CAROLINE *steps back a little as* ARRELSFORD *enters, and* MRS. VARNEY *faces him. Cannonading, etc.*)

ARRELSFORD (*roughly*). Is your daughter in the house?

MRS. VARNEY (*after a second's pause*). Certainly!

(*Cannonading, etc.*)

ARRELSFORD. I'll see her if you please!

MRS. VARNEY. I don't know that she'll care to receive you at present.

ARRELSFORD. What she cares to do at present is of small consequence! Shall I go up to her room with these men or will you have her come down here to me?

MRS. VARNEY. Neither one nor the other until I know your business.

(*Effect of passing cavalry and artillery.*)

ARRELSFORD (*excitedly*). My business! You'll know mighty quick! It's a very simple matter Mrs. Varney! Got a few questions to ask!—Listen to that!

(*Cannonading becomes heavy.*) Now you know what "Attack To-night Plan Three" means! Now you know!

MRS. VARNEY. Is that—Is that the attack they meant!

ARRELSFORD. That's the attack, Madam! They're breaking through our lines at Cemetery Hill! That was PLAN THREE! We're rushing over the reserves but they may not get there in time! —Now if you please I'll see Miss Varney!

(*Cannonading, etc.* CAROLINE *has gone to door as if going out, but turns near door to hear what* ARRELSFORD *is saying.*)

MRS. VARNEY. What has my daughter to do with this?

ARRELSFORD. Do with it! She did it!

MRS. VARNEY (*astonished*). What!

ARRELSFORD. Do you hear what I say—she did it!

(*Noise of passing Cavalry Officers going by singly.*)

MRS. VARNEY. Impossible!

ARRELSFORD. Impossible or not as you choose!—We had him there—in his own trap—under arrest—*under arrest you understand*—when she brought in that Commission!

MRS. VARNEY (*horrified*). You don't mean she—

ARRELSFORD. I mean she put the game in his hands! He got the wires! His cursed dispatch went through! As soon as I got to headquarters they saw the trick! They rushed the guard back—the scoundrel had got away!

But we're after him hot, an' if she knows where he is— (*About to turn toward door*) I'll get it out of her!

(*Cannonading, etc.*)

MRS. VARNEY. You don't suppose my daughter would—

ARRELSFORD. I suppose anything!

MRS. VARNEY. I'll not believe it!

ARRELSFORD. We can't stop for what you believe! (*Turns to go.*)

(*Alarm bells gradually cease.*)

MRS. VARNEY. Let me speak to her!

(*Passing cavalry effect has died away by this time.*)

ARRELSFORD. I'll see her myself!

CAROLINE (*as* ARRELSFORD *turns to go toward stairway, she confronts him just within the door, almost on cue of his last speech*). Where is your order for this?

ARRELSFORD (*stopped by* CAROLINE, *after an instant's surprise*). I've got a word or two to say to you—after I've been upstairs!

CAROLINE. Show me your order for going upstairs!

ARRELSFORD. Department business— I don't require an order! (*Moves as if to pass her.*)

CAROLINE (*stepping in his way again*). Oh, you've made a great mistake about that! This is a private house! It isn't the telegraph office! If you want to go up any stairs or see anybody about anything you'll have to bring an order! I don't know much —but I know *something*—an' that's it! (*She turns, and exits, and runs up the stairway.*)

(*Light cannonading, etc.*)

ARRELSFORD (*turns sharply to* MRS. VARNEY). Am I to understand, Madam, that you—

(*Loud ringing of doorbell in distant part of house, followed almost immediately by the sound of heavy door outside and tramp of many feet in the hallway. The sound of cavalry begins again.* ARRELSFORD *and* MRS. VARNEY *turn.* SERGEANT *and four* MEN *enter at door.* MEN *are halted.* SERGEANT *advances to* MRS. VARNEY. ARRELSFORD *steps back a little.*)

SERGEANT (*touching his cap roughly*). Are you the lady that lives here, ma'am?

MRS. VARNEY. I am Mrs. Varney!

SERGEANT. I've got an order to search the house! (*Showing* MRS. VARNEY *the order.*)

ARRELSFORD (*coming quickly forward*). Just in time!—I'll go through the house if you please!

SERGEANT (*roughly*). You can't go through on this order—it was issued to me.

MRS. VARNEY. You were sent here to—

SERGEANT. Yes, ma'am! Sorry to trouble you but we'll have to be quick about it! If we don't get him here we've got to follow down Franklin Street—he's over this way somewhere! (*Turns, about to give orders to* MEN.)

MRS. VARNEY. Who? Who is it you—

SERGEANT (*turning hurriedly*). Man named Thorne—Cap'n of Artillery— that's what he went by! (*Turns to his* MEN.) Here—this way! That room in there! (*Indicating room up center*) Two of you outside! (*Pointing to windows*) Cut off those windows.

(*Two* MEN *run into room and two off at windows as indicated, throwing open curtains and windows as they do so.* MRS. VARNEY *stands aside.* SERGEANT *glances quickly round the room, pushing desk out and looking behind it, etc. Keep cavalry effects on and flashes intermittently during this business. Also occasional low thunder of distant artillery. Cavalry effects distant, as if going down a street several blocks away. During this,* ARRELSFORD *goes to*

door and gives an order to his MEN. *Then he exits.* MEN *who came with* ARRELSFORD *exit after him. As the cannonading begins again, the two* MEN *who went off at door to search, re-enter shoving the old Negro* JONAS *roughly into the room. He is torn and dirty and shows signs of rough handling. They force him down center a little way and he stands crouching.*)

SERGEANT (*to* MEN). Where did you get that?

PRIVATE. Hiding in a closet, sir.

SERGEANT (*to* JONAS). What are you doing in there? If you don't answer me we'll kick the life out of you! (*Short pause. To* MRS. VARNEY) Belongs to you, I reckon?

MRS. VARNEY. Yes—but they want him for carrying a message—

SERGEANT (*interrupting*). Well, if they want him they can come an' get him—we're looking for someone else! (*Motions to* MEN.) Throw him back in there!

(MEN *shove* JONAS *off. Other* MEN *re-enter from windows at right.*) Here—this room! Be quick now! Cover that door!

(*Two* MEN *have quick business of searching. The other two* MEN *stand on guard by the door.*) Sorry to disturb you, ma'am!

(*Bell rings in distant part of house.*)

MRS. VARNEY. Do what you please—I have nothing to conceal!

(*Sound of heavy outside door. Cannonading, etc.*)

ORDERLY (*calling outside*). Here! Lend a hand, will you!

(*Two* MEN *at door exit to help someone outside. Enter the* ORDERLY *who took* WILFRED *away in Act Two, coming on hurriedly at door from the hall. Stands just below door—a few steps into room. He is splashed with foam and mud from hard riding. He sees* SERGEANT, *and salutes.* SERGEANT *salutes* ORDERLY *and goes over, looking out window.* MRS. VARNEY, *upon seeing the* ORDERLY, *utters a low cry of alarm.*) I've brought back the boy, ma'am!

MRS. VARNEY (*starting forward*). Oh! What do you— What—

ORDERLY. We never got out there at all! The Yankees made a raid down at Mechanicsville not three miles out! The Home Guard was goin' by on the dead run to head 'em off, an' before I knew it he was in with 'em riding like mad! There was a bit of a skirmish an' he got a clip across the neck—nothing at all, ma'am—he rode back all the way an'— (*Cavalry effects die away gradually.*)

MRS. VARNEY (*moving toward center*). Oh—Wilfred! He's—he's hurt!

ORDERLY. Nothing bad, ma'am—don't upset yourself!

MRS. VARNEY (*starts toward the door*). Where did you— (*Stops on seeing* WILFRED.)

(*Enter* WILFRED *at door left supported by the two* MEN. *He is pale and has a bandage about his neck.* MRS. VARNEY, *after the slight pause on his entrance, goes to him at once.*) Wilfred!

WILFRED (*weak voice—motioning* MRS. VARNEY *away*). It's all right—it's all right—you don't understand! (*Tries to free himself from the* MEN *who are supporting him.*) What do you want to hold me like that for? (*Frees himself and walks a little unsteadily.*) —You see—I can walk all right! (MRS. VARNEY *comes down anxiously on his right and holds him.* WILFRED *turns and sees his mother and takes her hand with an effort to do it in as casual a manner as possible.*) How-dy-do, Mother!—Didn't expect me back so soon, did you?—Tell you how it was— (*Turns and*

sees ORDERLY. *To* ORDERLY) Don't you go away now—I'm going back with you—just wait till I rest up about a minute.—See here! They're ringing the bells to call out the reserves! (*Starting weakly toward door*) That settles it—I'll go right now!

(*Cannonading, etc.*)

MRS. VARNEY (*gently holding him back*). No, no, Wilfred—not now!

(*Note:* WILFRED *must get well over to right center when he speaks to* MRS. VARNEY, *and not move back to left more than a step or two, in order to be near the couch.*)

(*The cannonading sounds more loudly.*)

WILFRED (*weakly*). Not now!—You hear that—you hear those bells—and tell me—not now!—I— (*Sways a little.*) I— (MRS. VARNEY *supports him tenderly.*)

SERGEANT (*quick undertone to* MEN). Stand by there!

(WILFRED *faints.* MRS. VARNEY *supports him, but almost immediately the two* MEN *come to her assistance.* SERGEANT *and two* MEN *push the couch forward and they quickly lay him on it with his head on the right.* MRS. VARNEY *goes to head of couch and holds* WILFRED's *head as they lay him down. Cannonading and other effects gradually cease.*)

SERGEANT (*to one of the* MEN). Find some water, will you? (*To* MRS. VARNEY) Put his head down ma'am—put his head down an' he'll be all right in a minute.

(*A* PRIVATE *hurries off at door to dining room on order to get water.* SERGEANT *gets a chair and puts it back of couch.* MRS. VARNEY *goes back of couch attending to* WILFRED. PRIVATE *re-enters with basin of water and gives it to* MRS. VARNEY.)

SERGEANT (*to* MEN). This way now!

(MEN *move quickly to door.* SER-
GEANT *gives quick directions to* MEN *at
door. All exit at door, one or two going right and* SERGEANT *with most of
men going up the stairway.* ORDERLY *is
left standing a little below door, exactly as he was.* MRS. VARNEY *is kneeling
back of* WILFRED *and bathing his head
tenderly—using her handkerchief.*)

ORDERLY (*after brief pause*). If there
ain't anything else, ma'am, I'd better
report back.

MRS. VARNEY. Yes—don't wait!—The
wound is dressed, isn't it?

ORDERLY. Yes, ma'am—I took him to
the Winder Hospital—they said he'd
be on his feet in a day or two—he
only wants to keep quiet a bit.

MRS. VARNEY. Tell the General just
how it happened!

ORDERLY (*touching cap*). I sure will,
ma'am. (*He turns and hurries off to
the hall.*)

(*Short pause.* MRS. VARNEY *gently
bathing* WILFRED'S *head and wrists.
Sound of alarm bells dies away excepting that from a very distant one which
continues to ring in muffled tones.*
CAROLINE *appears coming down the
stairway, absent-mindedly, stopping
when partway down because she sees
someone on couch with* MRS. VARNEY
*bathing his head. She looks more in-
tently. Then suddenly starts and runs
down the rest of the way and into the
room, stopping dead when a little way
in and looking across at what is going
on.* MRS. VARNEY *does not see her at
first.* CAROLINE *stands motionless—face
very white.* MRS. VARNEY *after a moment's pause sees* CAROLINE.)

MRS. VARNEY (*rising quickly*). Caroline, dear! (*Goes to* CAROLINE.) It's
nothing! (*Holds* CAROLINE, *though the
girl seems not to know it, her face expressionless and her eyes fixed on* WIL-
FRED.) He's hardly hurt at all! There

—there—don't you faint too, dear!

CAROLINE (*very low voice*). I'm not
going to faint! (*Sees the handkerchief
in* MRS. VARNEY'S *hand.*) Let me—
(*Takes the handkerchief and goes
across, toward front of couch. Turns
to* MRS. VARNEY.) —I can take care of
him—I don't need anybody here at
all! (*Goes toward* WILFRED.)

MRS. VARNEY. But Caroline—

CAROLINE (*still with a strange quiet;
looks calmly at* MRS. VARNEY). Mrs.
Varney—there's a heap o' soldiers goin' round upstairs—looking' in all the
rooms. I reckon you'd better go an'
attend to 'em.

MRS. VARNEY. Upstairs! Why I
didn't know they—

CAROLINE. Well, they did.—I was
keepin' 'em quiet as long as I could.

MRS. VARNEY. I—I must go up and
see to it! (*Turns and moves up left
center. Turns back.*) You know what
to do, dear!

CAROLINE. Oh, yes! (*Dropping down
on the floor beside* WILFRED *in front
of couch.*)

MRS. VARNEY. Bathe his forehead—
he isn't badly hurt!—I won't be long!
(*Exits hurriedly, closing the portieres
or curtains together after her.*)

(CAROLINE *on her knees close to*
WILFRED, *tenderly bathing his forehead and smoothing his hair.* WILFRED
soon begins to show signs of reviving.)

CAROLINE (*speaking to* WILFRED *in
low tone as he revives, not a continued
speech, but with pauses*). Wilfred
dear!—Wilfred! You're not hurt much,
are you?—Oh, no—you're not! There,
there!—You'll feel better in just a
minute!—Yes—just a minute!

WILFRED (*weakly, before he realizes
what has happened*). Is there—are you
—(*Looks round with wide-open eyes.*)

CAROLINE. Oh, Wilfred—don't you
know me?

WILFRED (*looks at her for a moment before speaking; voice weak, but clear and audible throughout this scene with* CAROLINE). What are you talking about? Of course I know you!—Say—what am I doing anyhow—taking a bath?

CAROLINE. No, no!—You see Wilfred—you just fainted a little an'—

WILFRED. Fainted!

(CAROLINE *nods*.)

I fainted! (*A weak attempt to rise, begins to remember.*) Oh— (*Sinks back weakly.*) —Yes, of course!—I was in a fight with the Yanks—an' got knocked— (*Begins to remember that he was wounded. He thinks about it a moment, then looks strangely at* CAROLINE.)

CAROLINE (*after looking at* WILFRED *in silence*). Oh—what is it?

WILFRED. I'll tell you one thing right yere! I'm not going to load you up with a cripple! Not much!

CAROLINE. Cripple!

WILFRED. I reckon I've got an arm knocked off, haven't I?

CAROLINE (*quickly*). No, no! You haven't Wilfred! (*Shaking head emphatically*) They're both on all right!

WILFRED (*after thinking a moment, weak voice*). Maybe I had a hand shot away?

CAROLINE. Oh, no—not a single one!

WILFRED. Are my—are my ears on all right?

CAROLINE (*looks on both sides of his head*). Yes—they're all right, Wilfred—you needn't trouble about them a minute!

WILFRED (*thinks a moment, then turns his eyes slowly upon her*). How many legs have I got left?

CAROLINE (*looks to see*). All of 'em —Every one!

(*Last alarm bell ceases.*)

WILFRED (*after pause*). Then—if

there's enough of me left to—to amount to anything— (*Looks in* CAROLINE'S *face a moment.*) you'll take charge of it just the same?—How about that?

CAROLINE (*after pause*). That's all right too! (CAROLINE *suddenly buries her face on his shoulder.* WILFRED *gets hold of her hand and kisses it.* CAROLINE *suddenly raises her head and looks at him.*) I tried to send you a telegram—an' they wouldn't let me!

WILFRED. Did you?

(CAROLINE *nods.*)

What did you say in it? (*Pause*) Tell me what you said!

CAROLINE. It was something nice! (*Looks away.*)

WILFRED. It was, eh? (CAROLINE *nods with her head turned away from him.* WILFRED *reaches up and turns her head toward him again.*) You're sure it was something nice!

CAROLINE. Well, I wouldn't have gone to work an' telegraphed if it was something bad, would I?

WILFRED. Well if it was good, why didn't you send it?

CAROLINE. Goodness gracious! How could I when they wouldn't let me!

WILFRED. Wouldn't let you!

CAROLINE. I should think not! (*Moves back a little for* WILFRED'S *getting up.*) Oh, they had a terrible time at the telegraph office!

WILFRED. Telegraph office. (*Tries to recollect.*) Telegr—were you there when— (*Raising himself.*)

(*Alarm bell begins to ring again in distant part of the town.* CAROLINE *moves back a little, frightened—without getting up—watching him.* WILFRED *suddenly tries to get up.*) That was it!—They told me at the hospital! (*Attempts to rise.*)

(*The cannonading becomes louder.*)

CAROLINE (*rising*). Oh—you mustn't!

(She tries to prevent him from rising.)

WILFRED *(gets partly on his feet and pushes* CAROLINE *away with one hand, holding to the chair near the desk for support with the other).* He gets hold of our Department Telegraph—sends out a false order—weakens our defense at Cemetery Hill—an' they're down on us in a minute! An' she gave it to him!—My sister Edith! She gave him the Commission that allowed him to do it!

CAROLINE. But you don't know how the—

WILFRED *(imperiously).* I know this —if the General was here he'd see her! The General isn't here—I'll attend to it!

(Sounds of cannon. WILFRED *begins to feel a dizziness and holds to the desk or chair near it for support.* CAROLINE *starts toward him in alarm. He braces himself erect again with an effort and motions her off. She stops. Weakly, but with clear voice, and commandingly, he continues.)*
Send her to me!

*(CAROLINE *stands almost frightened with her eyes upon him.* MRS. VARNEY *comes down the stairway and in the door.* CAROLINE *hurries toward her in a frightened way—with a glance back at* WILFRED.)*

CAROLINE. He wants to see Edith!

MRS. VARNEY *(going toward* WIL-FRED). Not now, Wilfred—you're too weak and ill!

WILFRED. Tell her to come here!

MRS. VARNEY. It won't do any good —she won't speak!

WILFRED. I don't *want* her to speak —I'm going to speak to *her!*

MRS. VARNEY. Some other time!

WILFRED *(leaves the desk or chair that he held to and moves toward door, as if to pass his mother and* CAROLINE). Very well—if you won't send her to me—I'll—

MRS. VARNEY *(stopping him).* There, there! If you insist I'll call her!

WILFRED. I insist!

(Cannonading.)

MRS. VARNEY *(turns toward door and goes a few steps, stops, then turns back to* CAROLINE). Stay with him, dear!

WILFRED *(weak voice but commandingly).* No!—I'll see her alone!

*(MRS. VARNEY *looks at him an instant. Sees that he means what he says. Motions* CAROLINE *to come.* CAROLINE *looks at* WILFRED *a moment, then turns and slowly goes to the door where* MRS. VARNEY *is waiting for her. Looks sadly back at* WILFRED *again, and then goes out with* MRS. VARNEY *and up the stairway.* WILFRED *stands motionless an instant as he was when the two ladies left the room. Noise of approaching men—low shouts, steps on gravel, etc., outside, begins in distance. On this,* WILFRED *turns and moves up center looking off to right. Then moves up into the doorway, but does not open the door. Alarm bell ceases. Low sound of distant voices and the tramp of hurrying feet outside quickly growing louder and louder. When it is on strong,* THORNE *appears springing over balustrade of veranda above window and instantly runs forward into the room, backing close against right wall below window and holding curtain between him and the window as he does so. A stand with vase is thrown over with this movement and crashes down in front of lower window. He stands there panting—face pale—eyes hunted and desperate and revolver clutched in right hand held at ready. His left hand is bandaged roughly. He has no hat or coat, hair is disheveled, shoes dusty, trousers and shirt torn and soiled. As*

the noise of his pursuers dies away, he turns into the room and makes a rapid start across, looking quickly about as if searching for someone. WILFRED—*who has been watching him from the doorway—turns quickly, as* THORNE *crosses, coming right of him and seizing him by right arm and shoulder.*)

WILFRED (*seizes hold of* THORNE'S *right arm and shoulder as* THORNE *crosses*). Halt! You're under arrest!

THORNE (*with a quick glance back at* WILFRED). Wait a minute! (*Shaking loose from* WILFRED) Wait a minute an' I'll go with you! (*Looking this way and that.*)

WILFRED (*a step toward* THORNE, *as if to follow*). Halt, I say! You're my prisoner!

THORNE (*turning and going quickly to* WILFRED). All right—prisoner—anything you like! (*Pushing his revolver into* WILFRED'S *hands*) Here—take this! Shoot the life out of me—but let me see my brother first!

WILFRED (*taking the revolver*). Your brother!

THORNE (*nods, breathless*). One look in his face—one look—that's all I ask!

WILFRED. Where is he?

THORNE (*breathless*). I don't know! (*Quick glance about. Points toward the door.*) Maybe they took him in there! (*Striding toward the door as he speaks.*)

WILFRED (*springing up between* THORNE *and the door and covering him with revolver*). What is he doing?

THORNE (*facing* WILFRED). What!

WILFRED (*still covering* THORNE). What's he doing in there?

THORNE. Nothing! . . . He's dead!

WILFRED (*looks at* THORNE *a moment. Then begins to back slowly up to door, keeping eyes on* THORNE *and revolver ready but not aimed. Opens*

door. *Quick look into the room. Faces* THORNE *again*). It's a lie!—There's no one there!—It's another trick of yours! (*Starts toward window—half backing so that he can still cover* THORNE *with revolver.*) Call in the Guard! Call the Guard! Captain Thorne is here in the house! (WILFRED *exits at window, calling the* GUARD. *His voice is heard outside, growing fainter and fainter in the distance.*)

(THORNE *stands an instant after* WILFRED *disappears—then springs to the door. Opens it and looks into the room, going partway off at the door. He glances this way and that within the room, then attitude of despair— left hand dropping from frame of door to his side as he comes to erect position—right hand retaining hold of knob of door. On* THORNE *standing erect,* EDITH *enters through the portieres of the door—expecting to find* WILFRED. *She stands just within the doorway.* THORNE *turns and comes out of room, closing the door as he does so. Turning away from the door— right hand still on the knob—he sees* EDITH *and stops motionless, facing her. A pause for an instant.*)

THORNE (*going toward* EDITH *a step or two*). You wouldn't tell me, would you! He was shot in this room—an hour ago—my brother Harry!—I'd like one look in his dead face before they send me the same way! Can't you tell me that much, Miss Varney? Where is he? If you won't speak to me perhaps you'll make some sign so I'll know? It's my brother, Miss Varney!

(EDITH *looks in his face an instant motionless—then turns and moves and stands near the table. As* EDITH *stops near table,* THORNE *turns away and goes toward window. Before he reaches it, there is a sudden burst of shouts and yells outside—short and* savage. THORNE *stops on the shouts and stands supporting himself a little by the upper wall or a door frame. He turns front with a grim smile, a flash from distant artillery action from window lighting his face for an instant.*)

(THORNE *continues.*) Ha!—They're on the scent at last! (*Muttering to himself*) They'll get me now—and then it won't take long to finish me off! (*Turns toward* EDITH.) And as that'll be the last of me— (*Moves toward her.*) As that'll be the last of me, Miss Varney— (*Comes near her.*) maybe you'll listen to one thing! We can't all die a soldier's death—in the roar of battle—our friends around us—under the flag we love!—No—not all! Some of us have orders for another kind of work—desperate—dare-devil work—the hazardous schemes of the Secret Service. We fight our battles alone—no comrades to cheer us on—ten thousand to one against us—death at every turn! If we win we escape with our lives—if we lose—dragged out and butchered like dogs—no soldier's grave—not even a trench with the rest of the boys—alone—despised—forgotten! These were my orders, Miss Varney—this is the death I die to-night—and I don't want you to think for one minute that I'm ashamed of it.

(*Sudden shouts and noise of many men running outside.* THORNE *swings round, walks in usual nonchalant manner, and stands waiting, leaning on side of door with outstretched right arm. He simply waits—his face utterly atonic—no attitude or expression of bravado martyrdom.* EDITH *moves and stands near mantel. The shouts and stamping of running feet grow quickly louder, gauged so that as* THORNE *stands motionless, squads of Confederate* SOLDIERS *rush in from both windows and from the hall—those on right headed by the* SERGEANT *who searched the house early in this act, and those on left by* CORPORAL. WILFRED VARNEY *with revolver still in his hand, enters at window in lead of others, letting men pass him. The* MEN *from both sides run savagely toward* THORNE *and stand each side of him with bayonets charged, hoping for the order to run him through.*)

SERGEANT. Halt! Halt! (*The* MEN *stand motionless.*)

WILFRED (*to* SERGEANT). There's your man, Sergeant—I hand him over to you!

SERGEANT (*advancing to* THORNE *and putting hand roughly on his shoulder*). Prisoner!

(*Cannonading, etc.*)

ARRELSFORD (*enters hurriedly, breaking through between men*). Where is he? (*Sees* THORNE.) Ah! We've got him, have we! (*Stands looking at* THORNE.)

SERGEANT. Young Varney here captured him, sir!

(*Enter* MRS. VARNEY *at door from stairway. She goes down left side.*)

ARRELSFORD. So!—Run down at last!

(THORNE *pays no attention to* ARRELSFORD. *He merely waits for the end of the disturbance.*)

Now you'll find out what it costs to play your little game with our Government Telegraph Lines! (*Turns to* SERGEANT.) Don't waste any time! Take him down the street and shoot him full of lead! Out with him!

(*Low shouts of approval from* MEN, *and general movement as if to start, the* SERGEANT *at same time shoving* THORNE *a little to swing him around toward left.*)

SERGEANT (*with other shouts*). Come along here!

WILFRED (*steps toward center, re-*

volver still in hand, speaking with all his force). No!

(MEN *and* OFFICERS *stand motionless.*)

Whatever he is—whatever he's done—he has a right to a trial!

(THORNE *turns and looks at* WILFRED.)

ARRELSFORD. General Tarleton said to me, "If you find him shoot him on sight!"

WILFRED. I don't *care* what General Tarleton said—I captured the man—he's in this house—and he's not going out without he's treated fair! (WILFRED *looks up toward* THORNE. *Their eyes meet. After an instant,* THORNE *turns away up stage, resting left hand against side of door frame.*)

ARRELSFORD (*suddenly, angrily*). Well—let him have it!—We'll give him a drum-head, boys—but it'll be the quickest drum-head ever held on earth!* (To* SERGEANT) Stack muskets here an' run 'em in for the court!

SERGEANT (*stepping a little down center and facing about—back to audience*). Fall in here!

(MEN *break positions each side and run up stage, falling quickly into a double rank just above* SERGEANT. THORNE *is up center above this double rank.*)

Fall in the Prisoner!

(MEN *separate, leaving space at center.* THORNE *steps down into position and stands.*)

Stack—arms!

(*Front rank* MEN *stack. Rear rank* MEN *pass pieces forward. Front rank* MEN *lay them on stacks.* SERGEANT *turns right to* MRS. VARNEY *and touches cap.*)

Where shall we find a vacant room, ma'am?

MRS. VARNEY. At the head of the stairs—there's none on this floor.

SERGEANT (*turning to* MEN). Escort —left face! (MEN *left face,* THORNE *obeying the order with them.*) Forward—march!—File left!

(SOLDIERS *with* THORNE *march rapidly out of the room and disappear up the stairway outside. The* SERGEANT *exits and goes up stairway after* MEN. ARRELSFORD *exits after* MEN, *following them closely up the stairway.*—WILFRED *follows and goes up the stairway with some effort.* MRS. VARNEY *exits.* EDITH *turns and goes slowly to window at right. Pauses a moment there, flashes of light from distant cannonading on her face. She stands in window —partly hidden by curtains—looking off. The door at center slowly opens a little way and the old Negro* JONAS *looks cautiously through from outside. Soon he opens the door and comes in almost crawling, and looking fearfully this way and that. After a moment, his eyes light on the stacks of muskets. He goes to one of them. Looks about fearfully, apprehensively. Hesitates an instant. During his next movements artillery and cavalry effects on strong. Cannon and musketry fire in distance—alarm bells on strong—begin as men go upstairs.* JONAS *makes up his mind. He drops down on knees by stack of muskets, snaps the breech lock of one without moving it from the stack—gets out the cartridge, looks at it, bites it with his teeth and looks at it again. Bites again and makes motions of getting the ball off and putting it in his pocket. Puts cartridge back in the musket, snaps the lock shut, and moves on to the next. Repeats the movement of taking the cartridge out, but is much quicker, biting off the ball at once. Repeats more rapidly and quickly with another musket, crawling quickly round the stack. Moves over to an-*

other stack. Make scene as rapid as the action will permit. As JONAS *gets well to work on muskets,* EDITH *turns at window and sees him. She stands motionless a moment—then comes down on right, and stands looking at him without moving.* JONAS *has worked around down stage on the stack, and has come to the lower side.* EDITH *stands near the desk and drops a book upon it, after the last musket but one, to make* JONAS *look up.* JONAS *looks up and sees* EDITH. *He stops. Effects of cannonading have gradually been dying down to a low distant rumble, and passing artillery and cavalry discontinued. Alarm bells in distance, however, are still heard.*)

JONAS (*after pause, very low voice*). Dhey's a-goin' ter shoot 'im—shoot 'im down like a dog, Missy—an' I couldn't b'ar to see 'em do dat! I wouldn't like to see 'im killed—I wouldn't like it noways! You won't say nuffin' 'bout dis—fer de sake of ole Jonas what was always so fond o' you—ebber sense ye was a little chile! (*He sees that* EDITH *does not appear angry, and goes on with his work of getting the bullet out of the last cartridge.*) Ye see—I jiss take away dis yer—an' den dar won't be no harm to 'im what-some-ebber—less'n day loads 'em up agin! (*Slowly hobbles to his feet as he speaks.*) When dey shoots—an' he jiss draps down, dey'll roll 'im over inter de gutter an' be off like dey was mad! Den I can be near by—an'— (*Suddenly thinks of something. A look of blank consternation comes over his face. He speaks in almost whisper.*) How's he goin' ter know! Ef he don't drap down dey'll shoot him agin—an' dey'll hab bullets in 'em nex' time! (*Anxiously glances around an instant.*) Dey'll hab bullets in 'em next time! (*Looks about. Suddenly to* EDITH) You tell

'im! *You* tell him, Missy—it's de onyest way! Tell 'im to drap down! (*Supplicatingly*) Do dis fur ole Jonas, honey—do it fur me—an' I'll be a slabe to ye ez long ez I lib! (*Slight pause. Sudden yell outside, from a dozen men shut inside a room on the floor above.* JONAS *starts and turns. Half whisper*) Dey's a-goin' ter kill 'im!

(*Noise of heavy tramp of feet outside—doors opening, etc.—An indistinct order or two before regular order heard.* JONAS *goes limping hurriedly to door.*)

SERGEANT (*outside, above*). Fall in! —Right face!—Forward—March!

JONAS (*at door*). Oh—tell 'im Missy! Tell 'im to drap down for God's sake! (*Exit* JONAS *at door, carefully closing it after him.*)

(*Cannonading is stronger. After an instant's pause,* EDITH *crosses and stands waiting near the table, her face quite expressionless. More cannonading.* WILFRED *enters at top of stairway, comes down the stairs and into the room. Enter* CAROLINE *as* WILFRED *goes down center. She hurries after him with an anxious glance up stairway and enters at door.*)

CAROLINE (*overtaking* WILFRED, *in a low voice*). What are they—going to do?

WILFRED. Shoot him!

CAROLINE. When?

WILFRED. Now.

CAROLINE (*low exclamation of pity*). Oh!

(WILFRED *goes below the lounge.* CAROLINE *follows and stands near him as* SOLDIERS *and others enter. Enter, coming down stairway,* SERGEANT, *followed by escort of* SOLDIERS. *They enter room at door and turn, marching to their former positions near the stacks of muskets.* ARRELSFORD *enters from above, down the stairway fol-*

lowing the escort of MEN. *He comes in through door.* MRS. VARNEY *enters at door.*)

SERGEANT. Halt! (MEN *halt.*) Left face! (MEN *face front.*)

(THORNE *enters at top of stairway and comes down unconcernedly and a trifle absently—for his thoughts of certain persons far away. He is followed by* CORPORAL *with his carbine.* THORNE *comes into position at front line of men.* CORPORAL *stands at left of* THORNE.)

(*After* THORNE *is in position*) Take—arms! (MEN *at once take muskets. All very quick.*) Carry—arms! (MEN *stand in line waiting.*) Fall in the Prisoner! (THORNE *walks in front of* MEN *and falls into position.*) Left—face! (THORNE *and* MEN *face to left on order.*) Forward—

EDITH. Wait!— (*Motion of hand to stop them without looking round. She controls her voice with difficulty.*) Who is the officer in command?

SERGEANT (*turning to* EDITH *and touching cap awkwardly*). I'm in command, Miss!

EDITH. I'd like to—speak to the prisoner!

SERGEANT. Sorry, Miss, but we haven't got *time!* (*Turns back to give order to* MEN.)

EDITH (*sudden turn on him and hand out*). Oh—Wait!

(SERGEANT *stops and turns slowly toward her again.*)

Only a word! (*Whispers it over to herself.*) Only a word!

(SERGEANT *hesitates an instant— turns to* MEN *and steps up a little.*)

SERGEANT. Right face!

(MEN *face to front again on order.* THORNE *obeying order with others.*) Fall out the Prisoner!

(THORNE *moves forward one step out of rank and stands motionless.*)

Now, Miss!

WILFRED (*starting indignantly toward center*). No!

(SERGEANT *turns in surprise.*)

CAROLINE (*holding to* WILFRED *and speaking in a low voice*). Oh, Wilfred —why can't she speak to him? She only wants to say good-by!

(WILFRED *looks at* CAROLINE. *Then with gesture to* SERGEANT *indicates that he may go on, and turns away with* CAROLINE.)

SERGEANT (*turning to* THORNE). The lady!

(THORNE *looks to the front as before. Then he turns slowly and looks at* SERGEANT. SERGEANT *motions with his head, indicating* EDITH. THORNE *walks down to her, stopping close on her right, standing in military position, faced in the same direction he walked, a little to left of front.* ARRELSFORD *looks at* EDITH *and* THORNE. CAROLINE, *with* WILFRED, *gives an occasional awed and frightened glance at* THORNE *and* EDITH. *No movement after the* SERGEANT's *order to "fall out the Prisoner" and* THORNE's *walk to* EDITH. EDITH, *after slight pause, speaks slowly, in almost a whisper and as if with an effort, but without apparent feeling, and without turning to* THORNE.)

EDITH (*voice for* THORNE *alone to hear. Slowly. Distinctly. Without inflection. A slight occasional tremor. Pauses as indicated*). One of the servants—has taken the musket balls—out of the guns! If you care to fall on the ground when they fire—you may escape with your life!

THORNE (*after motionless pause, speaks to* EDITH *in a low voice*). Do you wish me to do this?

EDITH (*low voice, without turning*). It's nothing to me.

THORNE (*with slight movement at*

the cue, turns slowly away. Brief pause. He turns toward EDITH *again and speaks in a very low voice*). Were you responsible in any way for—

(EDITH *shakes her head slightly without looking at him.*)

(THORNE *turns and walks right to center. Makes turn there and walks up center, and turns to face the* SERGEANT, *a little out of the way of bayonets in following scene.*) Sergeant— (*As if making an ordinary military report*) You'd better take a look at your muskets—they've been tampered with.

SERGEANT (*snatching musket from man nearest him*). What the— (*Quickly snaps it open. Cartridge drops to floor.* SERGEANT *picks it up and looks at it.*) Here!—(*Handing musket back to man, turns to squad and gives orders quickly as follows.*) Squad—ready!

(MEN *come in one movement from "carry" to position for loading.*) Draw—cartridge!

(MEN *draw cartridges, the click and snap of locks and levers ringing out simultaneously along the line.*) With ball cartridge—reload!

(MEN *quickly reload. Another rapid click of locks and levers down the line.*) Carry—arms!

(MEN *come to carry on the instant. Motionless. Eyes front.*) (*To* THORNE—*with off-hand salute*) Much obliged, sir!

THORNE (*low voice. Off-hand—as if of no consequence*). That's all right. (*Stands waiting for order to fall in.*)

WILFRED (*after* THORNE's *warning to officer about muskets, watches him with open admiration; suddenly walking up to* THORNE). I'd like to shake hands with you!

THORNE (*turns and looks at* WILFRED, *who is just below him a little to his right. A smile breaks gradually over his face*). Is this for yourself—or your father?

WILFRED (*earnestly*). For both of us, sir! (*Putting out his hand a little way;* THORNE *grasps his hand. They look into each other's faces a moment.* WILFRED *turns away and goes back of couch to* CAROLINE. THORNE *looks after* WILFRED *to front an instant—then turns.*) That's all, Sergeant!

SERGEANT (*lower voice than before*). Fall in the Prisoner!

(THORNE *steps to place in the line and turns front.*) Escort—left face!

(MEN *and* THORNE *left face.*) Forward ma—

(*Sharp cry of "Halt! Halt!" outside, followed by bang of heavy door.*) SERGEANT. Halt!

(MEN *stand motionless at left face. On seeing the* ORDERLY *approaching—just before he is on*) Right face!

(MEN *and* THORNE *face to front. An* AID—*wearing Lieutenant's uniform—enters quickly from the hall.* SERGEANT, *faced front just forward of his men, salutes.*—AID *salutes. More cannonading, etc.*)

AID. General Randolph's compliments, sir, and he's on the way with orders!

ARRELSFORD. What orders, Lieutenant?—Anything to do with this case?

AID (*no salute to* ARRELSFORD). I don't know what the orders are, sir. He's been with the President.

ARRELSFORD. I sent word to the Department we'd got the man and were going to drum-head him on the spot.

(WILFRED *and* CAROLINE *move unobtrusively to the upper side of couch.*)

AID. Then this must be the case, sir. I believe the General wishes to be present.

ARRELSFORD. Impossible! We've held the court and I've sent the finding to the Secretary! The messenger is to get his approval and meet us at the corner of Copley Street.

AID. I have no further orders, sir! (*Retires up with quick military movement and turns facing front. Stands motionless*)

(*The cannonading becomes louder. Sound of heavy door outside and the tread of the* GENERAL *as he strides across the hall.*)

SERGEANT (*low voice to* MEN). Present—arms!

(SERGEANT, ORDERLY, *etc., on salute. Enter* GENERAL RANDOLPH *at door, striding on hurriedly—returning salutes as he goes down, glancing about.* LIEUTENANT FORAY, *the* FIRST TELEGRAPH OPERATOR, *follows* GENERAL RANDOLPH *in at door. He stands waiting near door, faced front, military position.*)

SERGEANT (*low order to* MEN). Carry—arms!

(MEN *come to carry again.*)

GENERAL RANDOLPH. Ah, Sergeant!— (*Going down and across to right*) Got the prisoner in here have you?

SERGEANT (*saluting*). Just taking him out, sir.

GENERAL RANDOLPH. Prison?

SERGEANT. No, sir—to execute the sentence of the Court.

GENERAL RANDOLPH. Had his trial then?

ARRELSFORD (*stepping down with a salute*). All done according to regulations, sir—the finding has gone to the Secretary.

GENERAL RANDOLPH (*to* ARRELSFORD). Found guilty I judge?

ARRELSFORD. Found guilty, sir.—No time now for hanging—the Court ordered him shot.

GENERAL RANDOLPH. What were the grounds for this?

ARRELSFORD. Conspiracy against our government and the success of our arms by sending a false and misleading dispatch containing forged orders.

GENERAL RANDOLPH. Court's been misinformed—that dispatch was never sent.

(EDITH *looks up with sudden breathless exclamation.* WILFRED *turns with surprise. Others are greatly astonished.*)

ARRELSFORD (*coming down on right of* GENERAL). Why, General—the dispatch—I saw him—

GENERAL RANDOLPH. I say the dispatch wasn't sent! I expected to arrive in time for the trial and brought Foray here to testify. (*Calls to* LIEUTENANT FORAY *without looking round.*) Lieutenant!

(LIEUTENANT FORAY *comes quickly down, facing* GENERAL RANDOLPH. *Salutes.*)

Did Captain Thorne send out any dispatches after we left you with him in the office an hour ago?

LIEUTENANT FORAY. No, sir. I was just going to send one under his order, but he countermanded it.

GENERAL RANDOLPH. What were his words at the time?

LIEUTENANT FORAY. He said he refused to act under that Commission.

(EDITH *turns toward* THORNE *and her eyes are upon him for a moment.*)

GENERAL RANDOLPH. That will do, Lieutenant!

(LIEUTENANT FORAY *salutes and retires.*)

In addition we learn from General Chesney that no complete order was received over the wire—that Marston's Division was not withdrawn—that our position was not weakened in any way and the attack at that point has been repulsed. It's plain, therefore, that the Court has been acting under error.

The President for this reason finds himself compelled to disapprove the finding and it is set aside.

ARRELSFORD (*with great indignation*). General Randolph, this case was put in my hands and I—

GENERAL RANDOLPH (*interrupting bluffly, but without temper*). Well, I take it out of your hands! Report back to the War Office with my compliments!

ARRELSFORD (*turns and starts toward the door, but after proceeding a few steps stops and turns*). Hadn't I better wait and see—

GENERAL RANDOLPH. No—don't wait to see anything.

(ARRELSFORD *looks at* GENERAL RANDOLPH *an instant, then turns and, after raising his hat to the ladies, walks with dignity out at door and exits. Sound of heavy outside door, closed with force.* GENERAL RANDOLPH *is in front of couch.*)
Sergeant!

(SERGEANT *quickly to* GENERAL RANDOLPH *on salute.*)
Hold your men back there. I'll see the prisoner.

(SERGEANT *salutes, turns, marches straight up from where he is to the left division of the escort so that he is a little to left of* THORNE, *and turns front.*)

SERGEANT. Order—arms!

(*Squad obeys with precision.*)
Parade—rest!

(*Squad obeys order.*)
Fall out the Prisoner!

(THORNE *steps forward one step out of the rank and stands.*)
The General!

(THORNE *starts to* GENERAL RANDOLPH. *As* THORNE *steps forward on order, "The General," * EDITH *moves quickly and intercepts him about two-thirds of the way down, on his left.* THORNE, *stopped by* EDITH, *shows slight surprise for an instant, but quickly recovers and looks straight front.*)

EDITH (*to* THORNE, *as she meets him, impulsively, in a low voice*). Oh—why didn't you tell me!—I thought you sent it! I thought you—

GENERAL RANDOLPH (*surprised*). Miss Varney!

EDITH (*crossing* THORNE *to the* GENERAL). There's nothing against him, General Randolph!—He didn't send it so there's nothing to try him for now!

GENERAL RANDOLPH. You're very much mistaken, Miss Varney. The fact of his being caught in our lines without his uniform is enough to swing him off in ten minutes.

(EDITH *moans a little, at same time moving back from* GENERAL *a step.*)

GENERAL RANDOLPH. Cap'n Thorne—

(THORNE *steps down and faces the* GENERAL.)

or whatever your name may be—the President is fully informed regarding the circumstances of your case, and I needn't say that we look on you as a cursed dangerous character! There isn't any doubt whatever that you'd ought to be exterminated right now! —But considering the damned peculiarity of your behavior—and that you refused—*for some reason*—to send that dispatch when you might have done so, we've decided to keep you out of mischief some other way. The Sergeant will turn you over to Major Whitfield, sir!

(SERGEANT *salutes.*)
You'll be held as a prisoner of war!
(*Turns and goes a few steps.*)

EDITH (*turns suddenly to* THORNE, *coming down before him as he faces right. Looking in his face, she speaks in low voice*). Oh—that isn't nearly so bad!

THORNE (*holds her hand in his right*). No—?

EDITH. No!—Because—sometime—

THORNE (*low voice*). Ah—if it's sometime, there's nothing else in the world.

(*Slight pause.* EDITH *sees* MRS. VARNEY, *and goes to her,* THORNE *retaining her hand as she crosses—releasing it only when he has to.*)

EDITH. Mamma, won't you speak to him?

(MRS. VARNEY *and* EDITH *talk quietly.*)

WILFRED (*suddenly leaving* CAROLINE, *striding down from behind couch to* THORNE, *and extending hand*). I'd like to shake hands with you!

THORNE (*turning to* WILFRED). What —again? (*Taking* WILFRED's *hand.*)

(WILFRED, *shaking hands with* THORNE—*back to audience, laughing and very jovial about it.*)

CAROLINE (*coming quickly down on right of* THORNE). So would I! (*Holding out her hand.*)

(THORNE *lets go* WILFRED's *hand— now on his left—and takes* CAROLINE's.)

WILFRED. Don't you be afraid now— it'll be all right! They'll give you a parole and—

CAROLINE (*breaking in enthusiastically*). A parole! Goodness gracious— they'll give you *hundreds* of 'em! (*Turning away with funny little comprehensive gesture of both hands.*)

GENERAL RANDOLPH (*gruffly*). One moment, if you please!

(THORNE *turns at once, facing* GENERAL RANDOLPH. CAROLINE *and* WILFRED *go to the couch.* EDITH *stands.* MRS. VARNEY *is near table.*)

There's only one reason on earth why the President has set aside a certain verdict of death. You held up that false order and made a turn in our favor. We expect you to make the turn complete and enter our service.

THORNE (*after an instant's pause, quietly*). Why, General—that's impossible!

GENERAL RANDOLPH. You can give us your answer later!

THORNE. You have it now, sir.

GENERAL RANDOLPH. You'll very much regret that decision, sir. It means you'll be held a prisoner here and kept in close confinement until the Confederate Army marches into Washington!

THORNE. Why, General, you're making me a prisoner for life!

GENERAL RANDOLPH. Nothing of the kind, sir! You'll see it in another light before many days. And it wouldn't surprise me if Miss Varney had something to do with your change of views!

EDITH (*coming a little way toward center*). You're mistaken General Randolph—I think he's perfectly right!

(THORNE *turns to* EDITH.)

GENERAL RANDOLPH (*gruffly*). Oh, you do, eh! Very well—we'll see what a little prison life will do. (*A sharp order*) Sergeant!

(SERGEANT *comes down and salutes.*) Report with the prisoner to Major Whitfield! (*Turns away to front.*)

(SERGEANT *turns at once to* THORNE. THORNE *and* EDITH *are looking into each other's eyes.* THORNE *takes her hand and presses it against his breast.*)

THORNE (*low voice to* EDITH). What is it—love and good-by?

EDITH (*almost a whisper*). No, no— only the first—and that one every day —every hour—every minute—until we meet again!

THORNE. Until we meet again!

SERGEANT. Fall in the Prisoner!

(THORNE *turns and walks up, quick-*

ly taking his place in the Squad. EDITH *follows him a step or two, as he goes.*)

SERGEANT. Attention!

(*Squad comes to attention.*)

Carry—arms!

(*Squad comes to carry.*)

Escort—left—face!

(*Squad with* THORNE—*left face on the order.*)

Forward—march!

(*Escort with* THORNE *marches out at door to the hall.*)

THE GREAT DIVIDE

William Vaughn Moody

First presented by Margaret Anglin under the title *The Sabine Woman* at the Garrick Theatre in Chicago on April 12, 1906; and then as *The Great Divide* in New York on October 3 at the Princess Theatre.

PHILIP JORDAN	LON ANDERSON
POLLY JORDAN, *Philip's wife*	BURT WILLIAMS
MRS. JORDAN, *his mother*	DUTCH
RUTH JORDAN, *his sister*	A MEXICAN
WINTHROP NEWBURY	A CONTRACTOR
DR. NEWBURY, *Winthrop's father*	AN ARCHITECT
STEPHEN GHENT	A BOY

ACT ONE

Interior of PHILIP JORDAN's *cabin in southern Arizona, on a late afternoon in spring. A large room rudely built, adorned with blankets, pottery, weapons, and sacred images of the local Indian tribes, and hung with trophies of the chase, together with hunting-knives, saddles, bridles, nose-bags for horses, lariats, and other paraphernalia of frontier life. Through a long, low window at the back the desert is seen, intensely colored, and covered with the uncouth shapes of giant cacti, dotted with bunches of gorgeous bloom. The entrance door is on the left (from the spectator's standpoint), in a projecting elbow of the room; farther to the left is a door leading to the sleeping-quarters. On the right is a cook-stove, a cupboard for dishes and household utensils and a chimney-piece, over which hangs a bleached cow's skull supporting a rifle.*

At a rude table in the center sits PHILIP JORDAN, *a man of thirty-four, mending a bridle.* POLLY, *his wife, kneels before an open trunk, assisted in her packing by* WINTHROP NEWBURY, *a recent graduate of an Eastern medical college.* RUTH JORDAN, PHILIP's *sister, a girl of nineteen, stands at the window looking out.*

WINTHROP (*as he hands the last articles to* POLLY). What on earth possessed you to bring such a load of duds to Arizona?

POLLY. They promised me a good time, meaning one small shindig—one —in the three months I've spent in this unholy place.

PHILIP (*makes an impatient movement with the bridle; speaks gruffly*). You'd better hurry. It's getting late.

RUTH (*from the window*). It's getting cooler, which is more to the point. We can make the railroad easily by sunrise, with this delicious breeze blowing.

POLLY (*gives the finishing touches to the trunk and locks the lid*). There, at last! Heaven help the contents.

PHILIP (*gruffly, as he rises*). Give me a lift with the trunk, Win.

(*They carry the trunk outside.* POLLY, *with the aid of a cracked mirror, puts on her traveling-hat and cloak.*)

RUTH. My, Pollikins! You'll be the talk of all the jackrabbits and sage hens between here and the railroad.

POLLY. Phil is furious at me for going, and it *is* rather mean to sneak off for a visit in a grand house in San Francisco, when you poor dears have to slave on here. But really, I can't endure this life a day longer.

RUTH. It isn't in nature that you should. Fancy *that* (*She indicates* POLLY *with a grandiose gesture.*) nourishing itself on salt pork, chickory beans, and air-tight!

POLLY. Do you really mean to say that apart from your pride in helping your brother, making the project go, and saving the family fortunes, you really *enjoy* yourself here?

RUTH. Since Phil and I came out, one day has been more radiantly exciting than the other. I don't know what's the matter with me. I think I shall be punished for being so happy.

POLLY. Punished for being happy! There's your simonpure New Englander.

RUTH. True! I was discovered at the age of seven in the garret perusing *The Twelve Pillars and Four Cornerstones of a Godly Life.*

POLLY (*pointing at* RUTH's *heart, speaks with mock solemnity*). If Massachusetts and Arizona ever get in a mixup in there, woe be!—Are you ever going to have that coffee done?

RUTH. I hope soon, before you get me analyzed out of existence.

POLLY (*as* RUTH *busies herself at the stove*). The main point is this, my dear, and you'd better listen to what the old lady is a-tellin' of ye. Happiness is its own justification, and it's the sacreder the more unreasonable it is. It comes or it doesn't, that's all you can say about it. And when it comes, one has the sense to grasp it or one hasn't. There you have the Law and the Prophets.

(WINTHROP *and* PHILIP *enter from outside.* RUTH, *who has set out the coffee and sandwiches on the table, bows elaborately, with napkin over arm.*)

RUTH. *Messieurs et Mesdames!*

WINTHROP. Coffee! Well, rather, with an all-night ride in the desert ahead of us.

(*They drink their coffee,* PHILIP *standing sullenly apart.*)
Where do we get our next feed?

RUTH. With luck, at Cottonwood Wash.

WINTHROP. And how far may Cottonwood Wash be?

RUTH. Thirty miles.

WINTHROP (*sarcastically*). Local measurement?

POLLY (*poking* PHILIP). Phil, for Heaven's sake, say something. You diffuse the gloom of the Pit.

PHILIP. I've had my say out, and it makes absolutely no impression on you.

POLLY. It's the impression on the public I'm anxious about.

PHILIP. The public will have to excuse me.

POLLY. I *am* horribly sorry for you two poor dears, left alone in this dreadful place. When Dr. Newbury goes, I don't see how you'll support

life. I should like to know how long this sojourn in the wilderness is going to last, anyhow.

(*During the following,* RUTH *takes a candle from the shelf, lights it, and brings it to the table. The sunset glow has begun to fade.*)

RUTH. Till Cactus Fiber makes our eternal fortune.

WINTHROP. And how long will that be?

RUTH (*counts on her fingers*). Two years to pay back the money we raised on mother's estate, two years of invested profits, two years of hard luck and marking time, two years of booming prosperity. Say eight years!

POLLY. Shades of the tomb! How long do you expect to live?

RUTH. Forever!

(*The sound of a galloping horse is heard, muffled by the sand.*)

WINTHROP. Listen. What's that?

(*A boy of fifteen, panting from his rapid ride, appears at the open door.*)

PHILIP (*rising and going toward the door*). What's the matter?

BOY. I've come for the doctor.

PHILIP. Who wants the doctor?

BOY. Your man Sawyer, over to Lone Tree.—He's broke his leg.

RUTH. Broken his leg! Sawyer? Our foreman?

PHILIP. There's a nice piece of luck! —How did it happen?

BOY. They was doin' some Navajo stunts on horseback, pullin' chickens out of the sand at a gallop and takin' a hurdle on the upswing. Sawyer's horse renigged, and lunged off ag'in' a 'dobe wall. Smashed his leg all to thunder.

(WINTHROP *looks vaguely about for his kit and traveling necessaries, while* POLLY *gives the boy food, which he accepts shyly as he goes outside with* PHILIP. RUTH *has snatched saddle and bridle from their peg.*)

RUTH. I'll have Buckskin saddled for you in a jiffy. How long will it take you to set the leg?

WINTHROP. Perhaps an hour, perhaps three.

RUTH. It's a big detour, but you can catch us at Cottonwood Wash by sunrise, allowing three hours for Sawyer. Buckskin has done it before. (*She goes out.*)

POLLY (*pouting*). This will spoil all our fun! Why can't the creature wait till you get back?

WINTHROP. Did you ever have a broken leg?

POLLY. Well, no, not exactly a leg. But I've had a broken heart! In fact, I've got one now, if you're not going with us.

WINTHROP. To tell you the truth, mine is broken too. (*Pause*) Did you ever dream of climbing a long hill, and having to turn back before you saw what was on the other side? (POLLY *nods enthusiastically.*) I feel as if I'd had my chance tonight to see what was over there, and lost it.

POLLY. You'll excuse me if it sounds personal, Dr. Newbury, but did you expect to discern a—sort of central figure in the outrolled landscape?

WINTHROP (*embarrassed, repenting of his sentimental outburst*). No. That is—

POLLY (*with a sweep of her arm*). Oh, I see. Just scenery! (*She laughs and goes into the inner room, left.* RUTH *re-enters. The sky has partly faded and a great full moon begins to rise.*)

RUTH. Buckskin is ready, and so is the moon. The boy knows the trails like an Indian. He will bring you through to Cottonwood by daylight.

WINTHROP (*taking heart*). We shall have the ride back together, at any rate.

RUTH. Yes.—I would go with you,

and try to do something to make poor Sawyer comfortable, but we haven't another horse that can do the distance. (*She holds out her hand.*) Good-by.

WINTHROP (*detaining her hand*). Won't you make it up to me? (*He draws her toward him.*)

RUTH (*gently but firmly*). No, Win. Please not.

WINTHROP. Never?

RUTH. Life is so good just as it is! Let us not change it.

(*He drops her hand, and goes out, without looking back.* POLLY *re-enters. The women wave* WINTHROP *good-by.*)

POLLY (*takes* RUTH *by the shoulders and looks at her severely*). Conscience clear?

RUTH (*humoring her*). Crystal!

POLLY (*counts on her fingers*). Promising young physician, charming girl, lonely ranch, horseback excursions, spring of the year!

RUTH. Not guilty.

POLLY. Gracious! Then it's not play, it's earnest.

RUTH. Neither the one nor the other. It's just your little blonde romantic noddle. (*She takes* POLLY's *head between her hands and shakes it as if to show its emptiness.*) Do you think if I wanted to flirt, I would select a youth I've played hookey with, and seen his mother spank? (*Suddenly sobered*) Poor dear Win! He's so good, so gentle and chivalrous. But— (*With a movement of lifted arms, as if for air*) —ah, me, he's—finished! I want one that isn't finished!

POLLY. Are you out of your head, you poor thing?

RUTH. You know what I mean well enough. Winthrop is all rounded off, a completed product. But the man I sometimes see in my dreams is— (*Pausing for a simile*) —well, like this country out here, don't you know—? (*She breaks off, searching for words, and makes a vague outline in the air, to indicate bigness and incompletion.*)

POLLY (*dryly*). Yes, thank you. I do know. Heaven send you joy of him!

RUTH. Heaven won't, because, alas, he doesn't exist! I am talking of a sublime abstraction—of the glorious unfulfilled—of the West—the Desert.

POLLY (*lifts RUTH's chin, severely*). We haven't by chance, some spring morning, riding over to the trading-station or elsewhere—just by the merest chance *beheld* a sublime abstraction—say in blue overalls and jumper? (*RUTH shakes her head.*) Honest?

(*More emphatic head-shaking. POLLY drops RUTH's chin with a shrug of the shoulders. PHILIP enters.*)

RUTH (*putting on her riding-hat*). Is Pinto saddled?

PHILIP. Pinto is gone.

RUTH (*astonished*). Gone where?

PHILIP. To that Mexican blow-out over at Lone Tree. Every man-jack on the ranch has disappeared, without leave asked or notice given, except this paper which I just found nailed to the factory door.

(*RUTH takes the note and reads it anxiously. Then she slowly removes her hat and lays it away.*)
What are you up to now? We've no time to lose!

RUTH (*with quiet determination*). I am not going.

POLLY (*as PHILIP turns in surprise*). Not going?

RUTH. I must stay and look after the ranch.

PHILIP. Oh, come, that's out of the question!

RUTH. We have put all mother's money into this venture. We can't take any risks.

PHILIP. The men will be back to-morrow. It's not to be thought of—your staying here all alone.

POLLY (*seats herself with decision*). One thing is certain: either Ruth goes or I stay.

PHILIP (*takes off his hat and sets down the provision basket*). That suits me perfectly!

POLLY (*hysterical*). But I can't stay! I won't stay! I shall go mad if I spend another night in this place.

RUTH. No, you mustn't stay. You would never get us worked up to the point of letting you go, another time. (*She lifts POLLY, and with arm around her waist leads her to the door.*)

PHILIP. I refuse to leave you here alone, just to satisfy a whim of Polly's. That's flat!

RUTH. But, Phil, you forget the stores you're to fetch back. They will be dumped out there on the naked sand, and by tomorrow night— (*She blows across her palm, as if scattering thistledown.*)

PHILIP. Well, what of it? A few hundred dollars' worth of stuff!

RUTH. A few hundred dollars means sink or swim with us just now.—Besides, there's poor Sawyer. He'll be brought back here tomorrow, and nobody to nurse him. Then inflammation, fever, and good-by Sawyer.

(*PHILIP, with a gesture of accepting the inevitable, picks up the grain-sacks and basket.*)

POLLY (*at the door, embracing RUTH*). Good-by, dear. Aren't you really afraid to stay?

RUTH. I'm awfully sorry to miss the fun, but as for danger, the great Arizona Desert is safer than Beacon Hill.

POLLY. You're sure?

RUTH. If marauders prowl, I'll just fire the blunderbuss out the window, and they won't stop running this side of the Great Divide.

POLLY (*kissing her*). Good-by, dear.

RUTH. Good-by.

(POLLY *goes out.*)

PHILIP (*pausing beside* RUTH, *at the door*). Mind you put out the light early. It can be seen from the Goodwater Trail. There's no telling what riff-raff will be straggling back that way after the dance.

RUTH. Riff-raff! They're my sworn knights and brothers.

PHILIP. In that case, what makes you uneasy about the property?

RUTH. Oh, property! That's different.

PHILIP. Well, you mind what I say and put out the light.

RUTH. Yours for prudence! (*She puts her arm around his waist and draws him to her, kissing him tenderly.*) Good-by, Phil. (*He kisses her and starts to go. She still detains him. When she speaks again, her voice is softened and awed.*) What a lovely night! Who would ever think to call this a desert, this moonlit ocean of flowers? What millions of cactus blooms have opened since yesterday!

PHILIP (*looking at her dubiously*). What's the matter with you tonight?

RUTH. Nothing. Everything. Life!— I don't know what's got into me of late. I'm just drunk with happiness the whole time.

PHILIP. Well, you're a queer one.— Good-by, I shall get back as soon as horse-flesh will do it. (*He goes out.*)

RUTH (*as the rumble of the wagon is heard*). Good-by! Good-by, Pollikins! Good-by! (*She takes the candle from the table and stands in the door for a time, then raises the light in one hand and waves her handkerchief with the other. She sets the candle again on the table, goes to the mantelshelf, and takes down a photograph.*) Dear Win! I forgot how disappointed you were going to be. (*Pause, during which she still gazes at the picture.*) Clear, kind heart! (*After a moment she replaces it brusquely on the mantel-shelf, and raises her arms above her head with a deep breath. She stands thus, with arms crossed behind her head, looking at the photograph. Her gaze becomes amused and mischievous; she points her finger at the picture and whispers mockingly.*) Finished! Finished! (*She begins to prepare for bed, taking down her hair, and recoiling it loosely during the following. She hums a tune vaguely and in snatches, then with a stronger rhythm; at last she sings.*)

Heart, wild heart,
Brooding apart,
Why dost thou doubt, and why art
    thou sullen?
Flower and bird
Wait but thy word—

(*She breaks off, picks up a photograph from the table, and looks at it for a moment in silence.*) Poor little mother! You look out at me with such patient, anxious eyes. There are better days coming for you, and it's troublesome me that's bringing them. Only you trust me!

(*A man's face appears at the edge of the window, gazing stealthily in. As* RUTH *turns, he disappears. She lays down the picture and sings again.*)

This is the hour,
And thine is the power.
Heart, high heart, be brave to begin
    it.
Dare you refuse?
Think what we lose!
Think what we gain—

(*The words grow indistinct as she takes up the candle and passes into* the other room, from which her voice sounds from time to time in interrupted song. The man again appears, shading his face with a peaked Mexican hat so as to see into the darkened room. He turns and waves his hand as if signaling distant persons to approach, then enters through the open door. He looks cautiously about the room, tiptoes to the inner door and listens, then steals softly out, and is seen again at the window, beckoning. RUTH re-enters, carrying the candle. She is shod in moccasins, and clad in a loose, dark sleeping-dress, belted at the waist, with wide, hanging sleeves and open throat. As she crosses to the table she sings.)

Heart which the cold
Long did enfold—
Hark, from the dark eaves the night
     thaw drummeth!
Now as a god,
Speak to the sod,
Cry to the sky that the miracle
     cometh!

(She passes her hand over a great bunch of wild flowers on the table.) Be still, you beauties! You'll drive me to distraction with your color and your odor. I'll take a hostage for your good behavior. (She selects a red flower, puts it in the dark mass of her hair, and looks out at the open door.) What a scandal the moon is making, out there in that great crazy world! Who but me could think of sleeping on such a night? (She sits down, folds the flowers in her arms, and buries her face in them. After a moment she starts up, listens, goes hurriedly to the door, and peers out. She then shuts and bolts the door, draws the curtains before the window, comes swiftly to the table, and blows out the light.

The room is left in total darkness. There are muttering voices outside, the latch is tried, then a heavy lunge breaks the bolt. A man pushes in, but is hurled back by a taller man, with a snarling oath. A third figure advances to the table, and strikes a match. As soon as the match is lighted, RUTH levels the gun, which she has taken from its rack above the mantel. There is heard the click of the hammer, as the gun misses fire. It is instantly struck from her hand by the first man [DUTCH], who attempts to seize her. She evades him, and tries to wrest a pistol from a holster on the wall. She is met by the second man [SHORTY], who frustrates the attempt, pocketing the weapon. While this has been going on the third man [GHENT] has been fumbling with the lamp, which he has at last succeeded in lighting. All three are dressed in rude frontier fashion; the one called SHORTY is a Mexican half-breed, the others are Americans. GHENT is younger than DUTCH, and taller, but less powerfully built. All are intoxicated, but not sufficiently so to incapacitate them from rapid action. The MEXICAN has seized RUTH and attempts to drag her toward the inner room. She breaks loose, and flies back again to the chimney-piece, where she stands at bay. GHENT remains motionless and silent by the table, gazing at her.)

DUTCH (uncorking a whiskey flask). Plucky little catamount. I drink its health. (Drinks.)

RUTH. What do you want here?

DUTCH (laughs, with sinister relish). Did you hear that, Steve? (He drinks again, and reaches out the flask to RUTH.) Take one, and pull in its purty little claws, eh? Jolly time. No more fuss and fury. (RUTH reaches for a knife, hidden behind the elbow of the *chimney.* DUTCH *wrests the knife from her and seizes her in his arms.*) Peppery little devil!

(*With desperate strength she breaks from his clutch and reels from him in sickness of horror.* GHENT *remains gazing at her in a fascinated semi-stupor. Meanwhile, after closing the door, the* MEXICAN *has taken dice from his pocket, and, throwing them into a small vase on the table, shakes them and holds out the vase to* DUTCH. *He takes it and turns to* GHENT; *the latter has moved a step or two toward* RUTH, *who in her retreat has reached the chimney-piece and stands at bay.*)

DUTCH. Come, get into the game, curse you, Steve! This is going to be a free-for-all, by God! (*As he rattles the dice,* RUTH *makes a supplicating gesture to* GHENT.)

RUTH. Save me! save me! (*Her gesture is frozen by his advancing toward her. She looks wildly about, shrinking from him, then with sudden desperate resolution speaks.*) Save me, and I will make it up to you! (GHENT *again advances; she goes on pantingly, as she stands at bay.*) Don't touch me! Listen! Save me from these others, and from yourself, and I will pay you—with my life.

GHENT (*with dull wonder*). With—your life?

RUTH. With all that I am or can be.

GHENT. What do you mean?— (*Pause*) You mean you'll go along with me out of this? Stick to me—on the square?

RUTH (*in a tragic whisper*). Yes.

GHENT. On the dead square?

RUTH. Yes.

GHENT. You won't peach, and spoil it?

RUTH. No.

(*Pause, during which he looks at her fixedly.*)

GHENT. Give me your hand on it!

(*She gives him her hand. The other men, at the table, have drawn their weapons, and hold them carelessly, but alert to the slightest suspicious movement on the part of* GHENT.)

DUTCH (*as* GHENT *turns to them*). Shorty and me's sittin' in this game, and interested, eh, Shorty?

(*The* MEXICAN *nods.* GHENT *comes slowly to the table, eyeing the two.* DUTCH *holds out the vase containing the dice.*)

Shake for her!

GHENT. Shake how?

DUTCH. Any damn way! Sole and exclusive rights. License to love and cherish on the premises!

(GHENT *takes the vase, shakes the dice meditatively, is about to throw, then sets the vase down. He searches through his pockets and produces a few bills and a handful of silver, which he lays on the table.*)

GHENT. There's all I've got in my clothes. Take it, and give me a free field, will you?

DUTCH (*leaning over the table to* GHENT *in plaintive remonstrance*). You don't mean me, Steve!

GHENT (*to the* MEXICAN). Well, you, then!

(*The* MEXICAN *spreads the money carelessly with his left hand to ascertain its amount, then thrusts it away with a disgusted grunt of refusal.*)

DUTCH. Don't blame you, Shorty! A ornery buck of a dirt-eatin' Mojave'd pay more 'n that for his squaw.

(RUTH *covers her face shudderingly.* GHENT *stands pondering, watching the two men under his brows, and slowly gathering up the money. As if on a sudden thought, he opens his shirt, and unwinds from his neck a string of gold nuggets in the rough, strung on a leather thread.*)

GHENT. Well, it ain't much, that's sure. But there's a string of gold nuggets I guess is worth some money. (*He throws it on the table, speaking to both men.*) Take that, and clear out.

DUTCH (*draws up angrily*). I've give you fair warning!

GHENT. We'll keep everything friendly between me and you. A square stand-up shoot, and the best man takes her.

DUTCH (*mollified*). Now you're comin' to!

GHENT (*to the* MEXICAN). Then it's up to you, and you'd better answer quick!

THE MEXICAN (*eyeing* GHENT *and* RUTH, *points to the gun lying on the floor*). I take him, too.

GHENT. No, you don't. You leave everything here the way you found it.

THE MEXICAN. Alla right. (*He pockets the chain and starts for the door.*)

GHENT. Hold on a minute. You've got to promise to tie the man who falls, on his horse, and take him to Mesa Grande. Bargain? And mouth shut, mind you, or— (*He makes a sign across his throat.*)

THE MEXICAN (*nods*). Alla right. (*He goes out.*)

GHENT (*motioning toward the door*). Outside.

DUTCH (*surprised*). What for?

GHENT (*sternly*). Outside!

(*They move toward the door.* DUTCH *stops and waves his hand to* RUTH.)

DUTCH. Don't worry, my girl. Back soon.

GHENT (*threateningly*). Cut that out!

DUTCH. What's eatin' you? She ain't yours yet, and I guess she won't be, not till hell freezes over. (*He taps his pistol and goes out.* GHENT *picks up the rifle which has previously missed fire; he unloads it, throws it on the window-seat, and follows* DUTCH. RUTH *stands beside the table, listening. Four shots are heard. After a short time* GHENT *appears and watches from the door the vanishing horses. He comes to the table opposite* RUTH.)

RUTH (*in a low voice*). Is he dead?

GHENT. No; but he'll stay in the coop for a while.

(*She sinks down in a chair.* GHENT *seats himself at the other side of the table, draws a whiskey flask from his pocket, and uncorks it awkwardly, using only his right hand.*)

RUTH (*as he is about to drink*). Don't!

GHENT (*lowers the bottle and looks at her in a dazed way*). Is this on the square?

RUTH. I gave you my promise.

(*Gazing at her, he lets the bottle sink slowly by his side; the liquor runs out, while he sits as if in a stupor.* RUTH *glances toward the door, and half starts from her seat, sinking back as he looks up.*)

GHENT. Give me a drink of water.

(*She brings the water from a bucket in the corner. He sets the empty bottle on the table, drinks deeply of the water, takes a handkerchief from his neck, wets it, and mops his face.*)

GHENT. Where are your folks?

RUTH. My brother has gone out to the railroad.

GHENT. Him and you ranching it here by yourselves?

RUTH. Yes.

GHENT. Write him a note. (*He shoves paper, pen, and ink before her.*) Fix it up any way you like.

RUTH. Tell me first what you mean to do with me.

GHENT (*ponders awhile in silence*). Have you got a horse to ride?

RUTH. Yes.

GHENT. We can reach San Jacinto

before sunup. Then we're off for the Cordilleras. I've got a claim tucked away in them hills that'll buy you the city of Frisco some day, if you have a mind to it!

(*She shrinks and shudders.*)

What you shivering at?

(RUTH *does not answer, but begins to write.* GHENT, *still using only one hand, takes a pistol from his pocket, examines it, and lays it carelessly on the table, within* RUTH's *reach. He rises and goes to the fireplace, takes a cigarette from his pocket and lights it, and examines the objects on the mantel-shelf.* RUTH *stops writing, takes up the pistol, then lays it down, as he speaks without turning round.*)

Read what you've written.

(RUTH, *about to read, snatches up the pistol again, rises, and stands trembling and irresolute.*)

Why don't you shoot? (*He turns round deliberately.*) You promised on the square, but there's nothing square about this deal. You ought to shoot me like a rattlesnake!

RUTH. I know that.

GHENT. Then why don't you?

RUTH (*slowly*). I don't know.

GHENT. I guess you've got nerve enough, for that or anything.—Answer me; why not?

RUTH. I don't—know.—You laid it there for me.—And—you have no right to die.

GHENT. How's that?

RUTH. You must live—to pay for having spoiled your life.

GHENT. Do you think it is spoiled?

RUTH. Yes.

GHENT. And how about your life?

RUTH. I tried to do it.

GHENT. To do what?

RUTH. To take my life. I ought to die. I have a right to die. But I cannot, I cannot! I love my life, I must

live. In torment, in darkness—it doesn't matter. I want my life. I will have it! (*She drops the weapon on the table, pushes it toward him, and covers her eyes.*) Take it away! Don't let me see it. If you want me on these terms, take me, and may God forgive you for it; but if there is a soul in you to be judged, don't let me do myself violence. (*She sinks down by the table, hiding her face in her hands.*) O God have pity on me!

(GHENT *puts the pistol back into his belt, goes slowly to the outer door, opens it, and stands for some moments gazing out. He then closes the door, and takes a step or two toward the table. As he speaks,* RUTH's *sobs cease, she raises her head and looks strangely at him.*)

GHENT. I've lived hard and careless, and lately I've been going downhill pretty fast. But I haven't got so low yet but what I can tell one woman from another. If that was all of it, I'd be miles away from here by now, riding like hell for liquor to wash the taste of shame out of my mouth. But that ain't all. I've seen what I've been looking the world over for, and never knew it.—Say your promise holds, and I'll go away now.

RUTH. Oh, yes, go, go! You will be merciful. You will not hold me to my cruel oath.

GHENT. And when I come back?

(RUTH *does not answer. He takes a step nearer.*)

And when I come back?

RUTH. You never—could—come back.

GHENT. No, I guess I never could.

RUTH (*eager, pleading*). You *will* go?

GHENT. For good?

RUTH. Yes.

GHENT. Do you mean that?

RUTH (*wildly*). Yes, yes, ten thousand times!

GHENT. Is that your last word?

RUTH. Yes. (*Pause. She watches him with strained anxiety.*) Oh, why did you come here tonight?

GHENT. I come because I was blind-drunk and sun-crazy, and looking for damnation the nearest way. That's why I come. But that's not why I'm staying. I'm talking to you in my right mind now. I want you to try and see this thing the way it is.

RUTH. Oh, that is what I want you to do! You did yourself and me a hideous wrong by coming here. Don't do us both a more hideous wrong still! I was in panic fear. I snatched at the first thing I could. Think what our life would be, beginning as we have begun! Oh, for God's pity go away now, and never come back! Don't you see there can never be anything between us but hatred, and misery, and horror?

GHENT (*hardening*). We'll see about that!—Are you ready to start?

(RUTH, *conscious for the first time of her undress condition, shrinks, and folds her gown closer about her neck.*) Go, and be quick about it.

(*She starts toward her room; he detains her.*) Where's your saddle?

(*She points at it and goes out.* GHENT *picks up the note she has written, reads it, and stands for a moment in reflection before laying it down. He gets more water from the bucket, drinks deeply, mops his face, and rolls up the sleeve of his left arm, which is soaked with blood. He tries awkwardly to stanch a wound in his forearm, gives it up in disgust, and rolls down his sleeve again. He reads the note once more, then takes* RUTH's *saddle and bridle from the wall and goes out.* RUTH *comes in; her face is white and haggard, but her manner determined and collected. She comes to the table,*

and sees the bloody handkerchief and basin of water. As GHENT enters, she turns to him anxiously.*)

RUTH. You are hurt.

GHENT. It's no matter.

RUTH. Where?

(*He indicates his left arm. She throws off her hooded riding-cloak, and impulsively gathers together water, towels, liniment, and bandages; she approaches him, quite lost in her task, flushed and eager.*) Sit down.—Roll up your sleeve.

(*He obeys mechanically. She rapidly and deftly washes and binds the wound, speaking half to herself, between long pauses.*) Can you lift your arm?—The bone is not touched.—It will be all right in a few days.—This balsam is a wonderful thing to heal.

GHENT (*watching her dreamily, as she works*). What's your name?

RUTH. Ruth—Ruth—Jordan. (*Long pause*) There, gently.—It must be very painful.

(*He shakes his head slowly, with half-humorous protest.*)

GHENT. It's not fair!

RUTH. What isn't fair?

GHENT. To treat me like this. It's not in the rules of the game.

RUTH (*as the sense of the situation again sweeps over her*). Binding your wound? I would do the same service for a dog.

GHENT. Yes, I dare say. But the point is, I ain't a dog; I'm a human—the worst way!

(*She rises and puts away the liniment and bandages. He starts up with an impulsive gesture.*) Make this bad business over into something good for both of us! You'll never regret it! I'm a strong man! (*He holds out his right arm, rigid.*) I used to feel sometimes, before I went to the bad, that I could take the world like that and tilt her over. And I can do it, too, if you say the word! I'll put you where you can look down on the proudest. I'll give you the kingdoms of the world and all the glory of 'em.

(*She covers her face with her hands. He comes nearer.*)

Give me a chance, and I'll make good. By God, girl, I'll make good!—I'll make a queen of you. I'll put the world under your feet!

(RUTH *makes a passionate gesture, as if to stop her ears.*)

What makes you put your hands over your ears like that? Don't you like what I'm saying to you?

RUTH (*taking the words with difficulty*). Do you remember what that man said just now?

GHENT. What about?

RUTH. About the Indian—and—his squaw.

GHENT. Yes. There was something in it, too. I was a fool to offer him that mean little wad.

RUTH. For—me!

GHENT. Well, yes, for you, if you want to put it that way.

RUTH. But—a chain of nuggets—that comes nearer being a fair price?

GHENT. Oh, to buy off a greaser!

RUTH. But to buy the soul of a woman—one must go higher. A mining-claim! The kingdoms of the world and all the glory of them! (*Breaking down in sudden sobs*) Oh, be careful how you treat me! Be careful! I say it as much for your sake as mine. Be careful!

GHENT (*turns from her, his bewilderment and discomfiture translating itself into gruffness*). Well, I guess we'll blunder through.—Come along! We've no time to lose.—Where are your things?

(*At her gesture, he picks up the saddle-pack which she has brought out of the bedroom with her, and starts toward the door.*)

RUTH (*taking a hammer from the window-ledge and handing it to* GHENT). Fix the bolt. My brother must not know.

(*He drives in the staple of the bolt, while she throws the blood-stained water and handkerchief into the fire. He aids her in replacing the weapons on the walls, then takes the saddle-pack and stands at the door, waiting. She picks up her mother's picture, and thrusts it in her bosom. After standing a moment in hesitation, she takes the picture out, kisses it, lays it on the mantel, face down. She extinguishes the lamp, and goes out hastily. He follows, closing the door.*)

ACT TWO

STEPHEN GHENT's *home, in the Cordilleras. At the right, crowning a rude terrace, is an adobe cabin, stained a pale buff, mellowed to ivory by sun and dust. Over it clamber vines loaded with purple bloom. The front of the cabin is turned at an angle toward the spectator, the farther side running parallel with the brink of a canyon, of which the distant wall and upper reaches are crimsoned by the afternoon light. In the level space before the rocky terrace is a stone table and seats, made of natural rocks roughly worked with the chisel. The rude materials have manifestly been touched by a refined and artistic hand, bent on making the most of the glorious background. Against the rocks on the left stands a large hand-loom of the Navajo type, with weaving-stool, and a blanket half woven. On the table lies a half-finished Indian basket, and heaps of colored weaving-materials lie in a heap on the ground. Cactus plants in blossom fill the niches of the rocks and lift their fantastic forms above the stones which wall the canyon brink. At one point this wall is broken, where a path descends into the canyon.*

LON ANDERSON, *a venerable-looking miner, with gray hair and beard, sits smoking before the cabin.* BURT WIL-LIAMS, *a younger man, peeps up over the edge of the canyon, from the path.*

BURT. Hello, Lon. Is the missus inside?

(*Lon smokes on, without looking at the questioner.*)
Look here, I put a nickel in you, you blame rusty old slot-machine. Push out something!

LON (*removes his pipe deliberately*). What you wantin' off'n her now? A music lesson or a headache powder?

BURT. Boss's waitin' down at the mine, with a couple o' human wonders he's brought back with him from wherever he's been this time. Something doin' on the quiet.

LON. You can tell him his wife ain't nowheres about.

(BURT *produces an enormous bandanna from his pocket, mounts the wall, and waves it. He sits on the wall and smokes for a moment in silence, looking down into the canyon, as if watching the approaching party. He points with his pipe at the cabin.*)

BURT. Funny hitch-up—this here one —I think.

LON (*after a pause*). How much you gittin' a day now?

BURT. Same little smilin' helpless three and six-bits.

LON. Anything extry for thinkin'?

BURT. Nope! Throwed in.

(*They smoke again.* BURT *glances down to reassure himself, then points at the loom and basket.*)
Queer business—this rug-weavin' and basket-makin', ain't it?—What d' ye s'pose she wants to sit, day in and day out, like a half-starved Navajo, slavin' over them fool things fur?—Boss ain't near, is he? Don't keep her short of ice-cream sodas and trolley-rides, does 'e?

(LON *rises and approaches* BURT, *regarding him grimly.*)
Saw 'er totin' a lot o' that stuff burro-back over to the hotel week 'fore last. —An' Dod Ranger—you know what a disgustin' liar Dod is—he tells how he was makin' tests over in the cross-canyon, an' all of a sudden plump he comes on her talkin' to a sawed-off Mexican hobo, an' when- she sees Dod, she turns white 's a sheet.

LON (*with suppressed ferocity*). You tell Dod Ranger to keep his mouth shet, and you keep yourn shet too— or by Jee—hosophat, I'll make the two of ye eat yer Adam's-apples and swaller the core!

BURT. Oh, git down off'n yer hind legs, Lon! Nobody's intendin' any disrespect.

LON. You boys keep yer blatherin' tongues off'n her! Or you'll get mixed up with Alonzo P. Anderson— (*He taps his breast.*) —so 's it'll take a coroner to untangle ye!

BURT (*deprecatingly*). I guess I'd stick up fur 'er 's quick as you would, come to that.

LON. Well, we don't need no stickin' up fur 'er. What we need is less tongue. (*He leans down and speaks lower.*) Especially when the boss is round. You tell the boys so.

(BURT *looks at him in surprise and is about to speak;* LON *makes a warn-*

ing signal, indicating the approach of the party below. BURT *descends, saluting* GHENT *respectfully.*)

GHENT (*peeping up over the edge of the canyon*). Coast clear, eh, Lon?

LON. Yes, sir.

GHENT. Where is she?

LON (*points along the brink of the canyon*). Kind o' think she went out to Look-off Ledge.—Guess she didn't expect you back to-day.

GHENT (*speaking below*). Come up, gentlemen. (GHENT *emerges from the canyon, followed by an* ARCHITECT, *a dapper young Easterner, and a* CONTRACTOR, *a bluff Western type.* GHENT *is neatly dressed in khaki, with riding-boots and broad felt hat. He has a prosperous and busy air, and is manifestly absorbed in the national game of making money.*) Take a seat.

CONTRACTOR (*seats himself by the table*). Don't care if I do. That new stage of yours just jumped stiff-legged from the go-off. And the trail up here from the mine is a good deal of a proposition for the seedentary.

ARCHITECT (*as he takes in the stupendous view*). What a wonderful place! Even better than you described it.

GHENT. Yes. My wife picked it out. —Let's see your plans.

(*He removes basket from the table, where the* ARCHITECT *unrolls several sheets of blue paper.*)

ARCHITECT. I have followed your instructions to the letter. I understand that nothing is to be touched except the house.

GHENT. Not a stone, sir; not a head of cactus. Even the vines you've got to keep, exactly as they are.

ARCHITECT (*smiling*). That will be a little difficult.

GHENT. You can put 'em on a temporary trellis.—A little pains will do it.

CONTRACTOR. Maybe, with a man to shoo the masons off with a shot-gun.

GHENT (*over the plans*). Provide a dozen men, if necessary, with machine guns.

CONTRACTOR. As you please, Mr. Ghent. The owner of the Verde Mine has a right to his whims, I reckon.

ARCHITECT. I have designed the whole house in the Spanish style, very broad and simple. This open space where we stand— (*Points to the plans.*) —I have treated as a semi-enclosed *patio*, with arcaded porches.

GHENT (*dubiously*). Good.

ARCHITECT. This large room fronting the main arcade is the living room.

GHENT. I guess we'll have 'em all living rooms. This place is to be lived in, from the word go.

ARCHITECT (*humoring him*). To be sure, everything cheerful and open.— Here on the left of the inner court is the library and music room.

GHENT. I'm afraid we won't have much use for that. My wife don't go in much for frills. I used to play the concertina once, but it was a long while ago.

ARCHITECT. It can be used for other purposes. For instance, as a nursery, though I had put that on the other side.

GHENT (*embarrassed and delighted*). Um, yes, nursery.—Stamping-ground for the—?

(*The* ARCHITECT *nods; the* CONTRACTOR *follows suit, with emphasis.* LON *nods solemnly over his pipe.*) Good.

(*The* ARCHITECT *bends over to make a note with his pencil.* GHENT *restrains him and says somewhat sheepishly in his ear.*) You can leave it music room on the map.

ARCHITECT (*continuing his explanation*). This wing—

(GHENT, *interrupting him, holds the plan at arm's length, with head on one side and eyes squinted, as he looks from the drawings to the cabin and surroundings.*)

GHENT. Looks a little—*sprawly* on paper. I had sort of imagined something more—more up in the air, like them swell tepees on the Hill in Frisco. (*He makes a grandiose outline of high roofs and turrets in the air.*)

ARCHITECT. I think this is more harmonious with the surroundings.

CONTRACTOR (*in answer to* GHENT'*s inquiring look*). Won't look so showy from the new hotel across yonder. (*He points to the left, down the curve of the canyon wall.*)

GHENT. What's your estimate on this plan, now you've seen the location?

CONTRACTOR. It's a long way to haul the stuff.—Say somewheres between twenty and twenty-five thousand. Twenty-five will be safe.

GHENT (*slightly staggered*). That's a big lot of money, my friend!

CONTRACTOR (*with cold scorn*). I thought we was talkin' about a *house!* I can build you a good sheep-corral for a right smart less.

GHENT. Well, I guess we don't want any sheep-corrals.

CONTRACTOR. I should think not, with the Verde pumping money at you the way they tell she does.

GHENT (*holds up the plans again and looks at them in perplexed silence*). I'll tell you, gentlemen, I'll have to consult my wife about this before I decide. The fact is, I've been working the thing out on the sly, up to now.

CONTRACTOR. Expect to build it of an afternoon, while the lady was takin' her see-ester [siesta]?

GHENT. I thought I'd smuggle her off somewhere for a while. (*He is silent a moment, pondering.*) No! It's her house, and she must O.K. the plans before ground is broke. (*He looks along the canyon rim.*) Would you mind waiting a few minutes till I see if I can find her? (*He starts irresolutely, then turns back.*) Or, better still, leave the plans, and I'll see you at the hotel tomorrow morning. I haven't been over there since it was opened. I'd like to know what they're making of it.

CONTRACTOR (*astonished*). Hain't been over to the Buny Visty yet?

GHENT. Too busy.

CONTRACTOR. Well, you'll find it an up-to-date joint, and chock full of tourist swells and lungers.

GHENT. Good-afternoon, gentlemen. You'll excuse me. You can find your way back all right? Take the left-hand path. It's better going.

(*The* ARCHITECT *bows ceremoniously, the* CONTRACTOR *nods.* GHENT *disappears along the canyon brink behind the cabin.*)

ARCHITECT (*has been examining the work on the loom, and has then picked up the unfinished basket, admiringly*). What a beautiful pattern! I say, this is like those we saw at the hotel. (*To* LON) May I ask who is making this?

(LON *smokes in silence; the* ARCHITECT *raises his voice, slightly sharp.*) May I ask who is making this?

LON (*benignly*). You kin, my friend, you kin!

ARCHITECT. Well, then, the question is put.

LON. And very clear-put, too. You'd ought to be in the law business, young man. (*He gets up deliberately.*) Or some other business that'd take up all yer time.

ARCHITECT (*between wrath and*

amusement). Well, I'll be hanged! *(He follows his companion down the canyon path, stopping a moment at the brink to look round with a professional air at the house and surroundings, then at* LON.) Tart old party!

(He descends. LON *crosses to the table, looks over the plans, makes outlines in the air in imitation of* GHENT, *then shakes his head dubiously, as he rolls up the plans.* RUTH *appears, emerging from the canyon path. She wears the same dress as at the close of Act One, with a dark scarflike handkerchief thrown over her head. She is pale and exhausted. She sinks on the rocks at the edge of the canyon.)*

LON *(approaching her, anxiously).* It's too much fer you, ma'am. You'd oughter let me go. *(He brings her a glass of water from an Indian waterjar before the cabin.)*

RUTH *(tasting the water).* Oh, I thought I should never get back! *(She leans against a rock, with closed eyes, then rouses herself again.)* Lon, take the glass, and see if you can make out any one down yonder, on the nearer trail. I—I thought some one was following me.

LON *(speaks low).* Excuse me askin', Mis' Ghent, but is that dod-blamed Mexican a-botherin' you again?

RUTH. No. He has gone away, for good. It's some one I saw at the hotel —some one I used to know.—Look if you can make out a man's figure, coming up.

LON *(takes the glass from the niche in the rocks, and scans the canyon path).* Can't see nothin' but a stray burro, an' he ain't got no figger to speak of.—Might be t' other side o' Table Rock, down in the pinyon scrub.

*(*RUTH *gets up with an effort, takes the glass and looks through it, then lays it on the ledge.)*

Excuse me, ma'am, but—Mister Ghent come home this afternoon.

RUTH *(startled).* Where is he?

LON. Huntin' for you down Look-off Ledge way. I 'lowed you was there, not knowin' what else to say.

RUTH. Thank you, Lon.—You can go now.

(He goes down the canyon path. RUTH *looks once more through the glass, then crosses to the table, where she sits down and begins to finger the roll of plans.* GHENT *re-enters. He approaches with soft tread and bends over* RUTH. *She starts up with a little cry, avoiding his embrace.)*

You frightened me.—When did you come back?

GHENT. An hour ago.

RUTH. Was your journey successful?

GHENT. Yes. But my homecoming— that looks rather like a failure. *(Pause)* I expected to find you out on the bluff.

RUTH. Lon was mistaken. I had gone the other way. *(As she stands at the table, she begins to unroll the plans.)* What are these papers?

GHENT. Haven't you one word of welcome for me, after five days?

*(*RUTH *remains silent, with averted head, absently unrolling the packet.)* Not a look even? *(He waits a moment, then sighs and seats himself moodily by the table.)*

I never can remember! After I've been away from you for twelve hours, I forget completely.

RUTH. Forget what?

GHENT. How it stands between us. It's childish, but for the life of me I can't help it.—After I've been away a few hours, this place gets all lit up with bright colors in my mind, like— *(Searching for a simile)* —well, like a

Christmas tree! I dare say a Christmas tree don't amount to much in real life, but I saw one once, in a play—I was a little mining-camp roust-about, so high—and ever since it has sort of stood to me for the gates o' glory.

RUTH (*with a hysterical laugh*). A Christmas tree! (*She bows her head in her hands, and repeats the words, as if to herself, in a tone in which bitterness has given place to tragic melancholy.*) A Christmas tree!

(GHENT, *watching her moodily, crumples up the plans and throws them upon the ground. He goes toward the cabin, hesitates, turns, and comes back to the table, where* RUTH *still sits with buried head. He draws from his pocket a jewel-case, which he opens and lays before her.*)

GHENT. There is a little present I brought home for you. And here are some more trinkets. (*He takes out several pieces of jewelry and tumbles them together on the table.*) I know you don't care much for these things, but I had to buy something, the way I was feeling. And these papers— (*Picks them up and spreads them out on the table.*) —these mean that you're not to live much longer in a mud shanty, with pine boxes for furniture. These are the drawings for a new house that I want to talk over with you. (*He points at the map and speaks glibly, trying to master his discomfiture at her lack of interest.*) Spanish style, everything broad and simple! Large living-room opening on inner court. Library and music-room, bless your heart. Bedroom; kitchen and thereunto pertaining. Wing where the proprietor retires to express his inmost feelings. General effect sprawly, but harmonious with the surroundings. Twenty thousand estimated, twenty-five limit. Is she ours?

RUTH (*in a dead, flat tone*). How much did you say the house is to cost?

GHENT. Twenty-five thousand dollars at the outside.

RUTH. And these—trinkets?

GHENT. Oh, I don't know.—A few hundred.

RUTH (*draws the plans toward her and pours the jewels in a heap upon them from her lifted hands*). Twenty-five thousand dollars and the odd hundreds! (*She laughs suddenly and jarringly.*) My price has risen! My price has risen! (*She laughs again, as she rises from the table and looks down the canyon path.*) Keep those displayed to show to our visitors! My honor is at stake. (*She points down the path.*) There is one coming now!

GHENT. Visitors? What visitors?

RUTH. Only an old school friend of mine; a Mr. Winthrop Newbury.

GHENT. What are you talking about? Are you crazy? (*He joins her, where she stands looking down into the canyon.*) This fellow, is he really what you say?

(RUTH *nods, with unnaturally bright eyes and mocking smile.*) What does this mean?

RUTH. It means that he caught sight of me, an hour ago, in the hotel.

GHENT. In the hotel? What were you doing there?

RUTH (*with biting calm*). Nothing wicked—as yet. They don't pay twenty-five thousand dollars over there—at least not yet!

(GHENT *turns sharply, as if stung by a physical blow. She raises her hands to him, in a swift revulsion of feeling.*) Oh, don't judge me! Don't listen to me! I am not in my right mind.

GHENT (*sweeps the jewels together, and throws them over the cliff*). Do you want me to be here, while you see him? (*She does not answer.*) Won't you answer me?

RUTH (*again cold*). Act as you think best.

GHENT. It's a question of what will be easiest for you.

RUTH. Oh, it's all easy for me!

(GHENT *stands irresolute, then raises his hand in a gesture of perplexity and despair, and goes into the house, closing the door.* WINTHROP NEWBURY *appears at the top of the canyon path, looks curiously about, catches sight of* RUTH's *averted figure, and rushes toward her.*)

WINTHROP. Ruth! Is it really you!

(RUTH *starts involuntarily toward him, stretching out her arms. As he advances, she masters herself, and speaks in a natural voice, with an attempt at gaiety, as she takes his hand.*)

RUTH. Well, of all things! Winthrop Newbury! How did you find your way to this eagle's nest?

WINTHROP. I—we saw you—we caught a glimpse of you at the hotel, but we weren't sure. We followed you, but lost you in the canyon.

RUTH. We? Who is we?

WINTHROP. Your brother and his wife.

RUTH (*turning the shock, which she has been unable to conceal, into conventional surprise*). Philip and Polly here!

WINTHROP. They took the other turn, down there where the path forks. We didn't know which way you had gone.

RUTH. Yes, but why on earth are they here at all?

WINTHROP. They are on their way East. They stopped over to see me.

RUTH. To see you? Are you—living here?

WINTHROP. I have been here only a week. (*He starts impulsively, trying to break through the conventional wall which she has raised between them.*) Ruth—for God's sake—!

RUTH (*interrupting him, with exaggerated animation*). But tell me! I am all curiosity. How do you happen to be here—of all places?

WINTHROP. What does it matter? I am here. We have found you, after all these miserable months of anxiety and searching. O Ruth—why—

RUTH. I have acted badly, I know. But I wish not to talk of that. Not now. I will explain everything later. Tell me about yourself—about Philip and Polly—and mother. I am thirsty for news. What have you been doing all these months, since—our queer parting?

WINTHROP (*solemnly*). Looking for you. (*Pause*) O Ruth—how could you do it? How could you do it?

RUTH (*touches him on the arm and looks at him with dumb entreaty, speaking low*). Winthrop!

WINTHROP (*in answer to her unspoken words*). As you will.

RUTH (*resumes her hard, bright tone*). You haven't told me about Mother. How is she?

WINTHROP. Well. Or she will be, now. Ruth, you ought at least to have written to her. She has suffered cruelly.

RUTH (*quickly, with a nervous uplift of her arms*). Yes, yes, I know that! —And you are—settled here? You mean to remain?

WINTHROP. I am the physician at the End-of-the-Rainbow Mines, three miles below. At least I—I am making a trial of it. (*Pause*) How pale and worn you are.—Don't turn away. Look at me.

(*She flinches, then summons her courage and looks him steadily in the face.*)

You are—you are ill—I fear you are desperately ill!

RUTH (*moving away nervously*). Nonsense. I was never better in my life. (*She goes toward the canyon brink.*) You haven't praised our view. We are very proud of it.

WINTHROP (*following her*). Yes, very fine. Magnificent.

RUTH. But you're not looking at it at all! Do you see that bit of smoke far down yonder? That is the stamp mill of the Rio Verde Mine.

WINTHROP (*compelling himself to follow her lead*). Yes—the Rio Verde. One of the big strikes of the region. Dispute about the ownership, I believe.

RUTH. None that I ever heard of, and I ought to know. For— (*She makes a sweeping bow.*) —we are the Rio Verde, at your service.

WINTHROP. You—your—husband is the owner of the Verde Mine?

RUTH. No less!

WINTHROP (*embarrassed*). We found the record of your marriage at San Jacinto. The name was Ghent—Stephen Ghent.

RUTH. Yes. He will be so glad to see some of my people.

(WINTHROP's *eyes have fallen on the basket at the foot of the table. He picks it up, examines it curiously, and looks meaningly at* RUTH, *who snatches it from his hand and throws it over the cliff.*) A toy I play with! You know I always have to keep my hands busy pottering at some rubbishy craft or other.

WINTHROP (*is about to speak, but checks himself; he points at the loom*). And the blanket, too?

RUTH. Yes, another fad of mine. It is really fascinating work. The Indian women who taught me think I am a wonder of cleverness.

WINTHROP. So do—the women—over there. (*He points across the canyon.*)

RUTH (*flushing*). Ah, yes, you saw some of my stuff at the hotel. You know how vain I am. I had to show it.

WINTHROP. Perhaps. But why should the wife of the man who owns the Verde Mine *sell* her handiwork, and under such—such vulgar conditions?

RUTH (*brilliantly explanatory*). To see if it *will* sell, of course! That is the test of its merit.

(*He looks at her in mute protest, then with a shake of the head, rises and puts on his hat.*)

WINTHROP. Do you want to see the others?

RUTH. Why, yes, to be sure I do. How should I not?

WINTHROP. You haven't seemed very anxious—these last eight months.

RUTH. True. I have been at fault. I so dread explanations. And Phil's tempests of rage! Poor boy, he must feel sadly ill-used.

WINTHROP. He does. (*Hesitates.*) If there is any reason why you would rather he didn't see you, just now—

RUTH. There is no reason. At least, none valid.

WINTHROP. Then I will bring them up.

RUTH. By all means. (*She holds out her hand, smiling.*) Auf wiedersehen!

(WINTHROP *releases her hand and goes toward the canyon path. He waves, and turns to* RUTH.)

WINTHROP. They are just below.

(*As* RUTH *advances he takes her hand and looks searchingly into her eyes.*) For old friendship's sake, won't you give me one human word before they come? At least answer me honestly one human question?

RUTH (*keeping up her hard, bright gaiety*). In the great lottery of a woman's answers there is always one such prize!

WINTHROP (*dejectedly, as he drops her hand*). It's no use, if that is your mood.

RUTH. My mood! Your old bugbear! I am as sober-serious as my stars ever let me be.

WINTHROP. Did you, that night you bade me good-by, know that—this was going to happen?

RUTH (*cordially explanatory*). No. It was half accident, half wild impulse. Phil left me at the ranch alone. My lover came, impatient, importunate, and I—went with him.

WINTHROP. And your—this man—to whom you are married—pardon me, you don't need to answer unless you wish—for how long had you known him?

RUTH (*solemnly, as she looks him straight in the eyes*). All my life! And for aeons before.

(*He looks at her for a moment, then goes toward the canyon path.* POLLY's *voice is heard calling.*)

POLLY (*not yet visible*). Win! Win!

WINTHROP (*calls down the canyon*). Come up! Come up!

(RUTH *goes past him down the canyon path. In a moment she reappears, with* POLLY. *They are laughing and talking as they come.*)

POLLY. Ruth!

RUTH. Dear old Polly!

POLLY. You *naughty* girl!

RUTH. If our sins must find us out, you are the kind of Nemesis I choose.

POLLY. My! But you're a shady character. And sly!

(PHILIP *appears.* RUTH *hurries to embrace him, while* POLLY, *fanning herself with her handkerchief, examines the house and surroundings with curiosity.*)

RUTH. O Phil!—Dear old man! (*She covers his face lightly with her hands.*) No scolding, no frowns. This is the finding of the prodigal, and she expects a robe and a ring.

POLLY (*seating herself on a rock*). Heavens, what a climb!—I'm a rag.

RUTH (*motions to the men to be seated*). The cabin wouldn't hold us all, but there's one good thing about this place; there's plenty of outdoors.

WINTHROP (*looking about*). I should say there was!

POLLY. To think of our practical Ruth doing the one really theatrical thing known in the annals of Milford Corners, Mass.!—And what a setting! My dear, your stage arrangements are perfect.

RUTH. In this case Providence deserves the credit. We may have come here to have our pictures taken, but we stayed to make a living.

(PHILIP *has drawn apart, gloomy and threatening.* POLLY *keeps up her heroic efforts to give the situation a casual and humorous air.*)

POLLY (*with jaunty challenge*). Well, where is he?

RUTH. Who?

POLLY. He!

(RUTH *points at the cabin, smiling.*) Well, produce him!

RUTH (*following, with gratitude in her eyes, the key of lightness and raillery which* POLLY *has struck*). You insist?

POLLY. Absolutely.

RUTH. Oh, very well! (*She goes up the rocky incline, and enters the cabin, calling: "Steve! Steve!"* POLLY *goes to* PHILIP, *and shakes him.*)

POLLY. Now, you behave! (*Indicates* WINTHROP) He's behaving.

(RUTH *reappears in the doorway, followed by* GHENT.)

RUTH (*with elaborate gaiety, as they descend the rocks*). Well, Stephen, since they've run us to earth, I suppose we must put a good face on it, and acknowledge them.—This is Polly, of whom I've talked so much. Polly the irresistible. Beware of her! *(POLLY shakes his hand cordially.)* And this is—my brother Philip.

(GHENT extends his hand, which PHILIP pointedly ignores. RUTH goes on hastily, to cover the insult.) And this is my old school friend, Winthrop Newbury. *(They shake hands.)*

WINTHROP *(to PHILIP, formally explanatory)*. Mr. Ghent is the owner of the famous Verde Mine.

GHENT. Part owner, sir. I hadn't the capital to develop with, so I had to dispose of a half-interest.

WINTHROP. Isn't there some litigation under way?

RUTH *(looking at GHENT, surprised)*. Litigation?

GHENT. Yes—a whole rigmarole.

POLLY *(catching at a straw to make talk)*. Heaven help you if you have got entangled in the law! I can conceive of nothing more horrible or ghastly than a court of law; unless *(she glances at PHILIP)* it is that other court of high justice, which people hold in private to judge their fellows, from hearsay and half-knowledge!

RUTH *(keeping up the play desperately, as she blesses POLLY with a look)*. But there must be law, just the same, and penalties and rewards and all that. Else what's the use of being good?

POLLY. Like you—for instance!

RUTH. Well, yes, like me!

POLLY. You are not good, you are merely magnificent. I want to be magnificent! I want to live on the roof of the world and own a gold mine! *(To GHENT)* Show me where the sweet thing is.

GHENT. We can get a better view of the plant from the ledge below. Will you go down?

(GHENT, POLLY, and WINTHROP go down the canyon path. RUTH takes PHILIP by the arm, to lead him after.)

PHILIP. No. We must have a word together, before the gabble begins again. Winthrop has given me your explanation, which explains nothing.

RUTH *(trying to keep up the light tone)*. Hasn't that usually been the verdict on explanations of my conduct?

PHILIP. Don't try to put me off! Tell me in two words how you came to run away with this fellow.

RUTH *(hardening)*. Remember to whom you are speaking, and about whom.

PHILIP. I got your note, with its curt announcement of your resolve. Later, by mere accident, we found the record of your marriage at San Jacinto—if you call it a marriage, made hugger-mugger at midnight by a tipsy justice of the peace. I don't want to question its validity. I only pray that no one will. But I want to know how it came to be made, in such hurry and secrecy —how it came to be made at all, for that matter. How did you ever come to disgrace yourself and your family by clandestine meetings and a hedge-row marriage with a person of this class? And why, after the crazy leap was taken, did you see fit to hide yourself away without a word to me or your distracted mother? Though that, perhaps, is easier to understand!

RUTH. The manner of your questions absolves me from the obligation to answer them.

PHILIP. I refuse to be put off with any such patent subterfuge.

RUTH. Subterfuge or not, it will have to suffice, until you remember that my right to choose my course in life is unimpeachable, and that the man whose destiny I elect to share cannot be insulted in my presence.

PHILIP. Very well, I can wait. The truth will come out some day. Meanwhile, you can take comfort from the fact that your desertion at the critical moment of our enterprise has spelled ruin for me.

RUTH (*overwhelmed*). Philip, you don't mean—!

PHILIP. Absolute and irretrievable ruin.

RUTH. Then you are going back East—for good!

PHILIP. Yes.

RUTH. But—mother's money! What will she do? (PHILIP *shrugs his shoulders.*) Is everything gone—everything?

PHILIP. I shall get something from the sale. Perhaps enough to make a fresh start, somewhere, in some small way.

RUTH (*comes to him, and lays her arms on his shoulders*). Phil, I am sorry, sorry!

(*He caresses her; she bursts into suppressed convulsive weeping and clings to him, hiding her face in his breast.*)

PHILIP. Ruth, you are not happy! You have made a hideous mistake. Come home with me. (RUTH *shakes her head.*) At least for a time. You are not well. You look really ill. Come home with us, if only for a month.

RUTH. No, no, dear Phil, dear brother! (*She draws down his face and kisses him; then lifts her head, with an attempt at lightness.*) There! I have had my cry, and feel better. The excitement of seeing you all again is a little too much for me.

PHILIP. If there is anything that you want to tell me about all this, tell me now.

RUTH. Oh, there will be plenty of time for explanations and all that! Let us just be happy now in our reunion.

PHILIP. There will not be plenty of time. We leave tomorrow morning.

RUTH. Then you will take me on trust—like a dear good brother. Perhaps I shall never explain! I like my air of mystery.

PHILIP. Remember that if you ever have anything to complain of—in your life—it is my right to know it. The offender shall answer to me, and dearly, too.

RUTH (*takes his head between her hands, and shakes it, as with recovered gaiety*). Of course they will, you old fire-eater!

PHILIP (*pointing to the blanket on the loom*). Ruth, at least tell me why—

(RUTH *does not see his gesture, as she is looking at the others, who come up from below. The men linger in the background,* GHENT *pointing out objects in the landscape.*)

RUTH (*to* POLLY, *who advances*). Well, what do you think of us, in a bird's-eye view?

POLLY. In a bird's-eye view you are superb! (*She draws* RUTH *to her, and speaks in a lower tone.*) And looked at near, you are an enthralling puzzle.

RUTH (*half to herself*). If you only knew how much!

POLLY (*taking* RUTH *by the chin as in Act One*). So you *had*—just by chance—riding over to the trading-station or so—met the glorious unfulfilled—in blue overalls and a jumper! I thought so!

(RUTH *bows her head in a spasm of pain.* POLLY, *who does not see her face, goes on teasingly.*)

I see now what you meant about wanting one that wasn't finished. This one certainly isn't finished. But when he is, he'll be grand!

(RUTH *moves away with averted head.* POLLY *follows her, peeping round to view her face.*) Don't sulk! I meant nothing disrespectful. On the contrary, I'm crazy about him. (*In a louder tone*) And now that I've seen the outside of you, I *must* peep into that fascinating little house!

RUTH (*to* GHENT, *who has drawn nearer*). Polly wants to go inside the cabin. I can't let her until we have shown her what it's going to be. (*With* GHENT'*s aid, she spreads out the plans, which* POLLY *examines with curiosity.*) These are the plans for our new house. You call us magnificent. We will show you that we are not. We are overwhelming!

WINTHROP (*looking at his watch*). I am afraid we must be getting back. It grows dark very suddenly in the canyon.

RUTH (*to* POLLY). Well, then you may come in, if you will promise to view the simple present in the light of the ornate future.

(POLLY *goes in.* RUTH, *lingering at the door for an instant, looks back anxiously at the men.*)

PHILIP (*curtly, to* GHENT). If you will permit me, I should like a word with you.

GHENT. Certainly.

(WINTHROP *effaces himself, making and lighting a cigarette, as he looks out over the canyon.*)

PHILIP. In deference to my sister's wishes, I refrain from asking you for the explanation which is due me. (GHENT *bows in silence.*) But there is one thing which I think I am at liberty to question.

GHENT. Do so.

PHILIP. I hear of your interest in a valuable mine. I hear of plans for an elaborate house. Why, then, is my sister compelled to peddle her own handiwork in a public caravansary?

GHENT. What do you mean? I don't understand you.

PHILIP (*points at the loom*). Her rugs and baskets are on sale in the corridor of the hotel, fingered and discussed by the tourist mob.

GHENT (*astonished*). This can't be true!

PHILIP. It is, however.

GHENT. I know nothing of it. I've had to be away a great deal. I knew she worked too hard over these things, but I took it for a mere pastime. Perhaps—No, I can't understand it at all!

PHILIP. I advise you to make inquiries. She has taken pains to conceal her identity, but it is known, nevertheless, and the subject of public curiosity.

(POLLY *and* RUTH *come out from the cabin.*)

POLLY (*to* PHILIP). Take me away quickly, or I shall never enjoy upholstery again! (*To* RUTH) Please change your mind, dear, and come with us for the night.

RUTH. No. I will see you in the morning.

WINTHROP. We leave by the early stage.

RUTH (*looking at him quickly*). You, too?

WINTHROP. Yes, I have decided so.

RUTH. I will be there in good time, trust me. (*She kisses* POLLY *and* PHILIP.) Good-by, till morning. (*Gives her hand to* WINTHROP.) Good-by.

(PHILIP *ignores* GHENT *pointedly in the leave-takings.* POLLY *bids him farewell with corresponding cordiality.*)

POLLY. Good-by, Mr. Ghent. (*As they descend the canyon path, she is heard chatting enthusiastically.*) Oh, Phil, you ought to have seen the in-

side of that delightful little house!
(*Her voice is heard for some time, indistinctly.* RUTH, *at the top of the path, waves to them as they descend.*)

GHENT (*looks long at her, with deep gratitude*). God bless you! (*She sits down on the rocks of the cabin terrace. He walks up and down in anxious thought. Once or twice, he makes as if to speak. At length, he stops before her.*) You must go in and lie down. You are worn out.

RUTH (*rousing herself*). No, there is something I must tell you first.

GHENT (*points at the rug*). It's about this—work you have been doing?

RUTH (*slightly startled*). You know of that?

GHENT. Your brother told me. I should have found it out tomorrow anyhow. (*Pause*) Have you wanted money?

RUTH. Yes.

GHENT. I thought I—I thought you had enough. I have often begged you to take more.

RUTH. I haven't spent what you gave me. It is in there. (*She points toward the house.*)

GHENT (*astonished*). You haven't spent—any of it?

RUTH. A little. Nothing for myself.

GHENT. But there has been no need to save, not after the first month or two. You surely knew that!

RUTH. Yes, I knew it. It was not economy.

GHENT (*slowly*). You haven't been willing to take money from me?

RUTH. No. I know it was small of me, but I couldn't help it. I have paid for everything.—I have kept account of it—oh, to the last dreadful penny! These clothes are the ones I wore from my brother's house that night. This shelter—you know I helped to raise that with my own hands. And—and some things I paid for secretly, from the little hoard I brought away with me. You were careless; you did not notice.

GHENT (*sits down, dizzy from the shock of her words*). I must try to grasp this! (*There is a silence, during which he sits perfectly motionless. At last he turns to her.*) Why—why did you stand up so plucky, so splendid, just now? Put a good face on everything about our life? Call me by my first name and all that—before your own people?

RUTH. We are man and wife. Beside that, my own people are as strangers.

GHENT (*eagerly*). You say that? You can still say that?

RUTH (*looks up, startled*). Can't you? (*She awaits his answer tensely.*)

GHENT (*desperately*). Oh, I don't know. I can't say or think anything, after what you have just told me!

RUTH (*wails*). You can't say it! And it isn't true! It is we who are strangers. —Worse, a thousand times worse!

GHENT (*rises and stands over her*). Don't let us dash ourselves to hell in one crazy minute! (*He pauses and hesitates. When he speaks again it is with wistful tenderness.*) Ruth, do you remember our journey here? (*She lifts her head, looking at him with white, thirsty face.*) I thought—it seemed to me you had—begun to care for me.

RUTH. That night, when we rode away from the justice's office at San Jacinto, and the sky began to brighten over the desert—the ice that had gathered here— (*She touches her heart.*) —began to melt in spite of me. And when the next night and the next day passed, and the next, and still you spared me and treated me with beautiful rough chivalry, I said to myself, "He has heard my prayer to him. He knows what a girl's heart is." As you rode before me down the arroyos, and up over the mesas, through the dazzling sunlight and the majestic silence, it seemed as if you were leading me out of a world of little codes and customs into a great new world.—So it was for those first days.—And then—and then—I woke, and saw you standing in my tent-door in the starlight! I knew before you spoke that we were lost. You hadn't had the strength to save us!

GHENT (*huskily*). Surely it hasn't all been—hateful to you? There have been times, since that.—The afternoon we climbed up here. The day we made the table; the day we planted the vines.

RUTH (*in a half whisper*). Yes!—Beautiful days! (*She puts her hands suddenly before her face and sobs.*) Oh, it was not my fault! I have struggled against it. You don't know how I have struggled!

GHENT. Against what? Struggled against what?

RUTH. Against the hateful image you had raised up beside your own image.

GHENT. What do you mean?

RUTH. I mean that sometimes—often —when you stand there before my eyes, you fade away, and in your place I see—the Other One!

GHENT. Speak plainly, for God's sake! I don't understand this talk.

RUTH (*looking steadfastly, as at an invisible shape, speaks in a horrified whisper*). There he stands behind you now!—The human beast, that goes to its horrible pleasure as not even a wild animal will go—*in pack, in pack!*

(GHENT, *stung beyond endurance, rises and paces up and down.* RUTH *continues in a broken tone, spent by the violence of her own words.*)
I have tried—Oh, you don't know how

I have tried to save myself from these thoughts.—While we were poor and struggling I thought I could do it.—Then— (*She points toward the canyon.*) —then that hole down there began belching its stream of gold. You began to load me with gifts—to force easy ways upon me—

GHENT. Well, what else did I care to make money for?

RUTH (*does not answer for a moment, then speaks slowly, taking the words with loathing upon her tongue*). Every time you give me anything, or talk about the mine and what it is going to do there rings in my ears that dreadful sneer: "A dirt-eating Mojave would pay more than that for his squaw!" (*She rises, lifting her arms.*) I held myself so dear! And you bought me for a handful of gold, like a woman of the street! You drove me before you like an animal from the market!

(GHENT *has seated himself again, elbows on knees and face in his hands.* RUTH *takes slowly from her bosom the nugget chain and holds it crumpled up in her palm. Her tone is quiet, almost matter-of-fact.*)
I have got back the chain again.

GHENT (*looks up*). Chain?—What chain?

RUTH (*in the same tone, as she holds it up, letting it unwind*). The one you bought me with.

GHENT (*dumbfounded*). Where the devil—? Has that fellow been around here?

RUTH. It would have had no meaning for me except from his hand.

GHENT. So that's what you've been doing with this rug-weaving and basket-making tomfoolery?

(RUTH *does not answer, but continues looking at the chain, running it through her fingers and weighing it in her hand.*)

How long has this been going on?

RUTH. How long?—How long can one live without breathing? Two minutes? A few lifetimes. How long!

GHENT. It was about a month after we came here that you began to potter with this work.

RUTH (draws her hand about her neck as if loosening something there; convulsively). Since then this has been round my neck, round my limbs, a chain of eating fire. Link by link I have unwound it. You will never know what it has cost me, but I have paid it all. Take it and let me go free. (She tries to force it upon him, with wailing entreaty.) Take it, take it, I beseech you!

GHENT (holding himself under stern control). You are killing yourself. You mustn't go on this way. Go and rest. We will talk of this tomorrow.

RUTH. Rest! Tomorrow! Oh, how little you have understood of all I have said! I know it is only a symbol— a make-believe. I know I am childish to ask it. Still, take it and tell me I am free.

GHENT (takes the chain reluctantly, stands for a moment looking at it, then speaks with iron firmness). As you say, your price has risen. This is not enough. (He throws the chain about her neck and draws her to him by it.) You are mine, mine, do you hear? Now and forever! (He starts toward the house. She holds out her hand blindly to detain him.)

RUTH (in a stifled voice). Wait! There is—something else.

(He returns to her, anxiously, and stands waiting. She goes on, touching the chain.)

It isn't only for my sake I ask you to take this off me, nor only for your sake. There is—another life—to think of.

GHENT (leaning to look into her averted face). Ruth!—Is it true?— Thank God!

RUTH. Now, will you take this off me?

GHENT (starts to do so, then draws back). No. Now less than ever. For now, more than ever, you are mine.

RUTH. But—how yours? Oh, remember, have pity! How yours?

(PHILIP appears at the head of the canyon path. Hearing their voices, he waits, half concealed.)

GHENT. No matter how! Bought if you like, but mine! Mine by blind chance and the hell in a man's veins, if you like! Mine by almighty Nature, whether you like it or not!

RUTH. Nature! Almighty Nature! (She takes the chain slowly from her neck.) Not yours! By everything my people have held sacred! (She drops the chain.) Not yours! Not yours! (She turns slowly. PHILIP has come forward, and supports her as she sinks half fainting upon his neck.)

PHILIP (to GHENT). I came back to get my sister for the night.—I don't know by what ugly spell you have held her, but I know, from her own lips, that it is broken. (To RUTH) Come! I have horses below.

GHENT. No!

PHILIP (measuring him). Yes. (Pause.)

GHENT. Let her say!

RUTH (looks long at GHENT, then at the house and surroundings; at last, she turns to her brother). Take me— with you. Take me—home!

(PHILIP, supporting her, leads her down the canyon path. GHENT stands gazing after them as they disappear below the rim. He picks up the chain and goes back, looking down after the descending figures. The sunset light has faded, and darkness has begun to settle over the mountain world.)

ACT THREE

Sitting room of MRS. JORDAN's *house at Milford Corners, Massachusetts. An old-fashioned New England interior, faded but showing signs of former distinction. The walls are hung with family portraits, several in clerical attire of the eighteenth century, one in the uniform of the Revolutionary War. Doors open right and left. At the back is a fireplace, flanked by windows, the curtains of which are drawn. On the left is a small table, with a lamp, books, and magazines; on the right, near the fireplace, a sewing table, with lamp and sewing basket. A bookcase and a writing desk occupy opposite corners of the room, forward.*
WINTHROP *and* PHILIP *stand near the desk, chatting.* POLLY *is reading a newspaper at the table.* RUTH *sits before the grate, sewing; her face is turned away toward the fire.*

———

PHILIP (*offers* WINTHROP *his cigar case*). Have another cigar.

WINTHROP. Well, as a celebration. (*Takes one and lights it.*)

PHILIP. Rather small business for the Jordan family, to be celebrating a bare escape from the poorhouse.

WINTHROP. Where did you scare up the benevolent uncle? I never heard of him before.

PHILIP. Nor I, scarcely. He's always lived abroad.

WINTHROP (*strolling about, peeps over* POLLY's *shoulder; to* PHILIP, *with a scandalized gesture*). Stock reports!

PHILIP. Her latest craze.

WINTHROP. Last week it was Japanese Samurai.

POLLY (*crushingly*). And next week it will be—Smart Alecks.

(*The door on the left opens, and*

MRS. JORDAN *enters, with* DR. NEWBURY. *During the preceding conversation,* RUTH *has sat sewing, paying no heed to the chatter.* MRS. JORDAN *and the doctor look at her as they come in, but she does not look up.*)

MRS. JORDAN. Sit down, Doctor, at least for a moment.

DR. NEWBURY (*seats himself,* MRS. JORDAN *near him*). I can never resist such an invitation, in this house.

MRS. JORDAN. Dear Doctor, you've been a wonderful friend to me and mine all these years, since poor Josiah was taken.

DR. NEWBURY. But just when you needed help most—

MRS. JORDAN. I know how gladly you would have offered it, if you could.

DR. NEWBURY. Your brother-in-law in England was able to redeem the property?

MRS. JORDAN (*hastily*). Yes, yes.—But what we are to do for the future, with my little capital gone— (*She speaks lower.*) Oh, that dreadful West! If my children had only stayed where they were born and bred. (*She glances at* RUTH, *who has let her sewing fall in her lap and sits staring into the fire.*)

DR. NEWBURY (*sotto voce*). Poor child.

POLLY (*looks up from the newspaper excitedly, holding her finger at a place on the sheet*). I say, Phil! Win! Look here.

(PHILIP *and* WINTHROP, *who have been chatting and smoking apart, come to the table.*)

PHILIP. What is it now?

POLLY (*tapping on the paper*). Something about your Arizona scheme.

PHILIP (*bending over her, reads*). "Alleghany pig-iron, 93¾, National Brick—"

POLLY (*pointing*). No, there!

PHILIP. "Arizona Cactus Fiber, 84." (*He picks up the paper, astounded.*) Cactus Fiber listed! Selling at 84! (*He tosses the paper to* WINTHROP.) This is the last straw!

MRS. JORDAN (*who has been listening anxiously*). What does it mean, Phil?

PHILIP. Only that the people who bought our plant and patents for a song, have made a fortune out of them.

(RUTH *has resumed her needlework.* WINTHROP *offers her the paper, with his finger at the line. She takes it, looks at it vaguely, and lays it on the table.*)

POLLY (*leaning across*). Doesn't that interest you?

RUTH (*tonelessly*). Oh, yes. (*She rises, lays her work aside, and goes toward the door.*)

DR. NEWBURY (*as she passes him*). Won't you bid me good night, my child?

RUTH (*giving him her hand*). Good night, Doctor.

DR. NEWBURY (*shaking his finger*). Remember, no more moping! And from tomorrow, outdoors with you.

(RUTH *looks at him vacantly, attempting to smile. She moves toward the door, which* WINTHROP *opens for her.*)

WINTHROP (*holding out his hand*). You must bid me good night, too, and good-by.

RUTH (*with a faint kindling of interest*). Are you going away?

WINTHROP. Only back to Boston. Some time, when you are stronger, you will come down and see our new sailors' hospital.

RUTH. Yes.—Good-by. (*She goes out,* WINTHROP *closing the door.*)

WINTHROP (*to* DR. NEWBURY). I must be going along, father. Good night,

everybody! (*Patting* PHILIP's *shoulder*) Hard luck, old man! (*He goes out by the hall door on the right,* PHILIP *accompanying him.*)

DR. NEWBURY (*looking after his son*). Brave boy! Brave boy! He keeps up a good show.

MRS. JORDAN. You think he still grieves over her?

DR. NEWBURY. Ah, poor chap! He's made of the right stuff, if he is mine.

MRS. JORDAN. Let us not talk of it. It is too sad, too dreadful.

(PHILIP *re-enters.*)

DR. NEWBURY. About part of it we must talk. (*He speaks so as to include* PHILIP *and* POLLY *in the conversation.*) Mrs. Jordan, I don't want to alarm you, but your daughter—I may as well put it bluntly—is in a dangerous state.

MRS. JORDAN (*frightened*). Doctor, I thought she seemed so much stronger.

DR. NEWBURY. She is, so far as her body is concerned.

(MRS. JORDAN *sits in an attitude of nervous attention, gazing at the doctor as if trying to formulate one of many questions pressing upon her.* PHILIP *comes forward and sits by the table, near them.*)

PHILIP. Don't you think that the routine of life which she has taken up will soon restore her to a normal state of mind?

DR. NEWBURY. Perhaps.—I hope so.— I would have good hope of it, if it were not for her attitude toward her child.

MRS. JORDAN (*overwhelmed*). You noticed that, too! I haven't spoken to you of it, because—I haven't been willing to see it myself.

PHILIP. I can't see that there is anything particularly strange in her attitude. She takes care of the brat scrupulously enough.

POLLY. Brat!

MRS. JORDAN. Brat! (*To* DR. NEW-BURY, *after a reproachful gaze at* PHILIP) With the most watchful, the minutest care, but— (*She speaks in a constrained voice, with a nervous glance at the door.*) —exactly as if it were a piece of machinery!—Phil, do please lay down that paper-knife before you break it! Your father brought that to me from India. (*He obeys, but picks it up again absent-mindedly, after a few seconds.*) Pardon me, Doctor. She goes about her daily business, and answers when she is spoken to, but as for her really being here— (*She breaks out.*) Doctor, what *shall* we do?

DR. NEWBURY. She must be roused from this state, but how to do it, I don't know.

POLLY (*rising, with heightened color and nervous emphasis*). Well, I do!

MRS. JORDAN (*looking at her with frightened interrogation*). Polly—?

POLLY. What she needs is her husband, and I have sent for him!

PHILIP (*inarticulate with surprise and anger*). You—!

POLLY. Yes, I. He's been here a week. And he's an angel, isn't he, mother?

(PHILIP *snaps the paper-knife in two, flings the pieces to the floor, and rises, pale with rage.*)

MRS. JORDAN (*gathering up the pieces with a wail*). Oh, Phil! How could you! One of my most precious relics!

PHILIP (*to* MRS. JORDAN). Is this true, or is it another of her tedious jokes?

POLLY (*protesting*). Oh, my dear, tedious!

MRS. JORDAN (*wipes her eyes, after ruefully fitting the broken pieces of the knife together and laying them tenderly on the table*). You don't deserve to have me answer you, but it is true.

PHILIP. Was this action taken with your knowledge?

MRS. JORDAN. I do not expect to be spoken to in that tone. Polly telegraphed merely the facts. He came at his own instance.

PHILIP. But you have consented to enter into relations with him?

MRS. JORDAN. I have seen him several times.

POLLY (*triumphantly*). And yesterday we showed him the baby! Such fun, wasn't it, mother?

MRS. JORDAN (*wiping her eyes, sheepishly*). Yes, it was rather—enjoyable.

PHILIP. He can't be in this town. I should have heard of it.

POLLY. We've hid him safe.

PHILIP. Where?

POLLY. Never mind. He's on tap, and the sooner we turn on the spigot the better, is what I think. Doctor, what do you think?

DR. NEWBURY. Let me ask you again to state your view of Ruth's case. I don't think I quite grasp your view.

POLLY (*pluming herself, doctrinaire*). Well! Here on the one hand is the primitive, the barbaric woman, falling in love with a romantic stranger, who, like some old Viking on a harry, cuts her with his two-handed sword from the circle of her kinsmen, and bears her away on his dragon ship toward the midnight sun. Here on the other hand is the derived, the civilized woman, with a civilized nervous system, observing that the creature eats bacon with his bowie knife, knows not the manicure, has the conversation of a preoccupied walrus, the instincts of a jealous caribou, and the endearments of a dancing crab in the mating season.

MRS. JORDAN. Polly! What ideas! What language!

DR. NEWBURY. Don't be alarmed, Mrs.

Jordan. The vocabulary has changed since our day, and—the point of view has shifted a little. (*To* POLLY) Well?

POLLY. Well, Ruth is one of those people who can't live in a state of divided feeling. She sits staring at this cleavage in her life, like—like that man in Dante, don't you know, who is pierced by the serpent, and who stands there in hell staring at his wound, yawning like a sleepy man.

MRS. JORDAN. Oh, Polly, do please try not to get our heads muddled up with literature!

POLLY. All I mean is that when she married her man she married him for keeps. And he did the same by her.

(PHILIP *rises, with uncontrollable impatience, and goes back to the mantelpiece, against which he leans, nervously tearing a bit of paper to pieces.*)

DR. NEWBURY. Don't you think that a mere difference of cultivation, polish—or—or something of that sort—is rather small to have led to a rupture, and so painful a one, too?

POLLY (*a little nonplussed*). Well, yes, perhaps it does *look* small. But we don't know the particulars; and men *are* such *colossal* brutes, you know, dear doctor!

DR. NEWBURY (*judicially*). Yes, so they are, so they are!

POLLY. And then her pride! You know when it comes to pride, Ruth would make Lucifer look like a charity-boy asking for more soup.

DR. NEWBURY. I think perhaps the plan should be tried. (*After a pause*) Yes, I think so decidedly.

PHILIP. I call this a plot against her dignity and peace of mind!

DR. NEWBURY (*rising*). Well, this conspirator must be going. (*He shakes hands with* POLLY *and* MRS. JORDAN, *takes his hat and stick.* PHILIP *remains*

plunged in angry reflection. DR. NEWBURY *taps* PHILIP *jestingly on the shoulder with the tip of his cane.*) When you have lived as long as I have, my boy, you'll—you'll be just as old as I am! (*He goes out,* POLLY *accompanying him to the door.* PHILIP, *disregarding his mother's conciliatory look and gesture as he passes her, goes out.* POLLY *stretches her arms and draws a deep breath as the door closes after him.*)

MRS. JORDAN (*looking at her severely*). Pray what does that mean?

POLLY. Oh, Phil is such a walking thundercloud, these days. It's a relief to get rid of him.

MRS. JORDAN. Have you done what you could to make his life brighter?

POLLY. I never had a chance. He has always been too much wrapped up in Ruth to think of me.

MRS. JORDAN. How can you say such a thing? What do you suppose he married you for?

POLLY. Heaven knows! What do they ever do it for? It is a most curious and savage propensity. But immensely interesting to watch.

MRS. JORDAN (*with a despairing gesture*). If you hold such heathenish views, why are you so bent on bringing those two together?

POLLY (*soberly*). Because they represent—what Philip and I have missed.

MRS. JORDAN. And pray what have "Philip and I" missed?

POLLY. Oh, we're all right. But we're not like those two.

MRS. JORDAN. I should hope not!

POLLY. Even I believe that now and then a marriage is made in heaven. This one was. They are predestined lovers!

MRS. JORDAN (*mournfully, hypnotized by the evangelical note*). I pray it may be so. (*She looks suspiciously at* POLLY.) You wretched girl! Predestined lovers and marriages made in heaven, after all you've just been saying about how impossible he is.

POLLY. He is quite impossible, but he's the kind we can't resist, any of us. He'd only have to crook his little finger at me.

MRS. JORDAN (*lifting her hands in despair*). What are you young women coming to! (*Pause*) He seems to be a good man.

POLLY (*delighted*). Oh, he's *good!* So is a volcano between eruptions. And commonplace, too, until you happen to get a glimpse down one of the old volcanic rifts in his surface, and see—far below—underneath the cold lava-beds—fire, fire, the molten heart of a continent!

MRS. JORDAN. I only hope you have some vague general notion of what you are talking about.

POLLY. Amen.—And now let's consider when, where, and how we are to hale this dubious pair together.

MRS. JORDAN. One thing is sure, it mustn't be here.

POLLY. Why not?

MRS. JORDAN. On Philip's account.

POLLY. Oh, bother Philip!—Wasn't that the doorbell?

MRS. JORDAN. Yes. You had better go.

POLLY (*goes out; after a moment, she re-enters, excitedly*). It's Mr. Ghent!

MRS. JORDAN (*amazed*). Mr. Ghent?

(POLLY *nods enthusiastically.* GHENT *enters. He is conventionally dressed, a black string tie and the broad-brimmed hat which he carries being the only suggestions of Western costume remaining.* MRS. JORDAN *receives him in a flutter of excitement and alarm.*) Mr. Ghent—! Surely at this hour—!

GHENT. I beg your pardon. There was no other way. I am going West

tonight.—Can I see you alone?

MRS. JORDAN (*looks at* POLLY, *who goes out, pouting*). Going West tonight?

GHENT. Yes. Trouble at the mine.

MRS. JORDAN. Isn't your business partner competent to attend to it?

GHENT. He's competent to steal the whole outfit. In fact, is doing it, or has done it already.

MRS. JORDAN (*vaguely alarmed*). And —my property here? Is that involved in the danger?

GHENT. Certainly not.

MRS. JORDAN (*relieved*). I have gone through such months of misery at the thought of losing the dear old place!— If Ruth only knew that we owe the very roof over our heads to you—

GHENT. Well, she isn't to know, that's understood, isn't it? Besides, it's nothing to speak of. Glad if you think it a service. She wouldn't.

MRS. JORDAN. You mean—?

GHENT. I mean that if she knew about it, she wouldn't stay here overnight.

MRS. JORDAN. Sit down. (*She motions him to a seat at the table; she sits near him, speaking with nervous impulsiveness.*) Tell me what is the trouble between you! It has all been a dreadful mystery from the beginning!

GHENT. Is it a mystery that a woman like your daughter—? (*He stops and sinks into gloomy thought.*)

MRS. JORDAN. Should have chosen you?—Pardon me, I don't mean anything unkind—

(*He makes a gesture of brusque exoneration.*)

But having chosen—and broken faith with her brother to do it—

GHENT (*nervously*). Let's drop that! (*Pause*) Mrs. Jordan, you come of the old stock. Do you believe in the devil?

MRS. JORDAN. Perhaps not in the sense you mean.

GHENT (*tapping his breast*). I mean the devil inside of a man—the devil in the heart!

MRS. JORDAN. Oh, yes. We are all forced by our lives to believe in that.

GHENT. Our lives! (*He looks slowly round the room.*) How long have you lived here?

MRS. JORDAN. For thirty years, in this house. Before I was married I lived in the old house down the road yonder, opposite the church.

GHENT (*to himself*). Think of it!

MRS. JORDAN. What did you say?

GHENT (*gathers himself together*). Mrs. Jordan, I want you to promise that what I put in your hands from time to time comes to your daughter as if from another source.

MRS. JORDAN. You are going away for good?

GHENT. Yes.

MRS. JORDAN. You give her up?

GHENT. A man can't give up what isn't his.

MRS. JORDAN. What isn't his? She is your wife.

GHENT. No. Never has been.

MRS. JORDAN (*terrified*). Oh, pitiful heavens!

GHENT. I beg your pardon.—I was only trying to say—I used to think that when a couple was married, there they were, man and wife, and that was the end of it. I used to think that when they had a child, well, sure enough it was their child, and all said.—And there's something in that, too. (*He stares before him, smiting the table and speaking with low intensity.*) Damn me if there ain't something eternal in it! (*He sits for a moment more in gloomy thought.*) Do you think she'll make up to the young one, after a bit.

MRS. JORDAN. Oh, surely! To think otherwise would be too dreadful!

GHENT. I'd give a good deal to know.—It's kind of lonesome for the little rooster, sitting out there all by himself on the world's doorstep!—I must see her for a minute before I go.—Do your best for me.

MRS. JORDAN. I will do what I can.

GHENT. You can put it as a matter of business. There is a matter of business I want to talk over with her, if I can get up the gumption.

MRS. JORDAN. Hadn't you better tell me what it is?

GHENT. Well, it's about your son Philip. That little scheme he started out in my country—the Cactus Fiber industry.

MRS. JORDAN. Yes?

GHENT. I believe he thinks his sister's going away when she did queered his game.

MRS. JORDAN. It was a severe blow to him in every way. She was the life and soul of his enterprise.

GHENT. I want her to give him back the Cactus Fiber outfit, worth something more than when he dropped it.

MRS. JORDAN. Give it back to him? She?

GHENT (*takes papers from his pocket*). Yes. I happened to hear it was knocking around for nothing in the market, and I bought it—for the house, really. Hated to see that go to the dogs. Then I looked over the plant, and got a hustler to boom it. I thought as a matter of transfer to cancel her debt, or what she thinks her debt— (*Pause.*)

MRS. JORDAN (*fingering the paper with hesitation*). Mr. Ghent, we really can't accept such a thing. Your offer is quixotic.

GHENT. Quix—what?

MRS. JORDAN. Quixotic, it really is.

GHENT (*doubtfully*). I guess you're right. It depends on the way you look at it. One way it looks like a pure business proposition—so much lost, so much made good. The other way it looks, as you say, quix—um—. Anyway, there are the papers! Do what you think best with them. (*He lays the papers on the table, and picks up his hat.*)

MRS. JORDAN. Wait in the parlor. (*He opens the hall door.*) The second door on the left.

(*With an awkward bow to* MRS. JORDAN, *he partly closes the door after him, when the inner door opens and* RUTH *appears. She goes to the sewing table and picks up her sewing. Her mother, with a frightened glance at the half-open hall door, draws her back and kisses her.* GHENT, *unseen by* RUTH, *remains standing, with his hand on the door-knob.*)

MRS. JORDAN. Ruth, you are a brave girl, and I will treat you like one.—Your husband is here.

RUTH. Here?—Where?

(GHENT *pushes the door open, and closes it behind him.* RUTH, *sinking back against the opposite wall, stares at him blankly.*)

MRS. JORDAN. He is leaving for the West again tonight. He has asked to see you before he goes.

(RUTH *covers her face with her hands, then fumbles blindly for the latch of the door. Her mother restrains her.*)

It is your duty to hear what he has to say. You owe that to the love you once bore him.

RUTH. He killed my love before it was born!

MRS. JORDAN. It is your duty to hear him, and part with him in a Christian spirit, for our sakes, if not for your own.

RUTH. For whose sake?

MRS. JORDAN. For mine and your brother's.—We owe it to him, as a family.

GHENT (*raising his hand restrainingly*). Mrs. Jordan—!

RUTH. Owe!

MRS. JORDAN. We owe it to him, for what he has done and wishes to do.

RUTH. What he has done?—Wishes to do?

MRS. JORDAN. Yes, don't echo me like a parrot! He has done a great deal for us, and is anxious to do more, if you will only let him.

RUTH. What is this? Explain it to me quickly.

MRS. JORDAN (*with growing impatience*). Don't think to judge your mother!

RUTH. I demand to hear what all this is! Tell me.

MRS. JORDAN (*losing control of herself*). He has kept us from being turned into the street!

(GHENT, *who has tried dumbly to restrain her, turns away in stoic resignation to his fate.*) He has given us the very roof over our heads!

RUTH. You said that Uncle—

MRS. JORDAN. Well, it was not your uncle! I said so to shield you in your stubborn and cold-hearted pride.

RUTH. Is there more of this?

MRS. JORDAN. Yes, there *is* more. You wronged your brother to follow your own path of willful love, and now you wrong him again by following your own path of willful aversion. Here comes your husband, offering to make restitution—

RUTH. What restitution?

MRS. JORDAN. He has bought Philip's property out there, and wants you to give it back to him.

RUTH (*stands motionless for a mo-*

ment, *then looks vacantly about,
speaking in a dull voice, as at first*).
I must go away from this house.

MRS. JORDAN. You don't understand.
He claims nothing. He is going away
himself immediately. Whatever this
dreadful trouble is between you, you
are his wife, and he has a right to
help you and yours.

RUTH. I am not his wife.

MRS. JORDAN. Ruth, don't frighten
me. He said those same words—

RUTH. He said—what?

MRS. JORDAN. That you were not
his wife.

RUTH. He said—that?

MRS. JORDAN. Yes, but afterward he
explained—

RUTH (*flaming into white wrath*).
Explained! Did he explain that when
I was left alone that night at the
ranch he came—with two others—and
when gun and knife had failed me,
and nothing stood between me and
their drunken fury, I sold myself to
the strongest of them, hiding my head
behind the name of marriage? Did
he explain that between him and the
others money clinked— (*She raps on
the table.*) —my price in hard money
on the table? And now that I have
run away to the only refuge I have on
earth, he comes to buy the very house
where I have hidden, and every miserable being within it!• (*Long pause.
She looks about blankly and sinks
down by the table.*)

MRS. JORDAN (*cold and rigid*). And
you—married him—after that? (*She
turns away in horror-stricken judgment.*) You ought to have—died—first!

(PHILIP *opens the door and enters,
staring at* GHENT *with dislike and
menace.*)

Oh, Philip, she has told me!—You
can't imagine what horrors!

(RUTH *rises, with fright in her face,*

and approaches her brother to restrain him.*)

PHILIP. Horrors? What horrors?

MRS. JORDAN. It was your fault! You
ought never to have left her alone in
that dreadful place! She—she married
him—to save herself—from—Oh, horrible!

PHILIP (*waits an instant, the truth
penetrating his mind slowly; then,
with mortal rage in his face, he starts
toward* GHENT). You—dog!

RUTH (*throws herself in* PHILIP's
path). No, no, no!

PHILIP. Get out of my way. This is
my business now.

RUTH. No, it is mine. I tell you it is
mine.

PHILIP. We'll see whose it is. I said
that if the truth ever came out, this
man should answer to me, and now,
by God, he shall answer! (*With another access of rage he tries to thrust*
RUTH *from his path.* MRS. JORDAN, *terrified at the storm she has raised,
clings desperately to her son's arm.*)

RUTH. I told him long ago it should
be between us. Now it shall be between us.

MRS. JORDAN. Philip! For my sake,
for your father's sake! Don't, don't!
You will only make it worse. In pity's
name, leave them alone together. Leave them alone—together!

(*They force* PHILIP *back to the door,
where he stands glaring at* GHENT.)

PHILIP (*to* GHENT). My time will
come. Meanwhile, hide behind the
skirts of the woman whose life you
have ruined and whose heart you have
broken. Hide behind her. It is the
coward's privilege. Take it.

(PHILIP, *with* MRS. JORDAN *still clinging to his arm, goes out,* RUTH *closing
the door after them. She and* GHENT
*confront each other in silence for a
moment, across the width of the room.*)

RUTH. God forgive me! You never can.

GHENT. It was a pity—but—you were in a corner. I drove you to it, by coming here.

RUTH. It was base of me—base!

GHENT. The way your mother took it showed me one thing.—I've never understood you, because—I don't understand your people.

RUTH. You mean—her saying I ought to have died rather than accept life as I did?

GHENT. Yes.

RUTH. She spoke the truth. I have always seen it.

GHENT. Ruth, it's a queer thing for me to be saying, but—it seems to me, you've never seen the truth between us.

RUTH. What is the truth—between us?

GHENT. The truth is— (*He pauses, then continues with a disconsolate gesture.*) Well, there's no use going into that. (*He fumbles in his pocket, and takes from it the nugget chain, which he looks at in silence for a time, then speaks in quiet resignation.*) I've got here the chain, that's come, one way and another, to have a meaning for us. For you it's a bitter meaning, but, all the same, I want you to keep it. Show it some day to the boy, and tell him—about me. (*He lays it on the desk and goes toward the door.*)

RUTH. What is the truth—between us?

GHENT. I guess it was only of myself I was thinking.

RUTH. What is it—about yourself?

GHENT (*after a pause*). I drifted into one of your meetinghouses last Sunday; not knowing where else to go, and I heard a young fellow preaching about what he called "The Second Birth." A year and a half ago I should have thought it was all hocus-pocus, but you can believe me or not, the way he went on he might have been behind the door that night in that little justice den at San Jacinto, saying to the Recording Angel: "Do you see that rascal? Take notice! There ain't an ounce of bone or a drop of blood in him but what's new man!"

RUTH. You think it has been all my fault—the failure we've made of our life?

GHENT. It's been no failure. However it is, it's been our life, and in my heart I think it's been—all—right!

RUTH. All right! Oh, how can you say that? (*She repeats the words with a touch of awe and wonder.*) All right!

GHENT. Some of it has been wrong, but as a whole it has been right—right! I know that doesn't happen often, but it has happened to us, because— (*He stops, unable to find words for his idea.*) —because—because the first time our eyes met, they burned away all that was bad in our meeting, and left only the fact that we had met—pure good—pure joy—a fortune of it—for both of us. Yes, both of us! You'll see it yourself some day.

RUTH. If you had only heard my cry to you, to wait, to cleanse yourself and me—by suffering and sacrifice—before we dared begin to live! But you wouldn't see the need!— Oh, if you could have felt for yourself what I felt for you! If you could have said, "The wages of sin is death!" and suffered the anguish of death, and risen again purified! But instead of that, what you had done fell off from you like any daily trifle.

GHENT (*steps impulsively nearer her, sweeping his hand to indicate the portraits on the walls*). Ruth, it's these fellows are fooling you! It's they who keep your head set on the wages of sin, and all that rubbish. What have we got to do with suffering and sacrifice? That may be the law for some, and I've tried hard to see it as our law, and thought I had succeeded. But I haven't! Our law is joy, and selfishness; the curve of your shoulder and the light on your hair as you sit there says that as plain as preaching. —Does it gall you the way we came together? You asked me that night what brought me, and I told you whiskey, and sun, and the devil. Well, I tell you now I'm thankful on my knees for all three! Does it rankle in your mind that I took you when I could get you, by main strength and fraud? I guess most good women are taken that way, if they only knew it. Don't you want to be paid for? I guess every wife is paid for in some good coin or other. And as for you, I've paid for you not only with a trumpery chain, but with the heart in my breast, do you hear? That's one thing you can't throw back at me— the man you've made of me, the life and the meaning of life you've showed me the way to! (RUTH's *face is hidden in her hands, her elbows on the table. He stands over her, flushed and waiting. Gradually the light fades from his face. When he speaks again, the ring of exultation which has been in his voice is replaced by a sober intensity.*) If you can't see it my way, give me another chance to live it out in yours. (*He waits, but she does not speak or look up. He takes a package of letters and papers from his pocket, and runs them over, in deep reflection.*) During the six months I've been East—

RUTH (*looking up*). Six months? Mother said a week!

GHENT. Your sister-in-law's telegram was forwarded to me here. I let her think it brought me, but as a matter of fact, I came East in the next train after yours. It was rather a low-lived thing to do, I suppose, hanging about and bribing your servant for news— (RUTH *lets her head sink in her hands. He pauses and continues ruefully.*) I might have known how that would strike you! Well, it would have come out sooner or later.—That's not what I started to talk about.—You ask me to suffer for my wrong. Since you left me I *have* suffered—God knows! You ask me to make some sacrifice. Well— how would the mine do? Since I've been away they've as good as stolen it from me. I could get it back easy enough by fighting; but supposing I don't fight. Then we'll start all over again, just as we stand in our shoes, and make another fortune—for our boy.

(RUTH *utters a faint moan as her head sinks in her arms on the table. With trembling hands,* GHENT *caresses her hair lightly, and speaks between a laugh and a sob.*)
Little mother! Little mother! What does the past matter, when we've got the future—and him?

(RUTH *does not move. He remains bending over her for some moments, then straightens up, with a gesture of stoic despair.*)
I know what you're saying there to yourself, and I guess you're right. Wrong is wrong, from the moment it happens till the crack of doom, and all the angels in heaven, working overtime, can't make it less or different by a hair. That seems to be the law. I've learned it hard, but I guess I've learned it. I've seen it written in mountain letters across the continent of this life.—Done is done, and lost is lost, and smashed to hell is smashed to hell. We fuss and potter and patch

up. You might as well try to batter down the Rocky Mountains with a rabbit's heartbeat! (*He goes to the door, where he turns.*) You've fought hard for me, God bless you for it.— But it's been a losing game with you from the first!—You belong here, and I belong out yonder—beyond the Rockies, beyond—the Great Divide! (*He opens the door and is about to pass out.* RUTH *looks up with streaming eyes.*)

RUTH. Wait!

(*He closes the door and stands waiting for her to speak.* RUTH *masters herself and goes on, her eyes shining, her face exalted.*)

Tell me you know that if I could have followed you, and been your wife, without struggle and without bitterness, I would have done it.

GHENT (*solemnly*). I believe you would.

RUTH. Tell me you know that when I tore down with bleeding fingers the life you were trying to build for us, I did it only—because—I loved you!

GHENT (*comes slowly to the table, looking at her with bewilderment*). How was that?

RUTH. Oh, I don't wonder you ask! Another woman would have gone straight to her goal. You might have found such a one. But instead you found me, a woman in whose ears rang night and day the cry of an angry Heaven to us both—"Cleanse yourselves!" And I went about doing it in the only way I knew— (*She points at the portraits on the wall.*) —the only way my fathers knew—by wretchedness, by self-torture, by trying blindly to pierce your careless heart with pain. And all the while you— Oh, as I lay there and listened to you, I realized it for the first time— you had risen, in one hour, to a wholly new existence, which flooded the present and the future with brightness, yes, and reached back into our past, and made of it—made of all of it —something to cherish! (*She takes the chain, and comes closer.*) You have taken the good of our life and grown strong. I have taken the evil and grown weak, weak unto death. Teach me to live as you do! (*She puts the chain about her neck.*)

GHENT (*puzzled, not yet realizing the full force of her words*). Teach you—to live—as I do?

RUTH. And teach—him!

GHENT (*unable to realize his fortune*). You'll let me help make a kind of a happy life for—the little rooster?

RUTH (*holds out her arms, her face flooded with happiness*). And for us! For us!

THE NEW YORK IDEA

Langdon Mitchell

First produced at the Hackett Theatre in New York on November 18, 1906.

PHILIP PHILLIMORE

MRS. PHILLIMORE, *his mother*

THE REVEREND MATTHEW PHILLIMORE, *his brother*

GRACE PHILLIMORE, *his sister*

MISS HENEAGE, *his aunt*

WILLIAM SUDLEY, *his cousin*

MRS. VIDA PHILLIMORE, *his divorced wife*

BROOKS, *her footman*

BENSON, *her maid*

SIR WILFRID CATES-DARBY

JOHN KARSLAKE

MRS. CYNTHIA KARSLAKE, *his divorced wife*

NOGAM, *his valet*

TIM FIDDLER

THOMAS, *the* PHILLIMORES' *family servant*

ACT ONE

Living room in the house of PHILIP PHILLIMORE in New York. Five o'clock of an afternoon of May. The general air and appearance of the room is that of an old-fashioned, decorous, comfortable interior. There are no electric lights and no electric bells. Two bell ropes as in old-fashioned houses. The room is in dark tones inclining to somber and of old-fashioned elegance.

The curtain rises, disclosing MISS HENEAGE, MRS. PHILLIMORE, and THOMAS. MISS HENEAGE is a solidly built, narrow-minded woman in her sixties. She makes no effort to look younger than she is, and is expensively but quietly dressed, with heavy elegance. She commands her household and her family connection, and on the strength of a large and steady income feels that her opinion has its value. MRS. PHILLIMORE is a semi-professional invalid, refined and unintelligent. Her movements are weak and fatigued. Her voice is habitually plaintive and she is entirely a lady without a trace of being a woman of fashion. THOMAS is an easy-mannered, but entirely respectful family servant, un-English both in style and appearance. He has no deportment worthy of being so called, and takes an evident interest in the affairs of the family he serves. MISS HENEAGE, seated at the tea table, faces the footlights. MRS. PHILLIMORE is seated at the left side of the table. THOMAS stands near by. The table is set for tea. There is a vase with flowers, a silver match box, and a large old-fashioned tea urn on the table. The Evening Post is on the table. MISS HENEAGE and MRS. PHILLIMORE both have cups of tea. MISS HENEAGE sits up very straight, and pours tea for GRACE, who has just entered. She is a pretty and fashionably dressed girl of twenty. She speaks superciliously, coolly, and not too fast. She sits on the sofa, and does not lounge, wearing a gown suitable for spring visiting, hat, parasol, and gloves.

GRACE (as she crosses and sits down). I never in my life walked so far and found so few people at home. (She pauses, taking off her gloves, and somewhat querulously continues.) The fact is the nineteenth of May is ridiculously late to be in town.

MISS HENEAGE. Thomas, Mr. Phillimore's sherry?

THOMAS. The sherry, ma'am. (THOMAS indicates a table where the decanter is set.)

MISS HENEAGE. Mr. Phillimore's Post?

THOMAS (pointing to the Evening Post on the tea table). The Post, ma'am.

MISS HENEAGE (indicates the cup). Miss Phillimore.

(THOMAS takes a cup of tea to GRACE. There is silence while they all sip tea. THOMAS goes back, fills the sherry glass, remaining round and about the tea table. They all drink tea during the following scene.)

GRACE. The Dudleys were at home. They wished to know when my brother Philip was to be married, and where and how?

MISS HENEAGE. If the Dudleys were persons of breeding, they'd not intrude their curiosity upon you.

GRACE. I like Lena Dudley.

MRS. PHILLIMORE (slowly and gently). Do I know Miss Dudley?

GRACE. She knows Philip. She expects an announcement of the wedding.

MRS. PHILLIMORE. I trust you told her that my son, my sister, and myself are all of the opinion that those who have been divorced should remarry with modesty and without parade.

GRACE. I told the Dudleys, Philip's wedding was here, tomorrow.

MISS HENEAGE (*to* MRS. PHILLIMORE, *picking up a sheet of paper from the table*). I have spent the afternoon, Mary, in arranging and listing the wedding gifts and in writing out the announcements of the wedding. I think I have attained a proper form of announcement. (*She takes the sheet of note paper and gives it to* THOMAS.) Of course, the announcement Philip himself made was quite out of the question. (GRACE *smiles.*) However, there is mine. (*She points to the paper.* THOMAS *gives the list to* MRS. PHILLIMORE *and moves away.*)

GRACE. I hope you'll send an announcement to the Dudleys.

MRS. PHILLIMORE (*reading plaintively, ready to make the best of things*). "Mr. Philip Phillimore and Mrs. Cynthia Dean Karslake announce their marriage, May twentieth, at three o'clock, Nineteen A, Washington Square, New York." (*She replaces paper on* THOMAS's *salver.*) It sounds very nice.

(THOMAS *hands the paper to* MISS HENEAGE.)

MISS HENEAGE. In my opinion it barely escapes sounding nasty. However, it is correct. The only remaining question is—to whom the announcement should not be sent.

(*Exit* THOMAS.)

I consider an announcement of the wedding of two divorced persons to be in the nature of an intimate communication. It not only announces the wedding—it also announces the divorce. (*She returns to her teacup.*) The person I shall ask counsel of is Cousin William Sudley. He promised to drop in this afternoon.

GRACE. Oh! We shall hear all about Cairo.

MRS. PHILLIMORE. William is judicious.

(*Re-enter* THOMAS.)

MISS HENEAGE (*with finality*). Cousin William will disapprove of the match unless a winter in Cairo has altered his moral tone.

THOMAS (*announces*). Mr. Sudley.

(*Enter* WILLIAM SUDLEY, *a little, oldish gentleman. He is and appears thoroughly insignificant. But his opinion of the place he occupies in the world is exalted. Though he is filled with self-importance, his manners, voice, presence are all those of a man of breeding.*)

MRS. PHILLIMORE *and* MISS HENEAGE (*they rise and greet* SUDLEY; *a little tremulously*). My dear William!

(*Exit* THOMAS.)

SUDLEY (*shakes hands with* MRS. PHILLIMORE, *soberly glad to see them*). How d'ye do, Mary? A very warm May you're having, Sarah.

GRACE (*comes to him*). Dear Cousin William!

MISS HENEAGE. Wasn't it warm in Cairo when you left? (*She will have the strict truth, or nothing; still, on account of* SUDLEY's *impeccable respectability, she treats him with more than usual leniency.*)

SUDLEY (*sitting down*). We left Cairo six weeks ago, Grace, so I've had no news since you wrote in February that Philip was engaged. (*Pause*) I need not to say I consider Philip's engagement excessively regrettable. He is a judge upon the Supreme Court bench with a divorced wife—and such a divorced wife!

GRACE. Oh, but Philip has succeeded in keeping everything as quiet as possible.

SUDLEY (*acidly*). No, my dear! He has not succeeded in keeping his former wife as quiet as possible. We had not been in Cairo a week when who should turn up but Vida Phillimore. She went everywhere and did everything no woman should!

GRACE (*unfeignedly interested*). Oh, what did she do?

SUDLEY. She "did" Cleopatra at the tableaux at Lord Errington's! She "did" Cleopatra, and she did it robed only in some diaphanous material of a nature so transparent that—in fact she appeared to be draped in moonshine.

(MISS HENEAGE *indicates the presence of* GRACE. *She rises.*)

That was only the beginning. As soon as she heard of Philip's engagement, she gave a dinner in honor of it! Only divorcées were asked! And she had a dummy—yes, my dear, a dummy—at the head of the table. He stood for Philip—that is he sat for Philip! (*He rises and goes up to table.*)

MISS HENEAGE (*irritated and disgusted*). Ah!

MRS. PHILLIMORE (*with dismay and pain*). Dear me!

MISS HENEAGE (*confident of the value of her opinion*). I disapprove of Mrs. Phillimore.

SUDLEY (*taking cigarette*). Of course you do, but has Philip taken to Egyptian cigarettes in order to celebrate my winter at Cairo?

GRACE. Those are Cynthia's.

SUDLEY (*thinking that no one is worth knowing whom he does not know*). Who is Cynthia?

GRACE. Mrs. Karslake— She's staying here, Cousin William. She'll be down in a minute.

SUDLEY (*shocked*). You don't mean to tell me—?

MISS HENEAGE. Yes, William, Cynthia is Mrs. Karslake—Mrs. Karslake has no New York house. I disliked the publicity of a hotel in the circumstances, and accordingly when she be-

came engaged to Philip I invited her here.

SUDLEY (*suspicious and distrustful*). And may I ask *who* Mrs. Karslake is?

MISS HENEAGE (*with confidence*). She was a Deane.

SUDLEY (*walking about the room, sorry to be obliged to concede good birth to any but his own blood*). Oh, oh—well the Deanes are extremely nice people. (*Going to table*) Was her father J. William Deane?

MISS HENEAGE (*nodding, still more secure*). Yes.

SUDLEY (*giving in with difficulty*). The family is an old one. J. William Deane's daughter? Surely he left a very considerable—

MISS HENEAGE. Oh, fifteen or twenty millions.

SUDLEY (*determined not to be dazzled*). If I remember rightly she was brought up abroad.

MISS HENEAGE. In France and England—and I fancy brought up with a very gay set in very gay places. In fact she is what is called a "sporty" woman.

SUDLEY (*always ready to think the worst*). We might put up with that. But you don't mean to tell me Philip has the—the—the—assurance to marry a woman who has been divorced by—

MISS HENEAGE. Not at all. Cynthia Karslake divorced her husband.

SUDLEY (*gloomily, since he has less fault to find than he expected*). She divorced him! Ah! (*He sips his tea.*)

MISS HENEAGE. The suit went by default. And, my dear William, there are many palliating circumstances. Cynthia was married to Karslake only seven months. There are no— (*Glancing at* GRACE) —no hostages to fortune! Ahem!

SUDLEY (*still unwilling to be pleased*). Ah! What sort of a young woman is she?

GRACE (*with the superiority of one who is not too popular*). Men admire her.

MISS HENEAGE. She's not conventional.

MRS. PHILLIMORE (*showing a faint sense of justice*). I am bound to say she has behaved discreetly ever since she arrived in this house.

MISS HENEAGE. Yes, Mary—but I sometimes suspect that she exercises a degree of self-control—

SUDLEY (*glad to have something against someone*). She claps on the lid, eh? And you think that perhaps some day she'll boil over? Well, of course, fifteen or twenty millions—but who's Karslake?

GRACE (*very superciliously*). He owns Cynthia K. She's the famous mare.

MISS HENEAGE. He's Henry Karslake's son.

SUDLEY (*beginning to make the best of it*). Oh! Henry! Very respectable family. Although I remember his father served a term in the Senate. And so the wedding is to be tomorrow?

MRS. PHILLIMORE (*assenting*). Tomorrow.

SUDLEY (*rising, his respectability to the front when he thinks of the ceremony;* GRACE *rises*). Tomorrow. Well, my dear Sarah, a respectable family with some means. We must accept her. But on the whole, I think it will be best for me not to see the young woman. My disapprobation would make itself apparent.

GRACE (*whispering to* SUDLEY). Cynthia's coming. (*He doesn't hear.*)

(CYNTHIA *enters, absorbed in reading a newspaper. She is a young creature in her twenties, small and highbred, full of the love of excitement and sport. Her manner is wideawake and keen, and she is evidently in no fear of the opinion of others. Her dress is exceed-* ingly elegant, but with the elegance of a woman whose chief interests lie in life out of doors. There is nothing horsy in her style, and her expression is youthful and ingenuous.)

SUDLEY (*sententiously and determinedly epigrammatic*). The uncouth modern young woman, eight feet high, with a skin like a rhinoceros and manners like a cave dweller—an habitué of the race track and the divorce court—

GRACE (*aside to* SUDLEY). Cousin William!

SUDLEY. Eh, oh!

CYNTHIA (*coming down, reading, immersed, excited, trembling; lowers the paper to catch the light*). "Belmont favorite—six to one—Rockaway—Rosebud, and Flying Cloud. Slow track—raw wind—hm, hm, hm— At the half, Rockaway forged ahead, when Rosebud under the lash made a bold bid for victory—neck by neck—for a quarter—when Flying Cloud slipped by the pair and won on the post by a nose in one forty nine!" (*Speaking with the enthusiasm of a sport*) Oh, I wish I'd seen the dear thing do it. Oh, it's Mr. Sudley! You must think me very rude. How do you do, Mr. Sudley? (*She goes to* SUDLEY.)

SUDLEY (*bowing without cordiality*). Mrs. Karslake.

(*Pause;* CYNTHIA *feels he should say something. As he says nothing, she speaks again.*)

CYNTHIA. I hope Cairo was delightful? Did you have a smooth voyage?

SUDLEY (*pompously*). You must permit me, Mrs. Karslake—

CYNTHIA (*with good temper, somewhat embarrassed, and talking herself into ease*). Oh, please don't welcome me to the family. All that formal part is over, if you don't mind. I'm one of the tribe now! You're coming to our wedding tomorrow?

SUDLEY. My dear Mrs. Karslake, I think it might be wiser—

CYNTHIA (*still with cordial good temper*). Oh, but you must come! I mean to be a perfect wife to Philip and all his relations! That sounds rather miscellaneous, but you know what I mean.

SUDLEY (*very sententiously*). I am afraid—

CYNTHIA (*gay and still covering her embarrassment*). If you don't come, it'll look as if you were not standing by Philip when he's in trouble! You'll come, won't you—but of course you will.

SUDLEY (*after a self-important pause*). I will come, Mrs. Karslake. (*After a pause*) Good afternoon. (*In a tone of sorrow and light compassion*) Good-by, Mary. Good afternoon, Sarah. (*Sighing*) Grace, dear. (*To* MISS HENEAGE) At what hour did you say the alimony commences?

MISS HENEAGE (*quickly and commandingly to cover his slip*). The ceremony is at 3 P.M., William.

(SUDLEY *goes toward the door.*)

MRS. PHILLIMORE (*with fatigued voice and manner as she rises*). I am going to my room to rest awhile. (MRS. PHILLIMORE *goes up.*)

MISS HENEAGE (*to* SUDLEY). Oh, William, one moment—I entirely forgot! I've a most important social question to ask you! (*She goes slowly to the door with him.*) In regard to the announcements of the wedding—whom they shall be sent to and whom not. For instance—the Dudleys—

(*Exeunt* SUDLEY *and* MISS HENEAGE, *talking.*)

CYNTHIA. So that's Cousin William?

GRACE. Don't you like him?

CYNTHIA (*calmly sarcastic*). Like him? I love him. He's so generous. He couldn't have received me with

more warmth if I'd been a mulatto.

(THOMAS *re-enters.* PHILLIMORE *enters.* PHILIP PHILLIMORE *is a self-centered, short-tempered, imperious member of the respectable fashionables of New York. He is well and solidly dressed and in manner and speech evidently a man of family. He is accustomed to being listened to in his home circle and from the bench, and it is practically impossible for him to believe that he can make a mistake.*)

GRACE (*outraged*). Really you know — (CYNTHIA *sits at the table.*) Philip!

(PHILIP *nods to* GRACE *absent-mindedly. He is in his working suit and looks tired. He comes down silently, crosses to tea table, and bends over and kisses* CYNTHIA *on forehead. He goes to his chair, which* THOMAS *has moved to suit him. He sits, and sighs with satisfaction.*)

PHILIP. Ah, Grace! (*Exit* GRACE.) Well, my dear, I thought I should never extricate myself from the courtroom. You look very debonair!

CYNTHIA. The tea's making. You'll have your glass of sherry?

PHILIP (*the strain of the day has evidently been severe*). Thanks! (*Taking it from* THOMAS; *sighing*) Ah!

CYNTHIA. I can see it's been a tiring day with you.

PHILIP (*as before*). Hm! (*He sips the sherry.*)

CYNTHIA. Were the lawyers very long-winded?

PHILIP (*almost too tired for speech*). Prolix to the point of somnolence. It might be affirmed without inexactitude that the prolixity of counsel is the somnolence of the judiciary. I am fatigued, ah! (*A little suddenly, awaking to the fact that his orders have not been carried out to the letter*) Thomas! My *Post* is not in its usual place!

CYNTHIA. It's here, Philip.

(THOMAS *gets it.*)

PHILIP. Thanks, my dear. (*Opening the Post*) Ah! This hour with you—is —is really the—the— (*Absently*) — the one vivid moment of the day. (*Reading*) Hm—shocking attack by the President on vested interests. Hm— too bad—but it's to be expected. The people insisted on electing a desperado to the presidential office—they must take the holdup that follows. (*Pause; he reads.*) Hm! His English is lacking in idiom, his spelling in conservátism, his mind in balance, and his character in repose.

CYNTHIA (*amiable but not very sympathetic*). You seem more fatigued than usual. Another glass of sherry, Philip?

PHILIP. Oh, I ought not to—

CYNTHIA. I think you seem a little more tired than usual.

PHILIP. Perhaps I am. (*She pours out sherry.* PHILIP *takes the glass.*) Ah, this hour is truly a grateful form of restful excitement. (*Pause*) You, too, find it—eh? (*He looks at* CYNTHIA.)

CYNTHIA (*with veiled sarcasm*). Decidedly.

PHILIP. Decidedly what, my dear?

CYNTHIA (*as before*). Restful.

PHILIP. Hm! Perhaps I need the calm more than you do. Over the case today I actually—eh— (*Sipping*) — slumbered. I heard myself do it. That's how I know. A dressmaker sued on seven counts. (*Reading newspaper*) Really, the insanity of the United States Senate—you seem restless, my dear. Ah—um—have you seen the evening paper? I see there has been a lightning change in the style or size of hats which ladies— (*He sweeps a descriptive motion with his hands, giving paper to* CYNTHIA, *then moves his glass, reads, and sips.*)

CYNTHIA. The lamp, Thomas.

(THOMAS *blows out the alcohol lamp on the tea table with difficulty. He blows twice. Each time he moves* PHILIP *starts. He blows again.*)

PHILIP (*irritably*). Confound it, Thomas! What are you puffing and blowing at—?

THOMAS. It's out, ma'am—yes, sir.

PHILIP. You're excessively noisy, Thomas!

THOMAS (*in a fluster*). Yes, sir—I am.

CYNTHIA (*soothing* THOMAS's *wounded feelings*). We don't need you, Thomas.

THOMAS. Yes, ma'am.

PHILIP. Puffing and blowing and shaking and quaking like an automobile in an ecstasy!

(*Exit* THOMAS.)

CYNTHIA (*not unsympathetically*). Too bad, Philip! I hope my presence isn't too agitating?

PHILIP. Ah—it's just because I value this hour with you, Cynthia—this hour of tea and toast and tranquillity. It's quite as if we were married—happily married—already.

CYNTHIA (*admitting that married life is a blank, begins to look through paper*). Yes, I feel as if we were married already.

PHILIP (*not recognizing her tone*). Ah! It's the calm, you see.

CYNTHIA (*as before*). The calm? Yes—yes, it's—it's the calm.

PHILIP (*sighing*). Yes, the calm—the halcyon calm of—of second choice. Hm! (*He reads and turns over leaves of paper.* CYNTHIA *reads. Pause.*) After all, my dear—the feeling which I have for you—is—is—eh—the market is in a shocking condition of plethora! Hm— hm—and what are you reading?

CYNTHIA (*embarrassed*). Oh, eh— well—I—eh—I'm just running over the sporting news.

PHILIP. Oh! (*He looks thoughtful.*)

CYNTHIA (*beginning to forget* PHILIP *and to remember more interesting matters*). I fancied Hermes would come in an easy winner. He came in nowhere. Nonpareil was ridden by Henslow—he's a rotten bad rider. He gets nervous.

PHILIP (*reading still*). Does he? Hm! I suppose you do retain an interest in horses and races. Hm—I trust some day the—ah—law will attract— Oh— (*Turning a page*) —here's the report of my opinion in that dressmaker's case —Haggerty *vs.* Phillimore.

CYNTHIA. Was the case brought against you? (*Puzzled.*)

PHILIP (*a little uncomfortable*). Oh —no. The suit was brought by Haggerty, Miss Haggerty, a dressmaker, against the—in fact, my dear, against the former Mrs. Phillimore. (*Pause; he reads.*)

CYNTHIA (*curious about the matter*). How did you decide it?

PHILIP. I was obliged to decide in Mrs. Phillimore's favor. Haggerty's plea was preposterous.

CYNTHIA. Did you—did you meet the —the—former—?

PHILIP. No.

CYNTHIA. I often see her at afternoon teas.

PHILIP. How did you recognize—

CYNTHIA. Why— (*Opening paper*) —because Mrs. Vida Phillimore's picture appears in every other issue of most of the evening papers. And I must confess I was curious. But I'm sure you find it very painful to meet her again.

PHILIP (*slowly, considering*). No— would you find it so impossible to meet Mr.—

CYNTHIA (*much excited and aroused*). Philip! Don't speak of him. He's nothing. He's a thing of the past. I never think of him. I forget him!

PHILIP (*somewhat sarcastic*). That's extraordinarily original of you to forget him.

CYNTHIA (*gently, and wishing to drop the subject*). We each of us have something to forget, Philip—and John Karslake is to me— Well, he's dead!

PHILIP. As a matter of fact, my dear, he *is* dead, or the next thing to it—for he's bankrupt. (*Pause.*)

CYNTHIA. Bankrupt? (*Excited and moved*) Let's not speak of him. I mean never to see him or think about him or even hear of him!

(*He assents. She reads her paper. He sips his tea and reads his paper. She turns a page, starts, and cries out.*)

PHILIP. God bless me!

CYNTHIA. It's a picture of—of—

PHILIP. John Karslake?

CYNTHIA. Picture of him, and one of me, and in the middle between us Cynthia K!

PHILIP. Cynthia K?

CYNTHIA (*excited*). My pet riding mare! The best horse he has! She's an angel even in a photograph! Oh! (*Reading*) "John Karslake drops a fortune at Saratoga." (*Rises and goes up and down excitedly.* PHILIP *takes paper and reads.*)

PHILIP (*unconcerned, as the matter hardly touches him*). Hem—ah—advertises country place for sale—stables, famous mare, Cynthia K—favorite riding mare of former Mrs. Karslake who is once again to enter the arena of matrimony with the well-known and highly respected judge of—

CYNTHIA (*sensitive and much disturbed*). Don't! Don't, Philip, please don't!

PHILIP. My dear Cynthia—take another paper—here's my *Post!* You'll find nothing disagreeable in the *Post.*

CYNTHIA (*takes the paper; after reading, sits near table*). It's much worse in the *Post.* "John Karslake sells the former Mrs. Karslake's jewels—the famous necklace now at Tiffany's, and the sporty ex-husband sells his wife's portrait by Sargent"! Philip, I can't stand this. (*Puts the paper on table.*)

PHILIP. Really, my dear, Mr. Karslake is bound to appear occasionally in print—or even you may have to meet him.

(*Enter* THOMAS.)

CYNTHIA (*determined and distressed*). I won't meet him! I won't meet him. Every time I hear his name or Cynthia K's I'm so depressed.

THOMAS (*announcing with something like reluctance*). Sir, Mr. Fiddler. Mr. Karslake's trainer.

(*Enter* FIDDLER. *He is an English horse trainer, a wide-awake, stocky, well-groomed little cockney. He knows his own mind and sees life altogether through a stable door. Well-dressed for his station, and not young.*)

CYNTHIA (*excited and disturbed*). Fiddler? Tim Fiddler? His coming is outrageous!

FIDDLER. A note for you, sir.

CYNTHIA (*impulsively*). Oh, Fiddler —is that you?

FIDDLER. Yes'm!

CYNTHIA (*in a half whisper, still speaking on impulse*). How is she! Cynthia K? How's Planet II and the colt and Golden Rod? How's the whole stable? Are they well?

FIDDLER. No'm—we're all on the bum. (*Aside*) Ever since you kicked us over!

CYNTHIA (*reproving him, though pleased*). Fiddler!

FIDDLER. The horses is just simply gone to Egypt since you left, and so's the guv'nor.

CYNTHIA (*putting an end to* FIDDLER). That will do, Fiddler.

FIDDLER. I'm waiting for an answer, sir.

CYNTHIA. What is it, Philip?

PHILIP (*uncomfortable*). A mere matter of business. (*Aside to* FIDDLER) The answer is, Mr. Karslake can come. The—the coast will be clear. (*Exit* FIDDLER.)

CYNTHIA (*amazed; rising*). You're not going to see him?

PHILIP. But Karslake, my dear, is an old acquaintance of mine. He argues cases before me. I will see that you do not have to meet him.

(CYNTHIA *crosses in excited dejection. Enter* MATTHEW. *He is a High Church clergyman to a highly fashionable congregation. His success is partly due to his social position and partly to his elegance of speech, but chiefly to his inherent amiability, which leaves the sinner in happy peace and smiles on the just and unjust alike.*)

MATTHEW (*most amiably*). Ah, my dear brother!

PHILIP. Matthew. (*Meeting him.*)

MATTHEW (*nodding to* PHILIP). Good afternoon, my dear Cynthia. How charming you look! (CYNTHIA *sits at the tea table. To* CYNTHIA) Ah—why weren't you in your pew yesterday? I preached a most original sermon. (*He lays his hat and cane on the divan.*)

THOMAS (*aside to* PHILIP). Sir, Mrs. Vida Phillimore's maid called you up on the telephone, and you're to expect Mrs. Phillimore on a matter of business.

PHILIP (*astonished and disgusted*). Here, impossible! (*To* CYNTHIA) Excuse me, my dear! (*Exit* PHILIP, *much embarrassed, followed by* THOMAS.)

MATTHEW (*coming down to chair, happily and pleasantly self-important*). No, really, it was a wonderful sermon, my dear. My text was from Paul—"It is better to marry than to burn." It was a strictly logical sermon. I argued— that, as the grass withereth, and the flower fadeth, there is nothing final in nature; not even death! And, as there is nothing final in nature, not even death—so then if death is not final—why should marriage be final? (*Gently*) And so the necessity of—eh—divorce! You see? It was an exquisite sermon! All New York was there! And all New York went away happy! Even the sinners—if there were any! I don't often meet sinners—do you?

CYNTHIA (*indulgently, in spite of his folly, because he is kind*). You're such a dear, delightful pagan! Here's your tea!

MATTHEW (*sipping his tea*). Why, my dear—you have a very sad expression!

CYNTHIA (*a little bitterly*). Why not?

MATTHEW (*with sentimental sweetness*). I feel as if I were of no use in the world when I see sadness on a young face. Only sinners should feel sad. You have committed no sin!

CYNTHIA (*impulsively*). Yes, I have!

MATTHEW. Eh?

CYNTHIA. I committed, the unpardonable sin—whe—when I married for love!

MATTHEW. One must not marry for anything else, my dear!

CYNTHIA. Why am I marrying your brother?

MATTHEW. I often wonder why. I wonder why you didn't choose to remain a free woman.

CYNTHIA (*going over the ground she has often argued with herself*). I meant to; but a divorcée has no place in society. I felt horridly lonely! I wanted a friend. Philip was ideal as a friend—for months. Isn't it nice to bind a friend to you?

MATTHEW. Yes—yes! (*He sets down the teacup.*)

CYNTHIA (*growing more and more excited and moved as she speaks*). To marry, a friend—to marry on prudent,

sensible grounds—a man—like Philip? That's what I should have done first, instead of rushing into marriage—because I had a wild, mad, sensitive, sympathetic—passion and pain and fury—of I don't know what—that almost strangled me with happiness!

MATTHEW (*amiable and reminiscent*). Ah—ah—in my youth—I—I too!

CYNTHIA (*coming back to her manner of every day*). And besides—the day Philip asked me I was in the dumps! And now—how about marrying only for love?

(*Re-enter* PHILIP.)

MATTHEW. Ah, my dear, love is not the only thing in the world!

PHILIP (*speaking as he enters*). I got there too late; she'd hung up.

CYNTHIA. Who, Philip?

PHILIP. Eh—a lady—eh—

(*Enter* THOMAS, *flurried, with card on salver.*)

THOMAS. A card for you, sir. Ahem—ahem—Mrs. Phillimore—that was, sir.

PHILIP. Eh?

THOMAS. She's on the stairs, sir. (*He turns. Enter* VIDA. THOMAS *announces her as being the best way of meeting the difficulty.*) Mrs. Vida Phillimore! (*Vida comes in slowly, with the air of a spoiled beauty. She stops just inside the door and speaks in a very casual manner. Her voice is languorous and caressing. She is dressed in the excess of the French fashion and carries an outré parasol. She smiles and comes, undulating, to the middle of the stage. Exit* THOMAS.)

VIDA. How do you do, Philip. (*Pause*) Don't tell me I'm a surprise! I had you called up on the 'phone and I sent up my card—and besides, Philip dear, when you have the—the—habit of the house, as unfortunately I have, you can't treat yourself like a stranger in a strange land. At least I can't—so here I am. My reason for coming was to ask you about that B. and O. stock we hold in common. (*To* MATTHEW, *condescendingly, the clergy being a class of unfortunates debarred by profession from the pleasures of the world*) How do you do? (*Pause. She then goes to the real reason of her visit.*) Do be polite and present me to your wife-to-be.

PHILIP (*awkwardly*). Cynthia—

CYNTHIA (*cheerfully, with dash, putting the table between her and* VIDA). We're delighted to see you, Mrs. Phillimore. I needn't ask you to make yourself at home, but will you have a cup of tea?

(MATTHEW *sits near the little table.*)

VIDA (*to* PHILIP). My dear, she's not in the least what I expected. I heard she was a dove! She's a very dashing kind of a dove! (*To* CYNTHIA; *coming to tea table*) My dear, I'm paying you compliments. Five lumps and quantities of cream. I find single life very thinning. (*To* PHILIP, *very calm and ready to be agreeable to any man*) And how well you're looking! It must be the absence of matrimonial cares—or is it a new angel in the house?

CYNTHIA (*outraged at* VIDA'*s intrusion but polite though delicately sarcastic*). It's most amusing to sit in your place. And how at home you must feel here in this house where you have made so much trouble—I mean tea. (*Rising*) Do you know it would be in much better taste if you would take the place you're accustomed to?

VIDA (*as calm as before*). My dear, I'm an intruder only for a moment; I shan't give you a chance to score off me again! But I must thank you, dear Philip, for rendering that decision in my favor—

PHILIP. I assure you—

VIDA (*unable to resist a thrust at the close of this speech*). Of course, you would like to have rendered it against me. It was your wonderful sense of justice, and that's why I'm so grateful —if not to you, to your Maker!

PHILIP (*feels that this is no place for his future wife; rises quickly and irascibly; to* CYNTHIA). Cynthia, I would prefer that you left us.

(MATTHEW *comes to the sofa and sits.*)

CYNTHIA (*determined not to leave the field first remains seated*). Certainly, Philip!

PHILIP. I expect another visitor who—

VIDA (*with flattering insistence, to* CYNTHIA). Oh, my dear—don't go! The truth is—I came to see you! I feel most cordially towards you—and really, you know, people in our position should meet on cordial terms.

CYNTHIA (*taking it with apparent calm, but pointing her remarks*). Naturally. If people in our position couldn't meet, New York society would soon come to an end.

(*Enter* THOMAS.)

VIDA (*calm, but getting her knife in too*). Precisely. Society's no bigger than a bandbox. Why, it's only a moment ago I saw Mr. Karslake walking—

CYNTHIA. Ah!

THOMAS (*announcing clearly; everyone changes place in consternation, amusement, or surprise;* CYNTHIA *moves to leave the stage but stops for fear of attracting* KARSLAKE'*s attention*). Mr. John Karslake!

(*Enter* KARSLAKE. *He is a powerful, generous personality, a man of affairs, breezy, gay, and careless. He gives the impression of being game for any fate in store for him. His clothes indicate sporting propensities and his taste in waistcoats and ties is brilliant.* KARS-

LAKE *sees first* PHILIP *and then* MAT-THEW. *Exit* THOMAS.)

PHILIP. How do you do?

JOHN (*very gay and no respecter of persons*). Good afternoon, Mr. Philli-more. Hello—here's the church. (*Crossing to* MATTHEW *and shaking hands. He slaps him on the back.*) I hadn't the least idea—how are you? By George, Your Reverence, that was a racy sermon of yours on divorce! What was your text? (*Seeing* VIDA *and bowing very politely*) Galatians 4:2: "The more the merrier," or "Who next?" (*Smiling*) As the whale said after Jonah!

(CYNTHIA *makes a sudden movement and turns her cup over.* JOHN *faces about quickly and they face each other.* JOHN *gives a frank start. A pause.*)

JOHN (*bowing; astounded, in a low voice*). Mrs. Karslake—I was not aware of the pleasure in store for me. I understood you were in the country. (*Recovering, crosses to chair.*) Perhaps you'll be good enough to make me a cup of tea—that is if the teapot wasn't lost in the scrimmage. (*Pause.* CYNTHIA, *determined to equal him in coolness, returns to the tea tray.*) Mr. Phillimore, I came to get your signature in that matter of Cox *vs.* Keely.

PHILIP. I shall be at your service, but pray be seated. (*He indicates a chair by tea table.*)

JOHN (*sitting beyond but not far from the tea table*). And I also understood you to say you wanted a saddle horse.

PHILIP. You have a mare called—eh —Cynthia K?

JOHN (*promptly*). Yes—she's not for sale.

PHILIP. Oh, but she's just the mare I had set my mind on.

JOHN (*with a touch of humor*). You want her for yourself?

PHILIP (*a little flustered*). I—eh—I sometimes ride.

JOHN (*sure of himself now*). She's rather lively for you, Judge. Mrs. Karslake used to ride her.

PHILIP. You don't care to sell her to me?

JOHN. She's a dangerous mare, Judge, and she's as delicate and changeable as a girl. I'd hate to leave her in your charge!

CYNTHIA (*eagerly, but in a low voice*). Leave her in mine, Mr. Karslake!

JOHN (*after slight pause*). Mrs. Karslake knows all about a horse, but— (*Turning to* CYNTHIA) Cynthia K's got rather tricky of late.

CYNTHIA (*haughtily*). You mean to say you think she'd chuck me?

JOHN (*with polite solicitude and still humorous; to* PHILIP). I'd hate to have a mare of mine deprive you of a wife, Judge. (*Rising*) She goes to Saratoga next week, C. W.

VIDA (*who has been sitting and talking to* MATTHEW *for lack of a better man, comes to talk to* KARSLAKE). C. W.?

JOHN (*rising as she rises*). Creditors willing.

VIDA (*crossing and sitting left of tea table*). I'm sure your creditors are willing.

JOHN. Oh, they're a breezy lot, my creditors. They're giving me a dinner this evening.

VIDA (*more than usually anxious to please*). I regret I'm not a breezy creditor, but I do think you owe it to me to let me see your Cynthia K! Can't you lead her around to my house?

JOHN. At what hour, Mrs. Phillimore?

VIDA. Say eleven? And you too might have a leading in my direction—771 Fifth Avenue.

(JOHN *bows.* CYNTHIA *hears and notes this.*)

CYNTHIA. Your cup of tea, Mr. Karslake.

JOHN. Thanks. (JOHN *gets tea and sips it.*) I beg your pardon—you have forgotten, Mrs. Karslake—very naturally it has slipped from your memory, but I don't take sugar.

(CYNTHIA, *furious with him and herself. He hands cup back. She makes a second cup.*)

CYNTHIA (*cheerfully; in a rage*). Sorry!

JOHN (*also apparently cheerful*). Yes, gout. It gives me a twinge even to sit in the shadow of a sugar maple! First you riot, and then you diet!

VIDA (*calm and amused; aside to* MATTHEW). My dear Matthew, he's a darling! But I feel as if we were all taking tea on the slope of a volcano!

(MATTHEW *sits.*)

PHILIP. It occurred to me, Mr. Karslake, you might be glad to find a purchaser for your portrait by Sargent?

JOHN. It's not my portrait. It's a portrait of Mrs. Karslake, and to tell you the truth—Sargent's a good fellow —I've made up my mind to keep it —to remember the artist by.

(CYNTHIA *is wounded by this.*)

PHILIP. Hm!

CYNTHIA (*hands second cup of tea to* JOHN; *with careful politeness*). Your cup of tea, Mr. Karslake.

JOHN (*rising and taking tea with courteous indifference*). Thanks—sorry to trouble you. (*He drinks the cup of tea standing by the tea table.*)

PHILIP (*to make conversation*). You're selling your country place?

JOHN. If I was long of hair—I'd sell that.

CYNTHIA (*excited; taken out of herself by the news*). You're not really selling your stable?

JOHN (*finishing his tea, he places empty cup on tea table and reseats himself*). Every gelding I've got—seven foals and a donkey! I don't mean the owner.

CYNTHIA (*still interested and forgetting the discomfort of the situation*). How did you ever manage to come such a cropper?

JOHN. Streak of blue luck!

CYNTHIA (*quickly*). I don't see how it's possible—

JOHN. You would if you'd been there. You remember the head man? (*Sits.*) Bloke?

CYNTHIA. Of course!

JOHN. Well, his wife divorced him for beating her over the head with a bottle of Fowler's Solution, and it seemed to prey on his mind. He sold me—

CYNTHIA (*horrified*). Sold a race?

JOHN. About ten races, I guess.

CYNTHIA (*incredulous*). Just because he'd beaten his wife?

JOHN. No. Because she divorced him.

CYNTHIA. Well, I can't see why that should prey on his mind! (*Suddenly remembers.*)

JOHN. Well, I have known men that it stroked the wrong way. But he cost me eighty thousand. And then Urbanity ran third in the thousand dollar stakes for two-year-olds at Belmont.

CYNTHIA (*throws remark in*). I never had faith in that horse.

JOHN. And, of course, it never rains monkeys but it pours gorillas! So when I was down at St. Louis on the fifth, I laid seven to three on Fraternity—

CYNTHIA. Crazy! Crazy!

JOHN (*ready to take the opposite view*). I don't see it. With her record she ought to have romped in an easy winner.

CYNTHIA (*pure sport*). She hasn't the stamina! Look at her barrel!

JOHN. Well, anyhow, Geranium

finished me!

CYNTHIA. You didn't lay odds on Geranium!

JOHN. Why not? She's my own mare—

CYNTHIA. Oh!

JOHN. Streak o' bad luck—

CYNTHIA (*plainly anxious to say "I told you so"*). Streak of poor judgment! Do you remember the day you rode Billy at a six-foot stone wall, and he stopped and you didn't, and there was a hornets' nest—

(MATTHEW *rises*.)

—on the other side, and I remember you were hot just because I said you showed poor judgment? (*She laughs at the memory. A general movement of disapproval. She remembers the situation.*) I beg your pardon.

MATTHEW (*rising to meet* VIDA; *hastily*). It seems to me that horses are like the fourth gospel. Any conversation about them becomes animated almost beyond the limits of the urbane!

(VIDA, *disgusted by such plainness of speech, rises and goes to* PHILIP, *who waves her to a chair*.)

PHILIP (*formally*). I regret that you have endured such reverses, Mr. Karslake.

(JOHN *quietly bows*.)

CYNTHIA (*concealing her interest, she speaks casually*). You haven't mentioned your new English horse—Pantomime. What did he do at St. Louis?

JOHN (*sitting*). Fell away and ran fifth.

CYNTHIA. Too bad. Was he fully acclimated? Ah, well—

JOHN. We always differed—you remember—on the time needed—

MATTHEW (*coming to* CYNTHIA, *speaking to carry off the situation as well as to get a tip*). Isn't there a— eh—a race tomorrow at Belmont Park?

JOHN. Yes. I'm going down in my auto.

CYNTHIA (*evidently wishing she might be going too*). Oh!

MATTHEW. And what animal shall you prefer? (*Covering his personal interest with amiable altruism*.)

JOHN. I'm backing Carmencita.

CYNTHIA (*gesture of despair*). Carmencita! Carmencita!

(MATTHEW *goes to* VIDA.)

JOHN. You may remember we always differed on Carmencita.

CYNTHIA (*disgusted at* JOHN's *dunderheadedness*). But there's no room for difference. She's a wild, headstrong, dissatisfied, foolish little filly. The deuce couldn't ride her—she'd shy at her own shadow—Carmencita. Oh, very well, then, I'll wager you—and I'll give you odds too—Decorum will come in first, and I'll lay three to one he'll beat Carmencita by five lengths! How's that for fair?

JOHN (*never forgetting the situation*). Sorry I'm not flush enough to take you.

CYNTHIA (*impetuously*). Philip dear, you lend John enough for the wager.

MATTHEW (*as nearly horrified as so soft a soul can be*). Ahem! Really—

JOHN. It's a sporty idea, Mrs. Karslake, but perhaps in the circumstances —

CYNTHIA (*her mind on her wager*). In what circumstances?

PHILIP (*with a nervous laugh*). It does seem to me there is a certain impropriety—

CYNTHIA (*remembering the conventions which, for a moment, had actually escaped her*). Oh, I forgot. When horses are in the air—

MATTHEW (*pouring oil on troubled waters; crossing, he speaks to* VIDA *at back of armchair, where she sits*). It's the fourth gospel, you see.

(*Enter* THOMAS *with a letter on a*

salver, which he hands to PHILIP.)

CYNTHIA (*meekly*). You are quite right, Philip. The fact is, seeing Mr. Karslake again— (*Laying on her indifference with a trowel*)—he seems to me as much a stranger as if I were meeting him for the first time.

MATTHEW (*aside to* VIDA). We are indeed taking tea on the slope of a volcano.

VIDA (*about to go, but thinks she will have a last word with* JOHN). I'm sorry your fortunes are so depressed, Mr. Karslake.

PHILIP (*looking at the card that* THOMAS *has just brought in*). Who in the world is Sir Wilfrid Cates-Darby?

(*General move.*)

JOHN. Oh—eh—Cates-Darby?

(PHILIP *opens letter which* THOMAS *has brought with card.*) That's the English chap I bought Pantomime of.

PHILIP (*to* THOMAS). Show Sir Wilfrid Cates-Darby in.

(*Exit* THOMAS. *The prospect of an Englishman with a handle to his name changes* VIDA'S *plans and instead of leaving the house, she goes to the sofa and sits there.*)

JOHN. He's a good fellow, Judge. Place near Epsom. Breeder. Over here to take a shy at our races.

THOMAS (*enters, announcing*). Sir Wilfrid Cates-Darby.

(*Enter* SIR WILFRID CATES-DARBY. *He is a highbred, sporting Englishman. His manner, his dress, and his diction are the perfection of English elegance. His movements are quick and graceful. He talks lightly and with ease. He is full of life and unsmiling good temper.*)

PHILIP (*to* SIR WILFRID *and referring to the letter of introduction in his hand*). I am Mr. Phillimore. I am grateful to Stanhope for giving me the opportunity of knowing you, Sir

Wilfrid. I fear you find it warm?

SIR WILFRID (*delicately mopping his forehead*). Ah, well—ah—warm, no—hot, yes! Deuced extraordinary climate yours, you know, Mr. Phillimore.

PHILIP (*conventional*). Permit me to present you to— (*The unconventional situation pulls him up short. It takes him a moment to decide how to meet it. He makes up his mind to pretend that everything is as usual, and presents* CYNTHIA *first.*) Mrs. Karslake. (SIR WILFRID *bows, surprised and doubtful*).

CYNTHIA. How do you do?

PHILIP. And to Mrs. Phillimore. (VIDA *bows nonchalantly but with a view to catching* SIR WILFRID'S *attention.* SIR WILFRID *bows and looks from her to* PHILIP.) My brother—and Mr. Karslake you know.

SIR WILFRID. How do, my boy? (*Half aside, to* JOHN) No idea you had such a charming little wife—What? Eh?

(KARSLAKE *goes up to speak to* MATTHEW *and* PHILIP *in the further room.*)

CYNTHIA. You'll have a cup of tea, Sir Wilfrid?

SIR WILFRID (*at table*). Thanks awfully. (*Very cheerfully*) I'd no idea old John had a wife! The rascal never told me!

CYNTHIA (*pouring tea and facing the facts*). I'm not Mr. Karslake's wife!

SIR WILFRID. Oh! Eh! I see— (*Business of thinking it out.*)

VIDA (*who has been ready for some time to speak to him*). Sir Wilfrid, I'm sure no one has asked you how you like our country?

SIR WILFRID (*going to* VIDA *and speaking, standing by her at sofa*). Oh, well, as to climate and horses I say nothing. But I like your American humor. I'm acquiring it for home purposes.

VIDA (*getting down to love as the basis of conversation*). Aren't you going to acquire an American girl for home purposes?

SIR WILFRID. The more narrowly I look the agreeable project in the face, the more I like it. Oughtn't to say that in the presence of your husband. (*He casts a look at* PHILIP, *who has gone into the next room.*)

VIDA (*cheerful and unconstrained*). He's not my husband!

SIR WILFRID (*completely confused*). Oh—eh—my brain must be boiled. You are—Mrs.—eh—ah—of course, now I see! I got the wrong names! I thought you were Mrs. Phillimore. (*He sits by her.*) And that nice girl, Mrs. Karslake! You're deucedly lucky to be Mrs. Karslake. John's a prime sort. I say, have you and he got any kids? How many?

VIDA (*horrified at being suspected of maternity but speaking very sweetly*). He's not my husband.

SIR WILFRID (*his good spirits all gone, but determined to clear things up*). Phew! Awfully hot in here! Who the deuce is John's wife?

VIDA. He hasn't any.

SIR WILFRID. Who's Phillimore's wife?

VIDA. He hasn't any.

SIR WILFRID. Thanks fearfully! (*To* MATTHEW, *whom he approaches; suspecting himself of having lost his wits.*) Would you excuse me, my dear and reverend sir—you're a churchman and all that—would you mind straightening me out?

MATTHEW (*most gracious*). Certainly, Sir Wilfred. Is it a matter of doctrine?

SIR WILFRID. Oh damme—beg your pardon—no, it's not words, it's women.

MATTHEW (*ready to be outraged*). Women!

SIR WILFRID. It's divorce. Now, the lady on the sofa—

MATTHEW. *Was* my brother's wife; he

divorced her—incompatibility—Rhode Island. The lady at the tea table *was* Mr. Karslake's wife; she divorced him —desertion—Sioux Falls. One moment —she is about to marry my brother.

SIR WILFRID (*cheerful again*). I'm out! Thought I never would be! Thanks!

VIDA (*laughs; not a whit discountenanced and ready to please*). Have you got me straightened out yet?

SIR WILFRID. Straight as a die! I say, you had lots of fun, didn't you? (*Going back to sofa*) And so *she's* Mrs. John Karslake?

VIDA (*calm, but secretly disappointed*). Do you like her?

SIR WILFRID. My word!

VIDA (*fully expecting personal flattery*). Eh?

SIR WILFRID. She's a box o' ginger!

VIDA. You haven't seen many American women!

SIR WILFRID. Oh, haven't I?

VIDA. If you'll pay me a visit tomorrow—at twelve, you shall meet a most charming young woman who has seen you once, and who admires you—ah!

SIR WILFRID. I'm there—what!

VIDA. Seven hundred and seventy-one Fifth Avenue.

SIR WILFRID. Seven seventy-one Fifth Avenue—at twelve.

VIDA. At twelve.

SIR WILFRID. Thanks! (*Indicating* CYNTHIA) She's a thoroughbred—you can see that with one eye shut. Twelve. (*Shaking hands*) Awfully good of you to ask me. (*He joins* JOHN.) I say, my boy, your former's an absolute certainty. (*To* CYNTHIA) I hear you're about to marry Mr. Phillimore, Mrs. Karslake?

(KARSLAKE *crosses to* VIDA; *they both go to sofa, where they sit.*)

CYNTHIA. Tomorrow, 3 P.M., Sir Wilfrid.

SIR WILFRID (*much taken with* CYN-
THIA, *he addresses her*). Afraid I've
run into a sort of family party, eh?
(*Indicating* VIDA) The past and the
future—awfully chic way you Americans have of asking your divorced
husbands and wives to drop in, you
know—celebrate a christenin', or the
new bride, or—

CYNTHIA. Do you like your tea
strong?

SIR WILFRID. Middlin'.

CYNTHIA. Sugar?

SIR WILFRID. One!

CYNTHIA. Lemon?

SIR WILFRID. Just torture a lemon
over it. (*He makes a gesture as of
twisting a lemon peel. She gives tea.*)
Thanks! So you do it tomorrow at
three?

CYNTHIA. At three, Sir Wilfrid.

SIR WILFRID. Sorry!

CYNTHIA. Why are you sorry?

SIR WILFRID. Hate to see a pretty woman married. Might marry her myself.

CYNTHIA. Oh, but I'm sure you don't
admire American women.

SIR WILFRID. Admire you, Mrs. Karslake—

CYNTHIA. Not enough to marry me,
I hope.

SIR WILFRID. Marry you in a minute!
Say the word. Marry you now—here.

CYNTHIA. You don't think you ought
to know me a little before—

SIR WILFRID. Know you? Do know
you.

CYNTHIA (*covers her hair with her
handkerchief*). What color is my hair?

SIR WILFRID. Pshaw!

CYNTHIA. You see! You don't know
whether I'm a chestnut or a strawberry
roan! In the States we think a few
months of friendship is quite necessary.

SIR WILFRID. Few months of moonshine! Never was a friend to a woman
—thank God, in all my life.

CYNTHIA. Oh—oh, oh!

SIR WILFRID. Might as well talk about
being a friend to a whisky and soda.

CYNTHIA. A woman has a soul, Sir
Wilfrid.

SIR WILFRID. Well, good whisky is
spirits—dozens o' souls!

CYNTHIA. You are so gross!

SIR WILFRID (*changing seat to above
table*). Gross? Not a bit! Friendship between the sexes is all fudge! I'm no
friend to a rose in my garden. I don't
call it friendship—eh—eh—a warm,
starry night, moonbeams and ilex trees,
"and a spirit who knows how" and all
that—eh— (*Getting closer to her*)
You make me feel awfully poetical, you
know—

(PHILIP *comes down, glances nervously at* CYNTHIA *and* SIR WILFRID,
and walks up again.)
What's the matter? But, I say—poetry
aside—do you, eh— (*Looking around
to place* PHILIP) Does he—y'know—
is he—does he go to the head?

CYNTHIA. Sir Wilfrid, Mr. Phillimore
is my sober second choice.

SIR WILFRID. Did you ever kiss him?
I'll bet he fined you for contempt of
court. Look here, Mrs. Karslake, if
you're marryin' a man you don't care
about—

CYNTHIA (*amused and excusing his
audacity as a foreigner's eccentricity*).
Really!

SIR WILFRID. Well, I don't offer myself—

CYNTHIA. Oh!

SIR WILFRID. Not this instant—

CYNTHIA. Ah!

SIR WILFRID. But let me drop in
tomorrow at ten.

CYNTHIA. What country and state of
affairs do you think you have landed
in?

SIR WILFRID. New York, by Jove!
Been to school, too. New York is

bounded on the north, south, east, and west by the state of Divorce! Come, come, Mrs. Karslake, I like your country. You've no fear and no respect—no can't and lots of can. Here you all are, you see—your former husband, and your new husband's former wife— sounds like Ollendoff! Eh? So there you are, you see! But, jokin' apart—why do you marry him? Oh well, marry him if you must! You can run around the corner and get a divorce afterwards—

CYNTHIA. I believe you think they throw one in with an ice-cream soda!

SIR WILFRID (*rising*). Damme, my dear lady, a marriage in your country is no more than a—eh—eh—what do you call 'em? A "thank you, ma'am." That's what an American marriage is —a "thank you, ma'am." Bump—bump —you're over it and on to the next.

CYNTHIA. You're an odd fish! What? I believe I like you!

SIR WILFRID. 'Course you do! You'll see me when I call tomorrow—at ten? We'll run down to Belmont Park, eh?

CYNTHIA. Don't be absurd!

VIDA (*has finished her talk with* JOHN, *and breaks in on* SIR WILFRID, *who has hung about* CYNTHIA *too long to suit her*). Tomorrow at twelve, Sir Wilfrid!

SIR WILFRID. Twelve!

VIDA (*shaking hands with* JOHN). Don't forget, Mr. Karslake—eleven o'clock tomorrow.

JOHN (*bowing assent*). I won't!

VIDA (*coming to the middle of the stage and speaking to* CYNTHIA). Oh, Mrs. Karslake, I've ordered Tiffany to send you something. It's a sugar bowl to sweeten the matrimonial lot! I suppose nothing would induce you to call?

CYNTHIA (*distantly and careless of offending*). Thanks, no—that is, is Cynthia K really to be there at eleven?

I'd give a gold mine to see her again.

VIDA. Do come!

CYNTHIA. If Mr. Karslake will accommodate me by his absence.

VIDA. Dear Mr. Karslake, you'll have to change your hour.

JOHN. Sorry, I'm not able to.

CYNTHIA. I can't come later, for I'm to be married.

JOHN. It's not as bad as that with me, but I am to be sold up—sheriff, you know. Can't come later than eleven.

VIDA (*to* CYNTHIA). Any hour but eleven, dear.

CYNTHIA (*perfectly regardless of* VIDA, *and ready to vex* JOHN *if possible*). Mrs. Phillimore, I shall call on you at eleven—to see Cynthia K. I thank you for the invitation. Good afternoon.

VIDA (*aside to* JOHN, *crossing to speak quietly to him*). It's mere bravado; she won't come.

JOHN. You don't know her.

(*Pause. There is general embarrassment.* SIR WILFRID *plays with his eyeglass.* JOHN *is angry;* CYNTHIA *is triumphant;* MATTHEW *is embarrassed;* VIDA *is irritated;* PHILIP *is puzzled; everybody is at odds.*)

SIR WILFRID (*for the first time being a witness to the pretty complications of divorce, he speaks to* MATTHEW). Do you have it as warm as this ordinarily?

MATTHEW (*for whom these moments are more than usually painful, and wiping his brow*). It's not so much the heat as the humidity.

JOHN (*looking at watch; he is glad to be off*). I shall be late for my creditors' dinner.

SIR WILFRID (*coming down*). Creditors' dinner.

JOHN (*reading note*). Fifteen of my sporting creditors have arranged to give me a blowout at Sherry's, and I'm expected right away or sooner. And by the way, I was to bring my friends—if I had any. So now's the time to stand by me! Mrs. Phillimore?

VIDA. Of course!

JOHN (*ready to embarrass* CYNTHIA, *if possible, and speaking as if he had quite forgotten their former relations*). Mrs. Karslake—I beg your pardon. Judge? (PHILIP *declines.*) No? Sir Wilfrid?

SIR WILFRID. I'm with you!

JOHN (*to* MATTHEW). Your Reverence?

MATTHEW. I regret—

SIR WILFRID. Is it the custom for creditors—

JOHN. Come on, Sir Wilfrid!

(THOMAS *opens the door.*)
Good night, Judge—Your Reverence—

SIR WILFRID. Is it the custom—

JOHN. Hang the custom! Come on—I'll show you a gang of creditors worth having!

(*Exit* SIR WILFRID *with* JOHN, *preceded by* VIDA. MATTHEW *crosses the stage, smiling, as if pleased, in a Christian way, with this display of generous gaiety. He looks at his watch.*)

MATTHEW. Good gracious! I had no idea the hour was so late. I've been asked to a meeting with Maryland and Iowa, to talk over the divorce situation. (*Exit. His voice is heard off the stage.*) Good afternoon! Good afternoon!

(CYNTHIA *is evidently much excited. The outer door slams.* PHILIP *comes down the stage slowly.* CYNTHIA *stands, her eyes wide, her breathing rapid, until* PHILIP *speaks, when she seems suddenly to realize her position. There is a long pause.*)

PHILIP (*with a superior air*). I have seldom witnessed a more amazing cataclysm of jocundity! Of course, my dear, this has all been most disagreeable for you.

CYNTHIA (*excitedly*). Yes, yes, yes!

PHILIP. I saw how much it shocked your delicacy.

CYNTHIA (*distressed and moved*). Outrageous.

PHILIP (*sits*). Do be seated, Cynthia. (*Taking up paper; quietly*) Very odd sort of an Englishman—that Cates-Darby!

CYNTHIA. Sir Wilfrid? Oh, yes! (PHILIP *settles down to paper. To herself*) Outrageous! I've a great mind to go at eleven—just as I said I would!

PHILIP. Do sit down, Cynthia!

CYNTHIA. What? What?

PHILIP. You make me so nervous—

CYNTHIA. Sorry—sorry. (*She sits down and, seeing the paper, she takes it, looking at the picture of* JOHN KARSLAKE.)

PHILIP (*sighing with content*). Ah! now that I see him, I don't wonder you couldn't stand him. There's a kind of—ah—spontaneous inebriety about him. He is incomprehensible! If I might with reverence cross-question the Creator, I would say to him: "Sir, to what end or purpose did you create Mr. John Karslake?" I believe I should obtain no adequate answer! However— (*Sighing*) —at last we have peace—and the *Post!* (PHILIP, *settling himself, reads paper;* CYNTHIA *looks at her paper, occasionally looking across at* PHILIP.) Forget the dust of the arena—the prolixity of counsel—the involuntary fatuity of things in general. (*Pause. He reads.*) Compose yourself!

(MISS HENEAGE, MRS. PHILLIMORE, *and* GRACE *enter.* CYNTHIA *sighs without letting her sigh be heard. She tries to compose herself. She glances at paper and then hearing* MISS HENEAGE, *starts slightly.* MISS HENEAGE *and* MRS. PHILLIMORE *stop at table.*)

MISS HENEAGE (*carries a sheet of paper*). There, my dear Mary, is the announcement as I have now reworded it. I took William's suggestion.

(MRS. PHILLIMORE *takes and casually reads it.*)

I also put the case to him, and he was of the opinion that the announcement should be sent *only* to those people who are really *in* society. (*She sits near table.* CYNTHIA *braces herself to bear the Phillimore conversation.*)

GRACE. I wish you'd make an exception of the Dudleys.

(CYNTHIA *rises and crosses to chair by the table.*)

MISS HENEAGE. And of course that excludes the Oppenheims—the Vance-Browns.

MRS. PHILLIMORE. It's just as well to be exclusive.

GRACE. I do wish you'd make an exception of Lena Dudley.

MISS HENEAGE. We might, of course, include those new Girardos and possibly—possibly the Paddingtons.

GRACE. I do wish you would take in Lena Dudley.

(*They are now sitting.*)

MRS. PHILLIMORE. The mother Dudley is as common as a charwoman and not nearly as clean.

PHILIP (*sighing, his own feelings as usual to the fore*). Ah! I certainly am fatigued!

(CYNTHIA *begins to slowly crush the newspaper she has been reading with both hands, as if the effort of self-repression were too much for her.*)

MISS HENEAGE (*making the best of a gloomy future*). We shall have to ask the Dudleys sooner or later to dine, Mary—because of the elder girl's marriage to that dissolute French marquis.

MRS. PHILLIMORE (*plaintively*). I don't like common people any more than I like common cats and, of course, in my time—

MISS HENEAGE. I think I shall include the Dudleys.

MRS. PHILLIMORE. You think you'll include the Dudleys?

MISS HENEAGE. Yes, I think I will include the Dudleys!

(*Here* CYNTHIA *gives up. Driven desperate by their chatter, she has slowly rolled her newspaper into a ball and at this point tosses it violently to the floor and bursts into hysterical laughter.*)

MRS. PHILLIMORE. Why, my dear Cynthia—compose yourself.

PHILIP (*hastily*). What is the matter, Cynthia?

(*They speak together.*)

MISS HENEAGE. Why, Mrs. Karslake, what is the matter?

GRACE (*comes quickly forward, saying*). Mrs. Karslake!

ACT TWO

MRS. VIDA PHILLIMORE'S *boudoir. The room is furnished to please an empty-headed, pleasure-loving, and fashionable woman. The furniture, the ornaments, what pictures there are, are all witness to taste up-to-date. Two French windows open on to a balcony, from which the trees of Central Park can be seen. There is a table between them; a mirror and a scent bottle upon it. A lady's writing table stands between two doors, nearer center of stage. There is another door near an open fireplace, which is filled with potted plants and andirons not in use. Over it is a tall mirror. On the mantelpiece are French clock, candelabra, and vases. On a line with the fireplace, a lounge, gay with silk pillows. A florist's box, large and long, filled with American Beauty roses is on a low table near the head of the lounge. Small tables and light chairs are here*

and there. At rise of the curtain, BEN-
SON *is seen looking about her. She is a
neat and pretty little English lady's
maid in black silk and a thin apron.
She comes down the stage still looking
about her and inspects the flower box,
then goes to the door of* VIDA'S *room
and speaks to her.*

———

BENSON. Yes, ma'am, the flowers
have come.

(*She holds the door open.* VIDA, *in a
morning gown, enters slowly. She is
smoking a cigarette in as aesthetic a
manner as she can and is evidently
turned out in her best style for conquest.*)

VIDA (*speaking with her back to the
audience, always calm and, though
civil, a little disdainful of her servant*).
Terribly garish light, Benson. Pull down
the— (BENSON *obeys.*) Lower still—
that will do. (*As she speaks, she goes
about the room, giving the furniture a
push here and there, arranging vases,
etc.*) Men hate a clutter of chairs and
tables. (*Stopping and taking up hand
mirror, standing with back to audience.*) I really think I'm too pale for
this light.

BENSON (*quickly, understanding what
is implied*). Yes, ma'am. (*Exits.*)

VIDA (*sits at the table. Knock at the
door*). Come!

BROOKS (*enters, an ultra-English
footman in plush and calves*). Any
horders, m'lady?

VIDA (*incapable of remembering the
last man or of considering the new
one*). Oh—of course! You're the new—

BROOKS. Footman, m'lady.

VIDA (*as a matter of form*). Your
name?

BROOKS. Brooks, m'lady.

(*Re-enter* BENSON *with rouge.*)

VIDA (*carefully giving instructions

while she keeps her eyes on the glass
and is rouged by* BENSON). Brooks, I
am at home to Mr. Karslake at eleven,
not to anyone else till twelve, when I
expect Sir Wilfrid Cates-Darby. (BROOKS
is inattentive, watching BENSON.)

BROOKS. Yes, m'lady.

VIDA (*calm, but wearied by the ignorance of the lower classses*). And I
regret to inform you, Brooks, that in
America there are no ladies, except
salesladies!

BROOKS (*without a trace of compre-
hension*). Yes, m'lady.

VIDA. I am at home to no one but the
two names I have mentioned. (BROOKS
*bows and goes out. She dabs on rouge
while* BENSON *holds glass.*) Is the men's
club room in order?

BENSON. Perfectly, ma'am.

VIDA. Whisky and soda?

BENSON. Yes, ma'am, and the ticker's
been mended. The British sporting
papers arrived this morning.

VIDA (*looking at her watch, which
lies on the dressing table*). My watch
has stopped.

BENSON (*glancing at the French
clock on the chimney piece*). Five to
eleven, ma'am.

VIDA (*getting promptly to work*).
Hm, hm, I shall be caught. (*Rises.*)
The box of roses, Benson! (BENSON
*brings the box of roses, uncovers the
flowers, and places them at* VIDA'S *side.*)
My gloves—the clippers, and the vase!
(*Each of these things* BENSON *places in
turn within* VIDA'S *range where she sits
on the sofa. She has the long box of
roses at her side on a small table, a vase
of water on the floor by her side. She
cuts the stems and places the roses in
the vase. When she feels that she has
reached a picturesque position, in which
any onlooker would see in her a creature filled with the love of flowers and
of her fellow man, she says*) There!

(*The door opens and* BROOKS *enters;* VIDA *nods to* BENSON.)

BROOKS (*announcing stolidly*). Sir John Karslake.

(*Enter* JOHN, *dressed in very nobby riding togs. He comes in gaily and forcibly.* BENSON *gives way as he comes down. Exeunt* BROOKS *and* BENSON. JOHN *stops near the table.* VIDA, *from this point on, is busied with her roses.*)

VIDA (*languorously, but with a faint suggestion of humor*). Is that really you, Sir John?

JOHN (*lively and far from being impressed by* VIDA). I see now where we Americans are going to get our titles. Good morning! You look as fresh as paint. (*He takes chair.*)

VIDA (*facing the insinuation with gentle pain*). I hope you don't mean that? I never flattered myself for a moment you'd come. You're riding Cynthia K?

JOHN (*who has laid his gloves and riding crop on the table*). Fiddler's going to lead her round here in ten minutes!

VIDA. Cigars and cigarettes! Scotch? (*She indicates that he will find them on a small table up stage.*)

JOHN. Scotch! (*Going up quickly to the table and helping himself to scotch and seltzer.*)

VIDA. And now *do* tell me all about her! (*Putting in her last roses; she keeps one rosebud in her hand, of a size suitable for a man's buttonhole.*)

JOHN (*as he drinks*). Oh, she's an adorable creature—delicate, highbred, sweet-tempered—

VIDA (*showing her claws for a moment*). Sweet-tempered? Oh, you're describing the horse! By "her," I meant —

JOHN (*irritated by the remembrance of his wife*). Cynthia Karslake? I'd rather talk about the last tornado. (*Sits.*)

VIDA (*soothing the savage beast*). There is only one thing I want to talk about, and that is, *you!* Why were you unhappy?

JOHN (*still cross*). Why does a dollar last such a short time?

VIDA (*with curiosity*). Why did you part?

JOHN. Did you ever see a schooner towed by a tug? Well, I parted from Cynthia for the same reason that the hawser parts from the tug—I couldn't stand the tug.

VIDA (*sympathizing*). Ah! (*Pause.*)

JOHN (*still cross*). Awful cheerful morning chat.

VIDA (*excusing her curiosity and coming back to love as the only subject for serious conversation*). I must hear the story, for I'm anxious to know why I've taken such a fancy to you!

JOHN (*very nonchalantly*). Why do *I* like you?

VIDA (*doing her best to charm*). I won't tell you—it would flatter you too much.

JOHN (*not a bit impressed by* VIDA *but as ready to flirt as another*). Tell me!

VIDA. There's a rose for you. (*Giving him the one she has in her hand.*)

JOHN (*saying what is plainly expected of him*). I want more than a rose—

VIDA (*putting this insinuation by*). You refuse to tell me—?

JOHN (*once more reminded of* CYNTHIA, *speaks with sudden feeling*). There's nothing to tell. We met, we loved, we married, we parted; or at least we wrangled and jangled. (*Sighing*) Ha! Why weren't we happy? Don't ask me why! It may have been *partly* my fault!

VIDA (*with tenderness*). Never!

JOHN (*his mind on* CYNTHIA). But I believe it's all in the way a girl's brought up. Our girls are brought up to be ignorant of life—they're ignorant of life. Life is a joke, and marriage is a picnic, and a man is a shawl-strap— 'Pon my soul, Cynthia Deane—no, I can't tell you! (*During the following, he walks about in his irritation.*)

VIDA (*gently*). Please tell me!

JOHN. Well, she was an heiress, an American heiress—and she'd been taught to think marriage meant burnt almonds and moonshine and a yacht and three automobiles, and she thought —I don't know what she thought, but I tell you, Mrs. Phillimore, marriage is three parts love and seven parts forgiveness of sins.

VIDA (*flattering him as a matter of course*). She never loved you.

JOHN (*on whom she has made no impression at all*). Yes, she did. For six or seven months there was not a shadow between us. It was perfect, and then one day she went off like a pistol shot! I had a piece of law work and couldn't take her to see Flashlight race the Maryland mare. The case meant a big fee, big kudos, and in sails Cynthia, Flashlight mad! And will I put on my hat and take her? No—and bang she goes off like a stick o' dynamite—what did I marry her for—and words— pretty high words, until she got mad, when she threw over a chair and said, oh, well—marriage was a failure, or it was with me, so I said she'd better try somebody else. She said she would and marched out of the room.

VIDA (*gently sarcastic*). But she came back!

JOHN. She came back, but not as you mean. She stood at the door and said, "Jack, I shall divorce you." Then she came over to my study table, dropped her wedding ring on my law papers, and went out. The door shut, I laughed; the front door slammed, I damned. (*Pause. He crosses to the window.*) She

never came back. (*He comes back to where* VIDA *sits. She catches his hands.*)

VIDA (*hoping for a contradiction*). She's broken your heart.

JOHN. Oh no! (*He crosses to the chair by the lounge.*)

VIDA (*encouraged, begins to play the game again*). You'll never love again!

JOHN (*speaking to her from the foot of her sofa*). Try me! Try me! Ah, no, Mrs. Phillimore, I shall laugh, live, love, and make money again! And let me tell you one thing—I'm going to rap her one over the knuckles. She had a stick of a Connecticut lawyer, and he —well, to cut a legal story short, since Mrs. Karslake's been in Europe, I have been quietly testing the validity of the decree of divorce. Perhaps you don't understand?

VIDA (*letting her innate shrewdness appear*). Oh, about a divorce, everything!

JOHN. I shall hear by this evening whether the divorce will stand or not.

VIDA. But it's today at three she marries—you won't let her commit bigamy?

JOHN (*shaking his head*). I don't suppose I'd go as far as that. It may be the divorce will hold, but, anyway, I hope never to see her again. (*He sits beside her, facing up the stage as she faces down.*)

VIDA. Ah, my poor boy, she has broken your heart. (*Believing that this is her psychological moment, she lays her hand on his arm but draws it back as soon as he attempts to take it.*) Now don't make love to me.

JOHN (*bold and amused but never taken in*). Why not?

VIDA (*with immense gentleness*). Because I like you too much! (*More gaily*) I might give in and take a notion to like you still more!

JOHN. Please do!

VIDA (*with gush, and determined to

be womanly at all hazards). Jack, I believe you'd be a lovely lover!

JOHN (*as before*). Try me!

VIDA (*not hoping much from his tone*). You charming, tempting, delightful fellow, I could love you without the least effort in the world—but no!

JOHN (*playing the game*). Ah, well, now *seriously!* Between two people who have *suffered* and made their own mistakes—

VIDA (*playing the game too, but not playing it well*). But you see, you don't really love me!

JOHN (*still ready to say what is expected*). Cynthia—Vida, no man can sit beside you and look into your eyes without feeling—

VIDA (*speaking the truth as she sees it, seeing that her methods don't succeed*). Oh! That's not love! That's simply—well, my dear Jack, it's beginning at the wrong end. And the truth is you hate Cynthia Karslake with such a whole-hearted hate that you haven't a moment to think of any other woman.

JOHN (*with sudden anger*). I hate her!

VIDA (*very softly and most sweetly*). Jack—Jack, I could be as foolish about you as—oh, as foolish as anything, my dear! And perhaps some day—perhaps some day you'll come to me and say, Vida, I am totally indifferent to Cynthia—and then—

JOHN. And then?

VIDA (*the ideal woman in mind*). Then, perhaps, you and I may join hands and stroll together into the Garden of Eden. It takes two to find the Garden of Eden, you know—and once we're on the inside, we'll lock the gate.

JOHN (*gaily, and seeing straight through her veneer*). And lose the key under a rosebush!

VIDA (*agreeing very softly*). Under a rosebush! (*Very soft knock*) Come!

(JOHN *rises quickly. Enter* BENSON *and* BROOKS.)

BROOKS (*stolid and announcing*). My lady—Sir Wilf—

(BENSON *stops him with a sharp movement and turns toward* VIDA.)

BENSON (*with intention*). Your dressmaker, ma'am. (BENSON *waves* BROOKS *to go. Exit* BROOKS, *very haughtily.*)

VIDA (*wonderingly*). My dressmaker, Benson? (*With quick intelligence*) Oh, of course, show her up. Mr. Karslake, you won't mind for a few minutes using my men's club room? Benson will show you! You'll find cigars and the ticker, sporting papers, whisky; and, if you want anything special, just phone down to my chef.

JOHN (*looking at his watch*). How long?

VIDA (*very anxious to please*). Half a cigar! Benson will call you.

JOHN (*practical*). Don't make it too long. You see, there's my sheriff's sale on at twelve and those races this afternoon. Fiddler will be here in ten minutes, remember!

(*Door opens.*)

VIDA (*to* JOHN). Run along! (*Exit* JOHN. VIDA *suddenly practical, and with a broad gesture to* BENSON.) Everything just as it was, Benson! (BENSON *whisks the roses out of the vase and replaces them in the box. She gives* VIDA *scissors and empty vases, and when* VIDA *finds herself in precisely the same position which preceded* JOHN'S *entrance, she says*) There!

(*Enter* BROOKS, *as* VIDA *takes a rose from the basket.*)

BROOKS (*stolidly*). Your ladyship's dressmaker! M'lady!

(*Enter* SIR WILFRID *in morning suit with boutonniere.*)

VIDA (*with tender surprise and busy with the roses*). Is that really you, Sir Wilfrid! I never flattered myself for an instant that you'd remember to come.

SIR WILFRID (*coming to her above end of sofa*). Come? 'Course I come! Keen to come see you. By Jove, you know, you look as pink and white as a huntin' mornin'.

VIDA (*ready to make any man as happy as possible*). You'll smoke?

SIR WILFRID. Thanks! (*He watches her as she trims and arranges the flowers.*) Awfully long fingers you have! Wish I was a rose, or a ring, or a pair of shears! I say, d'you ever notice what a devil of a fellow I am for originality, what? (*Unlike* JOHN, *he is evidently impressed by her.*) You've got a delicate little den up here! Not so much low livin' and high thinkin', as low lights and no thinkin' at all, I hope—eh?

(*By this time* VIDA *has filled a vase with roses and rises to sweep by him and if possible make another charming picture to his eyes.*)

VIDA. You don't mind my moving about?

SIR WILFRID (*impressed*). Not if you don't mind my watchin'. (*He sits on the sofa.*) And sayin' how well you do it.

VIDA. It's most original of you to come here this morning. I don't quite see why you did. (*She places the roses here and there, as if to see their effect, and leaves them on a small table near the door through which her visitors entered.*)

SIR WILFRID. Admiration.

VIDA (*sauntering slowly toward the mirror as she speaks*). Oh, I saw that you admired her! And of course she did say she was coming here at eleven! But that was only bravado! She won't come, and besides, I've given orders to admit no one!

SIR WILFRID. May I ask you— (*He throws this in in the middle of her speech, which flows gently and steadily on.*)

VIDA. And indeed, if she came now, Mr. Karslake has gone, and her sole object in coming was to make him uncomfortable. (*She goes toward the table, stopping a half minute at the mirror to see that she looks as she wishes to look.*) Very dangerous symptom, too, that passionate desire to make one's former husband unhappy! But I can't believe that your admiration for Cynthia Karslake is so warm that it led you to pay me this visit a half hour too early in the hope of seeing—

SIR WILFRID (*rising; most civil, but speaking his mind like a Briton*). I say, would you mind stopping a moment! (*She smiles.*) I'm not an American, you know; I was brought up not to interrupt. But you Americans, it's different with you! If somebody didn't interrupt you, you'd go on forever.

VIDA (*passes him to tantalize*). My point is you come to see Cynthia—

SIR WILFRID (*believes she means it*). I came hopin' to see—

VIDA (*as before*). Cynthia!

SIR WILFRID (*perfectly single-minded and entirely taken in*). But I would have come even if I'd known—

VIDA (*evading him while he follows*). I don't believe it!

SIR WILFRID (*as before*). Give you my word I—

VIDA (*the same*). You're here to see her! And of course—

SIR WILFRID (*determined to be heard because, after all, he's a man*). May I have the—eh—the floor? (VIDA *sits in a chair.*) I was jolly well bowled over with Mrs. Karslake, I admit that, and I hoped to see her here, but—

VIDA (*talking nonsense and knowing it*). You had another object in coming. In fact, you came to see Cynthia, and you came to see me! What I really long to know is why you wanted to see *me*!

For, of course, Cynthia's to be married at three! And, if she wasn't she wouldn't have you!

SIR WILFRID (*not intending to wound; merely speaking the flat truth*). Well, I mean to jolly well ask her.

VIDA (*indignant*). To be your wife?

SIR WILFRID. Why not?

VIDA (*as before*). And you came here, to my house—in order to ask her—

SIR WILFRID (*truthful even on a subtle point*). Oh, but that's only my first reason for coming, you know.

VIDA (*concealing her hopes*). Well, now I *am* curious—what is the second?

SIR WILFRID (*simply*). Are you feelin' pretty robust?

VIDA. I don't know!

SIR WILFRID (*crossing to buffet*). Will you have something, and then I'll tell you!

VIDA (*gaily*). Can't I support the news without—

SIR WILFRID (*trying to explain his state of mind, a thing he has never been able to do*). Mrs. Phillimore, you see it's this way. Whenever you're lucky, you're too lucky. Now, Mrs. Karslake is a nipper and no mistake, but as I told you, the very same evenin' and house where I saw her— (*He attempts to take her hand.*)

VIDA (*gently rising and affecting a tender surprise*). What!

SIR WILFRID (*rising with her*). That's it! You're over! (*He suggests with his right hand the movement of a horse taking a hurdle.*)

VIDA (*very sweetly*). You don't really mean—

SIR WILFRID (*carried away for the moment by so much true womanliness*). I mean I stayed awake for an hour last night, thinkin' about you.

VIDA (*speaking to be contradicted*). But you've just told me—that Cynthia—

SIR WILFRID (*admitting the fact*). Well, she did—she did bowl my wicket, but so did you—

VIDA (*taking him very gently to task*). Don't you think there's a limit to— (*She sits.*)

SIR WILFRID (*roused by so much loveliness of soul*). Now, see here, Mrs. Phillimore! You and I are not bottle babies, eh, are we? You've been married and—I—I've knocked about, and we both know there's a lot of stuff talked about—eh, eh, well, you know—the one and only—that a fellow can't be awfully well smashed by two at the same time, don't you know! All rubbish! You know it, and the proof of the puddin's in the eatin', I am!

VIDA (*as before*). May I ask where I come in?

SIR WILFRID. Well, now, Mrs. Phillimore, I'll be frank with you. Cynthia's my favorite, but you're runnin' her a close second in the popular esteem!

VIDA (*laughing, determined not to take offense*). What a delightful, original, fantastic person you are!

SIR WILFRID (*frankly happy that he has explained everything so neatly*). I knew you'd take it that way!

VIDA. And what next, pray?

SIR WILFRID. Oh, just the usual—eh —thing—the—eh—the same old question, don't you know. Will you have me if she don't?

VIDA (*a shade piqued but determined not to risk showing it*). And you call that the same old usual question?

SIR WILFRID. Yes, I know, but—but will you? I sail in a week; we can take the same boat. And—eh—eh—my dear Mrs.—mayn't I say Vida, I'd like to see you at the head of my table.

VIDA (*with velvet irony*). With Cynthia at the foot?

SIR WILFRID (*practical, as before*). Never mind Mrs. Karslake. I admire her—she's—but you have your own points! And you're here, and so'm I! Damme, I offer myself and my affections, and I'm no icicle, my dear, tell you that for a fact, and, and in fact what's your answer!

(VIDA *sighs and shakes her head.*) Make it yes! I say, you know, my dear Vida— (*He catches her hands.*)

VIDA (*slips them from him*). Unhand me, dear villain! And sit further away from your second choice! What can I say? I'd rather have *you* for a lover than any man I know! You must be a lovely lover!

SIR WILFRID. I am! (*He makes a second effort to catch her fingers.*)

VIDA. Will you kindly go further away and be good!

SIR WILFRID (*quite forgetting* CYNTHIA). Look here, if you say yes, we'll be married—

VIDA. In a month!

SIR WILFRID. Oh no—this evening!

VIDA (*incapable of leaving a situation unadorned*). This evening! And sail in the same boat with *you?* And shall we sail to the Garden of Eden and stroll into it and lock the gate on the inside and then lose the key—under a rosebush?

SIR WILFRID (*pausing and, after consideration, saying*). Yes; yes, I say— that's too clever for me! (*He draws nearer to her to bring the understanding to a crisis.*)

VIDA (*a soft knock at the door*). My maid—come!

SIR WILFRID (*swinging out of his chair and going to sofa*). Eh?

BENSON (*enters; to* VIDA). The new footman, ma'am—he's made a mistake. He's told the lady you're at home.

VIDA. What lady?

BENSON. Mrs. Karslake; and she's on the stairs, ma'am.

VIDA. Show her in.

(SIR WILFRID *has been turning over the roses. On hearing this, he faces about with a long-stemmed one in his hand. He uses it in the following scene to point his remarks.*)

SIR WILFRID (*to* BENSON, *who stops*). One moment! (*To* VIDA) I say, eh—I'd rather not see her!

VIDA (*very innocently*). But you came here to see her.

SIR WILFRID (*a little flustered*). I'd rather not. Eh—I fancied I'd find you and her together—but her— (*Coming a step nearer*) —findin' me with you looks so dooced intimate—no one else, d'ye see, I believe she'd—draw conclusions—

BENSON. Pardon me, ma'am—but I hear Brooks coming!

SIR WILFRID (*to* BENSON). Hold the door!

VIDA. So you don't want her to know—?

SIR WILFRID (*to* VIDA). Be a good girl now—run me off somewhere!

VIDA (*to* BENSON). Show Sir Wilfrid the men's room.

(*Enter* BROOKS.)

SIR WILFRID. The men's room! Ah! Oh! Eh!

VIDA (*beckoning him to go at once*). Sir Wil — (*He hesitates then as* BROOKS *comes on, he flings off with* BENSON.)

BROOKS. Lady Karslake, milady!

VIDA. Anything more inopportune! I never dreamed she'd come—

(*Enter* CYNTHIA, *veiled. She comes down quickly.*)

My dear Cynthia, you don't mean to say— (*Languorously.*)

CYNTHIA (*rather short, and visibly agitated*). Yes, I've come.

VIDA (*polite but not urgent*). Do take off your veil.

CYNTHIA (*doing as* VIDA *asks*). Is no one here?

VIDA (*as before*). Won't you sit down?

CYNTHIA (*agitated and suspicious*). Thanks, no— That is, yes, thanks. Yes! You haven't answered my question? (CYNTHIA *waves her hand through the smoke, looks at the smoke suspiciously, looks for the cigarette.*)

VIDA (*playing innocence in the first degree*). My dear, what makes you imagine that anyone's here!

CYNTHIA. You've been smoking.

VIDA. Oh, puffing away!

CYNTHIA (*sees the glasses on the table*). And drinking—a pair of drinks? (*She sees* JOHN's *gloves on the table at her elbow.*) Do they fit you, dear? (VIDA *smiles;* CYNTHIA *picks up crop and looks at it and reads her own name.*) "Jack, from Cynthia."

VIDA (*without taking the trouble to double for a mere woman*). Yes, dear; it's Mr. Karslake's crop, but I'm happy to say he left me a few minutes ago.

CYNTHIA. He left the house?

(VIDA *smiles.*)

I wanted to see him.

VIDA (*with a shade of insolence*). To quarrel?

CYNTHIA (*frank and curt*). I wanted to see him.

VIDA (*determined to put* CYNTHIA *in the wrong*). And I sent him away because I didn't want you to repeat the scene of last night in my house.

CYNTHIA (*looks at* JOHN's *riding crop and is silent*). Well, I can't stay. I'm to be married at three, and I had to play truant to get here!

BENSON (*enters; to* VIDA). There's a person, ma'am, on the sidewalk.

VIDA. What person, Benson?

BENSON. A person, ma'am, with a horse.

CYNTHIA (*happily agitated*). It's Fiddler with Cynthia K. (*She goes up rapidly and looks out back through the window.*)

VIDA (*to* BENSON). Tell the man I'll be down in five minutes.

CYNTHIA (*looking down from the balcony with delight*). Oh, there she is!

VIDA (*aside to* BENSON). Go to the club room, Benson, and say to the two gentlemen I can't see them at present —I'll send for them when—

BENSON (*listening*). I hear someone coming.

VIDA. Quick!

(BENSON *leaves the door which opens, and* JOHN *enters.* JOHN *comes in slowly, carelessly.* VIDA *whispers to* BENSON.)

BENSON (*crosses, goes close to* JOHN, *and whispers*). Beg par—

VIDA (*under her breath*). Go back!

JOHN (*not understanding*). I beg pardon!

VIDA (*as before*). Go back!

JOHN (*the same*). Can't! I've a date! With the sheriff!

VIDA (*a little cross*). Please use your eyes.

JOHN (*laughing and flattering* VIDA). I am using my eyes.

VIDA (*fretted*). Don't you see there's a lovely creature in the room?

JOHN (*again taking the loud upper hand*). Of course there is.

VIDA. Hush!

JOHN (*teasingly*). But what I want to know is—

VIDA. Hush!

JOHN (*delighted at getting a rise*). —is when we're to stroll in the Garden of Eden—

VIDA. Hush!

JOHN. —and lose the key.

(*To put a stop to this, she lightly tosses her handkerchief into his face.*) By George, talk about attar of roses!

CYNTHIA (*up at window, excited and moved at seeing her mare once more*). Oh, she's a darling! (*She turns.*) A perfect darling! (JOHN *starts; he sees* CYN-THIA *at the same instant that she sees him.*) Oh! I didn't know you were here. (*Pause; then with take-it-or-leave-it frankness.*) I came to see *you!* (JOHN *looks extremely dark and angry;* VIDA *rises.*)

VIDA (*to* CYNTHIA, *most gently, and seeing there's nothing to be made of* JOHN). Oh, pray feel at home, Cynthia, dear! (*Stands by door; to* JOHN) When I've a nice street frock on, I'll ask you to present me to Cynthia K. (*Exits.*)

CYNTHIA (*agitated and frank*). Of course, I told you yesterday I was coming here.

JOHN (*irritated*). And I was to deny myself the privilege of being here?

CYNTHIA (*curt and agitated*). Yes.

JOHN (*ready to fight*). And you guessed I would do that?

CYNTHIA. No.

JOHN. What?

CYNTHIA (*speaks with agitation, frankness, and good will*). Jack—I mean, Mr. Karslake—no, I mean, Jack! I came because—well, you see, it's my wedding day—and—and—I—I —was rude to you last evening. I'd like to apologize and make peace with you before I go—

JOHN (*determined to be disagreeable*). Before you go to your last, long home!

CYNTHIA. I came to apologize.

JOHN. But you'll remain to quarrel!

CYNTHIA (*still frank and kind*). I will not quarrel. No! And I'm only here for a moment. I'm to be married at three, and just look at the clock! Besides, I told Philip I was going to Louise's shop, and I did—on the way here; but, you see, if I stay too long he'll telephone Louise and find I'm not there, and he might guess I was here. So you see I'm risking a scandal. And

now, Jack, see here, I lay my hand on the table, I'm here on the square, and —what I want to say is, why—Jack, even if we have made a mess of our married life, let's put by anger and pride. It's all over now and can't be helped. So let's be human, let's be reasonable, and let's be kind to each other! Won't you give me your hand? (JOHN *refuses.*) I wish you every happiness!

JOHN (*turning away, the past rankling*). I had a client once, a murderer; he told me he murdered the man, and he told me, too, that he never felt so kindly to anybody as he did to that man after he'd killed him!

CYNTHIA. Jack!

JOHN (*unforgiving*). You murdered my happiness!

CYNTHIA. I won't recriminate!

JOHN. And now I must put by anger and pride! I do! But not self-respect, not a just indignation—not the facts and my clear memory of them!

CYNTHIA. Jack!

JOHN. No!

CYNTHIA (*with growing emotion, and holding out her hand*). I give you one more chance! Yes, I'm determined to be generous. I forgive everything you ever did to me. I'm ready to be friends. I wish you every happiness and every —every—horse in the world! I can't do more than that! (*She offers her hand again.*) You refuse?

JOHN (*moved but surly*). I like wildcats and I like Christians, but I don't like Christian wildcats! Now I'm close-hauled, trot out your tornado. Let the tiger loose! It's the tamer, the man in the cage that has to look lively and use the red-hot crowbar! But by Jove, I'm out of the cage! I'm a mere spectator of the married circus! (*He puffs vigorously.*)

CYNTHIA. Be a game sport then! Our marriage was a wager; you wagered you could live with me. You lost; you paid with a divorce; and now is the time to show your sporting blood. Come on, shake hands and part friends.

JOHN. Not in this world! Friends with you, no! I have a proper pride. I don't propose to put my pride in my pocket.

CYNTHIA (*jealous and plain-spoken*). Oh, I wouldn't ask you to put your pride in your pocket while Vida's handkerchief is there. (JOHN *looks angered*.) Pretty little bijou of a handkerchief! (CYNTHIA *takes handkerchief out*.) And she is charming, and divorced, and reasonably well made-up.

JOHN. Oh well, Vida is a woman. (*Toying with handkerchief*) I'm a man, a handkerchief is a handkerchief, and as some old Aristotle or other said, whatever concerns a woman concerns me!

CYNTHIA (*not oblivious of him, but in a low voice*). Insufferable! Well, yes. (*She sits. She is too much wounded to make any further appeal.*) You're perfectly right. There's no possible harmony between divorced people! I withdraw my hand and all good feeling. No wonder I couldn't stand you. Eh? However, that's pleasantly past! But at least, my dear Karslake, let us have some sort of beauty of behavior! If we cannot be decent, let us endeavor to be graceful. If we can't be moral, at least we can avoid being vulgar.

JOHN. Well—

CYNTHIA. If there's to be no more marriage in the world—

JOHN (*cynical*). Oh, but that's not it; there's to be more and more and more!

CYNTHIA (*with a touch of bitterness*). Very well! I repeat then, if there's to be nothing but marriage and divorce, and remarriage and redivorce, at least, at least, those who *are* divorced can avoid the vulgarity of meeting each other here, there, and everywhere!

JOHN. Oh, that's where you come out!

CYNTHIA. I thought so yesterday, and today I know it. It's an insufferable thing to a woman of any delicacy of feeling to find her husband—

JOHN. Ahem—former!

CYNTHIA. *Once* a husband always—

JOHN (*still cynical*). Oh no! Oh dear, no.

CYNTHIA. To find her—to find the man she has once lived with—in the house of—making love to—to find you here!

(JOHN *smiles and rises*.)

You smile—but I say it should be a social axiom, no woman should have to meet her former husband.

JOHN (*cynical and cutting*). Oh, I don't know; after I've served my term I don't mind meeting my jailer.

CYNTHIA (JOHN *takes a chair near* CYNTHIA). It's indecent—at the horse show, the opera, at races and balls, to meet the man who once— It's not civilized! It's fantastic! It's half-baked! Oh, I never should have come here! (*He sympathizes, and she grows irrational and furious.*) But it's entirely your fault!

JOHN. My fault?

CYNTHIA (*working herself into a rage*). Of course. What business have you to be about—to be at large. To be at all!

JOHN. Gosh!

CYNTHIA (*as before*). To be where I am! Yes, it's just as horrible for you to turn up in my life as it would be for a dead person to insist on coming back to life and dinner and bridge!

JOHN. Horrid idea!

CYNTHIA. Yes, but it's *you* who behave just as if you were not dead, just as if I'd not spent a fortune on your funeral. You do; you prepare to bob up at afternoon teas—and dinners—and embarrass me to death with your extinct personality!

JOHN. Well, of course we *were* married, but it didn't quite kill me.

CYNTHIA (*angry and plain-spoken*). You killed yourself for me—I divorced you. I buried you out of my life. If any human soul was ever dead, you are! And there's nothing I so hate as a gibbering ghost.

JOHN. Oh, I say!

CYNTHIA (*with hot anger*). Go gibber and squeak where gibbering and squeaking are the fashion!

JOHN (*laughing and pretending to a coldness he does not feel*). And so, my dear child, I'm to abate myself as a nuisance! Well, as far as seeing you is concerned, for my part it's just like seeing a horse who's chucked you once. The bruises are O.K., and you see him with a sort of easy curiosity. Of course, you know, he'll jolly well chuck the next man! Permit me! (JOHN *picks up gloves, handkerchief, and parasol and gives her these as she drops them one by one in her agitation.*) There's pleasure in the thought.

CYNTHIA. Oh!

JOHN. And now may I ask you a very simple question? Mere curiosity on my part, but why did you come here this morning?

CYNTHIA. I have already explained that to you.

JOHN. Not your real motive. Permit me!

CYNTHIA. Oh!

JOHN. But I believe I have guessed your real — permit me — your real motive!

CYNTHIA. Oh!

JOHN (*with mock sympathy*). Cynthia, I am sorry for you.

CYNTHIA. H'm?

JOHN. Of course we had a pretty lively case of the fever—the mutual attraction fever, and we *were* married a very short time. And I conclude that's what's the matter with *you!* You see, my dear, seven months of married life is too short a time to cure a bad case of the fancies.

CYNTHIA (*in angry surprise*). What?

JOHN (*calm and triumphant*). That's my diagnosis.

CYNTHIA (*slowly and gathering herself together*). I don't think I understand.

JOHN. Oh yes, you do; yes, you do.

CYNTHIA (*with blazing eyes*). What do you mean?

JOHN. Would you mind not breaking my crop! Thank you! I mean— (*With polite impertinence*) —that ours was a case of premature divorce, and, ahem, you're in love with me still. (*He pauses.* CYNTHIA *has one moment of fury, then she realizes at what a disadvantage this places her. She makes an immense effort, recovers her calm, thinks hard for a moment more, and then has suddenly an inspiration.*)

CYNTHIA. Jack, some day you'll get the blind staggers from conceit. No, I'm not in love with you, Mr. Karslake, but I shouldn't be at all surprised if she were. She's just your sort, you know. She's a man-eating shark, and you'll be a toothsome mouthful. Oh come now, Jack, what a silly you are! Oh yes, you are, to get off a joke like that; me—in love with— (*She looks at him.*)

JOHN. Why are you here?

(*She laughs and begins to play her game.*)

Why are you here?

CYNTHIA. Guess! (*She laughs.*)

JOHN. Why are you—

CYNTHIA (*quickly*). Why am I here! I'll tell you. I'm going to be married. I had a longing, an irresistible longing to see you make an ass of yourself just once more! It happened!

JOHN (*uncertain and discomfited*). I know better!

CYNTHIA. But I came for a more serious purpose, too. I came, my dear fellow, to make an experiment on myself. I've been with you thirty minutes; and— (*She sighs with content.*) It's all right!

JOHN. What's all right?

CYNTHIA (*calm and apparently at peace with the world*). I'm immune.

JOHN. Immune?

CYNTHIA. You're not catching any more! Yes, you see, I said to myself, if I fly into a temper—

JOHN. You did!

CYNTHIA. If I fly into a temper when I see him, well, that shows I'm not yet so entirely convalescent that I can afford to have Jack Karslake at my house. If I remain calm I shall ask him to dinner.

JOHN (*routed*). Ask me if you dare! (*He rises.*)

CYNTHIA (*getting the whip hand for good*). Ask you to dinner? Oh, my dear fellow.

(JOHN *rises.*)

I'm going to do much more than that. (*She rises.*) We must be friends, old man! We must meet, we must meet often, we must show New York the way the thing should be done, and, to show you I mean it—I want you to be my best man and give me away when I'm married this afternoon.

JOHN (*incredulous and impatient*). You don't mean that! (*He puts back chair.*)

CYNTHIA. There you are! Always suspicious!

JOHN. You don't mean that!

CYNTHIA (*hiding her emotion under a sportswoman's manner*). Don't I? I ask you, come! And come as you are! And I'll lay my wedding gown to Cynthia K that you won't be there! If you're there, you get the gown, and if you're not, I get Cynthia K!

JOHN (*determined not be worsted*). I take it!

CYNTHIA. Done! Now, then, we'll see which of us two is the real sporting goods! Shake!

(*They shake hands on it.*)

Would you mind letting me have a plain soda? (JOHN *goes to the table, and, as he is rattled and does not regard what he is about, he fills the glass three-fourths full with whisky. He comes to* CYNTHIA *and gives her this. She looks him in the eye with an air of triumph.*) Thanks. (*Maliciously, as* VIDA *enters*) Your hand is a bit shaky. I think *you* need a little King William.

(JOHN *shrugs his shoulders, and as* VIDA *immediately speaks,* CYNTHIA *defers drinking.*)

VIDA (*to* CYNTHIA). My dear, I'm sorry to tell you your husband—I mean my husband—I mean Philip—he's asking for you over the phone. You must have said you were coming here. Of course I told him you were not here and hung up.

BENSON (*enters; to* VIDA). Ma'am, the new footman's been talking with Mr. Phillimore on the wire. (VIDA *makes a gesture of regret.*) He told Mr. Phillimore that his lady was here, and if I can believe my ears, ma'am, he's got Sir Wilfrid on the phone now!

SIR WILFRID (*comes from room, perplexed and annoyed*). I say y'know— extraordinary country; that old chap, Phillimore, he's been damned impertinent over the wire! Says I've run off with Mrs. Karslake—talks about "Louise"! Now who the dooce is Louise? He's comin' round here, too—I said Mrs. Karslake wasn't here— (*Seeing* CYNTHIA) Hello! Good job! What a liar I am!

BENSON (*to* VIDA). Mr. Fiddler, ma'-am, says the mare is gettin' very restive. (JOHN *hears this and moves at once. Exit* BENSON.)

JOHN (*to* VIDA). If that mare's restive, she'll break out in a rash.

VIDA (*to* JOHN). Will you take me?

JOHN. Of course. (*They go to the door.*)

CYNTHIA (*to* JOHN). Tata, old man! Meet you at the altar! If I don't, the mare's mine!

(SIR WILFRID *looks at her amazed.*)

VIDA (*to* CYNTHIA). Do the honors, dear, in my absence!

JOHN. Come along, come along, never mind them! A horse is a horse!

(*Exeunt* JOHN *and* VIDA, *gaily and in haste. At the same moment,* CYNTHIA *drinks what she supposes to be her glass of plain soda. As it is whisky straight, she is seized with astonishment and a fit of coughing.* SIR WILFRID *relieves her of the glass.*)

SIR WILFRID (*indicating contents of glass*). I say, do you ordinarily take it as high up—as seven fingers and two thumbs?

CYNTHIA (*coughs*). Jack poured it out. Just shows how groggy he was! And now, Sir Wilfrid— (*She gets her things to go.*)

SIR WILFRID. Oh, you can't go!

(*Enter* BROOKS.)

CYNTHIA. I am to be married at three.

SIR WILFRID. Let him wait. (*Aside to* BROOKS, *whom he meets near the door*) If Mr. Phillimore comes, bring his card up.

BROOKS (*going*). Yes, Sir Wilfrid.

SIR WILFRID (*to* BROOKS, *as before*). To me! (*He tips him.*)

BROOKS (*bowing*). To you, Sir Wilfrid. (*Exits.*)

SIR WILFRID (*returning to* CYNTHIA). I've got to have my innings, y'know!

(*He looks at her more closely.*) I say, you've been crying!

CYNTHIA. King William!

SIR WILFRID. You *are* crying! Poor little gal!

CYNTHIA (*tears in her eyes*). I feel all shaken and cold.

(*Enter* BROOKS, *with card.*)

SIR WILFRID (*astonished and sympathetic*). Poor little gal.

CYNTHIA (*as before*). I didn't sleep a wink last night. (*With disgust*) Oh, what is the matter with me?

SIR WILFRID. Why, it's as plain as a pikestaff! You— (BROOKS *has brought salver to* SIR WILFRID. *A card lies upon it.* SIR WILFRID *takes it and says aside to* BROOKS.) Phillimore? (BROOKS *assents. Aloud to* CYNTHIA, *calmly deceitful*) Who's Waldorf Smith? (CYNTHIA *shakes her head. To* BROOKS, *returning card to salver*) Tell the gentleman Mrs. Karslake is not here!

(*Exit* BROOKS.)

CYNTHIA (*aware that she has no business where she is*). I thought it was Philip!

SIR WILFRID (*telling the truth as if it were a lie*). So did I! (*With cheerful confidence*) And now, Mrs. Karslake, I'll tell you why you're cryin'. (*He sits beside her.*) You're marryin' the wrong man! I'm sorry for you, but you're such a goose. Here you are, marryin' this legal luminary. What for? You don't know! He don't know! But I do! You pretend you're marryin' him because it's the sensible thing; not a bit of it. You're marryin' Mr. Phillimore because of all the other men you ever saw he's the least like Jack Karslake.

CYNTHIA. That's a very good reason.

SIR WILFRID. There's only one good reason for marrying and that is because you'll die if you don't!

CYNTHIA. Oh, I've tried that!

SIR WILFRID. The Scripture says:

"Try, try again!" I tell you, there's nothing like a w'im!

CYNTHIA. What's that? W'im? Oh, you mean a *whim!* Do please try and say w*h*im!

SIR WILFRID (*for the first time emphasizing his* h *in the word*). W*h*im. You must have a w'im—w'im for the chappie you marry.

CYNTHIA. I had—for Jack.

SIR WILFRID. Your w'im wasn't w'im-my enough, my dear! If you'd had more of it, and tougher, it would ha' stood, y' know! Now, I'm not proposin'!

CYNTHIA (*diverted at last from her own distress*). I hope not!

SIR WILFRID. Oh, I will later! It's not time yet! As I was saying—

CYNTHIA. And pray, Sir Wilfrid, when will it be time?

SIR WILFRID. As soon as I see you have a w'im for me! (*Rising, he looks at his watch.*) And now, I'll tell you what we'll do! We've got just an hour to get there in; my motor's on the corner, and in fifty minutes we'll be at Belmont Park.

CYNTHIA (*her sporting blood fired*). Belmont Park!

SIR WILFRID. We'll do the races, and dine at Martin's—

CYNTHIA (*tempted*). Oh, if I only could! I can't! I've got to be married! You're awfully nice; I've almost got a "w'im" for you already.

SIR WILFRID (*delighted*). There you are! I'll send a telegram!

(*She shakes her head. He sits and writes at the table.*)

CYNTHIA. No, no, no!

SIR WILFRID (*reads what he writes*). "Off with Cates-Darby to races. Please postpone ceremony till seven-thirty."

CYNTHIA. Oh, no, it's impossible!

SIR WILFRID (*accustomed to have things go his way*). No more than breathin'! You can't get a w'im for me,

you know, unless we're together, so together we'll be!

(*Enter* JOHN KARSLAKE.)

And tomorrow you'll wake up with a jolly little w'im—(*Reads.*) "Postpone ceremony till seven-thirty." There. (*He puts on her cloak. Sees* JOHN.) Hello!

JOHN (*surly*). Hello! Sorry to disturb you.

SIR WILFRID (*cheerful as possible*). Just the man! (*Giving him the telegraph form*) Just step round and send it, my boy. Thanks!

(JOHN *reads it.*)

CYNTHIA. No, no, I can't go!

SIR WILFRID. Cockety-coo-coo-can't. I say, you must!

CYNTHIA (*positively*). No!

JOHN (*astounded*). Do you mean you're going —

SIR WILFRID (*very gay*). Off to the races, my boy!

JOHN (*angry and outraged*). Mrs. Karslake can't go with you there!

(CYNTHIA *starts, amazed at his assumption of marital authority and delighted that she will have an opportunity of outraging his sensibilities.*)

SIR WILFRID. Oho!

JOHN. An hour before her wedding!

SIR WILFRID (*gay and not angry*). May I know if it's the custom—

JOHN (*jealous and disgusted*). It's worse than eloping—

SIR WILFRID. —custom, y'know, for the husband-that-was to dictate—

JOHN (*thoroughly vexed*). By George, there's a limit!

CYNTHIA. What? What? What? (*Gathers up her things.*) What did I hear you say?

SIR WILFRID. Ah!

JOHN (*angry*). I say there's a limit—

CYNTHIA (*more and more determined to arouse and excite* JOHN). Oh, there's a limit, is there?

JOHN. There is! I bar the way! It

means reputation—it means—

CYNTHIA (*enjoying her opportunity*). We shall see what it means!

SIR WILFRID. Aha!

JOHN (*to* CYNTHIA). I'm here to protect your reputation—

SIR WILFRID (*to* CYNTHIA). We've got to make haste, you know.

CYNTHIA. Now, I'm ready—

JOHN (*to* CYNTHIA). Be sensible. You're breaking off the match—

CYNTHIA (*excitedly*). What's that to you?

SIR WILFRID. It's boots and saddles!

JOHN (*takes his stand between them and the door*). No thoroughfare!

SIR WILFRID. Look here, my boy—!

CYNTHIA (*catching at the opportunity of putting* JOHN *in an impossible position*). Wait a moment, Sir Wilfrid! Give me the wire! (*Facing him*) Thanks! (*She takes the telegraph form from him and tears it up.*) There! Too rude to chuck him by wire! But you, Jack, you've taken on yourself to look after my interests, so I'll just ask you, old man, to run down to the Supreme Court and tell Philip—nicely, you know—I'm off with Sir Wilfrid and where! Say I'll be back by seven, if I'm not later! And make it clear, Jack, I'll marry him by eight-thirty or nine at the latest! And mind *you're* there, dear! And now, Sir Wilfrid, we're off.

JOHN (*staggered and furious, giving way as they pass him*). I'm not the man to—to carry—

CYNTHIA (*quick and dashing*). Oh yes, you are.

JOHN. —a message from you.

CYNTHIA (*triumphant*). Oh, yes, you are; you're just exactly the man!

(*Exeunt* CYNTHIA *and* SIR WILFRID.)

JOHN. Great miracles of Moses!

ACT THREE

The same scene as that of Act One, but the room has been cleared of too much furniture and arranged for a wedding ceremony. The curtain rises on MRS. PHILLIMORE *reclining on the sofa,* MISS HENEAGE *is seated left of table,* SUDLEY *is seated at its right, while* GRACE *is on the sofa. There are cushions of flowers, alcove of flowers, flowers in vase, pink and white hangings, wedding bell of roses, calla lilies, orange blossoms, a ribbon of white stretched in front of an altar of flowers; two cushions for the couple to kneel on; two candelabra at each side of back of arch on pedestals. The curtain rises. There is a momentary silence, that the audience may take in these symbols of marriage. Every member of the Phillimore family is irritable, with suppressed irritation.*

SUDLEY (*impatiently*). All very well, my dear Sarah. But you see the hour. Twenty to ten! We have been here since half past two.

MISS HENEAGE. You had dinner?

SUDLEY. I did not come here at two to have dinner at eight and be kept waiting until ten! And, my dear Sarah, when I ask where the bride is—

MISS HENEAGE (*with forced composure*). I have told you all I know. Mr. John Karslake came to the house at lunch time, spoke to Philip, and they left the house together.

GRACE. Where is Philip?

MRS. PHILLIMORE (*feebly irritated*). I don't wish to be censorious or to express an actual opinion, but I must say it's a bold bride who keeps her future mother-in-law waiting for eight hours. However, I will not venture to— (MRS. PHILLIMORE *reclines again and fades away into silence.*)

GRACE (*sharply and decisively*). I do! I'm sorry I went to the expense of a silver ice pitcher.

(MRS. PHILLIMORE *sighs*. MISS HENEAGE *keeps her temper with an effort which is obvious. Enter* THOMAS.)

SUDLEY (*to* MRS. PHILLIMORE). For my part, I don't believe Mrs. Karslake means to return here or to marry Philip at all!

THOMAS (*to* MISS HENEAGE). Two telegrams for you, ma'am! The choir boys have had their supper.

(*Slight movement from everyone;* THOMAS *steps back.*)

SUDLEY (*rises*). At last we shall know!

MISS HENEAGE. From the lady! Probably! (MISS HENEAGE *opens telegram. She reads first one at a glance, laying it on salver again with a glance at* SUDLEY. THOMAS *passes salver to* SUDLEY, *who takes telegram.*)

GRACE. There's a toot now.

MRS. PHILLIMORE (*feebly confused*). I don't wish to intrude, but really I can't imagine Philip marrying at midnight.

(*As* SUDLEY *reads,* MISS HENEAGE *opens the second telegram but does not read it.*)

SUDLEY (*reads*). "Accident, auto struck"—something! "Gasoline"—did something—illegible, ah! (*Reads.*) "Home by nine forty-five! Hold the church!"

(*General movement from all.*)

MISS HENEAGE (*profoundly shocked*). "Hold the church!" William, she still means to marry Philip—and tonight, too!

SUDLEY. It's from Belmont Park.

GRACE (*making a great discovery*). She went to the races!

MISS HENEAGE. This is from Philip! (*She reads second telegram.*) "I arrive at ten o'clock. Have dinner ready."

(MISS HENEAGE *motions to* THOMAS *to withdraw. Exit* THOMAS. MISS HENEAGE *looks at her watch.*) They are both due now. (*Movement*) What's to be done? (*She rises.* SUDLEY *shrugs shoulders.*)

SUDLEY (*rising*). After a young woman has spent her wedding day at the races? Why, I consider that she has broken the engagement—and when she comes, tell her so.

MISS HENEAGE. I'll telephone Matthew. The choir boys can go home—her maid can pack her belongings—and when the lady arrives—

(*Very distant toot of an auto horn is heard coming nearer and nearer.* GRACE *flies up stage and looks out of door.* MRS. PHILLIMORE *does not know what to do or where to go.* SUDLEY *moves about excitedly.* MISS HENEAGE *stands ready to make herself disagreeable.*)

GRACE (*speaking rapidly and with excitement*). I hear a man's voice. Cates-Darby and brother Matthew.

(*Loud toot. Laughter and voices off back heard faintly.* GRACE *looks out of the door and leaves it rapidly.*)

MISS HENEAGE. Outrageous!

SUDLEY. Disgraceful!

MRS. PHILLIMORE (*partly rising as voices and horn are heard*). Shocking! I shall not take any part at all, in the— eh— (*She fades away.*)

MISS HENEAGE (*interrupting her*). Don't trouble yourself.

(*Voices and laughter grow louder.* CYNTHIA's *voice is heard.* SIR WILFRID *appears at the back. He turns and waits for* CYNTHIA *and* MATTHEW. *He carries wraps. He speaks to* CYNTHIA, *who is still off stage.* MATTHEW's *voice is heard and* CYNTHIA's. CYNTHIA *appears at back, followed by* MATTHEW. *As they appear,* CYNTHIA *speaks to* MATTHEW. SIR WILFRID *carries a newspaper and a parasol. The hat is the one she wore in Act Two. She is in getup for auto.*

Goggles, veil, an exquisite duster in latest Paris style. All three come down rapidly. As she appears, SUDLEY *and* MISS HENEAGE *exclaim, and there is a general movement.)*

SUDLEY. 'Pon my word!

GRACE. Hah!

MISS HENEAGE (*rising with shocked propriety*). Shocking!

(GRACE *remains standing above sofa.* SUDLEY *moves toward her.* MISS HENE-AGE *sits down again.* MRS. PHILLIMORE *reclines on sofa.* CYNTHIA *begins to speak as soon as she appears and speaks fluently to the end.*)

CYNTHIA. No! I never was so surprised in my life as when I strolled into the paddock and they gave me a rousing reception—old Jimmy Withers, Debt Gollup, Jack Deal, Monty Spiffles, the Governor, and Buckeye. All of my old admirers! They simply fell on my neck, and, dear Matthew, what do you think I did? I turned on the water main!

(*Movements and murmurs of disapprobation from the family.* MATTHEW *indicates a desire to go.*)

Oh, but you can't go!

MATTHEW. I'll return in no time!

CYNTHIA. I'm all ready to be married. Are they ready?

(MATTHEW *waves a pious, polite gesture of recognition to the family.*)

I beg everybody's pardon! (*She takes off her wrap and puts it on the back of a chair.*) My goggles are so dusty, I can't see who's who! (*To* SIR WILFRID) Thanks! You *have* carried it well! (*Takes parasol from* SIR WILFRID.)

SIR WILFRID (*aside to* CYNTHIA). When may I—?

CYNTHIA. See you next Goodwood!

SIR WILFRID (*imperturbably*). Oh I'm coming back!

CYNTHIA. Not a bit of use in coming back! I shall be married before you get here! Ta! Ta! Goodwood!

SIR WILFRID (*as before*). I'm coming back. (*He goes out quickly. More murmurs of disapprobation from family. Slight pause.*)

CYNTHIA (*beginning to take off her goggles and coming down slowly*). I do awfully apologize for being so late!

MISS HENEAGE (*importantly*). Mrs. Karslake—

SUDLEY (*importantly*). Ahem!

CYNTHIA (*lays down her goggles and sees their severity*). Dear me! (*She surveys the flowers and for a moment pauses.*) Oh good heavens! Why, it looks like a smart funeral!

(MISS HENEAGE *moves, then speaks in a perfectly ordinary natural tone, but her expression is severe.* CYNTHIA *immediately realizes the state of affairs in its fullness.*)

MISS HENEAGE (*to* CYNTHIA). After what has occurred, Mrs. Karslake—

CYNTHIA (*glances at table; sits at table, composed and good-tempered*). I see you got my wire—so you know where I have been.

MISS HENEAGE. To the racecourse.

SUDLEY. With a rowdy Englishman.

(CYNTHIA *glances at* SUDLEY, *uncertain whether he means to be disagreeable or whether he is only naturally so.*)

MISS HENEAGE. We concluded you desired to break the engagement!

CYNTHIA (*indifferently*). No! No! Oh! No!

MISS HENEAGE. Do you intend, despite our opinion of you—

CYNTHIA. The only opinion that would have any weight with me would be Mrs. Phillimore's. (*She turns expectantly to* MRS. PHILLIMORE.)

MRS. PHILLIMORE. I am generally a-sleep at this hour, and accordingly I will not venture to express any—eh—any—actual opinion. (*She fades away.* CYNTHIA *smiles.*)

MISS HENEAGE (*coldly*). You smile.

We simply inform you that as regards *us*, the alliance is not grateful.

CYNTHIA (*affecting gaiety and unconcern*). And all this because the gasoline gave out.

SUDLEY. My patience has given out!

GRACE. So has mine. I'm going. (*Exit* GRACE.)

SUDLEY (*vexed beyond civility; to* CYNTHIA). My dear young lady. You come here, to this sacred—eh—eh—spot—altar—odoriferous of the paddock—speaking of Spiffles and Buckeye, having practically eloped, having created a scandal and disgraced our family!

CYNTHIA (*as before*). How does it disgrace you? Because I like to see a highbred, clean, nervy, sweet little four-legged gee play the antelope over a hurdle!

MISS HENEAGE. Sister, it is high time that you— (*Turns to* CYNTHIA.)

CYNTHIA (*with quiet irony*). Mrs. Phillimore is generally asleep at this hour, and accordingly she will not venture to express—

SUDLEY (*spluttering with irritation*). Enough, madam—I *venture* to—to—to —to say you are leading a fast life.

CYNTHIA (*with powerful intention*). Not in this house! For six heavy weeks have I been laid away in the grave, and I've found it very slow indeed trying to keep pace with the dead!

SUDLEY (*despairingly*). This comes of horses!

CYNTHIA (*indignant*). Of what?

SUDLEY. C-c-caring for horses!

MISS HENEAGE (*with sublime morality*). What Mrs. Karslake cares for is—men.

CYNTHIA (*angry and gay*). What would you have me care for? The *Ornithorhynchus paradoxus?* Or *Pithacanthropus erectus?* Oh, I refuse to take you seriously.

(SUDLEY *begins to prepare to leave; he buttons himself into respectability and his coat.*)

SUDLEY. My dear madam, I take myself seriously—and madam, I—I retract what I have brought with me— (*He feels in his waistcoat pocket.*) —as a graceful gift, an Egyptian scarab—a —a—sacred beetle, which once ornamented the person of a — eh — mummy.

CYNTHIA (*getting even with him*). It should never be absent from your pocket, Mr. Sudley.

(SUDLEY *walks away in a rage.*)

MISS HENEAGE (*rising; to* SUDLEY). I've a vast mind to withdraw my—

CYNTHIA (*moves; interrupts, maliciously*). Your wedding present? The little bronze cat!

MISS HENEAGE (*moves, angrily*). Oh!

(*Even* MRS. PHILLIMORE *comes momentarily to life and expresses silent indignation.*)

SUDLEY (*loftily*). Sarah, I'm going.

(*Enter* PHILIP *with* GRACE. PHILIP *looks dusty and grim.* GRACE, *as they come in, speaks to him.* PHILIP *shakes his head. They pause up stage.*)

CYNTHIA (*emotionally*). I shall go to my room! However, all I ask is that you repeat to Philip— (*She comes suddenly on* PHILIP *and speaks to him in a low tone.*)

SUDLEY (*to* MISS HENEAGE, *determined to win*). As I go out, I shall do myself the pleasure of calling a hansom for Mrs. Karslake—

(PHILIP *comes down two or three steps.*)

PHILIP. As you go out, Sudley, have a hansom called, and when it comes, get into it.

SUDLEY (*furious and speaking to* PHILIP). Eh—eh—my dear sir, I leave you to your fate. (PHILIP *angrily points him the door.* SUDLEY *goes out.*)

MISS HENEAGE (*with weight*). Philip, you've not heard—

PHILIP (*interrupts*). Everything—from Grace!

(CYNTHIA *goes to the table.*)
My sister has repeated your words to me—and her own! I've told her what I think of her. (PHILIP *looks witheringly at* GRACE.)

GRACE. I shan't wait to hear any more. (*Exit* GRACE, *indignantly.*)

PHILIP. Don't make it necessary for me to tell you what I think of you. (PHILIP *gives his arm to his mother.* MISS HENEAGE *goes towards the door.*) Mother, with your permission, I desire to be alone. I expect you and Grace, Sarah, to be dressed and ready for the ceremony a half hour from now.

MISS HENEAGE. I shall come or not as I see fit. And let me add, my dear nephew, that a fool at forty is a fool indeed. (*Exit* MISS HENEAGE, *high and mighty, and much pleased with her quotation.*)

MRS. PHILLIMORE (*stupid and weary as usual, to* PHILIP, *as he leads her to the door*). My dear son—I won't venture to express—

(CYNTHIA *goes to the table.*)

PHILIP (*soothing a silly mother*). No, mother, don't! But I shall expect you, of course, at the ceremony. (*Exit* MRS. PHILLIMORE. PHILIP *takes the tone and assumes the attitude of the injured husband.*) It is proper for me to tell you that I followed you to Belmont. I am aware—I know with whom—in fact, *I know all!* (*Pauses. He indicates the whole censorious universe.*) And now let me assure you—I am the last man in the world to be jilted on the very eve of—of—everything with you. I won't be jilted.

(CYNTHIA *is silent.*)
You understand? I propose to marry you. I won't be made ridiculous.

CYNTHIA (*glancing at* PHILIP). Philip, I didn't mean to make you—

PHILIP. Why, then, did you run off to Belmont Park with that fellow?

CYNTHIA. Philip, I—eh—

PHILIP (*sitting at the table*). What motive? What reason? On our wedding day? Why did you do it?

CYNTHIA. I'll tell you the truth. I was bored.

PHILIP. Bored? In my company? (*In a gesture, gives up.*)

CYNTHIA. I was bored, and then—and besides, Sir Wilfrid asked me to go.

PHILIP. Exactly, and that was why you went. Cynthia, when you promised to marry me, you told me you had forever done with love. You agreed that marriage was the rational coming together of two people.

CYNTHIA. I know, I know!

PHILIP. Do you believe that now?

CYNTHIA. I don't know what I believe. My brain is in a whirl! But, Philip, I am beginning to be—I'm afraid—yes, I am afraid that one can't just select a great and good man—(*She indicates him.*) —and say: I will be happy with him.

PHILIP (*with dignity*). I don't see why not. You must assuredly do one or the other: You must either let your heart choose or your head select.

CYNTHIA (*gravely*). No, there's a third scheme; Sir Wilfrid explained the theory to me. A woman should marry whenever she has a whim for the man, and then leave the rest to the man. Do you see?

PHILIP (*furious*). Do I see? Have I ever seen anything else? Marry for whim! That's the New York idea of marriage.

CYNTHIA (*giving a cynical opinion*). New York ought to know.

PHILIP. Marry for whim and leave the rest to the divorce court! Marry for whim and leave the rest to the man. That was the former Mrs. Phillimore's idea. Only she spelled "whim" differently; she omitted the *w*. (*He rises in his anger.*) And now you—*you* take up with this preposterous—

(CYNTHIA *moves uneasily.*)

But, nonsense! It's impossible! A woman of your mental caliber— No. Some obscure, primitive, female *feeling* is at work corrupting your better judgment! What is it you *feel*?

CYNTHIA. Philip, you never felt like a fool, did you?

PHILIP. No, never.

CYNTHIA (*politely*). I thought not.

PHILIP. No, but whatever your feelings, I conclude you are ready to marry me.

CYNTHIA (*uneasy*). Of course, I came back. I am here, am I not?

PHILIP. You are ready to marry me?

CYNTHIA (*twisting in the coils*). But you haven't had your dinner.

PHILIP. Do I understand you refuse?

CYNTHIA. Couldn't we defer—?

PHILIP. You refuse?

CYNTHIA (*a slight pause, trapped and seeing no way out*). No, I said I'd marry you. I'm a woman of my word. I will.

PHILIP (*triumphant*). Ah! Very good, then. Run to your room.

(CYNTHIA *turns to* PHILIP.)

Throw something over you. In a half hour I'll expect you here! And, Cynthia, my dear, remember! I cannot cuculate like a wood pigeon, but—I esteem you!

CYNTHIA (*hopelessly*). I think I'll go, Philip.

PHILIP. I may not be fitted to play the lovebird, but—

CYNTHIA (*as before*). I think I'll go, Philip.

PHILIP. I'll expect you—in half an hour.

CYNTHIA (*with leaden despair*). Yes.

PHILIP. And, Cynthia, don't think any more about that fellow, Cates-Darby.

CYNTHIA (*amazed and disgusted by his misapprehension*). No. (*Exit* CYNTHIA.)

(THOMAS *enters from the opposite door.*)

PHILIP (*not seeing* THOMAS *and clumsily defiant*). And if I had that fellow, Cates-Darby, in the dock—!

THOMAS. Sir Wilfrid Cates-Darby.

PHILIP. Sir what—what—wh-who? (*Enter* SIR WILFRID *in evening dress.* PHILIP *looks* SIR WILFRID *in the face and speaks to* THOMAS.) Tell Sir Wilfrid Cates-Darby I am not at home to him. (THOMAS *embarrassed.*)

SIR WILFRID (*undaunted*). My dear Lord Eldon—

PHILIP (*speaks to* THOMAS, *as before*). Show the gentleman the door.

(*Pause.* SIR WILFRID *glances at door with a significant gesture.*)

SIR WILFRID (*goes to the door, examines it, and returns to* PHILIP). Eh— I admire the door, my boy! Fine, old, carved mahogany panel; but don't ask me to leave by it, for Mrs. Karslake made me promise I'd come, and that's why I'm here.

(THOMAS *exits.*)

PHILIP. Sir, you are—impudent!

SIR WILFRID (*interrupting*). Ah, you put it all in a nutshell, don't you?

PHILIP. To show your face here, after practically eloping with my wife!

SIR WILFRID (*pretending ignorance*). When were you married?

PHILIP. We're as good as married.

SIR WILFRID. Oh, pooh, pooh! You can't tell me that grace before soup is as good as a dinner! (*He takes cigar case out.*)

PHILIP. Sir—I—demand—

SIR WILFRID (*calmly carrying the

situation). Mrs. Karslake is *not* married. *That's* why I'm here. I am here for the same purpose *you* are: to ask Mrs. Karslake to be my wife.

PHILIP. Are you in your senses?

SIR WILFRID (*touching up his American cousin in his pet vanity*). Come, come, Judge—you Americans have no sense of humor. (*He takes a small jewel case from his pocket.*) There's my regards for the lady—and—(*Reasonably*) —if I must go, I will. Of course, I would like to see her, but—if it isn't your American custom—

THOMAS (*enters*). Mr. Karslake.

SIR WILFRID. Oh well, I say, if he can come, I can!

(*Enter* JOHN KARSLAKE *in evening dress, carrying a large and very smart bride's bouquet which he hands to* PHILIP. PHILIP *takes it because he isn't up to dropping it but gets it out of his hands as soon as he can.* PHILIP *is transfixed;* JOHN *comes to the front of the stage. Deep down, he is feeling wounded and unhappy. But, as he knows his coming to the ceremony on whatever pretext is a social outrage, he carries it off by assuming an air of its being the most natural thing in the world. He controls the expression of his deeper emotion, but the pressure of this keeps his face grave, and he speaks with force.*)

JOHN. My compliments to the bride, Judge.

PHILIP (*angry*). And you, too, have the effrontery?

SIR WILFRID. There you are!

JOHN (*pretending ease*). Oh, call it friendship—

(THOMAS *goes out.*)

PHILIP (*puts bouquet on table; ironically*). I suppose Mrs. Karslake—

JOHN. She wagered me I wouldn't give her away, and of course—

(*Throughout this scene* JOHN *hides the emotions he will not show behind a daring irony. He has* PHILIP *on his left, walking about in a fury;* SIR WILFRID *sits on the edge of the table, gay and undisturbed.*)

PHILIP (*taking a step toward* JOHN). You will oblige me—both of you—by immediately leaving—

JOHN (*smiling and going to* PHILIP). Oh, come, come, Judge—suppose I *am* here? Who has a better right to attend his wife's obsequies! Certainly I come as a mourner—for *you!*

SIR WILFRID. I say, is the custom?

JOHN. No, no—of course it's not the custom, no. But we'll make it the custom. After all, what's a divorced wife among friends?

PHILIP. Sir, your humor is strained!

JOHN. Humor, Judge?

PHILIP. It is, sir, and I'll not be bantered! Your both being here is—it is—gentlemen, there is a decorum which the stars in their courses do not violate.

JOHN. Now, Judge, never you mind what the stars do in their divorces! Get down to earth of the present day. Rufus Choate and Daniel Webster are dead. You must be modern. You must let peroration and poetry alone! Come along now. Why shouldn't I give the lady away?

SIR WILFRID. Hear! Hear! Oh, I beg your pardon!

JOHN. And why shouldn't we both be here? American marriage is a new thing. We've got to strike the pace, and the only trouble is, Judge, that the judiciary have so messed the thing up that a man can't be sure he *is* married until he's divorced. It's a sort of marry-go-round, to be sure! But let it go at that! Here we all are, and we're ready to marry my wife to you and start her on her way to him!

PHILIP (*brought to a standstill*).

Good Lord! Sir, you cannot trifle with monogamy!

JOHN. Now, now, Judge, monogamy is just as extinct as knee breeches. The new woman has a new idea, and the new idea is—well, it's just the opposite of the old Mormon one. Their idea is one man, ten wives, and a hundred children. Our idea is one woman, a hundred husbands, and one child.

PHILIP. Sir, this is polyandry.

JOHN. Polyandry? A hundred to one it's polyandry, and that's it, Judge! Uncle Sam has established consecutive polyandry, but there's got to be an interval between husbands! The fact is, Judge, the modern American marriage is like a wire fence. The woman's the wire—the posts are the husbands. (*He indicates himself and then* SIR WILFRID *and* PHILIP.) One—two—three! And if you cast your eye over the future you can count them, post after post, up hill, down dale, all the way to Dakota!

PHILIP. All very amusing, sir, but the fact remains—

JOHN (*going to* PHILIP, *as he moves away*). Now, now, Judge, I like you. But you're asleep; you're living in the Dark Ages. You want to call up Central. "Hello, Central! Give me the present time, 1906, New York!"

SIR WILFRID. Of course you do, and —there you are!

PHILIP (*heavily*). There I am not, sir! And— (*To* JOHN) —as for Mr. Karslake's ill-timed jocosity, sir, in the future—

SIR WILFRID. Oh, hang the future!

PHILIP. I begin to hope, Sir Wilfrid, that in the future I shall have the pleasure of hanging you! (*To* JOHN) And as to you, sir, your insensate idea of giving away your own—your former —my—your—oh! Good Lord! This is a nightmare! (*He turns to go in despair*.)

(*Enter* MATTHEW, *who, seeing* PHILIP, *speaks as he comes in from door*.)

MATTHEW (*to* PHILIP). My dear brother, Aunt Sarah Heneage refuses to give Mrs. Karslake away, unless you yourself—eh—

PHILIP (*as he exits*). No more! I'll attend to the matter! (*Exit. The choir boys are heard practicing in the next room*.)

MATTHEW (*mopping his brow*). How do you both do? My aunt has made me very warm. (*He rings the bell*.) You hear our choir practicing—sweet angel boys! Hm! Hm! Some of the family will not be present. I am very fond of you, Mr. Karslake, and I think it admirably Christian of you to have waived your—eh—your—eh—that is, now that I look at it more narrowly, let me say that in the excitement of pleasurable anticipation, I forgot, Karslake, that your presence might occasion remark—

(*Enter* THOMAS.)

Thomas! I left, in the hall, a small handbag or satchel containing my surplice.

THOMAS. Yes, sir. Ahem!

MATTHEW. You must really find the handbag at once.

(THOMAS *turns to go, when he stops, startled*.)

THOMAS. Yes, sir. (*Announcing in consternation*) Mrs. Vida Phillimore.

(*Enter* VIDA PHILLIMORE *in full evening dress. She steps gently to* MATTHEW.)

MATTHEW (*always piously serene*). Ah, my dear child! Now this is just as it should be! That is, eh— (*He comes to the front of the stage with her; she pointedly looks away from* SIR WILFRID.) That is, when I come to think of it—your presence might be deemed inauspicious.

VIDA. But, my dear Matthew, I had

to come. (*Aside to him*) I have a reason for being here.

(THOMAS *enters*.)

MATTHEW. But, my dear child—

THOMAS (*with sympathetic intention*). Sir, Mr. Phillimore wishes to have your assistance, sir—with Miss Heneage *immediately!*

MATTHEW. Ah! (*To* VIDA) One moment! I'll return. (*To* THOMAS) Have you found the bag with my surplice? (*He goes out with* THOMAS, *speaking.* SIR WILFRID *comes to* VIDA. JOHN *watches the door*.)

SIR WILFRID (*to* VIDA). You're just the person I most want to see!

VIDA (*with affected iciness*). Oh no, Sir Wilfrid, Cynthia isn't here yet! (*Crossing to table.* JOHN *comes toward her and she speaks to him with obvious sweetness*.) Jack, dear, I never was so ravished to see anyone.

SIR WILFRID (*taken aback*). By Jove!

VIDA (*very sweet*). I knew I should find you here!

JOHN (*annoyed but civil*). Now don't do that!

VIDA (*as before*). Jack!

(*They sit down*.)

JOHN (*civil but plain-spoken*). Don't do it!

VIDA (*in a voice dripping with honey*). Do what, Jack?

JOHN. Touch me with your voice! I have troubles enough of my own. (*He sits not far from her; the table is between them*.)

VIDA. And I know *who* your troubles are! Cynthia! (*From this moment* VIDA *gives up* JOHN *as an object of the chase and lets him into her other game*.)

JOHN. I hate her. I don't know why I came.

VIDA. You came, dear, because you couldn't stay away—you're in love with her.

JOHN. All right, Vida, what I feel may be *love*—but all I can say is, if I could get even with Cynthia Karslake—

VIDA. You can, dear—it's as easy as powdering one's face; all you have to do is to be too nice to me!

JOHN (*looks inquiringly at* VIDA). Eh!

VIDA. Don't you realize she's jealous of you? Why did she come to my house this morning? She's jealous—and all you have to do—

JOHN. If I can make her wince, I'll make love to you till the heavenly cows come home!

VIDA. Well, you see, my dear, if you make love to me it will— (*She delicately indicates* SIR WILFRID.) —cut both ways at once!

JOHN. Eh—what! Not Cates-Darby? (*Starting*) Is that Cynthia?

VIDA. Now don't get rattled and forget to make love to me.

JOHN. I've got the jumps. (*Trying to accept her instructions*) Vida, I adore you.

VIDA. Oh, you must be more convincing; that won't do at all.

JOHN (*listening*). Is that she now?

(*Enter* MATTHEW, *who goes to the inner room*.)

VIDA. It's Matthew. And, Jack dear, you'd best get the hang of it before Cynthia comes. You might tell me all about your divorce. That's a sympathetic subject. Were you able to undermine it?

JOHN. No. I've got a wire from my lawyer this morning. The divorce holds. She's a free woman. She can marry whom she likes.

(*The organ is heard, very softly played*.)

Is that Cynthia? (*He rises quickly*.)

VIDA. It's the organ!

JOHN (*overwhelmingly excited*). By George! I should never have come! I think I'll go. (*He crosses to go to the door.*)

VIDA (*rises and follows him remonstratingly*). When I need you?

JOHN. I can't stand it.

VIDA. Oh, but, Jack—

JOHN. Good night!

VIDA. I feel quite ill. (*Seeing that she must play her last card to keep him, pretends to faintness, sways and falls into his arms.*) Oh!

JOHN (*in a rage, but beaten*). I believe you're putting up a fake.

(*The organ swells as* CYNTHIA *enters sweepingly, dressed in full evening dress for the wedding ceremony.* JOHN, *not knowing what to do, holds* VIDA *up as a horrid necessity.*)

CYNTHIA (*speaking as she comes on, to* MATTHEW). Here I am. Ridiculous to make it a conventional thing, you know. Come in on the swell of the music and all that, just as if I'd never been married before. Where's Philip? (*She looks for* PHILIP *and sees* JOHN *with* VIDA *in his arms. She stops short.*)

JOHN (*uneasy and embarrassed*). A glass of water! I beg your pardon, Mrs. Karslake—

(*The organ plays on.*)

CYNTHIA (*ironical and calm*). Vida!

JOHN. She has fainted.

CYNTHIA (*as before*). Fainted? (*Without pause*) Dear, dear, dear, terrible! So she has.

(SIR WILFRID *takes flowers from a vase and prepares to sprinkle* VIDA'S *forehead with the water it contains.*) No, no, not her forehead, Sir Wilfrid, her frock! Sprinkle her best Paquin! If it's a real faint, she will not come to!

VIDA (*as her Paris importation is about to suffer, comes to her senses*). I almost fainted.

CYNTHIA. Almost!

VIDA (*using the stock phrase as a matter of course and reviving rapidly*).

Where am I?

(JOHN *glances at* CYNTHIA *sharply.*) Oh, the bride! I beg everyone's pardon. Cynthia, at a crisis like this, I simply couldn't stay away from Philip!

CYNTHIA. Stay away from Philip?

(JOHN *and* CYNTHIA *exchange glances.*)

VIDA. Your arm, Jack; and lead me where there is air.

(JOHN *and* VIDA *go into the further room;* JOHN *stands left of her. The organ stops.* SIR WILFRID *comes down. He and* CYNTHIA *are practically alone on the stage.* JOHN *and* VIDA *are barely within sight. You first see him take her fan and give her air; then he picks up a book and reads from it to her.*)

SIR WILFRID. I've come back.

CYNTHIA (*to* SIR WILFRID). Asks for air and goes to the green house. (CYNTHIA *crosses stage.* SIR WILFRID *offers her a seat.*) I know why you are here. It's that intoxicating little whim you suppose me to have for you. My regrets! But the whim's gone flat. Yes, yes, my gasoline days are over. I'm going to be garaged for good. However, I'm glad you're here; you take the edge off—

SIR WILFRID. Mr. Phillimore?

CYNTHIA (*sharply*). No, Karslake. I'm just waiting to say the words—

(*Enter* THOMAS.)

—"love, honor and obey" to Phillimore — (*Looks up back.*) —and at Karslake! (CYNTHIA *sees* THOMAS.) What is it? Mr. Phillimore?

THOMAS. Mr. Phillimore will be down in a few minutes, ma'am. He's very sorry, ma'am— (*Lowers his voice and comes nearer* CYNTHIA, *mindful of the respectabilities.*) —but there's a button off his waistcoat.

CYNTHIA (*excited, with irony; rising*). Button off his waistcoat!

(*Exit* THOMAS.)

SIR WILFRID (*delightedly*). Ah! So much the better for me.

(CYNTHIA *looks up back.*)

Now then, never mind those two! (CYNTHIA *moves restlessly.*) Sit down.

CYNTHIA. I can't.

SIR WILFRID. You're as nervous as—

CYNTHIA. Nervous! Of course I'm nervous! So would you be nervous if you'd had a runaway and smashup and you were going to try it again. (*Looking up back.* SIR WILFRID *is uneasy.*) And if someone doesn't do away with those calla lilies—the odor makes me faint! (SIR WILFRID *moves.*) No, it's not the lilies! It's the orange blossoms!

SIR WILFRID. Orange blossoms.

CYNTHIA. The flowers that grow on the tree that hangs over the abyss.

(SIR WILFRID *gets the vase of orange blossoms.*)

They smell of six o'clock in the evening. When Philip's fallen asleep, and the little boys are crying the winners outside, and I'm crying inside, and dying inside and outside and everywhere.

(SIR WILFRID *comes down.*)

SIR WILFRID. Sorry to disappoint you. They're artificial.

(CYNTHIA *shrugs her shoulders.*)

That's it! They're emblematic of artificial domesticity! And I'm here to help you balk it. (*He sits;* CYNTHIA *half rises and looks toward* JOHN *and* VIDA.) Keep still now, I've a lot to say to you. Stop looking—

CYNTHIA. Do you think I can listen to you make love to me when the man who—who—whom I most despise in all the world is reading poetry to the woman who—who got me into the fix I'm in!

SIR WILFRID (*leaning over the chair in which she sits*). What do you want to look at 'em for?

(CYNTHIA *moves.*)

Let 'em be and listen to me! Sit down; for damme, I'm determined.

CYNTHIA (*at the table; half to herself*). I won't look at them! I won't think of them. Beasts!

(SIR WILFRID *interposes between her and her view of* JOHN. *Enter* THOMAS.)

SIR WILFRID. Now then— (*He sits.*)

CYNTHIA. Those two *here!* It's just as if Adam and Eve should invite the snake to their golden wedding. (*She sees* THOMAS.) What is it, what's the matter?

THOMAS. Mr. Phillimore's excuses, ma'am. In a very short time— (*Exits.*)

SIR WILFRID. I'm on to you! You hoped for more buttons!

CYNTHIA. I'm dying of the heat; fan me.

SIR WILFRID (*as he fans* CYNTHIA). Heat! No! You're dying because you're ignorin' nature. Certainly you are! You're marryin' Phillimore!

(CYNTHIA *appears faint.*)

Can't ignore nature, Mrs. Karslake. Yes, you are; you're forcin' your feelin's.

(CYNTHIA *glances at him.*)

And what you want to do is to let yourself go a bit—up anchor and sit tight! I'm no seaman, but that's the idea!

(CYNTHIA *moves and shakes her head.*)

So just throw the reins on nature's neck, jump this fellow Phillimore, and marry me! (*He leans over to* CYNTHIA.)

CYNTHIA (*naturally, but with irritation*). You propose to me here, at a moment like this? When I'm on the last lap—just in sight of the goal—the gallows—the halter—the altar, I don't know what its name is! No, I won't have you! (*Looking toward* KARSLAKE *and* VIDA) And I won't have you stand near me! I won't have you talking to me in a low tone! (*As before*) Stand over there—stand where you are.

SIR WILFRID. I say—

CYNTHIA. I can hear you—I'm listening!

SIR WILFRID. Well, don't look so hurried and worried. You've got buttons and buttons of time. And now my offer. You haven't yet said you would—

CYNTHIA. Marry you? I don't even know you!

SIR WILFRID (feeling sure of being accepted). Oh—tell you all about myself. I'm no duke in a pickle o' debts, d'ye see? I can marry where I like. Some o' my countrymen are rotters, ye know. They'd marry a monkey, if poppa-up-the-tree had a corner in coconuts! And they do marry some queer ones, y'know.

(CYNTHIA looks up, exclaims and turns. SIR WILFRID turns.)

CYNTHIA. Do they?

SIR WILFRID. Oh, rather. That's what's giving your heiresses such a bad name lately. If a fellah's in debt he can't pick and choose, and then he swears that American gals are awfully fine lookers but they're no good when it comes to continuin' the race! Fair dolls in the drawin' room but no good in the nursery.

CYNTHIA (thinking of JOHN and VIDA and nothing else). I can see Vida in the nursery.

SIR WILFRID. You understand when you want a brood mare you don't choose a Kentucky mule.

CYNTHIA. I think I see one.

SIR WILFRID. Well, that's what they're saying over there. They say your gals run to talk— (He plainly remembers VIDA's volubility.) —and I have seen gals here that would chat life into a wooden Indian! That's what you Americans call being clever—all brains and no stuffin'! In fact, some of your American gals are the nicest boys I ever met.

CYNTHIA. So that's what you think?

SIR WILFRID. Not a bit what I think —what my countrymen think!

CYNTHIA. Why are you telling me?

SIR WILFRID. Oh, just explaining my character. I'm the sort that can pick and choose—and what I want is heart.

CYNTHIA (always having VIDA and JOHN in mind). No more heart than a dragonfly!

(The organ begins to play softly.)

SIR WILFRID. That's it, dragonfly. Cold as stone and never stops buzzing about and showin' off her colors. It's that American dragonfly girl that I'm afraid of, because, d'ye see, I don't know what an American expects when he marries; yes, but you're not listening!

CYNTHIA. I am listening. I am!

SIR WILFRID (speaking directly to her). An Englishman, ye see, when he marries, expects three things: love, obedience, and five children.

CYNTHIA. Three things! I make it seven!

SIR WILFRID. Yes, my dear, but the point is, will you be mistress of Traynham?

CYNTHIA (who has only half listened to him). No, Sir Wilfrid, thank you, I won't. (She turns to see JOHN crossing the drawing room at back with VIDA, apparently absorbed in what she says.) It's outrageous!

SIR WILFRID. Eh? Why, you're cryin'!

CYNTHIA (almost sobbing). I am not.

SIR WILFRID. You're not crying because you're in love with me?

CYNTHIA. I'm not crying—or if I am, I'm crying because I love my country. It's a disgrace to America— castoff husbands and wives getting together in a parlor and playing tag under a palm tree.

(JOHN, with intention and deter-

mined to stab CYNTHIA, *kisses* VIDA'*s hand.*)

SIR WILFRID. Eh! Oh! I'm damned! (*To* CYNTHIA) What do you think that means?

CYNTHIA. I don't doubt it means a wedding here at once—after mine!

(VIDA *and* JOHN *come down.*)

VIDA (*affecting an impossible intimacy to wound* CYNTHIA *and tantalize* SIR WILFRID). Hush, Jack—I'd much rather no one should know anything about it until it's all over!

CYNTHIA (*starts and looks at* SIR WILFRID). What did I tell you?

VIDA (*to* CYNTHIA). Oh, my dear, he's asked me to champagne and lobster at *your* house—his house! Matthew is coming!

(CYNTHIA *starts but controls herself.*) And you're to come, Sir Wilfrid. (VIDA *speaks, intending to convey the idea of a sudden marriage ceremony.*) Of course, my dear, I would like to wait for your wedding, but something rather —rather important to me is to take place, and I know you'll excuse me.

(*Organ stops.*)

SIR WILFRID (*piqued at being forgotten*). All very neat, but you haven't given me a chance even.

VIDA. Chance? You're not serious?

SIR WILFRID. I am!

VIDA (*striking while the iron is hot*). I'll give you a minute to offer yourself.

SIR WILFRID. Eh?

VIDA. Sixty seconds from now.

SIR WILFRID (*uncertain*). There's such a thing as bein' silly.

VIDA (*calm and determined*). Fifty seconds left.

SIR WILFRID. I take you—count fair. (*He hands her his watch and goes to where* CYNTHIA *stands.*) I say, Mrs. Karslake—

CYNTHIA (*overwhelmed with grief and emotion*). They're engaged; they're going to be married tonight over champagne and lobster at my house!

SIR WILFRID. Will you consider your —

CYNTHIA (*hastily, to get rid of him*). No, no, no, no! Thank you, Sir Wilfrid, I will not.

SIR WILFRID (*calm and not to be laid low*). Thanks awfully. (*Crosses to* VIDA. CYNTHIA *walks away*). Mrs. Phillimore—

VIDA (*gives him back his watch*). Too late! (*To* KARSLAKE) Jack dear, we must be off.

SIR WILFRID (*standing and making a general appeal for information*). I say, is it the custom for American girls— that sixty seconds or too late? Look here! Not a bit too late. I'll take you around to Jack Karslake's, and I'm going to ask you the same old question again, you know. (*To* VIDA) By Jove, you know in your country it's the pace that kills. (*Exeunt* SIR WILFRID *and* VIDA.)

JOHN (*gravely to* CYNTHIA, *who comes to the front of the stage*). Good night, Mrs. Karslake, I'm going; I'm sorry I came.

CYNTHIA. Sorry? Why are you sorry?

(JOHN *looks at her; she winces a little.*) You've got what you wanted. (*Pause*) I wouldn't mind your marrying Vida—

JOHN (*gravely*). Oh, wouldn't you?

CYNTHIA. —but I don't think you showed good taste in engaging yourselves *here.*

JOHN. Of course, I should have preferred a garden of roses and plenty of twilight.

CYNTHIA (*rushing into speech*). I'll tell you what you *have* done—you've thrown yourself away! A woman like that! No head, no heart! All languor and loose—loose frocks—she's the typical, worst thing America can do!

She's the regular American marriage worm!

JOHN. I have known others—

CYNTHIA (*quickly*). Not me. I'm not a patch on that woman. Do you know anything about her life? Do you know the things she did to Philip? Kept him up every night of his life—forty days out of every thirty—and then, without his knowing it, put brandy in his coffee to make him lively at breakfast.

JOHN (*banteringly*). I begin to think she is just the woman—

CYNTHIA (*unable to quiet her jealousy*). She is *not* the woman for *you!* A man with your bad temper—your airs of authority—your assumption of —of—everything. What you need is a good, old-fashioned, bread poultice woman! (CYNTHIA *comes to a full stop and faces* JOHN.)

JOHN (*sharply*). Can't say I've had any experience of the good, old-fashioned, bread poultice.

CYNTHIA. I don't care what you say! ·If you marry Vida Phillimore— You shan't do it. (*Tears of rage choking her*) No, I liked your father and for *his* sake, I'll see that his son doesn't make a donkey of himself a second time.

JOHN (*too angry to be amused*). Oh, I thought I was divorced. I begin to feel as if I had you on my hands still.

CYNTHIA. You have! You shall have! If you attempt to marry her, I'll follow you—and I'll find her—I'll tell Vida— (*He turns to her.*) I will. I'll tell Vida just what sort of a dance you led me.

JOHN (*quickly on her last word but speaking gravely*). Indeed! Will you? And *why* do you care what happens to me?

CYNTHIA (*startled by his tone*). I— I—ah—

JOHN (*insistently and with a faint hope*). *Why* do you *care?*

CYNTHIA. I don't. Not in your sense —

JOHN. How dare you then pretend—

CYNTHIA. I don't pretend.

JOHN (*interrupting her, proud, serious, and strong*). How dare you look me in the face with the eyes that I once kissed and pretend the least regard for me?

(CYNTHIA *recoils and looks away. Her own feelings are revealed to her clearly for the first time.*)

I begin to understand our American women now. Fireflies—and the fire they gleam with is so cold that a midge couldn't warm his heart at it, let alone a man. You're not of the same race as a man! You married me for nothing, divorced me for nothing, because you *are* nothing!

CYNTHIA (*wounded to the heart*). Jack! What are you saying?

JOHN (*with unrestrained emotion*). What—you feigning an interest in me, feigning a lie—and in five minutes— (*Gesture indicating altar*) Oh, you've taught me the trick of your sex—you're the woman who's not a woman!

CYNTHIA (*weakly*). You're saying terrible things to me.

JOHN (*low and with intensity*). You haven't been divorced from me long enough to forget—what you should be ashamed to remember.

CYNTHIA (*unable to face him and pretending not to understand him*). I don't know what you mean.

JOHN (*more forcibly and with manly emotion*). You're not able to forget me! You know you're not able to forget me; ask yourself if you are able to forget me, and when your heart, such as it is, answers "no," then—

(*The organ is plainly heard.*)

—well, then, prance gaily up to the altar and marry that, if you can!

(*He exits quickly.* CYNTHIA *crosses*

to armchair and sinks into it. She trembles as if she were overcome. Voices are heard speaking in the next room. Enter MATTHEW *and* MISS HENEAGE. *Enter* PHILIP. CYNTHIA *is so sunk in the chair they do not see her.* MISS HENEAGE *goes up to sofa back and waits. They all are dressed for an evening reception and* PHILIP *in the traditional bridegroom's rig.*)

MATTHEW (*as he enters*). I am sure you will do your part, Sarah—in a spirit of Christian decorum. (*To* PHILIP) It was impossible to find my surplice, Philip, but the more informal the better.

PHILIP (*with pompous responsibility*). Where's Cynthia?

MATTHEW (*gives glance around room*). Ah, here's the choir! (*He goes to meet it. Choir boys come in very orderly; divide and take their places, an even number on each side of the altar of flowers.* MATTHEW *vaguely superintends.* PHILIP *gets in the way of the bell. Moves out of the way. Enter* THOMAS.) Thomas, I directed you— One moment, if you please. (*He indicates table and chairs.* THOMAS *hastens to move the chairs and the table against the wall.* PHILIP *comes down.*)

PHILIP (*looking for her*). Where's Cynthia?

(CYNTHIA *rises.* PHILIP *sees her when she moves and crosses toward her, but stops. The organ stops.*)

CYNTHIA (*faintly*). Here I am.

(MATTHEW *comes down. The organ plays softly.*)

MATTHEW (*coming to* CYNTHIA). Ah, my very dear Cynthia, I knew there was something. Let me tell you the words of the hymn I have chosen:

Enduring love, sweet end of strife
Oh, bless this happy man and wife!

I'm afraid you feel—eh—eh!

CYNTHIA (*desperately calm*). I feel awfully queer—I think I need a Scotch.

(*The organ stops.* PHILIP *remains uneasily at a little distance.* MRS. PHILLIMORE *and* GRACE *enter back slowly, as cheerfully as if they were going to hear the funeral service read. They remain near the doorway.*)

MATTHEW. Really, my dear, in the pomp and vanity—I mean—ceremony of this—this unique occasion, there should be sufficient exhilaration.

CYNTHIA (*as before*). But there isn't! (*She sits.*)

MATTHEW. I don't think my bishop would approve of—eh—anything *before!*

CYNTHIA (*too agitated to know how much she is moved*). I feel very queer.

MATTHEW (*piously sure that everything is for the best*). My dear child—

CYNTHIA. However, I suppose there's nothing for it—now—but—to—to—

MATTHEW. Courage!

CYNTHIA (*desperate and with sudden explosion*). Oh, don't speak to me. I feel as if I'd been eating gunpowder and the very first word of the wedding service would set it off!

MATTHEW. My dear, your indisposition is the voice of nature.

(CYNTHIA *speaks more rapidly and with growing excitement,* MATTHEW *going toward the choir boys.*)

CYNTHIA. Ah—that's it—nature!

(MATTHEW *shakes his head.*)

I've a great mind to throw the reins on nature's neck.

PHILIP. Matthew! (*He moves to take his stand for the ceremony.*)

MATTHEW (*looking at* PHILIP; *to* CYNTHIA). Philip is ready.

(PHILIP *comes down. The organ plays "The Wedding March."*)

CYNTHIA (*to herself, as if at bay*) Ready? Ready? Ready?

MATTHEW. Cynthia, you will take

Miss Heneage's arm.

(MISS HENEAGE *comes down near table.*)

Sarah! (MATTHEW *indicates to* MISS HENEAGE *where* CYNTHIA *is.* MISS HENEAGE *advances a step or two.* MATTHEW *goes up and speaks in a low voice to choir.*) Now please don't forget, my boys. When I raise my hands so, you begin, "Enduring love; sweet end of strife."

(CYNTHIA *has risen. On the table is her long lace cloak. She stands by this table.* MATTHEW *assumes sacerdotal importance and takes his position inside the altar of flowers.*) Ahem! Philip! (*He indicates to* PHILIP *that he take his position.*) Sarah!

(CYNTHIA *breathes fast and supports herself on table.* MISS HENEAGE *goes toward her and stands for a moment looking at* CYNTHIA.) The ceremony will now begin.

(*The organ plays Mendelssohn's "Wedding March."* CYNTHIA *turns and faces* MISS HENEAGE. MISS HENEAGE *comes to* CYNTHIA *slowly and extends her hand in her readiness to lead the bride to the altar.*)

MISS HENEAGE. Mrs. Karslake!

PHILIP. Ahem!

(MATTHEW *steps forward two or three steps.* CYNTHIA *stands turned to stone.*)

MATTHEW. My dear Cynthia. I request you—to take your place.

(CYNTHIA *moves one or two steps across as if to go up to the altar. She takes* MISS HENEAGE's *hand, and slowly they walk toward* MATTHEW.) Your husband-to-be—is ready, the ring is in my pocket. I have only to ask you the—eh—necessary questions —and—eh—all will be blissfully over in a moment.

(*The organ is louder.*)

CYNTHIA (*at this moment, just as she reaches* PHILIP, *she stops, faces round, looks him,* MATTHEW, *and the rest in the face and cries out in despair*). Thomas! Call a hansom!

(THOMAS *exits and leaves door open.* MISS HENEAGE *crosses the stage.* MRS. PHILLIMORE *rises.* CYNTHIA *grasps her cloak on table.* PHILIP *turns and* CYNTHIA *comes forward and stops.*) I can't, Philip—I can't.

(*Whistle of hansom is heard off; the organ stops.*) It is simply a case of throwing the reins on nature's neck—up anchor— and sit tight!

(MATTHEW *crosses to* CYNTHIA.) Matthew, don't come near me! Yes, yes, I distrust you. It's your business, and you'd marry me if you could.

PHILIP (*watching her in dismay as she throws on her cloak*). Where are you going?

CYNTHIA. I'm going to Jack.

PHILIP. What for?

CYNTHIA. To stop his marrying Vida. I'm blowing a hurricane inside, a horrible, happy hurricane! I know myself—I know what's the matter with me. If I married you and Miss Heneage—what's the use of talking about it—he mustn't marry that woman. He shan't.

CYNTHIA (*has now all her wraps on; goes up rapidly; to* PHILIP). Sorry! So long! Good night and see you later. CYNTHIA *goes to door rapidly.*)

(MATTHEW, *in absolute amazement, throws up his arms.* PHILIP *is rigid.* MRS. PHILLIMORE *sinks into a chair.* MISS HENEAGE *is supercilious and unmoved.* GRACE *is the same. The choir, at* MATTHEW's *gesture, mistakes it for the concerted signal and bursts lustily into the Epithalamium.*)

Enduring love, sweet end of strife
Oh, bless this happy man and wife!

ACT FOUR

The scene is laid in JOHN KARS-LAKE's *study and smoking room. There is a bay window on the right. A door on the right leads to stairs and the front door of house, while a door at the back leads to the dining room. A fireplace is on the left and a mantel. A bookcase contains law books and sporting books. A full-length portrait of* CYNTHIA *is on the wall. Nothing of this portrait is seen by the audience except the gilt frame and a space of canvas. A large table with writing materials is littered over with law books, sporting books, papers, pipes, crops, and a pair of spurs. A wedding ring lies on it. There are three very low easy chairs. The general appearance of the room is extremely gay and garish in color. It has the easy confusion of a man's room. There is a small table on which is a woman's sewing basket. The sewing basket is open. A piece of rich fancywork lies on the table, as if a lady had just risen from sewing. On the corner are a lady's gloves. On a chair back is a lady's hat. It is a half hour later than the close of Act Three. Curtains are drawn over the window. A lamp on the table is lighted. Electric lights about the room are also lighted. One chair is conspicuously standing on its head.*

Curtain rises on NOGAM, *who busies himself at a table at the back. The door at the back is half open.*

SIR WILFRID (*coming in door*). Eh—what did you say your name was?

NOGAM. Nogam, sir.

SIR WILFRID. Nogam? I've been here thirty minutes. Where are the cigars?

(NOGAM *motions to a small table near the entrance door where the cigars are.*)

Thank you. Nogam, Mr. Karslake was to have followed us here immediately. (*He lights a cigar.*)

NOGAM. Mr. Karslake just now phoned from his club—

(SIR WILFRID *comes down the stage.*)

—and he's on his way home, sir.

SIR WILFRID. Nogam, why is that chair upside down?

NOGAM. Our orders, sir.

VIDA (*speaking as she comes on*). Oh, Wilfrid! (SIR WILFRID *turns.* VIDA *comes slowly down the stage.*) I can't be left longer alone with the lobster! He reminds me too much of Phillimore!

SIR WILFRID. Karslake's coming; stopped at his club on the way! (*To* NOGAM) You haven't heard anything of Mrs. Karslake—?

NOGAM (*surprised*). No, sir!

SIR WILFRID (*in an aside to* VIDA, *as they move to appear to be out of* NOGAM's *hearing*). Deucedly odd, ye know—for the Reverend Matthew declared she left Phillimore's house before *he* did—and she told him she was coming here!

(NOGAM *evidently takes this in.*)

VIDA. Oh, she'll turn up.

SIR WILFRID. Yes, but I don't see how the Reverend Phillimore had the time to get here and make us man and wife, don't y'know—

VIDA. Oh, Matthew had a fast horse and Cynthia a slow one—or she's a woman and changed her mind! Perhaps she's gone back and married Phillimore. And besides, dear, Matthew wasn't in the house four minutes and a half; only just long enough to hoop the hoop. (*She twirls her new wedding ring gently about her finger.*) Wasn't it lucky he had a ring in his pocket?

SIR WILFRID. Rather.

VIDA. And are you aware, dear, that Phillimore bought and intended it for Cynthia? Do come, (*She goes up to the door through which she entered.*) I'm desperately hungry! Whenever I'm married that's the effect it has! (VIDA *goes out.* SIR WILFRID *sees her through door but stops to speak to* NOGAM.)

SIR WILFRID. We'll give Mr. Karslake ten minutes, Nogam. If he does not come then, you might serve supper. (*He follows* VIDA.)

NOGAM (*to* SIR WILFRID). Yes, sir. (*Door opens.*)

FIDDLER (*enters; easy and business-like*). Hello, Nogam, where's the guv'nor? That mare's off her oats, and I've got to see him.

NOGAM. He'll soon be here.

FIDDLER. Who was the parson I met leaving the house?

NOGAM (*whispering*). Sir Wilfrid and Mrs. Phillimore have a date with the guv'nor in the dining room, and the reverend gentleman— (*He makes a gesture as of giving an ecclesiastical blessing.*)

FIDDLER (*amazed*). He hasn't spliced them?

(NOGAM *assents.*) He has? They're married? Never saw a parson could resist it!

NOGAM. Yes, but I've got another piece of news for you. Who do you think the Reverend Phillimore expected to find *here?*

FIDDLER (*proud of having the knowledge*). Mrs. Karslake? I saw her headed this way in a hansom with a balky horse only a minute ago. If she hoped to be in at the finish— (FIDDLER *is about to set chair on its legs.*)

NOGAM (*quickly*). Mr. Fiddler, sir, please to let it alone.

FIDDLER (*putting chair down in surprise*). Does it live on its blooming head?

NOGAM. Don't you remember? *She* threw it on its head when she left here, and he won't have it up. Ah,

that's it—hat, sewing basket, and all —the whole rig is to remain as it was when she handed him his knockout.

(*A bell rings outside.*)

FIDDLER. There's the guv'nor—I hear him!

NOGAM. I'll serve the supper. (*Taking letter from pocket and putting it on mantel*) Mr. Fiddler, would you mind giving this to the guv'nor? It's from his lawyer—his lawyer couldn't find him and left it with me. He said it was very important. (*Bell rings again. Speaking off to* SIR WILFRID.) I'm coming, sir! (NOGAM *goes out and shuts door.*)

(*Enter* JOHN KARSLAKE. *He looks downhearted, his hat is pushed over his eyes. His hands are in his pockets. He enters slowly and heavily. He sees* FIDDLER, *who salutes, forgetting the letter.* JOHN *slowly sits in armchair at the study table.*)

JOHN (*speaking as he walks to his chair*). Hello, Fiddler! (*Pause.* JOHN *throws himself into chair, keeping his hat on. Throws down his gloves, sighing.*)

FIDDLER. Came in to see you, sir, about Cynthia K.

JOHN (*drearily*). Damn Cynthia K!

FIDDLER. Couldn't have a word with you?

JOHN (*grumpy*). No!

FIDDLER. Yes, sir.

JOHN. Fiddler.

FIDDLER. Yes, sir.

JOHN. Mrs. Karslake—

(FIDDLER *nods.*) You used to say she was our mascot?

FIDDLER. Yes, sir.

JOHN. Well, she's just married herself to a—a sort of a man!

FIDDLER. Sorry to hear it, sir.

JOHN. Well, Fiddler, between you and me, we're a pair of idiots.

FIDDLER. Yes, sir.

JOHN. And now it's too late!

FIDDLER. Yes, sir—oh, beg your pardon, sir—your lawyer left a letter.

JOHN (*takes the letter, opens it, and reads it, indifferently at first; as he opens letter*). What's he got to say, more than what his wire said? Eh— (*As he reads, he is dumfounded.*) — what? Will explain. Error in wording of telegram. Call me up. (*Turning to telephone quickly*) The man can't mean that she's still— Hello! Hello! (JOHN *listens.*)

FIDDLER. Would like to have a word with you, sir—

JOHN. Hello, Central!

FIDDLER. That mare—

JOHN (*looks at letter, speaks into phone*). 33246a-38! Did you get it?

FIDDLER. That mare, sir, she's got a touch of malaria—

JOHN (*at the phone*). Hello, Central —33246a-38 — Clayton Osgood—yes, yes, and say, Central, get a move on you!

FIDDLER. If you think well of it, sir, I'll give her a tonic—

JOHN (*still at the phone*). Hello! Yes—yes—Jack Karslake. Is that you, Clayton? Yes—yes—well—

FIDDLER. Or if you like, sir, I'll give her—

JOHN (*turning on* FIDDLER). Shut up! (*To phone*) What was that? Not you—not you—a technical error? You mean to say that Mrs. Karslake is still —my— Hold the wire, Central—get off the wire! Get off the wire! Is that you, Clayton? Yes, yes—she and I are still— I got it! Good-by! (*He hangs up the receiver and falls back in the chair. For a moment he is overcome. He takes up the telephone book.*)

FIDDLER. All very well, Mr. Karslake, but I must know if I'm to give her a—

JOHN (*turning over the leaves of the telephone book in hot haste*). What's Phillimore's number?

FIDDLER. If you've no objections, I think I'll give her a—

JOHN (*as before*). L—M—N—O—P — It's too late! She's married by this! Married—and—my God—I—I am the cause. Phillimore—

FIDDLER. I'll give her—

JOHN. Give her Wheatena—give her Grape-Nuts—give her away! (FIDDLER *moves away.*) Only be quiet! Phillimore!

SIR WILFRID (*enters*). Hello! We'd almost given you up!

JOHN (*still in his agitation unable to find* PHILLIMORE's *number*). Just a moment! I'm trying to get Phillimore on the phone to—to tell Mrs. Karslake—

SIR WILFRID. No good, my boy—she's on her way here!

(JOHN *drops book and looks up dumfounded.*)

The Reverend Matthew was here, y'see —and he said—

JOHN (*rising, he turns*). Mrs. Karslake is coming here?

(SIR WILFRID *nods.*)

To this house? Here?

SIR WILFRID. That's right.

JOHN. Coming here? You're sure?

(SIR WILFRID *nods assent.*)

Fiddler, I want you to stay here, and if Mrs. Karslake comes, don't fail to let me know! Now then, for heaven's sake, what did Matthew say to you?

SIR WILFRID. Come along in and I'll tell you.

JOHN. On your life now, Fiddler, don't fail to let me—

(*Exeunt* JOHN *and* SIR WILFRID.)

VIDA (*voice off*). Ah, here you are!

FIDDLER. Phew!

(*There is a moment's pause, and* CYNTHIA *enters. She comes in very quietly, almost shyly, and as if she were uncertain of her welcome.*)

CYNTHIA. Fiddler! Where is he? Has he come? Is he here? Has he gone?

FIDDLER (*rattled*). Nobody's gone, ma'am, except the Reverend Matthew Phillimore.

CYNTHIA. Matthew? He's been here and gone?

(FIDDLER *nods assent.*)

You don't mean I'm too late? He's married them already?

FIDDLER. Nogam says he married them!

CYNTHIA. He's married them! Married! Married before I could get here! (*Sitting in armchair*) Married in less time than it takes to pray for rain! Oh, well, the church—the church is a regular quick marriage counter.

(*Voices of* VIDA *and* JOHN *heard in lighthearted laughter.*)

Oh!

FIDDLER. I'll tell Mr. Karslake—

CYNTHIA (*rising and going to the door through which* JOHN *left the stage; she turns the key in the lock and takes it out*). No—I wouldn't see him for the world! (*She comes down with key to the worktable.*) If I'm too late, I'm too late, and that's the end of it! (*She lays key on table and remains standing near it.*) I've come and now I'll go! (*Long pause.* CYNTHIA *looks about the room and changes her tone.*) Well, Fiddler, it's all a good deal as it used to be in my day.

FIDDLER. No, ma'am—everything changed, even the horses.

CYNTHIA (*absent-mindedly*). Horses—how are the horses? (*Throughout this scene she gives the idea that she is saying good-by to her life with* JOHN.)

FIDDLER. Ah, when husband and wife splits, ma'am, it's the horses that suffer. Oh yes, ma'am, we're all changed since you give us the go-by—even the guv'nor.

CYNTHIA. How's he changed?

FIDDLER. Lost his sharp for horses, and ladies, ma'am—gives 'em both the boiled eye.

CYNTHIA. I can't say I see any change; there's my portrait—I suppose he sits and pulls faces at me.

FIDDLER. Yes, ma'am, I think I'd better tell him of your bein' here.

CYNTHIA (*gently but decidedly*). No, Fiddler, no! (*She again looks about her.*) The room's in a terrible state of disorder. However, your new mistress will attend to that. (*Pause*) Why, that's not her hat!

FIDDLER. Yours, ma'am.

CYNTHIA. Mine! (*She goes to the table to look at it.*) Is that my workbasket? (*Pause*) My gloves?

(FIDDLER *assents.*)

And I suppose— (*She hurriedly goes to the writing table.*) My—yes, there it is: my wedding ring—just where I dropped it! Oh, oh, oh, he keeps it like this—hat, gloves, basket, and ring, everything just as it was that crazy, mad day when I— (*Glances at* FIDDLER *and breaks off.*) But for heaven's sake, Fiddler, set that chair on its feet!

FIDDLER. Against orders, ma'am.

CYNTHIA. Against orders?

FIDDLER. You kicked it over, ma'am, the day you left us.

CYNTHIA. No wonder he hates me with the chair in that state! He nurses his wrath to keep it warm. So, after all, Fiddler, everything is changed, and that chair is the proof of it. I suppose Cynthia K is the only thing in the world that cares a whinny whether I'm alive or dead. (*She breaks down and sobs.*) How is she, Fiddler?

FIDDLER. Off her oats, ma'am, this evening.

CYNTHIA. Off her oats! Well, she loves me, so I suppose she will die, or change, or—or something. Oh, she'll die, there's no doubt about that—she'll die.

(FIDDLER, *who has been watching his*

chance, takes the key off the table while she is sobbing, tiptoes up the stage, unlocks the door, and goes out. After he has done so, CYNTHIA *rises and dries her eyes.*)
There—I'm a fool—I must go—before —before—he— (*As she speaks her last word* JOHN *comes on.*)

JOHN. Mrs. Karslake!

CYNTHIA (*confused*). I—I—I just heard Cynthia K was ill—(JOHN *assents.* CYNTHIA *tries to put on a cheerful and indifferent manner.*) I—I ran round—I—and—and— (*Pausing, she turns and comes down.*) Well, I understand it's all over.

JOHN (*cheerfully*). Yes, it's all over.

CYNTHIA. How is the bride?

JOHN. Oh, she's a wonder.

CYNTHIA. Indeed! Did she paw the ground like the war horse in the Bible? I'm sure when Vida sees a wedding ring she smells the battle afar off. As for you, my dear Karslake, I should have thought once bitten, twice shy! But, you know best.

VIDA (*enters*). Oh, Cynthia, I've just been through it again, and I feel as if I were eighteen. There's no use talking about it, my dear, with a woman it's never the second time! And how nice you were, Jack, he never even laughed at us!

(*Enter* SIR WILFRID *with hat and cane.* VIDA *kisses* JOHN.)
That's the wages of virtue!

SIR WILFRID (*in time to see her kiss* JOHN). I say, is it the custom? Every time she does that, my boy, you owe me a thousand pounds. (*Seeing* CYNTHIA, *who approaches them, he looks at her and* JOHN *in turn.*) Mrs. Karslake. (*To* JOHN) And then you say it's not an extraordinary country.

(CYNTHIA *is more and more puzzled.*)

VIDA (*to* JOHN). See you next Derby,

Jack. (*Crossing to door. To* SIR WILFRID) Come along, Wilfrid! We really ought to be going. (*To* CYNTHIA) I hope, dear, you haven't married him! Phillimore's a tomb! Good-by, Cynthia —I'm so happy! (*As she goes*) Just think of the silly people, dear, that only have this sensation once in a lifetime! (*Exit* VIDA. JOHN *follows* VIDA *off.*)

SIR WILFRID (*to* CYNTHIA). Good-by, Mrs. Karslake. And I say, ye know, if you have married that dull old Phillimore fellah, why, when you've divorced him, come over and stay at Traynham! I mean, of course, ye know, bring your new husband. There'll be lots of horses to show you and a whole covey of jolly little Cates-Darbys. Mind you come! (*With real delicacy of feeling and forgetting his wife.*) Never liked a woman as much in my life as I did you!

VIDA (*outside, calling him*). Wilfrid, dear!

SIR WILFRID (*loyal to the woman who has caught him*). Except the one that's calling me!

(*Re-enter* JOHN. SIR WILFRID *nods to him and goes off.* JOHN *shuts the door and crosses the stage. A pause.*)

CYNTHIA. So you're not married?

JOHN. No. But I know that you imagined I was. (*Pause.*)

CYNTHIA. I suppose you think a woman has no right to divorce a man —and still continue to feel a keen interest in his affairs?

JOHN. Well, I'm not so sure about that, but I don't quite see how—

CYNTHIA. A woman can be divorced —and still— (JOHN *assents; she hides her embarrassment.*) Well, my dear Karslake, you've a long life before you in which to learn how such a state of mind is possible! So I won't stop to explain. Will you be kind enough to get me a cab? (*She moves to the door.*)

JOHN. Certainly. I was going to say I am not surprised at your feeling an interest in me. I'm only astonished that, having actually married Phillimore, you come here—

CYNTHIA (*indignantly*). I'm not married to him! (*A pause.*)

JOHN. I left you on the brink—made me feel a little uncertain.

CYNTHIA (*in a matter-of-course tone*).

I changed my mind—that's all.

JOHN (*taking his tone from her*). Of course. (*A pause*) Are you going to marry him?

CYNTHIA. I don't know.

JOHN. Does he know you—

CYNTHIA. I told him I was coming here.

JOHN. Oh! He'll turn up here, then —eh?

(CYNTHIA *is silent.*)

And you'll go back with him, I suppose?

CYNTHIA (*talking at random*). Oh—yes—I suppose so. I—I haven't thought much about it.

JOHN (*changing his tone*). Well, sit down; do. Till he comes—talk it over. (*He places the armchair more comfortably for her.*) This is a more comfortable chair!

CYNTHIA (*shamefacedly*). You never liked me to sit in that one!

JOHN. Oh well—it's different now. (CYNTHIA *crosses and sits down near the upset chair. There is a long pause.* JOHN *crosses the stage.*) You don't mind if I smoke?

CYNTHIA (*shaking her head*). No.

JOHN (*lights his pipe and sits on arm of chair*). Of course, if you find my presence painful, I'll—skiddoo. (*He indicates the door.* CYNTHIA *shakes her head.* JOHN *smokes pipe and remains seated.*)

CYNTHIA (*suddenly and quickly*). It's just simply a fact, Karslake, and that's all there is to it—if a woman has once been married—that is, the first man she marries—then—she may quarrel, she may hate him—she may despise him—but she'll always be jealous of him with other women. Always!

(JOHN *takes this as if he were simply glad to have the information.*)

JOHN. Oh— Hm! Ah—yes—yes. (*A pause.*)

CYNTHIA. You probably felt jealous of Phillimore.

JOHN (*reasonably, sweetly, and in doubt*). No-o! I felt simply: let him take his medicine. (*Apologetically.*)

CYNTHIA. Oh!

JOHN. I beg your pardon—I meant —

CYNTHIA. You meant what you said!

JOHN (*comes a step to her*). Mrs. Karslake, I apologize—I won't do it again. But it's too late for you to be out alone—Philip will be here in a moment—and of course, then—

CYNTHIA. It isn't what you *say*—it's —it's—it's everything. It's the entire situation. Suppose by any chance I don't marry Phillimore! And suppose I were seen at two or three in the morning leaving my former husband's house! It's all wrong. I have no business to be here! I'm going! You're perfectly horrid to me, you know—and—the whole place—it's so familiar, and so—so associated with—with—

JOHN. Discord and misery—I know—

CYNTHIA. Not at all with discord and misery! With harmony and happiness —with—with first love, and infinite hope—and—and—Jack Karslake, if you don't set that chair on its legs, I think I'll explode.

(JOHN *crosses the stage rapidly and sets chair on its legs. His tone changes.*)

JOHN (*while setting chair on its*

legs). There! I beg your pardon.

CYNTHIA (*nervously*). I believe I hear Philip. (*Rises.*)

JOHN (*going up to the window*). N-o! That's the policeman trying the front door! And now, see here, Mrs. Karslake—you're only here for a short minute, because you can't help yourself; but I want you to understand that I'm not trying to be disagreeable—I don't want to revive all the old unhappy—

CYNTHIA. Very well, if you don't—give me my hat. (JOHN *does so.*) And my sewing! And my gloves, please! (*She indicates the several ' articles which lie on the small table.*) Thanks! (CYNTHIA *throws the lot into the fireplace and returns to the place she has left near table.*) There! I feel better! And now—all I ask is—

JOHN (*laughs*). My stars, what a pleasure it is!

CYNTHIA. What is?

JOHN. Seeing you in a whirlwind!

CYNTHIA (*wounded by his seeming indifference*). Oh!

JOHN. No, but I mean a real pleasure! Why not? Time's passed since you and I were together—and—eh—

CYNTHIA. And you've forgotten what a vile temper I had!

JOHN (*reflectively*). Well, you did kick the stuffing out of the matrimonial buggy—

CYNTHIA (*pointedly but with good temper*). It wasn't a buggy; it was a break cart— (*She stands back of the armchair.*) It's all very well to blame me! But when you married me, I'd never had a bit in my mouth!

JOHN. Well, I guess I had a pretty hard hand. Do you remember the time you threw both your slippers out of the window?

CYNTHIA. Yes, and do you remember the time you took my fan from me

by force?

JOHN. After you slapped my face with it!

CYNTHIA. Oh, oh! I hardly touched your face! And do you remember the day you held my wrists?

JOHN. You were going to bite me!

CYNTHIA. Jack! I never! I showed my teeth at you! And I said I would bite you!

JOHN. Cynthia, I never knew you to break your word! (*He laughs casually.*) And anyhow—they were awfully pretty teeth!

(CYNTHIA, *though bolt upright, has ceased to seem pained.*) And I say—do you remember, Cyn— (*He leans over the armchair to talk to her.*)

CYNTHIA (*after a pause*). You oughtn't to call me Cyn—it's not nice of you. It's sort of cruel. I'm not—Cyn to you now.

JOHN. Awfully sorry; didn't mean to be beastly, Cyn. (CYNTHIA *turns quickly.* JOHN *stamps his foot.*) Cynthia! Sorry. I'll make it a commandment: thou shalt not Cyn!!

CYNTHIA (*laughs and wipes her eyes*). How can you, Jack? How can you?

JOHN. Well, hang it, my dear child, I—I'm sorry, but you know I always got foolish with you. Your laugh'd* make a horse laugh. Why, don't you remember that morning in the park before breakfast—when you laughed so hard your horse ran away with you!

CYNTHIA. I do, I do!

(*Both laugh. The door opens.* NOGAM *enters.*)

But what was it started me laughing? (*Laughing, sits down, and laughs again.*) That morning. Wasn't it somebody we met? (*Laughs.*) Wasn't it a man on a horse? (*Laughs.*)

* i.e., your laugh would.

JOHN (*laughing too*). Of course! You didn't know him in those days! But I did! And he looked a sight in the saddle!

(NOGAM, *trying to catch their attention, comes to right of table.*)

CYNTHIA. Who was it?

JOHN. Phillimore!

CYNTHIA. He's no laughing matter now. (*Sees* NOGAM.) Jack, he's here!

JOHN. Eh? Oh, Nogam?

NOGAM. Mr. Phillimore, sir—

JOHN. In the house?

NOGAM. On the street in a hansom, sir—and he requests Mrs. Karslake—

JOHN. That'll do, Nogam.

(*Exit* NOGAM. *Pause.* JOHN *from near the window.* CYNTHIA *faces audience.*) Well, Cynthia? (*He speaks almost gravely and with finality.*)

CYNTHIA (*trembling*). Well?

JOHN. It's the hour of decision; are you going to marry him? (*Pause*) Speak up!

CYNTHIA. Jack—I—I—

JOHN. There he is—you can join him. (*He points to the street.*)

CYNTHIA. Join Phillimore—and go home—with him—to his house, and Miss Heneage, and—

JOHN. The door's open. (*He points to the door.*)

CYNTHIA. No, no! It's mean of you to suggest it!

JOHN. You won't marry—

CYNTHIA. Phillimore—no. Never. (*Runs to window.*) No, never, never, Jack.

JOHN (*calls out of the window, having opened it*). It's all right, Judge. You needn't wait. (*Pause.* JOHN *comes down.* JOHN *bursts into laughter.* CYNTHIA *looks dazed. He closes door.*)

CYNTHIA. Jack!

(JOHN *laughs.*)

Yes, but I'm here, Jack.

JOHN. Why not?

CYNTHIA. You'll have to take me round to the Holland House!

JOHN. Of course I will! But, I say Cynthia, there's no hurry.

CYNTHIA. Why, I—I—can't stay here.

JOHN. No, of course you can't stay here. But you can have a bite, though. (CYNTHIA *shakes her head.* JOHN *places the small chair, which was upset, next to table.*) Oh, I insist. Just look at yourself—you're as pale as a sheet and—here, here. Sit right down. I insist! By George, you must do it! (CYNTHIA *crosses to chair beside table and sits.*)

CYNTHIA (*faintly*). I am hungry.

JOHN. Just wait a moment. (*Exits.*)

CYNTHIA. I don't want more than a nibble! (*Pause*) I am sorry to give you so much trouble.

JOHN. No trouble at all. (*He can be heard off the stage, busied with glasses and a tray.*) A hansom of course, to take you round to your hotel? (*Speaking as he comes down.*)

CYNTHIA (*to herself*). I wonder how I ever dreamed I could marry that man.

JOHN (*by table by this time*). Can't imagine! There!

CYNTHIA. I am hungry. Don't forget the hansom. (*She eats; he waits on her, setting this and that before her.*)

JOHN (*going to door; opens it and speaks off*). Nogam, a hansom at once.

NOGAM (*off stage*). Yes, sir.

JOHN (*back to above table; from here on he shows his feelings for her*) How does it go?

CYNTHIA (*faintly*). It goes all right. Thanks! (*Hardly eating at all.*)

JOHN. You always used to like anchovy. (CYNTHIA *nods and eats.*) Claret? (CYNTHIA *shakes her head.*) Oh, but you must!

CYNTHIA (*tremulously*). Ever so little. (*He fills her glass and then his.*) Thanks!

JOHN. Here's to old times. (*Raising glass.*)

CYNTHIA (*very tremulous*). Please not!

JOHN. Well, here's to your next husband.

CYNTHIA (*very tenderly*). Don't!

JOHN. Oh well, then, what shall the toast be?

CYNTHIA. I'll tell you— (*Pause*) — you can drink to the relation I am to you!

JOHN (*laughing*). Well—what relation are you?

CYNTHIA. I'm your first wife once removed!

JOHN (*laughing, he drinks*). I say, you're feeling better.

CYNTHIA. Lots.

JOHN (*reminiscent*). It's a good deal like those mornings after the races—isn't it?

CYNTHIA (*nodding*). Yes. Is that the hansom? (*Half rises.*)

JOHN (*going up to the window*). No.

CYNTHIA (*sitting again*). What is that sound?

JOHN. Don't you remember?

CYNTHIA. No.

JOHN. That's the rumbling of the early milk wagons.

CYNTHIA. Oh, Jack.

JOHN. Do you recognize it now?

CYNTHIA. Do I? We used to hear that —just at the hour, didn't we—when we came back from awfully jolly late suppers and things!

JOHN. H'm!

CYNTHIA. It must be fearfully late. I must go. (*She rises, croses to chair where she has left her cloak. She sees that JOHN will not help her and puts it on herself.*)

JOHN. Oh, don't go—why go?

CYNTHIA (*embarrassed and agitat-*

ed). All good things come to an end, you know.

JOHN. They don't need to.

CYNTHIA. Oh, you don't mean that! And, you know, Jack, if I were caught —seen at this hour, leaving this house, you know—it's the most scandalous thing anyone ever did my being here at all. Good-by, Jack! (*Pause; almost in tears.*) I'd like to say, I—I—I— well, I shan't be bitter about you here- after, and—(*Pause*) Thank you awful- ly, old man, for the fodder and all that! (*She turns to go out.*)

JOHN. Mrs. Karslake—wait—

CYNTHIA (*stopping to hear*). Well?

JOHN (*serious*). I've rather an ugly bit of news for you.

CYNTHIA. Yes?

JOHN. I don't believe you know that I have been testing the validity of the decree of divorce which you procured.

CYNTHIA. Oh, have you?

JOHN. Yes; you know I felt pretty warmly about it.

CYNTHIA. Well?

JOHN. Well, I've been successful. (*Pause*) The decree's been declared invalid. Understand?

CYNTHIA (*looking at him a moment; then speaking*). Not—precisely.

JOHN (*pause*). I'm awfully sorry— I'm awfully sorry, Cynthia, but you're my wife still. (*Pause.*)

CYNTHIA (*with rapture*). Honor bright? (*She sinks into the armchair.*)

JOHN (*nodding, half laughingly*). Crazy country, isn't it?

CYNTHIA (*nodding; pause*). Well, Jack—what's to be done?

JOHN (*gently*). Whatever you say.

NOGAM (*quietly enters*). Hansom, sir. (*Exits.* CYNTHIA *rises.*)

JOHN. Why don't you finish your supper?

CYNTHIA (*hesitates*). The — the — hansom—

JOHN. Why go to the Holland? After all—you know, Cyn, you're at home here.

CYNTHIA. No, Jack, I'm not at home here—unless—unless—

JOHN. Out with it!

CYNTHIA (*bursting into tears*). Unless I—unless I'm at home in your heart, Jack.

JOHN. What do you think?

CYNTHIA. I don't believe you want me to stay.

JOHN. Don't you?

CYNTHIA. No, no, you hate me still. You never can forgive me. I know you can't. For I can never forgive myself. Never, Jack, never, never! (*She sobs and he takes her in his arms.*)

JOHN (*very tenderly*). Cyn! I love you! (*Strongly*) And you've got to stay! And hereafter you can chuck chairs around till all's blue! Not a word now. (*He draws her gently to a chair.*)

CYNTHIA (*wiping her tears*). Oh, Jack! Jack!

JOHN. I'm as hungry as a shark. We'll nibble together.

CYNTHIA. Well, all I can say is, I feel that of all the improprieties I ever committed this—this—

JOHN. This takes the claret, eh? Oh, Lord, how happy I am!

CYNTHIA. Now don't say that! You'll make me cry more. (*She wipes her eyes.*)

JOHN (*takes out the wedding ring from his pocket; he lifts a wine glass, drops the ring into it and offers her the glass*). Cynthia!

CYNTHIA (*looking at it and wiping her eyes*). What is it?

JOHN. Benedictine!

CYNTHIA. Why, you know I never take it.

JOHN. Take this one for my sake.

CYNTHIA. That's not Benedictine. (*With gentle curiosity*) What is it?

JOHN (*slides the ring out of the glass and puts his arm about* CYNTHIA; *he slips the ring onto her finger and, as he kisses her hand, says*). Your wedding ring!

THE TRUTH

Clyde Fitch

Presented for the first time in Cleveland, Ohio,
on October 15, 1906; then at the Criterion
Theatre in New York on January 7, 1907.

WARDER

ROLAND

LINDON

SERVANT AT THE WARDERS'

BECKY WARDER

EVE LINDON

LAURA FRASER

MRS. GENEVIEVE CRESPIGNY

MESSENGER BOY

ACT ONE

At MRS. WARDER's, *New York. Thursday afternoon. An extremely attractive room, in the best of taste, with gray walls and dull soft-green moldings, old French chintz curtains, furniture painted to match the walls and covered with the same chintz. Some old colored engravings are on the mantelshelf, and a couple of eighteenth-century French portraits are on the wall. On the left is a mantel, and near it a large writing table against the back of a low sofa which faces the audience; on the table a telephone; an armchair and a small table on the left; a baby grand piano in the upper left corner of the room. Some consols and tables in the room; four windows at the back, through which one sees the park. Doors, right and left; books, photographs, flowers, etc., on the tables and consols.*

A smart, good-looking man-servant, JENKS, *shows in* MRS. LINDON *and* LAURA FRASER. *The former is a handsome, nervous, overstrung woman of about thirty-four, very fashionably dressed;* MISS FRASER, *on the contrary, a matter-of-fact, rather commonplace type of good humor—wholesomeness united to a kind sense of humor.* MRS. LINDON *is the sort of woman warranted to put any one on edge in the course of a few hours' consecutive association, while friction with* MISS FRASER *is equally certain to smooth down the raw edges.*

———

MRS. LINDON (*coming in to a chair near the center with quick determination*). You have no idea when Mrs. Warder will be in?

SERVANT. No, madam.

MRS. LINDON. She was lunching out?

SERVANT. Yes, madam.

LAURA (*with a movement to go*). Come! She may be playing bridge and not come home for hours.

MRS. LINDON (*firm, though irritable.*) I will wait till half-past five. (*To* SERVANT) If Mrs. Warder comes in before that, we will be here. (*Nervously she picks up a checkbook from the writing table, looks at it but not in it, and puts it down.*)

SERVANT. Very good, madam. (*Goes out.*)

LAURA (*goes to* MRS. LINDON). My dear, you must control yourself. That man, if he has half a servant's curiosity, could easily see you are excited.

MRS. LINDON. Yes, but think! She's been meeting Fred probably every day for the last two months, although she knew I had left his house, and always pretended to me she never saw him! (*Sitting beside the writing table.*)

LAURA (*sitting in a chair*). You shouldn't have come here at once. You should have waited till you had time to think over your information and calm yourself a little.

MRS. LINDON. I couldn't wait! Becky! One of my oldest friends! One of my bridesmaids!

LAURA. What!

MRS. LINDON. No, she wasn't, but she might have been; she was my next choice if any one had backed out.

LAURA. Probably Fred's appealing to her sympathy—you know your own husband!

MRS. LINDON (*with a disagreeable half-laugh*). Yes, I know him better than she does! What I don't like is her secrecy about it after I'd made her the confidante of my trouble!

LAURA. I thought *I* was that?

MRS. LINDON. You are—another! But you mustn't forget that I have gone to Becky in hysterics and begged her to make it up for me with Fred.

LAURA. Were you perfectly frank with her?

MRS. LINDON. Perfectly! I told her the truth, and more too! I told her I loved Fred in spite of his faults—Good Heavens! if a woman had to find a *faultless* man to love!—I've asked her advice. (*Rising nervously and going to the sofa.*)

LAURA. You haven't taken it!

MRS. LINDON. That doesn't make any difference! Who ever does? (*Sitting on the sofa*) She *owed* me her loyalty instead of flirting with Fred behind my back. (*She opens the cigar box on the writing table behind her and then bangs it shut.*)

LAURA. Perhaps she's really trying to make peace between you in her own way!

MRS. LINDON. Does it look like it? Actually telling me yesterday she wouldn't trust herself in his presence for fear she'd lose her control and tell him what she thought of him!—and all the time she had an appointment to meet him this afternoon—in the *Eden Musée*, if you please!

LAURA (*with comic disgust*). Oh! Horrors!

MRS. LINDON. Yes, in the chamber of them! If that isn't compromising!

LAURA. Eve!

MRS. LINDON. And Tom Warder so nice! Everybody likes him! (*Picks up stamp box and bangs it down.*)

LAURA. Including Becky. That's the point. Becky *loves* her own husband. What does she want of yours?

MRS. LINDON. She loved Tom Warder when she married him, but that was in 1903! Besides, Becky always liked having men fond of her whether she cared for them or not.

LAURA. Nonsense!

MRS. LINDON. She's what the French call an *allumeuse*—leads them on till they lose their heads, then she gets frightened and feels insulted!

LAURA. But you claim she *does* care for Fred!

MRS. LINDON. My dear, a magnetic man like Fred has a way of winding himself around a woman and keeping himself wound as long as he wishes! even when *she doesn't* wish—look at me! I'd give anything to throw him off for good, but I can't stop being in love with him!

LAURA (*who has moved over to the chair beside the sofa, pats* EVE's *hand*). Poor old Eve! Well, when she comes, what are you going to do?

MRS. LINDON. Give her one more chance to tell me the truth! I'll ask her outright when she saw Fred last.

LAURA. But if she keeps on with her "bluff" of not seeing him, you can't tell her she lies without making a horrid scene, and what good would that do?

MRS. LINDON. Exactly! She'd never acknowledge she was lying but just go on! I may appeal to Tom Warder himself! (*Rises and goes to mantel, looking at the flyleaves of two books on a table which she passes.*)

LAURA. No!

MRS. LINDON. Why not? We've been friends since babies.

LAURA. You *wouldn't!*

MRS. LINDON. I don't accuse Becky of anything dreadful! Besides, it will be for his good too, as well as mine—he knows Fred, and I'll wager anything he'll be as eager as I to stop any excess of friendship with him. (*Goes up to the window.*) Sh! here she is! and a man with her!

LAURA (*rises, excited, and joins her*). Who?

MRS. LINDON (*going to the other window*). I can't see.

LAURA (*joining her at the second window*). Suppose it should be—

MRS. LINDON. Exactly! If she hears I'm here, she'll never let him in. (*She starts with a new idea and goes to the door.*) The window in that hall juts out; perhaps we can see the front door from there. Come quickly! (*Tries to pull* LAURA *out.*)

LAURA. I don't approve of what you're doing at all.

MRS. LINDON. Oh, come!

(LAURA *and* EVE *go out and close the door behind them. The* SERVANT *shows in* BECKY *and* LINDON. BECKY *is a pretty, charming, volatile young woman, sprightly, vivacious, lovable. She is dressed ultrasmartly and in the best of taste.* LINDON *is dapper, rather good-looking, though not particularly strong in character, and full of a certain personal charm. He also wears very fashionable clothes. He is a man whose chief aim in life is to amuse himself.*)

SERVANT. Mrs. Lindon and Miss Fraser were waiting to see you, madam; they must have gone.

BECKY (*with a humorous raising of the eyebrows and a look to* LINDON). Oh!—I'm so sorry!

(*The* SERVANT *goes out.*)

LINDON. Gee! what a narrow escape.

LAURA (*off stage, pleading loudly*). Eve! Eve!! Come!!!

MRS. LINDON (*offstage, loudly*). I will not. I will run my own affairs my own way.

BECKY (*who has heard this, with an amused, mischievous expression*). They are there! Do you suppose they saw you?

(*They lower their voices slightly.*)

LINDON. Well—Eve can see through most things, but not through the walls! Good-by. (*He starts to hurry out, but* BECKY *stops him.*)

BECKY. You must come back! That's what I brought you home with me today for—to talk about Eve. This es-trangement has gone on long enough. I've come to the conclusion you're as much to blame as she is—or more.

LINDON. I like *that* from *you!*

BECKY. I mean it, and if she wants you back, you've got to go.

LINDON. Well, let me get a cocktail first.

BECKY. I'm serious.

LINDON. So'll I be if Eve comes in and catches me. (*Going.*)

BECKY (*going with him*). I'll let you out—but I expect you here again in half an hour. Do you understand? (*They go out. Offstage*) You're to come back at six.

LINDON (*offstage, at a distance*). All right.

(MRS. LINDON *comes in excitedly.*)

MRS. LINDON. I think it is Fred! Watch from the window! I'll stay here in case Becky comes in. (*She comes to the writing table.*) I'd like to scratch her eyes out!

LAURA (*comes in and goes to the sofa*). It *was* Fred.

MRS. LINDON (*gives a tigerish, half-controlled, hushed cry of rage*). The wretched little beast!

BECKY (*comes in with a start of surprise; she beams*). My dears! What a pleasant surprise! Why didn't Jenks tell me? Where in the world did you drop from? Laura, darling! (*She kisses* LAURA, *who is very unresponsive, having pressed* MRS. LINDON's *hand as she passed her.*)

MRS. LINDON. We heard you come in —we thought *with* some one—and as I'm rather upset, we went in there till you should be alone. If you are busy, don't let us interrupt.

BECKY (*shows that she is relieved when she hears they don't know* FRED *was there*). Oh, dear, no, I'm not busy. I came home alone—you must have heard me talking with the servant. I've been playing bridge since luncheon. (BECKY *and* LAURA *sit on the sofa.*) MRS. LINDON. Where?

BECKY. Clara Ford's, our usual four.

(LAURA *and* MRS. LINDON *exchange glances.*)

MRS. LINDON. Why! I saw her lunching at Sherry's.

BECKY (*quickly, after only a second's hesitation*). Yes, she couldn't play today, but it was her turn at her house, so we went all the same—and—er—er—Belle Prescott took her place.

(*Another surreptitious look passes between* LAURA *and* MRS. LINDON.)

LAURA. Did you win?

BECKY. Yes, a hundred and fifty!

LAURA. A hundred and fifty? Good!

MRS. LINDON (*who has seated herself in the chair beside the sofa*). Becky, Laura knows all my troubles; she's the bosom I weep them out on.

BECKY. Oh, come, I've gathered a few dewey diamonds off my laces! Well, how is Fred behaving? Has he shown any sign yet?

MRS. LINDON. Not one. I thought perhaps you'd have some news.

BECKY (*looking away*). I? How should I have? (*She leans over and smooths her skirt.* MRS. LINDON *exchanges a look with* LAURA.)

MRS. LINDON. You said two days ago for me to keep silent and wait, and Fred would make an advance.

BECKY. And so he will, I'm sure! unless you do what you threatened. (*To* LAURA) I tell Eve if she starts a suit for separation or does anything of that sort publicly, Fred may be furious and accept the situation, no matter how much of a bluff it might be on Eve's part.

LAURA. Very likely.

MRS. LINDON. I thought perhaps you meant to see Fred and have a talk with him?

BECKY. No! (MRS. LINDON *and* LAURA *exchange glances, as* BECKY, *rising, rings bell.*) What good would that do? To have the reconciliation mean anything it must be of his own volition. He must come for you, Eve, because he misses you, because he wants you back. (MRS. LINDON *joins* LAURA *on the sofa and talks in a loud and excited whisper to her as to* BECKY's *very evident prevarication.* SERVANT *enters;* BECKY *speaks to him aside, amusedly watching them, and then comes above table. As she comes back*) Well?

MRS. LINDON. I believe there's another woman in it!

BECKY (*laughing*). I knew she was jealous! (*To* MRS. LINDON) That's just the sort of thing that has made quarrels all along between you and Fred. (*She comes to her.*)

MRS. LINDON. Well, if you knew all I've had to forgive Fred, and all I have forgiven, you'd realize I had good reason always for my share of the quarrels.

BECKY. Listen to me, Eve. You're a luckier woman than you know!

MRS. LINDON (*startled*). How do you mean?

(LAURA *puts her hand on* MRS. LINDON's *shoulder to calm her.*)

BECKY. Because, instead of having the forgiveness always on his side, you have the blessed privilege of doing the forgiveness yourself. (MRS. LINDON *gives a falsetto snort.*) You may smile if you like—

MRS. LINDON (*interrupting*). Oh, no, thank you. I don't feel at all like smiling!

BECKY. Well, honestly, I envy you. (*Takes* MRS. LINDON's *hands in hers.* MRS. LINDON *looks once at* LAURA *questioningly, and back again quickly to* BECKY.) You know I love Tom with my whole heart—and it's a big heart for a little woman—and yet I keep him forgiving me—forgiving me something or other all the time. I'd be afraid his forgiveness would wear out, only it's in his soul instead of his body, and if our bodies wear out, our souls *don't*— do they? Already at the very beginning of our life together I owe him more dear forgiveness than I can ever repay, and believe me, Eve, such a debt would be unbearable for a woman unless she *adored* her husband.

MRS. LINDON. You've too much sentiment—I'm practical.

BECKY (*sitting down in a chair*). Does being practical give you one half the happiness my "sentiment" gives me?

MRS. LINDON. Nonsense! My sympathies are with the one who has the forgiving to do.

BECKY. You mean, like all selfish people, you sympathize with yourself, so you'll never be happy, even if you get Fred back.

MRS. LINDON (*startled, angry*). If? What do you mean by that? (*Looks at* BECKY, *then at* LAURA, *sharply, then back at* BECKY.)

BECKY (*smiling*). Say *when* instead! *when* you get Fred back. Trust me, teach yourself to be grateful that it is *you* who have to forgive, and not the other way round.

MRS. LINDON (*rises, facing* BECKY, *almost triumphantly, fully persuaded that she is in the wrong*). I knew when I came here you'd make excuses for him.

BECKY (*smiling*). You've misunderstood me. I'm *trying* to make them for you.

MRS. LINDON. Thank you. *You* need excuses more than I do.

LAURA (*rises, alarmed*). Eve!

MRS. LINDON. I am perfectly well aware that I made a very serious mistake in coming to *you* of all women!

BECKY (*rises*). In that case I think it best to consider the matter closed between us.

MRS. LINDON. You can think what you please, but I have no such intention!

LAURA. Eve! (*She sits again on the sofa.*) Really Becky has shown herself reasonable and kind, and you've said enough to-day. We'd better go.

BECKY. I should have to ask you to excuse me in any case, as I have an engagement in a few minutes.

MRS. LINDON (*looks meaningly at* LAURA, *to* BECKY). I intend to have the whole thing out now!

(WARDER *enters. He is a strong and sensible, unsuspicious man—no nerves and no "temperament," nothing subtle about him; he is straightforward and lovable.*)

WARDER. Oh, excuse me!

BECKY. No, come in, Tom; it's Laura and Mrs. Lindon.

(LAURA *and* MRS. LINDON *say "How do you do," as* WARDER *comes into the room. He greets them in turn.* BECKY *writes in pencil on a sheet of paper on the desk.*)

TOM. I wanted to ask Becky if she wished to go to a theatre to-night.

BECKY. Yes, I should like to. (*She indicates to* TOM *that she wants* MRS. LINDON *and* LAURA *to go, and having finished writing, comes to him.*) I'm sorry, but you really must excuse me. (*Slipping into* WARDER's *hand the note she had secretly written.*) Mrs. Lindon and Laura *are going.* What are *you* going to do now?

(MRS. LINDON *looks again meaningly at* LAURA.)

WARDER. I thought I'd go round to the club till dinner.

BECKY (*relieved*). That's right. I shall be engaged till half-past six—er— Mrs. Clayton is coming to see me about the Golf Club at Roslyn—and—lots of things. You needn't hurry back. (*She gives him an affectionate little squeeze of the arm and goes out. He looks down at the paper slyly and reads it.*)

MRS. LINDON (*rises and goes to* WARDER). Tom, if you've nothing in particular on at the club, would you give me half an hour?

LAURA (*rises and goes to* MRS. LINDON). Eve, you haven't the time yourself; you must come with me.

WARDER (*suppressing a smile as he finishes reading the note, he is a little embarrassed*). Well—really—Eve—I don't know—I'll tell you how it is—

MRS. LINDON. Oh, I don't mean here! I know Becky wrote you a note telling you not to let me stay, didn't she?

WARDER (*laughing*). She did—you see, she has an engagement. (*Reading from the paper, good-naturedly*) "Get rid of Eve, I want the room."

MRS. LINDON. At six o'clock. (*Glances meaningly at* LAURA.)

WARDER (*casually*). Is it?

MRS. LINDON. To see *Fred* in!

LAURA. Eve! be sensible!

WARDER. No, it's for Mrs. Clayton about Roslyn.

MRS. LINDON. Then why must she be rid of me? Georgia Clayton and I are the best of friends, and I have as much to do with Roslyn as Becky.

WARDER (*still pleasantly*). I suppose Becky has a good reason, if she cared to tell us.

MRS. LINDON. I *know* Becky has an appointment *here,* at *six,* with Fred.

LAURA. You don't *know* it, Eve!

MRS. LINDON. I *do.*

WARDER (*still pleasantly*). In any case that is Becky's and Fred's business, isn't it?

MRS. LINDON. You *know* Fred!

WARDER. Yes!

MRS. LINDON. Well?

WARDER. You don't want my opinion of Fred, at this late day! I also know Becky!

MRS. LINDON. Becky and Fred meet every single day.

LAURA (*interpolates*). She thinks so.

WARDER. What are you talking about?

MRS. LINDON. What I *know!* And if you'll wait here with me a few minutes now, in spite of what Becky said, you'll see *Fred* and not Mrs. Clayton arrive.

WARDER. If your husband is really coming, it was probably to spare you that Becky spoke of Mrs. Clayton, and I shouldn't think of embarrassing her by waiting.

MRS. LINDON (*disagreeably, irritatingly*). Oh, you don't mind, then?

WARDER. Almost any man, my dear Eve, would mind your husband meeting his wife every day! I only think you've been misinformed, or only half informed, that's all.

MRS. LINDON. You are aware that Fred and I have been separated for two months?

WARDER. Yes, Becky told me.

LAURA (*looking at her watch*). It's almost six now. Come, Eve.

WARDER (*going toward the door*). Yes, I'm afraid I must ask you— (*He rings the electric bell on wall beside the door.*)

MRS. LINDON (*going to him*). Tom, for the sake of our boy and girl friendship, walk home with me, and let me speak plainly.

LAURA (*on the other side of* WARDER). Mr. Warder, please don't go.

MRS. LINDON (*to* LAURA, *angry*). What do you mean? (*To* WARDER, *pleadingly*) I've no other man in the world to go to; I need advice. Won't you give me yours?

WARDER (*looks at her a moment, hes-*

itates, then says). My advice? Of course, if you wish that. (*The* SERVANT *appears in the doorway in answer to the bell. To* SERVANT) My hat and coat—and say to Mrs. Warder I'm walking home with Mrs. Lindon. (WARDER *goes out.*)

SERVANT. Yes, sir. (*Follows him out.*) (LAURA *looks significantly at* MRS. LINDON.)

LAURA. If you keep on, there soon won't be a soul left in New York whose advice you haven't asked and not taken!

MRS. LINDON. Well, it's my *own* trouble; I can do what I like with it. What are *you* going to do now? (*She sits in the armchair at the left.*)

LAURA (*going to her*). Don't tell him all you think you know about Becky.

MRS. LINDON. *Think!*

LAURA. It will be a very great mistake.

MRS. LINDON. Laura, I'll tell you the truth; I've had Fred watched by private detectives for over a month, and I have a list of dates and places of their meetings to more than prove what I say.

LAURA. How dreadful of you!

MRS. LINDON. Oh, wait till you get a husband, and then you'll sympathize more with a woman who is trying to keep one!

LAURA. But these places where they meet?

MRS. LINDON. Are respectable so far as I know. But *daily* meetings my dear, *daily!*

LAURA. And you'll tell Mr. Warder?

MRS. LINDON. I don't know yet how much I shall tell. What are you going to do now?

LAURA. Wait till tomorrow! Give yourself time to recover, to consider.

MRS. LINDON (*simply repeats*). What are you going to do now?

LAURA. Stay and see Becky.

MRS. LINDON (*rises, delighted*). Oh, do! Stay till Fred comes, and catch her!

LAURA. No, no! I've finished with this now. I don't sympathize with what you're going to do.

WARDER (*with hat and coat, in the doorway*). Ready?

MRS. LINDON. Yes.

WARDER. Good-by, Laura.

LAURA. Good-by. (MRS. LINDON *goes out with* WARDER. *After the outside door is heard to close,* BECKY *comes into the room hurriedly. She stops suddenly on seeing* LAURA, *turns and tries to steal out. Just as she gets to the door,* LAURA *catches her.*) Becky!

BECKY (*turns and their eyes meet; laughs, realizing she is caught*). Oh, you didn't go with them?

LAURA. No!

BECKY. Had enough of Eve to-day?

LAURA. Not enough of you.

BECKY (*sings instead of speaks*). "Thank you!" (*She puts her arm around* LAURA, *and they sit on the sofa.*)

LAURA. Becky, why won't you be frank with Eve?

BECKY. I was.

LAURA. No, you didn't tell the truth about seeing Fred.

BECKY. Oh, that!

LAURA. Yes, that!

BECKY. I may have seen him once or twice, that's all.

LAURA. Exactly what Eve says—you don't tell the truth!

BECKY. It's false! I never told a malicious lie in my life. I never told a fib that hurt anyone but myself!

LAURA. Tell Eve the truth. Make her have confidence in you. She says if you cross the ferry to Jersey City, you say you've been abroad.

BECKY (*laughing*). Well, so I *have!* Laura! I'm doing my best to make Eve happy. I can't do any more than my best, and if I do it at all, I must do it my own way!

LAURA. You've seen Fred today.

BECKY. No, I haven't.

LAURA. Becky! He came home with you just now!

BECKY. What makes you think so?

LAURA. I saw his back on the steps with you.

BECKY. Oh, I see—spying on me? Well, you made a mistake in the back.

LAURA. I know it was Fred Lindon.

BECKY. And I know it wasn't.

LAURA. You're not seeing him every day?

BECKY. Certainly not! But what affair is it of yours, if I do?

LAURA. We're all friends, and you're making Eve wildly jealous.

BECKY. That is entirely her own fault, not mine.

SERVANT (*enters, carrying a bill on a small silver tray*). Pardon me, madam, a man with a box and a bill to collect.

BECKY (*taking the bill*). A bandbox? (*She opens the bill.*)

SERVANT. Yes, madam.

BECKY (*to* LAURA). Oh, my dear, such a duck of a hat! And only sixty-five dollars. I saw it on my way here and couldn't resist buying. Are hats a passion with you?

LAURA (*uninterested*). Yes, rather.

BECKY. I told them to send it C.O. D., but I didn't suppose it would come till to-morrow and I haven't a cent!

LAURA. I thought you said you won a hundred and fifty at bridge?

BECKY. No, no, my dear, you misunderstood me, I lost. (*To* SERVANT) Tell the man if he can't leave the box, to take it back and call later; say Mrs. Warder is out.

SERVANT. Yes, madam. (*Goes out with the bill.*)

LAURA. You said you *won* at bridge!

BECKY. Oh, you tedious person! You hang on to anything like a terrier, don't you! I said I won because I didn't want Eve to think I'd lost; I never can bear to own up I've lost anything before Eve. (*Laughs, pulls* LAURA *by the arm.*) Good-by!

LAURA. I won't go yet.

BECKY (*urging her*). You must. I have an engagement.

LAURA. *With Fred Lindon!*

BECKY. It is not. (SERVANT *enters and announces "Mr. Lindon."* LINDON *follows. He is surprised to see* LAURA, *but instantly covers his surprise. Going to* LINDON, *quickly*) Oh, what a surprise!

LINDON. Surprise? Am I early?

BECKY (*indicating* LAURA). Sh! Yes, surprise. (LINDON *sees* LAURA *and makes an amused grimace.*) But I can only give you a very few minutes. I have an engagement, haven't I, Laura?

(LAURA *and* LINDON *shake hands.*)

LINDON. Oh, hello, Laura!

LAURA (*very dryly*). How d'you do, Fred?

LINDON. How's Eve?

LAURA (*embarrassed*). Very well—at least not very—yes, she is of course very well! (*Adds pointedly.*) She's just left here.

LINDON. Oh! sorry I missed her! Give her my regards when you see her, and say I'm glad she's well. (*He goes to the piano, sits on the bench, and plays.*)

LAURA (*rises indignant*). I shall do nothing of the kind. (*She starts to leave the room;* LINDON *runs what he is playing into "Good-by, Little Girl, Good-by."*)

BECKY (*offering her hand*). Good-by.

LAURA (*pretends not to see* BECKY's *hand*). Good-by. (*She goes out.*)

BECKY (*going to the piano*). They both saw you come back with me!

LINDON (*still playing, improvising;*

laughing). No! Did they?

BECKY (*laughing*). Yes, but it's no laughing matter! Eve is jealous.

LINDON (*stops playing*). What right has she? Did she expect me to sit alone in the drawing-room for two months straining my ears to hear her ring the front door bell? (*He continues playing.*)

BECKY. They know we've been meeting every day—at least they think so. *Have* we?

LINDON (*still playing*). No!

BECKY. Yes, we *have! Haven't* we?

LINDON (*stops playing*). Well, yes, if you want the truth.

BECKY (*goes to sofa and sits*). There's no use telling a story about it. I've nothing to be ashamed of—I did it with the best of motives.

LINDON (*goes to* BECKY). Oh, don't spoil it all, Becky, with motives! (*He leans over the arm of the sofa to talk to her.*)

BECKY (*laughs*). You know Eve mustn't be jealous of me!

LINDON (*earnestly*). Now you're not going to let her break up our little—

BECKY (*interrupting*). Fred, how much do you like me?

LINDON (*smiling*). I daren't tell you!

BECKY. No, I mean *really!*

LINDON. So do I!

BECKY. I believe you are fond of me.

LINDON. I am!

BECKY. And I like you to be.

LINDON (*placing his hand on hers on the sofa's arm*). Because?

BECKY (*slowly drawing her hand from his*). I like men to like me, even though it really means nothing.

LINDON (*rather chagrined*). Nothing?

BECKY (*amused*). I like it for myself, and besides I think it's a compliment to Tom!

LINDON (*mockingly*). Oh! Oh! I say!

Becky! (*He moves to the chair beside* BECKY *and, drawing it nearer, sits facing her.*)

BECKY. But with you there was a special reason.

LINDON (*is encouraged; draws a little nearer to her*). Yes?

BECKY. Of course you have perfectly understood why I've seen so much of you.

LINDON. You've been my friend.

BECKY. I've sympathized with you.

LINDON. You've been the only real glimpse of happiness I've had for months in my life.

BECKY. Don't be rhetorical! no man sounds sincere, when he talks pictures. I'll tell you why I wanted you to come back this afternoon.

LINDON (*taking her two hands*). To make me happy!

BECKY (*pulling her hands away, and patting his half seriously*). Yes (*He leans over toward her.*), by making you realize it's time you went to Eve and asked her to come back.

LINDON (*sinking back in his chair*). Nonsense; Eve's made a row and frightened you.

BECKY. How frightened me? I always meant when I'd got you where I wanted you, to influence you to make it up with Eve. She adores you!

LINDON. She has an odd way of showing it. (*He rises and leans against the mantel beside the sofa.*)

BECKY. You don't want every woman to show her love in the same way.

LINDON. I don't want any other woman to show me she loves me in Eve's way.

BECKY. Come now, you're unfair to Eve! I'm going to sympathize with her a little. Granted that she is jealous, granted that she doesn't always control her temper!—what woman worth while does!

LINDON (*laughing*). But she ought to trust me—as *you* do.

BECKY (*laughing*). Oh, I'm not your wife. I wouldn't trust you for a minute if I were married to you!

LINDON. How about Tom?

BECKY. Of course I trust Tom.

LINDON. And I trust Eve. (*Laughing.*)

BECKY. Oh! but it's not the same thing. You trust Eve because you don't care enough. I trust Tom because—well, in one little word, he is perfect and I adore him!

LINDON. Sounds boring!

BECKY. Eve's proved she loves you with a *big* love! She's proved it by forgiveness. That's the proof of a love it's not easy to get and even harder to deserve! You've got it— (*He moves toward her.*) we won't go into the deserving part! But if only half that she **says and one quarter of what everyone** else says of you is true, you ought to go on your knees to her in gratitude if she is willing to take you back.

LINDON (*sits on the arm of sofa, half laughing*). She will! She's left before.

BECKY. You love her, Fred?

LINDON (*casually*). No, I love you!

BECKY. Nonsense! I mean really! Promise me you'll go to Eve tomorrow and ask her to come back.

LINDON (*slides down on to sofa*). Not yet—give me another month!

BECKY. You'll lose her!

LINDON. No, there are certain things you can't lose—try as hard as you like!

BECKY. That isn't funny.

LINDON. She's been urging you to do this.

BECKY. Nothing of the sort! She's too proud. And she mustn't dream I've had anything to do with your going to her. No woman really wants to accept her happiness like a pauper at the Lady Bountiful hands of another woman. She might *think* she was grateful to me, but she wouldn't be! With a disposition like Eve's you'd have another quarrel inside a fortnight. No! Eve must think you've come to her spontaneously because you can't live without her. (*He whistles. She rises.*) You can whistle, but you'll never get another woman half so good to you as Eve! Make her think you want her back. Make *yourself* think you want her back, and you don't know how happy you'll be—first in making her happy, and second in finding you are yourself.

(*He takes hold of her hand; she draws it away quickly and sits in the armchair on the opposite side of the room.*)

LINDON. What are you doing away over there?

BECKY. Oh, I thought it was getting a little crowded on the sofa.

LINDON. And must I give up my visits with you?

BECKY. Of course.

LINDON. Oh, well, if that's the price, I don't want happiness; it costs too much!

BECKY. You won't need sympathy any more. You can write me a little note and say: "Becky, I thought I loved you, but it was only a heart being caught on the rebound. Thank you for being sensible and pitching the heart back! Thank you for seeing my real happiness was in making Eve happy."

LINDON. You know that doesn't sound like me!

BECKY. Not like your foolish *old you,* but like your sensible *new you,* who has found out you can have a woman friend without getting sued for damages—which has been your usual experience, I believe!

LINDON. Becky! Don't rob the graves!

BECKY. Well, will you go to Eve and beg her to come back?

LINDON (*rises*). No!

BECKY. Fred! The price of my friendship is your peace with Eve!

LINDON (*going to* BECKY). But if I consent, I may come to see you?

BECKY. Yes.

LINDON. Eve, my darling wife, forgive me! Come to my arms and stay there—for five minutes—consider it done! Where, tomorrow?

BECKY. The Metropolitan?

LINDON. No, let me come here tomorrow, and what time?

BECKY (*rises*). Four—but to say *Good-by!* (*She means it.*) *The* last visit!

LINDON. Oh! well, we won't cross that bridge till we come to it! and I'll make you a bet if you ever do send me away for good, do you know what will happen?

BECKY (*amused*). No, what?

LINDON. In a day or two you'd send for me to come again after all!

BECKY (*laughing*). Why?

LINDON. Because you like me better than you think you do!

BECKY (*going to the writing table*). Oh, really!!

LINDON (*following her*). Yes, really! and you know—though you may not acknowledge it to yourself, still you know just how strong my feeling is for you.

BECKY (*turning toward him*). But I do acknowledge it, and I am grateful and pleased to have you care for me. (*She pulls the chair beside the table in front of her.*)

LINDON (*pushing chair away*). "Care for you!"

BECKY (*pulling chair back*). Yes! and I want to show my appreciation by making you happy.

LINDON. Eve's jealousy has frightened you, but you'll forget it tomorrow!

BECKY (*really not understanding*).

How do you mean? (*She looks at him questioningly, innocently. He looks back knowingly with a half smile, not believing her. A pause.* WARDER *comes in left. He looks from one to the other, then speaks pleasantly.*)

WARDER. Oh! How are you, Lindon?

LINDON. Good evening, Warder.

(*Both men stand; on awkward pause.*)

BECKY (*sitting in the armchair*). Sit down, Tom.

(*He does so on the chair by the table.* LINDON *sits on the sofa. A moment's pause.*)

LINDON. Do you come up town generally as late as this?

WARDER. Oh, no, I've been up some time.

(*Second awkward pause.*)

BECKY. Did you get the theatre tickets?

WARDER. No, I forgot; I didn't go to the club, I'll telephone from here. (*Very casually*) Has Mrs. Clayton gone?

BECKY. Who?

WARDER. Mrs. Clayton. You said—

BECKY (*interrupting*). Mrs. Cl—? Oh! Yes! She's gone.

(*Awkward pause.*)

LINDON. Have you been to the club?

WARDER (*very casually*). No, I walked back with your wife to her mother's.

(*Awkward pause.* BECKY *and* LINDON *exchange glances.*)

LINDON (*half humorously*). I hear Eve is looking very well. (*Pause.*)

WARDER. By the way, will you have a whiskey and soda, a cocktail, or something?

BECKY. Or tea?

LINDON. Tea? poison to me! No, thanks, I must be getting on.

(*All rise; then, after a moment of embarrassment,* WARDER *speaks.*)

WARDER. Yes?

LINDON. I've an early, melancholy, bachelor's dinner at seven.

BECKY. It's your own fault! Think how well Eve looks in a dinner dress, and what a delightful hostess she always is.

LINDON. Yes, Eve's all right in a crowd! (*Shaking hands. To* WARDER) Forgive my domestic affairs intruding. Mrs. Warder has been kind enough to advise me a little! Good-by! (*Going.*)

WARDER. I'm sure her advice is good. You'd better take it!

LINDON. Perhaps!—but in homeopathic doses! (*To* BECKY) Good-by! (*To* WARDER) Bye, Warder. (*Laughing, he goes out.*)

(WARDER *and* BECKY, *alone, look at each other—*BECKY *questioningly,* WARDER *half puzzled.*)

BECKY. Well! Has Eve been weeping on *your* bosom, too?

WARDER. No, I think she *scratched* it, if she did anything!

BECKY (*half amused, half worried*). *How* do you mean? (*The* SERVANT *enters with a letter, which he gives to* BECKY.) When did this come?

SERVANT. A little while ago, but madam gave orders not to be interrupted. (*He goes out.*)

(WARDER *gives* BECKY *a quick, sharp look, which, however, she doesn't notice.*)

BECKY. From father! He can't want more money already!

WARDER. *You* sent him how much two days ago?

BECKY (*goes above the writing-table as she opens the letter*). *You* sent him, you generous darling, three hundred dollars. I had given him his allowance the beginning of the month.

WARDER. And gone already! Of course, he's been at the races this week! No more. Becky—is it true you've been seeing Lindon every day lately?

BECKY (*while she reads her letter*). No!—yes! (*Looks up at him.*) I mean no, certainly not!

WARDER (*smiling*). Which is it? or do I take my choice?

BECKY (*with a little laugh*). I've seen something of him. I'm sorry for him.—Father's in more trouble.

WARDER. That's an old story, and this is something new. Eve is jealous of you.

BECKY (*looks up at him*). Are you, of Fred Lindon?

WARDER. No!

BECKY (*goes quickly to him and kisses him and pushes him down on to the sofa*). Bless you! You're right, and that's my answer to Eve!—Father does want more money!

WARDER. We send no more till next month, not one penny. Come here! (*He makes her sit on the arm of the sofa beside him. She puts her arm about his neck and hugs him.* WARDER *continues.*) You haven't seen Lindon almost daily for the past month, have you?

BECKY. No.

WARDER. You haven't met him by appointment at the Metropolitan, *Eden Musée,* or any such places?

BECKY. Eve's jealousy gives her the most ridiculous ideas! When I have been with Mr. Lindon, it has been principally to talk about Eve, and entirely with the desire to try and reconcile them.

WARDER. Grant that! But it's not true about all these appointments?

BECKY. No!

WARDER (*with his arm about her waist*). I believe you love me better than all the world?

BECKY. Than all the world, and every world, and all the planets put together, Mars, Saturn, and Venus. Yes. I love you *even* more than Venus! (*Laughing and giving him another caress.*)

WARDER. I have every confidence in you and your motives. But I have none in Lindon's—so I want today's visit to be his last, my dear.

BECKY (*rising, a little uncomfortable*). All right.

WARDER. Own up, now, hasn't he tried to make love to you?

BECKY (*leaning on the back of the chair, facing him*). No!

WARDER. Not a bit?

BECKY (*smiling*). Well—maybe—just a tiny bit—but not in earnest.

WARDER (*rising, angrily*). I was sure of it! the damn puppy! Becky, I've heard him swear there's no such thing as a decent woman if a man goes about it in the right way!

BECKY. Oh, you men are always hard on another man whom women like.

WARDER. I know what I'm talking about *this* time, and you don't.

BECKY (*with dignity*). I judge by his behavior to me. He may have led me to believe he likes me very much—he ought to like me, I've been very nice to him—and I suppose it flattered me— (*Smiling*) it always does flatter me when men like me—and I think one feeling I have is pride that you have a wife whom other men admire! If Mr. Lindon has made—er—respectful love to me, that's a compliment to *you*. (WARDER *laughs, sincerely amused.*) But he has *not* insulted me.

WARDER (*smiling*). That's your fault. You are the kind of woman he doesn't believe exists, and he can't make up his mind just what tactics to adopt.

BECKY. He knows perfectly, unless he's deaf and blind, that my seeing him —a few times only—has been solely to reconcile him with Eve.

WARDER. That sort of man *is* deaf and blind except to his own rotten mental suggestions. He is incapable of believing in your philanthropic motive, so let it go, dear.

BECKY (*places the letter on the writing-table and sits behind it*). Eve has frightened you!

WARDER (*walks away*). Not a bit; I laughed at her fears that you were fascinated by her precious worm! But I do consider that unwittingly you have been playing a dangerous and—forgive me, darling—(*Going to her*) a very foolish game. Already some one believes you've been seeing Lindon every day. You haven't! But that doesn't make any difference! Every one will believe you have seen him twice a day in another month if you continue seeing him at all. No woman can have the "friendship" of a man like Lindon for long without —justly or unjustly—paying the highest price for it. (*He places his hand tenderly on her shoulder.*) You wouldn't know what the price was till the bill came in,—and then no matter how well you knew and those who love you knew you had not danced, all the same the world would make you pay the piper!

BECKY. I do your sex greater justice than you! I don't believe there's any man, no matter what he has been, whom some sincere woman can't waken to some good that is in him!

WARDER (*smiling*). That's all right, but you please let Eve wake up Lindon! (*He moves away.*) Had you made any arrangements to ring a little friendly alarm on him tomorrow?

BECKY. No! And that, of course, was Eve's suggestion!

WARDER. Well, never mind so long as it's understood his visits here are at an end. You don't expect him tomorrow, and should he come, you won't see him, eh?

BECKY. Exactly! (*Smiling*) When I told him today his visits were over, what do you think he said?

WARDER. I couldn't guess.

BECKY. He said I'd change my mind and send for him!

WARDER. And if you did, do you know what he would do?

BECKY. No—what?

WARDER. Consider it a signal of capitulation—and ten to one take you in his arms and kiss you!

BECKY (*rises*). He wouldn't dare!

WARDER. I'm not sure, but at any rate I am serious about one thing in this discussion.

BECKY (*goes to him and places her hands lovingly on his arms*). Our first "domestic row."

WARDER (*turns her about and holds her in his arms; she leans against him*). And last!

BECKY. Amen!

WARDER (*very seriously*). And I echo the sentiment, I know, of every sane husband in New York—Lindon's attentions to a man's wife are an insult, and as your husband I won't have them.

BECKY (*leaving his arms, pushes him playfully into a chair and sits near him in the corner of the sofa*). Well, give me my woman's last word. I still think you are unfair to him—but I love you all the same!!

WARDER. You'd better!

BECKY. I'm so afraid you'll get—not tired, but—well—too used to me!

WARDER. Not till I find you twice the same! Now—what about your father?

BECKY. He only wants fifty dollars, and says he must have it; let's send it.

WARDER. No, that's the way it's been always. Our "no" has always ended "yes," so of course he hasn't believed in it. This time it must stay "no."

BECKY (*plaintively*). You won't send it?

WARDER. No, and you mustn't.

BECKY. Oh, I haven't got a cent. But

he says he's in real trouble and he must have it.

WARDER. It's always the same thing! And we must put a stop to his inveterate, indiscriminate gambling. If we don't teach him the lesson he needs soon, before we know it he will be in real trouble that ten thousand times fifty dollars mightn't get him out of.

BECKY. But he promises not to—

WARDER (*interrupting*). My dear! He has given his word over and over again, and broken it twice as many times! If it isn't a race course, it's a bucket shop—or some cheap back door roulette table, and it's got to stop! Stop now!

BECKY. But, Tom—

WARDER (*interrupting*). Now, Becky! You know how hard it is for me to refuse you.

BECKY. It's only—

WARDER (*interrupting*). You must trust my judgment, and your father must learn, and a small matter of fifty dollars is a good chance to begin; it can't be so very serious! so that's ended. Very well, I'll ring when I'm ready.

BECKY (*half humorously, half discouragedly*). Yes, I guess it's ended!

WARDER. Now, will you try to realize that I only want to do what's best and right?

BECKY (*kisses him*). Yes, but I can't help feeling sorry for father. (*Smiling.*)

(*The* SERVANT *enters with a bill and a bandbox.*)

SERVANT. Beg pardon, madam, but the man has come back.

BECKY (*takes the bill*). Oh, my hat! Very well, I'll ring when I'm ready. Leave the box on the chair.

SERVANT (*puts bandbox on the chair at left*). Very good, madam. (*He goes out.*)

BECKY (*smiling, embarrassed*). I'm nearly as bad as father!

WARDER. Lose at bridge today?

BECKY. No, I didn't play today, but I couldn't resist a hat, my dear, the most adorable hat! (WARDER *laughs* "Oh, Becky.") No, honestly! Much more beautiful than the one I bought day before yesterday! I'm ashamed, but I did order it to come home, and I haven't a penny.

WARDER (*teasing her*). Send it back!

BECKY. Oh, you wouldn't be so heartless! and what would they think at the shop?

WARDER (*getting out his pocketbook*). How much is it?

BECKY (*hesitates a moment*). Fifty dollars!

WARDER (*with a slight quizzing look*). Just what your father wants.

BECKY. Yes! Give the money to father and I'll send back the bonnet.

WARDER. No, my darling. You know it isn't the money with your father, it's the principle of the thing. I've not got the money, I must write a check.

(WARDER *looks for the checkbook.* BECKY *quickly gets a checkbook from table and hides it behind her back.*)

BECKY. Your checkbook's upstairs. (*She rings the bell on the desk*).

WARDER. I thought perhaps yours was here?

BECKY. No, mine's used up, as usual!

WARDER. All right. (*He goes out, as the* SERVANT *enters.*)

BECKY (*opening the bandbox*). Send the man here, Jenks.

SERVANT. Yes, madam. (*He goes out.*)

BECKY (*takes out the hat and looks at it admiringly*). What a duck! (*Heaves a great sigh and puts it back and starts to retie the strings, as the* MAN *enters.*) I want you to take this back to Mme. Flora, and say Mrs. Warder is extremely sorry, but Mr. Warder has taken a violent dislike to the hat, so she cannot have it. She will be in later to choose another.

MAN. Yes, ma'am. (*He goes out with the bandbox.*)

(BECKY *sits down and starts to write a letter hurriedly.* WARDER *comes in with the check.* BECKY *hides the letter she is writing.*)

WARDER (*coming to the table*). Here's the check, all but the name of the payee. Where's the bill?

BECKY. Make it out to me, and I'll endorse it.

WARDER. Why?

BECKY. O dear! (*Half worried, half smiling*) I told you a sort of fib! The hat was only thirty-five dollars, but I wanted the extra fifteen for something else. Please don't be angry—

WARDER (*laughing*). I'm not angry, though you know I dislike even little fibs. Why didn't you tell me if you're hard up? I'll give you this and make out another for the bonnet shop.

BECKY. No, you needn't do that; the man's gone now for the change—I told him.

WARDER (*finishes the check and gives it to her*). Becky! you're not going to send this to your father? I forbid that.

BECKY. No, no, darling! (*Takes the check.*) And now you get dressed. I'll be up in a minute. You know it always takes you twice as long as it does me when you wear a white tie! It's a long play and begins early.

WARDER. I'll bet you I'll be dressed before you start! (*He hurries out.*)

BECKY (*rings the telephone on the desk*). Hello! Hello, 6304-72d. (*Writes on her interrupted letter with one hand and listens with the receiver in the other. After a moment*) Hello! 6304-72d? Is Mr. Lindon—yes, ask him to come to the 'phone and speak to 2759-38th. (*Listens as she writes.*) Hello! Is that you? Yes—yes—Oh (*Laughs.*), don't be silly! I called you to say I am very sorry, but our engagement for to-morrow is off! O double f! No, for good! For *Good!* (*She adds very quickly.*) Good-by! (*Hangs up the receiver and writes. In a moment the telephone bell rings furiously; at first she ignores it; then she makes a grimace at it; then she takes up the receiver.*) Hello! No, Central, I wasn't cut off. No, I don't want the number back, thank you, I hung up the receiver. I can't help that! You needn't re-connect us—say the line is busy! (*Hangs up the receiver.*) Mercy! when you don't want them!! (*Rings the electric bell on the desk, endorses the check, puts it in the letter, and seals the envelope. The* SERVANT *enters as she addresses letter.*) I want you to take this at once and put a special delivery stamp on it. I want it to reach my father in Baltimore to-night.

SERVANT. Yes, madam.

BECKY. Have you any idea whether it would be delivered there tonight or tomorrow morning?

SERVANT. One or the other, madam.

BECKY (*smiling*). That I know! Make haste.

(*The* SERVANT *goes out, as* WARDER, *all dressed, save that his tie hangs loose, rushes in. She rises quickly.*)

WARDER. Who's ready first?

BECKY (*laughing*). Oh, you've raced! But while you're tying your tie I'll—

WARDER (*interrupts*). No, I came down purposely to get you to tie it for me! (*He stands ready.*)

BECKY (*ties it during the following speeches*). You forgive me for telling you that little fib?

WARDER. Yes, if it's to be your last one.

BECKY. My *very* last.

WARDER. No more of those wicked little white lies, even, that you know you do amuse yourself with, and dis-tress me?

BECKY. No, no! Really! I've opened the cage door and let all the little white mice fibs out for good!

WARDER. And you do love me?

BECKY. Do you want to know how much I love you?

WARDER. Yes, how much?

BECKY. How deep is the ocean in its deepest spot?

WARDER. As deep as your love for me.

BECKY. Oh, that isn't fair! You're stealing my thunder! There! (*The tie is finished, and she pushes him playfully into the chair by the writing table.*) One good turn deserves another. (*With her arms about his neck, she slides on to his knee, like a child.*) I've let Per-kins go out, and you *must* hook me up the back.

(*And both laugh gayly as he em-braces her and the curtain falls.*)

ACT TWO

The same scene as Act One. Satur-day afternoon. BECKY *and* WARDER *are sitting on the sofa, both drinking coffee after lunch.* WARDER *puts his coffee cup on the table as the curtain rises.*

———

BECKY. Aren't you going to smoke, darling? (*Putting her coffee on the table behind her.*)

WARDER. Yes. (*Getting out a cigar.*)

BECKY. Give it to me. (*She takes it, and cuts the tip with a gold jewelled cutter which she wears on a chain about her neck.*) For six years you've not smoked a cigar in my presence that I haven't clipped, have you?

WARDER. No. And how about anybody else's cigars? That hasn't cut off any tips for—Lindon, I hope!

BECKY. No indeed! He only smokes

cigarettes.

WARDER (*amused*). Is that the only reason?

BECKY. Oh, you darling! I believe you are a little jealous of Lindon and I adore you for it. (*Hugging and kissing him.*)

WARDER. Well, you go on adoring, but I'm not a bit jealous of Lindon. (*Rises, and lights his cigar with a match from the table behind them.*)

BECKY. You're not going back to the office? It's Saturday.

WARDER. No—I think I'll have a game of racquets with Billy Weld.

BECKY. Do! You love it so. I've regretted their invitation to dine with them next week, Friday. I said we're going out of town.

WARDER. But we're not. We've people dining here, haven't we?

BECKY. Yes, but I think going out of town sounds so much more interesting. Besides, then they can't possibly be offended that they aren't asked here. Grace'll be consumed with curiosity, too, as to where we're going! (*Amused.*)

WARDER. But if they see us Friday?

BECKY. They'll think we haven't gone yet.

WARDER. But if Billy meets me down town Saturday morning?

BECKY. He'll think you took an early train back.

WARDER. The truth's so simple, so much easier—why not tell it?

BECKY. Don't worry, it'll be all right. I'm sorry I told you if you're going to worry!

WARDER (*goes to kiss her; she stops him; sitting beside her*). What's up?

BECKY. I've decided I kiss you too often. I'm a shopkeeper with only one line of goods—no variety, and I'm cheapening my wares. (WARDER *laughs.*) I don't want you to feel

you're getting a leftover stock of stale, shopworn kisses! I want you to feel the supply doesn't equal the demand. (*She kisses him. The* SERVANT *enters and they move apart.*)

SERVANT. Mrs. Lindon to see Mr. Warder.

BECKY (*to* WARDER). Eve! (*To* SERVANT) Ask her to come in here and have a cup of coffee and a cigarette.

SERVANT. Yes, madam. (*Goes out.*)

BECKY (*beaming*). Come to tell us of the reconciliation!

WARDER. Why she didn't let him go and be thankful! I don't see what she can love in a little outsider like Lindon!

BECKY. Thank Heaven all women don't love the same kind of a man! (*Steals a caress.*) Think what an awful fight there'd be!

SERVANT (*coming back*). Mrs. Lindon sends this message—she wishes to see *Mr.* Warder.

(BECKY *and* WARDER *look at each other, surprised and amused.* BECKY *makes a grimace.*)

WARDER. Very well, show Mrs. Lindon in.

SERVANT. Yes, sir. (*Goes out.*)

WARDER. More trouble!

BECKY. They've quarrelled again already! It must have been *his* fault.

(SERVANT *shows in* MRS. LINDON *and goes out.*)

MRS. LINDON (*to* WARDER, *not noticing* BECKY). How do you do?

WARDER. How do you do, Eve?

BECKY. How do you do, Eve! Sit down.

MRS. LINDON. I wish to see Tom for a moment, Becky.

BECKY. What for?

MRS. LINDON. I wish to see him alone.

BECKY. Why?

MRS. LINDON. That, Becky, is my affair—and *his* perhaps!

BECKY. Oh, really! I suppose I ought to become very jealous now, and do dreadful things. (*Smiles.*) But don't have me for a moment on your mind, Tom. (*Kisses her finger, puts it to Tom's lips, he kisses it, and she goes out.*)

WARDER. What is it, Eve? You know I have no earthly secrets from Becky.

MRS. LINDON. It's about her secrets from you!

WARDER. Nonsense! (*Half laughs.*)

MRS. LINDON (*sitting in the chair by the table*). I only hinted at things the other day—and only hinted at one-half the truth.

WARDER (*sitting on the sofa*). Excuse me, Eve, but you've got hold of the wrong half. I asked Becky outright— that is our way always. She denied practically all you said.

MRS. LINDON. You can't make me believe you've lived as long as you have with Becky Roland and not found out —she lies.

WARDER (*rises quickly in anger*). It's because you're a woman you dare say that to me, but you know I don't have to listen to you, so don't push our old friendship's claim too far.

MRS. LINDON. I said Becky and Fred met often on the sly.

WARDER (sitting again). Which isn't true!

MRS. LINDON. No! They meet *every day!*

WARDER. Eve, I think your trouble has gone to your brain.

MRS. LINDON (*still quietly, but with the quiet of the crater when the volcano is alive beneath*). I can prove to you that Becky has seen Fred every day and more than that! When we had our talk two days ago, they had agreed together that he was to go through a form of reconciliation with me for appearance' sake, and their meetings were

to continue. She had an appointment with him for yesterday.

WARDER. That I know isn't true, for she swore to me the opposite.

MRS. LINDON. Yes, you frightened her off and she broke the engagement by telephone, which made Fred perfectly furious!

WARDER (*rising, goes to mantel and knocks his cigar ashes into the grate; absolutely unconvinced, he continues with a cynical smile*). And how did you obtain this decidedly intimate information?

MRS. LINDON (*in an outburst, the volcano becoming a little active*). From him! I knew they hadn't met for two days—

WARDER (*interrupting*). How? (*He looks up curiously.*)

MRS. LINDON (*rises and turns away, a little ashamed*). I've had Fred watched for weeks!

WARDER (*astonished, rises*). You mean you've— (*He hesitates.*)

MRS. LINDON. Yes! (*Coming to the desk, and speaking across it to him*) I took their not meeting for a sign that after all Becky had given him up, and I had the impulse to go to him—to go back home. He turned on me like a wolf—said I'd meddled with his affairs once too often—that I'd frightened Becky into breaking off with him, that he had been on the point of making up with me for the reason I've told you, but now it was done for! I'd raised your suspicions, I'd given the whole thing away to everybody, and I could congratulate myself on having broken off his and my relations for good— forever! Oh, how could he insult me so when it was only his love I was asking for? (*She sinks down in the chair above the table, and buries her face in her hands and sobs.*)

WARDER (*forgets himself and ex-*

claims). But how can you—how can you still care for him after everything you've gone through? It's beyond my understanding! (*He throws his cigar angrily into the fireplace.*)

MRS. LINDON. The history of the world is full of women who love like me, but no men—I don't know why; but I suppose that's why you can't understand it. Why couldn't he realize it is for happiness not appearances I've been fighting? And now it's over, for I know when he means what he says—and he told me, like a low brute, I could go to—where you can imagine—for all he cares, or for all he'll ever live with me again. (*Her voice fills up again.*)

WARDER. I should think if you went to the address he proposed, it would insure at least an eventual meeting!

MRS. LINDON (*who has not heard and does not understand*). What?

WARDER. I beg your pardon! I made a foolish joke! Well? (*With a hearty long breath of relief*) Now do you feel better?

MRS. LINDON (*feebly, not understanding*). Better?

WARDER. Yes, now you've got it all "off your chest"? Tomorrow you'll be all right and ready to forgive again. Shall I call Becky? (*Going toward the bell beside the mantel.*)

MRS. LINDON (*rises*). You're going to accuse her before me?

WARDER (*stops and turns*). Accuse her? (*Laughs.*) No—I don't believe a word you've told me. I'd take Becky's unspoken denial against Fred's sworn statement any day.

MRS. LINDON (*going to him*). Then here's yesterday's report from the agency!—and Thursday's, and Thursday's includes the report of the telephone central who connected Becky with our house when she broke off the appointment with Fred—that telephone girl has told us many interesting things!

WARDER. Stop! Stop this! I won't listen to you—at any rate not behind Becky's back. I'm not a jealous, suspicious woman with good reason to believe the worst. I'm a straightforward, decent man, I hope, and I know I've every reason to believe absolutely in my wife, God bless her! (*He moves away and then turns upon her.*) Why have you come and told me this, anyway?

MRS. LINDON (*staggered*). Why—why?

WARDER (*angry*). Yes, why? to me of all people! I was the last person you should have told, as a matter of breeding, as a matter of tact, as a matter of the friendship you talk about.

MRS. LINDON. But that was just it!

WARDER. Do you dream what it would mean to me to shake even by a miserable tremor my confidence in my wife? But you haven't!

MRS. LINDON. I thought, and I still think, it's to your advantage to know.

WARDER (*with a complete change of voice, from anger to the tone one adopts with a silly child*). My dear Eve, while I don't for a minute excuse him, still I do now understand, perhaps, how even Fred Lindon must have found your ideas of devotion at times over the endurance line.

MRS. LINDON. You don't understand—I thought if you knew everything, together we could separate them —could arrange something.

WARDER. Eve! believe me, there's nobody to separate in this case; there's nothing, so far as I and mine are concerned, to arrange. (*He goes again to the bell by the mantel.*)

MRS. LINDON. Who are you going to ring for?

WARDER. You know.

MRS. LINDON (*stopping him quickly*). Not before me! I don't want to see her humiliated. I don't want a public revenge or triumph; that's not the feeling I have.

WARDER. What in the world do you mean? (*He rings.*) Becky will deny the—

MRS. LINDON (*interrupting*). Very likely! But these proofs are incompatible, and if that's her attitude, I shall go straight from your door to the divorce court. (*She places the envelope of reports on the table with a blow.*)

WARDER (*goes to her*). You're mad! If your proofs are all right, then Becky'll not deny, she'll explain them. You forget you can only see everything red now, but I'm sane and quiet and sure (*smiling*) and I see things in their true colors. You must be guided by me in this. (*He takes her hand almost cruelly and speaks strongly, with the manner and voice of the man who is and means to remain master.*) Do you understand that? (*She draws her hand away as if in pain.*) I beg your pardon. I am afraid you are one of those dangerous "well-meaning" persons who do more harm than the people who are purposely malicious. You are to take no step without my sanction.

(*BECKY comes in with a certain air of bravado.*)

BECKY. Excuse me, I heard the bell and I was waiting—am I right?

WARDER (*goes to her*). Come right in, dear.

BECKY. Well! has Eve thrown a bomb, or a trump card? Am I to be taken into the secret or conspiracy or what?

WARDER (*after a second's pause, in which he thinks how to begin*). Eve has convinced herself, and would convince me, of some very—(*He thinks for the word.*) wrong—worse than

wrong things, but I prefer to be convinced of the contrary by you. And I prefer to come to you with my confidence, my conviction complete. And together we'll try to keep Eve from harming others as well as herself and Lindon—the latter seems unavoidable. (MRS. LINDON *pushes her papers on the desk pointedly nearer to him. He ignores them.*) Eve says you've not been seeing Lindon often, but every day.

BECKY. Do you want me to deny it?

WARDER (*indulgently*). I want you to tell the truth.

BECKY. Of course the accusation and the idea behind it are absurd. (WARDER *turns and looks at* MRS. LINDON, *who meets his glance and then looks down at the evidence on the table, pushing the papers a little farther toward him. He does not follow her glance.* BECKY *half laughs.*) It's like a trial, isn't it? By what right does Eve—

MRS. LINDON (*interrupting*). The supreme right of any married woman who cares for her husband. Shall I be more explicit?

BECKY. No, you needn't trouble! What next, Tom?

WARDER. Eve claims you had an engagement with Fred—(*Hesitates, trying to remember the day.*)

MRS. LINDON (*quickly*). Day before yesterday.

WARDER. Which you broke off over the telephone.

BECKY. How does she know that? Does she tap our wire? Merciful Heavens, Eve, you've become so morbid over your trouble your mind's diseased on the subject of Fred—and everybody else apparently.

MRS. LINDON. Ha!

WARDER. But is this true, Becky?

BECKY (*to gain time*). Is what true?

WARDER. About this appointment with Fred which you broke over the—

BECKY (*interrupting*). Of course not!

WARDER (*who begins to doubt her*). If it were, you could easily explain it, I'm sure. (*Hoping to suggest this course to her.*)

BECKY (*her head lost*). Of course—but there's nothing to explain! The whole thing's false! What do you take me for, Eve? If you think I'm a home destroyer, you've made a mistake in the bird! And what do you mean by coming into my precious home and trying to make trouble for me? (*Sitting on the sofa, frightened and almost in tears.*)

WARDER. Wait a minute, Becky, it's partly my fault.

BECKY. It is not! I know whose fault it is, and I must say that, at last, I don't blame Fred Lindon!

MRS. LINDON. Oh!

BECKY. There! I'm sorry I said that. When I'm excited like this I speak the truth straight out, no matter what happens!

WARDER. Well really it was I who insisted on your joining us, against Eve's will. (*To* MRS. LINDON) Your way was best. It was my man's point of view—(*To* BECKY) and you are right, under the circumstances, no doubt, to answer as you do.

BECKY. My dear Tom, there's no other way to answer.

WARDER (*looks at her, then takes up the envelope containing the detective reports and holds them tightly in his hand. He comes down to* MRS. LINDON). If you will leave us alone, I will go over the whole matter with Becky—by ourselves will be much better.

MRS. LINDON. I need hardly tell you those papers are most valuable to me.

BECKY (*looking up, her curiosity aroused*). What papers? (*Nobody answers her. She tries to see.*)

MRS. LINDON. Will you promise me not to let them out of your hands till you put them back into mine?

WARDER. I will.

MRS. LINDON (*as she moves to go, stops*). You will find the entries which are of particular interest to you marked on the margin with a red cross!

WARDER (*satirically*). Thank you!

(BECKY *rises and rings for the* SERVANT. MRS. LINDON *goes out.*)

BECKY (*coming to meet* WARDER). I think I'm a pretty good-natured woman to let Eve—

WARDER (*stands before* BECKY *with his hands on her shoulders, making her look straight into his eyes*). Now be careful, dearest. You've married a man who doesn't understand a suspicious nature—who has every confidence in you and the deepest—a confidence that couldn't be easily disturbed; but once it was shaken, every unborn suspicion of all the past years would spring to life full-grown and strong at their birth, and God knows if my confidence could ever come back. It never has in any of the smaller trials of it I've made in my life. So you'll be careful, won't you, dearest? I mean even in little things. My faith in you is what gives all the best light to my life, but it's a live wire—neither you nor I can afford to play with it. (*Goes to the writing table and takes the papers out of* MRS. LINDON'S *envelope.*)

BECKY. Tom, you frighten me! Eve has made you jealous again. (*Goes to him and puts both arms about his neck.*) Now, my darling, I give you my word of honor I love only you and never have loved Fred Lindon and never could! Say you believe me!

WARDER. Haven't I always believed you?

BECKY. Ye—s.

WARDER. But if I find your word of

honor is broken in one thing, how can I ever trust it in another?

BECKY. Of course you can't—but you needn't worry, because it won't be broken.

WARDER. Then, now we're alone, tell me the truth, which you didn't tell me when you said you'd not seen Lindon often.

BECKY (*turns away*). It was the truth. I haven't—so very often.

WARDER. Not every day?

BECKY (*sits in the chair by the writing table*). How could I?

WARDER. Nor telephoned him Thursday, breaking off an engagement *after you told me absolutely you'd parted with him for good—and had no appointment?*

BECKY. Of course not! The idea! (*But she shows she is a little worried.*) Eve Lindon never could tell the truth!

WARDER. The telephone girl must have lied too or else the statement was made out of whole cloth. (*Throwing the envelope on the desk.*)

BECKY. What statement?

WARDER (*sitting on sofa*). From these detectives. (*He begins to look through the papers.*)

BECKY. Detectives! (*Stunned*) What detectives? (*Picks up envelope and looks at it, puts it back on desk.*)

WARDER. Eve's, who have shadowed her husband for the past two months.

BECKY (*thoroughly alarmed*). You don't mean—

WARDER (*interrupts, not hearing what* BECKY *says; his thoughts on the papers which he is reading, he speaks very quietly*). These certainly do make out a case of daily meetings for you two.

BECKY. It's not true!

WARDER. Though not so very many here. (*Turning over a fresh paper.*)

BECKY (*rises, gets above desk*). All!

All the meetings there have been—practically. This is simply awful! Eve is capable of making the most terrific scandal for nothing. Don't let her, Tom, will you? Tear those things up!

WARDER (*smiling indulgently, not taking her seriously*). Becky!

BECKY (*leaning over the table, stretches out her hand toward him*). Well, let me! Let me take them from you without your noticing till it's too late!

WARDER (*seriously*). You're not serious?

BECKY. I am!

WARDER. You heard me give Eve my word?

BECKY. To a mad woman like that, it doesn't count.

WARDER. I wonder just how much your word does count with you, Becky!

BECKY (*with great and injured dignity*). It counts everything!

WARDER. They seem to have hit on some very out-of-the-way places for your rendezvous. (*He smiles.*) Where is Huber's museum?

BECKY. Why, it's down on Fourteenth — (*She interrupts herself quickly.*) I don't know where it is! (*She moves away to collect herself.*)

WARDER (*still smiling*). And why the Washington Heights Inn in February? Or the *Eden Musée* ever?

BECKY. Of course someone else has been mistaken for me.

WARDER (*looks up*). Ah! yes, that's a very possible idea.

BECKY (*goes to the sofa and sits beside him*). Tom, don't read any more of the horrid things! Listen to me, don't let Eve go on. She'll ruin everything if she does. He'll never forgive her, never take her back.

WARDER (*reading and smiling*). I didn't know you skated!

BECKY. I always loved skating. I only

gave it up because it bored you. But I didn't skate then!

WARDER. When?

BECKY. I—I don't—oh, whenever that beast says!

WARDER. St. Nicholas Rink, Friday, February eighteenth. (*He has noticed the slip she made, but hides the fact; he speaks as he goes on reading.*) Eve and her husband have had a big row, and he swears he'll never see her again, not even in the other place, that she's come between you and him and that he'll never forgive. (*He finishes seriously, his bantering manner gone.*)

BECKY. Oh, how untrue! I don't believe he said any such thing. Eve's jealous mind has distorted something else. The reason for our friendship— (*He rises with a half-angry movement, goes above the table looking for the envelope.*) such as it is—was to bring Eve and him together.

WARDER. From *your* point of view.

BECKY. No, believe me, he isn't as bad as you think.

WARDER (*showing the papers*). And what about these? They agree with me.

BECKY. If you believe those papers about him, then you must believe them about me.

WARDER (*coming to her*). Heaven forbid, Becky! They would prove you a liar and a terrible one—which you're *not, are you?*

BECKY. How can you ask?

WARDER. If these were true—if I thought you had deceived me to such an extent—I could never trust you again so long as I lived, Becky.

BECKY. Shall you speak to Mr. Lindon about them?

WARDER. No, I wouldn't insult you by discussing you with Lindon, unless I was convinced every word and more here was true. I will see Eve tomorrow and perhaps get hold of these detectives

myself.

BECKY (*almost trembling with dread*). And now go and have your game. You need it! You're getting morbid. You'll be believing these beastly things if you don't get some exercise.

WARDER. What time is it?

BECKY (*she looks at clock on the mantel, and speaks with her face still away from him*). Three. When will you be back? (*She conceals her anxiety to hear his answer.*)

WARDER. Oh, six, I suppose.

BECKY (*facing him with a certain relief*). Not till six—you're sure?

WARDER. Yes, you know your father's coming and there's no necessity of my seeing him.

BECKY. Oh! I forgot all about father's telegram! If it's money, I'm to be firm?

WARDER. Absolutely.

BECKY (*taking hold of the envelope which he has in his left hand away from her*). What are you going to do with those?

WARDER. You heard me tell Eve they shouldn't go out of my hands except into hers. (*He gently, but firmly, removes her hand from the envelope.*)

BECKY. And you meant it?

WARDER. Don't you mean a promise you give like that?

BECKY. Yes, of course. . . .

WARDER (*taking out his keys*). I'm going to put them away in my room. I want to have a thorough, careful look through them later. Of course I can't let it rest here. The detectives must learn their mistake at once.

BECKY. Yes, of course. But you are going to the Welds' now for your game?

WARDER. Yes, good-by. (*Presses her hand. Gives her a tender but questioning look, but does not kiss her, and then goes out.*)

BECKY. He's begun to distrust me already. Dear God in Heaven, if I get out of this, I'll never tell another lie so long as I live! (*She turns to the window. Smiles to* WARDER *outside and throws him a kiss, but afterward her face at once assumes its frightened look. Coming from the window, she sinks upon the piano stool.*) He's got to save me! Now he can prove that he is worthy of a decent woman's friendship. (*She goes to the telephone and calls.*) Hello! Hello! (*She suddenly realizes.*) But I can't use the telephone! Central has told things already! (*She hangs up the receiver. The telephone bell rings.*) I must write him. (*The bell rings again. She takes up the receiver and speaks angrily.*) Hello? . . . No, I didn't ring. You've made a mistake. (*Hangs up the receiver.*) You telltale toad you! (*She writes.*) "If this note reaches you in time, please come over"—I ought to be able to get rid of father in half an hour—(*She looks up at the clock.*) "at half-past three." (*Seals note and addresses it.*) "Important." (*Which she underlines.*)

SERVANT (*entering left, announces*). Mr. Roland.

(ROLAND *is an elderly, dried-up little man with an air of the dandy jockey still clinging to him underneath his gray hairs and dyed moustache. A vivid carnation is in his buttonhole and a somewhat rusty springiness in his gait.*)

ROLAND (*coming in jauntily*). Hello, Beck!

BECKY (*with fictitious spirit*). Father! (*He starts to kiss her, forgetting the ever present cigarette in his mouth; then he stops to remove it, and does kiss her.*)

ROLAND. How are you?

BECKY. I'm awfully glad to see you, but you can't stay long. Excuse me just a moment. Jenks, I want you to ring for a messenger and give him— (*Stops.*) no, when he comes, send him to me. (*She has started to give* JENKS *the note, but changes her mind.* JENKS *bows and turns to leave.*)

ROLAND. I say, Becky, might I have a glass of brandy? I took coffee after lunch on the train and it's poisoned me. Must have been canned coffee!

BECKY. Very well, Jenks. (*The* SERVANT *goes out.*)

ROLAND (*lolling on the sofa*). What the devil did you mean by sending me fifty dollars instead of five hundred?

BECKY (*surprised*). I read it fifty! I never dreamed you'd ask for five hundred more! (*Going toward him.*)

ROLAND. I wrote five hundred and I must have it!

BECKY. My dear father, it's impossible. I tried as it was to get a little more from Tom, but he said "no," to send you the fifty dollars, with his love, but not one penny more, and to make you understand—and, Father, he means it—that for the future you must keep within your allowance.

(*The* SERVANT *enters with the brandy on a salver, and pours out a liqueur glass full.*)

ROLAND. But *you'll* help me?

BECKY (*sitting on the opposite end of the sofa*). No, he forbids it, and in the future I'm going to do what Tom wishes, and never deceive him even in a little thing again. (*To the* SERVANT *who hands the glass of brandy to* ROLAND.) The messenger boy hasn't come yet?

SERVANT. No, madam.

BECKY. If he doesn't come in five minutes, ring again.

SERVANT. Yes, madam. (*Starting to go,* ROLAND *stops him.*)

ROLAND. Not so fast! (*He points to the glass which he has emptied and the* SERVANT *pours out another glass.*

ROLAND *takes it and puts it on the table behind him. The* SERVANT *busies himself with gathering up the after-dinner coffee cups and trying to overhear all that he can.*)

BECKY. How is Mrs. Crespigny?

ROLAND. That woman will be the death or the marriage of me!

BECKY. Don't be absurd, Father! She's given you the most comfortable home you've had for years. In that letter she wrote me she said she'd been a real mother to you.

ROLAND. The *mother* is a blind, a false lead to hide her hand! her trumps are marriage.

BECKY. Nonsense! Mrs. Crespigny must realize the difference in your positions.

ROLAND. You haven't lived with her social souvenirs as I have for four years! (*The* SERVANT *starts to take up the glass which* ROLAND *has put aside, but the latter stops him. The* SERVANT *has delayed over his work as long as he dares in his desire to listen, and now goes out left.*) Becky, are you and Tom hungering for a mother-in-law?

BECKY. I don't know what you mean?

ROLAND. It's a question of five hundred dollars for me or a new Mrs. Roland!

BECKY (*astounded*). You don't mean you owe Mrs. Crespigny that money?

ROLAND. Well, I've not paid my board bill as regularly as I might have wished.

BECKY (*rises, indignant*). I'm ashamed of you!

ROLAND. I'm ashamed of myself, but shame won't pay bills; if it would, there'd have been many an unpaid debt washed off the slate in this world. (*The* SERVANT *returns with a* MESSENGER *boy.*)

SERVANT. The messenger, madam.

(BECKY *goes to the boy. During* BECKY's *talk with the* MESSENGER, ROLAND *fills his pocket with cigars from the box on the table.*)

BECKY. I want you to take this note to its address, but only leave it in case the gentleman is in. Do you understand?

MESSENGER. Yes, ma'am.

BECKY. And come back and tell me.

MESSENGER. Yes, ma'am. (*He goes out with the* SERVANT, *who has waited for him.*)

ROLAND. I confess, my child, I have flirted a little with the dame in question.

BECKY. Father!

ROLAND. I have, in a way, led her on!

BECKY. And you always told me my mother's memory was the one precious thing left, that you meant to keep always untouched by your life!

ROLAND. I don't deny, Becky, I'd be ashamed of it. I don't pretend Mrs. Crespigny would be a solace or a substitute; she would, at the best perhaps, be a resource — but what she threatens to become unless I pay is a legal necessity!

BECKY. *Could* she do that?

ROLAND. I have been obliged at times by desperate need of ready money to suggest to her certain things as probabilities which were barely remote possibilities! And unfortunately—*unfortunately*—once or twice in writing.

BECKY. She has compromising letters of yours?

ROLAND. She has a large collection of illustrated postal cards from every place I've been since I've lodged with her — they are her chief artistic dissipation — and a double set of Baltimore Duplicates, which I am afraid are the most foolish; as I am in the habit of making up with her in that way after little tiffs when she takes the stand of not being on speaking terms with me.

BECKY. Father! You've been a terrible idiot.

ROLAND. I have, my dear!

BECKY. Can't you get those cards back?

ROLAND. The rent due is "Mother's" price for them. (*Rising*) You will make Tom give it to me, won't you? and I'll promise not to make such a fool of myself again. (*Sitting on the arm of the sofa, drawing* BECKY *toward him and putting both his arms about her.*)

BECKY. Tom's idea now is that you deserve all you get. He'll say you deserve Mrs. Crespigny. (*Leaving him, she goes above the table.*)

ROLAND. Oh, come, she's not so bad as that!

BECKY. How old is she?

ROLAND. She has told me several ages. The general average would make her about forty-seven and a quarter.

BECKY. Pretty?

ROLAND. A fine figure of a woman and plays an A-one game of piquet.

BECKY. I see! When did her husband die?

ROLAND. He didn't die. He stole from the bank in which he was employed and went to jail, and she says for social reasons she was naturally obliged to take advantage of the divorce law. I have a suspicion myself he may have preferred jail!

BECKY (*comes quickly to him*). Father, I would never forgive you if you did such a thing! It's degrading to me and to my mother's memory for you to accept any sort of indulgence at that woman's hands! When we get her paid, you must leave her house.

ROLAND. That I can't and won't do, because I'm far too comfortable!

SERVANT (*entering announces*). Mrs. Crespigny!

ROLAND (*jumps up*). Mrs. who?

(MRS. CRESPIGNY *comes in flamboyantly. She is a woman past the age of uncertainty, dressed gaudily, with an hourglass figure; she has innumerable bracelets and bangles, and an imitation jewelled chain flaunts a heavy pair of lorgnettes, like a gargoyle hanging over a much-curved bust. Enormous wax pearls in her ears are in direct contrast to the dark beginnings of her otherwise russet-gold hair. Neither her shoes nor her stays fit, and both are too tight. She is brightly rouged, and yet the very failure of the façade reveals, somehow, the honest interior of a human if forlornly foolish female.*)

MRS. CRESPIGNY. Excuse me for intruding myself which I know is not social good form. Mis' Warder, I take it?

(BECKY *bows.*)

ROLAND (*angrily*). What do you mean by following me here?

MRS. CRESPIGNY (*after severe look at him, turns back to* BECKY). I want you to know the facts as between your father and me, and just how the matter is, and get your support that I done right! (*To* ROLAND) I know your daughter is a lady if you ain't, and being a lady myself I have a certain pride. (*To* BECKY) I've had a good deal of trouble persuading your father that though a lady sometimes takes in a paying guest she still holds her own in the social scale. I have friends of my own in the New York Smart Set! My niece married a Mr. Gubenhamers and lives in a perfectly elegant house of her own on Lennox Avenue. Do you know her? One thousand two hundred and fifty-three?

BECKY. No.

MRS. CRESPIGNY. Oh, don't you? Well, of course I know New York is big. Still, perhaps you know her husband's cousin, who is also in a way a

relation? You will know her by name—
Mrs. Otto Gurtz, President of the West
Side Ladies Saturday Afternoon Social
Gathering?

BECKY. No, I'm afraid I don't know
her.

MRS. CRESPIGNY. Well! I guess you
don't read the Harlem society notes in
the papers; if you did, you'd know what
she stands for socially.

BECKY. Suppose we keep to the reason of your visit — I understand my
father owes you money—(MRS.
CRESPIGNY *turns sharply to* ROLAND.)
and that you insist on being paid, which
is natural—

MRS. CRESPIGNY. A trumped-up
story! (*Going to* ROLAND) I guess I
done just about the right thing to chase
on here after you! I'm sorry to say it,
Mis' Warder, 'specially as it ain't exactly ladylike, but your father, with
all his superfine qualities, is a liar!
Yes, ma'am, between us two as ladies,
he's an ornery liar! (*Sinks into a chair
in tears.* ROLAND *lights a cigarette angrily and goes up to the window.*)

BECKY. Mrs. Crespigny, wouldn't it
be better to behave more like a lady
and talk less about one? Why break
into the house of a woman you don't
know and make a scene over a matter
of rent due you—

MRS. CRESPIGNY. It ain't the rent!
It's all a question of horses. When he
left my house this morning, he said he
was leaving for good unless I let him
have—

ROLAND (*interrupting her*). Mrs.
Crespigny! You're hysterical! You're
saying things you'll regret—

SERVANT (*entering*). The messenger
has come back, madam.

BECKY. Oh, I want to see that boy!
Excuse me a minute. (*She hurries out
and the* SERVANT *follows her.*)

ROLAND. I knew you were in the
train; that's why I stayed in the smok-
er. And it decided me to keep my
word never to go back to your house!
(*He sits determinedly in the armchair.*)

MRS. CRESPIGNY. And you told her
I was dunning you for the rent!

ROLAND. She has no more sympathy
with my betting than you have! I
wouldn't tell her the money was to put
on Wet Blanket, Monday!

MRS. CRESPIGNY (*rises and goes to
him*). No, you'd rather let her think I
was a grasping harpy, when you know,
if the truth's told, you owe me at least
five times five hundred dollars with
your borrowings and your losses at
cards!

ROLAND (*smilingly*). You haven't
won lately.

MRS. CRESPIGNY. Do you know why?

ROLAND. Oh, of course! You got out
of the wrong side of the bed or you
dreamed of a black horse!

MRS. CRESPIGNY (*pathetically and a
little ashamed*). No. I've let you win a-
purpose—because I was ashamed for
you to owe me any more money. I'm
trying to keep a little pride in you
somehow, even if I have to cheat to
do it. (*She almost breaks down again,
and turning away, takes a powder puff
from a little gilt box and powders her
nose to cover up the traces of tears.*)

ROLAND. Well, do you think it's pleasant for me to owe you money? A kind
friend like you! (*Going to the mantel
and flicking his cigarette ash in the
fireplace*) One reason I want to take
advantage of this tip for Monday is
pay you if I win.

MRS. CRESPIGNY. Yes, and then go
board somewhere else? Is that your
idea? Or to stay here?

ROLAND. Well, my daughter and her
husband want me. (*Leaning on the
mantel*) They say their home is my
home.

MRS. CRESPIGNY (*going toward him, alarmed*). But you won't stay, will you? I left word with Josephine to have your favorite meenoo cooked for a late supper in case you'd come back. We'll have a game tonight. I'll play you a rubber for the five hundred — it's against my conscience to give it to you outright for horse-racing.

ROLAND. *Loan* it to me!

MRS. CRESPIGNY. Yes, of course! I always mean loan. Oh, the flat'd be just too dreadful lonesome without you! Say you'll come back! Quick, before Mis' Warder comes in! Won't you?

ROLAND (*coming toward her*). Well, if you make it a personal favor to you in this way, I can't exactly refuse! And that ends the most serious quarrel we've had yet.

MRS. CRESPIGNY (*embarrassedly*). If we was man and wife, there wouldn't be any need of such quarrels. The money'd be yours then to do as you liked with.

ROLAND. Don't tempt me! You know you're a great deal too kind to me as it is and I'm no good to take as much advantage of you as I do.

MRS. CRESPIGNY. Oh, pshaw! Say! I wish you'd help me to get on the right side of your daughter. You're too delicate to say anything, but I always suspect it's her that stands between us.

BECKY (*coming back*). I'm very sorry, but you must go at once. I have an important engagement here in a few minutes and must change my dress. I will promise you, Mrs. Crespigny—

ROLAND (*interrupts*). I have made an arrangement with Mrs. Crespigny that is agreeable to her, without Tom's and your assistance—

BECKY (*alarmed*). Father, not—

ROLAND (*shakes his head*). It seems I exaggerated my indebtedness a little and Mrs. Crespigny exaggerated her

desire to be paid this month and—

MRS. CRESPIGNY. Yes, I was just mad clean through and would have said anything!

BECKY. Well, I'm glad it's settled, but it seems a pity you couldn't have accomplished it without the railway journey, especially as I must ask you to excuse me at once. (*She guides* MRS. CRESPIGNY *toward the door, but* MRS. CRESPIGNY, *instead of going out, makes a circle around an armchair and settles herself in it.* BECKY *goes despairingly to* ROLAND.)

MRS. CRESPIGNY. Oh, I don't regret the trip over, because I've been dying to meet you, Mis' Warder, ever since I had the pleasure of knowing your father in a taty taty sort of way. And we can catch the four-fifteen.

BECKY. Good! (*Crossing to her, and holding out her hand*) I'm sorry I can't ask you to stay.

MRS. CRESPIGNY. Oh, I can come over nearly any day! I've got such a perfectly lovely servant girl now. I give her every night out and she works like a dog all day—and you can trust her with everything! Can't you, Mr. Roland?

ROLAND. You can trust her with me all right.

(MRS. CRESPIGNY *laughs loudly.*)

BECKY. Father!

MRS. CRESPIGNY. Ain't he killing! Do you inherit his sense of humor? He can get anything he wants out of me with just one of them witticisms. (ROLAND *winks aside to* BECKY.) Of course, I won't say that he ain't an expensive boarder—(BECKY *sinks in a chair, discouraged.*)—but I consider he cuts both ways and at the finish the ends meets.

BECKY. I think I gather what you mean. I'm afraid you'll lose your train!

MRS. CRESPIGNY. I mean it's hard for

a lady what's got it in her blood, to take boarders, because usually the boarders is beneath what the lady's been accustomed to and she don't feel at home with 'em. Now with your father it's different, because he's a Roland and I'm a Crespigny.

BECKY. Oh, is that your own name? I thought—

ROLAND (*interrupting*). No, Mrs. Crespigny's maiden name was Ruggles.

MRS. CRESPIGNY. Yes, Mamma made what we'd call a messyliance, married beneath her, you know. But she never descended, nor allowed us to neither, to Papa's social level. Mamma was a O'Roorke. You know, one of them early high-toned families that came over from Amsterdam in the *Mayflower*.

BECKY. I see!

MRS. CRESPIGNY. Mamma often said to me, says she, "Jennie"—

BECKY (*with her patience exhausted, jumps up, interrupting her*). I must say good-by now—I've no time to dress. (*She hurries out.*)

MRS. CRESPIGNY (*rising*). Well, do you think I made any sort of a hit with her?

ROLAND. My dear friend, I've told you before, you're not quite my daughter's style.

MRS. CRESPIGNY. But why not? She seems real refined.

(ROLAND *groans.* WARDER *comes in. He does not see* MRS. CRESPIGNY *on his entrance.*)

WARDER. Hello, Father! I didn't think I was going to have this pleasure. I had an engagement to play racquets with Billy Weld, but he broke down in his motor somewhere between Tuxedo and here and I couldn't wait.

(MRS. CRESPIGNY *comes a few steps and beckons to* ROLAND *to introduce* WARDER.)

ROLAND. Mrs. Crespigny, Mr. Warder.

MRS. CRESPIGNY (*bows*). Pleased to make your acquaintance. (*She turns away with a rather grand manner.* WARDER *looks from her to* ROLAND *and shakes his head, then goes to the writing table with some letters he has brought in from the hall.*)

ROLAND. Excuse me one moment. (*Beckons to* MRS. CRESPIGNY *and whispers to her aside.*) Wait for me!

MRS. CRESPIGNY. In the hall?

ROLAND. Lord, no! At the station!

MRS. CRESPIGNY. Oh! (*Going, she turns at door to bid* WARDER *good-by.*) If you should ever be coming over to Baltimore, Mr. Warder, why just drop in! (*She goes out.*)

WARDER. Where's Becky?

ROLAND (*going to him*). She's upstairs. I just wanted to thank you for the money you sent me day before yesterday.

WARDER. What money?

ROLAND. The check for fifty dollars Becky mailed me.

WARDER (*starts, but controls it immediately*). Oh, a check for fifty dollars—

ROLAND. The joke on me is that what I wanted was five hundred! (*Digs* TOM *in ribs.*)

WARDER (*looking off where* BECKY *went, absorbed in his thoughts*). Oh, five hundred!

ROLAND. Yes, just five hundred. (*He looks at* WARDER, *and waits; hums a song and dances a few steps.*) Nothing doing, I suppose?

WARDER. No. Father, the fact is—

ROLAND. Yes, I know, Becky told me. Excuse me, I've got to catch a train. Good-by, my boy.

WARDER (*with his thoughts elsewhere*). Good-by!

(ROLAND *goes out whistling "Waiting*

at the Church." WARDER *stands a moment thinking, then takes out his key chain.*)

SERVANT (*entering, shows in* LINDON). Mr. Lindon to see Mrs. Warder, sir.

(WARDER *looks up with a start, which he immediately controls, and disguises completely his thoughts and emotions.*)

LINDON. How are you, Warder?

WARDER (*speaks very casually and pleasantly, with complete self-control*). Good afternoon, Lindon. (*Sees* SERVANT *about to go to* BECKY, *stops him.*) Jenks! (JENKS *goes to him.* WARDER *gives him a key from his chain.*) Go to my room and get me a large blue envelope from the upper right-hand drawer of the desk.

JENKS. Yes, sir. (*He goes out.*)

WARDER. Excuse me, Mrs. Warder is out. She'll be sorry.

LINDON (*surprised*). Out?

WARDER. Yes.

LINDON. But surely there must be some mistake?

WARDER. No, I'm sorry. I assure you she's out.

LINDON. Oh! Then do you mind if I wait?

WARDER. Is that scarcely worthwhile? I must be off at once, and I imagine Mrs. Warder is out for her usual bridge afternoon.

LINDON. I think, on the contrary, she must be surely coming back, and if you don't mind, I'll wait.

WARDER (*with an apparently good-natured laugh*). I don't like to insist against your apparently superior knowledge—

LINDON (*also smiling*). No, no, it's only a note I received a few moments ago at the club. Here it is. (*Takes it from his pocket.*) That she must see me this afternoon. You know your wife is kindly acting as intermediary between Eve and myself. It is in regard to that. (*He hands the note to* WARDER, *who glances at it and returns it without reading.*) As it only came half an hour ago, I feel sure Mrs. Warder must expect to return soon.

SERVANT (*entering with an envelope, which he gives to* WARDER). That is all I can find, sir.

WARDER (*humorously*). That's all I want, so it's all right. Jenks, am I wrong in understanding that Mrs. Warder is out?

SERVANT. Yes, sir. Mrs. Warder is in, sir.

WARDER. Oh! I beg your pardon, Lindon.

LINDON. That's all right.

WARDER (*to* JENKS). Jenks, say to Mrs. Warder, Mr. Lindon is here. You needn't say anything about me. I'm off.

SERVANT. Yes, sir. (*Goes out.*)

LINDON. I'm not driving you away, I hope.

WARDER. Oh, no, I have some important papers to go over. Make yourself comfortable. Good-by.

LINDON. Thanks, old man. Good-by. (*He sits on the sofa, as* WARDER *goes out.*)

LINDON. Well! She did send for you, Freddy, old son! Now's your chance!

SERVANT (*re-entering*). Mrs. Warder will be down at once.

LINDON. Thank you. (*The* SERVANT *goes out.* LINDON *goes to the piano and sings a verse of a song, "Everything comes to him who waits," etc. An idea comes to him. He weighs it, accepts it, smiles, and stops playing.*) I will! By George, I will! (*He rises.*)

(BECKY *hurries in and goes quickly toward him, crying, "Fred!" in a tone of distress and excitement. She leaves the door open behind her.* LINDON, *before she realizes what he is doing, has met her, taken her in his arms, and kissed her. She forces herself away from him, standing for a moment speechless with rage and astonishment.*)

LINDON. I told you, didn't I, Becky? (*Tries to embrace her again.*)

BECKY (*slowly and deliberately*). That's just exactly what Tom said you'd do!

LINDON. *What!*

BECKY. Ten to one, he said, if I sent for you again, you'd kiss me.

LINDON (*in alarm and astonishment*). Yes, but what—

BECKY. But I wouldn't believe him! I said, and I believed, he did you an injustice.

LINDON. So you talked me all over with him, did you! Then why did you send for me to-day?

BECKY. Because I was a fool, if you want the true treason!

LINDON. My dear Becky—

BECKY. Oh, you'll hear more and worse than that if you stay to listen! I advise you to go! You can't help me. I don't trust you. You might even make matters worse. It may have been all done purposely as it is.

LINDON. Oh!

BECKY. You see I'm ready to believe all I've heard of you, now that you've shown your true silly self to me in that one sickening moment, and I'd rather not be saved at all than be saved by you!

(*She leans for a second against the corner of the writing table.*)

LINDON. How saved? From what?

BECKY. Never mind! I only want to say one more thing to you and then go, please. But I want this to ring in your ears so long as you remember me! There is only one man in this world I love, and that's Tom, and there's only one man I despise and that's you! Lindon, Fred Lindon! You know who I mean! I know now what our friend-

ship meant to you and I wish I could cut out of my life every second of every hour I've spent with you! I've been a fool woman, and you've been a cad— but thank God, there are men in the world—real men—and one is my husband. Now go, please! Eve's a fool not to jump at the chance of getting rid of you and I shall tell her so. (*She turns away from him with a movement of dismissal.*)

LINDON (*going toward her*). Do! For that, at least, I shall thank you, as well as for our delightful friendship, which I am sorry to have end so contrary to my expectations.

BECKY (*with her eyes down, speaks in a low, shamed voice*). The room is too small for you and me at this moment,—which leaves?

(*He smiles, hesitates a moment, then sits in the armchair.* BECKY *gives a half-smothered exclamation of rage and starts to leave the room.* LINDON *rises quickly.*)

LINDON. No, no, I was only joking! I'm sorry you take the whole affair so seriously. Allow me. (*He bows and goes out.*)

BECKY (*stands quietly thinking a moment, then makes up her mind*). Eve herself is the one to help me! But I can't go to her till I'm sure she'll listen and understand—Laura! (*She sits by the table and takes up the receiver of the telephone.*) Seven O eight Plaza. Yes! It's a lady this time, so I hope you won't have to listen! Hello! Is Miss— Oh, is that you, Laura? Can you come over at once? I am in dreadful trouble! Oh, well, after dinner, then! No, I was going out, but I won't— it's too important. You were right—and Eve's right too. Never mind, I can't tell you over the 'phone. I'll explain everything tonight, only don't fail me. You can prevent a real catastrophe that has no need to happen.—Oh, that's all right, don't stop another minute, then. Thank you with all my heart. (*She hangs up the receiver, gives a long sigh, and sits worriedly thinking.* WARDER *comes in, serious but calm. Looking at him, half frightened, she makes a great effort to be natural, and to be in a good humor.*) Hello, Tom! Your game finished already?

WARDER. We didn't play. Weld didn't get back to town. Any callers?

BECKY. No.

WARDER. I thought I saw some one leaving—from the top of the street.

BECKY. Did you? Oh! it was probably father; he came.

WARDER. No, I spoke with your father some fifteen minutes ago. He told me about the money you gave him. (*A second's pause;* BECKY *looks down and then up at him.*)

BECKY. Are you angry?

WARDER. You gave me your word you wouldn't.

BECKY. But I was so sorry for him— that's why he came to-day, he said he must have it; I couldn't refuse him and you weren't here!

WARDER. He said you mailed him my check day before yesterday.

BECKY (*silent, trapped, frightened. A pause, then she speaks in a low voice*). I'm so sorry—(*A second's pause.*)

WARDER. It looked to me like Fred Lindon.

BECKY (*more frightened, realizing what is hanging over her, like a drowning person who cannot swim, flounders helplessly about in the next few speeches, trying to save herself by any and every means that she thinks may help her for the moment*). Well, I'll be honest, it *was* Fred Lindon!

WARDER (*anger getting the best of him*). After everything—your word of honor, Eve's accusations, my absolute desire—you sent for him to come and see you!

BECKY. No, no, you mustn't think that, Tom! He came of his own accord of course—I suppose to see if I would see him! I didn't know it!

WARDER (*wary, suspicious, to lead her on*). Then why did you see him? You could easily excuse yourself.

BECKY. No, you don't understand. (*She flounders hopelessly.*) I didn't know it was he! Don't you see?

WARDER. No, I don't see! (*Watches her with a face growing harder and harder with each lie she tells.*)

BECKY. But I'm telling you—it was just like this; I was upstairs and Jenks came—and said a gentleman wanted to see me in the drawing room. Just that, don't you see—a gentleman. (*She sees the doubting look in his face and mistaking it, tries to make her story more plausible.*) I was surprised too, and said "Who?" and Jenks said the gentleman gave no name— (*He turns sharply away from her, unable to face her as she tells the lies.*) Yes, I know it was funny—I thought so then. I suppose Jenks considered it a joke—and I suppose he didn't give his name for that very reason, for fear I wouldn't see him —(WARDER, *looking up as if to stop her, sees the door open and quickly closes it.*) Of course the moment I came into the room and saw who it was, I excused myself, and he left.

WARDER (*in a voice not loud but full of anger and emotion*). Lies! all of it! Every word a lie, and another and another and another!

BECKY (*breathless with fright, gasping*). Tom!

WARDER (*going to her*). You sent for him! (*She is too frightened to speak, but she shakes her head in a last desperate effort at denial.*) Don't shake your head! I know what I'm talking about and for the first time with you, I believe! (*She puts up her hands helplessly and backs away from him.*) I saw your note to him! (*She starts with a sense of anger added to her other emotions.*) I read it here, in this room; he gave it to me before you came down.

BECKY. The beast!

WARDER (*with biting satire*). You're going to misjudge him too!

BECKY. No, Tom, I'll tell you the truth and all of it!

WARDER. Naturally, now you've *got to!*

BECKY. No—wait! I did send for him —it was to tell him about those papers of Eve's.

WARDER. Yes, you must plan your escape together!

BECKY. No! because I still believed he was decent. I thought it was his duty, that he would claim it as his right, to prevent such a scandal as Eve threatened to make, which he knew I didn't deserve.

WARDER. Hah!

BECKY. You may sneer, but I don't! Yes, I broke my promise to you—what else could I do? You wouldn't let me send for him! And he came! And he did what you said he would. He took me in his arms before I could stop him, and kissed me. (*She bends over the back of the chair on which she is leaning, and sobs.*)

WARDER (*goes to her, speaking with bitter irony*). Charming! And you turned on him, of course! Played the shocked and surprised wife and ordered him out of the house!

BECKY. Yes. But I did! Why do you speak as if I didn't?

WARDER. Do you expect me to believe this, too?

BECKY (*facing him*). I don't expect, you've got to!

WARDER. Do you think you can go on telling lies forever and I'll go on blindly believing them as I have for three years?

BECKY. Even you couldn't have turned on him with more anger and disgust than I did!

WARDER. I couldn't believe you if I wanted to! You've destroyed every breath of confidence in me!

BECKY. It's the truth I'm telling you now!

WARDER. In everything—everything that has come up since my eyes were first forced half open—you have told me a lie!

BECKY. It's the truth! It's the truth!

WARDER (*continues, hardly hearing her*). The money to your father, the first lie, and today made a double one! All this rotten evidence of Eve's—another dozen! Your promise that Lindon's visit Thursday should be his last, the next!

BECKY. I meant it then—I meant it truthfully.

WARDER (*ignoring her interruption*). His visit after all today—that led of course to a mass of lies! And then the truth! He kissed you! And then another lie and another dozen to try and save yourself!

BECKY (*quietly, in a hushed, frightened voice*). By everything in this world and in the next that I hold dear and reverence, I've told you the truth at last.

WARDER. You don't know what's true when you hear it or when you speak it! I could never believe in you again! Never have confidence! How could I? Ask any man in the world, and his answer would be the same! (*He turns and goes away from her, to control his anger, which threatens to get the best of him.*)

BECKY (*sobbing*). No, no, Tom!

Don't! don't say that! You must believe in me! You must believe in me!

WARDER (*after a pause, collects himself and comes to the writing table*). Becky, you and I must say good-by to each other. We must finish separately. (*A silence. She looks at him in dumb horror and surprise.*) Do you understand?

BECKY (*in a low voice*). No!

WARDER. We must separate. Quietly —no fuss, no divorce unless you wish it. (*A pause, she does not answer. He goes toward her and repeats.*) No divorce unless you wish it.

BECKY (*with simple but deep pathos*). I love you.

WARDER. You must stay on in the house for the present, till you can make your plans. That will help keep the thing quiet, too.

BECKY. Tom! Do you really mean all you're saying? Do you realize what it must mean for me—for both of us?

WARDER. Yes.

BECKY. Tomorrow, perhaps—?

WARDER. No. I shall go to Boston tonight for a few days; when I come back, you may have settled on something. If you haven't, I can manage all right. I don't want to press you about that, only—

BECKY. I will not stay in your house one single day without you.

WARDER. You'll have to! My price for hushing up Lindon and Eve, and everyone else, is that you on your side act with dignity, and as I think wisest.

BECKY (*going to the armchair*). No! A woman like me whose heart is breaking, whether she's right or wrong, can't act like that. *She can't do it!* (*She sinks into the chair, bursting into tears.*)

WARDER (*beside her*). Try. For your sake as well as mine. Good-by, Becky.

BECKY (*with the tears choking her voice*). I told you the truth the last time. Oh, can't you believe me?

WARDER. No—good-by. (*Going.*)

BECKY. I love you and only you and you always—

WARDER (*turns in the doorway*). The club address will reach me! (*He goes out, closing the door behind him.*)

(BECKY *sits still a moment, thinking; then she goes to the writing table, rings the bell, and takes up a timetable. Her hands drop upon the table in utter dejection and her head lowers as the tears come again fast and thick.*)

SERVANT (*entering*). Yes, madam?

BECKY (*controlling her emotion and hiding as best she can the traces of it*). Tell Perkins to pack my small trunk and handbag. I am going to Baltimore to spend a day or so with my father.

SERVANT. Yes, madam.

BECKY. And then come back, please.

SERVANT. Very good, madam. (*Goes out.*)

BECKY (*takes up the telephone*). Hello! 708 Plaza. (*As she listens for the answer, she looks about the room, the control goes from her face, and the tears come once more; she brushes them away and tries to speak in a conventional tone without displaying her emotion, which is however plainly evident.*) Hello, I want Miss Fraser, please. . . . Oh, ask her to call me the minute she's free, please. Mrs. Warder. (*She hangs up the receiver and writes.*) "I am leaving now. You will at least believe that I cannot turn you out of your house, nor can I live in it one single day without you. It is ready waiting for you as I shall be all the rest of my life if you can ever again believe—" (*She stops as the SERVANT enters and comes to her.*)

SERVANT. Madam?

BECKY (*finishes writing silently, sealing the note*). Has Mr. Warder gone yet?

SERVANT. Only just this second went out, madam. He told me to pack his bag and meet him at the station with it.

BECKY (*rising*). Give this to Mr. Warder with his things. (*Gives the note.*)

SERVANT. Yes, madam. (*He goes out.*)

(*The telephone bell rings.*)

BECKY (*going to the table, sits, and takes up the receiver. Again she does her best to keep the emotion out of her voice, but only partly succeeds*). Hello! Laura? I'm so sorry, after all, I can't see you tonight. Tom has been called to —Chicago suddenly on business—yes, isn't it too bad? And I've had a telegram that Father isn't very well, so I am taking the five-twenty train to Baltimore. Yes, I'll write. No, I don't think he's seriously ill. Good-by! (*She hangs up the receiver, dropping her head on the table and sobbing heartbrokenly as the curtain falls.*)

ACT THREE

Saturday night. MR. ROLAND's *rooms in* MRS. CRESPIGNY's *flat in Baltimore. This is the parlor of a cheap flat, with the bedroom, through an arch, originally intended for the dining room and lit by a narrow window on a well. There is red paper on the walls and red gloves for the electric lights. An ugly set of furniture, with many tidies, a strange conglomeration of cheap feminine knickknacks, relieved by a sporting print or two, a frame of prize ribbons, and a few other masculine belongings which have been added to the original condition of the room, like a thin coat of paint. At back is a bow-window beside a sofa. On the left is the opening into the bedroom, and beside this a door leads to the hall. There is a center table with chairs on either side and a Morris chair down on the right. A sideboard in the upper left corner.* ROLAND *and* MRS. CRESPIGNY *are playing piquet at the center table. A "Teddy Bear" with a pink ribbon bow about its neck is sitting on the table near* MRS. CRESPIGNY. *They play on through part of the scene.* ROLAND *stops to light a cigarette, and* MRS. CRESPIGNY *takes advantage of the pause to powder her face and preen herself in a pocket mirror.*

MRS. CRESPIGNY. You don't think you smoke too many of them?

ROLAND. If my smoking is disagreeable to you, I might spend my evenings at the club.

MRS. CRESPIGNY. You know different! You can't make that an excuse for skinning out of spending your evenings at home. I only wish't I smoked 'em myself. I've read in the papers that real ladies do now—but I guess it's the fast set, and I always was conservative.

ROLAND (*playing*). Don't talk; study your cards. If you don't take care, you'll win!

MRS. CRESPIGNY. Will I? Excuse me, I wasn't thinking. (*She plays a card, and, as* ROLAND *takes the trick, she takes up her mirror and examines wrinkles.*) I believe I'll have massage. I heard of a fine massoor yesterday.

ROLAND. Masseuse, you mean, I hope.

MRS. CRESPIGNY. Massoor! Massoose is plural. The singular is massoor. You forget I was educated in New Orleans. (*She rises and goes to the sideboard and pours out a brandy and soda.*)

ROLAND. Where's my brandy and soda?

MRS. CRESPIGNY. I'm getting it. (*Bringing the glass down to the table.*)

ROLAND. That's a good girl. Thank you, Mrs. Crespigny.

MRS. CRESPIGNY. Ain't it funny, good friends as we've been for so long now, we've kep' on calling each other "Mr." and "Mrs."? S'pose it wouldn't be etiquay to call each other by our first names.

ROLAND. Etiquette.

MRS. CRESPIGNY. *Etiquay!* You can correct my English when you want to, but my French I've kep' pure since school, and I remember perfeckly—all words ending in e-t you pernounce A.

ROLAND. What is your first name?

MRS. CRESPIGNY. Genevieve, but I was always called Jenny by my first h—! I mean—I was always called Jenny by my schoolgirl friends.

ROLAND (*playing*). Very interesting.

MRS. CRESPIGNY (*playing*). I think your first name's real pretty!

ROLAND (*taking the trick*). Tut, tut! You're getting too skittish, Mrs. Crespigny.

MRS. CRESPIGNY (*laughs a little embarrassedly*). It's your fault!

ROLAND (*playing card, and laughing*). Then I apologize!

MRS. CRESPIGNY (*playing card, and giggling*). Oh, you needn't!

ROLAND (*laughing more at her than with her, but realizing that she will not know the difference*). I insist. (*He takes the trick.*)

MRS. CRESPIGNY. Anybody'd think we was engaged to be married or something of that sort, wouldn't they?

ROLAND. I hope not!

MRS. CRESPIGNY. Oh, I don't know! I remember some postal cards what I've read that might be construed to lean that way. (ROLAND *rises and gets a cigarette from the box on the table in the bow window.*) There was one from Atlantic City that was just too sweet for anything! You sent it after we had that ridickerlous quarrel on the board walk.

ROLAND. What about?

MRS. CRESPIGNY. I lost my self-respect and asked you to kiss me, 'cause you said you was grateful for the fifty dollars I gave you for your poker losses the night before. And you handed me back my money and said if that was the price of the loan— (*With a touch of futile emotion*) oh, how you hurt my feelings!

ROLAND (*coming back to his chair*). That was only a bluff! Come along, I'll play you a game for the whole bunch of postal cards. (*Takes up the second deck and shuffles.*)

MRS. CRESPIGNY (*rising, speaks rather grandly*). Nobody won't never get them postal cards from me except over my dead body. (*Cuts the cards, and* ROLAND *deals.*) And I intend to refer to 'em every chance I get in hopes that some day—just in a desperate fit, maybe—you'll up and marry me to stop me. (*Sits again.*)

ROLAND. Go on, play.

MRS. CRESPIGNY. You've owned up you're comfortable in my cute little flat—and I don't nag.

(*Both take up their hands, both play, and she takes trick.*)

ROLAND. You haven't the right, but as my wife—nay, nay, Pauline.

MRS. CRESPIGNY. You've got the best rooms here, and if you ever do pay any board, don't I lend it right back to you the next day?

ROLAND. Isn't it a little indelicate to remind me of that, Mrs. Crespigny? (*Playing.*)

MRS. CRESPIGNY (*getting a little angry*). Well, I guess the indelicacy's even! (*She plays and starts to take the trick. He stops her and takes it himself.*) Oh, excuse me, I'm at your beck and nod, and I've even so far forgot my family pride as to hint that you wasn't unacceptable to me in a nearer relation.

ROLAND. There you go again! Keep off the thin ice!

MRS. CRESPIGNY (*throws down her cards and loses her temper outright*). Well, why won't you marry me? I may have forgot my pride, but I never forget myself. You know you wouldn't dare step over the invisible line between the dumb-waiter and the bathroom what separates your apartment from mine in the flat.

ROLAND. One moment, please. Have I ever even hinted at taking the slightest advantage of your unprotected position in this house? (*He rises in mock dignity.*) Who's kept further from that invisible line, you or I?

MRS. CRESPIGNY. Well, I must say you've always behaved toward me like a perfect gentleman. (*He sits again and takes another cigarette.*) But jes' let's speak the truth—if you can about anything! (*He fumbles in his vest pockets.*) Matches? (*She rises, goes to the sideboard, and finding a box of matches, brings it back to the table. During the first part of the following speech she makes nervous and ineffectual efforts to strike matches, in each case breaking off the heads without any result.*) You know you ain't wanted at your clubs; that's why you first took to playin' evenings with me—that, and 'cause I was easy! You know that here in Baltimore you're called a tout, a brokendown gambler, and a has-been, but I've always hoped you was a will-be for me. (*Irritated by her repeated failures, he takes the matchbox from her and lights his cigarette with the first match he strikes.*) You know your old friends'd rather go 'round the block than stop and talk to you in the street. Yes, you know it as well as I do! And

you've lived off me, borrowed money of me, led me to caring for you, let me take care of you as if you was—my own child, and I've saved you from bein' a drunken sot! (*Her voice fills with tears, but her anger gets the best of her, and she finishes strongly, striking the table with her beringed hand as she leans across toward him.*) Now, why ain't I good enough for you?

ROLAND (*rising, really angry, and his dignity offended*). Mrs. Crespigny—

MRS. CRESPIGNY. Oh, you needn't get on your high horse or I'll win this rubber for the five hundred! I know you're worthless, and I know you don't always tell the truth, but through it all you've been a real gentleman to me, and I realized yesterday, when I thought you was gone for good, what it meant to me. I'm a decent woman, Mr. Roland, if I am a fool, and I swear I'm good enough for you!

ROLAND. So far as that goes, you're too good for me, but I've got others to consider. My daughter—

MRS. CRESPIGNY (*interrupting him*). Yes, I know she's against me. (*She sits again, and with determination.*) Well, I'm against her, and perhaps some day I'll have a chance to pay her back!

ROLAND. That's talking foolishly! In the first place, my allowance would stop the day I married.

MRS. CRESPIGNY. Well, haven't I got enough for two? It's looked mighty like it the last couple a years. (*She nervously takes the "Teddy Bear" from the table to hide her embarrassment at her boldness, and laying it flat on her knee, face downward, reties the pink bow on its neck.*)

ROLAND (*sitting, he gathers the cards together and shuffles them*). Come, come, here we are again on one of those useless discussions. Come along, give me another brandy and soda.

MRS. CRESPIGNY (*resignedly*). All right.(*Rises, and takes his glass, replacing the "Teddy Bear" on the table.*) This will be your second before twelve o'clock and it's got to be a little weakish. (*She goes to the sideboard. The front door-bell is heard ring.*) My goodness! who can that be? (*The bell rings again.*)

ROLAND. Don't know, old girl, but go on, I'll deal for you. (*He deals.*)

MRS. CRESPIGNY (*going to the table, cuts the cards*). I just love to have you call me "old girl"—it seems so nice and familiar.

(*The bell rings again, and* MRS. CRESPIGNY, *taking the "Teddy Bear" with her, places it on the side table and goes out.* ROLAND *deals. After a moment's pause,* BECKY *comes in, carrying a handbag. She enters with an air of bravado, which fades instantly that she observes* ROLAND *does not see her. But her pathetic, timid look vanishes immediately when he looks up.*)

ROLAND (*going on dealing, without looking up*). Who was it?

BECKY (*with forced gaiety*). Hello, Father!

ROLAND. Good Heavens!

BECKY (*putting her bag on the table*). Aren't you surprised?

ROLAND (*dryly*). Very.

BECKY. And pleased?

ROLAND. Where in the world did you come from?

BECKY. New York; the next train after you. Give me a kiss. How are you? (*Kisses him.*)

ROLAND. What have you come for? Where are you stopping?

BECKY. Here!

ROLAND. At what hotel?

BECKY. No hotel—here with you!

ROLAND. Nonsense! There's no place for you in the flat.

BECKY. Why not? I gave my check to the expressman and my trunk will be around in the morning.

ROLAND. These two rooms are all I have. (*Showing the opening to the left*) Take a look at the bedroom—a beastly, dark little hole with one window that doesn't look out—it looks in! The bedroom of the flat we use for a dining room. Mrs. Crespigny sleeps in the servant's room—so she tells me.

BECKY. Father!

ROLAND. Now you can see what nice sort of surroundings your poor old father's had to put up with these last years.

BECKY (*takes off her hat and cloak and puts them on sofa*). You have only yourself to blame! You could live splendidly on the allowance Tom makes you in the one club you've got left.

ROLAND. You needn't take off your things, you can't stay here.

BECKY. Oh, can't I? I've come to pay you a little visit, and here I stay to-night and several nights. (*Comes to the center table and starts to collect cards.*)

ROLAND. Be careful! That's Genevieve's hand and we must finish this sometime—I'm well ahead. (*Carefully places the cards, properly divided, on the table.*) And really, Becky, you can't stay here. You can go to a hotel if you want to, or back to New York. You're in the way here! I'm an old man; this sort of thing upsets me! There's no room and there's no bed for you. (*Crosses to the Morris chair and sits.*) What the devil do you mean, turning up here well toward midnight, and threatening to stay, when for years I've been trying to get you to come to Baltimore, and you know you were ashamed to come?

BECKY (*sitting in the chair, left of the center table*). That isn't true,

Father; I always said I'd come if you'd give up certain things.

ROLAND. Well, I haven't given them up, so why have you come? What's the joke? And where's Tom?

BECKY (*after a second's pause*). That's just it. Tom has been called to —San Francisco—suddenly—just after you left, on business—and the idea came to me, at last I'll make that visit to Father! It'll be a good chance for me to settle Mrs. Crespigny, too!

ROLAND. You couldn't have come at a more inopportune time! I was very busy this evening.

BECKY. Yes, I know—piquet with Mrs. C.! I'll finish it with you. (*Rises and goes to get the cards.*)

ROLAND. No, you won't! You'll go to a hotel for the night and I'll come and have a decent lunch with you tomorrow.

BECKY. I can't go to a hotel. I've come away without a penny. I had to borrow half the money for my ticket from Perkins.

ROLAND. Where is Perkins?

BECKY. In New York. I knew, of course, there'd be no place for her here.

ROLAND. Any of the hotel people here will trust you.

BECKY. I won't ask them. I forgot to get Tom's address, so I can't send to him for any money. I've got to stay with you, Father. (*She sits on the arm of the Morris chair and puts her arm about her father.*)

ROLAND. You're a very boring person!

BECKY. That's a kind welcome for a dear and only daughter!

ROLAND. And I'm not going to have myself made uncomfortable by you!

BECKY. Please let me stay for a day or two, maybe a little longer or maybe not so long. I'll promise not to be any trouble; I'll sleep on the sofa!

ROLAND. Humph! You don't know that sofa! That was made in the antebellum and the antespringum days! Even a cat couldn't sleep on it without chloroform.

BECKY. Well, I don't expect to sleep, Father, and if I don't, you won't know it. I've got to stay. (*Rises and goes away and stands by the table with her back toward him.*)

ROLAND (*looks at her, suddenly suspicious*). Becky, you're not telling me the truth. Something's the matter.

BECKY (*turning toward him, taking a high moral stand*). Really, Father!

ROLAND. There's something wrong. What is it?

BECKY. Nothing.

ROLAND. Oh, come, I'm your father, and I know the look in your eyes when you're not telling the truth; you get that look from me! You're telling me a lie—tell me the truth. What does it mean?

BECKY (*after a second's pause, bursts out with all her pent-up feelings, which she has been trying to hide*). I've left Tom.

ROLAND. How do you mean—"Left Tom"?

BECKY. Left him for good. I'll never live with him again.

ROLAND. Nonsense!

BECKY. Never! You don't understand. (*She sits again beside the table, leaning her elbows upon it and resting her face between her two hands.*)

ROLAND. No, I don't! and I don't want to!

BECKY. I've left his house in New York for good.

ROLAND. What's your reason? What's he done?

BECKY. He's deceived me.

ROLAND (*rising*). Tom! Never!

BECKY. Father, I can't go back to him; I can't! Don't ask me any more questions, only keep me with you—please, keep me with you. . . .

ROLAND (*going to her*). You're upset about matters. You've had a quarrel, that's all, and you're going back tonight.

BECKY. No. I've told him I'll never come back and I've come to stay—with you.

ROLAND. But I won't have it! In the first place, Mrs. Crespigny wouldn't have it either. She'd be jealous of your being here—and after all it's her flat. And I don't believe what you tell me about Tom.

BECKY. We can go somewhere else. Who is Mrs. Crespigny? (*Rises, and going to him takes hold of his sleeve.*) And I'm your daughter. Besides, Tom's allowance will stop. From now on you and I must get on together with the little money I have from Mother.

ROLAND. Nothing of the sort. Even if you did leave Tom, you can make him take care of you.

BECKY. I won't take any money from Tom! No more money! Do you hear me, Father?

ROLAND (*becoming more angry*). No, I don't hear you! And I have something to say about my end of all this, which is that you've got to go back to your husband before it's too late for him to take you back, and give him a chance to explain! You'll go back to Tom tonight! (*He goes determinedly to the sofa and gets her hat and cloak for her.*)

BECKY (*takes her hat from him and puts it on the center table with equal determination*). I shall sleep here, in **this room, tonight!**

ROLAND. You'll sleep in a Pullman car and wake up tomorrow, happy and in your right senses, in Jersey City.

BECKY (*moves back from him a little*). You can't turn me out!

(*A pause.* ROLAND *reads the real trouble in her face and becomes serious and sympathetic.*)

ROLAND. Becky, you don't really believe what you say about Tom? (*She lowers her head in assent.*) You *know*? (*She lowers her head again.*) There must be a mistake somewhere! (*Puts the cloak on the Morris chair.*) If I ever knew a man who loved his wife! Go back, Becky!

BECKY. It's impossible!

ROLAND (*going to her*). I speak to you with years of bitter experience behind me, and it's only what good there is left in me which is urging me to say this to you. I know in the end that you'll be nearer happiness than you ever can be any other way. Go back to Tom.

BECKY. No, no, I tell you, Father, I've left Tom for good! Keep me with you—

(*A knock on the door.*)

ROLAND. Come in!

(MRS. CRESPIGNY *comes in, and* BECKY *sinks down into the Morris chair.*)

MRS. CRESPIGNY (*worried*). It's getting pretty late! I didn't know as Mis' Warder knew the streetcar don't run past here after twelve thirty.

ROLAND. That's all right. Mrs. Warder is taking the one o'clock train to New York. We'll catch the last car.

MRS. CRESPIGNY (*relieved, smiles*). Oh, well, then, you've got plenty of time. I'd better let you have my latch-key, though. I'll leave it on the hall table. (*To* BECKY) Would you like anything? A glass of raspberry vinegar and a piece of jell cake?

BECKY. No, thanks.

MRS. CRESPIGNY (*offended*). Good evening.

BECKY. Good evening.

(MRS. CRESPIGNY *goes out.*)

Why did you say I was going? I'm not!

ROLAND. You are. If you love Tom, you'll go. (*He goes to her and puts his arm around her shoulder.*) Do you love Tom still?

BECKY. Yes, Father.

ROLAND. Then go back, Becky!

BECKY. No.

ROLAND. Your religion teaches you that the greatest love always carries with it the power of forgiveness.

BECKY (*eagerly*). Oh, it's what I want to believe. If it's only true—if it's only true of *us!*

ROLAND. You've got to *make* it true by going back! (*He moves away.*) Good God! you shan't repeat your mother's and my mistake and make a miserable failure of both your lives!

BECKY (*looks up surprised*). What mistake?

ROLAND (*quietly, ashamed*). Your mother left me, just as you want to leave Tom.

BECKY. Mother— (*Rises.*) left you?

ROLAND. And for the same reason, do you understand me—that you want to leave Tom.

BECKY. But you never told me!

ROLAND. No.

BECKY. How long before she died?

ROLAND. A year.

BECKY. And how long were you and Mother happy together?

ROLAND. A few months—not many.

BECKY. Tom and I have been blissfully happy for six years!

ROLAND. That's an argument for me! Go back!

BECKY. What a lot of lies you've always told me about yourself and Mother—all my life! You always said you were an ideal couple and that it was sorrow over her death that made you what you are!

ROLAND. I was ashamed when you found me out—I wanted some excuse to try and keep your sympathy and affection. Besides, what good would it have done to have told you the truth? (*He crosses to the table and, taking up a photograph of his wife, stands looking at it.*)

BECKY. If you had always told me the truth about everything, I think it would have saved me this night. I've about decided that the truth in everything is the best for everything in the end—if one could only learn to tell it.

ROLAND. You must begin young and you didn't.

BECKY. By whose fault? (ROLAND *turns away from her, feeling the sting.*) Tell me now about you and Mother. (*She sits again in the Morris chair.*)

ROLAND (*by the center table*). Well, your mother accused me as you do Tom. But it wasn't true of me, Becky! it wasn't true—then.

BECKY. I'm afraid I don't believe you, Father.

ROLAND. You don't believe me when, even now, after all these years, I tell you it wasn't true?

BECKY. No. I want to believe you, Father, but I can't! You've just admitted you've lied to me all my life about you and Mother! Why should I believe you would suddenly turn around and tell me the truth now?

ROLAND. At last, one trait in you like your mother! Do all that I could, swear by everything she or I held holy, I couldn't persuade her I was telling the truth!

BECKY. Perhaps you had already destroyed her confidence in you! You can do that, even with some one who loves you, in a day, in an hour, in even less!

ROLAND. It did look ugly against me, and your mother was already disappointed in me. I couldn't live up to her standard. (*He smiles.*) I was sort of good-looking when she married me—too foppish, perhaps—and I rode my own horses, generally to win, too—and what part of my income I didn't make on the race track I made with the ace and right bower! I promised your mother to give up the gambling side of it—but I couldn't, it was in my blood; I tried, Becky, but I failed. I lied to her about it and she found me out and began to distrust me. She was a crank on the subject of lying, anyway. One of those straightforward, narrow-minded, New England women who think everything that isn't the truth is a lie! I always hated the plain truth. I liked to trim it up a little.

BECKY (*with a nervous, pathetic little laugh*). Like me!

ROLAND. Yes. I remember how we used to laugh at you as a child! Almost the first words you spoke were fibs, and gad, the fairy stories you used to tell about yourself! (*Goes up to table.*)

BECKY. Yes. Do you remember the time, Father, after I'd been reading *Grimm's Fairy Tales* about the wicked **step-parents, how I told all over Balti**more you were my stepfather and beat me? It made me a real heroine, to the other children, and I loved it! And you found it out, and gave me my choice of being punished or promising never to tell another story! Do you remember?

ROLAND (*sits on the arm of the chair and puts his arm about her*). I could never bear to punish you!

BECKY. I always made up stories about everything. I didn't see any harm—*then*—

ROLAND. Well, your mother said I'd proved I couldn't tell the truth! She didn't often use plain and ugly words, but she called me a liar, and I've never heard the word since without hearing her voice and seeing her face as she said it!

BECKY. You loved her! Oh, I know how it must have hurt!

ROLAND. She wouldn't believe me, she wouldn't forgive, and she left me! I don't blame her; it was my own fault at bottom! But it's true as land and water, Becky, as true as you're my daughter, God help you, and that I've loved you in my useless, selfish old way, I *was true to your mother*. I loved her, and no other woman existed for me then. I was willing to own up I had broken my word and was a gambler! I was willing to own up I was a liar, even, and perhaps I deserved all I got, but I loved your mother, and when she went back on me and believed the one thing about me that wasn't true, I gritted my teeth like a damn fool and said, "To hell with women and to the dogs for me!"

BECKY. And it wasn't true! Father! I believe you, it wasn't true!

ROLAND. No, but it was true enough soon after! I kept my word to myself and gave her plenty of reasons not to love me afterward—and that was the beginning of the end of me.

BECKY. But if you'd only waited, if you'd only given her a chance, wouldn't she have realized?

ROLAND (*going to her, puts his hand on her shoulder*). Yes, and that's why you must go back to Tom tonight. Do you want to repeat your mother's and my story? Go back, Becky!

BECKY. I can't.

ROLAND. Well, I can tell you what Tom'll do if you put off going back to him till it's too late. He'll let you go, and help you to divorce him, so he can marry some other woman, your opposite, and be happy the rest of his life.

BECKY. Father! (BECKY *shows a new element, jealousy, added to her trouble.*)

ROLAND. Or else he'll grow hard and bitter about all women, and the gold years of a man's life will be brass in his mouth—thanks to you!

BECKY. Yes, and I'll live here with you and grow dowdy and slattern, till I'm slovenly all through—body and soul! I won't care how I look or what company I keep in place of the friends who will surely drop me. I'll take up your life here, and my face'll grow flabby and my heart dry and my spirit fogged, and I'll have nobody to thank for the dead end but myself!

ROLAND. But I won't have it! You've got to go back to Tom tonight! You were happy enough with him this afternoon! He's been a wonderful husband to you and I know the run of them! I don't blame him for not wanting me around—a father-in-law who was a disgrace to his wife. He did right to keep me here where I'm an old story and nobody cares. I'll own up to this now that you want to turn your back on him. But you shan't do it! You shan't break up his home with a beastly scandal and spoil your whole life and perhaps his, all in one hysterical hour! Listen! (*He goes to her and places his two hands on her shoulders.*) It's true that no one was to blame for what I've sunk to but myself. Still, it's also true that in the beginning, perhaps, a great deal of patience, and more forgiveness, might have made both your mother's life and mine a little more worth living! (*He turns aside, surprised by a welling up of an almost forgotten emotion.*)

BECKY. You don't dream how every word you say cuts and saws into me! But I can't go back!

ROLAND. You will. For if it comes down to this point, I won't keep you here!

BECKY. But I can't go to a hotel! I haven't any money.

ROLAND. I have enough for your ticket, and I'll take you to the station and send a telegram to Tom to expect you in the morning.

BECKY. No, I can't—I can't.

ROLAND (*sternly*). You've *got* to! You can't stay here and I won't give you a cent to stay anywhere else!

BECKY. You wouldn't turn me out into the streets!

ROLAND. Yes, I will, if I must to force you to go back to your husband. (*He gets her cloak.*)

BECKY (*rises, desperate*). Father!

ROLAND (*struck by her tone, pauses*). Well?

BECKY (*drops her head and with a great effort speaks, her voice sinking almost to a whisper*). I haven't left Tom—it's Tom's left me—

(*A pause. ROLAND stands looking at her and her cloak drops from his hand, as he slowly takes in what she means.*)

ROLAND. What do you say?

BECKY. Tom has left me—now you know why I can't go back.

ROLAND. What for?

BECKY. He called me what Mother called you. He's lost confidence in me. He believes— (*In agony of shame and grief*) there's some one else.

ROLAND. No wonder you made me worm out the truth! I wouldn't have believed it of you, Becky! I wouldn't have believed it of you!

BECKY (*frightened*). But it isn't true, Father!

ROLAND. Why didn't you tell me the right story in the beginning?

BECKY (*aghast*). Father! don't you believe me?

ROLAND. You denied it to him, I suppose?

BECKY. Of course.

ROLAND. And he turned you out all the same?

BECKY. He didn't turn me out; he

only refused to stay in the house with me. I came away!

ROLAND. Well, if your husband doesn't believe in you, how can you expect me to, who've known all your life you couldn't tell the truth?

BECKY. Father, I've told you the truth now! For God's sake, believe me, for if *you* won't believe me either, what will become of me?

ROLAND. I can help you better if you'll be honest with me. A man like Tom Warder isn't putting the wife he's been a slave to out of his life without good reason. (*He turns away from her.*)

BECKY. You said you knew the look in my face when I lied, because it was your look. (*Goes to him and stands close, facing him.*) Look in my face now and tell me what you see there. (*She speaks very simply and clearly.*) I love Tom and only Tom and never have loved any other man and have never been anything but faithful and true in my love for him. (ROLAND *stands silently looking into her face, still unconvinced.*) I stand with Tom exactly, Father, where you stood the day Mother left you—

(*His face begins to change. A knock on the door.*)

MRS. CRESPIGNY (*outside*). If Mis' Warder wants to catch that train, I hear the car coming!

BECKY (*breathlessly seizing hold of him with her two hands*). Father!

ROLAND. Mrs. Warder's changed her mind. She's stopping here tonight. (*Putting his arms about her.*)

BECKY. Father! (*Her tension gives way, and she lies limp in his arms, her slender body shaking with the emotion which now masters her as the curtain falls.*)

ACT FOUR

MR. ROLAND's *rooms in* MRS. CRESPIGNY's *flat, the following Monday. The sun pours in through the bow window; folded bedclothes and a pillow are placed neatly on one end of the sofa.* BECKY *and* ROLAND *are having coffee together at the center table. The cloth is soiled, other things in the room are in disorder, and everything is decidedly unappetizing.* ROLAND *is wearing a slovenly bathrobe; a newspaper is propped against the coffee pot before him.*

BECKY. How horrid and messy everything is!

ROLAND (*who is smoking a cigarette as he eats*). Oh, you'll get used to it. Before you know it you'll like things best this way.

BECKY. Not if I can help it. I shall fight against it.

ROLAND. You think so now; you've only had one day at it.

BECKY. To begin with, my dear father, you mustn't come to breakfast with me in that disgusting bathrobe.

ROLAND. If you imagine for a minute I'm going to let you come here and upset everything to rob me of my comfort, you'll have your hands full.

(MRS. CRESPIGNY *is heard playing a piano in a farther room through most of the scene. Her repertoire is varied, and consists of an old waltz, a coon song, the "Melody in F," and "Waiting at the Church."*)

BECKY (*with an effort at a smile*). It will be another fight then, Father, such as we used to have. Only this time I'm stronger by six years' life with a splendid character, which will help me bring you and myself up to Tom's level, rather than go down with you to this.

ROLAND (*to change the subject*). Have you written Tom?

BECKY (*sighing*). A hundred letters, I should think.

ROLAND. And no answer?

BECKY. No, there isn't time.

ROLAND. Yes, he could telegraph.

BECKY. But I didn't send any of the letters.

ROLAND (*looking up from his newspaper*). You aren't eating anything.

BECKY (*rising in disgust, goes and sits in Morris chair*). Father, we can't live here, can we? You must tell Mrs. Crespigny, and I'll find a little flat, just for us two—

ROLAND (*irritably*). I knew it would come to that! Not satisfied with upsetting Warder's existence and your own, you've got to come here and upset mine! No, sir! I'll marry Mrs. C. before I'll leave here.

BECKY. That's a threat I know you won't carry out. I've had two long, long nights to think things over. I wish I could die, but I know one can't die when one wants to. I know sorrow, however heartbreaking, doesn't kill— and I'm so horribly healthy I'll probably live forever. I may even have to stand aside and see Tom happy with some one else. Well, all the same I mean to live exactly as I would if I were still with Tom. I'm going to live as if every day, every hour, I was expecting him back. I'm going to live so that if he ever should come back to me —I will be ready to go home with him.

(*The music stops for a moment.*)

ROLAND. That's all very well for you, but I don't see why I should have to live a life to please Tom—just so you can leave me in the lurch when he comes back after you. The odds are pretty strong against his wanting me to go home with him too! I've never

ridden yet according to his rules, and I don't intend to begin now. (*Goes to far table in the bow window and takes a fresh cigarette and changes his paper for another.*)

BECKY (*rising, takes the bedclothes from the sofa*). Don't forget, Father, what little money we have is mine, so you'll have to live as I wish. And in the end I believe you'll thank me. (*She goes into the bedroom.*)

ROLAND. But in the beginning I'll damn you, and in the end too! I'm too old a leopard to change my spots. (*He makes himself comfortable in the Morris chair.*)

BECKY (*coming out of the bedroom*). I'm going to try just as hard as I can not to tell even little lies, no matter how small, just to see if I can't get into the habit of always telling the truth. Because he might come back, Father, don't you think so? Don't you think maybe he'll come back?

ROLAND. I'm doing my best to make him.

BECKY (*surprised and eager*). How?

ROLAND. Never mind how. I'll tell you if it works.

BECKY (*piling the breakfast dishes on the tray*). I hoped he'd answer the note I sent by Jenks, but he didn't. No; when Tom says a thing, he means it. I'm going out for a little while. (*She places the tray on the table.*)

ROLAND. Where?

BECKY. There's a small empty flat two doors below here; I'm going to look it over. I think it may do for us. (*She goes into the bedroom.*)

ROLAND. Don't be gone long, because I might need you.

BECKY (*in the bedroom*). For what?

ROLAND. To help receive Tom!

BECKY (*coming out quickly*). Father!

ROLAND. Don't get your expectations too high, but I telegraphed him yesterday to come here.

(*The piano is heard again, but stops during* BECKY's *long speech.*)

BECKY. If he wouldn't come for me, he wouldn't come because you asked him.

ROLAND. I feel if only you could get face to face with him, Becky, especially now when he's had time to think things over, to realize calmly, away from the heat of anger, that whatever your faults might be—

BECKY (*interrupts eagerly, going toward him*). Yes, yes—

ROLAND. Lack of love for him and faithlessness couldn't be among them.

BECKY. Yes, if I could see him! (*She kneels on the floor beside him, her arms on the arm of the chair.*) I feel that if there's left in the bottom of his heart—no matter how deep down—just a little love for me, if it's only the memory of what he once had, wouldn't my own love be some sort of a magnet to bring his back? If I could sit and talk to him, hold his hand, go back over our life a little, couldn't I make him see that I loved him—and only him, that what I'd done had been foolish—wrong not to do as he wished— but only *that* wrong—and that I've learned something by this terrible lesson? And if I promised to try with all my might and main not to lie any more, if I promised I wouldn't be discouraged with failure if he wouldn't be, but would keep on trying, wouldn't he on his side try to have a little confidence again? Wouldn't he let me come back into his life just for that trial anyway?...

ROLAND. I think so. A man like Warder can't get over loving a woman all in a moment, especially if he finds out before it's too late he's misjudged her. Wrong as you may have been, we know you're not so wrong as he thinks.

BECKY. But he won't come. You see you haven't heard from him—he won't come. (*She goes up to the bow window and looks out.*)

ROLAND. I'm a little worried myself. I told him to telegraph and said it was urgent.

BECKY. How—urgent?

ROLAND. Well, my dear, as you say, if I had simply said, "Come and see Becky," of course he wouldn't have paid any attention. I had to make the telegram so he would come.

BECKY. Yes, but how did you?

ROLAND. It was a stroke of genius! I said, "Becky is dying. Come at once!"

BECKY (*going to the sofa and sitting on it*). But I'm not dying. He'll find out as soon as he gets here.

ROLAND. No, he mustn't. My idea was that he would think you had tried to kill yourself—don't you see? It would rouse his sympathies—perhaps some remorse—and he would hurry on. (*Dropping the paper carelessly on the floor, he rises.*)

BECKY. But he hasn't!

ROLAND. He couldn't get here till this morning; still, I ought to have had an answer to the telegram. (*He goes into the bedroom.*)

BECKY (*rises and goes toward the opening*). And if he should come?

ROLAND (*coming out of the bedroom in his shirt sleeves, without the bathrobe*). Well, you must be careful not to give me away till you are solid with him again. You must be weak and ill— just getting over it—the doctor's saved you! Anyway, I thought that might bring him.

BECKY. I don't like it.

ROLAND (*going back into the bedroom offended*). I did my best!

BECKY. But it seems to me as if I would be telling Tom a lie again.

ROLAND. Not at all. I'm telling it.

And besides, doesn't the end justify the means?

BECKY. I think Tom'd call it a lie. I don't want to do it!

ROLAND. Well, if he comes in answer to my telegram, you've *got* to do it!

BECKY. No, Father, I won't!

ROLAND. Nonsense! You can't get out of it. And, good Heavens, why should you, if it's going to give you back what you want and prevent a terrible upheaval?

(*The piano is heard again.*)

BECKY. Well, anyway, he hasn't answered, so perhaps he won't come. I'm going out. (*Gets her hat from the table.*)

ROLAND. Don't be long in any case. He might have forgot to send word, or not have time, or even have suspected something and not answered purposely, and be coming all the same on this morning's train!

BECKY (*putting on her hat*). I'll see the flat and come straight back. (*She starts to go, stops and turns in the doorway.*) Thank you, Father, for trying to help me. If he only *will* come! (*She goes out.*)

ROLAND (*lighting another cigarette*). Move into another flat! To live with everything so filthy clean you can't be easy and let things go! Ta, ta to the bucket-shop, and never a cent to put on anything again! Nothing but cleanth and economy! No, no, Stephen Roland, not at your age. (*He stands gazing at a portrait of* MRS. CRESPIGNY *on the right wall, with a half-humorous expression of resignation, then crosses to the electric bell on the left wall.*) Listen, don't you hear wedding bells? (*He rings the bell.*) Do you hear them, Stephen! (*He rings again. The piano offstage stops.*) Wedding bells! (*He turns and walks toward the portrait again, nodding his head definitely. A knock on the door.*)

Come in—*Jennie!*

(MRS. CRESPIGNY *comes in.*)

MRS. CRESPIGNY. Did you ring?

ROLAND. I believe I did.

MRS. CRESPIGNY. What's the matter? My piano-playing disturb Mis' Warder?

ROLAND. Oh—is the pianola mended?

MRS. CRESPIGNY. Yes. The man said I worked the pedals too emotionally.

ROLAND. I wanted to see you.

MRS. CRESPIGNY (*pulling her belt down and her marcel wave out*). Well, I'm visible!

ROLAND. Mrs. Crespigny, I'm in trouble.

MRS. CRESPIGNY (*going to him*). Now look here, Mr. Roland, true as Gospel I can't let you have another cent, not before the first of the month. Your daughter's here now; you've got to go to her.

ROLAND. Not so fast, please! It isn't money. At least that isn't this moment's trouble. My daughter and her husband have quarrelled.

MRS. CRESPIGNY. I suspected something was wrong. (*She starts, aghast and angry at a new idea which comes to her.*) She don't mean to come here and live?

ROLAND. No, she wants to take me away to live with her.

MRS. CRESPIGNY. Didn't I always tell you she'd separate us if she could! Now show your character! I guess you're your own boss, ain't you? You won't go, Mr. Roland?

ROLAND. But you see if they don't make up their quarrel, my allowance stops and I won't have a cent. I'll have to live where my daughter wants me.

MRS. CRESPIGNY (*taking from the bosom of her shirtwaist a secondhand natural rose with a wired stem, and destitute of green leaves, she twists the wired part nervously about*). Why ain't one woman's money just as good as another's for you to live on?

ROLAND. Mrs. Crespigny, you've come straight to the point, and you've come pretty bluntly, but that's just as well in view of the poor figure I cut in the matter. (*He turns up toward the center table and places on it his newspaper, which he has picked up from the floor.*)

MRS. CRESPIGNY. Why, I think, considering your age, your figger's great!

ROLAND (*looking at her despairingly*). I spoke figuratively! Now I'm doing my best to bring about a reconciliation. Of course, if I succeed, I can keep on living here just as usual—I'll have my allowance.

MRS. CRESPIGNY. But if you don't bring about the reconciliation?...

ROLAND. Well, in that case, frankly, I should have to leave you or marry you!

MRS. CRESPIGNY (*going to the table*). Look here, Mr. Roland, I want this in black and white! Are you proposing to me?

ROLAND. Well, Mrs. Crespigny, in a way—

MRS. CRESPIGNY. But there's a string to it?

ROLAND. You know you have once or twice delicately suggested that a marriage wouldn't be altogether disagreeable to you, but it's a poor bargain for you, and in case the proposal should ever be definitely made, I want to be sure you know what you're getting!

MRS. CRESPIGNY. I guess I know well enough. I ain't lived in the same flat with you for four solid years without finding out whether or not you was worth it *to me*. I know your faults, Mr. Roland, but they're swell faults.

ROLAND (*he goes to the table in the window to get a cigarette*). Mrs. Crespigny, suppose you keep to the point, which is, if I marry—if you marry me, you do it with your eyes open. I'm to

have all the liberty I've ever had. None of my habits are to be interfered with, none of my ways of spending money.

MRS. CRESPIGNY. All right. I know I won't be marrying a hero, but I'll be getting a high-toned name and the company I want for keeps, for if once we're married, your daughter nor nobody else won't sneak you away from me, and you can't get nothing in this world for nothing. (*She sits at the right of the table with a lugubrious expression on her poor powdered face.*)

ROLAND. Very well, then (*Coming to her*) if there's no reconciliation today, we'll consider it settled without another word.

MRS. CRESPIGNY. And if she does make it up with her husband?

ROLAND. We'll let that stand for the present. I would still have my allowance and I wouldn't have to leave the flat.

MRS. CRESPIGNY. Then, so far as I'm concerned—and I don't make no bones about saying it—I'd rather they kep' separate.

ROLAND. Don't be selfish! I think you'll win without that. (*He lifts her head tenderly, smiling sweetly; then, as he turns away from her the sweetness fades, and he looks at least twenty years older.* MRS. CRESPIGNY, *happy but embarrassed, tears the faded rose to pieces, petal by petal.*) I don't understand it. I ought to have had a telegram long ago!

MRS. CRESPIGNY (*starts and rises*). A telegram! My stars! this telegram came before you was up and I forgot all about it. (*Giving him a telegram.*)

ROLAND. That won't do! You'll have to be more thoughtful than that! (*Reading the telegram*) He's coming! He's due here any minute! And Becky out! Quick! help me make this look like a sick room.

MRS. CRESPIGNY. A sick room?

ROLAND. I'll put this chair here for Becky to sit in! (*Moving the Morris chair near to the table.*)

MRS. CRESPIGNY. And I'll put a towel on the table. (*Getting one from the bedroom*) But why a sick room, Mr. Roland! Who's sick?

ROLAND. That's how I got him here. Telegraphed Becky was dying—and it's worked—he's coming!

MRS. CRESPIGNY. You ought to have some bottles for medicine!

ROLAND. Bottles? Here's a couple! (*Getting a whiskey bottle and a brandy bottle from the sideboard.*)

MRS. CRESPIGNY (*taking the bottles from him*). You don't want him to think she's been on a spree, do you? (*She puts them on the table.*) Put a glass of water on the table. (*He gets a glass from the sideboard.*) And I'll put this saucer and spoon on top—that'll look like homeopathic stuff. (*She places a saucer on the table and breathes on the spoon and polishes it on a corner of tablecloth.* ROLAND *gets a pillow and a blanket from the bedroom and arranges them in the Morris chair.*) Do you know what we ought to have on that table? An orange on a plate! I don't know why it is, but it always looks like sick folks, having an orange on a plate by 'em! Wait a minute. I've got a marble orange just like real. I'll get it. I'll take the tray. (MRS. CRESPIGNY *with the tray at the door*) Josephine! Josephine! Oh, never mind if your hands are in the suds! (ROLAND *gets a hassock, which he places in front of the Morris chair. He pulls down the window shades, takes the siphon, and fills the glass on the table, putting the saucer and spoon on top of it.* MRS. CRESPIGNY *enters with an imitation orange on a plate.*) Here it is! And I brought a knife with it—don't it look natural?

(*The front bell rings.*)

ROLAND. Becky!

MRS. CRESPIGNY. No—I let her take the key!

ROLAND. Maybe it's he! And Becky not back! Don't let Josephine open the door yet!

MRS. CRESPIGNY (*opens the door and calls*). Josephine! Josy! I'll tend door; you go on with your washing! (*She shuts the door.*)

ROLAND. Show him here—

MRS. CRESPIGNY. Huh, huh?

ROLAND. And I'll tell him the doctor's with Becky—

MRS. CRESPIGNY. Huh, huh?

ROLAND. Then you watch for her, and when she comes, knock on the door and tell me the doctor's gone—

MRS. CRESPIGNY (*doubtfully*). Huh, huh—

ROLAND. Then I'll go "to find out if she feels able to see him," and bring her in as if from her bedroom. (*He goes to the Morris chair and arranges the pillow and blanket.*)

MRS. CRESPIGNY. It's lucky I don't have to tell him all that! You know, I haven't got your—*imagination!* . . .

ROLAND. That's all right—you'll see —they'll be reconciled! (*Gets a fan from behind the book-rack on the back wall and puts it on the table.*)

MRS. CRESPIGNY. Reconciled!

ROLAND. Yes, yes, they'll be reconciled!

MRS. CRESPIGNY. *Our* marriage is as good as off then!

ROLAND. Yes, yes—I mean we'll see! (*The front bell rings again.*) Don't keep him waiting—he might get suspicious!

MRS. CRESPIGNY (*turning the matter over in her mind, speaks very abstractedly*). Our marriage is as good as off then! (*She goes out slowly, weighing this sudden complication in her affairs.*)

ROLAND. Well, you never know your luck! No, no, don't close the door! I'll be here, expecting him.

MRS. CRESPIGNY (*offstage*). How do you do? Won't you come right in?

(WARDER *enters.*)

ROLAND. So you've come, Tom?

WARDER (*very serious*). How is she, Father?

ROLAND. The doctor is with her now. Mrs. Crespigny will let me know when he's gone. I haven't let her know I telegraphed you.

WARDER. But will she get well? Is she no worse?

ROLAND. We have every hope of her getting well.

WARDER (*he turns aside to control a sudden flood of emotion*). Thank God!

ROLAND. I think a good deal now depends upon you. (WARDER *faces* ROLAND. ROLAND *goes to him.*) Are you ready to take my daughter back?

WARDER (*very quietly, soberly*). Yes.

ROLAND. For good?

WARDER. If I can only feel sure Becky will try—only *try*—to be straightforward and honest with me, that's all I ask. God knows what I've suffered these two days, and when your message came —oh, to have that on my shoulders too —it would have been more than a man could bear!

ROLAND. Whatever Becky's faults may have been, you did her one terrible injustice!

WARDER. Yes, I know that now! Becky—never! Father, hour after hour since the one in which I left her, I've paced up and down my room, or sat and gritted my teeth in the train, and thought—and thought—and *thought*— till the anger died out of me and I began to see things white and clear both ahead and behind me. And all the time Becky's final words kept ringing in my ears, and they rang *true:* "I love you,

and only you, and you always.". . . And the further away from the excitement and anger I got, the saner I grew. And as I passed over our life together, second by second of happiness, I found only proof after proof of her love for me! Yes, I did Becky one great injustice, and I want to ask her to forgive me.

ROLAND (*his better self moved, takes* WARDER'*s hand*). Tom—

WARDER. After all, life is made up of compromises and concessions, and if Becky will only try, and let me help her—

ROLAND. I believe you love her still?

WARDER. I can only answer you by saying that I want more than anything else in the world to believe in her again —to have at least the beginning of confidence. (*With a knock on the door,* MRS. CRESPIGNY *comes in, frightened at what she is going to do.* ROLAND *hesitates one moment, but his old habit soon reasserts itself.*)

ROLAND. The doctor gone? (MRS. CRESPIGNY *nods her head.*) Excuse me. (*He hurries out.*)

(MRS. CRESPIGNY *stands looking after* ROLAND, *evidently trying to nerve herself up to the task of telling* WARDER *the truth. She makes several ineffectual gasping efforts to speak, and finally gets started, rushing her words and not daring to speak slowly for fear she'd stop.*)

MRS. CRESPIGNY. I'm going to do something awful, and I only hope I won't be punished for it all the rest of my life. Lord knows, seems as if I'd been punished enough in advance. Can I trust you?

WARDER. In what way?

MRS. CRESPIGNY. As a gentleman. If I tell you something—something that you ought to know—will you promise to see it through and not let on I told you?

WARDER. I don't know if I can promise that. Is it anything you have a right to tell me?

MRS. CRESPIGNY (*going toward him*). It won't do you no harm to pertect me, and I give you my sacred word of honor it's the truth instead of the lie you've been told! And all I ask is that you'll pertect me as regards Mr. Roland.

WARDER (*astounded, bewildered, but his suspicions rearoused*). What lie? Go on. I give you the promise!

MRS. CRESPIGNY (*whispers*). She ain't sick!

WARDER. Who?

MRS. CRESPIGNY. Mis' Warder! She ain't been sick—that was all a story to get you here!

WARDER (*catching her two hands by the wrists and holding them tight, so she can't get away from him*). No! don't say that!

MRS. CRESPIGNY. Ssh! I will say it! It's true! The doctor wasn't here when you came! Mis' Warder was out and only came in when I knocked on the door just now!

WARDER. Do you realize what you're saying?

MRS. CRESPIGNY. Perfeckly!

WARDER. And you're telling me the truth?

MRS. CRESPIGNY. Keep your eyes open and judge for yourself, that's all! Maybe you think *that's* the truth! (*Snatching up the imitation orange from the table, she smashes it on the floor.* WARDER *moves to go; she stands in front of the door to stop him.*)

WARDER. Let me go! I won't stay for this brutal farce!

MRS. CRESPIGNY. You promised to pertect me, and if you go now Mr. Roland'll catch on, and I want him to marry me! Now you know—

WARDER. Was this his idea or hers?

MRS. CRESPIGNY. His, and she— (*Listens.*)

WARDER (*eagerly*). She what—

MRS. CRESPIGNY (*moving away from the door*). Ssh! they're here!

(WARDER *controls himself and goes to the other side of the room.* ROLAND *comes, bringing* BECKY, *who leans on him. Her eyes are down.* WARDER *stands immovable and watches.*)

ROLAND (*pointedly*). Thank you, Mrs. Crespigny.

(*She goes out unwillingly.* BECKY *looks up and sees* WARDER. *He stands motionless, watching her.*)

BECKY (*as she meets* WARDER's *eyes, breaks away from* ROLAND). No, Father! I can't do it! I won't do it!

ROLAND (*frightened*). Becky!

BECKY. No! I tell you it's only another lie and a revolting one!

ROLAND. You're ill! You don't know what you're saying!

BECKY. No, I'm not ill, and you know it, and I haven't been! And if I can't win his love back by the truth, I'll never be able to keep it, so what's the use of getting it back at all? (*The tears fill her eyes and her throat.*)

WARDER. Becky! (*He wants to go to her, but still holds himself back. His face shows his joy, but neither* BECKY *nor* ROLAND *sees this.*)

BECKY (*continues after a moment, pathetically*). I thought I might creep back, through pity, first into your life, and then into your heart again. But, after all, I can't do it. (*She sits in the Morris chair, hopelessly.*) Something's happened to me in these two days— even if I tell lies, I've learned to loathe them and be afraid of them, and all the rest of my life I'll try—

WARDER (*in a choked voice*). Thank God! (*He goes to her, almost in tears himself.* ROLAND *looks at* WARDER, *and realizes what it means; a smile comes over his own face, and at the same time his eyes fill with his almost-forgotten tears.*)

BECKY. You can't forgive me!

WARDER. We don't love people because they are perfect. (*He takes her*

two trembling hands in his, and she rises.)

BECKY. Tom!

WARDER. We love them because they are themselves. (*And he takes her in his arms close to him, as the final curtain falls.*)

THE WITCHING HOUR

Augustus Thomas

First presented at the Hackett Theatre in New York
on November 18, 1907.

JO, *a servant*

JACK BROOKFIELD, *professional gam-*
bler

TOM DENNING

HARVEY, *a servant*

MRS. ALICE CAMPBELL, *Jack's sister*

MRS. HELEN WHIPPLE, *Clay's mother*

VIOLA CAMPBELL

CLAY WHIPPLE

FRANK HARDMUTH

LEW ELLINGER

JUSTICE PRENTICE

JUSTICE HENDERSON

COLONEL BAYLEY

MR. EMMETT, *a reporter*

ACT ONE

The library and card-room at JACK BROOKFIELD's, Louisville.

There is a large doorway in the center, at the back, which leads into a hallway, in which the banister of a stairway that descends to the street level is seen. A second and smaller doorway is near the front in the wall to the left of the stage. This doorway leads to the dining room. The second plan of the left wall is occupied by a fireplace and mantel, surmounted by a marine painting. The fireplace is surrounded by a garde au feu club seat.

The rest of the left wall, as well as the rear wall on both sides of the center door and all of the right wall, is fitted with bookcases about five feet high, in which are books handsomely bound.

The walls above these bookcases are hung with heavy brocaded Genoese velvet of a deep maroon in color and loosely draped. The ceiling is of carved wood, gilded. On the wall velvet, at proper intervals, are paintings by celebrated modern artists. Some of these paintings are fitted with hooded electric lights. Such a fitting is above a noticeable Corot, which hangs to the right of the center door.

A dark-red rug of luxuriant thickness is on the floor. The furniture is simple, massive, and Colonial in type. It consists of a heavy sofa above the fireplace and running at right angles to the wall. A heavy table fitted with books is in the center; a smaller table for cards is at the stage right. Chairs are at both tables.

Above the center door is a marble bust of Minerva, surmounted by a bronze raven, lacquered black, evidently illustrating Poe's poem. The Antommarchi death-mask of Napoleon in bronze hangs on the dark wood fireplace. A bronze mask of Beethoven is on one of the bookcases and on another is a bust of Dante. A bronze Sphinx is on another bookcase.

The room is lighted by a standing lamp at the back and by the glow from the fireplace. Over the table, center, is suspended an electric lamp in a large bronze shade. This lamp, while not lighted, is capable of being turned on by a push button, which depends from it.

On the table, center, is a large paper-cutter made of an ivory tusk.

Empty stage. After a pause there is a sound of laughter and dishes, left.

Enter JO, sleek Negro of Pullman car variety, by stairway and center door. He goes to door, left, and pauses —laughter ceases.

———

JO. Massar Brookfield.

JACK (outside, left). Well, Jo?

JO. Mr. Denning, sah.

JACK. Ask Mr. Denning to come up.

JO. Yes, sah. (Exit center. More talk and laughter, left.)

(JACK enters left. He walks to center on way toward main door. Pauses. Returns, left.)

JACK (at door, left). Lew! I say—Lew—you ladies excuse Mr. Ellinger a moment?

HELEN, ALICE, VIOLA (outside). Oh—yes. Certainly.

(Enter LEW ELLINGER, from dining room, left.)

LEW. See me?

JACK. Tom Denning's here—he expects a game. My sister and Mrs. Whipple object to the pasteboards—so don't mention it before them.

LEW (anxiously). Not a word—but, Tom—?

JACK. I'll attend to Tom.

LEW. Good. (*Starts back to dining room.*)

(*Enter* TOM DENNING, *right center; he is fat, indolent type.*)

TOM. Hello, Lew. (LEW *stops and turns.* JACK *motions him out and* LEW *goes.*) What you got tonight? Young Rockefeller?

JACK. Some ladies—

TOM (*grinning*). What—

JACK (*sternly*). My sister and her daughter—and a lady friend of theirs.

TOM (*disappointed*). —No game?

JACK. Not until they go.

TOM (*getting a peek off into dining room*). Oh—chafing dish.

JACK. They've been to the opera.— I had Harvey brew them some terrapin.

TOM (*complaining*). My luck! (*His hands hang limp.*)

JACK. No, I think there's some left. (*Pause*) I'm going to take a long chance and introduce you, Tom, only don't say anything about poker before the ladies.

TOM. Thought you said your *sister*—

JACK. I did.

TOM. Well, she's on, isn't she?

JACK. But she doesn't like it—and my *niece*—my niece doesn't like it.

(*Enter* HARVEY, *old Negro servant, from dining room, left.*)

HARVEY. I've made some coffee, Mars Jack. You have it in the dining room or heah, sah?

JACK (*going*). I'll ask the ladies.

TOM. How are you, Harvey?

HARVEY (*bowing*). Mars Denning—

JACK (*who has paused at door, left*). Got some terrapin for Mr. Denning, Harvey?

HARVEY. Yas, sah. (*To* TOM) Yas, sah. (*Exit* JACK, *left*.)

TOM. They left some of the rum, too, I hope.

HARVEY. Couldn't empty my icebox

in one evening, Mars Denning. (*Starts off. Pause.*) De ladies getting up. (*Stands up stage in front of fire.* TOM *goes right. A pause.*)

JACK (*enters*). The ladies will have their coffee in here, Harvey.

HARVEY. Yes, sir.

(*Enter* ALICE. *She is smartly gowned and is energetic.*)

JACK. Alice—this is my friend, Mr. Denning—my sister—Mrs. Campbell.

ALICE. Mr. Denning.

(*Enter* HELEN *and* VIOLA. HELEN *is thoroughly feminine in type, and is young-looking for the mother of a boy of twenty.* VIOLA *is an athletic Kentucky girl.*)

HELEN. I never take coffee even after dinner and at this hour—never! (*Exit* HARVEY.)

JACK. Mrs. Whipple, may I present Mr. Denning?

HELEN (*bowing*). Mr. Denning.

TOM. Good-evening!

JACK. My niece, Miss Viola Campbell.

TOM. How are you? (VIOLA *bows*.)

JACK. Mr. Denning's just left the *foundry* and he's very hungry.

TOM. And thirsty—

JACK (*pushing him toward dining room*). Yes, and thirsty. Uncle Harvey's going to save his life.

TOM. Ha, ha! Excuse me! (*Exits.*)

ALICE. The foundry? (*Sits right of table.*)

JACK. Never did a day's work in his life. That's Tom Denning. (*Nods off.*)

VIOLA (*on sofa at fireplace*). Tom Denning's the name of the big race horse.

JACK. Yes—he's *named* after the race horse.

HELEN (*on sofa, beside* VIOLA). *What* does he do?

JACK. His father—father's in the packing business—Kansas City; this fellow has four men *shoveling* money away from him so he can breathe. (*Starts toward dining room.*)

ALICE (*in amused protest*). Oh, Jack!

JACK. Yes—I'm one of them—you'll find cigarettes in that box.

ALICE. Jack! (*Rises.*)

JACK (*apologizing*). Not *you*, Alice, but—

VIOLA (*protesting*). Well, certainly not for *me*, Uncle Jack?

JACK. Of course, not you . . .

HELEN. Thank you, Mr. Brookfield!

ALICE (*joining* JACK). My dear brother, you confuse the Kentucky ladies with some of your Eastern friends.

JACK. Careful, Alice. *Helen* lived in the East twenty years, remember.

HELEN. But even my *husband* didn't smoke.

JACK. No?

HELEN. *Never*—in his life—

JACK. In his *life?* Why make such a pessimistic distinction?

(HELEN *turns away right.*)

ALICE. Jack! (*After a look to* HELEN) How can you say a thing like that?

JACK. *She's* the man's widow—*I've got* to say it if any one does.

(*Enter* HARVEY *with coffee.*) Mr. Denning's got his tortoise, Uncle Harvey?

HARVEY (*offering tray to* HELEN). He's got the same as we all had, Mars Jack. Yas, sah. (*Laughs.*)

HELEN. None, thank you. (HARVEY *moves on.*)

JACK. I'll take it, Uncle Harvey. I think three or four of them'll help this head of mine.

ALICE (*taking coffee*). Why don't you let Viola cure your headache?

VIOLA (*taking coffee*). Yes, Uncle Jack.

JACK. No, the coffee'll fix it, I'm sure.

(*Exit* HARVEY.)

VIOLA. Sit here while you drink it.

JACK. No—no, Viola. It isn't enough for that. I'll conserve your mesmeric endowment for a real occasion. (*Swallows coffee in one mouthful.*)

VIOLA. Goodness! Just to please me?

JACK (*shaking head*). Don't want to spoil your awful stories. (*Exit to dining room.*)

HELEN. Is Viola a magnetic healer, too? (*Sits right of table.*)

VIOLA (*taking a book, and returning to the sofa, carrying also a large ivory tusk paper-cutter.*) Oh, no.

ALICE (*sitting left of table*). Yes— a remarkable one.

VIOLA. Only headaches, Mrs. Whipple. Those I *crush* out of my victims.

HELEN. I remember Jack used to have a wonderful ability that way as a young man.

VIOLA. He says only with the girls.

ALICE. We know better, don't we?

HELEN. Yes.

VIOLA. Well, for myself, I'd rather have Uncle Jack sit by me than any regular physician I ever saw.

HELEN. You mean if you were ill?

VIOLA. Of course.

ALICE. You must be very clear with Mrs. Whipple on that point, Viola, because she used to prefer your Uncle Jack to sit by her even when she wasn't ill.

HELEN (*to* VIOLA). But especially when ill, my dear. (*To* ALICE) And has he quit it?

ALICE. Yes—you know Jack went into politics for a while.

HELEN. Did he?

ALICE. *Local* politics—yes—something about the police didn't please him and then he quit all of his curative work.

HELEN. Why?

ALICE. Well, in politics, I believe

there's something unpleasant about the word "heeler."

HELEN. Oh!

VIOLA. Entirely different spelling, however.

HELEN. Our English language is so elastic in that way.

ALICE. Yes, the papers joked about his magnetic touch. The word "touch" is used offensively also. So Jack dropped the whole business.

HELEN. And Viola inherits the ability?

ALICE. Well, if one can inherit ability from an uncle.

HELEN. From a family.

ALICE. That's even more generous, but Viola is like Jack in every way in which a girl may resemble a man. Horses and boats and every kind of personal risk—and—

VIOLA (*rises*). I'm *proud* of it.

ALICE. And Jack spoils her.

VIOLA. Am I spoiled? (*Goes to back of table.*)

ALICE. He couldn't love her more if he were her father—

(*Enter* CLAY, *a boy of twenty.*)

CLAY (*pausing at door*). May I come in?

VIOLA. Certainly.

CLAY. Isn't this a jolly room, Mother?

HELEN. Beautiful.

CLAY (*waving hand above*). And the sleeping apartments are what I take pride in. Private bath to every bedroom, reading-lamps just over the pillows—

VIOLA. Haven't you seen the house, Mrs. Whipple?

HELEN. Not above this floor.

ALICE. Would it interest you? (*Rises and goes left.*)

HELEN. Very much.

ALICE (*at door of dining room*). Jack—

JACK (*outside*). Yes—

ALICE (*to* HELEN). Will I do as your guide?

HELEN (*rises*). Oh, yes.

(*Enter* JACK.)

ALICE. I want to show Helen over the house.

JACK. Do.

ALICE. The rooms are empty?

JACK. Empty, of course.

ALICE. Don't be too indignant, they're not always empty. (*To* HELEN) In *Jack's* house one is liable to find a belated pilgrim in any room.

HELEN (*laughing*). And a lady walking in unannounced would be something of a surprise, wouldn't she?

JACK. Well—two ladies would, certainly.

ALICE. Jack!

JACK. My dear sister—they *would*. Hard lines when the reputation of a man's house isn't respected by his own sister—ha! (*Exits left, with mock indignation.*)

HELEN (*smiling*). The same Jack.

ALICE. Intensified and confirmed! (*Pausing at door*) Will you come, too, Viola?

VIOLA. No, thank you, Mother.

(HELEN *looks at* ALICE. *She and* ALICE *go.*)

CLAY. What was Frank Hardmuth saying to you? (*He indicates the dining room.*)

VIOLA. When?

CLAY. At supper—and in the box at the theatre, too?

VIOLA. Oh—Frank Hardmuth—nobody pays any attention to him.

CLAY. I thought *you* paid a great deal of attention to what he was saying.

VIOLA. In the same theatre party a girl's got to listen—or leave the box.

CLAY. Some persons listen to the opera.

VIOLA. I told him that was what I wanted to do.

CLAY. Was he making love to you, Viola?

VIOLA. I shouldn't call it that.

CLAY. Would anybody else have called it that if they'd overheard it?

VIOLA. I don't think so.

CLAY. Won't you tell me what it was about?

VIOLA. I don't see why you ask.

CLAY. I asked because he seemed so much in earnest—and because *you* seemed so much in earnest.

VIOLA. Well?

CLAY. And Frank Hardmuth's a fellow that'll stand watching. (*Looks off left.*)

VIOLA (*smiling*). He stood a good deal tonight.

CLAY. I mean that he's a clever lawyer and would succeed in making a girl commit herself in some way to *him* before she knew it.

VIOLA. I think that depends more on the way the *girl* feels.

CLAY. Well—I don't want you to listen to Frank Hardmuth under the idea that he's the only chance in Kentucky.

VIOLA. Why, Clay Whipple—

CLAY. You know very well *I've* been courting you myself, Viola, don't you?

VIOLA. You haven't. You've been coming round like a big boy.

CLAY (*follows right*). Have I gone with any other girl—anywhere?

VIOLA. I don't know. (*Sits right.*)

CLAY. And I've spoken to your Uncle Jack about it.

VIOLA. To Uncle Jack?

CLAY. Yes.

VIOLA (*rises*). Nobody told you to speak to Uncle Jack.

CLAY. Mother did.

VIOLA. *Your* mother?

CLAY. Yes. Mother's got regular old-fashioned ideas about boys and young ladies and she said, "if you think

Viola *likes* you, the *honorable* thing to do is to speak to her guardian first."

VIOLA. Oh!—you *thought* that, did you?

CLAY. I certainly did.

VIOLA. I can't imagine why.

CLAY. I thought that because you're Jack Brookfield's niece, and nobody of his blood would play a game that isn't fair.

VIOLA. I wish you wouldn't always throw that up to me. (*Goes to sofa.*) 'Tisn't our fault if Uncle Jack's a sporting man. (*Sits.*)

CLAY (*following*). Why, Viola, I was praising him. I think your Uncle Jack the gamest man in Kentucky.

VIOLA. Nor that either. I don't criticize my Uncle Jack, but he's a lot better man than just a fighter or a card-player. I love him for his big heart.

CLAY. So do I. If I'd thought you cared I'd have said you were too much like him at heart to let a fellow come a-courtin' if you meant to refuse him—and that was all that was in my mind when I asked about Frank Hardmuth—and I don't care what Hardmuth said either, if it wasn't personal that way.

VIOLA. Frank Hardmuth's nothing to me.

CLAY. And he won't be? (*Pause*) Will he—? (*Pause*) Say that. Because I'm awfully in love with you.

VIOLA. Are you?

CLAY. You bet I am. Just Tom-fool heels over head in love with you.

VIOLA. You never said so.

CLAY. Mother said a boy in an architect's office had better wait till he was a partner—but I can't wait, Viola, if other fellows are pushing me too hard.

VIOLA (*rises*). Uncle Jack says you *are* a regular architect if there ever was one.

CLAY. It's what *you* think that

makes the difference to me.

VIOLA. Well, I think— (*Pause*) —Uncle Jack certainly *knows*.

CLAY. And an architect's just as good as a lawyer.

VIOLA. Every bit.

CLAY. Viola. (*Takes her in his arms.*)

VIOLA. Now—I don't *mind* tellin' you —he was speakin' for himself—Frank Hardmuth.

CLAY. By Jove—on this very night.

VIOLA. Yes.

CLAY. Seems like the Hand of Providence that I was here. Let's sit down. (*They sit.*) You've got confidence in me, haven't you?

VIOLA. Yes—I've always said to Mother—Clay Whipple'll make his mark some day—I should say I *had* confidence in you.

CLAY. Huh. (*Laughs.*) Of course the *big* jobs *pay*. Things like insurance buildings—but my heart's in domestic architecture—and if you don't laugh at me, I'll *tell* you something.

VIOLA. Laugh at you—about your work and your ambition! Why, Clay!

CLAY. I do most of the domestic interiors for the firm already—and whenever I plan a second floor or a staircase I can see *you* plain as day walkin' through the rooms—or saying good-night over the banisters.

VIOLA. Really? (CLAY *nods.*) You mean in your mind?

CLAY. No, with my eyes. Domestic architecture's the most poetic work a man can get into outside of *downright* poetry itself.

VIOLA. It must be if you can *see* it all that way.

CLAY. Every room—I can see your short sleeves as you put your hands on the banisters—and sometimes you push up your front hair with the back of your hand that way— (*Brushes his forehead.*)

VIOLA. Oh, this— (*Repeats the gesture.*) —all girls do that.

CLAY. But not just the same way as you do it. Yes, sir! I can see every little motion *you* make.

VIOLA. Whenever you care to think about me.

CLAY. Bless you, no—that's the trouble of it.

VIOLA. What trouble?

CLAY. The pictures of you—don't come just when I *want* them to come —and they don't go when I want them to go—especially in the dark.

VIOLA. Why, how funny.

CLAY. Sometimes I've had to light the gas in order to go to sleep.

VIOLA. Why, I never heard of anything like that.

CLAY. Well, it happens with me often. I designed this room for your Uncle Jack—but before I put a brush in my colorbox I saw this very Genoese velvet and the picture frames in their places—and that Corot right there—I've got kind of a superstition about that picture.

VIOLA (*rises*). A superstition! (*Regards the Corot.*)

CLAY. I said to Jack, have anything else you want on the other walls, but right there I want you to put a Corot that I've seen at a dealer's in New York—and he did it.

VIOLA. Uncle Jack generally has his own way about pictures.

CLAY. I only mean that he approved my taste in the matter—but my idea of this house really started *with*—and grew around that canvas of Corot's.

VIOLA. Then it isn't always *me* that you see?

CLAY. Always you when I think about a real house, you bet—a house for *me*—and you'll be there, won't you? (*Takes her in his arms.*)

VIOLA. Will I?

CLAY. Yes—say, "I will."

VIOLA. I will.

(*Re-enter* ALICE *and* HELEN.)

ALICE (*astonished*). Viola!

(VIOLA *goes left.*)

CLAY. I've asked her—Mother.

ALICE. Helen, you knew?

HELEN. Yes.

CLAY (*to* ALICE). And I asked Jack, too.

ALICE. You mean—

CLAY. We're engaged—if you say it's all right.

ALICE. And you—Viola?

VIOLA (*nodding*). Yes—

ALICE (*going to chair left of table*). Well, if Jack's been consulted and you *all* know of it—I should make a very hopeless minority.

CLAY. Why any minority?

ALICE. Only the necessary considerations. (*To* HELEN) Clay's prospects—his youth.

VIOLA. Why, he designs most of the work for his firm now.

CLAY. That is, dwellings.

HELEN. I should advise waiting—myself—until Clay is in the firm— (*To* CLAY) And I did advise delay in speaking to Viola herself.

CLAY. I'd 'a' waited, Mother, only Frank Hardmuth proposed to Viola *tonight!*

ALICE. Tonight?

VIOLA. At the opera.

ALICE (*to* HELEN). One isn't safe anywhere.

CLAY. You wouldn't want *him!* So you do consent, don't you?

ALICE. I think your mother and I should talk it over.

CLAY. Well, it's a thing a fellow doesn't usually ask his mother to arrange, but— (*Pause.*)

VIOLA. You mean privately?

ALICE. Yes.

CLAY. We can go to the billiard room, I suppose?

VIOLA. Come on.

CLAY. (*at the center door with* VIOLA). You know, Mother—how I feel about it. (*Exits with* VIOLA.)

HELEN. I supposed you had guessed it. (*Sits right of table.*)

ALICE. I had—but when the moment arrives after all, it's such a surprise that a mother can't act naturally.

HELEN. Clay is really very trustworthy for his years.

ALICE. There's only one thing to discuss. I haven't mentioned it because—well, because I've seen so little of you since it began and because the fault is in my own family.

HELEN. Fault?

ALICE. Yes—Jack's fault— (*Pause*) Clay is playing.

HELEN. You mean—

ALICE. Here with Jack's friends.

HELEN. Clay gambling!

ALICE (*wincing*). I don't quite get used to the word, though we've had a lifetime of it— (*Sits left of table.*) gambling.

HELEN. I shouldn't have thought Jack would do that—with *my* boy.

ALICE. Jack hasn't our feminine viewpoint, Helen—and, besides, Jack is calloused to it.

HELEN. You should have talked to Jack yourself.

ALICE. Talked to him? I did much more—that is, as much more as a sister dependent on a brother for support could do. You know Jack really *built* this place for me and Viola.

HELEN. I'd thought so—yes.

ALICE. Viola is the very core of Jack's heart—well, we both left the house and went into our little apartment and are there now. A woman can't do much more than that and still take her living from a man, can she?

HELEN. No—

ALICE. And it hurt him—hurt him past any idea.

HELEN. You did that because my Clay was—was playing here?

ALICE. Not entirely Clay—everybody! (*Pause—a distant burst of laughter comes from the men in the dining room.*) There isn't a better-hearted man nor an abler one in the State than Jack Brookfield, but I had my daughter to consider. There were two nights under our last city government when nothing but the influence of Frank Hardmuth kept the police from coming to this house and arresting everybody—think of it.

HELEN. Dreadful—

ALICE. Now, that's something, Helen, that I wouldn't tell a soul but you. *Viola* doesn't know it—but Jack's card-playing came between you and him years ago and you—*may* know it. (*Rises and looks toward dining room.*) You may even have some influence with Jack.

HELEN. I—ah, no.

ALICE. Yes—this supper tonight was Jack's idea for you. The box at the opera for you.

HELEN. Why, Jack didn't even sit with us.

ALICE. Also—for you—Jack Brookfield is a more notable character in Louisville to-day than he was twenty-two years ago. His company would have made you the subject of unpleasant comment. That's why he left us alone in the box.

HELEN. Isn't it a pity—a terrible pity! (*Laughter off left.* HELEN *rises.*)

(*Enter* HARDMUTH, JACK, DENNING, *and* LEW. HARDMUTH *is the aggressive prosecutor.*)

HARDMUTH. I tell the gentlemen we've left the ladies to themselves long enough, Mrs. Campbell.

ALICE. *Quite* long enough, Mr. Hardmuth.

DENNING. Where's the young lady? Jack's niece?

HELEN. In the billiard room, I believe.

DENNING (*to* HELEN, *disappointed*). Oh—Jack's been telling us what a great girl she is.

HARDMUTH. Some of us knew that without being told.

DENNING. And she's wonderfully like you—wonderfully.

HELEN. You compliment me—

JACK. Are you under the impression you're speaking to Viola's mother?

DENNING. Ain't I?

JACK. This lady is Mrs. Whipple.

DENNING. Oh, Clay's mother? (HELEN *bows.*) Well, your boy, Mrs. Whipple, plays in the hardest luck of all the people I ever sat next to.

HELEN. You mean—

JACK (*interrupting and putting his arm about* DENNING). You depreciate yourself, Tom. There's no hard luck in merely sitting next to you.

DENNING. Ha, ha.

HELEN (*to* ALICE). I think Clay and I should be going.

JACK (*consulting his watch*). Oh, no —only a little after twelve and no one ever goes to sleep here before two. (*To* DENNING) I told you to keep still about card games.

DENNING. I meant unlucky at billiards. *They're* all right, ain't they?

JACK. Oh—(*Walks away impatiently.*)

DENNING. Let's go and see the young lady play billiards with Clay. (*To* ALICE) I can see now your daughter resembles you. (*Moves up with* ALICE *toward door.* LEW *follows.*)

JACK. Shall we join them?

HELEN. I'd like it. (JACK *and* HELEN *start up.*)

HARDMUTH. Jack! Just a minute.

JACK (*to* HELEN). Excuse me—

DENNING (*to* ALICE *as they go*). No, Kansas City's my *home*, but I don't live there. (*Exit with* ALICE.)

JACK. Be right in, Lew.

(*Exit* HELEN *with* LEW.)

Well, Frank—

HARDMUTH. I took advantage of your hospitality, old man, tonight.

JACK. Advantage?

HARDMUTH. Yes—I've been talking to your niece.

JACK. Oh!

HARDMUTH. Proposed to her.

JACK. Yes?

HARDMUTH. Yes, Jack.

JO (*enters at back, from downstairs*). A gentleman called you on the telephone, sah.

JACK (*regarding watch*). Who?

JO. Judge Brennus—name sounds like. Holdin' the wire, sah.

JACK. I don't know any Judge Brennus.

JO. Says you don't know him, sah, but he's got to leave town in the mornin' and he'd be very much obliged if you'd see him tonight.

JACK. Did you tell him we were dark tonight?

JO. He didn't want no game. It's about a picture— a picture *you've* got.

JACK. A picture?

JO. He wants to look at it.

(JACK *looks at* HARDMUTH.)

HARDMUTH. It's a blind.

JACK (*consulting watch*). Well, this is a good night to work a blind on me. (*To* JO) Tell the gentleman I'll be up for half an hour.

JO. Yes, sah. (*Exit.*)

JACK. So you proposed to Viola?

HARDMUTH. Yes. How do you feel about that?

JACK. You know the story of the barkeeper asking the owner, "Is Grady good for a drink?"—"Has he had it?"

—"He has."—"He is."

HARDMUTH. Just that way, eh? (JACK *nods.*) Well—she hasn't answered me.

JACK (*musing*). Ha—

HARDMUTH. And under those conditions, how's Grady's credit with you?

JACK. Well, Frank, on any *ordinary* proposition you're aces with me. You know that.

HARDMUTH (*seated right of table*). But for the girl?

JACK. It's different.

HARDMUTH. Why?

JACK. She's only nineteen—you know.

HARDMUTH. My sister married at *eighteen*.

JACK. I mean *you're* thirty-five.

HARDMUTH. That's not an unusual difference.

JACK. Not an impossible difference, but I think unusual—and rather unadvisable.

HARDMUTH. That's what *you* think.

JACK. That's what I think.

HARDMUTH. But suppose the lady is willing to give that handicap? (*Pause—* JACK *shrugs his shoulders.*) What then?

JACK. Let's cross the bridge when we come to it.

HARDMUTH. You mean *you'd* still drag a little?

JACK (*pause*). Do you think Viola likes you well enough to say yes?

HARDMUTH. Let's cross *that* bridge when we come to it.

JACK. We have come to that one, Frank. There's another man in the running and I think she likes him.

HARDMUTH. You mean young Whipple? (*Rises, goes to fireplace.*) Well, he took second money in the box party tonight—at the supper table, too. I'll agree to take care of him, if you're with *me*.

JACK (*at table, center*). I think *he's* your biggest opposition.

HARDMUTH. But you. Can I count on you in the show-down?

JACK (*pause; sits right of table*). If Viola didn't care enough for you, Frank, to accept you in spite of everything, I shouldn't try to influence her in your favor.

LEW (*enters, center, from left*). I think a bum game of billiards is about as thin an entertainment for the outsiders as "Who's got the button?"

HARDMUTH (*meeting* LEW *up left center*). I've got a little business, Lew, with Jack for a minute.

LEW. Well, I can sit in by the bottle, can't I? (*Moves towards dining room.*)

JACK. Help yourself, Lew.

LEW. Such awful stage waits while they chalk their cues. (*Exits left.*)

HARDMUTH. But you wouldn't try to influence her against me.

JACK (*pause*). She's about the closest thing to me there *is*—that niece of mine.

HARDMUTH (*pause*). Well?

JACK. I'd protect her happiness to the limit of my ability.

HARDMUTH. If she likes me—or should come to like me—enough—her —happiness would be with *me*, wouldn't it? (*Sits again.*)

JACK. She might think so.

HARDMUTH. Well?

JACK. But she'd be mistaken. It would be a mistake, old chap.

HARDMUTH. I know twenty men— twelve to fifteen years older than their wives—all happy—wives happy, too.

JACK. 'T isn't just that.

HARDMUTH. What is it?

JACK. She's a fine girl—that niece of mine—not a blemish.

HARDMUTH. Well—

JACK. I want to see her get the best —the very best—in family—position— character—

HARDMUTH. Anything against the Hardmuths? (JACK *shakes head.*) I'm assistant district attorney—and next trip I'll be *the* district attorney.

JACK. I said character.

HARDMUTH. Character?

JACK. Yes.

HARDMUTH. You mean there's anything against my reputation?

JACK. No—I mean character pure and simple—I mean the moral side of you!

HARDMUTH. Well, by God!

JACK. You see, I'm keeping the *girl* in mind all the time.

HARDMUTH. *My morals!*

JACK. Let's say your moral fiber.

HARDMUTH (*rises*). Well, for richness this beats anything I've struck. Jack Brookfield talking to me about my moral fiber! (*Goes toward fire.*)

JACK. You asked for it.

HARDMUTH (*returns aggressively*). Yes—I did, and now I'm going to ask for the showdown. What do you mean by it?

JACK (*with fateful repression*). I mean—as long as you've called attention to the "richness" of Jack Brookfield talking to you on the subject— that Jack Brookfield is a professional gambler—people get from Jack Brookfield just what he promises—a square game. Do you admit that?

HARDMUTH. I admit that. Go on.

JACK (*rises, front of table*). You're the assistant prosecuting attorney for the city of Louisville; the people *don't* get from you just what *you* promised —not by a jugful—

HARDMUTH. I'm the *assistant* prosecuting attorney, remember—I promised to assist in prosecution, not to institute it.

JACK. I expect technical defense, old man, but this was to be a showdown.

HARDMUTH. Let's have it—I ask for particulars.

JACK. Here's one. You play *here* in my house and you know it's against the law that you've sworn to support.

HARDMUTH. I'll support the law whenever it's invoked. Indict me and I'll plead guilty.

JACK. This evasion is what I mean by lack of moral fiber.

HARDMUTH. Perhaps we're a little shy somewhere on mental fiber.

JACK. You make me say it, do you, Frank? Your duty, at least, is to keep secret the information of your office; contrary to that duty you've betrayed the secrets of your office to warn me and other men of this city when their game was in danger from the police.

HARDMUTH. You *throw* that up to me?

JACK (*sits on left end of table*). Throw nothing—you asked for it.

HARDMUTH. I stand by my friends.

JACK. Exactly—and you've taken an oath to stand by the people.

HARDMUTH. Do you know any sure politician that doesn't stand by his friends?

JACK. Not one.

HARDMUTH. Well, there!

JACK. But I don't know any sure politician that I'd tell my niece to marry.

HARDMUTH. That's a little too fine-haired for me! (*Turns to fire.*)

JACK. I think it is.

HARDMUTH (*returns*). I'll bet you a thousand dollars I'm the next prosecuting attorney of this city.

JACK. I'll take half of that if you can place it. I'll bet even money you're anything in politics that you go after for the next ten years.

HARDMUTH. Then I don't understand your kick.

JACK. But I'll give odds that the time'll come when you're way up there—full of honor and reputation

and pride—that somebody'll drop to you, Frank, and flosh! *You* for the down and outs.

HARDMUTH. Rot!

JACK. It's the same in every game in the world—the crook either gets too gay or gets too slow, or both, and the "come on" sees him make the pass. I've been pallbearer for three of the slickest men that ever shuffled a deck in Kentucky—just a little *too* slick, that's all—and they've always got it when it was hardest for the family.

HARDMUTH. So that'll be my finish, will it?

JACK. Sure.

HARDMUTH (*going back of table*). You like the moral fiber of this Whipple kid?

JACK. I don't know. (*Crosses to fireplace.*)

HARDMUTH. Weak as dishwater.

JACK. I don't think so.

HARDMUTH. I'll do him at any game you name.

JACK. He's only a boy—you should.

HARDMUTH. I'll do him at this game.

JACK. What game?

HARDMUTH. The girl! I thought I could count on you because—well, for the very tips you hold against me; but you're only her uncle, old man, after all. (*Swaggers down right.*)

JACK. That's all.

HARDMUTH. And if she says "yes"—

JACK. Frank! (*Comes to front of table. Pause. The men confront each other.*) Some day the truth'll come out—as to who murdered the governor-elect of this State.

HARDMUTH. Is there any doubt about that?

JACK. Isn't there?

HARDMUTH. The man who fired that shot's in jail.

JACK. I don't want my niece mixed up in it.

HARDMUTH (*angrily*). What do you mean by that?

(*Enter* HELEN, *center. An awkward pause.*)

The young people still playing?

HELEN. Yes.

HARDMUTH. I'll look 'em over. (*Exits.*)

HELEN. Won't you come, too?

JACK. I'd rather stay here with you.

HELEN. That gentleman that called after supper—

JACK. Mr. Denning—

HELEN. Yes. He seems to take pleasure in annoying Clay—

JACK (*seriously*). Yes—I know that side of Denning. (*Goes to door of dining room.*) Lew!

LEW. Yes.

JACK. I wish you'd go into the billiard room and look after Tom Denning.

LEW (*entering left*). What's he doing?

(JACK *turns to* HELEN.)

HELEN (*to* JACK). Commenting humorously—hiding the chalk and so on.

LEW (*as he goes up*). Lit up a little, I suppose.

JACK (*nodding*). Just "ride herd"[1] on him.

(*Exit* LEW.)

HELEN (*going left to sofa*). He doesn't seem much of a gentleman, this Mr. Denning.

JACK. He wasn't expected tonight.

HELEN. Is he one of your "clients"?

JACK (*smiling*). One of my "clients"?

HELEN. Clay meets him here?

JACK. Yes—*has* met him here.

HELEN. I didn't think you'd do that —Jack—with *my* boy.

JACK. Do what?

HELEN. Gamble.

JACK (*smiling*). It's no gamble with your boy, Helen—sure thing. He hasn't won a dollar!

HELEN. I'm glad you're able to smile over it.

JACK. Perhaps it would be more humorous to you if he'd won.

HELEN. If he plays—I'd rather see him win, of course.

JACK (*beside sofa*). That's what puts me in the *business*—winning. The thing that makes every gambler stick to it is winning occasionally. I've never let your boy get up from the table a dollar to the good and because he *was* your boy.

HELEN. Why let him play at all?

JACK. He'll play somewhere till he gets sick of it—or marries.

HELEN. Will marriage cure it?

JACK. It would have cured me—but you didn't see it that way.

HELEN. You made your choice.

JACK. I asked you to trust me—you wanted some ironclad pledge—well, my dear Helen—that wasn't the best way to handle a fellow of spirit. (*Goes front of table.*)

HELEN. So *you* chose the better way?

JACK. No choice—I stood pat—that's all.

HELEN. And wasted your life.

JACK (*sitting on edge of table*). That depends on how you look at it. You married a doctor who wore himself out in the Philadelphia hospitals. I've had three meals a day—and this place—and—a pretty fat farm and a stable with some good blood in it— and—

HELEN (*coming to him*). And every one of them, Jack, is a monument to the worst side of you.

JACK (*stands and takes her hands; he smiles*). Prejudice, my dear Helen.

---

[1] "Take care of," in the manner of a cowboy's rounding up a herd and keeping it out of trouble.

You might say that, if I'd earned these things in some respectable business combination that starved out all its little competitors—but I've simply furnished a fairly expensive entertainment—to eminent citizens—looking for rest.

HELEN. I know all the arguments of your—profession—Jack, and I don't pretend to answer them any more than I answer the arguments of reckless women who claim that they are more commendable than their sisters who make loveless marriages.

JACK (*goes to chair, right*). I'm not flattered by the implied comparison—still—

HELEN. I only feel sure that anything which the majority of good people condemn is wrong. (*Sits left of table.*)

JACK (*sits right of table*). I'm sorry—

HELEN. I'd be glad if you meant that —but you're not sorry.

JACK. I *am* sorry—I'm sorry not to have public respect—as long as you think it's valuable.

HELEN. I amuse you—don't I?

JACK (*elbows on knees*). Not a little bit—but you make me blue as the devil, if that's any satisfaction.

HELEN. I'd be glad to make you blue as the devil, Jack, if it meant discontent with what you're doing—if it could make you do better.

JACK. I'm a pretty old leopard to get nervous about my spots.

HELEN. Why are you blue?

JACK. You.

HELEN. In what way?

JACK. I had hoped that twenty years of charitable deeds had made you also charitable in your judgment.

HELEN. I hope it has.

JACK. Don't seem to ease up on my specialty.

HELEN. You called your conduct "wild oats" twenty years ago.

JACK. It was—but I found such an excellent market for my wild oats that I had to stay in that branch of the grain business. Besides, it has been partly your fault, you know.

HELEN (*plays with the ivory paper-knife, balancing it on the front edge of table*). Mine?

JACK. Your throwing me over for my wild oats—put it up to me to prove that they were a better thing than you thought.

HELEN. Well—having demonstrated that—

JACK. Here we are—

HELEN. Yes—here we are.

JACK. Back in the old town. Don't you think it would be rather a pretty finish, Helen, if despite all my—my leopard's spots—and despite that— (*Pause*) —that Philadelphia episode of yours—

HELEN. You call twenty years of marriage episodic?

JACK. I call any departure from the main story episodic.

HELEN. And the main story is—

JACK. You and I—

HELEN. Oh—

(*Paper-knife falls to floor—*JACK *rises and picks it up, stands in front of table left hand on* HELEN's—*his right gesticulating with paper-knife.*)

JACK. Wouldn't it be a pretty finish if you took my hand and I could walk right up to the camera and say, "I told you so"—? You know I always felt that you were coming back.

HELEN. Oh, did you?

JACK (*playfully, and going right center*). Had a candle burning in the window every night.

HELEN. You're sure it wasn't a red light?

JACK (*remonstrating*). Dear Helen! have some poetry in your composition. Literally "red light" of course—

but the real flame was here— (*Hand on breast*) —a flickering hope that somewhere—somehow—somewhen I should be at rest—with the proud Helen that loved and—rode away.

HELEN (*almost accusingly*). I—believe—you.

JACK. Of course you believe me.

HELEN. You had a way, Jack—when you were a boy at college, of making me write to you.

JACK. Had I? (*Goes back of table.*)

HELEN. You know you had—at nights—about this hour—I'd find it impossible to sleep until I'd got up and written to you—and two days later I'd get from you a letter that had crossed mine on the road. I don't believe the word "telepathy" had been coined then—but I guessed something of the force—and all these years, I've felt it—nagging! Nagging!

JACK. Nagging?

HELEN. Yes—I could not keep you out of my waking hours—out of my thought—but when I surrendered myself to sleep the *call* would come—and I think it was rather cowardly of you, really.

JACK (*back of table*). I plead guilty to having thought of you, Helen—lots —and it was generally when I was alone—late—my—clients gone. This room—

"Whose lights are fled,
Whose garlands dead,
And all but he departed."

HELEN. And as you say—here we are.

JACK. Well, what of my offer? Shall we say to the world—"We told you so"? What of my picturesque finish?

HELEN. You know my ideas—you've known them twenty-two years.

JACK. No modification?

HELEN. None!

JACK. I'll be willing to sell the tables. (*Points above to second floor.*) And—well—I don't think I could get interested in this bridge game that the real good people play—would you object to a gentleman's game of "draw" now and then?

HELEN. You called it a gentleman's game in those days.

JACK. No leeway at all?

HELEN. No compromise, Jack—no—

JACK. M— (*Pause*) I trust you won't consider my seeming hesitation uncomplimentary?

HELEN. Not unprecedented, at least.

JACK. You see it opens up a new line of thought—and— (*Passing his hand over forehead.*)

HELEN (*rising in sympathy*). And you have a headache, too—it isn't kind I'm sure.

(*Enter* JO.)

JACK. Oh, nothing—nothing. (*To* JO) Well?

JO. That gentleman, sah, about the picture.

JACK. I'll see him. (*Exit* JO.)

HELEN. A caller?

JACK. Won't be a minute—don't go away, because I think we can settle this question tonight, you and I.

HELEN. Please don't put me in the light of waiting for an answer.

JACK. Dear Helen—we're both past that—aren't we? If I can only be sure that I could be worthy of you. I'm the one that's waiting for an answer—from my own weak character and rotten irresolution.

(JACK *goes with* HELEN *to door, center, kisses her hand. She goes;* JACK *retains her hand as long as possible and when he lets it go, it falls limply to* HELEN'S *side as she disappears.*)

They say cards make a fellow superstitious. (*Pause*) Well—I—guess they do—

(*Enter* JO *and* JUSTICE PRENTICE.

PRENTICE *wears overcoat, carries cane and silk hat.*)

JACK. Judge de Brennus?

PRENTICE (*after amused look at* JO). Justice Prentice. (*Exit* JO.)

JACK. Oh, Justice Prentice! Good-evening!

PRENTICE. You are Mr. Brookfield?

JACK. Yes.

PRENTICE. I shouldn't have attempted so late a call but that a friend pointed you out tonight at the opera, Mr. Brookfield, and said that your habit was—well—

JACK. Not to retire immediately?

PRENTICE. Yes.

JACK. Will you be seated?

PRENTICE. I'm only passing through the city. I called to see a Corot that I understand you bought from Knoedler.

JACK. That's it.

PRENTICE. Oh—thank you. (*Starts.*) You don't object to my looking at it?

JACK. Not at all. (*Touches button, light shows on picture.*)

PRENTICE (*after regard*). That's it. (*Pause*) I thought at one time that I would buy this picture.

JACK. You know it, then?

PRENTICE. Yes. (*Pause*) Are you particularly attached to it, Mr. Brookfield?

JACK (*sitting*). I think not irrevocably. (*Takes pad of paper and figures mechanically.*)

PRENTICE. Oh. (*Pause, during which the* JUSTICE *looks at the picture.*) Do I understand that is what you paid for it, or what you intend to ask me for it?

JACK (*starts*). What?

PRENTICE. Sixty-five hundred.

JACK (*astonished*). I didn't speak the price, did I?

PRENTICE. Didn't you—oh. (*Pause*) I couldn't pay that amount.

JACK (*puzzled*). That's its price—however.

PRENTICE. I regret I didn't buy it from the dealer when I had my chance. (*Looks about at other pictures on back wall.*) I couldn't have given it so beautiful a setting, Mr. Brookfield, nor such kindred—but it would not have been friendless— (*At fireplace*) That's a handsome marine.

JACK. Yes.

PRENTICE. Pretty idea I read recently in an essay of Dr. van Dyke's. His pictures were for him his windows by which he looked out from his study onto the world. (*Pause*) Yes?

JACK. Quite so.

PRENTICE (*regarding a picture over dining room door*). M— Washington!

JACK (*again astonished*). What?

PRENTICE. My home is Washington— I thought you asked me?

JACK. No, I didn't.

PRENTICE. I beg your pardon—

JACK (*front of table; aside*). But I'm damned if I wasn't going to ask him.

PRENTICE (*viewing other pictures*). And the phases of your world, Mr. Brookfield, have been very prettily multiplied.

JACK. Thank you—may I offer you a cigar? (*Opens box on table.*)

PRENTICE. Thank you, I won't smoke.

JACK. Or a glass of wine?

PRENTICE. Nothing. I'll return to the hotel—first asking you again to excuse my untimely call.

JACK. I wish you'd sit down awhile.

PRENTICE. But I didn't know until I'd missed it from Knoedler's how large a part of my world—my dream world—I had been looking at through this frame. (*Regards the Corot again.*)

JACK. Well, if it's a sentimental matter, Mr. Justice, we might talk it over.

PRENTICE. I mustn't submit the

sentimental side of it, Mr. Brookfield, and where I have so—so intruded.

JACK. That's the big side of anything for me—the sentimental.

PRENTICE. I'm sure of it—and I mustn't take advantage of that knowledge.

JACK. You're sure of it?

PRENTICE. Yes.

JACK. Is that my reputation?

PRENTICE. I don't know your reputation.

JACK. Then, how are you sure of it?

PRENTICE (*impressively*). Oh—I see you—and—well, we have *met.*

JACK. Ah—

PRENTICE. Good-night. (*Going up.*)

JACK. One moment. (*Pause*) You said your address was Washington?

PRENTICE. Yes.

JACK. You thought at the time I was about to ask you that question?

PRENTICE. I thought you had asked it.

JACK. And you thought a moment before I had said sixty-five hundred for the picture?

PRENTICE. Yes.

JACK. Do you often—pick answers that way?

PRENTICE. Well, I think we all do—at times.

JACK. We all do?

PRENTICE. Yes—but we speak the answers only as we get older and less attentive and mistake a person's thought for his spoken word.

JACK. A person's thought?

PRENTICE. Yes.

JACK. Do you mean you know what I think?

PRENTICE (*returning to table*). I hadn't meant to claim any monopoly of that power. It's my opinion that every one reads the thoughts of others —that is, some of the thoughts.

JACK. Every one?

PRENTICE. Oh, yes.

JACK. That *I* do?

PRENTICE (*regarding him*). I should say *you* more generally than the majority of men.

JACK. There was a woman said something like that to me not ten minutes ago.

PRENTICE. A woman would be apt to be conscious of it.

JACK. You really believe that—that stuff? (*Sits left of table.*)

PRENTICE. Oh, yes—and I'm not a pioneer in the belief. The men who declare the stuff most stoutly are scientists who have given it most attention.

JACK. How do they prove it?

PRENTICE. They *don't* prove it—that is, not universally. Each man must do that for himself, Mr. Brookfield.

JACK. How—

PRENTICE (*pause; smiles*). Well, I'll tell you all I know of it. (*Becoming serious*) Every thought is active—that is, born of a desire—and travels from us—or it is born of the desire of someone else and comes to us. We send them out—or we take them in—that is all.

JACK. How do we know which we are doing?

PRENTICE. If we are idle and empty-headed, our brains are the playrooms for the thought of others—frequently rather bad. If we are active, whether benevolently or malevolently, our brains are workshops—*power-houses.* I was passively regarding the pictures; your active idea of the price—registered, that's all—so did your wish to know where I was from.

JACK. You say "*our* brains"—do you still include mine?

PRENTICE. Yes.

JACK. You said mine more than the majority of men's.

PRENTICE. I think so.

JACK. Why hasn't this whatever it is—effect—happened to me, then?

PRENTICE. It has.

JACK (*pause*). Why didn't I know it?

PRENTICE. Vanity? Perhaps.

JACK. Vanity?

PRENTICE. Yes—often some—friend has broached some independent subject and you have said, "I was just about to speak of that myself."

JACK. Very often, but—

PRENTICE. Believing the idea was your own—your vanity shut out the probably proper solution—that it was his.

JACK. Well, how, then, does a man tell which of his thoughts are his own?

PRENTICE. It's difficult. Most of his idle ones are not. When we drift we are with the current. To go against it or to make even an eddy of our own we must swim—Most everything less than that is hopeless.

JACK (*smiling*). Well—I haven't been exactly helpless.

PRENTICE. No one would call you so, Mr. Brookfield. (*Going*) You have a strong psychic—a strong hypnotic ability.

JACK (*smiling*). You think so?

PRENTICE. I know it.

JACK. This business? (*Makes slight pass after manner of the professional hypnotist.*)

PRENTICE (*smiling*). That business for the beginner, yes—

JACK. You mean that I could hypnotize anybody?

PRENTICE. Many persons—yes—but I wouldn't do it if I were you—

JACK. Why not?

PRENTICE. Grave responsibility.

JACK. In what way?

PRENTICE (*pause; smiles*). I'll send you a book about it—if I may.

JACK. Instructions?

PRENTICE. And cautions—yes— (*Goes up to picture again.*) If you tire of your Corot, I'd be glad to hear from you.

JACK. Why couldn't I save postage by just *thinking* another price?

PRENTICE. The laws on contracts haven't yet recognized that form of tender.

TOM (*enters, center; laughs and shows signs of drink*). I say, Jack—here's the greatest joke you ever saw— (*Sees the* JUSTICE.) Oh, excuse me.

LEW (*enters, following*). That won't do, Tom.— (*To* JACK) Excuse me, Jack, but I had to get him out of there.

JACK. I'll go downstairs with you, Mr. Justice. (*Exits with the* JUSTICE.)

TOM. Who's that old bird?

LEW. You'll offend Jack if you're not careful, Tom. You've got half a jag now.

TOM. J' ever see anything's as funny as that? He don't like my scarf-pin—ha, ha—well I don't like it—but my valet put it on me and what's difference—

HARDMUTH (*enters*). What was that?

TOM. My scarf-pin!

HARDMUTH. Scarf-pin?

TOM. Yes—he pushed me away from him and I said what's matter. He said I don't like your scarf-pin—ha, ha—I said don't? I don't like your face.

LEW. Very impolite with the ladies there.

HARDMUTH. Why should he criticize Tom's scarf-pin?

TOM. 'Zactly. I said I can change my scarf-pin—but I don't like your face.

CLAY (*enters from dining room, excitedly*). Where's Jack?

LEW. Saying good-night to some old gentleman below.

TOM (*interposing as* CLAY *starts up left center*). And I don't like your face.

CLAY. That's all right, Mr. Denning. (*Tries to pass.*) Excuse me.

TOM (*with scarf-pin in hand*). Excuse *me*. What's the matter with that scarf-pin?

CLAY. It's a cat's-eye and I don't like them, that's all—I don't like to look at them.

LEW. Let him alone, Tom.

TOM. Damn 'f 'ee ain't scared of it, ha, ha! (*Pushing pin in front of CLAY's face.*)

CLAY (*greatly excited*). Don't do that.

HARDMUTH (*sneering*). 'T won't bite you, will it?

CLAY (*averts his face*). Go away, I tell you.

TOM (*holds CLAY with left hand; has pin in right*). 'T will bite him—bow—wow—wow—

CLAY. Don't, I tell you—don't.

TOM (*still holding him*). Bow—wow—wow—

LEW. Tom!

HARDMUTH (*laughing*). Let them alone.

CLAY. Go away.

TOM. Bow—wow—

JACK (*enters*). What's the matter here?

TOM (*pursuing CLAY*). Wow—

(CLAY *in frenzy swings the large ivory paper-knife from table, blindly strikes TOM, who falls.*)

JACK. Clay!

CLAY (*horrified*). He pushed that horrible cat's-eye right against my face.

JACK. What cat's-eye?

HARDMUTH (*picks up the pin which DENNING has dropped*). Only playing with him—a scarf-pin.

LEW (*kneeling by DENNING*). He's out, Jack.

(*Enter JO.*)

CLAY. I didn't mean to hurt him; really I didn't mean that.

HARDMUTH (*taking the paper-cutter from CLAY*). The hell you didn't. You could kill a bull with that ivory tusk.

JACK. Put him on the window seat—give him some air.

ALICE (*enters, left center*). Jack, we're going now—all of us.

(*Enter HARVEY.*)

JACK (*turning to ALICE*). Wait a minute. (*To JO*) Help Mr. Ellinger there.

(JO, LEW, *and* HARVEY *carry off* TOM *into the dining room.*)

ALICE. What is it?

JACK. An accident—keep Helen and Viola out of these rooms.

ALICE. Hadn't we better go? Clay is with us.

CLAY. I can't go just now, Mrs. Campbell - (*Looks off.*) I hope it isn't serious—I didn't mean to hurt him, really. (*Exits left.*)

ALICE. A quarrel?

(LEW *enters and waves hand, meaning "All over."*)

HARDMUTH (*with paper-knife*). A murder!

(*Enter HELEN and VIOLA.*)

VIOLA. What's the matter?

(*Enter CLAY.*)

CLAY (*in panic and up right center; to HELEN*). Oh, Mother, I've killed him.

HELEN (*taking CLAY in her arms*). Killed him—whom?

HARDMUTH. Tom Denning.

CLAY. But I never meant it—Jack; I just struck—struck wild.

HARDMUTH. With this.

HELEN. With that! Oh, my boy!

JACK. That will do! Everybody—Lew, telephone Dr. Monroe it's an emergency case and to come in dressing-gown and slippers. (*Exit LEW, right center.*) Alice, I know you're not afraid of a sick man—or—that sort of thing. Help me and Jo. (*Leads ALICE, left. She braces herself.*) Viola, you take Mrs. Whipple upstairs and wait there.

HARDMUTH (*starting up right*). I'll notify the police.

HELEN. Oh!

JACK (*interposing*). *Stop!* You'll stay just where you are!

HARDMUTH. You tryin' to hide this thing?

JACK. The doctor'll tell us exactly what this thing is. And then the boy'll have the credit himself *of notifying the police.*

ACT TWO

The library-living room of JUSTICE PRENTICE, *Washington, D.C.*

The walls of this room are book-cases glassed quite to the ceiling, and filled with books mostly in sheepskin binding. This array is broken by a large bay window at the back, center, which is equipped with a window seat, and by two doors near the front of the stage, one on the right and one on the left.

At the left is also a fireplace with a log fire. In the upper left-hand corner of the room there is a buffet, fitted with glasses and decanters. A dark rug is on the floor.

The furniture of the room is dark oak in Gothic. It consists of a table and three chairs at the center, sofa and smaller table up right. The smaller table holds a lamp.

Over the buffet there is a small canvas by Rousseau showing a sunset.

JUSTICE PRENTICE and JUDGE HENDERSON are playing chess.

HENDERSON. Checkmate in three moves.

PRENTICE. I don't see that.

HENDERSON. Well, Knight to—

PRENTICE. Yes, yes, I see. Checkmate in three moves. That's one game each. Shall we play another?

HENDERSON. Let us look at the enemy. (*Draws watch.*) By Jove! Quarter of twelve. I guess Mrs. Henderson will be expecting me soon. (*Pause*) I'll play a rubber with you, and its result shall decide your position on the Whipple case.

PRENTICE. Why, Mr. Justice, I'm surprised at you. A United States Supreme Court decision—shaped by a game of chess. We'll be down to the level of the intelligent jurymen soon —flipping pennies for the verdict.

HENDERSON. And a very good method in just such cases as this. Well, if you won't play— (*Rises.*) —I'll have to go.

PRENTICE (*rises*). Not without another toddy.

HENDERSON. Yes.

PRENTICE (*at sideboard up left*). Oh, no. Come, now, don't you like this liquor?

HENDERSON. Immensely. Where did you say you got it?

PRENTICE. Kentucky. One lump?

HENDERSON. Only one!

PRENTICE. My old home, sir—and a bit of lemon?

HENDERSON. A piece of the peel—yes.

PRENTICE. They make it there.

HENDERSON. I'll pour the water.

PRENTICE. There, there, don't drown me.

HENDERSON. My folks were Baptists, you see. What do you say it costs you?

PRENTICE. Fifty cents a gallon.

HENDERSON. What!! I think I'll take water. (*Puts down glass.*)

PRENTICE. That's what it cost me. Its value I don't know. An old friend sends it to me. Fifty cents for express.

HENDERSON. Oh!

PRENTICE. That's different, isn't it?

HENDERSON (*recovers glass*). Very!

PRENTICE. He makes it down there. Why, it's in the same county in which this Whipple murder occurred.

HENDERSON. How about that point? We might as well admit it and remand the case.

PRENTICE. No. There's no constitutional point involved.

HENDERSON. A man's entitled to an open trial.

PRENTICE. Well, Whipple had it.

HENDERSON. No, he didn't. They wouldn't admit the public.

PRENTICE. Oh, come now; the courtroom was crowded and the Judge refused admission to others—only when there was danger of the floor breaking.

HENDERSON. But, my dear Mr. Justice, that would have been all right to limit the attendance—

PRENTICE. Well, that's all he did.

HENDERSON. Only he did it by having the sheriff issue tickets of admission. That placed the attendance entirely in the control of the prosecution and the defense is right in asking a rehearing.

PRENTICE. Oh, nonsense! Justice is a little too slow in my old State and I'm impatient with technical delays. It is two years since they openly assassinated the governor-elect and the guilty man is still at large.

HENDERSON. Why should the killing of Scovill bear on this case!

PRENTICE. It bears on me. I'm concerned for the fair fame of Kentucky.

HENDERSON. Well, if you won't, you won't and there's an end of it. (*Rings call bell.*)

PRENTICE. Have another?

HENDERSON. Not another drop.

(*Enter* SERVANT.)

Get my coat!

PRENTICE. A nightcap.

SERVANT. I beg pardon, sir.

PRENTICE. Speaking to the Justice. (*Exit* SERVANT.)

HENDERSON. No, I mustn't. Mrs. Henderson filed her protest against my coming home loaded and I've got to be moderate.

PRENTICE. Well, if you won't, you won't.

HENDERSON (*front of table, picks up book*). Hello! Reading the Scriptures in your old age?

PRENTICE. It does look like a Bible, doesn't it? That's a flexible binding I had put on a copy of Bret Harte. I admire him very much.

HENDERSON. I like some of his stuff.

PRENTICE. When I get home from the Capitol and you prosy lawyers, I'm too tired to read Browning and those heavy guns, so I take Bret Harte —very clever, I think; I was reading before you came— (*Takes book.*) —"A Newport Romance." Do you know it?

HENDERSON. I don't think I do.

PRENTICE. It's about an old house at Newport—that's haunted—a young girl in the colonial days dies of a broken heart in this house, it seems. Her sweetheart sailed away and left her—and here's the way Bret Harte tells of her coming back. (HENDERSON *sits.*) Oh, I'm not going to read all of it to you—only one verse. (*Looks at book.—Pause.*) Oh, I forgot to tell you that when this chap left the girl he gave her a little bouquet—understand? That's a piece of material evidence necessary to this summing up.

(HENDERSON *nods.* PRENTICE *reads.*)

"And ever since then when the clock strikes two,
She walks unbidden from room to room,
And the air is filled, that she passes through,

With a subtle, sad perfume.

The delicate odor of mignonette,
The ghost of a dead-and-gone bou-
    quet,
Is all that tells of her story; yet
Could she think of a sweeter way?"

Isn't that charming, eh?

HENDERSON. A very pretty idea.

PRENTICE. Beautiful to have a perfume suggest her. I suppose it appeals to me especially because I used
to know a girl who was foolishly fond
of mignonette.

HENDERSON. Well, you don't believe
in that stuff, do you?

PRENTICE. What stuff?

HENDERSON. That Bret Harte stuff—
the dead coming back—ghosts and so
forth?

PRENTICE. Yes, in one way I do. I
find as I get older, Judge, that the
things of memory become more real
every day—every day. Why, there are
companions of my boyhood that I
haven't thought of for years—that
seem to come about me—more tangi-
bly, or as much so as they were in life.

HENDERSON. Well, how do you account for that? Spiritualism?

PRENTICE. Oh, no. It's Time's perspective.

HENDERSON. Time's perspective?

PRENTICE. Yes. (Pause) I'll have to
illustrate my meaning. (Indicates a
painting.) Here's a sunset by Rousseau. I bought it in Paris last summer.
Do you see what an immense stretch
of land there is in it?

HENDERSON. Yes.

PRENTICE. A bird's-eye view of that
would require a chart reaching to the
ceiling. But see Rousseau's perspective. The horizon line isn't two inches
from the base.

HENDERSON. Well?

PRENTICE (returns to table). Well,
my dear Judge, that is the magic in
the perspective of Time. My boyhood's horizon is very near to my old
eyes now. The dimmer they grow, the
nearer it comes, until I think sometimes that when we are through with
it all—we got out almost as we entered
—little children.

HENDERSON (pause). That's a very
beautiful painting, Judge—a Russell,
you say?

PRENTICE. A Rousseau.

HENDERSON. Oh—

PRENTICE. Yes—cost me three thousand only, and a funny thing about
it: the canvas just fitted into the top
of my steamer trunk, and it came
through the custom-house without a
cent of duty. I completely forgot it.

HENDERSON. Your memory isn't so
retentive, then, as it seems?

PRENTICE. Not on those commercial
matters.

(Enter SERVANT with coat. In crossing front of table to HENDERSON, the
coat knocks a miniature from the
table to the floor.)

PRENTICE. You dropped your to-
bacco-box, I guess, Mr. Justice.

HENDERSON (examines pocket). No.

SERVANT (picks up miniature). It
was this picture, sir.

PRENTICE. My gracious—my gracious! It might have been broken.

SERVANT. Oh, it often falls when I'm
dusting, sir.

PRENTICE. Oh, does it? Well, I'll put
it away.

(Exit SERVANT.)

An ivory miniature by Wimar. I prize
it highly—old-fashioned portrait, see!
Gold back.

HENDERSON. A beautiful face.

PRENTICE (eagerly). Isn't it? Isn't it?
(Looks over HENDERSON's shoulder.)

HENDERSON. Very. What a peculiar

way of combing the hair—long, and over the ears.

PRENTICE. The only becoming way women ever wore their hair. I think the scrambly style they have now is disgraceful.

HENDERSON. Your mother?

PRENTICE. Dear, no, a young girl I used to know. Oh, don't smile, she's been dead a *good* thirty years—married and had a large family.

HENDERSON. Very sweet—very sweet, indeed.

PRENTICE. Isn't it?

(*Enter* SERVANT.)

Well?

SERVANT. Card, sir.

PRENTICE. Gentleman here? (*Takes card.*)

SERVANT. Yes, sir.

PRENTICE. I'll see him. (*Exit* SERVANT.)

HENDERSON. Call?

PRENTICE. Yes. The man owns a picture that I've been trying to buy—a Corot.

HENDERSON. Oh—another of these perspective fellows?

PRENTICE. Yes—his call doesn't surprise me, for he's been in my mind all day.

HENDERSON. Seems to be in a hurry for the money—coming at midnight.

PRENTICE. I set him the example—besides, midnight is just the shank of the evening for Mr. Brookfield. He's supposed to be a sporting man—ahem.

(*Enter* SERVANT *and* JACK. JACK *is paler and less physical than in first act.*)

PRENTICE. Good-evening.

JACK. You remember me, Mr. Justice?

PRENTICE. Perfectly, Mr. Brookfield —this is Justice Henderson.

HENDERSON. Mr. Brookfield.

JACK. Pleased to meet you, Mr. Justice. (*To* PRENTICE) I hope I'm not intruding.

HENDERSON. I'm just going, Mr. Brookfield. (*To* PRENTICE) Tomorrow?

PRENTICE. Tomorrow!

HENDERSON (*at door, inquiringly*). No constitutional point about it? Eh?

PRENTICE. None.

HENDERSON. Good-night.

PRENTICE. Good-night. (*To* JACK) Have a chair.

JACK. Thank you. (*Stands by chair left of table.*)

PRENTICE (*toward buffet*). I've some medicine here that comes directly from your city.

JACK. I don't think I will—if you'll excuse me.

PRENTICE. Ah— (*Pause. Smiles.*) Well, have you brought the picture?

JACK. The picture is still in Louisville—I—I'm in Washington with my niece.

PRENTICE. Yes?

JACK. And—a lady friend of hers. They're very anxious to meet you, Mr. Justice.

PRENTICE. Ah. (*Pause*) Well—I go to the Capitol at noon tomorrow and—

JACK. Tonight!—They're leaving the city tomorrow—as you were when I had the pleasure of receiving you.

PRENTICE. I remember.

JACK (*with watch*). They were to come after me in five minutes if I didn't return, and those five minutes, Mr. Justice, I hoped you would give to me.

PRENTICE. With pleasure. (*Sits right of table.*)

JACK (*plunging at once into his subject*). Those two books you sent me—

PRENTICE. Yes?

JACK. I want to thank you for them again—and to ask you how far you go—with the men that wrote them—

especially the second one. Do you believe that book?

PRENTICE. Yes.

JACK. You do?

PRENTICE. I do. I know the man who wrote it—and I believe him.

JACK. Did he ever do any of his stunts for you—that he writes about?

PRENTICE. He didn't call them "stunts," but he has given me many demonstrations of his ability—and mine.

JACK. For example?

PRENTICE. For example? He asked me to think of him steadily at some unexpected time and to think of some definite thing. A few days later—this room—two o'clock in the morning—I concentrated my thoughts—I mentally pictured him going to his telephone and calling me.

JACK. And did he do it?

PRENTICE. No— (Pause) —but he came here at my breakfast hour and told me that at two o'clock he had waked and risen from his bed—and walked to his 'phone in the hallway with an *impulse* to call me—and then had stopped—because he had no message to deliver and because he thought his imagination might be tricking him.

JACK. You hadn't given him any tip, such as asking him how he'd slept?

PRENTICE. None. Five nights after that I repeated the experiment.

JACK. Well?

PRENTICE. That time he called me.

JACK. What did he say?

PRENTICE. He said, "Old man, you ought to be in bed asleep and not disturbing honest citizens," which was quite true.

JACK. By Jove, it's a devilish creepy business, isn't it?

PRENTICE. Yes.

JACK. And if it's so—

PRENTICE. And it *is* so.

JACK. Pay a man to be careful what he thinks—eh?

PRENTICE. It will very well pay your type of man to do so.

JACK. I don't want to be possessed by any of these bughouse theories, but I'll be blamed if a few things haven't happened to me, Mr. Justice, since you started me on this subject.

PRENTICE. Along this line?

JACK. Yes. (Pause) And I've tried the other side of it, too.

PRENTICE. What other side?

JACK. The mesmeric business. (Pause. Makes passes.) I can do it.

PRENTICE. Then I should say, Mr. Brookfield, that for you the obligation for clean and unselfish thinking was doubly imperative.

JACK. Within this last year I've put people—well—practically asleep in a chair and I've made them tell me what a boy was doing—a mile away—in a jail.

PRENTICE. I see no reason to call clairvoyance a "bughouse" theory.

JACK. I only know that I do it.

PRENTICE. Yes—you have the youth for it—the glorious strength. Does it make any demand on your vitality?

JACK (passes hand over his eyes). I've fancied that a headache to which I'm subject is more frequent—that's all.

PRENTICE. But you find the ability—the power—increases—don't you?

JACK. Yes—in the last month I've put a man into a hypnotic sleep with half a dozen waves of the hand. (Makes pass.)

PRENTICE. Why any motion?

JACK. Fixed his attention, I suppose.

PRENTICE (shaking head). Fixes your attention. When in your own mind your belief is sufficiently trained, you won't need this. (Another slight pass.)

JACK. I won't?

PRENTICE. No.

JACK. What'll I do?

PRENTICE. Simply think. (*Pause*) You have a headache, for example.

JACK. I have a headache for a fact. (JACK *again passes hand over eyes and forehead.*)

PRENTICE. Well—some persons could cure it by rubbing your forehead.

JACK. I know that.

PRENTICE. Others could cure it by the passes of the hypnotist. Others by simply willing that it should— (*Pause*) —be cured.

JACK. Well, that's where I can't follow you—and your friend the author.

PRENTICE. You simply think your headache.

JACK. I know it aches.

PRENTICE. I think it doesn't.

JACK (*astonished*). What?

PRENTICE. I—think—it doesn't.

JACK (*pause*). Well, just this moment, it doesn't, but— (*Pause*) —isn't that—simply mental excitement—won't it come back?

PRENTICE. It won't come back today.

JACK. That's some comfort. The blamed things have made it busy for me since I've been studying this business.

PRENTICE. It is a two-edged sword—

JACK. You mean it's bad for a man who tries it?

PRENTICE. I mean that it constantly opens to the investigator new mental heights, higher planes—and every man, Mr. Brookfield, is ill in some manner who lives habitually on a lower level —than the light he sees.

SERVANT (*enters*). Two ladies, sir.

PRENTICE. Your friends?

JACK. I think so.

(PRENTICE *and* JACK *look at* SERVANT.)

SERVANT. Yes, sir.

PRENTICE. Ask them up. (*Exit* SERVANT.)

JACK. Thank you.

PRENTICE (*rises*). I'll put away Judge Henderson's glass.

JACK. They're Kentucky ladies, Mr. Justice.

PRENTICE (*indicating* JACK). But I don't want any credit for a hospitality I haven't earned.

JACK. I see.

(*Enter* SERVANT *with* HELEN *and* VIOLA.)

JACK. My niece, Miss Campbell.

PRENTICE. Miss Campbell.

JACK. And—

HELEN. One moment, Jack, I prefer to introduce myself.

PRENTICE. Won't you be seated, ladies?

(*Exit* SERVANT. HELEN *sits right of table.* VIOLA *goes to the window seat.* JACK *stands center.*)

HELEN. You are not a married man, Justice Prentice?

PRENTICE. I am not.

HELEN. But you have the reputation of being a very charitable one.

PRENTICE (*sits left of table*). That's pleasant to hear—what charity do you represent?

HELEN. None. I hardly know how to tell you my object.

PRENTICE. It's a personal matter, is it?

JACK (*back of table*). Yes, a very personal matter.

PRENTICE. Ah!

HELEN. I have here an autograph book—

PRENTICE (*to* JACK). I usually sign my autograph for those who wish it— at the—

HELEN. I did not come for an autograph, Justice Prentice, I have brought one.

PRENTICE. Well, I don't go in for that kind of thing very much. I have no collection—my taste runs more toward—

HELEN. The autograph I have brought is one of yours, written many years ago. It is signed to a letter. Will you look at it? (*Opens autograph book and gives small folded and old lace handkerchief from book to* VIOLA, *who joins her.*)

PRENTICE. With pleasure. (*Takes book.*) Is this the letter? Ah—(*Reads.*) "June 15, 1860." Dear me, that's a long time ago. (*Reads.*) "My dear Margaret: The matter passed satisfactorily—a mere scratch. Boland apologized.—Jim." What is this?

HELEN. A letter from you.

PRENTICE. And my dear Margaret—1860. Why, this letter—was it written to Margaret?

HELEN. To Margaret Price—

PRENTICE. Is it possible—well—well. (*Pause*) I wonder if what we call coincidences are ever mere coincidences. Margaret Price. Her name was on my lips a moment ago.

JACK. Really, Mr. Justice?

PRENTICE (*to* JACK). Yes. Did you know Margaret Price?

JACK. Yes. (*Looks at* HELEN—PRENTICE's *gaze follows.*)

HELEN. She was my mother—

PRENTICE. Margaret Price was—

HELEN. Was my mother.

PRENTICE. Why, I was just speaking of her to Justice Henderson whom you saw go out. Her picture dropped from the table here. (*Gets it.*) This miniature! Margaret Price gave it to me herself. And you are her daughter?

HELEN. Yes, Justice Prentice.

PRENTICE. Yes, I can see the likeness. At twenty you must have looked very like this miniature. (*Passes miniature to* HELEN.)

HELEN (*as* JACK *and* VIOLA *look at miniature*). I have photographs of myself that are very like this. (*To*

PRENTICE) And you were speaking of her just now?

PRENTICE. Not five minutes ago.—But be seated, please. (VIOLA *sits again at window.*) I'm very delighted to have you call.

HELEN. Even at such an hour?

PRENTICE. At any hour. Margaret Price was a very dear friend of mine; and to think, you're her daughter. And this letter 1860—what's this?

HELEN. Oh, don't touch that. It will break. It's only a dry spray of mignonette, pinned to the note when you sent it.

PRENTICE (*musingly*). A spray of mignonette.

HELEN. My mother's favorite flower and perfume.

PRENTICE. I remember. Well, well, this is equally astonishing.

JACK. Do you remember the letter, Mr. Justice?

PRENTICE. Perfectly.

JACK. And the circumstances it alludes to?

PRENTICE. Yes. It was the work of a romantic boy. I—I was very fond of your mother, Mrs.— by the way, you haven't told me your name.

HELEN. Never mind that now. Let me be Margaret Price's daughter for the present.

PRENTICE. Very well. Oh, this was a little scratch of a duel—they've gone out of fashion now, I'm thankful to say.

HELEN. Do you remember the cause of this one?

PRENTICE. Yes; Henry Boland had worried Margaret some way. She was frightened, I think, and fainted.

HELEN. And you struck him?

PRENTICE. Yes, and he challenged me.

HELEN. I've heard mother tell it. Do you remember what frightened her?

PRENTICE. I don't believe I do. Does the letter say?

HELEN. No. Try to think.

PRENTICE. Was it a snake or a toad?

HELEN. No—a jewel.

PRENTICE. A jewel? I remember now—a—a—cat's-eye. A cat's-eye jewel, wasn't it?

HELEN (*with excitement*). Yes, yes, yes. (*Weeping.*)

PRENTICE. My dear madam, it seems to be a very emotional subject with you.

HELEN. It is. I've so hoped you would remember it. On the cars I was praying all the way you would remember it. And you do—you do.

PRENTICE. I do.

VIOLA (*comes to* HELEN). Compose yourself, dear. Remember what depends on it.

PRENTICE. It is evidently something in which I can aid you.

HELEN. It is—and you will?

PRENTICE. There is nothing I would not do for a daughter of Margaret Price. You are in mourning, dear lady; is it for your mother?

HELEN. For my son.

PRENTICE (*to* JACK). How long has he been dead?

HELEN. He is not dead. Justice Prentice, my boy—the grandson of Margaret Price—is under a sentence of death.

PRENTICE. Sentence of death?

HELEN. Yes. I am the mother of Clay Whipple.

PRENTICE (*rises*). But, madam—

HELEN. He is to die. I come—

PRENTICE (*retreats toward second door*). Stop! You forget yourself. The case of Whipple is before the Supreme Court of the United States. I am a member of that body—I cannot listen to you.

HELEN. You must.

PRENTICE. You are prejudicing his chances. (*To* JACK) You are making it *necessary* for me to rule against him. (*To* HELEN) My dear madam, for the sake of your boy, do not do this. It is unlawful—without dignity or precedent. (*To* JACK) If the lady were not the mother of the boy I should call your conduct base—

VIOLA. But she is his mother.

HELEN (*following*). And Justice Prentice, I am the daughter of the woman you loved.

PRENTICE. I beg you to be silent.

JACK. Won't you hear us a moment?

PRENTICE. I cannot. I dare not—I must leave you. (*Going.*)

VIOLA. Why?

PRENTICE. I have explained—the matter is before the court. For me to hear you would be corrupt.

HELEN. I won't talk of the question before your court. That, our attorneys tell us, is a constitutional point.

PRENTICE. That is its attitude.

HELEN. I will not talk of that. I wish to speak of this letter.

JACK. You can listen to that, can't you, Mr. Justice?

PRENTICE. Do you hope for its influence indirectly?

HELEN. No; sit down, Justice Prentice, and compose yourself. I will talk calmly to you.

PRENTICE. My dear madam, my heart bleeds for you. (*To* JACK) Her agony must be past judicial measurement.

JACK. Only God knows, sir!

(HELEN *sits at table;* VIOLA *stands by her side;* PRENTICE *sits by the fire;* JACK *remains standing.*)

HELEN (*pause*). Justice Prentice.

PRENTICE. Mrs. Whipple.

HELEN. You remember this letter—you have recalled the duel. You remember—thank God—its cause?

PRENTICE. I do.

HELEN. You know that my mother's aversion to that jewel amounted almost to an insanity?

PRENTICE. I remember that.

HELEN. I inherited that aversion. When a child, the sight of one of them would throw me almost into convulsions.

PRENTICE. Is it possible?

HELEN. It is true. The physicians said I would outgrow the susceptibility, and in a measure I did so. But I discovered that Clay had inherited the fatal dislike from me.

JACK. You can understand that, Mr. Justice?

PRENTICE. Medical jurisprudence is full of such cases. Why should we deny them? Is nature faithful only in physical matters? You are like this portrait. Your voice *is* that of Margaret Price. Nature's behest should have also embraced some of the less apparent possessions, I think.

JACK. We urged all that at the trial, but they called it invention.

PRENTICE. Nothing seems more probable to me.

HELEN. Clay, my boy, had that dreadful and unreasonable fear of the jewel. I protected him as far as possible, but one night over a year ago, some men—companions—finding that the sight of this stone annoyed him, pressed it upon his attention. He did not know, Justice Prentice, he was not responsible. It was insanity, but he struck his tormentor and the blow resulted in the young man's death.

PRENTICE. Terrible—terrible!

HELEN. My poor boy is crushed with the awful deed. He is not a murderer. He was never that, but they have sentenced him, Justice Prentice—he—is to die. (*Rises impulsively.*)

JACK (*catching her*). Now—now—my dear Helen, compose yourself.

VIOLA (*embracing her*). You promised.

HELEN. Yes, yes, I will. (VIOLA *leads* HELEN *aside.*)

PRENTICE. All this was ably presented to the trial court, you say?

JACK. By the best attorneys.

PRENTICE. And the verdict?

JACK. Still was guilty. But, Mr. Justice, the sentiment of the community has changed very much since then. We feel that a new trial would result differently.

HELEN. When our lawyers decided to go to the Supreme Court, I remembered some letters of yours in this old book. Can you imagine my joy when I found the letter was on the very point of this inherited trait on which we rested our defense?

JACK. We have ridden twenty-four hours to reach you. The train came in only at ten o'clock.

HELEN. You—you are not powerless to help me. What is an official duty to a mother's love? To the life of my boy?

PRENTICE. My dear, dear madam, that is not necessary—believe me. This letter comes very properly under the head of new evidence. (*To* JACK) The defendant is entitled to a rehearing on that.

HELEN. Justice Prentice! Justice Prentice! (*Turns again to* VIOLA.)

VIOLA. There—there— (*Comforts* HELEN.)

PRENTICE. Of course, that isn't before us, but when we remand the case on this constitutional point—

HELEN. Then you will—you will remand it?

PRENTICE (*prevaricating*). Justice Henderson had convinced me on the point as you called. So I think there is no doubt of the decision.

HELEN. You can never know the light you let into my heart.

(VIOLA *returns the lace handker-chief to the book which* HELEN *opens for the purpose, closing it again on the handkerchief.*)

PRENTICE. What is that perfume? Have you one about you?

HELEN. Yes, on this handkerchief.

PRENTICE. What is it?

HELEN. Mignonette.

PRENTICE. Mignonette.

HELEN. A favorite perfume of mother's. This handkerchief of hers was in the book with the letter.

PRENTICE. Indeed.

HELEN. Oh, Justice Prentice, do you think I can save my boy?

PRENTICE (*to* JACK). On the rehearing I will take pleasure in testifying as to this hereditary aversion—and what I knew of its existence in Margaret Price.

JACK. May I tell the lawyers so?

PRENTICE. No. They will learn it in the court tomorrow. They can stand the suspense. I am speaking comfort to the mother's heart.

HELEN. Comfort. It is life!

PRENTICE (*to* JACK). Say nothing of this call, if you please. Nothing to any one.

JACK. We shall respect your instructions, Mr. Justice. My niece, who has been with Mrs. Whipple during this trouble, is the fiancée of the boy who is in jail.

PRENTICE. You have my sympathy, too, my dear.

VIOLA. Thank you. (*Goes to* PRENTICE *and gives him her hand.*)

PRENTICE. And now good-night.

VIOLA. Good-night. (*Goes to door where* JACK *joins her.*)

HELEN. Good-night, Justice Prentice. You must know my gratitude—words cannot tell it.

(*Exit* VIOLA.)

PRENTICE. Would you do me a favor?

HELEN. Can you ask it?

(JACK *waits at the door.*)

PRENTICE. If that was the handkerchief of Margaret Price, I'd like to have it.

(*With a moment's effort at self-control,* HELEN *gives* PRENTICE *the handkerchief. She does not dare to speak, but turns to* JACK *who leads her out.* PRENTICE *goes to the table and takes up the miniature. A distant bell tolls two.*)

PRENTICE. Margaret Price. People will say that she has been in her grave thirty years, but I'll swear her spirit was in this room tonight and directed a decision of the Supreme Court of the United States. (*Noticing the handkerchief which he holds, he puts it to his lips.*)

"The delicate odor of mignonette,
The ghost of a dead-and-gone bouquet,
Is all that tells of her story; yet
Could she think of a sweeter way?"

ACT THREE

Same scene as Act One. JACK *is sitting in the chair with his elbows on his knees, apparently in deep thought.*

———

HARVEY (*enters, left*). Mars Jack.

JACK. Well, Uncle Harvey?

HARVEY. 'Scuse me, sah, when you wants to be alone, but I'se awful anxious myself. Is dey any word from the court-house?

JACK. None, Uncle Harvey.

HARVEY. 'Cause Jo said Missus Campbell done come in, an' I thought she'd been to the trial, you know.

JACK. She has. You're not keeping anything from me, Uncle Harvey?

HARVEY. 'Deed, no, sah. Ah jes' like to ask you, Mars Jack, if I'd better have de cook fix sumpun' to eat—maybe de other ladies comin' too?

JACK. Yes, Uncle Harvey, but whether they'll want to eat or not'll depend on what word comes back with the jury.

HARVEY. Yes, sah. (*Exit left.*)

ALICE (*enters, right center; in astonishment and reproach*). Jack—

JACK. Well—

ALICE. Why are you here?

JACK. Well—I live here.

ALICE. But I thought you'd gone to Helen and Viola.

JACK. No.

ALICE. You should do so, Jack. Think of them alone when that jury returns—as it may at any moment—with its verdict.

JACK. The lawyers are there and Lew Ellinger is with them.

ALICE. But Helen—Helen needs you.

JACK. I may be useful here.

ALICE. How?

JACK. There's one man on that jury that I think is a friend.

ALICE. One man?

JACK. Yes.

ALICE. Out of a jury of twelve.

JACK. One man can stop the other eleven from bringing in an adverse verdict—and this one is with us.

ALICE. Would your going to Helen and Viola in the court-house stop his being with us?

JACK. Perhaps not, but it would stop my being with him.

ALICE. What? (*Looks about.*) I don't understand you.

JACK. Justice Prentice told me that he could sit alone in his room and make another man get up and walk to the telephone and call him by simply thinking steadily of that other man.

ALICE. Superstitious people imagine anything.

JACK. Imagine much—yes—but this isn't imagination.

ALICE. It's worse—Jack. I call it spiritualism.

JACK. Call it anything you like—spiritualism—or socialism—or rheumatism—it's there. I know nothing about it scientifically, but I've tried it on and it works, my dear Alice, it works.

ALICE. You've tried it on?

JACK. Yes.

ALICE. With whom?

JACK. With you.

ALICE. I don't know it if you have.

JACK. That is one phase of its terrible subtlety.

ALICE. When did you try it on?

JACK (*inquiringly*). That night, a month ago, when you rapped at my door at two o'clock in the morning and asked if I was ill in any way?

ALICE. I was simply nervous about you.

JACK. Call it "nervousness" if you wish to—but that was an experiment of mine—a simple experiment.

ALICE. Oh!

JACK. Two Sundays ago you went right up to the church door—hesitated, and turned home again.

ALICE. Lots of people do that.

JACK. I don't ask you to take stock in it, but that was another experiment of mine. The thing appeals to me. I can't help Helen by being at the court-house, but, as I'm alive and my name's Jack Brookfield, I do believe that my thought reaches that particular juryman.

ALICE. That's lunacy, Jack, dear.

JACK (*rises and walks*). Well, call it "lunacy." I don't insist on "rheumatism."

ALICE. Oh, Jack, the boy's life is in the balance. Bitter vindictive lawyers are prosecuting him, and I don't like my big strong brother, who used to meet men and all danger face to face, treating the situation with silly mind-cure methods—hidden alone in his rooms. I don't like it.

JACK. You can't acquit a boy of murder by having a strong brother thrash somebody in the court-rooms. If there was anything under the sun I could do with my physical strength, I'd do it; but there isn't. Now, why not try this? Why not, if I believe I can influence a juryman by my thought,—why not try?

(ALICE *turns away. Enter* JO, *right center.*)

JACK. Well?

JO. Mistah Hardmuth.

ALICE (*astonished*). Frank Hardmuth?

JO. Yes.

JACK. Here's one of the "bitter vindictive" men you want me to meet face to face. You stay here while I go and do it. (*Starts up.*)

HARDMUTH (*enters*). Excuse me, but I can't wait in an anteroom.

JACK. That'll do, Jo. (*Exit* JO.)

HARDMUTH. I want to see you alone.

JACK (*to* ALICE). Yes—

ALICE (*going*). What do you think it is?

JACK. Nothing to worry over. (*Conducts her to door. Exit* ALICE.)

HARDMUTH (*threateningly*). Jack Brookfield.

JACK. Well? (*Confronts* HARDMUTH.)

HARDMUTH. I've just seen Harvey Fisher—of the *Courier.*

JACK. Yes.

HARDMUTH. He says you've hinted at something associating me with the shooting of Scovill.

JACK. Right.

HARDMUTH. What do you mean?

JACK. I mean, Frank Hardmuth,

that you shan't hound this boy to the gallows without reckoning with me and the things I know of you.

HARDMUTH. I'm doing my duty as a prosecuting attorney.

JACK. You are, and a great deal more —you're venting a personal hatred.

HARDMUTH. That hasn't anything to do with this insinuation you've handed to a newspaper man, an insinuation for which anybody ought to kill you.

JACK. I don't deal in "insinuations." It was a charge.

HARDMUTH. A statement?

JACK. A charge! You understand English—a specific and categorical charge.

HARDMUTH. That I knew Scovill was to be shot.

JACK. That you knew it? No. That you planned it and arranged and *procured* his assassination.

HARDMUTH (*in low tone*). If the newspapers print that, I'll kill you—damn you, I'll kill you.

JACK. I don't doubt your willingness. And they'll print it—if they haven't done so already—and if they don't print it, by God, I'll print it myself and *paste it on the fences.*

HARDMUTH (*weakening*). What have I ever done to you, Jack Brookfield, except to be your friend?

JACK. You've been much too friendly. With this murder on your conscience, you proposed to take to yourself, as wife, my niece, dear to me as my life. As revenge for her refusal and mine, you've persecuted through two trials the boy she loved, and the son of the woman whose thought regulates the pulse of my heart, an innocent, unfortunate boy. In your ambition you've reached out to be the governor of this State, and an honored political party is seriously considering you for that office today.

HARDMUTH. That Scovill story's a lie—a political lie. I think you mean to be honest, Jack Brookfield, but somebody's strung you.

JACK. Wait! The man that's now hiding in Indiana—a fugitive from your feeble efforts at extradition—sat upstairs drunk and desperate—his last dollar on a case card. I pitied him. If a priest had been there he couldn't have purged his soul cleaner than poor Raynor gave it to me. If *he* put me on, am I strung?

HARDMUTH (*frightened*). Yes, you are. I can't tell you why, because this jury is out and may come in any moment and I've got to be there, but I can square it. So help me God, I can square it.

JACK. You'll have to square it.

(*Enter* ALICE, *from the left, followed by* PRENTICE. *The Justice carries a folded newspaper.*)

ALICE. Jack. (*Indicates* PRENTICE.)

PRENTICE. Excuse me, I—

HARDMUTH. Oh—Justice Prentice.

JACK. Mr. Hardmuth—the State's attorney.

PRENTICE. I recognize Mr. Hardmuth. I didn't salute him because I resent his disrespectful treatment of myself during his cross-examination.

HARDMUTH. Entirely within my rights as a lawyer and—

PRENTICE. Entirely—and never within the opportunities of a gentleman.

HARDMUTH. Your side foresaw the powerful effect on a local jury of any testimony by a member of the Supreme Court, and my wish to break that—

PRENTICE. Was quite apparent, sir,—quite apparent—but the testimony of every man is entitled to just such weight and consideration as that man's character commands. But it is not that disrespect which I resent. I am an old man—That I am unmarried—childless—without a son to inherit the vigor that time has reclaimed, is due to—a sentiment that you endeavored to ridicule, Mr. Hardmuth, a sentiment which would have been sacred in the hands of any true Kentuckian, which I am glad to hear you are not.

JACK. That's all.

HARDMUTH. Perhaps not. (*Exits.*)

PRENTICE. My dear Mr. Brookfield, that man certainly hasn't seen this newspaper?

JACK. No—but he knows it's coming.

PRENTICE. When I urged you as a citizen to tell anything you knew of the man, I hadn't expected a capital charge.

ALICE. What is it, Jack—what have you said?

JACK (*to* ALICE). All in the headlines—read it. (*Gives* ALICE *the paper. To* PRENTICE) That enough for your purpose, Justice Prentice?

PRENTICE. I never dreamed of an attack of that—that magnitude—Enough!

ALICE. Why—why did you do this, Jack?

JACK. Because I'm your big strong brother—and I had the information.

PRENTICE. It was necessary, Mrs. Campbell—necessary.

ALICE. Why necessary?

JACK. My poor sister, you don't think. If that jury brings in a verdict of guilty—what then?

ALICE. What then? I don't know.

JACK. An appeal to the governor—for clemency.

ALICE. Well?

JACK. Then we delay things until a new governor comes in. But suppose that new governor is Hardmuth himself.

ALICE. How can the new governor be Hardmuth?

PRENTICE. Nothing can stop it if he gets the nomination, and the convention is in session at Frankfort today with Mr. Hardmuth's name in the lead.

JACK (*indicating paper*). I've served that notice on them and they won't dare nominate him. That is, I think they won't.

ALICE. But to charge him with murder?

PRENTICE. The only thing to consider there is—have you your facts?

JACK. I have.

PRENTICE. Then it was a duty and you chose the psychological moment for its performance. "With what measure you mete—it shall be measured to you again." I have pity for the man whom that paper crushes, but I have greater pity for the boy he is trying to have hanged. (*Goes to* ALICE.) You know, Mrs. Campbell, that young Whipple is the grandson of an old friend of mine.

ALICE. Yes, Justice Prentice, I know that.

(*Enter* JO, *followed by* HELEN *and* VIOLA.)

JO. Mars Jack!

JACK (*turning*). Yes?

HELEN. Oh, Jack!— (*Comes down to* JACK. VIOLA *goes to* ALICE.)

JACK. What is it? (*Catches and supports* HELEN.)

VIOLA. The jury returned and asked for instructions.

JACK. Well?

HELEN. There's a recess of an hour.

VIOLA. The court wishes them locked up for the night, but the foreman said the jurymen were all anxious to get to their homes and he felt an agreement could be reached in an hour.

PRENTICE. Did he use exactly those words—"to their homes"?

VIOLA. "To their homes"—yes.

PRENTICE (*smiling at* JACK). There you are.

HELEN. What, Jack?

JACK. What?

PRENTICE. Men with vengeance or severity in their hearts would hardly say they're "anxious to get to their homes." They say, "the jury is anxious to get away," or "to finish its work."

HELEN. Oh, Justice Prentice, you pin hope upon such slight things.

PRENTICE. That is what hope is for, my dear Mrs. Whipple; the frail chances of this life.

VIOLA. And now, Uncle Jack, Mrs. Whipple ought to have a cup of tea and something to eat.

HELEN. Oh, I couldn't—we must go back at once.

VIOLA. Well, I could—I—I must.

ALICE. Yes—you must—both of you. (*Exits to dining room.*)

VIOLA (*returning to* HELEN). You don't think it's heartless, do you?

HELEN. You dear child. (*Kisses her.*)

VIOLA. You come, too.

HELEN (*refusing*). Please. (*Exit* VIOLA, *as* HELEN *sinks to sofa.*)

JACK. And now, courage, my dear Helen, it's almost over.

HELEN. At the other trial the jury delayed—just this way.

PRENTICE. Upon what point did the jury ask instruction?

HELEN. Degree.

PRENTICE. And the court?

HELEN. Oh, Jack, the Judge answered—guilty in the first degree, or not guilty.

PRENTICE. That all helps us.

HELEN. It does?

JACK. Who spoke for the jury?

HELEN. The foreman—and one other juryman asked a question.

JACK. Was it the man in the fourth chair—first row?

HELEN (*inquiringly*). Yes—?

JACK. Ah.

HELEN. Why?

JACK. I think he's a friend, that's all.

HELEN. I should die, Jack, if it wasn't for your courage. You won't get tired of it—will you—and forsake my poor boy—and me?

JACK (*encouragingly*). What do you think?

HELEN. All our lawyers are kindness itself, but—but—you—Jack—you somehow—

VIOLA (*enters*). Oh, Uncle Jack—here's a note our lawyer asked me to give to you—I forgot it until this minute.

JACK. Thank you. (*Takes note.*)

VIOLA. Please try a cup of tea.

HELEN. No—no—Viola.

(*Exit* VIOLA.)

What is it, Jack? Are they afraid?

JACK. It's not about the trial at all. (*Hands note to* PRENTICE.)

HELEN. Really?

JACK. Yes.

HELEN. But why don't you show it to us, then?

JACK (PRENTICE *returns note*). I will —if my keeping it gives you so much alarm as that. (*Turns on the large drop light and stands under it.*) Colonel Bayley says—"Dear Jack, I've seen the paper; Hardmuth will shoot on sight."

HELEN (*quickly to* JACK's *side*). Oh, Jack, if anything should happen to you—

JACK. "Anything" is quite as likely to happen to Mr. Hardmuth.

HELEN. But not even that—my boy has killed a man—and—you—Jack—you—well, you just mustn't let it happen, that's all.

JACK. I mustn't let it happen because—?

HELEN. Because—I—couldn't bear it.

(JACK *lifts her hand to his face and kisses it.*)

ALICE (*enters*). What was the letter, Jack?

JACK (*hands letter to* ALICE *as he passes, leading* HELEN *to door*). And, now I'll agree to do the best I can for Mr. Hardmuth if you'll take a cup of tea and a biscuit.

HELEN. There isn't time.

JACK. There's plenty of time if the adjournment was for an hour.

ALICE (*in alarm*). Jack!

JACK. Eh— (*Turns to* ALICE.) Wait one minute. (*Goes on to door with* HELEN.) Go. (*Exit* HELEN.)

ALICE (*as* JACK *returns*). He threatens your life.

JACK. Not exactly. Simply Colonel Bayley's opinion that he will shoot on sight.

ALICE (*impatiently*). Oh—

JACK. There is a difference, you know.

JO (*enters*). Mr. Ellinger, sah.

LEW (*enters; briskly*). Hello, Jack.

(*Exit* JO.)

JACK. Well, Lew?

LEW (*with newspaper*). Why, that's the damnedest thing— (*To* ALICE) I beg your pardon.

ALICE. Don't, please—some manly emphasis is a real comfort, Mr. Ellinger.

LEW. That charge of yours against Hardmuth is raisin' more h-h-high feeling than anything that ever happened.

JACK. I saw the paper.

LEW. You didn't see this—it's an extra. (*Reads.*) "The charge read to the convention in night session at Frankfort—Bill Glover hits Jim Macey on the nose—De Voe of Carter County takes Jim's gun away from him. The delegation from Butler get down to their stomachs and crawl under the benches—some statesmen go through the windows. Convention takes a recess till morning. Local sheriff swearin' in deputies to keep peace in the bar-rooms." That's all you've done.

JACK (to ALICE). Good! (To PRENTICE) Well, they can't nominate Mr. Hardmuth now.

LEW (to ALICE). I been hedgin'—I told the fellows I'd bet Jack hadn't said it.

JACK. Yes—I did say it.

LEW. In just those words—? (Reads.) "The poor fellow that crouched back of a window sill and shot Kentucky's governor deserves hanging less than the man whom he is shielding—the man who laid the plot of assassina-tion, the present prosecuting attorney by appointment—Frank Allison Hard-muth." Did you say that?

JACK. Lew, that there might be no mistake—I wrote it.

(LEW whistles; JACK takes the paper and scans it.)

LEW. Is it straight?

JACK. Yes. (Pushes hanging button and turns off the large drop-light).

LEW. He was in the plot to kill the governor?

JACK. He organized it.

LEW. Well, what do you think of that? And now he's runnin' for gov-ernor himself—a murderer?

JACK. Yes.

LEW (to PRENTICE). And for six months he's been houndin' every fel-low in Louisville that sat down to a game of cards. (JACK nods.) The damned rascal's nearly put me in the poorhouse.

JACK. Poor old Lew!

LEW (to PRENTICE). Why, before I could get to that court-house today I had to take a pair of scissors that I used to cut coupons with and trim the whiskers off o' my shirt cuffs. (To JACK) How long have you known this?

JACK. Ever since the fact.

PRENTICE. Mm—

LEW. Why do you spring it only now?

JACK. Because until now I lacked the character and the moral courage. I spring it now by the advice of Jus-tice Prentice to reach that conven-tion at Frankfort.

LEW. Well, you reached them.

PRENTICE. The convention was only a secondary consideration with me—my real object was this jury with whom Mr. Hardmuth seemed too powerful.

LEW. Reach the jury?

JACK (enthusiastically). The jury? Why, of course—the entire jury—and I was hoping for one man—

LEW. Why, they don't see the papers —the jury won't get a line of this.

JACK. I think they will.

LEW. You got 'em fixed?

JACK (indignantly). Fixed? No.

LEW. Then how will they see it?

PRENTICE (firmly and slowly to LEW, who is half dazed). How many people in Louisville have already read that charge as you have read it?

LEW. Thirty thousand, maybe, but—

PRENTICE. And five hundred thou-sand in the little cities and the towns. Do you think, Mr. Ellinger, that all those minds can be at white heat over that knowledge and none of it reach the thought of those twelve men? Ah, no—

JACK. To half a million good Ken-tuckians tonight Frank Hardmuth is a repulsive thing—and that jury's faith in him—is dead.

LEW (pause). Why, Jack, old man, you're dippy.

(ALICE turns away wearily, agreeing with LEW.)

PRENTICE. Then, Mr. Ellinger, I am

dippy, too.

(ALICE *turns back.*)

LEW. You mean you think the jury gets the public opinion—without anybody tellin' them or their reading it.

PRENTICE. Yes. (*Pause.* LEW *looks stunned.*) In every widely discussed trial the defendant is tried not alone by his twelve peers, but by the entire community.

LEW. Why, blast it! The community goes by what the newspaper says!

PRENTICE. That is often the regrettable part of it—but the fact remains.

JACK. And that's why you asked me to expose Frank Hardmuth?

PRENTICE. Yes.

LEW. Well, the public will think you did it because he closed your game.

JACK. Hardmuth didn't close my game.

LEW. Who did?

JACK (*pointing to* PRENTICE). This man.

PRENTICE (*to* JACK). Thank you.

LEW. How the he—er—heaven's name did he close it?

JACK. He gave my self-respect a slap on the back and I stood up. (*Exit.*)

LEW (*thoroughly confused; pause*). Stung! (*Turns to* PRENTICE.) So you are responsible for these—these new ideas of Jack's?

PRENTICE. In a measure. Have the ideas apparently hurt Mr. Brookfield?

LEW. They've put him out of business—that's all.

PRENTICE. Which business?

LEW. Why, this house of his.

PRENTICE. I see. But his new ideas? Don't you like them, Mr. Ellinger?

LEW. I love Jack Brookfield—love him like a brother—but I don't want even a brother askin' me if I'm sure I've "thought it over" when I'm startin' to take the halter off for a pleasant evenin'. Get my idea?

PRENTICE. I begin to.

LEW. In other words—I don't want to take my remorse first. It dampens fun. The other day a lady at the races said, "We've missed you, Mr. Ellinger." And I said, "Have you?— Well I'll be up this evening," and I'm pressing her hand and hanging on to it till I'm afraid I'll get the carriage grease on my coat—feelin' only about thirty-two, you know, then I turn round and Jack has those sleepy lamps on me—and "bla"— (*Turns and sinks on to sofa.*)

PRENTICE. And you don't go?

LEW (*bracing up*). I *do* go—as a matter of self-respect—but I don't make a hit. I'm thinking so much more about those morality ideas of Jack's than I am about the lady that it cramps my style and we never get past the weather, and "when did you last hear from So-and-so?" (*Rises.*) I want to reform all right. I believe in reform. But first I want to have the fun of fallin' and fallin' hard.

JO (*distant and outside*). 'Fore God, Mars Clay!

CLAY. Jo, is my mother here?

ALICE (*entering left*). Why, that's Clay.

(*Voices off continue together and approach.*)

LEW (*to* PRENTICE). It's the boy.

ALICE. His mother! (*Starts to call* HELEN, *then falters in indecision.*) Oh! (*The outside voices grow louder.*)

PRENTICE. Acquittal!

(*Enter* CLAY, *followed by* COLONEL BAYLEY, *his attorney.*)

ALICE. Clay, Clay!

CLAY. Oh, Mrs. Campbell. (ALICE *embraces him.*)

(*Enter* JACK, HELEN, *and* VIOLA.)

JACK (*seeing* CLAY *and speaking back to* HELEN). Yes.

HELEN (*as she enters*). My boy!

CLAY. Mother!

(*They embrace.* CLAY *slips to his knees with his face hidden in* HELEN's *lap, repeating her name.* HELEN, *standing, sways and is caught by* JACK. CLAY, *noting this weakness, rises and helps support her.*)

JACK (*rousing her*). He's free, Helen, he's free.

CLAY. Yes, Mother, I'm free.

(VIOLA, *who has crossed back of* CLAY *and* HELEN, *weeps on shoulder of* ALICE, *who comforts her.*)

HELEN. My boy, my boy!

(VIOLA *looks at them.* HELEN *sees* VIOLA *and turns* CLAY *toward her.* CLAY *takes* VIOLA *in his arms.*)

CLAY. Viola, my brave sweetheart!

VIOLA. It's really over?

CLAY. Yes.

JACK. It's a great victory, Colonel.

BAYLEY. Thank you.

JACK. If ever a lawyer made a good fight for a man's life, you did. Helen, Viola, you must want to shake this man's hand.

VIOLA. I could have thrown my arms around you when you made that speech.

BAYLEY (*laughing*). Too many young fellows crowding into the profession as it is.

HELEN (*taking his hand*). Life must be sweet to a man who can do so much good as you do.

BAYLEY. I couldn't stand it, you know, if it wasn't that my ability works both ways.

HARVEY (*enters, left*). Mars Clay.

CLAY. Harvey! Why, dear old Harvey. (*Half embraces* HARVEY *and pats him affectionately.*)

HARVEY. Yes, sah. Could—could you eat anything, Mars Clay?

CLAY. Eat anything! Why, I'm starvin', Harvey.

HARVEY. Ha, ha. Yes, sah. (*Exits quickly.*)

CLAY. But *you* with me, Mother—and *Viola.*

HELEN. My boy! Colonel! (*Turns to* BAYLEY. *Exeunt* CLAY, VIOLA, HELEN, BAYLEY, *and* ALICE *to dining room.*)

JACK (*alone with* PRENTICE, *picks up* BAYLEY's *letter; takes hold of push button over head*). I shall never doubt you again.

PRENTICE. Mr. Brookfield, never doubt yourself.

(*Enter* HARDMUTH. *He rushes down toward dining room and turns back to* JACK *who is under the lamp with his hand on its button.*)

HARDMUTH. You think you'll send me to the gallows, but, damn you, you go first yourself. (*Thrusts a derringer against* JACK's *body.*)

JACK. Stop! (*The big light flashes on above* HARDMUTH's *eyes. At* JACK's *"Stop,"* PRENTICE *inclines forward with eyes on* HARDMUTH *so that there is a double battery of hypnotism on him. A pause.*) You can't shoot—that —gun. You can't pull the trigger. (*Pause*) You can't even hold the gun. (*Pause. The derringer drops from* HARDMUTH's *hand.*) Now, Frank, you can go.

HARDMUTH (*recoiling slowly*). I'd like to know—how in hell you did that—to me.

ACT FOUR

The scene is the same as in Act Three. All the lights are on, including the large electric light. CLAY *and* VIOLA *seated on sofa near the fireplace.*

———

VIOLA. I must really say good-night and let you get some sleep.

CLAY. Not before Jack gets home. Our mothers have considerately left us alone together. They'll just as considerately tell us when it's time to part.

VIOLA. My mother said it was time half an hour ago.

CLAY. Wait till Jack comes in.

JO (*enters*). Mars Clay?

CLAY. Well, Jo?

JO. Dey's another reporter to see you, sah?

VIOLA. Send him away—Mr. Whipple won't see any more reporters.

CLAY (*rises*). Wait a minute—who is he? (JO *hands card.*) I've got to see this one, Viola.

VIOLA (*complaining*). Why "got to"?

CLAY. He's a friend—I'll see him, Jo.

JO. Yas, sah— (*Exit.*)

VIOLA (*rises*). You've said that all day—they're all friends.

CLAY. Well, they are—but this boy especially. It was fine to see you and mother and Jack when I was in that jail—great—but you were there daytimes. This boy spent hours on the other side of the bars helping me pass the awful nights. I tell you—death-cells would be pretty nearly hell if it wasn't for the police reporters—ministers ain't in it with 'em.

EMMETT (*a reporter, enters*). Good-evening.

CLAY. How are you, Ned? You know Miss Campbell?

EMMETT (*bowing*). Yes.

VIOLA. Good-evening.

CLAY. Have a chair.

EMMETT. Thank you. (*Defers to* VIOLA *who sits first on sofa. Pause.*) This is different. (*Looks around the room.*)

CLAY. Some.

EMMETT. Satisfied? The way we handled the story?

CLAY. Perfectly. You were just bully, old man.

EMMETT (*to* VIOLA). That artist of ours is only a kid—and they work him to death on the "Sunday"—so— (*Pause. To* CLAY) You understand.

CLAY. Oh—I got used to the—pictures a year ago.

EMMETT. Certainly. (*Pause*) Anything you want to say?

VIOLA. For the paper?

EMMETT. Yes.

CLAY. I think not.

(*Enter* HELEN *and* ALICE. EMMETT *rises.*)

HELEN. Clay, dear— (*Pause*) Oh—

CLAY. You met my mother?

EMMETT. No—

CLAY. Mother—this is Mr. Emmett of whom I've told you so often.

HELEN. Oh—the good reporter.

EMMETT (*to* CLAY). Gee! That'd be a wonder if the gang heard it. (*Taking* HELEN'S *hand as she offers it.*) We got pretty well acquainted—yes, 'm.

CLAY (*introducing* ALICE). Mrs. Campbell.

ALICE. Won't you sit down, Mr. Emmett?

EMMETT. Thank you. I guess we've covered everything, but the chief wanted me to see your son— (*Turns to* CLAY.) and see if you'd do the paper a favor?

CLAY. If possible—gladly—

EMMETT. I don't like the assignment because—well for the very reason that it was handed to me—and that is because we're more or less friendly.

JACK (*enters in fur coat, with cap and goggles in hand*). Well, it's a wonderful night outside.

ALICE. You're back early.

JACK. Purposely. (*To* EMMETT) How are you?

EMMETT (*rising*). Mr. Brookfield.

JACK. I thought you girls might like a little run in the moonlight before I put in the machine.

HELEN. Mr. Emmett has some message from his editor.

JACK. What is it?

EMMETT. There's a warrant out for Hardmuth—you saw that?

VIOLA. Yes, we saw that. (*Goes to* JACK.)

JACK. Tonight's paper—

EMMETT. If they get him and he comes to trial and all that, it'll be the biggest trial Kentucky ever saw.

CLAY. Well?

EMMETT. Well—the paper wants you to agree to report it for them—the trial—there'll be other papers after you, of course.

VIOLA. Oh, no—

EMMETT. Understand, Clay, I'm not asking it. (*To* VIOLA) I'm here under orders just as I'd be at a fire or a bread riot.

CLAY (*demurring*). And—of course—you understand, don't you?

EMMETT. Perfectly—and I told the chief myself you wouldn't see it.

CLAY. Paper's been too friendly for me to assume any—any—

JACK. Unnecessary dignity—

CLAY. Exactly—but—I just couldn't, you see—

EMMETT (*going*). Oh, leave it to me— I'll let 'em down easy.

CLAY. Thank you.

EMMETT. You expect to be in Europe or—

CLAY. But I don't.

(JACK *removes fur coat, puts it on chair up right center.*)

VIOLA. We're going to stay right here in Louisville—

CLAY. And work out my—my own future among the people who know me.

EMMETT. Of course—Europe's just to stall off the chief—get him on to some other dope—

HELEN (*rising*). But—

JACK (*interrupting*). It's all right.

HELEN (*to* JACK). I hate to begin with a falsehood.

EMMETT. Not your son—me—. Saw some copy on our telegraph desk, Mr. Brookfield, that'd interest you.

JACK. Yes.

EMMETT. Or maybe you know of it? Frankfort—

JACK. No.

EMMETT. Some friend named you in the caucus.

JACK. What connection?

EMMETT. Governor.

VIOLA (*to* EMMETT). Uncle Jack?

EMMETT. Yes, 'm—that is, for the nomination.

JACK. It's a joke.

EMMETT. Grows out of these Hardmuth charges, of course.

JACK. That's all.

EMMETT. Good-night— (*Bows.*) Mrs. Whipple—ladies— (*Exit.*)

CLAY (*going to door with* EMMETT). You'll make that quite clear, won't you?

EMMETT (*outside*). I'll fix it.

CLAY (*returning*). If it wasn't for the notoriety of it, I'd like to do that. (*Sits right of table.*)

HELEN (*reproachfully*). My son!

JACK. Why would you like to do it?

CLAY. To get even. I'd like to see Hardmuth suffer as he made me suffer. I'd like to *watch* him suffer and write of it.

JACK. That's a bad spirit to face the world with, my boy.

CLAY. I hate him. (*Goes to* VIOLA.)

JACK. Hatred is heavier freight for the shipper than it is for the consignee.

CLAY. I can't help it.

JACK. Yes, you can help it. Mr. Hardmuth should be of the utmost indifference to you. To hate him is weak.

VIOLA. Weak?

JACK. Yes, weak-minded. Hardmuth was in love with you at one time—he hated Clay. He said Clay was as weak as dishwater— (*To* CLAY) —and you were at that time. You've had your lesson—profit by it. Its meaning was self-control. Begin now if you're going to be the custodian of this girl's happiness.

HELEN. I'm sure he means to, Jack.

JACK. You can carry your hatred of Hardmuth and let it embitter your whole life—or you can drop it—so— (*Drops a book on table.*) The power that any man or anything has to annoy us we give him or it by our interest. Some idiot told your great-grandmother that a jewel with different colored strata in it was "bad luck"— or a "hoodoo"—she believed it, and she nursed her faith that passed the lunacy on to your grandmother.

HELEN. Jack, don't talk of that, please.

JACK. I'll skip one generation—but I'd like to talk of it.

ALICE. (*rising, comes to* HELEN). Why talk of it?

JACK. It was only a notion, and an effort of will can banish it.

CLAY. It was more than a notion.

JACK. Tom Denning's scarf-pin which he dropped there (*Indicates floor.*) was an exhibit in your trial— Judge Bayley returned it to me today. (*Puts hand in pocket.*)

VIOLA. I wish you wouldn't, Uncle Jack. (*Turns away.*)

JACK (*to* CLAY). You don't mind, do you?

CLAY. I'd rather not look at it—to-night.

JACK. You needn't look at it. I'll hold it in my hand and you put your hands over mine.

ALICE. I really don't see the use in this experiment, Jack.

JACK (*with* CLAY's *hand over his*). That doesn't annoy you, does it?

CLAY. I'm controlling myself, sir— but I feel the influence of the thing all through and through me.

HELEN. Jack!

(VIOLA *turns away in protest.*)

JACK. Down your back, isn't it, and in the roots of your hair—tingling—?

CLAY. Yes.

HELEN. Why torture him?

JACK. Is it torture?

CLAY (*with brave self-control*). I shall be glad when it's over.

JACK (*severely*). What rot! That's only my night-key—look at it. I haven't the scarf-pin about me.

CLAY. Why make me think it was the scarf-pin?

JACK. To prove to you that it's only thinking—that's all. Now, be a man— the cat's-eye itself is in that table drawer. Get it and show Viola that you're not a neuropathic idiot. You're a child of *the everlasting God* and nothing on the earth or under it can harm you in the slightest degree. (CLAY *opens drawer and takes pin.*) That's the spirit—look at it—I've made many a young horse do that to an umbrella. Now, give it to me. (*To* VIOLA) You're not afraid of it?

VIOLA. Why, of course I'm not.

JACK (*putting pin on her breast*). Now, if you want my niece, go up to that hoodoo like a man.

(CLAY *embraces* VIOLA.)

HELEN. Oh, Jack, do you think that will last?

JACK. Which—indifference to the hoodoo or partiality to my niece?

CLAY. They'll both last.

JACK. Now, my boy, drop your hatred of Hardmuth as you drop your fear of the scarf-pin. Don't look back—your life's ahead of you. Don't mount for the race over-weight.

JO (*enters*). Mr. Ellinger.

LEW (*enters*). I don't intrude, do I?

JACK. Come in.

LEW (*to* LADIES). Good-evening. Ah, Clay. (*Shakes hands with* CLAY.) Glad to see you looking so well. Glad to see you in such good company. (*To* JACK, *briskly*) I've got him.

JACK. Got whom?

LEW. Hardmuth. (*To* LADIES) Detectives been hunting him all day, you know.

HELEN. He's caught, you say?

LEW. No—but I've treed him— (*To* JACK) —and I thought I'd just have a word with you before passing the tip. (*To* LADIES) He's nearly put me in the poorhouse with his raids and closing laws, and I see a chance to get even.

JACK. In what way?

LEW. They've been after him nearly twenty-four hours—morning paper's going to offer a reward for him, and I understand the State will also. If I had a little help I'd hide him for a day or two and then surrender him for those rewards.

JACK. Where is Hardmuth? (*Sits at table.*)

LEW. Hiding.

JACK (*writing a note*). Naturally.

LEW. You remember Big George?

JACK. The darkey?

LEW. Yes—used to be on the door at Phil Kelly's?

JACK Yes.

LEW. He's there. In Big George's cottage—long story—Big George's wife —that is, she—well, his wife used to be pantry maid for Hardmuth's mother. When they raided Kelly's game, Big George pretended to turn State's evidence, but he really hates Hardmuth like a rattler—so it all comes back to me. You see, if I'd win a couple of hundred at Kelly's I used to slip George a ten going out. Your luck always stays by you if you divide a little with a nigger or a humpback—

and in Louisville it's easier to find a nigger—so—

JACK. He's there now?

LEW. Yes. He wants to get away. He's got two guns and he'll shoot before he gives up—so I'd have to con him some way. George's wife is to open the door to Kelly's old signal, you remember— (*Raps.*) —one knock, then two, and then one.

JACK. Where is the cottage?

LEW. Number 7 Jackson Street—little dooryard—border of arborvitae on the path.

JACK. One knock—then two—and then one— (*Rises with note written.*)

LEW. What you gonta do?

JACK. Send for him.

LEW. Who you gonta send?

JACK. That boy there.

CLAY. Me?

JACK. Yes.

HELEN. Oh. No—no.

JACK. And my niece.

VIOLA. What! To arrest a man?

JACK (*to* CLAY). My machine is at the door. Give Hardmuth this note. He'll come with you quietly. Bring him here. We'll decide what to do with him after that.

ALICE. I can't allow Viola on such an errand.

JACK. When the man she's promised to marry is going into danger—

VIOLA. If Mr. Hardmuth will come for that note—why can't I deliver it?

JACK. You may—if Clay'll let you.

CLAY (*quietly taking note as* JACK *offers it to* VIOLA). I'll hand it to him.

JACK. I hope so. (*Gives goggles and coat.*) Take these—remember—one rap, then two, then one.

CLAY. I understand—number seven—?

LEW. Jackson Street.

ALICE. I protest.

HELEN. So do I.

JACK (*to* CLAY *and* VIOLA). You're both of age. I ask you to do it. If you give Hardmuth the goggles, nobody'll recognize him and with a lady beside him you'll get him safely here.

CLAY. Come. (*Exits with* VIOLA.)

LEW (*following to door*). I ought to be in the party.

JACK. No—you stay here.

ALICE. That's scandalous.

JACK. But none of us will start the scandal, will we?

HELEN. Clay knows nothing of that kind of work—a man with two guns—think of it.

JACK. After he's walked barehanded up to a couple of guns a few times, he'll quit fearing men that are armed only with a scarf-pin.

HELEN (*hysterically*). It's cruel to keep constantly referring to that—that —mistake of Clay's—I want to forget it.

JACK (*going to* HELEN; *tenderly*). The way to forget it, my dear Helen, is not to guard it as a sensitive spot in your memory, but to grasp it as the wise ones grasp a nettle—crush all its power to harm you in one courageous contact. We think things are calamities and trials and sorrows— only names. They are spiritual gymnastics and have an eternal value when once you front them and make them crouch at your feet. Say once for all to your soul and thereby to the world—"Yes, my boy killed a man —because I'd brought him up a half-effeminate, hysterical weakling, but he's been through the fire and I've been through the fire, and we're both the better for it."

HELEN. I can say that truthfully, but I don't want to make a policeman of him, just the same. (*Exit to dining room.*)

ALICE (*following*). Your treatment's a little too heroic, Jack. (*Exit.*)

LEW. Think they'll fetch him?

JACK (*sits left of table*). Yes.

LEW. He'll come, of course, if he does, under the idea that you'll help him when he gets here.

JACK. Yes.

LEW. Pretty hard double-cross, but he deserves it. I've got a note of fifteen thousand to meet tomorrow, or, damn it, I don't think I'd fancy this man-hunting. I put up some Louisville-Nashville bonds for security, and the holder of the note'll be only too anxious to pinch 'em.

JACK. You can't get your rewards in time for that.

LEW. I know—and that's one reason I come to you, Jack. If you see I'm in a fair way to get a reward—

JACK. I'll lend you money, Lew.

LEW. Thank you. (JACK *takes checkbook and writes.*) I thought you would. If I lose those bonds they'll have me selling programs for a livin' at a grandstand. You see, I thought hatin' Hardmuth as you do, and your reputation bein' up through that stuff to the papers—

JACK. There. (*Gives check.*)

LEW. Thank you, old man. I'll hand this back to you in a week.

JACK (*rises*). You needn't.

LEW. What?

JACK. You needn't hand it back. It's only fifteen thousand and you've lost a hundred of them at poker in these rooms.

LEW. Never belly-ached, did I?

JACK. Never—but you don't owe me that fifteen.

LEW. Rot! I'm no baby—square game, wasn't it?

JACK. Perfectly.

LEW. And I'll sit in a square game any time I get a chance.

JACK. I know, Lew, all about that.

LEW. I'll play you for this fifteen

right away. (*Displays check.*)

JACK. No. (*Walks aside.*)

LEW. Ain't had a game in three weeks—and, besides, I think my luck's changin'? When Big George told me about Hardmuth I took George's hand before I thought what I was doin'—and you know what shakin' hands with a nigger does just before any play.

JACK (*resisting* LEW's *plea*). No, thank you, Lew.

LEW. My money's good as anybody else's, ain't it?

JACK. Just as good, but—

LEW. It ain't a phoney check, is it? (*Examines check.*)

JACK. The check's all right.

LEW (*taunting*). Losing your nerves?

JACK. No (*Pause*) — suppose you shuffle those and deal a hand. (*Indicates small table, right.*)

LEW. That's like old times; what is it—stud-horse or draw? (*Sits at table.*)

JACK (*goes to fireplace*). Draw if you say so.

LEW. I cut 'em?

JACK. You cut them.

LEW (*dealing two poker hands*). Table stakes—check goes for a thousand.

JACK. That suits me.

LEW (*taking his own cards*). Sit down.

JACK (*at other side of room looking into fire*). I don't need to sit down just yet.

LEW. As easy as that, am I?

JACK. Lew!

LEW. Yes?

JACK (*pause*). Do you happen to have three queens?

(LEW *looks at* JACK, *then carefully at back of his own cards, then at the deck.*)

LEW. Well, I can't see it.

JACK. No use looking—they're not marked.

LEW. Well, I shuffled 'm all right.

JACK. Yes.

LEW. And cut 'm? (JACK *nods.*) Couldn't 'a' been a cold deck?

JACK. No.

LEW. Then, how did you know I had three queens?

JACK. I didn't know it. I just thought you had.

LEW. Can you do it again?

JACK. I don't know. Draw one card.

LEW (*drawing one card from deck*). All right.

JACK (*pause*). Is it the ace of hearts?

LEW. It is.

JACK. Mm—turns me into a rotter, doesn't it? (*Comes gloomily to the big table.*)

LEW. Can you do that every time?

JACK. I never tried it until tonight—that is, consciously. I've always had luck and I thought it was because I took chances on a game—same as any player—but that don't look like it, does it?

LEW. Beats me.

JACK. And what a monster it makes of me—these years I've been in the business.

LEW. You say you didn't know it before?

JACK. I didn't know it—no—but—some things have happened lately that have made me think it might be so; that jury yesterday—some facts I've had from Justice Prentice. Telepathy of a very common kind—and I guess it's used in a good many games, old man, we aren't on to.

LEW. Well—have you told anybody?

JACK. No.

LEW (*excitedly*). Good! (*Rises and comes to* JACK.) Now, see here, Jack, if you can do that right along I know a game in Cincinnati where it'd be like takin' candy from children.

JACK. Good God! you're not suggesting that I keep it up?

LEW. Don't overdo it—no— (*Pause*) Or you show me the trick and *I'll* collect all right.

JACK (*slowly*). Lew— (*Pause*) Some of the fellows I've won from in this house have gone over to the park and blown their heads off.

LEW. Some of the fellows anybody wins from in any house go somewhere and blow their heads off.

JACK. True— (*Pause.*)

LEW. Three queens—before the draw —well, you could 'a' had me all right— and you won't tell me how you do it?

JACK. I don't know how I do it; the thought just comes to my mind stronger than any other thought.

LEW (*reprovingly*). God A'mighty gives you a mind like that and you won't go with me to Cincinnati. (*Goes to card table; studies cards.*)

JO (*enters*). Justice Prentice, sah.

JACK. Ask him to step up here.

JO. Yes, sah. (*Exit.*)

JACK (*goes to door, left*). Alice— Helen—Justice Prentice has called; I'd like you to join us.

LEW. Can the old man call a hand like that, too?

JACK. I'm sure he could.

LEW. And—are there others?

JACK. I believe there are a good many others who unconsciously have the same ability.

LEW. Well, it's a God's blessin' there's a sucker born every minute. I'm a widow and an orphan 'longside o' that. (*Throws cards in disgust onto table.*)

(*Enter* ALICE *and* HELEN.)

ALICE. Been losing, Mr. Ellinger?

LEW. Losing? I just saved fifteen thousand I was gonta throw 'way like sand in a rathole. I'm a babe eatin' spoon victuals and only gettin' half at that.

(*Enter* PRENTICE.)

JACK. Good-evening.

PRENTICE. Good-evening. (*Shakes hands with* ALICE *and* HELEN.)

JACK. I stopped at your hotel, Mr. Justice, but you were out.

(*Enter* VIOLA.)

ALICE (*anxiously*). Viola.

HELEN. Where's Clay?

VIOLA. Downstairs. Good-evening.

PRENTICE. Good-evening.

JACK (*to others*). Pardon. (*To* VIOLA.) Did the—gentleman come with you?

VIOLA. Yes.

(LEW *flutters and shows excitement.*)

JACK. Won't you ask Clay, my dear, to take him through the lower hall and into the dining room until I'm at liberty?

VIOLA. Certainly. (*Exit.*)

PRENTICE. I am keeping you from other appointments?

JACK. Nothing that can't wait.

PRENTICE. I am leaving for Washington in the morning.

JACK. We'll all be at the train to see you off.

PRENTICE. That's good, because I should like to say good-by to—to the young people—I can see them there— I shan't see you then, Mr. Ellinger— (*Goes to* LEW, *who stands at card table.*)

LEW. Good-by, Judge—you—you've given me more of a "turn over" than you know.

PRENTICE. Really?

LEW. I'd 'a' saved two hundred thousand dollars if I'd 'a' met you thirty years ago.

PRENTICE. Well, that's only about six thousand a year, isn't it?

LEW. That's so—and, damn it, I have lived. (*Smiles—looks dreamily into the past.*)

PRENTICE. Good-night. (*Exit* PRENTICE.)

JACK. Good-night—good-night.

ALICE. Is that Hardmuth in there? (*Points to dining room.*)

JACK. Yes.

ALICE. I don't want to see him.

JACK. Very well, dear, I'll excuse you.

ALICE (*going*). Come, Helen.

JACK (*at door, left*). Come in. (*To* HELEN, *who is going with* ALICE) Helen! I'd like *you* to stay.

HELEN. Me?

JACK. Yes.

(*Exit* ALICE. *Enter* CLAY, HARDMUTH, *and* VIOLA. VIOLA *lays automobile coat on sofa.* HARDMUTH *bows to* HELEN. HELEN *bows.*)

JACK. Your mother has just left us, Viola. You'd better join her.

VIOLA. Very well.

JACK (*taking her hand as she passes him*). And I want you to know —I appreciate very much, my dear, your going on this errand for me— you're the right stuff. (*Kisses her. Exit* VIOLA. *To* HARDMUTH) You're trying to get away?

HARDMUTH. This your note?

JACK. Yes.

HARDMUTH. You say you'll help me out of the State?

JACK. I will.

HARDMUTH. When?

JACK. Whenever you're ready.

HARDMUTH. I'm ready now.

JACK. Then I'll help you now.

LEW. Now?

JACK. Yes.

HELEN. Doesn't that render you liable in some way, Jack, to the law?

JACK. Yes— but I've been liable to the law in some way for the last twenty years. (*To* CLAY) You go down and tell the chauffeur to leave the machine and walk home. I'm going to run it myself and I'll turn it in.

CLAY. Yes, sir. (*Exit.*)

HARDMUTH. You're going to run it yourself?

JACK. Yes.

HARDMUTH. Where to?

JACK. Across the river, if that's agreeable to you—or any place you name.

HARDMUTH. Is anybody—waiting for you—across the river?

JACK. No.

HARDMUTH (*again with note*). This is all on the level?

JACK. Completely.

LEW. Why, I think you mean that.

JACK. I do.

LEW (*aggressively*). But I've got something to say, haven't I?

JACK. I hope not.

LEW (*quitting*). If you're in earnest, of course. But I don't see your game.

JACK. I'm not fully convinced of Mr. Hardmuth's guilt.

LEW. Why, he's running away?

(*Enter* CLAY.)

HARDMUTH. I know what a case they'd make against me, but I'm not guilty in any degree.

JACK. I want to do this thing for you, Frank—don't make it too difficult by any lying. When I said I wasn't fully convinced of your guilt, my reservation was one you wouldn't understand. (*To* CLAY) He gone?

CLAY. Yes.

JACK. My coat and goggles?

CLAY. Below in the reception room.

JACK. Thank you. I wish now you'd go to Viola and her mother and keep them wherever they are.

CLAY. All right. (*Exit.*)

JACK (*to* HARDMUTH). Hungry? (*Touches push button.*)

HARDMUTH. No, thank you.

JACK. Got money?

HARDMUTH. Yes.

(*Enter* JO.)

JACK. Jo, take Mr. Hardmuth below and lend him one of the fur coats.

(*To* HARDMUTH) I'll join you immediately.

(*Exit* HARDMUTH *with* JO.)

HELEN. What does it all mean, Jack?

JACK. Lew, I called that ace of hearts, didn't I?

LEW. And the three queens.

JACK. Because the three queens and the ace were in your mind.

LEW. I don't see any other explanation.

JACK. Suppose, instead of the cards there'd been in your mind a well-developed plan of assassination—the picture of a murder—

LEW. Did you drop to him that way?

JACK. No. Raynor told me all I know of Hardmuth—but here's the very *hell* of it. Long before Scovill was killed I thought he deserved killing and I thought it *could* be done just—as—it—was done.

HELEN. Jack!

JACK. I never breathed a word of it to a living soul, but Hardmuth planned it exactly as I dreamed it—and by God, a guilty thought is almost as criminal as a guilty deed. I've always had a considerable influence over that poor devil that's running away tonight, and I'm not sure that before the Judge of both of us the guilt isn't mostly mine.

HELEN. That's morbid, Jack, dear, perfectly morbid.

JACK. I hope it is—we'll none of us ever know—in this life—but we can all of us— (*Pause.*)

LEW. What?

JACK. Live as if it were true. (*Change of manner to brisk command*) I'm going to help him over the line—the roads are watched, but the police won't suspect me and they won't suspect Lew—and all the less if there's a lady with us— (*To* LEW) Will you go?

LEW. The limit.

JACK. Get a heavy coat from Jo.

LEW. Yes. (*Exit.*)

JACK (*alone with* HELEN). You know you said I used to be able to make you write to me when I was a boy at college?

HELEN. Yes.

JACK. And you were a thousand miles away—while this fellow—Hardmuth—was just at my elbow half the time.

HELEN. It can't help you to brood over it.

JACK. It can help me to know it, and make what amend I can. Will you go with me while I put this poor devil over the line?

HELEN (*taking* VIOLA's *fur coat*). Yes, I'll go with you.

JACK. Helen, you stood by your boy in a fight for his life.

HELEN. Didn't you?

JACK. Will you stand by *me* while I make my fight?

HELEN (*giving her hand*). You've made your fight, Jack, and you've won. (JACK *kisses her hand, which he reverently holds in both of his.*)

SALVATION NELL

"Man's Extremity is God's Opportunity"

Edward Sheldon

First presented at the Opera House, Providence, Rhode Island, November 12, 1908. The first New York performance was at the Hackett Theatre, November 17, 1908, and starred Mrs. Minnie Maddern Fiske.

JIM PLATT	MYRTLE HAWES
MAJOR WILLIAMS	SUSIE CALLAHAN
SID MCGOVERN	ROSIE HUBBELL
SQUIRT KELLY	PEGGY
KID CUMMINS	OLD MARY
JERRY GALLAGHER	MRS. SPRATT
AL MCGOVERN	MRS. FLANAGAN
JOE MADDEN	FRAU SCHMIDT
CHRIS JOHNSON	SALLY
CALLAHAN	MAMIE MCGONE
DENNY GRIFFEN	MAME MARSH
BLUMENTHAL	MRS. JACKSON
TOMMY BLAKE	MRS. MELLEN
MIKE O'ROURKE	MRS. BAXTER
DR. BENEDICT	JENNY
JIMMY SANDERS	PACKEY
BAXTER	MCGLONE
BRADLEY	A HOBO
PADDY	MINNIE
BOBBY	MRS. PHELAN
PETE	A MAN
TOM NELLIS	A POLICEMAN
MABEL	THREE ITALIAN MUSICIANS
NELL SANDERS	MEMBERS OF THE SALVATION BAND
SERGEANT PHILLIPS	TWO SALVATION COLOR-BEARERS
HALLELUJAH MAGGIE	AN ITALIAN ORGAN GRINDER
ENSIGN O'SULLIVAN	A GREEK POPCORN-MAN

ACT ONE

A bitterly cold Christmas Eve at Sid J. McGovern's Empire Bar in New York. To the right front is a door leading to Timmy Watson's poolrooms. It is half open; the sound of men's talk, the click of balls, laughter, and an occasional shout are heard. To the right, from front to back, is the bar itself. Behind is an arrangement of mirrors, with bottles of whiskey, glasses, etc. A telephone at the nearest end. In front of the bar is an irregular line of spittoons. There are brilliant Welsbach gas lights hung above, shedding a hard white light. Back, to left of bar, is the main entrance to the street; it consists of an inside pair of swinging doors and an outside door, thus forming a small vestibule. Back to left of entrance is a large, rather deep show window. It is brilliantly lighted; the audience can see the backs of the pictures (beer and whiskey advertisements and loose theatrical posters) which face the street outside. A streetlamp gives a dim idea of the exterior. Just to the left of the window, there stretches to the immediate foreground a slight partition, about eight feet high. It is ornamented on both sides with lithographic malt advertisements, highly colored. Toward the foreground end is a pair of swinging doors, connecting the two rooms. The space to the left is the ladies' buffet. There are two small windows on left, but very high to left front is a door leading directly to the alley. When it is opened, the sign "Family Entrance" can be seen stuck out above it. It is a step or two above the alley. In back of the ladies' buffet is a small doorway, leading down a flight of dark stairs to the basement. There

are Welsbach chandeliers in both rooms; the light is white and glaring —bare tables and kitchen chairs are scattered about the ladies' buffet. In the bar proper, against the partition, is a long, narrow table, covered by a solid, ragged, white cloth; on it are the various articles which make up a "free lunch"—sausages, cheese, pickles, crackers, etc. There are one or two chairs in the barroom, but not many.

As the curtain rises the stage makes a kaleidoscope-like effect. Behind the bar, SID MCGOVERN and SQUIRT BAXTER, his assistant, in white aprons much the worse for wear, are busily mixing and handing out drinks. The cash register rings continually as the money goes in and the change comes out. In front of the bar—leaning, chatting and laughing—are a number of shabby, ill-dressed, poor-looking men of all ages, already jovial with liquor. They come in and out of the entrance—mainly in —all through the act; so that at the end there are more than at the beginning. Groups are scattered about the room, drinking and talking, grabbing at the free lunch. Men saunter in from the poolrooms, have a drink, and return. Cheap cigars and clay pipes are smoked. Toward the back of the barroom, in the corner made by the wall and the partition, sit three ragged Italians in corduroys, bandanas about their necks, soft hats. They are playing some popular air on a violin, harp, and flute respectively; the result is thin and out of tune, but gay. In the ladies' buffet are four women. One of them, OLD MARY, is a sodden, wretched hag, already drunk, sitting huddled together in her chair; another is MRS. FLANAGAN, a fat old Irish woman with her shawl over her head; the remaining two, MABEL and SAL, are shabby, painted streetwalkers. One of these last secured a *customer. The assistant barkeeper rushes to the door occasionally to take their orders and bring them the drink. There is a rather confused noise of voices, laughter, banging of the door, cash register, bell, etc., heard above the tawdry music. The first scenes are to be played easily and swiftly, for a purely atmospheric effect.*

SID (*taking a coin*). Twenty-five. (*He rings the cash register and slams the change back on the counter. To* KID CUMMINS) Wot'll ye have?

KID (*a ragged and officious loafer*). Rye.

SID (*pouring*). Extra full for Chris'-mas Eve!—Next!

JERRY (*a drunken old man*). Hi! You damned dagos! Stop playin' them jigs or I'll crack yer jaws! T'hell wi' Spain—wow! (*He lurches, spilling his beer.*)

AL (*angrily*). Quit yer sloppin'—see?

OLD MARY (*to* SQUIRT). 'Nother—whiskey.

SQUIRT (*coolly*). Got yer cash with ye?

(*She shakes her head, drunkenly.*) Say, lemme introduce the door!

MABEL (*the successful streetwalker*). That's right, Squirt! Somethin' awful the way that old bat laps the booze. (*Turning her attention to her "feller,"* BLUMENTHAL) Dearie, let's have another rickey. I'm so dam' cold! (OLD MARY *reels on her way to the Family Entrance.*)

SQUIRT (*sternly*). Here now, none o' that! (*He bundles* OLD MARY *out, and rushes back to the bar, stopping only to take an order.*)

(*A burst of laughter from the pool-room.*)

JOE (*a tough, to another,* DENNY GRIFFEN). They're kidden' Old Billy again. Let's go in.

(*The two wander toward the pool-room at the right.*)

MRS. FLANAGAN (*waddling to the partition-door and shouting hoarsely*). Where's that drink, ye pie-faced mut? Here Oi've been waitin' twinty minutes whoile ye've sarved ivery other loidy on the primises!

SQUIRT (*at the bar*). Gettin' it now!

MRS. FLANAGAN (*in a sinister voice*). Wal, ye'd better! (*She waddles back to her seat. The other women titter.*)

KID (*eating free lunch*). Say, Sid, d'ye call these sausages? 'Tain't fit fer a dawg. I sh't'ink ye'd buck up yer grub on Chris'mas, anyways!

CHRIS JOHNSON (*another loafer at the free lunch table*). Swill—jus' plain swill! Have to get another drink t'wipe away the taste!

SID (*calling from the bar*). Shut yer face, Chris. (*To a man at the bar*) D'you say Manhattan? Yes, very cold —coldest Chris'mas weather fer six years! Good business, though! Ye-ep! Extra fine! (*He mixes a cocktail in an authoritative manner.*)

JERRY (*lurching toward the free lunch*). Where—pickles? (*In his effort to get one, he upsets the crock on the floor.*)

AL. Now ye done it! Spoilt my pants! (*He tries to wipe off his loud, checked trousers.*)

SID (*angrily*). That ain't no way to act! (*To* SQUIRT) Get him out—he'll make a mess in a minute. An' call Nell to wash up them pickles. (*To a man, in his professional tone*) Black Horse Rye? Here you are! Know a good thing when you see it!

SQUIRT (*tipping the wink to the crowd, as he speaks to the drunk*). That's all right, old boy—somebody wants ye in the street. (*He leads him to the door, then shoves him out.*)

AL. (*wiping his trousers with the*

edge of the tablecloth). Blame fool!

CHRIS. G'wan 'n put out some more pickles, Sid. We can't eat these!

SID *(laconically).* Ain't got no more! *(Calling to* SQUIRT *at the other end of the bar)* Two Milwaukees!

MABEL *(rising).* Say, dear, is my hat O.K.?

BLUMENTHAL *(calmly).* Great. Come on!

MABEL *(calling to* SQUIRT*).* Say Squirt—Jim Platt ain't come in tonight, is he?

SQUIRT. Naw!

BLUMENTHAL *(at the door).* It's past 'leven.

MABEL. Wot's yer rush? *(He grins slowly, takes her arm. They go toward the door. To* SAL*)* Tough luck! *(Tittering)* If I see any likely ducks, I'll send 'em in. S'long! *(She laughs loudly as she goes out. Then, as the door closes)* Gee, it's cold, ain't it?

SAL. Hell!

MRS. FLANAGAN *(severely).* Did yer shpake?

SAL *(petulantly).* Can't yer keep yer face shut? *(Glancing at her contemptuously)* If I owned this joint, I'd kick out every freckled mick as put her dirty nose inside the door!

MRS. FLANAGAN *(furiously).* Ye wad! I'll be doned if Oi shtay in the same room wid yes another minute! *(She finishes her drink, draws her shawl over her shoulders, and, with a parting scowl and a vituperative "good evenin," goes out, slamming the door behind her.)*

*(*O'ROURKE, *a policeman, enters the barroom.)*

O'ROURKE *(genially).* Good-avenin' to ye, gintlemen! Sure, it's a cold noight—too cold fer any man to walk up an' down—up an' down with niver a dhrop to help him along his— *(To* SID, *who, with a grin, has handed him a drink)* Thank ye, koindly!

SID *(shaking another drink, with a smile).* Say, Mike, we're not a goin' ter close up on time ternight—business too good!

O'ROURKE *(grinning).* Don' ye forgit Oi'm an orf'cer o' the law!

SID. Yes, but yer a friend o' mine first! *(Giving him another drink.)*

O'ROURKE *(with a wink, as he takes the glass).* Sure, Oi am, Sid. Ye got the roight idea! *(After drinking it at a gulp)* A-a-a-ah! *(He goes over to the free lunch. By this time* NELL *has finished cleaning up and is sticking bits of holly over the window and at the ends of the bar. The Italians have stopped playing and one of them is passing his hat around in a fawning manner.)* Oi was over to the Station an' Oi hear that at ileven-thirty they're a-makin' a raid on the farojoint down the block.

CHRIS. Madam's?

O'ROURKE. Madame Cloquette— though Oi knew her well when her name was just Maloney!

SID. They hain't ben pulled for more'n a year. It's about time—them girls been gettin' too flip—'specially Myrtle.

KID *(at the door).* Are they takin' 'em to the Station? Gee, I guess I stay!

O'ROURKE *(eating).* Ivery wan o' the loidy assistants'll get pinched along wid the ould woman.

(The talk and laughter breaks out again. Evidently the idea of the raid causes intense amusement. Exit O'ROURKE*)*

KID *(at the door of the poolroom).* Say! Raid on Cloquette's. 'Leven thirty! Wait for me, Charlie!

SUSIE CALLAHAN *(a little girl who enters boldly, a china pitcher in her hand, a shawl over her diminutive head, her voice loud and shrill).* A quart o' beer, an' Ma says she hopes you'll keep up your kind credit!

SID (*taking the pitcher*). You tell yer Ma I can't wait forever—I ain't no Pierpont Morgan! Do I look as if I was runnin' this bar fer my health?

SUSIE (*taking back the pitcher*). Say, Sid, quit yer kiddin! D'youse call this full? It's not hardly halfway up!

SID. Get along, or I'll change my mind!

SUSIE (*reproachfully*). You might a' done it fer us on Chris'mas Eve! Gee, yer a tightwad!

(*A laugh from the crowd about.*)

CHRIS JOHNSON (*a thumb in* SID'S *direction*). He won't give ye no presents!

SID. Beat it! Go hang up yer stockin' —if yer got one!

SUSIE (*shrilly*). Mebbe youse t'ink I'm green. They give me a pink stockin' over to the Mission 'cause I ain't ben late t' Sunday school once, an' it had an orange 'n a bag o' candy, an' a dime, but Pa pinched the dime's soon's I got home, an' I et the orange already so Ma couldn't give it to the kid 'n—

SID (*interrupting*). Did I tell youse to sneak? (*He seizes her arm.*)

SUSIE (*more shrilly again*). Leggo me or when Pa comes home I'll make him bust yer face. (*She darts out, amid a burst of laughter and the following lines.*)

CHRIS. S'long!

KID. Don't spill your booze!

AL. 'Ray for the kid!

CHRIS. Say, here's Jim!

(*As* SID, *with a grin, releases his hold,* SUSIE *raises her thumb to her nose and then flies toward the back door. A general laugh. Just as she reaches it, she bumps into* JIM PLATT, *who is coming through.*)

SUSIE. Get out o' my way, ye big chump! (*She darts out. The laughter sinks at her disappearance.*)

JIM (*a huge, coarsely good-looking, young brute in ragged clothes, now a trifle drunk*). Hello, Sid! (*He comes up to the bar.* SID *barely nods.*) Gimme a rye—full up, won't yer?

SID (*suspiciously*). Got the change? you hain't been workin' fer two weeks!

JIM. How d'jer know that?

SID. Yer girl told me.

JIM (*with a slow grin*). Which one?

SID. Which one? Listen to the blame slob! (*To* JIM, *with shake of the head*) Lord, how ye do it beats me!

JIM (*pleased*). Aw, go on!

SID. If ye want to know, it was Nell Sanders.

JIM. Nelly? Well, she didn't fired me!

SID (*coldly*). S'pose ye got fired again fer hittin' the booze—gimme yer dime!

JIM (*handing him the coin*). I only got one more!

SID (*snarling*). Ye lazy rum-hound! (*He goes to get him the drink.*)

KID (*calling over from the free lunch to* JIM *at the bar*). Say, Jim, you workin' these days?

JIM (*with a grin*). Naw, too cold! (*A pause.*)

KID. Mabel Keeney's been askin' where ye was!

JIM. Let her ask. I don't give a hoot!

CHRIS. Maudie Hayes was over here from Cloquette's an' she says all the girls are stuck on Jim. Say, Jim, tell us how ye work it!

JIM (*smiling, shamefacedly*). Tell nothin'—dunno myself!

KID (*lowering his voice and glancing at* AL). Well, ye'll have to buck up if ye want to keep yer girl here!

JIM (*turning*). Wot?

KID. Al's been layin' fer her!

JIM. The hell he has! (*Going to* AL *and seizing his arm*) I won't stand fer none o' this buttin'-in game, see?

AL. Yer off yer nut!

JIM. I am, am I? Then perhaps ye'd better keep out of my way!

AL. Wot d'yer live on, Jim, when yer girl ain't got a job?

JIM. That'll do fer you—understand?

CHRIS (*with jovial contempt*). Pickles an' whiskey! Jim's goin' t'eat Chris'mas dinner from this here table! (*Banging the free lunch counter.*)

AL (*to those about him, venomously*). Not if *I* know it!

JIM. Jump off your perch! I'll get better dinner tomorrow than's comin' t' *you*—that's a dead cinch! (*Chorus of "G'wan," "Aw," "Come off," "Where'll you get it,"* etc. *With a slow, reminiscent grin*) I met one o' them hymn-screechers an' she says to me, "D'youse want a ticket to the Salvation Army Chris'mas dinner?" 'Nd I said, "Lady," says I, "I'd give my pants fer one o' them very tickets —honest to Gawd I would." 'Nd she says, "Promise me to stop swearin' an' I'll give yer one." 'N I says to her, "Damn my soul if I don't!" an' then she cracks a smile 'nd hands me out the ticket, see? (*He gulps down the drink* SID *has placed before him.*)

KID. Where was she?

JIM (*licking his lip*). On the corner out here.

KID. Sort o' tall woman with gray hair an' a face like the kind mother used to make?

JIM. That's her!

KID. Thought so! It's Hallelujah Maggie! (*To* SID) 'Member the night she come in here an' give us hell? Oh, Lord! (*He is overcome at the recollection.*)

(*Enter* NELL. *She carries some dirty cloths, a scrubbing brush, and a bucket of soapy water.*)

SID (*to* NELL). Did ye throw out all that swill?

NELL. Yes, sir.

SID. An' cleaned out the back room?

NELL. Yes, sir.

SID. Then wipe up them pickles! Slow as tar in January!

NELL. Yes, sir! (*She begins wiping up the floor near the lunch table.*)

JIM (*to* SID *confidentially*). Say, Sid, does Nelly fit the bill round here? Works pretty hard, I s'pose?

JOE (*coming to the door of the poolroom and roaring to those about the bar*). Tom Blake's scrappin' three rounds wit' the Williams Street feather-weight. Got a ten-dollar pool. Come on!

CHRIS. Gee! (*He picks up his drink and starts hurriedly for the door.*)

SID (*loftily*). Nothin' but a chicken fight!

KID. Gimme my drink, Sid! (*He takes it and follows into the poolroom. The other men go too, carrying their glasses. In a few minutes, there are only three or four melancholy loafers hanging silently to the bar.*)

JIM (*insinuatingly*). Nelly gets two a week? Say, that's good o' you, Sid. Now if I was to make her say she'd do it for one-fifty, wouldn't yer pay me what ye owe her? It's over four dollars now!

SID. Pay *you*?

JIM. Aw, she won't care! (*Whining*) I've been out o' job two weeks an' only a dime in my pocket—s'elp me if I know where I'm goin' to sleep tonight—

SID (*with contempt*). Yer dirty son-of-a-gun, get out o' here!

NELL (*who has been listening in desperation*). Jim, won't ye come in there an' let me see yer fer a minute? (*To* SID) He means all right, Mr. McGovern—just let me talk to him! (SID *returns to the bar and his customers. There is a roar of delight from the poolroom. "That's it," "Paste him again" are heard above the din.*)

NELL. Won't yer come, Jim? I've gotter see ye!

JIM (*sullenly*). Wotcher want? (*He puts a coin on the bar.*) 'Nother rye, Sid. My last one!

SID (*savagely*). You bet it is! Say, Nell, wash up them tables in the buffet. Wot's the matter with yer, anyways?

(*She does not reply, but goes behind the bar, gets her bucket and cloths. She hesitates as she comes out, glancing at* JIM. *By this time, all but two or three customers should have gone.*)

JIM (*impatiently*). Wot's bitin' yer? Ain't I comin'? (*He takes up his drink and follows her a little unsteadily into the buffet where he sits heavily in one of the chairs, his legs spread out, his head a trifle fallen. She puts down the bucket and begins washing off the tables and the floor around them.*)

(*There is another uproar from the poolroom: "G'wan, Tommy," "Eat him alive," etc.*)

SID (*patronizingly*). Sounds like he was gettin' pulverized! (*He goes to the door of the poolroom and stands there for a moment looking in.*)

NELL (*nervously*). Jim, tell me where ye've ben these two weeks.

JIM (*drunkenly*). I—can't.

NELL. Why?

JIM (*same as before*). 'Cause, Nelly, my dear, 'cause I'm pretty close to bein'—dam' drunk!

NELL. I've been down t' yer place every day t' see if ye'd come back, Jim. Where was ye?

JIM. Lookin' fer work—over in Jersey.

NELL (*with sudden passion*). An' ye've lost yer job downtown!

JIM (*drinking*). They promised me a raise, too.

NELL. Couldn't ye've quit bein' loaded in work hours?

JIM (*savagely*). What! Didn't ye go lose yer own job in that hash-house? Wotter ye mean by roastin' me? *Youse* the one!

NELL (*rising to her knees and wringing out the cloths*). Ye know's well's me, Jim, they wouldn't keep me no more when they found out! (JIM *whistles.*) Jim, the woman where I lived, she wouldn't let me stay no longer at her place!

JIM (*dully*). Why not?

NELL. 'Cos she found out.

JIM. An' she kicked ye out, did she?

NELL. Yes! I can't go back there no more! She wouldn't let me in. So I'm livin' here. Down in the basement.

JIM (*pointing toward the bar*). Does he know?

NELL. I've kept it from him—but it's gettin' harder an' harder—

JIM (*brutally*). Aw come off! Ye needn't try that gag on *me!* I know how ye'v been monkeyin' around with Al McGovern.

NELL. Oh, I never! I never! (*She clenches her hands and rocks backward and forward.*)

JIM (*irritably*). Aw, dry up! You make me sick—you an' yer dam' kid story!

NELL (*suddenly drops her cloths*). Jim—don't go back on me—I ain't got no one else—I can't go on—alone—Jim!

(*From the poolroom comes a triumphant yell, whistles, etc. The men stream back into the bar.*)

SID. Wot did he do?

CHRIS. Tommy's most bust his jaw— Gee, it was a snap!

KID. Gimme another beer, Sid.

(*More men come in from the pool-room.* JIM *finishes his whiskey and rises unsteadily to his feet. He puts his hand heavily upon her shoulder.*)

JIM. How much cash hev ye?

NELL. I—I don't know.

JIM (*slowly*). Yer lyin'! Now ye go down n' bring me every dam' cent ye've got! If ye don't—I'll—I'll— (*Smiling with drunken devilishness*) Oh, you jus' wait 'n see wot I'll do to you!

NELL. What—do you want it for, Jim? Not whiskey?

JIM. Wot d'ye mean by talkin' back to me?

(NELL *wrings out her cloth and goes, without answering, to the door in the back of the buffet. She disappears downstairs.* JIM *sits again sluggishly.*)

(CALLAHAN, *a drunk, enters door center. Instantly, he is hailed with shouts.*)

CHRIS. Say, here's the feller what swiped the dime from his kid's stockin'!

(JIM *staggers to the door of the partition and listens to the talk indifferently.*)

JOE. Make him give it back!

CHRIS. Now, let the Mission hand out a drink fer a change! Gee, I'll bet they never thought that dime was goin' into Sid McGovern's cash register!

CALLAHAN (*smiling shamefacedly*). Straight rye, Sid. Fill her up good fer Chris'mas!

AL. G'wan, Callahan, yer ought to give half to the kid!

SID. Say—can't yer cough up some o' what yer wife owes me?

CALLAHAN (*still grinning*). Sid, I hain't got a cent but this here dime, straight goods!

(SID *takes the coin. He rings it up.*)

AL (*by now rather drunk himself*). Say, Nell—thought I seen her over

there a minute ago!

CHRIS (*laughing coarsely*). Got a good shape, eh?

AL. Fair, oh fair! Too thin for me, though. I like 'em soft an' round!

(*There is a laugh.*)

CHRIS. Jim Platt's got her on a string. How a booze-soaked bum like that can do it—

AL (*to the crowd*). Aw, he's got her, has he? Why, last night I caught her over there in the corner n' squeezed the life out o' her! She didn't mind—a slob like Jim Platt! (*He smiles with drunken self-approbation and cynicism, slowly shaking his head. Another laugh from the crowd.*)

JIM (*bursting through the door in the partition, where he has been leaning, listening to this*). That's a dam' lie!

(*Re-enter* NELL. *They do not notice her.*)

AL (*retiring behind the others*). Say, Uncle Sid, why don't ye kick him out?

SID (*to* JIM, *angrily*). You butt in here again, Mister Platt, and we'll see who owns this bar! Ain't I fed ye when yer couldn't get another bite in New York? Ain't I let yer sleep here when you'd've froze outside? 'N all ye ever do is to kick up a roughhouse!

(*Meanwhile,* NELL *has returned and is trying to pull* JIM *back into the buffet.* SID *mutters angrily and roughly polishes the bar with a cloth.*)

JIM (*heavily, seeing* NELL). Gimme — (*He follows her into the buffet. She pours the coins into his hand. Sitting, as he counts them over.*) Fifty—one—fifty—three more quarters—n' a dollar bill. (*Fiercely*) This ain't all! Yer keepin' it fer yourself! I'll bet that dam' little pet dawg o' Sid's, Al McGovern—how much's he been givin' ye?

NELL. N—nothin'!

JIM (*whose fury increases the more he thinks*). D'ye mean to say he hain't been makin' up to yer ever since I quit comin' here? D'ye mean to say he hain't never squeezed ye?

NELL (*looking down*). I can't keep out of his way. I try all the time just's hard's I can—

JIM. Like hell you do!

NELL. An' last night—I got away from him an' ran down 'n locked my door. An—an'—t— (*With sudden passion*) Jim, I can't stay here no more! An' she won't let me back to her place. Oh, what'll I do? (*She presses her twisted hands across her mouth.*)

JIM (*with drunken mournfulness*). I might a known it—I might a known it! A woman what'll let any man come along an' kiss an' squeeze her all he dam'—

NELL (*kneeling down beside him and putting her arms around his slouchy figure, her face against his shoulder*). I love you—I'd do anything in the world fer you—you know that! (*Looking up at him*) Jim, look at me—look at me jus' once! (*Her voice is beautifully and tragically sincere. He is somewhat touched; his arm, hanging limply, now slowly feels its way round her shoulders. He gives her one or two pats but does not move his head or reply. Suddenly burying her face against his side and clinging to him passionately.*) Oh, Jim— (*They remain thus for some moments, silently. His head nods and falls, but his arm rests loosely on her shoulders. She does not move.*)

(*Enter* TOMMY BLAKE, *the triumphant prize fighter, from the poolroom. He is dressed, but has a black eye, cuts. He is surrounded by friends; his arrival creates a sensation. Cries of* "Here he is," "Good work, old sock," "Ye done him up swell." TOMMY *advances proudly to the bar.*)

TOMMY. Black Horse Rye—best ye got—fer these foots an' myself!

SID. That's the ticket. (*Calling*) Say, Squirt, bring down them glasses! (*He begins giving out the drinks.*)

AL (*genially, glancing at his watch*). 'Leven-thirty. Wonder if anyone's put 'em wise over to Cloquette's!

CHRIS. Lord, I can just hear 'em squeal when they get into the street!

KID (*with a grin*). Say, I wouldn't mind bein' a cop! (*With a wink*) Gee, what a snap!

CHRIS. Has 'em on toast all right, all right!

(*A general laugh.* MAGGIE *enters suddenly through the back door and stands at the door, smiling. She is a tall, lank, gray-haired woman, with twinkling eyes and a kindly smile. She is dressed in the regulation Salvation Army uniform, with a woolen tippet wound around her neck, and heavy mittens.*)

MAGGIE. Hello boys! Hain't seen ye fer a month!

(*Chorus of* "Well Maggie," "Hallelujah," "Lord be praised," *etc.*)

SID (*grinning*). Wot'll yer have, Maggie? Manhattan or Martini?

MAGGIE (*pulling off her mittens and smiling cheerfully*). Gimme 'em mixed! My, but I'm cold!

AL. Say, Maggie, are we all goin' to hell?

MAGGIE (*cheerfully*). Sure! Yer on the 20th Century Limited, but I'm hopin' for a wreck!

SID (*calling out*). Everybody up an' have a drink on me! (*A rush to the bar*) This is fer your sweet sake, Maggie. Ain't ye pleased?

MAGGIE. The devil's in you, Sid McGovern, an' some day he'll up and tell yer so!

TOM NELLIS (*a drunken man, trying to sing, and succeeding in shrieking*).
"Glory, glory Hallelujah!
Glory—glo—ry—"
Wot's the matter with my voice? (*He lurches.* MAGGIE *pulls him to a chair.*)
MAGGIE. An' yer wife 'n kids waitin' fer you at home, Tom Nellis, with never a cent in their pockets an' the fire gone out!

SID (*raising his glass*). Hallelujah Maggie! May she never quit singin' hymns! No bar complete without her! Let her go!

(*They all drink amid howls of "Wow," "That's the stuff," "Amen"!*)

MAGGIE (*holding up her hands to gain silence*). Thank ye, boys, fer likin' me even if ye show it in a sinful way. But I didn't butt in to talk to ye this trip. We're a-goin' to have an open-air meetin' in 'bout half-an-hour right on the corner here, to cel'brate the comin' of Christ—over nineteen hundred years ago! 'N I wish ye'd step round. Cap'n Williams' goin' ter lead it—there's a young man for ye! Left money an' family an swell house on the Av'noo to join the Army! Why, I remember when ye couldn't pick up a paper without readin' 'bout the prizes he got in the horse show or the party his Ma gave the night before! He's a slick speaker, too—

SID (*interrupting good-naturedly*). A damned sight too swell! (*To the men*) 'Member old Joe Sessions? Lord, how he used to lap it up! Well, this here *Captain*, he turned him clean dippy! 'S a fact Old Joe never turns up here no more! One o' my best customers, too!

MAGGIE. Praise God fer that! Well, they're a-goin' to raid Cloquette's and I thought I'd try an' talk to the girls at the Station.

SID (*laughing*). Gee, I'd give a day's profit to see you talkin' pious to Myrtle Hawes!

MAGGIE. There's somethin' else! Cap'n Williams says he saw a girl last week, at one o' them meetin's down the street. She tol' him she lived here —in this bar. Who is she, Sid?

SID. Her name's Sanders, if that's the one. Does the scrubbin' round here!

MAGGIE. Any folks?

SID. Never heard her mention none.

MAGGIE. How long's she been here?

SID (*cleaning glasses*). 'Bout a month. Came from a hash-house on Tenth Avenue. Worked in a sweatshop on the East Side for the hell of a long time, too!

MAGGIE. That all ye know?

SID (*putting back glasses*). Sure!

MAGGIE. Well, the Major wants me to get her to come to the meetin' to-night. He said she had an awful sweet face— (*Looking round her*) Too sweet for this joint, I guess!

SID. She's cleaning up in there. (*Points to the buffet.*)

MAGGIE (*cheerfully*). All right. (*Giving her hand to the first man she sees*) God bless ye! (*To the next*) God bless ye, Tom. (*To a third*) I'm still prayin' fer ye, Chris. (*And so on. They all shake her hand heartily, saying: "Thanks," "Yer a good one, Maggie," "Keep it up," "Come again, old girl," etc. They are evidently sincere.*)

SID (*in the midst of this*). Listen! What's that!

(*A dead silence. There comes a faint sound of voices and the rattling of wheels outside.*)
They've started on Cloquette's.

(*There is a sudden movement toward the door.*)

KID (*at the window*). Wait a sec— that's so!

O'ROURKE (*at the outside door*). Come on! We got a squad of eight men an' the Sergeant. The ploice's full o' shports—three automobiles outside—'n ivry man, woman, and choild in the whole ward to look on!

(*There rises a roar of laughter from some distance away, then silence. All the men, galvanized to action, gulp down their drinks, and rush toward the door.*)

SQUIRT. Where's my hat?

JOE (*as he goes out*). Hell! It's cold!

DENNY GRIFFEN. Beat it! The whole thing'll be over!

TOM NELLIS (*over his shoulder*). Quit yer shovin'! This ain't no prize fight!

(*Finally they are all gone.*)

SID (*to* MAGGIE, *who is looking intently from the window*). Stay here a minute, will ye, Maggie? I want to get a look at Myrtle when she's pinched! (*Without waiting for a reply, he goes out hastily.*)

(MAGGIE, *with a sigh, leaves the window and walks toward the door of the 'ladies' buffet.'*)

JIM (*as if awakening*). Wot's doin'?

NELL. Somethin' down the block. They'll be right back!

JIM (*dully*). Where? (*He makes a movement as if to rise.*)

NELL (*trying to hold him*). Oh, stay here, Jim!

(MAGGIE *has opened the door and is looking at them.*)

JIM (*to* MAGGIE). Wot's up?

MAGGIE (*shortly*). Puttin' the lid on Cloquette's!

JIM (*eagerly*). Gee! (*He rises.*)

NELL. Will ye come back?

JIM (*facetiously*). It all depends on how long my cash lasts—see? (*He jams his hat on and starts for the main entrance.*)

NELL (*going to the partition door and calling after him*). I'll wait fer ye, Jim.

(*But he has already disappeared into the street. She droops and turns back to get her bucket, facing* MAGGIE.)

MAGGIE (*gently*). There's a Chris'mas meetin' tonight, jus' round the corner. Won't yer come?

NELL (*in a dry voice, beginning again at the tables*). Naw!

MAGGIE. Yer not happy. Anybody kin see that. Won't yer let us try an' help ye?

NELL (*bitterly*). Naw. (*She goes on with her work.*)

MAGGIE (*after a little pause*). It's him, ain't it?

(NELL *is silent. Pause.* MAGGIE *goes on solemnly.*)

Ye won't never have a moment's peace while yer carryin' that load on yer heart!

(NELL *is silent.*)

The heavy load o' sin! Oh, don't I know it's crushing ye down—down—down till ye can't hardly breathe or sleep or think! An' everywhere ye go it follows—nothin' ahead but black sufferin' until—

NELL (*passionately interrupting*). Keep still! I won't listen to ye!

MAGGIE. Because ye know it's true! (*Very gently*) My dearie, listen to Him as said, "Come unto me, all ye that are heavy laden, and I will give ye rest."

NELL (*in a low voice*). Who said that?

MAGGIE. Christ!—He died for every one of us—He knows an' pities every sinful, broken heart!

NELL (*dully*). Oh, he was all right, I s'pose, but what's he got to do with me? (*She resumes her washing.*)

(*There is another roar of laughter from outside, dying down to a long confused murmur of voices, broken by an occasional command or shout.* NELL *listens.*)

MAGGIE. Jus' come to the meetin'!

(NELL *is silent. Another roar in the*

street. SID *comes back into the bar, shivering with cold. He whistles as he begins washing the used glasses.*) Please!

(*Putting her arms around* NELL'S *shoulders*) I can't bear to think o' what's comin'! I want so much to save ye!

NELL (*dragging herself away roughly*). No one can do nothin' fer me!

SID (*calling out*). Ye there, Maggie?

MAGGIE (*calling*). Sure!

SID. Thought ye'd gone! Gee, ye oughter seen 'em lug out the old woman!

MAGGIE (*in a lower voice, to* NELL). P'raps this ain't God's time. But it's a-comin'—it's a-comin' sooner or later, an' then I want ye to remember that Ensign Maggie O'Sullivan, Corps. No. 11, 's waitin' fer a chance to do His work!

(*There is another laugh from the crowd, lasting longer and ending in hoots and howls.* SID *listens and goes out again, chuckling to himself, dancing in delighted interest. The Family Entrance door is flung open and* MISS MYRTLE HAWES *enters hurriedly. She is a pretty young woman—loud, sharp-tongued, and brazen; a long coat over her spangled evening dress, which is décolleté and stained with wine.*)

MYRTLE. Well, that was the neatest sneak I ever done in *my* life! Jerusalem! (*Seeing* NELL) Hello, Nelly! You come near seein' your little friend doin' the grand march to the police station with two cops! (*Noticing* MAGGIE, *with elaborate courtesy*) Oh, don't let me interrupt! (*She goes through the partition door into the barroom. Then calls back.*) Where's Sid?

NELL. I dunno!

MYRTLE (*returning to the buffet*). Thought they had me twice. Who's yer fren?

MAGGIE (*introducing herself*). Ensign— (*With an inquiring look at* NELL) O'Sullivan!

MYRTLE (*coolly*). Glad to meet yer. (*To* NELL) Say, gimme one o' them rags, the cleanest ye got. I've ruined my gown! (*To* MAGGIE, *conversationally*.) My name's Hawes—Miss Myrtle Hawes! (*To herself, as she examines the spots on the front of her dress*) Gee, ain't that a shame? (*Continuing*) Me an' Nell used to be kids together, didn't we, Nelly?

NELL (*bringing her the cloth*). Here.

(*There is another chorus of whoops from outside; the noise, though it dies down, continues in an undertone throughout the following scene.*)

MYRTLE (*unconcernedly*). Nothin' like furnishin' free vaudeville t' all the neighbors! (*Giggling*) I wish you could a-seen the expression on the Madam's face when the squad bust in! Not that I had a chance t' enjoy it long! (*Rubbing the spots*) She hit the table so hard my glass went smack in my lap.

MAGGIE (*looking at them*). You an' Nell used to know each other?

MYRTLE. Sure! We used to sew pants day in an' day out! Oh, them pants! Fifteen buttons, turn up at the bottom an' tape on the inside back seam. Oh, my Gawd! (*Giving* NELL *the cloth*) I guess that's all I kin get off now. (*Discovering a mirror and adjusting her hair*) Of course, soon's we got old er our paths changed. But even now I keep up an interest in Nell.

(SID *comes in the front door. As he opens it, the noise is more clearly heard.*)

(MYRTLE *calls.*) That you, Sid?

SID. Who's there?

MYRTLE (*smiling as she goes through into the barroom*). 'Evenin'! Pleased to see you!

SID. Gee! I thought they pinched the bunch.

MYRTLE. Not little Eva! No trip to the Station for mine! When they bust in, I faded double quick, gave five to the nigger not to put the lieuten'nt wise, an' beat it out the back into the alley. Then I crossed the lot on the corner an' sneaked round by Flannigan's to yer side door.

SID (*admiringly*). Slick work!

MYRTLE. Here's where I stay planted till the whole bunch clears out for the Station. (*Proudly*) All ye want in a case like this is a little nerve!

SID. You got it all right! But then, there ain't nothin' like experience! (*Calling*) Say, Nell, come in an' wash up them glasses! We'll have a crowd here in a minute!

MAGGIE (*following* NELL *into the barroom; to* MYRTLE). How many girls are goin' to the lock-up?

MYRTLE. Nine—includin' the Madam.

MAGGIE (*pulling on her mittens*). I'll be there when they land.

MYRTLE. That's sweet o' yer, but 'tain't no use—every blest' one o' them 's borey-eyed! As cashier, *I* can't absorb the sparklin' till late in the game. That's the only reason I had the sense to hook it!

MAGGIE (*to* MYRTLE). There's a Christmas meetin' up on the corner in 'bout half-an-hour. Would yer mind comin'?

MYRTLE. Is—what's his name?—that young feller goin' to speak?

MAGGIE. Major Williams? Sure!

MYRTLE (*drawling a little*). I seen him once. He's a corker on looks! (*Changing her manner*) But I can't come! Gawd, no! Hymns make my head ache!

MAGGIE (*restraining herself*). I'll go to the Station anyways. Ye never can tell when the Lord'll reach out his hand!

MYRTLE. Nor the law either! S'long! Give my love to Maud. They'll all get bailed out in the mornin'—only, it's a shame t' happen on Chris'mas Eve!

MAGGIE (*emphatically*). Yer right there! Good-by, Sid. (*To* NELL) I'll see you again. Remember what I told you! (*She waits for an answer from the girl, then goes out the front door, letting in as she does so an increased sound of the crowd.*)

SID. They're on the way to the Station. Get inside!

(MYRTLE *enters the buffet, where she stands at the partition door, occasionally peeking out. The crowd—hooting, shrieking, yelling—passes along the street in front of the saloon. Such cries as:* "Say, girls, ain't he cold," "Hooray for Cloquette's," "Look at the pink one, she's got the goods all right—all right," "Ye would would ye!" "Now will you be good," *etc., rise above the tumult.* SID *stands at the window, peering out, occasionally signaling with his hand to keep* MYRTLE *back. Finally the noise begins to die away in the opposite direction. He motions to her that the coast is clear.*) (*Behind the bar*) Yer'd better fade before they come back.

MYRTLE (*leaning over the bar*). Say, Sid—

SID (*leaning over with a meaning smile*). Wotcher want? I bet I know!

MYRTLE (*after a pause*). Quit yer gumdrops an' give me a dry Martini!

(SID *suddenly seizes her face and kisses her violently.*)

(MYRTLE *ostentatiously wipes her mouth.*) I said a dry one!

SID (*grinning*). I fergot! (*He begins busily mixing the drink.*)

MYRTLE (*eyeing him coldly, with dignity*). Just because a lady happens to be in trouble's no reason why a gent should treat her like she was a slimy gum-chewer!

SID (*coming around in front of the bar with the cocktail*). Yer no Shifty Sadie! (*With an expressive gesture*) Anybody could see that! Aw, no! (*He winks and gives her the drink, then softly puts his arm around her waist.*)

MYRTLE (*in well-feigned amazement*). Well, wouldn't that melt your rubbers! (*Reproachfully*) Ain't yer ashamed?

SID (*brazenly*). Who's ashamed?

MYRTLE (*cuttingly*). No one—if yer not! Say I ain't accustomed to bein' subjected to such treatment, an' the sooner you take yer arm from around my waist the better—*Mister* McGovern!

(*The noise again is heard, approaching rapidly, of men's voices and laughter.*)

(*Pulling herself away*) This is where I repeat my disappearin' act by special request!

SID. Come over later on! There won't be no cops here!

MYRTLE. It all depends—'cordin' to the state o' my health! (*She goes out by the Family Entrance, muffling herself up in her coat, just as the* MEN, *laughing and talking noisily, stream through the main door.* NELL, *who has been silently and unobtrusively washing behind the bar, keeps a quietly anxious lookout.*)

SID (*hospitable*). Quick work, weren't it?

AL. Gee. That little one yelled like a stuck hog when the big cop grabbed her arms!

CHRIS. I swear I thought I'd bust!

KID. An' 't hear the old lady curse! (*With a long whistle*) Lord, she could learn *me* a few! (*They are all getting their drinks at the bar. The Italians strike up "A Hot Time" in their cor-ner. Yells of "That's right," "Soak 'em," etc. A few sing the words boisterously.* NELL *is carrying her bucket into the buffet when she hears* JIM, *and turns.*)

JIM. Where's that whiskey, Sid? Don't yer take all night about it, either! (*JIM is at the end of the bar nearest the audience.* NELL *puts down her bucket by the door and crosses swiftly to where he is waiting. She pulls his sleeve.*)

NELL. Don't—not any more, Jim—

JIM (*shaking her off impatiently*). G'wan t' hell! Say, Sid, can't yer hurry it up?

SID (*sourly*). You wait yer turn, will ye? I ain't no machine!

JIM (*lurches towards the poolroom*). Send Squirt in here with it. I'm goin' t' have a game!

NELL. Yer only losin' money! (*NELL tries to intercept him, but he mutters an oath and puts her out of the way. She crosses again to where her bucket is, by the partition door.*)

AL (*to the men nearest him*). Cute little heifer, ain't she?

(*The men laugh and nudge him in coarse amusement.*)

KID. Go kiss her now, Al. Bet a quarter ye can't!

AL. Like t' know how she could stop me!

CHRIS. Go ahead! (*As* AL *hesitates*) Aw g'wan! Yer never done it!

AL (*emboldened by these taunts*). Didn't I? You just watch! (*NELL is wiping up the floor by the lunch table.* AL *goes to where she is bending over and puts his hand on her shoulder to steady himself. She stops wiping and shrinks at his touch. He says thickly.*) Jus' to show 'em you don't care!

NELL (*faintly*). Leggo o' me!

CHRIS (*laughing*). Al's got cold feet! (*General laugh.*)

AL. (*suddenly forcing her up, his arms around her*). Aw—come off! (*He kisses her again and again, in spite of her silent struggles. The men laugh and shout in ironical approval.*)

CHRIS. He's kissin' her ear!

KID. Try her mug for a change!

SQUIRT (*laughing*). Look out or she'll bit ye!

CHRIS. That's it—now ye got her goin'!

JIM (*as he enters from the poolroom*). Where's my drink? You—

NELL (*seeing him*). Jim—help me!

JIM (*suddenly seeing what is going on by the partition, and springing toward them with a choked roar*). Leggo that girl!

(*Before anyone can interfere, JIM has torn AL from the girl, struck him to the ground, and, choking and swearing, is kicking him brutally about the head, when, after a moment of stupefaction, the others rush in and drag him off. After one or two screams AL has become insensible; he lies, bloody and distorted, in a grotesque heap. NELL has silently fallen to her knees; she presses against the partition, her face averted and covered with her hands.*)

KID (*yelling*). Say, Jim—

SQUIRT. Get him away—

TOMMY. What the—

DENNY. Would ye look at that!

JIM (*continuing during business*). Ye dam' little sucker ye—crawlin' behin' yer uncle ev'ry time ye see me—I'll stamp yer face in—

KID. For Gawd's sake, grab his other arm!

CHRIS. Pull back his head somebody!

JIM (*continuing the roar*). Leggo o' me—jus' half a secon'—I'll finish him this trip! The dirty little scut—ye would lay for my girl, would ye? Hittin' it up—givin' her cash—kissin'

whenever I turn my back— (*He chokes.*) Oh, lemme kill him!

SID (*telephoning*). P'lice Station—3100 Orchard! (*Calling back*) Choke him off! I can't hear!

(*CHRIS and KID pull back JIM's head and cover his mouth with their hands. He continues to bellow unintelligibly during the following.*)

SID. Denny, run for a cop!

DENNY (*as he goes*). Ye'll need more'n one!

SID. Put some water on Al— (*At phone*) Station? Scrap at McGovern's bar—send an ambulance, too. Yes. (*Rings off, and coming around to AL.*)

DENNY (*outside*). S-a-y-, M-i-k-e!

SQUIRT (*to those who crowd about AL*). Get out o' the way!

JOE (*in an awed voice*). Has he croaked?

SQUIRT (*sharply*). Dunno! (*To the others*) Clear off—let him have some air.

TOM (*glancing drunkenly at JIM*). Ye dirty cuss—behin' his back, too!

JIM (*tearing away his head from CHRIS and KID, and continuing his stream of curses, this time toward NELL*). Ye dam' tart, ye! Youse the one's done all this! You secondhand, cracked piece o' damaged goods! Gawd, if they hadn't a-stopped me, I'd a-choked the life out o' ye! Soon's I'd finished with him!

SID (*looking up with a cruel laugh*). She certainly stung you slick!

JIM (*mouthing horribly*). Bawlin' an' whinin' an' swearin' as ye loved me — oh! (*He chokes again, and tries to get at her, his face crimson, his fingers crooked. They pull him back.*) Lemme get hold o' ye once, and ye'll never have a chance t' do me again. I'll fix ye soon's I get out, ye lyin' little bunch o' rags—ye can't skin me's easy 's all that. I'll— (*He stops at the entrance of the police, as described later. He again turns his attention to* AL.)

(NELL *has not moved; she seems trying to shrink through the wall. The noise of an ambulance, with its insistent bell and rattle of wheels, comes swiftly up the street.*)

JIM. There 'tis! Lift him up, so's his head won't bleed so fast!

(*The main door of the barroom opens and four men come in quickly, with an authoritative air*—O'BRIEN *and* BUTLER, *policemen;* DR. BENEDICT, *ambulance surgeon, and his* DRIVER, *with a stretcher.*)

O'BRIEN (*to* SID). What's happened?

SID (*shortly*). He— (*With a gesture toward* JIM) jumped on Al here from behin' an' killed him, I guess. That's all!

(DR. BENEDICT *is busying himself over* AL.)

DR. BENEDICT. Whiskey!

(*Some is brought him by* SQUIRT.)

O'BRIEN (*notebook in hand*). Name?

JIM (*sullenly*). Jim Platt.

O'BRIEN (*after a slight pause*). Address?

JIM. Hain't got none.

O'BRIEN. Put out your hands.

(*They handcuff him. He sullenly submits.*)

How is he, Doc?

DR. BENEDICT. Pretty bad! He may pull through. (*With a glance at* JIM) You've nabbed a nice one, all right!

O'BRIEN (*to* SID *sternly*). You, McGovern, and you Baxter, report at the Station at ten sharp tomorrow. It's the third time I've been down here, this winter. I hope it ends in losing your license—close up on the minute tonight, understand? (*Looking around*) Now I want two or three of you to come with me. You've all seen what happened? (*Without waiting for an answer*) What's your name?

JOE (*sullenly*). Joe Madden, but I—

O'BRIEN. You'll do. (*To* TOMMY BLAKE) Name?

TOMMY. Blake—Say, I didn't see nothin'—can't you see one o' me lamps is closed?

O'BRIEN (*interrupting*). Bring 'em along, Butler. (*To* DR. BENEDICT) Now, Doc, are you ready?

(BENEDICT, BUTLER, *and* DRIVER *have lifted* AL *on the stretcher. The crowd sullenly make way, as they go toward the door.*)

SID (*with a ghastly attempt at conciliatory facetiousness*). Oh, it's just a trifle, sir. I hope ye won't—

O'BRIEN (*interrupting him sternly*). Open that door!

(SID *obeys. The men with the stretcher and the officers with* JIM *and the witnesses pass out. The ambulance is heard starting up, and finally the sound dies away. A silent pause in the barroom. Everyone is afraid to speak.*)

SID (*grimly to* SQUIRT). Pull down them shades!

(SQUIRT *does so, while* SID *locks the outside door.*)

We're not a-goin' to have any more deadbeats in here tonight!

KID (*timidly*). Say, Sid, 'tain't our fault!

SID (*same as before*). I know whose fault it is! (*Clenching his hands*) Damn it—my license! (*After a pause, during which he looks at the motionless* NELL—*long, silently, and steadily.*) You—clear—out—see?

(*She does not answer, but huddles spasmodically against the partition.*)

Did ye hear what I said?

NELL (*slowly turning her head*). Yes, sir! (*She is pale and dry-eyed, her face slightly distorted.*)

SID (*threateningly*). I'll give you fifteen minutes to sneak it, an' if yer not gone by then, I'll kick ye out myself, s'elp my Gawd!

NELL (*after moving her lips a moment, unable to speak*). Wh—where'll I go?

SID. Out that door. Understand? I'll pay what I owe yer. (*He goes to the cash register.*)

CHRIS. Aw, say, 'twan't really her fault!

SID (*blazing up*). Shut yer dam' face! (*He pulls open the cash drawer and takes out some money; then returns to* NELL.)

NELL (*in the same dry voice*). Say, Mr. McGovern, won't yer wait until mornin'?

SID. Like hell I will! Four seventy-five. That's up to date and over. Now take yer duds and git!

(MYRTLE *comes in the Family Entrance during this and crosses to the partition door in time to hear the rest.* SID *turns to the bar.*)

MYRTLE (*to one of the silent spectators*). Say, been a scrap 'bout that girl?

CHRIS. Yesh! Al McGovern got laid out!

MYRTLE (*to* NELL). Come in here an' tell me 'bout it. (*Taking her by the arm into the buffet.*)

CHRIS (*timidly*). Gettin' colder, ain't it? Guess I'll have another rye. (*He puts his glass on the bar.*)

SID (*grimly*). I guess ye won't! (*To the others*) Beat it now—all of ye! They're keepin' tabs on me t'night! (*To the musicians*) There—that'll do for you—hike along!

MYRTLE (*to* NELL). He's bounced ye?

NELL (*dully*). Yes.

MYRTLE. 'Tain't no use talkin' to a fat man when he gits really mad!

NELL. I dunno!

MYRTLE. Any cash?

NELL (*in the same dazed manner*). Yes.

MYRTLE. How much?

NELL. Four seventy-five.

MYRTLE. That all?

NELL. Yes.

MYRTLE. Well, no girl can't live decent on that! (*Decidedly*) Yer've gotter come back with me.

NELL. What?

MYRTLE (*impatiently*). To Cloquette's. There ain't nothin' else fer ye now!

NELL. Ain't there?

MYRTLE (*imaginatively*). Why ye never would come before beats me! Ter stay scrubbin' round here an' hittin' it up with a regular bum—where's he been the last two weeks?

NELL. Over in Jersey—

MYRTLE. Jersey! (*She laughs.*) Yer easy meat, Nell! He's been hangin' around with that Keeney woman. I've watched him from my winder an'—

NELL. Oh! (*A cry.*)

MYRTLE (*soothingly*). Lie back! Lie back! What's the good o' gettin' sore? Now, here's your chance—that guy's out o' the way—no job— (*Looking at her critically*) You get a fair-sized pomp an' some decent duds an' a few drinks, why, yer'd be a different girl! Say, *you'll* make a hit! They're all crazy over blondes—an'—

NELL (*dully*). I gotter go! (*She suddenly begins beating her hands together.*)

MYRTLE (*soothingly*). So that's O.K. We've got it all fixed up! The Madam'll be tickled to death when she's bailed out in the mornin'! Go get your things! I'll wait here!

(NELL *obediently goes downstairs, at back of the buffet.*)

CHRIS (*the last man to go*). S'long, Sid!

SID (*laconically*). S'long!

KID (*just outside*). Come on! God, it's cold!

CHRIS (*as he departs*). Jus' twelve! Good beginnin' for Chris'mas, ain't it?

(*They disappear.*)

SID (*to himself*). Hell! (*To* SQUIRT) Got 'nough rye t'last over t'morrow?

SQUIRT (*not daring to catch his eye*). Dunno.

SID. Dam' it, didn't I tell ye t' look? Go lock them doors! (*He opens a trap and climbs down the cellar stairs, still grumbling to himself.* SQUIRT *goes into the buffet and locks the Family Entrance.*)

MYRTLE (*unconcernedly arranging her hair*). Sid's sort of peeved, ain't he?

SQUIRT. Ye'd better not let him catch ye!

MYRTLE. Lord, I can manage him! An' b'sides I'm waitin' fer Nelly. Say, Squirt, mix me two Vermouth cocktails, like a good kid, will ye?

SID (*calling from below*). Squirt! Bring down a candle! Think I can see in the dark?

SQUIRT (*to* MYRTLE). Wait a sec! (*Lights a candle at the bar and hastily goes down into trap.* MYRTLE *strolls into the main room and begins mixing the cocktails herself, whistling as she does so.*)

(MAGGIE *enters by main entrance.*)

MAGGIE (*to* MYRTLE). Where's that girl?

MYRTLE. Gettin' her things on.

MAGGIE. Wot for?

MYRTLE. That's my biz!

MAGGIE. Is she goin' with you?

MYRTLE (*still busy at the mirror*). What if she is?

MAGGIE. Where to?

MYRTLE. Where she'll learn to sing ragtime 'stead of hymns, see? (*She turns to greet* NELL, *who appears at back, a ragged shawl over her head and shoulders, a bundle in her hand, wrapped up in a blue checked apron.*)

MAGGIE. Yer hain't got her yet! (*Going swiftly to* NELL) I've seen your man at the Station.

NELL (*with a ray of hope*). Jim?

MAGGIE. He's down and out—dead drunk!

MYRTLE (*officiously*). Ready, Nell? We'll just have a drink before we start an'—

MAGGIE (*turning to* MYRTLE). I know what yer tryin' to do, an' ye'd better look out!

MYRTLE (*looking her opponent up and down*). Say, is this a joke?

MAGGIE (*putting her hands around* NELL). Lemme take care o' you, dearie! Yer not the first Hallelujah Maggie's helped bring to God!

MYRTLE (*angrily*). Doncher know this is the chance of her life?

MAGGIE (*glaring at* MYRTLE *over* NELL's *sunken head*). Yer right! It is the chance of her life—an' the Lord's given it!

MYRTLE. Oh, fudge! Say, Nell, are yer goin' with me or not?

MAGGIE. It's up to you, dearie—

NELL. Help me—help me—there ain't no one—else—

MAGGIE (*her face transfigured; her voice joyous*). There's Christ! Catch hold His hand, Nell. He's a-leanin' out to save ye! Come with me—they're jus' beginnin' the meetin'.

(NELL *flings her arms around* MAGGIE's *neck, almost sinking to her knees, and bursts into an agony of tears.*)

an' then I'll take ye home! (*Throwing up her face, impulsively*) Glory be to God! (*To* NELL) That's right, cry all ye want—every tear helps wash white your soul—Hallelujah—my dearie— (*She has led* NELL, *supporting her with one arm, to the main entrance, which she opens.* NELL *is trembling and weeping.*)

(*From the darkness outside comes a faint sound of the brass band playing* "*Glory, Glory, Hallelujah.*" *The door closes on* MAGGIE *and* NELL. *Meanwhile*

SQUIRT *and* SID *have emerged from the cellar, carrying a keg between them. The rest of the act goes on very quickly.*)

SID. Put it over there.

SQUIRT. Soon's I— (*He sees* MYRTLE *nonchalantly carrying her drinks into the buffet.*)

MYRTLE (*interrupting him haughtily*). Don't mention it—I made 'em myself!

SQUIRT (*following her*). Quarter, please!

MYRTLE (*over her shoulder*). There's a dime on the bar. Ye can keep the change!

(*The bell begins tolling twelve.*)

TOM (*who has been on the floor—half asleep—in front of the bar*). Twelve o'clock! (*He staggers to his feet, holding his empty glass.*) Here's t' Chris'mas—an'—Sid McGovern's bar!—

SID (*looking up*). Sh! Hold up, ye dam' fool!

(*There is a silence. From not far up the street comes the sound of voices and the band. The words are fairly distinct.*)

"Glory, glory, Hallelujah,
Glory, glory, Hallelujah,
Glory, glory, Hallelujah,
Our Lord was born Today!"

ACT TWO

The sitting room of NELL's *tenement flat, a night in July, eight years later. To the right, door leading to the bedroom with a framed text hanging over it. To the right, back, entrance door; stairs and landing, illuminated by one gas jet, seen when this door is opened. Two windows on* left, *with cheap, stiffly starched curtains. They are wide open. In corner—right back—is a gas stove with various cooking utensils hung neatly about; a small sink is next to it. To left of entrance door, an icebox. To front, left, a table with one or two books, a copy of the* War Cry, *a workbasket, a lamp with a white shade, etc., on the red-checked tablecloth. Several plain chairs about, a rocker by the table. Various texts, colored lithographs of General and Miss Booth in uniform on the walls. Telephone to right front. A clock on the false mantel-shelf—right—is ticking peacefully. Everything is neat and clean, homely but comfortable.* JIMMY's *clothes are hanging on one of the chairs.* NELL's *Salvation Army bonnet is on the table. The gas is lighted, but turned down low. During the first scene, the light comes from the lamp.*

As the curtain goes up, NELL—*dressed in Salvation Army uniform—is sitting in rocker by the table, with* JIMMY, *clad only in his night drawers, on her lap.* JIMMY *is a restless, quick little boy of eight; he is wriggling in her arms, evidently thinking of other things. She is holding him with one arm and reading aloud from an open Bible on the table.*

———

NELL (*reading earnestly, restraining* JIMMY *at the same time*). "—an' he that is holy, let him be made holy still. Behold I come quickly; an' my reward is with me to render to each man according as his work is—" (*To* JIMMY) Don't wriggle round so, Jimmy! (*Going on*) "I am the Alpha an' the Omega, the—"

JIMMY (*interrupting*). Is that Omega Oil—like what you rubbed on my knee?

NELL. No, dear, it means— (*Read-

ing) "the first an' the last, the beginning and the end. Blessed are they that wash their robes that they may have the right to come to the tree of life, an' may enter in by the gates o' the city. (*Running her eyes down the page. Going on*) "An' the Spirit an' the Bride, say, Come. An' he that heareth let him say, Come. An' he that is athirst, let him come; he that will, let him take the water of life freely."

JIMMY (*moving about restlessly*). Mamma, I want a drink o' water!

NELL (*soothing him*). In jus' a second, dear. (*Reading*) "He which testifieth these things saith, Yea: I come quickly!" (*As she closes the Bible*) "Amen: come, Lord Jesus!"

JIMMY (*querulously*). Ma—ma, I want a drink o' water!

NELL (*letting him slip from her lap*). All right. It's so hot I don't wonder you're thirsty! (*She goes to the icebox and gets him a drink in a china cup, poured from a small blue pitcher.*) What d'jer do ter-night when I was at the meetin'?

JIMMY (*excited at the remembrance*). Me an' Johnnie climbed down the fire escape! (*He rushes to the window to show how it was done.*) We got out here an' went right down t' the street. An' Johnnie bust one o' Mis' Riley's g'raniums. But I never bust a thing!

NELL (*severely*). Ye mustn't climb out on the fire escape again, Jimmy, d'ye hear me? It's a wonder ye didn't fall an' break yer neck! Now, remember!

JIMMY (*proudly*). Aw—'twas a cinch!

NELL. What else were you up to?

JIMMY. Johnnie an' me an' Susie had a meetin', too. I wouldn't let none of 'em say a word an' I prayed an' sang an' beat the drum all by myself, jus' like Major Will'ms!

NELL (*smiling as she gives him the water*). Ye oughter give the others a chance sometimes. Now, hurry up an' say yer prayers. Mother's tired tonight.

JIMMY. All right! (*Kneels down in a business-like way by her lap, shuts his eyes, raises his head, and then suddenly opens his eyes, saying earnestly.*) D'jer get me any candy?

NELL (*hurrying him*). Say yer prayers first!

JIMMY (*again resuming a pious attitude, speaking in a rapid, expressionless voice*). "Now I lay me down ter sleep I pray the Lord my soul ter keep'f I should die b'fore I wake, I pray the Lord my soul ter take!" (*Looking up eagerly*) Are they all-day suckers?

NELL (*shaking her head*). Yer ain't talked to yer heavenly Father yet!

JIMMY (*again shutting his eyes*). Oh, Lord, when I grow up, gimme—gimme— (*His feet begin wriggling as he thinks.*) —a real big drum—biggern anybody's else! An'—an' oh, Lord, make her have all-day suckers 'stead o' them choc'late creams that don't last hardly 'tall—an'—

NELL (*suggesting*). Ain't ye goin' to pray for me an' Dad?

JIMMY (*mechanically, as he twists about*). God bless Papa and Mama, an' help me ter be a good li'le boy for Chris' sake, Amen! (*Opening his eyes, in a relieved way*) Now gimme 'em! (*Climbing quickly over her lap to get candy, in a shrill triumph*) It *is* all-day suckers! (NELL *laughs and hugs him.*)

JIMMY. Ma—!

NELL (*smiling*). Yes, dear?

JIMMY. Ma, Mamie said Pa wouldn't come back no more, so why do I have to keep on prayin' fer him?

NELL (*kissing his hair*). Ye mustn't mind what Mamie says.

JIMMY (*persistently*). Is he comin' back?

NELL (*after a slight pause*). Yes, dear—sometime. So we must keep right on lovin' him jus' the same!

JIMMY (*resignedly*). All right. (*He chews a moment in silence*.) Is he nicer'n Major Will'ms?

NELL. Yes.

JIMMY. An' big?

NELL. Yes, big an' strong!

JIMMY (*hopefully*). Bigger'n Mamie's pa?

NELL. Yes.

JIMMY (*enthusiastically*). Gee, I wisht I could see him once!

NELL (*kissing him and carrying him toward room*). Come along to bed now. It's awful late fer little kids like you!

JIMMY (*whining*). No, it ain't!

(*They exit into inner room. Slight pause*.)

MAGGIE (*knocking at door and calling*). Oh, Nell!

NELL (*calling from inner room*). Come in, Maggie.

(*Enter* MAGGIE *from back; she is in uniform, bonnet, etc*.)

(NELL *calls from inner room*.) I'm jest puttin' Jimmy to bed an' gettin' out o' my uniform. It's so hot tonight!

JIMMY (*running to her*). Hello! Mama's got some all day suckers!

MAGGIE (*calling into room*). Ain't that fine? (*To* NELL) Feelin' bad?

NELL. Oh—no, I'm all right. Are ye jus' back?

MAGGIE. Yes. Old Ryan's come round at last!

NELL. Praise the Lord! (*To* JIMMY) Come along, Jimmy, an' quit yer foolin'! (*To* MAGGIE) Jus' wait till I put him in bed.

MAGGIE. All right. There's something I want to tell ye.

NELL. (*from the bedroom*). That's

nice— (*Suddenly*) Stop it, Jimmy! I don't want yer to do that again, now, d'yer hear? Let mother change her dress. (*Calling*) Maggie?

MAGGIE. Yeah?

NELL (*calling*). There's some lemon jelly in the icebox fer yer mother!

MAGGIE (*going to the icebox*). Thanks!

NELL. Now dear, lie still an' go t' sleep—jus' fer me, will ye?

JIMMY (*inside*). All right. (*Pause. A cry of "Ma" is heard from the bedroom*.)

NELL. Didn't I tell ye not to call me?

JIMMY (*plaintively*). Can't I have another drink o' water?

NELL. Ye don't want a drink of water!

JIMMY. Yer not goin' to shut the door, are ye?

NELL (*at door, appearing*). 'Course I am! (*She begins closing it*.)

JIMMY (*in the voice of a martyr*). Ye ain't never kissed me good night!

NELL (*relenting*). Didn't I? Well! (*She goes in and reappears almost immediately*.) Sleep tight, Jimmy! God bless ye! (*She smiles at him and shuts the door. Meanwhile,* MAGGIE *has put the jelly into one dish, covering it with another.* NELL *has changed her uniform to a simple light wrapper, and carries her brush and comb*.)

MAGGIE (*as* NELL *returns*). Mother'll like this; it looks real nice!

NELL. How do you like my wrapper?

MAGGIE. It's real cute! Turn 'round.

NELL. I got it in Grand Street for one fifteen. Their August sale. (*Letting down her hair*) Well, what's up?

MAGGIE (*trying to seem unconcerned*). Oh, it's nothin' much, I guess. Only I—

NELL. Go on!

MAGGIE (*as if changing the subject*).

How much time has Jim got—up the river?

NELL (*slightly surprised*). Two years more from next Chris'mas. It was a ten-year term, but you knew that!

MAGGIE (*uncomfortable*). So I did, dearie. But I jes' sort o' wanted to make sure. (*Brief pause*) Say—Nell!

NELL (*braiding her hair at mirror, her back to* MAGGIE). Yes?

MAGGIE. He— (*Hesitatingly*) Ain't there some way they can get out easier —by bein' real well behaved? Seems to me I've heard of men that—

NELL (*turning*). What do ye mean?

MAGGIE. Sometimes they take off two or three years—jes' fer good conduct!

NELL (*turning to mirror*). I guess Jim was never one o' them good-conducted ones!

MAGGIE. Ye can't always be sure, dearie! Strange things have happened!

NELL (*turning again, quickly*). Maggie!

MAGGIE (*soothingly*). Now, don't ye be gettin' all nervous now. Yer tired enough.

NELL. Maggie! Tell me!

MAGGIE (*resignedly*). Well, I saw Kid Cummins on my way from the Hall tonight—you remember Kid Cummins, don't yer? That red-haired feller used to be 'round Sid's all the time?

NELL. Yes. Go on!

MAGGIE. He's workin' in a shoe factory now—an' he said that one day las' week, he thought he saw Jim Platt comin' out o' a bum hotel on Granger Street. (NELL *lets fall a cup she has in her hand.*) Say—ain't that too bad!

NELL. He wasn't sure?

MAGGIE (*picking up pieces of the cup*). Mebbe I can mend it—no, it was growin' sort o' dark—he said, an' people change so in eight years!

NELL (*weakly*). Oh, Maggie—I'm afraid!

MAGGIE. There now, dearie, don't you bother! I most wish I'd never told ye at all, but I thought—'case anythin' did happen—

NELL. Maggie!

MAGGIE. What's the matter, dearie? He can't do nothin' to ye, an'—

NELL. I'm afraid!

MAGGIE (*catching her breath sharply*). Afraid! Afraid of what?

(*A knock at the door.*)

NELL (*starts, then stiffens and says, nervously*). Come in! (*She relaxes as* MYRTLE *enters, handsomely gowned and very distingué in her manner.*)

MYRTLE (*with assurance*). Hello, Nelly! (*Seeing* MAGGIE) How d'yer do, Mrs.—I can't remember yer name —it's so long ago since we had the *pleasure* o' meetin'!

NELL. Why, Myrtle! I couldn't hardly recognize ye!

MYRTLE (*holding out her hand in a society manner*). Yes, I noticed that! Same here!

MAGGIE (*who has turned to the icebox for her plate of jelly*). Mother'll be waitin' fer me, Nelly.

NELL (*accompanying her to the door*). Good night. Don't tell anyone what I said to ye!

MAGGIE. Trust me! An' I wouldn't bother no more 'bout it, if I was you!

NELL. I'll try— (*Smiling*) See ye in the mornin'!

MAGGIE (*outside on the landing*). Sure!

(NELL *closes the door and returns.*)

MYRTLE (*who is sitting in the rocker, fanning herself*). Turn up the lights, Nell, so I can snatch a look! (*As* NELL *turns up the gas*) Three flights o'stairs—I cert'nly thought my heart would go back on me b'fore I got t' the top! (*Glancing at* NELL, *who stands in the light*) My, but you've changed!

NELL. Yes. It's eight years ago las'

Chris'mas. Yes, I suppose I have changed a lot— (*To* MYRTLE) Are ye still at Cloquette's, Myrtle?

MYRTLE. Lord, no! I quit there almost soon's you cleared out from Sid's. After all, the position of cashier at even a first-class roulette joint ain't no place fer a lady!

NELL. That's right!

MYRTLE. I had a gentleman friend who used ter hang 'round Cloquette's —a dead swell sport—the real thing, yer know! Well, I gave him the roulette combination the Madam used to skin 'em all with. (*A pause*) Say, Nell, yer not listenin' ter me!

NELL. Yes—yes!

MYRTLE (*evasively*). Well, he was naturally kind o' grateful an' after he'd been rakin' it in fer near six months an' the Madam caught on, he set me up in a real elegant business on Sixth Av'noo, 'bout two blocks south o' Forty-second.

NELL. What in?

MYRTLE (*glibly*). "Slightly worn sealskin garments an' opera cloaks of all kinds. Spangles a speciality." That's my sign. I got two girls an' live over the store—supply a bunch o' these stock-companies actorines with clothes —oh, I'm fixed up, all right! Don't worry 'bout me!

NELL (*after a pause*) An' it's the business—that pays? (*She lays her hand on* MYRTLE's *arm.*)

MYRTLE. What d'ye— (*She encounters* NELL's *clear gaze and her own eyes fall, then, defiantly.*) Oh, I'm after the dollar, jus' like all the rest, if they'd only have more nerve to say so!

NELL (*with a sigh*). I see. I've prayed fer ye, Myrtle—often!

MYRTLE (*not overpleased*). Well, ye might spend yer spare time prayin' fer somebody that kin be saved! *I've* far too chick a figure!

NELL. Oh, Myrtle, you talk so!

MYRTLE (*sweetly*). Not that it's any reflection on yers, dear, although ye do wear a corset that ain't worthy of the name!

NELL (*with a faint smile*). I suppose that's so!

MYRTLE (*looking at a watch set in her bracelet*). It's gettin' near eleven. I gotter be movin' on. Miss Queenie St. John, a great friend o' mine— she's givin' a lobster lay-out at Shanley's, an' I promised I'd hit it up with 'em. Glad I seen ye!

NELL. How d'jer know I was here?

MYRTLE. Sid told me ye belonged to Corps No. 1, and I asked your address at the Hall. (*Importantly*) Oh, an' speakin' o' Sid, reminds me o' what I come t' see ye fer!

NELL (*startled*). Have ye seen Sid?

MYRTLE (*proudly*). Sometimes he sees me! Naturally, I don' associate no more with people o' his class!

NELL (*never taking her eyes from* MYRTLE's *face*). An' did Sid tell ye anythin' 'bout— (*She rises nervously.*)

MYRTLE (*complacently*). Ye've waked up at last, have ye? Well, I guess yer wise! It's yer old feller—the one that got eight years.

NELL. Has Sid seen him?

MYRTLE. Yes, he jus' cas'lly mentioned the fact that he'd come bummin' round in the same old way, askin' everyone where ye was!

NELL (*breathing quickly*). An' Sid told him! Sid told him, didn't he?

MYRTLE (*triumphantly*). *That's* where yer off! Sid chased him out an' never told him a thing!

NELL (*turning away with an involuntary little cry*). Oh!

MYRTLE. Ye don't mean ter say ye want t' take up with that guy *again?*

NELL. What right have ye got, Myrtle, to talk that way?

MYRTLE (*inquisitively*). Ye've never had dealin's with any other gent?

NELL. Myrtle!

MYRTLE (*soothingly*). O' course not! Yer a Cap'n in the Salvation Army, now, ain't ye? How's the young feller that looks like one o' these ready-made clothing ads?

NELL. Major Williams?

MYRTLE (*facetiously*). That's him! I give ye fair warnin', don't let *me* loose when he's round! Regular *affinity* sort o' eyes!

NELL. Oh, Myrtle, there's no use explainin' things, is there?

MYRTLE. I'm wise! An' I'm sure yer'll agree with me when I remark, jus' casual-like, that— (*Regarding the tip of her slipper*) —that love is grand!

NELL. I don't know what ye mean!

MYRTLE. Ain't she the enjaynoo! But how ye could demean yourself by livin' in a Rescue House, I don't understand!

NELL (*simply*). I was alone—I didn't have no one to go to.

MYRTLE (*in surprised reproach*). Why, ye had me!

NELL. I— (*Stops, realizing the futility.*) But what's it matter now?

MYRTLE (*impressively*). Well, anyway, I called there to see if I couldn't do somethin' to get ye out, fer yer own sake, Nell. "Rescue Home" sounds like it might be fer stray cats! An' if yer'll believe it, the female that ran the joint wouldn't let me inside the door. "Madam," I says to her, "I'm glad ye consider yer establishment no place fer a *lady!*"

NELL (*smiling a little*). Thanks, Myrtle, I know ye meant to be awful kind, but it was all right! (*There is a little knock at the door. NELL goes over and opens it. MAMIE is standing outside. NELL says kindly.*) Why, Mamie, ye oughter to been in bed long ago!

MAMIE (*delivering her message with assurance, eyeing* MYRTLE *the while*). Ma's compliments to ye, Mis' Sanders, an' would ye kindly step downstairs a second, 'cause Pa's tanked again an' actin' up somethin' fierce!

NELL (*to* MYRTLE). I'll be back in a minute! I'm the only one he'll listen to—d'ye mind?

MYRTLE. Not at all! Only, hurry up, I can't wait forever!

(*Exit* NELL, *closing door behind her. Left to herself,* MYRTLE *inspects her figure in the glass; straightens her hat, yawns, glances at pictures and finally discovers a photograph of* MAJOR WILLIAMS *in the place of honor on the false mantelpiece—the only photograph there. She gives a whistle and takes it nearer the light for a better look, then returns it to its place, humming a waltz tune unctuously. She goes to the table, looks at the titles of one or two books, brushes over the leaves of one of them, and finally sits down with it, her feet on another chair. She is fanning herself and reading languidly, when there is a knock at the door.*)

MYRTLE (*coming to quickly, withdrawing her feet, and adjusting her back hair.*) Come in!

(*Enter* MAJOR WILLIAMS *in Salvation Army uniform. He is a handsome young soldier, born a gentleman with the soul of an enthusiast. He carries a small bunch of roses done up in a newspaper. He puts them down unobtrusively.*)

MAJOR. I beg your pardon! I thought Mrs. Sanders was here.

MYRTLE (*graciously*). No, she's just stopped out t' calm down a drunk. Won't ye wait?

MAJOR. Thank you, I will.

MYRTLE. I'm here t' see her myself— just picked up one o' her books. (*Reading the title*) *Montgom'ry's Brief His-*

tory o' the United States. Excitin'!
Ain't it?

MAJOR (*twinkling*). A good many
people have found it so.

MYRTLE. 'Magine Nellie readin'
such truck! Bet my fall hat 'tain't
hers. (*Glances at the flyleaf; she looks
up.*) Oh, pardon me!

MAJOR. Occasionally Mrs. Sanders
is good enough to borrow my books!

MYRTLE. Then they're all yours?
This po'try book and the sermons—
and that other one—*The Vicar o'*
what-do-you-call-him?

MAJOR (*smiling*). All mine!

MYRTLE. Nell Sanders readin' po'try
an' sermons! (*Bursts into a fit of gig-
gles.*) Lord ye never can tell how people are goin' to turn out—can ye?

MAJOR. Never, I agree with you!
Perhaps that's why my life is so interesting, Miss—

MYRTLE. Hawes, my name's Hawes.
Say, that's a cute little photo you gave
her, ain't it?

MAJOR. Has she showed you?

MYRTLE. I'm dotty on the subject of
havin' my picture took! Yer oughter
seen my last ones, in a sheath gown
and my hair done à la Cleo dee Mes-
road. (*Meaningly*) An' then, I'm real
generous 'bout givin' them away.
(*Pause*) Mebbe ye'd like one. (*Giggling*) Now, spare my feelin's.

MAJOR (*dryly*). On such a brief acquaintance I really couldn't presume.

MYRTLE. Pity 'bout that. Oh, you
men are all alike!

MAJOR (*looks toward door*). I wonder when Mrs. Sanders—

MYRTLE. Oh, don't bother 'bout *me*
—I'm goin' as soon as she comes back!

MAJOR (*puzzled*). Really, I—

MYRTLE. Oh, I know yer both dyin'
fer a quiet chat. Far be it from me to
butt in. I've had troubles of my own,
and I understand just now—

MAJOR (*quietly*). How necessary it
is to mind one's affairs. I congratulate
you.

MYRTLE (*a little irritated*). So that's
your game, is it?

MAJOR (*blandly*). It would be if I
played it. But— (*Glancing at her*)
Sporting life no longer attracts me.

(MYRTLE *turns to retort angrily,
when* JIMMY *appears at the door of
the bedroom, right, his hands at his
blinking eyes.*)

JIMMY. Where's Ma?

MAJOR (*good-naturedly*). Hello Jimmy! What do you think you're doing?

JIMMY. I kicked the sheets right off
my bed, an' I can't find 'em in the
dark.

MAJOR (*picking him up and swinging him high above his head*). You
young sinner, you, if you do it again,
I'll court-martial you tomorrow morning. Understand?

JIMMY (*as he is swung to earth*).
O-o-h! Who's that lady?

MAJOR. "Where ignorance is bliss"
and so forth, Jimmy. Of course you
remember the quotation? (*Catching
him up again*) Come along!

(*They disappear into the bedroom
together, the* MAJOR *laughing and* JIM-
MY *gurgling ecstatically.*)

MAJOR (*within*). There you are!
Now, lie still or I'll spank you within
an inch of your life!

JIMMY (*confidently*). Ye will not!

MAJOR (*at the door*). How do you
know I won't?

JIMMY. 'Cause you said it so many
times before!

MAJOR (*laughing to himself*). You'd
better look out!

(*Slight distant thunder.*)

JIMMY. Say, it's goin' t' rain. Ma'll
get wet!

MAJOR. No, that's only because it's
such a hot night!

JIMMY. Major Will'ms!

MAJOR (*just as he is closing the door*). Yes?

JIMMY. I wish *you* were my papa!

MAJOR (*hastily*). Good night! (*He shuts the door and comes back, smiling.*)

MYRTLE (*yawning*). Cute little kid! Whose is it?

MAJOR (*looking at her*). Mrs. Sanders', naturally!

MYRTLE (*lazily*). Mrs. Sanders—*Mrs.* —is that what she calls herself?

MAJOR (*calmly*). Why not.

MYRTLE. Well, I never heard of no *Mr.* Sanders!

MAJOR (*clicking out his words*). Stop that!

MYRTLE (*easily*). The kid don't look like he was the son o' a jailbird, does he?

MAJOR (*contemptuously*). What do *you* know about it, anyway?

MYRTLE (*innocently*). Me? I was on deck at the time! Why, I thought everyone knew!

(*Enter* NELL *from back.*)

NELL (*to the* MAJOR). Oh, Major Williams! I—I—didn't know you was comin'! Excuse my lookin' so. (*She has stopped short at seeing him, greatly embarrassed.*)

MAJOR (*with unusual tenderness*). It's my fault for calling so late, but there was something I had to ask you so I thought I'd drop in on my way from the hall.

NELL. Oh, it don't matter. It's all right! (*To* MYRTLE) I'm sorry I kep' ye so long. D'ye have to go?

MYRTLE (*who has risen and is looking at her watch*). Yes, I must. Queenie—Miss St. John—jus' hates ter wait! Well, when ye happen to be over in civilization, drop in an' see my establishment, will ye? Sixth Av'noo—near Fortieth—don't forget!

NELL (*kindly*). No—I hope you'll come again, Myrtle.

MYRTLE. S'long, dear! (*Shaking hands. Then to the* MAJOR, *demurely*) Glad t'have met yer, Major! (*He nods silently.*) Don' bother—I'll get down all right! Good night!

NELL. Good night.

(*Exit* MYRTLE, *door at the back.*)

MAJOR (*to* NELL *as she turns*). Jimmy appeared while you were gone. I tucked him in again, but you'd better take a look and see if I did it right.

NELL. Oh, thank you! (*She goes into the bedroom, opening the door softly. The* MAJOR *sits down, left, passing his hand slowly over his forehead. Reenter* NELL, *closing door softly.*)

MAJOR. Is he asleep?

NELL. I think so. He does get so restless these hot nights.

MAJOR. Sit down, Mrs. Sanders, you must rest!

NELL (*very shyly*). Thanks. (*She sits down by the table and takes up some sewing.*)

MAJOR. Have you finished the books?

NELL. Not quite. I'm sort of slow this time.

MAJOR. Which do you like best?

NELL (*glancing at him, shyly*). The poetry, I guess.

MAJOR (*smiling*). I thought so. To tell you the truth, I do myself!

NELL (*again glancing awkwardly up at him*). Major—I—hope—you won't mind— (*Looking at her wrapper*) The uniform's so heavy in this awful hot weather, and ye see I didn't know.

MAJOR (*looking at her*). Mind—of course, I don't. In fact I—do you know this is the first time I've seen you without it?

NELL (*bending over her work*). Is that so?

MAJOR (*leaning forward*). Just now

you don't look a bit like—what is it they call you? "Salvation Nell"?

NELL. Don't I?

MAJOR. You're only a tired little woman darning stockings. There's all the difference in the world!

NELL. I *am* sort o' tired tonight—sort–o' (*Stops sewing, then goes on, bending her head.*)

MAJOR. What's the matter, Captain Nell?

NELL. Nothin'—did ye want to see me about anythin' particular, Major?

MAJOR (*leaning back*). Yes. Colonel Scott has wired for me to come up to Boston at once. It seems they're short of men. I'm going on the midnight train. Do you think you could take charge of my office tomorrow? I've left memorandums of all the important things in the desk. I'll be back by Friday, anyway.

NELL. Yes,—but—I'm sorry yer goin' away jest now!

MAJOR. Well—then—that's settled! (*Suddenly seeing the flowers on the kitchen table*) Oh, by the way, I have something here for you! (*He gets them.*)

NELL. Fer me?

MAJOR (*taking off the newspaper and presenting her with the roses*). I bought them from a poor old thing down the block. She's one of your finds, isn't she?

NELL. They're sweet. How d'jer know she was?

MAJOR. Because when she asked me where I was going, she chose the best on her tray, and insisted on wrapping them up in that newspaper. To "keep them clean," she said, "for Nelly."

NELL. Oh, they're lovely! I never had no one bring me flowers before. (*To him, simply*) Thank you, Major. (*She goes to the sink and puts the flowers in a white pitcher of water.*)

MAJOR. Leave out one.

NELL (*turning*). Leave one?

MAJOR. Two—perhaps!

NELL (*carrying the pitcher to mantel and then coming to him with the two roses, wonderingly*). Do ye want 'em?

MAJOR (*smiling*). No, but would you mind putting—let me see—one at your waist and one in your hair—over to the left?

NELL (*with a shy smile*). Seems like wastin' 'em—but if ye say so! (*She goes to the mirror and carries out his instruction. Then turning to him shyly*) Is that right?

MAJOR (*rising and going a step or two toward her, a note of passionate pity in his voice*). You—you break my heart!

NELL (*startled*). Why, Major?

MAJOR (*controlling himself*). I didn't mean that! Only—you ought to have grown up among the roses!

NELL. Oh, wouldn't that have been nice!

MAJOR. Did you know that woman who was here just now?

NELL. Yes, I knew her quite well—a long time ago.

MAJOR. I wouldn't have much to do with her, if I were you. She's a bad lot!

NELL. Well, that's the very sort o' person we—

MAJOR. You don't understand. She's been saying things about you—about your boy there! (*Going on quickly*) I don't want to know whether they're true or not. It can't make any difference to me, possibly. But I think you should be told. (*Stops and looks down.*)

NELL (*who is sewing calmly*). There's only one thing I kept back from ye—Major. Maggie an' me thought there wasn't no use in tellin' it—'count of Jimmy—it's—

MAJOR (*earnestly*). Don't explain, Mrs. Sanders!

NELL. I want to—now, Major. I—I wasn't married to Jim— (*Half to herself*) But it don't matter any more. Does it?

MAJOR (*tenderly*). No. He belongs to the part of your life that's ended. We all have—people—like that, Mrs. Sanders—people that belong to the life—that's—ended.

NELL (*after a pause, stopping her sewing*). Have you, too?

MAJOR (*after a slight pause*). Oh, yes!

NELL. But you come from a swell family! Maggie said yer father lives on Fifth Avenoo an's terrible rich an' —an' everything like that.

MAJOR (*a little bitterly*). Why, there's just as much misery on Fifth Avenue as there is on Tenth! But I thank God for it—it led me to salvation!

NELL (*timidly*). Then we're sort of alike, you an' me—ain't we? Even though we started from diff'rent places.

MAJOR (*tenderly*). The only difference was that I had every chance and you had none!

NELL (*nervously*). Major—I—I want ter ask ye to do somethin' fer me.

MAJOR. Yes?

NELL. I want to be transferred to some other city, right away.

MAJOR (*surprised*). Transferred—for good?

NELL (*looking down*). Yes.

MAJOR. But aren't you satisfied here? You have your little home—your friends—your are doing magnificent work—! Your—

NELL (*interrupting*). I—I—don't dare stay here no more. (*Rises suddenly and turns her back to him.*)

MAJOR (*quickly, after brief pause*). What's bothering you—Captain Nell?

NELL (*faintly*). It's—that man—Jimmy's father—

MAJOR (*quickly*). Yes.

NELL. He's come back!

MAJOR. You've seen him?

NELL. No—but I've heard—he's lookin' fer me everywhere—an'—I gotter get away.

MAJOR (*instantly*). You must stay and face him. There's nothing he can do to you. You're free—you've broken your chains long ago.

NELL. I pray God that's true.

MAJOR (*his voice softening*). But, after all, you're only a woman and you're alone—

NELL. Yes—yes, that's why I'm scared!

MAJOR (*tenderly*). Mrs. Sanders, won't you let me help you?

NELL. Ye have helped me, mor'n—anyone else.

MAJOR. That's not just what I mean. (*Pauses.*) I can never forget the night I first saw you—at that open air—eight years ago. Do you know why I sent Maggie to find. you at that third-rate bar?

NELL. Ye wanted to save me.

MAJOR. More than that! (*Solemnly*) I knew if once we had you—you could rise above us all. (*Simply*) And you have.

NELL (*distressed*). Oh—no!

MAJOR (*smiling*). Why, you're the very soul of the corps already.

NELL. Yer makin' fun of me again.

MAJOR. I've wanted you for eight years now, and—how can I put it? (*With change of tone*) You know—Captain Nell—when a lot of people are working toward the same goal, there're always one or two who reach it first. We can't tell why. Some call it Providence, some call it Genius, and some call it Foolishness—but there it is. That's the main thing. The great poet you've just been reading had it. And you have it too. You wonderful little wisp of humanity.

NELL. Really, I don't know what you mean, Major Williams.

MAJOR. Some day, Captain Nell, the old world will claim you as one of its immortal leaders—and then— (*With a touch of the whimsical*) please don't forget I was the first to say so.

NELL. Oh, Major Williams, I never thought I was anything—special.

MAJOR (*laughing gently*). My dear, your not knowing is the crown of it all—and now let's return to—

NELL (*earnestly*). Please won't you send me away? Out west—anywhere that's far.

MAJOR. No, I'm going to keep you here with me. I'm going to fight for you and stand by you, and drive away all these—these ghosts of suffering and sin and darkness! I'm going to bring you out into the sunshine! I'm going to show you that life's a happy thing, after all. You're too frail to go on alone; you're too little to struggle under that heavy load. Won't you let me carry half?

NELL. I can't hardly believe what you say.

MAJOR. I love you—I want you to— (*The door, back, opens, and* JIM *enters heavily. He is thin, pale, nervous, dirty, and unshaven. He walks with a shambling gait and uses stiff, suspicious gestures. His manner varies between sullenness and fierce, quiet bursts of rage. He stands with his hand on the knob. They, at the sound of the door, turn their heads; for a moment, all three look at each other.*)

NELL (*under her breath, as she springs to her feet*). Jim!

JIM (*after a slight pause, breathing hard*). Well, I've come back. (*Looking venomously at the* MAJOR) Hope I'm not buttin' in!

MAJOR (*to* NELL, *with quiet efficiency*). Shall I get him out?

(NELL, *her eyes fixed on* JIM, *does not appear to hear what he says. Her lips move a little, her hands are pressed together, as she goes a step or two nearer.*)

JIM (*to* MAJOR). Say, I want to talk to her by herself, an' I hain't got all the time in the world, neither!

MAJOR (*shortly*). What right have you to be here?

JIM (*fiercely*). 'Cause she's my girl—see?

MAJOR (*to* JIM). If I go, you'll come with me.

JIM (*in a rage*). Quit yer drip an' get ter hell outer here!

NELL. Please go, Major, I'm not afraid—now. It must be gettin' time fer yer train.

JIM. That's right! (*Looking at* NELL) She an' me ain't seen each other fer over eight years, an' we've got a good deal ter say! (*To* MAJOR) Now, beat it!

NELL (*in answer to a look from the* MAJOR). It's all right—it'll be better, perhaps, if I get through with it now.

MAJOR (*unwillingly*). Very well. I'll see you Friday.

NELL (*still looking at* JIM). Yes—good night.

MAJOR (*shaking hands*). I'm sorry I couldn't go on with what I was saying—but— (*He smiles at her half gaily, half tenderly.*)

NELL (*vaguely*). What you were—

MAJOR (*going to the door at back, and bowing to her, still smiling, and paying no attention to* JIM). Good night! (*Exit* MAJOR.)

NELL (*stepping forward just as the door closes*). Major, I— (*She clenches her hands and stops with a great effort.*)

MAJOR (*reappearing at the door*). Did you call?

NELL (*controlling herself, after a slight pause*). Nothin'. I forgot what I wanted to say.

MAJOR. You're sure it's all right?

NELL (*same as before*). Yes—real sure.

MAJOR. Good night, Mrs. Sanders. (*He closes the door.*)

JIM (*after a slight pause*). Swell friends, ain't ye?

NELL. How long have ye been out—Jim?

JIM. Six months.

NELL. Oh—an' I never knew!

JIM. Sid McGovern wouldn't tell me, what'd become of ye. I found out t'day from a guy in the lodgin'-house you'd got converted.

NELL. Ye look diff'rent—Jim.

JIM (*bitterly*). *I* ain't been in the Salvation Army! *I've* been in jail! (*Disgustedly*) An' now ye're wearin' all this sort o' stuff!

NELL. Eight years is a long time!

JIM (*savagely*). Yer right there—if yer spendin' it in Sing Sing!

NELL. Jim—after what you said ter me—that night—I didn't dare send word to ye—not even ter tell yer 'bout— (*Stops, squeezing her hands together.*)

JIM. 'Bout wot?

NELL. Jimmy—he's eight years old next April— (*She goes a step nearer him.*)

JIM (*disgustedly, after a short pause*). Hell!

NELL (*in sudden agony and horror*). Jim, what made ye try to find me?

JIM. That's a nice question t' ask a man!

NELL. Are ye goin' to—stay—in New York?

JIM. Naw, I'm leaving ter-morrer an' wot's more—I'm leavin' in a Pullman car!

NELL (*relieved*). Yer goin' away?

JIM. Yeh!

NELL. Have ye got a new job?

JIM (*slowly*). Yes, I got a new job.

NELL. Where?

JIM. Denver.

NELL (*nervously*). I 'spose it'd be hard on ye, stayin' here.

JIM (*bursting out into a short, almost hysterical laugh*). Hard! Say, that's a good one! Mebbe ye think a man has a soft snap when he comes outer jail! *Hard!* It's hell—that's what it is! I've been livin' in hell fer six months. (*Dropping his voice*) An' I won't do it no more!

(*Slight rumble of thunder in distance.*)

NELL. What d'yer mean?

JIM (*gradually becoming excited*). When I got out o' Sing Sing las' January, I wanted to buck up—an', an' go ahead—try an' live decent. All the boys up there said 'tain't no use, I might try jus's hard as I wanted, but I'd find in 'bout three weeks the world had the drop on me! I said *I'd* show 'em—an' I meant it, by Gawd, but every word they told me was true—dam' it! It's true!

NELL. What happened?

JIM. I went back to Casey's an' struck the old man fer a job at teamin'. He asked where I'd been. I thought I'd be straight—like a son-of-a-gun fool—so I told him, an' then he said—he said— (*His face works.*)

NELL. Well? Go on, Jim. What did he say?

JIM. He said "Once a convick, always a convick!" An'—he kicked me out! Said if I tried ter get a job at any Union place, he'd put 'em wise ter me!

NELL. Then what?

JIM (*controlling himself*). Ye can't get no steady hold-down without a reference. I worked 'round, did some haulin' down on West Street—but they found out somehow—then it was all up. I was sick fer nearly a month an' spent every cent I had. Then I got a little by shovelin' snow an' street cleaning, but I couldn't stand the work—it's awful hard—an'—an'— (*Breaking out*) They're all down on me! D'ye think they care wot *sent* me to Sing Sing? I've been there—I'm a convick—I can't never be no better— that's enough for them! I've squared *my* account with eight years o' sweat n' blood—It's all over. I'd paid it up, an' it's them that won't ferget an' call it off! Dam' 'em! Dam' 'em!

NELL (*gently*). I know, Jim, I know.

JIM (*after a pause*). I've picked swill-barrels ter keep on livin', I've laid out on the streets night after night; I've been run in fer a bum till they said they'd give me another term 'nless I bucked up. But what can I do? Who'd give me a job even if I was strong?

NELL. An' so—yer goin' t' Denver fer a new start?

JIM (*after a pause*). Yeah! (*A short pause. He turns to her as if seeing her for the first time.*) Nell, I never knew how much I wanted yer till now! Nearly nine years—sweetie! (*He makes a movement toward her.*)

NELL (*quickly retreating*). Jim, don't yer see? (*With a gesture of repulsion*) I'm through with all that!

JIM (*laughing with hungry passion*). Not while I'm around!

NELL. Ye mustn't talk that way to me, Jim, any more.

JIM (*coarsely*). Even if ye *are* in the Salvation Army, ye can't ferget we got a kid!

NELL. I don't ferget.

JIM. An' just 'cause I've struck it hard, ye needn't think I'll let *you* get

a swelled head—see?

NELL. Can't I make ye see, Jim, that everything's changed now?

JIM (*roughly*). I hain't kissed a woman for eight years! (*He goes toward her. She recovers herself with a supreme effort and smiles calmly, looking him straight in the eye as he approaches.*)

NELL (*in a matter-of-fact but slightly trembling voice, forcing a laugh*). Don't be a fool, Jim, if ye can help it! Now, what I want to know is— (*As he comes near she stands her ground bravely.*) —have ye had supper, Jim?

JIM (*very close to her*). Wot d' I care 'bout—

NELL (*distinctly*). Have ye had supper, Jim?

JIM. *Yer* the only sort o' supper I—

NELL. I thought not. (*For the first time her manner is assured. She has regained her poise and command of the situation.*) Ye don't look 's if yer'd had a square meal for weeks! (*She goes to the icebox and begins taking things out; then, during the following scene, begins preparing the supper.* JIM *sits down sullenly.* NELL *goes on cheerfully.*) Where ye been all evenin'? Loafin' 'roun'—goin' t' all the bars—same as ye used ter?

JIM (*growling*). Wot are ye jumpin' on me fer? Ain't I got a right t' do's I dam' want?

NELL (*pouring out some milk*). Oh, I'm not jumpin' on ye! (*Her tone deepening*) I was only thinkin' how little ye'd really changed! (*As she discovers an empty pan in the icebox*) There! I'm all out o' eggs! But I thought I had three left anyways!

JIM (*uneasily*). What in the hell's the diff? (*Follows her.*) I don't want—

NELL (*running to the window and leaning far out, calling down*). Maggie! Mag-gie! (*Pause.*)

MAGGIE (*from below*). Yeah?

NELL (*calling*). Have you got four eggs, Maggie?

MAGGIE. Not a one, I'm sorry.

NELL. Oh, I'll get 'em somewhere! Good night.

JIM. Aw—what do ye—

MAGGIE (*her voice disappearing as she goes inside*). Good night.

NELL (*suddenly, to herself*). Wait a minute. (*Looking across the street*) Yes, her light's burnin! (*To* JIM) Mis' Clingen, at 247, she borrowed some coffee o' me las' week. I'll jus' run over an' see if—ye see Jimmy an' me don't eat much when it's hot, but you men are different! (*At the door*) I'll be back in two minutes, Jim! Wait fer me! I hope I don't get caught in the rain. (*She smiles unconcernedly at him, then closes the door.*)

(JIM *sits still a minute, and then stealthily, with a certain fearfulness, begins walking about the room, glancing at the pictures, examining* NELL's *Salvation Army bonnet, etc. He begins at left, coming round to right. When he passes the icebox, he looks in, takes a pitcher, and drinks. He comes around the mantel shelf where he notices* MAJOR WILLIAMS' *photograph. He looks at it carefully, then puts it back with a gesture of contempt. Then goes on, till he comes to the bedroom door. He stands for a moment looking up at the text above, trying to decipher it, then opens the door in the same stealthy manner.*)

JIMMY (*his shrill voice coming from within*). I'm 'sleep. I'm 'sleep, jus's har's I kin be! (JIM *stands astonished, then moves suddenly to one side, so as not to be seen, his hand still on the knob.* JIMMY, *after a short pause*) Ma—! (*Another pause*) Who's that?

JIM. It's—yer ma's gone out fer a minute. Yer'd better go on sleepin'.

JIMMY (*inside*). Are you Major Williams?

JIM (*trying to soften his voice*). Naw. (*He begins gently closing the door.*)

JIMMY. I want 'nother drink!

JIM. Yer ma'll get it fer ye when she comes back—

JIMMY (*his voice getting nearer*). But I want it now! (*He suddenly appears, blinking, in the doorway, looking curiously up at* JIM. *There is a pause.* JIMMY, *active curiosity in his voice*) What's yer name?

JIM (*after a pause*). Jim.

JIMMY (*with delight*). Why, that's *my* name! Gee, we got the same names!

JIM. Sort o' queer, ain't it?

JIMMY. What's yer other name? Mebbe it's like mine, too!

JIM. Platt—my name's Jim Platt.

JIMMY. Mine's Jimmy Sanders. Ma says Jimmy is a nice name—nicern anybody else's! I think so, d'you?

JIM (*awkwardly*). I dunno.

JIMMY (*trotting to the icebox*). I want a drink awful bad! It's in there. Will ye get me a drink?

JIM (*lumbering after him*). Where?

JIMMY. Pull up the top. (JIM *opens the icebox.*) It's in a blue pitcher—it's my own pitcher.

JIM (*bringing out the pitcher he emptied before*). This it?

JIMMY. Yes. Now gimme a drink.

JIM. I'm sorry—but—I was thirsty an' I—drank it myself.

JIMMY. Outer *my* pitcher?

JIM. I didn't know it was your pitcher.

JIMMY. And there isn't none left fer me?

JIM (*looking in*). Not a da—not a drop!

JIMMY (*disconsolately*). I'm awful 'fraid yer a bad man!

JIM (*with a touch of roughness*). Aw, come off!

JIMMY. If Major Will'ms was here, he wouldn't let ye drink out o' my pitcher!

JIM (*grinning a little*). G'wan—! I'm biggern him!

JIMMY (*proudly*). Ye ain't biggern my pa.

JIM (*after a pause*). How d'yer know?

JIMMY. 'Cause Ma said he was big an' strong—biggern Major Will'ms an' Mamie's. papa—an' everybody!

JIM. Yer ma told ye that?

JIMMY. Yes, an' lots more things!

JIM. Wot?

JIMMY. Will yer give me an all-day sucker 'f I tell yer?

JIM. Where kin I get one?

JIMMY (*running and pointing up to the mantel shelf where* NELL *has put the bag*). Up there!

JIM (*taking two out of the bag*). Tell us first.

JIMMY (*standing first on one foot, then on the other*). Well, Ma said I was ter try an' be like pa 'cause he never did nothin' wrong—an' 'cause he was such a nice man. But I don't want ter *pray* fer him 'nless—'nless—

JIM. 'Nless wot?

JIMMY. 'Nless he's turrible big an' kin t'row me 'way 'way up—highern Major Will'ms, even!

JIM (*roughly*). *I* kin do that—lemme show yer! (*He bends over, holding the child between his knees; then tries to throw him up, but can raise him only about as high as his head. He staggers and has to stop.*)

JIMMY (*in disgust*). Lemme go! You can't do nowhere near's well's Major Will'ms! You can't do't at all. Gimme my all-day suckers!

JIM (*handing him the candy*). I've been sick; I hain't got my strength back.

JIMMY. *I* was sick too! I had the croup. (*Proudly*) They thought I was goin' ter die, only Mama wouldn't let me!

JIM (*rather contemptuously*). I s'pose yer ma's all ter the good? She never done nothing bad, did she?

JIMMY (*sucking*). Naw, but she says she did—once! An' that's why she put that there picture over the door.

JIM (*looking up and reading slowly*). "I have blotted out as a thick cloud thy"—wot's that? "transgressions 'n as a cloud thy sins—return unto Me; for I have redeemed thee."

(*A slight flash of lightning and distant thunder.*)

JIMMY. Aw! Look at that! (*He seizes* JIM's *hand for protection. Enter* NELL *from the back, as* JIM *finishes reading. She carries a paper bag in her hands.* JIMMY, *rushing to her*) Ma!

NELL. You bad child! What d'yer mean by gettin' out o' bed this way?.

JIMMY (*pointing to* JIM). He made me wak' up, 'cause he opened the door. An' he tried to swing me but he can't 'cause he's been sick. An' his name's Jimmy—jus' like mine!

NELL (*smiling as she puts down the bag carefully on the little kitchen table*). Ye must go back ter bed! It's dreadful late!

JIMMY (*clinging to her and whining*). Naw—please let me stay up jus' a li'le longer—?

NELL. No, I'm busy now. I'm going t' cook some coffee an' eggs for—

JIMMY. Fer Jim Platt?

NELL. Yes.

JIMMY (*entreatingly*). Aw—jus' a minute!

NELL (*picking him up and giving him to* JIM). Take him, Jim, he'll catch cold runnin' round in his bare feet. (*She goes on with her work.* JIM *sits down awkwardly in the rocker by the table, holding the child.*)

JIMMY (*to* JIM *sleepily*). Yer clo'es 's all dirty—an' so's yer face—but— (*He throws an arm carelessly around* JIM's *neck.*)

NELL. Stop talkin', Jimmy, or I'll put yer to bed! (*To* JIM, *as she works.*) Seems's if he took to ye right off, don't it? He's the greatest kid fer likin' an' not likin' people! When he was sick las' year, he wouldn't let the doctor come near him! Honest, it was awful hard t' pull him through!

JIM (*gruffly*). Looks all right, now.

NELL. Oh, he's strong 'nuff. I think he's a-goin' to be a big man like his dad. I never saw such han's an' feet on a child! Jus' look at 'em! An' he's always puttin' it over every other kid his size on the block!

JIM (*pleased*). Naw!

NELL. Why, only ter-night he got out the winder here an' climbed down the fire escape the whole way—ladder an' all!

JIM. He's a slick little kid!

NELL. He takes after you, Jim, more'n he does me. He's got yer eyes. Oh, I guess he'll be a good-looking one all right! (*She smiles at him cheerfully.*)

JIM (*regarding the child*). Aw—he don't look like me! Got a funny nose, ain't he? Sort o' pug!

NELL (*laughing*). They're always like that. You just wait! An' he's smart, too. They say at the kindergarten he won't play any o' the games 'nless he can be leader! An' he catches on that quick!

JIM (*grinning*). I bet he does!

NELL (*laughing merrily*). Yer oughter see when I take him over t' the Hall! He makes a dead track fer where the Ensign keeps the drum, an' 'nless I kin stop him in time he begins bangin' away right in the middle o' prayer meetin. (*Laughing*) It's jus'

awful the way he does.

JIM (*awkwardly, trying to lower his voice*). Say! He's asleep.

NELL (*lowering her voice*). Is he? Well, go put him in his crib, will ye? I don' want t' leave this. Be sure ye draw the sheet over him! It's so hot he don't need any more 'n that now. We're goin' to have a storm an' that'll cool things off, I guess.

JIM (*rising with the sleeping child, who sighs and nestles against him*). Jus' stick him down. 'S that 'll?

NELL. Yes, don't wake him if ye can help it. (JIM *slowly crosses to the bedroom door and disappears inside.* NELL *begins putting a plate, knife, fork, etc. on the front table. After a moment* JIM *returns.* NELL *is humming a little tune as she moves swiftly back and forth from the table to the stove. He watches her with growing anger in his face.* NELL, *cheerfully*) Did ye get him in without his wakin'?

JIM (*fiercely*). Aw—quit that slush! 'Tain't no use!

NELL (*surprised*). What do ye mean?

JIM (*bursting forth*). I don't want no supper!

NELL (*bringing the coffeepot to the table*). Don't ye?

JIM (*fiercely*). D'ye think I'm not on ter why ye went an' lef' me alone with the kid? Ye wanted to get me all calmed down an', an' mushy like, so ye could do's ye pleased! Well, ye nearly had me, but I'm wise ter ye now!

NELL (*reproachfully*). Wait till ye've had a bit t' eat an' then we kin talk all ye want!

JIM (*looking at the clock*). It's gettin' late! We'll talk now. Take back that grub.

NELL (*simply*). I thought yer'd like it!

JIM. That game ain't workin' no more!

NELL. Jus' take a cup o' coffee! Ye look awful hungry!

JIM. Ye do's I say!

(*For a moment they face each other. Then* NELL *turns to put the coffee on the table.*)

NELL (*inarticulately*). All right. I'm sorry— (*Suddenly she takes a deep breath, squares her shoulders, and faces him.*) Wait till I put out the stove. (*She goes quietly to the back and turns off the gas. Then washes her hands at the sink, dries them, and returns to him. A slight catch in her breath as she looks at him.*) Now, what is it?

JIM. Look a' here. Yer my girl, ain't ye?

NELL. I was—yer girl.

JIM. Well, yer are now, an' the sooner ye make up yer mind to't the better.

NELL. What d'ye want me ter do?

JIM. I said I was goin' t' Denver in the mornin'.

NELL. Ye came to say—good-by?

JIM. Naw. I came t' tell ye ye gotter go with me.

NELL. Why?

JIM. 'Cause I say so, see? (*Puts his hand on her shoulder.*)

NELL. How—how yer goin' t' raise the money?

JIM (*scowling*). Yer talk as if ye couldn't fork out a cent!

NELL. I got about fourteen dollars. That'll help a lot!

JIM. I'm no gazabo! I know how ye rake it in at every meetin'.

NELL (*looking at him, their eyes meet*). How yer goin' t' raise the money?

JIM (*with stealthy irritation*). That's *my* biz! You leave me be an' I'll 'tend to that! (*With sudden harshness*) You an' me's goin' ter Denver ter-morrer mornin'. Grasp it?

NELL (*drawing away from his hand*). You an' me—that all?

JIM. O' course!

NELL. And—what about—Jimmy?

JIM (*with disgust*). Wot's *he* gotter do with it? Ye don' suppose we kin lug 'round a kid, do yer?

NELL (*her voice growing a little louder*). Ye want t' go to Denver an' leave Jimmy behind?

JIM. That's wot I said!

NELL. No! I wouldn't stir a step.

JIM. Like hell ye wouldn't!

NELL (*laughing a little hysterically*). Wot d'ye think I'm made of?

JIM. Ye kin leave the kid with that old girl—wot's her name? The one's got hold o' you that night at Sid's.

NELL (*smiling oddly*). An' go off an' prob'ly never see him again!

JIM (*threateningly*). I hain't got time fer any lip, now. He's mine's much's he is yours!

NELL (*flaming*). He's not yours! He never has been yours an' never will be till ye do somethin' ter deserve him! He was born in the dark, poor little feller, but he'll grow up in the light— thank God. 'N I won't let anyone stand in his way!

JIM (*lamely*). I didn't know ye was so wild 'bout him. He's a cute little duck. Well, maybe we kin take him! How's that?

NELL (*faintly*). What about my work?

JIM. Yer *work*?

NELL. I'm Cap'n in the Salvation Army. Major Will'ms an' Maggie an' me do all the managin' o' Corps No. 1.

JIM. Ye don' call it *work* ter stand on street corners an' yell hymns, do ye?

NELL. That's only part of it.

JIM (*baffled and savage*). Ye didn't use ter be like this! I could do anythin' I liked with ye.

NELL. Yes, I know ye could.

JIM. There's a Salvation Army in Denver, ain't there?

NELL. Yes.

JIM. Well, go on "workin' " there! You'll get sick enough of it, with all the dough ye want an' swell livin'! I'll give yer jus' three weeks t' quit on yer own hook!

NELL. What d'yer mean by that?

JIM (*relapsing into sly irritation*). I ain't tellin' how, but you get wise to the fac' it's goin' t' happen! Now, looka here! (*Taking her by the shoulders*) When I say a thing, it goes! An' I've told yer we're leavin' fer Denver ter-morrer mornin' on the Lake Shore.

NELL. I can't—I won't!

JIM. Why not? Come on, spit it out!

NELL (*passionately*). Can't yer see, Jim? Ye must be blind!

JIM. See wot?

NELL. The diff'rence—now!

JIM. There ain't none! I've been in jail an' yer've been out—that's all! But ye b'long ter me yet, even if ye *are* gettin' stuck up! I don't leggo easy! Ye oughter know that by this time.

NELL. I can't go—'cause—'cause—

JIM (*between his teeth*). Well?

NELL (*wrenching herself free*). 'Cause now I know that right an' wrong ain't the same thing!

JIM. Come off!

NELL. I tell ye I'm through with all that!

JIM. Like hell ye are!

NELL (*panting*). I mean what I say. Now what are ye goin' ter do? Now what?

JIM (*after a pause*). Nell, mebbe I sized ye up wrong.

NELL. Mebbe ye did, Jim.

JIM. Ye have changed since that night at Sid's! I wouldn't think so t' first, 'cause—I know—

NELL. That *you* hadn't changed. No, yer just the same.

JIM. D'yer blame me? State Prison ain't 'sactly like the Salvation Army! Don' forget that!

NELL (*her voice softening*). I know, Jim.

JIM (*with rough tenderness*). They call ye Salvation Nell, don' they?

NELL. Yes, Jim.

JIM. An' ye spend yer time goin' round with all the ol' bums an' bats, tryin' ter convert 'em—make 'em different?

NELL. Yes.

JIM. Then why won' yer come with me? Don' I need yer more'n anyone else?

NELL. Jim—

JIM. Or don' ye care 'bout me no more? Nell—tell me! Don't ye care?

NELL (*almost whispering*). I care—more'n anythin' in the world!

JIM. Ye wouldn't find me no tough job. I've had hard luck ever since I was a kid no bigger'n Jimmy here! An' no one never—

NELL. *I* know, Jim, an'—an'—I'm not blamin' ye. I could cry when I think how little chance ye've had.

JIM. I never had none till now!

NELL. Now?

JIM. Ye know that! An' it's yer chance—it's yer's well's mine!

NELL (*turning away*). Mine!

JIM. I've done everythin' fer ye! I've gone ter hell for eight years, while ye've been gettin' salvation! An' I come out—an' find I'm forgot. Forgot—I wish t' Gawd, I could forget, Nelly, but I can't—can't—

NELL (*in agony*). If I could only know ye was speakin' the truth!

JIM. Look at me, Nelly, yer the only thing in the whole world that kin pull me up! I love yer—ye know that! Why I can't see ye without feelin' sick an' queer all over—I won't leave ye behind. Ye've got to come with me—Nellie—

NELL (*interrupting him as she retreats before him*). Jim, I feel myself slippin'—fallin'—

JIM. What's the diff' s'long as I catch you Nell? We'll go out together an' begin it all over. I'll make ye happy, I know. An' I'm not askin' ye to go back to that damn workin' round bars, cleanin' up the floors, sleepin' in the cellar—no—by Gawd! After t'night I'll have the cash to put ye where ye belong—live in the swell hotels, have yer own suite, yer own auto—go to the show and wear slick dresses—

NELL (*in terror*). Jim!

JIM. 'Cos after t'night I'll be a rich man—in a week I'll have thousands in my pockets. What are ye lookin' at me like that fer? You'll get yer share— don't ye worry about that—I'll—I'll—

NELL (*staring*). After t'night?

JIM. That's what I said, and I meant every damn word.

NELL (*piercingly*). Jim! *Now* I know why yer goin' away t'morrer mornin'!

(*There is occasional thunder and lightning.*)

JIM (*roughly*). Why, then?

NELL (*staring at him*). 'Cause after t'night—the p'lice'll be on yer tracks!

JIM (*raging*). You keep quiet. How d'jer catch on?

NELL. Yer face is tellin' me! Oh.

(*She suddenly sinks into the chair, throwing her arms on the table and burying her face in them.* JIM *stands looking at her sullenly. There is a pause.* NELL, *lifting her head and slowly pressing back the hair from her temples as she looks at him*) Tell me —about it, Jim.

JIM. I see myself!

NELL (*in a dry voice*). I've got the right ter know. Yer askin' me t' come an' live with ye.

JIM. Naw. I've let on too much already!

NELL. Ye'd a-told me everythin'— eight years ago.

JIM. Yer've changed since then.

NELL. Not so much—I'm beginnin' t' think— (*Pointing to the chair across the table*) Sit down, Jim, and gimme the whole thing!

JIM (*looking uncomfortably at the clock*). Naw! It's after 'leven. I can't waste no more time! (*He sits down. There is a brief pause.*)

NELL. Go on, Jim!

JIM. What's the use? There ain't much ter say 'bout it. Las' week I'd nearly gone under.

NELL. Well?

JIM. Well, I met Barney Hurdman, who got out o' Sing Sing same time's I did. He gave me a square meal—an' took me to his lodgin' house on Chatham Square.

NELL. McCoy's?

JIM. Yeah! How d'jer know?

NELL (*quietly*). We're down there a lot. Go on!

JIM (*fingering the workbag and not looking at her*). Well, the rest o' Barney's gang was there—an'—

NELL. An' you joined on?

JIM (*with sudden passion*). Damn it! That's my biz!

NELL. Ye joined on. Then what?

JIM. They had this job fixed up— the road. (*Looking up suddenly and angrily*) Say, I ain't goin' tell ye no more! 'S none o' yer biz anyways!

NELL (*who has not moved*). Up the road. Go on, Jim. Play square.

JIM (*sullenly*). They wanted another man an' so I— (*He pauses.*)

NELL. Where is it?

JIM. Irvington.

NELL. What are ye after?

JIM. Di'monds.

NELL. Is it goin' to come off tonight?

JIM. Yeah. They're havin' a party.

NELL. Any o' the gang inside?

JIM. Fisher's girl helps in the kitchen. She's goin' t' let us in.

NELL. How many are ye?

JIM. Four, countin' me.

NELL. Why d' they need you?

JIM. They're all bunched together an' the cops are wise!

NELL. O' course!

JIM (*beginning to warm up to the subject*). So *they* stay here—an' I skip with the sparklers. Then later on we all meet in Frisco an' div'vy up—see?

NELL (*quietly*). An' you've come back after nearly nine years t' tell me yer a thief!

JIM (*rising eagerly*). Dam' it, this is the first time an' the last. I tol' yer that, too! Don't ye b'lieve me?

NELL (*seizing his arm*). Jim, I won't let ye! It's a dirty game—ye know yer always thought so b'fore.

JIM. Ain't I been in jail? Wot's the good o' bein' pertikler?

NELL. Al McGovern was after yer girl. Stealin's diff'rent!

JIM. Ye get a longer term, that's all.

NELL. Jim, it's not you that's talkin' —it's the drink in ye!

JIM (*pulling himself away*). Aw—ring off! Wot's the diff' between me an' lots o' rich slobs that lift all the time? Things ain't wrong, 'nless yer get pinched, an' if ye got the cash, ye never are!

NELL (*instantly*). Don't yer fool yourself! Yer'll have the p'lice o' the whole country on yer trail! If an old hand like Jack Rutgers can't keep 'em off mor'n a week, how long'll they be gettin' you?

JIM. The Rutgers gang was too big. That's the only reason they got landed!

NELL (*laughing hysterically*). I see ye keepin' clear o' them! Yer'd show yer hand in three days. Yer not the right—

JIM. I'll risk it!

NELL. How d' ye know they're playin' ye square? They had it all fixed up before ye came in—there's somethin' queer 'bout that! I know they'll clear out an' leave yer in the gutter—jus' like young Allen! Ye remember him? He got twenty years.

JIM. Quit yer hot air! I'm a-leavin' with the haul, ain't I? That sounds if they was goin' to bounce me!

NELL (*going on*). An' ye've been out only six months! That means yer'll get an extra long term! Ye'll go up there sure as fate, Jim, an' spend ten— fifteen—twenty *more* years, breakin' stones—day in an' day out—till ye wish yer'd dropped dead the minute they got ye!

JIM (*savagely*). Trust me! It's all up if I get pinched—ye needn't bother 'bout that, but I won't be! I'll pull this thing through! I'm in it an' s'elp me Gawd, I'll stay in it till the bloddy end!

NELL (*desperately*). No yer won't! I'll stop ye myself!

JIM. Wot's that?

(*More lightning and thunder.*)

NELL. Yer've told me all 'bout it. I— I—know the whole thing—

JIM. S'posin' yer do?

NELL. I'll—I'll phone over t' the Station.

JIM (*snarling as he seizes her arm*). Ye dirty little *s.o.a.b.*! So that's wot yer after! Don't ye know I'd wring yer neck 'n less 'n minute 'fore I—

NELL (*flinging up her hand*). That won't do you no good, Jim—an' they'll hear you downstairs!

JIM. Promise me yer'll—

NELL. Ye can't make me promise nothin'!

JIM (*grinning with rage*). Can't I?

NELL. Ye know yer can't!

(*They face each other for a moment.*)

JIM (*pushing her away violently*). Aw—hell!

NELL (*imploringly*). Say yer'll drop it, Jim—!

JIM. I see myself!

NELL (*warningly*). I tell yer I'll 'phone the p'lice lieutenant! He knows me—an'

JIM (*suddenly self-possessed*). 'Phone away!

NELL (*desperately*). Jim—!

JIM. Go on, I don't give a rip! (*He whistles.*)

NELL (*turning toward the phone, right front*). I hate ter get yer gang nabbed—but—anythin's better—

JIM (*calmly*). How yer goin' to tell 'em you're caught on?

NELL (*stopping*). I'll say—I'll—I needn't say nothin'—they'll take my word! (*She goes nearer the telephone.*)

JIM. Wait an' see! S'pose ye *do* get Barney an' the rest landed, wot'll *they* say?

NELL. I—dunno—

JIM. I do!—They'll be wild! They'll know I spilt on 'em—they'll know I got 'em into the mess o' their lives— an' d'ye think they'll go to Sing Sing without draggin' me with 'em—I wonder!

NELL (*at the phone, turning*). —They couldn't prove it!

JIM. *Couldn't* they? It's a dead cinch. They know me. I know you, an' you're the one's put on the cops! How's that?

NELL (*swaying*). Oh!

JIM. Go ahead! You might's well tell the Station ye got one o' the bunch here now. It'll save time. Wotter yer waitin' for?

NELL (*realizing*). It's throwin' ye back in jail!

JIM (*grimly*). If they catch me alive!

NELL. Oh!

JIM. Go on—I want ter hear wot they say!

NELL (*wringing her hands*). I can't do it! An' I can't see ye lose yer soul. Oh, wot'll I do?

JIM. Anythin' ye want!

NELL (*entreatingly*). Jim, jus' give it up this once—jus' fer tonight!—Mebbe things'll seem different in the mornin'. Do't fer me, Jim. I've never asked nothin' from ye till now! Please, Jim, I know ye will. I hope ye'll be good ter me jus' this once, won't ye, won't ye?

JIM (*looking at the clock*). It's gettin' late. I gotter meet Barney up at the Grand Central in less'n an hour. If yer not goin' to do no phonin', I guess I'll move on.

NELL (*with a cry*). I can't help it then! I can't help it! (*She goes to the telephone.*) I done the best I could! (*She takes up the receiver.*) Madison 342. (*She looks back at* JIM, *who stands calmly watching her.*) Change yer mind, Jim—it ain't too late—I won't say another word— (*Suddenly, she turns to the phone, then looks back at* JIM.) Please—for God's sake, Jim!

JIM (*measuredly*). Mebbe it'll do yer a heap o' good ter think o' me down Sing Sing. Ye'll have all the fun o' the last eight years over again, an' ye kin say b'sides, "I done the whole thing myself this trip."

NELL (*swooningly*). Jim—?

JIM (*in a hard voice*). An' when the kid asks ye again where his pa is, ye kin say he got outer jail but ye sent him back in less'n six months— so he needn't bother no more 'bout him. That'll—

NELL (*suddenly drawn to the phone*). Hello—is this—the Station? I want ter speak t'—Lieutenant Andrews— (*Hurriedly turning to* JIM) Quick! It's yer last chance—say the word—jus' say the word—Jim!

JIM (*laughing recklessly*). It's up ter you! Go on! Say it—say it. I'd like to hear yer!

NELL (*turning suddenly to the phone*). Lieutenant Andrews? It's me —Nell Sanders—yes, Cap'n Sanders. I jus' wanted ter—ter—

JIM. I'm listenin'—wot's keepin' yer?

NELL (*holding on to the wall to keep herself from falling*). There's somethin'—I— (*Suddenly she hangs up the receiver and sinks to her knees. She bursts into a storm of hysterical sobbing.*) 'Tain't no use—I—can't!

JIM (*coming near her, in strong triumph*). No, ye can't, an' d'ye know why? It's 'cos ye love me, Nelly: ye love me more'n anythin' else in the world! Wot's the good o' tryin' ter fight it down—yer can't do it! It's stronger 'n you an' me an' all the Salvation Army bunched t'gether! It's got a strangle hold, Nelly, an' yer've gotter give in—there ain't nothin' else ter do! (*Laughing*) I knew it all along! (*Lifts her up.*) Ye let me kiss ye in the same ol' way—likes we used ter b'fore, an' that'll be the finish o' all this talkin' 'bout Gawd an' the devil an' Heaven an' Hell! (*He tries to gather* NELL *in his arms. She chokes and tears herself away, hurrying to the other side of the room.* JIM, *still laughing in triumph*) Ye don't want to now? (*Looking at the clock*) Well, mebbe yer're right! I'm pretty near late anyway. Now, listen, Nelly! Are ye listenin'?

NELL (*choking*). Yes—

JIM. I'll come fer ye at eight o'clock ter-morrer. The train goes at nine, an' that leaves plenty time to get over to the Grand Central. Don't bring no

more trunks'n ye kin help. Eight o'clock sharp—see?

NELL (*turning around desperately*). Jim, are ye goin' to—do it?

JIM (*kindly*). Say now—don't ye bother no more 'bout that. 'Tain't worth your while! (*Going toward the door and picking up his cap from the table*) Ye be ready, won' yer?

NELL (*almost at the end of her resources*). Jus' a minute! Yer've seen Jimmy! Ye know what a cute little feller he is—ye said so yerself! I want him t'grow up into a real fine man! I want him t'have ev'ry chance! (*Smiling pitifully*) You an' me didn't have no chance—did we, Jim? An' it ain't all our fault if we don't come quite up ter the mark. But it's different with Jimmy! (*Passionately*) Don't hit him down b'fore he gets started! Give him a show, Jim, that's all I'm askin'! Give him a show!

JIM. Ain't I goin' ter?

NELL (*her voice dying away—her eyes filling with tears*). Don't let him grow up the son of a—

JIM (*his good humor disappearing*). Dry up on that! (*In a momentary burst of anger at her obstinacy*) If I'm a thief, it's 'cause the Gawd yer always gassin' about's made things so I can't be anythin' else! (*Severely*) Good night! Don' keep me waitin' in the mornin'!

NELL. What's the good of sayin' that? You know I'm not goin'! (*Storm grows louder.*) Good-by, Jim!

JIM (*after a pause, looking at her darkly*). D'ye mean it?

NELL. Yes!

JIM. D'ye mean it?

NELL. Yes!

JIM. Yer goin' t'throw me over?

NELL (*whispering*). Yes. (*She turns to the mantel shelf unsteadily, clinging to it with both hands and bowing her head in front of the clock.* JIM *glares at her for a moment. He sees the photograph of the* MAJOR *and springs forward suddenly with a savage snarl.*)

JIM (*raging*). I know why yer doin' it! 'Tain't 'cause ye think it's wrong, it's 'cause ye've took another feller—that mush-head I found ye with—how long's *he* had you—huh? (*Turning her about violently*) An' me up in Sing Sing!

NELL (*terrified*). Jim!

JIM (*tearing down the photograph and destroying it*). Ye did it once with Al McGovern—an' now ye want to kick me out again! Well, ye can't do it—ye lyin' little— (*He flings the pitcher with the roses to the floor, where it breaks with a crash.*) Now ye tell me if it ain't so!

NELL (*facing him*). Yes—Jim—it is. He wants me to marry him!

JIM. Are ye goin' ter?

NELL. No. I won't marry him if ye'll give up this job t'night!

JIM (*glancing at the clock*). Twenty to twelve! I ought t' be leavin' this minute—Barney ain't the kind that waits!

NELL (*desperately*). I'll marry him, Jim—ye can blame it on yerself!

JIM (*tossing his head in disgust*). Aw—I see yer game, an' it don't work— (*He starts for the door.*)

NELL (*wildly*). Jim—I got one thing more! Stay here. I won't hold nothin' back—if ye'll only stay!

JIM (*harshly*). Wot d'ye mean? (*Turns at the door, breathing hard.*) I can't leave Barney—

NELL. Yes, ye can, Jim—I love ye—

JIM. Quit it! I'm goin'! (*He turns toward the door.*)

NELL (*with a cry*). Jim—! (*She runs across to him, holding out her shaking hands. He catches her as she reels.*) Stay here! Stay with me!

JIM (*half savagely, half passionately as he holds her up*). If this was t' come off any other night, an' I was here—alone with ye—d'ye think I wouldn't stay? Once I get my arms round ye so ye can't break away—an' kiss ye till—why, I can feel ye shakin' now at the very thought—

NELL (*her eyes closed*). Go on—kiss me—

JIM. Nelly, all right, I'll stay!

NELL. Then ye'll give up your job—t'night?

JIM (*recklessly*). Yes! Wot d' I care 'bout that now? Don't ye love me?

NELL (*clinging to him with sudden passion*). Oh, I do! I've felt it fer eight years—an' I didn't know—Jim! I'm not sorry—I'm glad! It's all over with me —an' I don't care, Jim—I love ye, Jim, an' I don't care!

JIM (*triumphantly*). That's my girl talkin'! I knew I'd find her—"Salvation Nell." She's got her finish—sweetie! (*Laughs as he kisses her.*)

(NELL *screams in horror.*)

We've kicked her out—dam' her! She'll never come back!

(NELL *breaks from him and stands staring at him.*)

(*He gives a cry of realization.*) Wot's the matter?

NELL. I wasn't doin' it t' save ye—I was doin' it b'cause I loved ye!

JIM. Ye can't back out now—

NELL (*in sudden agony*). God, why didn't ye help me? Where did ye go?

JIM (*with sudden access of fury*). I'm on! It's that other feller! But I'll kill ye before—

NELL (*dully*). Go ahead! I won't make a sound. Nobody'll hear ye. I ain't fit to live no longer!

JIM (*transfixed by a sudden thought*). Dam' it—ye've fooled me again! (*Pushing her off with a roar*) Where's my hat?

NELL. Yer goin' t' meet Barney?

JIM (*glancing at the clock and giving a sudden exclamation*). Quarter to twelve! If I can catch an uptown express— (*He turns hurriedly to the door, but* NELL *stands before it.*)

NELL. Jim—I—

JIM (*after glancing at the clock*). Move along—get out! (*He jams his hat on his head.*)

NELL. I'll call Maggie!

JIM (*under his breath*). We'll see about that! (*He rushes forward, takes her violently by the shoulders to throw her aside. She struggles frantically, twining her arms about him. Furious,* JIM *goes on.*) Leggo! Leggo! I say!

NELL (*screaming*). Maggie! Maggie!

JIM. Here—cut that out—!

NELL (*screaming*). Quick, Maggie!

JIM (*frenzied*). I'll fix ye then, ye dam' little fool! (*He suddenly frees one arm and strikes her on the head. Her body grows limp, and she falls to the floor in a heap.* JIM *runs to the door, softly opens it and listens. There is a silence. He turns to look at* NELL. *After a moment of hesitation, he comes quickly and tries to rouse her. In a low voice*) Buck up! 'Taint nothin'! (*He is seized by a sudden terror. He lifts her head quickly.*) Nelly—Nelly! (*He drops her head as if stung by some terrible thought.*)

MAGGIE (*voice from downstairs, coming anxiously through the half-open door*). Ne—ll! Oh, Ne—ll! (*A slight pause*) That you callin'?

(JIM *is kneeling, every muscle tense, over* NELL's *body, listening. Then, galvanized to action, he rushes to the window, looks out, then to the door, which he locks. After that, still silently and furtively, he turns down the gas. The lamplight falls upon the upper part of* NELL's *body.* JIM *glances at it with something like a groan; then*

crosses *swiftly to the window, where the rain has at last broken and is beating down in white sheets. He looks out, turns up his collar, climbs quietly to the fire escape, and disappears.* NELL *shows some signs of reviving consciousness. Meanwhile, as* JIM *makes his exit, there is knocking at the door.*)

MAGGIE (*outside, in an agitated voice*). Nell—what is it—somethin's happened? (*She knocks again.*)

NELL (*still dazed, rises to a sitting posture and suddenly remembers*). Jim, where are ye? I—I can't see—

(*There is a long quivering flash of lightning in which* NELL *can be seen staring at the emptiness about her, followed almost immediately by a terrific clap of thunder, seemingly just over her head.*)

NELL (*wildly*). He's gone—he's gone!

MAGGIE (*outside, her voice loud with terror, as she beats on the door*). Nell—open the door—it's me—Maggie! (*She redoubles her knocking.*)

(JIMMY, *wild with fright, runs in from the other room, and seeing his mother, rushes to her.*)

JIMMY (*as he enters*). Ma, I'm scared!

MAGGIE (*outside, calling frantically*). Help—Mis' Baxter! Help—help—Mis' Baxter! (*Her voice is heard as she rushes down the stairs for aid.*)

NELL (*seeing* JIMMY *for the first time and seizing him, her face suddenly transfigured*). Jimmy! Come on, Jimmy! We're goin' to pray—we're goin' t' pray for your dad, Jimmy, an' we're goin' t' save him! If we only believe—if we're only sure in our hearts—God'll do it! Now, Jimmy, pray hard—pray as ye never prayed in yer life b'fore—"Our Father who art in heaven, Hallowed be Thy name, Thy Kingdom come"—

(JIMMY, *his eyes shut tight, frown-*

ing earnestly, follows her in his high
intense little voice.)

"Thy Will be done"—

(*The fury of the storm continues.*)

ACT THREE

*A week later. On the West Side, be-
fore Corps No. 3, bars, pawnbrokers,
grocery stores, and other shops occupy
the first floors. Above are flats. The
center set, at back, represents the junc-
tion of three streets. On the right corner is the entrance to a half basement
bar, with several steps leading down
to it. A large window, filled with
posters, etc., and brilliantly lit, to front
of this entrance. The next store, going
still further front, is a poky little delicatessen shop. The windows filled with
cheeses, sausages, greens, etc. In front
of it on the sidewalk is a fruit and veg-
etable display. The delicatessen shop
is on the corner. Near this corner, to
the right, is the entrance to the flats,
which occupy the space over the bar
and the delicatessen shop. Two floors
of flats can be seen. There are fire escapes—on the side street—windows a-
lone on the street nearest front. A few
geraniums in pots on sills, etc. In fire
escapes and from one or two windows,
are underclothes, and aprons, etc.,
hung out to dry.*

*On the left corner, extending down
to the foreground and opposite the
bar and the delicatessen shop, is Corps
No. 1 Hall, a dingy brick building
with entrance on the side street leading up a flight of stairs. On either side
of the entrance are signs, painted
black and on white background. One
says: "The Salvation Army, Corps
No. 1. Meeting every evening at 8, on
Sunday 7 and 10:30 A.M. Sunday*

*School, 1:30 P.M. Public Service at 3
and 8. You are cordially invited." The
other sign reads "Sundays—10:30 A.M.
Sunday School, 8 P.M. Revival Service
in Building." Sidewalks go round
both these blocks. On both corners of
the street in the foreground are lamp
posts, as yet unlighted. There is a
sunset glow over the street. As the act
goes on, this gradually fades, lights
appear in the windows, etc., and at
last it is night.*

*As the curtain rises, it is about
seven o'clock on a hot July evening.
The street is filled more or less
through this act, people passing up
and down; an occasional delivery
wagon goes by. But all this is strictly
in the background. The side street
where all the action occurs is alive
with inhabitants who are out to enjoy
a breath of fresh air after a long hot
day.* WOMEN, *with bare arms and
faded wrappers loose about the neck,
sit on the fire escapes, holding babies
or hanging out the wash. On the left
front corner is a popcorn stand attended by a ragged* GREEK. *On the
right front, in the entrance to the flats,
lies a sleepy* HOBO. *On the sidewalk
in front of the Hall, several small
barefooted* URCHINS *are playing craps;
their loud shrill voices—"Aw, gee,
missed it!" "Yer turn." "Wotcher
lose?" "Gimme a swipe"—occasionally
ring out monotonously. In front of
the bar and delicatessen shop are two
groups of little* GIRLS; *one is sitting on
the curb, listening to a dime novel
read aloud. The other group is busily
engaged in gossip. Several of the little
girls carry babies. All of them are
bareheaded, barelegged, and ragged.
There are some* CHILDREN *about the
popcorn man, watching him at his
work. All these children cross and
recross the street at intervals. Three*

girls of about sixteen, dressed in taw-dry attempts at elegance, are walking up and down in front of the Hall, arm in arm. As they pass, they interrupt the little boys' game, much to the latter's shrill annoyance. On the cor-ner where the saloon is, under the arc light, stands a group of MEN, *talk-ing and laughing; occasionally one drops into the bar or comes out to join them. In front of the delicatessen shop, placidly knitting, sits* FRAU SCHMIDT, *a fat, kind old German woman.*

Just before and after the curtain goes up is heard the sound of the "Cavalleria Intermezzo," played on a cracked hand organ at the corner op-posite the bar. This lasts for a mo-ment or two, then stops, and the ITALIAN *wheels off his organ. As it stops there is heard more distinctly a subdued, continuous murmur of noise, and above all, the cries of the children at play, the women speaking to each other, the laughter of girls, the deep bass of the men's voices—all forming one general effect. As in Act One, the first scenes are played swiftly, for a purely atmospheric effect.*

———

PETE (*a little boy, to the girls who have swept through the game*). Aw cheese it—ye bugged my shot!

JENNY (*patronizingly*). Yer'll hert yerself yellin! (*To her companions*) An' then, Charlie says t' me, I cert'nly never seen anythin' better lookin'—

MRS. SPRATT (*raising a window over the delicatessen shop*). Mis' Hub—bell!

ROSIE HUBBELL (*on the pavement, screaming back*). Ma ain't come in yet!

MRS. SPRATT. My, that's funny— (*Her voice dies away as she withdraws. There is a loud laugh from the men at the corner over some joke.*)

PACKEY (*a newsboy, with a bundle of* Journals *under his arm, passes across the back of the set*). Extry! Ex-try! Latest news o' the big di'mond robb'ry! Extry!

SERGEANT PHILLIPS (*sitting before entrance of the Hall*). Hi!

PACKEY (*rushes up and sells him a paper, then goes on his way and dis-appears, yelling monotonously*). Ex-try! Di'mond thieves sail fer Europe! Extry! Extry! (*His voice dies away as the scene proceeds.*)

MAMIE MCGONE (*reading in a loud, expressionless voice*). " 'The fragrance of the roses is quite too oppressive my lord,' said Lady Angeela wit' a lovely smile. 'Let me return to the ballroom.' 'Not until I have told yer my sen-ti-ments, a-dor-able creecher, an' learned whether my future life is ter be a bow-er of bliss or cavern of despair,' answered the Dook, kneeling on bended knee—" (*Breaking off in admiration*) Aw, say, ain't that jus' grand?

PEGGY (*a little girl, who has been listening in rapt attention*). I wisht I could read 's well 's you!

MAMIE MCGONE (*proudly*). 'Tain't nothin'! (*Resuming*) "The orchestra began a low, sad waltz, an' while the music rose an' fell in dreamy cadence, Gerald—" (*Here the baby, which she is holding in the other arm, sets up a querulous howl. Angrily shaking it*) I can't read nothin' but the kid begins to howl!

BOBBY (*a fat little boy, who has come proudly down the street to the popcorn stand, followed by the other little boys. They have left the craps for a short time*). Gimme two bags! An' put in plenty o' butter!

PETE. Aw, say! Two bags!

PADDY. Where'd ye get the dough, Fatty?

PETE (*meaningly*). Say, Fatty, yer remember when I gave yer half my bananers!

PADDY (*as the buyer moves haughtily off*). Gee, yer a crackerjack!

PETE (*to the rest*). Say, le's— (*He nods and winks. Together, they make a rush at the fat boy.*)

BOBBY (*with a long scream as he rushes out, right, pursued by the rest, his bags clasped to his breast*). Ma! Ma!—

MRS. JACKSON (*coming out on the fire escape and calling to the floor below*). Mis' Me—llen! Mis' Me—llen! (*Her voice drops to a conventional level as* MRS. MELLEN, *another scantily-attired woman, emerges on the fire escape below.*) Hev' you got any o' that cuttlebone you was tellin' me 'bout this afternoon? Flossie hasn't sung a note for two days, an' he's droppin' his tail feather somethin' awful!

MRS. MELLEN (*disappearing*). Wait a sec! Mis' Jackson, an' I'll see!

JENNY (*on the opposite side of the street, after they have been laughing loudly*). Well, that beats me! Grace was so stuck on him, y'know! Honest to goodness, why she tol' me he was goin' ter give her a real engagement ring! 'Course, I tol' her that's what men always *said*, but—

(*They turn to resume their promenade.*)

PADDY (*to* PETE, *as they all come in, from right, eating the popcorn*). Think he'll tell the cop?

PETE. Naw! He knows I'd bust his mug! Say, it's yer turn, Pugsie! (*They resume their interrupted game.*)

MRS. MELLEN (*emerging and calling up*). Here 'tis! Ready?

MRS. JACKSON (*casually letting down a basket with a string attached to it*). Thanks! (*As she pulls it up*) My Carrie ain't down there, is she? No? She leaves

me the dishes ter do every night now!

MRS. MELLEN. Say, Mis' Jackson, can yer spare a little ice? I don't want my hamburger t' go bughouse overnight, an' I'm all out!

MRS. JACKSON. Not a bit! So hot t'day! Mebbe Mis' Stevens would have some! (*She goes inside. The woman below does likewise.*)

(MYRTLE HAWES *appears on the sidewalk, left. She is elaborately gowned, a huge hat, parasol, etc. Her manner is haughty, and she holds her skirts as though fearing contamination.* MC-GLONE *suddenly opens the door to the flats, extreme right, and falls over the sleeping* HOBO.)

MCGLONE (*startled*). Clear out, yer slob!

HOBO. Ye needn't stamp my head in!

(*The* HOBO *drifts away, right. The man turns up the street toward the saloon. By this time,* MYRTLE HAWES *is near the foreground. The little* GIRLS, *hitherto gossiping and reading, are now walking behind her in careful and delighted imitation. She stops and looks up at the entrance to the Hall.*)

MRS. SPRATT (*on the fire escape*). Say, look who's here!

MRS. PHELAN. Wait till I call Minnie! (*She disappears and presently returns with another woman. By this time,* MYRTLE *has the attention of the feminine neighborhood. She turns, crosses the street, carefully picking her way with skirts held high.*)

PETE (*shrilly*). Say, lady, where'd yer get them stockin's!

MYRTLE (*paying no attention, but addressing* FRAU SCHMIDT). This where the Salvation Army hangs out?

FRAU SCHMIDT (*knitting calmly*). It is!

MYRTLE. Meetin's on the corner? Hymns an' speakin' an' all that?

FRAU SCHMIDT. Efery efening!

MYRTLE. Cap'n Sanders sort o' runs things?

FRAU SCHMIDT. Wit' the Major!

MYRTLE. Cute little thing, ain't she?

FRAU SCHMIDT (*eagerly*). Ach, ja— wie eine Blume! So lofely! (*She raises her hands enthusiastically.*) Und so leedle! You know her?

MYRTLE (*with calmness*). Sure I do! But I've only seen her once these last five years!

FRAU SCHMIDT (*unbending*). Then shall she be so glad! But she is very white—vat you say, blue? The work is hard and she lof it too much! She is always tired! (*Tenderly*) Und so goot! (*Sighing, as she resumes her knitting.*) Ach—Gott!

MYRTLE (*meditatively*). Well, it cert'nly does seem funny!

FRAU SCHMIDT. I vatch her efery night. Perhaps—her, vat you say, luck? comes soon! The Major—when he sees her—there is lof in his smile!

MYRTLE (*interested*). I know! D'ye think she'll pull it off?

FRAU SCHMIDT (*bewildered*). Pull it—

MYRTLE (*impatiently*). Nab him— marry him, I mean! Or is he jus' stuck on her for the fun of it?

FRAU SCHMIDT. I do not know. But I hope—I hope always that it will happen. I would so much like to see her happy—vit' a smile!

MYRTLE (*impressed*). Well, wouldn't that freeze ye? (*She turns again to look at the Hall in a more respectful manner, and notices the little* GIRLS, *who are pacing up and down in a stately manner with pieces of kindling for parasols.*)

MRS. MELLEN (*above, cackling*). Look at the kids! Gee, they catch on quick!

MYRTLE (*in a slightly raised voice*). The little micks are so filthy an' dis-gustin'! (*Shrugging her shoulders*) But then, what can yer expect in the slums!

FRAU SCHMIDT. Nell Sanders is in the Hall now. If you longer wait the meeting will begin.

MYRTLE. Thanks. (*She crosses the street, then suddenly makes a vicious hit with her parasol at one peculiarly obnoxious child. The child, just escaping, dances insolently with a tantalizing "Yah—yah—yah—yah."*)

MRS. SPRATT (*from above*). I'll bet she never paid for them clothes!

MYRTLE (*to* BRADLEY, *a member of the band, who is on the point of going into the Hall*). Say, wait a second. (*Goes up to him.*) You b'long in here?

BRADLEY (*who is in uniform and carries a trombone case, goes in*). Yes, ma'am.

MYRTLE. Well, you tell Cap' Sanders —Cap'n Nell Sanders—understand?— that a lady wants ter speak to her.

BRADLEY (*civilly*). You kin come up if ye want.

MYRTLE (*decidedly*). No, thanks. I don't want t'interrupt no prayin' an' anyways life ain't worth while these hot nights if ye have t' climb a mile or two o' stairs!

BRADLEY. All right. I'll tell her. (*Brings a chair from just inside the doorway.*) Hev' a seat?

MYRTLE (*sitting down*). Don't mention it. You ain't got a evening paper, have ye?

BRADLEY. The Sergeant reads the Journal sometimes—here it is! (*He finds it and hands it to her.*)

MYRTLE. Thanks! I'm followin' the di'mond robbery. (*She is immediately absorbed in the contents. The man disappears into the Hall.*)

(*A few moments before this,* BAXTER, *one of the men in the group before the saloon, sees* MAME MARSH, *a cheaply dressed, gum-chewing girl, who is standing ostentatiously at the corner, front left. He has come up to her somewhat awkwardly, and seems to be persuading her to move on with him. After* MYRTLE's *past speech their dialogue is heard.*)

BAXTER. She'll see us—there'll be hell in a bottle! Let's go down an' have a drink at Carson's, nice an' quiet!

MAME. I guess this corner's free. I'll stay here till I find it ain't!

BAXTER (*seeing* MRS. BAXTER *open a window on right*). There she is! Aw, come on, Mame!

(MRS. BAXTER, *who has a baby in her arms, peers up and down the street.*)

MAME (*calling defiantly*). Good-even', Mis' Baxter! Lookin' fer yer husband?

BAXTER (*angrily*). Now ye done it!

MRS. BAXTER. So, there ye are! Jus' wait till I get ye!

MRS. JACKSON (*calling from the fire escape*). Scrap—scrap! Mis' Baxter an' that Marsh girl!

BAXTER (*nervously edging away*). Cut it out an' run, Mame! She'll rip ye up something fierce!

MAME (*insolently*). D'yer think I'd move for a dough-faced incubator like her? (*From the door to the flats, right, comes the outraged* MRS. BAXTER, *bare headed and furious. She rushes straight to the girl, amid a howl of* "Here she comes," "Paste her," "Scrap." *Everyone is gathered into a crowd.*)

MRS. BAXTER (*to* MAME). Wot d'yer mean by hangin' round after my man?

MAME. Ain't hangin' round—see?

MRS. BAXTER. Ye lie, ye fat-eyed bat!

MAME (*addressing the laughing crowd*). D'jever hear sech swell langwidge! (*To* MRS. BAXTER) Say, lemme give ye some advice—free of charge. If ye want to keep a man, quit wearin' yer hair like a peeled onion an' hevin'

yer waist go up in front—see? (*Tittering*) He—he! Got a shape like a bag o' cream cheese!

MRS. BAXTER. I'm a respectable married lady an' that's more'n you kin say, ye blacked up gutter-cat of a street picker! Ye know's well's me, ye two-for-a-nickle bunch o' lies, that my man wouldn't run after nobody 'nless she'd worked hard to get him— (*Suddenly seeing her husband trying to sneak off unseen*) Come back here, ye big brute, that never made a cent in all yer life an' me standin' over a washtub day in an' day out till my back's near breakin' while ye go an' pick up any pug-nosed grease-spot that happens ter be walkin'—

(*The girl, stung to action, hurls herself with a yell upon* MRS. BAXTER. *There ensues a combat, amid cries of delight from the crowd.* "Get hold her hair," "That's right," "Mash her good," "Trip her up," "Serves you right," *etc. The husband comes stealthily up behind his wife, suddenly lays hands on her; she turns on him, he gives her a black eye. The girl, laughing hysterically, begins to refurbish her toilette which has suffered considerable damage. Suddenly, almost as this happens, there is a pause in the laughter of the crowd, as it parts to let through a big* POLICEMAN.)

PETE (*shrilly*). Cheese it—de cop!

POLICEMAN (*separating the* BAXTERS). Here you—cut it out! Wot d'yer mean by smashin' the lady's face? (*To* MRS. BAXTER) Did he hand yer that one in the eye?

MRS. BAXTER (*venomously*). Yes, an' it's not the first time he's half killed me when he—

BAXTER (*reproachfully*). That's a nice way to talk—that is!

POLICEMAN (*his hand on* BAXTER's *collar, pulling him back*). Here—quit yer jawin'! We'll learn ye how ter treat yer wife!

BAXTER (*to his wife*). Now yer done it!

MRS. BAXTER (*to the* POLICEMAN). Wot'll he get?

POLICEMAN. Oh—two months—mebbe more!

MRS. BAXTER. Say, wotcher think I am? Goin' t'send my own man to the lockup? Can't yer keep out yer ugly mug when a lady an' gent settlin' their own private affairs? (*Aside to* BAXTER, *who attempts to speak*) Shut up, ye brute, or I'll hev' yer run in! (BAXTER *and* MAME *steal off.* MRS. BAXTER *to the* POLICEMAN) Say, you get out this street an' leave me an' my man alone or I'll scratch the spinach out yer jaw an' swear up an' down 'twas you as gave me this black eye! Now d'yer understan'? Mebbe yer'll come buttin' in again! (*Turns.*) An' as fer ye, ye lazy slob— (*Suddenly discovers that he has disappeared.*) Where's he gone to?

A MAN (*in the crowd, —uproariously*). He sneaked it with the other lady!

(*The crowd, suddenly becoming aware of the exquisite humor in the situation, burst into loud laughs.* MRS. BAXTER *clenches her hands and looks wildly around.*)

POLICEMAN (*departing as he laughs*). That'll hold ye fer a while, I guess—ho—ho!

THE CROWD (*amid their mirth*). That's one on yer.—Ye pasted her good, anyways!—He ain't worth it. My wife, won't let me.—Etc.

(MRS. BAXTER *lifts her hands with a gesture of hate and glances around at the grinning faces. Then, letting her arms fall, she turns, right, to go back to the flat. The crowd begins to disperse. The incident is ended for them, but as the woman reaches the curb,* she suddenly flops down and bursts into agonized tears.)

REMNANTS OF THE CROWD. Tain't no use bawlin'.—Dry up.—He'll come back! (*They turn away, chattering and laughing.*)

(NELL *comes out of the Hall quickly. She is in regular Salvation Army uniform, bonnet, etc. She goes past* MYRTLE, *not seeing her, and comes straight to the sobbing* MRS. BAXTER.)

NELL (*putting her hand on* MRS. BAXTER's *shoulder*). What's the matter, Mis' Baxter?

MRS. BAXTER (*her face in her hands, leaning on her knees*). G'wan! Leave me be! Oh, I wisht I was dead— (*She rebuffs* NELL, *fiercely.*)

NELL (*gently*). Is't yer man again?

MRS. BAXTER (*still sobbing*). It's always—him!

NELL (*comfortingly*). How's the baby?

(*Soft strains of a hand organ are heard.*)

MRS. BAXTER (*drying her eyes on her skirt*). I fergot the kid—it's time ter feed it! (*Rising*) Yer oughter seen him t'day, Cap'n! He crep halfway ter the winder all by hisself!

NELL. My, but that's a fine baby! Mrs. Baxter, you've got the finest baby in the ward. I don't think there's one to match him the whole length of Cherry Street!

MRS. BAXTER (*deprecatingly*). Mis' Simmon's baby weighs pounds more but then he ain't half so cute!

NELL (*smiling*). That's true as gospel, but don't tell Mis' Simmons I said so! Now, I'm goin' to come in tomorrow after my office work, and bring one of Jimmy's old jumpers. They're just the thing for a creepin' baby and yours is gettin' too big for dresses, Mis' Baxter!

MRS. BAXTER (*pleased and absorbed*).

D'ye think so, Cap'n? Ye see the kid only wears one o' them little white slips. It's so nice an' cool. An' awful easy to do up!

NELL (*going toward the door of the flat with* MRS. BAXTER). You jes' wait till yer see the jumpers! Honest, Jimmy was so glad to get into them—why, I remember as well as if it was yesterday when—

MRS. BAXTER (*at the door*). My man —he's off with that—

NELL (*interrupting*). You've got his baby, Mis' Baxter, an' that's the best of him!

MRS. BAXTER. I know! An' he'll come back—he always does! What's the likes o' *her* know 'bout holdin' onto a man? I'll keep some supper hot for him—the dirty brute! (*She disappears upstairs.*)

(*By this time, it has been gradually growing darker. The arc lights are now burning, strong white light is thrown on the groups at the corners, and, during this scene, a lamplighter lights the gas lights at the front corners. Lights begin to appear at various windows.*)

FRAU SCHMIDT. Nell!

(NELL, *who has accompanied* MRS. BAXTER *to the door and who is now returning to the Hall, looks back.*)

NELL. Yes? Oh, I didn't see you, Frau Schmidt. Gettin' cooler, isn't it?

FRAU SCHMIDT. There is a friend waiting for you, mein liebchen, ofer there.

NELL (*looking across the street*).— Why—oh! (*She hurries back.*) It *is* you, Myrtle! I didn't recognize you at first—it's gettin' so dark without the arc lights!

MYRTLE. I'm on my way to the People's Stock. It's *Sappho* this week—a swell play! Ever seen it? (NELL *shakes her head.*) Awful sad an' emotional, ye know! Miss De Vere D'Arcy's wearin'

some o' my mos' superb gowns! Say, Nell, can't ye dodge the meetin' an' come with me?

NELL. Oh, no—I—did the boy go by with the extras? I thought I heard him calling. Seems to me they ought to be—

MYRTLE. Aw, ferget it! Snatch a good time fer once in yer life!

NELL. It's good of you, Myrtle, but— the late edition ought to be out by now!

MYRTLE (*coaxing*). I want ye to see the gown Miss D'Arcy wears in the second ac'. Mauve spangles cut princess with a four-foot train, an' a big silver butterfly on the left shoulder! Hones' to goodness, it's worth ten meetin's just to see that one gown! I got it from a real prominent lady whose husbend went up the spout last May. By the time she's outer mournin', nobody'll be seen dead in a princess, so she—you'll come, Nell, won't ye?

NELL (*smiling*). Sorry, but I can't, Myrtle!

MYRTLE (*with a warning tone*). Yer gettin' sort o' green in the face from too much prayin'! Now a little goes a long way, *I* think—

NELL. Yes—don't it? A long way!

MYRTLE (*rising*). Well, if I can't make ye give yerself a treat, I s'pose I may as well be goin'!

NELL (*finding a paper on ground*). Oh, there it is! That's what I've been— (*She takes it and tries to read it.*) waitin' for. It's the last extra, isn't it? I wonder if the—

MYRTLE. Ye can't read in this light! Wot yer after? (*Pause*) Yer actin' awful nutty tonight. Don't yer hear me talkin' to you?

NELL (*still trying to read the paper*). Di'mond robbery. Myrtle, have they caught anyone?

MYRTLE. Naw! The detectives are

stung all the way round. The latest is, the whole gang's sailed for Europe. They think they spotted Hurdman at the dock, but he got off. It cer'nly makes interestin' readin', don't it?

NELL. Is that all—t'night?

MYRTLE. The fact is the p'lice are all up in the air; they don't know a thing about it. It's—

NELL. You're sure that's all? There ain't—there hasn't been nothin'—

MYRTLE (*continuing*). It's my private opinion that the gang's stayin' right here in the city, waitin' for the whole thing to blow over— (MAJOR WILLIAMS *enters from the Hall.* MYRTLE *stops. Distantly*) How'd ye do?

MAJOR (*after he has bowed slightly to* MYRTLE). Oh, there you are, Captain! I wanted to speak to you about Ensign Mark!

NELL. He's sick. I meant to have told ye. I'm forgettin' everythin' today!

MAJOR (*cheerfully*). That makes three men short. I'll tell Dick to bring the drum. They ought to practice a little before the meeting.

MYRTLE. Well, Nelly, I'm sorry ye won't come with me! (*Giggling a little nervously. To the* MAJOR) Awful hot, ain't it, this evenin'? Don't you let Nelly go have a sunstroke or anythin'! Will ye? (*To* NELL *as she lifts her skirts*) Say, Nell, in case ye ever need a real stylish weddin' gown, jus' remember Six Av'oo an' little Eva! (*Slight pause*) I got one I might a' used myself! (*She sighs.*) I've only rented it twice, so it's as good as new. You'd never notice the spots at night, and that's the main thing. Well, s'long! (*She trails away with a parting smile of exceeding sweetness. The* MAJOR *and* NELL *look at each other. He smiles sympathetically.*)

PADDY (*who has been for sometime staring at* NELL, *speaking in a hoarse voice*). Wotcher wear that sort o' lid for?

MAJOR (*smiling*). Because she spends her time helping anyone that will let her.

PADDY (*eagerly to* NELL). Say, would yer do somethin' fer me?

NELL. Yes, of course, I will, if I can! What do you want me to do?

PADDY. Well, there's a kid playin' craps down the corner, an' he owes me twenty cents but he won't pay me 'cause he's bigger'n me. (*A pause*) Say, will yer hold him while I bust his face? (*The* MAJOR *turns away suddenly, his shoulders shaking.*)

NELL (*who is troubled*). Oh, I couldn't do that! P'raps he hasn't got any money himself!

PADDY (*regretfully*). Yer don't know that kid!

MAJOR (*turning again*). Are you talking straight?

PADDY. Sure! He's a cheesy Ike, he is!

MAJOR (*whimsically*). Who says medieval life is dead? (*To* PADDY) Tomorrow morning you ask him again if he'll pay you—don't swear at him if you can help it! If he says no, invite him into the alley over there, and I'll bet on you every time!

PADDY. Will ye come an' see he don't do no sluggin' nor kickin'?

MAJOR. Of course I will! Just let me know when the battle is to be, and I'll bring it off according to the best Marquis of Queensberry style!

PADDY. You remember now! (*Suddenly catching sight of something on the corner, back, with a shrill whistle*) Aw—say! Lemme in the game! (*He rushes away toward the corner where the little* BOYS *again begin playing craps.*)

NELL (*walking about nervously*).

Yer not goin' ter help 'em fight—are you?

MAJOR. Indeed I am! There's nothing like it—when you're on the right side!

NELL. I never can tell when yer laughin' at me or when you're not!

MAJOR (*smiling*). What's the difference? (*Tenderly*) Sit down. You've been tired all day, and the meeting 'll take every bit of strength you have left!

NELL (*sitting down on the chair*). Oh, no, I'm all right!

MAJOR. I oughtn't to let you work half as hard!

NELL (*with a slight movement of her hands*). It ain't the work!

MAJOR (*suddenly*). Has that man been troubling you again? You told me he's left you for good and all.

NELL. I haven't seen him since that night!

MAJOR. He hasn't been bothering you in any way?

NELL. I don't know where he is—and it's jus' that that's killin' me!

MAJOR (*puzzled*). Why—Oh—I see. (*Sympathetically*) It's the uncertainty! (*She nods, speechless.*) But he's gone, really gone, Captain Nell! Think of him as if he were dead!

NELL. I can't—'nless I know he *is* dead!

MAJOR. Nerves, hard work, hot weather, Captain Nell, wherever he is, you've sent him there and he'll never come back!

NELL (*lashed to remembrance, with an involuntary cry*). Oh! (*A scream*) I know, I—sent him there an' he'll never come back!

MAJOR. What's the matter?

(NELL *controlling herself, and shaking her head. She cannot speak.*)

MAJOR (*sitting on the step beside* NELL's *chair*). I think you've been avoiding me this last week. I want to tell you something. I tried to that night at your flat, you know, but I didn't have a chance to finish. First, I want to tell you a little tale of the Hans Andersen type—you remember?

NELL. A story?

MAJOR. It's about a prince, of course, a prince foolish enough to believe that life was all beautiful and people all true. Well, one night he woke up from his dream, which had turned into a nightmare—and faced the world again. It wasn't very easy—for the fellow's heart was considerably damaged, and, as for his soul—why, he didn't have any!

NELL. Is that all?

MAJOR. Oh, no! One night he'd been through—well, what he called the hell of a time! Everything seemed a great bore, and the dawn found him sitting on a bench in a little park—rather conspicuous perhaps—in his palace clothes, but then he was beyond that. After a while he noticed that beside him sat another man not much older than himself—*he* wasn't a prince—oh, far from it! A sort—of—beggar, we'll say. Suddenly the beggar lifted his head from his hands and took something out of his pocket. The prince couldn't see clearly in the gray twilight, but he heard the beggar say to himself, "Well, time's up. S'long, old sport!" and the fellow just managed to knock up the man's hand before he could use what was in it. The spatterings burnt the prince's patent leather—no, I'm losing atmosphere! Well, the prince and the beggar had a long chat and it ended in their going to their—er—palace, and eating a great deal of breakfast!

NELL. And then what happened?

MAJOR. The beggar is now assisting in the care of the—royal motors—you see he's given up sitting on benches in the early mornings. And he's getting rather stout and very haughty!

NELL. And the prince, what happened to him?

MAJOR. After breakfast the prince found that they weren't nearly so unhappy as they fancied they were—talking with the beggar had cheered him up, no name! So he thought and thought—and at last decided to—well, to make a business of talking with beggars. And he did! Of course, the royal family didn't wholly approve of such eccentricities on the part of the kingdom's heir! In fact, they considered it quite insane!

NELL. Oh, no, he was very sensible!

MAJOR. I'm glad someone gives him a good word. And here comes the point of the whole story. You remember the prince's heart was cracked? Oh, yes, distinctly—a piece of damaged goods! Well, he never hoped to mend it. To tell you the truth, I expect he didn't want to—he rather liked it that way. But, after a while—he met a small person who always carried in her hand a marvelous little pot of patent cement—and—

NELL. But she was a beggar, too!

MAJOR. No, *she* was a good fairy! Just wait and see! She took his heart without so much as asking for it and after it had time to dry—there it was, as good as new! But the prince was quite polite, so he said, "Pray don't bother about returning it—keep it always, just as a souvenir." You see the crack was mended, after all!

NELL. It's a lovely story, Major—but, I don't want to hear any more!

MAJOR. I love Captain Nell!

NELL. You mustn't say things like that, Major. No, ye mustn't!

MAJOR. Why not?

NELL. I'm not good enough fer yer! Ye deserve somebody better—oh, much

better than I could ever dream o' bein'! And besides—

MAJOR. Besides what?

NELL. There's Jim! And now—I'd better tell ye something, Major Williams, I'm not good like what you think. I'm not strong! I can't walk in the straight path. I can't keep my eyes on God. It nearly kills me to say it—but—it's true!

MAJOR. Nonsense—now listen! (*A hand organ strikes up "Waltz Me Around Again, Willie." The* MAJOR *rises.*) I'll go on some other time! (*He makes a gesture toward the organ, which is surrounded by dancing children. By now, it is almost night. The street lamps and windows give practically all the light.*)

MRS. SPRATT (*calling to the children from the fire escape*). Sal-ly! Sal-ly!

SALLY (*stopping and screaming back*). What?

MRS. SPRATT. Where's the beer I sent ye fer?

SALLY (*who has a small tin pail in her hand, crossly*). I'm a-gettin' it! (*She goes into the bar, right.*)

(HALLELUJAH MAGGIE *comes out from the Hall and joins* NELL *and the* MAJOR.)

MAGGIE. It's after seven-thirty, Major. It's hot this evening! We oughter have a good open air!

MAJOR. I wish ninety in the shade and righteousness went together, but I'm afraid they don't!

MAGGIE (*smiling*). Cheer up! I got a feelin' in my bones they will ter night!

PETE (*from the corner, seeing* MAGGIE). Sa-ay, kids, here's the old girl!

(*All the children begin to gather about her. The* MAJOR *and* NELL, *smiling, exit into the Hall, left.*)

SUSIE (*with a baby*). Tell us a story!

MAGGIE (*kindly*). Too late now.

PADDY (*insinuatingly*). Tell us how

you gave 'em hell down in McCloskey's bar!

MAGGIE. I didn't give 'em hell. I offered 'em heaven! When you're grown up, you'll know the difference!

PEGGY (*calling shrilly to a companion across the street*). She's goin' ter tell us a story.

MAGGIE (*laughing*). Well, it was this way. I come into McCloskey's bar with a bundle of *War Cries* under my arm, an' McCloskey, he says ter me, "You get out o' this joint, Maggie O'Sullivan, or I'll sick this here bull-dawg on ye"—only his languidge was worse'n that. An' then he showed me a great big red-eyed bull-dawg, jus' tearin' at his chain, he was so wild ter get at me. But I says, "Jo Mc-Closkey," says I— (*She stops, looks hard at* JIM, *who has slouched down. She does not recognize him. He is in far worse condition than in the preceding act. Anguish, fear, terror that he may have killed* NELL *are revealed in every feature, tone, and gesture. He is changed utterly. After satisfying herself that she does not know this stranger, she continues.*) "Jo McCloskey," says I, "God is bigger than that bull-dawg"— (*Again she pauses and looks at* JIM, *now quite close to her.*)

JIM (*nervously noticing her interest*). Wot time's the meetin'? (*His voice is changed, hoarse and full of fear.*)

MAGGIE (*looking at him hard*). They'll be out directly with the band. Open air on this corner!

JIM (*still nervous*). Who's a-goin' ter speil?

MAGGIE (*trying to recall him*). Seem's if I'd seen yer before, but I can't—

JIM (*roughly in anguish and terror, almost a wild cry in his voice*). I ask ye— Who's goin' ter speil?

MAGGIE. Major Williams, Cap'n Sanders an' myself. Why?

(*A pause. The revulsion and the shock of relief almost overpower the man.*)

JIM (*faintly, weakly, falteringly*). Cap'n Sanders, did ye say?

MAGGIE. Sure! Salvation Nell!

JIM (*in the same tone*). She's all right? Nothin' the matter with her?

MAGGIE. She was sick a couple o' days las' week, but—

JIM. She's been 'round here? She weren't hurt bad?

MAGGIE (*puzzled*). Hurt? Say, wotter yer mean?

JIM (*pulling himself together*). Nothin'!

MAGGIE. I certainly hev seen you before! D'you remember where 't' was?

JIM (*in a surly tone*). How do *I* know? Might-a-been anywhere!

MAGGIE (*suddenly*). Wait! I got it! Yer Nell's old feller! Yer Jim!

JIM. Yeah—

MAGGIE (*looking at him*). Wotcher want 'round here?

JIM (*sullenly*). I want ter see her!

MAGGIE. Wot for?

JIM (*sullenly*). That's my biz!

MAGGIE. I tell ye she's been sick.

JIM. An' about three words from me'll get her well quicker 'n anything else!

PEGGY (*turning away disconsolately*). She ain't goin' ter finish the story!

(*The other* CHILDREN *follow suit with some mutterings. They are all soon playing again in the street.*)

MAGGIE. Ye can't see her now—she's goin' ter lead the meetin'!

(*Meanwhile the Major has entered, left, and has been peering about for* MAGGIE. *He sees her and crosses the street.*)

MAJOR (*as* JIM *slinks back into the*

shadow). Oh, Ensign, have you a key to the closet where Mark keeps his drum? I have to get it out for Dick. (*He sees* JIM. *Sharply*) Who's that?

MAGGIE (*confused*). That? Why, it's jus' man who—wanted to find out—

MAJOR (*decisively*). I know!

MAGGIE. I'll get the key. (*She exits into the Hall.*)

MAJOR (*to* JIM). Come out here where we can see each other. (JIM *slowly and sullenly obeys. The* MAJOR *continues firmly.*) What are you after?

JIM. I want to see—her! (*He makes a gesture toward the Hall.*)

MAJOR. What do you want to say?

JIM (*furiously*). Wotter you all buttin' in for? I want ter say what I dam' please, an' that's enough!

MAJOR (*still and cold*). She doesn't want to see you. Is that plain?

JIM. Dam' lie!

MAJOR. Clear out or I'll telephone for the police!

JIM (*sneering*). That's right! Crawl behind the cops! Ye hymn-singin' sissy, ye!

(*The* MAJOR *turns silently and quickly to cross the street.*)

JIM (*beseechingly*). Say, Mister, wait a sec'. Wot's yer hurry? I ain't said I wasn't goin'!

MAJOR (*turns to him and continues sharply*). Well?

JIM (*his voice breaking slightly*). I'll go, after I seen—after I seen that she's all right! There's somethin' I want t' tell her an' then I'm goin' fer keeps!

MAJOR. Is that the truth?

JIM (*angrily again*). I don't give a hoot in hell whether ye think I'm lyin' or not! Wot I want is five minutes with her! She's my girl! She was my girl before you ever laid eyes on her! An' she'll always be my girl, dam' ye! I don't care wot ye say!

MAJOR (*quietly*). Do you love her?

JIM (*sullenly*). Mebbe I do an' mebbe I don't!

MAJOR. If you love her you'll go off quietly and never let her see you again!

JIM (*furiously*). I know! Yer after her yerself! Of course ye want t' get me out the way, o' course! Well, I'm not goin'! See? I'm not goin' t' leave my girl fer any Gawd-blasted slob t' grab up 's soon's I'm out o' the way!

MAJOR (*quickly*). She's not your girl! You may have done what you wanted with her—back there—before her soul was born. But now, what do you know of her? Nothing, worse than nothing! If I told you she's found herself at last, if I told you she's rising to the heights of greatness, could you understand what I mean? Look at the glory of her future! Leading thousands toward the truth and the light— the head of an army that'll conquer the world! And you call her your girl!

JIM. Quit it!

MAJOR. Look at yourself! What are you, anyway? A barroom loafer, a big drunken, sodden animal, with no sense of anything, except a glass of whiskey! Now look here, pull yourself together, if you can, and then get out of her way. Don't try to soil her as she marches toward her splendid goal!

JIM (*breaking out*). I don't care! It may be so—all that! I know she's different now—and I ain't nothin' like her—but there's only one thing ye haven't said, an' that is, no matter what I am, she loves me just the same!

MAJOR (*fiercely*). *Loves* you?

JIM (*triumphantly*). She always has an' she always will, so d'ye think I'll go off an' hand her over to ye? My girl—I guess not!

MAJOR. Why did you say—this is the last time you want to see her?

JIM (*desperately*). It is! If she tells me to go—well, I'm goin'!—

MAJOR. You're lying!

JIM. I'm tellin' ye the truth! Only —when you say—it gets me so I don't know wot I'm doin'!

(*Band hymns begin softly in Hall.*)

MAJOR (*with sudden decision*). I believe you. Wait here! (*He offers his hand squarely.* JIM *refuses and turns away into the shadow of the doorway, as he mutters an oath. Meanwhile, all the girls, children, and loafers have gathered on the sidewalks to watch the Army set forth.*)

(*The color-bearers with the Army and U.S. flags, have come out first and stand with the colors crossed above the door. Following these, several* OFFICERS *and* SALVATIONISTS *of both sexes. Then come* NELL *and* MAGGIE.)

MAJOR (*as he stands under the street lamp, puts his hand on* NELL'S *arm*). Captain Nell, I want to ask you a question!

NELL. (*in sudden alarm*). What is it, Major Williams?

MAJOR (*controlling his voice*). Do you still love that man? (NELL *looks him full in the face and is silent. After a slight pause, he continues.*) I ought to have guessed it! (*Closing his lips firmly*) Then you must get ready for the hardest moment of your life!

NELL (*staring at him*). What do ye mean?

MAJOR (*tenderly*). You remember what Ensign Maggie keeps saying? "The readier you are to meet everything, the easier it will be for you when anything comes along." (*Taking both her hands in his*) Well, here's the chance to show God what eight years of salvation have done for you!

NELL (*with a cry*). They've got him!

MAJOR. What?

NELL. The police have got him!

MAJOR. He's here! (NELL *cries out again. She turns her eyes to him, as he continues.*) Across the street!

(*The hymn ceases. The* BAND *comes out from the Hall. The members of the band enter two by two, in uniform, carrying their instruments.*) Stay here while we're marching. (*Pats her hand.*) God bless you! God bless you! (*He releases her hand and joins the others, a little further back. Business of all upon stage. To leader of band*) That hymn ought to go faster. Remember now!

(*The* BAND *strikes up "Onward Christian Soldiers" and, preceded by the* OFFICERS, *marches, toward right back, amid cries of "Here we go!" "Forward March!" a few loud laughs, etc. Little children strut proudly behind, the Salvation Army turns to the right, and passes out of sight; the music gradually grows fainter. The crowd has followed it, so that now, with the exception of one or two loafers at the saloon corner, who soon disappear for a drink, the little side street is quite empty. A certain amount of life, however, is still going on in the background and in the windows and the doorways.* NELL *is left standing vaguely under the street light on the corner.* JIM *is under the shadow of* FRAU SCHMIDT'S *doorway, directly opposite her. As the music and the crowd's voices grow fainter, she crosses the street slowly and hesitatingly to where he is. Just as she reaches the opposite sidewalk, he comes out from the shadow into the glare of the street light directly above.*)

NELL (*whispering*). Jim?

JIM (*understanding her completely*). I wasn't in it, Nell. I swear t' Gawd I didn't go!

NELL (*weakly*). Oh— (*She staggers, but he catches her in his arms. She recovers herself and draws away.*) It's been a week—I didn't know anythin'—'cept what they had in the papers. Oh, Jim, I thank God!

JIM. It don't make no diff' to *you*, does it?

NELL (*smiling tearfully*). Where—have ye been?

JIM (*sullenly*). Bummin' around! Ye gave me cold feet that night—I dunno why—I never kept my date with Barney. Jus' let the whole thing go like a dam' kid!

NELL (*fervently*). I know what kept ye safe!

JIM (*roughly*). I thought I might a' laid ye out for keeps that trip, so I jus' come 'round ter—ter see! That's all!

NELL. Yer not all bad, Jim! There was somethin' that kept ye from harm that night.

JIM. Oh, ye had me on toast—I'm not sayin' ye hadn't, am I?

NELL. The good in ye knocked out the bad *once*! Ye can't ever forget it! Sometime ye'll save yer soul rememberin'!

JIM (*impatient of what he considers her personal triumph*). I tell ye, ye busted up my tracks fer fair, jus' when I was on the make! If ye hadn't got me dippy that night, I'd a-been a rich man t'day!

NELL. No, ye wouldn't—Jim!

JIM (*belligerently*). Yes, I would! A rich man! D'ye think they'll ever nab Barney! He's got 'em jus' where he wants—Europe! Shucks! He's in 'Frisco by this time, divvyin' up! (*Furiously*) An' if it weren't fer you, I'd be with him now gettin' my share!

NELL. Ye kept from sin that night! An' ye came back t' see if I was—Jim, God's guidin' ye! Ye've got t' go ahead!

JIM. Say, le's cut out that line o' talk. I got a job on a cattle boat goin' South. There's some fellers in New

Orleans that'll put me on t' all the hauls I can carry!

NELL. Ye've given up already? No, I won't believe it—God wouldn't let ye!

JIM. Well, I don't see how He can stop me!

NELL (*almost breaking down*). Oh, it can't be that way! There must be some chance left!

JIM. One thing more b'fore I go. Wot about that Major—that mug-faced slob that act 's if he owned you?

NELL. Jim—ye don't know—

JIM (*hoarsely*). I know that I'm a man an' he's one, too—dam' him! An' yer a woman—so b'fore I go, I want ye t' say, "Ye've been my feller, an' I'll never let no one take yer place."

NELL (*faintly*). There ain't no need!

JIM. I'll make ye say it b'fore I go!

NELL (*putting her hand on his arm and looking him full in the face*). Yer my Jim—an' no one'll ever take yer place!

JIM (*with a subdued cry, pressing her to him*). Nelly—I won't leave ye!

NELL (*gently disengaging herself and speaking tenderly, but firmly*). Yes, Jim, ye must! I see things clear now. I can't help ye—any more!

JIM (*hungrily*). I love ye, Nelly!

NELL (*sadly*). I know, Jim. An' as fer me, why I'd give up my soul, if it would do ye any good! But it wouldn't —not a bit! I've learnt that now!

JIM. Don't ye know how a man feels?

NELL. Oh, it seems as if I was talkin' from a long ways off an' nothin' I can say'll make much diff'rence! There's a river between us, Jim—an' there ain't no bridge!

JIM. Wot river?

NELL (*tenderly*). Ye wouldn't understand!

(*The music of the band is heard far away, gradually growing nearer.*)

I s'pose this is the last time we'll meet, Jim. If I could only make ye see just a little—before ye go!

JIM. See wot?

NELL. The reason why we have t' say "Good-by." Jim, d'ye remember how we met each other first?

JIM. Dunno's I do—it's a long time ago.

NELL. In that little eating place where I worked b'fore I came to Sid's. Ye used to come in ev'ry day an' sit at the same table. After a while I sort o' grew to expect ye. I think I'd been lovin' ye a long time b'fore I knew it myself—I was awful young then. One night ye came in drunk—the first time I'd seen ye that way! An'— (*She hesitates.*)

JIM (*interrupting*). Wot's the good o' remembering all that?

NELL (*going on*). An' I couldn't help myself, Jim! I did whatever ye wanted—always, without a single question! I thought that was what love meant!

JIM. I didn't treat ye bad, did I?

NELL. When ye hadn't been drinkin' it was all right. But then ye drank so much! Jim, there's only one time when we really were happy!

JIM. When was that?

NELL. The Sunday we went into the country. D'ye remember? It was in June some time, an' I had a day off. I'd saved up fer weeks t' get a new hat, an' thought it was awful stylish! We took our dinner with us—done up in a shoe box—an' we went across the river an' got a trolley way into the country! D'ye know, Jim, it was the first time I'd ever been out o' the city! Why, it seemed like heaven! Ye remember that big tree where we had our dinner? An' how ye talked t' that old farmer? An' me gettin' big bunches o' flowers t' take home with me? I made ye wear one in yer buttonhole, but ye didn't want to a bit! Why, that Sunday—I've never forgotten it! (*She goes off into a sort of revery.*)

JIM. Sure, I remember! That old jay-bird out there! Gee, it seems the hell of a long time since, don't it?

NELL. That was our only glimpse, Jim, of the green fields! Oh, how short it was!

JIM (*uncomfortable*). Nell, we couldn't a-kept *livin'* out there!

NELL. No, we had t' come back—t' the city streets, an' work—an' drink!

JIM. Ye talk's if *I* could help it!

NELL (*very tenderly*). Dear, I'm not blamin' you—I'm not even blamin' myself. We was just like heaps o' others. 'Twasn't our fault!

JIM. Well, what about it then?

NELL. After that awful fire at Sid's, I thought I hated you, Jim, an' underneath it all, I wanted ye in the same old way. Then I found God, an' when I came out into the light I was all diff'rent! D'ye know, Jim, what kept a-comin' to my mind then? Our day out there—across the river. Somehow I felt, "That's the real Jim. The other's —someone else, I don't know who." An' it was only then, Jim, I began t' love ye!

JIM (*incredulous*). Ye *began!*

NELL. I wanted t' save ye! (*After a pause, tenderly*) That's love!

JIM (*uncomfortably*). Lovin' ain't the same as prayin'!

NELL. I thought God would let me be the one to raise you up. But I know now that I can't. It's our love that stands between us!

JIM (*passionately*). I ain't got no one else but you!

NELL (*solemnly*). I can't save ye, Jim, but God will! He'll choose his time and place.

JIM (*wildly*). Wot d' I care 'bout bein' saved?

NELL.. All I can do 's my own work. God'll take care o' the rest! Ye can't get away from Him, Jim—sooner or later He'll lead ye to salvation, an' then I want ye t' remember one thing! We've lost each other in this life, but, dear, this life ain't all! Some day we'll meet soul to soul—oh, I believe it's comin', comin' with a hallelujah that'll break the skies! An' then, Jim, we'll be together—always!

JIM (with a despairing cry). But I want ye now!

NELL. (unsteadily as she holds out her hand). Good-by, Jim, until then!

JIM. D'ye know wot yer throwin' me into? D'ye know wot I'm goin' to do?

NELL.. I'll pray fer ye—Jim!

JIM (recklessly). Dam' yer prayers!

NELL. Don't let them be the last words—

JIM (between his teeth). Hell! (He turns his back and slouches away toward the bar, which he enters.)

(Just then the music breaks from around the corner and the BAND, OF-FICERS, etc., with the crowd trailing along beside and behind, appear on the side street. The BAND forms a circle, to the left, in front of the Hall, and nearly on the corner. The crowd is massed opposite the Hall and across the little side street. NELL stands under the street lamp, where JIM has left her. MAJOR WILLIAMS comes hastily to her before the music has stopped.)

MAJOR. Has he gone? Is it over?

NELL (turning suddenly at the sound of his voice). What? Yes—he's gone! Are they ready?

MAJOR. If you feel you can.

NELL (trying to smile). I'm all right—

MAJOR (reverently). God's light is in your eyes!

(Together, the MAJOR and NELL return to the circle made by the BAND; the OFFICERS stand within this circle.

There is a very simple portable pulpit for the speakers—more of a wooden box than anything else. The crowd is expectant and still. All through this scene, the speakers are characterized by utter unconsciousness, simplicity, and fervor. Occasionally, there are distracting noises—calls, laughs, rattling of wheels, etc.—in the street beyond; but these disturbances serve only to emphasize the street-corner enthusiasm and sincerity. The crowd is stolid but attentive. The BAND stops playing.)

(The MAJOR takes off his hat and slightly raises his head; his eyes close. The arc light falls upon his face as he continues.) Father, bless this meeting! Make us right in our hearts and our minds so that we can show Thy light to all here who stumble through the blackness of suffering and sin.

("That's right," "That's right!" is wrung from the lips of MAGGIE and other OFFICERS, all of whom are praying.)

Sin has touched us all! Blot it out, O, God, blot it out this night, and give Thy rest and Thy peace to every tired soul! Amen!

(His "Amen" is echoed aloud by NELL and the other OFFICERS, and a few members of the BAND. The MAJOR and the other MEN—officers, band, etc.—put on their hats. The crowd throughout has gazed quietly and attentively. The MAJOR glances at NELL; she steps forward simply and mounts the improvised pulpit. There is a rustle of interest in the crowd.)

NELL (earnestly and tenderly). My frien's, I've got nothin' new to say to ye; it's the old old story I've told ye so many times before. Christ was a poor man Himself, an' He chose poor people for His frien's. He knows how hard we have to work ter keep alive. He knows how strong an' terrible our temptations are. An' He pities us because we're His brothers an' sisters—every one of us, I don' care how wicked nor how low!

MAGGIE. Yes, yes!

NELL *(going on)*. The rich people have big, splendid churches to worship Him in, but we have our hearts an He likes them just as well, an' even though we *are* poor an' hungry an' sinful, He died to save us—He *has* saved us, if only we'll love an' b'lieve in Him more'n anythin' else!

MAJOR. Amen!

NELL. *(continuing)*. Ye can't get Christ by thinkin' or by askin' other people or by readin' lots o' books—the only way is t' open yer hearts an' feel Him enter in!

MAGGIE. Hallelujah!

MCGLONE *(emerging from the saloon, taking in the scene and howling back just as NELL goes on)*. Say! Come on out! Salvation Nell's givin' it to 'em again!

(During the following, the MEN, half drunk and laughing noisily, are beginning to come out from the bar, and to stand on the corner opposite NELL, under the other arc light. JIM is among the last to appear; he is heavy with drink and excitement. As she sees them—and finally JIM—her words take on a new intensity, a new fire. Before long it is evident that she is speaking to him alone.)

NELL. If everyone only let Christ do what He pleased with 'em, we'd have Heaven right here in N'York. The people that go to church all their lives and never done a thing to be ashamed of—well, p'raps they don't know Him as well's you an' me. He has to help us such an awful lot that we jus' naturally make friends with Him!

MAJOR. Hallelujah!

NELL *(increasing in feeling)*. Some of ye may say, we didn't get no chance, an' the world's against us, an' even with Christ on our side we haven't a show! But let me tell ye now that it's *you* Christ waits for! His followers and workers! *Your* souls are the souls that count! You've sunk to the bottom, you know the bitterness and the cruelty of life, an' it's to *you* Christ wants to show the beauty an' the glory an' the light. When you an' me who have fallen rise again, we're greater than our sins, we're bigger men and women than if we'd never sinned at all!

MAJOR *and* MAGGIE. Yes! Yes! Hallelujah!

NELL *(continuing)*. Don't ye think I know? Don't ye think I've borne it all myself? The black misery, the awful agony of body and soul together, an' then—Thank God! The knowledge that I was saved, the power to throw my past behind me, and walk in the Light—with my eyes on Heaven an' my back on Hell!

MAJOR. Praise the Lord!

MAGGIE. Hallelujah!

NELL. An' let me tell ye, my frien's, there's battles that's the same on Fifth Avenue as they are down here! Sometimes we find our sin—our terrible sin—is what we love most in the world! It seems as if we couldn't tear it off—it's flesh of our flesh an' soul of our soul! But, oh! when we've killed it with our own two hands, when we've conquered in that awful fight, when we've nailed our bleeding heart to the Cross itself—why it seems as if all the millions who have fought and conquered since time began stretch out their arms to us in pity! Those men an' women—down the river of the ages—they know, they understand! Because like us they've gone down into the darkest places an' found God's sunlight streaming there!

(*The* BAND *plays very softly and some of the* SALVATIONISTS *sing very softly throughout the following speech.*)

(*Her hands working*) "Though your sins be as scarlet, they shall be white as snow!" I didn't believe that once, but I know now that it's true! Oh, any of ye that's listenin' here tonight —that p'raps I'll never meet again till at the judgment bar of God! remember, it's Love that saves the world! They say it's strong as death, an' I know, ah, I know—it's strong as life! The Love that always pities, the Love that always forgives an' waits with open arms fer every wanderin' sinner to come an' know the joy that lasts for all eternity! (*Suddenly breaking into a passionate prayer of exaltation*) Oh, Christ, who some think can never feel the pains of age nor the secrets in a woman's soul—help all of us that need ye now, high and low, change our wickedness with yer own heart's blood, save us from ourselves—keep us pure an' clean an' strong forever—an' ever— O lamb of God who takes away the sins of the world! Amen. Amen. (*She stops, transfigured, her face still raised to the light which falls from the arc light above. At a word from the* MAJOR, *the hymn grows slightly louder. At the sound of the music,* NELL *recovers herself and steps from the little platform.* MAGGIE *hands her the tambourine as she passes.* MAJOR *mounts as she descends.*)

MAJOR (*to the crowd*). "Abide with Me." All sing while Captain Sanders takes the collection!

(NELL *passes through a crowd, which makes way for her, taking coins into the tambourine as she goes, until she has crossed the street and comes to where two* MEN *and* JIM *are standing on the corner. She silently offers them the tambourine in turn.*)

THE FIRST (*throwing in a bill*). Dam' it, yer all right!

THE SECOND (*shaking his head, his hands in his pockets*). Naw—I'm savin' my dough fer my wife! (*A laugh from the other men nearby.* NELL *turns her tambourine silently toward* JIM. *He looks in her face as he drops a coin.*)

JIM (*hoarsely*). Can't I see ye—after the meetin'? I want ye t' help me—

NELL. (*turning to him, her eyes blind with tears*). Ah!

JIM. I need ye—I need yer help!

NELL. Wait fer me, Jim. I'll meet ye here. I want ye to take me home. (*Holds out her hand, which he grasps. She passes from him toward the platform, where she joins the* MAJOR *and begins singing, her upraised face wet with tears.* JIM *stands looking after her, with longing and devotion in his figure.*)

THE SALVATIONISTS (*singing*).

Hold Thou Thy Cross before my
    closing eyes;
Shine through the gloom, and point
    me to the skies;
Heaven's morning breaks, and
    earth's black shadows flee:
In life, in death, O Lord, abide
    with me!

(JIM, *with an awkward gesture, takes off his hat and bows his head.*)

THE EASIEST WAY

Eugene Walter

First presented at the Hartford Opera House, Hartford, Connecticut, on December 31, 1908. The first New York performance was at the Belasco-Stuyvesant Theatre, under David Belasco's direction, on January 19, 1909, with Frances Starr as Laura Murdock.

LAURA MURDOCK   WILLARD BROCKTON

ELFIE ST. CLAIR   JOHN MADISON

ANNIE   JIM WESTON

ACT ONE

The scene is that of the summer country ranch house of MRS. WIL-LIAMS, *a friend of* LAURA MURDOCK's, *and a prominent society woman of Denver, perched on the side of Ute Pass, near Colorado Springs. The house is one of unusual pretentiousness, and to a person not conversant with conditions as they exist in this part of Colorado, the idea might be that such magnificence could not obtain in such a locality. At the left of stage, the house rises in the form of a turret, built of rough stone of a brown hue, two stories high, and projecting a quarter of the way out on the stage. The door leads to a small elliptical terrace built of stone, with heavy benches of Greek design, strewn with cushions, while over the top of one part of this terrace is suspended a canopy made from a Navajo blanket. The terrace is supposed to extend almost to the right of stage, and here it stops. The stage must be cut here so that the entrance of* JOHN *can give the illusion that he is coming up a steep declivity or a long flight of stairs. There are chairs at right and left, and a small table at left. There are trailing vines around the balustrade of the terrace, and the whole setting must convey the idea of quiet wealth. Up stage is supposed to be the part of the terrace overlooking the canyon, a sheer drop of two thousand feet, while over in the distance, as if across the canyon, one can see the rolling foothills and lofty peaks of the Rockies, with Pike's Peak in the distance, snow-capped and colossal. It is late in the afternoon, and as the scene progresses, the quick twilight of a canyon, beautiful in its tints of purple and amber, becomes later pitch black, and the curtain goes down on an absolutely black stage. The cyclorama, or semi-cyclorama, must give the perspective of greater distances, and be so painted that the various tints of twilight may be shown. AT RISE.* LAURA MURDOCK *is seen up right stage, leaning a bit over the balustrade of the porch and shielding her eyes with her hand from the late afternoon sun as she seemingly looks up the Pass to the left, as if expecting the approach of someone. Her gown is simple, girlish, and attractive, and made of summery, filmy stuff. Her hair is done up in the simplest fashion with a part in the center, and there is about her every indication of an effort to assume that girlishness of demeanor which has been her greatest asset through life.* WILLARD BROCKTON *enters from left; he is a man six feet or more in height, stocky in build, clean-shaven, and immaculately dressed. He is smoking a cigar, and upon entering takes one step forward and looks over toward* LAURA *in a semi-meditative manner.*

———

WILLARD. Blue?

LAURA. No.

WILLARD. What's up?

LAURA. Nothing.

WILLARD. A little preoccupied.

LAURA. Perhaps.

WILLARD. What's up that way?

LAURA. Which way?

WILLARD. The way you are looking.

LAURA. The road from Manitou Springs. They call it the trail out here.

WILLARD. I know that. You know I've done a lot of business west of the Missouri.

LAURA (*with a half-sigh*). No, I didn't know it.

WILLARD. Oh, yes; south of here in the San Juan country. Spent a couple of years there once.

LAURA (*still without turning*). That's interesting.

WILLARD. It was then. I made some money there. It's always interesting when you make money. Still —

LAURA (*still leaning in an absent-minded attitude*). Still what?

WILLARD. Can't make out why you have your eyes glued on that road. Someone coming?

LAURA. Yes.

WILLARD. One of Mrs. Williams' friends, eh? (*Goes up and sits down.*)

LAURA. Yes.

WILLARD. Yours too?

LAURA. Yes.

WILLARD. Man?

LAURA. Yes, a *real* man.

WILLARD (*catches the significance of this speech. He carelessly throws the cigar over the balustrade. He comes and leans on chair with his back to* LAURA. *She has not moved more than to place her left hand on a cushion and lean her head rather wearily against it, looking steadfastly up the Pass*). A real man. By that you mean —

LAURA. Just that — a real man.

WILLARD. Any difference from the many you have known?

LAURA. Yes, from all I have known.

WILLARD. So that is why you didn't come into Denver to meet me today, but left word for me to come out here?

LAURA. Yes.

WILLARD. I thought that I was pretty decent to take a dusty ride halfway across the continent in order to keep you company on your way back to New York, and welcome you to our home; but maybe I had the wrong idea.

LAURA. Yes, I think you had the wrong idea.

WILLARD. In love, eh?

LAURA. Yes, just that — in love.

WILLARD. A new sensation.

LAURA. No; the first conviction.

WILLARD. You have had that idea before. Every woman's love is the real one when it comes. Do you make a distinction in this case, young lady?

LAURA. Yes.

WILLARD. For instance, what?

LAURA. This man is poor — absolutely broke. He hasn't even got a (*Moves to armchair, leans over and draws with parasol on ground.*) good job. You know, Will, all the rest, including yourself, generally had some material inducement.

WILLARD. What's his business? (*Crosses to table and sits looking at magazine.*)

LAURA. He's a newspaper man.

WILLARD. H'm-m. Romance?

LAURA. Yes, if you want to call it that — romance.

WILLARD. Do I know him?

LAURA. How could you? You only came from New York today, and he has never been there.

(*He regards her with a rather amused, indulgent, almost paternal expression, in contrast to his big, bluff physical personality, with his iron-gray hair and his bulldog expression.* LAURA *looks more girlish than ever.*)

WILLARD. How old is he?

LAURA. Twenty-seven. You're forty-five.

WILLARD. No, forty-six.

LAURA. Shall I tell you about him? Huh? (*She goes to* WILLARD, *placing parasol on seat at the extreme left.*)

WILLARD. That depends.

LAURA. On what?

WILLARD. Yourself.

LAURA. In what way?

WILLARD. If it will interfere in the least with the plans I have made for you and for me.

LAURA. And have you made any particular plans for me that have anything particularly to do with you?

WILLARD. Yes, I have given up the lease of our apartment on West End Avenue, and I've got a house on Riverside Drive. Everything will be quiet and decent, and it'll be more comfortable for you. There's a stable near by, and your horses and car can be kept over there. You'll be your own mistress, and besides I've fixed you up for a new part.

LAURA. A new part! What kind of a part?

WILLARD. One of Charlie Burgess's shows, translated from some French fellow. It's been running over in Paris, Berlin, and Vienna, and all those places for a year or more, and appears to be an awful hit. It's going to cost a lot of money. I told Charlie he could put me down for a half interest, and I'd give all the money providing you got an important role. Great part, I'm told. Kind of a cross between a musical comedy and an opera. Looks as if it might stay in New York all season. So that's the change of plan. How does it strike you?

LAURA (goes to door, meditating; pauses in thought). I don't know.

WILLARD. Feel like quitting? (Turns to her.)

LAURA. I can't tell.

WILLARD. It's the newspaper man, eh?

LAURA. That would be the only reason.

WILLARD. You've been on the square with me this summer, haven't you? (Goes to table.)

LAURA (turns, looks at WILLARD). What do you mean by "on the square"?

WILLARD. Don't evade. There's only one meaning when I say that, and you know it. I'm pretty liberal. But you understand where I draw the line. You've not jumped that, have you, Laura?

LAURA. No, this has been such a wonderful summer, such a wonderfully different summer. Can you understand what I mean by that when I say "wonderfully different summer"? (Goes to WILLARD.)

WILLARD. Well, he's twenty-seven and broke, and you're twenty-five and pretty; and he evidently, being a newspaper man, has that peculiar gift of gab that we call romantic expression. So I guess I'm not blind, and you both think you've fallen in love. That it?

LAURA. Yes, I think that's about it; only I don't agree to the "gift of gab" and the "romantic" end of it. (Goes to table.) He's a man and I'm a woman, and we both have had our experiences. I don't think, Will, that there can be much of that element of what some folks call hallucination. (Sits on chair; takes candy-box on lap; selects candy.)

WILLARD. Then the Riverside Drive proposition and Burgess's show is off, eh?

LAURA. I didn't say that.

WILLARD. And if you go back on the Overland Limited day after tomorrow, you'd just as soon I'd go tomorrow or wait until the day after you leave?

LAURA (placing candy box back on table). I didn't say that, either.

WILLARD. What's the game?

LAURA. I can't tell you now.

WILLARD. Waiting for him to come?

LAURA. Exactly.

WILLARD. Think he is going to make a proposition, eh?

LAURA. I know he is.

WILLARD. Marriage?

LAURA. Possibly.

WILLARD. You've tried that once, and taken the wrong end. Are you going to play the same game again?

LAURA. Yes, but with a different card. (Picks up magazine off table.)

WILLARD. What's his name?

LAURA. Madison—John Madison. (*Slowly turning pages of magazine.*)

WILLARD. And his job?

LAURA. Reporter.

WILLARD. What are you going to live on—the extra editions?

LAURA. No, we're young, there's plenty of time. I can work in the meantime, and so can he; and then with his ability and my ability it will only be a matter of a year or two when things will shape themselves to make it possible.

WILLARD. Sounds well—a year off.

LAURA. If I thought you were going to make fun of me, Will, I shouldn't have talked to you. (*Throws down magazine, goes to door of house.*)

WILLARD. I don't want to make fun of you, but you must realize that after two years it isn't an easy thing to be dumped with so little ceremony. Maybe you have never given me any credit for possessing the slightest feeling, but even I can receive shocks from other sources than a break in the market.

LAURA (*goes to* WILLARD). It isn't easy for me to do this. You've been awfully kind, awfully considerate, but when I went to you it was just with the understanding that we were to be pals. You reserved the right then to quit me whenever you felt like it, and you gave me the same privilege. Now, if some girl came along who really captivated you in the right way, and you wanted to marry, it would hurt me a little,— maybe a lot —but I should never forget that agreement we made, a sort of two weeks' notice clause, like people have in contracts.

WILLARD (*he is evidently very much moved. Walks to end of seat, looks over the canyon.* LAURA *looks after him.* WILLARD *has his back to the audience. Long pause.*) I'm not hedging, Laura. If that's the way you want it

to be, I'll stand by just exactly what I said (*Turns to* LAURA.), but I'm fond of you, a damn sight fonder than I thought I was, now that I find you slipping away; but if this young fellow is on the square (LAURA *goes to* WILLARD, *taking his right hand.*) and he has youth and ability, and you've been on the square with him, why, all right. Your life hasn't had much in it to help you get a diploma from any celestial college, and if you can start out now and be a good girl, have a good husband, and maybe some day good children (LAURA *sighs.*), why, I'm not going to stand in the way. Only I don't want you to make any of those mistakes that you made before.

LAURA. I know, but somehow I feel that this time the real thing has come, and with it the real man. I can't tell you, Will, how much different it is, but everything I felt before seems so sort of earthly—and somehow this love that I have for this man is so different. It's made me want to be truthful and sincere and humble for the first time in my life. The only other thing I ever had that I cared the least bit about, now that I look back, was your friendship. We have been good pals, haven't we? (*Puts arms about* WILLARD.)

WILLARD. Yes, it's been a mighty good two years for me. I was always proud to take you around, because I think you one of the prettiest things in New York (LAURA *girlishly jumps into armchair.*), and that helps some, and you're always jolly, and you never complained. You always spent a lot of money, but it was a pleasure to see you spend it; and then you never offended me. Most women offend men by coming around looking untidy and sort of unkempt, but somehow you always knew the value of your beauty, and you always dressed up. I always thought that maybe some day the fellow would come along, grab you, and make you happy in a nice way, but I thought that he'd have to have a lot of money. You know you've lived a rather extravagant life for five years, Laura. It won't be an easy job to come down to cases and suffer for the little dainty necessities you've been used to.

LAURA. I've thought all about that, and I think I understand. (*Facing audience, leaning elbows on lap.*)

WILLARD. You know if you were working without anybody's help, Laura, you might have a hard time getting a position. As an actress you're only fair.

LAURA. You needn't remind me of that. That part of my life is my own. (*Goes up to seat.*) I don't want you to start now and make it harder for me to do the right thing. It isn't fair; it isn't square; and it isn't right. You've got to let me go my own way. (*Crosses to* WILLARD, *puts hand on his shoulder.*) I'm sorry to leave you, in a way, but I want you to know that if I go with John it changes the spelling of the word comradeship into love, and mistress into wife. Now, please don't talk any more. (*Crosses to post, takes scarf off chair.*)

WILLARD. Just a word. Is it settled?

LAURA (*impatiently*). I said I didn't know. I would know today—that's what I'm waiting for. Oh, I don't see why he doesn't come.

(WILLARD *turns, looking over the Pass.*)

WILLARD (*pointing up the Pass*). Is that the fellow coming up here?

LAURA (*quickly running toward the balustrade, speaks as she goes*). Where? (*Kneels on seat.*)

WILLARD (*pointing*). Up the road there. On that yellow horse.

LAURA (*looking*). Yes, that's John.

(*She waves her handkerchief and, putting one hand to her mouth, cries*) Hello!

JOHN (*off stage, giving the impression of being on the road winding up toward the house*). Hello, yourself!

LAURA (*same effect*). Hurry up, you're late.

JOHN (*same effect, a little louder*). Better late than never.

LAURA (*same effect*). Hurry up.

JOHN (*a little louder*). Not with this horse.

LAURA (*to* WILLARD, *with enthusiastic expression*). Now, Will, does he look like a yellow reporter?

WILLARD (*with a sort of sad smile*). He *is* a good-looking chap.

LAURA (*looking down again at* JOHN). Oh, he's just simply more than that. (*Turns quickly to* WILLARD.) Where's Mrs. Williams?

WILLARD (*motioning with thumb toward side of ranch house*). Inside, I guess, up to her neck in bridge.

LAURA (*goes hurriedly over to door*). Mrs. Williams! Oh, Mrs. Williams!

MRS. WILLIAMS (*heard off stage*). What is it, my dear?

LAURA. Mr. Madison is coming up the path.

MRS. WILLIAMS (*off stage*). That's good.

LAURA. Shan't you come and see him?

MRS. WILLIAMS (*same*). Lord, no! I'm six dollars and twenty cents out now, and up against an awful streak of luck.

LAURA. Shall I give him some tea?

MRS. WILLIAMS (*same*). Yes, do, dear; and tell him to cross his fingers when he thinks of me.

(*In the meantime,* WILLARD *has leaned over the balustrade, evidently surveying the young man, who is supposed to be coming up the path, with a great deal of interest. Underneath his stolid, businesslike demeanor of squareness, there is undoubtedly within his heart a very great affection for* LAURA. *He realizes that during her whole career he has been the only one who has influenced her absolutely. Since the time that they lived together he has always dominated, and he has always endeavored to lead her along a path that meant the better things of a Bohemian existence. His coming all the way from New York to Denver to accompany* LAURA *home was simply another example of his keen interest in the woman, and he suddenly finds that she has drifted away from him in a manner to which he could not in the least object, and that she had been absolutely fair and square in her agreement with him.* WILLARD *is a man who, while rough and rugged in many ways, possesses many of the finer instincts of refinement, latent though they may be, and his meeting with* JOHN *ought, therefore, to show much significance, because on his impressions of the young man depend the entire justification of his attitude in the play.*)

LAURA (*turning toward* WILLARD *and going to him, slipping her hand involuntarily through his arm and looking eagerly with him over the balustrade in almost girlish enthusiasm*). Do you like him?

WILLARD (*smiling*). I don't know him.

LAURA. Well, do you think you'll like him?

WILLARD. Well, I hope I'll like him.

LAURA. Well, if you hope you'll like him you ought to think you like him. He'll turn the corner of that rock in just a minute and then you can see him. Do you want to see him?

WILLARD (*almost amused at her girlish manner*). Why, yes — do you?

LAURA. Do I? Why, I haven't seen him since last night! There he is. (*Waves her hand.*) Hello, John! (*Gets candy box, throws pieces of candy at* JOHN.)

JOHN (*his voice very close now*). Hello, girlie! How's everything?

LAURA. Fine! Do hurry.

JOHN. Just make this horse for a minute. Hurry is not in his dictionary.

LAURA. I'm coming down to meet you.

JOHN. All — right.

LAURA (*turns quickly to* WILLARD). You don't care. You'll wait, won't you?

WILLARD. Surely.

(LAURA *hurriedly exits and disappears.*)

(*After a short interval,* LAURA *comes in more like a sixteen-year-old girl than anything else, pulling* JOHN *after her. He is a tall, finely built type of Western manhood, a frank face, a quick nervous energy, a mind that works like lightning, a prepossessing smile, and a personality that is wholly captivating. His clothes are a bit dusty from the ride, but are not in the least pretentious, and his leggings are of canvas and spurs of brass, such as are used in the army. His hat is off and he is pulled on to the stage from the entrance, more like a great big boy than a man. His hair is a bit tumbled, and he shows every indication of having had a rather long and hard ride.*)

LAURA. Hello, John!

JOHN. Hello, girlie!

(*Then she suddenly recovers herself and realizes the position that she is in. Both men measure each other for a moment in silence, neither flinching the least bit. The smile has faded from* JOHN's *face and the mouth droops into an expression of firm determination.* LAURA, *for a moment, loses her ingenuousness. She is the least bit fright-*

ened at finally placing the two men face to face, and speaks in a voice that trembles slightly from apprehension.)

LAURA. Oh, I beg your pardon! Mr. Madison, this is Mr. Brockton, a friend of mine from New York. You've often heard me speak of him; he came out here to keep me company when I go home.

JOHN (comes forward, extends a hand, looking WILLARD right in the eye). I am very glad to know you, Mr. Brockton.

WILLARD. Thank you.

JOHN. I've heard a great deal about you and your kindness to Miss Murdock. Anything that you have done for her in a spirit of friendliness I am sure all her friends must deeply appreciate, and I count myself in as one.

WILLARD (in an easy manner that rather disarms the antagonistic attitude of JOHN). Then we have a good deal in common, Mr. Madison, for I also count Miss Murdock a friend, and when two friends of a friend have the pleasure of meeting, I dare say that's a pretty good foundation for them to become friends too.

JOHN. Possibly. Whatever my opinion may have been of you, Mr. Brockton, before you arrived, now I have seen you — and I'm a man who forms his conclusions right off the bat — I don't mind telling you that you've agreeably surprised me. That's just a first impression, but they run kind o' strong with me.

WILLARD. Well, young man, I size up a fellow in pretty short order, and all things being equal, I think you'll do.

LAURA (radiantly). Shall I get the tea?

JOHN. Tea!

LAURA. Yes, tea. You know it must be tea — nothing stronger. (Goes to door.)

JOHN (looking at WILLARD rather comically). How strong are you for that tea, Mr. Brockton?

WILLARD. I'll pass; it's your deal, Mr. Madison.

JOHN. Mine! No, deal me out this hand.

LAURA. I don't think you're at all pleasant, but I'll tell you one thing — it's tea this deal or no game. (Goes to seat, picks up magazine, turns pages.)

WILLARD. No game then (goes to door), and I'm going to help Mrs. Williams; maybe she's lost nearly seven dollars by this time, and I'm an awful dub when it comes to bridge. (Exit.)

LAURA (tossing magazine on to seat, goes quickly to JOHN, and throws her arms around his neck in the most loving manner). JOHN!

(As the act progresses, the shadows cross the Pass and golden light streams across the lower hills and tops the snow-clad peaks. It becomes darker and darker, the lights fade to beautiful opalescent hues, until, when the curtain comes on the act, with JOHN and WILLARD on the scene, it is pitch dark, a faint glow coming out of the door. Nothing else can be seen but the glow of the ash on the end of each man's cigar as he puffs it in silent meditation.)

JOHN. Well, dear?

LAURA. Are you going to be cross with me?

JOHN. Why?

LAURA. Because he came?

JOHN. Brockton?

LAURA. Yes.

JOHN. You didn't know, did you?

LAURA. Yes, I did.

JOHN. That he was coming?

LAURA. He wired me when he reached Kansas City.

JOHN. Does he know?

LAURA. About us?

JOHN. Yes.

LAURA. I've told him.

JOHN. When?

LAURA. Today.

JOHN. Here?

LAURA. Yes.

JOHN. With what result?

LAURA. I think it hurt him.

JOHN. Naturally.

LAURA. More than I had any idea it would.

JOHN. I'm sorry. (Sits in armchair.)

LAURA. He cautioned me to be very careful and to be sure I knew my way.

JOHN. That was right.

LAURA (gets a cushion in each hand off seat; crosses to armchair, throws one cushion on ground, then the other on top of it, and kneels beside his chair; piano in house playing a Chopin nocturne). John.

JOHN. Yes.

LAURA. We've been very happy all summer.

JOHN. Very.

LAURA (rises, sits on arm of chair, her arm over back). And this thing has gradually been growing on us?

JOHN. That's true.

LAURA. I didn't think that when I came out here to Denver to play in a little stock company, it was going to bring me all this happiness, but it has, hasn't it?

JOHN. Yes.

LAURA (changing her position, sits on his lap, arms around his neck). And now the season's over and there is nothing to keep me in Colorado, and I've got to go back to New York to work.

JOHN. I know; I've been awake all night thinking about it.

LAURA. Well?

JOHN. Well?

LAURA. What are we going to do?

JOHN. Why, you've got to go, I suppose.

LAURA. Is it good-by?

JOHN. For a while, I suppose — it's good-by.

LAURA. What do you mean by a while? (LAURA turns JOHN's face to her, looks at him searchingly.)

JOHN. Until (Piano plays crescendo, then softens down.) I get money enough together, and am making enough to support you, then come and take you out of the show business and make you Mrs. Madison.

LAURA (tightens her arm around his neck, her cheek goes close to his own, and all the wealth of affection that the woman is capable of at times is shown; she seems more like a dainty little kitten purring close to its master; her whole thought and idea seem to be centered on the man whom she professes to love). John, that is what I want above everything else.

JOHN. But, Laura, we must come to some distinct understanding before we start to make our plans. We're not children.

LAURA. No, we're not.

JOHN. Now in the first place (LAURA rises.) we'll discuss you, and in the second place we'll discuss me. We'll keep nothing from each other (LAURA picks up cushions, places them on seat.), and we'll start out on this campaign (LAURA turns back and faces audience.) of decency and honor, fully understanding its responsibilities, without a chance of a comeback on either side.

LAURA (becoming very serious). You mean that we should tell each other all about each other, so, no matter what's ever said about us by other people, we'll know it first?

JOHN (rising). That's precisely what I'm trying to get at.

LAURA. Well, John, there are so many things I don't want to speak of even to you. It isn't easy for a woman to go back and dig up a lot of ugly memories and try to excuse them. (*Goes to front of table, picks up magazine, places it on table.*)

JOHN. I've known everything from the first; how you came to San Francisco as a kid and got into the show business, and how you went wrong, and then how you married, still a kid, and how your husband didn't treat you exactly right, and then how, in a fit of drunkenness, he came home and shot himself. (LAURA *buries her head in her hands, making exclamations of horror.* JOHN *goes to her as if sorry for hurting her, touches her on shoulder.*) But that's all past now, and we can forget that. And I know how you were up against it after that, how tough it was for you to get along. Then finally how you've lived, and — and that you and this man Brockton have been — well — never mind. I've known it all for months, and I've watched you. Now, Laura, the habit of life is a hard thing to get away from. You've lived in this way for a long time. If I ask you to be my wife you'll have to give it up; you'll have to go back to New York and struggle on your own hook until I get enough to come for you. I don't know how long that will be, but it *will* be. Do you love me enough to stick out for the right thing?

LAURA (*goes to him, puts her arms around him, kisses him once very affectionately, looks at him very earnestly*). Yes, I think this is my one great chance. I do love you and I want to do just what you said.

JOHN. I think you will. I'm going to make the same promise. Your life, dear girl, has been an angel's compared with mine. I've drunk whiskey, played bank, and raised hell ever since the time I could develop a thirst; and ever since I've been able to earn my own living I've abused every natural gift God gave me. The women I've associated with aren't good enough to touch the hem of your skirt, but they liked me, and (JOHN *goes to armchair, turns, then faces her.*) well — I must have liked them. My life hasn't been exactly loose, it's been all in pieces. I've never done anything dishonest. I've always gone wrong just for the fun of it, until I met you. (*Goes to her, takes her in his arms.*) Somehow then I began to feel that I was making an awful waste of myself.

LAURA. John!

JOHN. Some lovers place a woman on a pedestal and say, "She never has made a mistake." (*Taking her by each arm, he playfully shakes her.*) Well, we don't need any pedestals. I just know you never will make a mistake.

LAURA (*kissing him*). John, I'll never make you take those words back. (*Arms around his neck.*)

JOHN. That goes double. You're going to cut out the cabs and cafés, and I'm going to cut out the whiskey and all-night sessions (LAURA *releases him; he backs slightly away.*); and you're going to be somebody and I'm going to be somebody, and if my hunch is worth the powder to blow it up, we're going to show folks things they never thought were in us. Come on now, kiss me. (*She kisses him, tears are in her eyes. He looks into her face with a quaint smile.*)

JOHN. You're on, ain't you, dear?

LAURA. Yes, I'm on.

JOHN. Then (*Points toward door with his arm over her shoulder.*) call him.

LAURA. Brockton?

JOHN. Yes, and tell him you go back to New York without any travelling companion this season.

LAURA. Now?

JOHN. Sure.

LAURA. You want to hear me tell him?

JOHN (*with a smile*). We're partners, aren't we? I ought to be in on any important transaction like that, but it's just as you say.

LAURA. I think it would be right you should. I'll call him now.

JOHN. All right. (*Goes to stairway.*)

LAURA (*goes to door; twilight is becoming very much more pronounced; at door*). Mr. Brockton! Oh, Mr. Brockton!

WILLARD (*off stage*). Yes.

LAURA. Can you spare a moment to come out here?

WILLARD. Just a moment.

LAURA. You must come now.

WILLARD. All right. (*She waits for him, and, after a reasonable interval, he appears at door.*) Laura, it's a shame to lure me away from that mad speculation in there. I thought I might make my fare back to New York if I played until next summer. What's up?

LAURA. Mr. Madison wants to talk to you, or rather I do, and I want him to listen.

WILLARD (*his manner changing to one of cold, stolid calculation*). Very well. (*Comes down off step of house.*)

LAURA. Will.

WILLARD. Yes?

LAURA. I'm going home day after tomorrow on the Overland Limited.

WILLARD. I know.

LAURA. It's awfully kind of you to come out here, but under the circumstances I'd rather you'd take an earlier or a later train.

WILLARD. And may I ask what circumstances you refer to?

LAURA. Mr. Madison and I are going to be married. (*Pause*) He (WILLARD *looks inquiringly at* JOHN.) knows of your former friendship for me,

and he has the idea that it must end.

WILLARD. Then the Riverside Drive proposition, with Burgess's show thrown in, is declared off, eh?

LAURA. Yes; everything is absolutely declared off.

WILLARD. Can't even be friends any more, eh?

(JOHN *crosses and takes* LAURA's *arm, and leads her to a seat, his back is partly to audience.*)

JOHN. You could hardly expect Miss Murdock to be friendly with you under the circumstances. You could hardly expect me to (LAURA *puts scarf across her shoulders.*) sanction any such friendship.

WILLARD. I think I understand your position, young man, and I perfectly agree with you, that is — if your plans come out successfully.

JOHN. Thank you.

LAURA. Then everything is settled (*crossing in front of* JOHN, *facing* WILLARD, *back to audience*) just the way it ought to be — frankly and aboveboard?

WILLARD. Why, I guess so. If I was perfectly confident that this new arrangement was going to result happily for you both, I think it would be great, only I'm somewhat doubtful, for when people become serious and then fail, I know how hard those things hit, having *been* hit once myself.

JOHN. So you think we're making a wrong move and there isn't a chance of success.

WILLARD. No, I don't make any such gloomy prophecy. If you make Laura a good husband, and she makes you a good wife, and together you win out, I'll be mighty glad. As far as I am concerned I shall absolutely forget every thought of Laura's friendship for me.

LAURA. I thought you'd be just that

way. (*Goes to* WILLARD, *shakes hands.*)

WILLARD (*rising*). And now I must be off. (*Takes her by both hands and shakes them.*) Good-by, girlie! Madison, good luck. (*Crosses to* JOHN. *Shakes* JOHN's *hands, looks into his eyes.*) I think you've got the stuff in you to succeed if your foot don't slip.

JOHN. What do you mean by my foot slipping, Mr. Brockton?

WILLARD. You want me to tell you?

JOHN. I sure do.

WILLARD (*turns to* LAURA). Laura, run into the house and see if Mrs. Williams has won another quarter. (LAURA *sinks fearfully into chair.*) Madison and I are going to smoke a cigar and have a friendly chat, and when we get through I think we'll both be better off.

LAURA. You are sure that everything will be all right?

WILLARD. Sure.

(LAURA *looks at* JOHN *for assurance, he nods reassuringly, and she exits.*)

WILLARD. Have a cigar?

(*Servant in house places lamp on table inside house.*)

JOHN. No, I'll smoke my own. (*Sits in armchair.*)

WILLARD. What is your business? (*Sits.*)

JOHN. What's yours?

WILLARD. I'm a broker.

JOHN. I'm a reporter, so I've got something on you.

WILLARD. What kind?

JOHN. General utility, dramatic critic on Sunday nights.

WILLARD. Pay you well?

JOHN (*turns, looking at* WILLARD). That's pretty fresh. What's the idea?

WILLARD. I'm interested. I'm a plain man, Mr. Madison, and I do business in a plain way. Now if I ask you a few questions and discuss this matter with you in a frank way, don't get it in your head that I'm jealous or sore, but simply I don't want either of you people to make a move that's going to cost you a lot of pain and trouble. If you want me to talk sense to you, all right. If you don't we'll drop it now. What's the answer?

JOHN. I'll take a chance, but before you start I want to tell you that the class of people that you belong to I have no use for — they don't speak my language. You are what they call a manipulator of stocks; that means that you're living on the weaknesses of other people, and it almost means that you get your daily bread, yes, and your cake and your wine too, from the production of others. You're a "gambler under cover." Show me a man who's dealing bank, and he's free and aboveboard. You can figure the percentage against you, and then if you buck the tiger and get stung, you do it with your eyes open. With your financiers the game is crooked twelve months of the year, and from a business point of view, I think you are a crook. Now I guess we understand each other. If you've got anything to say, why, spill it.

WILLARD (*rises, goes toward* JOHN, *showing anger in his tones*). We are not talking business now, but women. How much money do you earn? (*Goes to chair left of table; gets it.*)

JOHN. Understand, I don't think it is any of your damn business, but I'm going through with you on this proposition, just to see how the land lays. But take my tip, you be mighty careful how you speak about the girl if you're not looking for trouble.

WILLARD. All right, but how much did you say you made? (*Carrying chair; sits.*)

JOHN. Thirty dollars a week.

WILLARD. Do you know how much Laura could make if she just took a job on her own merits?

JOHN. As I don't intend to share in her salary, I never took the trouble to inquire.

WILLARD. She'd get about forty dollars.

JOHN. That laps me ten.

WILLARD. How are you going to support her? Her cabs cost more than your salary, and she pays her week's salary for an everyday walking hat. She's always had a maid; her simplest gown flirts with a hundred-dollar note; her manicurist and her hairdresser will eat up as much as you pay for your board. She never walks when it's stormy, and every afternoon there's her ride in the park. She dines at the best places in New York, and one meal costs her more than you make in a day. Do you imagine for a moment that she's going to sacrifice these luxuries for any great length of time?

JOHN. I intend to give them to her.

WILLARD. On thirty dollars a week?

JOHN. I propose to go out and make a lot of money.

WILLARD. How?

JOHN. I haven't decided yet, but you can bet your sweet life that if I ever try and make up my mind that it's got to be, it's got to be.

WILLARD. Never have made it, have you?

JOHN. I have never tried.

WILLARD. Then how do you know you can?

JOHN. Well, I'm honest and energetic. If you can get great wealth the way you go along, I don't see why I can't earn a little.

WILLARD. There's where you make a mistake. Money-getting doesn't always come with brilliancy. I know a lot of fellows in New York who can paint a great picture, write a good play, and when it comes to oratory, they've got

me lashed to a pole; but they're always in debt. They never get anything for what they do. In other words, young man, they are like a skyrocket without a stick — plenty of brilliancy, but no direction, and they blow up and fizzle all over the ground.

JOHN. That's New York. I'm in Colorado, and I guess you know there is a difference.

WILLARD. I hope you'll make your money, because I tell you frankly that's the only way you can hold this girl. She's full of heroics now, self-sacrifice, and all the things that go to make up the third act of a play, but the minute she comes to darn her stockings, wash out her own handkerchiefs and dry them on the window, and send out for a pail of coffee and a sandwich for lunch, take it from me it will go Blah! (*Rises, goes to front of table, with chair, places it with back to him, braces his back on it, facing* JOHN.) You're in Colorado writing her letters once a day with no checks in them. That may be all right for some girl who hasn't tasted the joy of easy living, full of the good things of life, but one who for ten years has been doing very well in the way these women do is not going to let up for any great length of time. So take my advice if you want to hold her. Get that money quick, and don't be so damned particular how you get it either.

JOHN (*his patience is evidently severely tried; he approaches* WILLARD, *who remains impassive*). Of course you know you've got the best of me.

WILLARD. How?

JOHN. We're guests.

WILLARD. No one's listening.

JOHN. 'Tisn't that. If it was anywhere but here, if there was any way to avoid all the nasty scandal, I'd come a-shootin' for you, and you know it.

WILLARD. Gunfighter, eh?

JOHN. Perhaps. Let me tell you this. I don't know how you make your money, but I know what you do with it. You buy yourself a small circle of sycophants; you pay them well for feeding your vanity; and then you pose — pose with a certain frank admission of vice and degradation. And those who aren't quite as brazen as you call it manhood. Manhood? (*Goes slowly to armchair, sits.*) Why, you don't know what the word means. It's the attitude of a pup and a cur.

WILLARD (*angrily*). Wait a minute (*Goes to* JOHN.), young man, or I'll—

(JOHN *rises quickly. Both men stand confronting each other for a moment with fists clinched. They are on the very verge of a personal encounter. Both seem to realize that they have gone too far.*)

JOHN. You'll what?

WILLARD. Lose my temper and make a damn fool of myself. That's something I've not done for — let me see — why, it must be nearly twenty years — oh, yes, fully that. (*He smiles;* JOHN *relaxes and takes one step back.*)

JOHN. Possibly it's been about that length of time since you were human, eh?

WILLARD. Possibly — but you see, Mr. Madison, after all you're at fault.

JOHN. Yes?

WILLARD. Yes, the very first thing you did was to lose your temper. Now people who always lose their temper will never make a lot of money, and you admit that that is a great necessity — I mean now — to you.

JOHN. I can't stand for the brutal way you talk. (*Goes to seat, picks up newspaper, slams it down angrily on seat, and sits facing right, elbow on balustrade.*)

WILLARD. But you have got to stand it. The truth is never gentle. (*Goes and sits left of* JOHN.) Most conditions in life are unpleasant, and if you want to meet them squarely, you have got to realize the unpleasant point of view. That's the only way you can fight them and win.

JOHN (*turns to* WILLARD). Still, I believe Laura means what she says, in spite of all you say and the disagreeable logic of it. I think she loves me. If she should ever want to go back to the old way of getting along, I think she'd tell me so. So you see, Brockton, all your talk is wasted, and we'll drop the subject. (*Sits in armchair.*)

WILLARD. And if she should ever go back and come to me, I am going to insist that she let you know all about it. It'll be hard enough to lose her, caring for her the way you do, but it would hurt a lot more to be double-crossed.

JOHN (*sarcastically*). That's very kind. Thanks!

WILLARD. Don't get sore. It's common sense and it goes, does it not?

JOHN (*turns to* WILLARD). Just what goes?

WILLARD. If she leaves you first, you are to tell me, and if she comes to me, I'll make her let you know just when and why.

JOHN (*leaning on arm, facing* WILLARD; *his hand shoots out in a gesture of warning to* WILLARD). Look out!

WILLARD. I said common sense.

JOHN. All right.

WILLARD. Agreed? (*A pause.*)

JOHN. You're on.

(*By this time the stage is black and all that can be seen is the glow of the two cigars. Piano in the next room is heard.* JOHN *crosses slowly and deliberately to door, looks in, throws cigar away over the terrace, exits into house, closes doors, and, as* WILLARD *is seated on terrace, puffing cigar, the red coal of which is alone visible, a slow curtain falls.)*

ACT TWO

Six months have elapsed. The furnished room of LAURA MURDOCK, *second story back of an ordinary cheap theatrical lodginghouse in the theatre district of New York. The house is evidently of a type of the old-fashioned brownstone front, with high ceilings, dingy walls, and long, rather insecure windows. The woodwork is depressingly dark. The ceiling is cracked, the paper is old and spotted and in places loose. There is a door leading to the hallway. There is a large, old-fashioned wardrobe in which are hung a few old clothes, most of them a good deal worn and shabby, showing that the owner — LAURA MURDOCK — has had a rather hard time of it since leaving Colorado. The doors of this wardrobe must be equipped with springs so that they will open outward, and also furnished with wires so they can be controlled from the back. This is absolutely necessary, owing to business which is done during the progress of the act. The drawer in the bottom of the wardrobe is open. This is filled with a lot of rumpled tissue paper and other rubbish. An old pair of shoes is seen at the upper end of the wardrobe on the floor. At right center is an armchair over which is thrown an ordinary kimono, and on top of the wardrobe are a number of magazines and old books, and an unused parasol wrapped in tissue paper.*

The dresser, which is up stage and center against the flat, is in keeping with the general meanness, and its adornment consists of old postcards stuck in between the mirror and its frame, with some well-worn veils and ribbons hung on the side. On the dresser is a pincushion, a bottle of cheap perfume, purple in color and nearly empty; a common crockery match-holder containing matches, which must be practicable; a handkerchief box, powder box and puff, rouge box and rouge paw, hand mirror, small alcohol curling-iron heater, which must also be praticable, as it is used in business of act; scissors, curling tongs, hair comb and brush, and a small cheap picture of JOHN MADISON; *a small workbox containing a thimble and thread, and stuck in the pincushion are a couple of threaded needles. Directly to the left of the bureau, with the door to the outside closet intervening, is a broken-down washstand, on which is a basin half full of water, a bottle of tooth powder, toothbrushes and holder, soap and soapdish and other cheap toilet articles, and a small drinking-glass. Hung on the corner of the washstand is a soiled towel. One can see a pair of stockings hung on the rack across the top of the washstand. On the floor in front of the washstand is a pitcher half full of water, also a large waste water jar of the cheapest type.*

Below the washstand, and with the head against the flat, is an old wooden three-quarter bed, also showing the general decay of the entire room. Tacked on the head of this bed is a large photo of JOHN MADISON, *with a small bow of dainty blue ribbon at the top covering the tack. Under the photo are arranged half a dozen cheap artificial violets, in pitiful recognition of the girl's love for her absent sweetheart.*

Under the mattress at the head of the bed, is a heavy cardboard box about thirty inches long, seven inches wide, and four inches deep, containing about one hundred and twenty-five letters and eighty telegrams tied in about eight bundles, with dainty ribbon. One bundle must contain all practical letters of several closely written pages each, each letter having been opened. They must be written upon business paper and envelopes such as are used in newspaper offices and by business men. Under the pillow at the head of the bed, is carelessly thrown a woman's nightdress. Thrown on the bed is an **old book, open, face downward, and beside it is an apple which some-**one has been nibbling upon. Across the foot of the bed is a soiled quilt, untidily folded. The pillows are hollow in the center, as if having been used lately. At the foot of the bed is a small table with soiled and ink-stained cover, upon which are a cheap pitcher containing some withered carnations and a desk-pad, with paper, pen, ink, and envelopes scattered around.

Against the flat below the bed is an old mantelpiece and fireplace with iron grate, such as are used in houses of this type. On the mantelpiece are photos of actors and actresses, an old mantel clock in the center, in front of which is a box of cheap peppermint candy in large pieces, and a plate with two apples upon it; some cheap pieces of bric-a-brac and a little vase containing joss sticks, such as one might burn to improve the atmosphere of these dingy, damp houses. Below the mantelpiece is a thirty-six-inch theatre trunk, with theatre labels on it, in the tray of which are articles of clothing, a small box of thread, and a bundle of eight pawn tickets. Behind the trunk is a large cardboard box. Hanging from the ceiling directly over the table is a single-arm gasjet, from which is hung a turkey wishbone. On the jet is a little wire arrangement to hold small articles for heating. Beside the table is a chair. Under the bed is a pair of bedroom slippers and a box. Between the bed and the mantel is a small taborette on which is a book and a candlestick with the candle half burned. On the floor in front of the door is a slipper, also another in front of the dresser, as if they had been thrown carelessly down. On the wardrobe door is tacked another photo of JOHN MADISON.

In alcove is a table on which is a small oil stove, two cups, saucers, and plates, a box of matches, tin coffee-box, and a small Japanese teapot. On a **projection outside the window is a pint milk bottle half filled with milk,** and an empty benzine bottle, which is labeled. Both are covered with snow.

The backing shows a snow-covered street. In arranging the properties, it must be remembered that in the wardrobe is a box of Uneeda biscuits, with one end torn open. There is a door, opening inward, which leads into the hallway. The windows are at back, running from floor nearly to the ceiling. This window does not rise, but opens in the manner of the French or door window.

On the outside of the window is an iron guard such as is used in New York on the lower back windows. The rods running up and down are about four inches apart. There is a projection outside the window such as would be formed by a storm door in the basement; running the full length of the window and about thirty inches wide, raised about a foot from the floor in front and about nine inches in the back, there is opening inward a door at back leading into a small alcove, as has been mentioned before. The door is half glass, the glass part being the upper half of the door, and is ajar

when the curtain rises.
At rise of curtain, the stage is empty. After a pause, LAURA *enters, passes the dresser, places umbrella against wall, crosses to back of armchair, removes gloves, lays them over back of chair, takes off her coat and hat, hangs hat on end of wardrobe, and puts coat inside; notices old slipper in front of dresser and one on the extreme right and, with impatience, picks them up and puts them in wardrobe drawer. Then crosses to dresser, gets needle and thread off pincushion and mends small rip in glove, after which she puts gloves in top drawer of dresser, crosses to extreme end of dresser, and, standing, takes handkerchief out of box, takes up bottle containing purple perfume, holds it up so she can see there is only a small quantity left, sprinkles a drop on handkerchief carefully, so as not to use too much, looks at bottle again to see how much is left, places it on dresser; goes to side of bed, kneels on head of bed and looks lovingly at photo of* JOHN MADISON, *and finally pulls up the mattress and takes out box of letters, and opens it. She then sits down in Oriental fashion, with her feet under her, selects a bundle of letters, unties the ribbon, and takes out a letter, glances over it, puts it down in her lap, and again takes a long look at the picture of* JOHN MADISON. ANNIE *is heard coming upstairs.* LAURA *looks quickly towards the door, puts the letters back in box, and hurriedly places box under mattress and replaces pillows.* ANNIE *knocks on door.* LAURA *rises and goes to door.*

––––

LAURA. Come in.

(ANNIE, *a chocolate-colored Negress, enters. She is slovenly in appearance, but must not in any way denote the "mammy." She is the type one encounters in cheap theatrical lodginghouses. She has a letter in her hand, also a clean towel folded, and approaches* LAURA.)

LAURA. Hello, Annie.

ANNIE. Heah's yo' mail, Miss Laura.

LAURA (*taking letter*). Thank you! (*She looks at the address and does not open it.*)

ANNIE. One like dat comes every mornin', don't it? Used to all be postmarked Denver. Must 'a' moved. (*Trying to look over* LAURA'S *shoulder;* LAURA *turns, sees her;* ANNIE *looks away.*) Where is dat place called Goldfield, Miss Laura?

LAURA. In Nevada.

ANNIE. In *Nevada?*

LAURA. Yes, Nevada.

ANNIE (*draws her jacket closer around her, as if chilly*). Must be mighty smaht to write yuh every day. De pos'man brings it 'leven o'clock mos' always, sometimes twelve, and again sometimes tehn; but it comes every day, don't it?

LAURA. I know.

ANNIE (*goes to right of armchair, brushes it off, and makes an effort to read letter, leaning across chair*). Guess must be from yo' husban', ain't it?

LAURA. No, I haven't any.

ANNIE (*triumphantly*). Dat's what Ah tole Mis' Farley when she was down talkin' about you dis mornin'. She said if he all was yo' husban' he might do somethin' to help you out. Ah told her Ah didn't think you had any husban'. Den she says you ought to have one, you're so pretty.

LAURA. Oh, Annie!

ANNIE (*sees door open, goes and bangs it shut*). Der ain't a decent door in dis old house. Mis' Farley said yo' might have mos' any man you (*Hangs clean towel on washstand.*) wanted just for de askin', but Ah said yuh (*Takes newspaper and books off bed, places them on table.*) was too particular about the man yo'd want. Den she did a heap o' talkin'.

LAURA. About what? (*Places letter open on table, looks at hem of skirt, discovers a rip, rises, goes to dresser, gets needle, then to trunk; opens and takes thimble out, closes lid of tray, sits on it, and sews skirt during scene.*)

ANNIE (*at bed fussing around, folds nightgown, places it under pillow*). Well, you know, Mis' Farley, she's been havin' so much trouble wid her roomers. Yestuhday dat young lady on de second flo' front she lef'. She's goin' wiv some troupe on the road. She owed her room for three weeks and jus' had to leave her trunk. (*Fussing over table*) My! how Mis' Farley did scold her. Mis' Farley let on she could have paid dat money if she wanted to, but somehow Ah guess she couldn't— (*Reads letter on table.*)

LAURA (*sees her, angrily exclaims*). Annie!

ANNIE (*in confusion, brushing off table*).—for if she could she wouldn't have left her trunk, would she, Miss Laura? (*Crosses to armchair, picks up kimono off back.*)

LAURA. No, I suppose not. What did Mrs. Farley say about me?

ANNIE. Oh! nothin' much. (*Standing.*)

LAURA. Well, what?

ANNIE. She kinder say somethin' 'bout yo' bein' three weeks behind in yo' room rent, and she said she t'ought it was 'bout time yuh handed her somethin', seein' as how yuh must o' had some stylish friends when yuh come here.

LAURA. Who, for instance?

ANNIE. Ah don't know. Mis' Farley said some of 'em might slip yo' enough just to help yuh out. (*Pause*) Ain't yo'

got nobody to take care of you at all, Miss Laura? (*Hangs kimono over back of armchair.*)

LAURA. No! No one.

ANNIE. Dat's too bad.

LAURA. Why?

ANNIE. Mis' Farley says yuh wouldn't have no trouble at all gettin' any man to take care of yuh if yuh wanted to.

LAURA (*with sorrowful shudder*). Please (*Doors of wardrobe open very slowly.*) don't, Annie.

ANNIE. Dere's a gemman (*Playing with corner of tablecloth*) dat calls on one of de ladies from the Hippodrome, in de big front room downstairs. He's mighty nice, and he's been askin' 'bout you.

LAURA (*exasperated*). Oh, shut up!

ANNIE (*sees doors of wardrobe have swung open; she goes and slams them shut, them turns to* LAURA). Mis' Farley says—(*Doors have swung open again, hit her in the back. She turns and bangs them to with all her strength.*) Damn dat door! (*Goes to washstand, grabs basin which is half full of water, empties same into waste-jar, puts basin on washstand, and wipes out with soiled towel.*) Mis' Farley says if she don't get someone in the house dat has reg'lar money soon, she'll have to shut up and go to the po'house.

LAURA. I'm sorry; I'll try again to-day. (*Rises, crosses up to mantel, gets desk-pad, etc., and goes to table, sits.*)

ANNIE (*at back of bed, wiping basin with towel*). Ain't yo' got any job at all?

LAURA. No.

ANNIE. When yuh come here yuh had lots of money and yo' was mighty good to me. You know Mr. Weston?

LAURA. Jim Weston?

ANNIE. Yassum, Mr. Weston what goes ahead o' shows and lives on the top floor back; he says nobody's got jobs now. Dey're so many actors and actresses out o' work. Mis' Farley says she don't know how she's goin' to live. She said you'd been mighty nice up until three weeks ago, but yuh ain't got much left, have you, Miss Laura?

LAURA (*rising and going to the bureau*). No. It's all gone.

ANNIE. Mah sakes! All dem rings and things? You ain't done sold 'em? (*Sinks on bed.*)

LAURA. They're pawned. What did Mrs. Farley say she was going to do?

ANNIE. Guess maybe Ah'd better not tell. (*Goes to door hurriedly, carrying soiled towel.*)

LAURA. Please do. (*Goes to chair.*)

ANNIE. Yuh been so good to me, Miss Laura. Never was nobody in dis house what give me so much, and Ah ain't been gettin' much lately. And when Mis' Farley said yuh must either pay yo' rent or she would ask yuh for your room, Ah just set right down on de back kitchen stairs and cried. Besides, Mis' Farley don't like me very well since you've ben havin' yo' breakfasts and dinners brought up here.

LAURA. Why not? (*Takes kimono off chair-back, crosses up to dresser, puts kimono in drawer, takes out purse.*)

ANNIE. She has a rule in dis house dat nobody can use huh chiny or fo'ks or spoons who ain't boa'din' heah, and de odder day when yuh asked me to bring up a knife and fo'k she ketched me comin' upstairs, and she says, "Where yuh goin' wid all dose things, Annie?" Ah said, "Ah'm just goin' up to Miss Laura's room with dat knife and fo'k." Ah said, "Ah'm goin' up for nothin' at all, Mis' Farley, she jest wants to look at 'em, Ah guess." She said, "She wants to eat huh dinner wid em, Ah guess." Ah got real mad, and Ah told her if she'd give me mah pay Ah'd brush right out o' here;

dat's what Ah'd do, Ah'd brush right out o' here. (*Violently shaking out towel.*)

LAURA. I'm sorry, Annie, if I've caused you any trouble. Never mind, I'll be able to pay the rent tomorrow or next day anyway. (*She fumbles in purse, takes out a quarter, and turns to ANNIE.*) Here!

ANNIE. No, ma'am, Ah don' want dat. (*Making a show of reluctance.*)

LAURA. Please take it.

ANNIE. No, ma'am, Ah don' want it. You need dat. Dat's breakfast money for yuh, Miss Laura.

LAURA. Please take it, Annie, I might just as well get rid of this as anything else.

ANNIE (*takes it rather reluctantly*). Yuh always was so good, Miss Laura. Sho' yuh don' want dis?

LAURA. Sure.

ANNIE. Sho' yo' goin' to get plenty mo'?

LAURA. Sure.

MRS. FARLEY (*from downstairs*). Annie! Annie!

ANNIE (*going to door, opens it*). Dat's Mis' Farley. (*To* MRS. FARLEY) Yassum, Mis' Farley.

MRS. FARLEY. Is Miss Murdock up there?

ANNIE. Yassum, Mis' Farley, yassum!

MRS. FARLEY. Anything doin'?

ANNIE. Huh?

MRS. FARLEY. Anything doin'?

ANNIE (*at door*). Ah — Ah — hain't asked, Missy Farley.

MRS. FARLEY. Then do it.

LAURA (*coming to the rescue at the door, to* ANNIE). I'll answer her. (*Out of door to* MRS. FARLEY) What is it, Mrs. Farley.

MRS. FARLEY (*her voice softened*). Did ye have any luck this morning, dearie?

LAURA. No; but I promise you faithfully to help you out this afternoon or tomorrow.

MRS. FARLEY. Sure? Are you certain?

LAURA. Absolutely.

MRS. FARLEY. Well, I must say these people expect me to keep — (*Door closed.*)

(LAURA *quietly closes the door, and* MRS. FARLEY'S *rather strident voice is heard indistinctly.* LAURA *sighs and walks toward table, sits.* ANNIE *looks after her, and then slowly opens the door.*)

ANNIE. Yo' sho' dere ain't nothin' I can do fo' yuh, Miss Laura?

LAURA. Nothing.

(ANNIE *exits.* LAURA *sits down and looks at letter, opening it. It consists of several pages closely written. She reads some of them hurriedly, skims through the rest, and then turns to the last page, without reading, glances at it; lays it on table, rises.*)

LAURA. Hope, just nothing but hope. (*She crosses to bed, falls face down upon it, burying her face in her hands. Her despondency is palpable. As she lies there, a hurdy-gurdy in the street starts to play a popular air. This arouses her, and she rises, crosses to wardrobe, takes out box of crackers, opens window, gets bottle of milk off sill outside, places them on table, gets glass off washstand, at the same time humming the tune of the hurdy-gurdy when knock comes; she crosses quickly to dresser, powders nose. The knock is timidly repeated.*)

LAURA (*without turning, and in a rather tired tone of voice*). Come in.

(JIM WESTON, *a rather shabby theatrical advance agent of the old school, enters timidly, halting at the door and holding the knob in his hand. He is a man about forty years old, dressed in an ordinary manner, of medium height, and, in fact, has the* appearance of a once prosperous clerk who has been in hard luck. His relations with LAURA *are those of pure friendship. They both live in the same lodging-place, and both having been out of employment, they have naturally become acquainted.*)

JIM. Can I come in?

LAURA (*without turning*). Hello, Jim Weston. (*He closes door and enters.*) Any luck?

JIM. Lots of it.

LAURA. That's good. Tell me.

JIM. It's bad luck. Guess you don't want to hear.

LAURA. I'm sorry. Where have you been?

JIM. I kind o' felt around up at Burgess's office. I thought I might get a job there, but he put me off until tomorrow. Somehow those fellow always do business tomorrow.

(*Hurdy-gurdy dies out.*)

LAURA. Yes, and there's always today to look after.

JIM. I'm ready to give up. I've tramped Broadway for nine weeks until every piece of flagstone gives me the laugh when it sees my feet coming. Got a letter from the missis this morning. The kids got to have some clothes, there's measles in the town, and mumps in the next village. I've just got to raise some money or get some work, or the first thing you'll know I'll be hanging around Central Park on a dark night with a club.

LAURA. I know just how you feel. Sit down, Jim. (JIM *crosses and sits in chair near table.*) It's pretty tough for me (*Offers* JIM *glass of milk; he refuses; takes cracker.*), but it must be a whole lot worse for you with a wife and kids.

JIM. Oh, if a man's alone he can generally get along — turn his hand to anything; but a woman —

LAURA. Worse, you think?

JIM. I was just thinking about you and what Burgess said.

LAURA. What was that? (*Crosses to bed; sits, sipping milk.*)

JIM. You know Burgess and I used to be in the circus business together. He took care of the grafters when I was boss canvas man. I never could see any good in shaking down the rubes for all the money they had and then taking part of it. He used to run the privilege car, you know.

LAURA. Privilege car?

JIM. Had charge of all the pickpockets—dips we called 'em—surething gamblers, and the like. Made him rich. I kept sort o' on the level and I'm broke. Guess it don't pay to be honest —

LAURA (*turns to him and in a significant voice*). You don't really think that?

JIM. No, maybe not. Ever since I married the missis and the first kid come we figured the only good money was the kind folks worked for and earned; but when you can't get hold of that, it's tough.

LAURA. I know.

JIM. Burgess don't seem to be losing sleep over the tricks he's turned. He's happy and prosperous, but I guess he ain't any better now then he was then.

LAURA. Maybe not. I've been trying to get an engagement from him. There are half a dozen parts in his new attractions that I could do, but he has never absolutely said "no," but yet somehow he's never said "yes."

JIM. He spoke about you.

LAURA. In what way? (*Rising, stands behind* JIM's *chair.*)

JIM. I gave him my address and he seen it was yours, too. Asked if I lived in the same place.

LAURA. Was that all?

JIM. Wanted to know how you was getting on. I let him know you needed work, but I didn't tip my hand you was flat broke. He said something about you being a damned fool.

LAURA (*suddenly and interested*). How?

JIM. Well, Johnny Ensworth—you know he used to do the fights on the *Evening Journal;* now he's press agent for Burgess; nice fellow and way on the inside—he told me where you were in wrong.

LAURA. What have I done? (*Sits in armchair.*)

JIM. Burgess don't put up the money for any of them musical comedies—he just trails. Of course he's got a lot of influence, and he's always Johnny on the spot to turn any dirty trick that they want. There are four or five rich men in town who are there with the bank-roll, providing he engages women who ain't so very particular about the location of their residence, and who don't hear a curfew ring at eleven-thirty every night.

LAURA. And he thinks I am too particular?

JIM. That's what was slipped me. Seems that one of the richest men that is in on Mr. Burgess's address book is a fellow named Brockton from downtown some place. He's got more money than the Shoe and Leather National Bank. He. likes to play show business.

LAURA (*rises quickly*). Oh! (*Goes to wardrobe, gets hat, then to dresser, gets scissors with intention of curling feathers.*)

JIM. I thought you knew him. I thought it was just as well to tell you where he and Burgess stand. They're pals.

LAURA (*comes over to* JIM *and, with emphasis, goes to side of bed, puts hat and scissors on bed*). I don't want you to talk about him or any of them. I just want you to know that I'm trying to do everything in my power to go through this season without any more trouble. I've pawned everything I've got; I've cut every friend I knew. But where am I going to end? That's what I want to know—where am I going to end? (*To bed and sits.*) Every place I look for a position something interferes. It's almost as if I were blacklisted. I know I could get jobs all right if I wanted to pay the price, but I won't. I just want to tell you, I won't. No! (*Rises, goes to mantel, rests elbow.*)

JIM. That's the way to talk. (*Rises.*) I don't know you very well, but I've watched you close. I'm just a common ordinary showman who never had much money, and I'm going out o' date. I've spent most of my time with nigger minstrel shows and circuses, but I've been on the square. That's why I'm broke. (*Rather sadly*) Once I thought the missis would have to go back and do her acrobatic act, but she couldn't do that, she'd grown so damn fat. (*Goes to* LAURA.) Just you don't mind. It'll all come out right.

LAURA. It's an awful tough game, isn't it?

JIM (*during this speech,* LAURA *gets cup, pours milk back into bottle, closes biscuit-box, and puts milk on shed outside, biscuits into wardrobe, cup in alcove*). It's hell forty ways from the Jack. It's tough for me, but for a pretty woman with a lot o' rich fools jumping out o' their automobiles and hanging around stage doors, it must be something awful. I ain't blaming the women. They say "self-preservation is the first law of nature," and I guess that's right; but sometimes when the show is over and I see them fellows with their hair plastered back, smoking cigarettes in a (LAURA *goes to chair right of table and leans over back.*) holder long enough to reach from here to Harlem, and a bank roll that would bust my pocket and turn my head, I feel as if I'd like to get a gun and go a-shooting around this old town.

LAURA. Jim!

JIM. Yes, I do—you bet.

LAURA. That wouldn't pay, would it?

JIM. No, they're not worth the job of sitting on that throne in Sing Sing, and I'm too poor to go to Matteawan. But all them fellows under nineteen and over fifty-nine ain't much use to themselves or anyone else.

LAURA (*rather meditatively*). Perhaps all of them are not so bad.

JIM (*sits on bed*). Yes, they are—angels and all. Last season I had one of them shows where a rich fellow backed it on account of a girl. We lost money and he lost his girl; then we got stuck in Texas. I telegraphed: "Must have a thousand, or can't move." He just answered: "Don't move." We didn't.

LAURA. But that was business.

JIM. Bad business. It took a year for some of them folks to get back to Broadway. Some of the girls never did, and I guess never will.

LAURA. Maybe they're better off, Jim. (*Sits right of table.*)

JIM. Couldn't be worse. They're still in Texas. (*To himself*) Wish I knew how to do something else, being a plumber or a walking delegate; they always have jobs.

LAURA. Well, I wish I could do something else too, but I can't, and we've got to make the best of it.

JIM. I guess so. I'll see you this evening. I hope you'll have good news by that time. (*Business: Starts to exit, starts to open door; then retreats a step, with hand on doorknob. In a voice meant to be kindly*) If you'd like to go to the theatre tonight and take some other woman in the house, maybe I can get a couple of tickets for some of the shows. I know a lot of fellows who are working.

LAURA. No, thanks. I haven't anything to wear to the theatre, and I don't—

JIM (*with a smile, crosses to* LAURA *and puts arm around her*). Now you just cheer up! Something's sure to turn up. It always has for me, and I'm a lot older than you, both in years and in this business. There's always a break in hard luck sometime—that's sure.

LAURA (*smiling through her tears*). I hope so. But things are looking pretty hopeless now, aren't they?

JIM. I'll go down and give Mrs. F. a line o' talk and try to square you for a couple of days more anyway. But I guess she's laying pretty close to the cushion herself, poor woman.

LAURA. Annie says a lot of people owe her.

JIM. Well, you can't pay what you haven't got. And even if money was growing on trees, it's winter now. (JIM *goes towards door.*) I'm off. Maybe today is lucky day. So long!

LAURA. Good-by.

JIM. Keep your nerve. (*Exit.*)

LAURA. I will. (*She sits for a moment in deep thought, picks up the letter she received as if to read it, and then throws it down in anger. She buries her head in hands.*) I can't stand it— I just simply can't stand it.

MRS. FARLEY (*voice from off stage*). Miss Murdock—Miss Murdock.

LAURA (*brushing away tears, rises, goes to door, and opens it*). What is it?

MRS. FARLEY. There's a lady down here to see you.

ELFIE (*voice from off stage*). Hello, dearie, can I come up?

LAURA. Is that you, Elfie?

ELFIE. Yes; shall I come up?

LAURA. Why, certainly.

(*She waits at the door for a moment, and* ELFIE ST. CLAIR *appears. She is gorgeously gowned in the rather extreme style affected by the usual New York woman who is cared for by a gentleman of wealth and who has not gone through the formality of matrimonial alliance. Her conduct is always exaggerated and her attitude vigorous. Her gown is of the latest design, and, in every detail of dress, she shows evidence of most extravagant expenditure. She carries a handbag of gold, upon which are attached such trifles as a gold cigarette-case, a gold powder box, pencils, and the like.* ELFIE *throws her arms around* LAURA, *and both exchange kisses.*)

ELFIE. Laura, you old dear, I've just found out where you've been hiding, and came around to see you.

LAURA (*much brightened by* ELFIE'S *appearance*). Elfie, you're looking bully. How are you, dear?

ELFIE. Fine.

LAURA. Come in and sit down. I haven't much to offer, but—

ELFIE. Oh, never mind. It's such a grand day outside, and I've come around in my car to take you out (*sits right of table*). You know I've got a new one, and it can go some.

LAURA (*sits on arm of chair*). I'm sorry but I can't go out this afternoon, Elfie.

ELFIE. What's the matter?

LAURA. You see I'm staying home a good deal nowadays. I haven't been feeling very well and I don't go out much.

ELFIE. I should think not. I haven't seen you in Rector's or Martin's since you came back from Denver. Got a glimpse of you one day trailing up Broadway, but couldn't get to you—

you dived into some office or other. (*For the first time she surveys the room, rises, looks around critically, crossing to mantel.*) Gee! Whatever made you come into a dump like this? It's the limit.

LAURA (*standing back of the table*). Oh, I know it isn't pleasant, but it's my home, and after all—a home's a home.

ELFIE. Looks more like a prison. (*Takes candy from mantel, spits it out on floor.*) Makes me think of the old days of Child's sinkers and a hall bedroom.

LAURA. It's comfortable. (*Leaning hands on table.*)

ELFIE. Not! (*Sits on bed, trying bed with comedy effect.*) Say, is this here for an effect, or do you sleep on it?

LAURA. I sleep on it.

ELFIE. No wonder you look tired. Say, listen, dearie. What else is the matter with you anyway?

LAURA. Nothing.

ELFIE. Yes, there is. What happened between you and Brockton? (*Notices faded flowers in vase on table, takes them out, tosses them into fireplace, replaces them with gardenias which she wears.*) He's not broke, because I saw him the other day.

LAURA. Where?

ELFIE. In the park. Asked me out to luncheon, but I couldn't go. You know, dearie, I've got to be so careful. Jerry's so awful jealous—the old fool.

LAURA. Do you see much of Jerry nowadays, Elfie?

ELFIE. Not any more than I can help and be nice. He gets on my nerves. Of course, I've heard about your quitting Brockton.

LAURA. Then why do you ask? (*Crosses around chair right of table, stands.*)

ELFIE. Just wanted to hear from your own dear lips what the trouble was. Now tell me all about it. Can I smoke here? (*Takes cigarette case up, opens it, selecting cigarette.*)

LAURA. Surely. (*Gets matches off bureau, puts them on table.*)

ELFIE. Have one? (*Offers case.*)

LAURA. No, thank you. (*Sits in chair right of table, facing* ELFIE.)

ELFIE. H'm-m, h'm-m, hah! (*Lights cigarette.*) Now go ahead. Tell me all the scandal. I'm just crazy to know.

LAURA. There's nothing to tell. I haven't been able to find work, that is all, and I'm short of money. You can't live in hotels, you know, with cabs and all that sort of thing, when you're not working.

ELFIE. Yes, you can. I haven't worked in a year.

LAURA. But you don't understand, dear. I—I—Well, you know I—well, you know—I can't say what I want.

ELFIE. Oh, yes, you can. You can say anything to me—everybody else does. We've been pals. I know you got along a little faster in the business than I did. The chorus was my limit, and you went into the legitimate thing. But we got our living just the same way. I didn't suppose there was any secret between you and me about that.

LAURA. I know there wasn't then, Elfie, but I tell you I'm different now. I don't want to do that sort of thing, and I've been very unlucky. This has been a terribly hard season for me. I simply haven't been able to get an engagement.

ELFIE. Well, you can't get on this way. Won't (*Pauses, knocking ashes off cigarette to cover hesitation.*) Brockton help you out?

LAURA. What's the use of talking to you (*Rises and goes to fireplace.*), Elfie; you don't understand.

ELFIE (*puffing deliberately on ciga-*

rette and crossing her legs in almost a masculine attitude). No? Why don't I understand?

LAURA. Because you can't; you've never felt as I have.

ELFIE. How do you know?

LAURA *(turning impatiently).* Oh, what's the use of explaining?

ELFIE. You know, Laura, I'm not much on giving advice, but you make me sick. I thought you'd grown wise. A young girl just butting into this business might possibly make a fool of herself, but you ought to be on to the game and make the best of it.

LAURA *(going over to her angrily).* If you come up here, Elfie, to talk that sort of stuff to me, please don't. I was West this summer. I met someone, a real man, who did me a whole lot of good—a man who opened my eyes to a different way of going along—a man who—Oh, well, what's the use? You don't know—you don't know. *(Sits on bed.)*

ELFIE *(throws cigarette into fireplace).* I don't know, don't I? I don't know, I suppose, that when I came to this town from up state—a little burg named Oswego—and joined a chorus, that I didn't fall in love with just such a man. I suppose I don't know that then I was the best-looking girl in New York, and everybody talked about me? I suppose I don't know that there were men, all ages and with all kinds of money, ready to give me anything for the mere privilege of taking me out to supper? And I didn't do it, did I? For three years I stuck by this good man who was to lead me in a good way toward a good life. And all the time I was getting older, never quite so pretty one day as I had been the day before. I never knew then what it was to be tinkered with by hairdressers and manicures or a hundred and

one of those other people who make you look good. I didn't have to have them then. *(Rises, goes to table, facing* LAURA.*)* Well, you know, Laura, what happened.

LAURA. Wasn't it partly your fault, Elfie?

ELFIE *(speaking across table angrily).* Was it my fault that time made me older and I took on a lot of flesh? Was it my fault that the work and the life took out the color, and left the make-up? Was it my fault that other pretty young girls came along, just as I'd come, and were chased after, just as I was? Was it my fault the cabs weren't waiting any more and people didn't talk about how pretty I was? And was it my fault when he finally had me alone, and just because no one else wanted me, he got tired and threw me flat—cold flat *(Brings hand down on table.)*—and I'd been on the dead level with him. *(With almost a sob goes to bureau, powders nose, returns to table.)* It almost broke my heart. Then I made up my mind to get even and get all I could out of the game. Jerry came along. He was a has-been and I was on the road to be. He wanted to be good to me, and I let him. That's all.

LAURA. Still, I don't see how you can live that way. *(Lies on bed.)*

ELFIE. Well, you did, and you didn't kick.

LAURA. Yes, but things are different with me now. You'd be the same way if you were in my place.

ELFIE. No. I've had all the romance I want, and I'll stake you to all your love affairs. *(Goes back of bed, touches picture over bed.)* I am out to gather in as much coin as I can in my own way, so when the old rainy day comes along I'll have a little change to buy myself an umbrella.

LAURA (*rising and angry, goes to armchair*). What did you come here for? Why can't you leave me alone when I'm trying to get along?

ELFIE. Because I want to help you.

LAURA (*goes to upstage side of bed, angrily tosses quilt to floor, and sits on bed, in tears*). You can't help me. I'm all right—I tell you I am. What do you care anyway?

ELFIE (*sits on bed, facing* LAURA). But I do care. I know how you feel with an old cat for a landlady and living up here on a side street with a lot of cheap burlesque people. Why the room's cold (LAURA *rises, goes to window*.), and there's no hot water, and you're beginning to look shabby. You haven't got a job—chances are you won't have one. What does (*Indicating a picture on bed with thumb*) this fellow out there do for you? Send you long letters of condolences? That's what I used to get. When I wanted to buy a new pair of shoes or a silk petticoat, he told me how much he loved me; so I had the other ones resoled and turned the old petticoat. And look at you, you're beginning to show it. (*She surveys her carefully.*) I do believe there are lines coming in your face (LAURA *goes to dresser quickly, picks up hand mirror, looks at herself.*), and you hide in the house because you've nothing new to wear.

LAURA (*puts down mirror, crossing down to back of bed*). But I've got what you haven't got. I may have to hide my clothes, but I don't have to hide my face. And you with that man —he's old enough to be your father— a toddling dote hanging on your apron-strings, I don't see how you dare show your face to a decent woman.

ELFIE (*rises*). You don't!—but you did once and I never caught you hanging your head. You say he's old. I know he's old, but he's good to me. He's making what's left of my life pleasant. You think I like him. I don't —sometimes I hate him—but he understands; and you can bet your life his check is in my mail every Saturday night or there's a new lock on the door Sunday morning. (*Goes to fireplace.*)

LAURA. How can you say such things to me?

ELFIE (*goes to end of table*). Because I want you to be square with yourself. You've lost all that precious virtue women gab about. When you've got the name, I say get the game.

LAURA. You can go now, Elfie, and don't come back.

ELFIE (*gathering up muff, etc.*). All right, if that's the way you want it to be, I'm sorry. (*A knock on the door.*)

LAURA (*controlling herself after a moment's hesitation*). Come in.

ANNIE (*enters with a note, crosses, and hands it to* LAURA). Mis' Farley sent dis, Miss Laura.

LAURA (*takes the note and reads it; she is palpably annoyed*). There's no answer.

ANNIE. She tol' me not to leave until Ah got an answah.

LAURA. You must ask her to wait.

ANNIE. She wants an answah.

LAURA. Tell her I'll be right down— that it will be all right.

ANNIE. But, Miss Laura, she tol' me to get an answah. (*Exit reluctantly.*)

LAURA (*half to herself and half to* ELFIE). She's taking advantage of your being here. (*Standing near door.*)

ELFIE. How?

LAURA. She wants money—three weeks' room-rent. I presume she thought you'd give it to me.

ELFIE. Huh!

LAURA (*going to table*). Elfie, I've been a little cross; I didn't mean it.

ELFIE. Well?

LAURA. Could—could you lend me thirty-five dollars until I get to work?

ELFIE. Me?

LAURA. Yes.

ELFIE. Lend *you* thirty-five dollars?

LAURA. Yes; you've got plenty of money to spare.

ELFIE. Well, you certainly have got a nerve.

LAURA. You might give it to me. I haven't a dollar in the world, and you pretend to be such a friend to me!

ELFIE (*turning and angrily speaking across table*). So that's the kind of woman you are, eh? A moment ago you were going to kick me out of the place because I wasn't decent enough to associate with you. You know how I live. You know how I get my money— the same way you got most of yours. And now that you've got this spasm of goodness I'm not fit to be in your room; but you'll take my money to pay your debts. You'll let me go out and do this sort of thing for your benefit, while you try to play the grand lady. I've got your number now, Laura. Where in hell is your virtue anyway? You can go to the devil rich, poor, or any other way. I'm off! (ELFIE *rushes toward door; for a moment* LAURA *stands speechless, then bursts into hysterics.*)

LAURA. Elfie! Elfie! Don't go now! Don't leave me now! (ELFIE *hesitates with hand on doorknob.*) I can't stand it. I can't be alone. Don't go, please; don't go. (LAURA *falls into* ELFIE's *arms, sobbing. In a moment* ELFIE's *whole demeanor changes and she melts into the tenderest womanly sympathy, trying her best to express herself in her crude way.*)

ELFIE. There, old girl, don't cry, don't cry. You just sit down here and let me put my arms around you. (ELFIE *leads* LAURA *over to the armchair, places muff, etc., in chair, and*

sits LAURA *down in chair.* ELFIE *sits on arm of chair with her left arm behind* LAURA; *hugs* LAURA *to her.* LAURA *in tears and sobbing during scene.*) I'm awful sorry—on the level, I am. I shouldn't have said it. I know that. But I've got feelings too, even if folks don't give me credit for it.

LAURA. I know, Elfie. I've gone through about all I can stand.

ELFIE. Well, I should say you have— and more than I would. Anyway a good cry never hurts any woman. I have one myself, sometimes—under cover.

LAURA (*more seriously, recovering herself*). Perhaps what you said was true.

ELFIE. We won't talk about it. (*Wiping* LAURA's *eyes, kisses her.*)

LAURA (*with persistence*). But perhaps it was true, and, Elfie—

ELFIE. Yes.

LAURA. I think I've stood this just as long as I can. Every day is a living horror.

ELFIE (*looking around room*). It's the limit.

LAURA. I've got to have money to pay the rent. I've pawned everything I have, except the clothes on my back.

ELFIE. I'll give you all the money you need, dearie. Great Heavens, don't worry about that. Don't you care if I got sore and—and lost my head.

LAURA. No; I can't let you do that. (*Rises; goes to table.*) You may have been mad—awfully mad—but what you said was the truth. I can't take your money. (*Sits right of table.*)

ELFIE. Oh, forget that. (*Rises.*)

LAURA. Maybe—maybe if he knew about it — the suffering — he wouldn't blame me.

ELFIE. Who—the good man who wanted to lead you to the good life without even a breadbasket for an advance agent? Huh!

LAURA. Still he doesn't know how desperately poor I am.

ELFIE. He knows you're out of work, don't he?

LAURA (*turning to* ELFIE). Not exactly. I've let him think that I'm getting along all right.

ELFIE. Then you're a chump. Hasn't he sent you anything?

LAURA. He hasn't anything to send.

ELFIE. Well, what does he think you're going to live on?—asphalt croquettes with conversation sauce?

LAURA. I don't know—I don't know. (*Sobbing.*)

ELFIE (*goes to* LAURA, *puts arms around her*). Don't be foolish, dearie. You know there is somebody waiting for you—somebody who'll be good to you and get you out of this mess.

LAURA. You mean Will Brockton? (*Looking up.*)

ELFIE. Yes.

LAURA. Do you know where he is?

ELFIE. Yes.

LAURA. Well?

ELFIE. You won't get sore again if I tell you, will you?

LAURA. No—why? (*Rises.*)

ELFIE. He's downstairs—waiting in the car. I promised to tell him what you said.

LAURA. Then it was all planned, and —and—

ELFIE. Now, dearie, I knew you were up against it, and I wanted to bring you two together. He's got half of the Burgess shows, and if you'll only see him everything will be fixed.

LAURA. When does he want to see me?

ELFIE. Now.

LAURA. Here?

ELFIE. Yes. Shall I tell him to come up?

LAURA (*after a long pause, going around to bed*). Yes.

ELFIE (*suddenly becomes animated*). Now you're a sensible dear. I'll bet he's half frozen down there. (*Goes to door.*) I'll send him up. Look at you, Laura, you're a sight. (*Goes to* LAURA, *taking her by the hand, she leads her to washstand, takes towel and wipes* LAURA's *eyes.*) It'll never do to have him see you looking like this; come over here and let me fix your eyes. Now, Laura, I want you to promise me you won't do any more crying. (*Leads* LAURA *over to dresser, takes powder-puff and powders* LAURA's *face.*) Come over here and let me powder your nose. Now when he comes up you tell him he has got to blow us all off to a dinner tonight at Martin's, seven-thirty. Let me look at you. Now you're all right. (*After daubing* LAURA's *face with rouge paw,* ELFIE *takes* LAURA's *face in her hands and kisses her.*) Make it strong now, seven-thirty, don't forget, I'll be there. (*Goes to armchair, gathers up muff, etc.*) So long. (*Exit.*)

(*After* ELFIE's *exit,* LAURA *goes to wardrobe, pulls off picture of* JOHN, *takes picture of* JOHN *from dresser, carries both pictures over to bed, kneels on bed, pulls down picture at head of bed, places all three pictures under pillow.* WILLARD *is heard coming upstairs, and knocks.*)

LAURA. Come in.

(WILLARD *enters. His dress is that of a man of business, the time being about February. He is well groomed and brings with him the impression of easy luxury.*)

WILLARD (*as he enters*). Hello, Laura. (*There is an obvious embarrassment on the part of each of them. She rises, goes to him and extends her hand.*)

LAURA. I'm—I'm glad to see you, Will.

WILLARD. Thank you.

LAURA. Won't you sit down?

WILLARD (*regaining his ease of manner*). Thank you again. (*Puts hat and cane at end of wardrobe; removes overcoat and places it on back of armchair; sits in armchair.*)

LAURA (*sits right of table*). It's rather cold out, isn't it?

WILLARD. Just a bit sharp.

LAURA. You came with Elfie in the car?

WILLARD. She picked me up at Martin's; we lunched there.

LAURA. By appointment?

WILLARD. I'd asked her.

LAURA. Well?

WILLARD. Well, Laura.

LAURA. She told you?

WILLARD. Not a great deal. What do you want to tell me?

LAURA (*very simply, and avoiding his glance*). Will, I'm ready to come back.

WILLARD (*with an effort concealing his sense of triumph and satisfaction. Rises and goes to* LAURA.) I'm mighty glad of that, Laura. I've missed you like the very devil.

LAURA. Do we—do we have to talk it over much? (*She stands at table in front of bed.*)

WILLARD. Not at all unless you want to. I understand—in fact, I always have.

LAURA (*wearily*). Yes, I guess you always did. I didn't. (*Sits in front of table.*)

WILLARD. It will be just the same as it was before, you know.

LAURA. Yes.

WILLARD. I didn't think it was possible for me to miss anyone the way I have you. I've been lonely.

LAURA. That's nice in you to say that.

WILLARD. You'll have to move out of here right away. (*Moves to back of table and surveys room.*) This place is enough to give one the colly-wabbles.

If you'll be ready tomorrow I'll send my man over to help you take care of the luggage.

LAURA. Tomorrow will be all right, thank you.

WILLARD. And you'll need some money in the meantime. I'll leave this here. (*He takes a roll of bills and places it on the bureau.*)

LAURA. You seem to have come prepared. Did Elfie and you plan this all out?

WILLARD. Not planned—just hoped. I think you'd better go to some nice hotel now. Later we can arrange. (*Sits on side of bed.*)

LAURA. Will, we'll always be frank. I said I was ready to go. It's up to you —when and where.

WILLARD. The hotel scheme is the best, but, Laura—

LAURA. Yes?

WILLARD. You're quite sure this is in earnest. You don't want to change? You've time enough now.

LAURA. I've quite made up my mind. It's final.

WILLARD. If you want to work, Burgess has a nice part for you. I'll telephone and arrange if you say so.

LAURA. Thanks. Say I'll see him in the morning.

WILLARD. And, Laura, you know when we were in Denver, and—

LAURA (*rises hurriedly*). Please, please, don't speak of it.

WILLARD. I'm sorry, but I've got to. I told (*Rises.*) Madison (LAURA *turns her head.*)—pardon me, but I must do this—that if this time ever came I'd have you write him the truth. Before we go any further I'd like you to do that now.

LAURA. Say good-by? (*Turns to* WILLARD.)

WILLARD. Just that.

LAURA. I wouldn't know how to

begin. It will hurt him awfully deeply.

WILLARD. It'll be worse if you don't. He'll like you for telling him. It would be honest, and that is what he expects.

LAURA. Must I—now?

WILLARD. I think you should.

LAURA (goes to table and sits down). How shall I begin, Will?

WILLARD (standing back of table). You mean you don't know what to say?

LAURA. Yes.

WILLARD. Then I'll dictate.

LAURA. I'll do just as you say. You're the one to tell me now.

WILLARD. Address it the way you want to. (She complies.) I'm going to be pretty brutal. In the long run I think that is best, don't you?

LAURA. It's up to you.

WILLARD. Ready?

LAURA. Begin.

WILLARD (dictating). "All I have to say can be expressed in one word, 'good-by.' I shall not tell you where I've gone, but remind you of what Brockton told you the last time he saw you. He is here now (Pause) dictating this letter. What I am doing is voluntary—my own suggestion. Don't grieve. Be happy and successful. I do not love you."—

LAURA (puts pen down, looks at him). Will—please.

WILLARD. It has got to go just that way—"I do not love you." Sign it "Laura." (Does it.) Fold it, put it in an envelope—seal it—address it. Now shall I mail it?

LAURA. No. If you don't mind I'd sooner. It's sort of a last—message.

WILLARD (goes to armchair, gets coat, puts it on). All right. You're a little upset now, and I'm going. We are all to dine at Martin's tonight at seven-thirty. There'll be a party. Of course you'll come. (Gets hat and cane.)

LAURA. I don't think I can. You see—

WILLARD. I know, I guess there's enough there (Indicating money) for your immediate needs. Later you can straighten things up. Shall I send the car?

LAURA. Yes, please.

WILLARD. Good. It will be the first happy evening I've had in a long, long time. You'll be ready? (Approaches and bends over her as if to caress her.)

LAURA (shrinking away). Please don't. Remember, we don't dine until seven-thirty.

WILLARD. All right. (Exit.)

(For a moment LAURA sits silent, and then angrily rises, crosses up to dresser, gets alcohol lamp, crosses to table with lamp, lights same, and starts back to dresser. Knock at door.)

LAURA. Come in. (ANNIE enters, and stops.) That you, Annie?

ANNIE. Yassum.

LAURA. Mrs. Farley wants her rent. There is some money. (Tosses money on to table.) Take it to her.

ANNIE (goes to the table, examines the roll of bills, and is palpably surprised). Dey ain't nothin' heah, Miss Laura, but five great big one hundred dollah bills.

LAURA. Take two. And look in that upper drawer. You'll find some pawn tickets there.

ANNIE (complies). Yassum. (Aside) Dat's real money—dem's yellow backs sure.

LAURA. Take the two top ones and go get my lace gown and one of the hats. The ticket is for a hundred and ten dollars. Keep ten for yourself, and hurry.

ANNIE (aside). Ten for myself—I never see so much money (Her astonishment nearly overcoming her, to LAURA) Yassum, Miss Laura, yassum.

(*She goes toward door, and then turns to* LAURA.) Ah'm so mighty glad yo' out all yo' trouble, Miss Laura. I says to Mis' Farley now—

LAURA (*snapping her off*). Don't—don't. Go do as I tell you and mind your business. (ANNIE *turns sullenly and walks toward the door. At that moment,* LAURA *sees the letter, which she has thrown on the table.*) Wait a minute. I want you to mail a letter. (*By this time, her hair is half down, hanging loosely over her shoulders. Her waist is open at the throat, collar off, and she has the appearance of a woman's untidiness when she is at that particular stage of her toilet. Hands letter to* ANNIE, *but snatches it away as* ANNIE *turns to go. She glances at the letter long and wistfully, and her nerve fails her.*) Never mind.

(ANNIE *exits. Slowly* LAURA *puts the letter over the flame of the alcohol lamp and it ignites. As it burns, she holds it in her fingers, and when half consumed throws it into waste-jar, sits on side of bed watching letter burn, then lies down across bed on her elbows, her chin in her hands, facing audience. As the last flicker is seen, the curtain slowly descends.*)

ACT THREE

Two months have elapsed. The scene is at BROCKTON's *apartment in a hotel such as is not overparticular concerning the relations of its tenants. There are a number of these hotels throughout the theatre district of New York, and, as a rule, one will find them usually of the same type. The room in which this scene is placed is that of the general living room in one of the handsomest apartments in the building.*

The prevailing color is green, and there is nothing particularly gaudy about the general furnishings. They are in good taste, but without the variety of arrangement and ornamentation which would naturally obtain in a room occupied by people a bit more particular concerning their surroundings. Down stage and just right of center is a table about three feet square which can be used not only as a general center table, but also for service while the occupants are coming up stage, the room turns at a sharp angle of thirty-five degrees from 2 to 3, and this space is largely taken up by a large doorway. This is equipped with sliding doors and hung with green portieres, which are handsome and in harmony with the general scheme of the furnishings of the room. This entrance is to the sleeping room of the apartment. At the back of stage is a large window or alcove. The window is on the ordinary plan, and the view through it shows the back of another building of New York, presumably a hotel of about the same character. Green portieres are also hung on the windows. Down left is the entrance to the corridor of the hotel, and this must be so arranged that it works with a latchkey and opens upon a small hallway, which separates the apartment from the main hallway. This is necessary as the action calls for the slamming of a door and later the opening of the direct and intimate door of the apartment with a latchkey. At left of center is a sofa, and there is a general arrangement of chairs without overcrowding the apartment. Just below, where the right portiere is hung, is a long full-length mirror, such as women dress by. Against right flat is a large, lady's fancy dresser.

To the immediate left of the sliding doors, which go into the sleeping apart-

ment, is a lady's small writing desk, with a practical drawer on the right-hand side, in which is a pearl-handled 32-calibre revolver. The front of the desk is open at rise. On top of the desk is a desk lamp and a large box of candy, inside the desk is writing material, etc. In pigeonhole there is a small photo and frame, which ANNIE *places on the table when she removes the breakfast set. In front of center window in alcove is a small table on which is a parlor lamp, some newspapers, including the* New York Sun. *On the floor running between the desk and table is a large fur rug. In front of the table is a small gilt chair; in front of desk there is also a small gilt chair; there is a pianola piano, on top of which is a bundle of music rolls. In place, ready to play, is a roll of Negro tune called "Bon-Bon Buddie, My Chocolate Drop." On top of the piano, in addition to the music rolls, are a fancy lamp, a large basket of chrysanthemums, and two photos in frames, at the upper corner. Standing on the floor is a large piano lamp. On the sofa are cushions, and thrown over its back is a lady's opera-coat. On the sofa are also a fan and some small dinner favors.*

On the dresser are a lady's silver toilet set, including powder boxes, rouge boxes, manicuring implements, and a small plush black cat that might have been a favor at some time. Two little dolls hang on the side of the glass of the dresser, which also might have been favors. These are used later in the action, and are necessary.

When the curtain rises on this scene, it is noticeable that the occupants of the room must have returned rather late at night, after having dined, not wisely, but too well. In the alcove is a man's dress-coat and vest thrown on the cushions in a most careless manner, *a silk hat badly rumpled is near it. Over the top of sofa is an opera-cloak, and hung on the mirror is a huge hat, of the evening type, such as women would pay handsomely for. A pair of gloves is thrown on top of the pier glass. The curtains in the bay-window are half drawn, and the light shades are half drawn down the windows, so that when the curtain goes up the place is in a rather dim light. On the table are the remains of a breakfast, which is served in a boxlike tray such as is used in hotels.* LAURA *is discovered sitting near the table, her hair a bit untidy. She has on a very expensive negligee gown.* WILLARD, *in a business suit, is at the other side of the table, and both have evidently just about concluded their breakfast and are reading the newspapers while they sip their coffee.* LAURA *is intent in the scanning of her* Morning Telegraph, *while* WILLARD *is deep in the market reports of the* Journal of Commerce, *and in each instance these things must be made apparent.* WILLARD *throws down the paper rather impatiently.*

———

WILLARD. Have you seen the *Sun,* Laura?

LAURA. No.

WILLARD. Where is it?

LAURA. I don't know.

WILLARD (*in a loud voice*). Annie, Annie! (*A pause*) Annie! (*In an undertone, half directed to* LAURA) Where the devil is that nigger?

LAURA. Why, I suppose she's at breakfast.

WILLARD. Well, she ought to be here.

LAURA. Did it ever occur to you that she has got to eat just the same as you have?

WILLARD. She's your servant, isn't she?

LAURA. My maid.

WILLARD. Well, what have you got her for—to eat or to wait on you? Annie!

LAURA. Don't be so cross. What do you want?

WILLARD. I want the *Sun.* (*Pours out one half glass of water from bottle.*)

LAURA. I will get it for you. (*Rather wearily she gets up and goes to the table where there are other morning papers, she takes the* Sun, *hands it to him, goes back to her seat, reopens the* Morning Telegraph. *There is a pause.* ANNIE *enters from the sleeping room.*)

ANNIE. Do yuh want me, suh?

WILLARD. Yes, I did want you, but don't now. When I'm at home I have a man to look after me and I get what I want.

LAURA. For heaven's sake, Will, have a little patience. If you like your man so well you had better live at home, but don't come around here with a grouch and bulldoze everybody.

WILLARD. Don't think for a moment that there's much to come around here for. Annie, this room's stuffy.

ANNIE. Yassuh.

WILLARD. Draw those portieres. Let those curtains up. (ANNIE *lets up curtain.*) Let's have a little light. Take away these clothes and hide them. Don't you know that a man doesn't want to see the next morning anything to remind him of the night before. Make the place look a little respectable.

(*In the meantime,* ANNIE *scurries around, picking up the coat and vest, opera-cloak, etc., as rapidly as possible and throwing them over her arm without any idea of order. It is very apparent that she is rather fearful of the anger of* WILLARD *while he is in this mood.*)

WILLARD (*looking at her*). Be care-ful. You're not taking the wash off the line.

ANNIE. Yassuh. (*Exits in confusion.*)

LAURA (*laying down paper and looking at* WILLARD). Well, I must say you're rather amiable this morning.

WILLARD. I feel like hell.

LAURA. Market unsatisfactory?

WILLARD. No; head too big. (*He lights a cigar; as he takes a puff he makes an awful face.*) Tastes like punk. (*Puts cigar into cup.*)

LAURA. You drank a lot.

WILLARD. We'll have to cut out those parties. I can't do those things any more. I'm not as young as I was, and in the morning it makes me sick. How do you feel?

LAURA. A little tired, that's all. (*Rises, crosses to bureau.*)

WILLARD. You didn't touch anything?

LAURA. No.

WILLARD. I guess you're on the safe side. It was a great old party, though, wasn't it?

LAURA. Did you think so?

WILLARD. Oh, for that sort of a blowout. Not too rough, but just a little easy. I like them at night and I hate them in the morning. (*He picks up the paper and commences to glance it over in a casual manner, not interrupting his conversation.*) Were you bored?

LAURA. Yes; always at things like that.

WILLARD. Well, you don't have to go.

LAURA. You asked me.

WILLARD. Still, you could say no.

(LAURA *picks up paper, puts it on table, and goes back to the bureau.*)

LAURA. But you asked me.

WILLARD. What did you go for if you didn't want to?

LAURA. *You* wanted me to.

WILLARD. I don't quite get you.

LAURA. Well, Will, you have all my

time when I'm not in the theatre, and you can do with it just what you please. You pay for it. I'm working for you.

WILLARD. Is that all I've got—just your time?

LAURA (wearily). That and the rest. (LAURA goes to desk, gets "part," crosses to sofa, turning pages of "part.") I guess you know. (Goes to sofa and sits.)

WILLARD (looking at her curiously) Down in the mouth, eh? I'm sorry.

LAURA. No, only if you want me to be frank, I'm a little tired. You may not believe it, but I work awfully hard over at the theatre. Burgess will tell you that. I know I'm not so very good as an actress, but I try to be. (LAURA lies down on sofa.) I'd like to succeed, myself. They're very patient with me. Of course they've got to be—that's another thing you're paying for, but I don't seem to get along except this way.

WILLARD. Oh, don't get sentimental. If you're going to bring up that sort of talk, Laura, do it sometime when I haven't got a hangover, and then don't forget talk never does count for much.

(LAURA goes to mirror, picks up hat from box, puts it on, looks in mirror. She turns around and looks at him steadfastly for a minute. During this entire scene, from the time the curtain rises, she must in a way indicate a premonition of an approaching catastrophe, a feeling, vague but nevertheless palpable, that something is going to happen. She must hold this before her audience so that she can show to them, without showing to him, the disgust she feels. LAURA has tasted of the privations of self-sacrifice during her struggle, and she has weakly surrendered and is unable to go back, but that brief period of self-abnegation has shown to her most clearly the rottenness of the other sort of living. There is enough sentimentality and emotion in her character to make it impossible for her to accept this manner of existence as ELFIE does. Hers is not a nature of careless candor, but of dreamy ideals and better living, warped, handicapped, disillusioned, and destroyed by a weakness that finds its principal force in vanity. WILLARD resumes his newspaper in a more attentive way. The girl looks at him and expresses in pantomime, by the slightest gesture or shrug of the shoulders, her growing distaste for him and his way of living. In the meantime WILLARD is reading the paper rather carefully. He stops suddenly and then looks at his watch.)

LAURA. What time is it?

WILLARD. After ten.

LAURA. Oh.

(WILLARD, at this moment particularly, reads some part of the paper, turns to her with a keen glance of suspicion and inquiry, and then, for a very short moment, evidently settles in his mind a cross-examination. He has read in this paper a dispatch from Chicago, which speaks of JOHN MADISON having arrived there as a representative of a big Western mining syndicate which is going to open large operations in the Nevada gold-fields, and representing MR. MADISON as being on his way to New York with sufficient capital to enlist more, and showing him to be now a man of means. The attitude of LAURA and the coincidence of the dispatch bring back to WILLARD the scene in Denver, and later in New York, and with that subtle intuition of the man of the world he connects the two.)

WILLARD. I don't suppose, Laura, that you'd be interested now in knowing anything about that young fellow out in Colorado? What was his name—Madison?

LAURA. Do you know anything?

WILLARD. No, nothing particularly. I've been rather curious to know how he came out. He was a pretty fresh young man and did an awful lot of talking. I wonder how he's doing and how he's getting along. I don't suppose by any chance you have ever heard from him?

LAURA. No, no; I've never heard. (*Goes to bureau.*)

WILLARD. I presume he never replied to that letter you wrote?

LAURA. No.

WILLARD. It would be rather queer, eh, if this young fellow should (*Looks at paper.*) happen to come across a lot of money—not that I think he ever could, but it would be funny, wouldn't it?

LAURA. Yes, yes; it would be unexpected. I hope he does. It might make him happy.

WILLARD. Think he might take a trip East and see you act. You know you've got quite a part now.

LAURA (*impatiently*). I wish you wouldn't discuss this. Why do you mention it now? (*Going to table*) Is it because you were drinking last night and lost your sense of delicacy? You once had some consideration for me. What I've done I've done. I'm giving you all that I can. Please, please, don't hurt me any more than you can help. That's all I ask. (*Goes to mirror, back to table; sits.*)

WILLARD. Well, I'm sorry. I didn't mean that, Laura. I guess I am feeling a little bad today. Really, I don't want to hurt your feelings, my dear. (*He gets up, goes to her, puts his hands on her shoulders, and his cheek close to the back of her head. She bends forward and shudders a little bit. It is very easy to see that the life she is leading is becoming intolerable to her.*)

WILLARD. You know, dearie, I do a lot for you because you've always been on the level with me. I'm sorry I hurt you, but there was too much wine last night and I'm all upset. Forgive me.

(LAURA, *in order to avoid his caresses, has leaned forward, her hands are clasped between her knees, and she is looking straight outward with a cold, impassive expression.* WILLARD *regards her silently for a moment. Really in the man's heart there is an affection, and really he wants to try to comfort her; but he seems to realize that she has slipped away from the old environment and conditions, and that he simply bought her back; that he hasn't any of her affection, even with his money; that she evinces toward him none of the old camaraderie; and it hurts him, as those things always hurt a selfish man, inclining him to be brutal and inconsiderate.* WILLARD *crosses left to center, stands reading paper; bell rings, pause and second bell.* WILLARD *seizes upon this excuse to go up stage and over towards the door.*)

WILLARD (*after second bell*). Damn that bell. (*He continues on his way, he opens the door, leaves it open, and passes on to the outer door, which he opens.* LAURA *remains immovable and impassive with the same cold, hard expression on her face. He comes in slamming the outer door with effect, which one must have at this point of the play, because it is essential to a situation coming later. Enters the room, closes the door, and holds in his hand a telegram. Looks from newspaper to telegram.*)

WILLARD. A wire.

LAURA. For me?

WILLARD. Yes.

LAURA. From whom, I wonder. Perhaps Elfie with a luncheon engagement.

WILLARD (*handing to her*). I don't know. Here. (*Pauses; he faces her, looking at her. She opens it quickly. She reads it and as she does, gasps quickly with an exclamation of fear and surprise. This is what the dispatch says (it is dated at Buffalo and addressed to* LAURA): *"I will be in New York before noon. I'm coming to marry you, and I'm coming with a bankroll. I wanted to keep it secret and have a big surprise for you, but I can't hold it any longer, because I feel just like a kid with a new top. Don't go out, and be ready for the big matrimonial thing. All my love. John."*)

WILLARD. No bad news, I hope?

LAURA (*walking up stage rather hurriedly*). No, no—not bad news.

WILLARD. I thought you were startled.

LAURA. No, not at all.

WILLARD (*looking at paper about where he had left off*). From Elfie? (*Sits in armchair.*)

LAURA. No, just a friend.

WILLARD. Oh! (*He makes himself rather comfortable in the chair, and* LAURA *regards him for a moment from up stage as if trying to figure out how to get rid of him.*)

LAURA. Won't you be rather late getting down town, Will?

WILLARD. Doesn't make any difference. I don't feel much like the office now. Thought I might order the car and take a spin through the park. The cold air will do me a lot of good. Like to go?

LAURA. No, not today. I thought your business was important; you said so last night. (*Stands by sofa.*)

WILLARD. No hurry. Do you—er—want to get rid of me?

LAURA. Why should I?

WILLARD. Expecting someone?

LAURA. No—not exactly. (*Goes to window.*)

WILLARD. If you don't mind, I'll stay here. (*Lets curtain fly up.*)

LAURA. Just as you please. (*A pause. Goes to piano; plays.*) Will?

WILLARD. Yes.

LAURA. How long does it take to come from Buffalo?

WILLARD. Depends on the train you take.

LAURA. About how long?

WILLARD. Between eight and ten hours, I think. Someone coming?

LAURA. Do you know anything about the trains?

WILLARD. Not much. Why don't you find out for yourself? Have Annie get the timetable?

LAURA. I will. Annie! Annie! (*Rises from piano.* ANNIE *appears at doorway.*)

ANNIE. Yassum!

LAURA. Go ask one of the hall-boys to bring me a New York Central timetable.

ANNIE. Yassum!

(*Crosses the stage and exits through door.* LAURA *sits on arm of sofa.*)

WILLARD. Then you *do* expect someone, eh?

LAURA. Only one of the girls who used to be in the same company with me. But I'm not sure that she's coming here.

WILLARD. Then the wire was from her?

LAURA. Yes.

WILLARD. Did she say what train she was coming on?

LAURA. No.

WILLARD. Well, there are a lot of trains. About what time did you expect her in?

LAURA. She didn't say.

WILLARD. Do I know her?

LAURA. I think not. I met her while I worked in 'Frisco.

WILLARD. Oh! (*Resumes his paper.*)

(ANNIE *reenters with a timetable and hands it to* LAURA.)

LAURA. Thanks, take those breakfast things away, Annie. (*Sits on sofa.*)

(ANNIE *complies; takes them across stage, opens the door leading to the corridor, exits.* LAURA *in the meantime is studying the timetable.*)

LAURA. I can't make this out.

WILLARD. Give it here; maybe I can help you.

(LAURA *goes to table and sits opposite* WILLARD, *and hands him the timetable. He takes it and handles it as if he were familiar with it.*)

WILLARD. Where is she coming from?

LAURA. The West; the telegram was from Buffalo. I suppose she was on her way when she sent it.

WILLARD. There's a train comes in here at 9:30—that's the Twentieth Century, that doesn't carry passengers from Buffalo; then there's one at 11:41; one at 1:49; another at 3:45; another at 5:40; and another at 5:48 —that's the Lake Shore Limited, a fast train; and all pass through Buffalo. Did you think of meeting her?

LAURA. No. She'll come here when she arrives.

WILLARD. Knows where you live?

LAURA. She has the address.

WILLARD. Ever been to New York before?

LAURA. I think not.

WILLARD (*passing her the timetable*). Well, that's the best I can do for you.

LAURA. Thank you. (*Puts timetable in desk.*)

WILLARD (*takes up the paper again;* LAURA *looks at clock*). By George, this is funny.

LAURA. What?

WILLARD. Speak of the devil, you know.

LAURA. Who?

WILLARD. Your old friend Madison.

LAURA (*utters a slight exclamation and makes an effort to control herself*). What—what about him?

WILLARD. He's been in Chicago.

LAURA. How do you know?

WILLARD. Here's a dispatch about him.

LAURA (*coming quickly over to him, looking over his shoulder*). What— where—what's it about?

WILLARD. Well, I'm damned if he hasn't done what he said he'd do— see! (*Holds the paper so that she can see.* LAURA *takes paper.*) He's been in Chicago, and is on his way to New York. He's struck it rich in Nevada and is coming with a lot of money. Queer, isn't it? (LAURA *puts paper on table.*) Did you know anything about it? (*Lights cigarette.*)

LAURA. No, no; nothing at all. (*Goes to bureau.*)

WILLARD. Lucky for him, eh?

LAURA. Yes, yes; it's very nice.

WILLARD. Too bad he couldn't get this a little sooner, eh, Laura?

LAURA. Oh, I don't know—I don't think it's too bad. What makes you ask?

WILLARD. Oh, nothing. I suppose he ought to be here today. Are you going to see him if he looks you up?

LAURA. No, no; I don't want to see him. You know that, don't you, that I don't want to see him? What makes you ask these questions? (*Crosses to sofa and sits.*)

WILLARD. Just thought you might meet him, that's all. Don't get sore about it.

LAURA. I'm not. (*She holds the telegram crumpled in one hand.* WILLARD *lays down the paper, and regards* LAURA *curiously. She sees the expression on his face and averts her head in order not to meet his eye.*)

LAURA. What are you looking at me that way, for?

WILLARD. I wasn't conscious that I was looking at you in any particular way—why?

LAURA. Oh, nothing. I guess I'm nervous, too. (*Lies on sofa.*)

WILLARD. I dare say you are. (*A pause.*)

LAURA. Yes, I am. (WILLARD *goes to* LAURA.)

WILLARD. You know I don't want to delve into a lot of past history at this time, but I've got to talk to you for a moment.

LAURA. Why don't you do it some other time? I don't want to be talked to now. (*Rises.*)

WILLARD. But I've got to do it just the same.

LAURA (*trying to effect an attitude of resigned patience and resignation*). Well, what is it? (*Resuming seat on sofa.*)

WILLARD. You've always been on the square with me, Laura. That's why I've liked you a lot better than the other women.

LAURA. Are you going into all that again now, this morning? I thought we understood each other.

WILLARD. So did I, but somehow I think that maybe we *don't* quite understand each other.

LAURA. In what way? (*Turns to* WILLARD.)

WILLARD (*Looking her straight in the eye*). That letter I dictated to you the day that you came back to me, and left it for you to mail—did you mail it?

LAURA. Yes.

WILLARD. You're quite sure?

LAURA. Yes, I'm quite sure. I wouldn't say so if I wasn't.

WILLARD. And you didn't know Madison was coming East until you read about it in that newspaper?

LAURA. No—no, I didn't know.

WILLARD. Have you heard from him?

LAURA. No—no—I haven't heard from him. Don't talk to me about this thing. Why can't you leave me alone? I'm miserable enough as it is. (*Crossing to extreme right.*)

WILLARD (*crossing to table*). But I've got to talk to you. Laura, you're lying to me.

LAURA. What! (*She makes a valiant effort to become angry.*)

WILLARD. You're lying to me, and you've been lying to me, and I've trusted you. Show me that telegram!

LAURA. No.

WILLARD (*going over towards her*). Show me that telegram!

(LAURA *crosses up to doors leading into bedroom.*)

LAURA (*tears telegram in half*). You've no right to ask me.

WILLARD. Are you going to make me take it away (LAURA *crosses to window.*) from you? I've (*Crosses to sofa.*) never laid my hands on you yet.

LAURA. It's my business.

WILLARD. Yes, and it's mine.

(*During scene. Backing away from* WILLARD, *he is following her.* LAURA *backs against bureau.* WILLARD *grabs her and attempts to take telegram from her. She has put it in the front of waist. She slowly draws it out.*)

WILLARD. That telegram's from Madison. Give it here!

LAURA. No.

WILLARD. I'm going to find out where I stand. Give me that telegram, or I'll take it away from you.

LAURA. No.

WILLARD. Come on!

LAURA. I'll give it to you. *(Takes telegram out of waist, hands it to him. He takes it slowly, looking her squarely in the eye.* WILLARD *crosses to center and does not glance away while he slowly smooths it out so that it can be read; when he finally takes it in both hands to read it she staggers back a step or two weakly.)* WILLARD *(then reads the telegram aloud).* "I will be in New York before noon. I'm coming to marry you, and I'm coming with a bankroll. I wanted to keep it a secret and have a big surprise for you, but I can't hold it any longer, because I feel just like a kid with a new top. Don't go out, and be ready for the big matrimonial thing. All my love. John." Then you knew?

LAURA. Yes.

WILLARD. But you didn't know he was coming until this arrived?

LAURA. No.

WILLARD. And you didn't mail the letter *(Tossing telegram on table)*, did you?

LAURA. No.

WILLARD. What did you do with it?

LAURA. I—I burned it.

WILLARD. Why? (LAURA *is completely overcome and unable to answer.)* Why?

LAURA. I—I couldn't help it—I simply couldn't help it.

WILLARD. So you've been corresponding all this time.

LAURA. Yes.

WILLARD. And he doesn't know *(With a gesture around the room, indicating the condition in which they live)* about us?

LAURA. No.

WILLARD *(taking a step towards her).* By God, I never beat a woman in my life, but I feel as though I could wring your neck.

LAURA. Why don't you? You've done everything else. Why don't you?

WILLARD. Don't you know that I gave Madison my word that if you came back to me I'd let him know? Don't you know that I like that young fellow and I wanted to protect him, and did everything I could to help him? And do you know what you've done to me? You've made me out a liar—you've made me lie to a man—a man—you understand. What are you going to do now? Tell me—what are you going to do now? Don't stand there as if you've lost your voice—how are you going to square me?

LAURA. I'm not thinking about squaring you. What am I going to do for him?

WILLARD. Not what *you* are going to do for him—what am *I* going to do for him. Why, I couldn't have that young fellow think that I tricked him into this thing for you or all the rest of the women of your kind on earth. God! I might have known that you, and the others like you, couldn't be square. *(The girl looks at him dumbly. He glances at his watch, walks up stage, looks out of the window, comes down again, goes to the table, and looks at her acrosss it.)* You've made a nice mess of it, haven't you?

LAURA *(weakly).* There isn't any mess. Please go away. He'll be here soon. Please let *me* see him—please do that.

WILLARD. No, I'll wait. This time I'm going to tell him myself, and I don't care how tough it is.

LAURA *(immediately regaining all her vitality).* No, you mustn't do that. *(Crossing back of table to center)* Oh, Will, I'm not offering any excuse. I'm not saying anything, but I'm telling you the truth. I couldn't give him up—I couldn't do it. I love him.

WILLARD. Huh. (*Grins, goes to front of sofa.*)

LAURA. Don't you think so? I know you can't see what I see, but I do. And why can't you go away? Why can't you leave me this? It's all I ever had. He doesn't know. No one will ever tell him. I'll take him away. It's the best for him—it's the best for me. Please go.

WILLARD. Why—do you think that I'm going to let you trip him the way you tripped me? (*Crosses and sits in armchair.*) No. I'm going to stay right here until that young man arrives, and I'm going to tell him that it wasn't my fault. You were to blame.

LAURA. Then you are going to let him know. You're not going to give me a single, solitary chance?

WILLARD. I'll give you every chance that you deserve when he knows. Then he can do as he pleases, but there must be no more deception, that's flat.

(*LAURA goes and kneels beside WILLARD's chair.*)

LAURA. Then you must let me tell him—(WILLARD *turns away impatiently.*)—yes, you must. If I didn't tell him before, I'll do it now. You must go. If you ever had any regard for me —if you ever had any affection—if you ever had any friendship, please let me do this now. I want you to go— you can come back. Then you'll see —you'll know—only I want to try to make him understand that—that maybe if I am weak I'm not vicious. I want to let him know that I didn't want to do it, but I couldn't help it. Just give me the chance to be as good as I can be. (WILLARD *gives her a look.*) Oh, I promise you, I will tell him, and then—then I don't care what happens—only he must learn everything from me—please—please —let me do this—it's the last favor

I shall ever—ever ask of you. Won't you? (LAURA *breaks down and weeps.*)

WILLARD (*rising, looks at her a moment as if mentally debating the best thing to do. Crosses in front of table, stands facing her with back to audience.*) All right, I won't be unkind. I'll be back early this afternoon, and just remember, this is the time you'll have to go right through to the end. Understand?

LAURA. Yes, I'll do it—all of it. Won't you please go—now? (*Crosses; sits in armchair.*)

WILLARD. All right. (*He exits into the bedroom and immediately enters again with overcoat on his arm and hat in hand; he goes and turns.*) I am sorry for you, Laura, but remember you've got to tell the truth.

LAURA (*who is sitting in a chair looking straight in front of her with a set expression*). Please go. (WILLARD *exits.*)

(LAURA *sits in a chair in a state of almost stupefaction, holding this attitude as long as possible.* ANNIE *enters, and in a characteristic manner, begins her task of tidying up the room;* LAURA, *without changing her attitude and staring straight in front of her, her elbows between her knees and her chin on her hands.*)

LAURA. Annie!

ANNIE. Yassum.

LAURA. Do you remember in the boardinghouse—when we finally packed up—what you did with everything?

ANNIE. Yassum.

LAURA. You remember that I used to keep a pistol?

ANNIE. Yo' all mean dat one yo' say dat gemman out West gave yuh once?

LAURA. Yes.

ANNIE. Yassum, Ah 'membuh it.

LAURA. Where is it now?

ANNIE (*crosses to writing desk*). Last

Ah saw of it was in dis heah draw' in de writin' desk. (*This speech takes her across to desk; she opens the drawer, fumbles among a lot of old papers, letters, etc., and finally produces a small thirty-two calibre, and gingerly crosses to* LAURA.) Is dis it?

LAURA (*slowly turns around and looks at it*). Yes. Put it back. I thought perhaps it was lost. (ANNIE *complies when the bell rings.* LAURA *starts suddenly, involuntarily gathering her negligee gown closer to her figure, and at once she is under a great stress of emotion, and sways upon her feet to such an extent that she is obliged to put one hand out on to the table to maintain her balance. When she speaks, it is with a certain difficulty of articulation.*) See —who—that is—and let me know.

ANNIE (*turning*). Yassum. (*Opens the first door, and afterwards opens the second door.*)

ELFIE (*from off stage*). Hello, Annie —folks home?

ANNIE. Yassum, she's in.

(LAURA *immediately evinces her tremendous relief, and* ELFIE, *without waiting for a reply, has shoved* ANNIE *aside and enters,* ANNIE *following and closing the door.* ELFIE *is beautifully gowned in a morning dress with an overabundance of fur trimmings and all the furbelows that would accompany the extravagant raiment generally affected by a woman of that type.* ELFIE *approaching effusively.*)

ELFIE. Hello, dearie.

LAURA. Hello, Elfie. (*Sits on sofa.* ELFIE *puts muff, etc., on table.*)

ELFIE. It's a bully day out. (*Goes to bureau, looking in mirror.*) I've been shopping all morning long; just blew myself until I'm broke, that's all. My goodness, don't you ever get dressed? Listen. Talk about cinches. I copped out a gown, all ready made and fits me

like the paper on the wall, for $37.80. Looks like it might have cost $200. Anyway I had them charge $200 on the bill, and I kept the change. There are two or three more down town there, and I want you to go down and look them over. Models, you know, being sold out. I don't blame you for not getting up earlier. (*She sits at the table, not noticing* LAURA.) That was some party last night. I know you didn't drink a great deal, but gee! what an awful tide Will had on. How do you feel? (*Looks at her critically.*) What's the matter, are you sick? You look all in. What you want to do is this—put on your duds and go out for an hour. It's a perfectly grand day out. My Gaud! how the sun does shine! Clear and cold. (*A pause*) Well, much obliged for the conversation. Don't I get a "Good-morning," or a "How-dydo," or a something of that sort?

LAURA. I'm tired, Elfie, and blue— terribly blue.

ELFIE (*rises, goes to* LAURA). Well now, you just brace up and cut out all that emotional stuff. I came down to take you for a drive. You'd like it; just through the park. Will you go?

LAURA. Not this morning, dear; I'm expecting somebody.

ELFIE. A man?

LAURA (*finding it almost impossible to suppress a smile*). No, a gentleman.

ELFIE. Same thing. Do I know him?

LAURA. You've heard of him. (*At desk, looking at clock.*)

ELFIE. Well, don't be so mysterious. Who is he?

LAURA. What is your time, Elfie?

ELFIE (*looks at her watch*). Five minutes past eleven.

LAURA. Oh, I'm slow. I didn't know it was so late. Just excuse me, won't you, while I get some clothes on. He may be here any moment. Annie!

(*She goes up stage towards portieres.*)

ELFIE. Who?

LAURA. I'll tell you when I get dressed. Make yourself at home, won't you, dear?

ELFIE. I'd sooner hear. What is the scandal anyway?

LAURA (*as she goes out*). I'll tell you in a moment. Just as soon as Annie gets through with me.

ELFIE (*gets candy box off desk, sits on arm of sofa selecting candy; in a louder voice*). Do you know, Laura, I think I'll go back on the stage.

LAURA (*off stage*). Yes?

ELFIE. Yes, I'm afraid I'll have to. I think I need a sort of a boost to my popularity.

LAURA. How a boost, Elfie?

ELFIE. I think Jerry is getting cold feet. He's seeing a little too much of me (*Places candy box on sofa.*) nowadays.

LAURA. What makes you think that?

ELFIE. I think he is getting a relapse of that front-row habit. There's no use in talking, Laura, it's a great thing for a girl's credit when a man like Jerry can take two or three friends to the theatre, and when you make your entrance delicately point to you with his forefinger and say, "The third one from the front on the left belongs to muh." The old fool's hanging around some of these musical comedies lately, and I'm getting a little nervous every time rent day comes.

LAURA. Oh, I guess you'll get along all right, Elfie.

ELFIE (*with serene self-satisfaction*). Oh, that's a cinch (*Rises, goes to table, looking in dresser mirror at herself, and giving her hat and hair little touches.*), but I like to leave well enough alone, and if I had to make a change right now it would require a whole lot of thought and attention, to say nothing of the inconvenience, and I'm so nicely settled in my flat. (*She sees the pianola.*) Say, dearie, when did you get the piano player? I got one of them phonographs (*Goes to pianola, tries the levers, etc.*), but this has got that beat a city block. How does it work? What did it cost?

LAURA. I don't know.

ELFIE. Well, Jerry's got to stake me to one of these. (*Looks over the rolls on top. Mumbles to herself.*) "Tannhäuser, William Tell, Chopin." (*Then louder*) Listen, dear. Ain't you got anything else except all this highbrow stuff?

LAURA. What do you want?

ELFIE. Oh, something with a regular tune to it. (*Looks at empty box on pianola.*) Oh, here's one; just watch me tear this off. (*The roll is the tune of "Bon-Bon Buddie, My Chocolate Drop." She starts to play and moves the lever marked "Swell" wide open, increases the tempo, and is pumping with all the delight and enthusiasm of a child.*) Ain't it grand?

LAURA. Gracious, Elfie, don't play so loud. What's the matter?

ELFIE. I shoved over that thing marked "Swell." (*Stops and turns. Goes to center and stands.*) I sure will have to speak to Jerry about this. I'm stuck on that swell thing. Hurry up. (LAURA *appears.*) Gee! you look pale. (*And then in a tone of sympathy*) I'll just bet you and Will have had a fight, and he always gets the best of you, doesn't he, dearie? (LAURA *goes to dresser and busies herself.*) Listen. Don't you think you can ever get him trained? I almost threw Jerry down the stairs the other night and he came right back with a lot of American beauties and a check. I told him if he didn't look out I'd throw him downstairs every night. He's getting too damned independent and it's got me nervous. Oh, dear, I s'pose I will have to go back on the stage. (*Sits in armchair.*)

LAURA. In the chorus?

ELFIE. Well, I should say not! I'm going to give up my musical career. Charlie Burgess is putting on a new play, and he says he has a part in it for me if I want to go back. It isn't much, but very important—sort of a pantomime part. A lot of people talk about me and just at the right time I walk across the stage and make an awful hit. I told Jerry that if I went (LAURA *goes to sofa, picks up candy box, puts it upon desk, gets telegram off table and goes to right center.*) on he'd have to come across with one of those Irish crochet lace gowns. He fell for it. Do you know, dearie, I think he'd sell out his business just to have me back on the stage for a couple of weeks, just to give box parties every night for my entrance and *ex*-its.

LAURA (*seriously*). Elfie! (*Takes* ELFIE *by the hand, leads her over to sofa.* LAURA *sits,* ELFIE *standing.*)

ELFIE. Yes, dear.

LAURA. Come over here and sit down.

ELFIE. What's up?

LAURA. Do you know what I'm going to ask of you?

ELFIE. If it's a touch, you'll have to wait until next week. (*Sits opposite* LAURA.)

LAURA. No; just a little advice.

ELFIE (*with a smile*). Well, that's cheap, and Lord knows you need it. What's happened?

(LAURA *takes the crumpled and torn telegram that* WILLARD *has left on the table and hands it to* ELFIE. *The latter puts the two pieces together, reads it very carefully, looks up at* LAURA *about middle of telegram, and lays it down.*)

ELFIE. Well?

LAURA. Will suspected. There was something in the paper about Mr.

Madison—the telegram came—then we had a row.

ELFIE. Serious?

LAURA. Yes. Do you remember what I told you about that letter—the one Will made me write—I mean to John —telling him what I had done?

ELFIE. Yes, you burned it.

LAURA. I tried to lie to Will—he wouldn't have it that way. He seemed to know. He was furious.

ELFIE. Did he hit you?

LAURA. No; he made me admit that John didn't know, and then he said he'd stay here and tell himself that I'd made him lie, and then he said something about liking the other man and wanting to save him.

ELFIE. Save—shucks! He's jealous.

LAURA. I told him if he'd only go I'd —tell John myself when he came, and now you see I'm waiting—and I've got to tell—and—and I don't know how to begin—and—and I thought you could help me—you seem so sort of resourceful, and it means—it means so much to me. If John turned on me now I couldn't go back to Will, and, Elfie—I don't think I'd care to—stay here any more.

ELFIE. What! (*In an awestruck tone, taking* LAURA *in her arms impulsively.*) Dearie, get that nonsense out of your head and be sensible. I'd just like to see any two men who could make me think about—well—what you seem to have in your mind.

LAURA. But I don't know; don't you see, Elfie, I don't know. If I don't tell him Will will come back and he'll tell him, and I know John, and maybe— Elfie, do you know, I think John would kill him.

ELFIE. Well, don't you think anything about that. Now let's get (*Goes to armchair, draws it over a little, sits on arm.*) down to cases, and we haven't much time. Business is business, and love is love. You're long on love and I'm long on business, and between the two of us we ought to straighten this thing out. Now, evidently John is coming on here to marry you.

LAURA. Yes.

ELFIE. And you love him?

LAURA. Yes.

ELFIE. And as far as you know the moment that he comes in here it's quick to the justice and a big matrimonial thing.

LAURA. Yes, but you see how impossible it is—

ELFIE. I don't see anything impossible. From all you've said to me about this fellow there is only one thing to do.

LAURA. One thing?

ELFIE. Yes—get married quick. You say he has the money and you have the love, and you're sick of Brockton, and you want to switch and do it in the decent, respectable, conventional way, and he's going to take you away. Haven't you got sense enough to know that once you're married to Mr. Madison that Will Brockton wouldn't dare go to him, and if he did Madison wouldn't believe him. A man will believe a whole lot about his girl, but nothing about his wife.

LAURA (*turns and looks at her. There is a long pause*). Elfie (*Goes to table.*) —I—I don't think I could do like that to John. I don't think—I could deceive him.

ELFIE. You make me sick. The thing to do is to lie to all men (*Rises, pushes chair to table.*)—they all lie to you. Protect yourself. You seem to think that your happiness depends on this. Now do it. Listen. (*Touches* LAURA *to make her sit down;* LAURA *sits right of table;* ELFIE *sits on arm of chair left of table, elbows on table.*) Don't you realize that you and me, and all the

girls that are shoved into this life, are practically the common prey of any man who happens to come along? Don't you know that they've got about as much consideration for us as they have for any pet animal around the house, and the only way that we've got it on the animal is that we've got brains. This is a game, Laura, *not a sentiment.* Do you suppose this Madison (LAURA *turns to* ELFIE.)—now don't get sore—hasn't turned these tricks himself before he met you, and I'll gamble he's done it since. A man's natural trade is a heartbreaking business. Don't tell me about women breaking men's hearts. The only thing they can ever break is their bankroll. And besides, this is not Will's business; he has no right to interfere. You've been with him—yes, and he's been nice to you; but I don't think that he's given you any of the best of it. Now if you want to leave and go your own way and marry any Tom, Dick, or Harry that you want, it's nobody's affair but yours.

LAURA. But you don't understand—it's John. I can't lie to him.

ELFIE. Well, that's too bad about you. I used to have that truthful habit myself, and the best I ever got was the worst of it. All this talk about love and loyalty and constancy is fine and dandy in a book, but when a girl has to look out for herself, take it from me, whenever you've got that trump card up your sleeve just play it and rake in the pot. (*Takes* LAURA'*s hand affectionately.*) You know, dearie, you're just about the only one in the world I love.

LAURA. Elfie!

ELFIE. Since I broke away from the folks up state and they've heard things, there ain't any more letters coming to me with an Oswego postmark. Ma's gone, and the rest don't care. You're all

I've got in the world, Laura, and what I'm asking you to do is because I want to see you happy. I was afraid this thing was coming off, and the thing to do now is to grab your happiness, no matter how you get it nor where it comes from. There ain't a whole lot of joy in this world for you and me and the others we know, and what little you get you've got to take when you're young, because when those gray hairs begin to come, and the make-up isn't going to hide the wrinkles, unless you're well fixed it's going to be hell. You know what a fellow doesn't know doesn't hurt him, and he'll love you just the same and you'll love him. As for Brockton, let him get another girl; there're plenty 'round. Why, if this chance came to me I'd tie a can to Jerry so quick that you could hear it rattle all the way down Broadway. (*Rises, crosses back of table to* LAURA, *leans over back of chair, and puts arms around her neck very tenderly.*) Dearie, promise me that you won't be a damn fool.

(*The bell rings; both start.*)

LAURA (*rises*). Maybe that's John.

(ELFIE *brushes a tear quickly from her eye.*)

ELFIE. Oh! And you'll promise me, Laura?

LAURA. I'll try. (ANNIE *enters up stage from the adjoining room and crosses to the door.*) If that's Mr. Madison, Annie, tell him to come in. (*She stands near the table, almost rigid. Instinctively* ELFIE *goes to the mirror and rearranges her gown and hair as* ANNIE *exits.* ELFIE *turns to* LAURA.)

ELFIE. If I think he's the fellow when I see him, watch me and I'll tip you the wink. (*Kisses* LAURA, *crosses, puts on coat. She goes up stage.* LAURA *remains in her position. The doors are heard to open, and in a moment* JOHN enters. *He is dressed very neatly in a business suit and his face is tanned and weather-beaten. After he enters he stands still for a moment. The emotion that both he and* LAURA *go through is such that each is trying to control it,* LAURA *from the agony of her position and* JOHN *from the mere hurt of his affection. He sees* ELFIE *and forces a smile.*)

JOHN (*quietly*). Hello, Laura! I'm on time.

(LAURA *smiles and quickly crosses the stage and holds out her hand.*)

LAURA. Oh, John, I'm so glad—so glad to see you. (*They hold this position for a moment, looking into each other's eyes.* ELFIE *moves so as to take* JOHN *in from head to toe and is obviously very much pleased with his appearance. She coughs slightly.* LAURA *takes a step back with a smile.*) Oh, pardon me, John—one of my dearest friends, Miss St. Clair; she's heard a lot about you.

(ELFIE, *with a slight gush, in her most captivating manner, goes over and holds out her gloved hand laden with bracelets, and with her sweetest smile crosses to left center.*)

ELFIE. How do you do?

JOHN. I'm glad to meet you, I'm sure.

ELFIE (*still holding* JOHN's *hand*). Yes, I'm sure you are—particularly just at this time. (*To* LAURA) You know that old stuff about two's company and three (LAURA *smiles.*) is a crowd. Here's where I vamoose. (*Goes to door.*)

LAURA (*as* ELFIE *goes toward door*). Don't hurry, dear.

ELFIE (*with a grin*). No, I suppose not; just fall down stairs and get out of the way, that's all. (*Goes to* JOHN.) Anyway, Mr. Madison, I'm awfully glad to have met you, and I want to congratulate you. They tell me you're rich.

JOHN. Oh, no; not rich.

ELFIE. Well, I don't believe you— anyway I'm going. Ta-ta, dearie. Good-by, Mr. Madison.

JOHN. Good-by. (JOHN *crosses up to back of sofa, removes coat, puts it on sofa.*)

ELFIE (*goes to the door, opens it and turns.* JOHN'S *back is partly toward her and she gives a long wink at* LAURA, *snapping fingers to attract* LAURA'S *attention*). I must say, Laura, that when it comes to picking live ones, you certainly can go some. (*Exits.*)

(*After this remark both turn toward her and both smile. After* ELFIE *exits,* JOHN *turns to* LAURA *with a pleasant smile, and jerks his head towards the door where* ELFIE *has gone out.*)

JOHN. I bet she's a character.

LAURA. She's a dear.

JOHN. I can see that all right.

LAURA. She's been a very great friend to me.

JOHN. That's good, but don't I get a "how-dy-do," or a hand-shake, or a little kiss? You know I've come a long way.

(LAURA *goes to him and places herself in his arms; he kisses her affectionately. During all this scene between them the tenderness of the man is very apparent. As she releases herself from his embrace he takes her face in his hands and holds it up towards his.*)

JOHN. I'm not much on the love-making business, Laura, but I never thought I'd be as happy as I am now. (JOHN *and* LAURA *cross to right.* LAURA *kneels in armchair with back to audience,* JOHN *stands.*) I've been counting mileposts ever since I left Chicago, and it seemed like as if I had to go 'round the world before I got here.

LAURA. You never told me about your good fortune. If you hadn't telegraphed I wouldn't even have known you were coming.

JOHN. I didn't want you to. I'd made up my mind to sort of drop in here and give you a great big surprise —a happy one, I knew—but the papers made such a fuss in Chicago that I thought you might have read about it —did you?

LAURA. No.

JOHN. Gee! fixed up kind o' scrumptious, ain't you? (*Moves around, surveying rooms.*) Maybe you've been almost as prosperous as I have.

LAURA. You can get a lot of gilt and cushions in New York at half price, and besides, I've got a pretty good part now.

JOHN. Of course I know that, but I didn't think it would make you quite so comfortable. Great, ain't it?

LAURA. Yes.

JOHN (*standing beside her chair, with a smile*). Well, are you ready?

LAURA. For what, dear? (*Looking up at him.*)

JOHN. You know what I said in the telegram?

LAURA. Yes. (*Leans her head affectionately on his shoulder.*)

JOHN. Well, I meant it.

LAURA. I know.

JOHN. I've got to get back (JOHN *looks around, crosses behind table to chair, sits facing her across table.*), Laura, just as soon as ever I can. There's a lot of work to be done out in Nevada and I stole away to come to New York. I want to take you back. Can you go?

LAURA. Yes—when?

JOHN. This afternoon. We'll take the eighteen-hour train to Chicago, late this afternoon, and connect at Chicago with the Overland, and I'll soon have you in a home. (*Pause*) And here's another secret.

LAURA. What, dear?

JOHN. I've got that home all bought and furnished, and while you couldn't call it a Fifth Avenue residence, still it has got something on any other one in town.

LAURA. But, John, you've been so mysterious. In all your letters you haven't told me a single, solitary thing about your good luck.

JOHN. I've planned to take you out and show you all that.

LAURA. You should have told me, I've been so anxious.

JOHN. I waited until it was a dead-sure thing. You know it's been pretty tough sledding out there in the mining country, and it did look as if I never would make a strike; but your spirit was with me and luck was with me, and I knew if I could only hold out that something would come my way. I had two pals, both of them miners—they had the knowledge and I had the luck—and one day, clearing away a little snow to build a fire, I poked my toe into the dirt, and there was somethin' there, dearie, that looked suspicious. I called Jim—that's one of the men—and in less time than it takes to tell you there were three maniacs scratching away at old mother earth for all there was in it. We staked our claims in two weeks, and I came to Reno to raise enough money for me to come East. Now things are all fixed and it's just a matter of time. (*Taking* LAURA's *hand.*)

LAURA. So you're very, very rich, dear?

JOHN. Oh, not rich (*Releasing her hand he leans back in his chair.*), just heeled. I'm not going down to the Wall Street bargain counter and buy the Union Pacific, or anything like that; but we won't have to take the trip on tourists' tickets, and there's enough money to make us comfortable all the rest of our lives.

LAURA. How hard you must have worked and suffered.

JOHN. Nobody else ever accused me of that, but I sure will have to plead guilty to you. (*Rises, stands at upper side of table.*) Why, dear, since the day you came into my life hell-raising took a sneak out the back door and God poked His toe in the front, and ever since then I think He's been coming a little closer to me. I used to be a fellow without much faith and kidded everybody who had it, and I used to say to those who prayed and believed, "You may be right, but show me a message." You came along and you brought that little document in your sweet face and your dear love. Laura, you turned the trick for me, and I think I'm almost a regular man now.

(LAURA *turns away in pain; the realization of all she is to* JOHN *weighs heavily upon her. She almost loses her nerve, and is on the verge of not going through with her determination to get her happiness at any price.*)

LAURA. John, please, don't. I'm not worth it.

JOHN (*with a light air*). Not worth it? Why, you're worth (*Crossing behind table, stands behind* LAURA.) that and a whole lot more. And see how you've got on! Brockton told me you never could get along in your profession, but I knew you could. (*Back of* LAURA, *takes her by the shoulders, shakes her playfully.*) I knew what you had in you, and here you are. You see, if my foot hadn't slipped on the right ground and kicked up pay-dirt, you'd been all right. You succeeded and I succeeded, but I'm going to take you away; and after a while when things sort of smooth out, and it's all clear where the money's (*Crosses to sofa and sits.*) coming from, we're going to move back here, and go to Europe, and just have a great time, like a couple of good pals.

LAURA (*slowly crosses to* JOHN). But if I hadn't succeeded and if things —things weren't just as they seem— would it make any difference to you, John?

JOHN. Not the least in the world. (*He takes her in his arms and kisses her, drawing her on to sofa beside him.*) Now, don't you get blue. I should not have surprised you this way. It's taken you off your feet. (*He looks at his watch, rises, gets overcoat.*) But we've not any time to lose. How soon can you get ready?

LAURA (*kneeling on sofa, leaning over back*). You mean to go?

JOHN. Nothing else.

LAURA. Take all my things?

JOHN. All your duds.

LAURA. Why, dear, I can get ready most any time.

JOHN (*looking off into bedroom*). That your maid?

LAURA. Yes—Annie.

JOHN. Well, you and she can pack everything you want to take; the rest can follow later. (*Puts coat on.*) I planned it all out. There's a couple of the boys working down town— newspaper men on Park Row. Telephoned them when I got in and they're waiting for me. I'll just get down there as soon as I can. I won't be gone long.

LAURA. How long?

JOHN. I don't know just how long, but we'll make that train. I'll get the license. We'll be married and we'll be off on our honeymoon this afternoon. Can you do it?

(LAURA *goes up to him, puts her hands in his, and they confront each other.*)

LAURA. Yes, dear, I could do anything for you.

(*He takes her in his arms and kisses her again. Looks at her tenderly.*)

JOHN. That's good. Hurry now. I won't be long. Good-by.

LAURA. Hurry back, John.

JOHN. Yes. I won't be long. (*Exits.*)

LAURA (*stands for a moment looking after him, then she suddenly recovers herself and walks rapidly over to the dresser, picks up large jewel-case, takes doll that is hanging on dresser, puts them on her left arm, takes black cat in her right hand and uses it in emphasizing her words in talking to* ANNIE. *Places them all on table.*) Annie, Annie, come here!

ANNIE. Yassum. (*She appears at the door.*)

LAURA. Annie, I'm going away, and I've got to hurry.

ANNIE. Goin' away?

LAURA. Yes. I want you to bring both my trunks out here—I'll help you— and start to pack. We can't take everything (ANNIE *throws fur rug from across doorway into bedroom.*), but bring all the clothes out and we'll hurry as fast as we can. Come on.

(*Exit* LAURA *with* ANNIE. *In a very short interval she reappears, and both are carrying a large trunk between them. They put it down up stage, pushing sofa back.*)

ANNIE. Look out for your toes, Miss Laura.

LAURA. I can take two.

ANNIE. Golly, such excitement! (*Crosses to table, pushes it over further, also armchair.*) Wheah yuh goin', Miss Laura?

LAURA. Never mind where I'm going. I haven't any time to waste now talking. I'll tell you later. This is one time, Annie, that you've got to move. Hurry up.

(LAURA *pushes her in front of her.
They go out the same way and reappear with a smaller trunk.*)

ANNIE. Look out fo' your dress, Miss Laura.

(*These trunks are of the same type as those in Act Two. When the trunks are put down,* LAURA *opens one and commences to throw things out.* ANNIE *stands watching her.* LAURA *kneels in front of trunk, working and humming "Bon-Bon Buddie."*)

ANNIE. Ah nevah see you so happy, Miss Laura.

LAURA. I never was so happy. For Heaven's sake, go get something. Don't stand there looking at me. I want you to hurry.

ANNIE. I'll bring out all de fluffy ones first.

LAURA. Yes, everything.

(ANNIE *enters with armful of dresses and hatbox of tissue paper, dumps tissue paper on floor, puts dresses in trunk.*)

ANNIE (*goes out again; outside*). You goin' to take dat opera-cloak? (*Enters with more dresses, puts them on sofa, takes opera-cloak, spreads it on top of dresses on trunk.*) My, but dat's a beauty. I jest love dat crushed rosey one. (*Goes out.*)

LAURA. Annie, you put the best dresses on the foot of the bed and I'll get them myself. You heard what I said?

ANNIE (*off stage*). Yassum. (ANNIE *hangs dresses across bed in alcove.* LAURA *continues busily arranging the contents of the trunk, placing some garments here and some there, as if she were sorting them out.* WILLARD *quietly enters and stands at the door looking at her. He holds this position as long as possible, and when he speaks it is in a very quiet tone.*)

WILLARD. Going away?

LAURA (*starts, rises, and confronts him*). Yes.

WILLARD. In somewhat of a hurry, I should say.

LAURA. Yes.

WILLARD. What's the plan?

LAURA. I'm just going, that's all.

WILLARD. Madison been here?

LAURA. He's just left.

WILLARD. Of course you are going with him?

LAURA. Yes.

WILLARD. West?

LAURA. To Nevada.

WILLARD. Going—er—to get married?

LAURA. Yes, this afternoon.

WILLARD. So he didn't care, then?

LAURA. What do you mean when you say "he didn't care"?

WILLARD. Of course you told him about the letter, and how it was burned up, and all that sort of thing, didn't you?

LAURA. Why, yes.

WILLARD. And he said it didn't make any difference?

LAURA. He—he didn't say anything. We're just going to be married, that's all.

WILLARD. Did you mention my name and say that we'd been rather companionable for the last two months?

LAURA. I told him you'd been a very good friend to me.

(*During this scene* LAURA *answers* WILLARD *with difficulty, and to a man of the world it is quite apparent that she is not telling the truth.* WILLARD *looks over toward her in an almost threatening way.*)

WILLARD. How soon do you expect him back?

LAURA. Quite soon. I don't know just exactly how long he'll be.

WILLARD. And you mean to tell me that you kept your promise and told him the truth? (*Crossing to trunk.*)

LAURA. I—I—(*Then with defiance*) What business have you got to ask me that? What business have you got to interfere anyway? (*Goes to bed in alcove, gets dresses off foot, puts them on sofa.*)

WILLARD (*quietly*). Then you've lied again. You lied to him, and you just tried to lie to me now. I must say, Laura, that you're not particularly clever at it, although I don't doubt but that you've had considerable practice.

(*Gives her a searching look and slowly walks over to the chair at the table and sits down, still holding his hat in his hand and without removing his overcoat.* LAURA *sees* BROCKTON *sitting, stops and turns on him, laying dresses down.*)

LAURA. What are you going to do?

WILLARD. Sit down here and rest a few moments; maybe longer.

LAURA. You can't do that.

WILLARD. I don't see why not. This is my own place.

LAURA. But don't you see that he'll come back here soon and find you here?

WILLARD. That's just exactly what I want him to do.

LAURA (*with suppressed emotion almost on the verge of hysteria*). I want to tell you this. If you do this thing you'll ruin my life. You've done enough to it already. Now I want you to go. You've got to go. I don't think you've got any right to come here now, in this way, and take this happiness from me. I've given you everything I've got, and now I want to live right and decent, and he wants me to, and we love each other. Now, Will Brockton, it's come to this. You've got to leave this place, do you hear? You've got to leave this place. Please get out. (*Going to trunk.*)

WILLARD (*rises and comes to her*). Do you think I'm going to let a woman make a liar out of me? I'm going to stay right here. I like that boy, and I'm not going to let you put him to the bad.

LAURA. I want you to go. (*Slams trunk lid down, goes to dresser, opens drawer to get stuff out.*)

WILLARD. And I tell you I won't go. I'm going to show you up. I'm going to tell him the truth. It isn't you I care for—he's got to know.

LAURA (*slams drawer shut, loses her temper, and is almost tiger-like in her anger*). You don't care for me?

WILLARD. No.

LAURA. It isn't me you're thinking of?

WILLARD. No.

LAURA. Who's the liar now?

WILLARD. Liar?

LAURA. Yes, liar. You are. You don't care for this man, and you know it.

WILLARD. You're foolish.

LAURA. Yes, I am foolish and I've been foolish all my life, but I'm getting a little sense now. (*Kneels in armchair facing* WILLARD; *her voice is shaky with anger and tears.*) All my life, since the day you first took me away, you've planned and planned and planned to keep me, and to trick me and bring me down with you. When you came to me I was happy. I didn't have much, just a little salary and some hard work.

WILLARD. But like all the rest you found that wouldn't keep you, didn't you?

LAURA. You say I'm bad, but who's made me so? Who took me out night after night? Who showed me what these luxuries were? Who put me in the habit of buying something I couldn't afford? You did.

WILLARD. Well, you liked it, didn't you?

LAURA. Who got me in debt, and then, when I wouldn't do what you wanted me to, who had me discharged from the company, so I had no means of living? Who followed me from one place to another? Who, always entreating, tried to trap me into this life, and I didn't know any better?

WILLARD. You didn't know any better?

LAURA. I knew it was wrong—yes; but you told me everybody in this business did that sort of thing, and I was just as good as anyone else. Finally you got me and you kept me. Then when I went away to Denver, and for the first time found a gleam of happiness, for the first time in my life—

WILLARD. You're crazy.

LAURA. Yes, I am crazy. (*Rises angrily, crossing, sweeps table-cover off table, crosses to dresser, knocks bottles, etc., off upper end, turns, faces him, almost screaming.*) You've made me crazy. You followed me to Denver, and then when I got back you bribed me again. You pulled me down, and you did the same old thing until this happened. Now I want you to get out, you understand? I want you to get out.

WILLARD. Laura, you can't do this. (*Starts to sit on trunk.*)

LAURA (*screaming, going to WIL-LARD, she attempts to push him*). No, you won't; you won't stay here. You're not going to do this thing again. I tell you I'm going to be happy. I tell you I'm going to be married. (*He doesn't resist her very strongly. Her anger and her rage are entirely new to him. He is surprised and cannot understand.*) You won't see him; I tell you, you won't tell him. You've got no business to. I hate you. I've hated you for months. I hate the sight of your face. I've wanted to go, and now I'm going.

You've got to go, do you hear? You've got to get out—get out. (*Pushes him again.*)

WILLARD (*throwing her off,* LAURA *staggers to armchair, rises*). What the hell is the use of fussing with a woman? (*Exits.*)

LAURA (*hysterically*). I want to be happy, I'm going to be married, I'm going to be happy. (*Sinks down in exhausted state in front of trunk*).

ACT FOUR

The same scene as Act Three. It is about two o'clock in the afternoon.

When the curtain rises, there are two big trunks and one small one up stage. These are marked in the usual theatrical fashion. There are grips packed, umbrellas, and the usual paraphernalia that accompanies a woman when she is making a permanent departure from her place of living. All the bric-à-brac, etc., has been removed from dresser. On down-stage end of dresser is a small alligator bag containing nightdress, toilet articles, and bunch of keys. Some of the dresser drawers are half open, and old pieces of tissue paper and ribbons are hanging out. The writing desk has had all materials removed and is open, showing scraps of torn-up letters, and in one pigeonhole is a New York Central timetable; between desk and bay-window is a lady's hat-trunk containing huge picture hat. It is closed. Behind table is a suitcase with which ANNIE *is working when curtain rises. Under desk are two old millinery boxes around which are scattered old tissue paper, a pair of old slippers, a woman's shabby hat, old ribbon, etc. In front of window at end of pianola is thrown a lot of old empty boxes such as are used for stocking and shirt-waist boxes. The picture frame and basket of flowers have been removed from pianola. The stool is on top of pianola upside down. There is an empty White Rock bottle, with glass turned over it, standing between the legs of the stool. The big trunk is in front of sofa, and packed, and it has a swing tray under which is packed a fancy evening gown; the lid is down. On top of lid are an umbrella, lady's travelling-coat, hat, and gloves. On end of sofa are a large Gladstone bag packed and fastened, a smaller trunk (thirty-four inch), tray with lid. In tray are articles of wearing apparel. In end of tray is revolver wrapped in tissue paper. Trunk is closed, and supposed to be locked. Tossed across arm of armchair are a couple of violet cords. Down stage center is large piece of wide tan ribbon. The room has general appearance of having been stripped of all personal belongings. There are old magazines and tissue paper all over the place. Bearskin rug is thrown up against table in low window, the furniture is all on stage as used in Act Three. At rise* LAURA *is sitting on trunk, with clock in hand.* ANNIE *is on floor behind table fastening suitcase.* LAURA *is pale and perturbed.*

———

ANNIE. Ain't yuh goin' to let me come to yuh at all, Miss Laura?

LAURA. I don't know yet, Annie. I don't even know what the place is like that we're going to. Mr. Madison hasn't said much. There hasn't been time.

ANNIE. Why, Ah've done ma best for yuh, Miss Laura, yes, Ah have. Ah jest been with yuh ev'ry moment of ma time, an' (*Places suitcase on table.*) Ah worked for yuh an' Ah loved yuh, an' Ah doan' wan' to be left 'ere all alone in dis town 'ere New York. (LAURA *turns to door.* ANNIE *stoops, grabs up ribbon, hides behind her back.*) Ah ain't the kind of cullud lady knows many people. Can't yuh take me along wid yuh, Miss Laura?—yuh all been so good to me.

LAURA. Why, I told you to (*Goes to door, looks out, returns disappointedly.*) stay here and get your things together (ANNIE *hides ribbon in front of her waist.*), and then Mr. Brockton will probably want you to do something. Later I think he'll have you pack up just as soon as he finds I'm gone. I've got the address that you gave me. I'll let you know if you can come on.

ANNIE (*suddenly*). Ain't yuh goin' to give me anything at all jes' to remembuh yuh by? Ah've been so honest—

LAURA. Honest?

ANNIE. Honest, Ah have.

LAURA. You've been about as honest as most colored (*Goes to table, gets suitcase, to sofa, puts suitcase on sofa.*) girls are who work for women in the position that I am in. You haven't stolen enough to make me discharge you, but I've seen what you've taken. (*Sits on end of sofa.*)

ANNIE. Now, Miss Laura.

LAURA. Don't try to fool me. What you've got you're welcome to, but for Heaven's sake don't prate around here about loyalty and honesty. I'm sick of it.

ANNIE. Ain't yuh goin' to give me no recommendation?

LAURA (*impatiently looking around the room*). What good would my recommendation do? You can always go and get another position with people who've lived the way I've lived, and my recommendation to the other kind wouldn't amount to much.

ANNIE (*sits on trunk*). Ah can just see whah Ah'm goin',—back to dat boa'din'-house in Thirty-eighth Street fo' me. (*Crying.*)

LAURA. Now shut your noise. I don't want to hear any more. I've given you twenty-five dollars for a present. I think that's enough. (ANNIE *assumes a most aggrieved appearance.*)

ANNIE. Ah know, but twenty-five dollars ain't a home, and I'm (*Rises, goes to rubbish heap, picks up old slippers and hat, puts hat on head as she goes out, looks into pier-glass.*) losin' my home. Dat's jest my luck—every time I save enough money to buy my weddin' clothes to get married I lose my job. (*Goes out.*)

LAURA. I wonder where John is. We'll never be able to make that train. (LAURA *goes to window, then to desk, takes out timetable, crosses to armchair and spreads timetable on back, studies it, crosses impatiently to trunk, and sits nervously kicking feet. After a few seconds' pause, bell rings. She jumps up excitedly.*) That must be he, Annie —go quick.

(ANNIE *crosses and opens the door in the usual manner.*)

JIM (*from outside*). Is Miss Murdock in?

ANNIE. Yassuh, she's in.

(LAURA *is up stage and turns to receive visitor.* JIM *enters. He is nicely dressed in black and has an appearance of prosperity about him, but in other respects he retains the old drollness of enunciation and manner. He crosses to* LAURA *in a cordial way and holds out his hand.* ANNIE *crosses, after closing the door, and exits through the portieres into the sleeping-apartment.*)

JIM. How-dy-do, Miss Laura?

LAURA. Jim Weston, I'm mighty glad to see you.

JIM. Looks like as if you were going to move?

LAURA. Yes, I am going to move, and a long ways, too. How well you're looking—as fit as a fiddle.

JIM. Yes; I am feelin' fine. Where yer goin'? Troupin'?

LAURA. No, indeed.

JIM (*surveying the baggage*). Thought not. What's comin' off now? (*Takes off coat, puts coat and hat on trunk.*)

LAURA (*very simply*). I'm going to be married this afternoon.

JIM. Married?

LAURA. And then I'm going West.

JIM (*leaving the trunk and walking toward her and holding out his hands*). Now I'm just glad to hear that. Ye know when I heard how—how things was breakin' for ye—well, I ain't knockin' or anythin' like that, but me and the missis have talked ye over a lot. I never did think this feller was goin' to do the right thing by yer. Brockton never looked to me like a fellow would marry anybody, but now that he's goin' through just to make you a nice respectable wife, I guess everything must have happened for the best. (LAURA *averts her eyes. Both sit on trunk,* JIM *near* LAURA.) Y' see I wanted to thank you for what you did a couple of weeks ago. Burgess wrote me a letter and told me I could go ahead of one of his big shows if I wanted to come back, and offering me considerable money. He mentioned your name, Miss Laura, and I talked it over with the missis, and—well, I can tell ye now when I couldn't if ye weren't to be hooked up—we decided that I wouldn't take that job, comin' as it did from you (*Slowly*) and the way I knew it was framed up.

LAURA. Why not?

JIM (*embarrassed*). Well, ye see, there are three kids and they're all growing up, all of them in school, and the missis, she's just about forgot show business and she's playing a star part in the kitchen, juggling dishes and doing flip-flaps with pancakes; and we figgered that as we'd always gone along kinder clean-like, it wouldn't be good for the kids to take a job comin' from Brockton because you—you—well—you—

LAURA. I know. (*Rises, sits on arm of chair.*) You thought it wasn't decent. Is that it?

JIM. Oh, not exactly, only—well, you see I'm gettin' along pretty (*Rises, crosses to* LAURA.) good now. I got a little one-night stand theatre out in Ohio—manager of it, too. (*With a smile*) The town is called Gallipolis.

LAURA. Gallipolis?

JIM. Oh, that ain't a disease. It is the name of a town. Maybe you don't know much about Gallipolis, or where it is.

LAURA. No.

JIM. Well, it looks just like it sounds. We got a little house, and the old lady is happy, and I feel so good that I can even stand her cookin'. Of course we ain't makin' much money, but I guess I'm gettin' a little old-fashioned around theatres anyway. The fellows from newspapers and colleges have got it on me. Last time I asked a man for a job he asked me what I knew about the Greek drama, and when I told him I didn't know the Greeks had a theatre in New York he slipped me a laugh and told me to come in again on some rainy Tuesday. Then Gallipolis showed on the map, and I beat it for the West. (JIM *notices by this time the pain he has caused* LAURA, *and is embarrassed.*) Sorry if I hurt ye—didn't mean to; and now that yer goin' to be Mrs. Brockton, well, I take back all I said, and while I don't think I want to change my position, I wouldn't turn it down for —for that other reason, that's all.

LAURA (*with a tone of defiance in her voice*). But, Mr. Weston, I'm not going to be Mrs. Brockton.

JIM. No? (*Moves a little.*)

LAURA. No.

JIM. Oh—oh—

LAURA. I'm going to marry another man, and a good man.

JIM. The hell you are!

LAURA (*rises, puts hand on* JIM's *shoulder*). And it's going to be altogether different. I know what you meant when you said about the missis and the kids, and that's what I want —just a little home, just a little peace, just a little comfort, and—and the man has come who's going to give it to me. You don't want me to say any more, do you? (*Goes to door, opens it, and looks out, closes it, moves to* JIM.)

JIM (*emphatically, and with a tone of hearty approval*). No, I don't, and now I'm just going to put my mit out and shake yours and be real glad. I want to tell ye it's the only way to go along. I ain't never been a rival to Rockefeller, nor I ain't never made Morgan jealous, but since the day my old woman took her make-up off for the last time and walked out of that stage door to give me a little help and bring my kids into the world, I knew that was the way to go along; and if you're goin' to take that road, by Jiminy, I'm glad of it, for you sure do deserve it. I wish yer luck.

LAURA. Thank you.

JIM. I'm mighty glad you sidestepped Brockton. You're young (LAURA *sits on trunk.*) and you're pretty, and you're sweet, and if you've got the right kind of a feller there ain't no reason on earth why you shouldn't jest forget the whole business and see nothin' but laughs and a good time comin' to you, and the sun sort o' shinin' every twenty-four hours in the day. You know the missis feels just as if she knew you, after I told her about them hard times we had at Farley's boarding-house, so I feel that it's paid me to come to New York (*Picks up pin, puts it in lapel of coat.*) even if I didn't book anything but *East Lynne* and *Uncle Tom's Cabin.* (*Goes over to her.*) Now I'm goin'. Don't forget Gallipolis's (LAURA *helps him on with his coat.*) the name, and sometimes the mail does get there. I'd be awful glad if you wrote the missis a little note tellin' us how you're gettin' along, and if you ever have to ride on the Kanawha and Michigan just look out of the window when the train passes our town, because that is about the best you'll get.

LAURA. Why?

JIM. They only stop there on signal. And make up your mind that the Weston family is with you forty ways from the Jack day and night. Good-by, and God bless you.

LAURA. Good-by, Jim. I'm so glad to know you're happy, for it is good to be happy. (*Kisses him.*)

JIM. You bet. (*Moves toward the door. She follows him after they have shaken hands.*) Never mind, I can get out all right. (*Opens the door, and at the door*) Good-by, again.

LAURA (*very softly*). Good-by. (JIM *leaves and closes the door. She stands motionless until she hears the outer door slam.*) I wonder why he doesn't come. (*She goes up and looks out of the window and turns down stage, counting trunks; as she counts suitcase on table, bell rings; she crosses hurriedly to trunk.*) Hurry, Annie, and see who that is.

(ANNIE *enters, crosses, opens door, exits, opens the outer door.*)

ANNIE (*outside*). She's waitin' for yer, Mr. Madison.

(LAURA *hurries down to center of*

stage. JOHN *enters, hat in hand and his overcoat on arm, followed by* ANNIE. *He stops just as he enters and looks at* LAURA *long and searchingly.* LAURA *instinctively feels that something has happened. She shudders and remains firm.* ANNIE *crosses and exits. Closes doors.*)

LAURA (*with a little effort.* JOHN *places hat and coat on trunk*). Aren't you a little late, dear?

JOHN. I—I was detained downtown a few minutes. I think that we can carry out our plan all right.

LAURA (*after a pause*). Has anything happened?

JOHN. I've made all the arrangements. The men will be here in a few minutes for your trunks. (*Goes to coat, feels in pocket.*) I've got the railroad tickets and everything else, but—

LAURA. But what, John?

(*He goes over to her. She intuitively understands that she is about to go through an ordeal. She seems to feel that* JOHN *has become acquainted with something which might interfere with their plan. He looks at her long and searchingly. Evidently he too is much wrought up, but when he speaks to her it is with a calm dignity and force which show the character of the man.*)

JOHN. Laura.

LAURA. Yes?

JOHN. You know when I went downtown I said I was going to call on two or three of my friends in Park Row.

LAURA. I know.

JOHN. I told them who I was going to marry.

LAURA. Well?

JOHN. They said something about you and Brockton, and I found that they'd said too much, but not quite enough.

LAURA. What did they say?

JOHN. Just that—too much and not

quite enough. There's a minister waiting for us over on Madison Avenue. You see, then you'll be my wife. That's pretty serious business, and all I want now from you is the truth.

LAURA. Well?

JOHN. Just tell me that what they said was just an echo of the past—that it came from what had been going on before that wonderful day out in Colorado. Tell me that you've been on the level. I don't want their word, Laura— I just want yours.

(LAURA *summons all her courage, looks up into his loving eyes, shrinks a moment before his anxious face, and speaks as simply as she can.*)

LAURA. Yes, John, I have been on the level.

JOHN (*very tenderly*). I knew that, dear, I knew it. (*He takes her in his arms and kisses her. She clings to him in pitiful helplessness. His manner is changed to one of almost boyish happiness.*) Well, now everything's all ready let's get on the job. We haven't a great deal of time. Get your duds on.

LAURA. When do we go?

JOHN. Right away. The great idea is to get away.

LAURA. All right. (*Gets hat off trunk, crosses to bureau, puts it on.*)

JOHN. Laura, you've got trunks enough, haven't you? One might think we're moving a whole colony. (*Turns to her with a smile.*) And, by the way, to me you are a whole colony—anyway you're the only one I ever wanted to settle with.

LAURA. That's good. (*Takes bag off bureau, crosses to trunk, gets purse, coat, umbrella, as if ready to leave. She hurriedly gathers her things together, adjusting her hat and the like, and almost to herself in a low tone*) I'm so excited. (*Continues preparations.*) Come on.

(*In the meantime* JOHN *crosses by to get his hat and coat, and while the preparations are about to be completed and* LAURA *has said "Come on," she is transfixed by the noise of the slamming of the outer door. She stops as if she had been tremendously shocked, and a moment later the rattling of a latchkey in the inner door also stops* JOHN *from going any further. His coat is half on.* LAURA *looks toward the door, paralyzed with fright, and* JOHN *looks at her with an expression of great apprehension. Slowly the door opens, and* BROCKTON *enters with coat and hat on. As he turns to close the door after him,* LAURA, *pitifully and terribly afraid, retreats two or three steps, and lays coat, bag, purse and umbrella down in armchair, standing dazed.* BROCKTON *enters leisurely, paying no attention to anyone, while* JOHN *becomes as rigid as a statue, and follows with his eyes every move* BROCKTON *makes. The latter walks leisurely across the stage, and afterwards into the rooms through the portieres. There is a wait of a second. No one moves.* BROCKTON *finally reenters with coat and hat off, and throws back the portieres in such a manner as to reveal the bed and his intimate familiarity with the outer room. He goes down stage in the same leisurely manner and sits in a chair, opposite* JOHN, *crossing his legs.*)

WILLARD. Hello, Madison, when did you get in?

(*Slowly* JOHN *seems to recover himself. His right hand starts up toward the lapel of his coat and slowly he pulls his Colt revolver from the holster under his armpit. There is a deadly determination and deliberation in every movement that he makes.* WILLARD *jumps to his feet and looks at him. The revolver is uplifted in the air, as a Western man handles a gun, so that when it is snap-*

ped down with a jerk the deadly shot can be fired. LAURA *is terror-stricken, but before the shot is fired she takes a step forward and extends one hand in a gesture of entreaty.*)

LAURA (*in a husky voice that is almost a whisper*). Don't shoot.

(*The gun remains uplifted for a moment.* JOHN *is evidently wavering in his determination to kill. Slowly his whole frame relaxes. He lowers the pistol in his hand in a manner which clearly indicates that he is not going to shoot. He quietly puts it back in the holster, and* WILLARD *is obviously relieved, although he stood his ground like a man.*)

JOHN (*slowly*). Thank you. You said that just in time. (*A pause.*)

WILLARD (*recovering and in a light tone*). Well, you see, Madison, that what I said when I was—

JOHN (*threateningly*). Look out, Brockton, I don't want to talk to you.

(*The men confront.*)

WILLARD. All right.

JOHN (*to* LAURA). Now get that man out of here.

LAURA. John, I—

JOHN. Get him out. Get him out before I lose my temper or they'll take him out without his help.

LAURA (*to* WILLARD). Go—go. Please go.

WILLARD (*deliberately*). If that's the way you want it, I'm willing.

(*Exit* WILLARD *into the sleeping-apartment.* LAURA *and* JOHN *stand facing each other. He enters again with hat and coat on and passes over toward the door.* LAURA *and* JOHN *do not move. When he gets just a little to the left of the center of the stage* LAURA *steps forward and stops him with her speech.*)

LAURA. Now before you go, and to you both, I want to tell you how I've learned to despise him. John, I know you don't believe me, but it's true—it's true. I don't love anyone in the world but just you. I know you don't think that it can be explained—maybe there isn't any explanation. I couldn't help it. I was so poor, and I had to live, and he wouldn't let me work, and he's only let me live one way, and I was hungry. Do you know what that means? I was hungry and didn't have clothes to keep me warm, and I tried, oh, John, I tried so hard to do the other thing—the right thing,—but I couldn't.

JOHN. I—I know I couldn't help much, and perhaps I could have forgiven you if you hadn't lied to me. That's what hurt. (*Turning to* WILLARD *and approaching until he can look him in the eyes*) I expected you to lie, you're that kind of a man. You left me with a shake of the hand and you gave me your word, and you didn't keep it. Why should you keep it? Why should anything make any difference with you? Why, you pup, you've no right to live in the same world with decent folks. Now you make yourself scarce, or take it from me, I'll just kill you, that's all.

WILLARD. I'll leave, Madison, but I'm not going to let you think that I didn't do the right thing with you. She came to me voluntarily. She said she wanted to come back. I told you that when I was in Colorado, and you didn't believe me, and I told you that when she did this sort of thing I'd let you know. I dictated a letter to her to send to you, and I left it sealed and stamped in her hands to mail. She didn't do it. If there's been a lie she told it. I didn't. (JOHN *turns to her. She hangs her head and averts her eyes in a mute acknowledgment of guilt. The revelation hits* JOHN *so hard that he sinks on the trunk, his head fallen to his breast. He is utterly limp and whipped. There is a moment's silence.*)

WILLARD (*goes to* JOHN). You see! Why, my boy, whatever you think of me or the life I lead, I wouldn't have had this come to you for anything in the world. (JOHN *makes an impatient gesture.*) No, I wouldn't. My women don't mean a whole lot to me because I don't take them seriously. I wish I had the faith and the youth to feel the way you do. You're all in and broken up, but I wish I could be broken up just once. I did what I thought was best for you because I didn't think she could ever go through the way you wanted her to. I'm sorry it's all turned out bad. (*Pause*) Good-by.

(*He looks at* JOHN *for a moment as if he was going to speak.* JOHN *remains motionless. The blow has hit him harder than he thought.* WILLARD *exits. The first door closes. In a moment the second door is slammed.* JOHN *and* LAURA *look at each other for a moment. He gives her no chance to speak. The hurt in his heart and his accusation are shown by his broken manner. A great grief has come into his life and he doesn't quite understand it. He seems to be feeling around for something to say, some way to get out. His head turns toward the door. With a pitiful gesture of the hand he looks at her in all his sorrow.*)

JOHN. Well? (*Rises.*)

LAURA. John, I—(*Takes off hat, places it on table.*)

JOHN. I'd be careful what I said. Don't try to make excuses. I understand.

LAURA. It's not excuses. I want to tell you what's in my heart, but I can't; it won't speak, and you don't believe my voice.

JOHN. You'd better leave it unsaid.

LAURA. But I must tell. I can't let you go like this. (*She goes over to him and makes a weak attempt to put her arms around him. He takes her arms and puts them back to her side.*) I love you. I—how can I tell you—but I do, I do, and you won't believe me.

(*He remains silent for a moment and then takes her by the hand, leads her over to the chair and places her in it.*)

JOHN. I think you do as far as you are able; but, Laura, I guess you don't know what a decent sentiment is. (*He gathers himself together. His tone is very gentle and very firm, but it carries a tremendous conviction, even with his grief ringing through his speech.*) Laura, you're not immoral, you're just unmoral, kind o' all out of shape, and I'm afraid there isn't a particle of hope for you. When we met neither of us had any reason to be proud, but I thought that you thought that it was the chance of salvation which sometimes comes to a man and a woman fixed as we were then. What had been had been. It was all in the great to-be for us, and now, how you've kept your word! What little that promise meant, when I thought you handed me a new lease of life!

LAURA (*in a voice that is changed and metallic. She is literally being nailed to the cross*). You're killing me—killing me.

JOHN. Don't make such a mistake. In a month you'll recover. There will be days when you will think of me, just for a moment, and then it will be all over. With you it is the easy way, and it always will be. You'll go on and on until you're finally left a wreck, just the type of the common woman. And you'll sink until you're down to the very bed-rock of depravity. I pity you.

LAURA (*still in the same metallic tone of voice*). You'll never leave me to do that. I'll kill myself.

JOHN. Perhaps that's the only thing left for you to do, but you'll not do it. It's easier to live. (*Gets hat and coat, turns, looks at her,* LAURA *rising at the same time.*)

LAURA. John, I said I'd kill myself, and I mean it. If it's the only thing to do, I'll do it, and I'll do it before your very eyes. (*She crosses quickly, gets keys out of satchel, opens trunk, takes gun out of trunk, stands facing* JOHN, *waiting a moment.*) You understand that when your hand touches that door I'm going to shoot myself. I will, so help me God!

JOHN (*stops and looks at her*). Kill yourself? (*Pause*) Before me? (*Pause*) All right. (*Raising his voice*) Annie, Annie!

ANNIE (*enters*). Yes, sir.

JOHN (LAURA *looks at* JOHN *in bewilderment*). You see your mistress there has a pistol in her hand?

ANNIE (*frightened*). Yassuh—

JOHN. She wants to kill herself. I just called you to witness that the act is entirely voluntary on her part. Now, Laura, go ahead.

LAURA (*nearly collapsing, drops the pistol to the floor*). John, I—can't—

JOHN. Annie, she's evidently changed her mind. You may go.

ANNIE. But, Miss Laura, Ah—

JOHN (*peremptorily*). You may go. (*Bewildered and not understanding,* ANNIE *exits through the portieres. In that same gentle tone, but carrying with it an almost frigid conviction.*) You didn't have the nerve. I knew you wouldn't. For a moment you thought the only decent thing for you to do was to die, and yet you couldn't go through. I am sorry for you—more sorry than I can tell. (*He takes a step towards the door.*)

LAURA. You're going—you're going?

JOHN. Yes.

LAURA. And — and — you never thought that perhaps I'm frail, and weak, and a woman, and that now, maybe, I need your strength, and you might give it to me, and it might be better. I want to lean on you,—lean on you, John. I know I need someone. Aren't you going to let me? Won't you give me another chance?

JOHN. I gave you your chance, Laura.

LAURA (*throws arms around his neck*). Give me another.

JOHN. But you leaned the wrong way. Good-by. (*He pulls away and goes out, slamming both doors.*)

LAURA (*screaming*). John—John—I —(*She sits on trunk weeping in loud and tearful manner, rises in a dazed fashion, starts to move, sees gun, utters loud cry of mingled despair and anger, grabs up gun, crossing to bureau, opens up-stage drawer, throws gun in, slams drawer shut, calling*) Annie! Annie!

ANNIE (*appears through the portieres*). Ain't yuh goin' away, Miss Laura?

LAURA (*suddenly arousing herself, and with a defiant voice*). No, I'm not. I'm going to stay right here. (ANNIE *crosses and opens trunk, takes out handsome dress, crosses, hangs it over back of armchair, crosses up to hat trunk, takes out hat.* LAURA *takes it from her, crosses to trunk, starts to unpack it.*) Open these trunks, take out those clothes, get me my prettiest dress. Hurry up. (*She goes before the mirror.*) Get my new hat, dress up my body and paint up my face. It's all they've left of me. (*To herself*) They've taken my soul away with them.

ANNIE (*in a happy voice*). Yassum, yassum.

LAURA (*who is arranging her hair*). Doll me up, Annie.

ANNIE. Yuh goin' out, Miss Laura?

LAURA. Yes. I'm going to Rector's to make a hit, and to hell with the rest.

(*At this moment the hurdy-gurdy in the street, presumably immediately under her window, begins to play the tune of "Bon-Bon Buddie, My Chocolate Drop." There is something in this ragtime melody which is particularly and peculiarly suggestive of the low life, the criminality and prostitution that constitute the night excitement of that section of New York City known as the Tenderloin. The tune, its association, is like spreading before* LAURA's *eyes a panorama of the inevitable depravity that awaits her. She is torn from every ideal that she so weakly endeavored to grasp, and is thrown into the mire and slime at the very moment when her emancipation seems to be assured. The woman, with her flashy dress in one arm and her equally exaggerated type of picture hat in the other, is nearly prostrated by the tune and the realization of the future as it is terrifically conveyed to her. The Negress, in the happiness of serving* LAURA *in her questionable career, picks up the melody and hums it as she unpacks the finery that has been put away in the trunk.*)

LAURA (*with infinite grief, resignation, and hopelessness*). O God—O my God. (*She turns and totters toward the bedroom. The hurdy-gurdy continues, with the Negress accompanying it.*)

THE SCARECROW
A Tragedy of the Ludicrous

Percy MacKaye

First presented at Middlesex Theatre, Middletown, Connecticut, December 30, 1910. First New York presentation on January 17, 1911 at the Garrick Theatre.

JUSTICE GILEAD MERTON

GOODY RICKBY (*"Blacksmith Bess"*)

LORD RAVENSBANE (*"Marquis of Oxford, Baron of Wittenberg, Elector of Worms, and Count of Cordova"*), *their hypothetical son*

DICKON, *a Yankee improvisation of the Prince of Darkness*

RACHEL MERTON, *niece of the Justice*

MISTRESS CYNTHIA MERTON, *sister of the Justice*

RICHARD TALBOT, ESQUIRE, *betrothed to Rachel*

SIR CHARLES REDDINGTON, *Lieutenant-Governor*

MISTRESS REDDINGTON
AMELIA REDDINGTON } *his daughters*

CAPTAIN BUGBY, *the Governor's Secretary*

MINISTER DODGE

MISTRESS DODGE, *his wife*

REV. MASTER RAND, *of Harvard College*

REV. MASTER TODD, *of Harvard College*

MICAH, *a servant of the Justice*

THE BOY (EBENEZER)

Place: A town in Massachusetts.

Time: Late seventeenth century.

ACT ONE

The interior of a blacksmith shop. On the right of the stage, toward the center, is a forge. On the left stands a loft, from which are hanging dried cornstalks, hay, and the yellow ears of cattle-corn. Toward the rear is a wide double door, closed when the curtain rises. Through this door—when later it is opened—is visible a New England landscape in the late springtime: a distant wood; stone walls, high elms, a well-sweep; and, in the near foreground, a ploughed field, from which the green shoots of early corn are just appearing. The blackened walls of the shop are covered with a miscellaneous collection of old iron, horseshoes, and cart-wheels, the usual appurtenances of a smithy. In the right-hand corner, however, is an array of things quite out of keeping with the shop proper: musical instruments, puppets, tall clocks, and fantastical junk. Conspicuous amongst these articles is a large standing mirror, framed grotesquely in old gold and curtained by a dull stuff, embroidered with peaked caps and crescent moons.

Just before the scene opens, a hammer is heard ringing briskly upon steel. As the curtain rises there is discovered, standing at the anvil in the flickering light of a bright flame from the forge, a woman—powerful, ruddy, proud with a certain masterful beauty, white-haired (as though prematurely), bare-armed to the elbows, clad in a dark skirt (above her ankles), a loose blouse, open at the throat; a leathern apron and a workman's cap. The woman is GOODY RICKBY. *On the anvil she is shaping a piece of iron. Beside her stands a framework of iron formed like the ribs and backbone of a man.*

For a few moments she continues to ply her hammer, amid a shower of sparks, till suddenly the flame on the forge dies down.

———

GOODY RICKBY. Dickon! More flame.

A VOICE (*above her*). Yea, Goody.

(*The flame in the forge spurts up high and suddenly.*)

GOODY RICKBY. Nay, not so fierce.

THE VOICE (*at her side*). Votre pardon, madame. (*The flame subsides.*) Is that better?

GOODY RICKBY. That will do. (*With her tongs, she thrusts the iron into the flame; it turns white-hot.*) Quick work; nothing like brimstone for the smithy trade. (*At the anvil, she begins to weld the iron rib onto the framework.*) There, my beauty! We'll make a stout set of ribs for you. I'll see to it this year that I have a scarecrow can outstand all the nor'easters that blow. I've no notion to lose my corn-crop this summer. (*Outside, the faint cawings of crows are heard. Putting down her tongs and hammer,* GOODY RICKBY *strides to the double door, and flinging it wide open, lets in the gray light of dawn. She looks out over the fields and shakes her fist.*) So ye're up before me and the sun, are ye? (*Squinting against the light*) There's one! Nay, two. Aha!

> One for sorrow,
> Two for mirth—

Good! This time we'll have the laugh on our side. (*She returns to the forge, where again the fire has died out.*) Dickon! Fire! Come, come, where be thy wits?

THE VOICE (*sleepily from the forge*). 'Tis early, dame.

GOODY RICKBY. The more need— (*Takes up her tongs.*)

THE VOICE (*screams*). Ow!

GOODY RICKBY. Ha! Have I got thee? (*From the blackness of the forge she pulls out with her tongs, by the right ear, the figure of a devil, horned and tailed. In general aspect, though he resembles a medieval familiar demon, yet the suggestions of a goatish beard, a shrewdly humorous smile, and [when he speaks] the slightest of nasal drawls, remotely simulate a species of Yankee rustic.* GOODY RICKBY *substitutes her fingers for the tongs.*) Now, Dickon!

DICKON. *Deus!* I haven't been nabbed like that since St. Dunstan tweaked my nose. Well, sweet Goody?

GOODY RICKBY. The bellows!

DICKON (*going slowly to the forge*). Why,'tis hardly dawn yet. Honest folks are still abed. It makes a long day.

GOODY RICKBY (*working while* DICKON *plies the bellows*). Aye, for your black pets, the crows, to work in. That's why we must be at it early. You heard 'em. We must have this scarecrow of ours out in the field at his post before sunrise. Here, I've made the frame strong, so as to stand the weather; *you* must make the body lifelike so as to fool the crows. This year, we must make 'em think it's a real human crittur.

DICKON. To fool the philosophers is my speciality, but the crows—hm!

GOODY RICKBY. Pooh! That staggers thee!

DICKON. Madame Rickby, prod not the quick of my genius. I am Phidias, I am Raphael, I am the Lord God!— You shall see— (*Demands with a gesture.*) Yonder broomstick.

GOODY RICKBY (*fetching him a broom from the corner*). Good boy!

DICKON (*straddling the handle*). Ha, ha! gee up! my Salem mare. (*Then, pseudo-philosophically*) A broomstick —that's for imagination! (*He begins to construct the scarecrow, while* GOODY RICKBY, *assisting, brings the constructive parts from various nooks and corners.*) We are all pretty artists, to be sure, Bessie. Phidias, he sculptures the gods; Raphael, he paints the angels; the Lord God, he creates Adam; and Dickon—fetch me the poker—aha! Dickon! What doth Dickon? He nullifies 'em all; he endows the Scarecrow! A poker: here's his conscience. There's two fine legs to walk on,—imagination and conscience. Yonder flails now! The ideal — the *beau idéal*, dame — that's what we artists seek. The apotheosis of scarecrows! And pray, what's a scarecrow? Why, the antithesis of Adam.— "Let there be candles!" quoth the Lord God, sitting in the dark. "Let there be candle-extinguishers," saith Dickon. "I am made in the image of my maker," quoth Adam. "Look at yourself in the glass," saith Goodman Scarecrow. (*Taking two implements from* GOODY RICKBY) Fine! fine! here are flails—one for wit, t'other for satire. *Sapristi!* with two such arms, my lad, how thou wilt work thy way in the world!

GOODY RICKBY. You talk as if you were making a real mortal, Dickon.

DICKON. To fool a crow, Goody, I must fashion a crittur that will first deceive a man.

GOODY RICKBY. He'll scarce do that without a head. (*Pointing to the loft*) What think ye of yonder jack-o'-lantern? 'Twas made last Hallowe'en.

DICKON. Rare, my Psyche! We shall collaborate. Here! (*Running up the ladder, he tosses down a yellow hollowed pumpkin to* GOODY RICKBY, *who catches it. Then rummaging forth an armful of cornstalks, ears, tassels, dried squashes, gourds, beets, etc., he descends and throws them in a heap on the floor.*) Whist! (*As he drops them*) Gourd, carrot, turnip, beet—the anatomy.

GOODY RICKBY (*placing the pumpkin on the shoulders*). Look!

DICKON. O *Johannes Baptista!* What wouldst thou have given for such a head! I helped Salome to cut his off, dame, and it looked not half so appetizing on her charger. Tut! Copernicus wore once such a pumpkin, but it is rotten. Look at his golden smile! Hail, Phœbus Apollo!

GOODY RICKBY. 'Tis the finest scarecrow in town.

DICKON. Nay, poor soul, 'tis but a skeleton yet. He must have a man's heart in him. (*Picking a big red beet from among the cornstalks, he places it under the left side of the ribs.*) Hush! Dost thou hear it *beat?*

GOODY RICKBY. Thou merry rogue!

DICKON. Now for the lungs of him. (*Snatching a small pair of bellows from a peg on the wall*) That's for eloquence! He'll preach the black knaves a sermon on theft. And now— (*Here, with* GOODY RICKBY's *help, he stuffs the framework with the gourds, corn, etc., from the loft, weaving the husks about the legs and arms.*) Here goes for digestion and inherited instincts! More corn, Goody. Now he'll fight for his own flesh and blood!

GOODY RICKBY (*laughing*). Dickon, I am proud of thee.

DICKON. Wait till you see his peruke. (*Seizing a feather duster made of crow's feathers*) Voici! Scalps of the enemy! (*Pulling them apart, he arranges the feathers on the pumpkin, like a gentleman's wig.*) A rare conqueror!

GOODY RICKBY. Oh, you beauty!

DICKON. And now a bit of comfort for dark days and stormy nights. (*Taking a piece of corn-cob with the kernels on it,* DICKON *makes a pipe, which he puts into the scarecrow's mouth.*) So! There, Goody! I tell thee, with yonder brand-new coat and

breeches of mine—those there in my cupboard!—we'll make him a lad to be proud of. (*Taking the clothes, which* GOODY RICKBY *brings—a pair of fine scarlet breeches and a gold-embroidered coat with ruffles of lace—he puts them upon the scarecrow. Then, eying it like a connoisseur, makes a few finishing touches.*) Why, dame, he'll be a son to thee.

GOODY RICKBY. A son? Aye, if I had but a son!

DICKON. Why, here you have him. (*To the scarecrow*) Thou wilt scare the crows off thy mother's cornfield—won't my pretty? And send 'em all over t'other side the wall to her dear neighbor's, the Justice Gilead Merton's.

GOODY RICKBY. Justice Merton! Nay, if they'd only peck his eyes out, instead of his corn.

DICKON (*grinning*). Yet the Justice was a dear friend of "Blacksmith Bess."

GOODY RICKBY. Aye, "Blacksmith Bess"! If I hadn't had a good stout arm when he cast me off with the babe, I might have starved for all his worship cared.

DICKON. True, Bessie; 'twas a scurvy trick he played on thee—and on me, that took such pains to bring you together—to steal a young maid's heart—

GOODY RICKBY. And then toss it away like a bad penny to the gutter! And the child—to die! (*Lifting her hammer in rage*) Ha! If I could get the worshipful Justice Gilead into my power again— (*She drops the hammer sullenly on the anvil.*) But no! I shall beat my life away on this anvil, whilst my justice clinks his gold, and drinks his port to a fat old age. Justice! Ha—justice of God!

DICKON. Whist, dame! Talk of angels and hear the rustle of their relatives.

GOODY RICKBY (*turning, watches out-*

side a girl's figure approaching). His niece—Rachel Merton! What can she want so early? Nay, I mind me; 'tis the mirror. She's a maid after our own hearts, boy—no Sabbath-go-to-meeting airs about *her!* She hath read the books of the *magi* from cover to cover, and paid me good guineas for 'em, though her uncle knows naught on't. Besides, she's in love, Dickon.

DICKON (*indicating the scarecrow*). Ah? With *him?* Is it a rendezvous?

GOODY RICKBY (*with a laugh*). Pff! Begone!

DICKON (*shakes his finger at the scarecrow*). Thou naughty rogue! (*Then, still smiling slyly, with his head placed confidentially next to the scarecrow's ear, as if whispering, and with his hand pointing to the maiden outside,* DICKON *fades away into air.* RACHEL *enters, nervous and hesitant.* GOODY RICKBY *makes her a curtsy, which she acknowledges by a nod, half absent-minded.*)

GOODY RICKBY. Mistress Rachel Merton—so early! I hope your uncle, our worshipful Justice, is not ill?

RACHEL. No, my uncle is quite well. The early morning suits me best for a walk. You are—quite alone?

GOODY RICKBY. Quite alone, mistress. (*Bitterly*) Oh, folks don't call on Goody Rickby—except on business.

RACHEL (*absently, looking round in the dim shop*). Yes—you must be busy. Is it—is it here?

GOODY RICKBY. You mean the—

RACHEL (*starting back, with a cry*). Ah! who's that?

GOODY RICKBY (*chuckling*). Fear not, mistress; 'tis nothing but a scarecrow. I'm going to put him in my cornfield yonder. The crows are so pesky this year.

RACHEL (*draws her skirts away with a shiver*). How loathsome!

GOODY RICKBY (*vastly pleased*). He'll do.

RACHEL. Ah, here!—This is *the* mirror?

GOODY RICKBY. Yea, mistress, and a wonderful glass it is, as I told you. I wouldn't sell it to most comers, but seeing how you and Master Talbot—

RACHEL. Yes; that will do.

GOODY RICKBY. You see, if the town folks guessed what it was, well—You've heard tell of the gibbets on Salem Hill? There's not many in New England like you, Mistress Rachel. You know enough to approve some miracles—outside the Scriptures.

RACHEL. You are quite sure the glass will do all you say? It—never fails?

GOODY RICKBY. Ah, now, mistress, how could it? 'Tis the glass of truth—(*Insinuatingly*) —the glass of true lovers. It shows folks just as they are; no shams, no varnish. If a wolf should dress himself in a white sheep's wool, this glass would reflect the black beast inside it.

RACHEL (*with awe*). The black beast! But what of the sins of the soul, Goody? Vanity, hypocrisy, and—and inconstancy? Will it surely reveal them?

GOODY RICKBY. I have told you, my young lady. If it doth not as I say, bring it back and get your money again. Oh, trust me, sweeting, an old dame hath eyes in her heart yet. If your lover be false, this glass shall pluck his fine feathers!

RACHEL (*with aloofness*). 'Tis no question of that. I wish the glass to—to amuse me.

GOODY RICKBY (*laughing*). Why, then, try it on some of your neighbors.

RACHEL. You ask a large price for it.

GOODY RICKBY (*shrugs*). I run risks. Besides, where will you get another?

RACHEL. That is true. Here, I will

buy it. That is the sum you mentioned, I believe? (*She hands a purse to* GOODY RICKBY, *who opens it and counts over some coin.*)

GOODY RICKBY. Let see; let see.

RACHEL. Well?

GOODY RICKBY. Good: 'tis good. Folks call me a witch, mistress. Well—harkee—a witch's word is as good as a justice's gold. The glass is yours—with my blessing.

RACHEL. Spare yourself that, dame. But the glass: how am I to get it? How will you send it to me—quietly?

GOODY RICKBY. Trust me for that. I've a willing lad that helps me with such errands; a neighbor o' mine. (*Calls.*) Ebenezer!

RACHEL. (*startled*). What! is he here?

GOODY RICKBY. In the hayloft. The boy's an orphan; he sleeps there o' times. Ebenezer!

(*A raw, disheveled country boy appears in the loft, slides down the ladder, and shuffles up sleepily.*)

THE BOY. Evenin'.

RACHEL. (*drawing* GOODY RICKBY *aside*). You understand; I desire no comment about this purchase.

GOODY RICKBY. Nor I, mistress, be sure.

RACHEL. Is he—?

GOODY RICKBY (*tapping her forehead significantly*). Trust his wits who hath no wit; he's mum.

RACHEL. Oh!

THE BOY (*gaping*). Job?

GOODY RICKBY. Yea, rumple-head! His job this morning is to bear yonder glass to the house of Justice Merton—the big one on the hill; to the side door. Mind, no gabbing. Doth he catch?

THE BOY (*nodding and grinning*). 'E swallows.

RACHEL. But is the boy strong enough?

GOODY RICKBY. Him? (*Pointing to the anvil*) Ebenezer!

(*The* BOY *spits on his palms, takes hold of the anvil, lifts it, drops it again, sits on it, and grins at the door, just as* RICHARD TALBOT *appears there, from outside.*)

RACHEL. Gracious!

GOODY RICKBY. Trust him. He'll carry the glass for you.

RACHEL. I will return home at once, then. Let him go quietly to the side door, and wait for me. Good-morning. (*Turning, she confronts* RICHARD.)

RICHARD. Good-morning.

RACHEL. Richard!—Squire Talbot, you—you are abroad early.

RICHARD. As early as Mistress Rachel. Is it pardonable? I caught sight of you walking in this direction, so I thought it wise to follow, lest— (*Looks hard at* GOODY RICKBY.)

RACHEL. Very kind. Thanks. We can return together. (*To* GOODY RICKBY) You will make sure that I receive the—the article.

GOODY RICKBY. Trust me, mistress. (*She curtsies to* RICHARD.)

RICHARD (*bluntly, looking from one to the other*). What article?

(RACHEL *ignores the question and starts to pass out.* RICHARD *frowns at* GOODY RICKBY, *who stammers.*)

GOODY RICKBY. Begging your pardon, sir?

RICHARD. What article? I said. (*After a short, embarrassed pause, more sternly*) Well?

GOODY RICKBY. Oh, the article! Yonder old glass, to be sure, sir. A quaint piece, your honor.

RICHARD. Rachel, you haven't come here at sunrise to buy—that thing?

RACHEL. Verily, "that thing," and at sunrise. A pretty time for a pretty purchase. Are you coming?

RICHARD (*in a low tone*). More witchcraft nonsense? Do you realize this is serious?

RACHEL. Oh, of course. You know I am desperately mystical, so pray let us not discuss it. Good-by.

RICHARD. Rachel, just a moment. If you want a mirror, you shall have the prettiest one in New England. Or I will import you one from London. Only—I beg of you—don't buy stolen goods.

GOODY RICKBY. Stolen goods?

RACHEL (*aside to* RICHARD). Don't! don't!

RICHARD (*to* GOODY RICKBY). Can you account for this mirror—how you came by it?

GOODY RICKBY. I'll show ye! I'll show ye! Stolen—ha!

RICHARD. Come, old swindler, keep your mirror, and give this lady back her money.

GOODY RICKBY. I'll damn ye both, I will!—Stolen!

RACHEL (*imploringly*). Will you come?

RICHARD. Look you, old Rickby; this is not the first time. Charm all the broomsticks in town, if you like; bewitch all the tables and saucepans and mirrors you please; but gull no more money out of young girls. Mind you! We're not so enterprising in this town as at Salem; but—*it may come to it!* So look sharp! I'm not blind to what's going on here.

GOODY RICKBY. Not blind, Master Puritan? Oho! You can see through all my counterfeits, can ye? So! you would scrape all the wonder out'n the world, as I've scraped all the meat out'n my punkin-head yonder! Aha! wait and see! Afore sundown, I'll send ye a nut to crack, shall make your orthodox jaws ache. Your servant, Master Deuteronomy!

RICHARD (*to* RACHEL, *who has seized his arm*). We'll go.

(*Exeunt* RICHARD *and* RACHEL.)

GOODY RICKBY (*calls shrilly after them*). Trot away, pretty team; toss your heads. I'll unhitch ye and take off your blinders.

THE SLOUCHING BOY (*capering and grimacing in front of the mirror, shrieks with laughter*). Ohoho!

GOODY RICKBY (*returning, she mutters savagely*). "Stolen goods"! (*Screams.*) Dickon! Stop laughing.

THE BOY. O Lord! O Lord!

GOODY RICKBY. What tickles thy mirth now?

THE BOY. For to think that the soul of an orphan innocent, what lives in a hayloft, should wear horns.

(*On looking into the mirror, the spectator perceives therein that the reflection of the slouching boy is the horned demon figure of* DICKON, *who performs the same antics in pantomime within the glass as the boy does without.*)

GOODY RICKBY. Yea; 'tis a wise devil that knows his own face in the glass. But hark now! thou must find me a rival for this cock-squire—dost hear? A rival, that shall steal away the heart of his Mistress Rachel.

DICKON. And take her to church?

GOODY RICKBY. To church or to hell. All's one.

DICKON. A rival! (*Pointing at the glass*) How would *he* serve—in there? Dear Ebenezer! Fancy the deacons in the vestry, Goody, and her uncle, the Justice, when they saw him escorting the bride to the altar, with his tail round her waist!

GOODY RICKBY. Tut, tut! Think it over in earnest, and meantime take her the glass. Wait, we'd best fold it up small, so as not to attract notice on the road. (DICKON, *who has already drawn the curtains over the glass, grasps one side of the large frame,* GOODY RICKBY *the other.*) Now! (*Pushing their shoulders against the two sides, the frame disappears and* DICKON *holds in his hand a mirror about a foot square, of the same design.*) So! Be off! And mind, a rival for Richard!

DICKON.

For Richard a rival,
Dear Goody Rickby
Wants Dickon's connival:
Lord! What can the trick be?

(*To the scarecrow*) By-by, Sonny; take care of thy mother. (DICKON *slouches out with the glass, whistling.*)

GOODY RICKBY. Mother! Yea, if only I had a son—the Justice Merton's and mine! If the brat had but lived now to remind him of those merry days, which he has forgotten. Zooks, wouldn't I put a spoke in his wheel! But no such luck for me! No such luck!

(*As she goes to the forge, the stout figure of a man appears in the doorway behind her. Under one arm he carries a large book, in the other hand a gold-headed cane. He hesitates, embarrassed.*)

THE MAN. Permit me, madam.

GOODY RICKBY (*turning*). Ah, him— Justice Merton!

JUSTICE MERTON (*removing his hat, steps over the sill, and lays his great book on the table; then with a supercilious look, he puts his hat firmly on again*). Permit me, dame.

GOODY RICKBY. You!

(*With confused, affected hauteur, the* JUSTICE *shifts from foot to foot, flourishing his cane. As he speaks,* GOODY RICKBY, *with a shrewd, painful expression, draws slowly backward toward the door, left, which opens into an inner room. Reaching it, she opens it part way, stands facing him,* and listens.)

JUSTICE MERTON. I have had the honor—permit me—to entertain suspicions; to rise early, to follow my niece, to meet just now Squire Talbot; to hear his remarks concerning—hem!— you, dame! to call here—permit me— to express myself and inquire—

GOODY RICKBY. Concerning your waistcoat? (*Turning quickly, she snatches an article of apparel which hangs on the inner side of the door, and holds it up.*)

JUSTICE MERTON (*starting, crimson*). Woman!

GOODY RICKBY. You left it behind— the last time.

JUSTICE MERTON. I have not the honor to remember—

GOODY RICKBY. The one I embroidered?

JUSTICE MERTON. 'Tis a matter of—

GOODY RICKBY. Of some two-and-twenty years. (*Stretching out the narrow width of the waistcoat.*) Will you try it on now, dearie?

JUSTICE MERTON. Unconscionable! Un-un-unconscionable witch!

GOODY RICKBY. Witchling—thou used to say.

JUSTICE MERTON. Pah! pah! I forget myself. Pride, permit me, goeth before a fall. As a magistrate, Rickby, I have already borne with you long! The last straw, however, breaks the camel's back.

GOODY RICKBY. Poor camel!

JUSTICE MERTON. You have soiled, you have smirched, the virgin reputation of my niece. You have inveigled her into notions of witchcraft; already the neighbors are beginning to talk. 'Tis a long lane which hath no turning, saith the Lord. Permit me—as a witch, thou art judged. Thou shalt hang.

A VOICE (*behind him*). And me, too?

JUSTICE MERTON (*turns about and stares*). I beg pardon.

THE VOICE (*in front of him*). Not at all.

JUSTICE MERTON. Did—did somebody speak?

THE VOICE. Don't you recognize my voice? *Still and small,* you know. If you will kindly let me out, we can chat.

JUSTICE MERTON (*turning fiercely on* GOODY RICKBY). These are thy sorceries. But I fear them not. The righteous man walketh with God. (*Going to the book which lies on the table.*) Satan, I ban thee! I will read from the Holy Scriptures! (*Unclasping the Bible, he flings open the ponderous covers.*)

DICKON (*steps forth in smoke*). Thanks; it was stuffy in there.

JUSTICE MERTON (*clasping his hands*). Dickon!

DICKON (*moving a step nearer on the table*). Hullo, Gilly! Hullo, Bess!

JUSTICE MERTON. Dickon! No! No!

DICKON. Do ye mind Auld Lang Syne —the chorus that night, Gilly? (*Sings.*)

Gil-ead, Gil-ead,
Gil-ead Merton,
He was a silly head, silly head,
Certain,
When he forgot to steal a bed-
Curtain.

Encore, now!

JUSTICE MERTON. No, no, be merciful! I will not harm her; she shall not hang; I swear it, I swear it! (DICKON *disappears.*) I swear—ah! Is he gone? Witchcraft! Witchcraft! I have witnessed it. 'Tis proved on thee, slut. I swear it: thou shalt hang. (*Exit wildly.*)

GOODY RICKBY. Ay, Gilead! I shall hang *on*! Ahaha! Dickon, thou angel! Ah, Satan! Satan! For a son now!

DICKON (*reappearing*). Videlicet, in law—a bastard. *N'est ce pas?*

GOODY RICKBY. Yea, in law and in justice, I should 'a' had one now. Worse luck that he died.

DICKON. One-and-twenty years ago? (GOODY RICKBY *nods.*) Good; he should be of age now. One-and-twenty—a pretty age, too, for a rival. Haha!— For arrival?—Marry, he shall arrive, then; arrive and marry and inherit his patrimony—all on his birthday! Come, to work!

GOODY RICKBY. What rant is this?

DICKON. Yet, Dickon, it pains me to perform such an anachronism. All this medievalism in Massachusetts!—These old-fashioned flames and alchemic accompaniments, when I've tried so hard to be a native American product; it jars. But *che vuole!* I'm naturally middle-aged. I haven't been really myself, let me think—since 1492!

GOODY RICKBY. What art thou mooning about?

DICKON (*still impenetrable*). There was my old friend in Germany, Dr. Johann Faustus; he was nigh such a bag of old rubbish when I made him over. Ain't it trite! No, you can't teach an old dog like me new tricks. Still, a scarecrow! that's decidedly local color. Come, then; a Yankee masterpiece! (*Seizing* GOODY RICKBY *by the arm, and placing her before the scarecrow, he makes a bow and wave of introduction.*) Behold, madam, your son —illegitimate; the future affianced of Mistress Rachel Merton, the heir-elect, through matrimony, of Merton House —Gilead Merton second, Lord Ravensbane! Your lordship—your mother.

GOODY RICKBY. Dickon! Can you do it?

DICKON. I can—try.

GOODY RICKBY. You will create him for me?— (*Wickedly*) —and for Gilead!

DICKON. I will—for a kiss.

GOODY RICKBY (*about to embrace him*). Dickon!

DICKON (*dodging her*). Later. Now, the waistcoat.

GOODY RICKY (*handing it*). Rare! Rare! He shall go wooing in 't—like his father.

DICKON (*shifting the scarecrow's gold-trimmed coat, slips on the embroidered waistcoat and replaces the coat*). Stand still, Jack! So, my macaroni.[1] *Perfecto!* Stay—a walking-stick!

GOODY RICKY (*wrenching a spoke out of an old rickety wheel*). Here: the spoke for Gilead. He used to take me to drive in the chaise it came out of.

DICKON (*placing the spoke as a cane, in the scarecrow's sleeve, views him with satisfaction*). Sic! There, Jacky! *Filius fit non nanscitur.*—Sam Hill! My Latin is stale. "In the beginning, was the—gourd!" Of these thy modest ingredients may thy spirit smack! (*Making various mystic passes with his hands,* DICKON *intones, now deep and solemn, now with fanciful shrill rapidity, this incantation.*)

Flail, flip;
Broom, sweep;
Sic itur!
Cornstalk
And turnip, talk!
Turn crittur!

Pulse, beet;
Gourd, eat;
Ave Hellas!
Poker and punkin,
Stir the old junk in;
Breathe, bellows!

Corn-cob,
And crow's feather,
End the job;
Jumble the rest o' the
  rubbish together;
Dovetail and tune 'em.
  E pluribus unum!

(*The scarecrow remains stock still.*) The devil! Have I lost the hang of it? Ah! Hullo! He's dropped his pipe. What's a dandy without his 'baccy! (*Picking up the pipe, he shows it to* GOODY RICKBY, *pointing into the pipe-bowl.*) 'Tis my own brand, Goody: brimstone. Without it he'd be naught but a scarecrow. (*Restoring the corn-cob pipe to the scarecrow's mouth*) 'Tis the life and breath of him. So; hand me yon hazel switch, Goody. (*Waving it*) Presto!

Brighten, coal,
I' the dusk between us!
Whiten, soul!
Propinquat Venus!

(*A whiff of smoke puffs from the scarecrow's pipe.*)

Sic! Sic! *Jacobus!* (*Another whiff*) Bravo!

(*The whiffs grow more rapid and the thing trembles.*)

GOODY RICKBY. Puff! puff, manny, for thy life!

DICKON. *Fiat, foetus!*—Huzza! *Noch einmal!* Go it! (*Clouds of smoke issue from the pipe, half fill the shop, and envelop the creature, who staggers.*[2])

GOODY RICKBY. See! See his eyes!

DICKON (*beckoning with one finger*). *Veni fili! Veni!* Take 'ee first step, *bambino!*—Toddle!

(*The* SCARECROW *makes a stiff lurch forward and falls sidewise against the*

---

1 *macaroni*, dandy; concerning whom Dickon later exclaims, *Filius fit non nascitur*, "A son is made, not born."—*Sic*, thus; *sic itur*, thus is the way; *ave*, hail; *E pluribus unum!*, one out of many; *Propinquat Venus!* Venus approach!; *Veni filius*, Come, son!; *Fiat, foetus*, let there be offspring; *Noch einmal* (German) , once more.

2 At Dickon's words "Go it" the living actor, concealed by the smoke, and disguised, has substituted himself for the elegantly clad effigy. His make-up, of course, approximates to the latter, but the grotesque contours of his expression gradually, throughout the remainder of the act, become refined and sublimated till, at the *finale*, they are of a lordly and distinguished caste.

anvil, propped half-reclining against which he leans rigid, emitting fainter puffs of smoke in gasps.)

GOODY RICKBY *(screams).* Have a care! He's fallen.

DICKON. Well done, Punkin Jack! Thou shalt be knighted for that! *(Striking him on the shoulder with the hazel rod)* Rise, Lord Ravensbane!

(The SCARECROW *totters to his feet, and makes a forlorn rectilinear salutation.)*

GOODY RICKBY. Look! He bows.—He flaps his flails at thee. He smiles like a tik-doo-loo-roo!

DICKON *(With a profound reverence, backing away).* Will his lordship deign to follow his tutor?

(With hitches and jerks, the SCARECROW *follows* DICKON.*)*

GOODY RICKBY. O Lord! Lord! the style o' the broomstick!

DICKON *(holding ready a high-backed chair).* Will his lordship be seated and rest himself? *(Awkwardly the* SCARECROW *half falls into the chair; his head sinks sideways, and his pipe falls out.* DICKON *snatches it up instantly and restores it to his mouth.)* Puff! Puff, *puer;* 'tis thy life. *(The* SCARECROW *puffs again.)* Is his lordship's tobacco refreshing?

GOODY RICKBY. Look now! The red color in his cheeks. The beet juice is pumping, oho!

DICKON *(offering his arm).* Your lordship will deign to receive an audience? *(The* SCARECROW *takes his arm and rises.)* The Marchioness of Rickby, your lady mother, entreats leave to present herself.

GOODY RICKBY *(curtsying low).* My son!

DICKON *(holding the pipe, and waving the hazel rod).* Dicite! Speak! *(The* SCARECROW, *blowing out his last*

mouthful of smoke, opens his mouth, gasps, gurgles, and is silent.)* In principio erat verbum!* Accost thy mother!

(The SCARECROW, *clutching at his side in a struggle for coherence, fixes a pathetic look of pain on* GOODY RICKBY.*)*

THE SCARECROW. Mother!

GOODY RICKBY *(with a scream of hysterical laughter, seizes both* DICKON's *hands and dances him about the forge).* O, Beelzebub! I shall die!

DICKON. Thou hast thy son. *(*DICKON *whispers in the* SCARECROW's *ear, shakes his finger, and exits.)*

GOODY RICKBY. He called me "Mother." Again, boy, again.

THE SCARECROW. From the bottom of my heart—Mother.

GOODY RICKBY. "The bottom of his heart"!—Nay, thou killest me.

THE SCARECROW. Permit me, madam!

GOODY RICKBY. Gilead! Gilead himself! Waistcoat, "permit me," and all; thy father over again, I tell thee.

THE SCARECROW *(with a slight stammer).* It gives me—I assure you—lady —the deepest happiness.

GOODY RICKBY. Just so the old hypocrite spoke when I said I'd have him. But thou hast a sweeter deference, my son.

(Re-enter DICKON; *he is dressed all in black, save for a white stock—a suit of plain elegance.)*

DICKON. Now, my lord, your tutor is ready.

THE SCARECROW *(to* GOODY RICKBY).* I have the honor—permit me—to wish you—good-morning. *(Bows and takes a step after* DICKON, *who, taking a three-cornered cocked hat from a peg, goes toward the door.)*

GOODY RICKBY. Whoa! Whoa, Jack! Whither away?

DICKON *(presenting the hat).* Deign to reply, sir.

THE SCARECROW. I go—with my tutor—Master Dickonson—to pay my respects—to his worship—the Justice —Merton—to solicit—the hand—of his daughter—the fair Mistress—Rachel. (*With another bow*) Permit me.

GOODY RICKBY. Permit ye? God speed ye! Thou must teach him his tricks, Dickon.

DICKON. Trust me, Goody. Between here and Justice Merton's, I will play the mother-hen, and I promise thee, our bantling shall be as stuffed with compliments as a callow chick with caterpillars. (*As he throws open the big doors, the cawing of crows is heard again.*) Hark! your lordship's retainers acclaim you on your birthday. They bid you welcome to your majority. Listen! "Long live Lord Ravensbane! Caw!"

GOODY RICKBY. Look! Count 'em, Dickon.

One for sorrow, Two for mirth,
Three for a wedding,
Four for a birth—

Four on 'em! So! Good luck on thy birthday! And see! There's three on 'em flying into the Justice's field.

—Flight o' the crows
Tells how the wind blows!—

A wedding! Get thee gone. Wed the girl, and sting the Justice. Bless ye, my son!

THE SCARECROW (*with a profound reverence*). Mother—believe me—to be —your ladyship's—most devoted—and obedient—son.

DICKON (*prompting him aloud*). Ravensbane.

THE SCARECROW (*donning his hat, lifts his head in hauteur, shakes his lace ruffle over his hand, turns his* shoulder, nods slightly, and speaks for the first time with complete mastery of his voice*). Hm! Ravensbane! (*With one hand in the arm of* DICKON, *the other twirling his cane* [*the converted chaise-spoke*], *wreathed in halos of smoke from his pipe, the fantastical figure hitches elegantly forth into the daylight, amid louder acclamations of the crows.*)

ACT TWO

The same morning. JUSTICE MERTON's *parlor, furnished and designed in the style of the early colonial period. On the right wall hangs a portrait of the* JUSTICE *as a young man; on the left wall, an old-fashioned looking-glass. At the right of the room stands the Glass of Truth, draped—as in the blacksmith shop—with the strange, embroidered curtain. In front of it are discovered* RACHEL *and* RICHARD; RACHEL *is about to draw the curtain.*

RACHEL. Now! Are you willing?

RICHARD. So you suspect me of dark, villainous practices?

RACHEL. No, no, foolish Dick.

RICHARD. Still, I am to be tested; is that it?

RACHEL. That's it.

RICHARD. As your true lover.

RACHEL. Well, yes.

RICHARD. Why, of course, then, I consent. A true lover always consents to the follies of his lady-love.

RACHEL. Thank you, Dick; I trust the glass will sustain your character. Now; when I draw the curtain—

RICHARD (*staying her hand*). What if I be false?

RACHEL. Then, sir, the glass will reflect you as the subtle fox that you are.

RICHARD. And you—as the goose?

RACHEL. Very likely. Ah! but, Richard, dear, we mustn't laugh. It may prove very serious. You do not guess—you do not dream all the mysteries—

RICHARD (*shaking his head, with a grave smile*). You pluck at too many mysteries. Remember our first mother Eve!

RACHEL. But this is the glass of truth; and Goody Rickby told me—

RICHARD. Rickby, forsooth!

RACHEL. Nay, come; let's have it over. (*She draws the curtain, covers her eyes, steps back by* RICHARD's *side, looks at the glass, and gives a joyous cry.*) Ah! there you are, dear! There we are, both of us—just as we have always seemed to each other, true. 'Tis proved. Isn't it wonderful?

RICHARD. Miraculous! That a mirror bought in a blacksmith shop, before sunrise, for twenty pounds, should prove to be actually—a mirror!

RACHEL. Richard, I'm so happy.

(*Enter* JUSTICE MERTON *and* MISTRESS MERTON.)

RICHARD (*embracing her*). Happy, art thou, sweet goose? Why, then, God bless Goody Rickby.

JUSTICE MERTON. Strange words from you, Squire Talbot.

(RACHEL *and* RICHARD *part quickly;* RACHEL *draws the curtain over the mirror;* RICHARD *stands stiffly.*)

RICHARD. Justice Merton! Why, sir, the old witch is more innocent, perhaps, than I represented her.

JUSTICE MERTON. A witch, believe me, is never innocent. (*Taking their hands, he brings them together and kisses* RACHEL *on the forehead.*) Permit me, young lovers. I was once young myself, young and amorous.

MISTRESS MERTON (*in a low voice*). Verily!

JUSTICE MERTON. My fair niece, my worthy young man, beware of witchcraft.

MISTRESS MERTON. And Goody Rickby, too, brother?

JUSTICE MERTON. That woman shall answer for her deeds. She is proscribed.

RACHEL. Proscribed? What is that?

MISTRESS MERTON (*examining the mirror*). What is this?

JUSTICE MERTON. She shall hang.

RACHEL. Uncle, no! Not merely because of my purchase this morning?

JUSTICE MERTON. Your purchase?

MISTRESS MERTON (*pointing to the mirror*). That, I suppose.

JUSTICE MERTON. What! you purchased that mirror of her? You brought it here?

RACHEL. No, the boy brought it; I found it here when I returned.

JUSTICE MERTON. What! From her shop? From her infamous den, into my parlor! (*To* MISTRESS MERTON) Call the servant. (*Himself calling*) Micah! Away with it! Micah!

RACHEL. Uncle Gilead, I bought—

JUSTICE MERTON. Micah, I say! Where is the man?

RACHEL. Listen, Uncle. I bought it with my own money.

JUSTICE MERTON. Thine own money! Wilt have the neighbors gossip? Wilt have me, thyself, my house, suspected of complicity with witches?

(*Enter* MICAH.)

Micah, take this away.

MICAH. Yes, sir; but, sir—

JUSTICE MERTON. Out of my house!

MICAH. There be visitors.

JUSTICE MERTON. Away with—

MISTRESS MERTON (*touching his arm*). Gilead!

MICAH. Visitors, sir; gentry.

JUSTICE MERTON. Ah!

MICAH. Shall I show them in, sir?

JUSTICE MERTON. Visitors! In the morning? Who are they?

MICAH. Strangers, sir. I should judge they be very high gentry; lords, sir.

ALL. Lords!

MICAH. At least, one on 'em, sir. The other—the dark gentleman—told me they left their horses at the inn, sir.

MISTRESS MERTON. Hark! (*The faces of all wear suddenly a startled expression.*) Where is that unearthly sound?

JUSTICE MERTON (*listening*). Is it in the cellar?

MICAH. 'Tis just the dog howling, madam. When he spied the gentry he turned tail and run below.

MISTRESS MERTON. Oh, the dog!

JUSTICE MERTON. Show the gentlemen here, Micah. Don't keep them waiting. A lord! (*To* RACHEL) We shall talk of this matter later.—A lord! (*Turning to the small glass on the wall, he arranges his peruke and attire.*)

RACHEL (*to* RICHARD). What a fortunate interruption! But, dear Dick! I wish we needn't meet these strangers now.

RICHARD. Would you really rather we were alone together?

(*They chat aside, absorbed in each other.*)

JUSTICE MERTON. Think of it, Cynthia, a lord!

MISTRESS MERTON (*dusting the furniture hastily with her handkerchief*). And such dust!

RACHEL (*to* RICHARD). You know, dear, we need only be introduced, and then we can steal away together.

MICAH (*re-enters, announcing*). Lord Ravensbane: Marquis of Oxford, Baron of Wittenberg, Elector of Worms, and Count of Cordova; Master Dickonson.

(*Enter* RAVENSBANE *and* DICKON.)

JUSTICE MERTON. Gentlemen, permit me, you are excessively welcome. I am deeply gratified to meet—

DICKON. Lord Ravensbane, of the Rookeries, Somersetshire.

JUSTICE MERTON. Lord Ravensbane —his lordship's most truly honored.

RAVENSBANE. Truly honored.

JUSTICE MERTON (*turning to* DICKON). His lordship's—?

DICKON. Tutor.

JUSTICE MERTON (*checking his effusiveness*). Ah, so!

DICKON. Justice Merton, I believe.

JUSTICE MERTON. Of Merton House. —May I present—permit me, your lordship—my sister, Mistress Merton.

JUSTICE MERTON. And my—and my— (*Under his breath*)—Rachel! (RACHEL *remains with a bored expression behind* RICHARD.)—My young neighbor, Squire Talbot, Squire Richard Talbot of—of—

RICHARD. Of nowhere, sir.

RAVENSBANE (*nods*). Nowhere.

JUSTICE MERTON. And permit me, Lord Ravensbane, my niece—Mistress Rachel Merton.

RAVENSBANE (*bows low*). Mistress Rachel Merton.

RACHEL (*curtsies*). Lord Ravensbane.

(*As they raise their heads, their eyes meet and are fascinated.* DICKON *just then takes* RAVENSBANE'S *pipe and fills it.*)

RAVENSBANE. Mistress Rachel!

RACHEL. Your lordship!

(DICKON *returns the pipe.*)

MISTRESS MERTON. A pipe! Gilead!— in the parlor!

JUSTICE MERTON (*frowns silence*). Your lordship—ahem! —has just arrived in town?

DICKON. From London, via New Amsterdam.

RICHARD (*aside*). Is he staring at you? Are you ill, Rachel?

RACHEL (*indifferently*). What?

JUSTICE MERTON. Lord Ravensbane

honors my humble roof.

DICKON (*touches* RAVENSBANE'S *arm*). Your lordship—"roof."

RAVENSBANE (*starting, turns to* MERTON). Nay, sir, the roof of my father's oldest friend bestows generous hospitality upon his only son.

JUSTICE MERTON. Only son—ah, yes! Your father—

RAVENSBANE. My father, I trust, sir, has never forgotten the intimate companionship, the touching devotion, the unceasing solicitude for his happiness which you, sir, manifested to him in the days of his youth.

JUSTICE MERTON. Really, your lordship, the—the slight favors which—hem! some years ago, I was privileged to show your illustrious father—

RAVENSBANE. Permit me!—Because, however, of his present infirmities—for I regret to say that my father is suffering a temporary aberration of mind—

JUSTICE MERTON. You distress me!

RAVENSBANE. My lady mother has charged me with a double mission here in New England. On my quitting my home, sir, to explore the wideness and the mystery of this world, my mother bade me be sure to call upon his worship, the Justice Merton; and deliver to him, first, my father's remembrances; and secondly, my mother's epistle.

DICKON (*handing* JUSTICE MERTON *a sealed document*). Her ladyship's letter, sir.

JUSTICE MERTON (*examining the seal with awe, speaks aside to* MISTRESS MERTON). Cynthia!—a crested seal!

DICKON. His lordship's crest, sir: rooks rampant.

JUSTICE MERTON (*embarrassed, breaks the seal*). Permit me.

RACHEL (*looking at* RAVENSBANE). Have you noticed his bearing, Richard: what personal distinction! what inbred nobility! Every inch a true lord!

RICHARD. He may be a lord, my dear, but he walks like a broomstick.

RACHEL. How dare you! (*Turns abruptly away; as she does so, a fold of her gown catches in a chair.*)

RAVENSBANE. Mistress Rachel—permit me. (*Stooping, he extricates the fold of her gown.*)

RACHEL. Oh, thank you.

(*They go aside together.*)

JUSTICE MERTON (*to* DICKON, *glancing up from the letter*). I am astonished—overpowered!

RICHARD (*to* MISTRESS MERTON). So Lord Ravensbane and his family are old friends of yours?

MISTRESS MERTON (*monosyllabically*). I never heard the name before, Richard.

RAVENSBANE (*to* RACHEL, *taking her hand after a whisper from* DICKON). Believe me, sweet lady, it will give me the deepest pleasure.

RACHEL. Can you really tell fortunes?

RAVENSBANE. More than that; I can bestow them.

(RAVENSBANE *leads* RACHEL *off, left, into an adjoining room, the door of which remains open.* RICHARD *follows them.* MISTRESS MERTON *follows him, murmuring,* "Richard!" DICKON *stands where he can watch them in the room off scene, while he speaks to the* JUSTICE.)

JUSTICE MERTON (*to* DICKON, *glancing up from the letter*). I am astonished—overpowered! But is her ladyship really serious? An offer of marriage!

DICKON. Pray read it again, sir.

JUSTICE MERTON (*reads*). "To the Worshipful, the Justice Gilead Merton, Merton House.

"My Honorable Friend and Benefactor:

"With these brief lines I commend to you our son"—*our* son!

DICKON. She speaks likewise for his young lordship's father, sir.

JUSTICE MERTON. Oh! of course. (*Reads.*) "In a strange land, I entrust him to you as to a father." Honored, believe me! "I have only to add my earnest hope that the natural gifts, graces, and inherited fortune"—ah—!

DICKON. Twenty thousand pounds—on his father's demise.

JUSTICE MERTON. Ah!—"fortune of this young scion of nobility will so propitiate the heart of your niece, Mistress Rachel Merton, as to cause her to accept his proffered hand in matrimony" — but — but — but Squire Talbot is betrothed to—well, well, we shall see—"in matrimony, and thus cement the early bonds of interest and affection between your honored self and his lordship's father; not to mention, dear sir, your worship's ever grateful and obedient admirer,

"ELIZABETH,
"Marchioness of R."

Of R.! of R.! Will you believe me, my dear sir, so long is it since my travels in England!—I visited at so many—hem! noble estates—permit me, it is so awkward, but—

DICKON (*with his peculiar intonation of the First Act*). Not at all.

RAVENSBANE (*calls from the adjoining room*). Dickon, my pipe!

(DICKON *glides away.*)

JUSTICE MERTON (*starting in perturbation; to* DICKON). Permit me, one moment; I did not catch your name.

DICKON. My name? Dickonson.

JUSTICE MERTON (*with a gasp of relief*). Ah, Dickonson! Thank you, I mistook the word.

DICKON. A compound, your worship. (*With a malignant smile*) Dickon-(*Then, jerking his thumb toward the next room*) son! (*Bowing*) Both at your service.

JUSTICE MERTON. Is he—he there?

DICKON. Bessie's brat; yes; it didn't die, after all, poor suckling! Dickon weaned it. Saved it for balm of Gilead. Raised it for joyful homecoming. Prodigal's return! Twenty-first birthday! Happy son! Happy father!

JUSTICE MERTON. My—son!

DICKON. Felicitations!

JUSTICE MERTON (*faintly*). What—what do you want?

DICKON. Only the happiness of your dear ones—the union of these young hearts and hands.

JUSTICE MERTON. What! he will dare—an illegitimate—

DICKON. Fie, fie, Gilly! Why, the brat is a lord now.

JUSTICE MERTON. Oh, the disgrace! Spare me that, Dickon. And she is innocent; she is already betrothed.

DICKON. Twiddle-twaddle! 'Tis a brilliant match; besides, her ladyship's heart is set upon it.

JUSTICE MERTON. Her ladyship—?

DICKON. The Marchioness of Rickby!

JUSTICE MERTON (*glowering*). Rickby!—I had forgotten.

DICKON. Her ladyship has never forgotten. So, you see, your worship's alternatives are most simple. Alternative one: advance his lordship's suit with your niece as speedily as possible, and save all scandal. Alternative two: impede his lordship's suit, and—

JUSTICE MERTON. Don't, Dickon! don't reveal the truth; not disgrace now!

DICKON. Good; we are agreed, then?

JUSTICE MERTON. I have no choice.

DICKON (*cheerfully*). Why, true; we ignored that, didn't we?

MISTRESS MERTON (*re-entering*). This young lord—Why, Gilead, are you ill?

JUSTICE MERTON (*with a great effort, commands himself*). Not in the least.

MISTRESS MERTON. Rachel's deportment, my dear brother—I tell you, they are fortune-telling!

JUSTICE MERTON. Tush! Tush!

MISTRESS MERTON. Tush? "Tush" to me? Tush! (*She goes out.*)

(RAVENSBANE *and* RACHEL *re-enter from the adjoining room, followed shortly by* RICHARD.)

RACHEL. I am really at a loss. Your lordship's hand is so very peculiar.

RAVENSBANE. Ah! Peculiar.

RACHEL. This, now, is the line of life.

RAVENSBANE. Of life, yes?

RACHEL. But it begins so abruptly, and see! it breaks off and ends nowhere. And just so here with this line —the line of—of love.

RAVENSBANE. Of love. So; it breaks?

RACHEL. Yes.

RAVENSBANE. Ah, then, that must be the *heart* line.

RACHEL. Why, Lord Ravensbane, your pulse. Really, if I am cruel, you are quite heartless. I declare I can't feel your heart beat at all.

RAVENSBANE. Ah, mistress, that is because I have just lost it.

RACHEL (*archly*). Where?

RAVENSBANE (*faintly*). Dickon, my pipe!

RACHEL. Alas! my lord, are you ill?

DICKON (*restoring the lighted pipe to* RAVENSBANE, *speaks aside*). Pardon me, sweet young lady, I must confide to you that his lordship's heart is peculiarly responsive to his emotions. When he feels very ardently, it quite stops. Hence the use of his pipe.

RACHEL. Oh! Is smoking, then, necessary for his heart?

DICKON. Absolutely—to equilibrate the valvular palpitations. Without his pipe—should his lordship experience, for instance, the emotion of love—he might die.

RACHEL. You alarm me!

DICKON. But this is for you only, Mistress Rachel. We may confide in you?

RACHEL. Oh, utterly, sir.

DICKON. His lordship, you know, is so sensitive.

RAVENSBANE (*to* RACHEL). You have given it back to me. Why did you not keep it?

RACHEL. What, my lord?

RAVENSBANE. My heart.

RICHARD. Intolerable! Do you approve of *this*, sir? Are Lord Ravensbane's credentials satisfactory?

JUSTICE MERTON. Eminently, eminently.

RICHARD. Ah! So her ladyship's letter is—

JUSTICE MERTON. Charming; charming. (*To* RAVENSBANE) Your lordship will, I trust, make my house your home.

RAVENSBANE. My home, sir.

RACHEL (*to* DICKON, *who has spoken to her*). Really? (*To* JUSTICE MERTON) Why, Uncle, what is this Master Dickonson tells us?

JUSTICE MERTON. What! What! he has revealed—

RACHEL. Yes, indeed.

JUSTICE MERTON. Rachel! Rachel!

RACHEL (*laughingly to* RAVENSBANE). My uncle is doubtless astonished to find you so grown.

RAVENSBANE (*laughingly to* JUSTICE MERTON). I am doubtless astonished, sir, to be so grown.

JUSTICE MERTON (*to* DICKON). You have—

DICKON. Merely remarked, sir, that your worship had often dandled his lordship—as an infant.

JUSTICE MERTON (*smiling lugubriously*). Quite so—as an infant merely.

RACHEL. How interesting! Then you must have seen his lordship's home in England.

JUSTICE MERTON. As you say.

RACHEL (*to* RAVENSBANE). Do describe it to us. We are so isolated here from the grand world. Do you know, I always imagine England to be an enchanted isle, like one of the old Hesperides, teeming with fruits of solid gold.

RAVENSBANE. Ah, yes! my mother raises them.

RACHEL. Fruits of gold?

RAVENSBANE. Round like the rising sun. She calls them—ah! punkins.

MISTRESS MERTON. "Punkins"!

JUSTICE MERTON (*aside, grinding his teeth*). Scoundrel! Scoundrel!

RACHEL (*laughing*). Your lordship pokes fun at us.

DICKON. His lordship is an artist in words, mistress. I have noticed that in whatever country he is traveling, he tinges his vocabulary with the local idiom. His lordship means, of course, not pumpkins, but pomegranates.

RACHEL. We forgive him. But, your lordship, please be serious and describe to us your hall.

RAVENSBANE. Quite serious: the hall. Yes, yes; in the middle burns a great fire—on a black—ah! black altar.

DICKON. A Druidical heirloom. His lordship's mother collects antiques.

RACHEL. How fascinating!

RAVENSBANE. Fascinating! On the walls hang pieces of iron.

DICKON. Trophies of Saxon warfare.

RAVENSBANE. And rusty horseshoes. (*General Murmurs:* "Horseshoes!")

DICKON. Presents from the German Emperor. They were worn by the steeds of Charlemagne.

RAVENSBANE. Quite so; and broken cartwheels.

DICKON. Relics of British chariots.

RACHEL. How medieval it must be! (*To* JUSTICE MERTON) And to think you never described it to us!

MISTRESS MERTON. True, brother; you have been singularly reticent.

JUSTICE MERTON. Permit me; it is impossible to report all one sees on one's travels.

MISTRESS MERTON. Evidently.

RACHEL. But surely your lordship's mother has other diversions besides collecting antiques. I have heard that in England ladies followed the hounds; and sometimes— (*Looking at her aunt and lowering her voice*) —they even dance.

RAVENSBANE. Dance—ah, yes; my lady mother dances about the—the altar; she swings high a hammer.

DICKON. Your lordship, your lordship! Pray, sir, check this vein of poetry. Lord Ravensbane symbolizes as a hammer and altar a golf-stick and tee—a Scottish game, which her ladyship plays on her Highland estates.

RICHARD (*to* MISTRESS MERTON). What do you think of this?

MISTRESS MERTON (*with a scandalized look toward her brother*). He said to me "tush."

RICHARD (*to* JUSTICE MERTON, *indicating* DICKON). Who is this magpie?

JUSTICE MERTON (*hisses in fury*). Satan!

RICHARD. I beg pardon!

JUSTICE MERTON. Satan sir—makes you jealous.

RICHARD (*bows stiffly*). Good-morning. (*Walking up to* RAVENSBANE) Lord Ravensbane, I have a rustic colonial question to ask. Is it the latest fashion to smoke incessantly in ladies' parlors, or is it—medieval?

DICKON. His lordship's health, sir, necessitates—

RICHARD. I addressed his lordship.

RAVENSBANE. In the matter of fashions, sir— (*Hands his pipe to be refilled.*) My pipe, Dickon!

(*While* DICKON *holds his pipe—*

somewhat *longer than usual*—RAVENS-
BANE, *with his mouth open as if about
to speak, relapses into a vacant stare.*)
RICHARD. Well?

DICKON (*as he lights the pipe for* RAV-
ENSBANE, *speaks suavely and low as if
not to be overheard by him*). Pardon
me. The fact is, my young pupil is
sensitive; the wound from his latest
duel is not quite healed; you observe
a slight lameness, an occasional—absence of mind.

RACHEL. A wound—in a real duel?

DICKON (*aside*). You, mistress, know
the *true* reason—his lordship's heart.

RICHARD (*to* RAVENSBANE, *who is still
staring vacantly into space*). Well, well,
your lordship. (RAVENSBANE *pays no attention.*) You were saying—? (DICKON
returns the pipe.) —in the matter of
fashions, sir—?

RAVENSBANE (*regaining slowly a look
of intelligence, draws himself up with
affronted hauteur*). Permit me! (*Puffs
several wreaths of smoke into the air.*)
I *am* the fashions.

RICHARD (*going*). Insufferable! (*He
pauses at the door.*)

MISTRESS MERTON (*to* JUSTICE MER-
TON). Well—what do you think of that?

JUSTICE MERTON. Spoken like King
Charles himself.

MISTRESS MERTON. Brother! brother!
is there nothing wrong here? (*Going
out, she passes* DICKON, *starts at a look
which he gives her, and goes out,
flustered. Following her,* JUSTICE MER-
TON *is stopped by* DICKON, *and led off
by him.*)

RACHEL (*to* RAVENSBANE). I—object to
the smoke? Why, I think it is charming.

RICHARD (*who has returned from
the door, speaks in a low, constrained
voice*). Rachel!

RACHEL. Oh!—you?

RICHARD. You take quickly to European fashions.

RACHEL. Yes? To what one in particular?

RICHARD. Two; smoking and flirtation.

RACHEL. Jealous?

RICHARD. Of an idiot? I hope not.
Manners differ, however. Your confi-
dences to his lordship have evidently
not included—your relation to me.

RACHEL. Oh, our relations!

RICHARD. Of course, since you wish
him to continue in ignorance—

RACHEL. Not at all. He shall know
at once. Lord Ravensbane!

RAVENSBANE. Fair mistress!

RICHARD. Rachel, stop! I did not
mean—

RACHEL (*to* RAVENSBANE). My uncle
did not introduce to you with sufficient elaboration this gentleman.
Will you allow me to do so now?

RAVENSBANE. I adore Mistress Rachel's elaborations.

RACHEL. Lord Ravensbane, I beg to
present Squire Talbot, my *betrothed.*

RAVENSBANE. Betrothed! Is it—(*Noticing* RICHARD'S *frown*)—Is it pleasant?

RACHEL (*to* RICHARD). Are you satisfied?

RICHARD (*trembling with feeling*).
More than satisfied. (*Exit.*)

RAVENSBANE (*looking after him*).
Ah! Betrothed is *not* pleasant.

RACHEL. Not always.

RAVENSBANE (*anxiously*). Mistress
Rachel is not pleased?

RACHEL (*biting her lip, looks after
RICHARD*). With him.

RAVENSBANE. Mistress Rachel will
smile again?

RACHEL. Soon.

RAVENSBANE (*ardent*). Ah! What can
Lord Ravensbane do to make her
smile? See! will you puff my pipe? It
is very pleasant. (*Offering the pipe.*)

RACHEL (*smiling*). Shall I try? (*Takes
hold of it mischievously.*)

(*Enter* JUSTICE MERTON *and* DICKON.)

JUSTICE MERTON (*in a great voice*). Rachel!

RACHEL. Why, Uncle!

JUSTICE MERTON (*speaks suavely to* RAVENSBANE). Permit me, your lordship —Rachel, you will kindly withdraw for a few moments; I desire to confer with Lord Ravensbane concerning his mother's—her ladyship's letter— (*Obsequiously to* DICKON) —that is, if you think, sir, that your noble pupil is not too fatigued.

DICKON. Not at all; I think his lordship will listen to you with much pleasure.

RAVENSBANE (*bowing to* JUSTICE MERTON, *but looking at* RACHEL). With much pleasure.

DICKON. And in the meantime, if Mistress Rachel will allow me, I will assist her in writing those invitations which your worship desires to send in her name.

JUSTICE MERTON. Invitations—from my niece?

DICKON. To his Excellency, the Lieutenant-Governor; to your friends, the Reverend Masters at Harvard College, etc., etc.; in brief, to all your worship's select social acquaintance in the vicinity—to meet his lordship. It was so thoughtful in you to suggest it, sir, and believe me, his lordship appreciates your courtesy in arranging the reception in his honor for this afternoon.

RACHEL (*to* JUSTICE MERTON). This afternoon! Are we really to give his lordship a reception? And will it be here, Uncle?

DICKON (*looking at him narrowly*). Your worship said here, I believe?

JUSTICE MERTON. Quite so, sir; quite so, quite so.

DICKON. Permit me to act as your scribe, Mistress Rachel.

RACHEL. With pleasure. (*With a* curtsy *to* RAVENSBANE.) Till we meet again! (*Exit.*)

DICKON (*aside to* JUSTICE MERTON). I advise nothing rash, Gilly; the brat has a weak heart. (*Aside, as he passes* RAVENSBANE) Remember, Jack! Puff! Puff!

RAVENSBANE (*staring at the door*). She is gone.

JUSTICE MERTON. Impostor! You, at least, shall not play the lord and master to my face.

RAVENSBANE. Quite—gone!

JUSTICE MERTON. I know with whom I have to deal. If I be any judge of my own flesh and blood—permit me—you shall quail before me.

RAVENSBANE (*dejectedly*). She did not smile— (*Joyously*) She smiled!

JUSTICE MERTON. Affected rogue! I know thee. I know thy feigned pauses, thy assumed vagaries. Speak; how much do you want?

RAVENSBANE (*ecstatically*). Ah! Mistress Rachel!

JUSTICE MERTON. Her! Scoundrel, if thou dost name her again, my innocent—my sweet maid! If thou dost— thou godless spawn of temptation— mark you, I will put an end— (*Reaching for a pistol that rests in a rack on the wall,—the intervening form of* DICKON *suddenly appears, pockets the pistol, and exits.*)

DICKON. I beg pardon; I forgot something.

JUSTICE MERTON (*sinking into a chair*). God, Thou art just! (*He holds his head in his hands and weeps.*)

RAVENSBANE (*for the first time, since* RACHEL'S *departure, observing* MERTON). Permit me, sir, are you ill?

JUSTICE MERTON (*recoiling*). What art thou!

RAVENSBANE (*monotonously*). I am Lord Ravensbane: Marquis of Oxford, Baron of Wittenberg, Elector of

Worms, and— (*As* JUSTICE MERTON *covers his face again*) Shall I call Dickon? (*Walking quickly toward the door, calls.*) Dickon!

JUSTICE MERTON (*starting up*). No, do not call him. Tell me: I hate thee not; thou wast innocent. Tell me!—I thought thou hadst died as a babe.— Where has Dickon, our tyrant, kept thee these twenty years?

RAVENSBANE (*with gentle courtesy*). Master Dickonson is my tutor.

JUSTICE MERTON. And why has thy mother—Ah, I know well; I deserve all. But yet, it must not be published now! I am a justice now, an honored citizen—and my young niece—Thy mother will not demand so much.

RAVENSBANE. My mother is the Marchioness of Rickby.

JUSTICE MERTON. Yes, yes; 'twas well planned, a clever trick. 'Twas skillful of her. But surely thy mother gave thee commands to—

RAVENSBANE. My mother gave me her blessing.

JUSTICE MERTON. Ah, 'tis well, then. Young man, my son, I too will give thee my blessing, if thou wilt but go —go instantly—go with half my fortune—but leave me my honor—and my Rachel?

*RAVENSBANE. Rachel? Rachel is yours? No, no, Mistress Rachel is mine. We are ours.

JUSTICE MERTON (*pleadingly*). Consider the disgrace—you, an illegitimate —and she—oh, think what thou art!

RAVENSBANE (*monotonously, puffing smoke at the end*). I am Lord Ravensbane: Marquis of Oxford, Baron of Wittenberg, Elector of Worms, and Count—

JUSTICE MERTON (*wrenching the pipe from* RAVENSBANE'S *hand and lips*). Devil's child! Boor! Buffoon! (*Flinging the pipe away*) I will stand thy insults no longer. If thou hast no heart—

RAVENSBANE (*putting his hand to his side, staggers*). Ah! my heart!

JUSTICE MERTON. Hypocrite! Thou canst not fool me. I am thy father.

RAVENSBANE (*faintly, stretches out his hand to him for support*). Father!

JUSTICE MERTON. Stand away. Thou mayst break thy heart and mine and the devil's, but thou shalt not break Rachel's.

RAVENSBANE (*faintly*). Mistress Rachel is mine— (*He staggers again, and falls, half reclining, upon a chair. More faintly he speaks, beginning to change expression.*) Her eyes are mine; her smiles are mine. (*His eyes close.*)

JUSTICE MERTON. Good God! Can it be—his heart? (*With agitated swiftness, he feels and listens at* RAVENSBANE'S *side.*) Not a motion; not a sound! Yea, God, Thou art good! 'Tis his heart. He is—ah! he is my son. Judge Almighty, if he should die now; may I not be still a moment more and make sure? No, no, my son—he is changing. (*Calls.*) Help! Help! Rachel! Master Dickonson! Help! Richard! Cynthia! Come hither!

(*Enter* DICKON *and* RACHEL.)

RACHEL. Uncle!

JUSTICE MERTON. Bring wine. Lord Ravensbane has fainted.

RACHEL. Oh! (*Turning swiftly to go*) Micah, wine.

DICKON (*detaining her*). Stay! His pipe! Where is his lordship's pipe?

RACHEL. Oh, terrible!

(*Enter, at different doors,* MISTRESS MERTON *and* RICHARD.)

MISTRESS MERTON. What's the matter?

JUSTICE MERTON (*to* RACHEL). He threw it away. He is worse. Bring the wine.

MISTRESS MERTON. Look! How strange he appears!

RACHEL (*searching distractedly*). The pipe! His lordship's pipe! It is lost, Master Dickonson.

DICKON (*stooping, as if searching, with his back turned, having picked up the pipe, is filling and lighting it*). It must be found. This is a heart attack, my friends; his lordship's life depends on the nicotine. (*Deftly he places the pipe in* RACHEL'S *way.*)

RACHEL. Thank God! Here it is. (*Carrying it to the prostrate form of* RAVENSBANE, *she lifts his head and is about to put the pipe in his mouth.*) Shall I—shall I put it in?

RICHARD. No! not you.

RACHEL. Sir!

RICHARD. Let his tutor perform that office.

RACHEL. (*lifting* LORD RAVENSBANE'S *head again*). My lord!

RICHARD *and* JUSTICE MERTON (*together*). Rachel!

DICKON. Pardon me, Mistress Rachel; give the pipe at once. Only a token of true affection can revive his lordship now.

RICHARD (*as* RACHEL *puts the pipe to* RAVENSBANE'S *lips*). I forbid it, Rachel.

RACHEL (*watching only* RAVENSBANE). My lord—my lord!

MISTRESS MERTON. Give him air; unbutton his coat.

(RACHEL *unbuttons* RAVENSBANE'S *coat, revealing the embroidered waistcoat.*) Ah, Heavens! What do I see?

JUSTICE MERTON (*looks, blanches, and signs silence to* MISTRESS MERTON). Cynthia!

MISTRESS MERTON (*aside to* JUSTICE MERTON, *with deep tensity*). That waistcoat! that waistcoat! Brother, hast thou never seen it before?

JUSTICE MERTON. Never, my sister.

DICKON. See! He puffs—he revives. He is coming to himself.

RACHEL (*as* RAVENSBANE *rises to his feet*). At last!

DICKON. Look! he is restored.

RACHEL. God be thanked!

DICKON. My lord, Mistress Rachel has saved your life.

RAVENSBANE (*taking* RACHEL'S *hand*). Mistress Rachel is mine; we are ours.

RICHARD. Dare to repeat that.

RAVENSBANE (*looking at* RACHEL). Her eyes are mine.

RICHARD (*flinging his glove in his face*). And that, sir, is yours.

RACHEL. Richard!

RICHARD. I believe such is the proper fashion in England. If your lordship's last dueling wound is sufficiently healed, perhaps you will deign a reply.

RACHEL. Richard! Your lordship!

RAVENSBANE (*stops, picks up the glove, pockets it, bows to* RACHEL, *and steps close to* RICHARD). Permit me! (*He blows a puff of smoke full in* RICHARD'S *face.*)

ACT THREE

The same day. Late afternoon. The same scene as Act Two.

RAVENSBANE *and* DICKON *discovered at table, on which are lying two flails.* RAVENSBANE *is dressed in a costume which, composed of silk and jewels, subtly approximates in design to that of his original grosser composition. So artfully, however, is this contrived that, to one ignorant of his origin, his dress would appear to be merely an odd personal whimsy; whereas, to one initiated, it would stamp him grotesquely as the apotheosis of scarecrows.*

DICKON *is sitting in a pedagogical*

attitude; RAVENSBANE *stands near him, making a profound bow in the opposite direction.*

RAVENSBANE. Believe me, ladies, with the true sincerity of the heart.

DICKON. Inflection a little more lachrymose, please: "The *true* sincerity of the *heart.*"

RAVENSBANE. Believe me, ladies, with the *true* sincerity of the *heart.*

DICKON. Prettily, prettily! Next!

RAVENSBANE *(changing his mien, as if addressing another person).* Verily, sir, as that prince of poets, the immortal Virgil, has remarked: *"Adeo in teneris consuescere multum est."*[3]

DICKON. *Basta!* The next.

RAVENSBANE *(with another change to courtly manner).* Trust me, your Excellency, I will inform his Majesty of your courtesy.

DICKON. "His Majesty" more emphatic. Remember! You must impress all of the guests this afternoon. But continue, Cobby, dear; the retort now to the challenge!

RAVENSBANE *(with a superb air).* The second, I believe.

DICKON. Quite so, my lord.

RAVENSBANE. Sir! the local person whom you represent has done himself the honor of submitting to me a challenge to mortal combat. Sir! Since the remotest times of my feudal ancestors, in such affairs of honor, choice of weapons has ever been the—

DICKON. Prerogative!

RAVENSBANE. Prerogative of the challenged. Sir! This right of etiquette must be observed. Nevertheless, believe me, I have no selfish desire that my superior—

DICKON. Attainments!

RAVENSBANE. Attainments in this art should assume advantage over my challenger's ignorance. I have, there-

---

[3] "So strong is habit in tender years."—Virgil, *Georgics,* Book II, line 272.

fore, chosen those combative utensils most appropriate both to his own humble origin and to local tradition. Permit me, sir, to reveal my choice. *(Pointing grandly to the table)* There are my weapons!

DICKON. Delicious! O thou exquisite flower of love! How thy natal composites have burst in bloom!—The pumpkin in thee to a golden collarette; thy mop of crow's wings to these raven locks; thy broomstick to a lordly limp; thy corn-silk to these pale-tinted tassels. Verily in the gallery of scarecrows, thou art the Apollo Belvedere!

RAVENSBANE. Mistress Rachel—I may see her now?

DICKON. Romeo! Romeo! Was ever such an amorous puppet show!

RAVENSBANE. Mistress Rachel!

DICKON. Wait; let me think! Thou art wound up now, my pretty apparatus, for at least six-and-thirty hours. The wooden angel Gabriel that trumpets the hours on the big clock in Venice is not a more punctual manikin than thou with my speeches. Thou shouldst run, therefore,—

RAVENSBANE *(frowning darkly at* DICKON). Stop talking; permit me! A tutor should know his place.

DICKON *(rubbing his hands).* Nay, your lordship is beyond comparison.

RAVENSBANE *(in a terrible voice).* She will come? I shall see her?

(Enter MICAH.)

MICAH. Pardon, my lord.

RAVENSBANE *(turning joyfully to* MICAH). Is it she?

MICAH. Captain Bugby, my lord, the Governor's secretary.

DICKON. Good. Squire Talbot's second. Show him in.

RAVENSBANE *(flinging despairingly into a chair).* Ah! ah!

MICAH *(lifting the flails from the*

table). Beg pardon, sir; shall I remove—

DICKON. Drop them; go.

MICAH. But, sir—

DICKON. Go, thou slave!

(*Exit* MICAH. DICKON *hands* RAVENS-
BANE *a book.*)
Here, my lord; read. You must be
found reading.

RAVENSBANE (*in childlike despair*).
She will not come! I shall not see her!
(*Throwing the book into the fire-
place*) She does not come!

DICKON. Fie, fie, Jack; thou must
not be breaking thy Dickon's apron-
strings with a will of thine own.
Come!

RAVENSBANE. Mistress Rachel.

DICKON. Be good, boy, and thou
shalt see her soon.

(*Enter* CAPTAIN BUGBY.)
Your lordship was saying—Oh! Captain Bugby?

CAPTAIN BUGBY (*nervous and awed*).
Captain Bugby, sir, ah! at Lord
Ravensbane's service—ah!

DICKON. I am Master Dickonson, his
lordship's tutor.

CAPTAIN BUGBY. Happy, sir.

DICKON (*to* RAVENSBANE). My lord,
this gentleman waits upon you from
Squire Talbot. (*To* CAPTAIN BUGBY)
In regard to the challenge of this
morning, I presume?

CAPTAIN BUGBY. The affair, ah! the
affair of this morning, sir.

RAVENSBANE (*with his former superb
air—to* CAPTAIN BUGBY). The second,
I believe?

CAPTAIN BUGBY. Quite so, my lord.

RAVENSBANE. Sir! the local person
whom you represent has done himself
the honor of submitting to me a challenge to mortal combat. Sir! Since the
remotest times of my feudal ancestors,
in such affairs of honor, choice of
weapons has ever been the pre-pre-
(DICKON *looks at him intensely.*) prerogative of the challenged. Sir! this
right of etiquette must be observed.

CAPTAIN BUGBY. Indeed, yes, my lord.

DICKON. Pray do not interrupt. (*To*
RAVENSBANE) Your lordship: "observed."

RAVENSBANE. —observed. Nevertheless, believe me, I have no selfish
desire that my superior a-a-at-attain-
ments in this art should assume
advantage over my challenger's ignorance. I have, therefore, chosen those
combative utensils most appropriate
both to his own humble origin and
to local tradition. Permit me, sir, to
reveal my choice. (*Pointing to the
table*) There are my weapons!

CAPTAIN BUGBY (*looking, bewildered*). These, my lord?

RAVENSBANE. Those.

CAPTAIN BUGBY. But these are—are
flails.

RAVENSBANE. Flails.

CAPTAIN BUGBY. Flails, my lord?—Do
I understand that your lordship and
Squire Talbot—

RAVENSBANE. Exactly.

CAPTAIN BUGBY. But your lordship—
flails!

(DICKON'*s intense glance focusses on*
RAVENSBANE'*s face with the faintest of
smiles.*)

RAVENSBANE. My adversary should
be deft in their use. He has doubtless
wielded them frequently on his barn
floor.

CAPTAIN BUGBY. Ahaha! I understand now. Your lordship—ah! is a wit.
Haha! Flails!

DICKON. His lordship's satire is
poignant.

CAPTAIN BUGBY. Indeed, sir, so keen
that I must apologize for laughing at
my principal's expense. But— (*Soberly
to* RAVENSBANE) —my lord, if you will
deign to speak one moment seriously—

RAVENSBANE. Seriously?

CAPTAIN BUGBY. I will take pleasure in informing Squire Talbot—ah! as to your *real* preference for—

RAVENSBANE. For flails, sir. I have, permit me, nothing further to say. Flails are final. (*Turns away haughtily.*)

CAPTAIN BUGBY. Eh! What! Must I really report—?

DICKON. Lord Ravensbane's will is inflexible.

CAPTAIN BUGBY. And his wit, sir, incomparable. I am sorry for the Squire, but 'twill be the greatest joke in years. Ah! will you tell me—is it— (*Indicating* RAVENSBANE's *smoking*) —is it the latest fashion?

DICKON. Lord Ravensbane is always the latest.

CAPTAIN BUGBY. Obliged servant, sir. Aha! Such a joke as—O Lord! flails! (*Exit.*)

DICKON (*gayly to* RAVENSBANE). Bravo, my pumpky dear! That squelches the jealous betrothed. Now nothing remains but for you to continue to dazzle the enamored Rachel, and so present yourself to the Justice as a pseudo-son-nephew-in-law.

RAVENSBANE. I may go to Mistress Rachel?

DICKON. She will come to you. She is reading now a poem from you, which I left on her dressing-table.

RAVENSBANE. She is reading a poem from me?

DICKON. With your pardon, my lord, I penned it for you. I am something of a poetaster. Indeed, I flatter myself that I have dictated some of the finest lines in literature.

RAVENSBANE. Dickon! She will come?

DICKON. She comes!

(*Enter* RACHEL, *reading from a piece of paper.* DICKON *draws* RAVENSBANE *back.*)

RACHEL (*reads*). "To Mistress R——, enchantress:—

"If faith in witchcraft be a sin,
Alas! what peril he is in
Who plights his faith and love in thee,
Sweetest maid of sorcery.

"If witchcraft be a whirling brain,
A roving eye, a heart of pain,
Whose wound no thread of fate can stitch,
How hast thou conjured, cruel witch,—

With the brain, eye, heart, and total mortal residue of thine enamored.

"JACK LANTHORNE,
" (LORD R——.) "

(DICKON *goes out.*)

RACHEL. "To Mistress R——, enchantress:" R! It *must* be. R—— must mean—

RAVENSBANE (*with passionate deference*). Rachel!

RACHEL. Ah! How you surprised me, my lord.

RAVENSBANE. You are come again; you are come again.

RACHEL. Has anything happened? Oh, my lord, I have been in such terror. Promise me that there shall be—no duel!

RAVENSBANE. No duel.

RACHEL. Oh, I am so gratefully happy!

RAVENSBANE. I know I am only a thing to make Mistress Rachel happy. Ah! look at me once more. When you look at me, I live.

RACHEL. It is strange, indeed, my lord, how the familiar world, the daylight, the heavens themselves have changed since your arrival.

RAVENSBANE. This is the world; this is the light; this is the heavens themselves. Mistress Rachel is looking at me.

RACHEL. For me, it is less strange, perhaps. I never saw a real lord before. But you, my lord, must have seen so many, many girls in the great world.

RAVENSBANE. No, no; never.

RACHEL. No other girls before to-day, my lord!

RAVENSBANE. Before to-day? I do not know; I do not care. I was not—here. To-day I was born—in your eyes. Ah! my brain whirls!

RACHEL (*smiling*).

"If witchcraft be a whirling brain,
A roving eye, a heart of pain,—"

(*In a whisper*) My lord, do you really believe in witchcraft?

RAVENSBANE. With all my heart.

RACHEL. And approve of it?

RAVENSBANE. With all my soul.

RACHEL. So do I—that is, innocent witchcraft; not to harm anybody, you know, but just to feel all the dark mystery and the trembling excitement —the way you feel when you blow out your candle all alone in your bedroom and watch the little smoke fade away in the moonshine.

RAVENSBANE. Fade away in the moonshine.

RACHEL. Oh, but we mustn't speak of it. In a town like this, all such mysticism is considered damnable. But your lordship understands and approves? I am so glad! Have you read the *Philosophical Considerations* of Glanville, the *Saducismus Triumphatus,* and the *Presignifications of Dreams?* What kind of witchcraft, my lord, do you believe in?

RAVENSBANE. In all yours.

RACHEL. Nay, your lordship must not take me for a real witch. I can only tell fortunes, you know—like this morning.

RAVENSBANE. I know; you told how my heart would break.

RACHEL. Oh, that's palmistry, and that isn't always certain. But the surest way to prophesy—do you know what it is?

RAVENSBANE. Tell me.

RACHEL. To count the crows. Do you know how?

One for sorrow—

RAVENSBANE. Ha, yes!—

Two for mirth!

RACHEL.

Three for a wedding—

RAVENSBANE.

Four for a birth—

RACHEL. And five for the happiest thing on earth!

RAVENSBANE. Mistress Rachel, come! Let us go and count five crows.

RACHEL (*delightedly*). Why, my lord, how did *you* ever learn it? I got it from an old Goody here in town— a real witchwife. If you will promise not to tell a secret, I will show you.— But you must promise!

RAVENSBANE. I promise.

RACHEL. Come, then. I will show you a real piece of witchcraft that I bought from her this morning—the glass of truth. There! Behind that curtain. If you look in, you will see— But come; I will show you. (*They put their hands on the cords of the curtain.*) Just pull that string, and—ah!

DICKON (*stepping out through the curtain*). My lord, your pipe.

RACHEL. Master Dickonson, how you frightened me!

DICKON. So excessively sorry!

RACHEL. But how did you—?

DICKON. I believe you were showing his lordship—

RACHEL (*turning hurriedly away*). Oh, nothing; nothing at all.

RAVENSBANE (*sternly to* DICKON). Why do you come?

DICKON (*handing back* RAVENSBANE's *pipe filled*). Allow me. (*Aside*) 'Tis high time you came to the point, Jack; 'tis near your lordship's reception. Woo and win, boy; woo and win.

RAVENSBANE (*haughtily*). Leave me.

DICKON. Your lordship's humble, very humble. (*Exit.*)

RACHEL (*shivering*). My dear lord, why do you keep this man?

RAVENSBANE. I—keep this man?

RACHEL. Pardon my rudeness—I cannot endure him.

RAVENSBANE. You do not like him? Ah, then, I do not like him also. We will send him away—you and I.

RACHEL. You, my lord, of course; but I—

RAVENSBANE. You will be Dickon! You will be with me always and light my pipe. And I will live for you, and fight for you, and kill your betrothed!

RACHEL (*drawing away*). No, no!

RAVENSBANE. Ah! but your eyes say "yes." Mistress Rachel leaves me; but Rachel in her eyes remains. Is it not so?

RACHEL. What can I say, my lord! It is true that since my eyes met yours, a new passion has entered into my soul. I have felt—but 'tis so impertinent, my lord, so absurd in me, a mere girl, and you a nobleman of power— yet I have felt it irresistibly, my dear lord,—a longing to help you, I am so sorry for you—so sorry for you! I pity you deeply.—Forgive me; forgive me, my lord!

RAVENSBANE. It is enough.

RACHEL. Indeed, indeed, 'tis so rude of me,—'tis so unreasonable.

RAVENSBANE. It is enough. I grow— I grow—I grow! I am a plant; you give it rain and sun. I am a flower; you give it light and dew; I am a soul, you give it love and speech. I grow. Toward you—toward you I grow!

RACHEL. My lord, I do not understand it, how so poor and mere a girl as I can have helped you. Yet I do believe it is so; for I feel it so. What can I do for you?

RAVENSBANE. Be mine. Let me be yours.

RACHEL. But, my lord—do I love you?

RAVENSBANE. What is "I love you"? Is it a kiss, a sigh, an embrace? Ah! then, you do not love me.—"I love you": is it to nourish, to nestle, to lift up, to smile upon, to make greater —a worm? Ah! then, you love me.

(*Enter* RICHARD *at left back, unobserved.*)

RACHEL. Do not speak so of yourself, my lord; nor exalt me so falsely.

RAVENSBANE. Be mine.

RACHEL. A great glory has descended upon this day.

RAVENSBANE. Be mine.

RACHEL. Could I but be sure that this glory is love—Oh, *then*! (*Turns toward* RAVENSBANE.)

RICHARD (*stepping between them*). It is *not* love; it is witchcraft.

RACHEL. Who are you?—Richard?

RICHARD. You have, indeed, forgotten me? Would to God, Rachel, I could forget you.

RAVENSBANE. Ah, permit me, sir—

RICHARD. Silence! (*To* RACHEL) Against my will, I am a convert to your own mysticism; for nothing less than damnable illusion could so instantly wean your heart from me to— this. I do not pretend to understand it; but that it is witchcraft I am convinced; and I will save you from it.

RACHEL. Go; please go.

RAVENSBANE. Permit me, sir; you have not replied yet to flails!

RICHARD. Permit *me*, sir. (*Taking something from his coat*) My answer is—bare cob! (*Holding out a shelled corn-cob*) Thresh this, sir, for your antagonist. 'Tis the only one worthy of your lordship. (*Tosses it contemptuously toward him.*)

RAVENSBANE. Upon my honor, as a man—

RICHARD. As a *man*, forsooth! Were you, indeed, a man, Lord Ravensbane, I would have accepted your weapons, and flailed you out of New England. But it is not my custom to chastise runagates from asylums, or to banter further words with a natural and a ninny.

RACHEL. Squire Talbot! Will you leave my uncle's house?

RAVENSBANE. One moment, mistress: —I did not wholly catch the import of this gentleman's speech, but I fancy I have insulted him by my reply to his challenge. One insult may perhaps be remedied by another. Sir, permit me to call *you* a ninny, and to offer you— (*Drawing his sword and offering it*) —swords.

RICHARD. Thanks; I reject the offer.

RAVENSBANE (*turning away despondently*). He rejects it. Well!

RACHEL (*to* RICHARD). And *now* will you leave?

RICHARD. At once. But one word more. Rachel—Rachel, have you forgotten this morning and the Glass of Truth?

RACHEL (*coldly*). No.

RICHARD. Call it a fancy now if you will. I scoffed at it; yes. Yet *you* believed it. I loved you truly, you said. Well, have I changed?

RACHEL. Yes.

RICHARD. Will you test me again—in the glass?

RACHEL. No. Go; leave us.

RICHARD. I will go. I have still a word with your aunt.

RAVENSBANE (*to* RICHARD). I beg your pardon, sir. You said just now that had I been a man—

RICHARD. I say, Lord Ravensbane, that the straight fiber of a true man never warps the love of a woman. As for yourself, you have my contempt and pity. Pray to God, sir, pray to God to make you a man. (*Exit, right.*)

RACHEL. Oh! it is intolerable! (*To* RAVENSBANE) My dear lord, I do believe in my heart that I love you, and if so, I will with gratitude be your wife. But, my lord, strange glamors, strange darknesses reel, and bewilder my mind. I must be alone; I must think and decide. Will you give me this tassel?

RAVENSBANE (*unfastening a silk tassel from his coat and giving it to her*). Oh, take it.

RACHEL. If I decide that I love you, that I will be your wife—I will wear it this afternoon at the reception. Good-bye. (*Exit, right.*)

RAVENSBANE. Mistress Rachel!—

(*He is left alone. As he looks about gropingly, and raises his arms in vague prayer,* DICKON *appears from the right and watches him, with a smile.*) God, are you here? Dear God, I pray to you —make me to be a man! (*Exit, left.*)

DICKON. Poor Jacky! Thou shouldst 'a' prayed to t' other one.

(*Enter, right,* JUSTICE MERTON.)

JUSTICE MERTON (*to* DICKON). Will you not listen? Will you not listen!

DICKON. Such a delightful room!

JUSTICE MERTON. Are you merciless?

DICKON. And such a living portrait of your Worship! The waistcoat is so beautifully executed.

JUSTICE MERTON. If I pay him ten thousand pounds—

(*Enter, right,* MISTRESS MERTON, *who goes toward the table. Enter, left,* MICAH.)

MISTRESS MERTON. Flails! Flails in the parlor!

MICAH. The minister and his wife

have turned into the gate, madam.

MISTRESS MERTON. The guests! Is it so late?

MICAH. Four o'clock, madam.

MISTRESS MERTON. Remove these things at once.

MICAH. Yes, madam. (*He lifts them, and starts for the door where he pauses to look back and speak.*) Madam, in all my past years of service at Merton House, I never waited upon a lord till to-day. Madam, in all my future years of service at Merton House, I trust I may never wait upon a lord again.

MISTRESS MERTON. Micah, mind the knocker.

MICAH. Yes, madam. (*Exit at left back. Sounds of a brass knocker outside.*)

MISTRESS MERTON. Rachel! Rachel! (*Exit, left.*)

JUSTICE MERTON (*to* DICKON). So you are contented with nothing less than the sacrifice of my niece!

(*Enter* MICAH.)

MICAH. Minister Dodge, your Worship; and Mistress Dodge. (*Exit.*)

(*Enter the* MINISTER *and his wife.*)

JUSTICE MERTON (*stepping forward to receive them*). Believe me, this is a great privilege.—Madam! (*Bowing.*)

MINISTER DODGE (*taking his hand*). The privilege is ours, Justice; to enter a righteous man's house is to stand, as it were, on God's threshold.

JUSTICE MERTON (*nervously*). Amen, amen. Permit me—ah! Lord Ravensbane, my young guest of honor, will be here directly—permit me to present his lordship's tutor, Master Dickonson; the Reverend Master Dodge, Mistress Dodge.

MINISTER DODGE (*offering his hand*). Master Dickonson, sir—

DICKON (*barely touching the minister's fingers, bows charmingly to his wife*). Madam, of all professions in the world, your husband's most allures me.

MISTRESS DODGE. 'Tis a worthy one, sir.

DICKON. Ah! Mistress Dodge, and so arduous—especially for a minister's wife. (*He leads her to a chair.*)

MISTRESS DODGE (*accepting the chair*). Thank you.

MINISTER DODGE. Lord Ravensbane comes from abroad?

JUSTICE MERTON. From London.

MINISTER DODGE. An old friend of yours, I understand.

JUSTICE MERTON. From London, yes. Did I say from London? Quite so; from London.

(*Enter* MICAH.)

MICAH. Captain Bugby, the Governor's secretary. (*Exit.*)

(*Enter* CAPTAIN BUGBY. *He walks with a slight lameness, and holds daintily in his hand a pipe, from which he puffs with dandy deliberation.*)

CAPTAIN BUGBY. Justice Merton, your very humble servant.

JUSTICE MERTON. Believe me, Captain Bugby.

CAPTAIN BUGBY (*profusely*). Ah, Master Dickonson! my dear friend Master Dickonson—this is, indeed—ah! How is his lordship since—aha! but discretion! Mistress Dodge—her servant! Ah! yes— (*Indicating his pipe with a smile of satisfaction*) —the latest, I assure you; the very latest from London. Ask Master Dickonson.

MINISTER DODGE (*looking at* CAPTAIN BUGBY). These will hatch out in the springtime.

CAPTAIN BUGBY (*confidentially to* DICKON). But really, my good friend, may not I venture to inquire how his lordship—ah! has been in health since the—ah! since—

DICKON (*impressively*). Oh! quite, quite!

(*Enter* MISTRESS MERTON; *she joins* JUSTICE MERTON *and* MINISTER DODGE.)

CAPTAIN BUGBY. You know, I informed Squire Talbot of his lordship's epigrammatic retort—his retort of—shh! ha haha! Oh, that reply was a stiletto; 'twas sharper than a sword-thrust, I assure you. To have conceived it — 'twas inspiration, but to have expressed it—oh! 'twas genius. Hush! "Flails"! Oh! It sticks me now in the ribs. I shall die with concealing it.

MISTER DODGE (*to* MISTRESS MERTON). 'Tis true, mistress; but if there were more like your brother in the parish, the conscience of the community would be clearer.

(*Enter* MICAH.)

MICAH. The Reverend Master Rand of Harvard College; the Reverend Master Todd of Harvard College. (*Exit.*)

(*Enter two elderly, straight-backed divines.*)

JUSTICE MERTON (*greeting them*). Permit me, gentlemen; this is fortunate—before your return to Cambridge.

(*He conducts them to* MISTRESS MERTON *and* MINISTER DODGE, *center. Seated left,* DICKON *is ingratiating himself with* MISTRESS DODGE; CAPTAIN BUGBY, *laughed at by both parties, is received by neither.*)

CAPTAIN BUGBY (*puffing smoke toward the ceiling*). Really, I cannot understand what keeps his Excellency, the Lieutenant-Governor, so long. He has two such charming daughters, Master Dickonson—

DICKON (*to* MISTRESS DODGE). Yes, yes; such suspicious women with their charms are an insult to the virtuous ladies of the parish.

CAPTAIN BUGBY. How, sir!

MISTRESS DODGE. And to think that she should actually shoe horses herself!

CAPTAIN BUGBY (*piqued, walks another way*). Well!

REV. MASTER RAND (*to* JUSTICE MERTON). It would not be countenanced in the college yard, sir.

REV. MASTER TODD. A pipe! Nay, *mores inhibitae!*

JUSTICE MERTON. 'Tis most unfortunate, gentlemen; but I understand 'tis the new vogue in London.

(*Enter* MICAH.)

MICAH. His Excellency, Sir Charles Reddington, Lieutenant-Governor; the Mistress Reddingtons.

CAPTAIN BUGBY. At last!

MISTRESS MERTON (*aside*). Micah. (MICAH *goes to her.*)

(*Enter* SIR CHARLES, MISTRESS REDDINGTON, *and* AMELIA REDDINGTON.)

JUSTICE MERTON. Your Excellency, this is, indeed, a distinguished honor.

SIR CHARLES (*shaking hands*). Fine weather, Merton. Where's your young lord?

THE TWO GIRLS (*curtsying*). Justice Merton, Mistress Merton. (MICAH *goes out.*)

CAPTAIN BUGBY. Oh, my dear Mistress Reddington! Charming Mistress Amelia! You are so very late, but you shall hear—hush!

MISTRESS REDDINGTON (*noticing his pipe*). Why, what is this, Captain?

CAPTAIN BUGBY. Oh, the latest, I assure you, the very latest. Wait till you see his lordship.

AMELIA. What! isn't he here? (*Laughing*) La, Captain! Do look at the man!

CAPTAIN BUGBY. Oh, he's coming directly. Quite the mode—what? (*He talks to them aside, where they titter.*)

SIR CHARLES (*to* DICKON). What say? Traveling for his health?

DICKON. Partially, your Excellency;

but my young pupil and master is a singularly affectionate nature.

THE TWO GIRLS (*to* CAPTAIN BUGBY). What! flails—really! (*They burst into laughter among themselves.*)

DICKON. He has journeyed here to Massachusetts peculiarly to pay this visit to Justice Merton—his father's dearest friend.

SIR CHARLES. Ah! knew him abroad, eh?

DICKON. In Rome, your Excellency.

MISTRESS DODGE (*to* JUSTICE MERTON). Why, I thought it was in London.

JUSTICE MERTON. London, true, quite so; we made a trip together to Lisbon—ah! Rome.

DICKON. Paris, was it not, sir?

JUSTICE MERTON (*in great distress*). Paris, Paris, very true; I am—I am—sometimes I am—

(*Enter* MICAH, *right.*)

MICAH (*announces*). Lord Ravensbane.

(*Enter right,* RAVENSBANE *with* RACHEL.)

JUSTICE MERTON (*with a gasp of relief*). Ah! his lordship is arrived.

(*Murmurs of "his lordship" and a flutter among the girls and* CAPTAIN BUGBY.)

CAPTAIN BUGBY. Look!—Now!

JUSTICE MERTON. Welcome, my lord!

(*To* SIR CHARLES) Your Excellency, let me introduce—permit me—

RAVENSBANE. Permit *me;* (*Addressing her*) Mistress Rachel!—Mistress Rachel will introduce—

RACHEL (*curtsying*). Sir Charles, allow me to present my friend, Lord Ravensbane.

MISTRESS REDDINGTON (*aside to* AMELIA). Her *friend*—did you hear?

SIR CHARLES. Mistress Rachel, I see you are as pretty as ever. Lord Ravensbane, your hand, sir.

RAVENSBANE. Trust me, your Excellency, I will inform his Majesty of your courtesy.

CAPTAIN BUGBY (*watching* RAVENSBANE *with chagrin*). On my life! he's lost his limp.

RAVENSBANE (*apart to* RACHEL). You said: "A great glory has descended upon this day."

RACHEL (*shyly*). My lord!

RAVENSBANE. Be sure—O mistress, be sure—that this glory is love.

SIR CHARLES. My daughters, Fanny and Amelia—Lord Ravensbane.

THE TWO GIRLS (*curtsying*). Your lordship!

SIR CHARLES. Good girls, but silly.

THE TWO GIRLS. Papa!

RAVENSBANE. Believe me, ladies, with the *true* sincerity of the *heart.*

MISTRESS REDDINGTON. Isn't he perfection!

CAPTAIN BUGBY. What said I?

AMELIA (*giggling*). I can't help thinking of flails.

SIR CHARLES (*in a loud whisper aside to* JUSTICE MERTON). Is it congratulations for your niece?

JUSTICE MERTON. Not—not precisely.

DICKON (*to* JUSTICE MERTON). Your worship—a word. (*Leads him aside.*)

RAVENSBANE (*whom* RACHEL *continues to introduce to the guests, to* MASTER RAND). Verily, sir, as that prince of poets, the immortal Virgil, has remarked: "*Adeo in teneris consuescere multum est.*"[4]

REV. MASTER TODD. His lordship is evidently a university man.

REV. MASTER RAND. Evidently most accomplished.

JUSTICE MERTON (*aside to* DICKON). A song! Why, it is beyond all bounds of custom and decorum.

DICKON. Believe me, there is no such flatterer to win the maiden heart as

4 So strong is custom in the young.

music.

JUSTICE MERTON. And here; in this presence! Never!

DICKON. Nevertheless, it will amuse me vastly, and you will announce it.

JUSTICE MERTON (with hesitant embarrassment, which he seeks to conceal). Your Excellency and friends, I have great pleasure in announcing his lordship's condescension in consenting to regale our present company—with a song.

SEVERAL VOICES (in various degrees of amazement and curiosity). A song!

MISTRESS MERTON. Gilead! What is this?

JUSTICE MERTON. The selection is a German ballad—a particular favorite at the court of Prussia, where his lordship last rendered it. His tutor has made a translation which is entitled—

DICKON. "The Prognostication of the Crows."

ALL. Crows!

JUSTICE MERTON. And I am requested to remind you that in the ancient heathen mythology of Germany, the crow or raven, was the fateful bird of the god Woden.

CAPTAIN BUGBY. How prodigiously novel!

MINISTER DODGE (frowning). Unparalleled!

SIR CHARLES. A ballad! Come now, that sounds like old England again. Let's have it. Will his lordship sing without music?

JUSTICE MERTON. Master Dickonson, hem! has been—persuaded—to accompany his lordship on the spinet.

AMELIA. How delightful!

REV. MASTER RAND (aside to TODD). Shall we remain?

REV. MASTER TODD. We must.

RAVENSBANE (to RACHEL). My tassel, dear mistress; you do not wear it?

RACHEL. My heart still wavers, my lord. But whilst you sing, I will decide.

RAVENSBANE. Whilst I sing? My fate, then, is waiting at the end of a song?

RACHEL. At the end of a song.

DICKON (calling to RAVENSBANE). Your lordship!

RAVENSBANE (starting, turns to the company). Permit me.

(DICKON sits, facing left, at the spinet. At first, his fingers in playing give sound only to the soft tinkling notes of that ancient instrument; but gradually, strange notes and harmonies of an aërial orchestra mingle with, and at length drown, the spinet. The final chorus is produced solely by fantastic symphonic cawings, as of countless crows, in harsh but musical accord. During the song RICHARD enters. DICKON's music, however, does not cease but fills the intervals between the verses. To his accompaniment, amid the whispered and gradually increasing wonder, resentment, and dismay of the assembled guests, RAVENSBANE, with his eyes fixed upon RACHEL, sings.)

Baron von Rabentod arose;
(The golden sun was rising)
Before him flew a flock of crows:
    Sing heigh! Sing heigh!
        Sing heigh! Sing—

"Ill speed, ill speed thee, baron-wight;
Ill speed thy palfrey pawing!
Blithe is the morn but black the night
That hears a raven's cawing."
        (Chorus.)
    Caw! Caw! Caw!

MISTRESS DODGE (whispers to her husband). Did you hear them?

MINISTER DODGE. Hush!

AMELIA (sotto voce). What can it be?

CAPTAIN BUGBY. Oh, the latest, be sure.

DICKON. You note, my friends, the accompanying harmonics; they are an intrinsic part of the ballad, and may not be omitted.

RAVENSBANE (*sings*).

The baron reckèd not a pin;
(For the golden sun was rising)
He rode to woo, he rode to win;
Sing heigh! Sing heigh!
Sing heigh! Sing—

He rode into his prince's hall
Through knights and damsels
flow'ry:
"Thy daughter, prince, I bid thee
call;
I claim her hand and dowry."

(*Enter* RICHARD. MISTRESS MERTON *seizes his arm nervously.*)

SIR CHARLES (*to* CAPTAIN BUGBY). This gentleman's playing is rather ventriloquistical.

CAPTAIN BUGBY. Quite, as it were.

REV. MASTER TODD. This smells unholy.

REV. MASTER RAND (*to* TODD). Shall we leave?

RAVENSBANE (*sings*).

"What cock is this, with crest so
high,
That crows with such a pother?"
"Baron von Rabentod am I;
Methinks we know each other."

"Now welcome, welcome, dear guest
of mine,
So long why didst thou tarry?
Now, for the sake of auld lang syne,
My daughter thou shalt marry."

AMELIA (*to* BUGBY). And he kept right on smoking!

MINISTER DODGE (*who, with* RAND *and* TODD, *has risen uneasily*). This smacks of witchcraft.

RAVENSBANE (*sings*).

The bride is brought, the priest as
well;
(The golden sun was passing)
They stood beside the altar rail;
Sing ah! Sing ah!
Sing ah! Sing—

"Woman, with this ring I thee wed."
What makes his voice so awing?
The baron by the bride is dead:
Outside the crows were cawing.
(*Chorus, which grows tumultuous,
seeming to fill the room with the invisible birds.*)
Caw! Caw! Caw!

(*The guests rise in confusion.* DICKON *still plays delightedly, and the strange music continues.*)

MINISTER DODGE. This is no longer godly.—Justice Merton! Justice Merton, sir!—

RAVENSBANE (*to* RACHEL, *who holds his tassel in her hand*). Ah! and you have my tassel!

RACHEL. See! I will wear it now. You yourself shall fasten it.

RAVENSBANE. Rachel! Mistress!

RACHEL. My dear lord!

(*As* RAVENSBANE *is placing the silken tassel on* RACHEL'S *breast to fasten it there,* RICHARD, *by the mirror, takes hold of the curtain strings.*)

RICHARD. I told you—witchcraft, like murder will out! Lovers! Behold yourselves! (*He pulls the curtain back.*)

RACHEL (*looking into the glass, screams and turns her gaze fearfully upon* RAVENSBANE). Ah! Do not look!

DICKON (*who, having turned round from the spinet, has leaped forward, now turns back again, biting his finger).* Too late!

(*In the glass are reflected the figures of* RACHEL *and* RAVENSBANE—RACHEL *just as she herself appears, but* RAVENSBANE *in his essential form of a scarecrow, in every movement reflecting* RAVENSBANE'S *motions. The thing in the glass is about to pin a wisp of corn-silk on the mirrored breast of the maiden.*)

RAVENSBANE. What is there?

RACHEL (*looking again, starts away from* RAVENSBANE). Leave me! Leave me!—Richard! (*She faints in* RICHARD'S *arms.*)

RAVENSBANE. Fear not, mistress, I will kill the thing. (*Drawing his sword, he rushes at the glass. Within, the scarecrow, with a drawn wheel-spoke, approaches him at equal speed. They come face to face and recoil.*) Ah! ah! Fear'st thou me? What art thou? Why, 'tis a glass. Thou mockest me? Look, look, mistress, it mocks me! O God, no! no! Take it away. Dear God, do not look!—It is I!

ALL (*rushing to the doors*). Witchcraft! Witchcraft!

(*As* RAVENSBANE *stands frantically confronting his abject reflection, struck in a like posture of despair, the curtain falls.*)

ACT FOUR

The same. Night. The moon, shining in broadly at the window, discovers RAVENSBANE *alone, prostrate before the mirror. Raised on one arm to a half-sitting posture, he gazes fixedly at the vaguely seen image of the scarecrow prostrate in the glass.*

———

RAVENSBANE. All have left me—but not thou. Rachel has left me; her eyes have turned away from me; she is gone. All that I loved, all that loved me, have left me. A thousand ages— a thousand ages ago, they went away; and thou and I have gazed upon each other's desertedness. Speak! and be pitiful! If thou art I, inscrutable image, if thou dost feel these pangs thine own, show then self-mercy; speak! What art thou? What am I? Why are we here? How comes it that we feel and guess and suffer? Nay, though thou answer not these doubts, yet mock them, mock them aloud, even as there, monstrous, thou counterfeitest mine actions. Speak, abject enigma!—Speak, poor shadow, thou— (*Recoiling wildly*) Stand back, inanity! Thrust not thy mawkish face in pity toward me. Ape and idiot! Scarecrow!—to console me! Haha!—A flail and broomstick! a cob, a gourd and pumpkin, to fuse and sublimate themselves into a mage-philosopher, who discourseth metaphysics to itself—itself, God! Dost Thou hear? Itself! For even such am I—I whom Thou madest to love Rachel. Why, God—haha! dost Thou dwell in this thing? Is it Thou that peerest forth *at* me—*from* me? Why, hark then; Thou shalt listen, and answer—if Thou canst. Between the rise and setting of a sun, I have walked in this world of Thine. I have been thrilled with wonder; I have been calmed with knowledge; I have trembled with joy and passion. Power, beauty, love have ravished me. Infinity itself, like a dream, has blazed before me with the certitude of prophecy; and I have cried, "This world, the heavens, time itself, are mine to conquer," and I have thrust forth mine arm to wear Thy shield forever—and lo! for my shield Thou reachest me— a mirror, and whisperest: "Know thyself! Thou art—a scarecrow: a tinkling clod, a rigmarole of dust, a lump of ordure, contemptible, superfluous, inane!" Haha! Hahaha! And with such scarecrows Thou dost people a planet! O ludicrous! Monstrous! Ludicrous! At least,. I thank Thee, God! at least this breathing bathos can laugh at itself. Though hast vouchsafed to me, Spirit, —hahaha!—to know myself. Mine, mine is the consummation of man—even self-contempt! (*Pointing in the glass with an agony of derision*) Scarecrow! Scarecrow! Scarecrow!

THE IMAGE IN THE GLASS (*more and more faintly*). Scarecrow! Scarecrow! Scarecrow!

(RAVENSBANE *throws himself prone upon the floor, beneath the window, sobbing. There is a pause of silence, and the moon shines brighter.—Slowly then* RAVENSBANE, *getting to his knees, looks out into the night.*)

RAVENSBANE. What face are you, high up through the twinkling leaves? Do you not, like all the rest, turn, aghast, your eyes away from me—me, abject enormity, groveling at your feet? Gracious being, do you not fear —despise me? O white peace of the world, beneath your gaze the clouds glow silver, and the herded cattle, slumbering far afield, crouch—beautiful. The slough shines lustrous as a bridal veil. Beautiful face, you are Rachel's, and you have changed the world. Nothing is mean, but you have made it miraculous; nothing is loathsome, nothing ludicrous, but you have converted it to loveliness, that even this shadow of a mockery myself, cast by your light, gives me the clear assurance I am a man. Rachel, mistress, mother, out of my suffering you have brought forth my soul. I am saved!

THE IMAGE IN THE GLASS. A very pretty sophistry.

(*The moonlight grows dimmer, as at the passing of a cloud.*)

RAVENSBANE. Ah! what voice has snatched you from me?

THE IMAGE. A most poetified pumpkin!

RAVENSBANE. Thing! dost thou speak at last? My soul abhors thee.

THE IMAGE. I *am* thy soul.

RAVENSBANE. Thou liest.

THE IMAGE. Our daddy Dickon and our mother Rickby begot and conceived us at sunrise, in a Jack-o'lantern.

RAVENSBANE. Thou liest, torturing illusion. Thou art but a phantom in a glass.

THE IMAGE. Why, very true. So art thou. *We* are a pretty phantom in a glass.

RAVENSBANE. It is a lie. I am no longer thou. I feel it; I am a man.

THE IMAGE.

And prithee, what's a man?
Man's but a mirror,
Wherein the imps and angels play charades,
Make faces, mope, and pull each other's hair—
Till crack! the sly urchin
Death shivers the glass,
And the bare coffin boards show underneath.

RAVENSBANE. Yea! if it be so, thou coggery! if both of us be indeed but illusions, why, now let us end together. But if it be not so, then let *me* for evermore be free of thee. Now is the test—the glass! (*Springing to the fireplace, he seizes an iron crosspiece from the andirons.*) I'll play your urchin Death and shatter it. Let's see what shall survive! (*He rushes to strike the glass with the iron.* DICKON *steps out of the mirror, closing the curtain.*)

DICKON. I wouldn't, really!

RAVENSBANE. Dickon! dear Dickon! is it you?

DICKON. Yes, Jacky! it's dear Dickon, and I really wouldn't.

RAVENSBANE. Wouldn't what, Dickon?

DICKON. Sweep the cobwebs off the sky with thine aspiring broomstick. When a man questions fate, 'tis bad digestion. When a scarecrow does it, 'tis bad taste.

RAVENSBANE. At last, you will tell me the truth, Dickon! Am I, then—that thing?

DICKON. You mustn't be so skeptical. Of course you're that thing.

RAVENSBANE. Ah me despicable! Rachel, why didst thou ever look upon me?

DICKON. I fear, cobby, thou hast never studied woman's heart and hero-worship. Take thyself now. I remarked to Goody Bess, thy mother, this morning, as I was chucking her thy pate from the hayloft, that thou wouldst make a Mark Antony or an Alexander before night.

RAVENSBANE. Cease! cease! in pity's name. You do not know the agony of being ridiculous.

DICKON. Nay, Jacky, all mortals are ridiculous. Like you, they were rummaged out of the muck; and like you, they shall return to the dunghill. I advise 'em, like you, to enjoy the interim, and smoke.

RAVENSBANE. This pipe, this ludicrous pipe that I forever set to my lips and puff! Why must I, Dickon? Why?

DICKON. To avoid extinction—merely. You see, 'tis just as your fellow in there (Pointing to the glass) explained. You yourself are the subtlest of mirrors, polished out of pumpkin and pipe-smoke. Into this mirror the fair Mistress Rachel has projected her lovely image, and thus provided you with what men call a soul.

RAVENSBANE. Ah! then, I have a soul—the truth of me? Mistress Rachel has indeed made me a man?

DICKON. Don't flatter thyself, cobby. Break thy pipe, and whiff—soul, Mistress Rachel, man, truth, and this pretty world itself, go up in the last smoke.

RAVENSBANE. No, no! not Mistress Rachel.

DICKON. Mistress Rachel exists for your lordship merely in your lordship's pipe-bowl.

RAVENSBANE. Wretched, niggling caricature that I am! All is lost to me—lost!

DICKON. "Paradise Lost" again! Always blaming it on me. There's that gaunt fellow in England has lately wrote a parody on me when I was in the apple business.

RAVENSBANE (falling on his knees and bowing his head). O God! I am so contemptible!

(Enter, at door back, GOODY RICKBY; her blacksmith garb is hidden under a dingy black mantle with peaked hood.)

DICKON. Good verse, too, for a parody! (Ruminating, raises one arm rhetorically above RAVENSBANE.)

—"Farewell, happy fields
Where joy forever dwells!
Hail, horrors; hail,
Infernal world! and thou, profoundest hell,
Receive thy new possessor."

GOODY RICKBY (seizing his arm). Dickon!

DICKON. Hullo! You, Bess!

GOODY RICKBY. There's not a minute to lose. Justice Merton and the neighbors have ended their conference at Minister Dodge's, and are returning here.

DICKON. Well, let 'em come. We're ready.

GOODY RICKBY. But thou toldst me they had discovered—

DICKON. A scarecrow in a mirror. Well? The glass is bewitched; that's all.

GOODY RICKBY. All? Witchcraft is hanging—that's all! And the mirror was bought of me—of me, the witch. Wilt thou be my hangman, Dickon?

DICKON. Wilt thou give me a kiss, Goody? When did ever thy Dickon desert thee?

GOODY RICKBY. But how, boy, wilt thou—

DICKON. Trust me, and thy son. When the Justice's niece is thy daughter-in-law, all will be safe. For the Justice will cherish his niece's family.

GOODY RICKBY. But when he knows—

DICKON. But he shall *not* know. How can he? When the glass is denounced as a fraud, how will he, or any person, ever know that we made this fellow out of rubbish? Who, forsooth, but a poet—or a devil—*would* believe it? You mustn't credit men with our imaginations, my dear.

GOODY RICKBY. Then thou wilt pull me through this safe?

DICKON. As I adore thee—and my own reputation.

GOODY RICKBY (*at the window*). I see their lanterns down the road.

DICKON. Stay, marchioness—his lordship! My lord—your lady mother.

GOODY RICKBY (*curtsying, laughs shrilly*). Your servant—my son! (*About to depart.*)

RAVENSBANE. Ye lie! both of you!—I was born of Rachel.

DICKON. Tut, tut, Jacky; you mustn't mix up mothers and prospective wives

at your age. It's fatal.

GOODY RICKBY (*excitedly*). They're coming! (*Exit.*)

DICKON (*calling after her*). Fear not; I'll overtake thee.

RAVENSBANE. She is coming; Rachel is coming, and I may not look upon her!

DICKON. Eh? Why not?

RAVENSBANE. I am a monster.

DICKON. Fie! fie! Thou shalt have her.

RAVENSBANE. Have her, Dickon?

DICKON. For lover and wife.

RAVENSBANE. For wife?

DICKON. For wife and all. Thou hast but to obey.

RAVENSBANE. Ah! who will do this for me?

DICKON. I!

RAVENSBANE. Dickon! Wilt make me a man—a man and worthy of her?

DICKON. Fiddlededee! I make over no masterpieces. Thy mistress shall be Cinderella, and drive to her palace with her gilded pumpkin.

RAVENSBANE. It is the end.

DICKON. What! You'll not?

RAVENSBANE. Never.

DICKON. Harkee, manikin. Hast thou learned to suffer?

RAVENSBANE (*wringing his hands*). O God!

DICKON. *I* taught thee. Shall I teach thee further?

RAVENSBANE. Thou canst not.

DICKON. Cannot—ha! What if I should teach Rachel, too?

RAVENSBANE. Rachel!—Ah! now I know thee.

DICKON (*bowing*). Flattered.

RAVENSBANE. Devil! Thou wouldst not torment Rachel?

DICKON. Not if my lord—

RAVENSBANE. Speak! What must I do?

DICKON. *Not* speak. Be silent, my lord, and acquiesce in all I say.

RAVENSBANE. I will be silent.

DICKON. And acquiesce?

RAVENSBANE. I will be silent.

(*Enter* MINISTER DODGE, *accompanied by* SIR CHARLES REDDINGTON, CAPTAIN BUGBY, *the* REVEREND MASTERS RAND *and* TODD, *and followed by* JUSTICE MERTON, RICHARD, MISTRESS MERTON, *and* RACHEL. RICHARD *and* RACHEL *stand somewhat apart,* RACHEL *drawing close to* RICHARD *and hiding her face. All wear their outer wraps, and two or three hold lanterns, which, save the moon, throw the only light upon the scene. All enter solemn and silent.*)

MINISTER DODGE. Lord, be Thou present with us, in this unholy spot.

SEVERAL MEN'S VOICES. Amen.

DICKON. Friends! Have you seized her?

MINISTER DODGE. Stand from us.

DICKON. Sir, the witch! Surely you did not let her escape?

ALL. The witch!

DICKON. A dame in a peaked hood. She has but now fled the house. She called herself—Goody Rickby.

ALL. Goody Rickby!

MISTRESS MERTON. She here!

DICKON. Yea, mistress, and hath confessed all the damnable art, by which all of us have lately been so terrorized.

JUSTICE MERTON. What confessed she?

MINISTER DODGE. What said she?

DICKON. This: It appeareth that, for some time past, she hath cherished revengeful thoughts against our honored host, Justice Merton.

MINISTER DODGE. Yea, he hath often righteously condemned her!

DICKON. Precisely! So, in revenge, she bewitched yonder mirror, and this very morning unlawfully inveigled this sweet young lady into purchasing it.

SIR CHARLES. Mistress Rachel!

MINISTER DODGE (*to* RACHEL). Didst thou purchase that glass?

RACHEL (*in a low voice*). Yes.

MINISTER DODGE. From Goody Rickby?

RACHEL. Yes. (*Clinging to* RICHARD) O Richard!

MINISTER DODGE. But the image; what was the damnable image in the glass?

DICKON. A familiar devil of hers—a sly imp, who wears to mortal eyes the shape of a scarecrow. It seems she commanded this devil to reveal himself in the glass as my lord's own image, that thus she might wreck Justice Merton's family felicity.

MINISTER DODGE. Infamous!

DICKON. Indeed, sir, it was this very devil whom but now she stole here to consult withal, when she encountered me, attendant here upon my poor prostrate lord, and—held by the wrath in my eye—confessed it all.

SIR CHARLES. Thunder and brimstone! Where is this accursed hag?

DICKON. Alas—gone, gone! If you had but stopped her.

MINISTER DODGE. I know her den—the blacksmith shop. Let us seize her there!

SIR CHARLES (*starting*). Which way?

MINISTER DODGE. To the left.

SIR CHARLES. Go on, there.

MINISTER DODGE. My honored friends, come with us. Heaven shield, with her guilt, the innocent!

(*Exeunt all but* RICHARD, RACHEL, DICKON, *and* RAVENSBANE.)

DICKON. So, then, dear friends, this strange incident is happily elucidated. Bygones, therefore, be bygones. The future brightens—with orange-blossoms. Hymen and Felicity stand with us here ready to unite two amorous and bashful lovers. His lordship is reticent; yet to you alone, of all beau-

tiful ladies, Mistress Rachel—
RAVENSBANE (*in a mighty voice*).
Silence!
DICKON. My lord would—
RAVENSBANE. Silence! Dare not to
speak to her!
DICKON (*biting his lip*). My babe is
weaned. (*He steps back, and disappears, left, in the dimness.*)
RACHEL (*still at* RICHARD'*s side*). Oh,
my lord, if I have made you suffer—
RICHARD (*appealingly*). Rachel!
RAVENSBANE (*approaching her, raises
one arm to screen his face*). Gracious
lady! let fall your eyes; look not upon
me. If I dare now speak once more to
you, 'tis because I would have you
know—Oh, forgive me!—that I love
you.
RICHARD. Sir! This lady has renewed
her promise to be my wife.
RAVENSBANE. Your wife, or not, I
love her.
RICHARD. Zounds!
RAVENSBANE. Forbear, and hear me!
For one wonderful day I have gazed
upon this, your world. A million
forms—of trees, of stones, of stars, of
men, of common things—have swum
like motes before my eyes; but one
alone was wholly beautiful. That
form was Rachel: to her alone I was
not ludicrous; to her I also was beautiful. Therefore, I love her.
RICHARD. Sir!
RAVENSBANE. You talk to me of
mothers, mistresses, lovers, and wives
and sisters, and you say men love
these. What is love? The night and
day of the world—the *all* of life, the
all which must include both you and
me and God, of whom you dream.
Well, then, I love you, Rachel. What
shall prevent me? Mistress, mother,
wife—thou art all to me!
RICHARD. My lord, I can only reply
for Mistress Rachel, that you speak

like one who does not understand
this world.
RAVENSBANE. O God! Sir, and do
you? If so, tell me—tell me before it
be too late—why, in this world, such
a thing as *I* can love and talk of love.
Why, in this world, a true man and
woman, like you and your betrothed,
can look upon this counterfeit and
be deceived.
RACHEL *and* RICHARD. Counterfeit?
RAVENSBANE. Me—on me—the igno-
miny of the earth, the laughing-stock
of the angels!
RACHEL. Are you not Lord Ravensbane?
RAVENSBANE. No, I am *not* Lord Ravensbane. I am a nobleman of husks,
bewitched from a pumpkin. I am Lord
Scarecrow!
RACHEL. Ah me, the image in the
glass was true?
RAVENSBANE. Yes, true. It is the glass
of truth— Thank God for you, dear.
DICKON (*his face only reappearing in
the mirror, speaks low*). Remember! if
you dare—Rachel shall suffer for it.
RAVENSBANE. You lie. She is above
your power.
DICKON. Still, thou darest not—
RAVENSBANE. Fool, I dare. (RAVENS-
BANE *turns to* RACHEL. *While he speaks,*
DICKON'*s face slowly fades and disappears.*) Mistress, this pipe is I. This in-
termittent smoke holds, in its nebula,
Venus, Mars, the world. If I should
break it—Chaos and the dark! And
this of me that now stands up will sink
jumbled upon the floor—a scarecrow.
See! I break it. (*He breaks the pipe in
his hands, and flings the pieces to the
ground; then turns, agonized, to* RA-
CHEL.) Oh, Rachel, could I have been
a man—! (*He sways, staggering.*)
RACHEL. Richard! Richard! support
him. (*She draws the curtain of the mirror, just opposite which* RAVENSBANE

has sunk upon the floor. At her cry, he starts up faintly and gazes at his reflection, which is seen to be a normal image of himself.)
Look, look: the glass!
    RAVENSBANE. Who is it?
    RACHEL. Yourself, my lord—'tis the glass of truth.

    RAVENSBANE *(his face lighting with an exalted joy, starts to his feet, erect, before the glass).* A man! *(He falls back into the arms of the two lovers.)* Rachel! *(He dies.)*
    RICHARD *(bending over him).* Dead!
    RACHEL *(with an exalted look).* But a man!

A CATALOG OF SELECTED
DOVER BOOKS
IN ALL FIELDS OF INTEREST

A CATALOG OF SELECTED DOVER
BOOKS IN ALL FIELDS OF INTEREST

100 BEST-LOVED POEMS, Edited by Philip Smith. "The Passionate Shepherd to His Love," "Shall I compare thee to a summer's day?" "Death, be not proud," "The Raven," "The Road Not Taken," plus works by Blake, Wordsworth, Byron, Shelley, Keats, many others. 96pp. 5³⁄₁₆ x 8¼. 0-486-28553-7

100 SMALL HOUSES OF THE THIRTIES, Brown-Blodgett Company. Exterior photographs and floor plans for 100 charming structures. Illustrations of models accompanied by descriptions of interiors, color schemes, closet space, and other amenities. 200 illustrations. 112pp. 8⅜ x 11. 0-486-44131-8

1000 TURN-OF-THE-CENTURY HOUSES: With Illustrations and Floor Plans, Herbert C. Chivers. Reproduced from a rare edition, this showcase of homes ranges from cottages and bungalows to sprawling mansions. Each house is meticulously illustrated and accompanied by complete floor plans. 256pp. 9⅜ x 12¼.
0-486-45596-3

101 GREAT AMERICAN POEMS, Edited by The American Poetry & Literacy Project. Rich treasury of verse from the 19th and 20th centuries includes works by Edgar Allan Poe, Robert Frost, Walt Whitman, Langston Hughes, Emily Dickinson, T. S. Eliot, other notables. 96pp. 5³⁄₁₆ x 8¼. 0-486-40158-8

101 GREAT SAMURAI PRINTS, Utagawa Kuniyoshi. Kuniyoshi was a master of the warrior woodblock print — and these 18th-century illustrations represent the pinnacle of his craft. Full-color portraits of renowned Japanese samurais pulse with movement, passion, and remarkably fine detail. 112pp. 8⅜ x 11. 0-486-46523-3

ABC OF BALLET, Janet Grosser. Clearly worded, abundantly illustrated little guide defines basic ballet-related terms: arabesque, battement, pas de chat, relevé, sissonne, many others. Pronunciation guide included. Excellent primer. 48pp. 4³⁄₁₆ x 5¾.
0-486-40871-X

ACCESSORIES OF DRESS: An Illustrated Encyclopedia, Katherine Lester and Bess Viola Oerke. Illustrations of hats, veils, wigs, cravats, shawls, shoes, gloves, and other accessories enhance an engaging commentary that reveals the humor and charm of the many-sided story of accessorized apparel. 644 figures and 59 plates. 608pp. 6 ⅛ x 9¼.
0-486-43378-1

ADVENTURES OF HUCKLEBERRY FINN, Mark Twain. Join Huck and Jim as their boyhood adventures along the Mississippi River lead them into a world of excitement, danger, and self-discovery. Humorous narrative, lyrical descriptions of the Mississippi valley, and memorable characters. 224pp. 5³⁄₁₆ x 8¼. 0-486-28061-6

ALICE STARMORE'S BOOK OF FAIR ISLE KNITTING, Alice Starmore. A noted designer from the region of Scotland's Fair Isle explores the history and techniques of this distinctive, stranded-color knitting style and provides copious illustrated instructions for 14 original knitwear designs. 208pp. 8⅜ x 10⅞. 0-486-47218-3

Browse over 9,000 books at www.doverpublications.com

ALICE'S ADVENTURES IN WONDERLAND, Lewis Carroll. Beloved classic about a little girl lost in a topsy-turvy land and her encounters with the White Rabbit, March Hare, Mad Hatter, Cheshire Cat, and other delightfully improbable characters. 42 illustrations by Sir John Tenniel. 96pp. 5⅜₆ x 8¼.　　　　　0-486-27543-4

AMERICA'S LIGHTHOUSES: An Illustrated History, Francis Ross Holland. Profusely illustrated fact-filled survey of American lighthouses since 1716. Over 200 stations — East, Gulf, and West coasts, Great Lakes, Hawaii, Alaska, Puerto Rico, the Virgin Islands, and the Mississippi and St. Lawrence Rivers. 240pp. 8 x 10¾.

0-486-25576-X

AN ENCYCLOPEDIA OF THE VIOLIN, Alberto Bachmann. Translated by Frederick H. Martens. Introduction by Eugene Ysaye. First published in 1925, this renowned reference remains unsurpassed as a source of essential information, from construction and evolution to repertoire and technique. Includes a glossary and 73 illustrations. 496pp. 6⅛ x 9¼.　　　　　0-486-46618-3

ANIMALS: 1,419 Copyright-Free Illustrations of Mammals, Birds, Fish, Insects, etc., Selected by Jim Harter. Selected for its visual impact and ease of use, this outstanding collection of wood engravings presents over 1,000 species of animals in extremely lifelike poses. Includes mammals, birds, reptiles, amphibians, fish, insects, and other invertebrates. 284pp. 9 x 12.　　　　　0-486-23766-4

THE ANNALS, Tacitus. Translated by Alfred John Church and William Jackson Brodribb. This vital chronicle of Imperial Rome, written by the era's great historian, spans A.D. 14-68 and paints incisive psychological portraits of major figures, from Tiberius to Nero. 416pp. 5⅜₆ x 8¼.　　　　　0-486-45236-0

ANTIGONE, Sophocles. Filled with passionate speeches and sensitive probing of moral and philosophical issues, this powerful and often-performed Greek drama reveals the grim fate that befalls the children of Oedipus. Footnotes. 64pp. 5⅜₆ x 8 ¼.　　　　　0-486-27804-2

ART DECO DECORATIVE PATTERNS IN FULL COLOR, Christian Stoll. Reprinted from a rare 1910 portfolio, 160 sensuous and exotic images depict a breathtaking array of florals, geometrics, and abstracts — all elegant in their stark simplicity. 64pp. 8⅜ x 11.　　　　　0-486-44862-2

THE ARTHUR RACKHAM TREASURY: 86 Full-Color Illustrations, Arthur Rackham. Selected and Edited by Jeff A. Menges. A stunning treasury of 86 full-page plates span the famed English artist's career, from *Rip Van Winkle* (1905) to masterworks such as *Undine, A Midsummer Night's Dream,* and *Wind in the Willows* (1939). 96pp. 8⅜ x 11.

0-486-44685-9

THE AUTHENTIC GILBERT & SULLIVAN SONGBOOK, W. S. Gilbert and A. S. Sullivan. The most comprehensive collection available, this songbook includes selections from every one of Gilbert and Sullivan's light operas. Ninety-two numbers are presented uncut and unedited, and in their original keys. 410pp. 9 x 12.

0-486-23482-7

THE AWAKENING, Kate Chopin. First published in 1899, this controversial novel of a New Orleans wife's search for love outside a stifling marriage shocked readers. Today, it remains a first-rate narrative with superb characterization. New introductory Note. 128pp. 5⅜₆ x 8¼.　　　　　0-486-27786-0

BASIC DRAWING, Louis Priscilla. Beginning with perspective, this commonsense manual progresses to the figure in movement, light and shade, anatomy, drapery, composition, trees and landscape, and outdoor sketching. Black-and-white illustrations throughout. 128pp. 8⅜ x 11.　　　　　0-486-45815-6

Browse over 9,000 books at www.doverpublications.com

THE BATTLES THAT CHANGED HISTORY, Fletcher Pratt. Historian profiles 16 crucial conflicts, ancient to modern, that changed the course of Western civilization. Gripping accounts of battles led by Alexander the Great, Joan of Arc, Ulysses S. Grant, other commanders. 27 maps. 352pp. 5⅜ x 8½.   0-486-41129-X

BEETHOVEN'S LETTERS, Ludwig van Beethoven. Edited by Dr. A. C. Kalischer. Features 457 letters to fellow musicians, friends, greats, patrons, and literary men. Reveals musical thoughts, quirks of personality, insights, and daily events. Includes 15 plates. 410pp. 5⅜ x 8½.   0-486-22769-3

BERNICE BOBS HER HAIR AND OTHER STORIES, F. Scott Fitzgerald. This brilliant anthology includes 6 of Fitzgerald's most popular stories: "The Diamond as Big as the Ritz," the title tale, "The Offshore Pirate," "The Ice Palace," "The Jelly Bean," and "May Day." 176pp. 5⅜ x 8½.   0-486-47049-0

BESLER'S BOOK OF FLOWERS AND PLANTS: 73 Full-Color Plates from Hortus Eystettensis, 1613, Basilius Besler. Here is a selection of magnificent plates from the *Hortus Eystettensis,* which vividly illustrated and identified the plants, flowers, and trees that thrived in the legendary German garden at Eichstätt. 80pp. 8⅜ x 11.
0-486-46005-3

THE BOOK OF KELLS, Edited by Blanche Cirker. Painstakingly reproduced from a rare facsimile edition, this volume contains full-page decorations, portraits, illustrations, plus a sampling of textual leaves with exquisite calligraphy and ornamentation. 32 full-color illustrations. 32pp. 9⅜ x 12¼.   0-486-24345-1

THE BOOK OF THE CROSSBOW: With an Additional Section on Catapults and Other Siege Engines, Ralph Payne-Gallwey. Fascinating study traces history and use of crossbow as military and sporting weapon, from Middle Ages to modern times. Also covers related weapons: balistas, catapults, Turkish bows, more. Over 240 illustrations. 400pp. 7¼ x 10⅜.   0-486-28720-3

THE BUNGALOW BOOK: Floor Plans and Photos of 112 Houses, 1910, Henry L. Wilson. Here are 112 of the most popular and economic blueprints of the early 20th century — plus an illustration or photograph of each completed house. A wonderful time capsule that still offers a wealth of valuable insights. 160pp. 8⅜ x 11.
0-486-45104-6

THE CALL OF THE WILD, Jack London. A classic novel of adventure, drawn from London's own experiences as a Klondike adventurer, relating the story of a heroic dog caught in the brutal life of the Alaska Gold Rush. Note. 64pp. 5³⁄₁₆ x 8¼.
0-486-26472-6

CANDIDE, Voltaire. Edited by Francois-Marie Arouet. One of the world's great satires since its first publication in 1759. Witty, caustic skewering of romance, science, philosophy, religion, government — nearly all human ideals and institutions. 112pp. 5³⁄₁₆ x 8¼.   0-486-26689-3

CELEBRATED IN THEIR TIME: Photographic Portraits from the George Grantham Bain Collection, Edited by Amy Pastan. With an Introduction by Michael Carlebach. Remarkable portrait gallery features 112 rare images of Albert Einstein, Charlie Chaplin, the Wright Brothers, Henry Ford, and other luminaries from the worlds of politics, art, entertainment, and industry. 128pp. 8⅜ x 11.   0-486-46754-6

CHARIOTS FOR APOLLO: The NASA History of Manned Lunar Spacecraft to 1969, Courtney G. Brooks, James M. Grimwood, and Loyd S. Swenson, Jr. This illustrated history by a trio of experts is the definitive reference on the Apollo spacecraft and lunar modules. It traces the vehicles' design, development, and operation in space. More than 100 photographs and illustrations. 576pp. 6¾ x 9¼. 0-486-46756-2

Browse over 9,000 books at www.doverpublications.com

CATALOG OF DOVER BOOKS

A CHRISTMAS CAROL, Charles Dickens. This engrossing tale relates Ebenezer Scrooge's ghostly journeys through Christmases past, present, and future and his ultimate transformation from a harsh and grasping old miser to a charitable and compassionate human being. 80pp. 5³⁄₁₆ x 8¼. 0-486-26865-9

COMMON SENSE, Thomas Paine. First published in January of 1776, this highly influential landmark document clearly and persuasively argued for American separation from Great Britain and paved the way for the Declaration of Independence. 64pp. 5³⁄₁₆ x 8¼. 0-486-29602-4

THE COMPLETE SHORT STORIES OF OSCAR WILDE, Oscar Wilde. Complete texts of "The Happy Prince and Other Tales," "A House of Pomegranates," "Lord Arthur Savile's Crime and Other Stories," "Poems in Prose," and "The Portrait of Mr. W. H." 208pp. 5³⁄₁₆ x 8¼. 0-486-45216-6

COMPLETE SONNETS, William Shakespeare. Over 150 exquisite poems deal with love, friendship, the tyranny of time, beauty's evanescence, death, and other themes in language of remarkable power, precision, and beauty. Glossary of archaic terms. 80pp. 5³⁄₁₆ x 8¼. 0-486-26686-9

THE COUNT OF MONTE CRISTO: Abridged Edition, Alexandre Dumas. Falsely accused of treason, Edmond Dantès is imprisoned in the bleak Chateau d'If. After a hair-raising escape, he launches an elaborate plot to extract a bitter revenge against those who betrayed him. 448pp. 5³⁄₁₆ x 8¼. 0-486-45643-9

CRAFTSMAN BUNGALOWS: Designs from the Pacific Northwest, Yoho & Merritt. This reprint of a rare catalog, showcasing the charming simplicity and cozy style of Craftsman bungalows, is filled with photos of completed homes, plus floor plans and estimated costs. An indispensable resource for architects, historians, and illustrators. 112pp. 10 x 7. 0-486-46875-5

CRAFTSMAN BUNGALOWS: 59 Homes from "The Craftsman," Edited by Gustav Stickley. Best and most attractive designs from Arts and Crafts Movement publication — 1903–1916 — includes sketches, photographs of homes, floor plans, descriptive text. 128pp. 8¼ x 11. 0-486-25829-7

CRIME AND PUNISHMENT, Fyodor Dostoyevsky. Translated by Constance Garnett. Supreme masterpiece tells the story of Raskolnikov, a student tormented by his own thoughts after he murders an old woman. Overwhelmed by guilt and terror, he confesses and goes to prison. 480pp. 5³⁄₁₆ x 8¼. 0-486-41587-2

THE DECLARATION OF INDEPENDENCE AND OTHER GREAT DOCUMENTS OF AMERICAN HISTORY: 1775-1865, Edited by John Grafton. Thirteen compelling and influential documents: Henry's "Give Me Liberty or Give Me Death," Declaration of Independence, The Constitution, Washington's First Inaugural Address, The Monroe Doctrine, The Emancipation Proclamation, Gettysburg Address, more. 64pp. 5³⁄₁₆ x 8¼. 0-486-41124-9

THE DESERT AND THE SOWN: Travels in Palestine and Syria, Gertrude Bell. "The female Lawrence of Arabia," Gertrude Bell wrote captivating, perceptive accounts of her travels in the Middle East. This intriguing narrative, accompanied by 160 photos, traces her 1905 sojourn in Lebanon, Syria, and Palestine. 368pp. 5⅜ x 8½. 0-486-46876-3

A DOLL'S HOUSE, Henrik Ibsen. Ibsen's best-known play displays his genius for realistic prose drama. An expression of women's rights, the play climaxes when the central character, Nora, rejects a smothering marriage and life in "a doll's house." 80pp. 5³⁄₁₆ x 8¼. 0-486-27062-9

Browse over 9,000 books at www.doverpublications.com

CATALOG OF DOVER BOOKS

DOOMED SHIPS: Great Ocean Liner Disasters, William H. Miller, Jr. Nearly 200 photographs, many from private collections, highlight tales of some of the vessels whose pleasure cruises ended in catastrophe: the *Morro Castle, Normandie, Andrea Doria, Europa,* and many others. 128pp. 8⅞ x 11¼. 0-486-45366-9

THE DORÉ BIBLE ILLUSTRATIONS, Gustave Doré. Detailed plates from the Bible: the Creation scenes, Adam and Eve, horrifying visions of the Flood, the battle sequences with their monumental crowds, depictions of the life of Jesus, 241 plates in all. 241pp. 9 x 12. 0-486-23004-X

DRAWING DRAPERY FROM HEAD TO TOE, Cliff Young. Expert guidance on how to draw shirts, pants, skirts, gloves, hats, and coats on the human figure, including folds in relation to the body, pull and crush, action folds, creases, more. Over 200 drawings. 48pp. 8¼ x 11. 0-486-45591-2

DUBLINERS, James Joyce. A fine and accessible introduction to the work of one of the 20th century's most influential writers, this collection features 15 tales, including a masterpiece of the short-story genre, "The Dead." 160pp. 5³⁄₁₆ x 8¼. 0-486-26870-5

EASY-TO-MAKE POP-UPS, Joan Irvine. Illustrated by Barbara Reid. Dozens of wonderful ideas for three-dimensional paper fun — from holiday greeting cards with moving parts to a pop-up menagerie. Easy-to-follow, illustrated instructions for more than 30 projects. 299 black-and-white illustrations. 96pp. 8⅜ x 11. 0-486-44622-0

EASY-TO-MAKE STORYBOOK DOLLS: A "Novel" Approach to Cloth Dollmaking, Sherralyn St. Clair. Favorite fictional characters come alive in this unique beginner's dollmaking guide. Includes patterns for Pollyanna, Dorothy from *The Wonderful Wizard of Oz,* Mary of *The Secret Garden,* plus easy-to-follow instructions, 263 black-and-white illustrations, and an 8-page color insert. 112pp. 8¼ x 11. 0-486-47360-0

EINSTEIN'S ESSAYS IN SCIENCE, Albert Einstein. Speeches and essays in accessible, everyday language profile influential physicists such as Niels Bohr and Isaac Newton. They also explore areas of physics to which the author made major contributions. 128pp. 5 x 8. 0-486-47011-3

EL DORADO: Further Adventures of the Scarlet Pimpernel, Baroness Orczy. A popular sequel to *The Scarlet Pimpernel,* this suspenseful story recounts the Pimpernel's attempts to rescue the Dauphin from imprisonment during the French Revolution. An irresistible blend of intrigue, period detail, and vibrant characterizations. 352pp. 5³⁄₁₆ x 8¼. 0-486-44026-5

ELEGANT SMALL HOMES OF THE TWENTIES: 99 Designs from a Competition, Chicago Tribune. Nearly 100 designs for five- and six-room houses feature New England and Southern colonials, Normandy cottages, stately Italianate dwellings, and other fascinating snapshots of American domestic architecture of the 1920s. 112pp. 9 x 12. 0-486-46910-7

THE ELEMENTS OF STYLE: The Original Edition, William Strunk, Jr. This is the book that generations of writers have relied upon for timeless advice on grammar, diction, syntax, and other essentials. In concise terms, it identifies the principal requirements of proper style and common errors. 64pp. 5⅜ x 8½. 0-486-44798-7

THE ELUSIVE PIMPERNEL, Baroness Orczy. Robespierre's revolutionaries find their wicked schemes thwarted by the heroic Pimpernel — Sir Percival Blakeney. In this thrilling sequel, Chauvelin devises a plot to eliminate the Pimpernel and his wife. 272pp. 5³⁄₁₆ x 8¼. 0-486-45464-9

Browse over 9,000 books at www.doverpublications.com

AN ENCYCLOPEDIA OF BATTLES: Accounts of Over 1,560 Battles from 1479 B.C. to the Present, David Eggenberger. Essential details of every major battle in recorded history from the first battle of Megiddo in 1479 B.C. to Grenada in 1984. List of battle maps. 99 illustrations. 544pp. 6½ x 9¼. 0-486-24913-1

ENCYCLOPEDIA OF EMBROIDERY STITCHES, INCLUDING CREWEL, Marion Nichols. Precise explanations and instructions, clearly illustrated, on how to work chain, back, cross, knotted, woven stitches, and many more — 178 in all, including Cable Outline, Whipped Satin, and Eyelet Buttonhole. Over 1400 illustrations. 219pp. 8⅜ x 11¼. 0-486-22929-7

ENTER JEEVES: 15 Early Stories, P. G. Wodehouse. Splendid collection contains first 8 stories featuring Bertie Wooster, the deliciously dim aristocrat and Jeeves, his brainy, imperturbable manservant. Also, the complete Reggie Pepper (Bertie's prototype) series. 288pp. 5⅜ x 8½. 0-486-29717-9

ERIC SLOANE'S AMERICA: Paintings in Oil, Michael Wigley. With a Foreword by Mimi Sloane. Eric Sloane's evocative oils of America's landscape and material culture shimmer with immense historical and nostalgic appeal. This original hardcover collection gathers nearly a hundred of his finest paintings, with subjects ranging from New England to the American Southwest. 128pp. 10⅝ x 9. 0-486-46525-X

ETHAN FROME, Edith Wharton. Classic story of wasted lives, set against a bleak New England background. Superbly delineated characters in a hauntingly grim tale of thwarted love. Considered by many to be Wharton's masterpiece. 96pp. 5³⁄₁₆ x 8 ¼. 0-486-26690-7

THE EVERLASTING MAN, G. K. Chesterton. Chesterton's view of Christianity — as a blend of philosophy and mythology, satisfying intellect and spirit — applies to his brilliant book, which appeals to readers' heads as well as their hearts. 288pp. 5⅜ x 8½. 0-486-46036-3

THE FIELD AND FOREST HANDY BOOK, Daniel Beard. Written by a co-founder of the Boy Scouts, this appealing guide offers illustrated instructions for building kites, birdhouses, boats, igloos, and other fun projects, plus numerous helpful tips for campers. 448pp. 5³⁄₁₆ x 8¼. 0-486-46191-2

FINDING YOUR WAY WITHOUT MAP OR COMPASS, Harold Gatty. Useful, instructive manual shows would-be explorers, hikers, bikers, scouts, sailors, and survivalists how to find their way outdoors by observing animals, weather patterns, shifting sands, and other elements of nature. 288pp. 5⅜ x 8½. 0-486-40613-X

FIRST FRENCH READER: A Beginner's Dual-Language Book, Edited and Translated by Stanley Appelbaum. This anthology introduces 50 legendary writers — Voltaire, Balzac, Baudelaire, Proust, more — through passages from *The Red and the Black, Les Misérables, Madame Bovary,* and other classics. Original French text plus English translation on facing pages. 240pp. 5⅜ x 8½. 0-486-46178-5

FIRST GERMAN READER: A Beginner's Dual-Language Book, Edited by Harry Steinhauer. Specially chosen for their power to evoke German life and culture, these short, simple readings include poems, stories, essays, and anecdotes by Goethe, Hesse, Heine, Schiller, and others. 224pp. 5⅜ x 8½. 0-486-46179-3

FIRST SPANISH READER: A Beginner's Dual-Language Book, Angel Flores. Delightful stories, other material based on works of Don Juan Manuel, Luis Taboada, Ricardo Palma, other noted writers. Complete faithful English translations on facing pages. Exercises. 176pp. 5⅜ x 8½. 0-486-25810-6

Browse over 9,000 books at www.doverpublications.com

FIVE ACRES AND INDEPENDENCE, Maurice G. Kains. Great back-to-the-land classic explains basics of self-sufficient farming. The one book to get. 95 illustrations. 397pp. 5⅜ x 8½. 0-486-20974-1

FLAGG'S SMALL HOUSES: Their Economic Design and Construction, 1922, Ernest Flagg. Although most famous for his skyscrapers, Flagg was also a proponent of the well-designed single-family dwelling. His classic treatise features innovations that save space, materials, and cost. 526 illustrations. 160pp. 9⅜ x 12¼.
0-486-45197-6

FLATLAND: A Romance of Many Dimensions, Edwin A. Abbott. Classic of science (and mathematical) fiction — charmingly illustrated by the author — describes the adventures of A. Square, a resident of Flatland, in Spaceland (three dimensions), Lineland (one dimension), and Pointland (no dimensions). 96pp. 5³⁄₁₆ x 8¼.
0-486-27263-X

FRANKENSTEIN, Mary Shelley. The story of Victor Frankenstein's monstrous creation and the havoc it caused has enthralled generations of readers and inspired countless writers of horror and suspense. With the author's own 1831 introduction. 176pp. 5³⁄₁₆ x 8¼. 0-486-28211-2

THE GARGOYLE BOOK: 572 Examples from Gothic Architecture, Lester Burbank Bridaham. Dispelling the conventional wisdom that French Gothic architectural flourishes were born of despair or gloom, Bridaham reveals the whimsical nature of these creations and the ingenious artisans who made them. 572 illustrations. 224pp. 8⅜ x 11. 0-486-44754-5

THE GIFT OF THE MAGI AND OTHER SHORT STORIES, O. Henry. Sixteen captivating stories by one of America's most popular storytellers. Included are such classics as "The Gift of the Magi," "The Last Leaf," and "The Ransom of Red Chief." Publisher's Note. 96pp. 5³⁄₁₆ x 8¼. 0-486-27061-0

THE GOETHE TREASURY: Selected Prose and Poetry, Johann Wolfgang von Goethe. Edited, Selected, and with an Introduction by Thomas Mann. In addition to his lyric poetry, Goethe wrote travel sketches, autobiographical studies, essays, letters, and proverbs in rhyme and prose. This collection presents outstanding examples from each genre. 368pp. 5⅜ x 8½. 0-486-44780-4

GREAT EXPECTATIONS, Charles Dickens. Orphaned Pip is apprenticed to the dirty work of the forge but dreams of becoming a gentleman — and one day finds himself in possession of "great expectations." Dickens' finest novel. 400pp. 5³⁄₁₆ x 8¼.
0-486-41586-4

GREAT WRITERS ON THE ART OF FICTION: From Mark Twain to Joyce Carol Oates, Edited by James Daley. An indispensable source of advice and inspiration, this anthology features essays by Henry James, Kate Chopin, Willa Cather, Sinclair Lewis, Jack London, Raymond Chandler, Raymond Carver, Eudora Welty, and Kurt Vonnegut, Jr. 192pp. 5⅜ x 8½. 0-486-45128-3

HAMLET, William Shakespeare. The quintessential Shakespearean tragedy, whose highly charged confrontations and anguished soliloquies probe depths of human feeling rarely sounded in any art. Reprinted from an authoritative British edition complete with illuminating footnotes. 128pp. 5³⁄₁₆ x 8¼. 0-486-27278-8

THE HAUNTED HOUSE, Charles Dickens. A Yuletide gathering in an eerie country retreat provides the backdrop for Dickens and his friends — including Elizabeth Gaskell and Wilkie Collins — who take turns spinning supernatural yarns. 144pp. 5⅜ x 8½. 0-486-46309-5

CATALOG OF DOVER BOOKS

HEART OF DARKNESS, Joseph Conrad. Dark allegory of a journey up the Congo River and the narrator's encounter with the mysterious Mr. Kurtz. Masterly blend of adventure, character study, psychological penetration. For many, Conrad's finest, most enigmatic story. 80pp. 5³⁄₁₆ x 8¼. 0-486-26464-5

HENSON AT THE NORTH POLE, Matthew A. Henson. This thrilling memoir by the heroic African-American who was Peary's companion through two decades of Arctic exploration recounts a tale of danger, courage, and determination. "Fascinating and exciting." — *Commonweal.* 128pp. 5⅜ x 8½. 0-486-45472-X

HISTORIC COSTUMES AND HOW TO MAKE THEM, Mary Fernald and E. Shenton. Practical, informative guidebook shows how to create everything from short tunics worn by Saxon men in the fifth century to a lady's bustle dress of the late 1800s. 81 illustrations. 176pp. 5⅜ x 8½. 0-486-44906-8

THE HOUND OF THE BASKERVILLES, Arthur Conan Doyle. A deadly curse in the form of a legendary ferocious beast continues to claim its victims from the Baskerville family until Holmes and Watson intervene. Often called the best detective story ever written. 128pp. 5³⁄₁₆ x 8¼. 0-486-28214-7

THE HOUSE BEHIND THE CEDARS, Charles W. Chesnutt. Originally published in 1900, this groundbreaking novel by a distinguished African-American author recounts the drama of a brother and sister who "pass for white" during the dangerous days of Reconstruction. 208pp. 5⅜ x 8½. 0-486-46144-0

THE HUMAN FIGURE IN MOTION, Eadweard Muybridge. The 4,789 photographs in this definitive selection show the human figure — models almost all undraped — engaged in over 160 different types of action: running, climbing stairs, etc. 390pp. 7⅞ x 10⅝. 0-486-20204-6

THE IMPORTANCE OF BEING EARNEST, Oscar Wilde. Wilde's witty and buoyant comedy of manners, filled with some of literature's most famous epigrams, reprinted from an authoritative British edition. Considered Wilde's most perfect work. 64pp. 5³⁄₁₆ x 8¼. 0-486-26478-5

THE INFERNO, Dante Alighieri. Translated and with notes by Henry Wadsworth Longfellow. The first stop on Dante's famous journey from Hell to Purgatory to Paradise, this 14th-century allegorical poem blends vivid and shocking imagery with graceful lyricism. Translated by the beloved 19th-century poet, Henry Wadsworth Longfellow. 256pp. 5³⁄₁₆ x 8¼. 0-486-44288-8

JANE EYRE, Charlotte Brontë. Written in 1847, *Jane Eyre* tells the tale of an orphan girl's progress from the custody of cruel relatives to an oppressive boarding school and its culmination in a troubled career as a governess. 448pp. 5³⁄₁₆ x 8¼.
0-486-42449-9

JAPANESE WOODBLOCK FLOWER PRINTS, Tanigami Kônan. Extraordinary collection of Japanese woodblock prints by a well-known artist features 120 plates in brilliant color. Realistic images from a rare edition include daffodils, tulips, and other familiar and unusual flowers. 128pp. 11 x 8¼. 0-486-46442-3

JEWELRY MAKING AND DESIGN, Augustus F. Rose and Antonio Cirino. Professional secrets of jewelry making are revealed in a thorough, practical guide. Over 200 illustrations. 306pp. 5⅜ x 8½. 0-486-21750-7

JULIUS CAESAR, William Shakespeare. Great tragedy based on Plutarch's account of the lives of Brutus, Julius Caesar and Mark Antony. Evil plotting, ringing oratory, high tragedy with Shakespeare's incomparable insight, dramatic power. Explanatory footnotes. 96pp. 5³⁄₁₆ x 8¼. 0-486-26876-4

Browse over 9,000 books at www.doverpublications.com

THE JUNGLE, Upton Sinclair. 1906 bestseller shockingly reveals intolerable labor practices and working conditions in the Chicago stockyards as it tells the grim story of a Slavic family that emigrates to America full of optimism but soon faces despair. 320pp. 5³⁄₁₆ x 8¼. 0-486-41923-1

THE KINGDOM OF GOD IS WITHIN YOU, Leo Tolstoy. The soul-searching book that inspired Gandhi to embrace the concept of passive resistance, Tolstoy's 1894 polemic clearly outlines a radical, well-reasoned revision of traditional Christian thinking. 352pp. 5³⁄₁₆ x 8¼. 0-486-45138-0

THE LADY OR THE TIGER?: and Other Logic Puzzles, Raymond M. Smullyan. Created by a renowned puzzle master, these whimsically themed challenges involve paradoxes about probability, time, and change; metapuzzles; and self-referentiality. Nineteen chapters advance in difficulty from relatively simple to highly complex. 1982 edition. 240pp. 5⅜ x 8½. 0-486-47027-X

LEAVES OF GRASS: The Original 1855 Edition, Walt Whitman. Whitman's immortal collection includes some of the greatest poems of modern times, including his masterpiece, "Song of Myself." Shattering standard conventions, it stands as an unabashed celebration of body and nature. 128pp. 5³⁄₁₆ x 8¼. 0-486-45676-5

LES MISÉRABLES, Victor Hugo. Translated by Charles E. Wilbour. Abridged by James K. Robinson. A convict's heroic struggle for justice and redemption plays out against a fiery backdrop of the Napoleonic wars. This edition features the excellent original translation and a sensitive abridgment. 304pp. 6⅛ x 9¼. 0-486-45789-3

LILITH: A Romance, George MacDonald. In this novel by the father of fantasy literature, a man travels through time to meet Adam and Eve and to explore humanity's fall from grace and ultimate redemption. 240pp. 5⅜ x 8½. 0-486-46818-6

THE LOST LANGUAGE OF SYMBOLISM, Harold Bayley. This remarkable book reveals the hidden meaning behind familiar images and words, from the origins of Santa Claus to the fleur-de-lys, drawing from mythology, folklore, religious texts, and fairy tales. 1,418 illustrations. 784pp. 5⅜ x 8½. 0-486-44787-1

MACBETH, William Shakespeare. A Scottish nobleman murders the king in order to succeed to the throne. Tortured by his conscience and fearful of discovery, he becomes tangled in a web of treachery and deceit that ultimately spells his doom. 96pp. 5³⁄₁₆ x 8¼. 0-486-27802-6

MAKING AUTHENTIC CRAFTSMAN FURNITURE: Instructions and Plans for 62 Projects, Gustav Stickley. Make authentic reproductions of handsome, functional, durable furniture: tables, chairs, wall cabinets, desks, a hall tree, and more. Construction plans with drawings, schematics, dimensions, and lumber specs reprinted from 1900s *The Craftsman* magazine. 128pp. 8⅛ x 11. 0-486-25000-8

MATHEMATICS FOR THE NONMATHEMATICIAN, Morris Kline. Erudite and entertaining overview follows development of mathematics from ancient Greeks to present. Topics include logic and mathematics, the fundamental concept, differential calculus, probability theory, much more. Exercises and problems. 641pp. 5⅜ x 8½. 0-486-24823-2

MEMOIRS OF AN ARABIAN PRINCESS FROM ZANZIBAR, Emily Ruete. This 19th-century autobiography offers a rare inside look at the society surrounding a sultan's palace. A real-life princess in exile recalls her vanished world of harems, slave trading, and court intrigues. 288pp. 5⅜ x 8½. 0-486-47121-7

Browse over 9,000 books at www.doverpublications.com

THE METAMORPHOSIS AND OTHER STORIES, Franz Kafka. Excellent new English translations of title story (considered by many critics Kafka's most perfect work), plus "The Judgment," "In the Penal Colony," "A Country Doctor," and "A Report to an Academy." Note. 96pp. 5³⁄₁₆ x 8¼. 0-486-29030-1

MICROSCOPIC ART FORMS FROM THE PLANT WORLD, R. Anheisser. From undulating curves to complex geometrics, a world of fascinating images abound in this classic, illustrated survey of microscopic plants. Features 400 detailed illustrations of nature's minute but magnificent handiwork. The accompanying CD-ROM includes all of the images in the book. 128pp. 9 x 9. 0-486-46013-4

A MIDSUMMER NIGHT'S DREAM, William Shakespeare. Among the most popular of Shakespeare's comedies, this enchanting play humorously celebrates the vagaries of love as it focuses upon the intertwined romances of several pairs of lovers. Explanatory footnotes. 80pp. 5³⁄₁₆ x 8¼. 0-486-27067-X

THE MONEY CHANGERS, Upton Sinclair. Originally published in 1908, this cautionary novel from the author of *The Jungle* explores corruption within the American system as a group of power brokers joins forces for personal gain, triggering a crash on Wall Street. 192pp. 5⅜ x 8½. 0-486-46917-4

THE MOST POPULAR HOMES OF THE TWENTIES, William A. Radford. With a New Introduction by Daniel D. Reiff. Based on a rare 1925 catalog, this architectural showcase features floor plans, construction details, and photos of 26 homes, plus articles on entrances, porches, garages, and more. 250 illustrations, 21 color plates. 176pp. 8⅜ x 11. 0-486-47028-8

MY 66 YEARS IN THE BIG LEAGUES, Connie Mack. With a New Introduction by Rich Westcott. A Founding Father of modern baseball, Mack holds the record for most wins — and losses — by a major league manager. Enhanced by 70 photographs, his warmhearted autobiography is populated by many legends of the game. 288pp. 5⅜ x 8½. 0-486-47184-5

NARRATIVE OF THE LIFE OF FREDERICK DOUGLASS, Frederick Douglass. Douglass's graphic depictions of slavery, harrowing escape to freedom, and life as a newspaper editor, eloquent orator, and impassioned abolitionist. 96pp. 5³⁄₁₆ x 8¼. 0-486-28499-9

THE NIGHTLESS CITY: Geisha and Courtesan Life in Old Tokyo, J. E. de Becker. This unsurpassed study from 100 years ago ventured into Tokyo's red-light district to survey geisha and courtesan life and offer meticulous descriptions of training, dress, social hierarchy, and erotic practices. 49 black-and-white illustrations; 2 maps. 496pp. 5⅜ x 8½. 0-486-45563-7

THE ODYSSEY, Homer. Excellent prose translation of ancient epic recounts adventures of the homeward-bound Odysseus. Fantastic cast of gods, giants, cannibals, sirens, other supernatural creatures — true classic of Western literature. 256pp. 5³⁄₁₆ x 8¼. 0-486-40654-7

OEDIPUS REX, Sophocles. Landmark of Western drama concerns the catastrophe that ensues when King Oedipus discovers he has inadvertently killed his father and married his mother. Masterly construction, dramatic irony. Explanatory footnotes. 64pp. 5³⁄₁₆ x 8¼. 0-486-26877-2

ONCE UPON A TIME: The Way America Was, Eric Sloane. Nostalgic text and drawings brim with gentle philosophies and descriptions of how we used to live — self-sufficiently — on the land, in homes, and among the things built by hand. 44 line illustrations. 64pp. 8⅜ x 11. 0-486-44411-2

ONE OF OURS, Willa Cather. The Pulitzer Prize–winning novel about a young Nebraskan looking for something to believe in. Alienated from his parents, rejected by his wife, he finds his destiny on the bloody battlefields of World War I. 352pp. 5³⁄₁₆ x 8¼. 0-486-45599-8

ORIGAMI YOU CAN USE: 27 Practical Projects, Rick Beech. Origami models can be more than decorative, and this unique volume shows how! The 27 practical projects include a CD case, frame, napkin ring, and dish. Easy instructions feature 400 two-color illustrations. 96pp. 8¼ x 11. 0-486-47057-1

OTHELLO, William Shakespeare. Towering tragedy tells the story of a Moorish general who earns the enmity of his ensign Iago when he passes him over for a promotion. Masterly portrait of an archvillain. Explanatory footnotes. 112pp. 5³⁄₁₆ x 8¼. 0-486-29097-2

PARADISE LOST, John Milton. Notes by John A. Himes. First published in 1667, *Paradise Lost* ranks among the greatest of English literature's epic poems. It's a sublime retelling of Adam and Eve's fall from grace and expulsion from Eden. Notes by John A. Himes. 480pp. 5³⁄₁₆ x 8¼. 0-486-44287-X

PASSING, Nella Larsen. Married to a successful physician and prominently ensconced in society, Irene Redfield leads a charmed existence — until a chance encounter with a childhood friend who has been "passing for white." 112pp. 5⅜ x 8½. 0-486-43713-2

PERSPECTIVE DRAWING FOR BEGINNERS, Len A. Doust. Doust carefully explains the roles of lines, boxes, and circles, and shows how visualizing shapes and forms can be used in accurate depictions of perspective. One of the most concise introductions available. 33 illustrations. 64pp. 5⅜ x 8½. 0-486-45149-6

PERSPECTIVE MADE EASY, Ernest R. Norling. Perspective is easy; yet, surprisingly few artists know the simple rules that make it so. Remedy that situation with this simple, step-by-step book, the first devoted entirely to the topic. 256 illustrations. 224pp. 5⅜ x 8½. 0-486-40473-0

THE PICTURE OF DORIAN GRAY, Oscar Wilde. Celebrated novel involves a handsome young Londoner who sinks into a life of depravity. His body retains perfect youth and vigor while his recent portrait reflects the ravages of his crime and sensuality. 176pp. 5³⁄₁₆ x 8¼. 0-486-27807-7

PRIDE AND PREJUDICE, Jane Austen. One of the most universally loved and admired English novels, an effervescent tale of rural romance transformed by Jane Austen's art into a witty, shrewdly observed satire of English country life. 272pp. 5³⁄₁₆ x 8¼. 0-486-28473-5

THE PRINCE, Niccolò Machiavelli. Classic, Renaissance-era guide to acquiring and maintaining political power. Today, nearly 500 years after it was written, this calculating prescription for autocratic rule continues to be much read and studied. 80pp. 5³⁄₁₆ x 8¼. 0-486-27274-5

QUICK SKETCHING, Carl Cheek. A perfect introduction to the technique of "quick sketching." Drawing upon an artist's immediate emotional responses, this is an extremely effective means of capturing the essential form and features of a subject. More than 100 black-and-white illustrations throughout. 48pp. 11 x 8¼. 0-486-46608-6

RANCH LIFE AND THE HUNTING TRAIL, Theodore Roosevelt. Illustrated by Frederic Remington. Beautifully illustrated by Remington, Roosevelt's celebration of the Old West recounts his adventures in the Dakota Badlands of the 1880s, from round-ups to Indian encounters to hunting bighorn sheep. 208pp. 6¼ x 9¼. 0-486-47340-6

THE RED BADGE OF COURAGE, Stephen Crane. Amid the nightmarish chaos of a Civil War battle, a young soldier discovers courage, humility, and, perhaps, wisdom. Uncanny re-creation of actual combat. Enduring landmark of American fiction. 112pp. 5³⁄₁₆ x 8¼.   0-486-26465-3

RELATIVITY SIMPLY EXPLAINED, Martin Gardner. One of the subject's clearest, most entertaining introductions offers lucid explanations of special and general theories of relativity, gravity, and spacetime, models of the universe, and more. 100 illustrations. 224pp. 5⅜ x 8½.   0-486-29315-7

REMBRANDT DRAWINGS: 116 Masterpieces in Original Color, Rembrandt van Rijn. This deluxe hardcover edition features drawings from throughout the Dutch master's prolific career. Informative captions accompany these beautifully reproduced landscapes, biblical vignettes, figure studies, animal sketches, and portraits. 128pp. 8⅜ x 11.   0-486-46149-1

THE ROAD NOT TAKEN AND OTHER POEMS, Robert Frost. A treasury of Frost's most expressive verse. In addition to the title poem: "An Old Man's Winter Night," "In the Home Stretch," "Meeting and Passing," "Putting in the Seed," many more. All complete and unabridged. 64pp. 5³⁄₁₆ x 8¼.   0-486-27550-7

ROMEO AND JULIET, William Shakespeare. Tragic tale of star-crossed lovers, feuding families and timeless passion contains some of Shakespeare's most beautiful and lyrical love poetry. Complete, unabridged text with explanatory footnotes. 96pp. 5³⁄₁₆ x 8¼.   0-486-27557-4

SANDITON AND THE WATSONS: Austen's Unfinished Novels, Jane Austen. Two tantalizing incomplete stories revisit Austen's customary milieu of courtship and venture into new territory, amid guests at a seaside resort. Both are worth reading for pleasure and study. 112pp. 5⅜ x 8½.   0-486-45793-1

THE SCARLET LETTER, Nathaniel Hawthorne. With stark power and emotional depth, Hawthorne's masterpiece explores sin, guilt, and redemption in a story of adultery in the early days of the Massachusetts Colony. 192pp. 5³⁄₁₆ x 8¼.
                     0-486-28048-9

THE SEASONS OF AMERICA PAST, Eric Sloane. Seventy-five illustrations depict cider mills and presses, sleds, pumps, stump-pulling equipment, plows, and other elements of America's rural heritage. A section of old recipes and household hints adds additional color. 160pp. 8⅜ x 11.   0-486-44220-9

SELECTED CANTERBURY TALES, Geoffrey Chaucer. Delightful collection includes the General Prologue plus three of the most popular tales: "The Knight's Tale," "The Miller's Prologue and Tale," and "The Wife of Bath's Prologue and Tale." In modern English. 144pp. 5³⁄₁₆ x 8¼.   0-486-28241-4

SELECTED POEMS, Emily Dickinson. Over 100 best-known, best-loved poems by one of America's foremost poets, reprinted from authoritative early editions. No comparable edition at this price. Index of first lines. 64pp. 5³⁄₁₆ x 8¼. 0-486-26466-1

SIDDHARTHA, Hermann Hesse. Classic novel that has inspired generations of seekers. Blending Eastern mysticism and psychoanalysis, Hesse presents a strikingly original view of man and culture and the arduous process of self-discovery, reconciliation, harmony, and peace. 112pp. 5³⁄₁₆ x 8¼.   0-486-40653-9

SKETCHING OUTDOORS, Leonard Richmond. This guide offers beginners step-by-step demonstrations of how to depict clouds, trees, buildings, and other outdoor sights. Explanations of a variety of techniques include shading and constructional drawing. 48pp. 11 x 8¼.   0-486-46922-0

SMALL HOUSES OF THE FORTIES: With Illustrations and Floor Plans, Harold E. Group. 56 floor plans and elevations of houses that originally cost less than $15,000 to build. Recommended by financial institutions of the era, they range from Colonials to Cape Cods. 144pp. 8⅜ x 11. 0-486-45598-X

SOME CHINESE GHOSTS, Lafcadio Hearn. Rooted in ancient Chinese legends, these richly atmospheric supernatural tales are recounted by an expert in Oriental lore. Their originality, power, and literary charm will captivate readers of all ages. 96pp. 5⅜ x 8½. 0-486-46306-0

SONGS FOR THE OPEN ROAD: Poems of Travel and Adventure, Edited by The American Poetry & Literacy Project. More than 80 poems by 50 American and British masters celebrate real and metaphorical journeys. Poems by Whitman, Byron, Millay, Sandburg, Langston Hughes, Emily Dickinson, Robert Frost, Shelley, Tennyson, Yeats, many others. Note. 80pp. 5³⁄₁₆ x 8¼. 0-486-40646-6

SPOON RIVER ANTHOLOGY, Edgar Lee Masters. An American poetry classic, in which former citizens of a mythical midwestern town speak touchingly from the grave of the thwarted hopes and dreams of their lives. 144pp. 5³⁄₁₆ x 8¼.
0-486-27275-3

STAR LORE: Myths, Legends, and Facts, William Tyler Olcott. Captivating retellings of the origins and histories of ancient star groups include Pegasus, Ursa Major, Pleiades, signs of the zodiac, and other constellations. "Classic." — Sky & Telescope. 58 illustrations. 544pp. 5⅜ x 8½. 0-486-43581-4

THE STRANGE CASE OF DR. JEKYLL AND MR. HYDE, Robert Louis Stevenson. This intriguing novel, both fantasy thriller and moral allegory, depicts the struggle of two opposing personalities — one essentially good, the other evil — for the soul of one man. 64pp. 5³⁄₁₆ x 8¼. 0-486-26688-5

SURVIVAL HANDBOOK: The Official U.S. Army Guide, Department of the Army. This special edition of the Army field manual is geared toward civilians. An essential companion for campers and all lovers of the outdoors, it constitutes the most authoritative wilderness guide. 288pp. 5³⁄₁₆ x 8¼. 0-486-46184-X

A TALE OF TWO CITIES, Charles Dickens. Against the backdrop of the French Revolution, Dickens unfolds his masterpiece of drama, adventure, and romance about a man falsely accused of treason. Excitement and derring-do in the shadow of the guillotine. 304pp. 5³⁄₁₆ x 8¼. 0-486-40651-2

TEN PLAYS, Anton Chekhov. *The Sea Gull, Uncle Vanya, The Three Sisters, The Cherry Orchard,* and *Ivanov,* plus 5 one-act comedies: *The Anniversary, An Unwilling Martyr, The Wedding, The Bear,* and *The Proposal.* 336pp. 5³⁄₁₆ x 8¼. 0-486-46560-8

THE FLYING INN, G. K. Chesterton. Hilarious romp in which pub owner Humphrey Hump and friend take to the road in a donkey cart filled with rum and cheese, inveighing against Prohibition and other "oppressive forms of modernity." 320pp. 5⅜ x 8½. 0-486-41910-X

THIRTY YEARS THAT SHOOK PHYSICS: The Story of Quantum Theory, George Gamow. Lucid, accessible introduction to the influential theory of energy and matter features careful explanations of Dirac's anti-particles, Bohr's model of the atom, and much more. Numerous drawings. 1966 edition. 240pp. 5⅜ x 8½. 0-486-24895-X

TREASURE ISLAND, Robert Louis Stevenson. Classic adventure story of a perilous sea journey, a mutiny led by the infamous Long John Silver, and a lethal scramble for buried treasure — seen through the eyes of cabin boy Jim Hawkins. 160pp. 5³⁄₁₆ x 8¼.
0-486-27559-0

Browse over 9,000 books at www.doverpublications.com

THE TRIAL, Franz Kafka. Translated by David Wyllie. From its gripping first sentence onward, this novel exemplifies the term "Kafkaesque." Its darkly humorous narrative recounts a bank clerk's entrapment in a bureaucratic maze, based on an undisclosed charge. 176pp. 5³⁄₁₆ x 8¼. 0-486-47061-X

THE TURN OF THE SCREW, Henry James. Gripping ghost story by great novelist depicts the sinister transformation of 2 innocent children into flagrant liars and hypocrites. An elegantly told tale of unspoken horror and psychological terror. 96pp. 5³⁄₁₆ x 8¼. 0-486-26684-2

UP FROM SLAVERY, Booker T. Washington. Washington (1856-1915) rose to become the most influential spokesman for African-Americans of his day. In this eloquently written book, he describes events in a remarkable life that began in bondage and culminated in worldwide recognition. 160pp. 5³⁄₁₆ x 8¼. 0-486-28738-6

VICTORIAN HOUSE DESIGNS IN AUTHENTIC FULL COLOR: 75 Plates from the "Scientific American – Architects and Builders Edition," 1885-1894, Edited by Blanche Cirker. Exquisitely detailed, exceptionally handsome designs for an enormous variety of attractive city dwellings, spacious suburban and country homes, charming "cottages" and other structures — all accompanied by perspective views and floor plans. 80pp. 9¼ x 12¼. 0-486-29438-2

VILLETTE, Charlotte Brontë. Acclaimed by Virginia Woolf as "Brontë's finest novel," this moving psychological study features a remarkably modern heroine who abandons her native England for a new life as a schoolteacher in Belgium. 480pp. 5³⁄₁₆ x 8¼. 0-486-45557-2

THE VOYAGE OUT, Virginia Woolf. A moving depiction of the thrills and confusion of youth, Woolf's acclaimed first novel traces a shipboard journey to South America for a captivating exploration of a woman's growing self-awareness. 288pp. 5³⁄₁₆ x 8¼. 0-486-45005-8

WALDEN; OR, LIFE IN THE WOODS, Henry David Thoreau. Accounts of Thoreau's daily life on the shores of Walden Pond outside Concord, Massachusetts, are interwoven with musings on the virtues of self-reliance and individual freedom, on society, government, and other topics. 224pp. 5³⁄₁₆ x 8¼. 0-486-28495-6

WILD PILGRIMAGE: A Novel in Woodcuts, Lynd Ward. Through startling engravings shaded in black and red, Ward wordlessly tells the story of a man trapped in an industrial world, struggling between the grim reality around him and the fantasies his imagination creates. 112pp. 6⅛ x 9¼. 0-486-46583-7

WILLY POGÁNY REDISCOVERED, Willy Pogány. Selected and Edited by Jeff A. Menges. More than 100 color and black-and-white Art Nouveau–style illustrations from fairy tales and adventure stories include scenes from Wagner's "Ring" cycle, *The Rime of the Ancient Mariner, Gulliver's Travels,* and *Faust.* 144pp. 8⅜ x 11.
0-486-47046-6

WOOLLY THOUGHTS: Unlock Your Creative Genius with Modular Knitting, Pat Ashforth and Steve Plummer. Here's the revolutionary way to knit — easy, fun, and foolproof! Beginners and experienced knitters need only master a single stitch to create their own designs with patchwork squares. More than 100 illustrations. 128pp. 6½ x 9¼. 0-486-46084-3

WUTHERING HEIGHTS, Emily Brontë. Somber tale of consuming passions and vengeance — played out amid the lonely English moors — recounts the turbulent and tempestuous love story of Cathy and Heathcliff. Poignant and compelling. 256pp. 5³⁄₁₆ x 8¼. 0-486-29256-8